T0189303

Lecture Notes in Computer Science　　10529

Commenced Publication in 1973
Founding and Former Series Editors:
Gerhard Goos, Juris Hartmanis, and Jan van Leeuwen

More information about this series at http://www.springer.com/series/7410

Wieland Fischer · Naofumi Homma (Eds.)

Cryptographic Hardware and Embedded Systems – CHES 2017

19th International Conference
Taipei, Taiwan, September 25–28, 2017
Proceedings

 Springer

Editors
Wieland Fischer
Infineon Technologies
Neubiberg, Bayern
Germany

Naofumi Homma
Tohoku University
Sendai-shi
Japan

ISSN 0302-9743   ISSN 1611-3349   (electronic)
Lecture Notes in Computer Science
ISBN 978-3-319-66786-7   ISBN 978-3-319-66787-4   (eBook)
DOI 10.1007/978-3-319-66787-4

Library of Congress Control Number: 2017951309

LNCS Sublibrary: SL4 – Security and Cryptology

Printed on acid-free paper

This Springer imprint is published by Springer Nature
The registered company is Springer International Publishing AG
The registered company address is: Gewerbestrasse 11, 6330 Cham, Switzerland

Preface

The 19th International Conference on Cryptographic Hardware and Embedded Systems (CHES 2017) was held in Taipei, Taiwan, during September 25–28, 2017. The conference was sponsored by the *International Association for Cryptologic Research.*

CHES 2017 received 130 submissions. Each paper was anonymously reviewed by at least four Program Committee members in a double-blind peer-review process. Submissions co-authored by PC members received at least five reviews. With the help of 212 external reviewers our 48 Program Committee members wrote a total of 552 reviews. CHES continued the policy that submissions needed to closely match the final versions published by Springer in length and format. Additionally, the new paper submission policy from last year was applied whereby authors needed to indicate conflicts of interest with Program Committee members. A rebuttal process complemented again the review process and the Program Committee finally selected 33 papers for publication in these proceedings.

Of the two papers that were nominated for the CHES 2017 best paper award, the Program Committee decided to give the award to *Nanofocused X-Ray Beam to Reprogram Secure Circuits* by Stéphanie Anceau, Pierre Bleuet, Jessy Clédière, Laurent Maingault, Jean-luc Rainard, and Rémi Tucoulou. The second nominee was *High-Order Conversion from Boolean to Arithmetic Masking* by Jean-Sébastien Coron. Together with *Blockcipher-Based Authenticated Encryption: How Small Can We Go?* by Avik Chakraborti, Tetsu Iwata, Kazuhiko Minematsu, and Mridul Nandi all three papers were invited to submit extended versions to the *Journal of Cryptology.*

The technical program was completed by an invited talk by Shih-Lien Lu from TSMC about *HW Security: A Foundry Perspective.* Furthermore, CHES 2017 also featured a poster session, which was kindly chaired by Oscar Reparaz. As in previous years, two tutorials on the first day of the conference were held: one by Colin O'Flynn on *Side Channel Live!* and one by Tim Güneysu on *Post-Quantum Cryptography for Embedded Systems.*

Many people contribute to such a big conference. First of all, we would like to thank all the authors who submitted their excellent research to CHES 2017. After all, it is their results that the conference is about and without them, it would not exist. We are very much indebted to the members of the Program Committee and their external reviewers for their effort over an extended period of time to select the papers for the program. The review process and the editing of the final proceedings were greatly supported by the software written by Shai Halevi. We further thank the general chairs, Chen-Mou Cheng and Bo-Yin Yang, for organizing all aspects of the conference in such a great location. A special thanks goes to Peter Schwabe who provided us with his pleasant website. We always could count on his prompt support. We are grateful to

Emmanuel Prouff, Thomas Baignères, Matthieu Finiasz, Pascal Paillier, and Matthieu Rivain, who organized our CHES challenge and to Oscar Reparaz, who served as the poster session chair. We are also grateful for the financial support received from our many generous sponsors.

July 2017

Wieland Fischer
Naofumi Homma

CHES 2017

19th Conference on Cryptographic Hardware and Embedded Systems

Taipei, Taiwan,
September 25–28, 2017
Sponsored by the *International Association for Cryptologic Research*

General Chairs

Chen-Mou Cheng	National Taiwan University, Taiwan
Bo-Yin Yang	Academia Sinica, Taiwan

Program Chairs

Wieland Fischer	Infineon Technologies, Germany
Naofumi Homma	Tohoku University, Japan

Program Committee

Diego Aranha	University of Campinas, Brazil
Josep Balasch	KU Leuven, Belgium
Lejla Batina	Radboud University, The Netherlands
Olivier Benoit	Qualcomm Technologies, Inc., USA
Daniel J. Bernstein	University of Illinois at Chicago, USA
Guido Marco Bertoni	STMicroelectronics, Italy
Tung Chou	Technische Universiteit Eindhoven, The Netherlands
Christophe Clavier	Université de Limoges, France
Elke De Mulder	Rambus, Cryptography Research Division, USA
Hermann Drexler	Giesecke & Devrient, Germany
Thomas Eisenbarth	Worcester Polytechnic Institute, USA
Junfeng Fan	Open Security Research, China
Viktor Fischer	Hubert Curien Laboratory, University of Lyon, France
Pierre-Alain Fouque	Université de Rennes 1, France
Berndt Gammel	Infineon Technologies, Germany
Benedikt Gierlichs	KU Leuven, Belgium
Christophe Giraud	Oberthur Technologies, France
Jorge Guajardo	Robert Bosch LLC, Research and Technology Center, USA
Sylvain Guilley	TELECOM-ParisTech and Secure-IC, France

Gizem Çetin
Colin Chaigneau
Ou Changhai
Urbi Chatterjee
Chien-Ning Chen
Cong Chen
Jiun-Peng Chen
Abdelkarim Cherkaoui
Brice Colombier
John Connor
Edouard Cuvelier
Joan Daemen
Wei Dai
Nilanjan Datta
Eloi de Chérisey
Ruan de Clercq
Nicolas Debande
He Debiao
Jeroen Delvaux
Jérémie Detrey
Yarkin Doroz
Milos Drutarovsky
Cécile Dumas
Karim Eldefrawy
Zhang Fan
Benoît Feix
Francesc Fons
Tom Forest
Marc Fyrbiak
Georges Gagnerot
Adriano Gaibotti
Flavio Garcia
Benoît Gérard
Gilbert Goodwill
Dahmun Goudarzi
Vincent Grosso
Giuseppe Guagliardo
Oscar Guillen
Berk Gulmezoglu
Patrick Haddad
Carl-Daniel Hailfinger
Zhang Hailong
Mike Hamburg
Nabil Hamzi
Helena Handschuh
Francisco Rodríguez
  Henríquez

Lars Hoffmann
Yohei Hori
Li Huiyun
Michael Hutter
Dirmanto Jap
Jérémy Jean
Anthony Journault
Bernhard Jungk
Koray Karabina
Elif Bilge Kavun
Ilya Kizhvatov
Roman Korkikian
Archanaa
  Santhana Krishnan
Tanja Lange
Sandra Lisa Lattacher
Wen-Ding Li
Zheng Liu
Weiqiang Liu
David Lubicz
Aaron Lye
Takanori Machida
Pieter Maene
Cédric Marchand
Mark Marson
Pedro Maat Massolino
Philippe Maurine
Silvia Mella
Filippo Melzani
Wil Michiels
Jelena Milosevic
Xiaoyu Min
Tarik Moataz
Maria Chiara Molteni
Thorben Moos
Sumio Morioka
Daisuke Moriyama
Nicky Mouha
Ugo Mureddu
Bruce Murray
Köksal Mus
Zakaria Najm
Kashif Nawaz
Ventzislav Nikov
Tobias Oder
Naoki Ogura
Thomaz Oliveira

Jheyne N. Ortiz
Elisabeth Oswald
Erdinç Öztürk
Paolo Palmieri
Kostas Papgiannopoulos
Sikhar Patranabis
Conor Patrick
Sylvain Pelissier
Hervé Pelletier
Fernando Magno Quintao
  Pereira
Ludovic Perret
Edoardo Persichetti
Mert D. Pesé
Jonathan Petit
Oto Petura
Christian Pilato
Thomas Plos
Christina Plump
Thomas Pöppelmann
Ilia Polian
Yuriy Polyakov
Axel Poschmann
Romain Poussier
Emmanuel Prouff
Jürgen Pulkus
Prasanna Ravi
Christof Rempel
Guénaël Renault
Joost Renes
Oscar Reparaz
Léo Reynaud
Bastian Richter
Franck Rondepierre
Sujoy Sinha Roy
Debapriya Basu Roy
Vladimir Rožić
Sayandeep Saha
Durga Prasad Sahoo
Kazuo Sakiyama
Peter Samarin
Niels Samwel
Manuel San Pedro
Pascal Sasdrich
Alexander Schaub
Falk Schellenberg
Alexander Schlösser

Contents

Side Channel Analysis I

A Side-Channel Assisted Cryptanalytic Attack Against QcBits.   3
  Mélissa Rossi, Mike Hamburg, Michael Hutter, and Mark E. Marson

Improved Blind Side-Channel Analysis by Exploitation of Joint
Distributions of Leakages.   24
  Christophe Clavier and Léo Reynaud

Convolutional Neural Networks with Data Augmentation Against
Jitter-Based Countermeasures: Profiling Attacks Without Pre-processing   45
  Eleonora Cagli, Cécile Dumas, and Emmanuel Prouff

CacheZoom: How SGX Amplifies the Power of Cache Attacks   69
  Ahmad Moghimi, Gorka Irazoqui, and Thomas Eisenbarth

Higher Order Countermeasures

High-Order Conversion from Boolean to Arithmetic Masking.   93
  Jean-Sébastien Coron

Reconciling $d + 1$ Masking in Hardware and Software.   115
  Hannes Gross and Stefan Mangard

Changing of the Guards: A Simple and Efficient Method
for Achieving Uniformity in Threshold Sharing   137
  Joan Daemen

Generalized Polynomial Decomposition for S-boxes with Application
to Side-Channel Countermeasures   154
  *Dahmun Goudarzi, Matthieu Rivain, Damien Vergnaud,
  and Srinivas Vivek*

Emerging Attacks I

Nanofocused X-Ray Beam to Reprogram Secure Circuits.   175
  *Stéphanie Anceau, Pierre Bleuet, Jessy Clédière, Laurent Maingault,
  Jean-luc Rainard, and Rémi Tucoulou*

Novel Bypass Attack and BDD-based Tradeoff Analysis Against All
Known Logic Locking Attacks   189
    Xiaolin Xu, Bicky Shakya, Mark M. Tehranipoor, and Domenic Forte

Post Quantum Implementations

McBits Revisited.   213
    Tung Chou

High-Speed Key Encapsulation from NTRU.   232
    Andreas Hülsing, Joost Rijneveld, John Schanck, and Peter Schwabe

FPGA-based Key Generator for the Niederreiter Cryptosystem
Using Binary Goppa Codes   253
    Wen Wang, Jakub Szefer, and Ruben Niederhagen

Cipher & Protocol Design

Blockcipher-Based Authenticated Encryption: How Small Can We Go?.   277
    Avik Chakraborti, Tetsu Iwata, Kazuhiko Minematsu, and Mridul Nandi

GIMLI : A Cross-Platform Permutation   299
    Daniel J. Bernstein, Stefan Kölbl, Stefan Lucks,
    Pedro Maat Costa Massolino, Florian Mendel, Kashif Nawaz,
    Tobias Schneider, Peter Schwabe, François-Xavier Standaert,
    Yosuke Todo, and Benoît Viguier

GIFT: A Small Present: Towards Reaching the Limit
of Lightweight Encryption   321
    Subhadeep Banik, Sumit Kumar Pandey, Thomas Peyrin, Yu Sasaki,
    Siang Meng Sim, and Yosuke Todo

Making Password Authenticated Key Exchange Suitable
for Resource-Constrained Industrial Control Devices   346
    Björn Haase and Benoît Labrique

Security Evaluation

Back to Massey: Impressively Fast, Scalable and Tight Security
Evaluation Tools.   367
    Marios O. Choudary and P.G. Popescu

Fast Leakage Assessment.   387
    Oscar Reparaz, Benedikt Gierlichs, and Ingrid Verbauwhede

FPGA Security

Your Rails Cannot Hide from Localized EM: How Dual-Rail Logic Fails
on FPGAs   403
    Vincent Immler, Robert Specht, and Florian Unterstein

How to Break Secure Boot on FPGA SoCs Through Malicious Hardware . . .   425
    Nisha Jacob, Johann Heyszl, Andreas Zankl, Carsten Rolfes,
    and Georg Sigl

Emerging Attacks II

Illusion and Dazzle: Adversarial Optical Channel Exploits Against Lidars
for Automotive Applications.   445
    Hocheol Shin, Dohyun Kim, Yujin Kwon, and Yongdae Kim

Hacking in the Blind: (Almost) Invisible Runtime User Interface Attacks. . . .   468
    Luka Malisa, Kari Kostiainen, Thomas Knell, David Sommer,
    and Srdjan Capkun

On the Security of Carrier Phase-Based Ranging.   490
    Hildur Ólafsdóttir, Aanjhan Ranganathan, and Srdjan Capkun

Side Channel Analysis II

Single-Trace Side-Channel Attacks on Masked Lattice-Based Encryption   513
    Robert Primas, Peter Pessl, and Stefan Mangard

A Systematic Approach to the Side-Channel Analysis of ECC
Implementations with Worst-Case Horizontal Attacks   534
    Romain Poussier, Yuanyuan Zhou, and François-Xavier Standaert

Sliding Right into Disaster: Left-to-Right Sliding Windows Leak   555
    Daniel J. Bernstein, Joachim Breitner, Daniel Genkin,
    Leon Groot Bruinderink, Nadia Heninger, Tanja Lange,
    Christine van Vredendaal, and Yuval Yarom

Encoding Techniques

Faster Homomorphic Function Evaluation Using Non-integral
Base Encoding   579
    Charlotte Bonte, Carl Bootland, Joppe W. Bos, Wouter Castryck,
    Ilia Iliashenko, and Frederik Vercauteren

Hiding Secrecy Leakage in Leaky Helper Data.   601
    Matthias Hiller and Aysun Gurur Önalan

Efficient Implementations

Very High Order Masking: Efficient Implementation and Security
Evaluation   623
    Anthony Journault and François-Xavier Standaert

PRESENT Runs Fast: Efficient and Secure Implementation in Software.   644
    Tiago B.S. Reis, Diego F. Aranha, and Julio López

FourQ on Embedded Devices with Strong Countermeasures Against
Side-Channel Attacks   665
    Zhe Liu, Patrick Longa, Geovandro C.C.F. Pereira, Oscar Reparaz,
    and Hwajeong Seo

Bit-Sliding: A Generic Technique for Bit-Serial Implementations
of SPN-based Primitives: Applications to AES, PRESENT and SKINNY   687
    Jérémy Jean, Amir Moradi, Thomas Peyrin, and Pascal Sasdrich

Author Index   709

Side Channel Analysis I

A Side-Channel Assisted Cryptanalytic Attack Against QcBits

Mélissa Rossi[2,3,4(✉)], Mike Hamburg[1], Michael Hutter[1], and Mark E. Marson[1]

[1] Rambus Cryptography Research,
425 Market Street, 11th Floor, San Francisco, CA 94105, USA
{mike.hamburg,michael.hutter,mark.marson}@cryptography.com
[2] Thales Communications & Security, Paris, France
[3] Département d'informatique de l'ENS,
École normale supérieure, CNRS, PSL Research University,
75005 Paris, France
melissa.rossi@ens.fr
[4] INRIA, Paris, France

Abstract. QcBits is a code-based public key algorithm based on a problem thought to be resistant to quantum computer attacks. It is a constant-time implementation for a quasi-cyclic moderate density parity check (QC-MDPC) Niederreiter encryption scheme, and has excellent performance and small key sizes. In this paper, we present a key recovery attack against QcBits. We first used differential power analysis (DPA) against the syndrome computation of the decoding algorithm to recover partial information about one half of the private key. We then used the recovered information to set up a system of noisy binary linear equations. Solving this system of equations gave us the entire key. Finally, we propose a simple but effective countermeasure against the power analysis used during the syndrome calculation.

Keywords: QcBits · Post-quantum cryptography · McEliece · Niederreiter · QC-MDPC codes · Side-channel analysis · Differential power analysis · Noisy binary linear equations · Learning parity with noise

1 Introduction

1.1 Quantum Computers and Post-Quantum Cryptography

The security of the most commonly-used public key cryptosystems is based on the difficulty of either the integer factorization problem or the discrete logarithm problem. Unfortunately, both of these problems can be efficiently solved using quantum computers [36]. Progress in quantum computing has been steady, and many believe that practical quantum computers will become a reality

---

M. Rossi—This work was done while the author was at Rambus Cryptography Research.

W. Fischer and N. Homma (Eds.): CHES 2017, LNCS 10529, pp. 3–23, 2017.
DOI: 10.1007/978-3-319-66787-4_1

within the next 20 years [12,28]. In fact, the National Security Agency (NSA) and the National Institute of Standards and Technology (NIST) have both issued announcements calling for the standardization and transition to post-quantum public key algorithms in the near future [12,33]. A European initiative, PQCRYPTO, sponsored by the European Commission under its Horizon 2020 Program, published a report entitled "Initial Recommendation of long-term secure post-quantum systems" [1]. This report recommends the development of cryptography which is resistant to quantum computers. These concerns about quantum computers have given research in post-quantum cryptography a great deal of momentum in the past few years. Some of the most promising directions include cryptosystems based on lattices, error correcting codes, hash functions, and multivariate quadratic equations. The mathematical problems upon which these cryptosystems are based are expected to remain intractable even in the presence of quantum computers [7].

In this paper, we analyze and successfully attack a code-based post-quantum public key cryptosystem called QcBits [13]. QcBits (pronounced "quick-bits") is a variant of the McEliece public-key cryptosystem [24] based on quasi-cyclic (QC) moderate density parity check (MDPC) codes [26]. Although the McEliece cryptosystem in its original form is still regarded as secure, the public keys for the originally proposed parameters are very large. On the other hand, cryptosystems based on QC-MDPC codes have much smaller and simpler public and private keys. The quasi-cyclic form allows the public and private keys to be completely defined by the first rows of their matrices.

However, it is precisely the quasi-cyclic structure and moderate density of the private key which allows our attack to succeed. The QcBits secret parity check matrix is the concatenation of two sparse circulant matrices, denoted $\boldsymbol{H}_0$ and $\boldsymbol{H}_1$. We first used differential power analysis (DPA) against $\boldsymbol{H}_0$ to narrow down the locations of its nonzero elements. This gave us enough information to set up a system of noisy binary linear equations, which we could solve with high probability. Solving these equations gave us both the exact matrix $\boldsymbol{H}_0$, as well as the other matrix $\boldsymbol{H}_1$.

1.2   Previous Related Work

The first code-based public key cryptosystem is due to McEliece [24]. Its security is based on the difficulty of decoding a random linear code. It has been extensively analyzed since being proposed, and is still regarded as secure in its original form using Goppa codes. The main drawback of this construction is the size of the public keys. For the originally proposed parameters these keys contain about 500 Kbits. This drawback motivated the search for secure code-based cryptosystems with more manageable key sizes [19,23,29,38]. Unfortunately, most of the proposed McEliece variants using codes other than Goppa codes have turned out to be insecure [14,22,25,27,34,39]. Using QC-MDPC codes to replace Goppa codes in the McEliece cryptosystem was first suggested by Misoczki et al. in 2013 [26], and appears to be a promising choice. Some hardware implementations of this scheme followed in 2013 [18] and 2014 [42].

QC-MDPC codes are characterized by moderate density parity check matrices in quasi-cyclic form. The quasi-cyclic form allows both the public key and private key matrices to be completely defined by their first rows, leading to much smaller key sizes. Also, because of the way the public generator matrix is constructed, there is no need for scrambling and permutation matrices. Instead, the generator matrix is directly presented as a public key in its systematic form. In [1], the PQCRYPTO group recommends the QC-MDPC scheme for further study.

QC-MDPC McEliece was originally designed to be secure against chosen plaintext attacks (CPA) but not against chosen ciphertext attacks (CCA). To achieve security against adaptive chosen ciphertext attacks, some transformations were proposed in [4,20]. A hybrid CCA-secure encryption protocol using QC-MDPC Niederreiter was proposed by Persichetti [32] and implemented by Von Maurich et al. [43]. QcBits is an implementation of a variant of this protocol due to Chou in [13]. It operates in a constant time and has very good speed results and small keys sizes.

Another issue with the QC-MDPC cryptosystems is that they have a non-negligible probability of decryption failure, with the failure rate depending on the security parameters. The failure rate was around 10^{-7} in Misoczki et al. original proposal [26], and is even worse for constant-time decoders. In [16], Guo et al. take advantage of the decryption failures to recover the secret key of Misoczki's original version in minutes. Preliminary work was done to improve constant-time decoding algorithms in [10], but they did not improve the failure rate below 10^{-7}. For CCA-secure versions of QC-MDPC cryptosystems, Guo et al. proposed a more complex version of their attack that requires at most 350 million decryptions and has a time complexity of $2^{39.7}$. QcBits is CCA-secure but it has a more advanced constant-time decoder [13]. Chou claims a failure rate of 10^{-8} for the 80-bit secure version. Guo et al. still estimate the time complexity for attacking QcBits to be $2^{55.3}$, but to our knowledge have not run the attack. They have not provided estimates against the 128-bit secure version. They proposed drastically reducing the decoding failure probability as countermeasure against this attack, but no details about how to do so have been published.

Side-channel attacks against code-based schemes have focused more on the original version of the McEliece cryptosystem based on Goppa Codes. Timing leakages were first studied in [41]. This was followed by Strenzke and Shoufan et al., who performed a key recovery attack using timing analysis [37,40]. Heyse et al. performed a simple power analysis (SPA) attack against software implementations of classic McEliece algorithm [17]. In [11], Chen et al. describe a differential power analysis (DPA) [21] key recovery attack against a QC-MDPC FPGA McEliece implementation. To our knowledge, no DPA attacks have been performed on CCA-secure constant-time versions of QC-MDPC McEliece.

Our attack also includes solving a learning parity with noise (LPN) problem. We set up and solve a system of noisy binary linear equations to complete the key recovery. Solving such systems has a long history in cryptanalysis, with many different methods used depending upon the specifics of the problem.

See Belaid *et al.* in [2,3] for recent examples of such attacks. Our system of equations has very low noise. We therefore used an elementary method which, for very low noise systems (1%), was shown in [35] to be more efficient than the Blum-Kalai-Wasserman (BKW) algorithm [9].

1.3   Our Contribution

In this paper we present a side-channel assisted cryptanalytic attack against QcBits. In contrast to Guo *et al.*'s attack in [16], our attack focuses on the first step of the decoding process, and is independent of its failure probability. Our attack only requires us to observe a small number of decryptions (about 200 power traces for the implementation we analyzed), and we need to analyze less than 1% of each trace. Our attack also works for both the 80-bit and 128-bit security versions.

Our attack consists of two steps:

1. A DPA attack targeting the syndrome computation of the decryption operation. The operation uses half of the private key, and during this step we recover some information about that half of the key. Because of the way in which the implementation leaks, there is some ambiguity as to the exact location of the nonzero elements of the key.
2. A linear algebra computation which takes advantage of the sparseness of the private key and succeeds with high probability. We repeat this operation (varying the equations slightly each time) until the computation succeeds. This allows us to recover the entire secret key.

The number of traces required in the first step will of course depend upon the implementation and hardware on which it is run. The amount of work required for the second step will depend on how much information is recovered in the first step. For the implementation and hardware we used for our analysis, the DPA attack required about 200 power traces in Step 1. The work factors in Step 2 were 2^{24} for the 80-bit security version, and 2^{27} for the 128-bit security version. See Sect. 4 for details.

1.4   Paper Roadmap

In Sect. 2, we describe the QcBits cryptosystem introduced by Chou in [13]. In Sect. 3, we describe the DPA attack we used to recover information about the private key. In Sect. 4, we present the algebraic attack we implemented recovering the entire private key. In Sect. 5, we describe a simple countermeasure to help protect against our attack. Finally, in Sect. 6, we summarize our results and discuss future research.

2   Description of the **QcBits** Cryptosystem

2.1   Definitions

Definition 1 (Circulant matrix). *A $r \times r$ matrix is a **circulant matrix** if its rows are successive cyclic shifts of its first one.*

Definition 2 (Quasi-cyclic matrix). *A matrix $H = (H_0, ..., H_m)$ is a **quasi-cyclic (QC) matrix** if the submatrices $H_0, ..., H_m$ are circulant matrices.*

Definition 3 (QC-MDPC code). *An (n, r, w)-**QC-MDPC code** is a binary linear code with n-bit codewords and dimension r which is defined by a QC Moderate Density Parity Check (MDPC) matrix H.*

$$\mathcal{C} = \{x \in \mathbb{F}_2^n | H \cdot x^T = 0\}. \tag{1}$$

In other words, the codewords are all the vectors in the right nullspace of H which is QC and has a "moderate density". "Moderate" here means that H has a constant row weight $w = O(\sqrt{n.\log(n)})$.

2.2 QC-MDPC Codes Used for QcBits

QcBits uses (n, r, w)-QC-MDPC binary codes with $n = 2r$. The parity check matrix in its QC-MDPC form is then composed of 2 square sparse circulant matrices

$$H = (H_0, H_1) \in \mathbb{F}_2^{r \times n} \tag{2}$$

The generator matrix in its systematic form is the $r \times n$ binary matrix

$$G = (I, P) \tag{3}$$

where I is the $r \times r$ identity matrix and P is an $r \times r$ dense binary circulant matrix

$$P = (H_1^{-1} \cdot H_0)^T \tag{4}$$

The reader can easily verify that $H \cdot G^T = 0$, so the rows of G form a basis for the codewords. An r-bit data vector x is encoded by multiplying it by G:

$$c = x \cdot G. \tag{5}$$

Let e be a n-bit error vector, and $\hat{c}$ the corrupted codeword

$$\hat{c} = c \oplus e = x \cdot G \oplus e. \tag{6}$$

In the general case, decoding a corrupted codeword (i.e., removing its errors) from a random binary linear code is an NP-hard problem [5]. However, if the QC-MDPC parity check matrix $H = (H_0, H_1)$ is known and the Hamming weight of e is not too large, there are efficient algorithms for decoding corrupted QC-MDPC codewords. There is no known efficient algorithm if the two sparse circulant matrices H_0 and H_1 are not known. The most commonly-used decoding algorithm is the probabilistic bit-flipping algorithm introduced by Gallager in [15]. See Sect. 2.3 for details.

For the bit-flipping decoding algorithm on QC-MDPC codes, the maximum allowed number of bit errors, denoted t, is an estimated value. In [26] the authors determined values for QC-MDPC code parameters (n, r, w, t) which would provide the desired security levels, while keeping the probability of a decoding failure as low as possible ($<10^{-7}$). The parameters they selected are shown in Table 1.

Table 1. Proposed QC-MDPC instances with security level

n	r	w	t	Bits of security
9602	4801	90	84	80
19714	9857	142	134	128

For the remainder of this paper, we focus on QC-MDPC codes with the two parameter sets (n, r, w, t) from Table 1. The private key of QcBits is the QC-MDPC parity check matrix $\boldsymbol{H}_{priv}$:

$$\boldsymbol{H}_{priv} = (\boldsymbol{H}_0, \boldsymbol{H}_1) \tag{7}$$

where $\boldsymbol{H}_0, \boldsymbol{H}_1 \in \mathbb{F}_2^{r \times r}$ are randomly generated circulant matrices with weight $\frac{w}{2}$ in each row. The private key is sparse, so only the indices of the nonzero values of the first row are stored. Knowing the private key, one can use the bit-flipping decoding algorithm to recover a codeword which has been corrupted by up to t errors.

The public key is computed directly from the private key $\boldsymbol{H}_{priv}$ as the dense circulant $r \times r$ matrix $\boldsymbol{P}$:

$$\boldsymbol{P} = (\boldsymbol{H}_1^{-1} \cdot \boldsymbol{H}_0)^T. \tag{8}$$

Knowing $\boldsymbol{P}$ allows anyone to build the generator matrix in its systematic form $\boldsymbol{G}_{pub}$ and a parity check matrix $\boldsymbol{H}_{pub}$:

$$\boldsymbol{G}_{pub} = (\boldsymbol{I}, \boldsymbol{P}), \tag{9}$$

$$\boldsymbol{H}_{pub} = (\boldsymbol{P}^T, \boldsymbol{I}). \tag{10}$$

2.3   QcBits Encryption and Decryption Algorithms

QcBits is an hybrid CCA-secure encryption protocol based on Niederreiter [29]. Unlike McEliece cryptosystem, Niederreiter uses the parity-check matrix rather than the generator matrix for the encryption. QcBits uses the following cryptographic primitives. See [13] for more details.

1. A hash function denoted $Hash$. QcBits uses Keccak [31];
2. A symmetric stream cipher denoted ($Senc$,$Sdec$). QcBits uses Salsa20 [8];
3. An authentication function denoted (Tag,$Check$). QcBits uses Poly1305 [6].

The encryption of a message m using QcBits is shown in Algorithm 1.

Algorithm 1. QcBits encryption

Data: Plaintext m, Public matrix P

Result: Ciphertext $(c|d|g)$

1 $e \leftarrow \$$ // Drawing a random n-bit error vector with Hamming weight t
2 $key \leftarrow Hash(e)$;
3 $c^T \leftarrow (I, P^{-T}) \cdot e^T \in \mathbb{F}_2^r$;
4 $d \leftarrow Senc(key, m)$;
5 $g \leftarrow Tag(key)$;
6 Return $(c|d|g)$;

The reader can verify that $(c|0) \in \mathbb{F}_2^n$ is a codeword corrupted with the error e. The encrypted message d has the size of the plaintext m, as it is encrypted with a stream cipher. The message authenticator g is 16 bytes in length.

We next describe the bit-flipping algorithm, which is used by the decryption algorithm. Given a vector that is at most t errors away from a codeword, the bit flipping algorithm attempts to recover the codeword (or equivalently the error) using a sequence of iterations. During each iteration the algorithm decides which of the n positions of the input vector are most likely to be wrong, and inverts those bits. The resulting vector then becomes the input to the next iteration. In QcBits, the bit-flipping algorithm performs a total of $j_{max} = 6$ iterations. It uses the precomputed thresholds $Thresh[0, \ldots, 5] = [29, 27, 25, 24, 23, 23]$ in each iteration to determine which bits should be flipped. The bit-flipping process is shown in Algorithm 2.

Algorithm 2. Bit Flipping

Data: $H_{priv} \in \mathbb{F}_2^{r \cdot n}, x \in \mathbb{F}_2^n$

Result: Corrected codeword v

1 $v \leftarrow x$;
2 $S \leftarrow H_{priv} \cdot v^T$ // Syndrome computation;
3 **for** $j \in \{0, j_{max}\}$ **do**
4   **for** $i \in \{0, ..., n - 1\}$ **do**
5          $\sigma_i \leftarrow \langle S, h_i \rangle \in \mathbb{Z}$ // h_i denotes the i-th column of H;
6   **if** $\sigma_i \geq Thresh[j]$ **then**
7              $v_i \leftarrow v_i \oplus 1$
8   **end**
9   **end**
10     $S \leftarrow H_{priv} \cdot v^T$
11 **end**
12 Return the codeword v

Algorithm 3 shows the decryption process. First, $(c|0) \in \mathbb{F}_2^n$ gets decoded. The bit-flipping returns the error e. Then, the decryption hashes e to compute the symmetric key, verifies the tag g, and decrypts the second part of the ciphertext, d.

Algorithm 3. QcBits decryption

Data: Ciphertext $(c|d|g)$, Private key $H_{priv} = (H_0, H_1)$
Result: Plaintext m or $\perp$

1   $s \leftarrow (c \mid 0) \in \mathbb{F}_2^n$;
2   $e \leftarrow$ Bit-Flipping$(H_{priv}, s) \oplus s$;
3   $key \leftarrow Hash(e)$;
4   **if** $Check(key, g)$ **then**
5 | Return $m \leftarrow Sdec(key, d)$
6   **else**
7 | Return $\perp$
8   **end**

We performed our side-channel attack against the use of the secret parity check matrix H_{priv} during Step 2 in Algorithm 2. This gave us enough information after just a few decryptions to complete the cryptanalytic attack. This is in contrast to the attack of Guo *et al.*, who obtained information about the key during the low-probability failures of Algorithm 3. We describe our attack in the next two sections.

3   Differential Power Analysis Attack Against QcBits

In this section, we describe how we used DPA to recover some partial information about the secret matrix H_0. Our attack targets the syndrome calculation at the start of the bit-flipping algorithm, and recovers partial information about H_0.

3.1   General Leakage Model

We analyzed the C code of QcBits and identified the syndrome computation of the bit-flipping decoding (Step 2 in Algorithm 2) as a candidate for a DPA attack:

$$H_{priv} \cdot \begin{pmatrix} c^T \\ 0 \end{pmatrix} = (H_0, H_1) \cdot \begin{pmatrix} c^T \\ 0 \end{pmatrix} = H_0 \cdot c^T \tag{11}$$

where $c \in \mathbb{F}_2^r$ is the first part of the ciphertext. We will focus our attention on this computation.

Let $\{x_0, ..., x_{(\frac{w}{2}-1)}\}$ denote the unknown indices of the nonzero elements of h_0, the first row of H_0. Because H_0 is a circulant, it is uniquely defined by the x_i, and is represented in QcBits as a list of these indices. Due to its structure, the matrix H_0 can be decomposed as a sum of $\frac{w}{2}$ rotation matrices

$$H_0 = R_{x_0} + ... + R_{x_{(\frac{w}{2}-1)}}. \tag{12}$$

Multiplying $\boldsymbol{c}^T$ by $\boldsymbol{R}_{x_i}$, $0 \leq i \leq \frac{w}{2} - 1$, results in a left circular shift of $\boldsymbol{c}$ by x_i positions:

$$\boldsymbol{R}_{x_i} \cdot \boldsymbol{c}^T = \boldsymbol{r}_{x_i}(\boldsymbol{c})^T. \tag{13}$$

Hence the multiplication in Eq. 11 can be accomplished by computing the rotated ciphertexts $\boldsymbol{r}_{x_i}(\boldsymbol{c})$, $0 \leq i \leq \frac{w}{2} - 1$, and XORing them all together:

$$\boldsymbol{H}_0 \cdot \boldsymbol{c}^T = \bigoplus_{i=0}^{\frac{w}{2}-1} \boldsymbol{r}_{x_i}(\boldsymbol{c})^T. \tag{14}$$

In fact, this is how the multiplication is performed in the QcBits implementation. In a loop, each rotated vector $\boldsymbol{r}_{x_i}(\boldsymbol{c})$ is stored into a temporary memory location as it is calculated, and then XORed with the partial XOR sum from the previous loop iteration:

$$S_i = S_{i-1} \oplus \boldsymbol{r}_{x_i}(\boldsymbol{c}) = \bigoplus_{j=0}^{i-1} \boldsymbol{r}_{x_j}(\boldsymbol{c}) \oplus \boldsymbol{r}_{x_i}(\boldsymbol{c}). \tag{15}$$

Our side-channel analysis model assumes that the power consumption of the device depends on whether the leftmost bit (bit position 0) of each rotated vector $\boldsymbol{r}_{x_i}(\boldsymbol{c})$ is either 0 or 1 when it is stored to memory. Note that bit x_i of $\boldsymbol{c}$ is rotated into bit position 0 by $\boldsymbol{r}_{x_i}$ and into bit position 1 by $\boldsymbol{r}_{x_{i-1}}$. We therefore expect the device to leak for multiple guesses near the correct value, with the number of guesses exhibiting leaks related to the native word size of the device.

3.2   The Experiment Setup

We used the reference C version of QcBits[1] with 80 and 128 bits of security. We ported the code to run on ChipWhisperer evaluation platform designed by Colin O'Flynn [30]. The ChipWhisperer is a board composed of a programmable chip (Atmel AVR XMEGA128) and an on-board power-measurement circuit that can be connected to a PC via USB interface. An open-source python software is available that can be used to communicate with the chip, for example, to send encryption or decryption commands to the AVR. In order to measure the power consumption, the board features an analog to digital converter (OpenADC) that allows synchronous clocking to the AVR's clock. The clock frequency is fixed at 7.37 MHz. The signal is amplified with up to 55 dB gain and the power traces were sampled at a 96 MS/s rate.

We then generated a set of N known, random values $\{c_0, ..., c_{N-1}\} \in \mathbb{F}_2^r$. These were padded with zeros and passed to the bit-flipping Algorithm 2. Since they were randomly generated, the zero-padded values were almost certainly not codewords corrupted by at most t errors. As we were attacking the syndrome calculation at the beginning of the bit-flipping algorithm, however, we were not concerned with whether these values could be decoded properly. If properly formed ciphertext was required by the implementation, it could have been computed using the public-key information.

---

[1] Available at http://www.win.tue.nl/~tchou/qcbits/.

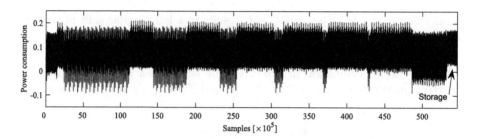

Fig. 1. Power trace of the first rotated ciphertext computation.

Figure 1 shows a typical power trace during the computation of one cipher-text rotation $r_{x_i}(c)$ in QcBits. After the computation, the result is stored into memory, which can be seen in the power trace at the very end of the rotation operation. Figure 2 zooms into the store operation where the first 64-bits of the rotated value are written to memory. Because the XMEGA is an 8-bit architecture, we can observe eight different power patterns which are related to the storing of each 8-bit value from internal registers into internal RAM. We collected 13,000 traces of that operation for each key index, which was sufficient for our analyses. To characterize the leakage behavior of the device, we analyzed 25 different key indices, varying both the secret value and the loop iteration in which it gets XORed into the partial sum in Eq. 15.

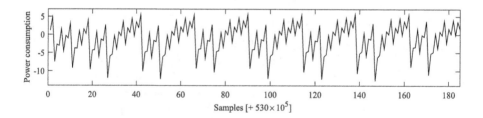

Fig. 2. Storing of the first 64 bits of the result of the rotation.

We attacked the unknown values $\{x_0, \ldots, x_{(\frac{w}{2}-1)}\}$ sequentially using standard DPA. We first made guesses for all possible values for the unknown x_0. Given the size of the secret matrix $\boldsymbol{H}_0$ this is clearly an exhaustible parameter. For each of those guesses, we sorted the traces T_j into two partitions based on whether the leftmost bit of the each rotated vector $\{r_{x_0}(c_0), \ldots, r_{x_0}(c_{N-1})\}$ was a zero or a one. We averaged the traces in the two partitions separately and computed the difference of the averages. Large spikes in the difference trace indicated a leak of information. As will be discussed in the next section, multiple guesses for each x_i exhibited significant leaks. This is due to how the algorithm was implemented, and how the hardware on the evaluation board leaked. We discuss how we resolved this ambiguity in Sect. 4. The DPA process is then repeated for each of the unknowns x_i.

3.3   DPA Results

Figure 3 shows the result of the DPA targeting for all possible values x_i using 500 power traces on the 80-bit version. The device clearly shows a significant leakage around the correct index (value $2,000$ in this experiment). However, it also shows that there are other indices leaking, for example, the indices $1,985$ up to $2,000$ show similar Difference of Mean (DoM) values. We performed DPA attacks targeting other unknown indices of $\boldsymbol{h}_0$ and identified a particular leakage model. For a given secret index x_i, the device always leaks for 16 consecutive guesses starting at index

$$y_i = \lfloor \frac{(x_i - 1) \bmod r}{64} \rfloor \cdot 64 + 1, \tag{16}$$

which is $\lfloor \frac{2000-1}{64} \rfloor \cdot 64 + 1 = 1985$ in our example.

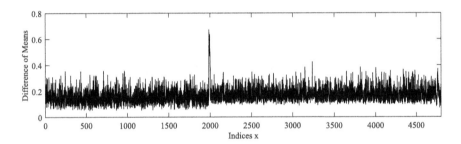

Fig. 3. Maximum Difference of Means (DoM) using 500 traces over all possible values x_i. Significant difference is observed for around the correct index 2000.

This gives us 64 different possible values for x_i. Complicating matters is that there isn't always a DPA peak for the correct secret index because the device leaks only for 16 consecutive guesses. For example, if $x_i = 2030$, then $y_i = \lfloor \frac{2030-1}{64} \rfloor \cdot 64 + 1 = 1985$ and the device will show leaks only for the 16 consecutive guesses from ($1,985$ to $2,000$). Fortunately, more information is available if we look at the times at which the leaks occur.

We observed that the leak corresponding to y_i can appear in one of 8 different time locations corresponding to the 8-bit AVR memory-store operations. These 8 positions can be seen in Fig. 4. The upper plot shows the DPA results for the indices $1,985$ to $1,992$ (drawn in black) and other index values from 0 to $1,984$ (drawn in gray). The lower plot shows the results for the indices $1,993$ to $2,000$, and other index values from $2,001$ to $4,800$. The leakage occurs during two 8-bit AVR memory-store operations near sample points 146 and 172. We discovered that the time location at which the leak for guess y_i occurs gives us more information about the correct value x_i.

Let $q_i \in \{0, ..., 7\}$ denote the location at which the leak corresponding to guess y_i occurs. It turns out that q_i is related to x_i by Eq. 17:

$$q_i = 7 - \lfloor \frac{(x_i - 1) \bmod 64}{8} \rfloor \in \{0, ..., 7\}. \tag{17}$$

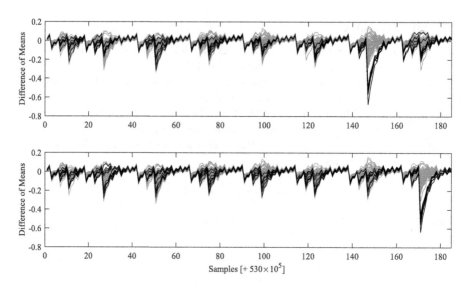

Fig. 4. Upper plot shows the DPA result using indices from 1,985 to 1,992 (drawn in black), the lower plot shows the result using indices from 1,993 to 2,000 (drawn in black). Other indices are drawn in gray.

In our example, $q_i = 7 - \lfloor \frac{2000-1 \mod 64}{8} \rfloor = 6^{th}$ position. In Fig. 4, we see that the leak corresponding to $y_i = 1985$, in the upper plot, is in the 6th location.

Hence, using power analysis we were able to recover a pair of values (y_i, q_i) which narrows down the choice of x_i to one of 8 possible values. Given (y_i, q_i), there are only 8 possible values for x_i which satisfy both Eqs. 16 and 17:

$$x_i \in Z_i = [y_i + (7 - q_i) \times 8, \ y_i + (7 - q_i) \times 8 + 7]. \tag{18}$$

In our example we measured $(y_i, q_i) = (1985, 6)$, and therefore deduce that $Z_i = [1993, 2000]$.

3.4   About the Index Search Intervals Z_i

We denote by α the length of index search intervals Z_i. In a sense, α represents the precision of the DPA analysis. Our attack gave us search intervals of length $\alpha = 8$, which actually equals to the word width of the underlying AVR architecture. We assume that on other devices, with different architectures and word lengths, our attack could yield search intervals with different lengths. For example, on a 64-bit device, the search interval could have length $\alpha = 64$. We will see in Sect. 4 that the algebraic part of the attack is not feasible for such a large value of α. In this case, we recommend looking for ways to improve the precision of the power analysis step to reduce the size of the search intervals, or using a stronger method than we did for solving the noisy system of equations.

It may be the case that different secret indices lie in the same interval Z_i. We denote by β the total number of unique search intervals Z_i. Note that β satisfies

$\beta \le \frac{w}{2}$. In our experiments, we needed around 100–200 traces to identify all β intervals of size $\alpha = 8$ containing the nonzero elements of h_0. Figure 5 illustrates the intervals recovered.

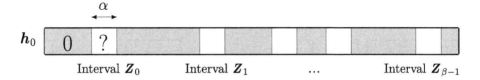

h_0 α 0   ?

Interval Z_0 Interval Z_1 ...   Interval $Z_{\beta-1}$

Fig. 5. Partial knowledge of h_0 after the DPA attack.

4 Recovering the Rest of the Key

In this section we describe how we used the partial information discovered by our DPA attack to recover the rest of the key. A brute force attack could take up to $\alpha^{\frac{w}{2}}$ calculations, which would be infeasible. However, the sparseness of the private key enables a much more efficient attack.

We simply choose a large number of private key bit positions at random, and hope that all the bits in those positions are 0. Since over 99% of the private key bits are 0, our guess will be correct with non-negligible probability. Combined with the information recovered in the DPA attack, this will give us enough linear equations to solve for the private key. A more sophisticated attack might work with less information recovered, but our attack is sufficient for α up to 32.

4.1 Cryptanalytic Attack Using Partial Information of Secret Key

Recall that the public key is $P = (H_1^{-1} \cdot H_0)^T$. Setting $Q = P^{-1}$ we rearrange and write

$$Q \cdot H_0^T = H_1^T. \tag{19}$$

The matrices H_0 and H_1 are sparse circulants defined by their first rows h_0 and h_1 respectively. We can therefore write 19 as the system of linear equations

$$Q \cdot h_0^T = h_1^T \tag{20}$$

where Q is dense and known, h_0 is sparse and partially known as shown in Fig. 5, and h_1 is sparse and unknown.

We now use the information we recovered about h_0 to help us completely solve the system of Eq. in 20. First, we know the β intervals $\{Z_0, ..., Z_{\beta-1}\}$ of length α which contain all the nonzero entries of h_0. All the entries of h_0 outside these intervals are known to be zero. We can therefore remove from our system of equations the zero-valued entries of h_0, and the corresponding columns of Q. This leaves us with a new system of equations

$$Q' \cdot h_0'^T = h_1^T \tag{21}$$

where $h_0' = (Z_0, ..., Z_{\beta-1})$ is the vector of length $\alpha\beta$ obtained by concatenating the variables in the intervals containing the nonzero entries of h_0, and Q' is the $r \times \alpha\beta$ matrix obtained by removing from Q the columns corresponding to the zero-valued entries of h_0. This step is illustrated in Fig. 6 below. We use the color gray to represent the removed variables.

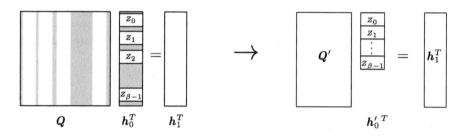

Fig. 6. Removing the columns of Q

The DPA attack allows us to know if two or more secret indices lie in the same interval Z_i. We therefore know the number of nonzero values of each interval of h_0 and use this information to add parity equations to the system. Let b_i denote the number of nonzero values of the interval Z_i modulo 2. Then

$$b_i = (1, 1, ..., 1) \cdot Z_i^T. \tag{22}$$

There will be exactly β such equations. Let $b = (b_0, ..., b_{\beta-1})$ and W be the $\beta \times \alpha\beta$ matrix which for row i, $0 \le i < \beta$, has ones in positions j for $i \cdot \alpha \le j < (i+1) \cdot \alpha$ and zeros elsewhere. We can then extend our system of equations to include the parity equations by appending W to the bottom of Q' and appending b to h_1. The new extended $(r + \beta) \times \alpha\beta$ system of equations is shown in Fig. 7 below.

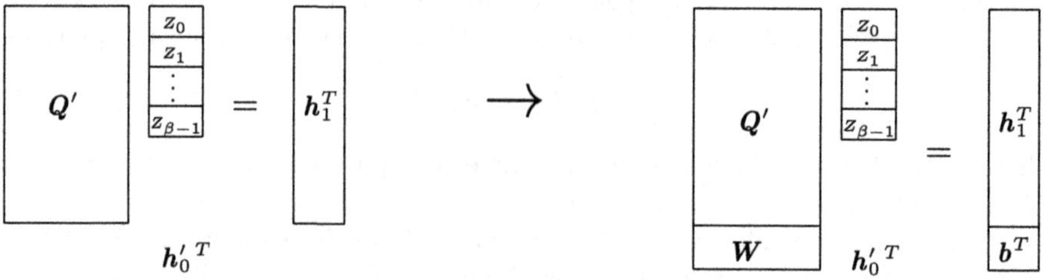

Fig. 7. Adding the parity equations

We don't know the vector h_1. However, it is generated to be an extremely sparse vector and the entries are zero with probability $1 - \frac{w}{2r} > 0.99$. Suppose we create a square $\alpha\beta \times \alpha\beta$ system of equations by randomly selecting $\beta(\alpha - 1)$ entries from $\boldsymbol{h}_1$, and keeping the corresponding rows of $\boldsymbol{Q}'$. We also retain all the parity information $\boldsymbol{W}$ and $\boldsymbol{b}$. Then the probability p that all the randomly selected entries from $\boldsymbol{h}_1$ are zero is

$$p = \frac{\text{number of } \boldsymbol{h}_1 \text{ for which guess is right}}{\text{total possible number of } \boldsymbol{h}_1} \tag{23}$$

$$= \frac{\binom{r-\beta(\alpha-1)}{\frac{w}{2}}}{\binom{r}{\frac{w}{2}}} = \frac{(r - \beta(\alpha - 1))!(r - \frac{w}{2})!}{r!(r - \beta(\alpha - 1) - \frac{w}{2})!} \tag{24}$$

The expected number of attempts before finding a subvector of $\boldsymbol{h}_1$ with all zeros entries is $\frac{1}{p}$. Table 2 gives an estimation of this, using the parameters proposed for QcBits and assuming the worst case of $\beta = \frac{w}{2}$.

Table 2. Approximate number of attempts in the worst case

$\alpha =$	8	16	32	64
80-bit	22	950	2^{23}	2^{58}
128-bit	40	3500	2^{26}	2^{64}

The last step in the attack proceeds as follows. We randomly select $\beta(\alpha - 1)$ entries of $\boldsymbol{h}_1$, and guess that they are all zero. We also extract the corresponding rows of $\boldsymbol{Q}'$ and denote the resulting matrix $\boldsymbol{Q}''$. We retain all the parity information $\boldsymbol{W}$ and $\boldsymbol{b}$ as well, giving us a square $\alpha\beta \times \alpha\beta$ system of equations. This process is shown in Fig. 8 below. Here the color gray represents the rows that we keep.

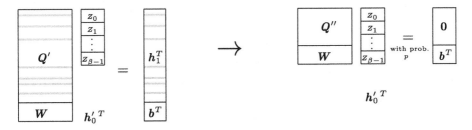

Fig. 8. Selecting random positions in $\boldsymbol{h}_1$ and corresponding rows of $\boldsymbol{Q}'$

Finally, we solve the system of equations

$$\begin{pmatrix} \boldsymbol{Q}'' \\ \boldsymbol{W} \end{pmatrix} \cdot {\boldsymbol{h}_0'}^T = \begin{pmatrix} \boldsymbol{0} \\ \boldsymbol{b}^T \end{pmatrix} \tag{25}$$

If all the selected entries of h_1 are actually zero, then the correct value of h_0' is among the solutions. We then look for a solution vector $h_0'^T$ with weight exactly $\frac{w}{2}$, and we also check that $Q \cdot h_0^T$ has weight exactly $\frac{w}{2}$. If this is the case, we have found h_0, and h_1 can be computed directly from it. If this is not the case, the selected entries of h_1 are not all zero and a suitable solution will not be found. We then keep repeating the final step with different random subvectors of h_1 until a solution is found.

4.2   Attack Complexity

To compute the attack's complexity, we include the cost of repeatedly solving $\alpha\beta \times \alpha\beta$ systems of binary linear equations. For our estimates, we assume the worst case, in which $\beta = \frac{w}{2}$. As for solving the system, Vassilevska Williams has an algorithm which can solve such a system with complexity $\left(\frac{w\alpha}{2}\right)^{2.373}$ [44]. Hence the average total complexity of the algebraic part of our attack is

$$\frac{1}{p} \cdot \left(\frac{w\alpha}{2}\right)^{2.373} \tag{26}$$

In our experiments, the DPA attack gave us $\alpha = 8$. Hence, the total average complexity of our key recovery attack is 2^{24} for the 80-bit security version, and 2^{27} for the 128-bit security version.

4.3   Experimental Results

We verified the algebraic part of our attack using SAGE on one core of a 2.9 GHz Core i5 MacBook Pro. We tested the attack for $\alpha \in \{8, 16, 32\}$. For $\alpha \in \{8, 16\}$ we had a 100% success rate with a bounded number of iterations. We successfully recovered the secret key in each test, with at most 10, 000 iterations. For $\alpha = 32$ with 80 bits of security, the expected time in the worst case of $\beta = \frac{w}{2}$ is around 16 h. For $\alpha = 32$ with 128 bits of security, and $\alpha = 64$, we estimated the expected times based on our experiments with the other α values.

The results are shown in Table 3, and the times shown exclude the preparation step of computing the initial matrix Q'. Since the main loop of the attack is based on guessing subsets of the equations until a guess is correct, it is completely parallelizable. Thus the results should scale inversely with the number of cores used to perform the attack.

Table 3. Approximate solving times in SAGE on one core

$\alpha =$	8	16	32	64
80 bits	0.4 s	15 s	16 h	≈530 years
128 bits	2 s	4 min	≈ 7 days	≈790,000 years

5   Attack Countermeasure

We propose a simple masking technique to help defend against side channel attacks during the syndrome calculation in QcBits. Since QC-MDPC codes are linear, the XOR of two codewords is another codeword. Also, all codewords are in the nullspace of the parity check matrix $\boldsymbol{H}_{priv}$. We can therefore mask the corrupted codeword $(\boldsymbol{c}|\boldsymbol{0})$ by XORing it with a random codeword $\boldsymbol{c}_m$ before passing it to the syndrome calculation. This does not change the outcome of the syndrome calculation since

$$\boldsymbol{H}_{priv} \cdot ((\boldsymbol{c}|\boldsymbol{0}) \oplus \boldsymbol{c}_m)^T = \boldsymbol{H}_{priv} \cdot (\boldsymbol{c}|\boldsymbol{0})^T \oplus \boldsymbol{H}_{priv} \cdot \boldsymbol{c}_m^T = \boldsymbol{H}_{priv} \cdot (\boldsymbol{c}|\boldsymbol{0})^T. \quad (27)$$

It does effectively mask the DPA leak we exploited, however. Figure 9 shows the difference of means for all possible guesses for x_i with this countermeasure implemented. In contrast to Fig. 3, there is no significant spike for any of the guesses.

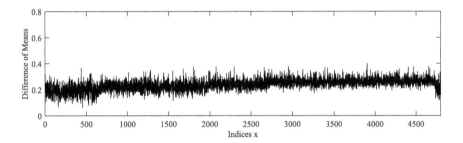

Fig. 9. Maximum Difference of Means (DoM) using 500 traces over all possible values x_i when the countermeasure is enabled. The right key index is 2000.

This countermeasure is of course only effective during the syndrome calculation. Additional side-channel countermeasures would be required to protect the private key during other calculations such as the bit flipping algorithm.

6   Conclusions

In this paper we described a key recovery attack against QcBits. We first performed power analysis to recover partial information about the key. We then used that information to set up and solve a system of noisy binary linear equations. Solving that system recovered the entire key. Finally, we proposed a simple countermeasure which was effective against the power analysis we performed in the attack.

QcBits has sparse, highly structured private keys. The sparseness is required for the decoding algorithm to work. The quasi-circulant nature of the keys is essential for small key sizes and efficient calculations. We exploited both these features in our attack. Another characteristic of QcBits and other code-based algorithms is that the Hamming weight of the noise added to codewords during encryption must be modest enough that the corrupted word can be decoded.

Many proposals for post-quantum cryptography are based on noisy linear systems: lattices, learning with errors or error-correcting codes. In terms of side-channel resilience, these systems have an important difference from systems based on number-theoretic problems. Leaking a few bits of a number-theoretic system may open up a new avenue of attack, but it usually doesn't directly contribute to solving the underlying hard problem. For noisy linear systems, leaking a few bits of the secret is likely to directly erode the difficulty of the underlying hard problem. Therefore designers and analysts may wish to consider the risks of side-channel analysis when evaluating post-quantum cryptographic algorithms.

References

1. Augot, D., Batina, L., Bernstein, D.J., Bos, J., Buchmann, J., Castryck, W., Dunkelman, O., Güneysu, T., Gueron, S., Hülsing, A. , Lange, T., Emam Mohamed, M.S., Rechberger, C., Schwabe, P., Sendrier, N., Vercauteren, F., Yang, B.-Y.: Initial recommendations of long-term secure post-quantum systems (2015). http://pqcrypto.eu.org/docs/initial-recommendations.pdf. 4, 5
2. Belaïd, S., Coron, J.-S., Fouque, P.-A., Gérard, B., Kammerer, J.-G., Prouff, E.: Improved side-channel analysis of finite-field multiplication. In: Güneysu, T., Handschuh, H. (eds.) CHES 2015. LNCS, vol. 9293, pp. 395–415. Springer, Heidelberg (2015). doi:10.1007/978-3-662-48324-4_20. 6
3. Belaïd, S., Fouque, P.-A., Gérard, B.: Side-channel analysis of multiplications in $GF(2^{128})$ - application to AES-GCM. In: Sarkar, P., Iwata, T. (eds.) ASIACRYPT 2014. LNCS, vol. 8874, pp. 306–325. Springer, Heidelberg (2014). doi:10.1007/978-3-662-45608-8_17. 6
4. Bellare, M., Desai, A., Pointcheval, D., Rogaway, P.: Relations among notions of security for public-key encryption schemes. In: Krawczyk, H. (ed.) CRYPTO 1998. LNCS, vol. 1462, pp. 26–45. Springer, Heidelberg (1998). doi:10.1007/BFb0055718. 5
5. Berlekamp, E.R., McEliece, R.J., van Tilborg, H.C.: On the inherent intractability of certain coding problems. IEEE Trans. Inf. Theory **24**(3), 384–386 (1978). 7
6. Bernstein, D.J.: The Poly1305-AES message-authentication code. In: Gilbert, H., Handschuh, H. (eds.) FSE 2005. LNCS, vol. 3557, pp. 32–49. Springer, Heidelberg (2005). doi:10.1007/11502760_3. 8
7. Bernstein, D.J., Buchmann, J., Dahmen, E. (eds.): Post-Quantum Cryptography. Springer, Heidelberg (2009). 4
8. Bernstein, D.J., Schwabe, P.: New AES software speed records. In: Chowdhury, D.R., Rijmen, V., Das, A. (eds.) INDOCRYPT 2008. LNCS, vol. 5365, pp. 322–336. Springer, Heidelberg (2008). doi:10.1007/978-3-540-89754-5_25. 8
9. Blum, A., Kalai, A., Wasserman, H.: Noise-tolerant learning, the parity problem, and the statistical query model. In: Frances Yao, F., Luks, E.M. (eds.) Proceedings of the Thirty-Second Annual ACM Symposium on Theory of Computing, Portland, OR, USA, 21–23 May 2000, pp. 435–440. ACM (2000). 6
10. Chaulet, J., Sendrier, N.: Worst case QC-MDPC decoder for McEliece cryptosystem. In: IEEE International Symposium on Information Theory, ISIT 2016, Barcelona, Spain, 10–15 July 2016, pp. 1366–1370. IEEE (2016). 5

11. Chen, C., Eisenbarth, T., Maurich, I., Steinwandt, R.: Differential power analysis of a McEliece cryptosystem. In: Malkin, T., Kolesnikov, V., Lewko, A.B., Polychronakis, M. (eds.) ACNS 2015. LNCS, vol. 9092, pp. 538–556. Springer, Cham (2015). doi:10.1007/978-3-319-28166-7_26. 5

12. Chen, L., Jordan, S., Liu, Y.-K., Moody, D., Peralta, R., Perlner, R., Smith-Tone, D.: Report on post-quantum cryptography. National Institute of Standards and Technology (NIST), NISTIR 8105 Draft, U.S. Department of Commerce, February 2016. 4

13. Chou, T.: QcBits: constant-time small-key code-based cryptography. In: Gierlichs, B., Poschmann, A.Y. (eds.) CHES 2016. LNCS, vol. 9813, pp. 280–300. Springer, Heidelberg (2016). doi:10.1007/978-3-662-53140-2_14. 4, 5, 6, 8

14. Couvreur, A., Corbella, I.M., Pellikaan, R.: A polynomial time attack against algebraic geometry code based public key cryptosystems. In: 2014 IEEE International Symposium on Information Theory, Honolulu, HI, USA, 29 June–4 July 2014, pp. 1446–1450. IEEE (2014). 4

15. Gallager, R.G.: Low-density parity-check codes. IRE Trans. Information Theory 8(1), 21–28 (1962). 7

16. Guo, Q., Johansson, T., Stankovski, P.: A key recovery attack on MDPC with CCA security using decoding errors. Cryptology ePrint Archive, Report 2016/858 (2016). http://eprint.iacr.org/2016/858. 5, 6

17. Heyse, S., Moradi, A., Paar, C.: Practical power analysis attacks on software implementations of McEliece. In: Sendrier, N. (ed.) PQCrypto 2010. LNCS, vol. 6061, pp. 108–125. Springer, Heidelberg (2010). doi:10.1007/978-3-642-12929-2_9. 5

18. Heyse, S., Maurich, I., Güneysu, T.: Smaller keys for code-based cryptography: QC-MDPC McEliece implementations on embedded devices. In: Bertoni, G., Coron, J.-S. (eds.) CHES 2013. LNCS, vol. 8086, pp. 273–292. Springer, Heidelberg (2013). doi:10.1007/978-3-642-40349-1_16. 4

19. Janwa, H., Moreno, O.: McEliece public key cryptosystems using algebraic-geometric codes. Des. Codes Crypt. 8(3), 293–307 (1996). 4

20. Kobara, K., Imai, H.: Semantically secure McEliece public-key cryptosystems - conversions for McEliece PKC. In: Kim, K. (ed.) PKC 2001. LNCS, vol. 1992, pp. 19–35. Springer, Heidelberg (2001). doi:10.1007/3-540-44586-2_2. 5

21. Kocher, P., Jaffe, J., Jun, B.: Differential power analysis. In: Wiener, M. (ed.) CRYPTO 1999. LNCS, vol. 1666, pp. 388–397. Springer, Heidelberg (1999). doi:10.1007/3-540-48405-1_25. 5

22. Landais, G., Tillich, J.-P.: An efficient attack of a McEliece cryptosystem variant based on convolutional codes. Cryptology ePrint Archive, Report 2013/080 (2013). http://eprint.iacr.org/2013/080. 4

23. Löndahl, C., Johansson, T.: A new version of McEliece PKC based on convolutional codes. In: Chim, T.W., Yuen, T.H. (eds.) ICICS 2012. LNCS, vol. 7618, pp. 461–470. Springer, Heidelberg (2012). doi:10.1007/978-3-642-34129-8_45. 4

24. McEliece, R.J.: A public-key system based on algebraic coding theory. DSN Progress Report 44, pp. 114–116 (1978). 4

25. Minder, L., Shokrollahi, A.: Cryptanalysis of the Sidelnikov cryptosystem. In: Naor, M. (ed.) EUROCRYPT 2007. LNCS, vol. 4515, pp. 347–360. Springer, Heidelberg (2007). doi:10.1007/978-3-540-72540-4_20. 4

26. Misoczki, R., Tillich, J.-P., Sendrier, N., Barreto, P.S.L.M.: MDPC-McEliece: new McEliece variants from moderate density parity-check codes. In: Proceedings of the 2013 IEEE International Symposium on Information Theory, Istanbul, Turkey, 7–12 July 2013, pp. 2069–2073. IEEE (2013). 4, 5, 7

27. Monico, C., Rosenthal, J., Shokrollahi, A.: Using low density parity check codes in the McEliece cryptosystem. In: IEEE International Symposium on Information Theory, ISIT 2000, p. 215 (2000). 4

28. Mosca, M.: Cybersecurity in an era with quantum computers: will we be ready? Cryptology ePrint Archive, Report 2015/1075 (2015). http://eprint.iacr.org/2015/1075. 4

29. Niederreiter, H.: Knapsack-type cryptosystems and algebraic coding theory. Probl. Control Inf. Theory **15**, 159–166 (1986). 4, 8

30. O'Flynn, C., Chen, Z.D.: ChipWhisperer: an open-source platform for hardware embedded security research. In: Prouff, E. (ed.) COSADE 2014. LNCS, vol. 8622, pp. 243–260. Springer, Cham (2014). doi:10.1007/978-3-319-10175-0_17. 11

31. Peeters, M., Van Assche, G., Bertoni, G., Daemen, J.: Keccak and the SHA-3 standardization (2013). http://csrc.nist.gov/groups/ST/hash/sha-3/documents/Keccak-slides-at-NIST.pdf. 8

32. Persichetti, E.: Secure and anonymous hybrid encryption from coding theory. In: Gaborit, P. (ed.) PQCrypto 2013. LNCS, vol. 7932, pp. 174–187. Springer, Heidelberg (2013). doi:10.1007/978-3-642-38616-9_12. 5

33. Schneier, B.: NSA plans for a post-quantum world (2015). https://www.schneier.com/blog/archives/2015/08/nsa_plans_for_a.html. 4

34. Sendrier, N.: On the concatenated structure of a linear code. Appl. Algebra Eng. Commun. Comput. **9**(3), 221–242 (1998). 4

35. Seurin, Y.: Primitives et protocoles cryptographiques à sécurité prouvée. Ph.D. thesis, Université de Versailles Saint-Quentin-en-Yvelines (2009). Sect. 3.5.7. 6

36. Shor, P.W.: Algorithms for quantum computation: discrete logarithms and factoring. In: Proceedings of the 35th FOCS, pp. 124–134. IEEE Computer Society Press, November 1994. 3

37. Shoufan, A., Strenzke, F., Molter, H.G., Stöttinger, M.: A timing attack against patterson algorithm in the McEliece PKC. In: Lee, D., Hong, S. (eds.) ICISC 2009. LNCS, vol. 5984, pp. 161–175. Springer, Heidelberg (2010). doi:10.1007/978-3-642-14423-3_12. 5

38. Sidelnikov, V.M.: A public-key cryptosystem based on binary Reed-Muller codes. Discret. Math. Appl. **4**(3), 191–208 (1994). 4

39. Sidelnikov, V.M., Shestakov, S.O.: On insecurity of cryptosystems based on generalized Reed-Solomon codes. Discret. Math. Appl. **2**(4), 439–444 (1992). 4

40. Strenzke, F.: A timing attack against the secret permutation in the McEliece PKC. In: Sendrier, N. (ed.) PQCrypto 2010. LNCS, vol. 6061, pp. 95–107. Springer, Heidelberg (2010). doi:10.1007/978-3-642-12929-2_8. 5

41. Strenzke, F., Tews, E., Molter, H.G., Overbeck, R., Shoufan, A.: Side channels in the McEliece PKC. In: Buchmann, J., Ding, J. (eds.) PQCrypto 2008. LNCS, vol. 5299, pp. 216–229. Springer, Heidelberg (2008). doi:10.1007/978-3-540-88403-3_15. 5

42. von Maurich, I., Güneysu, T.: Lightweight code-based cryptography: QC-MDPC McEliece encryption on reconfigurable devices. In: Fettweis, G., Nebel, W. (eds.) Design, Automation & Test in Europe Conference & Exhibition, DATE 2014, Dresden, Germany, 24–28 March 2014, pp.1–6. European Design and Automation Association (2014). 4

43. Maurich, I., Heberle, L., Güneysu, T.: IND-CCA secure hybrid encryption from QC-MDPC Niederreiter. In: Takagi, T. (ed.) PQCrypto 2016. LNCS, vol. 9606, pp. 1–17. Springer, Cham (2016). doi:10.1007/978-3-319-29360-8_1. 5

44. Williams, V.V.: Multiplying matrices faster than Coppersmith-Winograd. In: Karloff, H.J., Pitassi, T. (eds.) Proceedings of the 44th Symposium on Theory of Computing Conference, STOC 2012, New York, NY, USA, 19–22 May 2012, pp. 887–898. ACM (2012). 18

Improved Blind Side-Channel Analysis by Exploitation of Joint Distributions of Leakages

Christophe Clavier$^{(\boxtimes)}$ and Léo Reynaud

Université de Limoges, XLIM-CNRS, Limoges, France
christophe.clavier@unilim.fr, leo.reynaud@xlim.fr

Abstract. Classical side-channel analysis include statistical attacks which require the knowledge of either the plaintext or the ciphertext to predict some internal value to be correlated to the observed leakages.

In this paper we revisit a blind (i.e. leakage-only) attack from Linge et al. that exploits joint distributions of leakages. We show – both by simulations and concrete experiments on a real device – that the maximum likelihood (ML) approach is more efficient than Linge's distance-based comparison of distributions, and demonstrate that this method can be easily adapted to deal with implementations protected by first-order Boolean masking. We give example applications of different variants of this approach, and propose countermeasures that could prevent them.

Interestingly, we also observe that, when the inputs are known, the ML criterion is more efficient than correlation power analysis.

Keywords: Unknown plaintext · Joint distributions · Maximum likelihood

1 Introduction

Cryptographic implementations of embedded products like smartcards are known to be vulnerable to statistical side-channel analysis such as Differential Power Analysis [12], Correlation Power Analysis [1] or Mutual Information Analysis [7]. These side-channel analyses are divide-and-conquer attacks where the whole key is recovered by chunks of few bits (e.g. one byte) at a time. This is possible because the device produces a measurable leakage like power consumption or electromagnetic emanation which depends at any instant on the internal value manipulated by the processor. When this value only depends on a public information – like the plaintext or the ciphertext – and a small piece of the key, a so-called subkey, it is possible to validate or invalidate an hypothesis about the subkey by correlating the leakage with a prediction of the internal value.

While these statistical analyses all require the knowledge of the input or the output to be correlated with, there are some use cases or protocols where this information is either not available or not exploitable. This is the case for the derivation of the session key that is used to compute application cryptograms

© International Association for Cryptologic Research 2017
W. Fischer and N. Homma (Eds.): CHES 2017, LNCS 10529, pp. 24–44, 2017.
DOI: 10.1007/978-3-319-66787-4_2

in the EMV payment scheme [4, p. 128] (see also left of Fig. 8). In this case the attacker does not know the output (session key) and the input only varies on its first two bytes, so that he can expect to recover only the two corresponding bytes of the master key.

To deal with situations where neither the plaintext nor the ciphertext are available, Linge et al. introduced the concept of joint distribution analysis [16]. In the case of the AES cipher, the idea is to exploit the fact that the joint distribution of the Hamming weight of a byte m and that of $y = S(m \oplus k)$ depends on k so that this key byte value can be retrieved (at any round) by comparing the distance between the observed experimental distribution of $(HW(m), HW(y))$ and all 2^8 theoretical ones. Linge et al. also proposed a so-called *slice* method to convert leakages to Hamming weights. While Le Bouder [14] presented an alternative approach – based on the maximum likelihood (ML) criterion – to Linge's distance-based comparison of distributions, she did not provide any comparison between both methods. In this paper we build upon [14,16] and provide the following contributions: (i) we propose a novel way to estimate Hamming weights based on variance analysis, (ii) we compare the ML and distance-based methods using both the slice and the variance analysis ways of obtaining Hamming weights, (iii) we present new variants that improve the attack by exploiting other and/or more points of interest, (iv) we adapt the blind joint distribution analysis to implementations featuring Boolean masking countermeasure. Our work is supported by experimental results based both on simulations and on real traces.

Another related work by Hanley et al. [11] presents a template-based attack by joint distribution analysis in the blind context. This work differs from our's as it requires a profiling phase on a similar device with known key where the unknown input assumption does not hold. Also, and contrarily to our work, the adaptation of their attack to masked implementations is only applicable on the first round. In the context of blind fault analysis, Korkikian et al. [13] and Li et al. [15] also exploit the joint distribution of $(HW(m), HW(y))$ with the distance-based and ML methods respectively.

This paper is organized as follows. In Sect. 2 we introduce the notations used in the paper and present the original joint distribution analysis from Linge et al. In Sect. 3 we describe the ML criterion and compare it to Linge's distance-based method. Section 4 considers how the different variants of our attacks can be adapted to implementations protected by first-order Boolean masking. We then depart from the unknown plaintext scenario in Sect. 5 to further assess the efficiency of the ML criterion and compare it with classical CPA. Concrete experiments on side-channel traces captured from a real device are presented in Sect. 6 and their results compared to simulation figures. We then provide several application examples of our attacks in Sect. 7 and discuss which kind of countermeasures could prevent them. Section 8 finally concludes this work.

2   Background and Original Linge's Attack

The attacks presented in this paper assume a software implementation of a block cipher, and without loss of generality we will consider the AES [18].

For these attacks one needs to measure the leakages corresponding to some specific internal byte states. We thus assume that the attacker is able to locate precisely the points of interest related to these variables. This means that an attacker facing an implementation hardened by random delays or other types of time randomization must have been able to preprocess the traces and remove the effect of these desynchronizations. When the traces are aligned, identifying the points of interest may not be an easy task. Since the attacker does not know the plaintext, the statistical T-test or other tests that partition the trace set based on a plaintext dependent value [3,8,9,17] can not be used. Although, it is still possible to identify instants where the device shows a high activity from the peaks on the trace of standard deviations such as depicted in Fig. 2. Such traces do not provide any clue by themselves about which kind of internal data leaks, but this information may be guessed based on reasonable assumptions about the implementation.

2.1 Notations

We are mainly concerned with three kinds of internal AES states that we generically call m, x and y, and respectively correspond to:

m : the input byte of the XOR operation with the key byte k during the AddRoundKey function,

x : the result of the XOR operation with the key byte $(x = m \oplus k)$, which is the input of the S-Box during the subsequent SubBytes function,

y : the output of the S-Box $(y = S(x) = S(m \oplus k))$ during the SubBytes function.

Note that, except if explicitly stated, we do not assume any particular byte number or any particular round number for m, x and y.

2.2 The Original Attack

The joint distribution analysis proposed by Linge et al. [16] considers the case of two state bytes m and y which are seen as random variables. Assuming uniformly distributed plaintexts, the probability distributions of both m and y – considered separately – are uniform and independent on the key. Though, this is totally different for the joint distribution of the couple (m, y). Indeed this joint distribution actually depends on k. The core idea of Linge's attack is that if the joint distribution of (m, y) depends on the key then it should be also true for the joint distribution of their Hamming weights $(\mathrm{HW}(m), \mathrm{HW}(y))$. We can thus consider 2^8 theoretical distributions of $(\mathrm{HW}(m), \mathrm{HW}(y))$, one per value of k, that we call models and which we denote by $\mathcal{M}_k$. As an illustrative example, Fig. 1 shows models $\mathcal{M}_{39}$ and $\mathcal{M}_{167}$ which clearly appear to be different.

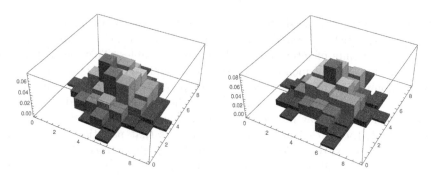

Fig. 1. Joint distributions of $(HW(m), HW(y))$ for $k = 39$ (left) and for $k = 167$ (right)

Since we assume the Hamming weight leakage model, an attacker able to infer the Hamming weights of m and y from two corresponding series of leakages ℓ_m and ℓ_y can generate an empirical distribution of $(HW(m), HW(y))$ issued from the device. We denote this distribution by $\mathcal{D}$. As this empirical distribution should converge to the model corresponding to the key used in the device, one can compare $\mathcal{D}$ with each model $\mathcal{M}_k$ and select the one that achieves the best match. To sum up, Linge's attack comprises three steps:

Computing the models. One computes the theoretical distribution $\mathcal{M}_k$ for each key candidate. This is simply a matter of considering all possible inputs m, derive the value $y = S(m \oplus k)$, counting how many times each couple $(HW(m), HW(y))$ appears, and normalizing in order to obtain the probability distribution. These models are independent from the device and can thus be computed beforehand.

Obtaining the empirical distribution $\mathcal{D}$. Given a large set of traces corresponding to encryptions with random inputs, one measures the leakages ℓ_m and ℓ_y at the two previously identified points of interest. These couples of leakages must be converted to couples of Hamming weights in $\{0, \ldots, 8\} \times \{0, \ldots, 8\}$ in order to comply with the domain of the models. Finally, counting the number of occurrences of each observed Hamming weight couple, and normalizing by the total number of observations, allows to generate the empirical distribution $\mathcal{D}$.

Comparing $\mathcal{D}$ with the models. Linge et al. proposed to compare the empirical distribution to the theoretical ones based on some distance. The closest model $\mathcal{M}_k$ to $\mathcal{D}$ provides the best candidate for the secret. They studied a large panel of 65 distances and selected four of them for giving better results in the presence of errors in estimating the Hamming weights.

A tricky task in this attack is the conversion from leakages to Hamming weights. Linge et al. proposed a simple method that assigns Hamming weights by "slices" of the sorted list of leakages in accordance to their relative probabilities. Given a set of leakages measured at a given point of interest, if we consider them sorted in ascending order, it is reasonable to think that the smallest ones would correspond to a Hamming weight $h = 0$ and the largest ones to $h = 8$. How many leakages should correspond to each Hamming weight slice may be estimated by the theoretical proportion of each of them: given the leakages of n random values, one assigns $h = 0$ to the $\frac{n}{256}\binom{8}{0}$ smallest ones, $h = 1$ to the $\frac{n}{256}\binom{8}{1}$ immediately larger ones, and so on, up to $h = 8$ to the $\frac{n}{256}\binom{8}{8}$ largest leakages.

3   Improved Joint Distribution Analysis

The attack presented in Sect. 2.2 does not require the knowledge of neither the plaintext nor the ciphertext. This remarkable property results from the fact that the analysis is *local*: the information used to "correlate" with the S-Box output y is self-contained in the trace since it comes from the leakage of m instead of from its value. The important benefit from this is that the attack applies at any arbitrary round, and not solely on the first or last one. On the other side, instead of using the exact value of the input – as in classical attacks – this information is replaced by a noisy estimation of its Hamming weight. This makes this attack less efficient than classical ones (in term of number of traces) and motivates the need to exploit the available information as efficiently as possible.

In this section we recall an improved method to exploit the joint distribution of leakages at points m-y which is based on the maximum likelihood criterion [14]. The idea is to compute for each key hypothesis the probability of this key given the observed leakages. The attacker then selects the most probable one. In this approach the noisy leakage must be converted to a noisy Hamming weight which does not require to be an integer value since the noise is modeled as being distributed according to a centered Gaussian law with variance σ^2. Section 3.2 discusses several ways to convert the original leakages to real-valued Hamming weights.

3.1   Maximum Likelihood Criterion

We consider a noisy measurement (h_m, h_y) of a couple of Hamming weights (h_m^*, h_y^*) corresponding to the values manipulated at points of interest related to m and y. That means $h_m^* = \mathrm{HW}(m)$ and $h_y^* = \mathrm{HW}(y) = \mathrm{HW}(S(m \oplus k))$. We have $h_m = h_m^* + \omega_m$ and $h_y = h_y^* + \omega_y$ where ω_m and ω_y are two independent and centered Gaussian noises with standard deviations σ_m and σ_y respectively[1]. The probability of the key given a single observation of Hamming weights can be derived from Bayes formula as:

$$\Pr(k|(h_m, h_y)) = \frac{\Pr((h_m, h_y)|k) \cdot \Pr(k)}{\Pr((h_m, h_y))}$$

---

[1] The assumption that the distribution of the noise is Gaussian is not restrictive. If it is not, one uses the same equations given in this section, except that Eq. (3) must be consequently adapted to the actual (or supposed) distribution of the noise.

Note that in this equation the denominator $\Pr((h_m, h_y))$ is a normalization term that does not depend on the key. We can simply ignore it since we are just interested in comparing the probabilities to each other instead of actually computing their values[2]. We so have

$$\Pr(k|(h_m, h_y)) \propto \Pr((h_m, h_y)|k) \cdot \Pr(k)$$

where the term $\Pr(k)$ corresponds to the uniform distribution in the case of a first observation of (h_m, h_y) and more generally to the posterior distribution computed based upon the already exploited Hamming weights couples. The probability of the key given a set of observations $((h_m, h_y)_i)_{i=1\ldots n}$ can then be derived in the following iterative way:

$$\Pr(k|((h_m, h_y)_i)_{i=1\ldots n} \leftarrow \Pr((h_m, h_y)_n|k) \cdot \Pr(k|((h_m, h_y)_i)_{i=1\ldots n-1} \qquad (1)$$

Considering that the observed Hamming weights can be issued from any possible actual ones, the multiplicative term $\Pr((h_m, h_y)|k)$ can be computed thanks to the law of total probabilities as:

$$\Pr((h_m, h_y)|k) = \sum_{h_m^*, h_y^*} \Pr((h_m, h_y)|(h_m^*, h_y^*)) \cdot \Pr((h_m^*, h_y^*)|k) \qquad (2)$$

The second term of the product comes from the same precomputed models as exploited in the original method, while the first term is simply the probability of the noise that accounts for the observation:

$$\Pr((h_m, h_y)|(h_m^*, h_y^*)) = \Pr(\omega_m = h_m - h_m^*) \cdot \Pr(\omega_y = h_y - h_y^*)$$

$$= \left(\frac{1}{\sigma_m \sqrt{2\pi}} e^{-\frac{1}{2}\left(\frac{h_m - h_m^*}{\sigma_m}\right)^2} \right) \cdot \left(\frac{1}{\sigma_y \sqrt{2\pi}} e^{-\frac{1}{2}\left(\frac{h_y - h_y^*}{\sigma_y}\right)^2} \right) \qquad (3)$$

Equations (1) to (3) allow to compute the probability distribution of the key given the observed Hamming weights. This exploits the full information that can be derived from the measurements. Based on this distribution, the attacker simply selects the key with highest probability.

3.2 Estimating the Hamming Weights

Section 2.2 describes Linge's "slice" method for converting leakages to Hamming weights. While clever and quite simple to apply, its main drawback is that it estimates Hamming weights as integers, so that the process may arbitrarily assign two different Hamming weights to two quite near (possibly even equal) leakages. While such integer values can be used in Eqs. (1) to (3), we see this threshold effect as undesirable since the maximum likelihood method can take advantage of a more smooth estimation without such rounding inaccuracies. We now propose two methods for converting real-valued leakages to real-valued Hamming weights.

---

[2] For sake of simplicity, we continue to use the notation $\Pr(\cdot)$ in the next equations while this actually denotes a term which is proportional to the actual probability.

Linear Regression. According to the linear model $\ell = \alpha\,\mathrm{HW}(v) + \beta$, it is possible to estimate the Hamming weight from the leakage ℓ as soon as we know – or have estimated – the values of the constant coefficients α and β. Linear regression infers from two series $(\ell_i)_i$ and $(\mathrm{HW}(v_i))_i$ of leakages and corresponding Hamming weights the coefficients α and β of the linear relationship that best fits the set of points. Unfortunately this requires the knowledge of the byte values v_i corresponding to each leakage l_i. This means that this method preferably applies during a characterization phase on a known-key device, the inferred coefficient values being subsequently used for the attack on a similar target device with an unknown key.

Variance Analysis. As for linear regression, our second method for converting leakages to Hamming weights also estimates α and β. However, as far as we know this is the first proposed method that can estimate these coefficients without the knowledge of the key or the plaintexts/ciphertexts. It does not need them because it is not required to know which v_i corresponds to which ℓ_i.

From a large set of execution traces with varying inputs it is possible to compute the variance (or the standard deviation) of the leakage at each instant. Usually, this variance trace clearly shows two kinds of time samples. Those for which the variance is low, which correspond to a low activity of the device, or at least to a constant activity independent from the algorithm input. At these instants we consider that the variance level reflects the variance of the measurement noise on the leakage. On the other hand when the activity is related to a data that depends on the algorithm input, then the variance is quite larger as it also includes that of the manipulated data. This is illustrated in Fig. 2 where three groups of 16 peaks correspond to the standard deviation when m, x and y bytes are manipulated, while the initial portion up to time sample 30 000 corresponds to a low activity process.

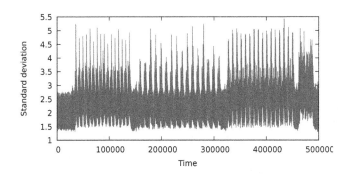

Fig. 2. Standard deviation trace computed on 1000 executions

From the measurement of the variance levels both on a quiet part and at the point of interest for the attack, one can derive the coefficient α of the leakage model. The noisy leakage expresses as: $\ell = \alpha \, \mathrm{HW}(v) + \beta + \omega$. Due to the independence of the noise from the data, we have:

$$\mathrm{Var}(\ell) = \mathrm{Var}(\alpha \, \mathrm{HW}(v) + \beta) + \mathrm{Var}(\omega) = \alpha^2 \, \mathrm{Var}(\mathrm{HW}(v)) + \mathrm{Var}(\omega) \qquad (4)$$

As v is a random byte value the variance of its Hamming weight is equal to 8 times the variance of a uniformly distributed bit, that is $\mathrm{Var}(\mathrm{HW}(v)) = 8 \times \frac{1}{4} = 2$. We can now derive α from Eq. (4):

$$\alpha = \pm\sqrt{((\mathrm{Var}(\ell) - \mathrm{Var}(\omega))/2} \qquad (5)$$

Once α is known, the value of β can be inferred from the model as $\beta = \mathrm{E}(\ell) - \alpha \, \mathrm{E}(\mathrm{HW}(v)) = \mathrm{E}(\ell) - 4\alpha$, where $\mathrm{E}(\ell)$ is estimated by the average leakage at the considered point of interest. Finally, from α and β, a leakage ℓ can be converted to the estimated Hamming weight $h = \frac{(\ell - \beta)}{\alpha}$.

3.3   Experimental Results

In this section we provide experimental results that compare the original distance-based method with that based on the ML criterion. We performed simulations where m is generated at random uniformly and $y = S(m \oplus k)$ is derived from m and from the key byte to be recovered (k is drawn at random for each run). We generated our observations by adding two independent Gaussian noises with same variance to $\mathrm{HW}(m)$ and $\mathrm{HW}(y)$.

Based on the sets of real-valued Hamming weights $(h_m)_i$ and $(h_y)_i$, we computed integer versions of them suitable for applying the distance method. To that end we applied Linge's slice method to the real-valued Hamming weights in a same manner as if they were original leakages. Note that applying the slice method to the real-valued Hamming weights is strictly equivalent to applying it to the leakages from which they are supposed to be linearly derived.

The left part of Fig. 3 presents the results in terms of the average rank of the correct key based on 10 000 runs with a medium noise level of $\sigma = 1.0$. Drawings in plain line style refer to the "slice" way to derive integer Hamming weights from real-valued ones. Blue, green and gray lines refer to the Inner Product, to the Pearson χ^2 and to the Euclidean distances respectively. Red lines refer to the ML criterion for which we also show in dotted line style the results when using directly the real-valued Hamming weights. In the case of the ML we used the same noise level $\sigma = 1.0$ for the attack phase as we used to generate the observations.

We can clearly see that IP and Euclidean distances do not give good results whereas the Pearson χ^2 based distance gives better ones. Also, ML strongly outperforms all distance-based methods, particularly when used with original real values. For the maximum likelihood the average rank is about 5 with 1000 observations, and below 2 with only 2000 observations.

These simulation results demonstrate that the maximum likelihood approach is superior to the distance based one in two respects: (i) it is intrinsically better when compared with the same observations (integer Hamming weights generated by the slice process) and further, (ii) it can take great advantage of real-valued Hamming weight estimations that can be directly inferred from the measured leakage.

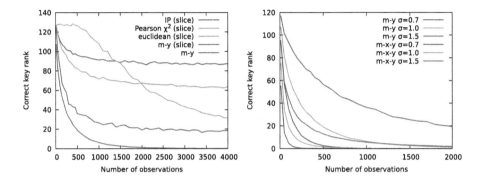

Fig. 3. Left: comparison of original distance method and m-y maximum likelihood ($\sigma = 1.0$). Right: comparison of m-y and m-x-y variants for different levels of noise. (Color figure online)

Variants with More Points of Interest. While the joint Hamming weights distribution analysis has been presented in Sect. 3.1 with two observed leakages (namely m and y), it is possible to use more of them if available. For example we can use the joint leakage from the three points of interest of m, $x = m \oplus k$ and $y = S(m \oplus k)$. Such so-called m-x-y attack is a straightforward generalization of the m-y attack where the theoretical models contain values of $\Pr((h_m^*, h_x^*, h_y^*)|k)$ instead of $\Pr((h_m^*, h_y^*)|k)$, where the summation of Eq. (2) is over all triplets $(h_m^*, h_x^*, h_y^*)^3$, and where the conditional probability of the observation in Eq. (3) includes an extra term corresponding to $\Pr(\omega_x = h_x - h_x^*)$.

The right part of Fig. 3 compares both m-y (plain lines) and m-x-y (dotted lines) variants of the maximum likelihood attack with three noise levels $\sigma=0.7$ (blue), $\sigma=1.0$ (green) and $\sigma=1.5$ (red). Notice that for a same noise level the m-x-y attack is quite more efficient than the m-y one. This is because the observation of h_x brings extra information that helps to further discriminate candidate keys. We also observe that the effect of the noise is important as it requires about five times more observations to get the same reliability on the key for $\sigma=1.5$ than for $\sigma=1.0$.

It is also possible to use other points of interest. For example, the y value is subsequently used in the MixColumns operation. Thus, depending on the implementation, there may exist instants where $2y$ and $3y$ are also manipulated. We have studied variants of the attack where these variables are included in the analysis. This results in attacks of types m-y-$2y$, m-y-$3y$, m-y-$2y$-$3y$ and the

---

[3] While this can be viewed as a multiplication by 9 of the terms in the summation, it is worth to note that $\Pr((h_m^*, h_x^*, h_y^*)|k)$ is non null for at most 256 triplets.

same ones with x also. The simulation results show that adding more variables to the analysis always gives better results, but this gain is smaller for $3y$ than for x, and even smaller for $2y$ [4].

Variant m-x. We now present a particular variant of the joint distribution analysis which involves only the leakages of m and x. This variant is special in the sense that if one computes the theoretical models for all possible k then one observes that they form classes of indistinguishable models, with each class being specific to the Hamming weight of k. That means that the distribution of $(\mathrm{HW}(m), \mathrm{HW}(m \oplus k))$ only depends on $\mathrm{HW}(k)$. This property is not so surprising, and comes from the fact that the XOR operation acts on bits independently from each other and that the Hamming weight function is invariant by any permutation of the bits.

There are two practical consequences of this property. First, the amount of information that can be retrieved from a m-x joint distribution analysis is less than for the m-y variant (about 2.5 bits instead of 8 bits on average). The second consequence is that the m-x attack retrieves $h_k = \mathrm{HW}(k)$ more efficiently than the m-y attack retrieves k. This is due not only to the fact that there are only 9 models to distinguish from, but also to the fact the those models are more different from each other.

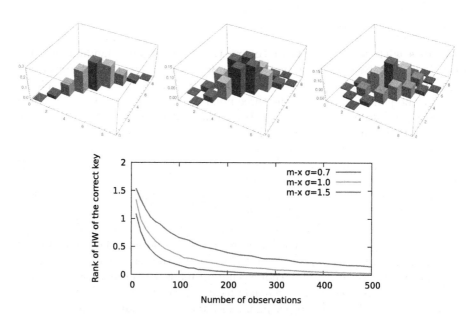

Fig. 4. Top: joint distributions of $(\mathrm{HW}(m), \mathrm{HW}(x))$ for $\mathrm{HW}(k)$ equal to 0, 1 and 2. Bottom: simulation results of the m-x variant for different noise levels.

---

[4] This last observation can be explained by the fact that information brought by y and $2y$ are somewhat redundant. Indeed their Hamming weights are quite correlated since they are equal for all $y < 128$ values for which $2y$ is equal to $y \ll 1$.

As an illustrative example, the top of Fig. 4 shows the models $\mathcal{M}_{h_k}$ for values 0, 1 and 2 of h_k. One can observe that these distributions show a characteristic pattern made of respectively 1, 2 and 3 parallel and linear structures like "walls".

Simulation results for the m-x variant are presented on the bottom of Fig. 4. The correct Hamming weight of the key is "first ranked" (arbitrarily, say a mean rank less than 0.2) with less than 100, 200 and 500 traces for noise levels σ equal to 0.7, 1.0 and 1.5 respectively.

4   Implementations Protected by Boolean Masking

Both Linge's and the maximum likelihood methods presented in Sect. 3 require a non protected implementation. Notably, they can not recover the key in the presence of the Boolean masking countermeasure [10,19]. This defense technique prevents from classical statistical attacks by XOR-masking all intermediate state bytes of the ciphering path with a random mask byte which is refreshed at every execution. To do so, it is necessary to generate a modified S-Box S' designed to produce a masked version $y' = y \oplus r_{out}$ of the normal output $y = S(x)$ when it receives a masked input $x' = x \oplus r_{in}$. The modified S-Box is thus defined as $y' = S'(x') = S(x' \oplus r_{in}) \oplus r_{out}$. From the measured leakages $\ell_{m'}$ and $\ell_{y'}$ the attacker infers a masked couple $(\mathrm{HW}(m'), \mathrm{HW}(y'))$ which is differently distributed than the couple $(\mathrm{HW}(m), \mathrm{HW}(y))$ based on which the models are defined.

4.1   Variants m-y and m-x-y

Figure 5 presents different options for implementing the Boolean masking countermeasure. We focus here on the area involving the XOR with the key and the S-Box. These schemes differ according to whether the key itself is masked or not, and whether the input and output masks of the S-Box are the same or not.

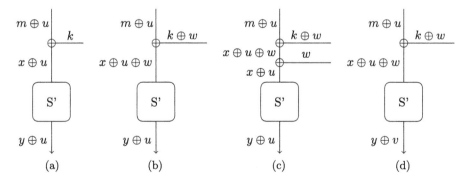

Fig. 5. Examples of Boolean masking schemes

When an attacker performs the first-order joint distribution analysis on an implementation protected by first-order Boolean masking, he generates an empirical distribution of masked couples $(\mathrm{HW}(m'), \mathrm{HW}(y'))$ and "compares"[5] it to a distribution of non masked couples $(\mathrm{HW}(m), \mathrm{HW}(y))$. The consequence is that the empirical distribution will not match the models even for the correct key.

In the case where m and y are masked by the same value (schemes a, b and c of Fig. 5), it is possible to recover the consistency between both empirical and theoretical distributions if we define the models as being distributed according to the distribution of masked couples with an uniformly distributed m and an uniformly distributed mask u.

Thus, it is possible to adapt the joint distribution attack to such masked implementations and the only modification consists in creating the models in a way that fits with the distribution of the couples of masked Hamming weights. Precisely, there still exists 256 models $\mathcal{M}_k$, one per key byte, and each model contains the conditional probabilities $\Pr((\mathrm{HW}(m'), \mathrm{HW}(y'))|k)$. But in this case, these probabilities are computed by counting the number of occurrences of each couple of Hamming weights when both m and the mask u range over all byte values. These models still mutually differ but they are much more similar to each other than for the non-masked case. This is illustrated on the top of Fig. 6 which presents the models for the same example keys than those presented in Fig. 1. We verified that all 256 models are different from each other.

The greater similarity between theoretical distributions in the masked case induces a much larger number of observations that are needed to distinguish between them. This is due to the fact that one must wait longer before the empirical distribution converges toward its model.

Notice that a m-x-y variant of such second-order joint distribution analysis is also possible provided that all three intermediate state bytes are masked by the same value. This is notably the case for schemes a and c of Fig. 5. We present experimental results for both m-y and m-x-y variants of the second-order joint distribution analysis (with ML criterion) on the bottom of Fig. 6. These simulation results were obtained by averaging the rank of the correct key over 1000 runs with a noise level equal to $\sigma=1.0$.

Here also the m-x-y variant is more efficient than the m-y one. We also observe that the number of traces needed to recover the key is much more than for the first-order attack. Nevertheless, this demonstrates that joint distribution analysis also works on masked implementations provided that relevant variables are masked by the same value.

4.2 Variant m-x

We have seen in Sect. 3.3 that the m-x variant is particular in the sense that it allows to recover the Hamming weight of k instead of k itself. Another remarkable and important property of this variant is that it is exactly as efficient when applied to masked values $m' = m \oplus u$ and $x' = x \oplus u$ as it is when applied

---

[5] This comparison is either explicit (Linge's distances) or implicit (ML).

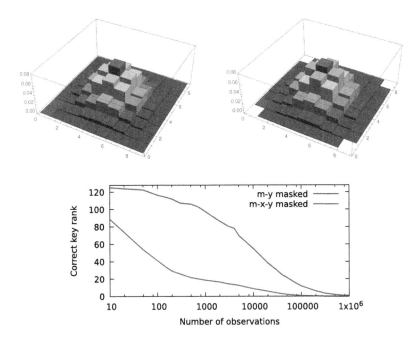

Fig. 6. Top: joint distributions of $(\mathrm{HW}(m'), \mathrm{HW}(y'))$ for $k = 39$ (left) and $k = 167$ (right). Bottom: comparison of second-order m-x and m-x-y variants ($\sigma = 1.0$)

directly to m and x. This means that masking is totally useless with respect to this attack. The reason is that both joint distributions of $(\mathrm{HW}(m), \mathrm{HW}(x))$ and $(\mathrm{HW}(m'), \mathrm{HW}(x'))$ are the same. This is because both series of (m, x) and (m', x') are the same in a permuted order, so are equal the series of their Hamming weights.

We stress on the importance of this special behavior: even an implementation protected by Boolean masking is vulnerable to the m-x variant which can recover the Hamming weight of the key byte with about only few hundreds traces. Again, this is only true if m and x are masked by the same value, which is the case of schemes a and c of Fig. 5.

5   Joint Distribution Analysis with Knowledge of the Plaintext

As stated by Eq. (2), the joint distribution analysis with ML criterion uses the conditional distributions $\Pr((h_m^*, h_y^*)|k)$ of the Hamming weights given the key. These models are built in a precomputation phase by counting, for the given key, the number of occurrences of each Hamming weight couple (or triplet for a m-x-y attack) for all possible values of m, and possibly all values of the mask u in the case of a masked implementation.

In this section we study how to adapt this attack to the classical case where the plaintext is known from the attacker. Of course, contrarily to the blind context, the attack is now feasible only on the first round.

5.1   First-Order Attack

When m is known it is no more useful to include h_m in the observation, and we work with the probability distribution of h_y^* (or of (h_x^*, h_y^*) for a m-x-y attack) for given values of k and m. Note that in this case the distribution is degenerated as a unique h_y^* value (or a unique (h_x^*, h_y^*) couple) resulting from k and m. Though, the computation of the probability distribution of k given the observations remains feasible in a similar way by summing over only h_y^* (or (h_x^*, h_y^*)) in Eq. (2).

We have simulated the m-y attack on 1000 runs and compared it with the classical CPA. Results are presented on the left part of Fig. 7 for σ noise levels of 1.0, 3.0 and 5.0 respectively. We note that retrieving the key by the ML method is slightly more efficient than by CPA. On the other hand, CPA does not require the determination of the point of interest.

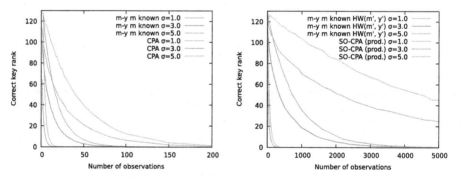

Fig. 7. Left: comparison of m-y attack (with m known) to CPA. Right: comparison of 2nd-order m-y attack (with m known) to 2nd-order CPA. Variant with points of interest $m' = m \oplus u$ and $y' = y \oplus u$.

5.2   Second-Order Attack

In the case of a masked implementation, a first option is also to straightforwardly adapt the attack to the knowledge of m. The attack takes m' and y' as points of interest. For each couple (k, m) we precompute a corresponding model that gives the distribution of $(h_{m'}^*, h_{y'}^*)$ when only the mask u varies.

As an alternative method, one can substitute the observation of m' by that of the random value that masks y. The two points of interest are then u and $y' = y \oplus u$, and the models correspond to the distribution of $(h_u^*, h_{y'}^*)$. A great advantage of this variant is that it applies even when two independent masks are added to m and y. On the other hand, it requires to identify the point of interest of the mask, which may be difficult.

We have simulated both variants on 1000 runs. In each case we compare the ML method with the 2nd-order CPA where the combination of the leakages (centered product[6]) is correlated with $\text{HW}(m \oplus y)$ in the first case, and with $\text{HW}(y)$ in the second case. Both variants give almost the same results, which is not surprising as when m is known, the information brought by $m' = m \oplus u$ and by u are essentially the same. The right part of Fig. 7 presents the results for the variant which exploits m' and y'. Note that the ML method finds the key somewhat earlier than 2nd-order CPA.

6 Concrete Experiments

In this section we present concrete experiments on side-channel traces captured from a real device. We have implemented two versions of a software AES on an Arduino Uno 8-bit microcontroller. The first version does not feature any countermeasure while the other one implements Boolean masking with the same mask on m, x and y.

We present two attacks: a m-y attack with unknown plaintext on the naive implementation, and a m-y attack with known plaintext on the masked implementation (variant with points of interest on m' and y').

Traces were acquired on a Lecroy WaveRunner oscilloscope with a sampling rate of 5 GS/s. The 1000 traces for the first attack and the 200 traces for the second one were perfectly aligned and the points of interest were blindly determined based on the highest peaks of the standard deviation trace. Figure 2 shows the computed trace that was used for the first attack. It clearly shows three groups of 16 peaks. The points of interest corresponding to m and y bytes were easily identified by assuming that the three groups correspond to manipulations of m, x and y respectively. For the second attack the points of interest for m' and y' where identified similarly based on a standard deviation trace that exhibits four groups of peaks corresponding to successive manipulations of m, m', x' and y'.

We used the variance analysis method of Sect. 3.2 to derive α and β coefficients at each point of interest. Based on the first part of the standard deviation trace of Fig. 2, we have estimated the standard deviation (in leakage unit[7]) of the noise by visual inspection, and we choose the value 2.0 which approximately lies in the middle of the vertical range. This procedure resulted in the same estimated value for the second attack.

Notice that when α is derived from Eq. (5), the attacker must decide its sign. If he does not know which sign is correct for α_m nor for α_y, he must perform the attack four times, and the four sorted lists of key candidates must be interleaved when trying to find to correct whole key by key enumeration. In our case, a prior

---

[6] Given two leakages ℓ_1 and ℓ_2 the *centered product* combining function computes $f(\ell_1, \ell_2) = (\ell_1 - \text{E}(\ell_1)) \times (\ell_2 - \text{E}(\ell_2))$. The *absolute value of centered difference* combining function defined by $g(\ell_1, \ell_2) = |(\ell_1 - \text{E}(\ell_1)) - (\ell_2 - \text{E}(\ell_2))|$ has also been considered but shows to be less efficient than the centered product.

[7] σ of the noise on the leakage and that on the Hamming weight are equal up to the factor $|\alpha|$. It is thus expressed in leakage unit or in bit unit according to the context.

characterization of the device revealed that α is negative for all points of interest as explained in Appendix A.

Table 1 gives the ranks of correct key bytes for the m-y attack with unknown plaintexts on the unprotected implementation. For comparison purpose the attack has also been performed with the distance-based method using Inner Product and Euclidean distances[8]. Except for six bytes, the maximum likelihood always finds the correct key in the first 10 positions, whereas the distance based attacks are quite less efficient. Note that the standard deviation of the noise (in bit unit) was more or less equal to $\sigma = 0.7$ for each byte. Simulations show that for this noise level the average rank is about 58 for the Inner Product, about 29 for the Euclidean distance, and close to 0.25 for the maximum likelihood.

Table 1. Rank of the correct key byte for a m-y attack with unknown plaintexts on an unprotected implementation (1000 traces)

Byte	0	1	2	3	4	5	6	7	8	9	10	11	12	13	14	15
In. Prod	0	0	167	29	45	187	192	45	77	108	36	124	5	104	64	147
Eucl. Dist	1	80	210	106	3	62	186	17	38	68	194	48	27	120	21	116
ML (slice)	1	1	29	0	1	46	1	0	1	32	36	19	26	67	66	28
ML (var.)	0	2	6	1	1	17	1	0	1	19	5	15	4	40	19	13

Similarly, Table 2 gives the ranks of correct key bytes for the m-y attack with known plaintexts on the masked implementation. ML and centered product 2nd-order CPA give similar almost perfect results. For comparison, we also provide results for the absolute value of centered difference combining function which show to be globally less efficient.

Table 2. Rank of the correct key byte for a m-y attack with known plaintexts on a masked implementation (200 traces)

Byte	0	1	2	3	4	5	6	7	8	9	10	11	12	13	14	15
SO-CPA (abs. diff.)	0	5	1	213	0	109	0	75	0	0	0	58	0	1	3	0
SO-CPA (product)	0	0	6	64	0	16	0	0	1	0	0	2	0	0	0	0
ML (variance)	1	0	0	12	0	5	0	0	0	0	0	9	0	0	0	0

---

[8] The Pearson χ^2 distances were impossible to compute due to an insufficient number of traces.

7   Applications and Possible Countermeasures

7.1   Applications

We now present three applications of the attacks presented in this paper.

1. Our first application relates to the AES-based[9] EMV session key derivation function depicted on the left of Fig. 8. As Linge et al. already noted
   this scheme resists to classical side-channel analyses like DPA or CPA. An
   attacker who wants to recover the master key would target the first AES.
   Unfortunately, its output is not known since this is the session key. It is thus
   impossible to perform an attack at the last round. It is also impossible to
   attack the first round except on the first two key bytes since the 14 remaining input bytes are constant. Linge et al. also observed that, contrarily to
   DPA and CPA, joint distribution analysis can be used to recover the master key. Indeed after two rounds all state bytes can be considered to vary
   uniformly. It is thus possible to apply their attack e.g. at the third round to
   retrieve the value of K_3. While Linge's attack is restricted to naive implementations, our m-y and m-x-y variants presented in Sect. 4.1 can do the same
   on implementations protected by first-order Boolean masking.
2. EMV session key derivation can also be attacked by the m-x variant. Since this
   variant only recovers the Hamming weights of the key bytes, applying it on the
   16 bytes of a round key is not sufficient as this brings an average of only about
   20 bits of information. Instead we can perform the attack at all rounds, which
   recovers the Hamming weights of all 176 bytes of the expanded key. While
   this is much more information about the key, one would wonder whether this
   information can be efficiently exploited to retrieve the ciphering key K. It has
   been shown [2] that a branch-and-bound like algorithm can recover K quite
   efficiently from part of these Hamming weights. This algorithm can also deal
   with some errors in the estimation of the Hamming weights. It is thus possible

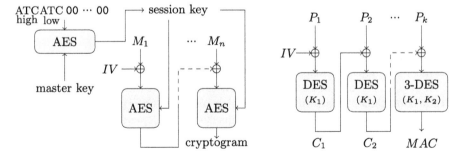

Fig. 8. Left: EMV session key derivation scheme. Right: ISO/IEC 9797-1 MAC scheme
using 3-DES algorithm.

---

[9] EMV scheme also allows to use the Triple DES function.

to recover an AES key on a Boolean masked implementation with no extra cost compared to a naive one.

3. In [6] Feix et al. show that a fixed key used to compute a cryptogram with the standard scheme ISO/IEC 9797-1 MAC algorithm using 3-DES algorithm can be compromised even if the DES itself is implemented in a secure way. The right part of Fig. 8 shows how the MAC value is computed from a k-bloc plaintext $P = (P_1, \ldots, P_k)$ and a 112-bit secret key $K = (K_1, K_2)$. Their attack obtains side-channel information outside the DES function, at the protocol level. Precisely, if an attacker fixes the first n plaintext blocks and lets P_{n+1} vary, then the fixed value of the intermediate ciphertext block C_n can be recovered by correlating, byte per byte, the known value P_{n+1} with the leakage of $C_n \oplus P_{n+1}$. Once C_n is known, K_1 can be retrieved by a 56-bit exhaustive search against a known plaintext/ciphertext pair. Once K_1 is known, K_2 is also recovered by a 56-bit exhaustive search.

A proposed fix to this attack, which consists in applying a Boolean masking on all plaintext blocks, has later been proven vulnerable to 2nd-order analysis [5] if the masks do not have maximal entropy. The authors show that one can jeopardize a masked implementation in the two following cases: (i) a *same* 8-byte mask block $M = (R_0, R_1, \ldots, R_7)$ is used to mask all P_i blocks, or (ii) all P_i are masked with different mask blocks $M_i = (R_i, R_i, \ldots, R_i)$ made of a *same* repeated random byte. They notice that the attack does not work when all mask blocks $M_i = (R_{i,0}, \ldots, R_{i,7})$ are different and made of different bytes, and consequently recommend this full entropy masking.

In the case of careful Boolean masking with full entropy, we observe that both P_{n+1} and $P_{n+1} \oplus C_n$ are still masked by the same value M_{n+1}. It is then possible to mount an m-x type joint distribution analysis[10] which reveals the Hamming weights of each C_n byte. One can obtain similar information for several plaintexts $(P_1, \ldots, P_n)$ and use them all in the exhaustive search phase. More precisely, any key candidate that complies with the Hamming weights of the first pair will be checked against those of the second one, and so on.

7.2 Possible Countermeasures

As stated in Sects. 4.1 and 4.2, it is possible to apply the joint distribution analysis to implementations protected by first-order masking. Yet, a requirement for all m-y, m-x-y and m-x variants is that the targeted variables are all masked with a same value. As a result, the masking scheme d of Fig. 5 is not vulnerable to our attacks since m, x and y are all masked by independent random values. We thus recommend this masking scheme or any other one which would share the same property.

---

[10] A classical second-order CPA on the pair of leakages of $(P_{n+1} \oplus M_{n+1}, P_{n+1} \oplus M_{n+1} \oplus C_n)$ is not possible in this case as it would imply to correlate the combination of these leakages with the Hamming weight of C_n which does not vary.

We also recommend any countermeasure that introduces time randomization – like random delays or shuffling of independent operations – and spoils the notion of point of interest or make them difficult to identify.

8 Conclusion

We demonstrated that the maximum likelihood method better exploits couples of Hamming weights in Linge's joint distribution analysis. Given a set of observed couples of Hamming weights it computes the posterior probability of each key candidate and selects the most probable of them. We have studied the non trivial problem of inferring Hamming weights from leakages and described a new method based on variance analysis that does not require the knowledge of the key and the plaintexts/ciphertexts (contrarily to linear regression).

We compared the ML approach to Linge's technique based on distances between distributions and showed, by simulations and concrete experiments, that it recovers the key value more efficiently. We derived several variants – m-x-y, m-x and others – of the original m-y attack and adapted the generation of theoretical models to make this attack work in the presence of Boolean masking. We noticed a remarkable property of the m-x attack that applies equally well on naive and masked implementations.

We proposed new applications of our attacks that can threaten the EMV session key derivation even on protected implementations, and we proposed implementation guidelines in order to thwart our attacks or at least make them quite difficult.

As future works, it could be interesting to study how the ML criterion can deal with non Gaussian noises and with non linear leakage functions.

Acknowledgements. The authors would like to thank Yanis Linge, Antoine Wurcker and Benoit Feix for fruitful discussions about the attacks presented in this paper.

References

1. Brier, E., Clavier, C., Olivier, F.: Correlation power analysis with a leakage model. In: Joye, M., Quisquater, J.-J. (eds.) CHES 2004. LNCS, vol. 3156, pp. 16–29. Springer, Heidelberg (2004). doi:10.1007/978-3-540-28632-5_2
2. Clavier, C., Marion, D., Wurcker, A.: Simple power analysis on AES key expansion revisited. In: Batina, L., Robshaw, M. (eds.) CHES 2014. LNCS, vol. 8731, pp. 279–297. Springer, Heidelberg (2014). doi:10.1007/978-3-662-44709-3_16
3. Durvaux, F., Standaert, F.-X.: From improved leakage detection to the detection of points of interests in leakage traces. In: Fischlin, M., Coron, J.-S. (eds.) EURO-CRYPT 2016. LNCS, vol. 9665, pp. 240–262. Springer, Heidelberg (2016). doi:10.1007/978-3-662-49890-3_10
4. EMV Co. EMV Integrated Circuit Card Specifications for Payment Systems, Book 2, Security and Key Management, Version 4.3, November 2011

5. Feix, B., Ricart, A., Timon, B., Tordella, L.: Defeating embedded cryptographic protocols by combining second-order with brute force. In: Lemke-Rust, K., Tunstall, M. (eds.) CARDIS 2016. LNCS, vol. 10146, pp. 23–38. Springer, Cham (2017). doi:10.1007/978-3-319-54669-8_2
6. Feix, B., Thiebeauld, H.: Defeating ISO9797-1 MAC Algo 3 by Combining Side-Channel and Brute Force Techniques. IACR Cryptology ePrint Archive, Report 2014/702 (2014)
7. Gierlichs, B., Batina, L., Tuyls, P., Preneel, B.: Mutual information analysis. In: Oswald, E., Rohatgi, P. (eds.) CHES 2008. LNCS, vol. 5154, pp. 426–442. Springer, Heidelberg (2008). doi:10.1007/978-3-540-85053-3_27
8. Gierlichs, B., Lemke-Rust, K., Paar, C.: Templates vs. stochastic methods. In: Goubin, L., Matsui, M. (eds.) CHES 2006. LNCS, vol. 4249, pp. 15–29. Springer, Heidelberg (2006). doi:10.1007/11894063_2
9. Goodwill, G., Jun, B., Jaffe, J., Rohatgi, P.: A testing methodology for side-channel resitance validation. In: NIST Non-invasing Attack Testing Workshop (2011)
10. Goubin, L., Patarin, J.: DES and differential power analysis the "Duplication" method. In: Koç, Ç.K., Paar, C. (eds.) CHES 1999. LNCS, vol. 1717, pp. 158–172. Springer, Heidelberg (1999). doi:10.1007/3-540-48059-5_15
11. Hanley, N., Tunstall, M., Marnane, W.P.: Unknown plaintext template attacks. In: Youm, H.Y., Yung, M. (eds.) WISA 2009. LNCS, vol. 5932, pp. 148–162. Springer, Heidelberg (2009). doi:10.1007/978-3-642-10838-9_12
12. Kocher, P., Jaffe, J., Jun, B.: Differential power analysis. In: Wiener, M. (ed.) CRYPTO 1999. LNCS, vol. 1666, pp. 388–397. Springer, Heidelberg (1999). doi:10.1007/3-540-48405-1_25
13. Korkikian, R., Pelissier, S., Naccache, D.: Blind fault attack against SPN ciphers. In: Tria, A., Choi, D. (eds.) Fault Diagnosis and Tolerance in Cryptography - FDTC 2014, pp. 94–103. IEEE Computer Society Press (2014)
14. le Bouder, H.: Un formalisme unifiant les attaques physiques sur circuits cryptographiques et son exploitation afin de comparer et rechercher de nouvelles attaques. Ph.D. thesis, École Nationale Supérieure des Mines de Saint-Étienne (2014)
15. Li, Y., Chen, M., Liu, Z., Wang, J.: Reduction in the number of fault injections for blind fault attack on SPN block ciphers. ACM Trans. Embed. Comput. Syst. 16(2), 55:1–55:20 (2017)
16. Linge, Y., Dumas, C., Lambert-Lacroix, S.: Using the joint distributions of a cryptographic function in side channel analysis. In: Prouff, E. (ed.) COSADE 2014. LNCS, vol. 8622, pp. 199–213. Springer, Cham (2014). doi:10.1007/978-3-319-10175-0_14
17. Mather, L., Oswald, E., Bandenburg, J., Wójcik, M.: Does my device leak information? An a priori statistical power analysis of leakage detection tests. In: Sako, K., Sarkar, P. (eds.) ASIACRYPT 2013. LNCS, vol. 8269, pp. 486–505. Springer, Heidelberg (2013). doi:10.1007/978-3-642-42033-7_25
18. National Institute of Standards and Technology. Advanced Encryption Standard (AES). Federal Information Processing Standard #197 (2001)
19. Schramm, K., Paar, C.: Higher order masking of the AES. In: Pointcheval, D. (ed.) CT-RSA 2006. LNCS, vol. 3860, pp. 208–225. Springer, Heidelberg (2006). doi:10.1007/11605805_14

A   Determination of the Sign of α

The sign of α indicates whether the leakage function linearly increases ($\alpha > 0$) or decreases ($\alpha < 0$) with the Hamming weight of the data. Experiments on our device with known plaintexts and a known key demonstrated that positive CPA peaks always occur on the descending part of the leakage during the clock cycle, while negative peaks always occur on its ascending part. This is clearly visible in Fig. 9 where the power consumption and the CPA traces are depicted in red and green respectively.

On the same figure one can notice that the standard deviation peaks (in blue) may occur either on positive or negative CPA peaks. Deciding whether a standard deviation peak corresponds to a positive or negative α value simply consists in observing whether it matches with a falling or a raising edge of the leakage respectively. In the experiments described in Sect. 6 we observed that the selected points of interest – defined by the highest standard deviation peaks – always correspond to the ascending part of the clock cycle leakage, which means a negative α value.

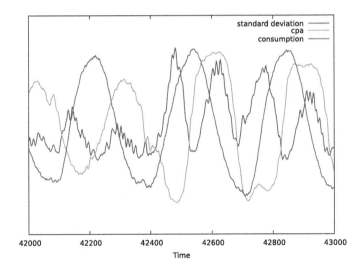

Fig. 9. Relation between the correlation sign and the raising/falling part of the leakage (Color figure online)

Convolutional Neural Networks with Data Augmentation Against Jitter-Based Countermeasures

Profiling Attacks Without Pre-processing

Eleonora Cagli[1,2,4]($\boxtimes$), Cécile Dumas[1,2], and Emmanuel Prouff[3,4]

[1] Univ. Grenoble Alpes, 38000 Grenoble, France
[2] CEA, LETI, MINATEC Campus, 38054 Grenoble, France
{eleonora.cagli,cecile.dumas}@cea.fr
[3] Safran Identity and Security, Issy-les-Moulineaux, France
emmanuel.prouff@ssi.gouv.fr
[4] Sorbonne Universités, UPMC Univ Paris 06, POLSYS, UMR 7606, LIP6,
75005 Paris, France

Abstract. In the context of the security evaluation of cryptographic implementations, *profiling attacks* (aka *Template Attacks*) play a fundamental role. Nowadays the most popular Template Attack strategy consists in approximating the information leakages by Gaussian distributions. Nevertheless this approach suffers from the difficulty to deal with both the traces misalignment and the high dimensionality of the data. This forces the attacker to perform critical preprocessing phases, such as the selection of the points of interest and the realignment of measurements. Some software and hardware countermeasures have been conceived exactly to create such a misalignment. In this paper we propose an end-to-end profiling attack strategy based on the Convolutional Neural Networks: this strategy greatly facilitates the attack roadmap, since it does not require a previous trace realignment nor a precise selection of points of interest. To significantly increase the performances of the CNN, we moreover propose to equip it with the data augmentation technique that is classical in other applications of Machine Learning. As a validation, we present several experiments against traces misaligned by different kinds of countermeasures, including the augmentation of the clock jitter effect in a secure hardware implementation over a modern chip. The excellent results achieved in these experiments prove that Convolutional Neural Networks approach combined with data augmentation gives a very efficient alternative to the state-of-the-art profiling attacks.

Keywords: Side-Channel Attacks · Convolutional Neural Networks · Data augmentation · Machine learning · Jitter · Trace misalignment · Unstable clock

E. Prouff—This work has been finalized when the author was working at ANSSI, France.

W. Fischer and N. Homma (Eds.): CHES 2017, LNCS 10529, pp. 45–68, 2017.
DOI: 10.1007/978-3-319-66787-4_3

1 Introduction

To prevent Side-Channel Attacks (SCA), manufacturers commonly implement countermeasures that create misalignment in the measurements sets. The latter countermeasures are either implemented in hardware (unstable clock, random hardware interruption, clock stealing) or in software (insertion of random delays through dummy operations [8,9], shuffling [31]). Until now two approaches have been developed to deal with misalignment problems. The first one simply consists in adapting the number of side-channel acquisitions (usually increasing it by a factor which is linear in the misalignment effect). Eventually an integration over a range of points [21] can be made, which guarantees the extraction of the information over a single point, at the cost of a linear increase of the noise, that may be compensated by the increase of the acquisitions. The second one, which is usually preferred, consists in applying realignment techniques in order to limit the desynchronization effects. Two realignment techniques families might be distinguished: a signal-processing oriented one (*e.g.* [24,30]), more adapted to hardware countermeasures, and a probabilistic-oriented one (*e.g.* [11]), conceived for the detection of dummy operations, *i.e.* software countermeasures.

Among the SCAs, *profiling attacks* (aka Template Attacks, TA for short) play a fundamental role in the context of the security evaluation of cryptographic implementations. Indeed the profiling attack scenario allows to evaluate their worst-case security, admitting the attacker is able to characterize the device leakages by means of a full-knowledge access to a device identical to the one under attack. Such attacks work in two phases: first, a leakage model is estimated during a so-called *profiling phase*, then the profiled leakage model is exploited to extract key-dependent information in the proper *attack phase*. Approximating the information leakage by a Gaussian distribution is today the most popular approach for the profiling, due to its theoretical optimality when the noise tends towards infinity. Nevertheless the performances of such a classical TA highly depend on some preliminary phases, such as the traces realignment or the selection of the Points of Interest (PoIs). Indeed the efficiency/effectiveness of the Gaussian approximation is strongly impacted by the dimension of the leakage traces at input.

In this paper we propose the use of a Convolutional Neural Network (CNN) as a comprehensive profiling attack strategy. Such a strategy, divided into a learning phase and a proper attack phase, can replace the entire roadmap of the state of the art attacks: for instance, contrary to a classical TA, any trace preprocessing such as realignment or the choice of the PoIs are included in the learning phase. Indeed we will show that the CNNs implicitly perform an appropriate combination of the time samples and are robust to trace misalignment. This property makes the profiling attacks with CNNs efficient and easy to perform, since they do not require critical preprocessings. Moreover, since the CNNs are less impacted than the classical TA by the dimension of the traces, we can *a priori* expect that their efficiency outperforms (or at least perform as well as) the classical TAs. Indeed, CNNs can extract information from a large range of points while, in practice, Gaussian TAs are used to extract information on some previously dimensionality-reduced data (and dimensionality reduction never raises the informativeness of the data [10]). This claim, and more generally the soundness and the efficiency of our approach, will be proven by several experiments throughout this paper.

To compensate some undesired behaviour of the CNNs, we propose as well to embed them with *Data Augmentation* (DA) techniques [28,32], recommended in the machine learning domain for improving performances: the latter technique consists in artificially generating traces in order to increase the size of the profiling set. To do so, the acquired traces are distorted through plausible transformations that preserve the label information (*i.e.* the value of the handled sensitive variable in our context). Actually, in this paper we propose to turn the misalignment problem into a virtue, enlarging the profiling trace set *via* a random shift of the acquired traces and another typology of distortion that together simulate a clock jitter effect. Paradoxically, instead of trying to realign the traces, we propose to further misalign them (a much easier task!), and we show that such a practice provides a great benefit to the CNN attack strategy.

This contribution makes part of the transfer of methodology in progress in last years from the machine learning and pattern recognition domain to the side-channel analysis one. Recently the strict analogy between template attacks and the supervised classification problem as been depicted [15], while the deployment of Neural Networks (NNs) [22,23,33] and CNNs [20] to perform profiled SCAs has been proposed. Our paper aims to pursue this line of works.

This paper focuses over the robustness of CNNs to misalignment, thus considerations about other kinds of countermeasures, such as masking, are left apart. Nevertheless, the fact that CNNs usually applies non-linear functions to the data makes them potentially (and practically, as already experienced in [20]) able to deal with such a countermeasure as well.

The paper is organized as follows: in Sect. 2 we recall the classical TA roadmap, we introduce the MLP family of NNs, we describe the NN-based SCA and we finally discuss the practical aspects of the training phase of an NN. In Sect. 3 the basic concepts of the CNNs are introduced, together with the description of the deforming functions we propose for the data augmentation. In Sect. 4 we test the CNNs against some software countermeasures, in order to validate our claim of robustness to the misalignment caused by shifting. Experiments against hardware countermeasures are described in Sect. 5, proving that the CNN are robust to deformations due to the jitter.

2   Preliminaries

2.1   Notations

Throughout this paper we use calligraphic letters as $\mathcal{X}$ to denote sets, the corresponding upper-case letter X to denote random variables (random vectors if in bold $\mathbf{X}$) over $\mathcal{X}$, and the corresponding lower-case letter x (resp. $\mathbf{x}$ for vectors) to denote realizations of X (resp. $\mathbf{X}$). The i-th entry of a vector $\mathbf{x}$ is denoted by

$\mathbf{x}[i]$. Side-channel traces will be viewed as realizations of a random column vector $\mathbf{X} \in \mathbb{R}^D$. During their acquisition, a target sensitive variable $Z = f(P, K)$ is handled, where P denotes some public variable, e.g. a plaintext, and K the part of secret key the attacker aims to retrieve. The value assumed by such a variable is viewed as a realization $z \in \mathcal{Z} = \{z^1, z^2, \ldots, z^{|\mathcal{Z}|}\}$ of a discrete finite random variable Z. We will sometimes represent the values $z^i \in \mathcal{Z}$ via the so-called *one-hot encoding* representation, assigning to z^i a $|\mathcal{Z}|$-dimensional vector, with all entries equal to 0 and the i-th entry equal to 1: $z^i \to \mathbf{z}^i = (0, \ldots, 0, \underbrace{1}_{i}, 0, \ldots, 0)$.

2.2 Profiling Side-Channel Attack

A profiling SCA is composed of two phases: a profiling (or *characterization*, or *training*) phase, and an attack (or *matching*) phase. During the first one, the attacker estimates the probability:

$$\Pr[\mathbf{X}|Z = z] \, , \tag{1}$$

from a *profiling set* $\{\mathbf{x}_i, z_i\}_{i=1,\ldots,N_p}$ of size N_p, which is a set of traces $\mathbf{x}_i$ acquired under known value z_i of the target. The potentially huge dimensionality of $\mathbf{X}$ lets such an estimation a very complex problem, and the most popular way adopted until now to estimate the conditional probability is the one that led to the well-established Gaussian TA [5] (aka *Quadratic Discriminant Analysis* [12]). To perform the latter attack, the adversary priorly exploits some statistical tests (*e.g.* SNR or T-Test) and/or dimensionality reduction techniques (*e.g.* Principal Component Analysis, Linear Discriminant Analysis [12], Kernel Discriminant Analysis [4]) to select a small portion of PoIs or an opportune combination of them. Then, denoting $\varepsilon(\mathbf{X})$ the result of such a dimensionality reduction, the attacker assumes that $\varepsilon(\mathbf{X})|Z$ has a multivariate Gaussian distribution, and estimates the mean vector $\boldsymbol{\mu}_z$ and the covariance matrix $\boldsymbol{\Sigma}_z$ for each $z \in \mathcal{Z}$ (*i.e.* the so-called templates). In this way the pdf (1) is approximated by the Gaussian pdf with parameters $\boldsymbol{\mu}_z$ and $\boldsymbol{\Sigma}_z$. The attack phase eventually consists in computing the likelihood of the *attack set* $\{\mathbf{x}_i\}_{i=1,\ldots,N}$ for each template and in sorting the key candidates $k \in \mathcal{K}$ with respect to their score d_k defined such that:

$$d_k = \prod_{i=1}^{N} \Pr[Z = f(p_i, k)|\varepsilon(\mathbf{X}) = \varepsilon(\mathbf{x}_i)] = \prod_{i=1}^{N} \frac{\Pr[\varepsilon(\mathbf{X}) = \varepsilon(\mathbf{x}_i)|Z = f(p_i, k)]}{\Pr[Z = f(p_i, k))]}, \tag{2}$$

where (2) is obtained *via* Bayes' Theorem under the hypothesis that acquisitions are independent.[1]

Traces misalignment affects the approach above. In particular, if not treated with a proper realignment, it makes the PoI selection harder, obliging the

---

[1] In TA the profiling set and the attack set are assumed to be different, namely the traces $\mathbf{x}_i$ involved in (2) have not been used for the profiling.

attacker to consider a wide range of points for the characterization and matching (the more effective the misalignment, the wider the range), directly or after a previous *integration* [7] or a dimension reduction methods.[2] As we will see in the next section, neural networks, and in particular the CNNs, are able to efficiently and simultaneously address the PoI selection problem and the misalignment issue. More precisely, they can be trained to search for informative weighted combinations of leakage points, in a way that is robust to traces misalignment.

2.3   Neural Networks and the Multi-layer Perceptron

The classification problem is the most widely studied one in machine learning, since it is the central building block for all other problems, e.g. detection, regression, etc. [3] It consists in taking an input, *e.g.* a side-channel trace $\mathbf{x}$, and in assigning it a label $z \in \mathcal{Z}$, *e.g.* the value of the target variable handled during the acquisition. In the typical setting of a supervised classification problem, a *training set* is available, which is a set of data already assigned to the right label. The latter set exactly corresponds to the profiling set in the side-channel context.

Neural networks (NN) are nowadays the privileged tool to address the classification problem. They aim at constructing a function $F \colon \mathbb{R}^D \to \mathbb{R}^{|\mathcal{Z}|}$ that takes data $\mathbf{x} \in \mathbb{R}^D$ and outputs vectors $\mathbf{y} \in \mathbb{R}$ of scores. The classification of $\mathbf{x}$ is done afterwards by choosing the label z^i such that $i = \mathrm{argmax}\ \mathbf{y}[i]$. In general F is obtained by combining several simpler functions, called *layers*. An NN has an *input layer* (the identity over the input datum $\mathbf{x}$), an output layer (the last function, whose output is the scores vector $\mathbf{y}$) and all other layers are called *hidden* layers. The nature (the number and the dimension) of the layers is called the *architecture* of the NN. All the parameters that define an architecture, together with some other parameters that govern the training phase, have to be carefully set by the attacker, and are called *hyper-parameters*. The so-called *neurons*, that give the name to the NNs, are the computational units of the network and essentially process a scalar product between the coordinates of its input and a vector of *trainable weights* (or simply *weights*) that have to be *trained*. Each layer processes some neurons and the outputs of the neuron evaluations will form new input vectors for the subsequent layer. The training phase consists in an automatic tuning of the weights and it is done *via* an iterative approach which locally applies the Stochastic Gradient Descent algorithm [13] to minimize a *loss function* quantifying the classification error of the function F over the training set. We will not give further details about this classical optimization approach, and the interested reader may refer to [13].

In this paper we focus on the family of the *Multi-Layer Perceptrons* (MLPs). They are associated with a function F that is composed of multiple linear functions and some non-linear *activation functions* which are efficiently-computable and whose derivatives are bounded and efficient to evaluate. To sum-up, we can express an MLP by the following equation:

---

[2] The latter techniques being themselves very sensible to misalignment effect.

$$F(\mathbf{x}) = \mathbf{s} \circ \lambda_n \circ \sigma_{n-1} \circ \lambda_{n-1} \circ \cdots \circ \lambda_1(\mathbf{x}) = \mathbf{y} \, , \tag{3}$$

where:

- the λ_i functions are the so-called *Fully-Connected* (FC) layers and are expressible as affine functions: denoting $\mathbf{x} \in \mathbb{R}^D$ the input of an FC, its output is given by $A\mathbf{x} + \mathbf{b}$, being $A \in \mathbb{R}^{D \times C}$ a matrix of weights and $\mathbf{b} \in \mathbb{R}^C$ a vector of biases. These weights and biases are the trainable weights of the FC layer.[3]
- the σ_i are the so-called *activation functions* (ACT): an activation function is a non-linear real function that is applied independently to each coordinate of its input,
- s is the so-called *softmax*[4] function (SOFT): $\mathbf{s}(\mathbf{x})[i] = \frac{e^{\mathbf{x}[i]}}{\sum_j e^{\mathbf{x}[j]}}$.

Examples of ACT layers are the *sigmoid* $f(\mathbf{x})[i] = (1 + e^{-\mathbf{x}[i]})^{-1}$ or the *rectified linear unit* (ReLU) $f(\mathbf{x})[i] = max(0, \mathbf{x}[i])$. In general they do not depend on trainable weights.

The role of the *softmax* is to renormalise the output scores in such a way that they define a probability distribution $\mathbf{y} = \Pr[Z|\mathbf{X} = \mathbf{x}]$.

In this way, the computed output does not only provide the most likely label to solve the classification problem, but also the likelihood of the remaining $|\mathcal{Z}| - 1$ other labels. In the profiling SCA context, this form of output allows us to enter it in (2) (setting the preprocessing function ε equal to the identity) to rank key candidates; actually (3) may be viewed as an approximation of the pdf in (1).[5] We can thus rewrite (2) as:

$$d_k = \prod_{i=1}^{N} F(\mathbf{x}_i)[f(p_i, k)]. \tag{4}$$

We refer to [19] for an (excellent) explication over the relationship between the softmax function and the Bayes theorem.

2.4   Practical Aspects of the Training Phase and Overfitting

The goal of the training phase is to tune the weights of the NN. The latter ones are first initialized with random values and are afterwards updated by applying several times the same process: a batch of traces chosen in random order goes through the network to obtain its score, the loss function is computed from this

---

[3] They are called *Fully-Connected* because each i-th input coordinate is *connected* to each j-th output via the $A[i, j]$ weight. FC layers can be seen as a special case of the linear layers in general *Feed-Forward* networks, in which not all the connections are present. The absence of some (i, j)-th connections can be formalized as a constraint for the matrix A consisting in forcing to 0 its (i, j)-th coordinates.

[4] To prevent underflow, the log-softmax is usually preferred if several classification outputs must be combined.

[5] Remarkably, this places SCAs based on MLP as a particular case of the classical profiling attack that exploits the maximum likelihood as distinguisher.

score and finally the loss is reduced by modifying the trainable parameters. A good choice for the size of the batch is a value as large as possible but which avoids computational performances drop. An iteration over the entire training set is called *epoch*. To monitor the training of an NN and to evaluate its performances it is a good practice to separate the labelled data into 3 sets:

- the proper *training set*, which is actually used to train the weights (in general it contains the greatest part of the labelled data)
- a *validation set*, which is observed in general at the end of each epoch to monitor the training
- a *test set*, which is kept unobserved during the training phase and which is involved to finally evaluate the performances of the trained NN.

For our experiments we will use the attack traces as test set, while we will split the profiling traces into a training set and a validation set.[6]

The Accuracy is the most common metric to both monitor and evaluate an NN. It is defined as the successful classification rate reached over a dataset. The *training accuracy*, the *validation accuracy* and the *test accuracy* are the successful classification rates achieved respectively over the training, the validation and the test sets. At the end of each epoch it is useful to compute and to compare the training accuracy and the validation accuracy. For some trained models we will measure in this paper (see *e.g.* Table 1) the following two additional quantities:

- the *maximal training accuracy*, corresponding to the maximum of the training accuracies computed at the end of each epoch
- the *maximal validation accuracy*, corresponding to the maximum of the validation accuracies computed at the end of each epoch.

In addition to the two quantities above, we will also evaluate the performances of our trained model, by computing a *test accuracy*. Sometimes it is useful to complete this evaluation by looking at the so-called *confusion matrix* (see the bottom part of Fig. 5). Indeed the latter matrix enables, in case of misclassification, for the identification of the classes which are confused. The confusion matrix corresponds to the distribution over the couples *(true label, predicted label)* directly deduced from the results of the classification on the test set. A test accuracy of 100% corresponds to a diagonal confusion matrix.

---

[6] The way how the profiling set is split into training and validation sets might induce a bias in the learned model. A good way to get rid of such a bias is to apply a *cross-validation* technique, *e.g.* a *10-fold cross-validation*. The latter one consists in partitioning the profiling set into 10 sub-sets, and in performing 10 times the training while choosing each time one of the sub-sets for the validation and the union of the 9 other ones for the training. An average over the performances of the 10 obtained models gives a more robust estimation of the accuracies and performances. Results of this papers do not make use of such a cross-validation technique.

On the Need to Also Consider the Guessing Entropy. The accuracy metric is perfectly adapted to the machine learning classification problem, but corresponds in side-channel language to the success rate of a Simple Attack, *i.e.* an attack where a single attack trace is available. When the attacker can acquire several traces for varying plaintexts, the accuracy metric is not sufficient alone to evaluate the attack performance. Indeed such a metric only takes into account the label corresponding to the maximal score and does not consider the other ones, whereas an SCA through (4) does (and therefore exploits the full information).

To take this remark into account, we will always associate the test accuracy to a side-channel metric defined as the minimal number $N^\star$ of side-channel traces that makes the *guessing entropy* (the average rank of the right key candidate) be permanently equal to 1 (see *e.g.* Table 1). We will estimate such a guessing entropy through 10 independent attacks.

As we will see in the sections dedicated to our attack experiments, applying Machine Learning in a context where at the same time (1) the model to recover is complex and (2) the amount of exploitable measurements for the training is limited, may be ineffective due to some overfitting phenomena.

Overfitting. Often the training accuracy is higher than the validation one. When the gap between the two accuracies is excessive, we assist to the *overfitting* phenomenon. It means that the NN is using its weights to *learn by heart* the training set instead of detecting significant discriminative features. For this reason its performances are poor over the validation set, which is new to it. Overfitting occurs when an NN is excessively complex, *i.e.* when it is able to express an excessively large family of functions. In order to keep the NN as complex as wished and hence limiting the overfitting, some *regularization* techniques can be applied. For example, in this paper we will propose the use of the *Data Augmentation* (DA) [28] that consists in artificially adding observations to the training set. Moreover we will take advantage of the *early-stopping* technique [26] that consists in well choosing a stop condition based on the validation accuracy or on the validation loss (*i.e.* the value taken by the loss function over the validation set).

3 Convolutional Neural Networks

In this section we describe the layers that turn an MLP into a Convolutional Neural Network (CNN), and we explain how the form of these layers makes the CNNs robust to misalignment. Then we will specify the Data Augmentation that can be applied in our context, in order to deal with overfitting.

3.1 Description of the CNNs

The CNNs complete the classical principle of MLP with two additional types of layers: the so-called *convolutional* layer based on a convolutional filtering, and a *pooling* layer. We describe these two particular layers hereafter.

Convolutional (CONV) Layers are linear layers that share weights across space. The representation is given in Fig. 1(a).[7] To apply a convolutional layer to an input trace, V small column vectors, called *convolutional filter*, of size W are slid over the trace.[8] The column vectors form a window which defines a linear transformation of W consecutive points of the trace into a new vector of V points. The coordinates of the window (viewed as a matrix) are among the trainable weights and are constrained to be unchanged for every input window. This constraint is the main difference between a CONV layer and an FC layer; it allows the former to learn shift-invariant features. The reason why several filters are applied is that we expect each filter to extract a different kind of characteristic from the input. As one goes along convolutional layers, higher-level abstraction features are expected to be extracted. These high-level features are arranged side-by-side over an additional data dimension, the so-called *depth*.[9] This is this geometric characteristic that makes CNNs robust to temporal deformations [18].

To avoid complexity explosion due to this depth increasing, the insertion of pooling layers is recommended.

Pooling (POOL) Layers are non-linear layers that reduce the spatial size in order to limit the amount of neurons, and by consequence the complexity of the minimization problem (see Fig. 1(b)). As the CONV layers, they make some filters slide across the input. Filters are 1-dimensional, characterised by a length W, and usually the stride (see footnote 5) is chosen equal to their length; for example in Fig. 1(b) both the length and the stride equal 3, so that the selected segments of the input do not overlap. In contrast with convolutional layers, the pooling filters do not contain trainable weights. They only slide across the input to select a segment, then a pooling function is applied: the most common pooling functions are the *max-pooling* which outputs the maximum values within the segment and the *average-pooling* which outputs the average of the coordinates of the segment.

Common architecture. The main block of a CNN is a CONV layer γ directly followed by an ACT layer σ. The former locally extracts information from the input thanks to filters and the latter increases the complexity of the learned classification function thanks to its non-linearity. After some $(\sigma \circ \gamma)$ blocks, a POOL layer δ is usually added to reduce the number of neurons: $\delta \circ [\sigma \circ \gamma]^{n_2}$. This new block is repeated in the neural network until obtaining an output of reasonable size. Then, some FC are introduced in order to obtain a global result

---

[7] CNNs have been introduced for images [18]. So, usually, layer interfaces are arranged in a 3D-fashion (height, weight and depth). In Fig. 1(a) we show a 2D-CNN (length and depth) adapted to 1D-data as side-channel traces are.

[8] The amount of units by which the filter shifts across the trace is called *stride*. In Fig. 1(a) the stride equals 1.

[9] Ambiguity: NNs with many layers are sometimes called *Deep Neural Networks*, where the *depth* corresponds to the number of layers.

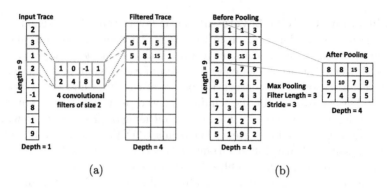

Fig. 1. (a) Convolutional filtering: $W = 2$, $V = 4$, stride $= 1$. (b) Max-pooling layer: $W =$ stride $= 3$.

which depends on the entire input. To sum-up, a common convolutional network can be characterized by the following formula:[10]

$$s \circ [\lambda]^{n_1} \circ [\delta \circ [\sigma \circ \gamma]^{n_2}]^{n_3}. \tag{5}$$

Layer by layer it increases depth through convolution filters, adds non-linearity through activation functions and reduces spatial (or temporal, in the side-channel traces case) size through pooling layers. Once a deep and narrow representation has been obtained, one or more FC layers are connected to it, followed by a softmax function. An example of CNN architecture is represented in Fig. 2.

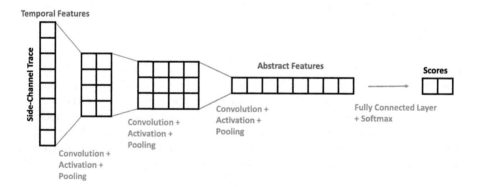

Fig. 2. Common CNN architecture

---

[10] where each layer of the same type appearing in the composition is not to be intended as exactly the same function (e.g. with same input/output dimensions), but as a function of the same form.

3.2   Data Augmentation

As pointed out in Sect. 2.4, it is sometimes necessary to manage the overfitting phenomenon, by applying some regularization techniques. As we will see in Sects. 4 and 5 this will be the case in our experiments: indeed we will propose a quite deep CNN architecture, flexible enough to manage the misalignment problems, but trained over some relatively small training sets. This fact, combined with the high number of weights exploited by our CNN implies that the latter one will *learn by heart* each element of the training set, without catching the truly discriminant features of the traces.

Among all regularization techniques, we choose to concentrate priorly on the Data Augmentation [28], mainly for two reasons. First, it is well known that the presence of misalignment forces to increase the number of acquisitions. In other terms, misalignment may provoke a lack of data phenomenon on the adversary side. In the machine learning domain such a lack is classically addressed thanks to the DA technique, and its benefits are widely proved. For example, many image recognition competition winners made use of such a technique (*e.g.* the winner of ILSVRC-2012 [17]). Second, the DA is controllable, meaning that the deformations applied to the data are chosen, thus fully characterized. It is therefore possible to fully determine the addition of complexity induced to the classification problem. In our opinion, other techniques add constraints to the problem in a more implicit way, *e.g.* the dropout [14] or the ℓ_2-norm regularization [3].

Data augmentation consists in artificially generating new training traces by deforming those previously acquired. The deformation is done by the application of transformations that preserve the label information (*i.e.* the value of the handled sensitive variable in our context). We choose two kinds of deformations, that we denote by *Shifting* and *Add-Remove*.

*Shifting Deformation (*SH$_{T^\star}$*)* simulates a random delay effect of maximal amplitude $T^\star$, by randomly selecting a shifting window of the acquired trace, as shown in Fig. 3. Let D denote the original size of the traces. We fix the size of the input layer of our CNN to $D' = D - T^\star$. Then the technique SH$_{T^\star}$ consists (1) in drawing a uniform random $t \in [0, T^\star]$, and (2) in selecting the D'-sized window starting from the t-th point. For our study, we will compare the SH$_T$ technique for different values $T \leq T^\star$, without changing the architecture of the CNN (in particular the input size D'). Notably, $T \leq T^\star$ implies that $T^\star - T$ time samples will never have the chance to be selected. As we suppose that the information is localized in the central part of the traces, we choose to center the shifting windows, discarding the heads and the tails of the traces (corresponding to the first and the last $\frac{T^\star - T}{2}$ points).

Add-Remove Deformation (AR) simulates a clock jitter effect (Fig. 3). We will denote by AR$_R$ the operation that consists (1) in inserting R time samples, whose positions are chosen uniformly at random and whose values are the arithmetic mean between the previous time sample and the following one, (2) in suppressing R time samples, chosen uniformly at random.

The two deformations can be composed: we will denote by SH$_T$AR$_R$ the application of a SH$_T$ followed by a AR$_R$.

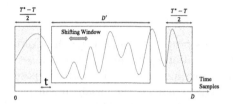 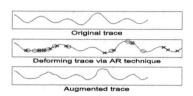

Fig. 3. Left: Shifting technique for DA. Right: Add-Remove technique for DA (added points marked by red circles, removed points marked by black crosses). (Color figure online)

4   Application to Software Countermeasures

In this section we present a preliminary experiment we have performed in order to validate the shift-invariance claimed by the CNN architecture, recalled in Sect. 3.1. In this experiment a single leaking operation was observed through the side-channel acquisitions, shifted in time by the insertion of a random number of dummy operations. A CNN-based attack is run, successfully, without effectuating any priorly realignment of the traces. We also performed a second experiment in which we targeted two leaking operations.

We believe (and we discuss it in more details in Appendix A) that dealing with dummy operations insertion does not represent an actual obstacle for an attacker nowadays. Thus, the experiment we present in this section is not expected to be representative of real application cases. Actually, we think that the CNNs bring a truly great advantage with respect to the state-of-the-art TAs in presence of hardware-flavoured countermeasures, such as augmented jitter effects. We refer to Sect. 5 for experiments in such a context.

CNN-based Attack Against Random Delays. For this experiment, we implemented, on an Atmega328P microprocessor, a uniform Random Delay Interrupt (RDI) [29] to protect the leakage produced by a single target operation. Our RDI simply consists in a loop of r *nop* instructions, with r drawn uniformly in $[0, 127]$.

Some acquired traces are reported in the left side of Fig. 4, the target peak being highlighted with a red ellipse. They are composed of $3,996$ time samples, corresponding to an access to the AES-Sbox look-up table stored in NVM. For the training, we acquired only $1,000$ traces and 700 further traces were acquired as validation data. Our CNN has been trained to classify the traces according to the Hamming weight of the Sbox output; namely, our labels are the 9 values taken by $Z = \mathrm{HW}(\mathrm{Sbox}(P \oplus K))$. This choice has been done to let each class contain more than only a few (i.e. about $1,000/256$) training traces.[11] Since Z is assumed to take 9 values and the position of the leakage depends on a random r ranging over 128 values, it is clear that the $1,000$ training traces do not encompass

---

[11] For Atmega328P devices, the Hamming weight is known to be particularly relevant to model the leakage occurring during register writing [2].

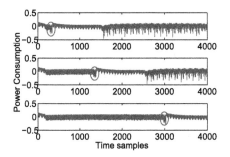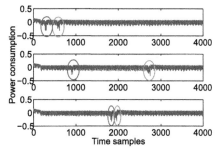

Fig. 4. Left: one leakage protected by single uniform RDI. Right: two leaking operations protected by multiple uniform RDI. (Color figure online)

the full $9 \times 128 = 1,152$ possible combinations $(z, r) \in [0, 8] \times [0, 127]$. We undersized the training set by purpose, in order to establish whether the CNN technique, equipped with DA, is able to catch the meaningful shift-invariant features without having been provided with all the possible observations.

For the training of our CNN, we applied the SH_T data augmentation, selecting $T^\star = 500$ and $T \in \{0, 100, T^\star\}$; this implies that the input dimension of our CNN is reduced to $3,496$. Our implementation is based on Keras library [1] (version 1.2.1), and we run the trainings over an ordinary computer equipped with a gamers market GPU, as specified in Sect. 5.2. For the CNN architecture, we chose the following architecture:

$$s \circ [\lambda]^1 \circ [\delta \circ [\sigma \circ \gamma]^1]^4, \tag{6}$$

i.e. (5) with $n_1 = n_2 = 1$ and $n_3 = 4$. To accelerate the training we introduced a *Batch Normalization* layer [16] after each pooling δ. The network transforms the $3,496 \times 1$ inputs in a 1×256 list of abstract features, before entering the last FC layer $\lambda : \mathbb{R}^{256} \to \mathbb{R}^9$. Even if the ReLU activation function [25] is classically recommended for many applications in literature, we obtained in most cases better results using the hyperbolic tangent. We trained our CNN by batches of size 32. In total the network contained $869,341$ trainable weights. The training and validation accuracies achieved after each epoch are depicted in Fig. 5 together with the confusion matrices that we obtained from the test set. Applying the early-stopping principle recalled in Sect. 2.4, we automatically stopped the training after 120 epochs without decrement of the loss function evaluated over the validation set, and kept as final trained model the one that showed the minimal value for the loss function evaluation. Concerning the learning rate, i.e. the factor defining the size of the steps in the gradient descent optimization (see [13]) we fixed the beginning one to 0.01 and reduced it by a factor of $\sqrt{0.1}$ after 5 epochs without validation loss decrement.

Table 1 summarizes the obtained results. For each trained model we can compare the maximal training accuracy achieved during the training with the maximal validation accuracy (see Sect. 2.4 for the definition of these accuracies).

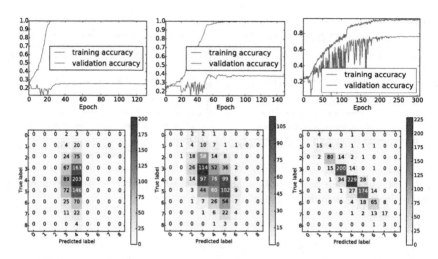

Fig. 5. One leakage protected via single uniform RDI: accuracies vs epochs and confusion matrices obtained with our CNN for different DA techniques. From left to right: SH_0, SH_{100}, SH_{500}.

Table 1. Results of our CNN, for different DA techniques, in presence of an uniform RDI countermeasure protecting. For each technique, 4 values are given: in position a the maximal training accuracy, in position b the maximal validation accuracy, in position c the test accuracy, in position d the value of $N^\star$ (see Sect. 2.4 for definitions).

		SH_0		SH_{100}		SH_{500}	
a	b	100%	25.9%	100%	39.4%	**98.4%**	**76.7%**
c	d	27.0%	> 1000	31.8%	101	**78.0%**	**7**

This comparison gives an insight about the risk of overfitting for the training.[12] Case SH_0 corresponds to a training performed without DA technique. When no DA is applied, the overfitting effect is dramatic: the training set is 100%-successfully classified after about 22 epochs, while the test accuracy only achieves 27%. The 27% is around the rate of uniformly distributed bytes showing an Hamming weight of 4.[13] Looking at the corresponding confusion matrix we remark that the CNN training has been biased by the binomial distribution of the training data, and almost always predicts the class 4. This essentially means that no discriminative feature has been learned in this case, which is confirmed by the fact that the trained model leads to an unsuccessful attack ($N^\star > 1,000$).

---

[12] The validation accuracies are estimated over a 700-sized set, while the test accuracies are estimated over 100,000 traces. Thus the latter estimation is more accurate, and we recall that the test accuracy is to be considered as the final CNN classification performance.

[13] We recall that the Hamming weight of uniformly distributed data follows a binomial law with coefficients $(8, 0.5)$.

Table 2. Results of our CNN in presence of uniform RDI protecting two leaking operations. See the caption Table 1 for a legend.

		First operation		Second operation	
a	b	95.2%	79.7%	96.8%	81.0%
c	d	76.8%	7	82.5%	6

Remarkably, the more artificial shifting is added by the DA, the more the over-fitting effect is attenuated; for SH_T with *e.g.* $T = 500$ the training set is never completely learnt and the test accuracy achieves 78%, leading to a guessing entropy of 1 with only $N^\star = 7$ traces.

These results confirm that our CNN model is able to characterize a wide range of points in a way that is robust to RDI.

Two Leaking Operations. In this section we study whether our CNN classi-fier suffers from the presence of multiple leaking operations with the same power consumption pattern. This situation occurs for instance any time the same oper-ation is repeated several successive times over different pieces of data (*e.g.* the SubByte operation for a software AES implementation is often performed by 16 successive look-up table access). To start our study we performed the same exper-iments as in Sect. 4 over a second traces set, where two look-up table accesses leak, each preceded by a random delay. Some examples of this second traces set are given in the right side of Fig. 4, where the two leaking operations being highlighted by red and green ellipses. We trained the same CNN as in Sect. 4, once to classify the first leakage, and a second time to classify the second leak-age, applying SH_{500}. Results are given in Table 2. They show that even if the CNN transforms spatial (or temporal) information into abstract discriminative features, it still holds an ordering notion: indeed if no ordering notion would have been held, the CNN could no way discriminate the first peak from the second one.

5   Application to Hardware Countermeasures

A classical hardware countermeasure against side-channel attacks consists in introducing instability in the clock. This implies the cumulation of a deforming effect that affects each single acquired clock cycle, and provokes traces misalign-ment on the adversary side. Indeed, since clock cycles do not have the same duration, they are sampled during the attack by a varying number of time sam-ples. As a consequence, a simple translation of the acquisitions is not sufficient in this case to align w.r.t. an identified clock cycle. Several realignment tech-niques are available to manage this kind of deformations, *e.g.* [30]. The goal of this paper is not to compare a new realignment technique with the existing ones, but to show that we can get rid of the realignment pre-processing exploiting the end-to-end attack strategy provided by the CNN approach.

5.1   Performances over Artificial Augmented Clock Jitter

In this section we present the results that we obtained over two datasets named *DS_low_jitter* and *DS_high_jitter*. Each one contains $10,000$ labelled traces, used for the training/profiling phase (more precisely, $9,000$ are used for the training, and $1,000$ for the validation), and $100,000$ attack traces. The traces are composed of $1,860$ time samples. The two datasets have been obtained by artificially adding a simulated jitter effect over some synchronized original traces. The original traces were measured on the same Atmega328P microprocessor used in the previous section. We verified that they originally encompass leakage on 34 instructions: 2 *nops*, 16 loads from the NVM and 16 accesses to look-up tables. For our attack experiments, it is assumed that the target is the first look-up table access, *i.e.* the 19th clock cycle. As in the previous section, the target is assumed to take the form $Z = \mathrm{HW}(\mathrm{Sbox}(P \oplus K))$. To simulate the jitter effect each clock pattern has been deformed[14] by adding r new points if $r > 0$ (resp. removing r points if $r < 0$), with $r \sim \mathcal{N}(0, \sigma^2)$.[15] For the *DS_low_jitter* dataset, we fixed $\sigma^2 = 4$ and for the *DS_high_jitter* dataset we fixed $\sigma^2 = 36$. As an example, some traces of *DS_low_jitter* are depicted in the left-hand side of Fig. 6: the cumulative effect of the jitter is observable by remarking that the desynchronization raises with time. Some traces of *DS_high_jitter* are depicted as well in the right-hand side of Fig. 6. For both datasets we did not operate any PoI selection, but entered the entire traces into our CNN.

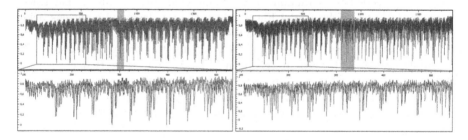

Fig. 6. Left: some traces of the *DS_low_jitter* dataset, a zoom of the part highlighted by the red rectangle is given in the bottom part. Right: some traces (and the relative) of the *DS_high_jitter* dataset. The interesting clock cycle is highlighted by the grey rectangular area.

We used the same CNN architecture (6) as in previous section. We assisted again to a strong overfitting phenomenon and we successfully reduced it by applying the DA strategy introduced in Sect. 3.2. This time we applied both the shifting deformation SH_T with $T^\star = 200$ and $T \in \{0, 20, 40\}$ and the add-remove deformation AR_R with $R \in \{0, 100, 200\}$, training the CNN model using the 9

---

[14] The 19th clock cycle suffers from the cumulation of the previous 18 deformations.

[15] This deformation is not the same of the proposed AR technique for the DA.

combinations $SH_T AR_R$. We performed a further experiment with much higher DA parameters, *i.e.* $SH_{200} AR_{500}$, to show that the benefits provided by the DA are limited: as expected, too much deformation affects the CNN performances (indeed results obtained with $SH_{200} AR_{500}$ will be worse than those obtained with *e.g.* $SH_{40} AR_{200}$).

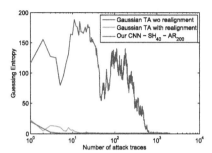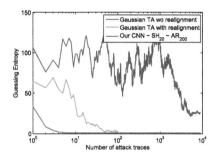

Fig. 7. Comparison between a Gaussian template attack, with and without realignment, and our CNN strategy, over the *DS_low_jitter* (left) and the *DS_high_jitter* (right).

The results we obtained are summarized in Table 3. Case $SH_0 AR_0$ corresponds to a training performed without DA technique (and hence serves as a reference suffering from the overfitting phenomenon). It can be observed that as the DA parameters raise, the validation accuracy increases while the training accuracy decreases. This experimentally validates that the DA technique is efficient in reducing overfitting. Remarkably in some cases, for example in the *DS_low_jitter* dataset case with $SH_{100} AR_{40}$, the best validation accuracy is higher than the best training accuracy. In Fig. 8 the training and validation accuracies achieved in this case epoch by epoch are depicted. It can be noticed that the unusual relation between the training and the validation accuracies does not only concern the maximal values, but is almost kept epoch by epoch. Observing the picture, we can be convinced that, since this fact occurs at many epochs, this is not a consequence of some unlucky inaccurate estimations. To interpret this phenomenon we observe that the training set contains both the original data and the augmented ones (*i.e.* deformed by the DA) while the validation set only contains non-augmented data. The fact that the achieved training accuracy is lower than the validation one, indicates that the CNN does not succeed in learning how to classify the augmented data, but succeeds to extract the features of interest for the classification of the original data. We judge this behaviour positively. Concerning the DA techniques we observe that they are efficient when applied independently and that their combination is still more efficient.

According to our results in Table 3, we selected the model issued using the $SH_{200} AR_{40}$ technique for the *DS_low_jitter* dataset and the one issued using the $SH_{200} AR_{20}$ technique for the *DS_higher_jitter*. In Fig. 7 we compare their performances with those of a Gaussian TA possibly combined with a realignment technique. To tune this comparison, several state-of-the-art Gaussian TA have

Table 3. Results of our CNN in presence of artificially-generated jitter countermeasure, with different DA techniques. See the caption of Table 1 for a legend.

DS_low_jitter								
a	b	SH_0		SH_{20}		SH_{40}		SH_{200}
c	d							
AR_0		100.0%	68.7%	99.8%	86.1%	98.9%	84.1%	
		57.4%	14	82.5%	6	83.6%	6	
AR_{100}		87.7%	88.2%	82.4%	88.4%	81.9%	89.6%	
		86.0%	6	87.0%	5	87.5%	6	
AR_{200}		83.2%	88.6%	81.4%	86.9%	**80.6%**	**88.9%**	
		86.6%	6	85.7%	6	**87.7%**	**5**	
AR_{500}								85.0% / 88.6%
								86.2% / 5

DS_high_jitter								
a	b	SH_0		SH_{20}		SH_{40}		SH_{200}
c	d							
AR_0		100%	45.0%	100%	60.0%	98.5%	67.6%	
		40.6%	35	51.1%	9	62.4%	11	
AR_{100}		90.4%	57.3%	76.6%	73.6%	78.5%	76.4%	
		50.2%	15	72.4%	11	73.5%	9	
AR_{200}		83.1%	67.7%	**82.0%**	**77.1%**	82.6%	77.0%	
		64.0%	11	**75.5%**	**8**	74.4%	8	
AR_{500}								83.6% / 73.4%
								68.2% / 11

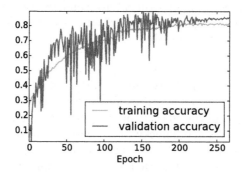

Fig. 8. Training of the CNN model with DA $SH_{100}AR_{40}$. The training classification problem becomes harder than the real classification problem, leading validation accuracy constantly higher than the training one.

been tested. In particular, for the selection of the PoIs, two approaches have been applied: first we selected from 3 to 20 points maximising the estimated instantaneous SNR, secondly we selected sliding windows of 3 to 20 consecutive points covering the region of interest. For the template processing, we tried (1) the classical approach [5] where a mean and a covariance matrix are estimated for each class, (2) the *pooled* covariance matrix strategy proposed in [6] and (3) the stochastic approach proposed in [27]. In this experiment, the leakage is concentrated in peaks that are easily detected by their relatively high amplitude, so we use a simple method that consists in first detecting the peaks above a chosen threshold, then keeping all the samples in a window around these peaks. The results plotted in Fig. 7 are the best ones we obtained (via the stochastic approach over some 5-sized windows). Results show that the performances of the CNN approach are much higher than those of the Gaussian templates, both with and without realignment. This confirms the robustness of the CNN approach with respect to the jitter effect: the selection of PoIs and the realignment integrated in the training phase are effective.

5.2   Performances on a Secure Smartcard

As a last (but most challenging) experiment we deployed our CNN architecture to attack an AES hardware implementation over a modern secure smartcard (secure implementation on 90 nm technology node). On this implementation, the architecture is designed to optimize the area, and the speed performances are not the major concern. The architecture is here minimal, implementing only one hardware instance of the SubByte module. The AES SubByte operation is thus executed serially and one byte is processed per clock cycle. To protect the implementation, several countermeasures are implemented. Among them, a hardware mechanism induces a strong jitter effect which produces an important traces' desynchronization. The bench is set up to trig the acquisition of the trace on a peak which corresponds to the processing of the first byte. Consequently, the set of traces is aligned according to the processing of the first byte while the other bytes leakages are completely misaligned. To illustrate the effect of this misalignment, the SNR characterizing the (aligned) first byte and the (misaligned) second byte are computed (according to the formula given in [4]) using a set of 150,000 traces labelled by the value of the SubByte output (256 labels). These SNRs are depicted in the top part of Fig. 9. The SNR of the first byte (in green) detects a quite high leakage, while the SNR of the second byte (in blue) is nullified. A zoom of the SNR of the second peak is proposed in the bottom-left part of Fig. 9. In order to confirm that the very low SNR corresponding to the second byte is only due to the desynchronization, the patterns of the traces corresponding to the second byte have been resynchronized using a peak-detection-based algorithm, quite similar to the one applied for the experiments of Sect. 5.1. Then the SNR has been computed onto these new aligned traces and has been plot in red in the top-left part of Fig. 9; this SNR is very similar to that of the first byte. This clearly shows that the leakage information is contained into the trace but is efficiently hidden by the jitter-based countermeasure.

We applied the CNN approach onto the rough set of traces (without any alignement). First, a 2,500-long window of the trace has been selected to input CNN. The window, identified by the vertical cursors in the bottom part of Fig. 9, has been selected to ensure that the pattern corresponding to the leakage of the second byte is inside the selection. At this step, it is important to notice that such a selection is not at all as meticulous as the selection of PoIs required by a classical TA approach. The training phase has been performed using 98,000

labelled traces; 1,000 further traces have been used for the validation set. We
performed the training phase over a desktop computer equipped with an Intel
Xeon E5440 @2,83GHz processor, 24Gb of RAM and a GeForce GTS 450 GPU.
Without data augmentation each epoch took about 200s.[16] The training stopped
after 25 epochs. Considering that in this case we applied an early-stopping strategy that stopped training after 20 epochs without validation loss decrement, it
means that the final trainable weights are obtained after 5 epochs (in about
15 min). The results that we obtained are summarized in Table 4. They prove
not only that our CNN is robust to the misalignment caused by the jitter but
also that the DA technique is effective in raising its efficiency. A comparison
between the CNN performances and the best results we obtained over the same
dataset applying the realignment-TA strategy in the right part of Fig. 9. Beyond
the fact that the CNN approach slightly outperforms the realignment-TA one,
and considering that both case-results shown here are surely non-optimal, what
is remarkable is that the CNN approach is potentially suitable even in cases
where realignment methods are impracticable or not satisfying. It is of particular interest in cases where sensitive information does not lie in proximity of
peaks or of easily detectable patterns, since many resynchronization techniques
are based on pattern or peak detection. If the resynchronization fails, the TA
approach falls out of service, while the CNN one remains a further weapon in
the hands of an attacker.

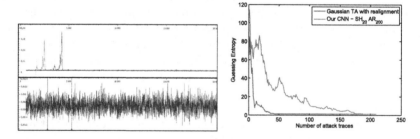

Fig. 9. Top Left: in green the SNR for the first byte; in blue the SNR for the second
byte; in red the SNR for the second byte after a trace realignment. Bottom Left: a zoom
of the blue SNR trace. Right: comparison between a Gaussian template attack with
realignment, and our CNN strategy, over the modern smart card with jitter. (Color
figure online)

Table 4. Results of our CNN over the modern smart card with jitter.

		SH_0AR_0		$SH_{10}AR_{100}$		$SH_{20}AR_{200}$	
a	b	35.0%	1.1%	12.5%	1.5%	**10.4%**	**2.2%**
c	d	1.2%	137	1.3%	89	**1.8%**	**54**

---

[16] Raising to about 2,000 seconds when $SH_{20}DA_{200}$ data augmentation is performed
(data are augmented online during training).

6   Conclusions

In this paper we have proposed an end-to-end profiling attack approach, based on the CNNs. We claimed that such a strategy would be robust to trace misalignment, and we successfully verified our claim by performing CNN-based attacks against different kinds of misaligned data. This property represents a great practical advantage compared to the state-of-the-art profiling attacks, that require a meticulous trace realignment in order to be efficient. It represents also a solution to the problem of the selection of points of interest issue: CNNs efficiently manage high-dimensional data, allowing the attacker to simply select large windows. In this sense, the experiments described in Sect. 5.2 are very representative: our CNN retrieves information from a large window of points instead of an almost null instantaneous SNR. To guarantee the robustness to trace misalignment, we used a quite complex architecture for our CNN, and we clearly identified the risk of overfitting phenomenon. To deal with this classical issue in machine learning, we proposed two Data Augmentation techniques adapted to misaligned side-channel traces. All the experimental results we obtained have proved that they provide a great benefit to the CNN strategy.

Acknowledgements. This work has been partially funded by the H2020-DS-LEIT-2016 project REASSURE. The authors would like to thank Charles Guillemet for the fruitful discussions about this work.

References

1. Keras library. https://keras.io/
2. Belaïd, S., Coron, J.-S., Fouque, P.-A., Gérard, B., Kammerer, J.-G., Prouff, E.: Improved side-channel analysis of finite-field multiplication. In: Güneysu, T., Handschuh, H. (eds.) CHES 2015. LNCS, vol. 9293, pp. 395–415. Springer, Heidelberg (2015). doi:10.1007/978-3-662-48324-4_20
3. Bishop, C.M.: Pattern Recognition and Machine Learning. Springer, Heidelberg (2006)
4. Cagli, E., Dumas, C., Prouff, E.: Kernel discriminant analysis for information extraction in the presence of masking. In: Lemke-Rust, K., Tunstall, M. (eds.) CARDIS 2016. LNCS, vol. 10146, pp. 1–22. Springer, Cham (2017). doi:10.1007/978-3-319-54669-8_1
5. Chari, S., Rao, J.R., Rohatgi, P.: Template attacks. In: Kaliski, B.S., Koç, K., Paar, C. (eds.) CHES 2002. LNCS, vol. 2523, pp. 13–28. Springer, Heidelberg (2003). doi:10.1007/3-540-36400-5_3
6. Choudary, O., Kuhn, M.G.: Efficient template attacks. In: Francillon, A., Rohatgi, P. (eds.) CARDIS 2013. LNCS, vol. 8419, pp. 253–270. Springer, Cham (2014). doi:10.1007/978-3-319-08302-5_17
7. Clavier, C., Coron, J.-S., Dabbous, N.: Differential power analysis in the presence of hardware countermeasures. In: Koç, Ç.K., Paar, C. (eds.) CHES 2000. LNCS, vol. 1965, pp. 252–263. Springer, Heidelberg (2000). doi:10.1007/3-540-44499-8_20
8. Coron, J.-S., Kizhvatov, I.: An efficient method for random delay generation in embedded software. In: Clavier, C., Gaj, K. (eds.) CHES 2009. LNCS, vol. 5747, pp. 156–170. Springer, Heidelberg (2009). doi:10.1007/978-3-642-04138-9_12

9. Coron, J.-S., Kizhvatov, I.: Analysis and improvement of the random delay countermeasure of CHES 2009. In: Mangard, S., Standaert, F.-X. (eds.) CHES 2010. LNCS, vol. 6225, pp. 95–109. Springer, Heidelberg (2010). doi:10.1007/978-3-642-15031-9_7

10. Cover, T.M., Thomas, J.A.: Elements of Information Theory. Wiley, New York (2012)

11. Durvaux, F., Renauld, M., Standaert, F.-X., van Oldeneel tot Oldenzeel, L., Veyrat-Charvillon, N.: Efficient removal of random delays from embedded software implementations using Hidden Markov models. In: Mangard, S. (ed.) CARDIS 2012. LNCS, vol. 7771, pp. 123–140. Springer, Heidelberg (2013). doi:10.1007/978-3-642-37288-9_9

12. Fisher, R.A.: The use of multiple measurements in taxonomic problems. Ann. Eugen. **7**(7), 179–188 (1936)

13. Goodfellow, I., Bengio, Y., Courville, A.: Deep Learning. MIT Press, Cambridge (2016). http://www.deeplearningbook.org

14. Hinton, G.E., Srivastava, N., Krizhevsky, A., Sutskever, I., Salakhutdinov, R.: Improving neural networks by preventing co-adaptation of feature detectors. CoRR, abs/1207.0580 (2012)

15. Hospodar, G., Gierlichs, B., De Mulder, E., Verbauwhede, I., Vandewalle, J.: Machine learning in side-channel analysis: a first study. J. Crypt. Eng. **1**(4), 293–302 (2011)

16. Ioffe, S., Szegedy, C.: Batch normalization: accelerating deep network training by reducing internal covariate shift. CoRR, abs/1502.03167 (2015)

17. Krizhevsky, A., Sutskever, I., Hinton, G.E.: ImageNet classification with deep convolutional neural networks. In: Pereira, F., Burges, C.J.C., Bottou, L., Weinberger, K.Q. (eds.) Advances in Neural Information Processing Systems, vol. 25, pp. 1097–1105. Curran Associates Inc. (2012)

18. LeCun, Y., Bengio, Y., et al.: Convolutional networks for images, speech, and time series. In: The Handbook of Brain Theory and Neural Networks, vol. 3361(10) (1995)

19. Lin, H.W., Tegmark, M.: Why does deep and cheap learning work so well? arXiv preprint arXiv:1608.08225 (2016)

20. Maghrebi, H., Portigliatti, T., Prouff, E.: Breaking cryptographic implementations using deep learning techniques. In: Carlet, C., Hasan, M.A., Saraswat, V. (eds.) SPACE 2016. LNCS, vol. 10076, pp. 3–26. Springer, Cham (2016). doi:10.1007/978-3-319-49445-6_1

21. Mangard, S.: Hardware countermeasures against DPA – a statistical analysis of their effectiveness. In: Okamoto, T. (ed.) CT-RSA 2004. LNCS, vol. 2964, pp. 222–235. Springer, Heidelberg (2004). doi:10.1007/978-3-540-24660-2_18

22. Martinasek, Z., Hajny, J., Malina, L.: Optimization of power analysis using neural network. In: Francillon, A., Rohatgi, P. (eds.) CARDIS 2013. LNCS, vol. 8419, pp. 94–107. Springer, Cham (2014). doi:10.1007/978-3-319-08302-5_7

23. Martinasek, Z., Zeman, V.: Innovative method of the power analysis. Radioengineering **22**(2), 586–594 (2013)

24. Nagashima, S., Homma, N., Imai, Y., Aoki, T., Satoh, A.: DPA using phase-based waveform matching against random-delay countermeasure. In: IEEE International Symposium on Circuits and Systems, ISCAS 2007, pp. 1807–1810. IEEE (2007)

25. Nair, V., Hinton, G.E.: Rectified linear units improve restricted boltzmann machines. In: Proceedings of the 27th International Conference on Machine Learning (ICML 2010), pp. 807–814 (2010)

26. Prechelt, L.: Early stopping — but when? In: Montavon, G., Orr, G.B., Müller, K.-R. (eds.) Neural Networks: Tricks of the Trade. LNCS, vol. 7700, pp. 53–67. Springer, Heidelberg (2012). doi:10.1007/978-3-642-35289-8_5
27. Schindler, W., Lemke, K., Paar, C.: A stochastic model for differential side channel cryptanalysis. In: Rao, J.R., Sunar, B. (eds.) CHES 2005. LNCS, vol. 3659, pp. 30–46. Springer, Heidelberg (2005). doi:10.1007/11545262_3
28. Simard, P.Y., Steinkraus, D., Platt, J.C., et al.: Best practices for convolutional neural networks applied to visual document analysis. In: ICDAR, vol. 3, pp. 958–962. Citeseer (2003)
29. Tunstall, M., Benoit, O.: Efficient use of random delays in embedded software. In: Sauveron, D., Markantonakis, K., Bilas, A., Quisquater, J.-J. (eds.) WISTP 2007. LNCS, vol. 4462, pp. 27–38. Springer, Heidelberg (2007). doi:10.1007/978-3-540-72354-7_3
30. Woudenberg, J.G.J., Witteman, M.F., Bakker, B.: Improving differential power analysis by elastic alignment. In: Kiayias, A. (ed.) CT-RSA 2011. LNCS, vol. 6558, pp. 104–119. Springer, Heidelberg (2011). doi:10.1007/978-3-642-19074-2_8
31. Veyrat-Charvillon, N., Medwed, M., Kerckhof, S., Standaert, F.-X.: Shuffling against side-channel attacks: a comprehensive study with cautionary note. In: Wang, X., Sako, K. (eds.) ASIACRYPT 2012. LNCS, vol. 7658, pp. 740–757. Springer, Heidelberg (2012). doi:10.1007/978-3-642-34961-4_44
32. Wong, S.C., Gatt, A., Stamatescu, V., McDonnell, M.D.: Understanding data augmentation for classification: when to warp? In: 2016 International Conference on Digital Image Computing: Techniques and Applications (DICTA), pp. 1–6. IEEE (2016)
33. Yang, S., Zhou, Y., Liu, J., Chen, D.: Back propagation neural network based leakage characterization for practical security analysis of cryptographic implementations. In: Kim, H. (ed.) ICISC 2011. LNCS, vol. 7259, pp. 169–185. Springer, Heidelberg (2012). doi:10.1007/978-3-642-31912-9_12

A   Discussion about Software Countermeasures

The goal of the experiences performed in in Sect. 4 was to verify the shift-invariance property claimed by the CNN architecture. We achieved this objective by considering the case of a simple countermeasure, the uniform RDI, which consists in injecting shifts in side-channel traces. We remark that this kind of countermeasure is nowadays considered defeated, e.g. thanks to resynchronization by *cross-correlation* [24]. The complexity of the state-of-the-art resynchronization techniques strongly depends on the variability of the shift. When the latter variability is low, i.e. when attacks are judge to be applicable, multiple random delays are recommended. It has even been proposed to adapt the probabilistic distributions of the random delays to achieve good compromises between the countermeasure efficiency and the chip performance overhead [8,9]. Attacks have already been shown even against this multiple RDI kind of countermeasures, e.g. [11]. The latter attack exploits some Gaussian templates to classify the leakage of each instruction; the classification scores are used to feed a Hidden Markov Model (HMM) that describes the complete chip execution, and the Viterbi algorithm is applied to find the most probable sequence of states for the HMM and to remove the random delays. We remark that this HMM-based attack exploits Gaussian templates to feed the HMM model, and the accuracy of such templates is affected by other misalignment reasons, *e.g.* clock jitter. We believe that our CNN approach proposal for operation classification, is a valuable alternative to the Gaussian template one, and might even provide benefits to the HMM performances, by *e.g.* improving the robustness of the attack in presence of both RDI and jitter-based countermeasures. This robustness w.r.t. of misalignment caused by the clock jitter is analysed in Sect. 5.

CacheZoom: How SGX Amplifies the Power of Cache Attacks

Ahmad Moghimi$^{(\boxtimes)}$, Gorka Irazoqui, and Thomas Eisenbarth

Worcester Polytechnic Institute, Worcester, MA, USA
{amoghimi,girazoki,teisenbarth}@wpi.edu

Abstract. In modern computing environments, hardware resources are commonly shared, and parallel computation is widely used. Parallel tasks can cause privacy and security problems if proper isolation is not enforced. Intel proposed SGX to create a trusted execution environment within the processor. SGX relies on the hardware, and claims runtime protection even if the OS and other software components are malicious. However, SGX disregards side-channel attacks. We introduce a powerful cache side-channel attack that provides system adversaries a high resolution channel. Our attack tool named *CacheZoom* is able to virtually track all memory accesses of SGX enclaves with high spatial and temporal precision. As proof of concept, we demonstrate AES key recovery attacks on commonly used implementations including those that were believed to be resistant in previous scenarios. Our results show that SGX cannot protect critical data sensitive computations, and efficient AES key recovery is possible in a practical environment. In contrast to previous works which require hundreds of measurements, this is the first cache side-channel attack on a real system that can recover AES keys with a minimal number of measurements. We can successfully recover AES keys from T-Table based implementations with as few as ten measurements.

1   Motivation

In the parallel computing environment, processes with various trust and criticality levels are allowed to run concurrently and share system resources. Proliferation of cloud computing technology elevated these phenomena to the next level. Cloud computers running many different services authored by various providers process user information on the same hardware. Traditionally, the operating system (OS) provides security and privacy services. In cloud computing, cloud providers and the hypervisor also become part of the Trusted Computing Base (TCB). Due to the high complexity and various attack surfaces in modern computing systems, keeping an entire system secure is usually unrealistic [19,33].

One way to reduce the TCB is to outsource security-critical services to Secure Elements (SE), a separate trusted hardware which usually undergoes rigorous auditing. Trusted Platform Modules (TPM), for example, provide services such as cryptography, secure boot, sealing data and attestation beyond the authority of the OS [39]. However, SEs come with their own drawbacks: they are static

© International Association for Cryptologic Research 2017
W. Fischer and N. Homma (Eds.): CHES 2017, LNCS 10529, pp. 69–90, 2017.
DOI: 10.1007/978-3-319-66787-4_4

components and connected to the CPU over an untrusted bus. Trusted Execution Environments (TEE) are an alternative, which provide similar services within the CPU. A TEE is an isolated environment to run software with a higher trust level than the OS. The software running inside a TEE has full access to the system resources while it is protected from other applications and the OS. Examples include ARM TrustZone [4] and Intel Software Guard eXtensions (SGX) [29]. Intel SGX creates a TEE on an untrusted system by only trusting the hardware in which the code is executed. Trusted code is secured in an *enclave*, which is encrypted and authenticated by the hardware. The CPU decrypts and verifies enclave code and data as it is moved into the cache. That is, enclaves are logically protected from malicious applications, the OS, and physical adversaries monitoring system buses. However, Intel SGX is not protected against attacks that utilize hardware resources as a side channel [28]. And indeed, first proposed works showing that microarchitectural side channels can be exploited include attacks using page table faults [52] and the branch prediction unit [34].

Caches have become a very popular side channel in many scenarios, including mobile [35] and cloud environments [26]. Reasons include that Last Level Cache (LCC) attacks perform well in cross-core scenarios on Intel machines. Another advantage of cache attacks are the high *spatial* resolution they provide. This high spatial resolution, combined with a good temporal resolution, have enabled attacks on major asymmetric implementations, unless they are optimized for constant memory accesses. For symmetric cryptography, the scenario is more challenging. A software AES implementation can be executed in a few hundred cycles, while a `Prime+Probe` cycle on the LLC takes about 2000 cycles to monitor a single set. To avoid the undersampling, synchronized attacks first prime, trigger a single encryption and then probe, yielding at best one observation per encryption [37]. Higher resolution is only possible in OS adversarial scenarios.

1.1   Our Contribution

We demonstrate not only that Intel SGX is vulnerable to cache attacks, but show that with SGX, the quality of information retrieved is significantly improved. The improved resolution enables attacks that are infeasible in previous scenarios, e.g., cloud environments. We utilize all the capabilities that SGX assumes an attacker has, i.e., full access to OS resources. We construct a tool[1] named *CacheZoom* that is able to interrupt the victim every few memory accesses, thereby collecting high-resolution information about all memory accesses that the target enclave makes by applying `Prime+Probe` attack in the L1 cache. The usage of core-private resources does not reduce the applicability of the attack, as the compromised OS schedules both victim and attacker in the same core.

While tracking memory accesses of enclave with high temporal and spatial resolution has many adversarial scenarios, we demonstrate the power of this side channel by attacking several AES implementations. Further, we show that

---

[1] *CacheZoom* source and data sets: https://github.com/vernamlab/CacheZoom.

adopted countermeasures in popular cryptographic libraries, like cache prefetching and implementations with small memory footprint, not only do not prevent attacks, but can facilitate attacker's observation. In short, this work:

- Presents a powerful and low-noise side channel implemented through the L1 cache. We exploit several capabilities corresponding to the compromised OS. This side channel can be applied against TEEs to recover fine grained information about memory accesses, which often carry sensitive data.
- Demonstrates the strength of our side channel by recovering AES keys with fewer traces than ever in previous attacks, and further, by attacking implementations considered resistant against cache attacks.
- Shows that some of the countermeasures that were supposed to protect AES implementations, e.g. prefetching and S-box implementations, are not effective in the context of SGX. In fact, prefetching can even ease the retrieval of memory traces.

2 Background

This section covers topics that help understand the side channel used to retrieve sensitive information. We discuss the basic functionality of Intel SGX and possible microarchitectural attacks that can be deployed against it.

2.1 How Intel SGX Works

Intel introduced SGX, a new subset of hardware instructions that allows execution of software inside isolated environments called *enclaves* with the release of Skylake generation. Enclaves are isolated from other components running on the same hardware, including OSs. SGX has recently gained attention of the security community and various SGX-based solutions have been proposed [5,7,44].

Enclave modules can be shipped as part of an untrusted application and can be utilized by untrusted components of the application. The untrusted component interacts with the system software, which dedicates specific trusted memory regions for the enclave. After that, the authenticity, integrity and confidentiality of enclave are provided and measured by the hardware. Any untrusted code base, including the OS, has no control over the trusted memory region. Untrusted applications can only use specific instructions to call the trusted component through predefined interfaces. This design helps developers to benefit from the hardware isolation for security critical applications.

SGX is designed to protect enclaves from malicious users that gain root access to an OS. Memory pages belonging to an enclave are encrypted in DRAM and protected from a malicious OS snooping on them. Pages are only decrypted when they are processed by the CPU, e.g., when they are moved to the caches. In short, SGX assumes only the hardware to be trusted; any other agent is considered susceptible of being malicious. Upon enclave creation, virtual memory pages that can only map to a protected DRAM region (called the Enclave Page Cache) are reserved. The OS is in charge of the memory page mapping; however, SGX detects any malicious mapping performed by it. In fact, any malicious action from the OS will be stored by SGX and is verifiable by third party agents.

2.2   Microarchitectural Attacks in SGX

Despite all the protection that SGX offers, the documentation specifically claims that side channel attacks were not considered under the threat scope of its design. In fact, although dealing with encrypted memory pages, the cache utilization is performed similar to decrypted mode and concurrently to any other process in the system. This means that the hardware resources can be utilized as side channels by both malicious enclaves and OSs. While enclave-to-enclave attacks have several similarities to cross-VM attacks, malicious OS-to-enclave attacks can give attackers a new capability not observed before: virtually unlimited temporal resolution. The OS can interrupt the execution of enclave processes after every small number of memory accesses to check the hardware utilization, as just the TLB (but no other hardware resources) is flushed during context switches. Further, while cross-core attacks gained huge popularity in others scenarios for not requiring core co-residency, a compromised OS can assign an enclave any affinity of its choice, and therefore use any core-private resource. Thus, while SGX can prevent untrusted software to perform Direct Memory Access (DMA) attacks, it also gives almost full resolution for exploitation by hardware side channels. For instance, an attacker can exploit page faults to learn about the memory page usage of the enclave. Further she can create contention and snoop on the utilization of any core-private and core-shared resource, including but not limited to Branch Prediction Units (BPUs), L1 caches or LLCs [1,36,41]. Further, although applicable in other scenarios [10], enclave execution mode does not update the Hardware Performance Counters, and these can not provide (at least directly) information about the isolated process.

From the aforementioned resources, cache gives the most information. Unlike page faults, which at most will give a granularity of 4 kB, cache hits/misses can give 64 byte utilization granularity. In addition, while other hardware resources like Branch Prediction Units (BPU) can only extract branch dependent execution flow information, cache attacks can extract information from any memory access. Although most prior work targets the LLC for being shared across cores, this is not necessary in SGX scenarios, local caches are as applicable as LLC attacks. Further, because caches are not flushed when the enclave execution is interrupted, the OS can gain almost unlimited timing resolution.

2.3   The Prime+Probe Attack

The Prime+Probe attack was first introduced as a spy process capable of attacking core-private caches [41]. It was later expanded to recover RSA keys [2], keystrokes and ElGamal keys across VMs [43,55]. As our attack is carried out in the L1 caches, we do not face some hurdles (e.g. slices) that an attacker would have to overcome. The Prime+Probe attack stages include:

- **Prime:** in which the attacker fills the entire cache or a small portion of it with her own dummy data.
- **Victim Access:** in which the attacker waits for the victim to make accesses to particular sets in the cache, hoping to see key dependent cache utilization. Note that, in any case, victim accesses to primed sets will evict at least one of the attackers dummy blocks from the set.
- **Probe:** in which the attacker performs a per-set timed re-access of the previously primed data. If the attacker observes a high probe time, she deduces that the cache set was utilized by the victim. On the contrary, if the attacker observes low access times, she deduces that all the previously primed memory blocks still reside in the cache, i.e., it was not utilized by the victim.

Thus, the `Prime+Probe` methodology allows an attacker to guess the cache sets utilized by the victim. This information can be used to mount a full key recovery attack if the algorithm has key-dependent memory accesses translated into different cache set accesses.

3   Related Work

Timing side-channel attacks have been studied for many years. On a local area network, the timing of the decryption operation on a web server could reveal information about private keys stored on the server [15]. Timing attacks are capable of breaking important cryptography primitives, such as exponentiation and factorization operations of Diffie-Hellman and RSA [32]. More specifically, **microarchitectural timing side channels** have been explored extensively [21]. The first attacks proposed were based on the timing difference between local core-private cache misses and hits. Generally, cache timing attacks are based on the fact that a spy process can measure the differences in memory access times. These attacks are proposed to recover cryptography keys of ciphers such as DES [50], AES [11] and RSA [42]. Although there exist solutions to make cryptographic implementation resistant to cache attacks [13,41], most of these solutions result in worse performance. Further, cache attacks are capable of extracting information from non-cryptographic applications [56].

More recent proposals applied **cache side channels on shared LLC**, a shared resource among all the cores. This is important as, compared to previous core-private attacks, LLC attacks are applicable even when attacker and victim reside in different cores. The Flush+Reload [8,53] attack on LLC is only applicable to systems with shared memory. These side channels can be improved by performance degradation [3,24]. Flush+Reload can be applied across VMs [31], in Platform as a service (PaaS) clouds [56] and on smartphones [35]. The Flush+Reload is constrained by the memory deduplication requirement. On the other hand, `Prime+Probe` [36], shows that in contrast to the previous core-private cache side channels and the Flush+Reload attack, practical attacks can be performed without memory deduplication or a core co-residency requirement. The `Prime+Probe` attack can be implemented from virtually any cloud virtual machines running on the same hardware. The attacker can identify where a particular VM is located on the cloud infrastructure such as Amazon EC2, create VMs until a co-located one is found [43,54] and perform cross-VM Prime+Probe attacks [30]. Prime+Probe can also be mounted from a browser using JavaScript [40] and as a malicious smartphone application [35]. In addition to caches, other microarchitectural components such as **Branch Target Buffers (BTB)** are vulnerable to side channels [1,34]. BTB can be exploited to determine if a branch has been taken by a target process or not, e.g. to bypass Address Space Layout Randomization (ASLR) [20].

Security of Intel SGX has been analyzed based on the available public resources [17]. A side channel resistant TCB is proposed in the literature [18]. However, the proposed solution requires significant changes to the design of the processor. Similar to Intel SGX, ARM TrustZone is vulnerable to cache side-channel attacks [35]. Control-Channel attacks [52] have been proposed using the page-fault mechanism. An adversarial OS can introduce page faults to a target application and, based on the timing of the accessed page, the execution flow of a target can be inferred at page size granularity. Page fault side channels are effective on SGX and can be defeated using software solutions [48] or by exploiting Intel Transactional Synchronization Extensions (TSX) [47]. Race conditions between two running threads inside an enclave can be exploited [51]. SGX-Shield [46] proposes protection by adding ASLR protection and introduces software diversity inside an enclave. Several Cache attacks on SGX have recently and concurrently been shown, e.g. on AES [22] and RSA [12]. While those works also exploit core co-location and L1 cache leakage, they fall short of exposing the full temporal and spatial resolution and thus focus on known vulnerable implementations and attack styles. An enclave-to-enclave attack through LLC in a different adversarial scenario [45], as well as methods to detect privileged side-channel attacks from within an enclave [16] have concurrently been proposed.

4   Creating a High-Resolution Side Channel on Intel SGX

We explain how to establish a high resolution channel on a compromised OS to monitor an SGX enclave. We first describe attacker capabilities, then our main design goals and how our malicious kernel driver is implemented. We finally test the resolution of our proposed side channel.

4.1   Attacker Capabilities

In our attack, we assume that the adversary has root access to a Linux OS running SGX. The attacker is capable of installing kernel modules and configuring boot properties of the machine. As consequence of root access, the attacker can read the content of static binary on the disk, observe which symmetric cipher and implementation is used, and *identify offset of tables that static data from the victim binary will occupy.*[2] Although the attacker can observe the binary,

---

[2] If the enclave binary is obfuscated, position of tables needs to be reconstructed using reverse engineering methods, e.g. by analyzing cache access patterns [26].

she has no knowledge of the cipher key used during the encryption. In addition, the attacker is capable of synchronizing the enclave execution with CacheZoom. These assumptions are reasonable, as SGX promises a trusted environment for execution on untrusted systems. Symmetric keys can be generated at runtime from a secure random entropy (using *RDRAND* instruction) and/or transferred through a public secure channel without the attacker knowledge.

4.2   CacheZoom Design

To create a high bandwidth channel with minimal noise, **(1)** we need to isolate the attackers' malicious spy process code and the target enclave's trusted execution from the rest of the running operations and **(2)** we need to perform the attack on small units of execution. By having these two elements, even a comparably small cache like L1 turns into a high capacity channel. Note that our spy process monitors the L1D data cache, but can also be implemented to monitor the L1I instruction cache or LLC. Our spy process is designed to profile all the sets in the L1D cache with the goal of retrieving maximum leakage. In order to avoid noise, we dedicate one physical core to our experimental setup, i.e., to the attacker `Prime+Probe` code and the victim enclave process. All other running operations on the system, including OS services and interrupts, run on the remaining cores. Furthermore, CacheZoom forces the enclave execution to be interrupted in short time intervals, in order to identify all enclave memory accesses. Note that, the longer the victim enclave runs without interruption, the higher the number of accesses made to the cache, implying higher noise and less temporal resolution. CacheZoom should further reduces other possible sources of noise, e.g., context switches. The main purpose is that the attacker can retrieve most of the secret dependent memory accesses made by the target enclave. Since the L1 cache is virtually addressed, knowing the offset with respect to a page boundary is enough to know the accessed set.

4.3   CacheZoom Implementation

We explain technical details behind the implementation of CacheZoom, in particular, how the noise sources are limited and how we increase the time resolution to obtain clean traces.

Enclave-Attack Process Isolation. Linux OS schedules different tasks among available logical processors by default. The main scheduler function `__schedule` is triggered on every tick of the logical processor's local timer interrupt. One way to remove a specific logical processor from the default scheduling algorithm is through the kernel boot configuration `isolcpus` which accepts a list of logical cores to be excluded from scheduling. To avoid a logical core from triggering the scheduling algorithm on its local timer interrupt, we can use `nohz_full` boot configuration option. Recall that reconfiguring the boot parameters and restarting the OS is included in our attackers capabilities. However, these capabilities are not necessary, as we can walk through the kernel task tree structure and turn the PF_NO_SETAFFINITY flag off for all tasks. Then, by dynamically calling the kernel sched_setaffinity interface for every task, we are able to force all the running kernel and user tasks to execute on specific cores. In addition to tasks and kernel threads, interrupts also need to be isolated from the target core. Most of the interrupts can be restricted to specific cores except for the non-maskable interrupts (NMIs), which can't be avoided. However, in our experience, their occurrence is negligible and does not add considerable amount of noise.

CPU frequency has a more dynamic behavior in modern processors. Our target processor has **Speedstep** technology which allows dynamic adjustment of processor voltage and **C-state**, which allows different power management states. These features, in addition to hyper-threading (concurrent execution of two threads on the same physical core), make the actual measurement of cycles through *rdtsc* less reliable. Cache side channel attacks that use this cycle counter are affected by the dynamic CPU frequency. In non-OS adversarial scenarios, these noise sources have been neglected thus forcing the attacker to do more measurements. In our scenario, these processor features can be disabled through the computer BIOS setup or can be configured by the OS to avoid unpredictable behavior. In our attack, we simply disable every second logical processor to practically avoid hyper-threading. To maintain a stable frequency in spite of the available battery saving and frequency features, we set the CPU scaling governor to **performance** and limit the maximum and minimum frequency range.

Increasing the Time Resolution. Aiming at reducing the number of memory accesses made by the victim between two malicious OS interrupts, we use the local APIC programmable interrupt, available on physical cores. The APIC timer has different programmable modes but we are only interested in the **TSC-Deadline** mode. In TSC deadline mode, the specified TSC value will cause the local APIC to generate a timer IRQ once the CPU reaches it. In the Linux kernel, the function lapic_next_deadline is responsible for setting the next deadline on each interrupt. The actual interrupt handler routine for this IRQ is local_apic_timer_interrupt. In order to enable/disable our attack, we install hooks on these two functions. By patching the null function calls, available for the purpose of live patching, we can redirect these functions to the malicious routines in our kernel modules at runtime.

```
ffffffff81050900 lapic_next_deadline          ffffffff81050c90 local_apic_timer_interrupt
ffffffff81050900: callq  null_sub1            ffffffff81050c90:  callq  null_sub2
```

In the modified lapic_next_deadline function, we set the timer interrupt to specific values such that the running target enclave is interrupted every short period of execution time. In the modified local_apic_timer_interrupt, we first probe the entire 64 sets of the L1D cache to gather information of the previous execution unit and then prime the entire 64 sets for the next one. After each probe, we store the retrieved cache information to a separate buffer. Our kernel driver is capable of performing 50000 circular samplings. To avoid unnecessarily sampling, we need to synchronize with the target enclave execution. For this purpose, we enable the hooks just before the call to the enclave interface and disable it right after.

4.4 Testing the Performance of CacheZoom

Our experimental setup is a Dell Inspiron 5559 laptop with Intel(R) Skylake Core(TM) i7-6500U processor running Ubuntu 14.04.5 LTS and SGX SDK 1.7. Our target processor has 2 hyper-threaded physical cores. Each physical core has 32 kB of L1D and 32 kB of L1I local cache memory. The L1 cache, used as our side channel, is 8 way associative and consists of 64 sets.

Even though Skylake processors use an adaptive LRU cache replacement policy and the adaptive behavior is undocumented [23], our results show that we can still use the pointer chasing eviction set technique [36] to detect memory accesses. In the specific case of our L1D cache, the access time for chasing 8 pointers associated to a specific set is about 40 cycles on average. In order to test the resolution of our side channel, we took an average of 50000 samples of all the sets and varied the number of evictions from 0 to 8. The results can be seen in Fig. 1, where the access time is increased by roughly 5 cycles for every additional eviction. Thus, our results show that our eviction set gives us an accurate measurement on the number of evicted lines from a specific set.

Our isolated CPU core and the L1D eviction set have the minimal possible noise and avoid noises such as CPU frequency, OS and enclave noise; however, the actual noise from the context switch between enclave process and attacker interrupt is mostly unavoidable. The amount of noise that these unwanted memory accesses add to the observation can be measured by running an enclave with an empty loop under our attack measurement. Our results, presented in Fig. 2, show that every set has a consistent number of evictions. Among the 64 sets, there are only 4 sets that get filled as a side effect of the context switch memory accesses. For the other sets, we observed either 0 or less than 8 unwanted accesses. Due to the consistency of the number of evictions per set, we can conclude that only sets that get completely filled are obscure and do not leak any information, 4 out of 64 sets in our particular case. An example of the applied noise ex-filtration process can be observed in Fig. 3, in which the enclave process was consecutively accessing different sets. The left hand figure shows the hit access map, without

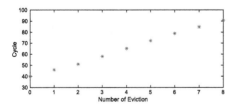

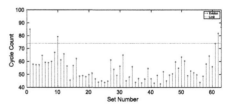

Fig. 1. Average cycle count per number of evictions in a set.

Fig. 2. Average cycle count for each set. Variations are due to channel noise: 4 sets are unusable for attacks.

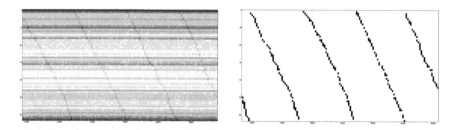

Fig. 3. Cache hit map before (left) and after (right) filtering for context switch noise. Enclave memory access patterns are clearly visible once standard noise from context switch has been eliminated

taking into account the appropriate set threshold. The right hand figure shows the access pattern retrieved from the enclave once the context switch noise access has been taking into account and removed.

5   Attack on AES

The following gives a detailed description of different implementation styles for AES to help the reader understand the attacks that we later perform:

5.1   Cache Attacks on Different AES Implementations

AES is a widely used block cipher that supports three key sizes from 128 bit to 256 bits. Our description and attacks focus on the 128-bit key version, AES-128, but most attacks described can be applied to larger-key versions as well. AES is based on 4 main operations: AddRoundKey, SubBytes, ShiftRows and Mix-Columns. The main source of leakage in AES comes from the state-dependent table look ups for the SubBytes operation. These look-ups result in secret-dependent memory accesses, which can be exploited by cache attacks.

S-box: Software implementations that implement the 4 stages independently base the SubBytes operation in a 256 entry substitution table, each entry being 8 bits long. In this implementation, a total of a 160 accesses are performed to the S-box during a 128-bit AES encryption, 16 accesses per round. We refer to this implementation style as the *S-box* implementation.

4 T-tables: To achieve a better performance, some implementations combine the MixColumns and SubBytes in a single table lookup. At the cost of bigger pre-computed tables (and therefore, more memory usage) the encryption time can be significantly reduced. The most common type uses 4 T-tables: 256 entry substitution tables, each entry being 32 bits long. The entries of the four T-tables are the same bytes but rotated by 1, 2 and 3 positions, depending on the position of the input byte in the column of the AES state. We refer to this style as *T-table implementation*. We refer to this as the 4 T-table implementation.

Large T-table Aiming at improving the memory usage of T-table based implementations, some designs utilize a single 256 entries T-table, where each entry is 64 bits long. Each entry contains two copies of the 32 bit values typically observed with regular size T-tables. This design reads each entry *with a different byte offset*, such that the values from the 4 T-tables can be read from a single bigger T-table. The performance of the implementation is comparable, but requires efficient non word-aligned memory accesses. We refer to this as the Large T-table implementation.

Depending on the implementation style, implementations can be more susceptible to cache attacks or less. The resolution an attacker gets depends on the cache line size, which is 64 bytes on our target architecture. For the **S-box** implementation, the S-box occupies a total of 4 cache lines (256 bytes). That is, an attacker able to learn for each observed access to a table entry at most two bits. Attacks relying on probabilistic observations of the S-box entries not being accessed during an entire encryption [31] would observe such a case with a probability of $1.02 \cdot 10^{-20}$, making a micro-architectural attack nearly infeasible. For a **4 T-tables** implementation, each of the T-tables gets 40 accesses per encryption, 4 per round, and occupies 16 cache lines. Therefore, the probability of a table entry not being accessed in an entire encryption is 8%, a fact that was exploited in [31] to recover the full key. In particular, all these works target either the first or the last round to avoid the MixColumns operation. In the first round, the intermediate state before the MixColumns operation is given by $s_i^0 = T_i[p_i \oplus k_i^0]$, where p_i and k_i^0 are the plaintext and first round key bytes i, T_i is the table utilization corresponding to byte i and s_i^0 is the intermediate state before the MixColumns operation in the first round. We see that, if the attacker knows the table entry being utilized x_i and the plaintext he can derive equations in the form $x_i = p_i \oplus k_i^0$ to recover the key. A similar approach can be utilized to mount an attack in the last round where the output is in the form $c_i = T_i[s_i^9] \oplus k_i^{10}$. The maximum an attacker can learn, however, is 4 bit per lookup, if each lookup can be observed separately. The scenario for attacks looking at accesses to a single cache line for an entire encryption learn a lot less, hence need significantly more measurements.

For a Large T-table implementation, the T-table occupies 32 cache lines, and the probability of not accessing an entry is reduced to 0.6%. This, although not exploited in a realistic attack, could lead to key recovery with sufficiently many measurements. An adversary observing each memory access separately, however, can learn 5 bits per access, as each cache line contains only 8 of the larger entries.

Note that an attacker that gets to observe every single access of the aforementioned AES implementations would succeed to recover the key with significantly fewer traces, as she gets to know the entry accessed at every point in the execution. This scenario was analyzed in [6] with simulated cache traces. Their work focuses on recovering the key based on observations made in the first and second AES rounds establishing relations between the first and second round keys. As a result, they succeed on recovering an AES key from a 4 T-table implementation with as few as six observed encryptions in a noise free environment.

5.2   Non-vulnerable AES Implementations

There are further efficient implementations of AES that are not automatically susceptible to cache attacks, as they avoid secret-dependent memory accesses. These implementation styles include bit-sliced implementations [38], implementations using vector instructions [25], constant memory access implementations and implementations using AES instruction set extensions on modern Intel CPUs [27]. However, they all come with their separate drawbacks. The bit-sliced implementations need data to be reformatted before and after encryption and usually show good performance only if data is processed in large chunks [9]. Constant memory access implementations also suffer from performance as the number of memory accesses during an encryption significantly increases. While hardware support like AES-NI combines absence of leakage with highest performance, it is only an option if implemented and if the hardware can be trusted [49], and further might be disabled in BIOS configuration options.

5.3   Cache Prefetching as a Countermeasure

In response to cache attacks in general and AES attacks in particular, several cryptographic library designers implement cache prefetching approaches, which just load the key dependent data or instructions to the cache prior to their possible utilization. In the case of AES, this simply means loading all the substitution tables to the cache, either once during the encryption (at the beginning) or before each round of AES. Prefetching takes advantage of the low temporal resolution that an attacker obtains when performing a regular non-OS controlled attack, as it assumes that an attacker cannot probe faster than the prefetching. Translated to AES, prefetching assumes that a cache attack does not have enough temporal granularity to determine which positions in the substitution table have been used if they are prefetched, e.g., at the beginning of each round.

An example of the implications that such a countermeasure will have on a typical cache attack can be observed in Fig. 4. The `Prime+Probe` process cannot be executed within the execution of a single AES round. Thanks to prefetching, the attacker is only able to see cache hits on all the Table entries. We analyze whether those countermeasures, implemented in many cryptographic libraries, resist the scenario in which an attacker fully controls the OS and can interrupt the AES process after every small number of accesses. As it was explained in Sect. 2, attacking SGX gives a malicious OS adversary almost full temporal resolution, which can reverse the effect of prefetching mechanisms.

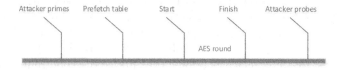

Fig. 4. Prefetching and the timeline effect for a regular `Prime+Probe` attack.

6 CacheZooming SGX-Based AES

We use CacheZoom to retrieve secret keys of different implementations of AES running inside an enclave. As mentioned in Sect. 4.1, we assume no knowledge of the encryption key, but to have access to the enclave binary, and thus to the offset of the substitution tables. We further assume the enclave is performing encryptions over a set of known plaintext bytes or ciphertext bytes.

6.1 T-Table Implementations

Our first attacks target the T-table implementations. To recover the AES key from as few traces as possible, we recover the memory access pattern of the first 2 rounds of the AES function. A perfect single trace first round attack reveals at most the least significant 4 and 5 bits of each key byte in 4 T-table (16 entries/cache line) and Large T-table implementations (8 entries/cache line) respectively. As we want to retrieve the key with the minimal number of traces, we also retrieve the information from the accesses in the second round and use the relation between the first and second round key. In particular, we utilize the relations described in [6], who utilized simulated data to demonstrate the effectiveness of their AES key recovery algorithm.

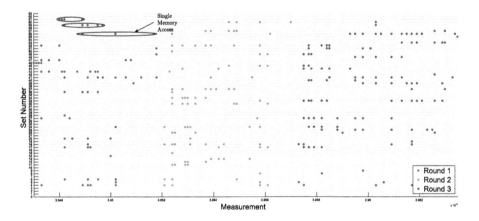

Fig. 5. Memory footprint of the AES execution inside enclave.

In our specific practical attack, we face three problems: (**1**) Even in our high resolution attack, we have noise that adds false positives and negatives to our observed memory access patterns. (**2**) Our experiments show that the out-of-order execution and parallel processing of memory accesses does not allow for a full serialization of the observed memory accesses. (**3**) Separating memory accesses belonging to different rounds can be challenging. These first two facts can be observed in Fig. 5, which shows 16 memory accesses to each round of a 4

T-table (4 access per table) AES. Due to our high resolution channel and the out-of-order execution of instructions, we observe that we interrupt the out-of-order execution pipeline while a future memory access is being fetched. Thus, interrupting the processor and evicting the entire L1D cache on each measurement forces the processor to repeatedly load the cache line memory until the target read instruction execution completes. Hence, attributing observed accesses to actual memory accesses in the code is not trivial. Although this behavior adds some confusion, we show that observed accesses still have minimal order that we can take into account. As for the third fact, it involves thorough visual inspection of the collected trace. In particular, we realized that every round start involves the utilization of a substantially higher number of sets than the rest, also observable in Fig. 5.

In the first implementation of our key recovery algorithm, we just use the set access information without taking into account the ordering of our observed accesses. Recall that we have access to the binary executed by the enclave, and thus, we can map each set number to its corresponding T-table entry. This means that all our accesses can be grouped on a T-table basis. Duplicated accesses to a set within a round are not separated and are considered part of the same access. After applying this filter to the first and second round traces, we apply the key recovery algorithm, as explained in [6]. The accuracy of our measurements with respect to the aforementioned issues can be seen in Table 1. For the 4 T-table implementation, 55% of the accesses correspond to true accesses (77% of them were ordered), 44% of them were noisy accesses and 56% of the true accesses were missed. For the single Large T-table implementation, 75% of the T-table accesses corresponded to true accesses (67% ordered), 24% were noisy accesses and 12% of the true accesses were missed. The quality of the data is worse in the 4 T-table case because they occupy larger number of sets and thus include more noisy lines, as explained in Fig. 2.

With these statistics and after applying our key recovery algorithms with varying number of traces we obtained the results presented in Fig. 6. If we do not consider the order in our experiments, we need roughly 20 traces (crosses

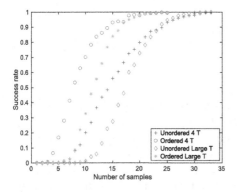

Table 1. Statistics on recovered memory accesses for T-table implementations.

Implementation	4 T-table	Large T-table
True Positive	55%	75%
False Positive	44%	24%
False Negative	56%	12%
Ordered	77%	67%

Fig. 6. Key recovery success rate.

and diamonds) to get the entire correct key with 90% probability in both the 4 T-table and single T-table implementations.

To further improve our results, we attempt to utilize the partial order of the observed accesses. We obtain the average position for all the observed accesses to a set within one round. These positions are, on average, close to the order in which sets were accessed. The observed order is then mapped to the order in which each T-table should have been utilized. Since this information is not very reliable, we apply a score and make sure misorderings are not automatically discarded. After applying this method, the result for our key recovery algorithm can be observed again in Fig. 6, for which we needed around 15 traces for the 4 T-table implementation (represented with stars) and 12 traces for the single Large T-table implementation (represented circles) to get the key with 90% probability. Thus, we can conclude that using the approximate order helped us to recover the key with fewer traces.

Cache Prefetching, as explained in Sect. 5, is implemented to prevent passive attackers from recovering AES keys. CacheZoom, in theory, should bypass such a countermeasure by being able to prime the cache after the T-tables are prefetched. The observation of a trace when cache prefetching is implemented before every round can be observed in Fig. 7. We can see how cache prefetching is far from preventing us to recover the necessary measurements. In fact, it eases the realization of our attack, as we now can clearly distinguish accesses belonging to different rounds, allowing for further automation of our key recovery step. Thus, CacheZoom not only bypasses but further benefits from mechanisms that mitigated previous cache attacks.

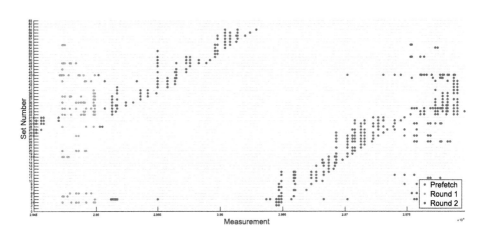

Fig. 7. Memory footprint of the AES execution inside an enclave with prefetch countermeasure. The prefetch is clearly distinguishable and helps to identify the start of each round. Further, it also highlights out-of-order execution and in-order completion.

6.2   S-Box Implementation

S-box implementation is seen as a remedy to cache attacks, as all S-box accesses use only a very small number of cache lines (typically 4). With 160 S-Box accesses per encryption, each line is loaded with a very high likelihood and thus prevents low resolution attackers from gaining information. Adding a prefetch for each round does not introduce much overhead and also prevents previous attacks that attempted interrupting the execution [14,24]. However, CacheZoom can easily distinguish S-box accesses during the rounds, but due to the out-of order execution, it is not possible to distinguish accesses for different byte positions in a reliable manner. However, one distinguishable feature is the number of accesses each set sees during a round. We hypothesize that the number of observed accesses correlates with the number of S-box lookups to that cache line. If so, a classic DPA correlating the observed accesses to the predicted accesses caused by one state byte should recover the key byte. Hence we followed a classic DPA-like attack on the last round, assuming known ciphertexts.

   The model used is rather simple: for each key byte k, the accessed cache set during the last round for a given ciphertext byte c is simply given as $set = S^{-1}(x \oplus k) \gg 6$, i.e. the two MSBs of the corresponding state byte before the last SubBytes operation. The access profile for a state byte position under an assumed key k and given ciphertext bytes can be represented by a matrix A where each row corresponds to a known ciphertext and each column indicates whether that ciphertext resulted in an access to the cache line with the same column index. Hence, each row has four entries, one per cache line, where the cache line with an access is set to one, and the other three columns are set to zero (since that state byte did not cause an access). Our leakage is given as a matrix L, where each row corresponds to a known ciphertext and each column to the number of observed accesses to one of the 4 cache lines. A correlation attack can then be performed by computing the correlation between A and L, where A is a function of the key hypothesis. We used synthetic, noise-free simulation data for the last AES round to validate our approach, where accesses for 16 bytes are accumulated over 4 cache lines for numerous ciphertexts under a set key. The synthetic data shows a best expectable correlation of about .25 between noise-free cumulative accesses L and the correct accesses for a single key byte A. As little as 100 observations yield a first-order success rate of 93%.

   Next, we gathered hundreds of measurements using CacheZoom. Note that due to a lack of alignment, the collection of a large number of observations and the extraction of the last round information still requires manual intervention. When performing the key recovery attack, even 200 observations yielded 4–5 key bytes correctly. However, the first-order success rate only increases very slowly with further measurements. We further observed that (1) more traces always recover later key bytes first and (2) key ranks for earlier lookups are often very low, i.e. the correct key does not even yield a high correlation. To analyze this behavior, we simply correlated the expected leakage A for each byte position to the observed leakage L. The result is shown in Fig. 8. It can be observed that the correlation for the later key bytes is much stronger than for the earlier key bytes. This explains why later key bytes are much easier to recover. The plot also shows a comparison of using the absolute number of observed accesses (ranging between 10 and 80 observed accesses per round, blue) an the relative number of accesses per cache set (amber) after removing outliers.

Results for the best and the worst key guess are shown in Fig. 9. For k_{15} (amber), the correlation for the correct key guess is clearly distinguishable. For k_0 however, the correct key guess does not show any correlation with the used 1500 observations. In summary, 500 traces are sufficient to recover 64 key bits, while 1500 recover 80 key bits reliably. While full key recovery will be challenging, recovering 12 out of 16 key bytes is easily possible with thousands of observations. The remaining key bytes can either be brute-forced or can be recovered by exploiting leakage from the second last round.

Next, we explain the reason why we believe bytes processed first are harder to recover. The Intel core i7 uses deep pipelines and speculative out-of-order execution. Up to six micro-instructions can be dispatched per clock cycle, and several instructions can also complete per cycle. As a result, getting order information for the accesses is difficult, especially if 16 subsequent S-box reads are spread over only 4 cache lines. While execution is out-of-order, each instruction and its completion state are tracked in the CPU's reorder buffer (ROB). Instruction results only affect the system state once they are completed *and* have reached the top of the ROB. That is, micro-ops *retire* in-order, even though they *execute* out-of-order. The result of micro-ops that have completed hence do not immediately affect the system. In our case, if the previous load has not yet been serviced, the subsequent completed accesses cannot retire and affect the system until the unserviced load is also completed.

Every context switch out of an enclave requires the CPU to flush the out-of order execution pipeline of the CPU [17]. Hence CacheZoom's interrupt causes a pipeline flush in the CPU, all micro-ops on the ROB that are not at the top and completed will be discarded. Since our scheduler switches tasks very frequently, many loads cannot retire and thus the same load operation has to be serviced repeatedly. This explains why we see between 9 and 90 accesses to the S-box cache lines although there are only 16 different loads to 4 different cache lines.

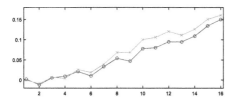

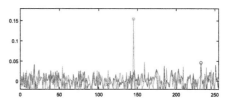

Fig. 8. Correlation between observed and expected accesses caused by one byte position. Leakage is stronger for later bytes. Correlation of observed (blue) vs. relative accesses (amber).

Fig. 9. Correlation of key values for the best (k_{15}, amber) and worst (k_0, blue) key bytes with 1500 traces. The guess with the highest correlation (o) and the correct key (x) match only for k_{15}. (Color figure online)

The loads for the first S-box are, however, the least affected by preceding loads. Hence, they are the most likely to complete and retire from the ROB after a single cache access. Later accesses are increasingly likely to be serviced more than once, as their completion and retirement is dependent on preceding loads. Since our leakage model assumes such behavior (in fact, we assume one cache access per load), the model becomes increasingly accurate for later accesses.

7 Conclusion

This work presented CacheZoom, a new tool to analyze memory accesses of SGX enclaves. To gain maximal resolution, CacheZoom combines a L1 cache `Prime+Probe` attack with OS modifications that greatly enhance the time resolution. SGX makes this scenario realistic, as both a modified OS and knowledge of the unencrypted binary are realistic for enclaves. We demonstrate that CacheZoom can be used to recover key bits from all major software AES implementations, including ones that use prefetches for each round as a cache-attack countermeasure. Furthermore, keys can be recovered with as few as 10 observations for T-table based implementations. For the trickier S-box implementation style, 100s of observations reveal sufficient key information to make full key recovery possible. Prefetching is in this scenario beneficial to the adversary, as it helps identifying and separating the accesses for different rounds. A list of libraries that contain vulnerable implementations can be found at Table 2.

CacheZoom serves as evidence that security-critical code needs constant execution flows and secret-independent memory accesses. As SGX's intended use is the protection of sensitive information, enclave developers must thus use the necessary care when developing code and avoid microarchitectural leakages. For AES specifically, SGX implementations must feature constant memory accesses. Possible implementation styles are thus bit-sliced or vectorized-instruction-based implementations or implementations that access all cache lines for each look-up.

Table 2. Vulnerable implementations in popular current cryptographic libraries. These implementations can be configured through compile/runtime settings.

Library	Vulnerable implementations
OpenSSL 1.1.0f	`aes_core.c` T-table, `aes_x86core.c` Large T-table, S-box and prefetching configurable through AES_COMPACT_IN_INNER_ROUNDS, AES_COMPACT_IN_OUTER_ROUNDS
WolfCrypt 3.11.0	`aes.c` T-Table with prefetching before the first round
Mozilla NSS 3.30.2	`rijndael.c` T-Table and S-box configurable through RIJNDAEL_GENERATE VALUES_MACRO
Nettle 3.3	`aes-encrypt-internal.asm` T-table
Libtomcrypt 1.17	`aes.c` T-table
Libgcrypt 1.7.7	`rijndael.c` T-table, S-box for the last round with prefetching
MbedTLS 2.4.2	`aes.c` T-table, S-box for the last round

Acknowledgments. This work is supported by the National Science Foundation, under the grant CNS-1618837. *CacheZoom* source repository and data sets are available at https://github.com/vernamlab/CacheZoom.

References

1. Aciiçmez, O., Koç, Ç.K., Seifert, J.P.: On the power of simple branch prediction analysis. In: Proceedings of the 2nd ACM Symposium on Information, Computer and Communications Security, pp. 312–320. ACM (2007)
2. Aciiçmez, O., Schindler, W.: A vulnerability in RSA implementations due to instruction cache analysis and its demonstration on openSSL. In: Malkin, T. (ed.) CT-RSA 2008. LNCS, vol. 4964, pp. 256–273. Springer, Heidelberg (2008). doi:10. 1007/978-3-540-79263-5_16
3. Allan, T., Brumley, B.B., Falkner, K., van de Pol, J., Yarom, Y.: Amplifying side channels through performance degradation. In: Proceedings of the 32nd Annual Conference on Computer Security Applications, pp. 422–435. ACM (2016)
4. ARM TrustZone. https://www.arm.com/products/security-on-arm/trustzone. Accessed 25 June 2017
5. Arnautov, S., Trach, B., Gregor, F., Knauth, T., Martin, A., Priebe, C., Lind, J., Muthukumaran, D., O'Keeffe, D., Stillwell, M.L., et al.: SCONE: Secure linux containers with Intel SGX. In: 12th USENIX Symposium on Operating Systems Design and Implementation (OSDI 2016). USENIX Association (2016)
6. Ashokkumar, C., Giri, R.P., Menezes, B.: Highly efficient algorithms for AES key retrieval in cache access attacks. In: 2016 IEEE European Symposium on Security and Privacy (EuroS&P), pp. 261–275. IEEE (2016)
7. Baumann, A., Peinado, M., Hunt, G.: Shielding applications from an untrusted cloud with haven. ACM Trans. Comput. Syst. (TOCS) 33(3) (2015)
8. Benger, N., Pol, J., Smart, N.P., Yarom, Y.: "Ooh Aah.. Just a Little Bit" : A small amount of side channel can go a long way. In: Batina, L., Robshaw, M. (eds.) CHES 2014. LNCS, vol. 8731, pp. 75–92. Springer, Heidelberg (2014). doi:10.1007/ 978-3-662-44709-3_5
9. Bernstein, D.J., Schwabe, P.: New AES software speed records. In: Chowdhury, D.R., Rijmen, V., Das, A. (eds.) INDOCRYPT 2008. LNCS, vol. 5365, pp. 322–336. Springer, Heidelberg (2008). doi:10.1007/978-3-540-89754-5_25
10. Bhattacharya, S., Mukhopadhyay, D.: Who watches the watchmen?: Utilizing performance monitors for compromising keys of RSA on intel platforms. In: Güneysu, T., Handschuh, H. (eds.) CHES 2015. LNCS, vol. 9293, pp. 248–266. Springer, Heidelberg (2015). doi:10.1007/978-3-662-48324-4_13
11. Bonneau, J., Mironov, I.: Cache-collision timing attacks against AES. In: Goubin, L., Matsui, M. (eds.) CHES 2006. LNCS, vol. 4249, pp. 201–215. Springer, Heidelberg (2006). doi:10.1007/11894063_16
12. Brasser, F., Müller, U., Dmitrienko, A., Kostiainen, K., Capkun, S., Sadeghi, A.R.: Software Grand Exposure: SGX Cache Attacks are Practical (2017). arXiv preprint arXiv:1702.07521
13. Brickell, E., Graunke, G., Neve, M., Seifert, J.P.: Software mitigations to hedge AES against cache-based software side channel vulnerabilities. IACR Cryptology ePrint Archive 2006, vol. 52 (2006)
14. Briongos, S., Malagón, P., Risco-Martín, J.L., Moya, J.M.: Modeling side-channel cache attacks on AES. In: Proceedings of the Summer Computer Simulation Conference, p. 37. Society for Computer Simulation International (2016)

15. Brumley, D., Boneh, D.: Remote timing attacks are practical. Comput. Netw. **48**(5), 701–716 (2005)
16. Chen, S., Zhang, X., Reiter, M.K., Zhang, Y.: Detecting privileged side-channel attacks in shielded execution with déjá vu. In: Proceedings of the 2017 ACM on Asia Conference on Computer and Communications Security, pp. 7–18. ACM (2017)
17. Costan, V., Devadas, S.: Intel SGX explained. Technical report, Cryptology ePrint Archive, Report 2016/086 (2016). https://eprint.iacr.org/2016/086
18. Costan, V., Lebedev, I., Devadas, S.: Sanctum: Minimal hardware extensions for strong software isolation. USENIX Security, vol. 16, pp. 857–874 (2016)
19. Dahbur, K., Mohammad, B., Tarakji, A.B.: A survey of risks, threats and vulnerabilities in cloud computing. In: Proceedings of the 2011 International Conference on Intelligent Semantic Web-Services and Applications, p. 12. ACM (2011)
20. Evtyushkin, D., Ponomarev, D., Abu-Ghazaleh, N.: Jump over ASLR: Attacking branch predshared cache attictors to bypass ASLR. In: IEEE/ACM International Symposium on Microarchitecture (MICRO) (2016)
21. Ge, Q., Yarom, Y., Cock, D., Heiser, G.: A Survey of Microarchitectural Timing Attacks and Countermeasures on Contemporary Hardware. IACR Eprint (2016)
22. Götzfried, J., Eckert, M., Schinzel, S., Müller, T.: Cache attacks on intel SGX. In: EUROSEC, pp. 2–1 (2017)
23. Gruss, D., Maurice, C., Mangard, S.: Rowhammer.js: A remote software-induced fault attack in javascript. In: Caballero, J., Zurutuza, U., Rodríguez, R.J. (eds.) DIMVA 2016. LNCS, vol. 9721, pp. 300–321. Springer, Cham (2016). doi:10.1007/978-3-319-40667-1_15
24. Gullasch, D., Bangerter, E., Krenn, S.: Cache games-bringing access-based cache attacks on AES to practice. In: 2011 IEEE Symposium on Security and Privacy, pp. 490–505. IEEE (2011)
25. Hamburg, M.: Accelerating AES with vector permute instructions. In: Clavier, C., Gaj, K. (eds.) CHES 2009. LNCS, vol. 5747, pp. 18–32. Springer, Heidelberg (2009). doi:10.1007/978-3-642-04138-9_2
26. İnci, M.S., Gulmezoglu, B., Irazoqui, G., Eisenbarth, T., Sunar, B.: Cache attacks enable bulk key recovery on the cloud. In: Gierlichs, B., Poschmann, A.Y. (eds.) CHES 2016. LNCS, vol. 9813, pp. 368–388. Springer, Heidelberg (2016). doi:10.1007/978-3-662-53140-2_18
27. Intel: Intel® Data Protection Technology with AES-NI and Secure Key. http://www.intel.com/content/www/us/en/architecture-and-technology/advanced-encryption-standard-aes-/data-protection-aes-general-technology.html
28. ISCA 2015 tutorial slides for Intel ® SGX.https://software.intel.com/sites/default/files/332680-002.pdf. Accessed: 25 June 2017
29. Intel SGX. https://software.intel.com/en-us/sgx. Accessed: 25 June 2017
30. Irazoqui, G., Eisenbarth, T., Sunar, B.: S $ A: A shared cache attack that works across cores and defies VM sandboxing-and its application to AES. In: 2015 IEEE Symposium on Security and Privacy, pp. 591–604. IEEE (2015)
31. Irazoqui, G., Inci, M.S., Eisenbarth, T., Sunar, B.: Wait a minute! A fast, cross-VM attack on AES. In: Stavrou, A., Bos, H., Portokalidis, G. (eds.) RAID 2014. LNCS, vol. 8688, pp. 299–319. Springer, Cham (2014). doi:10.1007/978-3-319-11379-1_15
32. Kocher, P.C.: Timing attacks on implementations of diffie-hellman, RSA, DSS, and other systems. In: Koblitz, N. (ed.) CRYPTO 1996. LNCS, vol. 1109, pp. 104–113. Springer, Heidelberg (1996). doi:10.1007/3-540-68697-5_9

33. Langner, R.: Stuxnet: Dissecting a cyberwarfare weapon. IEEE Secur. Priv. **9**(3), 49–51 (2011)
34. Lee, S., Shih, M.W., Gera, P., Kim, T., Kim, H., Peinado, M.: Inferring Fine-grained Control Flow Inside SGX Enclaves with Branch Shadowing. Technical report, arxiv Archive 2016 (2017). https://arXiv.org/pdf/1611.06952.pdf
35. Lipp, M., Gruss, D., Spreitzer, R., Mangard, S.: Armageddon: Last-level cache attacks on mobile devices. arXiv preprint (2015). arXiv:1511.04897
36. Liu, F., Yarom, Y., Ge, Q., Heiser, G., Lee, R.B.: Last-level cache side-channel attacks are practical. In: IEEE Symposium on Security and Privacy (2015)
37. Liu, W., Di Segni, A., Ding, Y., Zhang, T.: Cache-timing attacks on AES. New York University (2013)
38. Matsui, M., Nakajima, J.: On the power of bitslice implementation on intel core2 processor. In: Paillier, P., Verbauwhede, I. (eds.) CHES 2007. LNCS, vol. 4727, pp. 121–134. Springer, Heidelberg (2007). doi:10.1007/978-3-540-74735-2_9
39. Morris, T.: Trusted platform module. In: van Tilborg, H.C.A., Jajodia, S. (eds.) Encyclopedia of Cryptography and Security, pp. 1332–1335. Springer, Heidelberg (2011)
40. Oren, Y., Kemerlis, V.P., Sethumadhavan, S., Keromytis, A.D.: The spy in the sandbox: Practical cache attacks in javascript and their implications. In: Proceedings of the 22nd ACM SIGSAC Conference on Computer and Communications Security, pp. 1406–1418. ACM (2015)
41. Osvik, D.A., Shamir, A., Tromer, E.: Cache attacks and countermeasures: The case of AES. In: Pointcheval, D. (ed.) CT-RSA 2006. LNCS, vol. 3860, pp. 1–20. Springer, Heidelberg (2006). doi:10.1007/11605805_1
42. Percival, C.: Cache missing for fun and profit (2005)
43. Ristenpart, T., Tromer, E., Shacham, H., Savage, S.: Hey, you, get off of my cloud: exploring information leakage in third-party compute clouds. In: Proceedings of the 16th ACM Conference on Computer and Communications Security, pp. 199–212. ACM (2009)
44. Schuster, F., Costa, M., Fournet, C., Gkantsidis, C., Peinado, M., Mainar-Ruiz, G., Russinovich, M.: VC3: trustworthy data analytics in the cloud using SGX. In: 2015 IEEE Symposium on Security and Privacy. IEEE (2015)
45. Schwarz, M., Weiser, S., Gruss, D., Maurice, C., Mangard, S.: Malware guard extension: Using SGX to conceal cache attacks (2017). arXiv preprint arXiv:1702.08719
46. Seo, J., Lee, B., Kim, S., Shih, M.W., Shin, I., Han, D., Kim, T.: SGX-Shield: Enabling address space layout randomization for SGX programs. In: Proceedings of the 2017 Annual Network and Distributed System Security Symposium (NDSS), San Diego, CA (2017)
47. Shih, M.W., Lee, S., Kim, T., Peinado, M.: T-SGX: Eradicating controlled-channel attacks against enclave programs. In: Proceedings of the 2017 Annual Network and Distributed System Security Symposium (NDSS), San Diego, CA (2017)
48. Shinde, S., Chua, Z.L., Narayanan, V., Saxena, P.: Preventing page faults from telling your secrets. In: Proceedings of the 11th ACM on Asia Conference on Computer and Communications Security, pp. 317–328. ACM (2016)
49. Takehisa, T., Nogawa, H., Morii, M.: AES Flow Interception: Key Snooping Method on Virtual Machine-Exception Handling Attack for AES-NI-. IACR Cryptology ePrint Archive 2011, vol. 428 (2011)
50. Tsunoo, Y., Saito, T., Suzaki, T., Shigeri, M., Miyauchi, H.: Cryptanalysis of DES implemented on computers with cache. In: Walter, C.D., Koç, Ç.K., Paar, C. (eds.) CHES 2003. LNCS, vol. 2779, pp. 62–76. Springer, Heidelberg (2003). doi:10.1007/978-3-540-45238-6_6

51. Weichbrodt, N., Kurmus, A., Pietzuch, P., Kapitza, R.: AsyncShock: Exploiting synchronisation bugs in intel SGX enclaves. In: Askoxylakis, I., Ioannidis, S., Katsikas, S., Meadows, C. (eds.) ESORICS 2016. LNCS, vol. 9878, pp. 440–457. Springer, Cham (2016). doi:10.1007/978-3-319-45744-4_22
52. Xu, Y., Cui, W., Peinado, M.: Controlled-channel attacks: Deterministic side channels for untrusted operating systems. In: 2015 IEEE Symposium on Security and Privacy, pp. 640–656. IEEE (2015)
53. Yarom, Y., Falkner, K.: Flush+reload: a high resolution, low noise, L3 cache side-channel attack. In: 23rd USENIX Security Symposium (USENIX Security 14), pp. 719–732 (2014)
54. Zhang, Y., Juels, A., Oprea, A., Reiter, M.K.: Homealone: Co-residency detection in the cloud via side-channel analysis. In: 2011 IEEE Symposium on Security and Privacy, pp. 313–328. IEEE (2011)
55. Zhang, Y., Juels, A., Reiter, M.K., Ristenpart, T.: Cross-VM side channels and their use to extract private keys. In: Proceedings of the 2012 ACM conference on Computer and Communications Security, pp. 305–316. ACM (2012)
56. Zhang, Y., Juels, A., Reiter, M.K., Ristenpart, T.: Cross-tenant side-channel attacks in PaaS clouds. In: Proceedings of the 2014 ACM SIGSAC Conference on Computer and Communications Security, pp. 990–1003. ACM (2014)

Higher Order Countermeasures

Higher Order Contributions

High-Order Conversion from Boolean to Arithmetic Masking

Jean-Sébastien Coron[(✉)]

University of Luxembourg, Luxembourg, Luxembourg
jean-sebastien.coron@uni.lu

Abstract. Masking with random values is an effective countermeasure against side-channel attacks. For cryptographic algorithms combining arithmetic and Boolean masking, it is necessary to switch from arithmetic to Boolean masking and vice versa. Following a recent approach by Hutter and Tunstall, we describe a high-order Boolean to arithmetic conversion algorithm whose complexity is independent of the register size k. Our new algorithm is proven secure in the Ishai, Sahai and Wagner (ISW) framework for private circuits. In practice, for small orders, our new countermeasure is one order of magnitude faster than previous work.

We also describe a 3rd-order attack against the 3rd-order Hutter-Tunstall algorithm, and a constant, 4th-order attack against the t-th order Hutter-Tunstall algorithms, for any $t \geq 4$.

1 Introduction

The Masking Countermeasure. Masking is a very common countermeasure against side channel attacks, first suggested in [CJRR99, GP99]. It consists in masking every variable x into $x' = x \oplus r$, where r is a randomly generated value. The two shares x' and r are then manipulated separately, so that a first-order attack that processes intermediate variables separately cannot succeed. However first-order masking is vulnerable to a second-order attack combining information on the two shares x' and r; see [OMHT06] for a practical attack. Boolean masking can naturally be extended to n shares, with $x = x_1 \oplus \cdots \oplus x_n$; in that case an implementation should be resistant against t-th order attacks, in which the adversary combines leakage information from at most $t < n$ variables. It was shown in [CJRR99, PR13, DDF14] that under a reasonable noisy model, the number of noisy samples required to recover a secret x from its shares x_i grows exponentially with the number of shares.

Security Model. The theoretical study of securing circuits against side-channel attacks was initiated by Ishai, Sahai and Wagner (ISW) [ISW03]. In this model, the adversary can probe at most t wires in the circuit, but he should not learn anything about the secret key. The authors show that any circuit C can be transformed into a new circuit C' of size $\mathcal{O}(t^2 \cdot |C|)$ that is resistant against such

© International Association for Cryptologic Research 2017
W. Fischer and N. Homma (Eds.): CHES 2017, LNCS 10529, pp. 93–114, 2017.
DOI: 10.1007/978-3-319-66787-4_5

an adversary. The construction is based on secret-sharing every variable x into n shares with $x = x_1 \oplus \cdots \oplus x_n$, and processing the shares in a way that prevents a t-limited adversary from leaning any information about the initial variable x, for $n \geq 2t + 1$.

The approach for proving security is based on simulation: instead of considering all possible t-uples of probes, which would be unfeasible since this grows exponentially with t, the authors show how to simulate any set of t wires probed by the adversary, from a proper subset of the input shares of the transformed circuit C'. Since any proper subset of the input shares can be simulated without knowledge of the input variables of the original circuit (simply by generating random values), one can then obtain a perfect simulation of the t probes. This shows that the t probes do not bring any additional information to the attacker, since he could simulate those t probes by himself, without knowing the secret key.

In this paper, all our constructions are proven secure in the ISW model. More precisely, we use the refined t-SNI security notion introduced in [BBD+16]. This enables to show that a particular gadget can be used in a full construction with $n \geq t + 1$ shares, instead of $n \geq 2t + 1$ for the weaker definition of t-NI security (as used in the original ISW security proof). The t-SNI security notion is a very practical definition that enables modular proofs; this is done by first considering the t-SNI security of individual gadgets and then composing them inside a more complex construction.

Boolean vs. Arithmetic Masking. Boolean masking consists in splitting every variable x into n shares x_i such that $x = x_1 \oplus x_2 \oplus \cdots \oplus x_n$, and the shares are then processed separately. However some algorithms use arithmetic operations, for example IDEA [LM90], RC6 [CRRY99], XTEA [NW97], SPECK [BSS+13] and SHA-1 [NIS95]. In that case it can be advantageous to use arithmetic masking. For example, if the variable $z = x + y \bmod 2^k$ must be computed securely for some parameter k, a first-order countermeasure with arithmetic shares consists in writing $x = A_1 + A_2$ and $y = B_1 + B_2$ for arithmetic shares A_1, A_2, B_1, B_2. Then instead of computing $z = x + y$ directly, which would leak information on x and y, one can add the shares separately, by letting $C_1 \leftarrow A_1 + B_1$ and $C_2 \leftarrow A_2 + B_2$; this gives the two arithmetic shares C_1 and C_2 using $z = x + y = A_1 + A_2 + B_1 + B_2 = C_1 + C_2$. Note that throughout the paper all additions and subtractions are performed modulo 2^k for some k; for example for SHA-1 we have $k = 32$.

When combining Boolean and arithmetic masking, one must be able to convert between the two types of masking; obviously the conversion algorithm itself must be secure against side-channel attacks. More precisely, a Boolean to arithmetic conversion algorithm takes as input n shares x_i such that:

$$x = x_1 \oplus x_2 \oplus \cdots \oplus x_n$$

and one must compute n arithmetic shares A_i such that:

$$x = A_1 + A_2 + \cdots + A_n \pmod{2^k}$$

without leaking information about x.

Prior Work. The first Boolean to arithmetic conversion algorithms were described by Goubin in [Gou01], with security against first-order attacks only. Goubin's Boolean to arithmetic algorithm is quite elegant and has complexity $\mathcal{O}(1)$, that is independent of the register size k. The arithmetic to Boolean conversion is more complex and has complexity $\mathcal{O}(k)$; this was later improved to $\mathcal{O}(\log k)$ in [CGTV15]; however in practice for $k = 32$ the number of operations is similar.

The first conversion algorithms secure against high-order attacks were described in [CGV14], with complexity $\mathcal{O}(n^2 \cdot k)$ for n shares and k-bit addition in both directions, with a proof of security in the ISW model.[1] The authors of [CGV14] also describe an alternative approach that use Boolean masking only and employ secure algorithms to perform the arithmetic operations directly on the Boolean shares, with the same asymptotic complexity; they show that for HMAC-SHA-1 this leads to an efficient implementation.

Recently, Hutter and Tunstall have described in [HT16] a high-order Boolean to arithmetic conversion algorithm with complexity independent of the register size k (as in Goubin's original algorithm). However no proof of security is provided, except for second-order and third-order attacks. The complexity of the algorithm for n shares is $\mathcal{O}(2^{n/2})$, but for small values of n the algorithm is much more efficient than [CGV14, CGTV15], at least by one order of magnitude[2].

Our Contributions. In this paper our contributions are as follows:

- We describe a high-order Boolean to arithmetic conversion algorithm with complexity independent of the register size k, using a similar approach as in [HT16], but with a proof of security in the ISW model. Our algorithm achieves security against attacks of order $n-1$ for n shares, for any $n \geq 3$. Our conversion algorithm has complexity $\mathcal{O}(2^n)$, instead of $\mathcal{O}(n^2 \cdot k)$ in [CGV14], but for small values of n it is one order of magnitude more efficient. In Sect. 6 we report the execution times we achieved for both algorithms, using 32-bit registers.
- We describe a 4th order attack against the t-th order Hutter-Tunstall algorithm (with $n = t + 1$ shares), for any $t \geq 4$. We also describe a 3rd order attack for $t = 3$. This implies that the conversion algorithm in [HT16] cannot offer more than second-order security[3].

Source Code. A proof-of-concept implementation of our high-order conversion algorithm, using the C language, is available at: http://pastebin.com/CSn67PxQ

---

[1] This can also be improved to $\mathcal{O}(n^2 \cdot \log k)$ using [CGTV15].

[2] In [HT16] the authors claim that the complexity of their algorithm is $\mathcal{O}(n^2)$, but it is actually $\mathcal{O}(2^{n/2})$, because it makes 2 recursive calls to the same algorithm with $n - 2$ shares.

[3] Our attacks apply on the version posted on 22-Dec-2016 of [HT16]; it has been updated since then.

2   Security Definitions

In this section we recall the t-NI and t-SNI security definitions from [BBD+16]. For simplicity we only provide the definitions for a simple gadget taking as input a single variable x (given by n shares x_i) and outputting a single variable y (given by n shares y_i). Given a vector of n shares $(x_i)_{1 \leq i \leq n}$, we denote by $x_{|I} := (x_i)_{i \in I}$ the sub-vector of shares x_i with $i \in I$.

Definition 1 (t-NI security). *Let G be a gadget taking as input $(x_i)_{1 \leq i \leq n}$ and outputting the vector $(y_i)_{1 \leq i \leq n}$. The gadget G is said t-NI secure if for any set of t intermediate variables, there exists a subset I of input indices with $|I| \leq t$, such that the t intermediate variables can be perfectly simulated from $x_{|I}$.*

Definition 2 (t-SNI security). *Let G be a gadget taking as input $(x_i)_{1 \leq i \leq n}$ and outputting $(y_i)_{1 \leq i \leq n}$. The gadget G is said t-SNI secure if for any set of t intermediate variables and any subset $\mathcal{O}$ of output indices such that $t + |\mathcal{O}| < n$, there exists a subset I of input indices with $|I| \leq t$, such that the t intermediate variables and the output variables $y_{|\mathcal{O}}$ can be perfectly simulated from $x_{|I}$.*

The t-NI security notion corresponds to the original security definition in the ISW probing model; based on the ISW multiplication gadget, it allows to prove the security of a transformed circuit with $n \geq 2t + 1$ shares. The stronger t-SNI notion allows to prove the security with $n \geq t + 1$ shares only [BBD+16]. The difference between the two notions is as follows: in the stronger t-SNI notion, the size of the input shares subset I can only depend on the number of probes t and is independent of the number of output variables $|\mathcal{O}|$ that must be simulated (as long as the condition $t + |\mathcal{O}| < n$ is satisfied). For a complex construction involving many gadgets (as the one considered in this paper), this enables to easily prove that the full construction is t-SNI secure, based on the t-SNI security of its components.

3   Goubin's First-Order Conversion and Previous Works

3.1   Goubin's Algorithm

We first recall Goubin's first-order algorithm for conversion from Boolean to arithmetic masking [Gou01]. The algorithm is based on the affine property of the function $\Psi(x_1, r) : \mathbb{F}_{2^k} \times \mathbb{F}_{2^k} \to \mathbb{F}_{2^k}$

$$\Psi(x_1, r) = (x_1 \oplus r) - r \pmod{2^k}$$

As mentioned previously, all additions and subtractions are performed modulo 2^k for some parameter k, so in the following we omit the mod 2^k. Moreover we grant higher precedence to xor than addition, so we simply write $\Psi(x_1, r) = x_1 \oplus r - r$.

Theorem 1 (Goubin [Gou01]). *The function $\Psi(x_1, r)$ is affine with respect to r over $\mathbb{F}_2$.*

Thanks to the affine property of Ψ, the conversion from Boolean to arithmetic masking is relatively straightforward. Namely given as input the two Boolean shares x_1, x_2 such that

$$x = x_1 \oplus x_2$$

we can write:

$$
\begin{aligned}
x &= x_1 \oplus x_2 - x_2 + x_2 \\
&= \Psi(x_1, x_2) + x_2 \\
&= \left[(x_1 \oplus \Psi(x_1, r \oplus x_2)) \oplus \Psi(x_1, r) \right] + x_2
\end{aligned}
$$

for random $r \leftarrow \{0,1\}^k$. Therefore one can compute

$$A \leftarrow (x_1 \oplus \Psi(x_1, r \oplus x_2)) \oplus \Psi(x_1, r)$$

and get the two arithmetic shares A and x_2 of

$$x = A + x_2 \pmod{2^k}$$

The conversion algorithm is clearly secure against first-order attacks, because the left term $\Psi(x_1, r \oplus x_2)$ is independent of x_2 (thanks to the mask r), and the right term $\Psi(x_1, r)$ is also independent from x_2. The algorithm is quite efficient as it requires only a constant number of operations, independent of k.

3.2 t-SNI Variant of Goubin's Algorithm

In this paper our goal is to describe a high-order conversion algorithm from Boolean to arithmetic masking, with complexity independent of the register size k, as in Goubin's first-order algorithm above. Moreover we will use Goubin's first-order algorithm as a subroutine, for which the stronger t-SNI property recalled in Sect. 2 is needed. However it is easy to see that Goubin's algorithm recalled above does not achieve the t-SNI security notion. This is because by definition the output share x_2 in $x = A + x_2$ is the same as the input share in $x = x_1 \oplus x_2$; therefore if we take $O = \{2\}$ in Definition 2, we need to set $I = \{2\}$ to properly simulate x_2; this contradicts the t-SNI bound $|I| \leq t$, since in that case for $t = 0$ we should have $I = \emptyset$.

However, it is straightforward to modify Goubin's algorithm to make it t-SNI: it suffices to first refresh the 2 input shares x_1, x_2 with a random s. We obtain the following first-order t-SNI Boolean to arithmetic algorithm (Algorithm 1).

Lemma 1 (GoubinSNI). *Let x_1, x_2 be the inputs of Goubin's algorithm (Algorithm 1) and let A_1 and A_2 be the outputs. Let t be the number of probed variables and let $O \subset \{1,2\}$, with $t + |O| < 2$. There exists a subset $I \subset \{1,2\}$, such that all probed variables and $A_{|O}$ can be perfectly simulated from $x_{|I}$, with $|I| \leq t$*

Proof. We distinguish two cases. If $t = 0$, then the variable s is not probed by the adversary, and therefore both $A_2 = a_2 = x_2 \oplus s$ and $A_1 = x - A_2 = x - x_2 \oplus s$ have

---

Algorithm 1. GoubinSNI: Boolean to arithmetic conversion, t-SNI variant

---

Input: x_1, x_2 such that $x = x_1 \oplus x_2$
Output: A_1, A_2 such that $x = A_1 + A_2$
1: $s \leftarrow \{0,1\}^k$
2: $a_1 \leftarrow x_1 \oplus s$
3: $a_2 \leftarrow x_2 \oplus s$
4: $r \leftarrow \{0,1\}^k$
5: $u \leftarrow a_1 \oplus \Psi(a_1, r \oplus a_2)$
6: $A_1 \leftarrow u \oplus \Psi(a_1, r)$
7: $A_2 \leftarrow a_2$
8: **return** A_1, A_2

---

the uniform distribution separately; therefore any of these 2 output variables can be perfectly simulated with $I = \emptyset$.

If $t = 1$, then we must have $O = \emptyset$. It is easy to see that any single intermediate variable can be perfectly simulated from the knowledge of either x_1 or x_2, as in Goubin's original conversion algorithm, which gives $|I| \leq t$ as required.   □

Complexity Analysis. We see that Algorithm 1 requires 2 random generations, 2 computations of Ψ, and 5 xors, for a total of 11 operations. In particular, the complexity of Goubin's algorithm is independent of the register size k.

3.3   High-Order Conversion Between Boolean and Arithmetic Masking

The first conversion algorithms secure against high-order attacks were described in [CGV14], with complexity $\mathcal{O}(n^2 \cdot k)$ for n shares and k-bit addition in both directions. The algorithms in [CGV14] are proven secure in the ISW probing model [ISW03], with $n \geq 2t + 1$ shares for security against t probes. The arithmetic to Boolean conversion proceeds by recursively applying a $n/2$ arithmetic to Boolean conversion on both halves, and then performing a Boolean-protected arithmetic addition:

$$
\begin{aligned}
A &= A_1 + \cdots + A_{n/2} + A_{n/2+1} + \cdots + A_n \\
&= x_1 \oplus \cdots \oplus x_{n/2} + y_1 \oplus \cdots \oplus y_{n/2} \\
&= z_1 \oplus \cdots \oplus z_n
\end{aligned}
$$

The arithmetic addition can be based on Goubin's recursion formula [Gou01] with complexity $\mathcal{O}(k)$ for k-bit register. This can be improved to $\mathcal{O}(\log k)$ by using a recursion formula based on the Kogge-Stone carry look-ahead adder (see [CGTV15]); however for $k = 32$ the number of operations is similar. In both cases the recursion formula only uses Boolean operation, so it can be protected with n shares with complexity $\mathcal{O}(n^2 \cdot k)$ or $\mathcal{O}(n^2 \cdot \log k)$. For the other direction, *i.e.* Boolean to arithmetic, it is based on the above arithmetic to Boolean conversion, and it has also complexity $\mathcal{O}(n^2 \cdot k)$ (and $\mathcal{O}(n^2 \cdot \log k)$ with Kogge-Stone).

Recently, Hutter and Tunstall have described in [HT16] a different technique for high-order Boolean to arithmetic conversion, with complexity independent of the register size k (as in Goubin's original algorithm). However no proof of security is provided, except for second-order and third-order attacks. The complexity of their algorithm for n shares is $\mathcal{O}(2^{n/2})$, but for small values of n the algorithm is much more efficient than [CGV14, CGTV15], at least by one order of magnitude. In [HT16] the authors claim that the complexity of their algorithm is $\mathcal{O}(n^2)$, but it is easy to see that it must be $\mathcal{O}(2^{n/2})$, because it makes 2 recursive calls to the same algorithm with $n - 2$ shares.

However, in this paper we describe a 4th order attack against the t-th order Hutter-Tunstall algorithm (with $n = t+1$ shares), for any $t \geq 4$; we also describe a 3rd order attack for $t = 3$; see Sect. 5. This implies that the conversion algorithm in [HT16] cannot offer more than second-order security. In particular, we have not found any attack against the second-order Boolean to arithmetic conversion specified in [HT16, Algorithm 2].

4   High-order Conversion from Boolean to Arithmetic Masking

In this section, we describe our main contribution: a high-order conversion algorithm from Boolean to arithmetic masking, with complexity independent of the register size k, with a proof of security in the ISW model for $n \geq t + 1$ shares against t probes (t-SNI security).

4.1   A Simple but Insecure Algorithm

To illustrate our approach, we first describe a simple but insecure algorithm; namely we explain why it fails to achieve the t-SNI security property. We start from the n shares x_i such that

$$x = x_1 \oplus \cdots \oplus x_n$$

and we must output n shares A_i such that

$$x = A_1 + \cdots + A_n \pmod{2^k}$$

Our tentative conversion algorithm $\mathcal{C}_n$ is defined recursively, using a similar approach as in [HT16], and works as follows:

1. We write

$$x = x_2 \oplus \cdots \oplus x_n + (x_1 \oplus x_2 \oplus \cdots \oplus x_n - x_2 \oplus \cdots \oplus x_n)$$

which gives using $\Psi(x_1, u) = x_1 \oplus u - u$:

$$x = x_2 \oplus \cdots \oplus x_n + \Psi(x_1, x_2 \oplus \cdots \oplus x_n)$$

From the affine property of the Ψ function, we obtain:

$$x = x_2 \oplus \cdots \oplus x_n + (n \wedge 1) \cdot x_1 \oplus \Psi(x_1, x_2) \oplus \cdots \oplus \Psi(x_1, x_n)$$

Therefore we let $z_1 \leftarrow (n \wedge 1) \cdot x_1 \oplus \Psi(x_1, x_2)$ and $z_i \leftarrow \Psi(x_1, x_{i+1})$ for all $2 \le i \le n - 1$. This gives:

$$x = x_2 \oplus \cdots \oplus x_n + z_1 \oplus \cdots \oplus z_{n-1}$$

2. We then perform two recursive calls to the Boolean to arithmetic conversion algorithm $\mathcal{C}_{n-1}$, with $n - 1$ shares. This gives:

$$x = A_1 + \cdots + A_{n-1} + B_1 + \cdots + B_{n-1}$$

3. We reduce the number of arithmetic shares from $2n - 2$ to n by some additive grouping, letting $D_i \leftarrow A_i + B_i$ for $1 \le i \le n - 2$, and $D_{n-1} \leftarrow A_{n-1}$ and $D_n \leftarrow B_{n-1}$. This gives as required:

$$x = D_1 + \cdots + D_n$$

This terminates the description of our tentative algorithm. We explain why this simple algorithm is insecure. Namely if the adversary probes the $n - 1$ variables z_i, since each z_i reveals information about both x_1 and x_{i+1}, those $n - 1$ variables reveal information about x. More precisely, from the probed z_i's the adversary can compute:

$$z_1 \oplus \cdots \oplus z_{n-1} = \Psi(x_1, x_2 \oplus \cdots \oplus x_n)$$

Letting $u = x_2 \oplus \cdots \oplus x_n$ and $v = x_n$, for $n \ge 3$ we can assume that the two variables u and v are uniformly and independently distributed. Therefore the adversary obtains the two variables:

$$\Psi(x_1, u) = x_1 \oplus u - u, \quad \Psi(x_1, v) = x_1 \oplus v - v$$

and one can check that the distribution of $(\Psi(x_1, u), \Psi(x_1, v))$ depends on $x = x_1 \oplus u$. Therefore, the $n-1$ probes leak information about x. Moreover, due to the recursive definition of the above algorithm, the number of required probes can be decreased by probing within the recursive calls, instead of the z_i's. Namely if the adversary probes only $n - 2$ variables within $\mathcal{C}_{n-1}$, this reveals information about the $n - 1$ variables z_i's, which in turn reveals information about x, as explained above.

The attack can be applied recursively down to a single probe. Namely one can check experimentally (for small k and n) that for randomly distributed $x_1, \ldots, x_n$, some intermediate variables in the recursion have a distribution that depends on $x = x_1 \oplus \cdots \oplus x_n$; hence the algorithm is actually vulnerable to a first-order attack.

Algorithm 2. RefreshMasks

Input: $x_1, \ldots, x_n$

Output: $y_1, \ldots, y_n$ such that $y_1 \oplus \cdots \oplus y_n = x_1 \oplus \cdots \oplus x_n$

1: $y_n \leftarrow x_n$
2: **for** $i = 1$ to $n - 1$ **do**
3:     $r_i \leftarrow \{0,1\}^k$
4:     $y_i \leftarrow x_i \oplus r_i$
5:     $y_n \leftarrow y_n \oplus r_i$ ▷ $y_{n,i} = x_n \oplus \bigoplus_{j=1}^{i} r_j$
6: **end for**
7: **return** $y_1, \ldots, y_n$

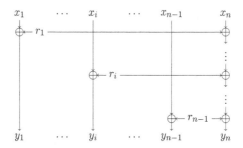

Fig. 1. The RefreshMasks algorithm, with the randoms r_i accumulated on the last column.

4.2 Mask Refreshing

To prevent the above attack (and any other attack), we must perform some mask refreshing on the intermediate shares. We use the same RefreshMasks procedure as in [RP10]; see Algorithm 2, and Fig. 1 for an illustration.

In the RefreshMasks algorithm above we denote by $y_{n,i}$ the intermediate variables in the accumulated sum, namely for $1 \leq i \leq n - 1$:

$$y_{n,i} = x_n \oplus \bigoplus_{j=1}^{i} r_j$$

We add 3 applications of RefreshMasks in the previous conversion algorithm. The first application is to first expand the n input shares x_i into $n + 1$ shares, so that we can now have n variables of the form $z_i = \Psi(x_1, x_{i+1})$ instead of only $n - 1$; this is to prevent the adversary from recovering all variables z_i's. However, one must still compress to $n - 1$ variables for the recursive application of the conversion algorithm with $n - 1$ shares. This is done by using two RefreshMasks (one for each recursive application) followed by xoring the last two shares into one, to get $n - 1$ shares. As will be seen in the next sections, we obtain a t-SNI conversion algorithm; this is essentially based on a careful analysis of the security properties of RefreshMasks.

4.3 Secure Conversion from Boolean to Arithmetic Masking

We are now ready to describe our new high-order conversion algorithm from Boolean to arithmetic masking; as previously, our algorithm $\mathcal{C}_n$ is defined recursively. We start from the n shares:

$$x = x_1 \oplus \cdots \oplus x_n$$

If $n = 2$, we apply the t-SNI variant of Goubin's first order algorithm, as described in Algorithm 1. For $n \geq 3$, we proceed as follows.

1. We first perform a $(n + 1)$-RefreshMasks of the n shares x_i's and $x_{n+1} = 0$, so that we obtain the following $n + 1$ shares:

$$a_1, \ldots, a_{n+1} \leftarrow \mathsf{RefreshMasks}_{n+1}(x_1, \ldots, x_n, 0)$$

   Therefore we still have $x = a_1 \oplus \cdots \oplus a_{n+1}$. We can write as previously using $\Psi(a_1, u) = a_1 \oplus u - u$:

$$x = a_2 \oplus \cdots \oplus a_{n+1} + (a_1 \oplus \cdots \oplus a_{n+1} - a_2 \oplus \cdots \oplus a_{n+1})$$
$$= a_2 \oplus \cdots \oplus a_{n+1} + \Psi(a_1, a_2 \oplus \cdots \oplus a_{n+1})$$

2. Thanks to the affine property of Ψ, this gives as previously:

$$x = a_2 \oplus \cdots \oplus a_{n+1} + (\overline{n \wedge 1}) \cdot a_1 \oplus \Psi(a_1, a_2) \oplus \cdots \oplus \Psi(a_1, a_{n+1})$$

   Therefore, we let $b_1 \leftarrow (\overline{n \wedge 1}) \cdot a_1 \oplus \Psi(a_1, a_2)$ and $b_i \leftarrow \Psi(a_1, a_{i+1})$ for all $2 \leq i \leq n$. This gives:

$$x = a_2 \oplus \cdots \oplus a_{n+1} + b_1 \oplus \cdots \oplus b_n$$

3. We perform a RefreshMasks of the a_i's and of the b_i's, letting:

$$c_1, \ldots, c_n \leftarrow \mathsf{RefreshMasks}(a_2, \ldots, a_{n+1})$$
$$d_1, \ldots, d_n \leftarrow \mathsf{RefreshMasks}(b_1, \ldots, b_n)$$

   Therefore we still have:

$$x = c_1 \oplus \cdots \oplus c_n + d_1 \oplus \cdots \oplus d_n$$

4. We compress from n shares to $n-1$ shares, by xoring the last two shares of the c_i's and d_i's. More precisely we let $e_i \leftarrow c_i$ and $f_i \leftarrow d_i$ for all $1 \leq i \leq n - 2$, and $e_{n-1} \leftarrow c_{n-1} \oplus c_n$ and $f_{n-1} \leftarrow d_{n-1} \oplus d_n$. Therefore we still have:

$$x = e_1 \oplus \cdots \oplus e_{n-1} + f_1 \oplus \cdots \oplus f_{n-1}$$

5. We perform two recursive calls to the Boolean to arithmetic conversion algorithm $\mathcal{C}_{n-1}$:

$$A_1, \ldots, A_{n-1} \leftarrow \mathcal{C}_{n-1}(e_1, \ldots, e_{n-1})$$
$$B_1, \ldots, B_{n-1} \leftarrow \mathcal{C}_{n-1}(f_1, \ldots, f_{n-1})$$

   This gives:

$$x = A_1 + \cdots + A_{n-1} + B_1 + \cdots + B_{n-1}$$

6. We reduce the number of arithmetic shares from $2n-2$ to n by some additive grouping, letting $D_i \leftarrow A_i + B_i$ for $1 \le i \le n-2$, and $D_{n-1} \leftarrow A_{n-1}$ and $D_n \leftarrow B_{n-1}$. This gives as required:

$$x = D_1 + \cdots + D_n \pmod{2^k}$$

This completes the description of the algorithm. For clarity we also provide a formal description in Appendix A.

Theorem 2 (Completeness). *The C_n Boolean to arithmetic conversion algorithm, when taking $x_1, \ldots, x_n$ as input, outputs $D_1, \ldots, D_n$ such that $x_1 \oplus \cdots \oplus x_n = D_1 + \cdots + D_n \pmod{2^k}$.*

Proof. The proof is straightforward from the above description. The completeness property holds for $n = 2$ with Goubin's conversion algorithm. Assuming that completeness holds for $n - 1$ shares, we obtain:

$$\sum_{i=1}^{n} D_i = \sum_{i=1}^{n-1} A_i + \sum_{i=1}^{n-1} B_i = \bigoplus_{i=1}^{n-1} e_i + \bigoplus_{i=1}^{n-1} f_i = \bigoplus_{i=1}^{n} c_i + \bigoplus_{i=1}^{n} d_i = \bigoplus_{i=2}^{n+1} a_i + \bigoplus_{i=1}^{n} b_i$$

$$= \bigoplus_{i=2}^{n+1} a_i + \Psi\left(a_1, \bigoplus_{i=2}^{n+1} a_i\right) = \bigoplus_{i=1}^{n+1} a_i = \bigoplus_{i=1}^{n} x_i$$

and therefore completeness holds for n shares.   □

Complexity Analysis. We denote by T_n the number of operations for n shares. We assume that random generation takes unit time. We have $T_2 = 11$ (see Sect. 3.2). The complexity of RefreshMasks with n shares is $3n - 3$ operations. From the recursive definition of our algorithm, we obtain:

$$T_n = [3 \cdot (n + 1) - 3] + [2 \cdot n + 3] + [2 \cdot (3n - 3)] + 2 + 2 \cdot T_{n-1} + [n - 2]$$
$$= 2 \cdot T_{n-1} + 12 \cdot n - 3$$

This gives:

$$T_n = 14 \cdot 2^n - 12 \cdot n - 21$$

Therefore, the complexity of our algorithm is exponential in n, namely $\mathcal{O}(2^n)$, instead of $\mathcal{O}(n^2 \cdot k)$ in [CGV14]; however for small values of n our conversion algorithm is one order of magnitude more efficient; see Sect. 6 for implementation results.

Security. The following theorem shows that our conversion algorithm achieves the t-SNI property. This means that our conversion algorithm is secure against any adversary with at most $n-1$ probes in the circuit. Moreover thanks to the t-SNI property, our conversion algorithm can be used within a larger construction (for example a block-cipher, or HMAC-SHA-1), so that the larger construction also achieves the t-SNI property.

Theorem 3 (*t*-SNI of C_n). *Let* $(x_i)_{1\leq i\leq n}$ *be the input and let* $(D_i)_{1\leq i\leq n}$ *be the output of the Boolean to arithmetic conversion algorithm* C_n. *For any set of* t *intermediate variables and any subset* $O \subset [1, n]$, *there exists a subset* I *of input indices such that the* t *intermediate variables as well as* $D_{|O}$ *can be perfectly simulated from* $x_{|I}$, *with* $|I| \leq t$.

The rest of the section is devoted to the proof of Theorem 3. The proof is based on a careful analysis of the properties of the RefreshMasks algorithm. In the next section, we start with three well known, basic properties of RefreshMasks.

4.4   Basic Properties of RefreshMasks

The lemma below shows that RefreshMasks achieves the *t*-NI property in a straightforward way, for any $t < n$.

Lemma 2 (*t*-NI of RefreshMasks). *Let* $(x_i)_{1\leq i\leq n}$ *be the input of Refresh-Masks and let* $(y_i)_{1\leq i\leq n}$ *be the output. For any set of* t *intermediate variables, there exists a subset* I *of input indices such that the* t *intermediate variables can be perfectly simulated from* $x_{|I}$, *with* $|I| \leq t$.

Proof. The set I is constructed as follows. If for some $1 \leq i \leq n - 1$, any of the variables x_i, r_i or y_i is probed, we add i to I. If x_n or y_n or any intermediate variable $y_{n,j}$ is probed, we add n to I. Since we add at most one index to I per probe, we must have $|I| \leq t$.

The simulation of the probed variable is straightforward. All the randoms r_i for $1 \leq i \leq n - 1$ can be simulated as in the real algorithm, by generating a random element from $\{0, 1\}^k$. If y_i is probed, then we must have $i \in I$, so it can be perfectly simulated from $y_i = x_i \oplus r_i$ from the knowledge of x_i. Similarly, if any intermediate variable $y_{n,j}$ is probed, then $n \in I$, so it can be perfectly simulated from x_n. Therefore all probes can be perfectly simulated from $x_{|I}$. □

Remark 1. It is easy to see that RefreshMasks does not achieve the *t*-SNI property. Namely with $t = 1$ we can probe $y_{n,1} = x_n \oplus r_1$ and additionally require the simulation of the output variable $y_1 = x_1 \oplus r_1$. We have $y_{n,1} \oplus y_1 = x_n \oplus x_1$, hence the knowledge of both x_1 and x_n is required for the simulation of the two variables, which contradicts the bound $|I| \leq t$.

The following lemma shows that any subset of $n - 1$ output shares y_i of RefreshMasks is uniformly and independently distributed, when the algorithm is not probed.

Lemma 3. *Let* $(x_i)_{1\leq i\leq n}$ *be the input and let* $(y_i)_{1\leq i\leq n}$ *be the output of Refresh-Masks. Any subset of* $n - 1$ *output shares* y_i *is uniformly and independently distributed.*

Proof. Let $S \subsetneq [1, n]$ be the corresponding subset. We distinguish two cases. If $n \notin S$, we have $y_i = x_i \oplus r_i$ for all $i \in S$, and therefore those y_i's are uniformly and independently distributed. If $n \in S$, let $i^* \notin S$. We have $y_i = x_i \oplus r_i$ for all $i \in S \setminus \{n\}$. Moreover:

$$y_n = \left(x_n \oplus \bigoplus_{i=1, i \neq i^*}^{n-1} r_i \right) \oplus r_{i^*}$$

where r_{i^*} is not used in another y_i for $i \in S$. Therefore the $n - 1$ output y_i's are uniformly and independently distributed. □

The following lemma, whose proof is also straightforward, shows that when RefreshMasks is not probed, the distribution of the n output shares y_i's can be perfectly simulated from the knowledge of $x_1 \oplus \cdots \oplus x_n$ only; that is, the knowledge of the individual shares x_i's is not required.

Lemma 4. *Let $(x_i)_{1 \leq i \leq n}$ be the input and let $(y_i)_{1 \leq i \leq n}$ be the output of Refresh-Masks. The distribution of $(y_i)_{1 \leq i \leq n}$ can be perfectly simulated from $x_1 \oplus \cdots \oplus x_n$.*

Proof. We have $y_i = x_i \oplus r_i$ for all $1 \leq i \leq n - 1$ and:

$$y_n = x_n \oplus \bigoplus_{i=1}^{n-1} r_i = \left(\bigoplus_{i=1}^{n} x_i \right) \oplus \left(\bigoplus_{i=1}^{n-1} y_i \right)$$

Therefore we can perfectly simulate the output $(y_i)_{1 \leq i \leq n}$ by letting $y_i \leftarrow \{0, 1\}^k$ for all $1 \leq i \leq n - 1$ and $y_n \leftarrow \left(\bigoplus_{i=1}^{n} x_i \right) \oplus \left(\bigoplus_{i=1}^{n-1} y_i \right)$. □

4.5   Property of the Initial RefreshMasks

The lemma below gives the first non-trivial property of RefreshMasks. We consider the first RefreshMasks of our conversion algorithm C_n described in Sect. 4.3, taking as input $n + 1$ input shares x_i (instead of n), but with $x_{n+1} = 0$. The lemma below is a refinement of the basic t-NI lemma (Lemma 2); namely we show that if at least one of the output variables y_j is probed, then it can be simulated "for free", that is without increasing the size of the input index I. More precisely, we get the bound $|I| \leq t - 1$ under that condition, instead of $|I| \leq t$ in Lemma 2. This stronger bound will be used for the security proof of our conversion algorithm; namely at Step 2 in Sect. 4.3 the adversary can probe t of the variables $b_i = \Psi(a_1, a_{i+1})$, whose simulation then requires the knowledge of $t + 1$ variables a_i. Thanks to the stronger bound, this requires the knowledge of only t input shares x_i (instead of $t + 1$), as required for the t-SNI bound.

Below we actually prove a slightly stronger lemma: if we fix $x_{n+1} = 0$, then we can always simulate the t probes from $x_{|I}$ with $|I| \leq t - 1$, except in the trivial case of the adversary probing the input x_i's only.

Lemma 5. *Let $x_1, \ldots, x_n$ be n inputs shares, and let $x_{n+1} = 0$. Consider the circuit $y_1, \ldots, y_{n+1} \leftarrow \mathsf{RefreshMasks}_{n+1}(x_1, \ldots, x_n, x_{n+1})$, where the randoms are accumulated on x_{n+1}. Let t be the number of probed variables. There exists a subset I such that all probed variables can be perfectly simulated from $x_{|I}$, with $|I| \le t - 1$, except if only the input x_i's are probed.*

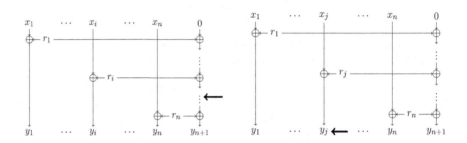

Fig. 2. Illustration of Lemma 5. Case 1 (left): the adversary has spent at least one probe on the last column for which $x_{n+1} = 0$, therefore we can have $|I| \le t - 1$. Case 2 (right): no intermediate variable is probed on the last column; therefore r_j can play the role of a one-time pad for the simulation of the probed y_j, hence x_j is not required and again $|I| \le t - 1$.

Proof. As illustrated in Fig. 2, we distinguish two cases. If x_{n+1} or y_{n+1} or any intermediate variable $y_{n+1,j}$ has been probed, we construct the set I as follows. If for some $1 \le i \le n$, any of the variables x_i, y_i or r_i is probed, we add i to I. In the construction of I we have omitted at least one probed variable (on the column of index $n + 1$), and therefore we must have $|I| \le t - 1$ as required. The simulation is then straightforward and proceeds as in Lemma 2. Namely all the randoms r_i are simulated as in the actual algorithm, and all probed variables x_i and y_i can be perfectly simulated from x_i, since in that case $i \in I$. The only difference is that $n + 1$ need not be in I since $x_{n+1} = 0$ by definition.

We now consider the second case. If neither x_{n+1} nor y_{n+1} nor any intermediate variable $y_{n+1,i}$ has been probed, we construct the set I as follows. By assumption, there exists an index j such that r_j or y_j or both have been probed, with $1 \le j \le n$; namely we have excluded the case of the adversary probing only the input x_i's. For all $1 \le i \le n$ and $i \ne j$, if x_i or r_i or y_i has been probed, we add i to I. Moreover if x_j has been probed, or if both r_j and y_j have been probed, we add j to I. From the construction of I, we must have $|I| \le t - 1$ as required. Namely either a single variable among r_j and y_j has been probed, and this probe does not contribute to I, or both r_j and y_j have been probed, and these two probes contribute to only one index in I.

The simulation of probed x_i, r_i or y_i is straightforward for $i \ne j$, from the knowledge of x_i. If $j \in I$, the simulation of x_j, r_j and y_j is also straightforward. If $j \notin I$, then either r_j or y_j has been probed (but not both). If r_j has been probed, it can be simulated by generating a random value. If y_j has been probed, since we have $y_j = x_j \oplus r_j$ and moreover r_j does not appear in the computation of any other probed variable (since in that case r_j has not been probed, nor any intermediate variable $y_{n+1,i}$), we can simulate y_j as a random value in $\{0,1\}^k$. Therefore all probed variables can be perfectly simulated from $x_{|I}$.   □

Remark 2. The lemma does not necessarily hold if we don't assume that $x_{n+1} = 0$, or if we only assume that $x_i = 0$ for some $i \neq n+1$. For example, assuming that $x_2 = 0$, the adversary can probe both $y_1 = x_1 \oplus r_1$ and $y_{n+1,1} = x_{n+1} \oplus r_1$, which gives $y_1 \oplus y_{n+1} = x_1 \oplus x_{n+1}$. Hence the knowledge of 2 input shares is required to simulate the 2 probes (including the output variable y_1), which contradicts the bound $|I| \leq t - 1$.

4.6   More Results on RefreshMasks

In this section we consider the properties of RefreshMasks required for the compression from n shares to $n - 1$ shares as performed at steps 3 and 4 of our conversion algorithm in Sect. 4.3. Namely if the adversary probes t of the variables f_i's, because of the last variable $f_{n-1} = d_{n-1} \oplus d_n$, this can require the knowledge of $t + 1$ of the variables d_i's. Without RefreshMasks the knowledge of $t + 1$ of the variables b_i's would be required, and eventually $t + 1$ of the input shares x_i's, which would contradict the t-SNI bound. In this section, we show that thanks to RefreshMasks we can still get the bound $|I| \leq t$ instead of $|I| \leq t + 1$.

We first prove two preliminary lemmas. The first lemma below is analogous to Lemma 5 and shows that when the randoms in RefreshMasks are accumulated on x_n, the corresponding output variable y_n can always be simulated "for free", that is, without increasing the size of the input index I; more precisely, if we require that y_n is among the t probes, then we can have $|I| \leq t - 1$ instead of $|I| \leq t$ in Lemma 2. This will enable to show that when a subsequent compression step to $n - 1$ shares is performed with $z_{n-1} \leftarrow y_{n-1} \oplus y_n$, we can still keep the bound $|I| \leq t$ instead of $|I| \leq t + 1$. Namely either the adversary does not probe $z_{n-1} = y_{n-1} \oplus y_n$ and he does not benefit from getting information on two variables with a single probe, or z_{n-1} is probed and we can apply Lemma 6 below with probed y_n; in both cases we get $|I| \leq t$ instead of $|I| \leq t + 1$. We provide the proof of Lemma 6 in the full version of this paper [Cor17].

Lemma 6. *Let $x_1, \ldots, x_n$ be the input of a RefreshMasks where the randoms are accumulated on x_n, and let $y_1, \ldots, y_n$ be the output. Let t be the number of probed variables, with $t < n$. If y_n is among the probed variables, then there exists a subset I such that all probed variables can be perfectly simulated from $x_{|I}$, with $|I| \leq t - 1$.*

Remark 3. The lemma does not hold for other output variables. For example the adversary can probe both $y_1 = x_1 \oplus r_1$ and $y_{n,1} = x_n \oplus r_1$. Since $y_1 \oplus y_{n,1} = x_1 \oplus x_n$, both x_1 and x_n are required for the simulation, which contradicts the bound $|I| \leq t - 1$.

In the previous lemma we have restricted ourselves to $t < n$ probes (including the probe on y_n). Namely if $t = n$, the adversary can probe all y_i's and learn $x_1 \oplus \cdots \oplus x_n = y_1 \oplus \cdots \oplus y_n$; therefore the simulation cannot be performed using a proper subset I of $[1, n]$. In Lemma 4 we have showed that when no intermediate variables of RefreshMasks are probed, the n output shares y_i can be simulated from the knowledge of $x_1 \oplus \cdots \oplus x_n$ only. The lemma below shows that this is essentially the best that the adversary can do: when the adversary has n probes, and if one of which must be y_n, then either all probes in the circuit can be simulated from $x_1 \oplus \cdots \oplus x_n$ only, or they can be simulated from $x_{|I}$ with $|I| \leq n - 1$. As previously this only holds if y_n must be among the n probes; namely without this restriction the attacker could probe the n input shares x_i directly and learn the value of the individual shares x_i (and not only the xor of the x_i's); see also Remark 4 below.

As previously, this will enable to show that when a subsequent compression step is performed with $z_{n-1} \leftarrow y_{n-1} \oplus y_n$, if the adversary has a total of $n - 1$ probes, then the simulation can be performed from $x_1 \oplus \cdots \oplus x_n$ only, or from $x_{|I}$ with $|I| \leq n - 1$. Namely either the adversary does not probe $z_{n-1} = y_{n-1} \oplus y_n$ and we can simulate from $x_{|I}$ with $|I| \leq n - 1$, or z_{n-1} is probed and we can apply Lemma 7 below with probed y_n. The proof of Lemma 7 can be found in the full version of this paper [Cor17].

Lemma 7. *Let $x_1, \ldots, x_n$ be the input of a RefreshMasks where the randoms are accumulated on x_n, and let $y_1, \ldots, y_n$ be the output. Let t be the number of probed variables, with $t = n$. If y_n is among the probed variables, then either all probed variables can be perfectly simulated from $x_1 \oplus \cdots \oplus x_n$, or there exists a subset I with $|I| \leq n - 1$ such that they can be perfectly simulated from $x_{|I}$.*

Remark 4. As previously, the lemma does not hold if any other output variable y_i is required to be probed instead of y_n. Namely the adversary can probe the n variables $y_1 = x_1 \oplus r_1$, $x_2, \ldots, x_{n-1}$ and $y_{n,1} = x_n \oplus r_1$. The xor of these n variables gives $x_1 \oplus \cdots \oplus x_n$, but the adversary also learns the individual shares $x_2, \ldots, x_{n-1}$. Whereas in Lemma 7, the adversary either learns $x_1 \oplus \cdots \oplus x_n$ and nothing else, or at most $n - 1$ of the shares x_i.

The lemma below is the main result of the section. As mentioned previously, it enables to show that when we perform the compression from n shares to $n - 1$ shares at steps 3 and 4 of our conversion algorithm from Sect. 4.3, we can still have the bound $|I| \leq t$ instead of $|I| \leq t + 1$ when $t < n$; and for $t = n - 1$, the simulation can be performed either from $x_1 \oplus \cdots \oplus x_n$, or from $x_{|I}$ with $|I| \leq n - 1$. We refer to the full version of this paper [Cor17] for the proof of Lemma 8.

Lemma 8. *Consider the circuit with $y_1, \ldots, y_n \leftarrow$ RefreshMasks$(x_1, \ldots, x_n)$, $z_i \leftarrow y_i$ for all $1 \leq i \leq n - 2$ and $z_{n-1} \leftarrow y_{n-1} \oplus y_n$. Let t be the number of probed variables. If $t < n - 1$, there exists a subset I with $|I| \leq t$ such that all probed variables can be perfectly simulated from $x_{|I}$. If $t = n - 1$, then either all probed variables can be perfectly simulated from $x_1 \oplus \cdots \oplus x_n$, or there exists a subset I with $|I| \leq n - 1$ such that they can be perfectly simulated from $x_{|I}$.*

Remark 5. The lemma does not hold if the two xored output variables of Refresh-Masks do not include y_n (when the randoms of RefreshMasks are accumulated on x_n). For example, if we let $z_1 \leftarrow y_1 \oplus y_2$ instead, the adversary could probe both $z_1 = y_1 \oplus y_2 = (x_1 \oplus r_1) \oplus (x_2 \oplus r_2)$ and $y_{n,2} = x_n \oplus r_1 \oplus r_2$, which gives $z_1 \oplus y_{n,2} = x_1 \oplus x_2 \oplus x_n$. Hence to simulate those 2 probes the knowledge of 3 shares is required, which contradicts the bound $|I| \le t$.

Note that the value $x_1 \oplus \cdots \oplus x_n$ in the above lemma corresponds to either $a_2 \oplus \cdots \oplus a_{n+1}$ or $b_1 \oplus \cdots \oplus b_n$ at Step 3 of our conversion algorithm from Sect. 4.3. In that case, the adversary has already spent $n - 1$ probes, and no other variable is probed. As shown in the next section, this enables to prove that these values can be simulated without knowing the input shares. Namely when the initial RefreshMasks is not probed, the distribution of $a_2 \oplus \cdots \oplus a_{n+1}$ is uniform because of Lemma 3, and can therefore be simulated by a random value. Similarly we have:

$$b_1 \oplus \cdots \oplus b_n = \Psi(a_1, a_2 \oplus \cdots \oplus a_{n+1}) = x - x \oplus a_1$$

where $x = x_1 \oplus \cdots \oplus x_n = a_1 \oplus \cdots \oplus a_{n+1}$. Since in that case the initial Refresh-Masks is not probed, the variable a_1 has the uniform distribution, hence the value $b_1 \oplus \cdots \oplus b_n$ can also be simulated by a random value.

4.7   Proof of Theorem 3

We refer to the full version of this paper [Cor17] for the proof of Theorem 3.

5   Cryptanalysis of the Hutter-Tunstall Boolean to Arithmetic Conversion Algorithm

In this section, we describe two attacks against the high-order Hutter-Tunstall Boolean to arithmetic conversion algorithm in [HT16], breaking all the conversion algorithms except the second-order algorithm. For clarity we will use the same notations as in [HT16] and denote by n the maximum number of probes in the circuit; therefore the conversion algorithm takes as input $n+1$ shares and outputs $n+1$ shares, instead of n in the previous sections. Following [HT16], we say that a countermeasures is of order n when it should be resistant against n probes (hence with $n+1$ shares as input and output).

Our two attacks are as follows:

- An attack of order 4 against the n-th order countermeasure, for $n \ge 4$.
- An attack of order n against the n-th order countermeasure, for $n \ge 3$.

Therefore the second attack is only useful for $n = 3$, as for $n \ge 4$ the first attack is of constant order 4. In particular, we show that our second attack can be applied against the third-order algorithm explicitly described in [HT16, Algorithm 3]. Our two attacks imply that the conversion algorithm in [HT16] cannot offer more than second-order security.

In the following we do not provide a full description of the conversion algorithm from [HT16]; for simplicity we only provide the relevant part leading to the attack; we refer to [HT16] for the full description.

5.1 Attack of Order 4 Against n-th Order Countermeasure

We have as input the $n + 1$ shares x', $r_1, \ldots r_n$, where:

$$x = x' \oplus r_1 \oplus \cdots \oplus r_n$$

We copy Eq. (24) from [HT16]:

$$\left(\bigoplus_{i=1}^{n-1} \kappa_i \right) - \left(\alpha \oplus \bigoplus_{i=1}^{n} r_i \right) = ((\neg n \wedge 1)\beta) \oplus \bigoplus_{i=1}^{n-1} \Psi(\beta, \delta_i) \oplus \Psi \left(\beta, \alpha \oplus r_n \oplus \bigoplus_{i=1}^{n-1} \delta_i \oplus r_i \right)$$

The above equation means that the variable

$$X = ((\neg n \wedge 1)\beta) \oplus \bigoplus_{i=1}^{n-1} \Psi(\beta, \delta_i) \oplus \Psi \left(\beta, \alpha \oplus r_n \oplus \bigoplus_{i=1}^{n-1} \delta_i \oplus r_i \right) \tag{1}$$

is explicitly computed, using a certain sequence of operations following from the right-hand side of the equation. From the affine property of the Ψ function, we have:

$$X = \Psi \left(\beta, \alpha \oplus \bigoplus_{i=1}^{n} r_i \right)$$

Letting $u := \alpha \oplus \bigoplus_{i=1}^{n} r_i$, we can write:

$$X = \Psi(\beta, u) = \beta \oplus u - u$$
$$x = x' \oplus \alpha \oplus u$$

Therefore, if the variable β is explicitly computed when evaluating (1), our attack works by probing the 4 variables β, X, α and x'. From β and $X = \beta \oplus u - u$, we obtain information about u. From α and x', this reveals information about $x = x' \oplus \alpha \oplus u$.

Alternatively, if the variable β is not explicitly computed[4], the variable $Y = \Psi(\beta, \delta_1)$ must still be explicitly computed when evaluating X. Therefore our attack works by probing the 4 variables Y, X, α and x'. We obtain the two variables:

$$X = \Psi(\beta, u), \quad Y = \Psi(\beta, \delta_1)$$

---

[4] In the concrete description of the third-order conversion algorithm in [HT16, Algorithm 3], the variable β is not explicitly computed when computing $\Psi(\beta, \delta_i) = \beta \oplus \delta_i - \delta_i$, by only computing $\beta \oplus \delta_i$ instead.

and one can check that for randomly distributed β, δ_1, the distribution of (X, Y) leaks information about u. Namely, the variable $Y = \Psi(\beta, \delta_1) = \beta \oplus \delta_1 - \delta_1$ leaks information about β, which combined with $X = \Psi(\beta, u) = \beta \oplus u - u$ leaks information about u. From α and x', this reveals information about $x = x' \oplus \alpha \oplus u$. Hence in both cases we obtain an attack of constant order 4 against the n-th order countermeasures for any $n \geq 4$.

5.2 Attack of Order n Against the n-th Order Countermeasure

We refer to the full version of this paper [Cor17] for the description of our second attack.

6 Operation Count and Implementation

As shown in Sect. 4.3, the number of operations of our Boolean to arithmetic conversion algorithm is given by $T_n = 14 \cdot 2^n - 12 \cdot n - 21$, so it has complexity $\mathcal{O}(2^n)$ independent of the register size k, while the conversion algorithm from [CGV14] has complexity $\mathcal{O}(k \cdot n^2)$. We summarize in Table 1 the operation count for [CGV14] (for $k = 32$) and for our new algorithm from Sect. 4.3. We see that for small orders t, our new countermeasure is at least one order of magnitude faster than previous work.

Table 1. Operation count for Boolean to arithmetic conversion algorithms, up to security order $t = 12$, with $n = t + 1$ shares.

B → A conversion	Security order t								
	1	2	3	4	5	6	8	10	12
Goubin [Gou01]	7								
Hutter-Tunstall [HT16]		31							
CGV, 32 bits [CGV14]		2 098	3 664	7 752	10 226	14 698	28 044	39 518	56 344
Our algorithm (Sect. 4.3)		55	155	367	803	1 687	7 039	28 519	114 511

We have also implemented the algorithm in [CGV14] and our new algorithm, in C on an iMac running a 3.2 GHz Intel processor, using the Clang compiler. We summarize the execution times in Table 2, which are consistent with the operation count from Table 1. This confirms that in practice for small orders, our new countermeasure is at least one order of magnitude faster than previous work.

Table 2. Running time in μs for Boolean to arithmetic conversion algorithms, up to security order $t = 12$, with $n = t + 1$ shares. The implementation was done in C on a iMac running a 3.2 GHz Intel processor.

B → A conversion	Security order t							
	2	3	4	5	6	8	10	12
CGV, 32 bits [CGV14]	1 593	2 697	4 297	5 523	7 301	10 919	15 819	21 406
Our algorithm (Sect. 4.3)	45	119	281	611	1 270	5 673	22 192	87 322

References

[BBD+16] Barthe, G., Belaïd, S., Dupressoir, F., Fouque, P.-A., Grégoire, B., Strub, P.-Y., Zucchini, R.: Strong non-interference and type-directed higher-order masking. In: Proceedings of the 2016 ACM SIGSAC Conference on Computer and Communications Security, Vienna, Austria, 24–28 October, pp. 116–129 (2016)

[BSS+13] Beaulieu, R., Shors, D., Smith, J., Treatman-Clark, S., Weeks, B., Wingers, L.: The SIMON and SPECK families of lightweight block ciphers. IACR Cryptology ePrint Archive **2013**, 404 (2013)

[CGTV15] Coron, J.-S., Großschädl, J., Tibouchi, M., Vadnala, P.K.: Conversion from arithmetic to boolean masking with logarithmic complexity. In: Leander, G. (ed.) FSE 2015. LNCS, vol. 9054, pp. 130–149. Springer, Heidelberg (2015). doi:10.1007/978-3-662-48116-5_7

[CGV14] Coron, J.-S., Großschädl, J., Vadnala, P.K.: Secure conversion between boolean and arithmetic masking of any order. In: Batina, L., Robshaw, M. (eds.) CHES 2014. LNCS, vol. 8731, pp. 188–205. Springer, Heidelberg (2014). doi:10.1007/978-3-662-44709-3_11

[CJRR99] Chari, S., Jutla, C.S., Rao, J.R., Rohatgi, P.: Towards sound approaches to counteract power-analysis attacks. In: Wiener, M. (ed.) CRYPTO 1999. LNCS, vol. 1666, pp. 398–412. Springer, Heidelberg (1999). doi:10.1007/3-540-48405-1_26

[Cor17] Coron, J.-S.: High-order conversion from boolean to arithmetic masking. Cryptology ePrint Archive, Report 2017/252 (2017). http://eprint.iacr.org/2017/252

[CRRY99] Contini, S., Rivest, R.L., Robshaw, M.J.B., Yin, Y.L.: Improved analysis of some simplified variants of RC6. In: Knudsen, L. (ed.) FSE 1999. LNCS, vol. 1636, pp. 1–15. Springer, Heidelberg (1999). doi:10.1007/3-540-48519-8_1

[DDF14] Duc, A., Dziembowski, S., Faust, S.: Unifying leakage models: from probing attacks to noisy leakage. In: Nguyen, P.Q., Oswald, E. (eds.) EUROCRYPT 2014. LNCS, vol. 8441, pp. 423–440. Springer, Heidelberg (2014). doi:10.1007/978-3-642-55220-5_24

[Gou01] Goubin, L.: A sound method for switching between boolean and arithmetic masking. In: Koç, Ç.K., Naccache, D., Paar, C. (eds.) CHES 2001. LNCS, vol. 2162, pp. 3–15. Springer, Heidelberg (2001). doi:10.1007/3-540-44709-1_2

[GP99] Goubin, L., Patarin, J.: DES and differential power analysis the "Duplication" method. In: Koç, Ç.K., Paar, C. (eds.) CHES 1999. LNCS, vol. 1717, pp. 158–172. Springer, Heidelberg (1999). doi:10.1007/3-540-48059-5_15

[HT16] Hutter, M., Tunstall, M.: Constant-time higher-order boolean-to-arithmetic masking. Cryptology ePrint Archive, Report 2016/1023 (2016). http://eprint.iacr.org/2016/1023. Version posted on 22 Dec 2016

[ISW03] Ishai, Y., Sahai, A., Wagner, D.: Private circuits: securing hardware against probing attacks. In: Boneh, D. (ed.) CRYPTO 2003. LNCS, vol. 2729, pp. 463–481. Springer, Heidelberg (2003). doi:10.1007/978-3-540-45146-4_27

[LM90] Lai, X., Massey, J.L.: A proposal for a new block encryption standard. In: Damgård, I.B. (ed.) EUROCRYPT 1990. LNCS, vol. 473, pp. 389–404. Springer, Heidelberg (1991). doi:10.1007/3-540-46877-3_35

[NIS95] NIST. Secure hash standard. In: Federal Information Processing Standard, FIPA-180-1 (1995)

[NW97] Needham, R.M., Wheeler, D.J.: Tea extentions. Technical report, Computer Laboratory, University of Cambridge (1997)

[OMHT06] Oswald, E., Mangard, S., Herbst, C., Tillich, S.: Practical second-order DPA attacks for masked smart card implementations of block ciphers. In: Pointcheval, D. (ed.) CT-RSA 2006. LNCS, vol. 3860, pp. 192–207. Springer, Heidelberg (2006). doi:10.1007/11605805_13

[PR13] Prouff, E., Rivain, M.: Higher-order side channel security and mask refreshing. In: Advances in Cryptology - EUROCRYPT 2013 - 32nd Annual International Conference on the Theory and Applications of Cryptographic Techniques, Athens, Greece, May 26–30, 2013. Proceedings, pp. 142–159 (2013)

[RP10] Rivain, M., Prouff, E.: Provably secure higher-order masking of AES. In: Mangard, S., Standaert, F.-X. (eds.) CHES 2010. LNCS, vol. 6225, pp. 413–427. Springer, Heidelberg (2010). doi:10.1007/978-3-642-15031-9_28

A   Formal Description of the High-order Boolean to Arithmetic Conversion

---

Algorithm 3. $\mathcal{C}_n$: high-order Boolean to Arithmetic Conversion

---

Input: $x_1, \ldots, x_n$
Output: $D_1, \ldots, D_n$ such that $x_1 \oplus \cdots \oplus x_n = D_1 + \cdots + D_n \pmod{2^k}$
 1: **if** $n = 2$ **then**
 2:     $D_1, D_2 \leftarrow \mathsf{GoubinSNI}(x_1, x_2)$
 3:     **return** D_1, D_2
 4: **end if**
 5: $a_1, \ldots, a_{n+1} \leftarrow \mathsf{RefreshMasks}_{n+1}(x_1, \ldots, x_n, 0)$
 6: $b_1 \leftarrow \overline{(n \wedge 1)} \cdot a_1 \oplus \Psi(a_1, a_2)$
 7: **for** $i = 2$ **to** n **do**
 8:     $b_i \leftarrow \Psi(a_1, a_{i+1})$
 9: **end for**
10: $c_1, \ldots, c_n \leftarrow \mathsf{RefreshMasks}_n(a_2, \ldots, a_{n+1})$
11: $d_1, \ldots, d_n \leftarrow \mathsf{RefreshMasks}_n(b_1, \ldots, b_n)$
12: $e_1, \ldots, e_{n-2} \leftarrow c_1, \ldots, c_{n-2}$ and $e_{n-1} \leftarrow c_{n-1} \oplus c_n$
13: $f_1, \ldots, f_{n-2} \leftarrow d_1, \ldots, d_{n-2}$ and $f_{n-1} \leftarrow d_{n-1} \oplus d_n$
14: $A_1, \ldots, A_{n-1} \leftarrow \mathcal{C}_{n-1}(e_1, \ldots, e_{n-1})$
15: $B_1, \ldots, B_{n-1} \leftarrow \mathcal{C}_{n-1}(f_1, \ldots, f_{n-1})$
16: **for** $i = 1$ **to** $n - 2$ **do**
17:     $D_i \leftarrow A_i + B_i$
18: **end for**
19: $D_{n-1} \leftarrow A_{n-1}$
20: $D_n \leftarrow B_{n-1}$
21: **return** $D_1, \ldots, D_n$

Reconciling $d + 1$ Masking in Hardware and Software

Hannes Gross$^{(\boxtimes)}$ and Stefan Mangard

Institute for Applied Information Processing and Communications (IAIK),
Graz University of Technology, Inffeldgasse 16a, 8010 Graz, Austria
{hannes.gross,stefan.mangard}@iaik.tugraz.at

Abstract. The continually growing number of security-related autonomous devices requires efficient mechanisms to counteract low-cost side-channel analysis (SCA) attacks. Masking provides high resistance against SCA at an adjustable level of security. A high level of SCA resistance, however, goes hand in hand with an increasing demand for fresh randomness which drastically increases the implementation costs. Since hardware based masking schemes have other security requirements than software masking schemes, the research in these two fields has been conducted quite independently over the last ten years. One important practical difference is that recently published software schemes achieve a lower randomness footprint than hardware masking schemes. In this work we combine existing software and hardware masking schemes into a unified masking algorithm. We demonstrate how to protect software and hardware implementations using the same masking algorithm, and for lower randomness costs than the separate schemes. Especially for hardware implementations the randomness costs can in some cases be halved over the state of the art. Theoretical considerations as well as practical implementation results are then used for a comparison with existing schemes from different perspectives and at different levels of security.

Keywords: Masking · Hardware security · Threshold Implementations · Domain-oriented masking · Side-channel analysis

1 Introduction

One of the most popular countermeasures against side-channel analysis attacks is Boolean masking. Masking is used to protect software implementations as well as hardware implementations. However, since it was shown that software based masking schemes (that lack resistance to glitches) are in general not readily suitable to protect hardware implementations [15], the research has split into masking for software implementations and masking for hardware implementations.

The implementation costs of every masking scheme is thereby highly influenced by two factors. At first, the number of shares (or masks) that are required to achieve d^{th}-order security, and second the randomness costs for the evaluation

© International Association for Cryptologic Research 2017
W. Fischer and N. Homma (Eds.): CHES 2017, LNCS 10529, pp. 115–136, 2017.
DOI: 10.1007/978-3-319-66787-4_6

of nonlinear functions. For the first one, there exists a natural lower bound of $d + 1$ shares in which every critical information needs to be split in order to achieve d^{th}-order security.

For the evaluation of nonlinear functions, the number of required fresh random bits have a huge influence on the implementation costs of the masking because the generation of fresh randomness requires additional chip area, power and energy, and also limits the maximum throughput. Recently proposed software based masking schemes require (with an asymptotic bound of $d(d + 1)/4$) almost half the randomness of current hardware based masking schemes.

Masking in hardware. With the Threshold Implementations (TI) scheme by Nikova *et al.* [16], the first provably secure masking scheme suitable for hardware designs (and therefore resistant to glitches) was introduced in 2006. TI was later on extended to higher-order security by Bilgin *et al.* [3]. However, the drawback in the original design of TI is that it requires at least $td + 1$ shares to achieve d^{th}-order (univariate [17]) security where t is the degree of the function. In 2015, Reparaz *et al.* [18] demonstrated that d^{th}-order security can be also achieved with only $d + 1$ shares in hardware. A proof-of-concept was presented at CHES 2016 by De Cnudde *et al.* [20] requiring $(d+1)^2$ fresh randomness. Gross *et al.* [11,12] introduced the so-called domain-oriented masking (DOM) scheme that lowers the randomness costs to $d(d + 1)/2$.

Masking in software. Secure masked software implementations with $d + 1$ shares exist all along [5,14,19]. However, minimizing the requirements for fresh randomness is still a demanding problem that continues to be researched. Since efficient implementation of masking requires decomposition of complex nonlinear functions into simpler functions, the reduction of randomness is usually studied on shared multiplications with just two shared input bits without a loss of generality.

In 2016, Belaïd *et al.* [2] proved an upper bound for the randomness requirements of masked multiplication of $O(d \log d)$ for large enough d's, and a lower bound to be $d + 1$ for $d \leq 3$ (and d for the cases $d \leq 2$). Furthermore, for the orders two to four, Belaïd *et al.* showed optimized algorithms that reach this lower bound and also introduced a generic construction that requires $\frac{d^2}{4} + d$ fresh random bits (rounded). Recently, Barthe *et al.* [1] introduced a generic algorithm that requires $\lceil \frac{d}{4} \rceil (d + 1)$ fresh random bits. Barthe *et al.*'s algorithm saves randomness in three of four cases over Belaïd *et al.*'s algorithm but for the remaining cases it requires one bit more.

Please note, even though Barthe *et al.* states that their parallelization consideration makes their algorithm more suitable for hardware designs, it stays unclear how these randomness optimized multiplication algorithms can be securely and efficiently implemented in hardware with regard to glitches.

Our Contribution. In this work we combine the most recent masking approaches from both software and hardware in a unified masking approach (UMA). The basis of the generic UMA algorithm is the algorithm of Barthe *et al.* which we combine with DOM [12]. The randomness requirements of UMA are in all cases less or equal to generic software masking approaches. As a non-generic optimization, for the second protection order, we also take the solution of Belaïd et al. into account.

We then show how the UMA algorithm can be efficiently ported to hardware and thereby reduce the asymptotic randomness costs from $d(d+1)/2$ to $d(d+1)/4$. Therefore, we analyze the parts of the algorithm that are susceptible to glitches and split the algorithm into smaller independent hardware modules that can be calculated in parallel. As a result, the delay in hardware is at most five cycles.

Finally, we compare the implementation costs and randomness requirements of UMA to the costs of DOM in a practical and scalable case study for protection orders up to 15, and analyze the SCA resistance of the UMA design with a t-test based approach.

2   Boolean Masked Multiplication

We use similar notations as Barthe et al. [1] to write the multiplication of two variables a and b. In shared form, the multiplication of $\boldsymbol{a} \cdot \boldsymbol{b}$ is given by Eq. 1 where the elements of the vectors $\boldsymbol{a}$ and $\boldsymbol{b}$ are referred to as the randomly generated sharing of the corresponding variable. For any possible randomized sharing, the equations $a = \sum_{i=0}^{d} a_i$ and $b = \sum_{j=0}^{d} b_j$ always needs to be fulfilled, where a_i and b_j refer to individual shares of $\boldsymbol{a}$ and $\boldsymbol{b}$, respectively.

$$q = \boldsymbol{a} \cdot \boldsymbol{b} = \sum_{i=0}^{d} \sum_{j=0}^{d} a_i b_j \tag{1}$$

In order to correctly implement this multiplication in shared form, Eq. 1 needs to be securely evaluated. In particular, summing up the multiplication terms $a_i b_j$ needs to result again in a correct sharing of the result q with $d+1$ shares, and needs to be performed in such a way that an attacker does not gain any information on the unshared variables a, b, or q. To achieve d^{th}-order security, an attacker with the ability to "probe" up to d signals during any time of the evaluation should not gain an advantage in guessing any of the multiplication variables. This model is often referred to as the so-called (d-)probing model of Ishai et al. [14] which is linked to differential side-channel analysis (DPA) attacks over the statistical moment that needs to be estimated by an attacker for a limited set of noisy power traces [7,19]. This task gets exponentially harder with increasing protection order d if the implementation is secure in the d-probing model [4].

However, directly summing up the terms $a_i b_j$ does not even achieve first-order security regardless of the choice for d. To make the addition of the terms secure, fresh random shares denoted as r in the following are required that are applied to the multiplication terms on beforehand. The number of required fresh random bits and the way and order in which they are used is essential for the correctness, security, and efficiency of the shared multiplication algorithm.

Barthe et al.'s Algorithm. A vectorized version of Barthe *et al.*'s algorithm is given in Eq. 2 where all operations are performed share-wise from left to right. Accordingly, the vector multiplication is the multiplication of the shares with the same share index, *e.g.* $ab = \{a_0b_0, a_1b_1, \ldots, a_db_d\}$. Additions in the subscript indicate an index offset of the vector modulo $d+1$ which equals a rotation of the vector elements inside the vector, *e.g.* $a_{+1} = \{a_1, a_2, \ldots, a_0\}$. Superscript indices refer to different and independent randomness vectors with a size of $d+1$ random bits for each vector.

$$q = ab + r^0 + ab_{+1} + a_{+1}b + r^0_{+1} + ab_{+2} + a_{+2}b$$
$$+ r^1 + ab_{+3} + a_{+3}b + r^1_{+1} + ab_{+4} + a_{+4}b \tag{2}$$
$$+ r^2 + ab_{+5} + a_{+5}b + r^2_{+1} + ab_{+6} + a_{+6}b \ldots$$

At the beginning of the algorithm, the q shares are initialized with the terms resulting from the share-wise multiplication ab. Then there begins a repeating sequence that ends when all multiplication terms were absorbed inside one of the shares of q. The first sequence starts with the addition of the random bit vector r^0. Then a multiplication term and mirrored term pair (a_ib_j and a_jb_i, where $i \neq j$) is added, before the rotated r^0_{+1} vector is added followed by the next pair of terms. The next (up to) four multiplication terms are absorbed using the same sequence but with a new random bit vector r^1. This procedure is repeated until all multiplication terms are absorbed. There are thus $\lceil \frac{d}{4} \rceil$ random vectors required with each a length of $d+1$ bits. So in total the randomness requirement is $\lceil \frac{d}{4} \rceil(d+1)$. In cases other than $d \equiv 0 \mod 4$, the last sequence contains less than four multiplication terms.

3   A Unified Masked Multiplication Algorithm

For the assembly of the unified masked multiplication algorithm (UMA) we extend Barthe *et al.*'s algorithm with optimizations from Belaïd *et al.* and DOM. We therefore differentiate between four cases for handling the last sequence in Barthe *et al.*'s algorithm: (1) if the protection order d is an integral multiple of 4 than we call the last sequence *complete*, (2) if $d \equiv 3 \mod 4$ we call it *pseudo-complete*, (3) if $d \equiv 2 \mod 4$ we call it *half-complete*, and (4) if $d \equiv 1 \mod 4$ we call it *incomplete*. We first introduce each case briefly before we give a full algorithmic description of the whole algorithm.

Complete and Pseudo-Complete. Complete and pseudo complete sequences are treated according to Barthe *et al.*'s algorithm. In difference to the complete sequence, the pseudo-complete sequence contains only three multiplication terms per share of q. See the following example for $d = 3$:

$$q = ab + r^0 + ab_{+1} + a_{+1}b + r^0_{+1} + ab_{+2}$$

Half-Complete. Half-complete sequences contain two multiplication terms per share of q. For handling this sequence we consider two different optimizations.

The first optimization requires d fresh random bits and is in the following referred to as Belaïd's optimization because it is the non-generic solution in [2] for the $d = 2$ case. An example for Belaïd's optimization is given in Eq. 3. The trick to save randomness here is to use the accumulated randomness used for the terms in the first functions to protect the last function of $\boldsymbol{q}$. It needs to be ensured that r_0^0 is added to r_1^0 before the terms $a_2 b_0$ and $a_0 b_2$ are added.

$$
\begin{aligned}
q_0 &= a_0 b_0 + r_0^0 + a_0 b_1 + a_1 b_0 \\
q_1 &= a_1 b_1 + r_1^0 + a_1 b_2 + a_2 b_1 \\
q_2 &= a_2 b_2 + r_0^0 + r_1^0 + a_2 b_0 + a_0 b_2
\end{aligned}
\tag{3}
$$

Unfortunately Belaïd's optimization can not be generalized to higher orders to the best of our knowledge. As a second optimization we thus consider the DOM approach for handling this block which is again generic. DOM requires one addition less for the last $\boldsymbol{q}$ function for $d = 2$ but requires one random bit more than the Belaïd's optimization (see Eq. 4) and thus the same amount as Barthe et $al.$'s original algorithm. However, for the hardware implementation in the next sections the DOM approach saves area in this case because it can be parallelized.

$$
\begin{aligned}
q_0 &= a_0 b_0 + r_0^0 + a_0 b_1 + r_2^0 + a_0 b_2 \\
q_1 &= a_1 b_1 + r_1^0 + a_1 b_2 + r_0^0 + a_1 b_0 \\
q_2 &= a_2 b_2 + r_2^0 + a_2 b_0 + r_1^0 + a_2 b_1
\end{aligned}
\tag{4}
$$

Incomplete. Incomplete sequences contain only one multiplication term per share of $\boldsymbol{q}$. Therefore, in this case one term is no longer added to its mirrored term. Instead the association of each term with the shares of $\boldsymbol{q}$ and the usage of the fresh random bits is performed according to the DOM scheme. An example for $d = 1$ is given in Eq. 5.

$$
\begin{aligned}
q_0 &= a_0 b_0 + r_0^0 + a_0 b_1 \\
q_1 &= a_1 b_1 + r_0^0 + a_1 b_0
\end{aligned}
\tag{5}
$$

3.1   Full Description of UMA

Algorithm 1 shows the pseudo code of the proposed UMA algorithm. The inputs of the algorithm are the two operands $\boldsymbol{a}$ and $\boldsymbol{b}$ split into $d + 1$ shares each. The randomness vector $\boldsymbol{r}^*$ (we use $*$ to make it explicit that r is a vector of vectors) contains $\lceil d/4 \rceil$ vectors with $d+1$ random bits each. Please note that all operations, including the multiplication and the addition, are again performed share-wise from left to right.

At first the return vector q is initialized with the multiplication terms that have the same share index for a and b at Line 1. In Line 2 to 4, the *complete* sequence are calculated according to Barthe et $al.$'s original algorithm. We use the superscript indices to address specific vectors of r^* and use again subscript

---

Algorithm 1. Unified masked multiplication algorithm (UMA)

Input: a, b, r^*
Output: q
    Initialize q:
1: $q = ab$
    Handle complete sequences:
2: **for** $i = 0 < \lfloor d/4 \rfloor$ **do**
3:    $q += r^i + ab_{+2i+1} + a_{+2i+1}b + r^i_{+1} + ab_{+2i+2} + a_{+2i+2}b$
4: **end for**
    Handle last sequence:
5: $l = \lfloor d/4 \rfloor$
      Pseudo-complete sequence:
6: **if** $d \equiv 3 \mod 4$ **then**
7:    $q += r^l + ab_{+2l+1} + a_{+2l+1}b + r^l_{+1} + ab_{+2l+2}$
    Half-complete sequence:
8: **else if** $d \equiv 2 \mod 4$ **then**
9:    **if** $d = 2$ **then**
10:      $z = \{r^l_0, r^l_1, r^l_0 + r^l_1\}$
11:      $q += z + ab_{+2l+1} + a_{+2l+1}b$
12:    **else**
13:      $q += r^l + ab_{+2l+1} + r^l_{+2l+2} + ab_{+2l+2}$
14:    **end if**
    Incomplete sequence:
15: **else if** $d \equiv 1 \mod 4$ **then**
16:    $z = \{r^l, r^l\}$
17:    $q += z + ab_{+2l+1}$
18: **end if**
19: **return** q

---

indices for indexing operations on the vector. Subscript indexes with a leading "+" denote a rotation by the given offset.

From Line 5 to 17 the handling of the remaining multiplication terms is performed according to the description above for the *pseudo-complete*, *half-complete*, and *incomplete* cases. In order to write this algorithm in quite compact form, we made the assumption that for the last random bit vector r^l only the required random bits are provided. In Line 10 where Belaïd's optimization is used for $d = 2$, a new bit vector z is formed that consists of the concatenation of the two elements of the vector r^l and the sum of these bits. So in total the z vector is again $d + 1$ (three) bits long. In similar way we handle the randomness in Line 16. We concatenate two copies of r^l of the length $(d + 1)/2$ to form z which is then added to the remaining multiplication terms.

Randomness requirements. Table 1 shows a comparison of the randomness requirements of UMA with other masked multiplication algorithms. The comparison shows that UMA requires in all generic cases the least amount of fresh randomness. With the non-generic Belaïd's optimization, the algorithm reaches the Belaïd *et al.*'s proven lower bounds of $d+1$ for $d > 2$ and of d for $d \leq 2$ below the fifth protection order.

Compared to Barthe *et al.*'s original algorithm, UMA saves random bits in the cases where the last sequence is *incomplete*. More importantly, since we target efficient higher-order masked hardware implementations in the next sections, UMA has much lower randomness requirements than the so far most randomness efficient hardware masking scheme DOM. Up to half of the randomness costs can thus be saved compared to DOM. In the next section we show how UMA can be securely and efficiently implemented in hardware.

Table 1. Randomness requirement comparison

d	UMA	Barthe *et al.*	Belaïd *et al.*	DOM
1	**1**	2	1	**1**
2	**3 (2^1)**	3	3 (2^1)	3
3	**4**	4	5 (4^1)	6
4	**5**	5	8 (5^1)	10
5	**9**	12	11	15
6	**14**	**14**	15	21
7	**16**	**16**	19	28
8	**18**	**18**	24	36
9	**25**	30	29	45
10	**33**	**33**	35	55
11	**36**	**36**	41	66
12	**39**	**39**	48	78
13	**49**	56	55	91
14	**60**	**60**	63	105
15	**64**	**64**	71	120

[1] Non-generic solution

4   UMA in Hardware

Directly porting UMA to hardware by emulating what a processor would do, *i.e.* ensuring the correct order of instruction execution by using registers in between every operation, would introduce a tremendous area and performance overhead over existing hardware masking approaches. To make this algorithm more efficient and still secure in hardware, it needs to be sliced into smaller portions of independent code parts than can be translated to hardware modules which can be evaluated in parallel.

Domain-Oriented Masking (DOM). To discuss the security of the introduced hardware modules in the presence of glitches, we use the same terminology as DOM [10] in the following. DOM interprets the sharing of any function

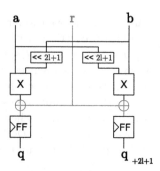

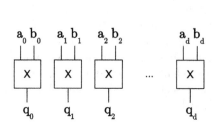

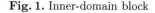

Fig. 1. Inner-domain block   **Fig. 2.** Incomplete block

in hardware as a partitioning of the circuit into $d + 1$ independent subcircuits which are also called domains. All shares of one variable are then associated with one specific domain according to their share index number (a_0 is associated with domain "0", a_1 with domain "1", et cetera.). By keeping the $d+1$ shares in their respective domains, the whole circuit is trivially secure against an attacker with the ability to probe d signals as required.

This approach is intuitively simple for linear functions that can be performed on each of the shares independently. To realize nonlinear functions, shared information from one domain needs to be sent to another domain in a secure way. This process requires the usage of fresh randomness without giving the attacker any advantage in probing all shares of any sensitive variable.

In the context of DOM, multiplication terms with the same share index (*e.g.* a_0b_0) are also called *inner-domain* terms. These terms and are considered uncritical since the combination of information inside one domain can never reveal two or more shares of one variable as the domain itself contains only one share per variable. Terms which consist of shares with different share index (*cross-domain* terms) that thus originate from different domains (*e.g.* a_0b_1) are considered to be more critical. Special care needs to be taken to ensure that at no point in time, *e.g.* due to timing effects (glitches), any two shares of one variable come together without a secure remasking step with fresh randomness in between.

Inner-domain block. The assignment of the inner-domain terms ($q = ab$) in Line 1 of Algorithm 1 can thus be considered uncritical in terms of dth-order probing security. Only shares with the same share index are multiplied and stored at the same index position of the share in q. The *inner-domain* block is depicted in Fig. 1 and consist of $d+1$ AND gates that are evaluated in parallel. Hence each share stays in its respective share domain. So even if the sharings of the inputs of a and b would be the same, this block does not provide a potential breach of the security because neither a_0a_0 nor b_0b_0, for example, would provide any additional information on a or b. We can thus combine the *inner-domain* block freely with any other secure masked component that ensures the same domain separation.

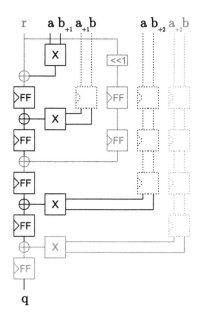

Fig. 3. Complete block (Color figure online)

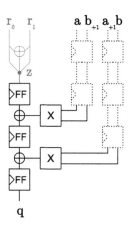

Fig. 4. Half-complete block (Belaïd opt.)

(Pseudo-)Complete blocks. For the security of the implementation in hardware, the order in which the operations in Line 3 (and Line 7) are performed is essential. Since the calculation of one *complete* sequence is subdivided by the addition of the random vector in the middle of this code line, it is quite tempting to split this calculation into two parts and to parallelize them to speed up the calculation.

However, if we consider Eq. 2, and omit the inner domain-terms that would be already calculated in a separate inner-domain block, a probing attacker could get (through glitches) the intermediate results from the probe $p_0 = r_0 + a_0 b_1 + a_1 b_0$ from the calculation of q_0 and $p_1 = r_0 + a_4 b_1 + a_1 b_4$ from the calculation of q_4. By combining the probed information from p_0 and p_1 the attacker already gains information on three shares of a and b. With the remaining two probes the attacker could just probe the missing shares of a or b to fully reconstruct them. The *complete* sequence and for the same reasons also the *pseudo-complete* sequence can thus not be further parallelized.

Figure 3 shows the vectorized *complete* block that consists of five register stages. Optional pipeline registers are depicted with dotted lines where necessary that make the construction more efficient in terms of throughput. For the *pseudo-complete* block, the last XOR is removed and the most right multiplier including the pipeline registers before the multiplier (marked green).

The security of this construction has already been analyzed by Barthe *et al.* [1] in conjunction with the inner-domain terms (which have no influence on the probing security) and for subsequent calculation of the sequences. Since the scope of the randomness vector is limited to one block only, a probing attacker does not gain any advantage (information on more shares than probes she uses) by combining intermediate results of different blocks even if they are calculated in parallel. Furthermore, each output of these blocks is independently and freshly masked and separated in $d+1$ domains which allows the combination with other blocks.

Half-complete block. Figure 4 shows the construction of the *half-complete* sequence in hardware when Belaïd's optimization is used for $d = 2$. The creation of the random vector z requires one register and one XOR gate. The security of this construction was formally proven by Belaïd et al. in [2]. For protection orders other than $d = 2$, we use instead the same DOM construction as we use for the incomplete block.

Incomplete block. For the *incomplete* block (and the half-complete block without Belaïd optimization) each random bit is only used to protect one multiplication term and its mirrored term. The term and the mirrored term are distributed in different domains to guarantee probing security. Figure 2 shows the construction of an *incomplete* block following the construction principles of DOM for two bits of q at the same time. For *half-complete* blocks (without Belaïd's optimization) two instances of the *incomplete* constructions are used with different indexing offsets and the resulting bits are added together (see Line 13). No further registers are required for the XOR gate at the output of this construction because it is ensured by the registers that all multiplication terms are remasked by r before the results are added. For a more detailed security discussion we refer to the original paper of Gross *et al.* [10].

Assembling the UMA AND Gate. Figure 5 shows how the UMA AND gate is composed from the aforementioned building blocks. Except the *inner-domain* block which is always used, all other blocks are instantiated and connected depending on the given protection order which allows a generic construction of the masked AND gate from $d = 0$ (no protection) to any desired protection order. Connected to the *inner-domain* block, there are $\lfloor \frac{d}{4} \rfloor$ *complete* blocks, and either one or none of the *pseudo-complete*, *half-complete*, or *incomplete* blocks.

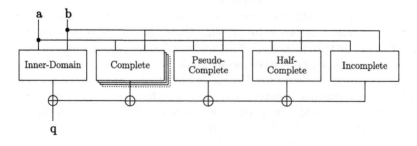

Fig. 5. Fully assembled UMA AND gate

Table 2. Overview on the hardware costs of the different blocks

Block	AND $\cdot(d+1)$	XOR $\cdot(d+1)$	FF $\cdot(d+1)$ w/o pipel.	Pipelined	Delay [Cycles]
Inner-domain	1	$\lceil \frac{d}{4} \rceil$	0	0–10	0
Complete	4	5	5	7	5
Pseudo-complete	3	4	4	6	4
Half-complete:					
Belaïd's optimization	2	$2 + \frac{1}{3}$	3	3	3
DOM	2	3	2	2	1
Incomplete	1	1	1	1	1

Table 2 gives an overview about the hardware costs of the different blocks that form the masked AND gate. All stated gate counts need to be multiplied by the number of shares $(d + 1)$. The XOR gates which are required for connecting the different blocks are accounted to the *inner-domain* block. In case pipelining is used, the input shares of a and b are pipelined instead of pipelining the multiplication results inside the respective blocks. The required pipelining registers for the input shares are also added on the *inner-domain* block's register requirements, since this is the only fixed block of every masked AND gate. The number of pipelining registers are determined by the biggest delay required for one block. In case one or more *complete* blocks are instantiated, there are always five register stages required which gives a total amount of $10(d+1)$ input pipelining registers. However, for $d < 4$ the number of input pipelining register is always twice the amount of delay cycles of the instantiated block which could also be zero for the unprotected case where the masked AND gate consists only of the *inner-domain* block. The *inner-domain* block itself does not require any registers except for the pipelining case and thus has a delay of zero.

For the cost calculation of the UMA AND gate, the gate counts for the *complete* block needs to be multiplied by the number of instantiated *complete* blocks ($\lfloor \frac{d}{4} \rfloor$) and the number of shares $(d+1)$. The other blocks are instantiated at maximum one time. The *pseudo-complete* block in case $d \equiv 3 \mod 4$, the *half-complete* block in case $d \equiv 2 \mod 4$ (where Belaïd's optimization is only used for $d = 2$), and the *incomplete* block in case $d \equiv 1 \mod 4$.

Comparison with DOM. Table 3 shows a first comparison of the UMA AND gate with a masked AND gate from the DOM scheme. For the generation of these numbers we used Table 2 to calculate the gate counts for the UMA AND gate. For DOM, we used the description in [10] which gives us $(d+1)^2$ AND gates, $2d(d+1)$ XOR gates, and $(d + 1)^2$ registers ($- d - 1$, for the unpipelined variant). For calculating the gate equivalence, we used the 90 nm UMC library from Faraday as reference as we also use them for synthesis in Sect. 5. Accordingly, a two input AND gate requires 1.25 GE, an XOR gate 2.5 GE, and a D-type flip-flop with asynchronous reset 4.5 GE.

Table 3. Comparison of the UMA AND gate with DOM

d	UMA AND						DOM AND					
	AND	XOR	Registers		GE		AND	XOR	Registers		GE	
			Unpipel.	Pipel.	Unpipel.	Pipel.			Unpipel.	Pipel.	Unpipel.	Pipel.
1	4	4	2	6	24	42	4	4	2	4	24	33
2	9	10	9	27	77	157	9	12	6	9	68	82
3	16	20	16	56	142	322	16	24	12	16	134	152
4	25	30	25	85	219	489	25	40	20	25	221	244
5	36	48	36	108	327	651	36	60	30	36	330	357
6	49	70	49	133	457	835	49	84	42	49	460	492
7	64	88	72	184	624	1,128	64	112	56	64	612	648
8	81	108	90	216	776	1,343	81	144	72	81	785	826
9	100	140	110	250	970	1,600	100	180	90	100	980	1,025
10	121	176	132	286	1,185	1,878	121	220	110	121	1,196	1,246
11	144	204	168	360	1,446	2,310	144	264	132	144	1,434	1,488
12	169	234	195	403	1,674	2,610	169	312	156	169	1,693	1,752
13	196	280	224	448	1,953	2,961	196	364	182	196	1,974	2,037
14	225	330	270	510	2,321	3,401	225	420	210	225	2,276	2,344
15	256	368	304	592	2,608	3,904	256	480	240	256	2,600	2,672

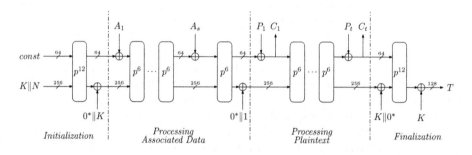

Fig. 6. Data encryption and authentication with Ascon

Since in both implementations AND gates are only used for creating the multiplication terms, both columns for the UMA AND gate construction and the DOM AND are equivalent. The gate count for the XORs is in our implementation is lower than for the DOM gate which results from the reduced randomness usage compared to DOM. The reduced XOR count almost compensates for the higher register usage in the unpipelined case. The difference for the 15th order is still only 8 GE, for example. However, the delay of the UMA AND gate is in contrast to the DOM AND gate, except for $d = 1$, not always one cycle but increases up to five cycles. Therefore, in the pipelined implementation more register are necessary which results in an increasing difference in the required chip area for higher protection orders.

5   Practical Evaluation on Ascon

To show the suitability of the UMA approach and to study the implications on a practical design, we decide on implementing the CAESAR candidate ASCON [6] one time with DOM and one time with the UMA approach. We decided on ASCON over the AES for example, because of its relatively compact S-box construction which allows to compare DOM versus UMA for a small percentage of non-linear functionality, but also for a high percentage of non-linear functionality if the S-box is instantiated multiple times in parallel. The design is for both DOM and UMA generic in terms of protection order and allows some further adjustments. Besides the different configuration parameters for the algorithm itself, like block sizes and round numbers, the design also allows to set the number of parallel S-boxes and how the affine transformation in the S-box is handled, for example.

ASCON is an authenticated encryption scheme with a sponge-like mode of operation as depicted in Fig. 6. The encryption and decryption work quite similar. At the beginning of the initialization the 320-bit state is filled with some cipher constants, the 128-bit key K, and the 128-bit nonce N. In the upcoming calculation steps, the state performs multiple rounds of the transformation p which consists of three substeps: (1) the addition of the round constant, (2) the nonlinear substitution layer, and (3) the linear transformation. For the ASCON-128 the initialization and the finalization takes 12 rounds and the processing of any data takes six rounds. The input data is subdivided into associated data (data that only requires authentication but no confidentiality) and plaintext or ciphertext data. The data is processed by absorbing the data in 64-bit chunks into the state and subsequently performing the state transformation. In the finalization step, a so-called tag is either produced or verified that ensures the authenticity of the processed data.

5.1   Proposed Hardware Design

An overview of the top module of our hardware design is given in Fig. 7 (left). It consists of a simple data interface to transfer associated data, plaintext or ciphertext data with ready and busy signaling which allows for simple connection

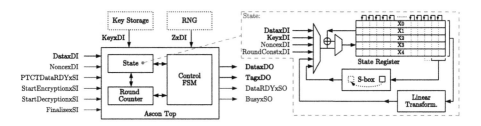

Fig. 7. Overview of the ASCON core (left) and the state module of the ASCON design (right)

with *e.g.* AXI4 streaming masters. Since the nonce input and the tag output have a width of 128 bit, they are transferred via a separate port. The assumptions taken on the key storage and the random number generator (RNG) are also depicted. We assume a secure key storage that directly transfers the key to the cipher core in shared form, and an RNG that has the capability to deliver as many fresh random bits as required by the selected configuration of the core.

The core itself consists of the *control FSM* and the *round counter* that form the control path, and the *state* module that forms the data path and is responsible for all state transformations. Figure 7 (right) shows a simplistic schematic of the state module. The state module has a separate FSM and performs the round transformation in four substeps:

(1) during *IDLE*, the initialization of the state with the configuration constants, the key, and the nonce is ensured.
(2) in the *ADD_ROUND_CONST* state the round constant is added, and optionally other required data is either written or added to the state registers like input data or the key. Furthermore, it is possible to perform the linear parts of the S-box transformation already in this state to save pipeline registers during the S-box transformation and to save one delay cycle. This option, however, is only used for the configuration of ASCON where all 64 possible S-box instances are instantiated.
(3) the *SBOX_LAYER* state provides flexible handling of the S-box calculation with a configurable number of parallel S-box instances. Since the S-box is the only non-linear part of the transformation, its size grows quadratically with the protection order and not linearly as the other data path parts of the design. The configurable number of S-boxes thus allows to choose a trade-off between throughput and chip area, power consumption, et cetera. During the S-box calculation the state registers are shifted and the S-box module is fed with the configured number of state slices with five bits each slice. The result of the S-box calculation is written back during the state shifting. Since the minimum delay of the S-box changes with the protection order and whether the DOM or UMA approach is used, the S-box calculation takes one to 70 cycles.
(4) in the *LINEAR_LAYER* state the whole linear part of the round transformation is calculated in a single clock cycle. The linear transformation simply adds two rotated copies of one state row with itself. It would be possible to breakdown this step into smaller chunks to save area. However, the performance overhead and the additional registers required to do so, would relativize the chip area savings especially for higher orders.

S-box construction. ASCONS's S-box is affine equivalent to the Keccak S-box and takes five (shared) bits as an input (see Fig. 8). The figure shows where the pipeline registers are placed in our S-box design (green dotted lines). The first pipeline stage (Stage 0, grey) is optionally already calculated in the *ADD_ROUND_CONST* stage. The registers after the XOR gate in State 0 are important for the glitch resistance and therefore for the security of the design. Without this registers, the second masked AND gate from the top (red paths),

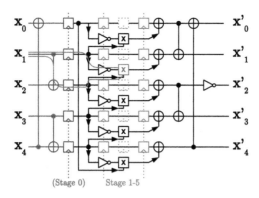

Fig. 8. ASCON's S-box module with optional affine transformation at input (grey) and variable number of pipeline registers (green) (Color figure online)

for example, could temporarily be sourced two times by the shares of x_1 for both inputs of the masked AND gate. Because the masked AND gate mixes shares from different domains, a timing dependent violation (glitch) of the d-probing resistance could occur. Note that the XOR gates at the output do not require an additional register stage because they are fed into one of the state registers. As long as no share domains are crossed during the linear parts of the transformation the probing security is thus given. We assure this by associating each share and each part of the circuit with one specific share domain (or index) and keeping this for the entire circuit.

The other pipelining registers are required because of the delay of the masked AND gates which is one cycle for the DOM gate, and up to five cycles for the UMA AND gate according to Table 2.

5.2   Implementation Results

All results stated in this section are post-synthesis results for a 90 nm Low-K UMC process with 1 V supply voltage and a 20 MHz clock. The designs were synthesized with the Cadence Encounter RTL compiler v14.20-s064-1. Figure 9 compares the area requirements of the UMA approach with DOM for the pipelined ASCON implementation with a single S-box instance. The figure on the left shows the comparison of single masked AND gates inside the ASCON design, while figure right compares the whole implementations of the design. Comparing this results with Table 3 reveals that the expected gate counts for DOM quite nicely match the practical results. For the UMA approach, on the other hand, the practical results are always lower than the stated numbers. The reduction results from the fact that the amount of required pipelining registers for the operands is reduced because the pipelining register are shared among the masked AND gates. This does not affect the DOM implementation because the multiplication results are always calculated within only one delay cycle.

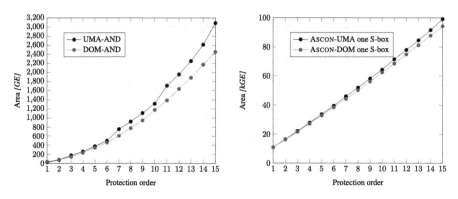

Fig. 9. UMA versus DOM area requirements for different protection orders. Left figure compares masked AND gates, right figure compares full ASCON implementations

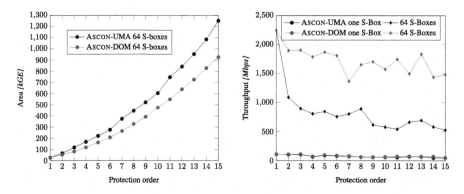

Fig. 10. UMA versus DOM area requirements for different protection orders and 64 parallel S-boxes (left) and throughput comparison in the right figure

The right figure shows that the difference for the single S-box ASCON implementation is relatively low especially for low protection orders, and seems to grow only linearly within the synthesized range for d between 1 and 15. For the first order implementation both designs require about 10.8 kGE. For the second order implementation the difference is still only about 200 GE (16.2 kGE for DOM versus 16.4 kGE). The difference grows with the protection order and is about 4.8 kGE for $d = 15$ which is a size difference of about 5%. The seemingly linear growth in area requirements for both approaches is observed because the S-box is only a relatively small part with 3–20% of the design which grows quadratically, while the state registers that grow linearly dominate the area requirements with 96–80%.

We also synthesized the design for 64 parallel S-boxes which makes the implementation much faster in terms of throughput but also has a huge impact on the area requirements (see Fig. 10). The characteristics for UMA and DOM look pretty similar to the comparison of the masked AND gates in Fig. 9 (left) and shows a quadratic increase with the protection order. The chip area is now between 28 kGE ($d = 1$) and 1,250 kGE ($d = 15$) for UMA and 926 kGE for DOM. The S-box requires between 55% and 92% of the whole chip area.

Throughput. To compare the maximum throughput achieved by our designs we calculated the maximum clock frequency for which our design is expected to work for typical operating conditions (1 V supply, and 25 °C) over the timing slack for the longest delay path. This frequency is then multiplied with the block size for our encryption (64 bits) divided by the required cycles for absorbing the data in the state of ASCON (for six consecutive round transformations).

The results are shown in Fig. 10. The throughput of both masking approaches with only one S-box instance is quite similar which can be explained with the high number of cycles required for calculating one round transformation (402–426 cycles for UMA versus 402 cycles for DOM). The UMA approach achieves a throughput between 48 Mbps and 108 Mbps, and the DOM design between 50 Mbps and 108 Mbps for the single S-box variants.

For 64 parallel S-boxes the gap between DOM and UMA increases because DOM requires only 18 cycles to absorb one block of data while UMA requires between 18 and 42 cycles which is a overhead of more than 130%. Therefore, also the throughput is in average more than halved for the UMA implementation. The UMA design achieves between 0.5 Gbps and 2.3 Gbps, and DOM ASCON between 1.5 Gbps and 2.3 Gbps.

Randomness. The amount of randomness required for the UMA and DOM designs can be calculated from Table 1 by multiplying the stated number by five (for the five S-box bits), and additionally with 64 in case of the 64 parallel S-box version. For the single S-box design, the (maximum) amount of randomness required per cycle for the UMA design is thus between 5 bits for $d = 1$ and 320 bits for $d = 15$, and for DOM between 5 bits and 600 bits. For the 64 parallel S-boxes design, the first-order designs already require 320 bits per cycle, and for the 15th-order designs the randomness requirements grow to 20 kbits and 37.5 kbits per cycle, respectively.

6   Side-Channel Evaluation

In order to analyze the correctness and the resistance of our implementations, we performed a statistical t-test according to Goodwill *et al.* [8] on leakage traces of the S-box designs of the UMA variants. We note that t-tests are unfeasible to prove any general statements on the security of a design (for all possible conditions and signal timings) as it would be required for a complete security verification. However, to the best of our knowledge there exist no tools which are suitable to prove the security of higher-order masked circuits in the presence of glitches in a formal way. T-tests only allow statements for the tested devices and under the limitations of the measurement setup. Many works test masked circuits on an FPGA and perform the t-test on the traces gathered from power measurements. This approach has the drawback that due to the relatively high noise levels the evaluation is usually limited to first and second-order multivariate t-tests. We use the recorded signal traces from the post-synthesis simulations of the netlists, which are noise-free and allows us to evaluate the designs up to the third-order. Because of the simplified signal delay model this evaluation covers only glitches resulting from cascaded logic gates and no glitches caused by different signal propagation times resulting from other circuit effects. We emphasize that we use this t-test based evaluation merely to increase the trust in the correctness and security of our implementation, and keep a formal verification open for future work.

The intuition of the t-test follows the idea that an DPA attacker can only make use of differences in leakage traces. To test that a device shows no exploitable differences, two sets of traces are collected per t-test: (1) a set with randomly picked inputs, (2) a set with fixed inputs and the according t-value is calculated. Then the t-value is calculated according to Eq. 6 where X denotes the mean of the respective trace set, S^2 is the variance, and N is the size of the set, respectively.

$$t = \frac{X_1 - X_2}{\sqrt{\frac{S_1^2}{N_1} + \frac{S_2^2}{N_2}}} \tag{6}$$

The null-hypothesis is that the means of both trace sets are equal, which is accepted if the calculated t-value is below the border of ± 4.5. If the t-value exceeds this border then the null-hypothesis is rejected with a confidence greater than 99.999% for large enough trace sets. A so-called centered product pre-processing step with trace points inside a six cycle time window is performed for higher-order t-tests. Beyond this time frame, the intermediates are ensured to be unrelated to the inputs. We thus combine multiple tracepoints by first normalizing the means of the trace points and then multiplying the resulting values with other normalized points inside the time window.

Results. Figure 11 shows the results of the t-tests for the time offsets which achieved the highest t-values for the UMA S-box implementations of Ascon. From top to bottom the figures show the results for different protection orders from $d = 0$ to $d = 3$, and from left to right we performed different orders of t-tests starting from first order up to third order. Above $d = 3$ and third-order t-tests the evaluation of the t-tests becomes too time intensive for our setup.

On the y-axis of the figures the t-values are drawn, and the y-axis denotes the used number of traces at a fraction of a million. The horizontal lines (green, inside the figures) indicate the ± 4.5 confidence border. The protection border between the figures (the red lines) separates the t-tests for which the protection order of the design is below the performed t-test (left) from the t-tests for which the test order is above (right).

As intended, the t-values for the masked implementations below the protection border do not show any significant differences even after one million noise-free traces. For the unprotected implementation (top, left figure), for example, the first-order t-test fails with great confidence even after only a couple of traces, and so do the second and third-order t-tests on the right. The first-order t-test

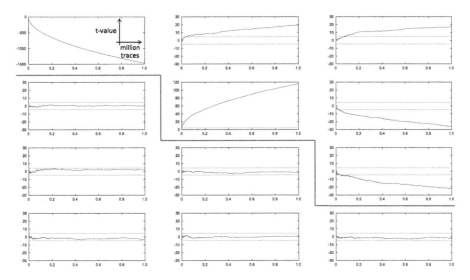

Fig. 11. T-test evaluation for different protection orders $d = 0 \ldots 3$ (from top to bottom) and for different t-test orders (first to third, from left to right) (Color figure online)

below of the first-order protected S-box does not show leakages anymore but the higher-order t-tests fail again as expected. The third-order implementation does not show any leakages anymore for the performed t-tests. We thus conclude that our implementations seem to be secure under the stated limitations.

7 Discussion on the Randomness Costs and Conclusions

In this work, we combined software and hardware based masking approaches into a unified masking approach (UMA) in order to save randomness and the cost involved. In practice, the generation of fresh randomness with high entropy is a difficult and costly task. It is, however, also difficult to put precise numbers on the cost of randomness generation because there exist many possible realizations. The following comparison should thus not be seen as statement of implementation results but reflects only one possible realization which serves as basis for the discussion.

A common and performant way to generate many random numbers with high entropy is the usage of PRNGs based on symmetric primitives, like ASCON for example. A single cipher design thus provides a fixed number of random bits, *e.g.* 64 bits in the case of ASCON, every few cycles. In the following comparison, we assume a one-round unrolled ASCON implementation resulting in six delay cycles and 7.1 kGE of chip area [13]. If more random bits are required, additional PRNGs are inserted, which increase the area overhead accordingly.

Figure 12 (left) shows the area results from Sect. 5 including the overhead cost for the required PRNGs. Starting with $d = 2$ for DOM, $d = 3$ for UMA for the

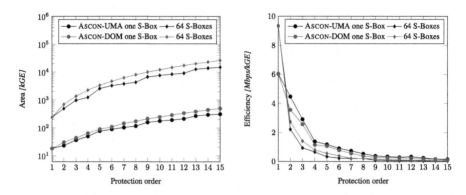

Fig. 12. UMA versus DOM area requirements including an area estimation for the randomness generation in the left figure, and an efficiency evaluation (throughput per chip area) on the right

single S-box variants, and for all of the 64 parallel S-box variants, one PRNG is no longer sufficient to reach the maximum possible throughput the designs offer. The randomness generation thus becomes the bottleneck of the design and additional PRNGs are required, which result in the chip area differences compared to Figs. 9 and 10, respectively. As depicted, both UMA variants require less chip area than their DOM pendants. However, this comparison does not take the throughput of the designs into account (see Fig. 10).

Figure 12 (right) compares the efficiency, calculated as throughput (in Mbps) over the chip area (in kGE). By using this metric, it shows that UMA is the more efficient scheme when considering the single S-box variants, while DOM is the more efficient solution for the 64 S-box variants. However, the practicality of the 64 S-box implementations with up to a few millions of GE and between 30 and 3,600 additional PRNGs is very questionable.

In practice, the most suitable approach for generating random bits and the constraints vary from application to application. While UMA seems to be the more suitable approach for low-area applications, DOM introduces less delay cycles which is a relevant constraint for performance oriented applications. To make our results comparable for future designs and under varying constraints, we make our hardware implementations available online [9].

Acknowledgements. This work has been supported by the Austrian Research Promotion Agency (FFG) under grant number 845589 (SCALAS), and has received funding from the European Unions Horizon 2020 research and innovation programme under grant agreement No 644052. The work has furthermore been supported in part by the Austrian Science Fund (project P26494-N15) and received funding from the European Research Council (ERC) under the European Unions Horizon 2020 research and innovation programme (grant agreement No 681402).

References

1. Barthe, G., Dupressoir, F., Faust, S., Grégoire, B., Standaert, F.-X., Strub, P.-Y.: Parallel implementations of masking schemes and the bounded moment leakage model. IACR Cryptology ePrint Archive 2016:912 (2016)
2. Belaïd, S., Benhamouda, F., Passelègue, A., Prouff, E., Thillard, A., Vergnaud, D.: Randomness complexity of private circuits for multiplication. In: Fischlin, M., Coron, J.-S. (eds.) EUROCRYPT 2016. LNCS, vol. 9666, pp. 616–648. Springer, Heidelberg (2016). doi:10.1007/978-3-662-49896-5_22
3. Bilgin, B., Gierlichs, B., Nikova, S., Nikov, V., Rijmen, V.: Higher-order threshold implementations. In: Sarkar, P., Iwata, T. (eds.) ASIACRYPT 2014. LNCS, vol. 8874, pp. 326–343. Springer, Heidelberg (2014). doi:10.1007/978-3-662-45608-8_18
4. Chari, S., Jutla, C.S., Rao, J.R., Rohatgi, P.: Towards sound approaches to counteract power-analysis attacks. In: Wiener, M. (ed.) CRYPTO 1999. LNCS, vol. 1666, pp. 398–412. Springer, Heidelberg (1999). doi:10.1007/3-540-48405-1_26
5. Coron, J., Prouff, E., Rivain, M., Roche, T.: Higher-order side channel security and mask refreshing. IACR Cryptology ePrint Archive 2015:359 (2015)
6. Dobraunig, C., Eichlseder, M., Mendel, F., Schläffer, M.: Ascon v1.2. Submission to the CAESAR competition (2016). http://competitions.cr.yp.to/round3/asconv 12.pdf
7. Faust, S., Rabin, T., Reyzin, L., Tromer, E., Vaikuntanathan, V.: Protecting circuits from leakage: the computationally-bounded and noisy cases. In: Gilbert, H. (ed.) EUROCRYPT 2010. LNCS, vol. 6110, pp. 135–156. Springer, Heidelberg (2010). doi:10.1007/978-3-642-13190-5_7
8. Goodwill, G., Jun, B., Jaffe, J., Rohatgi, P.: A testing methodology for side-channel resistance validation. In: NIST Non-Invasive Attack Testing Workshop (2011)
9. Gross, H.: DOM and UMA masked hardware implementations of Ascon (2017). https://github.com/hgrosz/ascon_dom
10. Gross, H., Mangard, S., Korak, T.: An efficient side-channel protected AES implementation with arbitrary protection order. In: Handschuh, H. (ed.) CT-RSA 2017. LNCS, vol. 10159, pp. 95–112. Springer, Cham (2017). doi:10.1007/978-3-319-52153-4_6
11. Gross, H., Mangard, S., Korak, T.: Domain-oriented masking: compact masked hardware implementations with arbitrary protection order. Cryptology ePrint Archive, Report 2016/486 (2016). http://eprint.iacr.org/2016/486
12. Gross, H., Mangard, S., Korak, T.: Domain-oriented masking: compact masked hardware implementations with arbitrary protection order. In: Proceedings of the 2016 ACM Workshop on Theory of Implementation Security, TIS 2016, p. 3. ACM, New York (2016)
13. Groß, H., Wenger, E., Dobraunig, C., Ehrenhofer, C.: Suit up! - made-to-measure hardware implementations of ASCON. In: DSD 2015, Madeira, Portugal, 26–28 August 2015, pp. 645–652 (2015)
14. Ishai, Y., Sahai, A., Wagner, D.: Private circuits: securing hardware against probing attacks. In: Boneh, D. (ed.) CRYPTO 2003. LNCS, vol. 2729, pp. 463–481. Springer, Heidelberg (2003). doi:10.1007/978-3-540-45146-4_27
15. Mangard, S., Schramm, K.: Pinpointing the side-channel leakage of masked AES hardware implementations. In: Goubin, L., Matsui, M. (eds.) CHES 2006. LNCS, vol. 4249, pp. 76–90. Springer, Heidelberg (2006). doi:10.1007/11894063_7
16. Nikova, S., Rechberger, C., Rijmen, V.: Threshold implementations against side-channel attacks and glitches. In: Ning, P., Qing, S., Li, N. (eds.) ICICS 2006. LNCS, vol. 4307, pp. 529–545. Springer, Heidelberg (2006). doi:10.1007/11935308_38

17. Reparaz, O.: A note on the security of higher-order threshold implementations. IACR Cryptology ePrint Archive 2015:001 (2015)
18. Reparaz, O., Bilgin, B., Nikova, S., Gierlichs, B., Verbauwhede, I.: Consolidating masking schemes. In: Gennaro, R., Robshaw, M. (eds.) CRYPTO 2015. LNCS, vol. 9215, pp. 764–783. Springer, Heidelberg (2015). doi:10.1007/978-3-662-47989-6_37
19. Rivain, M., Prouff, E.: Provably secure higher-order masking of AES. In: Mangard, S., Standaert, F.-X. (eds.) CHES 2010. LNCS, vol. 6225, pp. 413–427. Springer, Heidelberg (2010). doi:10.1007/978-3-642-15031-9_28
20. De Cnudde, T., Reparaz, O., Bilgin, B., Nikova, S., Nikov, V., Rijmen, V.: Masking AES with $d + 1$ shares in hardware. In: Gierlichs, B., Poschmann, A.Y. (eds.) CHES 2016. LNCS, vol. 9813, pp. 194–212. Springer, Heidelberg (2016). doi:10.1007/978-3-662-53140-2_10

Changing of the Guards: A Simple and Efficient Method for Achieving Uniformity in Threshold Sharing

Joan Daemen[1,2(✉)]

[1] Radboud University, Nijmegen, The Netherlands
J.Daemen@science.ru.nl
[2] STMicroelectronics, Diegem, Belgium

Abstract. Since they were first proposed as a countermeasure against differential power analysis (DPA) and differential electromagnetic analysis (DEMA) in 2006, threshold schemes have attracted a lot of attention from the community concentrating on cryptographic implementations. What makes threshold schemes so attractive from an academic point of view is that they come with an information-theoretic proof of resistance against a specific subset of side-channel attacks: first-order DPA. From an industrial point of view they are attractive as a careful threshold implementation forces adversaries to DPA of higher order, with all its problems such as noise amplification. A threshold scheme that offers the mentioned provable security must exhibit three properties: correctness, incompleteness and uniformity. A threshold scheme becomes more expensive with the number of shares that must be implemented and the required number of shares is lower bound by the algebraic degree of the function being shared plus 1. Defining a correct and incomplete sharing of a function of degree d in $d+1$ shares is straightforward. However, up to now there is no generic method to achieve uniformity and finding uniform sharings of degree-d functions with $d+1$ shares has been an active research area. In this paper we present a generic, simple and potentially cheap method to find a correct, incomplete and uniform $d+1$-share threshold scheme of any S-box layer consisting of degree-d invertible S-boxes. The uniformity is not implemented in the sharings of the individual S-boxes but rather at the S-box layer level by the use of feedforward and some expansion of shares. When applied to the KECCAK-p nonlinear step χ, its cost is very small.

Keywords: Side-channel attacks · Threshold schemes · Uniformity · KECCAK

1 Introduction

Systems such as digital rights management (DRM) or banking cards try to offer protection against adversaries that have physical access to platforms performing cryptographic computations, allowing them to measure computation time, power

© International Association for Cryptologic Research 2017
W. Fischer and N. Homma (Eds.): CHES 2017, LNCS 10529, pp. 137–153, 2017.
DOI: 10.1007/978-3-319-66787-4_7

consumption or electromagnetic radiation. Adversaries can use this side channel information to retrieve cryptographic keys. A particularly powerful attack against implementations of cryptographic algorithms is differential power analysis (DPA) introduced by Kocher et al. [20]. This attack can exploit even the weakest dependence of the power consumption (or electromagnetic radiation) on the value of the manipulated data by combining the measurements of many computations to improve the signal-to-noise ratio. The simplest form of DPA is first-order DPA, that exploits the correlation between the data and the power consumption. To make side channel attacks impractical, system builders implement countermeasures, often multiple at the same time.

In threshold schemes, as proposed by Rijmen et al. [23–25] one represents each sensitive variable by a number of shares (typically denoted by $d + 1$) such that their (usually) bitwise sum equals that variable. These shares are initially generated in such a way that any subset of d shares gives no information about the sensitive variable. Functions (S-boxes, mixing layers, round functions ...) are computed on the shares of the inputs resulting in the output as a number of shares. Threshold schemes must be *correct*: the sum of the output shares equals the result of applying the implemented function on the sum of the input shares. Another essential property of a threshold implementation of a function is *incompleteness*: each output share shall be computed from at most d input shares, or equivalently, in the computation of each output share at least one input share is not used. Incompleteness guarantees that each individual output share computation cannot leak information about sensitive variables. The resulting output is then typically subject to some further computation, again in the form of separate and incomplete computation on shares. For these subsequent computations to not leak information about the sensitive variables, the output of the previous stage must still be uniform. Therefore, in an iterative cryptographic primitive such as a block cipher, we need a threshold implementation of the round function that yields a uniformly shared output if its input is uniformly shared. This property of the threshold implementation is called *uniformity*.

Threshold schemes form a good protection mechanism against DPA. In particular, using it allows building cryptographic hardware that is guaranteed to be unattackable with first-order DPA, assuming certain leakage models of the cryptographic hardware at hand and for a plausible definition of "first order". De Cnudde et al. have an interesting work [13] on such assumptions and their validity in the real world. Still, threshold schemes remain a very attractive technique for building cipher implementations that offer a high level of resistance against DPA and differential electromagnetic analysis (DEMA).

Constructing an incomplete threshold implementation of a non-linear function is rather straightforward and can be done in the following way. One can express the function algebraically as the sum of monomials. Then one replaces each shared variable by the sum of its shares. Subsequently, one can work out the expressions resulting in a larger number of monomials, where the factors are bits (or in general, components) of the shares. A monomial of degree d can have factors from at most d shares. So if there are $d + 1$ shares, such a monomial is incomplete: there is at least one share missing. It follows that to build an incomplete sharing of a function of algebraic degree d, it suffices to take $d+1$ shares. Clearly, the implementation cost of a function increases exponentially with its degree: a monomial of degree d requires $d+1$ shares and explodes into the sum of $(d+1)^d$ monomials. To reduce the implementation cost, Stoffelen applies techniques for representing S-boxes with minimum number of nonlinear operations [31]. Kutzner et al. on the other hand factor S-boxes of some degree as the composition of functions of lower algebraic degree [21]. Such techniques, combined with tower field representation, are also applied in the sharing of the AES S-box, that natively has algebraic degree 7. We refer again to De Cnudde et al. for an example [14]. These publications demonstrate that these techniques are quite powerful, but serial composition comes at a prize. It requires the insertion of registers (or latches) between the combinatorial circuits that increase latency.

Constructing a correct, incomplete and uniform sharing is widely perceived as a challenge and an important research problem. Several publications have been devoted to the classification of 3, 4 and 5-bit S-boxes with respect to cryptographic properties, and the minimum number of shares for which a uniform sharing is known is an important criterion. Examples include the study of Bilgin et al. [8] and that of Božilov et al. [10]. Other papers propose solutions, sometimes only partial, for large classes of S-boxes. We refer again to Bilgin et al. [9], Kutzner et al. [21], and Beyne et al. [5]. A well-known example of an S-box that is problematic in this context is the KECCAK S-box, known as χ. It has algebraic degree 2 and no uniform incomplete 3-share threshold implementations is known. We proposed a number of different solutions with varying degrees of efficiency in [6]. One solution is the transition from 3 to 4 or even 5 shares. Another is the compensation of loss of uniformity by injecting fresh randomness. As argued by Reparaz et al. [29], this technique brings the threshold scheme in the realm of private circuits as proposed by Ishai et al. [19].

Given a non-uniform threshold implementation, it is not immediate how to exploit its non-uniformity in an attack. We made a start in explorations in that direction in [16,17]. However, uniformity of a threshold implementation is essential in its information-theoretical proof of resistance against first-order DPA. In short, if one has a uniform sharing, one does not have to give additional arguments why the threshold scheme would be secure against first-order DPA.

In this paper we present a simple and efficient technique for building a threshold implementation with $d+1$ shares of any invertible S-box layer of degree d that is correct, incomplete and uniform. When applied to the nonlinear layer in KECCAK, χ, it can be seen as the next logical step of the methods discussed in Sect. 3 of our paper [6]. In that method 4 fresh random bits must be introduced every round to restore uniformity. The added value of the technique in this paper is that it no longer needs any fresh randomness and that it can convert a correct and incomplete sharing of any S-box into a correct, incomplete and uniform sharing of a layer of such S-boxes.

1.1   The "Changing of the Guards" Idea in a Nutshell

The basic method can be summarized as follows:

- The shared S-boxes are arranged in a linear array. These sharings must be correct and incomplete.
- Each share at the output of S-box i is made uniform by bitwise adding to it one or two shares from the input of S-box $i - 1$.
- The state is augmented with d dummy components, called *guards*, to be added to the output of the first S-box in the array.
- The new value of the guards are taken from the input of the last S-box in the array.
- Uniformity is proven by giving an algorithm that computes the shared input from the shared output of this mapping.

For threshold sharings that have a so-called multi-transformation property, the guards can be reduced in size and so does the amount of bits fed forward.

1.2   Notation

Assume we have a nonlinear mapping that consists of a layer of invertible S-boxes. We denote the width of the S-boxes by n and their total number by m. So the layer operates on an array of $n \times m$ bits. We denote the input as $x = (x_1, x_2, x_3, \ldots x_m)$ and the output as $X = (X_1, X_2, X_3, \ldots X_m)$, with each of the x_i and X_i an n-bit array.

In general the S-boxes can differ per position. We denote the S-box at position i by S_i, so $X_i = S_i(x_i)$.

We denote addition in GF(2) by $+$.

1.3   Overview of the Paper

In Sect. 2 we explain and prove the soundness of the method applied to the simplest possible case. In Sect. 3 we formulate the method for a more general case and in Sect. 4 we apply it to the nonlinear layer used in KECCAK, KEYAK and KETJE. Finally in Sect. 5 we discuss some implementation aspects.

2   The Basic Method Applied to 3-Share Threshold Schemes

Assume the same S-box is used for all positions and its algebraic degree is 2 over GF(2), that we denote by S. In that case it is trivial to find a correct and incomplete threshold scheme with 3 shares S by substituting the terms in the algebraic expression of the S-box by their sum as components and appropriately distributing the monomials over the three shares of the S-box sharing. We denote the three shares that represent x_i by a_i, b_i and c_i, with $x_i = a_i + b_i + c_i$. Likewise, we denote the three shares that represent X_i by A_i, B_i and C_i, with

$X_i = A_i + B_i + C_i$. The sharing of S consists of three functions from $2n$ to n bits, that we denote as (S_a, S_b, S_c). Correctness is satisfied if:

$$S_a(b_i, c_i) + S_b(a_i, c_i) + S_c(a_i, b_i) = S(a_i + b_i + c_i).$$

Incompleteness is implied by the fact that each of the three elements of (S_a, S_b, S_c) take only two shares as inputs. In this scheme our m-component input x is represented by triplet (a, b, c) with three shares.

At the basis of our "Changing of the Guards" technique for achieving uniformity is the expansion of the shared representation. In particular, for the input we expand share b with an additional dummy component that we denote as b_0 and do the same for c. In this sharing x is represented by (a, b, c) where a has m components and both b and c have $m + 1$ components. A triplet (a, b, c) is a uniform sharing of x if all possible values (a, b, c) compliant with x are equiprobable. As there are $2^{(3m+2)n}$ possible triplets (a, b, c) and being compliant with x requires the satisfaction of mn independent linear binary equations, there are exactly $2^{(3m+2)n-mn} = 2^{2(m+1)n}$ encodings (a, b, c) of any particular value x. The same holds for the sharing (A, B, C) of the output X.

Definition 1. *The* Changing of the Guards *sharing of an S-box layer where (S_a, S_b, S_c) is a sharing of S, mapping (a, b, c) to (A, B, C), is given by:*

$$
\begin{aligned}
A_i &= S_a(b_i, c_i) + b_{i-1} + c_{i-1} && for\ i > 0 \\
B_i &= S_b(a_i, c_i) + c_{i-1} && for\ i > 0 \\
C_i &= S_c(a_i, b_i) + b_{i-1} && for\ i > 0 \\
B_0 &= c_m \\
C_0 &= b_m
\end{aligned}
$$

The sharing is depicted in Fig. 1.

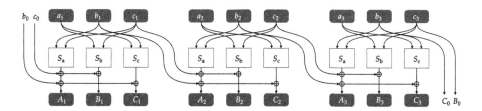

Fig. 1. Changing of the Guards sharing applied to simple S-box layer.

We can now prove the following theorem.

Theorem 1. *If S is an invertible S-box and (S_a, S_b, S_c) is a correct and incomplete sharing of S, the sharing of Definition 1 is a correct, incomplete and uniform sharing of an S-box layer with S as component.*

Proof. Correctness follows from the correctness of the S-box sharing and the fact that each input components that is fed forward to the output of its neigboring components is added twice. We have for all $i > 0$:

$$
\begin{aligned}
A_i + B_i + C_i &= S_a(b_i, c_i) + b_{i-1} + c_{i-1} + S_b(a_i, c_i) + c_{i-1} + S_c(a_i, b_i) + b_{i-1} \\
&= S_a(b_i, c_i) + S_b(a_i, c_i) + S_c(a_i, b_i) \\
&= S(a_i + b_i + c_i).
\end{aligned}
$$

For incompleteness, we see in Definition 1 that the computation of A_i does not involve components of a, the one of B_i does not involve components of b and the one of C_i does not involve components of c. Note that making this statement valid for component $i = 0$ necessitates the *swap* when expressing the output guards from the input shares of the last S-box: $(C_0, B_0) = (b_m, c_m)$.

For uniformity, we observe that for each input x or each output X there are exactly $2^{2(m+1)n}$ valid sharings. If the mapping of Definition 1 is an invertible mapping from (a, b, c) to (A, B, C), it implies that if (a, b, c) is a uniform sharing of x, then (A, B, C) is a uniform sharing of X. It is therefore sufficient to show that the mapping of Definition 1 is invertible. We will do that by giving a method to compute (a, b, c) from (A, B, C).

We compute the components of (a, b, c) starting from index m down to 0. First we compute the shares b_m and c_m from the output guards. We have $b_m = C_0$ and $c_m = B_0$. Then we use the correctness property to compute the component x_m from $X_m = A_m + B_m + C_m$ by applying the inverse S-box yielding $a_m = x_m + b_m + c_m$. From this we compute the output components of the S-box. This allows us again to compute b_{m-1} and c_{m-1}. Concretely, we can iterate the following loop for i going from m down to 1:

$$
\begin{aligned}
a_i &= S^{-1}(A_i + B_i + C_i) + b_i + c_i \\
b_{i-1} &= S_c(a_i, b_i) + C_i \\
c_{i-1} &= S_b(a_i, c_i) + B_i.
\end{aligned}
$$

$\square$

The term "guards" refers to the dummy components b_0 and c_0 that are there to guard uniformity and that are "changed" to B_0 and C_0 by the shared implementation of the S-box layer.

The cost of this method is the addition of 4 XOR gates per bit of x and the expansion of the representation by $2n$ bits. The cost of additional XOR gates is typically not negligible but still relatively modest compared to the gates in the S-box sharing. For a typical S-box layer the expansion of the state is very small.

When applying this method to an iterated cipher that has a round function consisting of an S-box layer and a linear layer, one can do the following. The sharing of the S-box layer maps (a, b, c) to (A, B, C) and the linear layer is applied to the shares separately. In the linear mapping the guard components B_0 and C_0 are simply mapped to the components b_0 and c_0 of the next round by the identity.

It is likely that the *swapping* that takes place between the guards is not necessary, but it does simplify the proof for the incompleteness aspect.

3   Generalization to Any Invertible S-box Layer

Here we give a method for an S-box layer with only restriction that the component S-boxes have the same width and are all invertible. So this includes the case that the S-boxes are different and even the case that they have different algebraic degrees. We assume the maximum degree over all S-boxes of the layer is d and so we can produce a correct and incomplete threshold scheme with $d+1$ shares. We denote the shares by x^0 to x^d and component j of share i by x_i^j.

In the generalization there are d guard components instead of two. Similarly to the three-share implementation, there is no guard for the first share (a or x^0). The schedule for adding shares from the neighboring S-box is somewhat more complicated. There are four cases, depending on the index j of the output share considered:

$j > 2$: add input shares $j - 1$ and $j - 2$ of its neighboring S-box;
$j = 2$: add input share 1 of its neighboring S-box;
$j = 1$: add input share d of its neighboring S-box;
$j = 0$: add input shares d and $d - 1$ of its neighboring S-box.

Clearly, input shares with index 0 are not added to the neighboring S-box output share. All other input shares are added to exactly two output shares of the neighboring S-box. We depict the treatment of the output of shared S-box of index i for a threshold scheme with 6 shares in Fig. 2. The S-box inputs have been omitted for not crowding the picture. We now provide the more formal definition.

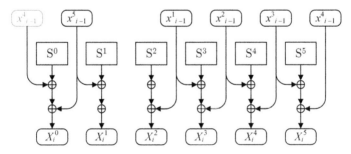

Fig. 2. Example of the generic method, depicting treatment of output of shared S-box i.

Definition 2. *The* Changing of the Guards *sharing of an S-box layer with* $(S_i^0, S_i^1, \ldots, S_i^d)$ *a sharing of S_i, mapping $(x^0, x^1, x^2, \ldots, x^d)$ to $(X^0, X^1, X^2, \ldots, X^d)$, is given by (with $x_i \setminus x_i^j$ denoting the vector of d elements $x_i^{j'}$ for $j' \neq j$):*

$$X_i^0 = S_i^0(x_i \setminus x_i^0) + x_{i-1}^{d-1} + x_{i-1}^d \qquad\qquad for\ i > 0$$
$$X_i^1 = S_i^1(x_i \setminus x_i^1) + x_{i-1}^d \qquad\qquad for\ i > 0$$
$$X_i^2 = S_i^2(x_i \setminus x_i^2) + x_{i-1}^1 \qquad\qquad for\ i > 0$$
$$\cdots$$

$$X_i^j = S_i^j(x_i \setminus x_i^j) + x_{i-1}^{j-2} + x_{i-1}^{j-1} \qquad\qquad for\ i > 0$$

$$\dots$$

$$X_i^d = S_i^d(x_i \setminus x_i^d) + x_{i-1}^{d-2} + x_{i-1}^{d-1} \qquad\qquad for\ i > 0$$

$$X_0^j = x_m^{j+1} \qquad\qquad for\ j > 0$$

$$X_0^d = x_m^1$$

We can now prove the following theorem.

Theorem 2. *Let S be an S-box layer consisting of invertible n-bit S-boxes S_i with $1 \le i \le m$, where the S-boxes S_i may be different and where d is the maximum degree over all these S-boxes. Let $(S_i^0, S_i^1, \dots S_i^d)$ with $1 \le i \le m$ be correct and incomplete sharing of S_i with $d+1$ shares. Then the sharing of Definition 2 is a correct, incomplete and uniform sharing of the S-box layer with S_i as components.*

Proof. Correctness follows from the correctness of the individual S-box sharings and the fact that each input component that is fed forward to the output of its neigboring components is added twice. We have for all $i > 0$:

$$\sum_j X_i^j = \left(\sum_j S_i^j(x_i \setminus x_i^j) \right) + \left(\sum_{j>2} x_{i-1}^{j-2} + x_{i-1}^{j-1} \right) + \left(x_{i-1}^{d-1} + x_{i-1}^d \right) + \left(x_{i-1}^d \right) + \left(x_{i-1}^1 \right)$$

$$= S_i(x_i) + \left(\sum_{0<j<d-1} x_{i-1}^j \right) + \left(\sum_{1<j<d} x_{i-1}^j \right) + x_{i-1}^{d-1} + x_{i-1}^1$$

$$= S_i(x_i).$$

For incompleteness, we see in Definition 2 that the computation of X_i^j does not involve components of x^j as in the S-box input x_i^j is excluded and the inputs of the neighboring S-box that are added are taken from shares $j-1$ and $j-2$ (modulo $d+1$ for $j < 2$). Moreover, there is a (cyclic) swap taking place in the mapping from the input shares of the last S-box to the output guards to ensure this.

For uniformity, it is again sufficient to show that the mapping of Definition 2 is invertible. We give a method to compute $(x^0, x^1, x^2, \dots, x^d)$ from $(X^0, X^1, X^2, \dots, X^d)$.

We compute the components of $(x^0, x^1, x^2, \dots, x^d)$ starting from index m down to 0. From Definition 2 it is immediate that $x_m^1 = X_0^d$ and then $x_m^2 = X_0^1, x_m^3 = X_0^2, x_m^4 = X_0^3, \dots x_m^d = X_0^{d-1}$. Then we can iterate the following loop for i going from m down to 1:

$$x_i^0 = S_i^{-1}\left(\sum_j X_i^j\right) + \sum_{j>0} x_i^j$$

$$x_{i-1}^d = S_i^1(x_i \setminus x_i^j) + X_i^1$$

$$x_{i-1}^1 = S_i^2(x_i \setminus x_i^2) + X_i^2$$

$$x_{i-1}^2 = S_i^3(x_i \setminus x_i^3) + X_i^3 + x_{i-1}^1$$
$$x_{i-1}^3 = S_i^4(x_i \setminus x_i^4) + X_i^4 + x_{i-1}^2$$
$$\cdots$$
$$x_{i-1}^{d-1} = S_i^d(x_i \setminus x_i^j) + X_i^d + x_{i-1}^{d-2} .$$

$\square$

As said, our method applies also to heterogeneous S-box layers, i.e., S-box layers with different S-boxes. Such layers are quite rare in modern cryptography, especially after the benefits of symmetry became clear. The block cipher DES [26] is a notable exception to this, but one may argue whether that is a modern cipher. In any case, one may ask how the method applies to S-box layer in the DES F-function as it consists of non-invertible S-boxes. Remarkably, as was stated by Boss et al. [11] and mathematically explained by the same team [12], in Feistel networks where the S-box layer is embedded in a function whose output is (bitwise) added to part of the state, uniformity is achieved automatically. Basically, thanks to the Feistel construction the shared round function is a permutation and hence uniform. So, if the algebraic degree of the S-box layer is d, it is sufficient to represent the state by $d + 1$ shares and have a threshold implementation for the S-boxes that is correct and incomplete.

4   Application to the Sharing χ' for Keccak

KECCAK-p is the permutation underlying our hash function KECCAK [2,28], our authenticated encryption schemes KEYAK [4] and KETJE [3] and is defined in the KECCAK reference [2] and NIST standard [28].

4.1   The Sharing χ' of the Nonlinear Layer in Keccak

The nonlinear layer in KECCAK-p is called χ. It has algebraic degree 2 over GF(2) and operates independently on 5-bit rows. If we denote the elements of a row by x^0 to x^4, the mapping χ applied to a single row is defined as (with addition and multiplication over GF(2) and indices $\ell \in \mathbb{Z}_5$ taken modulo 5):

$$X^\ell = x^\ell + (x^{\ell+1} + 1)x^{\ell+2} .$$

Note that the state of KECCAK-p is a three-dimensional array and we only represent the intra-row index here by ℓ for clarity as we look here at a single row.

In [1] we proposed a correct and incomplete sharing of χ with 3 shares and called it χ'. As she mapping χ operates independently on 5-bit rows and consequently χ' operates in parallel on 15-bit units. If we denote the three shares by a, b and c, χ' is defined as:

$$A^\ell = b^\ell + (b^{\ell+1} + 1)b^{\ell+2} + b^{\ell+1}c^{\ell+2} + b^{\ell+2}c^{\ell+1}, \tag{1}$$
$$B^\ell = c^\ell + (c^{\ell+1} + 1)c^{\ell+2} + c^{\ell+1}a^{\ell+2} + c^{\ell+2}a^{\ell+1}, \tag{2}$$
$$C^\ell = a^\ell + (a^{\ell+1} + 1)a^{\ell+2} + a^{\ell+1}b^{\ell+2} + a^{\ell+2}b^{\ell+1}, \tag{3}$$

4.2   The Multi-transformation Property

The mapping χ' has a remarkable property that we can exploit to reduce the overhead due to the "Changing of the Guards" method. We call this a *multi-transformation property*, inspired by the concept of multi-permutations proposed by Schnorr and Vaudenay [30]. Loosely speaking, an n-bit transformation has a multi-transformation property of order r if for any input, the bits in r specific positions in the input and the bits in $n - r$ specific positions in the output, with $r < n$, together fully determine the remaining $n - r$ bits of the input. We now give a more rigorous definition.

Definition 3 (Transformation property with respect to an index subset). *Let f be a transformation operating on vectors of n bits $(x_0, x_1, \ldots, x_{n-1})$ and let us denote the bits of $f(x_0, x_1, \ldots, x_{n-1})$ by $(x_n, x_{n+1}, \ldots, x_{2n-1})$. We can now represent f by a set $\mathcal{F}$ of 2^n vectors of the form $(x_0, x_1, \ldots, x_{2n-1})$. Let S be a subset with n elements of the set of indices of these vectors, i.e., $S \subset \mathbb{Z}_{2n}$. Then we say f has the transformation property with respect to S if the set $\mathcal{F}$ has no two elements that are equal in all components in S, or equivalently:*

$$\forall x \in \mathcal{F} : \#\{y \mid \forall i \in S : x_i = y_i\} = 1.$$

We call $r = \#(S \cap \mathbb{Z}_n)$ the order of the transformation property.

Clearly, any n-bit transformation f has a transformation property of order n with respect to $S = \mathbb{Z}_n$. So if it has the transformation property with respect to an additional set S, we call it a multi-transformation. Note that any permutation f has a transformation property of order 0 with respect $S = \mathbb{Z}_{2n} \setminus \mathbb{Z}_n$. In the context of this paper we are interested in finding a multi-transformation property in S-box threshold implementations that are not uniform and hence are not permutations.

4.3   Using the Multi-transformation Property of χ'

The mapping χ' restricted to a single row is a transformation operating on 15 bits. We can show it has a transformation property of order 6. The consequence of this is that we can reduce the size of the guards from 10 bits to 4 bits and the number of bitwise addition operations per row to 8.

We first need to introduce some notation. For a 5-bit vector s, let $\mathrm{L}(s) \triangleq (s^0, s^1, s^2)$ and $\mathrm{R}(s) \triangleq (s^3, s^4)$. Similarly, we define $\mathrm{L}(a, b, c) \triangleq (a^0, b^0, c^0, a^1, b^1, c^1, a^2, b^2, c^2)$ and $\mathrm{R}(a, b, c) \triangleq (a^3, b^3, c^3, a^4, b^4, c^4)$.

Lemma 1. *For any of the 2^{15} choices of $\mathrm{L}(A, B, C), \mathrm{R}(a, b, c)$, there is exactly one solution $\mathrm{L}(a, b, c), \mathrm{R}(A, B, C)$ such that $(A, B, C) = \chi'(a, b, c)$.*

Proof. We describe how to compute $L(a, b, c), R(A, B, C)$ from $L(A, B, C)$, $R(a, b, c)$. We rewrite each of the Eq. (1) by switching lefthand term and first terms on the righthand from side:

$$b^\ell = A^\ell + (b^{\ell+1} + 1)b^{\ell+2} + b^{\ell+1}c^{\ell+2} + b^{\ell+2}c^{\ell+1},$$
$$c^\ell = B^\ell + (c^{\ell+1} + 1)c^{\ell+2} + c^{\ell+1}a^{\ell+2} + c^{\ell+2}a^{\ell+1},$$
$$a^\ell = C^\ell + (a^{\ell+1} + 1)a^{\ell+2} + a^{\ell+1}b^{\ell+2} + a^{\ell+2}b^{\ell+1},$$

We can use these equations for computing (a^2, b^2, c^2) by taking $\ell = 2$. Clearly the first term on the righthand side is part of $L(A, B, C)$ and the remaining terms are expressed in terms of bits in $R(a, b, c)$. We can now use this equation with $\ell = 1$ to compute (a^1, b^1, c^1) using the acquired value of (a^2, b^2, c^2). This can be repeated for $\ell = 0$ giving us the full knowledge of (a, b, c). From (a, b, c) we can compute (A, B, C) using Eq. (1) and hence we also know $R(A, B, C)$.   □

We can use Lemma 1 to apply a variant of the "Changing of the Guards" method to χ' that requires less state expansion and XOR gates due to the feedforward. We call it χ''.

Definition 4. *The χ'' sharing of χ is given by:*

$$R(A_i) = R(\chi'_a(b_i, c_i)) + R(b_{i-1}) + R(c_{i-1}) \qquad for\ i > 0$$
$$R(B_i) = R(\chi'_b(a_i, c_i)) + R(c_{i-1}) \qquad for\ i > 0$$
$$R(C_i) = R(\chi'_c(a_i, b_i)) + R(b_{i-1}) \qquad for\ i > 0$$
$$L(A_i) = L(\chi'_a(b_i, c_i)) \qquad for\ i > 0$$
$$L(B_i) = L(\chi'_b(a_i, c_i)) \qquad for\ i > 0$$
$$L(C_i) = L(\chi'_c(a_i, b_i)) \qquad for\ i > 0$$
$$R(B_0) = R(c_m)$$
$$R(C_0) = R(b_m).$$

Here the indexing i assumes rows arranged in a one-dimensional array. In KECCAK-*p this is a two-dimensional array indexed by y and z. It is however simple to adopt a convention for converting this to a single-dimensional one, e.g. $i = y + 5z$.*

Note that $L(b_0)$, $L(c_0)$, $L(B_0)$ and $L(C_0)$ do not occur in the computations. We can therefore reduce the guards to their 2-bit right parts: $R(b_0)$, $R(c_0)$, $R(B_0)$ and $R(C_0)$.

The total expansion of the state reduces from 2 times the S-box width (totalling to 10 bits) to 4 bits. Moreover, there are only 8 XOR gates per S-box, i.e. 1.6 per native bit instead of 4 additional XOR gates per native bit. In the context of the χ' sharing the computational overhead is very small, as implementing Eq. (1) requires 9 XOR gates and 9 (N)AND gates per native bit. Note that the multi-transformation technique can be applied to other primitives that use a variant of χ as nonlinear layer.

We can now prove the following theorem.

Theorem 3. χ'' *as defined in Definition 4 is a correct, incomplete and uniform sharing of* χ.

Proof. Correctness and incompleteness is immediate. For proving uniformity we describe how to compute (a, b, c) from (A, B, C). We compute the components of (a, b, c) starting from index m down to 0. First we have $R(b_m) = R(C_0)$ and $R(c_m) = R(B_0)$. Then we can iterate the following loop going from m down to 1, computing $a_i, L(b_i), L(c_i)$ and $R(b_{i-1}), R(c_{i-1})$:

- $R(a_i) = R(S^{-1}(A_i + B_i + C_i)) + R(b_i) + R(c_i)$
- compute $L(a_i, b_i, c_i)$ from $L(A_i, B_i, C_i), R(a_i, b_i, c_i)$ using Lemma 1
- $R(b_{i-1}) = R(S_c(a_i, b_i)) + R(C_i)$
- $R(c_{i-1}) = R(S_b(a_i, c_i)) + R(B_i)$. $\square$

5 Implementation Aspects

In this section we discuss suitability of our method for decomposed S-boxes, parallel and serial architectures.

5.1 Compatibility with Serial Decomposition of S-boxes

To reduce the number of shares, one has proposed the serial decomposition of S-boxes in S-boxes of lower degree. Notably, Kutzner et al. decomposed all 4-bit S-boxes of algebraic degree 3 into component degree-2 mappings [21] in such a way that for each of the components a correct, incomplete and uniform 3-share threshold scheme can be found. One may wonder whether our method can be combined with such decomposition.

As a matter of fact, when "Changing of the Guards" is applied, the requirements on the decomposition due to sharing vanish: it suffices to find a decomposition of an invertible S-box as the series of two degree-2 S-boxes. If such a decomposition exists, but if no uniform sharing for one or both component S-boxes can be found, our method comes to the rescue. In Fig. 3 we illustrate it for the case that the "Changing of the Guards" is applied to both layers. Note that the uniformity of the composed mapping follows directly from the uniformity of the component mappings.

One can see that in between the two layers, there is a register or latch. This results in an increase of latency. The output guards of the first step are used as input guards for the second step. If one of the two layers would not require "Changing of the Guards", the guards would just skip that step. For example, if the first layer would not use the method, the incoming guards b_0, c_0 would not be used the first layer but directly in the second layer and the outcoming guards A_0, B_0 would be produced by the second layer.

In the case of more complex decompositions that combine serial and parallel composition, our "Changing of the Guards" cannot be readily applied. Especially if the decomposition contains building blocks that are not permutations. A well-known example of such decompositions are the ones applied to

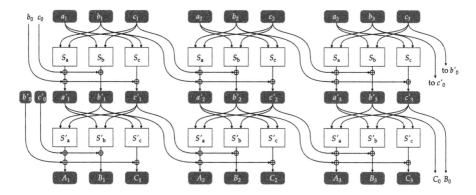

Fig. 3. Changing of the Guards applied to a layer of serially decomposed S-boxes.

the S-box of our cipher RIJNDAEL [15] by Moradi et al. [22] and Bilgin et al. [7]. As the RIJNDAEL S-box has algebraic degree 7 in GF(2) and hence would require 8 shares, a straightforward implementation of our proposed method would be very expensive. Due to the status of RIJNDAEL as worldwide block cipher standard [27], it would be interesting further work to find a decomposition of the RIJNDAEL S-box in terms of components that are all permutations of low algebraic degree.

5.2 Implementation Cost in Parallel Architectures

In a parallel architecture where the full round function is implemented in a block of combinatorial logic, the cost of the basic method is d XOR gates per bit plus d/m additional registers per bit. Introducing an extra share costs a single additional register per bit, plus possibly additional combinatorial logic. It follows that in parallel architectures the method becomes less and less interesting as d grows. It is at its best for protecting degree-2 functions, especially when a multi-transformation property can be exploited as in KECCAK. As a matter of fact, Bilgin et al. [6] compare KECCAK 4-share circuits with ones protected with a method that only differs from our method by the fact that the 4 bits of additional state are generated randomly every round, and hence the numbers reported there are expected to be very close to what we would achieve. A 4-share fully parallel implementation of KECCAK-f[1600] turns out to be about 20% more expensive than a 3-share *guards-like* one.

5.3 Implementation Cost in Serial Architectures

In serial architectures, the combinatorial logic can be limited to a fraction of the round function and one round takes multiple cycles. In the extreme case, this logic would only contain a single implementation of the (shared) S-box. In Fig. 4 we illustrate two cases to show that our method is compatible with such an architecture, both zooming in on the circuit implementing the shared S-box.

It can be seen that the combinatorial logic is extended with two registers (called *guard*) for keeping the inputs of the previous S-box computation. Figure 4 should give a good idea of how these circuits operate, but are not fully self-explanatory as we omit some details to not overload the pictures. The single-stage circuit operates as follows:

- The S-box input arrives in the boxes indicated by *in*. Depending on the architecture these can be registers, the output of another combinatorial block or a multiplexer.
- The operation of the guard registers:
  - At the beginning of the computation, they are initialized to random values (not depicted).
  - While processing an S-box layer, they get their input from the *in* boxes.
  - After processing the last S-box of a layer, they keep their value but swap contents (not depicted).
- The S-box output is presented in the boxes indicated by *out* for further processing or storage. The guards never leave the *guard* registers.

The two-stage circuit is a pipeline and operates similarly to the single-stage one, with the following refinements:

- During operation the first stage will always be one S-box ahead of the second stage. This implies that the processing of a layer of m S-boxes will take $m+1$ cycles.
- The guard register of the first stage operate similarly to the single-stage case. The only difference is that after the last S-box of a layer has been processed,

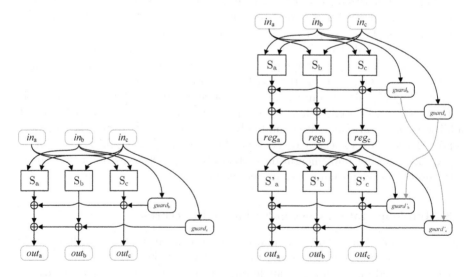

Fig. 4. Circuit for shared S-box computation in serial architecture, single-stage (left), two-stage (right)

they get their values from the guard registers of the second stage (not depicted to not overload the figure).

– The operation of the guard registers of the second stage:
  - At the beginning of the computation, they are initialized to random values (not depicted).
  - While processing an S-box layer, they get their input from the from the registers or latches, indicated by *reg*, in between the two stages.
  - After processing the last S-box of a stage, they get their value from the guard registers of the first stage.

In a serial implementation the guard registers have a higher relative overhead when comparing to the combinatorial circuit alone. However, when the real estate for keeping the state is also counted, an additional share is much more expensive than some additional XOR gates and guard registers. The exercise by Bilgin et al. [6] reports on 4-share serialized architectures that are 30% more expensive than a 3-share guards-like one.

6   Conclusions

In this paper we introduce a simple and low cost technique for achieving a 3-share correct, incomplete and uniform threshold implementation of the nonlinear layer in KECCAK. We have generalized this to a generic technique for achieving a $d+1$-share correct, incomplete and uniform threshold implementation of any S-box layer of invertible S-boxes that have degree at most d. Looking for S-boxes with uniform threshold implementations with the minimum $(d + 1)$ number of shares has therefore lost relevance. On the other hand, it becomes now interesting to look for S-boxes that have $d + 1$-share implementations with a suitable multi-transformation property, such as observed in the nonlinear layer of KECCAK.

Acknowledgements. I thank Gilles Van Assche, Vincent Rijmen, Begül Bilgin, Svetla Nikova and Ventzi Nikov for working with me on the paper [6], that already contained an idea very close to the "Changing of the Guards" technique, Guido Bertoni for inspiring discussions and finally Lejla Batina and Amir Moradi for useful feedback on earlier versions of this text.

References

1. Bertoni, G., Daemen, J., Peeters, M., Van Assche, G.: Building power analysis resistant implementations of KECCAK. In: Second SHA-3 Candidate Conference, August 2010
2. Bertoni, G., Daemen, J., Peeters, M., Van Assche, G.: The KECCAK reference, January 2011. http://keccak.noekeon.org/
3. Bertoni, G., Daemen, J., Peeters, M., Van Assche, G., Van Keer, R.: CAESAR submission: KETJE v2, September 2016. http://ketje.noekeon.org/
4. Bertoni, G., Daemen, J., Peeters, M., Van Assche, G., Van Keer, R.: CAESAR submission: KEYAK v2, document version 2.2, September 2016. http://keyak.noekeon.org/

5. Beyne, T., Bilgin, B.: Uniform first-order threshold implementations. IACR Cryptology ePrint Archive 2016:715 (2016)
6. Bilgin, B., Daemen, J., Nikov, V., Nikova, S., Rijmen, V., Assche, G.: Efficient and First-Order DPA resistant implementations of KECCAK. In: Francillon, A., Rohatgi, P. (eds.) CARDIS 2013. LNCS, vol. 8419, pp. 187–199. Springer, Cham (2014). doi:10.1007/978-3-319-08302-5_13
7. Bilgin, B., Gierlichs, B., Nikova, S., Nikov, V., Rijmen, V.: A more efficient AES threshold implementation. In: Pointcheval, D., Vergnaud, D. (eds.) AFRICACRYPT 2014. LNCS, vol. 8469, pp. 267–284. Springer, Cham (2014). doi:10.1007/978-3-319-06734-6_17
8. Bilgin, B., Nikova, S., Nikov, V., Rijmen, V., Stütz, G.: Threshold implementations of all 3×3 and 4×4 S-boxes. In: Prouff, E., Schaumont, P. (eds.) CHES 2012. LNCS, vol. 7428, pp. 76–91. Springer, Heidelberg (2012). doi:10.1007/978-3-642-33027-8_5
9. Bilgin, B., Nikova, S., Nikov, V., Rijmen, V., Tokareva, N.N., Vitkup, V.: Threshold implementations of small S-boxes. Cryptogr. Commun. $7(1)$, 3–33 (2015)
10. Božlov, D., Bilgin, B., Sahin, H.: A note on 5-bit quadratic permutations' classification. IACR Trans. Symmetric Cryptol. $2017(1)$, 398–404 (2017)
11. Boss, E., Grosso, V., Güneysu, T., Leander, G., Moradi, A., Schneider, T.: Strong 8-bit S-boxes with efficient masking in hardware. In Gierlichs, B., Poschmann, A.Y. (eds.) [18], pp. 171–193 (2016)
12. Boss, E., Grosso, V., Güneysu, T., Leander, G., Moradi, A., Schneider, T.: Strong 8-bit sboxes with efficient masking in hardware extended version. J. Cryptogr. Eng. $7(2)$, 149–165 (2017)
13. De Cnudde, T., Bilgin, B., Gierlichs, B., Nikov, V., Nikova, S., Rijmen, V.: Does coupling affect the security of masked implementations? IACR Cryptology ePrint Archive 2016:1080 (2016)
14. De Cnudde, T., Reparaz, O., Bilgin, B., Nikova, S., Nikov, V., Rijmen, V.: Masking AES with d + 1 shares in hardware. In: Gierlichs, B., Poschmann, A.Y. (eds.) [18], pp. 194–212 (2016)
15. Daemen, J., Rijmen, V.: The Design of Rijndael — AES, the Advanced Encryption Standard. Springer, Heidelberg (2002)
16. Daemen, J.: Spectral characterization of iterating lossy mappings. IACR Cryptology ePrint Archive 2016:90 (2016)
17. Daemen, J.: Spectral characterization of iterating lossy mappings. In: Carlet, C., Hasan, M.A., Saraswat, V. (eds.) SPACE 2016. LNCS, vol. 10076, pp. 159–178. Springer, Cham (2016). doi:10.1007/978-3-319-49445-6_9
18. Gierlichs, B., Poschmann, A.Y. (eds.) Cryptographic Hardware and Embedded Systems - CHES 2016–Proceedings of the 18th International Conference, Santa Barbara, CA, USA, 17–19 August 2016. LNCS, vol. 9813. Springer (2016)
19. Ishai, Y., Sahai, A., Wagner, D.: Private circuits: securing hardware against probing attacks. In: Boneh, D. (ed.) CRYPTO 2003. LNCS, vol. 2729, pp. 463–481. Springer, Heidelberg (2003). doi:10.1007/978-3-540-45146-4_27
20. Kocher, P., Jaffe, J., Jun, B.: Differential power analysis. In: Wiener, M. (ed.) CRYPTO 1999. LNCS, vol. 1666, pp. 388–397. Springer, Heidelberg (1999). doi:10.1007/3-540-48405-1_25
21. Kutzner, S., Nguyen, P.H., Poschmann, A.: Enabling 3-share threshold implementations for all 4-Bit S-boxes. In: Lee, H.-S., Han, D.-G. (eds.) ICISC 2013. LNCS, vol. 8565, pp. 91–108. Springer, Cham (2014). doi:10.1007/978-3-319-12160-4_6

22. Moradi, A., Poschmann, A., Ling, S., Paar, C., Wang, H.: Pushing the limits: a very compact and a threshold implementation of AES. In: Paterson, K.G. (ed.) EUROCRYPT 2011. LNCS, vol. 6632, pp. 69–88. Springer, Heidelberg (2011). doi:10.1007/978-3-642-20465-4_6

23. Nikova, S., Rechberger, C., Rijmen, V.: Threshold implementations against side-channel attacks and glitches. In: Ning, P., Qing, S., Li, N. (eds.) ICICS 2006. LNCS, vol. 4307, pp. 529–545. Springer, Heidelberg (2006). doi:10.1007/11935308_38

24. Nikova, S., Rijmen, V., Schläffer, M.: Secure hardware implementation of non-linear functions in the presence of glitches. In: Lee, P.J., Cheon, J.H. (eds.) ICISC 2008. LNCS, vol. 5461, pp. 218–234. Springer, Heidelberg (2009). doi:10.1007/978-3-642-00730-9_14

25. Nikova, S., Rijmen, V., Schläffer, M.: Secure hardware implementation of nonlinear functions in the presence of glitches. J. Cryptol. **24**(2), 292–321 (2011)

26. NIST: Federal information processing standard 46, data encryption standard (DES), October 1999

27. NIST: Federal information processing standard 197, advanced encryption standard (AES), November 2001

28. NIST: Federal information processing standard 202, SHA-3 standard: permutation-based hash and extendable-output functions, August 2015. doi:10.6028/NIST.FIPS.202

29. Reparaz, O., Bilgin, B., Nikova, S., Gierlichs, B., Verbauwhede, I.: Consolidating masking schemes. In: Gennaro, R., Robshaw, M. (eds.) CRYPTO 2015. LNCS, vol. 9215, pp. 764–783. Springer, Heidelberg (2015). doi:10.1007/978-3-662-47989-6_37

30. Schnorr, C.P., Vaudenay, S.: Parallel FFT-hashing. In: Anderson, R.J. (ed.) FSE 1993. LNCS, vol. 809, pp. 149–156. Springer, Heidelberg (1994). doi:10.1007/3-540-58108-1_18

31. Stoffelen, K.: Optimizing S-box implementations for several criteria using SAT solvers. In: Peyrin, T. (ed.) FSE 2016. LNCS, vol. 9783, pp. 140–160. Springer, Heidelberg (2016). doi:10.1007/978-3-662-52993-5_8

Generalized Polynomial Decomposition for S-boxes with Application to Side-Channel Countermeasures

Dahmun Goudarzi[1,2($\boxtimes$)], Matthieu Rivain[1], Damien Vergnaud[2], and Srinivas Vivek[3]

[1] CryptoExperts, Paris, France
{dahmun.goudarzi,matthieu.rivain}@cryptoexperts.com
[2] ENS, CNRS, INRIA, PSL Research University, Paris, France
damien.vergnaud@ens.fr
[3] University of Bristol, Bristol, UK
sv.venkatesh@bristol.ac.uk

Abstract. Masking is a widespread countermeasure to protect implementations of block-ciphers against side-channel attacks. Several masking schemes have been proposed in the literature that rely on the *efficient* decomposition of the underlying s-box(es). We propose a generalized decomposition method for s-boxes that encompasses several previously proposed methods while providing new trade-offs. It allows to evaluate $n\lambda$-bit to $m\lambda$-bit s-boxes for any integers $n, m, \lambda \geq 1$ by seeing it a sequence of m n-variate polynomials over $\mathbb{F}_{2^\lambda}$ and by trying to minimize the number of multiplications over $\mathbb{F}_{2^\lambda}$.

Keywords: S-box decomposition · Multiplicative complexity · Side-channel countermeasure · Masking · Software implementation · Block-cipher

1 Introduction

Implementing cryptographic algorithms in constrained embedded devices is a challenging task. In the 1990s, Kocher *et al.* [Koc96,KJJ99] showed that one may often use the physical leakage of the underlying device during the algorithm execution (e.g., the running-time, the power consumption or the electromagnetic radiations) to recover some secret information. Side-channel analysis is the class of cryptanalytic attacks that exploit such physical emanations to hinder the strength of the underlying cryptography.

One of the most common technique to protect implementations against side-channel attacks is to mask internal secret variables. This so-called *masking* technique [GP99,CJRR99] splits every sensitive data manipulated by the algorithm (which depends on the secret key and possibly on other variables known to the attacker) into $d + 1$ shares (where $d \geq 1$, the *masking order*, plays the role of a

© International Association for Cryptologic Research 2017
W. Fischer and N. Homma (Eds.): CHES 2017, LNCS 10529, pp. 154–171, 2017.
DOI: 10.1007/978-3-319-66787-4_8

security parameter). The first d shares are usually generated uniformly at random and the last one is computed so that the combination of the $d+1$ shares for some group law is equal to the initial value. With this technique, the attacker actually needs the whole set of $d+1$ shares to learn any information on the initial value. Since each share's observation comes with noise, the higher is the order d, the more complex is the attack [CJRR99, PR13]. This masking approach permits to achieve provable security in formal security models, notably the *probing security model* [ISW03] and the *noisy leakage model* [PR13, DDF14].

Most symmetric cryptographic algorithms manipulate binary data $x \in \{0,1\}^n$ (for some integer $n \geq 1$) and the natural group law used for masking is the Boolean XOR $\oplus$ over $\mathbb{F}_2$ (or more generally addition in the finite field $\mathbb{F}_{2^n}$ or in the vector space $\mathbb{F}_2^n$). Using this Boolean masking, each sensitive data x is thus split into $d+1$ shares $x_0, \ldots, x_d$ whose addition returns the initial value (i.e. $x = x_0 \oplus x_1 \oplus \cdots \oplus x_d$). One can then compute securely any linear function f of the sensitive value x since a sharing of $y = f(x)$ is readily obtained by computing $y_i = f(x_i)$ for $i \in \{0, \ldots, d\}$ (such that $y = y_0 \oplus y_1 \oplus \cdots \oplus y_d$). It is unfortunately not so easy to compute a sharing of $f(x)$ for non-linear functions f but solutions were proposed for multiplication (e.g. see [ISW03, RP10, BBP+16]). However, if the evaluation cost of linear function is linear in d, the best known algorithms for multiplication have $O(d^2)$ computational complexity.

In practice, iterative block cipher (such as AES) apply several time a round function to an internal state composed itself usually of a linear round key addition, of linear operations to ensure diffusion and of non-linear operations (usually called s-boxes) to ensure confusion. The main issue to provide secure implementation of block ciphers is thus to provide an efficient and secure way to mask the s-box(es). The most widely-used solution is to consider their representation as polynomial functions over finite fields $\mathbb{F}_{2^n}$ (using Lagrange's interpolation theorem) and to find an efficient way to evaluate this polynomial using a minimal number of multiplications. In this paper, we present a generalization of known methods and we obtain new interesting construction for efficiency/memory trade-offs.

1.1   Related Work

The first generic method to mask any s-box at any masking order d was proposed in 2012 by Carlet, Goubin, Prouff, Quisquater and Rivain [CGP+12] (following prior work by Rivain and Prouff for the AES block cipher [RP10]). The core idea is to split into simple operations over $\mathbb{F}_{2^n}$ (namely, addition, multiplication by constant, squaring and regular multiplication of two distinct elements), the evaluation of the polynomial representation of the s-box. Among these operations, only the regular multiplication of two distinct elements is non-linear (since squaring over a characteristic 2 finite field is actually linear), and one can use the secure multiplication algorithms mentioned above [ISW03, RP10, BBP+16] to evaluate them. Since these operations have $O(d^2)$ complexity, it is interesting to propose an evaluation scheme of the polynomial with as few as possible regular multiplications. Carlet *et al.* [CGP+12] defined the *masking complexity* (also known as *multiplicative complexity* and *non-linear complexity*) of an s-box as the minimal number of such multiplications necessary to evaluate the corresponding polynomial and they adapted known methods for polynomial evaluation based on *addition chains* (see [CGP+12] for details).

This technique was later improved by Roy and Vivek in [RV13] using *cyclotomic cosets addition chains*. They notably presented a polynomial evaluation method for the DES s-boxes that requires 7 non-linear multiplications (instead of 10 in [CGP+12]). They also presented lower-bound on the length of such a chain and showed that the multiplicative complexity of the DES s-boxes is lower bounded by 3. In 2014, Coron, Roy and Vivek [CRV14] proposed an heuristic method which may be viewed as an extension of the ideas developed in [CGP+12] and [RV13]. The so-called CRV method considers the s-box as a polynomial over $\mathbb{F}_{2^n}$ and has heuristic multiplicative complexity $O(2^{n/2}/\sqrt{n})$ instead of $O(2^{n/2})$ proven multiplicative complexity for the previous methods. They also proved a matching lower bound of $\Omega(2^{n/2}/\sqrt{n})$ on the multiplicative complexity of any generic method to evaluate n-bit s-boxes. For all the tested s-boxes their method is at least as efficient as the previous proposals and it often requires less non-linear multiplications (e.g. only 4 for the DES s-boxes).

In [GR16], Goudarzi and Rivain introduced a new method to decompose an s-box into a circuit with low multiplicative complexity. One can see their approach as a way to model the s-box as a polynomial over $\mathbb{F}_2^n$ (instead of $\mathbb{F}_{2^n}$) and it consists in applying masking at the Boolean level by bitslicing the s-boxes within a block cipher round. The proposed decomposition then relies on the one proposed by Coron *et al.* [CRV14] and extends it to efficiently deal with several coordinate functions. The schemes from [ISW03, RP10, BBP+16] can then be used to secure bitwise multiplication and the method allows to compute all the s-boxes within a cipher round at the same time.

Finally, in [PV16], Pulkus and Vivek generalized and improved Coron *et al.* technique [CRV14] by working over slightly larger fields than strictly needed (i.e. they considered the s-box as a polynomial over $\mathbb{F}_{2^t}$ instead of $\mathbb{F}_{2^n}$, where $t \geq n$). Their technique permits notably to evaluate DES s-boxes with only 3 non-linear multiplications over $\mathbb{F}_{2^8}$ (compared to 4 over $\mathbb{F}_{2^6}$ with Coron *et al.* method [CRV14]).

1.2   Our Results

We propose a generalized decomposition method for s-boxes that unifies these previously proposed methods and provides new median case decompositions. More precisely, in our approach any $n\lambda$-bit s-box for some integers $n \geq 1$ and $\lambda \geq 1$ can be seen as a polynomial (or a vector of $m \geq 1$ polynomials) over $\mathbb{F}_{2^\lambda}^n$. We first prove a lower bound of $\Omega(2^{\lambda n/2}\sqrt{m/\lambda})$ for the complexity of any method to evaluate $n\lambda$-bit to $m\lambda$-bit s-boxes. We then describe our generalized decomposition method for which we provide concrete parameters to achieve decomposition for several triplet (n, m, λ) and for exemplary s-boxes of popular block ciphers (namely PRESENT [BKL+07], SC2000 [SYY+02], CLEFIA [SSA+07] and KHAZAD [BR00]).

Depending on the s-box, our generalized method allows one to choose the parameters n, m and λ to obtain the best possible s-box decomposition in terms of multiplications over $\mathbb{F}_{2^\lambda}$. In particular, for 8×8 s-boxes, the CRV decomposition method [CRV14] ($n = 1$, $m = 1$, $\lambda = 8$) and the bitslice decomposition method [GR16] ($n = 8$, $m = 8$, $\lambda = 1$) are special cases of this generalized decomposition method. The implementation results provided in Sect. 6 (8×8 s-boxes on a 32-bit ARM architecture) show that our method is comparable with [CRV14] while being more space efficient. It is therefore a good alternative to prior techniques and can be effectively implemented in software on devices with limited resources.

In the full version of this paper, we generalize the method further by exploring the problem of decomposing arbitrary (n, m)-bit s-boxes over an arbitrary field $\mathbb{F}_{2^\lambda}$. Namely we do not require that λ divides the s-box input and output bit-lengths. This allows us to also integrate, in addition to [CRV14, GR16], the method of [PV16] that considers decomposition when $\lambda \geq n$.

2   Preliminaries

2.1   Notations and Notions

Let λ be a positive integer. Then $\mathbb{F}_{2^\lambda}$ denotes the finite field with 2^λ elements. Let $\mathcal{F}_{\lambda,n}$ be the set of functions from $\mathbb{F}_{2^\lambda}^n$ to $\mathbb{F}_{2^\lambda}$. Using Lagrange's interpolation theorem, any function $f \in \mathcal{F}_{\lambda,n}$ can be seen as a multivariate polynomial over $\mathbb{F}_{2^\lambda}[x_1, x_2, \ldots, x_n]/(x_1^{2^\lambda} - x_1, x_2^{2^\lambda} - x_2, \ldots, x_n^{2^\lambda} - x_n)$:

$$f(x) = \sum_{u \in [0, 2^\lambda - 1]^n} a_u\, x^u , \tag{1}$$

where $x = (x_1, x_2, \ldots, x_n)$, $x^u = x_1^{u_1} \cdot x_2^{u_2} \cdot \ldots \cdot x_n^{u_n}$, and $a_u \in \mathbb{F}_{2^\lambda}$ for every $u = (u_1, \ldots, u_n) \in [0, 2^\lambda - 1]^n$.

The *multiplicative complexity* of a function in $\mathcal{F}_{\lambda,n}$ (also called the non-linear complexity) is defined as the minimal number of $\mathbb{F}_{2^\lambda}$-multiplications required to evaluate it.

2.2   S-box Characterization

In the following, an s-box S is characterized with respect to 3 parameters: the number of input elements n; the number of output elements m; and the bit-size of the elements λ. In other words, an s-box with λn input bits and λm outputs bits is represented as follows:

$$S(x) = (f_1(x), f_2(x), \ldots, f_m(x)), \tag{2}$$

where functions $f_1, f_2, \ldots, f_m \in \mathcal{F}_{\lambda,n}$ are called the *coordinate functions* of S.

As mentioned in the introduction, Roy and Vivek presented in [RV13] lower-bound on the length of cyclotomic coset addition chains and used it to derive a logarithmic lower bound on the multiplicative complexity of an s-box (i.e. on the minimal number of such multiplications necessary to evaluate the corresponding polynomial). Coron *et al.* [CRV14] improved this lower bound and showed that the non-linear complexity of any generic method to evaluate n-bit s-boxes when seen as a polynomial defined over $\mathbb{F}_{2^n}$ is in $\Omega(2^{n/2}/\sqrt{n})$.

In the following section, we generalize their approach and provide a new lower bound on the multiplicative complexity of a sequence of n-variate polynomials over $\mathbb{F}_{2^\lambda}$. Following [RV13], we define the multiplicative complexity notion for such a sequence as follows:

Definition 1 (Polynomial chain). *Let $\lambda \geq 1$, $n \geq 1$ and $m \geq 1$ be three integers and let $f_1, \ldots, f_m \in \mathbb{F}_{2^\lambda}[x_1, \ldots, x_n]$ be a sequence of n-variate polynomials over $\mathbb{F}_{2^\lambda}$. A polynomial chain $\boldsymbol{\pi}$ for $(f_1, \ldots, f_m)$ is a sequence $\boldsymbol{\pi} = (\pi_i)_{i \in \{-n, \ldots, \ell\}}$ and a list $(i_1, \ldots, i_m) \in \{-n, \ldots, \ell\}^m$ with*

$$\pi_{-n} = x_n, \; \pi_{1-n} = x_{n-1}, \; \ldots, \; \pi_{-1} = x_1, \; \pi_0 = 1,$$

$$\pi_{i_j} = f_j(x_1, \ldots, x_n) \bmod (x_1^{2^\lambda} + x_1, \ldots, x_n^{2^\lambda} + x_n), \; \forall j \in \{1, \ldots, m\},$$

and such that for every $i \in \{1, \ldots, \ell\}$, one of the following condition holds:

1. *there exist j and k in $\{-n, \ldots, i-1\}$ such that $\pi_i = \pi_j \cdot \pi_k$;*
2. *there exist j and k in $\{-n, \ldots, i-1\}$ such that $\pi_i = \pi_j + \pi_k$;*
3. *there exists j in $\{-n, \ldots, i-1\}$ such that $\pi_i = \pi_j^2$;*
4. *there exists j in $\{-n, \ldots, i-1\}$ and $\alpha \in \mathbb{F}_{2^\lambda}$ such that $\pi_i = \alpha \cdot \pi_j$.*

Given such a polynomial chain $\boldsymbol{\pi}$ for $(f_1, \ldots, f_m)$, the multiplicative complexity of $\boldsymbol{\pi}$ is the number of times the first condition holds in the whole chain $\boldsymbol{\pi}$. The multiplicative complexity of $(f_1, \ldots, f_m)$ over $\mathbb{F}_{2^\lambda}$, denoted $\mathcal{M}(f_1, \ldots, f_m)$ is the minimal multiplicative complexity over all polynomial chains for $(f_1, \ldots, f_m)$.

Remark 1. The multiplicative complexity is similar to the classical circuit complexity notion in which we do not count the linear operations over $\mathbb{F}_{2^\lambda}$ (namely addition, scalar multiplication and squaring operations). For any sequence of n-variate polynomials $f_1, \ldots, f_m \in \mathbb{F}_{2^\lambda}[x_1, \ldots, x_n]$ we obviously have:

$$\mathcal{M}(f_1, \ldots, f_m) \leq \mathcal{M}(f_1) + \cdots + \mathcal{M}(f_m)$$

3   Multiplicative Complexity Lower Bound

In the next section, we will provide a heuristic method which given a sequence of n-variate polynomials over $\mathbb{F}_{2^\lambda}$ provides an evaluation scheme (or a circuit) with "small" multiplicative complexity. Following, Coron *et al.* [CRV14], Proposition 1 provides a $\Omega(2^{n\lambda/2}\sqrt{m/\lambda})$ lower bound on this multiplicative complexity. As in [CRV14], the proof is a simple combinatorial argument inspired by [PS73].

Proposition 1. *Let $\lambda \geq 1$, $n \geq 1$ and $m \geq 1$ be three integers. There exists $f_1, \ldots, f_m \in \mathbb{F}_{2^\lambda}[x_1, \ldots, x_n]$ a sequence of n-variate polynomials over $\mathbb{F}_{2^\lambda}$ such that $\mathcal{M}(f_1, \ldots, f_m) \geq \sqrt{\frac{m2^{n\lambda}}{\lambda}} - (2n + m - 1)$.*

Proof. We consider a sequence of n-variate polynomials $f_1, \ldots, f_m$ in the algebra $\mathbb{F}_{2^\lambda}[x_1, \ldots, x_n]$ with multiplicative complexity $\mathcal{M}(f_1, \ldots, f_m) = r$ for some integer $r \geq 1$. If we consider only the non-linear operations in a polynomial chain of minimal multiplicative complexity $\boldsymbol{\pi} = (\pi_i)_{i \in \{-n, \ldots, \ell\}}$, we can see that there exists indices $m_0, m_1, \ldots, m_{n+r+(m-1)}$ with $m_i \in \{-n, \ldots, \ell\}$ for $i \in \{0, \ldots, n + r + (m-1)\}$ such that

- $m_j = -j - 1$ for $j \in \{0, \ldots, n - 1\}$
  (i.e. $\pi_{m_j} = \pi_{-j-1} = x_{j+1}$ for $j \in \{0, \ldots, n-1\}$);
- for $k \in \{n, \ldots, n + r - 1\}$, there exist field elements $\beta_k, \beta'_k \in \mathbb{F}_{2^\lambda}$ and $\beta_{k,i,j}, \beta'_{k,i,j} \in \mathbb{F}_{2^\lambda}$ for $(i, j) \in \{0, \ldots, k-1\} \times \{0, \ldots, \lambda - 1\}$ such that

$$\pi_{m_k} = \left(\beta_k + \sum_{i=0}^{k-1} \sum_{j=0}^{\lambda-1} \beta_{k,i,j} \pi_{m_i}^{2^j} \right) \cdot \left(\beta'_k + \sum_{i=0}^{k-1} \sum_{j=0}^{\lambda-1} \beta'_{k,i,j} \pi_{m_i}^{2^j} \right)$$

$$\mod (x_1^{2^\lambda} + x_1, \ldots, x_n^{2^\lambda} + x_n);$$

- for $k \in \{n + r, \ldots, n + r + (m-1)\}$ there exist field elements $\beta_k \in \mathbb{F}_{2^\lambda}$ and $\beta_{k,i,j} \in \mathbb{F}_{2^\lambda}$ for $(i, j) \in \{0, \ldots, n + r - 1\} \times \{0, \ldots, \lambda - 1\}$ such that

$$f_{k+1-(n+r)} = \pi_{m_k} = \beta_k + \sum_{i=0}^{n+r-1} \sum_{j=0}^{\lambda-1} \beta_{k,i,j} \pi_{m_i}^{2^j} \mod (x_1^{2^\lambda} + x_1, \ldots, x_n^{2^\lambda} + x_n).$$

The total number of parameters β in this evaluation scheme of P is simply equal to:

$$\sum_{k=n}^{n+r-1} 2 \cdot (1 + k \cdot \lambda) + m(1 + (n+r) \cdot \lambda) = r^2 \lambda + r(\lambda m + 2\lambda n - \lambda + 2) + \lambda mn + m$$

and each parameter can take any value in $\mathbb{F}_{2^\lambda}$. The number of sequence of n-variate polynomials $f_1, \ldots, f_m \in \mathbb{F}_{2^\lambda}[x_1, \ldots, x_n]$ with multiplicative complexity $\mathcal{M}(f_1, \ldots, f_m) = r$ is thus upper-bounded by $2^{\lambda(r^2\lambda + r(\lambda m + 2\lambda n - \lambda + 2) + \lambda mn + m)}$.

Since the total number of sequence of n-variate polynomials $f_1, \ldots, f_m \in \mathbb{F}_{2^\lambda}[x_1, \ldots, x_n]$ defined $\mod (x_1^{2^\lambda} + x_1, \ldots, x_n^{2^\lambda} + x_n)$ is $((2^\lambda)^{2^{n\lambda}})^m$, in order to be able to evaluate all such polynomials with at most r non-linear multiplications, a necessary condition is to have

$$r^2 \lambda + r(\lambda m + 2\lambda n - \lambda + 2) + \lambda mn + m \geq m 2^{n\lambda}$$

and therefore

$$r^2 \lambda + r(\lambda m + 2\lambda n - \lambda + 2) - (m 2^{n\lambda} - \lambda mn - m) \geq 0.$$

Eventually, we obtain

$$r \geq \frac{\sqrt{\lambda 4 \, m 2^{n\lambda} + (\lambda m + 2\lambda n - \lambda + 2)^2} - (\lambda m + 2\lambda n - \lambda + 2)}{2\lambda} \tag{3}$$

and

$$r \geq \frac{\sqrt{4\lambda m 2^{n\lambda} - 2(\lambda m + 2\lambda n - \lambda + 2)}}{2\lambda} \geq \sqrt{\frac{m 2^{n\lambda}}{\lambda}} - (2n + m - 1).$$

$\square$

4   Generalized Decomposition Method

In this section, we propose a generalized decomposition method for s-boxes that aims at encapsulating previously proposed methods and at providing new median case decompositions. Depending on the s-box, we can then choose the parameters n, m and λ in order to obtain the best possible s-box decomposition in terms of multiplications over $\mathbb{F}_{2^\lambda}$. In particular, for 8×8 s-boxes, the CRV decomposition method [CRV14] ($n = 1$, $m = 1$, $\lambda = 8$) and the bitslice decomposition method [GR16] ($n = 8$, $m = 8$, $\lambda = 1$) are special cases of this generalized decomposition method.

4.1   Decomposition of a Single Coordinate Function

Let us define the *linear power class* of a function $\phi \in \mathcal{F}_{\lambda,n}$, denoted by $\mathcal{C}_\phi$, as the set

$$\mathcal{C}_\phi = \{\phi^{2^i} : i = 0, \ldots, \lambda - 1\}. \tag{4}$$

Intuitively, $\mathcal{C}_\phi$ corresponds to the set of functions in $\mathcal{F}_{\lambda,n}$ that can be computed from ϕ using only the squaring operation. It is not hard to see that $\{\mathcal{C}_\phi\}_\phi$ are equivalence classes partitioning $\mathcal{F}_{\lambda,n}$. For any set $\mathcal{B} \subseteq \mathcal{F}_{\lambda,n}$, let us define the *linear power closure* of $\mathcal{B}$ as the set

$$\overline{\mathcal{B}} = \bigcup_{\phi \in \mathcal{B}} \mathcal{C}_\phi$$

and the *linear span* of $\mathcal{B}$ as the set

$$\langle \mathcal{B} \rangle = \left\{ \sum_{\phi \in \mathcal{B}} a_\phi \phi \mid a_\phi \in \mathbb{F}_{2^\lambda} \right\}.$$

Let f be a function in $\mathcal{F}_{\lambda,n}$. The proposed decomposition makes use of a basis of functions $\mathcal{B} \subseteq \mathcal{F}_{\lambda,n}$ and consists in writing f as:

$$f(x) = \sum_{i=0}^{t-1} g_i(x) \cdot h_i(x) + h_t(x), \tag{5}$$

where $g_i, h_i \in \langle \overline{\mathcal{B}} \rangle$ and $t \in \mathbb{N}$. By definition, the functions g_i and h_i can be written as

$$g_i(x) = \sum_{j=1}^{|\mathcal{B}|} \ell_j(\varphi_j(x)) \quad \text{and} \quad h_i(x) = \sum_{j=1}^{|\mathcal{B}|} \ell'_j(\varphi_j(x)),$$

where the ℓ_j, ℓ'_j are *linearized polynomials* over $\mathcal{F}_{\lambda,n}$ (i.e. polynomials for which the exponents of all the constituent monomials are powers of 2) and where $\{\varphi_j\}_{1 \leq j \leq |\overline{\mathcal{B}}|} = \overline{\mathcal{B}}$. We now explain how to find such a decomposition by solving a linear system.

Solving a Linear System. In the following, we shall consider a basis $\mathcal{B}$ such that $1 \in \mathcal{B}$ and we will denote $\mathcal{B}^* = \mathcal{B} \setminus \{1\} = \{\phi_1, \phi_2, \ldots, \phi_{|\mathcal{B}|-1}\}$. We will further heuristically assume $|\mathcal{C}_{\phi_i}| = \lambda$ for every $i \in \{1, 2, \ldots, |\mathcal{B}| - 1\}$. We then get $|\overline{\mathcal{B}}| = 1 + \lambda|\mathcal{B}^*| = 1 + \lambda(|\mathcal{B}| - 1)$.

We first sample t random functions g_i from $\langle \overline{\mathcal{B}} \rangle$. This is simply done by picking $t \cdot |\overline{\mathcal{B}}|$ random coefficients $a_{i,0}, a_{i,j,k}$ of $\mathbb{F}_{2^\lambda}$ and setting $g_i = a_{i,0} + \sum_{j,k} a_{i,j,k}\phi_j^{2^k}$ for every $i \in [0, t-1]$ where $1 \leq k \leq \lambda$ and $1 \leq j \leq |\mathcal{B}| - 1$. Then we search for a family of $t + 1$ functions $\{h_i\}_i$ satisfying (5). This is done by solving the following system of linear equations over $\mathbb{F}_{2^\lambda}$:

$$A \cdot c = b \tag{6}$$

where $b = (f(e_1), f(e_2), \ldots, f(e_{2^{n\lambda}}))^{\mathsf{T}}$ with $\{e_i\} = \mathbb{F}_{2^\lambda}^n$ and where A is a block matrix defined as

$$A = (\mathbf{1}|A_0|A_1| \cdots |A_t), \tag{7}$$

where $\mathbf{1}$ is the all-one column vector and where

$$A_i = (A_{i,0}|A_{i,1| \cdots |A_{i,|\mathcal{B}|-1}}) \tag{8}$$

with

$$A_{i,0} = (g_i(e_1), g_i(e_2), \ldots, g_i(e_{2^{n\lambda}}))^{\mathsf{T}} \tag{9}$$

for every $i \in [0, t]$, with

$$A_{i,j} = \begin{pmatrix} \phi_j(e_1) \cdot g_i(e_1) & \phi_j^2(e_1) \cdot g_i(e_1) & \cdots & \phi_j^{2^{\lambda-1}}(e_1) \cdot g_i(e_1) \\ \phi_j(e_2) \cdot g_i(e_2) & \phi_j^2(e_2) \cdot g_i(e_2) & \cdots & \phi_j^{2^{\lambda-1}}(e_2) \cdot g_i(e_2) \\ \vdots & \vdots & \ddots & \vdots \\ \phi_j(e_{2^{n\lambda}}) \cdot g_i(e_{2^{n\lambda}}) & \phi_j^2(e_{2^{n\lambda}}) \cdot g_i(e_{2^{n\lambda}}) & \cdots & \phi_j^{2^{\lambda-1}}(e_{2^{n\lambda}}) \cdot g_i(e_{2^{n\lambda}}) \end{pmatrix}, \tag{10}$$

for every $i \in [0, t-1]$ and $j \in [1, |\mathcal{B}| - 1]$, and with

$$A_{t,j} = \begin{pmatrix} \phi_j(e_1) & \phi_j^2(e_1) & \cdots & \phi_j^{2^{\lambda-1}}(e_1) \\ \phi_j(e_2) & \phi_j^2(e_2) & \cdots & \phi_j^{2^{\lambda-1}}(e_2) \\ \vdots & \vdots & \ddots & \vdots \\ \phi_j(e_{2^{n\lambda}}) & \phi_j^2(e_{2^{n\lambda}}) & \cdots & \phi_j^{2^{\lambda-1}}(e_{2^{n\lambda}}) \end{pmatrix}, \tag{11}$$

for every $j \in [1, |\mathcal{B}| - 1]$.

It can be checked that the vector c, solution of the system, gives the coefficients of the h_i's over the basis $\overline{\mathcal{B}}$ (plus the constant term in first position). A necessary condition for this system to have a solution whatever the target vector b (*i.e.* whatever the coordinate function f) is to get a matrix A of full rank. In particular, the following inequality must hold:

$$(t+1)|\overline{\mathcal{B}}| + 1 \geq 2^{n\lambda} . \tag{12}$$

Another necessary condition to get a full-rank matrix is that the squared linear power closure $\overline{\mathcal{B}} \times \overline{\mathcal{B}}$ spans the entire space $\mathcal{F}_{\lambda,n}$. More details about the choice of such basis are discussed in the following.

4.2 S-box Decomposition

Let $\mathcal{S}\colon x \mapsto (f_1(x), f_2(x), \ldots, f_m(x))$ be an s-box. We could apply the above decomposition method to each of the m coordinate functions f_i, which could roughly result in multiplying by m the multiplicative complexity of a single function in $\mathcal{F}_{\lambda,n}$. As suggested in [BMP13, GR16], we can actually do better: the product involved in the decomposition of a coordinate function can be added to the basis for the subsequent decompositions. Specifically, we start with some basis $\mathcal{B}_1$ and, for every $i \geq 1$, we look for a decomposition

$$f_i(x) = \sum_{j=0}^{t_i-1} g_{i,j}(x) \cdot h_{i,j}(x) + h_{i,t_i}(x), \tag{13}$$

where $t_i \in \mathbb{N}$ and $g_{i,j}, h_{i,j} \in \langle \overline{\mathcal{B}_i} \rangle$. Once such a decomposition has been found, we carry on with the new basis $\mathcal{B}_{i+1}$ defined as:

$$\mathcal{B}_{i+1} = \mathcal{B}_i \cup \{g_{i,j} \cdot h_{i,j}\}_{j=0}^{t_i-1}. \tag{14}$$

This update process implies that, for each decomposition, the basis grows and hence the number t_i of multiplicative terms in the decomposition of f_i might decrease. In this context, the necessary condition on the matrix rank (see (12)) is different for every i. In particular, the number t_i of multiplications at step i satisfies:

$$t_i \geq \frac{2^{n\lambda} - 1}{\lambda|\mathcal{B}_i^*| + 1} - 1 , \tag{15}$$

where as above $\mathcal{B}_i^*$ stands for $\mathcal{B}_i \setminus \{1\}$.

4.3 Basis Selection

Let us recall that the basis $\mathcal{B}_1$ needs to be such that the squared basis $\overline{\mathcal{B}}_1 \times \overline{\mathcal{B}}_1$ spans the entire space $\mathcal{F}_{\lambda,n}$, *i.e.* $\langle \overline{\mathcal{B}}_1 \times \overline{\mathcal{B}}_1 \rangle = \mathcal{F}_{\lambda,n}$ in order to have a solvable linear system. This is called the *spanning property* in the following. This property can be rewritten in terms of linear algebra. For every $\mathcal{S} \subseteq \mathcal{F}_{\lambda,n}$, let us define $\mathrm{Mat}(\mathcal{S})$

as the $(\lambda n \times |\mathcal{S}|)$-matrix for which each column corresponds to the evaluation of one function of $\mathcal{S}$ in every point of $\mathbb{F}_{2^\lambda}^n$, that is

$$
\mathrm{Mat}(\mathcal{S}) = \begin{pmatrix}
\varphi_1(e_1) & \varphi_2(e_1) & \cdots & \varphi_{|\mathcal{S}|}(e_1) \\
\varphi_1(e_2) & \varphi_2(e_2) & \cdots & \varphi_{|\mathcal{S}|}(e_2) \\
& & & \\
\vdots & \vdots & \ddots & \vdots \\
& & & \\
\varphi_1(e_{2^{n\lambda}}) & \varphi_2(e_{2^{n\lambda}}) & \cdots & \varphi_{|\mathcal{S}|}(e_{2^{n\lambda}})
\end{pmatrix}, \tag{16}
$$

where $\{\varphi_1, \varphi_2, \ldots, \varphi_{|\mathcal{S}|}\} = \mathcal{S}$. Then, we have

$$
\langle \overline{\mathcal{B}}_1 \times \overline{\mathcal{B}}_1 \rangle = \mathcal{F}_{\lambda,n} \iff \mathrm{rank}(\mathrm{Mat}(\overline{\mathcal{B}}_1 \times \overline{\mathcal{B}}_1)) = 2^{\lambda n}. \tag{17}
$$

To construct the basis $\mathcal{B}_1$, we proceed as follows. We start with the basis composed of all monomials of degree 1 plus unity, *i.e.* the following basis:

$$
\mathcal{B}_1 = \{1, x_1, x_2, \ldots, x_n\}. \tag{18}
$$

Then, we iterate $\mathcal{B}_1 \leftarrow \mathcal{B}_1 \cup \{\phi \cdot \psi\}$, where ϕ and ψ are randomly sampled from $\langle \overline{\mathcal{B}}_1 \rangle$ until reaching a basis with the desired cardinality and satisfying $\mathrm{rank}(\mathrm{Mat}(\overline{\mathcal{B}}_1 \times \overline{\mathcal{B}}_1)) \geq 2^{\lambda n}$. We add the constraint that, at each iteration, a certain amount of possible products are tried and only the best product is added to the basis, namely the one inducing the greatest increase in the rank of $\mathrm{Mat}(\overline{\mathcal{B}}_1 \times \overline{\mathcal{B}}_1)$. To summarize, the construction of the basis $\mathcal{B}_1$ is given in the following algorithm:

Algorithm 1. $\mathcal{B}_1$ construction algorithm

Input: Parameters λ, n, and N
Output: A basis $\mathcal{B}_1$ such that $\langle \overline{\mathcal{B}}_1 \times \overline{\mathcal{B}}_1 \rangle = \mathcal{F}_{\lambda,n}$
1. $\mathcal{B}_1 = \{1, x_1, x_2 \ldots, x_n\}$
2. $\mathrm{rank} = 0$
3. **while** $\mathrm{rank} < 2^{n\lambda}$ **do**
4.   **for** $i = 1$ to N **do**
5. $\phi, \psi \xleftarrow{\$} \langle \overline{\mathcal{B}}_1 \rangle$
6. $\mathcal{S}_i \leftarrow \mathcal{B}_1 \cup \{\phi \cdot \psi\}$
7. $r_i \leftarrow \mathrm{rank}(\mathrm{Mat}(\mathcal{S}_i \times \mathcal{S}_i))$
8.   **end for**
9. $j \leftarrow \mathrm{argmax}\ r_i$
10.   **if** $r_j = \mathrm{rank}$ **then**
11.   **return** error
12.   **end if**
13. $\mathrm{rank} \leftarrow r_j$
14. $\mathcal{B}_1 \leftarrow \mathcal{S}_j$
15. **end while**
16. **return** $\mathcal{B}_1$

Remark 2. In [GR16], the starting basis $\mathcal{B}_1$ is constructed from a basis $\mathcal{B}_0$ that has the spanning property by design. In practice, the optimal parameters for s-boxes are always obtained by taking $\mathcal{B}_1 = \mathcal{B}_0$ and could be improved with a smaller basis. Our experiments showed that we can achieve a smaller basis $\mathcal{B}_1$ with the spanning property (hence slightly improving the optimal parameters from [GR16]) with a random generation as described above. For instance, in the Boolean case applied on a 8-bit s-box, Algorithm 1 easily finds a basis $\mathcal{B}_1$ of 26 elements (involving 17 multiplications) instead of 31 by taking $\mathcal{B}_1 = \mathcal{B}_0$ as in [GR16].

4.4   Optimal Parameters

Assuming that satisfying the lower bound on t_i (see (15)) is sufficient to get a full-rank system, we can deduce optimal parameters for our generalized decomposition method. Specifically, if we denote $s_i = |\mathcal{B}_i^*|$, we get a sequence $(s_i)_i$ that satisfies

$$\begin{cases} s_1 = r + n \\ s_{i+1} = s_i + t_i \quad \text{with} \quad t_i = \left\lceil \frac{2^{n\lambda}-1}{\lambda s_i + 1} \right\rceil - 1 \end{cases} \tag{19}$$

for $i = 1$ to $m-1$, where r denotes the number of multiplications involved in the construction of the first basis $\mathcal{B}_1$ (the n *free* elements of $\mathcal{B}_1$ being the monomials $x_1, x_2, \ldots, x_n$). From this sequence, we can determine the optimal multiplicative complexity of the method C^* which then satisfies

$$C^* = \min_{r \geq r_0}(r + t_1 + t_2 + \cdots + t_m) , \tag{20}$$

where r_0 denotes the minimal value of r for which we can get an initial basis $\mathcal{B}_1$ satisfying the spanning property (that is $\langle \overline{\mathcal{B}}_1 \times \overline{\mathcal{B}}_1 \rangle = \mathcal{F}_{\lambda,n}$) and where the t_i's are viewed as functions of r according to the sequence (19).

Table 1 provides a set of optimal parameters r, t_1, t_2, ..., t_m and corresponding C^* for several s-box sizes and several parameters λ and $n = m$ (as for bijective s-boxes). For the sake of completeness, we included the extreme cases $n = 1$, *i.e.* standard CRV method [CRV14], and $\lambda = 1$, *i.e.* Boolean case [GR16]. We obtain the same results as in [CRV14] for the standard CRV method. For the Boolean case, our results slightly differ from [GR16]. This is due to our improved generation of $\mathcal{B}_1$ (see Remark 2) and to our bound on the t_i's (see (15)) which is slightly more accurate than in [GR16].

Table 2 gives the size of the smallest randomised basis we could *achieve* using Algorithm 1 for various parameters. The number of tries made was $N = 1000$ before adding a product of random linear combination to the current basis.

5   Experimental Results

In this section, we report the concrete parameters for random and specific s-boxes achieved using our generalized decomposition method. Table 3 compares

Table 1. Theoretical optimal parameters for our decomposition method.

(λ, n)	$|\mathcal{B}_1|$	r	$t_1, t_2, \ldots, t_n$	C^*
4-bit s-boxes				
(1,4)	7	2	2,1,1,1	7
	8	3	1,1,1,1	7
	9	4	1,1,1,1	8
(2,2)	4	1	2,1	4
	5	2	1,1	4
	6	3	1,1	5
(4,1)	3	1	1	2
	4	2	1	3
6-bit s-boxes				
(1,6)	14	7	4,3,2,2,2,2	22
	15	8	4,3,2,2,2,2	23
(2,3)	8	4	4,2,2	12
	9	5	3,2,2	12
	10	6	3,2,2	13
(3,2)	6	3	3,2	8
	7	4	3,2	9
	8	5	2,2	9
(6,1)	4	2	3	5
	5	3	2	5
	6	4	2	6
8-bit s-boxes				
(1,8)	24	17	9,7,6,5,4,4,4,3	59
	25	18	9,7,5,5,4,4,4,3	59
	28	19	9,6,5,5,4,4,4,3	59
	29	20	8,6,5,5,4,4,4,3	59
	30	21	8,6,5,5,4,4,4,3	60
(2,4)	15	9	9,5,4,4	31
	16	10	8,5,4,4	31
	17	11	8,5,4,3	31
	18	12	7,5,4,3	31
	19	13	7,5,4,3	32
(4,2)	8	5	8,4	17
	9	6	7,4	17
	10	7	6,4	17
	11	8	6,3	17
	12	9	5,3	17
	13	10	5,3	18
(8,1)	5	3	7	10
	6	4	6	10
	7	5	5	10
	8	6	4	10
	9	7	3	10
	10	8	3	11

(λ, n)	$|\mathcal{B}_1|$	r	$t_1, t_2, \ldots, t_n$	C^*
9-bit s-boxes				
(1,9)	35	25	14,10,8,7,6,6,5,5,5	91
	36	26	14,10,8,7,6,6,5,5,5	92
	37	27	13,10,8,7,6,6,5,5,5	92
(3,3)	13	9	13,6,5	33
	14	10	12,6,5	33
	15	11	11,6,5	33
	16	12	11,6,5	34
(9,1)	8	6	7	13
	9	7	6	13
	10	8	6	14
10-bit s-boxes				
(1,10)	49	38	20,14,12,10,9,8,8,7,7,7	140
	50	39	20,14,12,10,9,8,8,7,7,7	141
	51	40	20,14,12,10,9,8,8,7,7,7	142
(2,5)	25	19	20,11,9,7,7	73
	26	20	20,11,9,7,7	74
	27	21	19,11,9,7,7	74
(5,2)	13	10	16,7	33
	14	11	15,7	33
	15	12	14,7	33
	16	13	13,7	33
	17	14	12,7	33
	18	15	11,7	33
	19	16	11,7	34
(10,1)	9	7	12	19
	10	8	11	19
	11	9	10	19
	12	10	9	19
	13	11	8	19
	14	12	7	19
	15	13	7	20

the achievable parameters vs. the optimal estimate for random s-boxes. Note that in the table, the parameters $|\mathcal{B}_1|$, r, $t_1, t_2, \ldots, t_n$ correspond to the parameters in the achievable decomposition for randomly chosen s-boxes. The last column gives the probability of obtaining a successful decomposition for random S-boxes and for randomly chosen coefficients in the basis computation as well as the

Table 2. Achievable smallest randomised basis computed according to Algorithm 1.

	4-bit s-boxes			5-bit s-boxes		6-bit s-boxes				7-bit s-boxes	
(λ, n)	(1,4)	(2,2)	(4,1)	(1,5)	(5,1)	(1,6)	(2,3)	(3,2)	(6,1)	(1,7)	(7,1)
$|\mathcal{B}_1|$	7	4	3	10	4	14	8	6	4	19	4
r	2	1	1	4	2	7	4	3	2	11	2

	8-bit s-boxes				9-bit s-boxes			10-bit s-boxes			
(λ, n)	(1,8)	(2,4)	(4,2)	(8,1)	(1,9)	(3,3)	(9,1)	(1,10)	(2,5)	(5,2)	(10,1)
$|\mathcal{B}_1|$	26	14	8	5	35	13	5	49	25	11	6
r	17	9	5	3	25	9	3	38	19	8	4

decomposition step. In all the cases 10 trials each were made to compute the probabilities except for the decomposition of 8-bit S-boxes over $\mathbb{F}_{2^2}$ where 100 trials each were made.

In the experiments, successive basis elements were added by products of random linear combinations of elements from the current basis. The basis $\mathcal{B}_1$ was chosen such that the corresponding matrix for the first coordinate function resulted in full rank (implying that the spanning property of the basis $\mathcal{B}_1$ was satisfied). The basis was successively updated with the t_i products formed in the decomposition step of the ith coordinate function. While the parameter t_1 is invariant of the chosen s-box, the other t_i are indeed dependent on it. As we see from Table 3, the probabilities increase with the size of the field used for the decomposition.

Table 3. Optimal and achievable parameters for random s-boxes.

Optimal/Achievable	(λ, n)	$|\mathcal{B}_1|$	r	$t_1, t_2, \ldots, t_n$	C^*	proba.
4-bit s-boxes						
Optimal	(2,2)	5	2	1,1	4	-
Achievable	(2,2)	5	2	1,1	4	0.2
6-bit s-boxes						
Optimal	(2,3)	8	4	4,2,2	12	-
Achievable	(2,3)	8	4	5,2,2	13	0.3
Optimal	(3,2)	6	3	3,2	8	-
Achievable	(3,2)	6	3	4,2	9	0.9
8-bit s-boxes						
Optimal	(2,4)	16	11	8,5,4,3	31	-
Achievable	(2,4)	16	11	9,6,5,3	34	0.02
Optimal	(4,2)	10	7	6,4	17	-
Achievable	(4,2)	10	7	7,4	18	1.0
9-bit s-boxes						
Optimal	(3,3)	15	11	11,6,5	33	-
Achievable	(3,3)	15	11	14,6,5	36	0.8

Table 4 gives the concrete parameters to achieve decomposition for s-boxes of popular block ciphers (namely PRESENT [BKL+07], DES S1 and S8 [DES77], SC2000 S6 [SYY+02], CLEFIA S0 and S1 [SSA+07] and KHAZAD [BR00]). Note that for all the cases considered the parameters from Table 4 yield a decomposition. As above, the last column of the table gives the success probability over the random choice of the coefficients in the basis computation as well as the decomposition step. In all the cases 10 trials each were made to compute the probabilities except for the decomposition of 8-bit S-boxes over $\mathbb{F}_{2^2}$ where 100 trials each were made.

Table 4. Achievable parameters to decompose specific s-boxes.

s-box		(λ, n)	$|\mathcal{B}_1|$	r	$t_1, t_2, \ldots, t_n$	C^*	proba.
4-bit s-boxes							
PRESENT	[BKL+07]	(2,2)	5	2	1,1	4	0.3
(6,4)-bit s-boxes							
DES S1	[DES77]	(2,3)	7	4	5,2	11	0.3
DES S8	[DES77]	(2,3)	7	4	5,2	11	0.5
6-bit s-boxes							
SC2000 S6	[SYY+02]	(2,3)	8	4	5,2,2	13	0.2
SC2000 S6	[SYY+02]	(3,2)	6	3	4,2	9	0.8
8-bit s-boxes							
CLEFIA S0	[SSA+07]	(4,2)	10	7	7,4	18	1.0
CLEFIA S0	[SSA+07]	(2,4)	16	11	9,5,4,3	32	0.01
CLEFIA S1	[SSA+07]	(4,2)	10	7	7,4	18	1.0
CLEFIA S1	[SSA+07]	(2,4)	16	11	9,6,5,3	34	0.01
KHAZAD	[BR00]	(4,2)	10	7	7,4	18	1.0
KHAZAD	[BR00]	(2,4)	16	11	9,5,4,3	32	0.02

6   Implementation

Based on our generic decomposition method, we now describe our implementation of an s-box layer protected with higher-order masking in ARM v7. We focused our study on the common scenario of a layer applying 16 8-bit s-boxes to a 128-bit state. We apply our generalized decomposition with parameters $n = m = 2$ and $\lambda = 4$ (medium case) to compare the obtained implementation to the ones for the two extreme cases:

- **Plain field case** ($\lambda = 8$, $n = 1$): standard CRV decomposition [CRV14];
- **Boolean case** ($\lambda = 1$, $n = 8$): Boolean decomposition from [GR16].

Our implementation is based on the decomposition obtained for the CLEFIA S0 s-box with parameters $(r, t_1, t_2) = (7, 7, 4)$. Note that it would have the same performances with any other 8-bit s-box with the same decomposition parameters (which we validate on all our tested random 8-bit s-boxes). The input (x_1, x_2) of each s-box is shared as $([x_1], [x_2])$ where

$$[x_i] = (x_{i,1}, x_{i,2}, \ldots, x_{i,d}) \quad \text{such that} \quad \sum_{j=1}^{d} x_{i,j} = x_i. \tag{21}$$

Note that for those chosen parameters (n, m, λ), the input x_1 and x_2 are 4-bit elements, *i.e.* the inputs of the 8-bit s-boxes are split into 2. The output of the computation is a pair $([y_1], [y_2])$ where y_1 and y_2 are the two 4-bit coordinates of the s-box output.

We start from a basis that contains the input sharings $\{[z_1], [z_2]\} = \{[x_1], [x_2]\}$. Then for $i = 3$ to 21 each of the 18 multiplications is performed between two linear combinations of the elements of the basis, that is

$$[z_i] = [u_i] \odot [v_i] , \tag{22}$$

where $\odot$ denotes the ISW multiplication with refreshing of one of the operand (see [GR17] for details) and where

$$u_{i,j} = \sum_{k<i} \ell_{i,k}(z_{k,j}) \quad \text{and} \quad v_{i,j} = \sum_{k<i} \ell'_{i,k}(z_{k,j}) \text{ for every } j \in [1, d], \tag{23}$$

for some linearized polynomials $\ell_{i,k}$ and $\ell'_{i,k}$ obtained from the s-box decomposition. Once all the products have been computed, the output sharings $[y_1]$ and $[y_2]$ are simple linear combinations of the computed $[z_i]$.

To make the most of the 32-bit architecture, the s-box evaluations are done eight-by-eight since we can fill a register with eight 4-bit elements. The ISW-based multiplications can then be parallelized as suggested in [GR17] except for the field multiplications between two shares. To perform those multiplications, we simply need to unpack the eight 4-bit elements in each 32-bit operand, and then to sequentially perform the 8 field multiplications. These field multiplications are fully tabulated which only takes 0.25 KB of ROM on $\mathbb{F}_{16}$ (following the results of [GR17]). Using such a degree-8 parallelized ISW multiplication allows to improve by 58% the asymptotic gain compared to 8 serials ISW multiplications [GR17].

Table 5. Performances in clock cycles.

	CRV [GR17]	Bitslice Decomposition [GR16]	Our implementations
	$4 \times 4 /\!/$ s-boxes	$16 /\!/$ s-boxes	$2 \times 8 /\!/$ s-boxes
Clock Cycle	$2576\, d^2 + 5476\, d + 2528$	$656\, d^2 + 19786\, d + 5764$	$2757\, d^2 + 17671\, d + 2402$
Code size	27.5 KB	4.6 KB	8.7 KB
RAM	$80d$ bytes	$644d$ bytes	$92d$ bytes
Random usage	$28d^2 - 28$ bytes	$61d^2 - 61$ bytes	$28d^2 - 28$ bytes

We compare our results with the bitslice implementation from [GR16] and the CRV-based optimized implementation from [GR17]. The former evaluates 16 s-boxes in parallel (based on bitslicing), whereas the latter performs 4 times 4 s-boxes in parallel (by filling 32-bits registers with four 8-bit elements). Table 5 summarizes the obtained performances in terms clock cycles, RAM consumption, and the random usage (needed by both the ISW multiplication and the refreshing procedure) with respect to the masking order d and in terms of code size (including the look-up tables).

These results show that our implementation is slightly less efficient in terms of timings (Fig. 1). However, it provides an interesting tradeoff in terms of memory consumption. Indeed the bitslice implementation has the drawback of being quite consuming in terms of RAM (with $644d$ bytes needed) and the CRV-based implementation has the drawback of having an important code size (27.5 KB) which is mainly due to the *half-table* multiplication and the tabulation linearized polynomials over $\mathbb{F}_{256}$. Our implementation offers a nice alternative when both RAM and code size are constrained. It also needs the same amount of randomness than the CRV decomposition and more than twice less than the bitslice decomposition.

Additionally, implementations based on our medium case decomposition might provide further interesting tradeoffs on smaller (8-bit or 16-bit) architectures where bitslice would be slowed down and where the optimized CRV-based implementation from [GR17] might be too consuming in terms of code size.

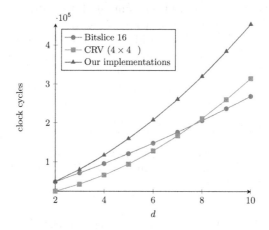

Fig. 1. Timings for $n = 8$.

Acknowledgements. We would like to thank Jürgen Pulkus for helpful discussions regarding choosing basis elements as random products. We would also like to thank the anonymous reviewers of CHES 2017 for valuable feedback that helped to improve the paper. Srinivas Vivek's work was partially supported by the European Union's H2020 Programme under grant agreement number ICT-644209 (HEAT).

References

[BBP+16] Belaïd, S., Benhamouda, F., Passelègue, A., Prouff, E., Thillard, A., Vergnaud, D.: Randomness complexity of private circuits for multiplication. In: Fischlin, M., Coron, J.-S. (eds.) EUROCRYPT 2016. LNCS, vol. 9666, pp. 616–648. Springer, Heidelberg (2016). doi:10.1007/978-3-662-49896-5_22

[BKL+07] Bogdanov, A., Knudsen, L.R., Leander, G., Paar, C., Poschmann, A., Robshaw, M.J.B., Seurin, Y., Vikkelsoe, C.: PRESENT: an ultra-lightweight block cipher. In: Paillier, P., Verbauwhede, I. (eds.) CHES 2007. LNCS, vol. 4727, pp. 450–466. Springer, Heidelberg (2007). doi:10.1007/978-3-540-74735-2_31

[BMP13] Boyar, J., Matthews, P., Peralta, R.: Logic minimization techniques with applications to cryptology. J. Cryptol. **26**(2), 280–312 (2013)

[BR00] Barreto, P., Rijmen, V.: The Khazad legacy-level block cipher. First Open NESSIE Workshop, KU-Leuven (2000). http://www.cosic.esat.kuleuven.ac.be/nessie/

[CGP+12] Carlet, C., Goubin, L., Prouff, E., Quisquater, M., Rivain, M.: Higher-order masking schemes for S-Boxes. In: Canteaut, A. (ed.) FSE 2012. LNCS, vol. 7549, pp. 366–384. Springer, Heidelberg (2012). doi:10.1007/978-3-642-34047-5_21

[CJRR99] Chari, S., Jutla, C.S., Rao, J.R., Rohatgi, P.: Towards sound approaches to counteract power-analysis attacks. In: Wiener, M. (ed.) CRYPTO 1999. LNCS, vol. 1666, pp. 398–412. Springer, Heidelberg (1999). doi:10.1007/3-540-48405-1_26

[CRV14] Coron, J.-S., Roy, A., Vivek, S.: Fast evaluation of polynomials over binary finite fields and application to side-channel countermeasures. In: Batina, L., Robshaw, M. (eds.) CHES 2014. LNCS, vol. 8731, pp. 170–187. Springer, Heidelberg (2014). doi:10.1007/978-3-662-44709-3_10

[DDF14] Duc, A., Dziembowski, S., Faust, S.: Unifying leakage models: from probing attacks to noisy leakage. In: Nguyen, P.Q., Oswald, E. (eds.) EUROCRYPT 2014. LNCS, vol. 8441, pp. 423–440. Springer, Heidelberg (2014). doi:10.1007/978-3-642-55220-5_24

[DES77] Data encryption standard. National Bureau of Standards, NBS FIPS PUB 46, U.S. Department of Commerce, January 1977

[GP99] Goubin, L., Patarin, J.: DES and differential power analysis the "Duplication" method. In: Koç, Ç.K., Paar, C. (eds.) CHES 1999. LNCS, vol. 1717, pp. 158–172. Springer, Heidelberg (1999). doi:10.1007/3-540-48059-5_15

[GR16] Goudarzi, D., Rivain, M.: On the multiplicative complexity of boolean functions and bitsliced higher-order masking. In: Gierlichs, B., Poschmann, A.Y. (eds.) CHES 2016. LNCS, vol. 9813, pp. 457–478. Springer, Heidelberg (2016). doi:10.1007/978-3-662-53140-2_22

[GR17] Goudarzi, D., Rivain, M.: How fast can higher-order masking be in software? In: Coron, J.-S., Nielsen, J.B. (eds.) EUROCRYPT 2017. LNCS, vol. 10210, pp. 567–597. Springer, Cham (2017). doi:10.1007/978-3-319-56620-7_20

[ISW03] Ishai, Y., Sahai, A., Wagner, D.: Private circuits: securing hardware against probing attacks. In: Boneh, D. (ed.) CRYPTO 2003. LNCS, vol. 2729, pp. 463–481. Springer, Heidelberg (2003). doi:10.1007/978-3-540-45146-4_27

[KJJ99] Kocher, P., Jaffe, J., Jun, B.: Differential power analysis. In: Wiener, M. (ed.) CRYPTO 1999. LNCS, vol. 1666, pp. 388–397. Springer, Heidelberg (1999). doi:10.1007/3-540-48405-1_25

[Koc96] Kocher, P.C.: Timing attacks on implementations of Diffie-Hellman, RSA, DSS, and other systems. In: Koblitz, N. (ed.) CRYPTO 1996. LNCS, vol. 1109, pp. 104–113. Springer, Heidelberg (1996). doi:10.1007/3-540-68697-5_9

[PR13] Prouff, E., Rivain, M.: Masking against side-channel attacks: a formal security proof. In: Johansson, T., Nguyen, P.Q. (eds.) EUROCRYPT 2013. LNCS, vol. 7881, pp. 142–159. Springer, Heidelberg (2013). doi:10.1007/978-3-642-38348-9_9

[PS73] Paterson, M., Stockmeyer, L.J.: On the number of nonscalar multiplications necessary to evaluate polynomials. SIAM J. Comput. 2(1), 60–66 (1973)

[PV16] Pulkus, J., Vivek, S.: Reducing the number of non-linear multiplications in masking schemes. In: Gierlichs, B., Poschmann, A.Y. (eds.) CHES 2016. LNCS, vol. 9813, pp. 479–497. Springer, Heidelberg (2016). doi:10.1007/978-3-662-53140-2_23

[RP10] Rivain, M., Prouff, E.: Provably secure higher-order masking of AES. In: Mangard, S., Standaert, F.-X. (eds.) CHES 2010. LNCS, vol. 6225, pp. 413–427. Springer, Heidelberg (2010). doi:10.1007/978-3-642-15031-9_28

[RV13] Roy, A., Vivek, S.: Analysis and improvement of the generic higher-order masking scheme of FSE 2012. In: Bertoni, G., Coron, J.-S. (eds.) CHES 2013. LNCS, vol. 8086, pp. 417–434. Springer, Heidelberg (2013). doi:10.1007/978-3-642-40349-1_24

[SSA+07] Shirai, T., Shibutani, K., Akishita, T., Moriai, S., Iwata, T.: The 128-bit blockcipher CLEFIA (Extended Abstract). In: Biryukov, A. (ed.) FSE 2007. LNCS, vol. 4593, pp. 181–195. Springer, Heidelberg (2007). doi:10.1007/978-3-540-74619-5_12

[SYY+02] Shimoyama, T., Yanami, H., Yokoyama, K., Takenaka, M., Itoh, K., Yajima, J., Torii, N., Tanaka, H.: The block cipher SC2000. In: Matsui, M. (ed.) FSE 2001. LNCS, vol. 2355, pp. 312–327. Springer, Heidelberg (2002). doi:10.1007/3-540-45473-X_26

Emerging Attacks I

Nanofocused X-Ray Beam to Reprogram Secure Circuits

Stéphanie Anceau[1,2], Pierre Bleuet[1,2], Jessy Clédière[1,2(✉)],
Laurent Maingault[1,2], Jean-luc Rainard[1,2], and Rémi Tucoulou[3]

[1] University of Grenoble Alpes, 38000 Grenoble, France
[2] CEA, LETI, MINATEC Campus, 38054 Grenoble, France
{stephanie.anceau,pierre.bleuet,jessy.clediere,laurent.maingault,
jean-luc.rainard}@cea.fr
[3] ESRF, The European Synchrotron, 71 Avenue des Martyrs,
38043 Grenoble, France
tucoulou@esrf.fr

Abstract. Synchrotron-based X-ray nanobeams are investigated as a tool to perturb microcontroller circuits. An intense hard X-ray focused beam of a few tens of nanometers is used to target the flash, EEP-ROM and RAM memory of a circuit. The obtained results show that it is possible to corrupt a single transistor in a semi-permanent state. A simple heat treatment can remove the induced effect, thus making the corruption reversible. An attack on a code stored in flash demonstrates unambiguously that this new technique can be a threat to the security of integrated circuits.

Keywords: X-ray · Flash · EEPROM · RAM · ATmega · Circuit edit · MOS Stuck-At

1 Introduction

The need to increase the level of digital security standards requires a sustained research effort on new means of perturbations likely to disturb the processing of integrated circuits. The possibility of using visible and IR light was revealed by Skorobogatov and Anderson [1]. The physical phenomena have been studied and explained by the failure-analysis community [2–5]. Laser light can be synchronized and focused in order to induce transient faults. In the security-evaluation practice, these faults may give powerful results. Electromagnetic radiation perturbation allows a new breach that corrupts circuits [6–8]. Access to the circuit is less restrictive since depackaging is not necessarily required.

In order to further investigate the wavelength spectrum of perturbations, it is proposed here to study the effects of ionizing radiation like X-rays. For one thing, hard X-rays offer the great advantage of deeply penetrating through materials. Every embedded component within the chip can be reached compared to only the silicon substrate and doped regions with visible or IR light. X-ray interaction

© International Association for Cryptologic Research 2017
W. Fischer and N. Homma (Eds.): CHES 2017, LNCS 10529, pp. 175–188, 2017.
DOI: 10.1007/978-3-319-66787-4_9

with electronic circuits has been analyzed [9–12], but its use for security evaluation has been mainly restricted to die and package imaging, and an occasional mention as a perturbation means without practical or successful results [13,14]. Focusing exclusively on a selected area of the device under test may be seen as the ultimate goal of a perturbation technique and the lack of practical tests in the literature may be due to the difficulty to focus these high energy photons down to the nanoscale. The recent advent of third-generation synchrotron nano-probe beamlines makes possible to focus hard X-ray beams down to a few tens of nanometers. This paves the way to single transistor corruption during operando experiments. It must be mentioned that the work detailed hereafter is unprecedented, mostly because such beamlines have existed for only a few years; before that, only micro-focusing was possible, i.e. single-transistor irradiation was simply impossible.

The experimental setup, the physics of the X-ray interaction with MOS transistors and the possibility of using fluorescence techniques are detailed in Sect. 2. Experimental results are given on an ATmega1284P circuit in Sect. 3 for RAM, flash and EEPROM memory blocks. A real attack on this circuit for flash is reported in Sect. 4, demonstrating the possibility of permanently modifying the code of an application. The conclusion outlines all the potential of using X-ray in the security-testing domain.

2   Nanofocused X-Ray Beam

2.1   Experiment Setup

A very intense multi-keV X-ray nanobeam is required to perform single-transistor X-ray corruption, to profit from high penetration depth and locally create a sufficient number of photo-electrons to induce faults. Unfortunately, hard X-ray beams featuring decananometer resolution are unachievable today using laboratory systems. Moreover, the extreme brilliance of new third-generation synchrotron long beamlines, combined with high-efficiency X-ray focusing optics, offers completely new possibilities in terms of X-ray characterization and X-ray-based attacks. The work detailed in this paper is based entirely on the use of the ID16B beamline at the European Synchrotron Radiation Facility (ESRF) fully described by Martinez-Criado et al. [15]. For readers' convenience, the general principle of the X-ray microscope and essential numbers follow: the low-divergence X-ray source located in the main storage ring of the ESRF (844 m circumference) is demagnified using Kirkpatrick-Baez optics located 165 m from the source. This optical scheme produces a beam of $60 \times 60 \, \text{nm}^2$ (full width at half minimum [FWHM]) in the case of the results detailed in this paper, with a high monochromaticity (18 keV, $\Delta E/E \approx 10^{-4}$) and a photon flux of $2 \times 10^9 \, \text{ph/s}$. The brilliance is high enough to generate very locally a significant number of electrons (called X-ray beam induced current or XBIC) able to induce faults, and the probe is sufficiently local even for the latest nanoelectronic nodes. On top of that, a comfortable working space around the sample enables performing operando experiments and accommodating X-ray detectors. It operates in ambient air, i.e. with no vacuum constraint. It is therefore well suited for the experiment described here. A rough overview of the optical scheme is shown in Fig. 1, with horizontal and vertical planes of the beam, the characteristic distances in meters, and a picture of the space between the optics and the sample.

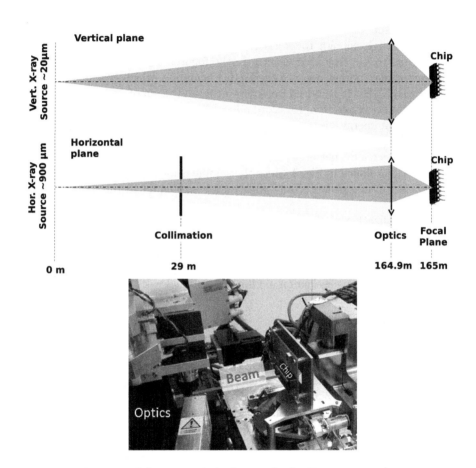

Fig. 1. ID16B setup. Schematic of the line with the X-ray source (sizes are given FWHM), optics (Kirkpatrick-Baez) and device under test (chip) in the focal plane. Space between optics and the chip.

There are nearly 50 synchrotrons worlwide, including three very large facilities (ESRF in Europe, APS in USA and Spring-8 in Japan) operating multi-GeV storage rings; very few beamlines in the world can operate sub-100 nm beams with hard X-rays.

2.2   Local Positioning on the Device Under Test by X-Ray Fluorescence

The ID16B test-bench is equipped with a long working distance optical microscope aligned with the X-ray beam and having its focal plane coplanar with the one from the X-ray microscope, allowing a pre-positioning on the sample surface (10 × magnification, field of view of $1 \times 1 \, \text{mm}^2$). Obviously, this visible-light microscope can be used only if the circuit packaging has been removed.

Although the visible-light microscope is ideal for pre-localization, its resolution is not high enough to precisely locate the transistors and therefore to place the one to be irradiated exactly in the focused X-ray beam. Fine-tuning is required using another asset of the ID16B beamline, which is scanning X-ray fluorescence (XRF). It is indeed possible to run a 2D scan of a region of interest (ROI) and, at every position, to record a local X-ray fluorescence spectrum using a multi-element energy-dispersive detector. A 2D map is obtained for each chemical element in the sample. These maps can be obtained either by selecting a peak in the spectra or, better, by fitting background and peaks using the PyMca software [16], as shown in Fig. 2. Since the sample is located in the common focal plane, it can be mapped precisely with a step size equal to the focused beam size.

XRF visualization mode can be particularly interesting when addressing an unknown circuit or when the attacker does not want to open the circuit's packaging. Results on ATmega1284P presented in this paper are obtained with a front-side opened circuit. However, it can also be performed without opening the package, as it was checked on a Thin Quad Flat Package (TQFP).

2.3   X-Ray Interaction

At 18 keV, the photoelectric effect is the main contributor driving the X-ray absorption in semiconductor materials. The absorption coefficient greatly varies with the atomic number (Z). A regular silicon chip is composed of very thin layers of possibly high-Z metals (W, Au) and thicker layers of small atomic number elements (Si, O, N), in which hard X-rays are weakly absorbed. They can therefore deeply penetrate into the device and reach logic gates with irradiation from the top surface or even through the package. After absorption, a high number of carriers are generated within the material. These localized carriers can deeply perturb an operating chip, especially when absorption occurs in the oxide layers. It should be noted that it is impossible to generate carriers in the oxide with an IR laser. Oxide band gaps are much larger than IR photon energy. Depending on the types of gates that are targeted, two effects are of interest with X-rays:

- charge trappings in insulating layers, inducing V_t shifts in MOS transistors
- photoemission of carriers stored in floating gates.

These effects have been extensively studied [9–12,17–28], especially for aerospace applications, in which radiation naturally occurs and prevents chips

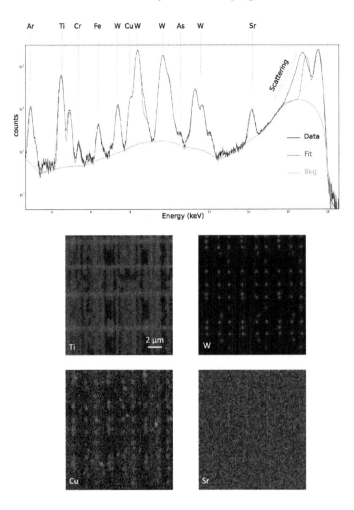

Fig. 2. Typical fluorescence spectrum (log scale) of the ATmega circuit (top). The energy unit is keV. It shows the sum of all measured spectra (black) and the corresponding fitted sum spectrum and background (blue and green, respectively). The scattering peak mismatch at 18 keV is due to multiple Compton scattering (only first-order Compton scattering is modeled). The Ar peak at low energy comes from the Ar naturally present in air. A selection of elemental 2D mappings for Ti, W, Cu and Sr is shown below. (Color figure online)

from functioning properly. This paper gives a short summary of the most important effects, focusing on the application for circuit perturbations and the two types of memory in the experiment.

Charge Trapping. Electron-hole pairs created by X-rays are separated by the electric field applied to the grid: electrons are drained away through the grid thanks to their higher mobility, while lower mobility holes move inside the oxide towards the transistor channel. Reaching the Si/SiO$_2$ interface, holes can be trapped into defect sites, which are numerous at this interface. This positive charge accumulated near the transistor channel results in a shift of $I_D(V_{GS})$ curves to lower gate voltages (Fig. 3). From an electrical point of view:

– a NMOS transistor becomes more easily conducting, even permanently conducting
– a PMOS transistor becomes less easily conducting, even permanently blocking.

This is a total ionizing dose (TID) effect: the more the device is irradiated, the more holes are trapped and curves shifted (Fig. 3). Also, trapped charges can escape when temperature is increased thanks to thermal excitation. Thermal annealing can restore normal behavior of irradiated devices. As a result, these faults can be viewed as "semi-permanent faults": "permanent" as its effect remains after irradiation has ceased, and "semi" because annealing can restore the chip to a normal-state.

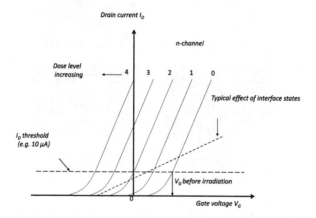

Fig. 3. Effect of dose level increasing (1 to 4, arbitrary unit) on $I_D(V_{GS})$ of a NMOS device (extracted from [29]). The more the dose is increased, the greater the shift of $I_D(V_{GS})$ curve toward lower gate voltages. The NMOS transistor becomes more easily conducting, even permanently-conducting.

Effects on Floating Gates. Floating gates are used in non-volatile memories, such as EEPROM and flash. A charge-storage element (floating gate) is placed between the silicon channel and the control gate (normal transistor gate). By changing the amount of electrons and holes in the floating gate, the threshold voltage of the transistor can be altered. For ATmega1284P, the state with positive or no charge in the floating gate is the erased state, whereas negative charges present in the floating gate are the programmed state of the cell.

This is the interpretation detailed in reference [12]:

- a first effect is very similar to the one that affects classical MOS transistors, resulting in a semi-permanent shift of $I_D(V_{GS})$ curves: the cell is then semi-permanently stuck in the erased state, but
- additionally, it is likely that the photoemission of the carriers in the floating gate gets enough energy from the radiation to escape from this storage-element potential. It is also possible that the positive charges created in the surrounding oxides are injected into the floating gate. The injected holes recombine with the stored electrons. This results in a decrease of the number of electrons in the floating gate, which induces the memory cell erasure.

If the first effect dominates, stuck-at faults of the cell will be observed and the cell cannot be programmed any more. If the second effect dominates, the cell will not be semi-permanently faulted, and can be reprogrammed as a normally erased cell.

3   Experimental Results

3.1   RAM

RAM in the ATmega128 uses a classic six-transistor cell, as shown in Fig. 4. It comprises two cross-coupled inverters (transistors NI1, PI1 and transistors NI2, PI2), and two access transistors (NA1, NA2) connecting inverters to the two-bit lines. Access-transistor grids are driven by the word line, allowing read-and-write operations. The inverters' PMOS (PI1, PI2) are weak transistors to facilitate writing operations.

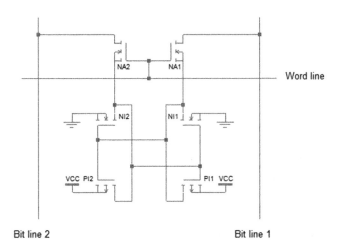

Fig. 4. Six-transistor RAM cell of the ATmega128.

Fig. 5. RAM faults. Background: SEM picture of etched RAM, showing transistor grids (metals are removed); colored dots: superimposed result of fluorescence mapping; red and green rectangles: irradiated transistors, causing the cell to be faulted at logical value 1 (red) or 0 (green); in yellow: addresses of corresponding RAM cells. (Color figure online)

The attack was directed at the ESRF bench targets' inverter's NMOS transistors. Accurate location of transistors to be targeted was obtained using fluorescence mapping, allowing localization of tungsten vias in the device. Superposition of fluorescence and SEM pictures (Fig. 5) show location of RAM transistors and allow precise focused irradiation of any individual transistors in a cell. If NMOS NI2 is irradiated, this becomes a conducting device, whatever the value applied to its grid. Inverter output is then stuck at logical value 0 and the cell value remains semi-permanently at 0. A heat annealing of 150 °C for one hour at ambient atmosphere restores normal behavior of NI2. Attacking NI1 transistor symmetrically causes the cell to become stuck at logical value 1. Experimental results are shown in Fig. 5. Several bit cells are targeted to semi-permanently have them stuck at logical value 0 or 1.

Every RAM cell of the circuit can be stuck at a desired value 0 or 1.

3.2   Non Volatile Memories

The ATmega1284P device has 128 KB of flash and four kilobytes of EEPROM for non volatile memories (NVM). Both memories have the same cell structure: a floating gate transistor dedicated to store the carriers and a second MOS transistor to select the cell.

The two memory blocks are tested with the same protocol. The chip was first erased (all bytes set to $0 \times FF$). With the help of a fluorescence image for localization inside the memory cell, the chip was irradiated by the nano beam for a few seconds. Reading the memory afterwards showed whether modification in the memory was successful or not.

Two types of memory modifications are observed:

- a whole column is reset
- a single bit is reset.

These two behaviors are explained by the physical effects described in Sect. 2.3. A whole column is reset if the beam affects the selection transistor of the cell. The NMOS transistor becomes conductive and the entire column is always read as logical value 0. This fault was semi-permanent: a thermal annealing (150 °C for one hour at ambient atmosphere) removes holes from defect sites to restore the transistor to its normal behavior. A single bit was reset when the beam was focused on the floating gate transistor. In this case, electrons stored in the floating gate were removed either by recombining with holes created in the neighboring oxides or by direct photoemission. The cell was emptied and reset. The transistor kept its normal operating conditions: the cell could be erased/programmed again. The semi-permanent effect on the floating gate transistor was not observed during this experiment. EEPROM and flash memory exhibited the same behavior.

This is an unprecedented demonstration of the ability to modify a single bit at any given address in an NVM memory. Targeting a specific address is possible with reverse-engineering of the memory mapping. Memory mapping (the relation between physical position and logical address) was retrieved after several irradiations over the memory surface. This mapping is presented in Fig. 6. It is possible to individually modify any data or program stored in the NVM from an attacker's point of view. An attack example using this feature is presented in Sect. 4.

3.3   Comparison with Laser Attacks

Compared to laser-induced faults, classically used in secured smart-card attacks, focused X-ray results in different kinds of faults:

- X-ray faults are semi-permanent: fault effect remains after irradiation has ceased. Normal operation can be restored with a thermal annealing or erasing NVM memory. Laser faults are fugitive, i.e. they are present only during laser irradiation.
- X-ray attacks can be used for "circuit editing": by individual irradiation, NMOS can be made always conductive, while PMOS can be blocked. Functions or parts of a device can be modified; for example, to deactivate security countermeasures or detectors. Moreover, X-rays penetrate regular protective shields that prevent focused ion beam (FIB) attacks.
- X-ray attacks can be used to directly modify non-volatile memories programming, while laser attacks can corrupt only NVM reading or writing.
- X-ray can be focused down to nanometric size, to target a single transistor, while laser is limited to micrometric scale (Rayleigh criterion).

4   Real Attack on Flash Program

In this investigation, a full attack path was performed to illustrate the feasibility of circuit reprogramming. An authentication program was stored in the flash boot sector in one ATmega1284P circuit. After start-up of the circuit, this program waited for a four-digit PIN sequence to be sent on UART0. Code analysis of the dumped assembly code [30] pointed out that the authentication relies on a single statement at flash address $0 \times 0000015c$:

```
0000015c:    b1 f6   BRNE.−84  ;0x10a <main+0x2e>
```

The branch if not equal (BRNE) statement catches the 9999 erroneous, presented PIN. Modifying the BRNE op-code to a branch if equal (BREQ) op-code would allow reversing the situation and accepting the 9999 erroneous PIN and rejecting the genuine PIN. Thus, without the correct PIN, an assailant would have a probability of 9999 of 10000 to pass the authentication (instead of one of 10000 previously).

Comparing the BRNE and BREQ op-codes Table 1 shows that a single-bit reset is needed in flash memory to modify the assembly. This bit reset can be performed by X-ray lighting of the floating gate transistor storing the bit value.

Table 1. Comparison of BRNE and BREQ op-code of ATmega circuit.

Instruction	hexadecimal code	binary code
BRNE .-84	$0 \times$ f6b1	1111011010110001
BREQ .-84	$0 \times$ f2b1	1111001010110001

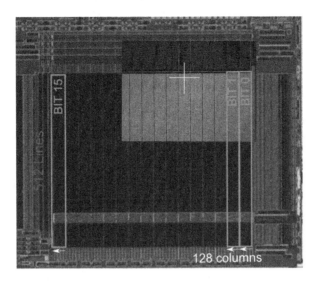

Fig. 6. Optical microscope images of the flash of an ATmega chip. The strip to attack should be chosen in one of the green rectangles. Then the nine most significant bits of the address correspond to the lines, whereas the seven least significant bits represent the column inside the green box. The position of the actual attack is shown by the yellow cross. The superimposed image corresponds to the ID16B's optical microscope view. (Color figure online)

Without the correct PIN, it is impossible to use the circuit: a well-implemented PIN-try counter limits the exhaustive search to a single PIN trial. With the results obtained in Sect. 3.2, it is possible to transform the code stored in flash in order to change the BRNE to BREQ at address $0 \times 0000015c$. The CPU address 16 bits of flash (words). Address $0 \times 0000015c$ corresponds to $0 \times \mathsf{ae} = 174 = 128 + 5 \times 8 + 6$. Thus, the targeted bit is stored on the second line, sixth strip and seventh column of the flash memory block. Figure 6 presents the routing of ATmega's flash memory and the position of the floating gate transistor holding the stored value to attack.

The X-ray beam is focused once on the desired bit of the target circuit for 500 ms. The first attempt was successful. The circuit was then permanently reprogrammed, and PIN security bypassed by choosing any incorrect PIN among the 9999 possibilities.

In order to perform such an attack, the code analysis must take into account the error model. For a flash memory block, this error model is a permanent reset of chosen bit(s).

5   Conclusion

Nano-focused X-ray beams turned out to be an efficient means of corrupting the integrity of integrated circuits. It has been shown that targeting a single

MOS transistor is possible. A RAM cell can be stuck at a logical value 0 or 1 semi-permanently, and a heat treatment can then remove the corruption. Discharging the floating gate can reset the flash and EEPROM cells. A real attack has been demonstrated on a flash cell to modify the secure start-up sequence of a programmed circuit. Fluorescence mapping at the nanoscale provided a very powerful opportunity to obtain a precise location in the layout of the circuit to successfully target the desired transistor.

The results presented in this paper were obtained on an ATmega circuit with an ancient technology (350 nm). Ongoing experiments are producing similar results with an up-to-date technology node: a microcontroller circuit in 45 nm has been tested. The size of the X-ray beam (60 nm) is not restrictive as soon as the distance between two transistors is increased. A single transistor will still be targeted in future technology nodes.

Results are presented for RAM, flash and EEPROM memory block. However, transistors in the logic part of a circuit can also be targeted. NMOS transistors can be made conductive and PMOS transistors blocked. The corresponding CMOS cell can be stuck at logical value 0 or 1 depending on the implemented functionality. For a complex cell, the Karnaugh map could be modified to a selected state. Although not tackled in this paper, this feature provides a new way to approach the circuit-editing technique and an alternative to the FIB system. Considering the fact that it is not necessary to open the package of the circuit and that the size of the technology node is not a constraint, X-ray circuit edit could play an important role.

In the context of security application, X-ray nanofocusing provides many opportunities for attacking electronic circuits. Among them, let's note the possibility to cause permanent faults in cryptographic algorithms, deactivation of counter measures, reprogramming of memories, etc. Nanofocused X-ray are a serious threat to circuit security. At present, access to third-generation synchrotron sources equipped with a nanofocus beamline is, obviously, a major concern. The work discussed here is completely exploratory and was performed through the so-called academic beamtime regulated by scientific committees, with time constraints incompatible with routine analyses. However, access to beamtime through the industrial channel is much easier and faster, making X-ray nanoprobe a new tool to corrupt circuits at the single transistor level.

Acknowledgements. The experiments were performed on beamline ID16B at the European Synchrotron Radiation Facility (ESRF), Grenoble, France.

Thanks to Olivier Hériveaux and Olivier Meynard for their pertinent contributions during days and nights at ID16B in May 2016.

References

1. Skorobogatov, S.P., Anderson, R.J.: Optical fault induction attacks. In: Kaliski, B.S., Koç, K., Paar, C. (eds.) CHES 2002. LNCS, vol. 2523, pp. 2–12. Springer, Heidelberg (2003). doi:10.1007/3-540-36400-5_2
2. Habing, D.H.: The use of lasers to simulate radiation-induced transients in semiconductor devices and circuits. IEEE Trans. Nucl. Sci. **12**, 91–100 (1965)

3. Henley, F.J.: Logic failure analysis of CMOS VLSI using a laser probe. In: 22nd Annual Reliability Physics Symposium, pp. 69–75 (1984)
4. Burns, D., Pronobis, M., Eldering, C., Hillman, R.: Reliability/design assessment by internal-node timing-margin analysis using laser photocurrent injection. In: 22nd Annual Proceedings on Reliability Physics 1984, pp. 76–82. IEEE (1984)
5. Hériveaux, L., Clédière, J., Anceau, S.: Electrical modeling of the effect of photoelectric laser fault injection on bulk CMOS design. In: 39th International Symposium for Testing and Failure Analysis ISTFA (2013)
6. Quisquatter, J.-J., Samyde, D.: Eddy current for magnetic analysis with active sensor. In: Proceedings of Esmart (2002)
7. Schmidt, J.-M., Hutter, M.: Optical and EM fault-attacks on CRT-based RSA: concrete results. In: 15th Austrian Workshop on Microelectronics, Austrochip (2007)
8. Poucheret, F., Tobich, K., Lisart, M., Chusseau, L., Robisson, B., Maurine, P.: Local and direct EM injection of power into CMOS integrated circuits. In: Fault Diagnosis and Tolerance in Cryptography, FDTC (2011)
9. Micheloni, R., Crippa, L., Marelli, A.: Inside NAND Flash Memories, pp. 537–571. Springer, Heidelberg (2010)
10. Oldham, T.R., McLean, F.B.: Total ionizing dose effects in MOS oxides and devices. IEEE Trans. Nucl. Sci. **50**, 483–499 (2003)
11. Oldham, T.R.: Ionizing Radiation Effect in MOS Oxides. Advances in Solid State Electronics and Technology (ASSET) Series. World Scientific, Singapore (1999)
12. Gerardin, S., Bagatin, M., Paccagnella, A., Grürmann, K., Gliem, F., Oldham, T.R., Irom, F., Nguyen, D.N.: Radiation effects in flash memories. IEEE Trans. Nucl. Sci. **60**(3), 1953–1969 (2013)
13. Bar-El, H., Choukri, H., Naccache, D., Tunstall, M., Whelan, C.: The Sorcerer's Apprentice Guide to Fault Attacks. IACR Cryptology ePrint Archive (2004)
14. Soucarros, M., Clédière, J., Dumas, C., Elbaz-Vincent, P.: Fault analysis and evaluation of a true random number generator embedded in a processor. J. Electron. Test. **29**(3), 367–381 (2013)
15. Martinez-Criado, G., Villanova, J., Tucoulou, R., Salomon, D., Suuronen, J.-P., Labouré, S., Guilloud, C., Valls, V., Barrett, R., Gagliardini, E., Dabin, Y., Baker, R., Bohic, S., Cohen, C., Morse, J.: ID16B: a hard X-ray nanoprobe beamline at the ESRF for nano-analysis. J. Synchrotron Radiat. **23**(1), 344–352 (2016)
16. ESRF. http://www.atmel.com/webdoc/avrassembler/
17. Ma, T.P., Dressendorfer, P.V.: Ionizing Radiation Effects in MOS Devices and Circuits. Wiley, New York (1989)
18. Shaneyfelt, M.R., Schwank, J.R., Fleetwood, D.M., Winokur, P.S., Hughes, K.L., Sexton, F.W.: Field dependence of interface trap buildup in polysilicon and metal gate MOS devices. IEEE Trans. Nucl. Sci. **37**(6), 16–32 (1990)
19. Caywood, J., Prickett, B.: Radiation-induced soft errors and floating gate memories. In: Proceedings of 21st Annual Reliability Physics Symposium, pp. 167–172 (1983)
20. Snyder, E., McWhorter, P., Dellin, T., Sweetman, J.: Radiation response of floating gate EEPROM memory cells. IEEE Trans. Nucl. Sci. **36**, 2131–2139 (1989)
21. McNulty, P., Yow, S., Scheick, L., Abdel-Kader, W.: Charge removal from FGMOS floating gates. IEEE Trans. Nucl. Sci. **49**, 3016–3021 (2002)
22. Cellere, G., Paccagnella, A., Visconti, A., Bonanomi, M.: Ionizing radiation effects on floating gates. Appl. Phys. Lett. **85**, 485–487 (2004)
23. Cellere, G., Paccagnella, A., Visconti, A., Bonanomi, M., Caprara, P., Lora, S.: A model for TID effects on floating gate memory cells. IEEE Trans. Nucl. Sci. **51**, 3753–3758 (2004)

24. Cellere, G., Paccagnella, A., Lora, S., Pozza, A., Tao, G., Scarpa, A.: Charge loss after 60 Co irradiation of flash arrays. IEEE Trans. Nucl. Sci. **51**, 2912–2916 (2004)
25. Wang, J., Samiee, S., Chen, H.-S., Huang, C.-K., Cheung, M., Borillo, J., Sun, S.-N., Cronquist, B., McCollum, J.: Total ionizing dose effects on flash-based field programmable gate array. IEEE Trans. Nucl. Sci. **51**, 3759–3766 (2004)
26. Wang, J., Kuganesan, G., Charest, N., Cronquist, B.: Biased-irradiation characteristics of the floating gate switch in FPGA. In: Proceedings of IEEE Radiation Effects Data Workshop, pp. 101–104, July 2006
27. Cellere, G., Paccagnella, A., Visconti, A., Bonanomi, M., Beltrami, S., Schwank, J., Shaneyfelt, M., Paillet, P.: Total ionizing dose effects in NOR and NAND flash memories. IEEE Trans. Nucl. Sci. **54**, 1066–1070 (2007)
28. Nguyen, D.N., Lee, C.I., Johnston, A.H.: Total ionizing dose effects on flash memories. In: IEEE Radiation Effect Data Workshop, p. 100 (1998)
29. Sharma, A.K.: Semiconductor memory radiation effects. In: Semiconductor Memories, Technology, Testing and Reliability, Chap. 7, p. 328. IEEE (1997)
30. ATMEL AVR Assembler. http://pymca.sourceforge.net/

Novel Bypass Attack and BDD-based Tradeoff Analysis Against All Known Logic Locking Attacks

Xiaolin Xu$^{(\boxtimes)}$, Bicky Shakya, Mark M. Tehranipoor, and Domenic Forte

ECE Department, University of Florida, Gainesville, USA
{xiaolinxu,tehranipoor,dforte}@ece.ufl.edu, bshakya@ufl.edu

Abstract. Logic locking has emerged as a promising technique for protecting gate-level semiconductor intellectual property. However, recent work has shown that such gate-level locking techniques are vulnerable to Boolean satisfiability (SAT) attacks. In order to thwart such attacks, several SAT-resistant logic locking techniques have been proposed, which minimize the discriminating ability of input patterns to rule out incorrect keys. In this work, we show that such SAT-resistant logic locking techniques have their own set of unique vulnerabilities. In particular, we propose a novel "bypass attack" that ensures the locked circuit works even when an incorrect key is applied. Such a technique makes it possible for an adversary to be oblivious to the type of SAT-resistant protection applied on the circuit, and still be able to restore the circuit to its correct functionality. We show that such a bypass attack is feasible on a wide range of benchmarks and SAT-resistant techniques, while incurring minimal run-time and area/delay overhead. Binary decision diagrams (BDDs) are utilized to analyze the proposed bypass attack and assess tradeoffs in security vs overhead of various countermeasures.

1 Introduction

With the globalization of semiconductor industry, many companies have relocated the fabrication of their integrated circuits (ICs) from trusted on-shore foundries to untrusted off-shore foundries. As a result of this realignment, companies as well as government agencies are now facing threats of intellectual property (IP) theft/piracy, counterfeiting, and IC overproduction [1]. Therefore, there is a critical need to develop technologies that tackle the threats associated with untrusted foundries. Towards this end, various countermeasures such as split manufacturing [2], IC metering [3] and logic locking [4,5] have been developed. Among these techniques, logic locking has emerged as a low-cost and effective solution. Basic logic locking works by embedding extra *key-gates* into the netlist

---

X. Xu and B. Shakya—Indicates equal contribution.

©IACR 2017. This article is the final version submitted by the author(s) to the IACR and to Springer-Verlag on June 26, 2017. The version published by Springer-Verlag is available at <DOI>.

© International Association for Cryptologic Research 2017
W. Fischer and N. Homma (Eds.): CHES 2017, LNCS 10529, pp. 189–210, 2017.
DOI: 10.1007/978-3-319-66787-4_10

of the circuit design. Proper operation of the circuit can only be ensured in the presence of the correct unlocking key. However, recent work has shown that early logic locking techniques are all vulnerable to *Boolean satisfiability (SAT) based attacks* [6]. In these SAT attacks, a small set of *discriminating input patterns (DIPs)* are obtained from the locked circuit netlist and incorrect keys that do not satisfy the DIP and the corresponding correct output are ruled out. In order to mitigate SAT attacks, several SAT-resistant countermeasures have been recently proposed [7,8].

In this paper, we show that the cutting-edge SAT-resistant logic locking techniques: SARLock and Anti-SAT, also possess their own critical vulnerability. In particular, we show that for any logic locking technique which is highly resistant to SAT attacks, it becomes more vulnerable to "bypass attacks" that can easily circumvent the effect of the SAT resistant locking scheme. In this novel yet simple attack, the logic locked circuit is embedded with a low-overhead bypass circuitry that enables the circuit to operate *even in the presence of an incorrect key*. Our main contributions in this paper can be summarized as follows:

- We present the bypass attack, which can be applied to recently proposed SAT-resistant logic locking techniques. Our attack uses the *same* set of assumptions/adversarial models as regular SAT attacks and can make the circuit operate correctly with any arbitrary key.
- We present the complete flow of the attack and show that it can thwart the state-of-the-art logic locking techniques: SARLock, Anti-SAT and hybrid versions of SARLock. We execute the attack on several benchmark circuits protected with these SAT-resistant logic locking methods. Further, we show that the original functionality of the circuit can be restored with area overheads linear to the number of patterns to bypass, and with minimal runtime required to execute the attack.
- We analyze logic locking techniques and SAT-resistant countermeasures in terms of existing attacks and the proposed attack. We show that bypass attack possesses a tradeoff with SAT attack, i.e., resistance to bypass decreases the resistance to SAT and resistance to SAT decreases the area overhead of the proposed attack. This leads to an interesting new way of assessing the security of logic locking schemes.
- Binary decision diagrams (BDDs) are introduced as a method to determine whether there exists a feasible complexity/overhead/attack resistance tradeoff for secure logic locking. The benefits and future challenges associated with BDD-based logic locking approaches are also discussed.

The rest of the paper is organized as follows. Section 2 reviews the background of conventional logic locking and the countermeasures against SAT attacks. Section 3 explains our bypass attack; in particular, the feasibility/scalability of our attack on different logic locking techniques is shown. Section 4 presents experimental results (delay/area overhead, computation time) of the attack on various benchmarks. Our proposed attack is also compared with the state-of-the-art. Section 5 presents the BDD-based approach for logic locking and tradeoff analysis. Section 6 concludes the paper.

2   Background and Related Work

Logic locking techniques modify the netlist of a circuit design by adding extra key controlled logic such that the circuit will only work correctly when the correct key (or keys) is applied to it; otherwise, the circuit's output is corrupted. The insertion of additional key gates into the original netlist obfuscates the functionality of the IC to an untrusted foundry and potentially prevents them from engaging in overproduction or IC piracy. Several techniques have been proposed over the years in order to perform logic locking, such as random locking [4] and fault analysis-based techniques [5]. Unfortunately, all these approaches are vulnerable to SAT attacks, as discussed below.

2.1   SAT Attacks on Logic Locking

In the SAT attack model [6], an attacker has access to: (1) *Logic Locked Netlist*: Such a netlist can be obtained from a malicious foundry or through reverse-engineering [9]. Simulations can also be readily performed on the netlist. (2) *Unlocked IC*: Such an IC can be purchased from the open market or through a malicious insider in the trusted design house. This IC can be used by the attacker as an oracle, i.e., one can check whether the output for a given key from the locked netlist is correct. In order to perform this attack within reasonable time, an attacker seeks to apply the minimum number of input patterns to the IC. Note that only combinational circuits (or sequential circuits in which all flip-flops are assumed to be accessible through the scan chain) are considered in such attacks [6].

Various attacks have been proposed based on this attack model to minimize the number of required input patterns. For example, in [10], automatic test pattern generation (ATPG) tools [11] are used to generate a set of inputs that can propagate (sensitize) the correct key to observable outputs in the circuit. In SAT-based attacks, such propagations are not required. Instead, the attacker iteratively finds a set of *distinguishing input patterns* (DIPs) for which two copies of the locked netlist, loaded with two wrong keys, produce different outputs. Since the unlocked IC is available to the attacker, he or she can then apply this pattern to the unlocked IC and find the correct output. The algorithm then iteratively uses these DIPs to guide a SAT solver to a correct key value. The algorithm terminates when no more DIPs can be found, which means that the remaining key is guaranteed to be the correct key. The results in [6] show that the algorithm quickly converges in little to no time, with a fairly small amount of DIPs.

2.2   Notation and Terminology

– A bold variable means a set of elements, and $|.|$ is used to denote the number of elements in a set. For example $\mathbf{K}$ stands for a key set with $|\mathbf{K}|$ possible keys, and K_i represents the ith element in this set;

- We denote the input/output relationship of the obfuscated logic circuit with: $Y = F(X, K)$, where Y denotes the primary output space of the circuit, X denotes the primary input space and K denotes the key input space; similarly, $Y = F(X, K)$ means that one primary output Y is generated by the circuit fed with one input vector X and key K;
- To keep it consistent with common SAT notation, an obfuscated logic circuit is expressed in conjunctive normal form (CNF) as $C(X, K, Y)$. $SAT(C(X, K, Y))$ is used to evaluate whether the CNF $C(X, K, Y)$ is true or false. $X = SAT\_Assignment(C(X, K, Y))$ refers to calling a SAT solver to find satisfying assignments X for the CNF $C(X, K, Y)$.
- The evaluation operation with X on the unlocked IC (i.e., applying DIPs and observing the correct output) is denoted by $eval(X)$.

2.3   SAT-Resistant Logic Locking

To strengthen the security of logic locking, various SAT-resistant techniques have been recently developed, most notably SARlock [7] and Anti-SAT [8]. Both these techniques attach additional logic to the circuit in order to reduce the number of wrong keys that can be ruled out by each DIP and, therefore, force the SAT attack to take an exponential number of iterations to find the correct key.

SARLock. In SARLock [7], *at most* one incorrect key value is ruled out by each DIP. This effect is brought about by a small comparator circuit that flips the circuit output for only one input pattern for a given (wrong) key. SARLock results in the worst case scenario for the attacker, as shown in the truth table of Fig. 1. For this particular circuit/Boolean function, there are, in total, $2^3 = 8$ possible key values: K_0–K_7. When the input pattern $\{1, 1, 1\}$ is applied, only K_7 can be identified as incorrect. To find the correct key, one has to iteratively search through 6 more DIPs and rule out the other wrong keys (K_0–K_5). On the other hand, it is possible to rule out all incorrect keys with one input pattern $\{1, 1, 0\}$ for a regular logic locked design.

SARLock+SLL. Though SARLock possesses strong resistance against SAT attacks, it cannot protect the circuit against other attacks that exploit its mode of implementation. For example, in a *removal attack*, an attacker can analyze the netlist and then identify and remove the SARLock gates from the design. To mitigate this vulnerability, the authors in [7] proposed a two-layer or hybrid logic-locking mechanism: SARLock + strong logic locking (SLL) [10]. This hybrid technique combines SARLock with regular logic locking (i.e., embedding of XOR/XNOR/MUX key-gates into the netlist), and also intertwines the two keys (SARLock key and SLL key) using permutations.

The SARLock+SLL scheme comprises of a $2n$-bit key, where n-bits are used for SARLock and n-bits are used for SLL. To understand the exact effect of such a hybrid scheme, we divide the whole key set (consisting of 2^{2n} keys) into *SLL set* and *SARlock set*. The SARLock set comprises of 2^n keys where the n SLL

Input Patterns	Golden output	Output patterns for different keys							
		Ko	K1	K2	K3	K4	K5	K6	K7
000	0	1	0	0	1	0	0	0	0
001	0	0	0	1	0	0	0	0	0
010	0	0	1	0	0	1	0	0	0
011	1	1	1	1	0	1	1	1	1
100	0	0	0	0	0	1	0	0	0
101	1	1	1	1	1	1	1	1	1
110	1	0	0	0	0	0	0	1	0
111	1	1	1	0	1	1	1	1	0

(a) Truth table of regular logic-lock design

Input Patterns	Golden output	Output patterns for different keys							
		Ko	K1	K2	K3	K4	K5	K6	K7
000	0	1	0	0	0	0	0	0	0
001	0	0	0	1	0	0	0	0	0
010	0	0	1	0	0	0	0	0	0
011	1	1	1	1	0	1	1	1	1
100	0	0	0	0	0	1	0	0	0
101	1	1	1	1	1	1	1	1	1
110	1	1	1	1	1	1	0	1	1
111	1	1	1	1	1	1	1	1	0

(b) Truth table of SARLock design

Fig. 1. Two truth tables of a logic design with 3-bit inputs. (a) shows that multiple wrong keys will be ruled out for each input pattern. (b) shows that with each input patterns, only one incorrect key value can be identified.

key bits are correct and the n SARLock key bits are incorrect. All the other keys $(2^{2n} - 2^n)$ are classified into a SLL set, as shown in Fig. 2. From the table, it can be seen that a single DIP can rule out multiple wrong keys in the SLL set. However, if a wrong key is in the SARLock set, then only one DIP can be found and *at most* one key in the SARLock set can be ruled out per iteration. As shown in Fig. 2, we can see that the SAT attack can easily rule out the keys $(K_0, K_1, K_2, K_3, K_4, K_5, K_6)$[1] in the SLL set with a small number of DIPs. However, the keys $(K_0^{SAR}, K_1^{SAR}, K_2^{SAR}, K_3^{SAR})$ in the SARLock set can only be ruled out one at a time per input pattern. Therefore, the SAT resistance of the hybrid scheme is only brought about by keys in the SARLock set. The keys in the SLL set only add a negligible amount of DIPs for the attack.

Input Patterns	Golden output	Output patterns for different keys										
		SLL set				SARLock set				SLL set		
		Ko	K1	K2	K3	Ko^SAR	K1^SAR	K2^SAR	K3^SAR	K4	K5	K6
000...000	0	1	1	0	1	1	0	0	0	0	1	1
000...001	1	0	0	0	0	0	0	0	0	0	0	0
000...011	0	1	1	0	0	0	0	0	0	0	1	0
...	...	...	...	...	...	...	...	...	...	...	...	...
111...100	0	1	0	1		0	1	0	0	1	1	0
111...101	1	1	0	1	0	1	1	1	1	1	0	0
111...110	0	1	0	0	1	1	1	1	1	1	1	1
111...111	1	1	1	0	0	1	1	1	1	1	0	1

Fig. 2. A truth table example of the SARLock+SLL mechanism. The strength of the SARLock+SLL scheme against SAT attack is provided only by the keys in the SARLock set. (Note that the key space is divided into SLL and SARLock sets for simplicity. In practice, the keys of the two sets are mixed with each other.)

---

[1] These sequential numbers are used to make it easier to visualize the entire key space.

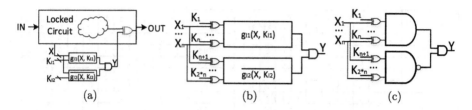

Fig. 3. Schematic of Anti-SAT: (a) shows the integration of Anti-SAT and a locked circuit. By using an XOR gate, the Anti-SAT block can flip the output if a wrong key is used. (b) illustrates the construction of Anti-SAT block, in which two complementary Boolean functions with n-bit inputs are employed. (c) shows an example of Anti-SAT implemented with AND and NAND gates.

Anti-SAT. In Anti-SAT [8], an Anti-SAT block is integrated into the circuit (see Fig. 3), which is composed of a pair of sub-blocks $B_1 = g_{l1}(X, K^{l1})$ and $B_2 = \overline{g_{l2}(X, K^{l2})}$. The two blocks share a common input X but two different keys K^{l1} and K^{l2}. The functionality of the two blocks g_{l1} and $\overline{g_{l2}}$ are complementary. Hence, they can also be denoted by g and $\bar{g}$. There is a one-bit output Y for the Anti-SAT block, which is generated by ANDing B_1 and B_2. Similar to SARLock, a wrong key applied on the Anti-SAT block will enable $Y = 1$ for some input pattern(s), and flip the correct outputs, as depicted in Fig. 3(a). Assuming the Boolean function g has n inputs, we denote the number of input patterns that make g evaluate to "1" as p. The authors in [8] prove that the decryption capability of the SAT attack is greatly limited if p is sufficiently close to 1 (or $2^n - 1$). A properly designed Anti-SAT block satisfying $p = 1$ forces an attacker to enumerate the largest number of possible keys to reveal the correct ones. They also note that natural candidates for g and $\bar{g}$ that satisfy $p = 1$ are AND and NAND respectively.

2.4 Other Attacks

Yasin *et al.* have proposed the use of cipher blocks (such as AES) for generating logic-locking keys [12], which are infeasible to break by SAT within reasonable time. However, due to the independence between the cipher block and the functional circuitry, it becomes trivial for the attacker to identify and circumvent the AES. To prevent similar vulnerabilities, Xie *et al.* propose functional and structural obfuscation techniques to enhance the security of Anti-SAT block [8]. However, it has been recently shown that although the Anti-SAT block can be hidden in the whole netlist, the attacker can still identify the flip signal Y generated by the Anti-SAT block, by analyzing the signal probability skew of the g and $\bar{g}$ blocks in the circuit [13]. This allows the attacker to set the flip signal of the Anti-SAT block to 0 and then apply the conventional SAT attack.

3   Bypass Attack: Definition and Methodologies

3.1   Adversarial Model/Capabilities

In this work, we follow the *same* adversarial model considered in most attacks on logic locking [6], i.e., the malicious party is in possession of the following: (1) The locked netlist; and (2) An unlocked IC, on which the attacker can apply input patterns and observe outputs. In practice, the attacker treats the locked netlist as a black box, and seeks to unlock the functionality of the design so that it can be pirated/overproduced.

3.2   Our Method: Bypass Attack

The main purpose of SAT attack is to reveal the correct key by iteratively applying DIPs. However, once all DIPs for any wrong key are known, an alternative for the attacker is to reverse the incorrect outputs instead of continuing with the search for the correct key(s). Taking the schematic in Fig. 4(a) as an example, if the DIPs that cause an incorrect output for a wrong key are known, then one can simply stitch a "bypass circuit" to monitor those DIPs and reverse the output back to the correct one. Such a bypass circuitry can be constructed with a comparator, which is stitched to the primary output of the circuit/logic cone. An example bypass circuit that monitors the DIP=$(0, 0, 0, 1)$ is shown in Fig. 4(b). When the circuit encounters this DIP, it can be used to trigger a signal

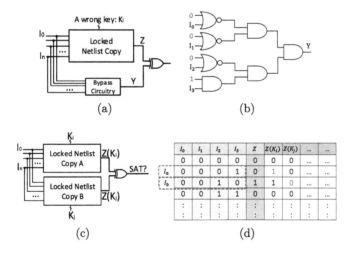

Fig. 4. (a) shows that for a locked netlist, a bypass circuit can be inserted to detect the DIP for the wrong key K_i. (b) shows an example bypass circuit block for correcting the flipped output in (d). When the input pattern (I_0, I_1, I_2, I_3) is $(0,0,0,1)$, a logic "Y=1" will be generated to flip the original wrong output. (c) denotes the construction of miter circuit, which will be then applied to the SAT Solver. (d) shows an example truth table for finding the DIPs.

$Y = 1$ that inverts the incorrect output. In summary, a bypass circuit ensures that the incorrect output can be inverted back; thereby nullifying the effect of a wrong key.

Miter Construction. The first step in our proposed bypass attack is constructing a miter circuit that can be fed into a SAT solver. The miter is constructed with two circuit copies: the first is a copy of the locked netlist with an incorrect key K_i and the second is the same locked netlist with another incorrect key K_j, as shown in Fig. 4(c). A SAT solver can then be used to find a DIP that causes the miter to evaluate to 1 (where the output of copy A does not equal the output of copy B). In the example in Fig. 4(d), the SAT solver should find and return the input pattern $I_a = (0, 0, 0, 1)$ or $I_b = (0, 0, 1, 0)$ where $Z(K_i) \neq Z(K_j)$, where Z is the output of the circuit copy. Further, calling the SAT solver again (while banning the previous solution) should return both input patterns I_a and I_b. Note that any input pattern which causes both $Z(K_i)$ and $Z(K_j)$ to evaluate to the same wrong logic value (e.g., $Z(K_i) = Z(K_j) = 0$ when $Z = 1$) will not be discovered by this miter construction.

Querying Unlocked IC. Once I_a and I_b are found, they can be applied on the unlocked IC to find the correct outputs. In Fig. 4(d), $Z = 0$ for I_a, and $Z = 1$ for I_b. With these observations, we can now see that for the locked netlist with key K_i, only input pattern I_a produces the incorrect output. Provided that standalone SARLock or Anti-SAT is applied (no SLL or structural/functional obfuscation), we can be certain that this is the only input pattern for which the circuit with wrong key K_i produces the wrong output. Similarly, for the locked netlist with wrong key K_j, I_b is the only pattern that produces the wrong output.

Bypass Circuitry Overhead. In terms of gates, the bypass circuitry overhead is a linear function of the number of DIPs N_{DIP} for the wrong key found above and the number of output bits flipped by the DIPs. Consider a circuit with N primary inputs. It would need N XNOR gates (or AND/NOR) for checking the inputs for the single DIP, $(N - 1)$ two input AND gates for determining a match between the DIP and input, and one XOR gate to flip the primary output when the input matches the DIP. In case the flip signal from the Anti-SAT/SARLock is not connected directly to the primary output (and instead, to an internal net), we can evaluate the number of primary outputs in the fan-in cone of the key input (say N_{out}), and embed N_{out} XOR gates into the N_{out} primary outputs. Thus we have the following expression:

$$Overhead = (2N - 1) \times N_{DIP} + N_{out} \tag{1}$$

The overhead across a set of benchmarks will be shown in Sect. 4.

In the sections below, we show how to apply this attack on SARLock, SAR-Lock+SLL, and Anti-SAT.

3.3 Bypass Attack on SARLock

In SARLock, there is only one DIP corresponding to each wrong key. In other words, though the wrong key is applied, the functionality of the circuit is just slightly different from that of an unlocked IC. This favors our bypass attack. Simply put, we can just apply any random key[2], and then identify the lone DIP with a SAT solver. By simply reversing the flipped output with a bypass circuitry, we can make the circuit (fed with a wrong key) regain its correct input-output behavior.

3.4 Bypass Attack on SARLock+SLL

Following the methodology of bypass attack on SARLock, we can pick up a random wrong key, identify all the DIPs and reverse them for SARLock+SLL. However, this is not a good choice in practice because for each key in the SLL set (as mentioned in Sect. 2.3), the number of DIPs is not a constant value. This would increase the overhead of the bypass circuit. Further, we would not be able to guarantee the correct functionality of the bypassed circuit (more on this will be discussed in Sect. 4). By analyzing the truth table in Fig. 2, we can make two conclusions:

1. For any two random keys K_i^{SAR} and K_j^{SAR} from the SARLock set, the Hamming Distance $HD(F(X, K_i^{SAR}), F(X, K_j^{SAR}))$ between their outputs[3] is 1 if the input X is a DIP. Here, $F(X, K_i^{SAR})$ denotes the output of the design for a primary input X and key input K_i^{SAR}. In other words, for any two (wrong) keys in SARLock set, *at most* 2 DIPs can be observed.
2. In a single iteration of the SAT attack, *at most* 1 incorrect key from the SARLock set can be ruled out using one DIP, but ≥ 2 wrong keys from SLL set can be ruled out.

These two observations imply that our approach should now be to first find a wrong key in the SARLock set and then implement our bypass attack. To realize this, we propose Algorithm 1[4], which is a modified version of the original SAT algorithm presented in [6]. In the original attack, the algorithm terminates when no further DIPs can be found. For the purpose of executing our bypass attack, the algorithm should instead terminate when all the wrong keys in the SLL set have been ruled out. In other words, the new algorithm stops when *no more DIPs which can rule out at least 2 wrong keys in a single iteration are found*[5]. The modified attack is shown in Algorithm 1. The main difference between this and the original SAT attack [6] lies between lines 2 and 11. In the modified

---

[2] The probability of getting the correct key in the first random try is extremely low, thus we do not consider this situation.

[3] "1" means the number of flipped outputs, not the number of flipped bits.

[4] Note that a paper recently accepted to GLSVLSI 2017 proposed a similar algorithm [14]. We developed Algorithm 1 independently.

[5] Note that when this condition is satisfied, some keys in the SARlock set might also have been ruled out, but all the keys in SLL set are already ruled out.

Algorithm 1. Ruling out the wrong keys in SLL set.

Prerequisite: C and $eval$ (as defined in Sect. 2.2)
Ensure: A wrong key candidate K^{SAR} in SARlock set
1: $i := 1$
2: $F_1^1 = C(X_1, K_1, Y_1) \wedge C(X_1, K_2, Y_2)$
3: $F_1^2 = C(X_1, K_3, Y_1) \wedge C(X_1, K_4, Y_2)$ {K_1, K_2, K_3 and $K4$ are 4 random key candidates}
4: $F_1 = F_1^1 \wedge F_1^2$ {F_1 is a SAT formula composed by 2 parts: F_1^1 and F_1^2}
5: **while** $SAT\big[F_i \wedge (Y_1 \neq Y_2) \wedge (K_1 \neq K_3) \wedge (K_2 \neq K_4)\big]$ **do**
6:    $X_i^d := SAT\_Assignment\Big((F_i \wedge (Y_1 \neq Y_2) \wedge (K_1 \neq K_3) \wedge (K_2 \neq K_4))\Big)$
7:    $Y_i^d := eval(X_i^d)$
8:    $F_{i+1}^1 = F_i^1 \wedge C(X_i^d, K_1, Y_i^d) \wedge C(X_i^d, K_2, Y_i^d)$
9:    $F_{i+1}^2 = F_i^2 \wedge C(X_i^d, K_3, Y_i^d) \wedge C(X_i^d, K_4, Y_i^d)$
10:    $i \leftarrow i + 1$
11:    $F_i = F_i^1 \wedge F_i^2$
12: **end while**
13: $K^{SAR} = K_1$ {when the algorithm terminates, any key remaining should be in $SARLock$ set}
14: **return** K^{SAR}

---

attack, a combinational miter is formed between four copies of the locked netlist, each with keys K_1, K_2, K_3, K_4, the same input X_i and outputs Y_1, Y_2 (lines 2, 3 and 4). A SAT solver is called to find a DIP X_i^d, that causes the four circuit copies to produce outputs such that $Y_1 \neq Y_2$ (line 6). This X_i^d is then applied on the unlocked circuit to obtain the correct output Y_i^d (line 7). After X_i^d and Y_i^d are obtained, these are added as constraints to the conjunctive normal form (CNF) circuit formula, so that in the next iteration, the keys K_1, K_2, K_3, K_4 will be chosen such that they are consistent with all the X_i^d and Y_i^d inputs/outputs observed thus far on the unlocked IC (line 8 and 9). In contrast to the original SAT algorithm, this algorithm will terminate when no more than 2 wrong keys can be ruled out within a single iteration (with one single DIP X_i^d). This implies that all the wrong keys in SLL set have been ruled out, and any key(s) left behind (K^{SAR}) should now be in the SARlock set. As stated earlier, in the SARlock set, the key bits corresponding to SLL gates are correct and the key bits corresponding to the SARLock block may or may not be correct. After this, K_{SAR} can be used to implement our bypass attack as previously discussed in Sect. 3.3 for SARLock. Note that once K_{SAR} is obtained, the area overhead required for the bypass attack will be the same as that of standalone SARLock.

3.5 Bypass Attack on Anti-SAT

In [8], two different modes of integration of the Anti-SAT block were proposed: *secure integration (SI)* and *random integration (RI)*. In *secure integration* mode, the n-bit inputs X of the Anti-SAT block are directly connected with the n-bit primary inputs (IN) of the original circuit, and output Y of the Anti-SAT block is connected to a randomly selected wire in the circuit that has high observability. In *random integration* mode, the inputs X and output Y of Anti-SAT are connected to several random internal wires of the original circuit. The authors also showed that the Anti-SAT block implemented with secure integration was more resistant to SAT attacks than random integration. In Appendix A, we describe the secure integration mode in more detail and also show that using secure integration makes it easier to apply the bypass attack. More specifically, we show that if an Anti-SAT block is implemented using secure integration (where $p = 1$), there exists one and only one DIP for any wrong key. This then implies that our bypass attack can be implemented on Anti-SAT in the exact same manner as on SARLock. However, for $p > 1$, the number of DIPs causing bit flips (N_{DIP}) increases and therefore, the overhead of the bypass attack increases (see Eq. 1). Thus, there is tradeoff between SAT-resistance attack complexity and bypass attack overhead.

In random integration mode, it cannot be guaranteed that there exists only one DIP per wrong key. Internal nets in wires are often correlated (to varying degrees), which prevents all possible input patterns from occurring at the input of the Anti-SAT block. Therefore, the *one bit flip per wrong key* assumptions holds only for a very limited subset of the entire input space. This brings about two effects.

- The SAT attack becomes easier, as only a limited subset of the entire input space triggers the Anti-SAT block. Therefore, the number of DIPs as well as the time required to execute the attack decrease significantly. Further, a large number of keys could turn out to be correct, because of the failure of the Anti-SAT block to trigger. This explanation is also supported by the results in [8], where it was shown that random integration was broken in far fewer iterations/less time than secure integration. We also performed a few experiments on random integration, where we varied the nodes chosen (as well as the number of nodes chosen) as inputs to the Anti-SAT block. While SAT attack execution time increased with the number of nodes chosen, it also varied significantly with the choice of nodes. For example, for the C3540 benchmark, a 32 bit Anti-SAT key resulted in a SAT attack time of 89 s (941 iterations) for one choice of 16 random nodes, and 616 s (2615 iterations) for yet another choice of nodes.
- Bypass attack becomes harder (or less feasible), as setting a random wrong key in the locked circuit could result in multiple bit flips for multiple input patterns. Depending on which wrong key is randomly chosen, the number of patterns (and therefore, the number of gates required to implement the bypass circuitry) could be prohibitively high. For example, when querying the miter circuit for the C3540 benchmark, we found that for some wrong keys, the SAT solver returned UNSAT immediately, indicating that no distinguishing patterns existed between the two circuits with the two wrong keys. For other key pairs, however, we found that the solver returned more than 50 K patterns as distinguishing.

In summary, our bypass attack works very good against secure integration (SI). Although the bypass attack also works on random integration (RI), its scalability in terms of area overhead depends on which internal nodes are selected.

4   Experimental Results and Discussion

In this section, we evaluate the performance and overhead of our approach. We also compare our technique with the current state-of-the-art.

4.1   Experimental Setup

We evaluate our method with a subset of benchmarks from the ISCAS, MCNC and EPFL benchmark sets [15,16]. For each benchmark, a primary output with at least 8 inputs in its transitive fan-in cone was chosen and all gates in such a cone were extracted to create a logic cone for locking. SARLock/Anti-SAT were implemented on the output cone, and then the bypass circuitry was embedded on the locked cone. As for the key length, for a benchmark with N inputs, the SARLock key length is N whereas the Anti-SAT (SI) key length is $2N$. We excluded random integration (RI) for Anti-SAT because of the aforementioned scalability issues of our bypass attack. For SARLock+SLL, we added 32 randomly inserted key gates which makes the key length $N + 32$. In terms of tools, we employed the Python extension of Cryptominisat [17] for finding the DIPs to bypass, and used the ABC synthesis tool [18] to estimate the area/delay overhead of the final bypassed circuit (after optimizing/resynthesizing them using the commands $strash \rightarrow refactor \rightarrow rewrite$).

Bypass Circuitry Overhead. The basis of our attack is that we are able to embed a bypass circuitry to circumvent SAT-resistant logic locking. However, the area/delay overhead consumed by the bypass circuitry itself cannot go unnoticed. Therefore, from an attacker's perspective, the relevant metrics for attack efficacy would be area and delay overhead from the bypass circuitry. Area and delay overhead are estimated by the increases in design gate count and number of levels in the output cone, respectively, from the original as well as locked design.

Table 1 shows the area/delay overhead from integrating the bypass circuitry on designs locked with SARLock and Anti-SAT. For most of the benchmarks, we can see that the there is actually a considerable improvement in area/delay overheads (compared to the locked designs). This is because we applied resynthesis to the bypassed circuit[6]. Since the bypassed design has hard-coded SARLock/Anti-SAT key values, resynthesis leads to a considerable portion of the locking circuitry being automatically eliminated/merged with other gates. However, there is a slight increase in area/delay overheads compared to the original design (as seen in the columns under "over original"). Note that these overheads scale

---

[6] Note that if resynthesis were not applied, we can expect to see an area overhead in line with Eq. 1, as shown in Fig. 5(b).

Table 1. Area, delay overheads for implementing bypass circuitry on SAT-resistant circuits.

Benchmark	Gate count	Cone gate count	SARLock						Anti-SAT					
			Locked Cone		Bypass (over locked)		Bypass (over original)		Locked Cone		Bypass (over locked)		Bypass (over original)	
			Area %	Cone Delay %	Area %	Cone Delay %	Area %	Cone Delay %	Area %	Cone Delay %	Area %	Cone Delay %	Area %	Cone Delay %
C432	160	105	83.13	29.03	−43.69	−32.5	3.13	−12.9	394.74	29.03	−23.23	−15	48.75	9.68
C880	383	80	44.19	110.53	−25.19	−52.5	0.78	0.00	50.5	111.11	−9.72	−10.53	26.11	88.89
C1908	880	522	15.36	37.04	−11.19	−27.03	0.11	0.00	18.11	37.04	−4.74	−21.62	9.55	7.41
C3540	1669	354	7.02	178.57	−4.38	−66.67	0.84	−7.14	8.26	178.57	−3.94	−30.77	2.22	92.86
C5315	2297	184	6.6	166.67	−5.86	−62.5	0.00	0.00	7.38	166.67	−6.51	−62.5	0.00	0.00
C7552	3512	493	10.08	476.47	−8.56	−77.55	−0.2	29.41	11.68	476.47	−9.76	−77.55	−0.2	29.41
apex2	1522	583	11.04	11.76	−3.68	−10.53	−0.33	0.00	11.67	11.76	−3.87	−10.53	−0.33	0.00
sqrt	16998	884	0.63	0.86	−0.61	−1.7	−0.01	−0.86	0.7	0.86	−0.33	0.43	0.33	1.29

mostly as a function of the number of primary inputs N in the circuit (see Eq. 1). For designs with few primary inputs and large number of gates, the overhead becomes negligible (e.g., $\approx 1\%$ area/delay overheads for benchmarks *apex2, sqrt*).

Attack Time. From the attacker's perspective, execution time is also important. The execution time to generate the DIPs to bypass for SARLock and Anti-SAT is < 2 s for all the benchmarks. Note that the scalability/run-time of our attack is limited only by the number of variables/clauses (from the circuit's CNF representation) that can be handled by the SAT solver (which only needs to be called twice for the two DIPs). Arbitrarily large sequential circuits could also be bypassed (provided there is scan access), because the SAT-resistant scheme is only applied to a few combinational logic cones in the circuit. These are usually much smaller than the entire circuit.

We also implemented Algorithm 1 using the Python wrapper for Cryptominisat, and used it to extract a bypass key for the hybrid version of SARLock (i.e., SARLock + SLL, with 32 bit XOR keys inserted randomly into the netlist). For the locked output cone of the C3540 benchmark, the code converged to the final key with the correct SLL portion in 442 iterations (i.e., 442 input-output observations). Similarly, for the C432 benchmark, the code took 651 iterations. For apex2, the number of iterations was 820. The run-time for the SAT solver on these benchmarks was on the order of 5–15 min. The run-times were higher as we used the Python wrapper for Cryptominisat (not the native C++ version). We do not present area/delay results for bypass attack on hybrid SARLock, as they are identical to the results for standalone SARLock (the bypass circuit only depends on the no. of inputs).

4.2   Comparison to State-of-the-Art

Table 2 shows a comparison of various logic locking countermeasures and applicable attacks, where a ✓ (✗) denotes that an attack can (can not) break a particular logic locking method. The table shows that SAT attack applies only to SLL. Removal attacks can apply to Anti-SAT and SARLock [13]. Bypass attack applies to all of the techniques except SLL. Note that the bypass attack may or may not scale to Anti-SAT (RI), which is why it has a ✓as well as ✗. Furthermore, bypass attack is complementary to both SAT and removal attacks.

– *SAT Attack:* The parameter p for Anti-SAT is directly proportional to N_{DIP}[7]. As discussed earlier, a low (high) value of p (and therefore, N_{DIP}) implies higher (lower) SAT resistance. However, the overhead of the bypass attack (see Eq. 1) increases linearly with N_{DIP} (and therefore, p). This implies that

---

[7] Note that in [8], p refers to the output one count of the function g. When p is very low (i.e., 1) or very high ($2^N - 1$, where N is the number of inputs to the Anti-SAT block), SAT attack becomes difficult. For values of p between 1 and $2^N - 1$, SAT resistance decreases. In the discussion here, a high value of p refers to $p \approx \frac{2^N - 1}{2}$.

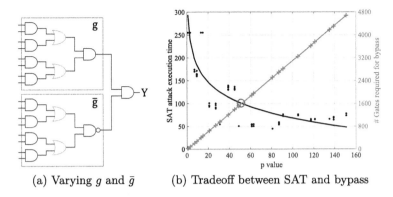

(a) Varying g and $\bar{g}$ (b) Tradeoff between SAT and bypass

Fig. 5. (a) Alternative Anti-SAT construction for g and $\bar{g}$ to vary p (by changing few AND gates to OR gates) (b) Trade-off between SAT resistance and bypass circuitry overhead on varying p. Each data point is a 16 key bit Anti-SAT block with varying p. Maximum value of p is 255. However, the graph is symmetric before and after $p \approx 127$. Therefore, only the first half is shown.

Table 2. A comparison of various logic locking techniques, attacks and countermeasures.

Attacks	Countermeasures				
	Regular Logic Lock (SLL)	SARLock	SARLock + SLL	Anti-SAT (SI)	Anti-SAT (RI)
SAT	✓	✗	✗	✗	✗
Removal	✗	✓	✗	✓	✓
Bypass	✗	✓	✓	✓	✗/✓

there is a tradeoff between these two attacks, which can be seen in Fig. 5. As one attack becomes more effective (i.e., time complexity of SAT decreases, bypass circuit overhead decreases), the other attack becomes less effective (i.e., time complexity of SAT increases, bypass circuit overhead increases).

It should also be noted that when p is modified by changing the construction of the Anti-SAT block (as shown in Fig. 5a), there is a chance that some patterns can be missed by the miter construction (as explained in Sect. 3). The number of patterns remaining undetected will depend on the key chosen for bypass, and the boolean function obtained by the modified Anti-SAT block. In any case, the trade-off observation still holds. A higher p value implies a higher chance of undetected patterns, higher overhead for bypass but also much lower SAT resistance.

- *Removal Attack:* Anti-SAT (RI) cannot always be efficiently attacked using bypass attack. However, it is vulnerable to removal attacks, if the Anti-SAT block is not obfuscated using additional key gates. Further, SAT resistance is also lowered as discussed in Sect. 3.5.

Therefore, for any secure logic locking scheme, all the aforementioned attacks need to be considered in unison.

5   Countermeasure Exploration and Trade-Off Assessment

5.1   Binary Decision Diagram

In order to better understand the tradeoffs discussed above (complementary nature of the attacks), we propose logic locking at the functional level using binary decision diagrams (BDDs) instead of at the netlist level. BDDs are graph-representations of Boolean functions that have been extensively used in the past decade for synthesis and formal verification. A BDD is able to represent the entire input space of a Boolean function in a compact form. An example of a BDD for a simple XOR function $Y = A \oplus B$ is shown in Fig. 6(a), where the variables A, B are represented as nodes. Dashed lines represent a variable (A, B) equaling logic '0' and solid lines represent a variable (A, B) equaling logic '1'.

Given a BDD representation of a combinational circuit, a simple logic locking scheme is shown in Fig. 6(b). K_1, K_2 are new variables added to the BDD. In this scheme, application of the correct key $\{K_1 = 0, K_2 = 0\}$ allows the BDD to exert the original circuit functionality f. Application of any other (wrong) key causes the circuit to perform functions f', f'', f''', and so forth which are different from the original function f, as shown in Fig. 6(c). In order to develop SAT attack resistance at the BDD level (for $p = 1$), we need to make sure that every wrong key value leads to a function f', f'', etc. that has Hamming Distance from f equal to 1. This causes a 1-bit flip when the wrong key is used. Further, any arbitrary values of p (or N_{DIP}) can be accommodated by the BDD.

We summarize the benefits of BDD-based logic locking below.

– *Balancing Bypass and SAT Resistance:* As shown in Fig. 5, there is clearly a tradeoff between SAT attack execution time and bypass attack feasibility. Since BDDs permit arbitrary values of p, it would be possible to find the

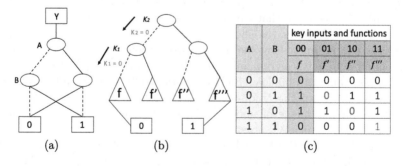

(a)   (b)   (c)

Fig. 6. (a) BDD representation of an XOR function. (b) Logic locking at the BDD Level. (c) Every wrong key value leads to a function that has Hamming Distance from f equal to 1.

point of intersection in Fig. 5. As a designer, this is the best-case scenario for logic locking, since it balances the highest SAT attack execution time with the highest bypass cost for the attacker. In addition, by knowing this point of intersection, the designer can determine whether logic locking provides enough protection against piracy.

– *Removal and Sensitization Attacks*: Unlike Anti-SAT/SARLock which inverts the circuit at a single net, BDD-based obfuscation represents the Boolean function as a digraph, embeds key gates and introduces the obfuscated functions as part of the original logic circuit. It would not be possible to isolate the original function f from the obfuscated functions f', f'', f'''. Therefore, there is no tradeoff involved for mitigating removal attacks. Further, sensitization attacks that try to propagate a single key value to the output are also difficult [10], as (i) all key values converge to the same BDD output and (ii) a key vector appears as a graph traversal path (not as individual key gates).

Therefore, BDDs could be viewed as a platform for simultaneously assessing all known threats against logic locking.

Table 3. BDD-based Logic Locking with SAT Resistance: Each benchmark was logic locked for SAT resistance with BDDs (w/ 10 bit key) and 32 key gates were then introduced to increase the key length. *Build/Lock Time* indicates the total time required to build the BDD for the selected output logic cone of the benchmark, and to introduce the 10-bit SAT-resistant locking.

Benchmark	Hybrid BDD Obfuscation			
	Area Overhead /%	Iterations for SAT Attack	SAT Attack Time (s)	Build/Lock Time (s)
C880	4090.72	1457	3049.3	1.08
C1908	3314.89	1268	1839.5	0.56
C3540	1286.9	1034	2161.3	3.18
dalu	1171.99	1075	821.6	0.56
apex2	535.58	1028	1789.9	0.37

However, we've also identified a shortcoming of BDD-based logic locking – area overhead. Table 3 shows the results from applying the proposed BDD-based logic locking scheme with SAT attack resistance. The BDD transformation of the original circuit and subsequent embedding of key inputs (10 bits long) was performed in the CUDD environment, using iterative ITE operations [19]. From the table, we can observe that the SAT attack tool takes a number of iterations that is, at the least, exponential in the size of the SAT-resistant key-length (i.e., # iterations $\geq 2^{10}$ for 10-bit key). Unfortunately, the area overheads are also observed to be extremely high. This is expected because for SAT resistance, every wrong key value ($2^n - 1$) leads to a separate BDD with a unique DIP. Although several BDD size reduction techniques exist (e.g., changing the variable orders as they appear in the BDD, BDD-based logic optimization), we noticed that for SAT resistance, the size of the locked BDD is almost always exponential in the key length, as seen in Fig. 7. Also, the BDD tool could read in and build a BDD for all the benchmarks in the ISCAS'85 benchmark set (with the exception of C6288, which is a multiplier). The node count for the BDD of the largest benchmark (C7552) was 16 K nodes, with regular sifting-based reordering and *without* any resynthesis of the BDD. Since this is clearly much bigger than the original gate count (3.5 K), it is recommended that BDD-based locking be performed on a per-output basis (i.e., extract transitive fan-in cone of an output, convert the cone to BDDs, lock and then merge with the cones of the other outputs which have not been converted to BDDs).

In order to further combat the area overhead limitation, three avenues can be pursued.

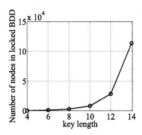

Fig. 7. Growth of no. of nodes (area) as a function of key length for SAT attack resistant BDD locking on the C5315 benchmark

- The SAT-resistant key can be shortened, and regular logic locking (i.e., embedding XOR, MUX key gates) can be performed on the circuit generated from BDD-based obfuscation. This prevents an attacker from brute forcing a short key. In fact, for the results in Table 3, we incorporated 32-bit XOR-based logic locking into the resultant circuit after BDD-based locking. However, the extra key gates introduced *do not* increase the circuit's SAT resistance capabilities. The SAT attack tool's solving time is only limited as a function of the Anti-SAT keys, not the regular logic locking keys (as these keys only add a minimal number of DIPs for the attack). Further, the attack in Algorithm 1 could be used to directly obtain keys in the SAT-resistant key space, which can then be used for bypass.
- Another option is to embed the BDD-based obfuscation on multiple outputs of the circuit, with a short key dedicated to each output. This allows the key length of the circuit to increase without exponential area blow-up. However, the number of DIPs required by the SAT attack will now be linear in the size of the key. For example, a circuit with outputs Y_1 and Y_2 is locked using the BDD-based approach. Output Y_1 and Y_2 are locked with keys K_1 and K_2 respectively. Provided that these outputs do not share any DIPs, the

number of iterations required by the SAT solver will now be lower bounded by $(2^{|K_1|} - 1) + (2^{|K_2|} - 1)$ iterations, and not $2^{|K_1|+|K_2|} - 1$. However, area will only grow linearly as a function of the number of locked outputs. Due to these reasons, there is again, an inherent tradeoff in SAT resistance and area overhead when doing BDD-based logic locking.

– The area overhead from BDD-based logic locking is also a direct result of sub-optimal logic synthesis from BDDs. Note that BDDs can be further optimized by better variable ordering or logic decomposition [20]. Unfortunately, techniques and tools for synthesizing circuits from BDDs are still scarce. More research in this domain could make BDD-based logic locking more feasible.

5.2 Parametric Tests

As shown in Fig. 4(a), the bypass attack is implemented by adding extra circuit to decrypt the locked netlist. The area and delay overhead of the bypassed IC copies would be different from the original (locked) ones, and therefore can be potentially identified by so called parametric tests such as side-channel measurements. As the original IC is larger, the detection becomes possible since the size of the bypass circuit also increases, as depicted in Fig. 5. However, there are several issues that prohibit the implementation of these parametric tests in practical scenarios:

1. The existence of process variations between different ICs would introduce uncertainty into side-channel leakage and limit the effectiveness of the parametric tests.
2. Motivation for consumers in the market to undertake such an effort is weak. Consumers usually want the cheapest chip, regardless of whether it contains pirated IP. Our results in Table 1 show that the pirated IP can perform even better (in terms of overhead) after re-synthesis than the obfuscated circuit.
3. It is already common practice for design houses to use reverse-engineering (RE) companies (e.g., TechInsights) to physically RE the IP of competitors for litigation purposes, which would be more effective than parametric tests.

With the reasons above, we argue that although it may be possible to use parametric tests as a countermeasure against bypass attacks, practical concerns like detection accuracy and cost would likely limit their applicability.

6 Conclusion

In this paper, we presented a novel bypass attack that can thwart SAT-resistant logic locking schemes. The only overhead from our attack is a small bypass logic that can be stitched onto the SAT-resistant circuit. We also assessed how all existing attacks on logic locking can complement each other. Specifically, high SAT attack resistance corresponds to low bypass resistance and vice-versa. The only Anti-SAT locking technique that is somewhat resistant to our bypass attack is still vulnerable to removal attacks. We also introduced a BDD-based logic locking approach for analyzing these competing attacks and simultaneously balancing them. Finally, we highlighted the challenges and future work required to make BDD (and in general, secure logic locking approaches) more practical.

Acknowledgment. This research is supported in part by Cisco Systems Inc, and by the AFOSR award number FA9550-14-1-0351.

References

1. Tehranipoor, M.M., Guin, U., Forte, U.: Counterfeit integrated circuits. In: Counterfeit Integrated Circuits, pp. 15–36. Springer, Heidelberg (2015)
2. Vaidyanathan, K., Liu, R., Sumbul, E., Zhu, Q., Franchetti, F., Pileggi, L.: Efficient and secure intellectual property (IP) design with split fabrication. In: 2014 IEEE International Symposium on Hardware-Oriented Security and Trust (HOST), pp. 13–18. IEEE (2014)
3. Alkabani, Y., Koushanfar, F.: Active hardware metering for intellectual property protection and security. In: USENIX security, Boston MA, USA, pp. 291–306 (2007)
4. Roy, J.A., Koushanfar, F., Markov, I.L.: Epic: Ending piracy of integrated circuits, vol. 43, pp. 30–38. IEEE (2010)
5. Rajendran, J., Zhang, H., Zhang, C., Rose, G.S., Pino, Y., Sinanoglu, O., Karri, R.: Fault analysis-based logic encryption. IEEE Trans. Comput. **64**(2), 410–424 (2015)
6. Subramanyan, P., Ray, S., Malik, S.: Evaluating the security of logic encryption algorithms. In: 2015 IEEE International Symposium on Hardware Oriented Security and Trust (HOST), pp. 137–143. IEEE (2015)
7. Yasin, M., Mazumdar, B., Rajendran, J.J.V., Sinanoglu, O.: SARLock: SAT attack resistant logic locking. In: 2016 IEEE International Symposium on Hardware Oriented Security and Trust (HOST), pp. 236–241, May 2016
8. Xie, Y., Srivastava, A.: Mitigating SAT attack on logic locking. In: Gierlichs, B., Poschmann, A.Y. (eds.) CHES 2016. LNCS, vol. 9813, pp. 127–146. Springer, Heidelberg (2016). doi:10.1007/978-3-662-53140-2_7
9. Torrance, R., James, D.: The state-of-the-art in IC reverse engineering. In: Clavier, C., Gaj, K. (eds.) CHES 2009. LNCS, vol. 5747, pp. 363–381. Springer, Heidelberg (2009). doi:10.1007/978-3-642-04138-9_26
10. Rajendran, J., Pino, Y., Sinanoglu, O., Karri, R.: Security analysis of logic obfuscation. In: Proceedings of the 49th Annual Design Automation Conference, pp. 83–89. ACM (2012)
11. Bushnell, M., Agrawal, V.: Essentials of Electronic Testing for Digital, Memory and Mixed-Signal VLSI Circuits, vol. 17. Springer, Heidelberg (2004)
12. Yasin, M., Rajendran, J.J., Sinanoglu, O., Karri, R.: On improving the security of logic locking. IEEE Trans. Comput.-Aided Des. Integr. Circuits Syst. **35**(9), 1411–1424 (2016)
13. Yasin, M., Mazumdar, B., Sinanoglu, O., Rajendran, J.: Security analysis of anti-SAT. In: 2017 22nd Asia and South Pacific Design Automation Conference (ASP-DAC), pp. 342–347. IEEE (2017)
14. Shen, Y., Zhou, H.: Double DIP: Re-evaluating security of logic encryption algorithms. In: Proceedings of the Great Lakes Symposium on VLSI 2017, GLSVLSI 2017, pp. 179–184. ACM, New York (2017)

15. Brglez, F.: A neutral netlist of 10 combinational benchmark circuits and a target translation in FORTRAN. In: ISCAS-85 (1985)
16. Amarú, L., Gaillardon, P.-E., De Micheli, G.: The EPFL combinational benchmark suite. In: Proceedings of the 24th International Workshop on Logic & Synthesis (IWLS), number EPFL-CONF-207551 (2015)
17. Soos, M.: Cryptominisat-a SAT solver for cryptographic problems (2009). http://www.msoos.org/cryptominisat4
18. Brayton, R., Mishchenko, A.: ABC: An academic industrial-strength verification tool. In: Touili, T., Cook, B., Jackson, P. (eds.) CAV 2010. LNCS, vol. 6174, pp. 24–40. Springer, Heidelberg (2010). doi:10.1007/978-3-642-14295-6_5
19. Somenzi, F.: CUDD: CU decision diagram package release 2.3.0. University of Colorado at Boulder (1998)
20. Yang, C., Ciesielski, M.: BDS: A BDD-based logic optimization system. IEEE Trans. Comput.-Aided Des. Integr. Circuits Syst. **21**(7), 866–876 (2002)

A   Bypass Attack on Anti-SAT with Secure Integration

Note that in this proof, we follow the notation and terminology in Sect. 2.2. Following the notation in [8], we denote the n-bit inputs to the Anti-SAT block with $\mathbf{X}$. In the *secure integration* mode, $\mathbf{X}$ are directly connected to the primary inputs ($\mathbf{IN}$, width of which might be larger than n) of the netlist, as shown in Fig. 3(a). If $(|\mathbf{IN}| - |\mathbf{X}|) > 0$, then those input wires not connected with Anti-SAT block become "don't cares" for it. The existence of such "don't cares" makes it easier for attackers, since $|\mathbf{X}|$ is not maximized, which means $|\mathbf{K}|$ is not maximized since $|\mathbf{K}| = |\mathbf{X}|$(as shown in Fig. 3(b) and (c)). If our attack works when $|\mathbf{IN}| = |\mathbf{X}|$ then it should also work when $|\mathbf{IN}| > |\mathbf{X}|$. Therefore, in the following discussion we shall simply assume that $|\mathbf{IN}| = |\mathbf{X}|$.

Lemma 1. *Given a wrong key to Anti-SAT of secure integration mode, for all n-bit input patterns: $\mathbf{X} = \mathbb{B}^n$, $\mathbb{B} = \{0,1\}$, there exists one and only one DIP.*

Proof. First of all, note that to make it more understandable, our proof is based on the same notation and terminology as [8]. Given a Boolean function $g(\mathbf{L})$ with n-bit inputs, we can divide the input vectors $\mathbf{L}$ into two sets: $\mathbf{L}^1$ and $\mathbf{L}^0$, which represent the inputs that make the Boolean function g equal to 1 and 0. If we denote $|\mathbf{L}^1| = p$, we can get:

$$\begin{aligned}
\mathbf{L}^1 &= \{\mathbf{L}|g(\mathbf{L}) = 1\}, \quad (|\mathbf{L}^1| = p) \\
\mathbf{L}^0 &= \{\mathbf{L}|g(\mathbf{L}) = 0\}, \quad (|\mathbf{L}^0| = 2^n - p)
\end{aligned} \tag{2}$$

We define all $2n$-bit keys for Anti-SAT with $\mathbf{K}=< \mathbf{K}^{l1}, \mathbf{K}^{l2} >= \mathbb{B}^{2n}$, $\mathbb{B} = \{0,1\}$, in which $\mathbf{K}^{l1}$ and $\mathbf{K}^{l2}$ stand for two n-bit key inputs connected to the Anti-SAT components g and $\overline{g}$ ($l1$ and $l2$ refer to the locations of g and its complementary function $\overline{g}$ in the netlist, as shown in Fig. 3). Assuming $\mathbf{X}^d$ denotes a set of DIPs, and $\mathbf{Y}^d$ stands for corresponding outputs of Anti-SAT, then for the wrong key set $\mathbf{WK}_i =< \mathbf{K}_i^{l1}, \mathbf{K}_i^{l2} >$ ruled out at the ith iteration of SAT attack by a DIP X_i^d and Y_i^d, we can get:

$$Y_i^d = g(X_i^d \oplus \mathbf{K}_i^{l1}) \wedge \overline{g(X_i^d \oplus \mathbf{K}_i^{l2})} = 1 \tag{3}$$

From Eqs. 2 and 3, we can deduce that:

$$(X_i^d \oplus \mathbf{K}_i^{l1}) \in \mathbf{L}^1 \quad and \quad (X_i^d \oplus \mathbf{K}_i^{l2}) \in \mathbf{L}^0 \tag{4}$$

Note that X_i^d is a input vector, thus $|\mathbf{K}_i^{l1}| = |\mathbf{L}^1| = p$. By defining the elements in $\mathbf{K}_i^{l1}$ as $\{K_{i\_1}^{l1}, K_{i\_2}^{l1}, \ldots K_{i\_p}^{l1}\}$, and corresponding XORed results in $\mathbf{L}^1$ as $\{L_1^1, L_2^1, \ldots L_p^1\}$, we can get:

$$(X_i^d \oplus K_{i\_o}^{l1}) = L_o^1 \in \mathbf{L}^1, \quad o \in [1, 2, \ldots p] \tag{5}$$

In Eq. 5, $K_{i\_o}^{l1}$ stands for a wrong key vector for g, thus according to the properties of XOR operation, the following equation holds true, $\forall X_j \in \mathbf{X}$, if $X_j \neq X_i^d$:

$$(X_i^d \oplus K_{i\_o}^{l1}) \neq (X_j \oplus K_{i\_o}^{l1}), \quad o \in [1, 2, \ldots p] \tag{6}$$

As proven in [8], if the output-one count p of Anti-SAT block g is sufficiently close to 1, attackers are forced to iterate *at least* 2^n keys to reveal the correct one(s). That is, the SAT-resistance capability of Anti-SAT is maximized when p is 1. The authors of [8] proposed to use AND and NAND gates to realize this goal, as shown in Fig. 3(c). This implies that $|\mathbf{K}_i^{l1}| = |\mathbf{L}^1| = 1$, if this wrong key $K_{i\_1}^{l1}$ is applied on the Boolean function g, then output becomes:

$$g(X \oplus K_{i\_1}^{l1}) = \begin{cases} 1, & \text{if } X = X_i^d \\ 0, & \text{otherwise} \end{cases} \tag{7}$$

The total number of 0 outputs from $g(\mathbf{X} \oplus K_{i\_1}^{l1})$ is $2^n - 1$, this means that for $2^n - 1$ input vectors of $\mathbf{X}$, the outputs $\mathbf{Y}$ of Anti-SAT block will be 0, i.e., the original outputs are not flipped. Note that there must exist *at least* one input corresponds to an output $Y = 1$, since otherwise, it violates the definition of a wrong key.

   Conclusion: in *secure integration* mode, there exists one and only one DIP for any wrong key.

Post Quantum Implementations

McBits Revisited

Tung Chou[(✉)]

Graduate School of Engineering, Osaka University Japan,
1-1, Yamadaoka, Suita, Osaka Prefecture 565-0871, Japan
blueprint@crypto.tw

Abstract. This paper presents a constant-time fast implementation for
a high-security code-based encryption system. The implementation is
based on the "McBits" paper by Bernstein, Chou, and Schwabe in 2013:
we use the same FFT algorithms for root finding and syndrome computation, similar algorithms for secret permutation, and bitslicing for
low-level operations. As opposed to McBits, where a high decryption
throughput is achieved by running many decryption operations in parallel, we take a different approach to exploit the internal parallelism
in one decryption operation for the use of more applications. As the
result, we manage to achieve a slightly better decryption throughput at
a much higher security level than McBits. As a minor contribution, we
also present a constant-time implementation for encryption and key-pair
generation, with similar techniques used for decryption.

Keywords: McEliece · Niederreiter · Bitslicing · Software implementation

1 Introduction

In recent years, due to the advance in quantum computing, cryptographers are
paying more and more attention to post-quantum cryptography. In particular,
NIST's call for proposal [16] serves as an announcement to declare that post-
quantum cryptography is going to be reality, and the whole world needs to
be prepared for that. Among other things, we need post-quantum public-key
encryption schemes, and the most promising candidates today are from code-
based cryptography and lattice-based cryptography.

In 1978, McEliece proposed his hidden-Goppa-code cryptosystem [13] as the
first code-based encryption system. Until today, almost 40 years of research has
been invested on cryptanalyzing the system, yet nothing has really shaken its
security. It has thus become one of the most confidence-inspiring post-quantum
encryption systems we have today, and it is important to evaluate how practical
the system is for deployment.

This work was supported by the Cisco University Research Program, by the National
Science Foundation under grant 1018836, and by the Netherlands Organisation for
Scientific Research (NWO) under grant 639.073.005. Permanent ID of this document:
a6d277b6724b21ae996418cbec02d682. Date: 2017.06.26.

© International Association for Cryptologic Research 2017
W. Fischer and N. Homma (Eds.): CHES 2017, LNCS 10529, pp. 213–231, 2017.
DOI: 10.1007/978-3-319-66787-4_11

Table 1. Number of cycles for decoding for McBits and our software.

reference	m	n	t	bytes	sec	perm	synd	key eq	root	all	arch
McBits [3]	13	6624	115	958482	252	23140	83127	102337	65050	444971	IB
	13	6960	119	1046739	263	23020	83735	109805	66453	456292	IB
This paper	13	8192	128	1357824	297	3783	62170	170576	53825	410132	IB
						3444	36076	127070	34491	275092	HW

In 2013, Bernstein, Chou, and Schwabe published the "McBits" paper [3], which presents a software implementation of Niederreiter's dual form [15] of the McEliece cryptosystem. McBits features (1) a very high decoding (and thus decryption) throughput which is an order of magnitude faster than the previous implementation by Biswas and Sendrier [8], and (2) full protection against timing attacks. These features are achieved by bitslicing non-conventional algorithms for decoding: they use the Gao–Mateer additive FFT [11] for the root-finding, the corresponding "transposed" FFT for syndrome computation, and a sorting network for secret permutation.

The decryption throughput McBits achieves, however, relies on the assumption that there are many decryption operations that can be run at the same time. This is a reasonable assumption for some applications, but not for the all applications. The user would be glad to have an implementation that is capable of decrypting efficiently, even when there is only one decryption operation at the moment.

The main contribution of this paper is that we show the assumption is NOT a requirement to achieve a high decryption throughput. Even better, our software actually achieves a slightly better decryption throughput than McBits, at a much higher security level. To achieve this, we need to have a deep understanding about the data flow in each stage of decoding algorithm in order to figure out what kind of internal parallelism there is and how it can be exploited.

Speeds. The decoding speed of our software, as well as those for the highest-security parameters in [3, Table 1], are listed in Table 1. Most notations here are the same as in [3, Table 1]: we use m to indicate the field size 2^m, n to denote the code length, and t to denote the number of errors. "Bytes" is the size of public keys in bytes; "Sec" is the (pre-quantum) security level reported by the https://bitbucket.org/cbcrypto/isdfq script from Peters [17], rounded to the nearest integer. We list the cycle counts for each stage of the decoding process as in [3, Table 1]: "perm" for secret permutation, "synd" for syndrome computation, "key eq" for key-equation solving, and "root" for root finding. In [3, Table 1] there are two columns for "perm": one stands for the initial permutation and one stands for the final permutation, but the cycle counts are essentially the same (we pick the timing for the initial permutation). Note that the column "all", which serves as an estimation for the KEM decryption time, is computed as

$$\text{"perm"} \times 2 + \text{"synd"} \times 2 + \text{"key eq"} + \text{"root"} \times 2.$$

Table 2. Cycle counts for key generation, encryption (for 59-byte messages), and decryption.

key-generation	encryption	decryption	arch
1552717680	312135	492404	IB
1236054840	289152	343344	HW

This is different from the "total" column in [3, Table 1] for decoding time, which is essentially

$$\text{"perm"} \times 2 + \text{"synd"} + \text{"key eq"} + \text{"root"}.$$

The difference is explained in Sect. 6 in detail. "Arch" indicates the microarchitecture of the platform: "IB" for Ivy Bridge and "HW" for Haswell.

We comment that the way we exploit internal parallelism brings some overhead that can be avoided when using external parallelism. In general such an overhead is hard to avoid since the data flow of the algorithm is not necessarily friendly for bitslicing internally. This is exactly the main reason why our software is slower in "key eq" than McBits (a minor reason is that we are using a larger t). Despite the extra overhead, we still perform better when it comes to "synd" and "root". The improvement on "perm" is mainly because of our use of an asymptotically faster algorithm. Our "all" speed ends up being better than McBits. We emphasize that the timings for McBits are actually 1/256 of the timings for 256 parallel decryption operations, while the timings for our software involve only one decryption operation.

For completeness, we also implement the complete KEM/DEM-like ([19]) encryption system as described in [3, Sect. 6]. The corresponding cycle counts for key generation, encryption, and decryption are presented in Table 2.

For comparison with lattice-based cryptosystems, NTRU Prime [4], which appears to be the fastest high-security NTRU-type system (that has a constant-time implementation) at the moment, takes

- 1 multiplications in $\mathbb{F}_{9829}[x]/(x^{739} - x - 1)$ for encryption and
- 2 multiplications in $\mathbb{F}_{9829}[x]/(x^{739} - x - 1)$ plus
  1 multiplication in $\mathbb{F}_3[x]/(x^{739} - x - 1)$ for decryption,

where each multiplication in $\mathbb{F}_{9829}[x]/(x^{739} - x - 1)$ takes around 50000 Haswell cycles. As other lattice-based cryptosystems, NTRU Prime has a relatively small public key size of 1232 bytes. Our system has a ciphertext overhead of only 224 bytes, while NTRU Prime takes at least 1141 bytes.

Parameter Selection. As shown in Table 1, we implement one specific parameter set $(m, n, t) = (13, 8192, 128)$, with 1357824-byte public keys and a 2^{297} security level. We explain below the reasons to select this parameter set.

The Gao–Mateer additive FFT evaluates the input polynomial at a predefined $\mathbb{F}_2$-linear subspace of $\mathbb{F}_{2^m}$. The parameter n indicates the size of the list of field elements that we need to evaluate at, so for $n = 2^m$ we can simply define the subspace as $\mathbb{F}_{2^m}$. In the case of $n < 2^m$, however, there is no way to define the subspace to fit arbitrary choice of the field elements (which is actually a part of the secret key), so the best we can do is still evaluate at the whole $\mathbb{F}_{2^m}$. In other words, having $n < 2^m$ would result in some redundant computation.

The parameter n also indicates the number of elements that we need to apply secret permutations on. The permutation algorithm we use, in its original form, requires that the number of elements to be a power of 2. The algorithm can be "truncated" to deal with an arbitrary number of elements, but this makes implementation difficult.

Having t close to the register size is convenient for bitslicing the FFT algorithms and the Berlekamp–Massey algorithm. We choose $t = 128$ to match the size of XMM registers in SSE-supporting architectures, as well as the size of the vector registers in the ARM-NEON architectures. Not having t close to the register size will not really affect the performance of FFTs: the algorithms are dominated by the t-irrelevant part as long as t is much smaller than 2^m. A bad value for t has more impact on the performance of the Berlekamp–Massey algorithm since we might waste many bits in the registers. Choosing $t = 128$ (after choosing $n = 2^m$) also forces the number of rows mt and number of columns $n - mt$ of the public-key matrix to be multiples of 128, which is convenient for implementing the encryption operation.

For the reasons stated above, some other nice parameters for (m, n, t) are

- $(12, 4096, 64)$ with 319488-byte public keys and a 2^{159} security level,
- $(12, 4096, 128)$ with 491520-byte public keys and a 2^{189} security level, and
- $(13, 8192, 64)$ with 765440-byte public keys and a 2^{210} security level.

We decided to select a parameter set that achieves at least a 2^{256} pre-quantum security level and thus presumably at least a 2^{128} post-quantum security level.

The reader might argue that such a high security level is not required for real applications. Indeed, even if quantum algorithms can take a square root on the security level, it still means that our system has a roughly 2^{150} post-quantum security level. In fact, we even believe that quantum algorithms will not be able to take a square root on the security: we believe there is a overhead of more than 2^{20} that needs to be added upon the square root. However, before the post-quantum security of our system is carefully analyzed, we think it is not a bad idea to implement a parameter set that is very likely to be an overkill and convince users that the system achieves a decent speed even in this case. Once careful analysis is done, our implementation can then be truncated to fit the parameters. The resulting implementation will have at least the same speed and a smaller key size.

Organization. The rest of this paper is organized as follows. Section 2 introduces the low-level building blocks used in our software. Section 3 describes how we implement the Beneš networks for secret permutations. Section 4 describes how we implement the Gao–Mateer FFT for root finding and the corresponding "transposed" FFT for syndrome computation. Section 5 introduces how we implement the Berlekamp–Massey algorithm for key-equation solving. Finally, Sect. 6 introduces how the components in Sects. 3, 4, 5 are combined to form the complete decryption, as well as how key generation and encryption are implemented.

2   Building Blocks

This section describes the low-level building blocks used in our software. We will use these building blocks as black boxes in the following sections. The implementation techniques behind these building blocks are not new. In particular, this section presents (1) how to use bitslicing to perform several field operations in parallel and (2) how to perform bit-matrix transposition in software. Readers who are familiar with these techniques may skip this section.

Individual Field Operations. The finite field $\mathbb{F}_{2^{13}}$ is constructed as $\mathbb{F}_2[x]/(g)$, where $g = x^{13}+x^4+x^3+x+1$. Let $z = x+(g)$. Each field element $\sum_{i=0}^{12} a_i z^i$ can then be represented as the integer $(a_{12}a_{11} \cdots a_0)_2$ in software. Field additions are carried out by XORs between integers. Field multiplications are carried out by the following C function.

```
typedef uint16_t gf;
gf gf_mul(gf in0, gf in1)
{
        uint64_t i, tmp, t0=in0, t1=in1, t;
        tmp = t0 * (t1 & 1);
        for (i = 1; i < 13; i++) tmp ^= (t0 * (t1 & (1 << i)));
        t = tmp & 0x1FF0000;
        tmp ^= (t >> 9) ^ (t >> 10) ^ (t >> 12) ^ (t >> 13);
        t = tmp & 0x000E000;
        tmp ^= (t >> 9) ^ (t >> 10) ^ (t >> 12) ^ (t >> 13);
        return tmp & ((1 << 13)-1);
}
```

The squaring function is written in a similar way. Computing the inverse of a field element is carried out by raising the element to the power $2^{13} - 2$ using 12 squarings and 4 multiplications.

Bitsliced Field Operations. The field multiplication function **gf_mul** and the field addition shown above are rather inefficient. The reason is that each logical instruction deals with only a small number of bits. For the algorithms used in our software, however, most of the time several field operations can be performed in parallel. We thus "bitslice" the field operations. The idea of bitslicing is to use bitwise logical operations to simulate w copies of a combinational circuit: the data for the ith copy is stored in the ith bits of the registers. In this way, the number of bits involved in each instruction can be improved to w. Bitslicing is also heavily used in [3]. We emphasize that for [3], the w copies are from w different decryption operations. For our software, the w copies are all from the same decryption operation.

```
void vec64_mul(uint64_t *h, uint64_t *f, uint64_t *g)
{
        int i, j;
        uint64_t r[2*13 - 1];
        for (i = 0; i < 2*13 - 1; i++)
                r[i] = 0;
        for (i = 0; i < 13; i++)
        for (j = 0; j < 13; j++)
                r[i+j] ^= r[i+j] ^ (f[i] & g[j]);
        for (i = 2*13-2; i >= 13; i--)
        {
                r[i - 9]  ^= r[i];
                r[i - 10] ^= r[i];
                r[i - 12] ^= r[i];
                r[i - 13] ^= r[i];
        }
        for (i = 0; i < 13; i++) h[i] = r[i];
}
```

Fig. 1. The C function for bitsliced multiplications in $\mathbb{F}_{2^{13}}[x]/(x^{13} + x^4 + x^3 + x + 1)$ using 64-bit words.

The function vec64_mul for bitsliced field multiplications using 64-bit words is shown in Fig. 1. One can of course use 128-bit or 256-bit words instead. According to Fog's well-known performance survey [10], on the Ivy Bridge architecture, the bitwise AND/XOR/OR instructions on the 128-bit registers (XMM registers) have a throughput of 3 per cycle, while for the 256-bit registers (YMM registers) the throughput is only 1. On Haswell, the instructions for the 256-bit registers have a throughput of 3 per cycle. We thus use the corresponding function vec128_mul for Ivy Bridge and use vec256_mul as much as possible for Haswell. Since both functions are heavily used in our software, they are written in qhasm [2] code for the best performance.

Many CPUs nowadays support the pclmulqdq instruction. The instruction essentially performs a multiplication between two 64-coefficient polynomials in $\mathbb{F}_2[x]$, so it can be used for field multiplications. Our multiplication function vec256_mul takes 138 Haswell cycles, which means a throughput of 1.86 field multiplications per cycle. The pclmulqdq instruction has a throughput of 1/2 on Haswell. We may perform 2 multiplications between 13-coefficient polynomials using one pclmulqdq instruction. However, non-bitsliced representations make it expensive to perform reductions modulo the irreducible polynomial g. On Ivy Bridge the throughput for pclmulqdq is only 1/8, which makes it even less favorable.

Transposing Bit Matrices. Bit-matrix transposition appears to be a well-known technique in computer programming. Perhaps due to the simplicity of the method, it is hard to trace who the credit belongs to. Below we give a brief review on the idea.

The task is to transpose a $w \times w$ bit matrix M, where w is a power of 2. The idea is to first divide the matrix into 4 $w/2 \times w/2$ submatrices, i.e., the left upper, right upper, left bottom, and right bottom submatrices. Then a "coarse-grained transposition" is performed on M, which simply interchanges the left bottom and right upper submatrices. Finally each block is transposed recursively, until we reach 1×1 matrices. The idea is depicted below.

$$M = \begin{pmatrix} M_{00} & M_{01} \\ M_{10} & M_{11} \end{pmatrix} \implies M' = \begin{pmatrix} M_{00} & M_{10} \\ M_{01} & M_{11} \end{pmatrix} \implies \begin{pmatrix} M_{00}^T & M_{10}^T \\ M_{01}^T & M_{11}^T \end{pmatrix} = M^T$$

The benefit of this approach is that it can be carried out efficiently in software. Suppose we are working on a w-bit machine, where the matrix is naturally represented as an array of w w-bit words in a row-major fashion. Observe that each of the first $w/2$ rows of M' is the concatenation of the first halves of two rows in M. Similarly, each of the second $w/2$ rows is the concatenation of the second halves of two rows in M. Therefore, each row in M' can be generated using a few logical operations. After this, in order to carry out operations in the recursive calls efficiently, the operations involving the upper two blocks can be handled together using logical operations on w-bit words. The same applies for the bottom two blocks. The C code for transposing 64×64 matrices is shown in Fig. 2.

```c
const uint64_t mask[6][2] =
{
  {0X5555555555555555, 0XAAAAAAAAAAAAAAAA},
  {0X3333333333333333, 0XCCCCCCCCCCCCCCCC},
  {0X0F0F0F0F0F0F0F0F, 0XF0F0F0F0F0F0F0F0},
  {0X00FF00FF00FF00FF, 0XFF00FF00FF00FF00},
  {0X0000FFFF0000FFFF, 0XFFFF0000FFFF0000},
  {0X00000000FFFFFFFF, 0XFFFFFFFF00000000}
};
for (j = 5; j >= 0; j--)
{
  s = 1 << j;
  for (p = 0; p < 32/s; p++)
  for (i = 0; i < s; i++)
  {
    idx0 = p*2*s + i;
    idx1 = p*2*s + i + s;
    x = (in[idx0] & mask[j][0]) | ((in[idx1] & mask[j][0]) << s);
    y = ((in[idx0] & mask[j][1]) >> s) | (in[idx1] & mask[j][1]);
    in[idx0] = x;
    in[idx1] = y;
  }
}
```

Fig. 2. The C code for transposing 64×64 bit matrices. The matrix to be transposed is stored in the array **in**. The transposition is performed in-place.

The same technique can be easily generalized to deal with non-square matrices. Our software makes use of functions for transposing 64×128 and 128×64 matrices, where instructions such as psrlq, psllq, psrld, pslld, psrlw, and psllw are used to shift the 128-bit registers.

3   The Beneš Network

As described in [3], a "permutation network" uses a sequence of conditional swaps to apply an arbitrary permutation to an input array S. Each conditional swap is a permutation-independent pair of indices (i, j) together with a permutation-dependent bit c; it swaps $S[i]$ with $S[j]$ if $c = 1$. Our software uses a specific type of permutation network, called the Beneš network [1], to perform secret permutations for the code-based encryption system.

The McBits paper uses a "sorting network" for the same purpose but notes that it takes asymptotically more conditional swaps than the Beneš network: $O(n \log^2 n)$ versus $O(n \log n)$ for array size $n = 2^m$. We found that the Beneš network is more favorable for our implementation because it is easier to use the internal parallelism due to its simple structure. This section introduces the structure of the Beneš network, as well as how it is implemented in our software.

Conditional Swaps: Structure. The Beneš network for 2^m elements consists of a sequence of $2m - 1$ stages, where each stage consists of exactly 2^{m-1} conditional swaps. The set of index pairs for these 2^{m-1} conditional swaps is defined as

$$\left\{ (\alpha \cdot 2^{s+1} + \beta, \; \alpha \cdot 2^{s+1} + 2^s + \beta) \mid 0 \leq \alpha < 2^{m-1-s}, \; 0 \leq \beta < 2^s \right\},$$

where s is stage-dependent. The sequence of s is defined as

$$m - 1, m - 2, \ldots, 1, 0, 1, \ldots, m - 2, m - 1.$$

To visualise the structure, the size-16 Beneš network is depicted in Fig. 3.

The Beneš network is often defined in a recursive way, in which case the size-2^m Beneš network is viewed as the combination of the first and last stage, plus 2 size-2^{m-1} Beneš networks in the middle. Also note that in some materials the sequence of s is defined as

$$0, 1, \ldots, m - 2, m - 1, m - 2, \ldots, 1, 0.$$

The two ways to define the sequence for s are equivalent up to a permutation of the array indices.

Conditional Swaps: Implementation. Consider the Beneš network for an array S of 2^m bits for some even m. We may consider S as a $m/2 \times m/2$ matrix M such that

$$M_{i,j} = S[i \cdot 2^{m/2} + j].$$

In each of the first and last $m/2$ stages, the index pairs always have an index difference that is a multiple of $2^{m/2}$. This implies that in each of these stages,

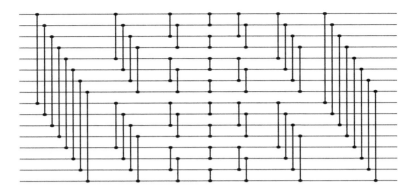

Fig. 3. The size-16 Beneš network with 7 stages. Each horizontal line represents an element in the array. Each vertical line segment illustrates a conditional swap involving the array elements corresponding to the end points.

$M_{i,j}$ is always conditionally swapped with $M_{i',j}$, where i' is a function of i. This implies that the conditional swaps can be carried out by performing bitwise logical operations between the rows (and the vectors formed by the corresponding conditions): a conditional swap between $M_{i,j}$ and $M_{i',j}$ with condition bit c can be carried out by 4 bit operations

$$(y \leftarrow M_{i,j} \oplus M_{i',j}; y \leftarrow cy; M_{i,j} \leftarrow M_{i,j} \oplus y; M_{i',j} \leftarrow M_{i',j} \oplus y),$$

as mentioned in [3]. Likewise, the $m - 1$ stages in the middle can be carried out by using bitwise logical operations between columns.

The Beneš network can be easily implemented on a machine with $m/2$-bit registers. The matrix M can be represented using an array of $m/2$ $m/2$-bit words in a row-major fashion. With such a representation, the conditional swaps between the rows can be performed by bitwise logical instructions between the words. To deal with the $m - 1$ stages in the middle, we transpose the bit matrix right after the first $m/2$ stages and right before the last $m/2$ stages (using the technique described in Sect. 2), to maintain a column-major representation of M during the $m - 1$ stages.

For our system it is required to permute $2^m = 2^{13}$ bits. We store these bits in a 64×128 matrix, and the same technique described above still applies.

4 The Gao–Mateer Additive FFT

Given a predefined $\mathbb{F}_2$-linear basis $\{\beta_1, \beta_2, \ldots, \beta_k\} \subset \mathbb{F}_{2^m}$ and an ℓ-coefficient input polynomial $f = \sum_{i=0}^{\ell-1} f_i x^i \in \mathbb{F}_{2^m}[x]$ such that $\ell \leq 2^k \leq 2^m$, the Gao–Mateer FFT evaluates f at all the subset sums of the basis. In other words, the FFT outputs the sequence $f(e_1), f(e_2), \ldots, f(e_{2^k})$, where

$$(e_1, e_2, e_3, e_4, e_5, \ldots) = (0, \beta_1, \beta_2, \beta_1 + \beta_2, \beta_3, \ldots).$$

Such an FFT will be called a size-2^k FFT.

Assuming that $\beta_k = 1$. The idea is to compute two polynomials $f^{(0)}$ and $f^{(1)}$ such that

$$f = f^{(0)}(x^2 + x) + x f^{(1)}(x^2 + x),$$

using the "radix conversion" described in [3, Sect. 3] (this is called "Taylor expansion" in [11]). Note that $f^{(0)}$ is a $\lceil \ell/2 \rceil$-coefficient polynomial, while $f^{(1)}$ is a $\lfloor \ell/2 \rfloor$-coefficient polynomial. Observe that $\alpha^2 + \alpha = (\alpha + 1)^2 + (\alpha + 1)$. This implies that once $t_0 = f^{(0)}(\alpha^2 + \alpha)$ and $t_1 = f^{(1)}(\alpha^2 + \alpha)$ are computed, $f(\alpha)$ can be computed as $t_0 + \alpha \cdot t_1$, and $f(\alpha + 1)$ can be computed as $f(\alpha) + t_1$. Observe that the output of the FFT is the sequence

$$f(e_1), f(e_2), \ldots, f(e_{2^{k-1}}), \quad f(e_1 + 1), f(e_2 + 1), \ldots, f(e_{2^{k-1}} + 1),$$

and $e_1, \ldots, e_{2^{k-1}}$ forms all subset sums of $\{\beta_1, \ldots, \beta_{k-1}\}$. Therefore, two FFT recursive calls are carried out to evaluate $f^{(0)}$ and $f^{(1)}$ at all subset sums of $\{\beta_1^2 + \beta_1, \ldots, \beta_{k-1}^2 + \beta_{k-1}\}$. Finally, $f(e_i)$ and $f(e_i + 1)$ are computed by using $f^{(0)}(e_i^2 + e_i)$ and $f^{(1)}(e_i^2 + e_i)$ from the recursive calls, for all i from 1 to 2^{k-1}.

In the case where $\beta_k \neq 1$, the task is reconsidered as evaluating $f(\beta_k x)$ at the subset sums of $\{\beta_1/\beta_k, \beta_2/\beta_k, \ldots, 1\}$. This is called "twisting" in [3]. Note that it takes $\ell - 1$ multiplications to compute $f(\beta_k x)$. To sum up, the Gao–Mateer additive FFT consists of 4 steps: (1) twisting, (2) radix conversion, (3) two FFT recursive calls, and (4) combining outputs from the recursive calls.

In order to find the roots of an error locator, we need to evaluate at every field element in $\mathbb{F}_{2^{13}}$. The corresponding basis is defined as

$$\{\beta_1 = z^{12}, \beta_2 = z^{11}, \ldots, \beta_{13} = 1\}.$$

Having $\beta_{13} = 1$ means that the first twisting can be skipped. Since we use $t = 128$, the error locator for our system is a 129-coefficient polynomial. However, for implementation of the FFT algorithm it is more convenient to have a 128-coefficient input polynomial. We therefore consider the error locator as $x^{128} + f$ and compute $\alpha^{128} + f(\alpha)$ for all $\alpha \in \mathbb{F}_{2^{13}}$. Below we explain how the Gao–Mateer additive FFT for root finding, as well as the corresponding "transposed" FFT for syndrome computation, are implemented in our software.

Radix Conversions and Twisting. As described in [3], the first step of the radix conversion is to compute polynomials Q and R from the $4n$-coefficient (n is a power of 2) input polynomial $f = \sum_{i=0}^{4n-1} f_i x^i$:

$$Q = (f_{2n} + f_{3n}) + \cdots + (f_{3n-1} + f_{4n-1})x^{n-1} + f_{3n}x^n + \cdots + f_{4n-1}x^{2n-1},$$
$$R = (f_0) + \cdots + (f_{n-1})x^{n-1}$$
$$+ (f_n + f_{2n} + f_{3n})x^n + \cdots + (f_{2n-1} + f_{3n-1} + f_{4n-1})x^{2n-1},$$

so that $f = Q(x^{2n} + x^n) + R$. Then Q and R are fed into recursive calls to obtain the corresponding $R^{(0)}, R^{(1)}, Q^{(0)}, Q^{(1)}$. Finally, the routine outputs $f^{(0)} = R^{(0)} + x^n Q^{(0)}$ and $f^{(1)} = R^{(1)} + x^n Q^{(1)}$. The recursion ends when we reach a 2-coefficient polynomial $f_0 + f_1 x$ in which case $f^{(0)} = f_0$ and $f^{(1)} = f_1$.

Here is a straightforward way to implement the routine. First of all, represent the input polynomial f as a $4n$-element array in of datatype gf (see Sect. 2) such that f_i is stored in in[i]. Then perform $4n$ XORs

```
for (i = 0; i < n; i++) in[2*n+i] ^= in[3*n+i];
for (i = 0; i < n; i++) in[1*n+i] ^= in[2*n+i];
```

to store R_i in in[i] and Q_i in in[2*n+i]. Likewise, the additions in the recursive calls can be carried out by in-place XORs between array elements. Eventually we have $f_i^{(0)}$ in in[2*i] and $f_i^{(1)}$ in in[2*i+1].

Representing the polynomials as arrays in gf is, however, expensive for twisting: as mentioned in Sect. 2, the function gf_mul is not efficient. Therefore in our software the polynomials are represented in bitsliced format. In this case, the additions can be simulated by using bitwise logical instructions and shifts. As a concrete example, let f be a 64-coefficient input polynomial in $\mathbb{F}_{2^{13}}[x]$, which is represented as a 13-element array of type uint64_t. Then the following code applies the radix conversion on f.

```
const uint64_t mask[5][2] =
{
  {0x8888888888888888, 0x4444444444444444},
  {0xC0C0C0C0C0C0C0C0, 0x3030303030303030},
  {0xF000F000F000F000, 0x0F000F000F000F00},
  {0xFF000000FF000000, 0x00FF000000FF0000},
  {0xFFFF000000000000, 0x0000FFFF00000000}
};
for (k = 4; k >= 0; k--)
for (i = 0; i < 13; i++)
{
  in[i] ^= (in[i] & mask[k][0]) >> (1 << k);
  in[i] ^= (in[i] & mask[k][1]) >> (1 << k);
}
```

In the end, the coefficients of $f^{(0)}$ are represented by the even bits of the words, while the coefficients of $f^{(1)}$ are represented by the odd bits.

The same technique can also be used to complete the radix conversions in the FFT recursive calls. Since a twisting operation simply multiplies f_i by β_k^i, they are carried out using bitsliced multiplications. See Fig. 4 for the code for all the radix conversions and twisting operations, including those in the FFT recursive calls. Note that the first twisting operation, which should take place before the first radix conversion, is already skipped in the code. Our software uses similar code but replaces 64-bit words by 128-bit words.

Butterflies. The reader might have noticed that the last 4 stages of Fig. 3 are similar to the well-known butterfly diagram for standard multiplicative FFTs. In a standard multiplicative FFT, f is written as $f^{(0)}(x^2) + x f^{(1)}(x^2)$ so that $f(\alpha)$ and $f(-\alpha)$ can be computed using $f^{(0)}(\alpha^2)$ and $f^{(1)}(\alpha^2)$ obtained from

```
for (j = 0; j <= 4; j++)
{
  for (i = 0; i < 13; i++)
  for (k = 4; k >= j; k--)
  {
    in[i] ^= (in[i] & mask[k][0]) >> (1 << k);
    in[i] ^= (in[i] & mask[k][1]) >> (1 << k);
  }
  vec64_mul(in, in, s[j]); // twisting
}
```

Fig. 4. The code for performing the twisting operations and radix conversion in the FFT for a 64-coefficient polynomial $f \in \mathbb{F}_{2^{13}}[x]$.

recursive calls. The similarity (between multiplicative FFTs and additive FFTs) in the ways of rewriting f results in the same "butterfly" structure.

In the case of a "full-size" additive FFT, where $\ell = 2^k$, the whole butterfly diagram has to be carried out. The technique used for carrying out the Beneš network (see Sect. 3) can be easily generalized to carry out the diagram. For decoding, however, ℓ is usually much smaller than $2^k = 2^m$. As the result, we only need to carry out the last $\log_2 \ell$ stages of the complete butterfly diagram.

As described in Sect. 3, we carry out the second half of the Beneš network by using a bit-matrix transposition in the middle. In the case of additive FFT butterflies, there will be m bit-matrix transpositions. The ideal case is that the ℓ is small enough so that the transpositions can be avoided. The corresponding code using 64-bit words for $m = 12$ is presented in Fig. 5. For the parameters $\ell = 128$ and $m = 13$, we are close to this ideal case but need to carry out 1 or 2 extra stages. The extra stages can be carried out by interleaving the 128-bit or 256-bit words.

```
for (i = 0; i <= 5; i++)
{
  s = 1 << i;
  for (j = 0; j < 64; j += 2*s)
  for (k = j; k < j+s; k++)
  {
    vec64_mul(tmp, out[k+s], consts[ consts_ptr + (k-j) ]);
    for (b = 0; b < 13; b++) out[k][b] ^= tmp[b];
    for (b = 0; b < 13; b++) out[k+s][b] ^= out[k][b];
  }
  consts_ptr += (1 << i);
}
```

Fig. 5. Butterflies in the additive FFT.

```
for (i = 5; i >= 0; i--)
{
  s = 1 << i;
  consts_ptr -= s;
  for (j = 0; j < 64; j += 2*s)
  for (k = j; k < j+s; k++)
  {
    for (b = 0; b < 13; b++) out[k][b] ^= out[k+s][b];
    vec64_mul(tmp, out[k], consts[ consts_ptr + (k-j) ]);
    for (b = 0; b < 13; b++) out[k+s][b] ^= tmp[b];
  }
}

                        :
                        :
                        :

for (j = 4; j >= 0; j--)
{
  vec64_mul(in, in, s[j]); // twisting
  for (k = j; k <= 4; k++)
  for (i = 0; i < 13; i++)
  {
    in[i] ^= (in[i] & (mask[k][1] >> (1 << k))) << (1 << k);
    in[i] ^= (in[i] & (mask[k][0] >> (1 << k))) << (1 << k);
  }
}
```

Fig. 6. Transposed FFT code with respect to Figs. 4 and 5.

The Bottom Level of Recursion. As shown in Fig. 4, when carrying out the radix conversions and twisting operations, we maintain a list of ℓ field elements. On the other hand, as shown in Fig. 5, when carrying out the FFT butterflies, we maintain a list of 2^m field elements. Apparently some operations are required to transit from the ℓ-element representation to the 2^m-element representation. This has to do with how the bottom level of recursion is defined.

The straightforward way to end the recursion is to check whether the input polynomial has only 1 coefficient; if so, the output is simply copies of the coefficient (the constant term). This is exactly the case for Figs. 4 and 5: after running the code in Fig. 4, we simply prepare the bitsliced representation of 64 copies of each elements and store them in out, and then Fig. 5 can be run to complete the FFT.

We do better by using the idea in [3, Sect. 3] to end the recursion when the input is a 2-coefficient polynomial. Let the input be $f = f_0 + f_1 x$ and the basis be $\{\beta_1, \ldots, \beta_k\}$. The idea is to first prepare a table containing $f_1 \beta_i$ for all i, and then each output element can be computed using at most one field addition. To implement the idea, we perform the radix conversions and twisting operations as in Fig. 4 but stop when we reach 2-coefficient polynomials. At this moment, the $\ell/2$ elements corresponding to f_0 would lie in the lower $\ell/2$ bits of the ℓ-bit words, while those for f_1 would lie in the higher $\ell/2$ bits. The outputs of the lowest-level FFTs can then be obtained by carrying out bitsliced multiplications and additions using bitwise logical operations between the $\ell/2$-bit words.

After this, we have the bitsliced representation (an array of m $\ell/2$-bit words) for the first output elements of the lowest level FFTs, the representation for the second output elements, and so on; in total there are $2^m/(\ell/2)$ such arrays. In order to group the output elements that belong to the same lowest-level FFT, we perform a sequence of m transpositions on $2^m/(\ell/2) \times (\ell/2) = 128 \times 64$ bit matrices, using the technique described in Sect. 2. Finally, the FFT butterflies can be performed using code similar to Fig. 5.

The Transposed Additive FFT. As described in [3, Sect. 4], a *linear algorithm* can be represented as a directed graph, and an algorithm that performs the transposed linear map can be obtained by reversing the edges in the graph. The way we implement the FFT makes it easy to imagine the structure of the graph and program the corresponding transposed FFT. As shown in Figs. 4 and 5, each inner loop in our FFT code essentially applies a simple linear operation on the values in in or out. In general it suffices to modify the loops to reverse the order that the inner loop is iterated and then replace the inner loop by its transpose. The transposed additive FFT code with respect to Figs. 4 and 5 is shown in Fig. 6 (the code for transposing the bottom level of recursion is skipped).

5   The Berlekamp-Massey Algorithm

The description of the original Berlekamp–Massey algorithm (BM) can be found in [12]. In each iteration of the algorithm, a field inversion has to be carried out. To perform the inversion in constant time, we may use the square-and-multiply algorithm, but this is rather expensive as discussed in Sect. 2. To avoid the problem, our implementation follows the inversion-free version of the algorithm as described in [21].

The algorithm begins with initializing polynomials $\sigma(x) = 1, \beta(x) = x \in \mathbb{F}_{2^m}[x]$, $\ell = 0 \in \mathbb{Z}$, and $\delta = 1 \in \mathbb{F}_{2^m}$. The input syndrome polynomial is denoted as $S(x) = \sum_{i=0}^{2t-1} S_i x^i$. Then in iteration k (from 0 to $2t - 1$), the variables are updated using operations in Fig. 7. Note that ℓ and δ are just an integer and a field element, and multiplying a polynomial by x (to update $\beta(x)$) is rather cheap. Therefore the algorithm is bottlenecked by computing d and updating $\sigma(x)$. We explain below how the algorithm is implemented in our software.

General Implementation Strategy. Assume that there are $(t+1)$-bit general-purpose registers on the target machine. For example, one can assume that $t = 63$ and that we are working on a 64-bit machine. We store polynomials $\sigma(x)$ and $\beta(x)$ in the bitsliced format, each using an array of m $(t + 1)$-bit words. The constant terms σ_0 and β_0 are stored in the most significant bits of the words; σ_1 and β_1 are stored in the second significant bits; and so on. We also use an array

$$d \leftarrow \sum_{i=0}^{t} \sigma_i S_{k-i}$$

$$\left[\sigma(x),\ \beta(x),\ \ell,\ \delta\right] \leftarrow \begin{cases} \left[\delta\sigma(x) - d\beta(x),\ x\beta(x),\ \ell,\ \delta\right], & d = 0 \text{ or } k < 2\ell. \\[2mm] \left[\delta\sigma(x) - d\beta(x),\ x\sigma(x),\ k - \ell + 1,\ d\right], & \text{otherwise.} \end{cases}$$

Fig. 7. Iteration k in the inversion-free BM.

S' of m (t+1)-bit words to store at most $t+1$ coefficients of $S(x)$. This array is maintained so that S_k is stored in the most significant bits of the words; S_{k-1} is stored in the second significant bits; and so on.

To compute d, we first perform a bitsliced field multiplication between $\sigma(x)$ and S'. The result is the bitsliced representation of $\sigma_0 S_k$, $\sigma_1 S_{k-1}$, ..., etc. The element d can then be computed as the parities of the m $(t+1)$-bit words. After this, S_{k+1} is inserted to the most significant bits of the words in S', which will be used in the next iteration.

To update $\sigma(x)$, we need to perform two scalar multiplications $\delta \cdot \sigma(x)$ and $d \cdot \beta(x)$. The bitsliced representations of $t+1$ copies of δ and d are first prepared, and then bitsliced multiplications are carried out to compute the products. Updating $\beta(x)$ is done by conditionally replacing the value of $\beta(x)$ by $\sigma(x)$ (which can be easily represented as logical operations) and then shifting each word to the right by one bit to simulate the multiplication by x.

The implementation strategy pretty much simulates the circuit presented in [21, Fig. 1]. Using the strategy, (each iteration of) the BM algorithm can be represented as a fixed sequence of instructions. In particular, the load and store instructions always use the same memory indices. As the result, the implementation is fully protected against timing attacks.

Haswell Implementation for $t = 128$. Exactly the same implementation strategy cannot be used for $t = 128$ on Haswell for there is no $(128 + 1)$-bit registers. To solve this problem, our strategy is to store σ_0 and S_k in two variables of datatype `gf`. The elements $\sigma_1, \ldots, \sigma_{128}$ and $S_{k-1}, \ldots, S_0$ are still stored in the bitsliced format, using two arrays of 128-bit words. To compute d, the product $\sigma_0 S_k$ is computed separately. Similarly, to update $\sigma(x)$, the product $\sigma_0 \delta$ is computed separately. Note that β_0 is always 0, so we simply store $\beta_1, \ldots, \beta_{128}$ in the bitsliced format.

We also need a way to update S' and $\beta(x)$ without generic shift instructions for 128-bit registers. Our solution is to make use of the `shrd` instruction. Given 64-bit registers r_1, r_0 as arguments, the `shrd` instruction is able to shift the least significant bit of r_1 into the most significant bit of r_0. Therefore, with 2 `shrd` instructions, we can shift a 128-bit word by one bit to the right. In particular, the second `shrd` shifts one bit into the most significant bit of the 128-bit word.

Therefore, we update S' by setting this bit to bits of S_k and update β by setting this bit to 0 or bits of σ_0 (depending on the condition).

To optimize the speed for Haswell, we combine the two `vec128_mul` function calls for $\delta \cdot \sigma(x)$ and $d \cdot \beta(x)$ to form one `vec256_mul`. As discussed in Sect. 2, this is better because 256-bit logical instructions have the same throughput as the 128-bit ones.

We also use 256-bit logical instructions to accelerate `vec128_mul`. A field multiplication can be viewed as a multiplication between 13-coefficient polynomials, followed by a reduction modulo g. Let the polynomials be f and f'; the idea is to split the polynomial multiplication into two parts $f(f'_0 + \cdots + f'_6 x^6)$ and $f(f'_7 + \cdots + f'_{12} x^5 + 0x^6)$. In this way, we create two bitsliced multiplications for computing d, and the two can be combined as what we do for $\delta \cdot \sigma(x)$ and $d \cdot \beta(x)$. Note that for combining the two products and the reduction part we still use 128-bit logical instructions. By using 256-bit logical instructions, we improve the cycle counts of `vec128_mul` from 137 to 94 Haswell cycles.

As a minor optimization, we also combine the computation of $\sigma_0 S_k$ and $\sigma_0 \delta$. This is achieved by using the upper 32 bits of the 64-bit variables in `gf_mul` for another multiplication. In this way, two field multiplications can be carried out in roughly the same time as `gf_mul`.

As discussed in Sect. 4, the input of the FFT function for root finding is the bitsliced representation of $f_0, \ldots, f_{127}$; f_{128} is not stored since it is assumed to be 1. In fact, at the end of the Berlekamp–Massey algorithm we have $f_i = \sigma_{128-i}$. Therefore we perform a field inversion for σ_0 and bitsliced multiplications to force a monic output polynomial for the Berlekamp–Massy algorithm.

6   The Complete Cryptosystem

In [3, Sect. 6] a complete public-key encryption system is described. The cryptosystem uses a KEM/DEM-like structure, where the KEM is based on the Niederreiter cryptosystem. To send a message, the sender first uses the receiver's Niederreiter public key to compute the syndrome of a random weight-t error vector. Then the error vector is hashed to obtain two symmetric keys. The first symmetric key is used for a stream cipher to encrypt the arbitrary-length message. The second symmetric key is used for a message authentication code to authenticate the output generated by the stream cipher. The syndrome, the stream-cipher output, and the authentication tag are then sent to the receiver.

The receiver first decodes the syndrome using the Niederreiter secret key. The resulting error vector is then hashed to obtain the symmetric keys, and the receiver verifies (using the tag) and decrypts the stream-cipher output. Note that the receiver can fail in decoding or verification. The decryption algorithm should be carefully implemented such that others cannot distinguish (for example, by using timing information) what kind of failure the receiver encounters.

We show below how key-pair generation, KEM encryption, and KEM decryption are implemented in our software.

Private-Key Generation. The private key of the system consists of two parts: (1) a sequence $(\alpha_1, \ldots, \alpha_n)$ of n distinct elements in $\mathbb{F}_{2^m}$ and (2) a square-free degree-t polynomial $g \in \mathbb{F}_{2^m}[x]$ such that $g(\alpha_i) \neq 0$ for all i.

For our implementation, g is generated as a uniform random degree-t monic irreducible polynomial in $\mathbb{F}_{2^m}[x]$. To generate g, we first generate a random element α in the extension field $\mathbb{F}_{2^{mt}}$. The polynomial g is then defined as the minimal polynomial of α in $\mathbb{F}_{2^m}[x]$, if the degree is t. To find the minimal polynomial, we view $\mathbb{F}_{2^{mt}}$ as the vector space $(\mathbb{F}_{2^m})^t$ and try to find linear dependency between $1, \alpha, \alpha^2, \ldots, \alpha^t$ using Gaussian elimination. A description of the algorithm can be found in, for example, [20, Sect. 17.2].

The benefit of this approach is that it is easy to make Gaussian elimination constant-time: [3] already shows how this can be achieved in the case of bit matrices. Note that the algorithm can fail to find a degree-t irreducible polynomial when $\alpha \in \mathbb{F}_{2^{mt'}}$ such that t' is a divisor of t. For our parameters $m = 13$ and $t = 128$ the probability of failure is only 2^{-832}.

Recall that we use $n = 2^m$. Let ϕ be a permutation function such that $\phi(e_1, \ldots, e_{2^m}) = (\alpha_1, \ldots, \alpha_{2^m})$, where $(e_1, \ldots, e_{2^m})$ is the stardard order of field elements introduced by the FFT (see Sect. 4). In our software, the permutation function is defined using the condition bits in the corresponding size-2^m Beneš network. Instead of generating the sequence α_i and then figure out the condition bits, the condition bits are generated as random bits in the current implementation; the reader may refer to [3, Sect. 5] for a brief discussion on this approach. We comment that there are $(2m-1)2^{m-1} = m2^m - 2^{m-1}$ condition bits in the Beneš network, while a list of 2^m field elements takes $m2^m$ bits. In other words, representing $(\alpha_1, \ldots, \alpha_n)$ as condition bits actually saves the size of secret keys.

Public-Key Generation. Let H be the bit matrix obtained by replacing each entry in the matrix

$$\begin{pmatrix} 1/g(\alpha_1) & 1/g(\alpha_2) & \cdots & 1/g(\alpha_n) \\ \alpha_1/g(\alpha_1) & \alpha_2/g(\alpha_2) & \cdots & \alpha_n/g(\alpha_n) \\ \vdots & \vdots & \ddots & \vdots \\ \alpha_1^{t-1}/g(\alpha_1) & \alpha_2^{t-1}/g(\alpha_2) & \cdots & \alpha_n^{t-1}/g(\alpha_n) \end{pmatrix}$$

by a column of m bits from the standard-basis representation. The receiver computes the row-reduced echelon form of H. If the result is of the form $[I|H']$, the public-key is set to H'; otherwise a new secret key is generated.

In our implementation, the images $g(e_1), \ldots, g(e_n)$ are first generated using the FFT implementation described in Sect. 4. After this, the inversions of all these images are computed, using Montgomery's trick [14] with bitsliced field multiplications. Now we have the bitsliced representation of the first row of the matrix

$$\begin{pmatrix} 1/g(e_1) & 1/g(e_2) & \cdots & 1/g(e_n) \\ e_1/g(e_1) & e_2/g(e_2) & \cdots & e_n/g(e_n) \\ \vdots & \vdots & \ddots & \vdots \\ e_1^{t-1}/g(e_1) & e_2^{t-1}/g(e_2) & \cdots & e_n^{t-1}/g(e_n) \end{pmatrix}.$$

The remaining rows are then computed one-by-one using bitsliced field multi-plications. Since all the rows are represented in the bitsliced format, the matrix can be easily viewed as the corresponding $mt \times n$ bit matrix. Then the Beneš network is applied to each row of the bit matrix to obtain H. Finally we follow [3, Sect. 6] to perform a constant-time Gaussian elimination. The public key is then the row-major representation of H' (one can of course use a column-major representation instead).

KEM Encryption. The KEM encryption begins with generating the error vector e of weight t. This is carried out by first generating a sequence of t random m-bit values, which indicates the positions of the errors. The t values are then checked for repetition. If a repetition is found, we simply regenerate the t random m-bit values; otherwise, we convert the indices into the error vector as a sequence of $n/8$ bytes.

To compute each bit of the syndrome, each 128-bit word in the corresponding row is first ANDed with the corresponding 128-bit word in the error vector. The 128-bit results are then XORed together to form one single 128-bit word. We make use of the popcnt instruction to compute the parity of the 128-bit word, and the syndrome bit is set to the parity. Finally, after processing all the rows of the public key, we deal with the identity matrix by XORing the first $mt/8$ bytes of the error vector into the syndrome.

KEM Decryption. As explained in [3], decoding consists of 5 stages: the initial permutation, syndrome computation, key-equation solving, root finding, and the final permutation. This is why the "total" column in [3, Table 1] is essentially

$$\text{"perm"} \times 2 + \text{"synd"} + \text{"key eq"} + \text{"root"}.$$

The "all" column in Table 1, however, is computed as

$$\text{"perm"} \times 2 + \text{"synd"} \times 2 + \text{"key eq"} + \text{"root"} \times 2.$$

In other words, we count one extra "root" and one extra "synd".

The reason we count "root" one more time is a matter of implementation choice. To perform syndrome computation, each of the 2^m input bits is required to be scaled by $1/g(\alpha)^2$, where α is the corresponding point for evaluation. Since $1/g(\alpha)^2$ depends only on g, [3] uses them as pre-computed values. This strategy saves time but enlarges the size of secret keys. We decide to save the size of secret keys and compute all $1/g(\alpha)^2$ on the fly, using "root" for computing $g(\alpha)$, Montgomery's trick for simultaneous inversions [14] with bitsliced multiplications, and bitsliced squarings.

The reason we count "synd" one more time is for re-encryption. A decoding algorithm is only required to decode when the input syndrome corresponds to an error vector of weight t. For KEM, however, we need additionally the ability to reject invalid inputs. We therefore check the weight of the error vector and perform "synd" again to compute the syndrome of the error vector. The decoding is considered successful only if the weight is exactly t and the syndrome matches the output of the first "synd" stage.

References

1. Beneš, V.E.: Mathematical Theory of Connecting Networks and Telephone Traffic. Academic Press, Cambridge (1965). §3
2. Bernstein, D.J.: qhasm software package (2007). http://cr.yp.to/qhasm.html. §2
3. Bernstein, D.J., Chou, T., Schwabe, P.: McBits: fast constant-time code-based cryptography. In: Bertoni, G., Coron, J.-S. (eds.) CHES 2013. LNCS, vol. 8086, pp. 250–272. Springer, Heidelberg (2013). doi:10.1007/978-3-642-40349-1_15. §1, §1, §1, §1, §1, §1, §1, §1, §2, §2, §3, §3, §4, §4, §4, §4, §4, §6, §6, §6, §6, §6, §6, §6
4. Bernstein, D.J., Chuengsatiansup, C., Lange, T., van Vredendaal, C.: NTRU Prime (2016). https://eprint.iacr.org/2016/461.pdf. §1
5. Bertoni, G., Coron, J.-S. (eds.): CHES 2013. LNCS, vol. 8086. Springer, Heidelberg (2013). See [3]
6. Biham, E. (ed.): FSE 1997. LNCS, vol. 1267. Springer, Heidelberg (1997). See [7]
7. Biham, E.: A fast new DES implementation in software, in [6], pp. 260–272 (1997)
8. Biswas, B., Sendrier, N.: McEliece cryptosystem implementation: theory and practice, in [9], pp. 47–62 (2008). §1
9. Buchmann, J., Ding, J. (eds.): Post-Quantum Cryptography. LNCS, vol. 5299. Springer, Heidelberg (2008). See [8]
10. Agner Fog: Instruction tables (2016). http://www.agner.org/optimize/instruction_tables.pdf. §2
11. Gao, S., Mateer, T.: Additive fast Fourier transforms over finite fields. IEEE Trans. Inf. Theory **56**, 6265–6272 (2010). http://www.math.clemson.edu/sgao/pub.html. §1, §4
12. Massey, J.L.: Shift-register synthesis and BCH decoding. IEEE Trans. Inf. Theory **15**, 122–127 (1969). §5
13. McEliece, R.J.: A public-key cryptosystem based on algebraic coding theory, JPL DSN Progress report, pp. 114–116 (1978). http://ipnpr.jpl.nasa.gov/progress_report2/42-44/44N.PDF. §1
14. Montgomery, P.L.: Speeding the Pollard and elliptic curve methods of factorization. Mathe. Comput. **48**, 243–264 (1987). http://www.jstor.org/stable/pdf/2007888.pdf. §6, §6
15. Niederreiter, H.: Knapsack-type cryptosystems and algebraic coding theory. Probl. Control Inf. Theory **15**, 159–166 (1986). §1
16. NIST: Submission Requirements and Evaluation Criteria for the Post-Quantum Cryptography Standardization Process (2016). http://csrc.nist.gov/groups/ST/post-quantum-crypto/documents/call-for-proposals-final-dec-2016.pdf. §1
17. Peters, C.: Information-set decoding for linear codes over $\mathbf{F}_q$. In: Sendrier, N. (ed.) PQCrypto 2010 [18]. LNCS, vol. 6061, pp. 81–94. Springer, Heidelberg (2010). doi:10.1007/978-3-642-12929-2_7. §1
18. Sendrier, N. (ed.): PQCrypto 2010. LNCS, vol. 6061. Springer, Heidelberg (2010). See [17]
19. Shoup, V.: A proposal for an ISO standard for public key encryption (version 2.1). http://www.shoup.net/papers. §1
20. Shoup, V. (ed.): A Computational Introduction to Number Theory and Algebra (Version 2). Cambridge University Press, Cambridge (2015). §6
21. Youzhi, X.: Implementation of Berlekamp-Massey algorithm without inversion. IEE Proc. I Commun. Speech Vision **138**, 138–140 (1991). §5, §5

High-Speed Key Encapsulation from NTRU

Andreas Hülsing[1]([✉]), Joost Rijneveld[2]([✉]), John Schanck[3,4]([✉]),
and Peter Schwabe[2]([✉])

[1] Department of Mathematics and Computer Science, Technische Universiteit
Eindhoven, Eindhoven, The Netherlands
andreas@huelsing.net
[2] Digital Security Group, Radboud University, Nijmegen, The Netherlands
joost@joostrijneveld.nl, peter@cryptojedi.org
[3] Institute for Quantum Computing, University of Waterloo, Waterloo, Canada
[4] Security Innovation, Wilmington, MA, USA
jschanck@uwaterloo.ca

Abstract. This paper presents software demonstrating that the 20-year-old NTRU cryptosystem is competitive with more recent lattice-based cryptosystems in terms of speed, key size, and ciphertext size. We present a slightly simplified version of textbook NTRU, select parameters for this encryption scheme that target the 128-bit post-quantum security level, construct a KEM that is CCA2-secure in the quantum random oracle model, and present highly optimized software targeting Intel CPUs with the AVX2 vector instruction set. This software takes only 307 914 cycles for the generation of a keypair, 48 646 for encapsulation, and 67 338 for decapsulation. It is, to the best of our knowledge, the first NTRU software with full protection against timing attacks.

Keywords: Post-quantum crypto · Lattice-based crypto · NTRU · CCA2-secure KEM · QROM · AVX2

1 Introduction

In December 2016, NIST issued a call for proposals for "post-quantum cryptography" [34] to select schemes for standardization. More specifically, NIST requests algorithms in three categories: public-key encryption, key exchange or key encapsulation mechanisms (KEMs), and digital signatures. Obviously, the central requirement is that proposed schemes are indeed "post-quantum", i.e., that they resist attacks by a large quantum computer.

This work has been supported by the European Commission through the ICT program under contract ICT-645622 (PQCRYPTO), and by the Netherlands Organisation for Scientific Research (NWO) through Veni 2013 project 13114. This work has also been supported by Canada's NSERC CREATE program. The Institute for Quantum Computing is supported in part by the Government of Canada and the Province of Ontario. Permanent ID of this document: 65dcfe39848495fe9b2423ac0a563d43. Date: June 26, 2017.

© International Association for Cryptologic Research 2017
W. Fischer and N. Homma (Eds.): CHES 2017, LNCS 10529, pp. 232–252, 2017.
DOI: 10.1007/978-3-319-66787-4_12

For encryption and key encapsulation, it seems that the most promising approach in terms of speed, key size, and ciphertext size is lattice-based cryptography. It is no coincidence that Google chose a lattice-based scheme, more specifically the NEWHOPE Ring-LWE-based key exchange [2], for their post-quantum TLS experiment [9]. It is also not surprising that various recent papers propose constructions and parameters, often together with implementations, for lattice-based encryption schemes and KEMs. See, for example, [2,3,7,8,13,14,17,35].

These schemes differ in terms of security notions (e.g., passive vs. active security), underlying hard problems (e.g., learning-with-errors vs. learning with rounding), structure of the underlying lattices (standard vs. ideal lattices), cryptographic functionality (encryption vs. key encapsulation), and performance in terms of speed and sizes.

Contributions of this paper. In this paper we take a step back and turn our attention to the "grandfather of lattice-based encryption schemes", namely NTRU [23], with the goal of constructing a CCA2-secure key encapsulation mechanism (KEM).

We start by reconsidering the textbook OW-CPA-secure NTRU encryption scheme and show how a restriction on parameters leads to a considerably simpler and more efficient key generation algorithm. We also reconsider the sample spaces for private key and message vectors. We avoid the commonly used fixed-weight sample spaces and propose a sampling algorithm that produces independent and identically distributed coefficients. These changes make constant-time noise sampling much more efficient without significantly impacting security.

We then carefully optimize NTRU parameters to achieve 128 bits of post-quantum security while at the same time eliminating the possibility of decryption failures. Next, we transform this optimized OW-CPA-secure scheme into a CCA2-secure KEM in the quantum-accessible random oracle model (QROM). To this end, we tweak a known transform by Dent [18] such that security can also be shown in the QROM without notably sacrificing efficiency.

We illustrate the performance of our NTRU-based KEM by providing a highly optimized implementation targeting Intel processors with AVX2 vector instructions, the same architectures targeted by the optimized NEWHOPE software described in [2]. To the best of our knowledge, our software is the first NTRU software with full timing-attack protection.

KEM vs. PKE and passive vs. active security. Achieving CCA2 security for an NTRU-based public key encryption scheme appears to require the use of complex padding mechanisms [27]. However, already [40] and [36] showed that most of this complexity can be avoided when constructing an NTRU-based CCA2-secure *KEM*. CCA2-secure KEMs are very versatile building blocks. Together with a CCA2-secure symmetric "data encapsulation mechanism" (DEM) they can be used for CCA2-secure public-key encryption of messages of arbitrary length [16]. They are, furthermore, the central building block in (authenticated) key exchange constructions (see, e.g., [31]), in particular those that do not rely on signatures for authentication. We note that the NTRU-based KEM we describe in this paper could be used in place of NEWHOPE in the key exchange setting considered in Google's post-quantum TLS experiment. As a potential benefit, the CCA2 security allows busy servers to cache and reuse ephemeral keys to reduce the number of CPU cycles spent on key generation. This is a common optimization in TLS libraries, but passively secure schemes like NEWHOPE or Frodo may not be secure when this optimization is deployed. See [2, Sect. 2].

Hasn't NTRU been superseded? From some recent papers on lattice-based cryptography one might get the impression that NTRU has been "superseded" by public-key encryption based on Ring-LWE [33] or by NTRU Prime [3]. For example, Kirchner and Fouque write in [30]: *"Since the practical cost of transforming a [sic] NTRU-based cryptosystem into a Ring-LWE-based cryptosystem is usually small, especially for key-exchange [...], we recommend to dismiss the former, in particular since it is known to be weaker."* Bernstein, Chuengsatiansup, Lange, and van Vredendaal write in [3]: *"Rings of the form $(\mathbb{Z}/q)[x]/(x^p-1)$, where p is a prime and q is a power of 2, are used in the classic NTRU cryptosystem, and have none of our recommended defenses."*

The statement by Kirchner and Fouque about NTRU being weaker than Ring-LWE is an asymptotic statement. It is actually not surprising that Ring-LWE is asymptotically a better choice than NTRU, because Ring-LWE-based (and LWE-based) cryptography has been designed, to a large extent, with asymptotic security statements in mind. However, these asymptotic results say little or nothing about the *concrete* security of parameters that have been proposed for actual use. See for example [10, Sect. 6]. NTRU on the other hand was designed with concrete security for concrete efficient parameters in mind and does not attempt to make asymptotic statements.

NTRU Prime can be seen as a variation of NTRU that uses a different ring (or, as the authors phrase it, that avoids *"rings with worrisome structure"*). Whether or not this choice of ring and other choices made in the design of NTRU Prime lead to a more or less secure scheme will need careful investigation. This is acknowledged by the authors, who state that they *"caution potential users that many details of Streamlined NTRU Prime are new and require careful security review"*.

To summarize, in this paper we do not argue for an order of preference among NTRU, NTRU Prime, and Ring-LWE. For concrete parameters aiming at a similar level of security and efficiency it is unclear which of the three will prove optimal in the long run. At the moment there are good reasons for and against choosing any of them. We focus on NTRU, the oldest of these schemes, with a track record of surviving 20 years of cryptanalysis.

A note on patents. One reason that NTRU is not more widely deployed is that there have been patents restricting its usage for most of its lifetime. The NTRU cryptosystem was patented in [24], and NTRU with "product-form keys" was patented in [25]. The former patent was due to expire on August 19, 2017, but in March of this year Security Innovation released both patents [38], placing NTRU into the public domain. Neither the present work nor the accompanying software makes use of product-form keys.

Availability of software. We place all software presented in this paper into the public domain to maximize reusability of our results. It is available for download at https://joostrijneveld.nl/papers/ntrukem.

2   Preliminaries

Minimal representatives. In describing NTRU it is useful to refer to quotient rings such as $\mathbb{Z}[x]/(8192, x^n - 1)$ and $\mathbb{Z}[x]/(3, x^n - 1)$. However, the scheme involves computations that are not well defined as maps on quotient rings. To avoid technical pitfalls around this issue, we describe all operations in $\mathbb{Z}[x]$ and introduce a "minimal representative" map to enact reduction modulo an ideal.

Let I be an ideal of $\mathbb{Z}[x]$ with $\mathbb{Z}[x]/I \cong (\mathbb{Z}/\ell)^m$ for some m, possibly ∞. The minimal representative map $[\cdot]_I : \mathbb{Z}[x] \to \mathbb{Z}[x]$ is defined such that $[a]_I \equiv a$ (mod I), deg $[a]_I < m$, and $[a]_I$ has coefficients in $[-\ell/2, \ell/2)$. When ℓ is even we use the convention that $[\ell/2]_I = -\ell/2$. We write $[1/a]_I$ to denote the minimal b for which $[ab]_I = 1$, if such an element exists.

Cyclotomic rings. We denote the dth cyclotomic polynomial by Φ_d. Note $\Phi_1 = x - 1$ and if d is prime $\Phi_d = 1 + x + x^2 + \cdots + x^{d-1}$. These are the only two cases we consider. We define

$$S_d := \mathbb{Z}[x]/(\Phi_d),$$
$$R_n := \mathbb{Z}[x]/(x^n - 1).$$

For prime n we have $x^n - 1 = \Phi_1 \Phi_n$ and $R_n \cong S_1 \times S_n$. We will occasionally need to lift elements of S_n/p to R_n for a fixed prime p. We do this by solving the system of congruences

$$\mathsf{Lift}_p(v) \equiv 0 \quad (\text{mod } \Phi_1)$$
$$\mathsf{Lift}_p(v) \equiv v \quad (\text{mod } (p, \Phi_n)).$$

Solutions are guaranteed to exist by the Chinese remainder theorem. We fix a particular solution

$$\mathsf{Lift}_p(v) := \left[\Phi_1 \left[v/\Phi_1 \right]_{(p,\Phi_n)} \right]_{(x^n-1)}.$$

An efficient algorithm for Lift_p may be found in the full version of this paper.

Coefficient embedding of R_n. The coefficient embedding identifies the monomial basis $\{1, x, x^2, \ldots, x^{n-1}\}$ of R_n as an orthonormal basis of $\mathbb{R}^n$. We write v_i for the ith coefficient of v and allow arithmetic modulo n in the index. We write $\langle \cdot, \cdot \rangle$ for the inner product on $\mathbb{R}^n$ and define the 2-norm and max-norm as usual: $|v|_2 = \sqrt{\langle v, v \rangle}$, and $|v|_\infty = \max_i |v_i|$.

For $a \in R_n$ we write $\bar{a}$ to denote the element with $\bar{a}_i = a_{-i}$ for all i. This "reversal" map reveals a connection between the multiplicative structure of R_n and the geometry of the coefficient embedding that we use in Lemma 1. Namely,

$$ab = \sum_{k=0}^{n-1} \sum_{i=0}^{n-1} a_{k-i} b_i x^k = \sum_{k=0}^{n-1} \langle x^k \bar{a}, b \rangle x^k.$$

Min-entropy. If ρ is a probability distribution on a finite set X, then the min-entropy of ρ is $\min\{-\log_2 \rho(x) : x \in X\}$.

eXtendable Output Functions (XOF). Our constructions make use of an extendable output function $\mathsf{XOF}(X, L, S)$, where X is the input bitstring, L is the desired output length in bits, and S is a context string (domain separator). As the XOF will be modeled as (quantum-accessible) random oracle in our security arguments, we require the instantiation of the XOF to be indistinguishable from a random oracle. The XOF can be instantiated, for example, using sponge constructions like SHAKE [5]. We often need a length value that is consistent with the security level for the scheme. We denote this μ. One may assume $\mu = 256$.

3   OW-CPA-secure NTRU Encryption

In this section we describe the key generation, encryption, and decryption routines for our OW-CPA-secure NTRU encryption scheme. We make several departures from previous instantiations. First, we work directly with S_n to avoid common security issues associated with the S_1 subring of R_n. While it is possible to instantiate NTRU directly in S_n, and not use R_n at all, we still lift elements of S_n to R_n to take advantage of convenient computational and geometric features of R_n. Second, we choose parameters so that decryption failures are completely eliminated, and we do this without restricting the key and message spaces. Finally, we eliminate any need for fixed-weight distributions like those used in [3,15,17,20,21,23,28]. All of our sampling routines are chosen to admit simple and efficient constant time implementations.

3.1   Parameters

NTRU is parameterized by an odd prime n and coprime positive integers p and q. The parameter n indexes R_n and S_n, hereafter denoted R and S. We define $\mathfrak{p} = (p, \Phi_n)$ and $\mathfrak{q} = (q, x^n - 1)$. Ciphertexts and public keys belong to the set of minimal representatives of $R/\mathfrak{q} = \mathbb{Z}[x]/\mathfrak{q}$. Messages, blinding polynomials, and private keys belong to the set of minimal representatives of $S/\mathfrak{p} = \mathbb{Z}[x]/\mathfrak{p}$, denoted

$$\mathcal{T} = \{a \in \mathbb{Z}[x] : a = [a]_{\mathfrak{p}}\}.$$

Private keys are restricted to non-negatively correlated elements of $\mathcal{T}$:

$$\mathcal{T}_+ = \{v \in \mathcal{T} : \langle xv, v \rangle \geq 0\}.$$

The correlation restriction is new to this work. It comes from the proof of correctness in Sect. 3.5.

In Sect. 3.5 we prove that our instantiation of NTRU is correct, i.e. that decryption failures are impossible, with $p = 3$ and $q = q(n)$ where $\log_2 q(n) = \lceil 7/2 + \log_2(n) \rceil$. With $p = 3$ and q as the smallest power of two providing correctness, n is our only free parameter.

A final restriction on parameters is that Φ_n must be irreducible modulo both p and q. This obviates invertibility tests during key generation and makes the process more amenable to a constant time implementation. A similar condition has been recommended since the original description of NTRU [22,23], but has not previously been a requirement. Streamlined NTRU Prime has an analogous requirement for q, but not for p [3]. This leaves us with only a handful of valid n in the range typical of recent NTRU and LWE instantiations. They are: $509, 557, 653, 677, 701, 773, 797, 821, 859, 907, 941$, and 1061. All of these satisfy $q(n) \in \{8192, 16384\}$. The largest for which $q(n) = 8192$ is $n = 701$. In Sect. 4 we show that the corresponding parameter set, $n = 701, p = 3, q = 8192$, is expected to provide 128-bit security in a post-quantum setting.

3.2 Key Generation

A private key for our OW-CPA-secure encryption scheme is a non-zero element $f \in \mathcal{T}$. A corresponding public key is $h \in R$ such that $[fh]_q$ has small coefficients. We generate h by sampling g in $\mathcal{T}$ and computing $h = [\Phi_1 g f_q]_q$ where $f_q = [1/f]_{(q,\Phi_n)}$. This ensures $[fh]_q = \Phi_1 g$.

Previous instantiations of NTRU have taken f to be a short element of R with an inverse in both R/p and R/q. With the parameters of the previous section, every non-zero element of $\mathcal{T}$ is invertible as an element of both S/p and S/q. Invertibility in S/p and S/q is sufficient for our decryption procedure, so we can forego tests for invertibility in R/p and R/q. Inverses must still be computed, but the process never fails.

The factor of Φ_1 in the definition of h ensures that h is equivalent to zero modulo (q, Φ_1). Previous instantiations of NTRU have taken $h = [g/f]_q$ and the value of h modulo (q, Φ_1) has been a security concern – one that is typically mitigated by sampling f and g from sets of fixed-weight vectors. To avoid complicated sampling routines, we allow f and g to take any value in $\mathcal{T}_+$.

Of course the exact distribution from which f and g are drawn affects security. Algorithm 1 makes use of a generic subroutine $\mathsf{Sample}\mathcal{T}_+$ that may be thought of as sampling from the uniform distribution on $\mathcal{T}_+$. In Sect. 3.4 we describe a non-uniform $\mathsf{Sample}\mathcal{T}_+$ routine that admits simple and efficient constant time implementation. Our security claims in Sect. 4 are relative to this non-uniform distribution. Implementations that sample from the uniform distribution on $\mathcal{T}_+$ may be able to claim a slightly higher security level.

Algorithm 1. KeyGen(*coins*)

1: $g = \mathsf{Sample}\mathcal{T}_+(\mathsf{XOF}(coins, \mu, \mathtt{randg}))$
2: $f = \mathsf{Sample}\mathcal{T}_+(\mathsf{XOF}(coins, \mu, \mathtt{randf}))$
3: $f_q = [1/f]_{(q,\Phi_n)}$
4: $h = [\Phi_1 g f_q]_q$
Output: Private key f, Public key h

3.3   OW-CPA Encryption

An NTRU public key determines an R-module of rank 2 that we denote by

$$L_h = \{(u, v) \in R^2 : v \equiv uh \pmod{q}\}. \tag{1}$$

Clearly $(1, h) \in L_h$, so $[L_h]_q$ is a set of exactly q^n distinct points in R^2. Elements of R^2 of the form $r(1, h) + (0, m) = (r, rh + m)$ will generally not be in L_h. The essential idea behind NTRU is that with suitable restrictions on r and m it is possible to recover m uniquely from $rh + m$.

In previous instantiations of NTRU, r and m have been chosen to have coefficients in $\{-1, 0, 1\}$ with a prescribed number of coefficients taking each value. We depart from this by letting r and m take arbitrary values in $\mathcal{T}$.

We also ensure that all ciphertexts are identical modulo (q, Φ_1). Toward this end we take encryption to be the map

$$(r, m) \mapsto [prh + \mathsf{Lift}_p(m)]_q.$$

Since h and $\mathsf{Lift}_p(m)$ are equivalent to 0 modulo (q, Φ_1) this achieves our goal.

Complete encryption and decryption routines are given by Algorithms 2 and 3. As with $\mathsf{Sample}\mathcal{T}_+$ in the previous section, $\mathsf{Sample}\mathcal{T}$ in Algorithm 2 is a generic sampling routine that may be thought of as sampling from the uniform distribution on $\mathcal{T}$. However, our security claims in Sect. 4 are with respect to the $\mathsf{Sample}\mathcal{T}$ instantiation described in Sect. 3.4, which does not sample the uniform distribution on $\mathcal{T}$.

Line 2 of Algorithm 2 is equivalent to the original NTRU encryption primitive [23] on the subring corresponding to S. The OW-CPA security [18, Definition 3] of this scheme is (trivially) equivalent to the assumption that random NTRU ciphertexts are hard to invert.

Algorithm 2. $\mathcal{E}(m, coins, h)$

1: $r = \mathsf{Sample}\mathcal{T}(coins)$
2: $e = [prh + \mathsf{Lift}_p(m)]_q$
Output: Ciphertext e.

Algorithm 3. $\mathcal{D}(e, f)$

1: $m' = \left[[ef]_q\, f^{-1}\right]_p$
Output: m'

3.4   Simplified Sampling

Sampling from the uniform distribution on $\mathcal{T}$ or $\mathcal{T}_+$ in constant time may be difficult or slow. In this section we present alternative distributions that admit simple and efficient constant time sampling routines. Our security analysis in Sect. 4 assumes that these simplified sampling routines are used. Implementations that sample from the uniform distribution on these spaces may be able to claim a slightly higher security level.

We first note that any routine for sampling from $\mathcal{T}$ can be transformed into a routine for sampling from $\mathcal{T}_+$ with at most a one bit loss in the min-entropy of its output distribution. Let v be an element of $\mathcal{T}$ and let w be the element obtained by flipping the signs of the even index coefficients of v. With the exception of $w_{n-1}w_0$, each product in the expansion of $\langle xw, w \rangle$ contains one even index term and one odd index term. Hence $\langle xw, w \rangle = 2v_{n-1}v_0 - \langle xv, v \rangle$. However, since $v \in \mathcal{T}$ we have $v_{n-1} = 0$ and in fact $\langle xw, w \rangle = -\langle xv, v \rangle$.

Our simplified SampleT$_+$ routine (Algorithm 4) draws v from $\mathcal{T}$ and then conditionally applies an even index sign flip to v if $\langle xv, v \rangle < 0$. While Algorithm 4 does not preserve the distribution of its SampleT subroutine, in the way that rejection sampling would, it does preserve expected length. Also note that the even index sign flip is an involution on $\mathcal{T}$, so the min-entropy of the output of SampleT$_+$, over a uniform choice of coins, is at most one bit less than the min-entropy of the output of SampleT.

Algorithm 4. SampleT$_+(coins)$

1: $v = $ SampleT$(coins)$
2: $s = \text{sign}(\langle xv, v \rangle)$
3: /* $s = \pm 1$, sign$(0) = 1$ */
4: **for** $i = 0$ **to** $(n-1)/2$ **do**
5:    $v_{2i} = s \cdot v_{2i}$
6: **end for**
Output: $v \in \mathcal{T}_+$

Algorithm 5. SampleT$(coins)$

1: $b = \text{XOF}(coins, 4n - 4, \textbf{expand})$
2: $v = 0$
3: **for** $i = 0$ **to** $n - 2$ **do**
4:    $v_i = [b_{4i} + b_{4i+1} - b_{4i+2} - b_{4i+3}]_p$
5: **end for**
Output: v

Our simplified SampleT routine (Algorithm 5) draws $n - 1$ coefficients independently from a centered binomial distribution[1] of parameter $t = 2$ and then reduces these coefficients modulo p. The process always consumes exactly $2t(n-1)$ random bits. The resulting distribution is centrally symmetric (for any value of p and t) and tends to the uniform distribution as t is increased. With $p = 3$ and $t = 2$, a coefficient drawn from this distribution is $-1, 0$, or 1 with probability $\frac{5}{16}$, $\frac{6}{16}$, and $\frac{5}{16}$ respectively. The expected length of the output is therefore $\sqrt{\frac{5}{8}(n-1)}$.

3.5 Correctness

The following lemma determines the parameters for which we can prove that $(\text{KeyGen}, \mathcal{E}, \mathcal{D})$ is a correct probabilistic encryption scheme. It also explains our use of $\mathcal{T}_+$. A similar statement with $g \in \mathcal{T}$ would require a factor of 2 rather than $\sqrt{2}$.

Lemma 1. For $r \in \mathcal{T}$ and $g \in \mathcal{T}_+$,

$$|\text{Lift}_p(r)g|_\infty \leq \sqrt{2} \max_{a \in \mathcal{T}} |a|_2^2.$$

---

[1] A centered binomial distribution of parameter t is defined as $\sum_{i=1}^{t} b_i - b_{t+i}$ where $b_1, b_2, \ldots, b_{2t}$ are uniform random bits.

Proof. We may write $\mathsf{Lift}_p(r) = [(x-1)\overline{v}]_{(x^n-1)}$ where $\overline{v} = [r/\varPhi_1]_{\mathfrak{p}} \in \mathcal{T}$. The quantity in question satisfies

$$|\mathsf{Lift}_p(r)g|_\infty = |\overline{v}(xg - g)|_\infty = \max_i |\langle x^i v, xg\rangle - \langle x^i v, g\rangle|.$$

To simplify the indexing we will assume wlog that the maximum is attained at $i = 0$. Let $\gamma = \langle v, g\rangle/|g|_2^2$, and let $\widetilde{v}$ denote the projection of v orthogonal to g, $\widetilde{v} = v - \gamma g$. Let $\eta = \langle g, xg\rangle/|g|_2^2$. Crucially, note that $g \in \mathcal{T}_+$ implies $\eta \in [0, 1]$. This gives us

$$
\begin{aligned}
|\langle v, xg\rangle - \langle v, g\rangle| &= |\langle \widetilde{v}, xg\rangle + \gamma\langle g, xg\rangle - \langle v, g\rangle| \\
&\le |\widetilde{v}|_2|xg|_2 + |\gamma\langle g, xg\rangle - \langle v, g\rangle| \\
&= |\widetilde{v}|_2|g|_2 + |\eta\langle v, g\rangle - \langle v, g\rangle| \\
&\le |\widetilde{v}|_2|g|_2 + |\langle v, g\rangle|.
\end{aligned}
$$

For an upper bound we may assume that $|v|_2 = |g|_2 = \max\{|a|_2 : a \in \mathcal{T}\}$. Then with θ as the angle between v and g we have $|\widetilde{v}|_2 = \sin(\theta)|v|_2$, hence

$$
\begin{aligned}
|\widetilde{v}|_2|g|_2 + |\langle v, g\rangle| &\le (\sin(\theta) + \cos(\theta)) \max_{a \in \mathcal{T}} |a|_2^2 \\
&\le \sqrt{2} \max_{a \in \mathcal{T}} |a|_2^2
\end{aligned}
$$

as claimed.   □

Theorem 1 (Correctness). *The algorithms* KeyGen, $\mathcal{E}$, *and* $\mathcal{D}$ *with parameters* $p = 3$ *and* $q > 8\sqrt{2}n$ *are a correct probabilistic encryption scheme.*

Proof. Let f, g, and h be as in Algorithm 1, and let h' be such that $h = [\varPhi_1 h']_{\mathfrak{q}}$. Fix a message $m \in \mathcal{T}$ and coins $c \in \{0, 1\}^\mu$. Let $e = \mathcal{E}(m, c, h)$. Note that we may write $e = [p\mathsf{Lift}_p(r)h' + \mathsf{Lift}_p(m)]_{\mathfrak{q}}$ for some $r \in \mathcal{T}$. The claim is that $[[ef]_{\mathfrak{q}}f^{-1}]_{\mathfrak{p}} = m$. It suffices to show that $[[ef]_{\mathfrak{q}}]_{\mathfrak{p}} = [\mathsf{Lift}_p(m)f]_{\mathfrak{p}}$. Toward this end, note that

$$
\begin{aligned}
ef &= [p\mathsf{Lift}_p(r)h' + \mathsf{Lift}_p(m)]_{\mathfrak{q}}f \\
&\equiv p\mathsf{Lift}_p(r)g + \mathsf{Lift}_p(m)f \pmod{\mathfrak{q}}.
\end{aligned}
$$

By definition of the minimal representative map, the claim holds if

$$[p\mathsf{Lift}_p(r)g + \mathsf{Lift}_p(m)f]_{\mathfrak{q}} = [p\mathsf{Lift}_p(r)g + \mathsf{Lift}_p(m)f]_{(x^n-1)}.$$

Only the reduction modulo q can obstruct this since $(x^n - 1) \subset \mathfrak{q}$. Hence it is sufficient to have

$$|p\mathsf{Lift}_p(r)g + \mathsf{Lift}_p(m)f|_\infty < q/2.$$

With $p = 3$ an element of $\mathcal{T}$ is of norm at most $n - 1$. By Lemma 1 we have

$$|3\mathsf{Lift}_p(r)g + \mathsf{Lift}_p(m)f|_\infty < 4\sqrt{2}n < q(n)/2,$$

and the claim follows.   □

4   NTRU Parameters for 128-bit Post-quantum Security

We claim that our $n = 701$ parameter set offers 128-bit security in a post-quantum setting. Recall that we have defined our KEM so that n is the only free parameter; for $n = 701$ we have $p = 3$ and $q = 8192$. The claim of 128-bit post quantum security is based on two separate numerical analyses. First, an analysis of the "known quantum" primal attack described in [2] with the cost model of the same paper. Second, an analysis of the hybrid attack [26] using the cost model of [21]. In the full version of this paper we review the cryptanalytic literature around NTRU and provide some insight into how security analyses of NTRU have evolved since 1996.

Both of our numerical analyses attempt to estimate the cost of lattice reduction on a sublattice of L_h (Eq. 1). Specifically, a lattice generated by a subset of the columns of

$$\left(\frac{q \cdot I_{n-1} \mid H}{0 \mid I_{n-1}} \right), \tag{2}$$

where column $0 \leq i < n - 1$ of H is given by $[x^i h]_{(q, \Phi_n)}$. The analyses also require estimates for the length of a shortest vector in L_h. For this we assume the distribution on f and g induced by Algorithm 5.

When optimized according to the success criteria of [2], the "known quantum" primal attack applies BKZ with blocksize 466 to the first 1283 columns of Eq. (2)[2]. The cost of BKZ-466 is dominated by a polynomial number of calls to an SVP solver in dimension 466. The quantum version of Laarhoven's hypercone filtering sieve solves SVP in dimension k at a cost of $(13/9)^{k/2 + o(k)}$ queries to a quantum search oracle [32, Sect. 14.2.10]. Following [2] we assume that the $o(k)$ term is positive for relevant values of k. Setting $k = 466$ and suppressing all subexponential factors, including the number of SVP calls made by BKZ, we obtain a cost of $(13/9)^{466/2} > 2^{123}$ queries. In [2] the overhead of converting the query cost into a quantum RAM model cost is absorbed into the $(13/9)^{o(k)}$ term. Our claim of 128 bit post-quantum security follows as long as a query has a quantum RAM model cost $\geq 2^5$. To see that this is the case we will briefly sketch the steps of the hypercone filtering sieve and what these queries involve.

With $k = 466$, each iteration of the sieve involves the enumeration of $> 2^{98}$ lattice points. A subset of these of size 2^{97} is put aside for later use. The remaining lattice points, of which there are $> 2^{97}$, are stored in a database that admits nearest-neighbor queries. Points are stored in a data structure called a filter bucket in order to facilitate these queries. Each point is stored in 2^{26} out of a total of 2^{97} filter buckets. The total number of point representations stored is therefore $> 2^{123}$. Having built this database, the attacker makes a nearest neighbor query for each of the reserved 2^{97} points. Let v be such a point. The search for a neighbor of v involves the construction of a list of points in filter buckets relevant to v. There are expected to be $\gtrsim 2^{26}$ filter buckets relevant to v, each containing $\gtrsim 2^{26}$ points. For the $(13/9)^{k/2}$ query cost estimate, one assumes

---

[2] If Sample$\mathcal{T}$ produced the uniform distribution on $\mathcal{T}$, then the attack would apply BKZ with blocksize 470 to the first 1285 columns of Eq. (2).

that this list of $\gtrsim 2^{52}$ points relevant to v is presented by a quantum-accessible oracle, O_v, and moreover, that quantum search finds a nearest neighbor of v after 2^{26} queries to O_v. Each query tests whether a point w is close to v; the test is performed in superposition over relevant w. Accessing the entries of w, in order to compute $||v - w||$, has a (quantum) RAM model cost that is at least linear in k (the dimension of v and w). The nearest neighbor search is repeated for each of the reserved points for a total quantum RAM model cost of at least $466 \cdot 2^{26} \cdot 2^{97} > 2^{131}$ operations.

We will now consider the cost of Howgrave-Graham's hybrid attack [26]. This analysis allows for a more direct comparison with recent security estimates for NTRU [21] and NTRU Prime [3]. As in [3,21] we use the BKZ 2.0 simulator of [12] to estimate the quality of the basis produced by BKZ-β after a fixed number of SVP calls.

In a slight departure from [3,21], we estimate the cost of solving SVP by enumeration in dimension β using a quasilinear fit to the experimental data of Chen and Nguyen [11]. Following [1] we use the trend line:

$$enum(\beta) = 0.18728 \cdot \beta \log_2(\beta) - 1.0192 \cdot \beta + 16.10. \tag{3}$$

Note that $enum(\beta)$ estimates the logarithm of the RAM cost for one SVP call.

After optimizing the attack parameters subject to the success criteria given in [21], we estimate that hybrid attack makes $> 2^{13}$ SVP calls in dimension 339. Each SVP call has a cost of $2^{enum(\beta)} > 2^{204}$ operations. The attack has a cost of $> 2^{217}$ operations. As described, this is an entirely pre-quantum attack. The meet-in-the-middle stage of the hybrid attack can be replaced by quantum search to reduce the storage requirements, but this does not change the estimated cost.

Following [17], we also consider the effect of a quadratic improvement in the cost of solving SVP by enumeration. We report the resulting cost in the "Quantum Enum" column of Table 1. Lastly, in the column labeled "Quantum Sieve", we report the cost of the hybrid attack when the quantum version of Laarhoven's hypercone filtering sieve is used within BKZ.

Table 1. Cost of the hybrid attack with various SVP subroutines.

SVP routine	Enum	Quantum Enum	Quantum Sieve
Dimension	925	1092	1144
Blocksize β	339	434	464
SVP calls	12250	11462	13128
SVP cost exponent	$enum(\beta)$	$enum(\beta)/2$	$\beta \log_2(13/9)$
Cost	2^{217}	2^{156}	2^{136}

Note that the cost estimates in Table 1 do not have the same units. The enumeration column has units of "bit operations." The quantum enumeration and quantum sieve columns have units of "quantum queries." Furthermore the queries required for quantum enumeration could potentially be replaced with polynomial space algorithms, while the quantum sieve requires exponential space.

5   CCA2-secure Key-Encapsulation Mechanism

We now show how to turn the above OW-CPA secure encryption into an IND-CCA2-secure KEM. Toward this end, we make use of a generic transform by Dent [18, Table 5]. Similar transforms have already been used for the NTRU-based KEMs described in [36,40] and [3]. This transform comes with a security reduction in the random oracle model. As we are interested in post-quantum security, we have to deal with the quantum-accessible random oracle model (QROM) [6]. As it turns out, Dent's transform can be viewed as the KEM version of the Fujisaki-Okamoto transform (FO) [19]. For this FO-transform there exists a security reduction in the QROM by Targhi and Unruh [41]. It just requires appending a hash to the ciphertext.

The basic working of the KEM-transform is as follows. First, a random string m is sampled from the message space of the encryption scheme. This string is encrypted using random coins, deterministically derived from m using a hash function, later modeled as a random oracle (RO) in the proof (we use a XOF to instantiate all ROs). The session key is derived from m by applying another RO. Finally, the ciphertext and the session key are output.

The decapsulation algorithm decrypts the ciphertext to obtain m, derives the random coins from m, and re-encrypts m using these coins. If the resulting ciphertext matches the received one, it generates the session key from m.

In the QROM setting, Targhi and Unruh had to add the hash of m to the ciphertext to make the proof go through. The reason is that in the QROM setting a reduction simulating the RO has no way to learn the actual content of adversarial RO queries. This issue can be circumvented by this additional hash using a length preserving RO. In the proof, the reduction simulates this RO using an invertible function. When it later receives a classical output of this RO, it can recover the corresponding input, inverting the function.

An unfortunate detail in our case is that message space elements are strictly larger than a single hash value. Appending the output of a length preserving function to the ciphertext would therefore significantly increase the encapsulation size. One might think of several ways to circumvent this issue, sadly all straight forward approaches fail. A first approach would be to append a hash of the coins used for SampleT instead of using its output. This does not work in the given setting as SampleT is not invertible. Hence, the receiver has no way to check the validity of the hash. A second approach would be as follows. Instead of deriving everything from the message, one could first compute a message digest using a XOF parameterized to be compressing. Then the coins used in the encryption, the encapsulated key, and the appended hash are all computed from this message digest. This makes the security reduction fail, as it becomes impossible for the reduction to verify if a given decapsulation query contains a valid ciphertext. The reduction would always return a valid decapsulation as it does not use decryption for this. Hence, the behavior of the reduction would significantly differ from the real security game. As none of these straightforward approaches work, we accept the increase of 141 bytes, which "only" accounts for 11% of the final encapsulation size. Users that do not consider a QROM proof necessary, can just omit this hash value. Alternatively, one could replace $\mathsf{Sample}\mathcal{T}$ with an efficiently invertible function. In that case the first approach described above becomes viable.

Algorithm 6. Encaps (h)	**Algorithm 7.** Decaps $((e_1, e_2), (f, h))$
1: $c_0 \leftarrow \{0,1\}^\mu$	1: $m = \mathcal{D}(e, f)$
2: $m = \mathsf{Sample}\mathcal{T}(c_0)$	2: $c_1 = \mathsf{XOF}(m, \mu, \mathtt{coins})$
3: $c_1 = \mathsf{XOF}(m, \mu, \mathtt{coins})$	3: $k = \mathsf{XOF}(m, \mu, \mathtt{key})$
4: $k = \mathsf{XOF}(m, \mu, \mathtt{key})$	4: $e_1' = \mathcal{E}(m, c_1, h)$
5: $e_1 = \mathcal{E}(m, c_1, h)$	5: $e_2' = \mathsf{XOF}(m, \mu, \mathtt{qrom})$
6: $e_2 = \mathsf{XOF}(m, \mu, \mathtt{qrom})$	6: **if** $(e_1', e_2') \neq (e_1, e_2)$ **then**
Output: Ciphertext (e_1, e_2),	7: $k = \bot$
session key k.	8: **end if**
	Output: Session key k

6   Implementation

With this work, we provide a portable reference implementation of the scheme described above, as well as an optimized implementation using vector instructions from the AVX2 instruction set. Both implementations run in constant time. The AVX2 implementation is tailored to the $n = 701, q = 8192, p = 3$ parameter set. This section highlights some of the relevant building blocks to consider when implementing the scheme, focusing on the AVX2 implementation. Recall that the AVX2 extensions provide 16 vector registers of 256 bits that support a wide range of SIMD instructions.

6.1   Polynomial Multiplication

It will come as no surprise that the most crucial implementation aspect is polynomial multiplication. As is apparent from the definition of the scheme, we require multiplication in R/q during key generation and during encryption and decryption. Additionally, decryption uses multiplication in S/p. Furthermore, we use multiplication of binary polynomials in order to perform inversion in S/q, which we will describe in Sect. 6.2.

Multiplication in R/q. The multiplication can be composed into smaller instances by combining Toom-Cook multiplication with Karatsuba's method[3].

---

[3] Note that, as is observed in [3], popular choices for the ring in Ring-LWE schemes typically make it convenient to use the NTT to perform multiplication. As was also the case in [3], however, our ring of choice is particularly unsuitable. In our case this is caused by q being a power of two, and the polynomials being of prime degree.

Consider that elements of R/q are polynomials with 701 coefficients in $\mathbb{Z}/8192$; 16 such coefficients fit in a vector register. With this in mind, we look for a sequence of decompositions that result in multiplications best suited for parallel computation.

By applying Toom-Cook to split into 4 limbs, we decompose into 7 multiplications of polynomials of degree 176. We decompose each of those by recursively applying two instances of Karatsuba to obtain 63 multiplications of polynomials of 44 coefficients. Consider the inputs to these multiplications as a matrix, rounding the dimensions up to 64 and 48. By transposing this matrix we can efficiently perform the 63 multiplications in a vectorized manner. Using three more applications of Karatsuba, we decompose first into 22 and 11 coefficients, until finally we are left with polynomials of degree 5 and 6. At this point a straight-forward schoolbook multiplication can be performed without additional stack usage.

The full sequence of operations is as follows. We first combine the evaluation step of Toom-4 and the two layers of Karatsuba. Then, we transpose the obtained 44-coefficient results by applying transposes of 16×16 matrices, and perform the block of 63 multiplications. The 88-coefficient products remain in 44-coefficient form (i.e. aligned on the first and 45th coefficient), allowing for easy access and parallelism during interpolation; limbs of 44 coefficients are the smallest elements that interact during this phase, making it possible to operate on each part individually and keep register pressure low.

A single multiplication in R/q costs 11 722 cycles. Of this, 512 cycles are spent on point evaluation, 3 692 cycles are used for the transposes, 4 776 are spent computing the 64-way parallel multiplications, and the interpolation and recomposition takes 2 742 cycles.

Multiplication in S/p. In this setting it appears to be efficient to decompose the multiplication by applying Karatsuba recursively five times, resulting in 243 multiplications of polynomials of degree 22. One could then bitslice the two-bit coefficients into 256-bit registers with only very minimal wasted space, and perform schoolbook multiplication on the 22-register operands, or even decide to apply another layer of Karatsuba.

For our implementation, however, we instead decide to use our R/q multiplication as though it were a generic $\mathbb{Z}[x]/(x^n - 1)$ multiplication. Even though in general these operations are not compatible, for our parameters it works out. After multiplication and summation of the products, each result is at most $701 \cdot 4 = 2804$, staying well below the threshold of 8192. While a dedicated S/p multiplication would out-perform this use of R/q multiplication, the choice of parameters makes this an attractive alternative at a reasonable cost.

Multiplication in $(\mathbb{Z}/2)[x]$. Dedicated processor instructions have made multiplications in $(\mathbb{Z}/2)[x]$ considerably easier. As part of the CLMUL instruction set, the PCLMULQDQ instruction computes a carry-less multiplication of two 64-bit quadwords, performing a multiplication of two 64-coefficient polynomials over $\mathbb{Z}/2$.

We set out to efficiently decompose into polynomials of degree close to 64, and do so by recursively applying a Karatsuba layer of degree 3 followed by a regular Karatsuba layer and a schoolbook multiplication. This reduces the full multiplication to 72 multiplications of 59-bit coefficients, which we perform using PCLMULQDQ. By interweaving the evaluation and interpolation steps with the multiplications, we require no intermediate loads and stores, and a single multiplication ends up measuring in at only 244 cycles.

6.2 Inverting Polynomials

Computing the inverse of polynomials plays an important role in key generation. We compute $[1/f]_{(q,\Phi_n)}$ when producing the public key, but also pre-compute $[1/f]_{(p,\Phi_n)}$ as part of the secret key, to be used during decryption.

Inversion in S/q. We compute $[1/f]_{(2,\Phi_n)}$ and then apply a variant of Newton iteration [39] in R/q to obtain $f_q \equiv f^{-1} \pmod{(q,\Phi_n)}$. It may not be the case that $f_q = [1/f]_{(q,\Phi_n)}$, however the difference this makes in the calculation of h is eliminated after the multiplication by Φ_1 in Line 4 of Algorithm 1. The Newton iteration adds an additional cost of eight multiplications in R/q on top of the cost of an inversion in $S/2$.

Finding an inverse in $S/2$ is done using $f^{2^{n-1}-1} \equiv 1 \pmod{(2,\Phi_n)}$, and thus $f^{2^{700}-2} \equiv f^{-1} \pmod{(2,\Phi_{701})}$ [29]. This exponentiation can be done efficiently using an addition chain, resulting in twelve multiplications and thirteen multi-squarings.

Performing a squaring operation in $(\mathbb{Z}/2)[x]$ is equivalent to inserting 0-bits between the bits representing the coefficients: the odd-indexed products cancel out in $\mathbb{Z}/2$. When working modulo (x^n-1) with odd n, the subsequent reduction of the polynomial causes the terms with degree exceeding x^n to wrap around and fill the empty coefficients. This allows us to express the problem of computing a squaring as performing a permutation on bits. More importantly: repeated squarings can be considered repeated permutations, which compose into a single bit permutation.

Rewording the problem to that of performing bit permutations allows for different approaches; both generically and for specific permutations. In order to aid in constructing routines that perform these permutations, we have developed a tool to simulate a subset of the assembly instructions related to bit movement. Rather than representing the bits by their value, we label them by *index*, making it significantly easier to keep track. The assembly code corresponding to the simulated instructions is generated as output. While we have used this tool to construct permutations that represent squarings, it may be of separate interest in a broader context — the source code is also available as part of this work.

We use two distinct generic approaches to construct permutation routines, based on pext/pdep (from the BMI2 instruction set), and on vshufb.

The first approach amounts to extracting and depositing bits that occur within the same 64-bit block in both the source and destination bit sequence, under the constraint that their order remains unchanged. By relabeling the bits according to their destination and using the patience sorting algorithm, we iteratively find the longest increasing subsequence in each block until all bits have been extracted. Note that the number of required bit extractions is equal to the number of piles patience sort produces. In order to minimize this, we examine the result for each possible rotated input, and rotate it according to the rotation that produces the least amount of disjunct increasing subsequences. Heuristically keeping the most recently used masks in registers allows us to reduce the number of load operations, as the BMI2 instructions do not allow operands from memory. Further improvements could include dynamically finding the right trade-off between rotating registers and re-using masks, as well as grouping similar extractions together. For the permutations we faced, these changes did not immediately seem to hold any promises for significant improvements.

The second approach uses byte-wise shuffling to position the bits within 256-bit registers. We examine all eight rotations of the input bytes and use `vshufb` to reposition the bytes (as well as `vpermq` to cross over between `xmm` lanes). The number of required shuffles is minimized by gathering bytes for all three destination registers at the same time, and where possible, rotation sequences are replaced by shifts (as the rotated bits often play no role in the bit deposit step, and shifts are significantly cheaper). Whereas the bit extraction approach works for well-structured permutations, it is beaten by the (somewhat more constant) shuffling-based method for the more dispersed results. While there is some potential for gain when hand-crafting permutations, it turns out to be non-trivial to beat the generated multi-squarings.

The multi-squaring routines vary around 235 cycles, with a single squaring taking only 58. Including converting from R/q to $S/2$, an inversion in $S/2$ costs 10 332 cycles. Combining this with the multiplication in R/q described above, the full procedure takes 107 726 cycles.

Inversion in S/p. Inversion in S/p is done using the 'Almost Inverse' algorithm described in [37] and [39]. However, the algorithm as described in [39] does not run in constant time. Notably, it performs a varying number of consecutive divisions and multiplications by x depending on the coefficients in f, and halts as soon as f has degree zero. We eliminate this issue by iterating through every term in f (i.e. including potential zero terms, up to the nth term), and always performing the same operations for each term (i.e. constant-time swaps and always performing the same addition, multiplied with a flag fixing the sign). See the full version of this paper for a listing in pseudo-code.

While the number of loop iterations is constant, the final value of the rotation counter k is not; the **done** flag may be set before the final iteration. We compensate for k after the loop has finished by rotating 2^i bits for each bit in the binary representation of k, and subsequently performing a constant-time move when the respective bit is set.

Benefiting from the width of the vector registers, we operate on bitsliced vectors of coefficients. This allows us to efficiently perform the multiplications and additions in parallel modulo 3, and makes register swaps comparatively easy. On the other hand, shifts are still fairly expensive, and two are performed

Table 2. Comparison of lattice-based KEMs and public-key encryption. Benchmarks were performed on an Intel Core i7-4770K (Haswell) if not indicated otherwise. Cycles are stated for key generation (**K**), encapsulation/encryption (**E**), and decapsulation/decryption (**D**) Bytes are given for secret keys (**sk**), public keys (**pk**), and ciphertexts (**c**). The column "ct?" indicates whether the software is running in constant time, i.e., with protection against timing attacks.

Scheme	PQ sec.	ct?		Cycles		Bytes
Passively secure KEMs						
BCNS [8]	78[a]	yes	**K:**	≈ 2 477 958	**sk:**	4096
			E:	≈ 3 995 977	**pk:**	4096
			D:	≈ 481 937	**c:**	4224
NEWHOPE [2]	255[a]	yes	**K:**	88 920	**sk:**	1792
			E:	110 986	**pk:**	1824
			D:	19 422	**c:**	2048
FRODO [7] (recommended parameters)	130[a]	yes	**K:**	≈ 2 938 000[b]	**sk:**	11 280
			E:	≈ 3 484 000[b]	**pk:**	11 296
			D:	≈ 338 000[b]	**c:**	11 288
CCA2-secure KEMs						
NTRU Prime [3]	129[a]	yes	**K:**	?[c]	**sk:**	1417
			E:	> 51488[c]	**pk:**	1232
			D:	?[c]	**c:**	1141
spLWE-KEM [13] (128-bit PQ parameters)	128[g]	?	**K:**	≈ 336 700[d]	**sk:**	?
			E:	≈ 813 800[d]	**pk:**	?
			D:	≈ 785 200[d]	**c:**	804
NTRU-KEM (this paper)	123[a]	yes	**K:**	307 914	**sk:**	1422
			E:	48 646	**pk:**	1140
			D:	67 338	**c:**	1281
CCA-secure public-key encryption						
NTRU ees743ep1 [21]	159[a]	no	**K:**	1 194 816	**sk:**	1 120
			E:	57 440	**pk:**	1 027
			D:	110 604	**c:**	980
Lizard [14] (recommended parameters)	128[g]	no	**K:**	≈ 97 573 000	**sk:**	466 944[f, h]
			E:	≈ 35 000	**pk:**	2 031 616[h]
			D:	≈ 80 800	**c:**	1 072

[a] According to the conservative estimates obtained by the approach from [2]
[b] Benchmarked on a 2.6 GHz Intel Xeon E5 (Sandy Bridge)
[c] The NTRU Prime paper reports benchmarks only for polynomial multiplication
[d] Benchmarked on "PC (Macbook Pro) with 2.6 GHz Intel Core i5"
[e] Benchmarked by eBACS [4] on Intel Xeon E3-1275 (Haswell)
[f] Unlike our scheme, the secret key does not include the public key required for decryption in the Targhi-Unruh transform
[g] According to the authors' analysis, i.e., not following [2]
[h] Derived from the implementation – can be compressed to $\frac{10}{16}$ of its size at a marginal increase in cost of **K**, **E** and **D** by representing each coefficient using $\log(q)$ bits

for each loop iteration to multiply and divide by x. With 159 606 cycles, the inversion remains a very costly operation that determines a large chunk of the cost of the key generation operation. There may still be some room for significant improvement, though, considering the fact that each instruction in the critical loop gets executed fourteen hundred times.

7   Results and Comparison

Table 2 gives an overview of the performance of various lattice-based encryption schemes and KEMs. As memory is typically not a big concern on the given platforms, concrete memory usage figures are often not available and we do not attempt to include this in the comparison. In the same spirit, our reference implementation uses almost 11 KiB of stack space and our AVX2 software uses over 43 KiB, but this should not be considered to be a lower bound. We performed our benchmarks on one core of an Intel Core i7-4770K (Haswell) at 3.5 GHz and followed the standard practice of disabling TurboBoost and hyperthreading. We warn the reader that direct comparison of the listed schemes and implementations is near impossible for various reasons: First of all, there are significant differences in the security level; however, at least most schemes aim at a level of around 128 bits of post-quantum security. More importantly, the passively secure KEMs have a very fast decapsulation routine, but turning them into CCA2-secure KEMs via the Targhi-Unruh transform would add the cost of encapsulation to decapsulation. Also, the level of optimization of implementations is different. For example, we expect that Frodo [7] or the spLWE-based KEM from [13] could be sped up through vectorization. Finally, not all implementations protect against timing attacks and adding protection may incur a serious overhead. However, the results show that carefully optimized NTRU is very competitive, even for key generation and even with full protection against timing attacks.

References

1. Albrecht, M.R., Player, R., Scott, S.: On the concrete hardness of learning with errors. IACR Cryptology ePrint Archive report 2015/046 (2015). https://eprint. iacr.org/2015/046. 242
2. Alkim, E., Ducas, L., Pöppelmann, T., Schwabe, P.: Post-quantum key exchange - a new hope. In: Holz, T., Savage, S. (eds.) Proceedings of the 25th USENIX Security Symposium. USENIX Association (2016). https://cryptojedi.org/papers/# newhope. 233, 234, 241, 248
3. Bernstein, D.J., Chuengsatiansup, C., Lange, T., van Vredendaal, C.: NTRU prime. IACR Cryptology ePrint Archive report 2016/461 (2016). https://eprint.iacr.org/ 2016/461. 233, 234, 236, 237, 242, 243, 244, 248
4. Bernstein, D.J., Lange, T.: eBACS: ECRYPT benchmarking of cryptographic systems. http://bench.cr.yp.to. 248
5. Bertoni, G., Daemen, J., Peeters, M., Van Assche, G.: The Keccak reference (2011). http://keccak.noekeon.org/. 236

6. Boneh, D., Dagdelen, Ö., Fischlin, M., Lehmann, A., Schaffner, C., Zhandry, M.: Random oracles in a quantum world. In: Lee, D.H., Wang, X. (eds.) ASI-ACRYPT 2011. LNCS, vol. 7073, pp. 41–69. Springer, Heidelberg (2011). doi:10. 1007/978-3-642-25385-0_3. https://eprint.iacr.org/2010/428. 243

7. Bos, J., Costello, C., Ducas, L., Mironov, I., Naehrig, M., Nikolaenko, V., Raghunathan, A., Stebila, D.: Frodo: take off the ring! Practical, quantum-secure key exchange from LWE. In: Kruegel, C., Myers, A., Halevi, S. (eds.) Conference on Computer and Communications Security - CCS 2016, pp. 1006–1018. ACM (2016). https://doi.org/10.1145/2976749.2978425. 233, 248, 249

8. Bos, J.W., Costello, C., Naehrig, M., Stebila, D.: Post-quantum key exchange for the TLS protocol from the ring learning with errors problem. In: Bauer, L., Shmatikov, V. (eds.) 2015 IEEE Symposium on Security and Privacy, pp. 553–570. IEEE (2015). https://eprint.iacr.org/2014/599. 233, 248

9. Braithwaite, M.: Experimenting with post-quantum cryptography. Posting on the Google Security Blog (2016). https://security.googleblog.com/2016/07/experimenting-with-post-quantum.html. 233

10. Chatterjee, S., Koblitz, N., Menezes, A., Sarkar, P.: Another look at tightness ii: practical issues in cryptography. IACR Cryptology ePrint Archive report 2016/360 (2016). https://eprint.iacr.org/2016/360. 234

11. Chen, Y.: Lattice reduction and concrete security of fully homomorphic encryption. Ph.D. thesis, l'Université Paris Diderot (2013).242

12. Chen, Y., Nguyen, P.Q.: BKZ 2.0: better lattice security estimates. In: Lee, D.H., Wang, X. (eds.) ASIACRYPT 2011. LNCS, vol. 7073, pp. 1–20. Springer, Heidelberg (2011). doi:10.1007/978-3-642-25385-0_1. http://www.iacr.org/archive/asiacrypt2011/70730001/70730001.pdf. 242

13. Cheon, J.H., Han, K., Kim, J., Lee, C., Son, Y.: A practical post-quantum public-key cryptosystem based on spLWE. In: Hong, S., Park, J.H. (eds.) ICISC 2016. LNCS, vol. 10157, pp. 51–74. Springer, Cham (2017). doi:10.1007/978-3-319-53177-9_3. https://eprint.iacr.org/2016/1055. 233, 248, 249

14. Cheon, J.H., Kim, D., Lee, J., Song, Y.: Lizard: cut off the tail! Practical post-quantum public-key encryption from LWE and LWR. IACR Cryptology ePrint Archive report 2016/1126 (2016). https://eprint.iacr.org/2016/1126. 233, 248

15. Consortium for Efficient Embedded Security. EESS #1: Implementation aspects of NTRUEncrypt and NTRUSign v. 2.0. http://grouper.ieee.org/groups/1363/lattPK/submissions/EESS1v2.pdf. 236

16. Cramer, R., Shoup, V.: Design and analysis of practical public-key encryption schemes secure against adaptive chosen ciphertext attack. SIAM J. Comput. **33**(1), 167–226 (2003). http://www.shoup.net/papers/cca2.pdf. 233

17. del Pino, R., Lyubashevsky, V., Pointcheval, D.: The whole is less than the sum of its parts: constructing more efficient lattice-based AKEs. In: Zikas, V., De Prisco, R. (eds.) SCN 2016. LNCS, vol. 9841, pp. 273–291. Springer, Cham (2016). doi:10. 1007/978-3-319-44618-9_15. https://eprint.iacr.org/2016/435. 233, 236, 242

18. Dent, A.W.: A designer's guide to KEMs. In: Paterson, K.G. (ed.) Cryptography and Coding 2003. LNCS, vol. 2898, pp. 133–151. Springer, Heidelberg (2003). doi:10.1007/978-3-540-40974-8_12. http://www.cogentcryptography.com/papers/designer.pdf. 233, 238, 243

19. Fujisaki, E., Okamoto, T.: Secure integration of asymmetric and symmetric encryption schemes. In: Wiener, M. (ed.) CRYPTO 1999. LNCS, vol. 1666, pp. 537–554. Springer, Heidelberg (1999). doi:10.1007/3-540-48405-1_34. 243

20. Hirschhorn, P.S., Hoffstein, J., Howgrave-Graham, N., Whyte, W.: Choosing NTRUEncrypt parameters in light of combined lattice reduction and MITM approaches. In: Abdalla, M., Pointcheval, D., Fouque, P.-A., Vergnaud, D. (eds.) ACNS 2009. LNCS, vol. 5536, pp. 437–455. Springer, Heidelberg (2009). doi:10. 1007/978-3-642-01957-9_27. https://eprint.iacr.org/2005/045. 236

21. Hoffstein, J., Pipher, J., Schanck, J.M., Silverman, J.H., Whyte, W., Zhang, Z.: Choosing parameters for NTRUEncrypt. In: Handschuh, H. (ed.) CT-RSA 2017. LNCS, vol. 10159, pp. 3–18. Springer, Cham (2017). doi:10.1007/ 978-3-319-52153-4_1. https://eprint.iacr.org/2015/708. 236, 241, 242, 248

22. Hoffstein, J., Pipher, J., Silverman, J.H.: NTRU: a new high speed public key cryptosystem (1996). Draft from at CRYPTO 1996 rump session. http://web. securityinnovation.com/hubfs/files/ntru-orig.pdf. 237

23. Hoffstein, J., Pipher, J., Silverman, J.H.: NTRU: a ring-based public key cryptosystem. In: Buhler, J.P. (ed.) ANTS 1998. LNCS, vol. 1423, pp. 267–288. Springer, Heidelberg (1998). doi:10.1007/BFb0054868. 233, 236, 237, 238

24. Hoffstein, J., Pipher, J., Silverman, J.H.: Public key cryptosystem method and apparatus. United States Patent 6081597 (2000). Application filed 19 August 1997. http://www.freepatentsonline.com/6081597.html. 234

25. Hoffstein, J., Silverman, J.H.: Speed enhanced cryptographic method and apparatus. United States Patent 7031468 (2006). Application filed 24 August 2001. http://www.freepatentsonline.com/7031468.html. 234

26. Howgrave-Graham, N.: A hybrid lattice-reduction and meet-in-the-middle attack against NTRU. In: Menezes, A. (ed.) CRYPTO 2007. LNCS, vol. 4622, pp. 150–169. Springer, Heidelberg (2007). doi:10.1007/978-3-540-74143-5_9. http://www.iacr.org/archive/crypto2007/46220150/46220150.pdf. 241, 242

27. Howgrave-Graham, N., Silverman, J.H., Singer, A., Whyte, W.: NAEP: provable security in the presence of decryption failures. Cryptology ePrint Archive, Report 2003/172 (2003). https://eprint.iacr.org/2003/172. 233

28. Howgrave-Graham, N., Silverman, J.H., Whyte, W.: Choosing parameter sets for NTRUEncrypt with NAEP and SVES-3. In: Menezes, A. (ed.) CT-RSA 2005. LNCS, vol. 3376, pp. 118–135. Springer, Heidelberg (2005). doi:10.1007/ 978-3-540-30574-3_10. https://eprint.iacr.org/2005/045. 236

29. Itoh, T., Tsujii, S.: A fast algorithm for computing multiplicative inverses in $GF(2^m)$ using normal bases. Inf. Comput. **78**(3), 171–177 (1988). https://sciencedirect.com/science/article/pii/0890540188900247. 246

30. Kirchner, P., Fouque, P.-A.: Comparison between subfield and straightforward attacks on NTRU. IACR Cryptology ePrint Archive report 2012/387 (2016). https://eprint.iacr.org/2016/717. 234

31. Krawczyk, H., Paterson, K.G., Wee, H.: On the security of the TLS protocol: a systematic analysis. In: Canetti, R., Garay, J.A. (eds.) CRYPTO 2013. LNCS, vol. 8042, pp. 429–448. Springer, Heidelberg (2013). doi:10.1007/978-3-642-40041-4_24. eprint.iacr.org/2013/339. 233

32. Laarhoven, T.: Search problems in cryptography. Ph.D. thesis, Eindhoven University of Technology (2015). http://www.thijs.com/docs/phd-final.pdf. 241

33. Lyubashevsky, V., Peikert, C., Regev, O.: On ideal lattices and learning with errors over rings. In: Gilbert, H. (ed.) EUROCRYPT 2010. LNCS, vol. 6110, pp. 1–23. Springer, Heidelberg (2010). doi:10.1007/978-3-642-13190-5_1. http://www.di.ens.fr/~lyubash/papers/ringLWE.pdf. 234

34. NIST. Post-quantum crypto project (2016). http://csrc.nist.gov/groups/ST/ post-quantum-crypto/. 232

35. Saarinen, M.-J.O.: Ring-LWE ciphertext compression and error correction: tools for lightweight post-quantum cryptography. IACR Cryptology ePrint Archive report 2016/461 (2016). https://eprint.iacr.org/2016/1058. 233

36. Sakshaugh, H.: Security analysis of the NTRUEncrypt public key encryption scheme. Master's thesis, Norwegian University of Science and Technology (2007). https://brage.bibsys.no/xmlui/handle/11250/258846. 233, 243

37. Schroeppel, R., Orman, H., O'Malley, S., Spatscheck, O.: Fast key exchange with elliptic curve systems. In: Coppersmith, D. (ed.) CRYPTO 1995. LNCS, vol. 963, pp. 43–56. Springer, Heidelberg (1995). doi:10.1007/3-540-44750-4_4. https://pdfs.semanticscholar.org/edc9/5e3d34f42deabe82ff3e9237266e30adc1a7.pdf. 247

38. Security Innovation. Security Innovation makes NTRUEncrypt patent-free (2017). https://www.securityinnovation.com/company/news-and-events/press-releases/security-innovation-makes-ntruencrypt-patent-free. 234

39. Silverman, J.H.: Almost inverses and fast NTRU key creation. Technical report #014, NTRU Cryptosystems (1999). Version 1. https://assets.onboardsecurity.com/static/downloads/NTRU/resources/NTRUTech014.pdf. 246, 247

40. Stam, M.: A key encapsulation mechanism for NTRU. In: Smart, N.P. (ed.) Cryptography and Coding 2005. LNCS, vol. 3796, pp. 410–427. Springer, Heidelberg (2005). doi:10.1007/11586821_27. 233, 243

41. Targhi, E.E., Unruh, D.: Quantum security of the Fujisaki-Okamoto and OAEP transforms. Cryptology ePrint Archive, Report 2015/1210 (2015). https://eprint.iacr.org/2015/1210. 243

FPGA-based Key Generator for the Niederreiter Cryptosystem Using Binary Goppa Codes

Wen Wang[1]([⊠]), Jakub Szefer[1]([⊠]), and Ruben Niederhagen[2]([⊠])

[1] Yale University, New Haven, CT, USA
{wen.wang.ww349,jakub.szefer}@yale.edu
[2] Fraunhofer Institute SIT, Darmstadt, Germany
ruben@polycephaly.org

Abstract. This paper presents a post-quantum secure, efficient, and tunable FPGA implementation of the key-generation algorithm for the Niederreiter cryptosystem using binary Goppa codes. Our key-generator implementation requires as few as 896,052 cycles to produce both public and private portions of a key, and can achieve an estimated frequency Fmax of over 240 MHz when synthesized for Stratix V FPGAs. To the best of our knowledge, this work is the first hardware-based implementation that works with parameters equivalent to, or exceeding, the recommended 128-bit "post-quantum security" level. The key generator can produce a key pair for parameters $m = 13$, $t = 119$, and $n = 6960$ in only 3.7 ms when no systemization failure occurs, and in $3.5 \cdot 3.7$ ms on average. To achieve such performance, we implemented an optimized and parameterized Gaussian systemizer for matrix systemization, which works for any large-sized matrix over any binary field $GF(2^m)$. Our work also presents an FPGA-based implementation of the Gao-Mateer additive FFT, which only takes about 1000 clock cycles to finish the evaluation of a degree-119 polynomial at 2^{13} data points. The Verilog HDL code of our key generator is parameterized and partly code-generated using Python and Sage. It can be synthesized for different parameters, not just the ones shown in this paper. We tested the design using a Sage reference implementation, iVerilog simulation, and on real FPGA hardware.

Keywords: Post-Quantum Cryptography · Code-based cryptography · Niederreiter key generation · FPGA · Hardware implementation

1 Introduction

Once sufficiently large and efficient quantum computers can be built, they will be able to break many cryptosystems used today: Shor's algorithm [22,23] can solve the integer-factorization problem and the discrete-logarithm problem in polynomial time, which fully breaks cryptosystems built upon the hardness of

Permanent ID of this document: 503b6c5d84a7a196a4fd4ce7034b06ba.
Date: 2017.06.26.

W. Fischer and N. Homma (Eds.): CHES 2017, LNCS 10529, pp. 253–274, 2017.
DOI: 10.1007/978-3-319-66787-4_13

these problems, e.g., RSA, ECC, and Diffie-Hellman. In addition, Grover's algorithm [10] gives a square-root speedup on search problems and improves brute-force attacks that check every possible key, which threatens, e.g., symmetric key ciphers like AES. However, a "simple" doubling of the key size can be used as mitigation for attacks using Grover's algorithm. In order to provide alternatives for the cryptographic systems that are threatened by Shor's algorithm, the cryptographic community is investigating cryptosystems that are secure against attacks by quantum computers using both Shor's and Grover's algorithm in a field called Post-Quantum Cryptography (PQC).

Currently, there are five popular classes of PQC algorithms: hash-based, code-based, lattice-based, multivariate, and isogeny-based cryptography [3, 21]. Most code-based public-key encryption schemes are based on the McEliece cryptosystem [16] or its more efficient dual variant developed by Niederreiter [18]. This work focuses on the Niederreiter variant of the cryptosystem using binary Goppa codes. There is some work based on QC-MDPC codes, which have smaller key sizes compared to binary Goppa codes [12]. However, QC-MDPC codes can have decoding errors, which may be exploited by an attacker [11]. Therefore, binary Goppa codes are still considered the more mature and secure choice despite their disadvantage in the key size. Until now, the best known attacks on the McEliece and Niederreiter cryptosystems using binary Goppa codes are generic decoding attacks which can be warded off by a proper choice of parameters [5].

However, there is a tension between the algorithm's parameters (i.e., the security level) and the practical aspects, e.g., the size of keys and computation speed, resulting from the chosen parameters. The PQCRYPTO project [20] recommends to use a McEliece cryptosystem with binary Goppa codes with binary field of size $m = 13$, adding $t = 119$ errors, code length $n = 6960$, and code rank $k = 5413$ in order to achieve 128-bit post-quantum security for public-key encryption when accounting for the worst-case impact of Grover's algorithm [1]. The classical security level for these parameters is about 266-bit [5]. This recommended parameter set results in a private key of about 13 kB, and a public key of about 1022 kB. These parameters provide maximum security for a public key of at most 1 MB [5]. Our tunable design is able to achieve these parameters, and many others, depending on the user's needs.

The Niederreiter cryptosystem consists of three operations: key generation, encryption, and decryption. In this paper, we are focusing on the implementation of the most expensive operation in the Niederreiter cryptosystem: the key generation. The industry PKCS #11 standard defines a platform-independent API for cryptographic tokens, e.g., hardware security modules (HSM) or smart cards, and explicitly contains functions for public-private key-pair generation [19]. Furthermore, hardware crypto accelerators, e.g., for IBM's z Systems, have dedicated key-generation functions. These examples show that efficient hardware implementations for key generation will also be required for post-quantum schemes. We selected FPGAs as our target platform since they are ideal for hardware development and testing; most parts of the hardware code can also be re-used for developing an ASIC design.

Due to the confidence in the Niederreiter cryptosystem, there are many publications on hardware implementations related to this cryptosystem, e.g., [13,15,24]. We are only aware of one publication [24] that presents a hardware implementation of the key-generation algorithm. The key-generation hardware design in [24], however, uses fixed, non-tunable security and design parameters, which do not meet the currently recommended post-quantum security level, and has a potential security flaw by using a non-uniform permutation, which may lead to practical attacks.

Contributions. This paper presents the first post-quantum secure, efficient, and tunable FPGA-based implementation of the key-generation algorithm for the Niederreiter cryptosystem using binary Goppa codes. The contributions are:

- a key generator with tunable parameters, which uses code-generation to generate vendor-neutral Verilog HDL code,
- a constructive, constant-time approach for generating an irreducible Goppa polynomial,
- an improved hardware implementation of Gaussian systemizer which works for any large-sized matrix over any binary field,
- a new hardware implementation of Gao-Mateer additive FFT for polynomial evaluation,
- a new hardware implementation of Fisher-Yates shuffle for obtaining uniform permutations, and
- design testing using Sage reference code, iVerilog simulation, and output from real FPGA runs.

Source code. The source code is available as Open Source at `http://caslab.csl.yale.edu/code/keygen`.

2 Niederreiter Cryptosystem and Key Generation

The first code-based public-key encryption system was given by McEliece in 1978 [16]. The private key of the McEliece cryptosystem is a randomly chosen irreducible binary Goppa code $\mathcal{G}$ with a generator matrix G that corrects up to t errors. The public key is a randomly permuted generator matrix $G^{\mathrm{pub}} = SGP$ that is computed from G and the secrets P (a permutation matrix) and S (an invertible matrix). For encryption, the sender encodes the message m as a codeword and adds a secret error vector e of weight t to get ciphertext $c = mG^{\mathrm{pub}} \oplus e$. The receiver computes $cP^{-1} = mSG \oplus eP^{-1}$ using the secret P and decodes m using the decoding algorithm of $\mathcal{G}$ and the secret S. Without knowledge of the code G, which is hidden by the secrets S and P, it is computationally hard to decrypt the ciphertext. The McEliece cryptosystem with correct parameters is believed to be secure against quantum-computer attacks.

In 1986, Niederreiter introduced a dual variant of the McEliece cryptosystem by using a parity check matrix H for encryption instead of a generator matrix [18]. For the Niederreiter cryptosystem, the message m is encoded as a

---

Algorithm 1. Key-generation algorithm for the Niederreiter cryptosystem.

Input : System parameters: m, t, and n.

Output: Private key $(g(x), (\alpha_0, \alpha_1, \ldots, \alpha_{n-1}))$ and public key K.

1 Choose a random sequence $(\alpha_0, \alpha_1, \ldots, \alpha_{n-1})$ of n distinct elements in $\mathrm{GF}(2^m)$.

2 Choose a random polynomial $g(x)$ such that $g(\alpha) \neq 0$ for all $\alpha \in (\alpha_0, \ldots, \alpha_{n-1})$.

3 Compute the $t \times n$ parity check matrix

$$
H = \begin{bmatrix}
1/g(\alpha_0) & 1/g(\alpha_1) & \cdots & 1/g(\alpha_{n-1}) \\
\alpha_0/g(\alpha_0) & \alpha_1/g(\alpha_1) & \cdots & \alpha_{n-1}/g(\alpha_{n-1}) \\
\vdots & \vdots & \ddots & \vdots \\
\alpha_0^{t-1}/g(\alpha_0) & \alpha_1^{t-1}/g(\alpha_1) & \cdots & \alpha_{n-1}^{t-1}/g(\alpha_{n-1})
\end{bmatrix}.
$$

4 Transform H to a $mt \times n$ binary parity check matrix H' by replacing each entry with a column of m bits.

5 Transform H' into its systematic form $[\mathbb{I}_{mt}|K]$.

6 Return the private key $(g(x), (\alpha_0, \alpha_1, \ldots, \alpha_{n-1}))$ and the public key K.

---

weight-t error vector e of length n; alternatively, the Niederreiter cryptosystem can be used as a key-encapsulation scheme where a random error vector is used to derive a symmetric encryption key. For encryption, e is multiplied with H and the resulting syndrome is sent to the receiver. The receiver decodes the received syndrome, and obtains e. Originally, Niederreiter used Reed-Solomon codes for which the system has been broken [25]. However, the scheme is believed to be secure when using binary Goppa codes. Niederreiter introduced a trick to compress H by computing the systemized form of the public key matrix. This trick can be applied to some variants of the McEliece cryptosystem as well.

We focus on the Niederreiter cryptosystem due to its compact key size and the efficiency of syndrome decoding algorithms. As the most expensive operation in the Niederreiter cryptosystem is key generation, it is often omitted from Niederreiter implementations on FPGAs due to its large memory demand. Therefore, our paper presents a new contribution by implementing the key-generation algorithm efficiently on FPGAs.

2.1 Key Generation Algorithm

Algorithm 1 shows the key-generation algorithm for the Niederreiter cryptosystem. The system parameters are: m, the size of the binary field, t, the number of correctable errors, and n, the code length. Code rank k is determined as $k = n - mt$. We implemented Step 2 of the key-generation algorithm by computing an irreducible Goppa polynomial $g(x)$ of degree t as the minimal polynomial of a random element r from a polynomial ring over $\mathrm{GF}(2^m)$ using a power sequence $1, r, \ldots, r^t$ and Gaussian systemization in $\mathrm{GF}(2^m)$ (see Sect. 5). Step 3 requires the evaluation of $g(x)$ at points $\{\alpha_0, \alpha_1, \ldots, \alpha_{n-1}\}$. To achieve high efficiency, we decided to follow the approach of [4] which evaluates $g(x)$ at all elements of $\mathrm{GF}(2^m)$ using a highly efficient additive FFT algorithm (see Sect. 4.2).

Table 1. Parameters and resulting configuration for the key generator.

Param.	Description	Size (bits)	Config.	Description	Size (bits)
m	Size of the binary field	13	$g(x)$	Goppa polynomial	120×13
t	Correctable errors	119	P	Permutation indices	8192×13
n	Code length	6960	H	Parity check matrix	1547×6960
k	Code rank	5413	K	Public key	1547×5413

Therefore, we evaluate $g(x)$ at all $\alpha \in \mathrm{GF}(2^m)$ and then choose the required α_i using Fisher-Yates shuffle by computing a random sequence $(\alpha_0, \alpha_1, \ldots, \alpha_{n-1})$ from a permuted list of indices P. For Step 5, we use the efficient Gaussian systemization module for matrices over $\mathrm{GF}(2)$ from [26].

2.2 Structure of the Paper

The following sections introduce the building blocks for our key-generator module in a bottom-up fashion. First, we introduce the basic modules for arithmetic in $\mathrm{GF}(2^m)$ and for polynomials over $\mathrm{GF}(2^m)$ in Sect. 3. Then we introduce the modules for Gaussian systemization, additive FFT, and Fisher-Yates shuffle in Sect. 4. Finally, we describe how these modules work together to obtain an efficient design for key generation in Sect. 5. Validation of the design using Sage, iVerilog, and Stratix V FPGAs is presented in Sect. 6 and a discussion of the performance is in Sect. 7.

2.3 Reference Parameters and Reference Platform

We are using the recommended parameters from the PQCRYPTO project [20] shown in Table 1 as reference parameters; however, our design is fully parameterized and can be synthesized for any other valid parameter selection.

Throughout the paper (except for Table 9), performance results are reported from Quartus-synthesis results for the Altera Stratix V FPGA (5SGXEA7N), including Fmax (maximum estimated frequency) in MHz, Logic (logic usage) in Adaptive Logic Modules (ALMs), Mem. (memory usage) in Block RAMs, and Reg. (registers). Cycles are derived from iVerilog simulation. Time is calculated as quotient of Cycles and Fmax. Time $\times$ Area is calculated as product of Cycles and Logic.

3 Field Arithmetic

The lowest-level building blocks in our implementation are $\mathrm{GF}(2^m)$ finite field arithmetic and on the next higher level $\mathrm{GF}(2^m)[x]/f$ polynomial arithmetic.

Table 2. Performance of different field multiplication algorithms for $GF(2^{13})$.

Algorithm	Logic	Reg.	Fmax (MHz)
Schoolbook algorithm	90	78	637
2-split Karatsuba algorithm	99	78	625
3-split Karatsuba algorithm	101	78	529
Bernstein	87	78	621

3.1 GF(2^m) Finite Field Arithmetic

$GF(2^m)$ represents the basic finite field in the Niederreiter cryptosystem. Our code for all the hardware implementations of $GF(2^m)$ operations is generated by code-generation scripts, which take in m as a parameter and then automatically generate the corresponding Verilog HDL code.

GF(2^m) Addition. In $GF(2^m)$, addition corresponds to a simple bitwise xor operation of two m-bit vectors. Therefore, each addition has negligible cost and can often be combined with other logic while still finishing within one clock cycle, e.g., a series of additions or addition followed by multiplication or squaring.

GF(2^m) Multiplication. Multiplication over $GF(2^m)$ is one of the most used operations in the Niederreiter cryptosystem. A field multiplication in $GF(2^m)$ is composed of a multiplication in $GF(2)[x]$ and a reduction modulo f, where f is a degree-m irreducible polynomial. For the case of $m = 13$, we use the pentanomial $f(x) = x^{13} + x^4 + x^3 + x + 1$ since there is no irreducible trinomial of degree 13. We are using plain schoolbook multiplication, which turns out to deliver good performance. Table 2 shows that the schoolbook version of $GF(2^{13})$ multiplication achieves a higher Fmax while requiring less logic compared to several of our implementations using Karatsuba multiplication [14,17]. The performance of the schoolbook version is similar to Bernstein's operation-count optimized code [2]. We combine multiplication in $GF(2)[x]$ and reduction modulo f such that one $GF(2^m)$ multiplication only takes one clock cycle.

GF(2^m) Squaring. Squaring over $GF(2^m)$ can be implemented using less logic than multiplication and therefore an optimized squaring module is valuable for many applications. However, in the case of the key-generation algorithm, we do not require a dedicated squaring module since an idle multiplication module is available in all cases when we require squaring. Squaring using $GF(2^m)$ multiplication takes one clock cycle.

GF(2^m) Inversion. Inside the $GF(2^m)$ Gaussian systemizer, elements over $GF(2^m)$ need to be inverted. An element $a \in GF(2^m)$ can be inverted by computing $a^{-1} = a^{|GF(2^m)|-2}$. This can be done with a logarithmic amount of squarings and multiplications. For example, inversion in $GF(2^{13})$ can be implemented using twelve squarings and four multiplications. However, this approach requires at least one multiplication circuit (repeatedly used for multiplications and squarings) plus some logic overhead and has a latency of at least several cycles in order to achieve high frequency. Therefore, we decided to use a pre-computed lookup table for the implementation of the inversion module. For inverting an element $\alpha \in \text{GF}(2^m)$, we interpret the bit-representation of α as an integer value and use this value as the address into the lookup table. For convenience, we added an additional bit to each value in the lookup table that is set high in case the input element α can not be inverted, i.e., $\alpha = 0$. This saves additional logic that otherwise would be required to check the input value. Thus, the lookup table has a width of $m+1$ and a depth of 2^m, and each entry can be read in one clock cycle. The lookup table is read-only and therefore can be stored in either RAM or logic resources.

3.2 $\text{GF}(2^m)[x]/f$ Polynomial Arithmetic

Polynomial arithmetic is required for the generation of the secret Goppa polynomial. $\text{GF}(2^m)[x]/f$ is an extension field of $\text{GF}(2^m)$. Elements in this extension field are represented by polynomials with coefficients in $\text{GF}(2^m)$ modulo an irreducible polynomial f. We are using a sparse polynomial for f, e.g., the trinomial $x^{119} + x^8 + 1$, in order to reduce the cost of polynomial reduction.

Polynomial Addition. The addition of two degree-d polynomials with $d+1$ coefficients is equivalent to pair-wise addition of the coefficients in $\text{GF}(2^m)$. Therefore, polynomial addition can be mapped to an xor operation on two $m(d+1)$-bit vectors and finishes in one clock cycle.

Polynomial Multiplication. Due to the relatively high cost of $\text{GF}(2^m)$ multiplication compared to $\text{GF}(2^m)$ addition, for polynomials over $\text{GF}(2^m)$ Karatsuba multiplication [14] is more efficient than classical schoolbook multiplication in terms of logic cost when the size of the polynomial is sufficiently large.

Given two polynomials $A(x) = \sum_{i=0}^{5} a_i x^i$ and $B(x) = \sum_{i=0}^{5} b_i x^i$, schoolbook polynomial multiplication can be implemented in hardware as follows: Calculate $(a_5 b_0, a_4 b_0, \ldots, a_0 b_0)$ and store the result in a register. Then similarly calculate $(a_5 b_i, a_4 b_i, \ldots, a_0 b_i)$, shift the result left by $i \cdot m$ bits, and then add the shifted result to the register contents, repeat for all $i = 1, 2, \ldots, 5$. Finally the result stored in the register is the multiplication result (before polynomial reduction). One can see that within this process, 6×6 $\text{GF}(2^m)$ multiplications are needed.

Karatsuba polynomial multiplication requires less finite-field multiplications compared to schoolbook multiplication. For the above example, Montgomery's six-split Karatsuba multiplication [17] requires only 17 field element multiplications over $\text{GF}(2^m)$ at the cost of additional finite field additions which are cheap for binary field arithmetic. For large polynomial multiplications, usually several levels of Karatsuba are applied recursively and eventually on some low level schoolbook multiplication is used. The goal is to achieve a trade-off between running time and logic overhead.

The multiplication of two polynomials of degree $d = t - 1$ is a key step in the key-generation process for computing the Goppa polynomial $g(x)$. Table 3 shows the results of several versions of polynomial multiplication for $t = 119$, i.e., $d = 118$, using parameterized six-split Karatsuba by adding zero-terms in

Table 3. Performance of different multiplication algorithms for degree-118 polynomials.

Algorithm	Mult.	Cycles	Logic	Times × Area	Fmax (MHz)
1-level Karatsuba 17 × (20 × 20)	20	377	11,860	$4.47 \cdot 10^6$	342
2-level Karatsuba 17 × 17 × (4 × 4)	16	632	12,706	$8.03 \cdot 10^6$	151
2-level Karatsuba 17 × 17 × (4 × 4)	4	1788	11,584	$2.07 \cdot 10^7$	254

order to obtain polynomials with 120 and 24 coefficients respectively. On the lowest level, we use parameterized schoolbook multiplication. The most efficient approach for the implementation of degree-118 polynomial multiplication turned out to be one level of six-split Karatsuba followed by schoolbook multiplication, parallelized using twenty $GF(2^{13})$ multipliers. Attempts using one more level of six-split Karatsuba did not notably improve area consumption (or even worsened it) and resulted in both more cycles and lower frequency. Other configurations, e.g., five-split Karatsuba on the second level or seven-split Karatsuba on the first level, might improve performance, but our experiments do not indicate that performance can be improved significantly.

In the final design, we implemented a one-level six-split Karatsuba multiplication approach, which uses a size-$\lceil \frac{d+1}{6} \rceil$ schoolbook polynomial multiplication module as its building block. It only requires 377 cycles to perform one multiplication of two degree-118 polynomials.

4   Key Generator Modules

The arithmetic modules are used as building blocks for the units inside the key generator, shown later in Fig. 2. The main components are: two Gaussian systemizers for matrix systemization over $GF(2^m)$ and $GF(2)$ respectively, Gao-Mateer additive FFT for polynomial evaluation, and Fisher-Yates shuffle for generating uniformly distributed permutations.

4.1   Gaussian Systemizer

Matrix systemization is needed for generating both the private Goppa polynomial $g(x)$ and the public key K. Therefore, we require one module for Gaussian systemization of matrices over $GF(2^{13})$ and one module for matrices over $GF(2)$. We use a modified version of the highly efficient Gaussian systemizer from [26] and adapted it to meet the specific needs for Niederreiter key generation. As in [26], we are using an $N \times N$ square processor array to compute on column blocks of the matrix. The size of this processor array is parameterized and can be chosen to either optimize for performance or for resource usage.

The design from [26] only supports systemization of matrices over $GF(2)$. An important modification that we applied to the design is the support of arbitrary binary fields — we added a binary-field inverter to the diagonal "pivoting" elements of the processor array and binary-field multipliers to all the processors. This results in a larger resource requirement compared to the $GF(2)$ version but the longest path still remains within the memory module and not within the computational logic for computations on large matrices.

4.2   Gao-Mateer Additive FFT

Evaluating a polynomial $g(x) = \sum_{i=0}^{t} g_i x^i$ at n data points over GF(2^m) is an essential step for generating the parity check matrix H. Applying Horner's rule is a common approach for polynomial evaluation. For example, a polynomial $f(x) = \sum_{i=0}^{7} f_i x^i$ of degree 7 can be evaluated at a point $\alpha \in$ GF(2^m) using Horner's rule as

$$f(\alpha) = f_7 \alpha^7 + f_6 \alpha^6 + \cdots + f_1 \alpha + f_0$$
$$= (((f_7 \alpha + f_6)\alpha + f_5)\alpha + f_4)\ldots)\alpha + f_0$$

using 7 field additions and 7 field multiplications by α. More generically speaking, one evaluation of a polynomial of degree d requires d additions and d multiplications. Evaluating several points scales linearly and is easy to parallelize. The asymptotic time complexity of polynomial evaluation of a degree-d polynomial at n points using Horner's rule is O$(n \cdot d)$.

In order to reduce this cost, we use a characteristic-2 additive FFT algorithm introduced in 2010 by Gao and Mateer [9], which was used for multipoint polynomial evaluation by Chou in 2013 [4]. This algorithm evaluates a polynomial at *all* elements in the field GF(2^m) using a number of operations logarithmic in the length of the polynomial. Most of these operations are additions, which makes this algorithm particularly suitable for hardware implementations. The asymptotic time complexity of additive FFT is O$\left(2^m \cdot \log_2(d)\right)$.

The basic idea of this algorithm is to write f in the form $f(x) = f^{(0)}(x^2 + x) + xf^{(1)}(x^2 + x)$, where $f^{(0)}(x)$ and $f^{(1)}(x)$ are two half-degree polynomials, using *radix conversion*. The form of f shows a large overlap between evaluating $f(\alpha)$ and $f(\alpha + 1)$. Since $(\alpha + 1)^2 + (\alpha + 1) = \alpha^2 + \alpha$ for $\alpha \in$ GF(2^m), we have:

$$f(\alpha) = f^{(0)}(\alpha^2 + \alpha) + \alpha f^{(1)}(\alpha^2 + \alpha)$$
$$f(\alpha + 1) = f^{(0)}(\alpha^2 + \alpha) + (\alpha + 1)f^{(1)}(\alpha^2 + \alpha).$$

Once $f^{(0)}$ and $f^{(1)}$ are evaluated at $\alpha^2 + \alpha$, it is easy to get $f(\alpha)$ by performing one field multiplication and one field addition. Now, $f(\alpha+1)$ can be easily computed using one extra field addition as $f(\alpha + 1) = f(\alpha) + f^{(1)}(\alpha^2 + \alpha)$. Additive FFT applies this idea recursively until the resulting polynomials $f^{(0)}$ and $f^{(1)}$ are 1-coefficient polynomials (or in another word, constants). During the recursive operations, in order to use the α and $\alpha+1$ trick, a *twisting* operation is needed for all the subspaces, which is determined by the new basis of $f^{(0)}$ and $f^{(1)}$. Finally, the 1-coefficient polynomials of the last recursion step are used to recursively evaluate the polynomial at all the 2^m data points over GF(2^m) in a concluding *reduction* operation.

Radix Conversion. Radix conversion converts a polynomial $f(x)$ of coefficients in GF(2^m) into the form of $f(x) = f^{(0)}(x^2 + x) + xf^{(1)}(x^2 + x)$. As a basic example, consider a polynomial $f(x) = f_0 + f_1 x + f_2 x^2 + f_3 x^3$ of 4 coefficients with basis $\{1, x, x^2, x^3\}$. We compute the radix conversion as follows: Write the coefficients as a list $[f_0, f_1, f_2, f_3]$. Add the 4th element to the 3rd element and add the new 3rd element to the 2nd element to obtain $[f_0, f_1 + f_2 + f_3, f_2 + f_3, f_3]$. This transforms the basis to $\{1, x, (x^2 + x), x(x^2 + x)\}$, we have

$$\begin{aligned} f(x) &= f_0 + (f_1 + f_2 + f_3)x + (f_2 + f_3)(x^2 + x) + f_3 x(x^2 + x) \\ &= \big(f_0 + (f_2 + f_3)(x^2 + x)\big) + x\big((f_1 + f_2 + f_3) + f_3(x^2 + x)\big) \\ &= f^{(0)}(x^2 + x) + x f^{(1)}(x^2 + x) \end{aligned}$$

with $f^{(0)}(x) = f_0 + (f_2 + f_3)x$ and $f^{(1)}(x) = (f_1 + f_2 + f_3) + f_3 x$.

For polynomials of larger degrees, this approach can be applied recursively: Consider a polynomial $g(x) = g_0 + g_1 x + g_2 x^2 + g_3 x^3 + g_4 x^4 + g_5 x^5 + g_6 x^6 + g_7 x^7$ of 8 coefficients. Write $g(x)$ as a polynomial with 4 coefficients, i.e.,

$$g(x) = (g_0 + g_1 x) + (g_2 + g_3 x)x^2 + (g_4 + g_5 x)x^4 + (g_6 + g_7 x)x^6.$$

Perform the same operations as above (hint: substitute x^2 with y and re-substitute back in the end) to obtain

$$\begin{aligned} g(x) &= (g_0 + g_1 x) + \big((g_2 + g_3 x) + (g_4 + g_5 x) + (g_6 + g_7 x)\big)x^2 \\ &\quad + \big((g_4 + g_5 x) + (g_6 + g_7 x)\big)(x^2 + x)^2 + (g_6 + g_7 x)x^2(x^2 + x)^2 \\ &= (g_0 + g_1 x) + \big((g_2 + g_4 + g_6) + (g_3 + g_5 + g_7)x\big)x^2 \\ &\quad + \big((g_4 + g_6) + (g_5 + g_7)x\big)(x^2 + x)^2 + (g_6 + g_7 x)x^2(x^2 + x)^2 \end{aligned}$$

with basis $\{1, x, x^2, x^3, (x^2 + x)^2, x(x^2 + x)^2, x^2(x^2 + x)^2, x^3(x^2 + x)^2\}$.

Now, recursively apply the same process to the 4-coefficient polynomials $g^{(L)}(x) = g_0 + g_1 x + (g_2 + g_4 + g_6)x^2 + (g_3 + g_5 + g_7)x^3$ and $g^{(R)}(x) = (g_4 + g_6) + (g_5 + g_7)x + g_6 x^2 + g_7 x^3$. This results in

$$\begin{aligned} g^{(L)}(x) &= g_0 + (g_1 + g_2 + g_3 + g_4 + g_5 + g_6 + g_7)x \\ &\quad + (g_2 + g_3 + g_4 + g_5 + g_6 + g_7)(x^2 + x) + (g_3 + g_5 + g_7)x(x^2 + x), \text{ and} \\ g^{(R)}(x) &= (g_4 + g_6) + (g_5 + g_6)x + (g_6 + g_7)(x^2 + x) + g_7 x(x^2 + x). \end{aligned}$$

Substituting $g^{(L)}(x)$ and $g^{(R)}(x)$ back into $g(x)$, we get

$$\begin{aligned} g(x) = g_0 \\ + (g_1 + g_2 + g_3 + g_4 + g_5 + g_6 + g_7)x \\ + (g_2 + g_3 + g_4 + g_5 + g_6 + g_7)(x^2 + x) \\ + (g_3 + g_5 + g_7)x(x^2 + x) \\ + (g_4 + g_6)(x^2 + x)^2 \\ + (g_5 + g_6)x(x^2 + x)^2 \\ + (g_6 + g_7)(x^2 + x)^3 \\ + (g_7)x(x^2 + x)^3. \end{aligned}$$

with basis $\{1, x, (x^2+x)^1, x(x^2+x)^1, \ldots, (x^2+x)^3, x(x^2+x)^3\}$. This representation can be easily transformed into the form of $g(x) = g^{(0)}(x^2+x) + xg^{(1)}(x^2+x)$.

In general, to transform a polynomial $f(x)$ of 2^k coefficients into the form of $f = f^{(0)}(x^2 + x) + xf^{(1)}(x^2 + x)$, we need 2^i size-2^{k-i}, $i = 0, 1, \ldots, k$ radix conversion operations. We will regard the whole process of transforming $f(x)$ into the form of $f^{(0)}(x^2 + x) + xf^{(1)}(x^2 + x)$ as one complete radix conversion operation for later discussion.

Twisting. As mentioned above, additive FFT applies Gao and Mateer's idea recursively. Consider the problem of evaluating an 8-coefficient polynomial $f(x)$ for all elements in GF(2^4). The field GF(2^4) can be defined as: GF(2^4) = $\{0, a, \ldots, a^3+a^2+a, 1, a+1, \ldots, (a^3+a^2+a)+1\}$ with basis $\{1, a, a^2, a^3\}$. After applying the radix conversion process, we get $f(x) = f^{(0)}(x^2+x) + xf^{(1)}(x^2+x)$. As described earlier, the evaluation on the second half of the elements ("$\ldots + 1$") can be easily computed from the evaluation results of the first half by using the α and $\alpha + 1$ trick (for $\alpha \in \{0, a, \ldots, a^3 + a^2 + a\}$). Now, the problem turns into the evaluation of $f^{(0)}(x)$ and $f^{(1)}(x)$ at points $\{0, a^2 + a, \ldots, (a^3 + a^2 + a)^2 + (a^3 + a^2 + a)\}$. In order to apply Gao and Mateer's idea again, we first need to *twist* the basis: By computing $f^{(0')}(x) = f^{(0)}((a^2 + a)x)$, evaluating $f^{(0)}(x)$ at $\{0, a^2 + a, \ldots, (a^3 + a^2 + a)^2 + (a^3 + a^2 + a)\}$ is equivalent to evaluating $f^{(0')}(x)$ at $\{0, a^2 + a, a^3 + a, a^3 + a^2, 1, a^2 + a + 1, a^3 + a + 1, a^3 + a^2 + 1\}$. Similarly for $f^{(1)}(x)$, we can compute $f^{(1')}(x) = f^{(1)}((a^2+a)x)$. After the twisting operation, $f^{(0')}$ and $f^{(1')}$ have element 1 in their new basis. Therefore, this step equivalently twists the basis that we are working with. Now, we can perform radix conversion and apply the α and $\alpha + 1$ trick on $f^{(0')}(x)$ and $f^{(1')}(x)$ recursively again.

The basis twisting for $f^{(0)}(x)$ and $f^{(1)}(x)$ can be mapped to a sequence of field multiplication operations on the coefficients. Let $\beta = \alpha^2 + \alpha$. f_i denotes the i-th coefficient of a polynomial $f(x)$. For a degree-7 polynomial $f(x)$, we get

$$[f_3^{(1')}, f_2^{(1')}, f_1^{(1')}, f_0^{(1')}, f_3^{(0')}, f_2^{(0')}, f_1^{(0')}, f_0^{(0')}]$$
$$= [\beta^3 f_3^{(1)}, \beta^2 f_2^{(1)}, \beta f_1^{(1)}, f_0^{(1)}, \beta^3 f_3^{(0)}, \beta^2 f_2^{(0)}, \beta f_1^{(0)}, f_0^{(0)}].$$

When mapping to hardware, this step can be easily realized by an entry-wise multiplication between the polynomial coefficients and powers of β, which are all independent and can be performed in parallel. Given a polynomial of 2^k coefficients from GF(2^m), each twisting step takes 2^k GF(2^m) multiplication operations. In our implementation, we use a parameterized parallel multiplier module that is composed of multiple GF(2^m) multipliers. The number of GF(2^m) multipliers is set as a parameter in this module, which can be easily adjusted to achieve an area and running time trade-off, as shown in Table 4.

Reduction. Evaluating a polynomial $f(x) \in$ GF(2^m)$[x]$ of 2^k coefficients at all elements in GF(2^m) requires k twisting and k radix conversion operations. The last radix conversion operation operates on 2^{k-1} polynomials of 2 coefficients of the form $g(x) = a + bx$. We easily write $g(x)$ as $g(x) = g^{(0)}(x^2+x) + xg^{(1)}(x^2+x)$ using $g^{(0)}(x) = a, g^{(1)}(x) = b$. At this point, we finish the recursive twist-then-radix-conversion process, and we get 2^k polynomials with only one coefficient.

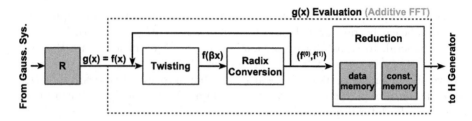

Fig. 1. Dataflow diagram of our hardware version of Gao-Mateer additive FFT. Functional units are represented as white boxes and memory blocks are represented as grey boxes.

Table 4. Performance of additive FFT using different numbers of multipliers for twist.

Multipliers							
Twist	Reduction	Cycles	Logic	Times × Area	Mem.	Reg.	Fmax (MHz)
4	32	1188	11,781	$1.39 \cdot 10^7$	63	27,450	399
8	32	1092	12,095	$1.32 \cdot 10^7$	63	27,470	386
16	32	1044	12,653	$1.32 \cdot 10^7$	63	27,366	373
32	32	1020	14,049	$1.43 \cdot 10^7$	63	26,864	322

Now we are ready to perform the reduction step. Evaluation of these 1-coefficient polynomials simply returns the constant values. Then by using $g(\alpha) = g^{(0)}(\alpha^2 + \alpha) + \alpha g^{(1)}(\alpha^2 + \alpha)$ and $g(\alpha + 1) = g(\alpha) + g^{(1)}(\alpha^2 + \alpha)$, we can recursively finish the evaluation of the polynomial f at all the 2^m points using $\lceil \log_2(t) \rceil$ recursion steps and 2^{m-1} multiplications in $GF(2^m)$ in each step.

Non-recursive Hardware Implementation. We mapped the recursive algorithm to a non-recursive hardware implementation shown in Fig. 1. Given a polynomial of 2^k coefficients, the twist-then-radix-conversion process is repeated for k times, and an array containing the coefficients of the resulting 1-coefficient polynomials is fed into the reduction module. Inside the reduction module, there are two memory blocks: A *data memory* and a *constants memory*. The data memory is initialized with the 1-coefficient polynomials and gets updated with intermediate reduction data during the reduction process. The constants memory is initialized with elements in the subspace of $f^{(0)}$ and $f^{(1)}$, which are pre-generated via Sage code. Intermediate reduction data is read from the data memory while subspace elements are read from the constants memory. Then the reduction step is performed using addition and multiplication submodules. The computed intermediate reduction results are then written back to the data memory. The reduction step is repeated until the evaluation process is finished and the final evaluation results are stored in the data memory.

Performance. Table 4 shows performance and resource-usage for our additive FFT implementation. For evaluating a degree-119 Goppa polynomial $g(x)$ at all the data points in $GF(2^{13})$, 32 finite filed multipliers are used in the reduction

Algorithm 2. Fisher-Yates shuffle

Output: Shuffled array A
Initalize: $A = \{0, 1, \ldots, n-1\}$
1 **for** i from $n-1$ downto 0 **do**
2   Generate j uniformly from range$[0, i]$
3   Swap $A[i]$ and $A[j]$

Table 5. Performance of the Fisher-Yates shuffle module for 2^{13} elements.

m	Size $(= 2^m)$	Cycles (avg.)	Logic	Time $\times$ Area	Mem.	Reg.	Fmax (MHz)
13	8192	23,635	149	$3.52 \cdot 10^6$	7	111	335

step of our additive FFT design in order to achieve a small cycle count while maintaining a low logic overhead. The twisting module is generated by a Sage script such that the number of multipliers can be chosen as needed. Radix conversion and twisting have only a small impact in the total cycle count; therefore, using only 4 binary filed multipliers for twisting results in good performance, with best Fmax. The memory required for additive FFT is only a small fraction of the overall memory consumption of the key generator.

4.3 Random Permutation: Fisher-Yates Shuffle

Computing a random list of indices $P = [\pi(0), \pi(1), \ldots, \pi(2^m - 1)]$ for a permutation $\pi \in S_{2^m}$ (here, S_i denotes the symmetric group on $\{0, 1, \ldots, i-1\}$), is an important step in the key-generation process. We compute P by performing Fisher-Yates shuffle [8] on the list $[0, 1, \ldots, 2^m - 1]$ and then using the first n elements of the resulting permutation. We choose Fisher-Yates shuffle to perform the permutation, because it requires only a small amount of computational logic. Algorithm 2 shows the Fisher-Yates shuffle algorithm.

We implemented a parameterized permutation module using a dual-port memory block of depth 2^m and width m. First, the memory block is initialized with contents $[0, 1, \ldots, 2^m - 1]$. Then, the address of port A decrements from $2^m - 1$ to 0. For each address A, a PRNG keeps generating new random numbers as long as the output is larger than address A. Therefore, our implementation produces a non-biased permutation (under the condition that the PRNG has no bias) but it is not constant-time. Once the PRNG output is smaller than address A, this output is used as the address for port B. Then the contents of the cells addressed by A and B are swapped. We improve the probability of finding a random index smaller than address A by using only $\lceil \log_2(A) \rceil$ bits of the PRNG output. Therefore, the probability of finding a suitable B always is at least 50%.

Since we are using a dual-port memory in our implementation, the memory initialization takes 2^{m-1} cycles. For the memory swapping operation, for each address A, first a valid address B is generated and data stored in address A and B is read from the memory in one clock cycle, then one more clock cycle is required

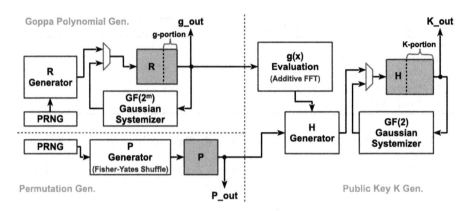

Fig. 2. Dataflow diagram of the key generator. Functional units are represented as white boxes and memory blocks are represented as grey boxes. The ports g_out and P_out are for the private-key data, and the port K_out is for the public-key data.

for updating the memory contents. On average, $2^{m-1} + \sum_{i=1}^{m} \sum_{j=0}^{2^{i-1}-1}(\frac{2^i}{2^i-j}+1)$ cycles are needed for our Fisher-Yates shuffle implementation. Table 5 shows performance data for the Fisher-Yates shuffle module.

5 Key Generator for the Niederreiter Cryptosystem

Using two Gaussian systemizers, Gao-Mateer additive FFT, and Fisher-Yates shuffle, we designed the key generator as shown in Fig. 2. Note that the design uses two simple PRNGs to enable deterministic testing. For real deployment, these PRNGs must be replaced with a cryptographically secure random number generator, e.g., [6]. We require at most m random bits per clock cycle per PRNG.

5.1 Private Key Generation

The private key consists of an irreducible Goppa polynomial $g(x)$ of degree t and a permuted list of indices P.

Goppa Polynomial $g(x)$. The common way for generating a degree-d irreducible polynomial is to pick a polynomial g of degree d uniformly at random, and then to check whether it is irreducible or not. If it is not, a new polynomial is randomly generated and checked, until an irreducible one is found. The density of irreducible polynomials of degree d is about $1/d$ [16]. When $d = t = 119$, the probability that a randomly generated degree-119 polynomial is irreducible gets quite low. On average, 119 trials are needed to generate a degree-119 irreducible polynomial in this way. Moreover, irreducibility tests for polynomials involve highly complex operations in extension fields, e.g., raising a polynomial to a power and finding the greatest common divisor of two polynomials. In the hardware key generator design in [24], the Goppa polynomial $g(x)$ was generated in this way, which is inefficient in terms of both time and area.

We decided to explicitly generate an irreducible polynomial $g(x)$ by using a deterministic, constructive approach. We compute the minimal (hence irreducible) polynomial of a random element in $GF(2^m)[x]/h$ with $\deg(h) = \deg(g) = t$: Given a random element r from the extension field $GF(2^m)[x]/h$, the minimal polynomial $g(x)$ of r is defined as the non-zero monic polynomial of least degree with coefficients in $GF(2^m)$ having r as a root, i.e., $g(r) = 0$. The minimal polynomial of a degree-$(t-1)$ element from field $GF(2^m)[x]/h$ is always of degree t and irreducible if it exists.

The process of generating the minimal polynomial $g(x) = g_0 + g_1 x + \cdots + g_{t-1} x^{t-1} + x^t$ of a random element $r(x) = \sum_{i=0}^{t-1} r_i x^i$ is as follows: Since $g(r) = 0$, we have $g_0 + g_1 r + \cdots + g_{t-1} r^{t-1} + r^t = 0$ which can be equivalently written using vectors as: $(1^T, r^T, \ldots, (r^{t-1})^T, (r^t)^T) \cdot (g_0, g_1, \ldots, g_{t-1}, 1)^T = 0$. Note that since $R = (1^T, r^T, \ldots, (r^{t-1})^T, (r^t)^T)$ is a $t \times (t+1)$ matrix while $g = (g_0, g_1, \ldots, g_{t-1}, 1)^T$ is a size-$(t+1)$ vector, we get

$$R \cdot g = \begin{bmatrix} 0 & r_{t-1} & \cdots & (r^t)_{t-1} \\ 0 & r_{t-2} & \cdots & (r^t)_{t-2} \\ \vdots & \vdots & \ddots & \vdots \\ 0 & r_1 & \cdots & (r^t)_1 \\ 1 & r_0 & \cdots & (r^t)_0 \end{bmatrix} \begin{pmatrix} g_0 \\ g_1 \\ \vdots \\ g_{t-1} \\ 1 \end{pmatrix} = 0.$$

Now, we can find the minimal polynomial of r by treating g as variable and by solving the resulting system of linear equations for g. By expanding this matrix-vector multiplication equation, we get t linear equations which uniquely determine the solution for $(g_0, g_1, \ldots, g_{t-1})$. Solving systems of linear equations can be easily transformed into a matrix systemization problem, which can be handled by performing Gaussian elimination on the coefficient matrix R.

In our hardware implementation, first a PRNG is used, which generates t random m-bit strings for the coefficients of $r(x) = \sum_{i=0}^{t-1} r_i x^i$. Then the coefficient matrix R is calculated by computing the powers of $1, r, \ldots, r^t$, which are stored in the memory of the $GF(2^m)$ Gaussian systemizer. We repeatedly use the polynomial multiplier described in Sect. 3.2 to compute the powers of r. After each multiplication, the resulting polynomial of t coefficients is written to the memory of the $GF(2^m)$ Gaussian systemizer. (Our Gaussian-systemizer module operates on column-blocks of width N_R. Therefore, the memory contents are actually computed block-wise.) This multiply-then-write-to-memory cycle is repeated until R is fully calculated. After this step is done, the memory of the $GF(2^m)$ Gaussian systemizer has been initialized with the coefficient matrix R.

After the initialization, the Gaussian elimination process begins and the coefficient matrix R is transformed into its reduced echelon form $[\mathbb{I}_t | g]$. Now, the right part of the resulting matrix contains all the unknown coefficients of the minimal polynomial g.

The part of memory which stores the coefficients of the Goppa polynomial $g(x)$ is shown as the "g-portion" in Fig. 2. Later the memory contents stored in

Table 6. Performance of the $GF(2^m)$ Gaussian systemizer for $m = 13$ and $t = 119$, i.e., for a 119×120 matrix with elements from $GF(2^{13})$.

N_R	Cycles	Logic	Time × Area	Mem.	Reg.	Fmax (MHz)
1	922,123	2539	$2.34 \cdot 10^9$	14	318	308
2	238,020	5164	$1.23 \cdot 10^9$	14	548	281
4	63,300	10,976	$6.95 \cdot 10^8$	13	1370	285

the g-portion are read out and sent to the $g(x)$ evaluation step, which uses the additive FFT module to evaluate the Goppa polynomial $g(x)$ at every point in field $GF(2^m)$.

Table 6 shows the impact of different choices for the Gaussian-systemizer parameter N_R for a matrix of size 119×120 in $GF(2^{13})$. N_R defines the size of the $N_R \times N_R$ processor array of the Gaussian systemizer [26] and implicitly the width of the memory that is used to store the matrix. It has an impact on the number of required memory blocks, because the synthesis tools usually require more memory blocks for wider memory words to achieve good performance. Furthermore, have to add zero-columns to the matrix to make the number of columns a multiple of N_R. However, for these parameters, the memory is used most efficiently for $N_R = 4$. When doubling N_R, the number of required cycles should roughly be quartered and the amount of logic should roughly be quadrupled. However, the synthesis results show a doubling pattern for the logic when $N_R = 1$, 2 and 4, which is probably due to some logic overhead that would vanish for larger N_R.

Random Permutation P. In our design, a randomly permuted list of indices of size 2^{13} is generated by the Fisher-Yates shuffle module and the permutation list is stored in the memory P in Fig. 2 as part of the private key. Later memory P is read by the H generator which generates a permuted binary form the parity check matrix. In our design, since $n \leq 2^m$, only the contents of the first n memory cells need to be fetched.

5.2   Public Key Generation

As mentioned in Sect. 2, the public key K is the systemized form of the binary version of the parity check matrix H. In [24], the generation of the binary version of H is divided into two steps: first compute the non-permuted parity check matrix and store it in a memory block A, then apply the permutation and write the binary form of the permuted parity-check matrix to a new memory block B, which is of the same size as memory block A. This approach requires simple logic but needs two large memory blocks A and B.

In order to achieve better memory efficiency, we omit the first step, and instead generate a permuted binary form H' of the parity check matrix in one step. We start the generation of the public key K by evaluating the Goppa polynomial $g(x)$ at all $\alpha \in GF(2^m)$ using the Gao-Mateer additive FFT module.

After the evaluation finishes, the results are stored in the data memory of the additive FFT module.

Now, we generate the permuted binary parity check matrix H' and store it in the memory of the GF(2) Gaussian systemizer. Suppose the permutation indices stored in memory P are $[p_0, p_1, \ldots, p_{n-1}, \ldots, p_{2^m-1}]$, then

$$
H' = \begin{bmatrix}
1/g(\alpha_{p_0}) & 1/g(\alpha_{p_1}) & \cdots & 1/g(\alpha_{p_{n-1}}) \\
\alpha_{p_0}/g(\alpha_{p_0}) & \alpha_{p_1}/g(\alpha_{p_1}) & \cdots & \alpha_{p_{n-1}}/g(\alpha_{p_{n-1}}) \\
\vdots & \vdots & \ddots & \vdots \\
\alpha_{p_0}^{t-1}/g(\alpha_{p_0}) & \alpha_{p_1}^{t-1}/g(\alpha_{p_1}) & \cdots & \alpha_{p_{n-1}}^{t-1}/g(\alpha_{p_{n-1}})
\end{bmatrix}.
$$

To generate the first column of H', the first element p_0 from P is fetched and stored in a register. Then, the corresponding polynomial evaluation value $g(\alpha_{p_0})$ is read out from the data memory of the additive FFT module. This value is then inverted using a GF(2^m) inverter. After inversion, we get $1/g(\alpha_{p_0})$ which is the first entry of the column. The second entry is calculated by a multiplication of the first entry row and α_{p_0}, the third entry again is calculated by a multiplication of the previous row and α_{p_0} and so on. Each time a new entry is generated, it is written to the memory of the GF(2) Gaussian systemizer (bit-wise, one bit per row). This computation pattern is repeated for all $p_0, p_1, \ldots, p_{n-1}$ until H' is fully calculated. After this step, the memory of the GF(2) Gaussian systemizer contains H' and the Gaussian systemization process is started. (Again, this process is actually performed on column-blocks of width N_H due to the architecture of the Gaussian systemizer.)

If a fail signal from the GF(2) Gaussian systemizer is detected, i.e., the matrix cannot be systemized, key generation needs to be restarted. Otherwise, the left part of the matrix has been transformed into a $mt \times mt$ identity matrix and the right side is the $mt \times k$ public key matrix K labeled as "K-portion" in Fig. 2.

Success Probability. The number of invertible $mt \times mt$ matrices over GF(2) is the order of the general linear group GL(mt, GF(2)), i.e., $\prod_{j=0}^{mt-1} 2^{mt} - 2^j$. The total number of $mt \times mt$ matrices over GF(2) is $2^{(mt)^2}$. Therefore, the probability of a random $mt \times mt$ matrix over GF(2) being invertible is $(\prod_{j=0}^{mt-1} 2^{mt} - 2^j)/2^{(mt)^2}$. For $mt = 13 \cdot 119 = 1547$, the probability is about 29%. Thus, on average we need about 3.5 attempts to successfully generate a key pair.

Performance. Table 7 shows the effect of different choices for parameter N_H on a matrix of size 1547×6960 in GF(2). Similar to the GF(2^m) Gaussian systemizer, N_H has an impact on the number of required memory blocks. When doubling N_H, the number of required cycles should roughly be quartered (which is the case for small N_H) and the amount of logic should roughly be quadrupled (which is the case for large N_H). The best time-area product is achieved for $N_H = 80$, because for smaller values the non-computational logic overhead is significant and for larger values the computational logic is used less efficiently. Fmax is mainly limited by the paths within the memory.

Table 7. Performance of the GF(2) Gaussian systemizer for a 1547×6960 matrix.

N_H	Cycles	Logic	Time × Area	Mem.	Reg.	Fmax (MHz)
10	150,070,801	826	$1.24 \cdot 10^{11}$	663	678	257
20	38,311,767	1325	$5.08 \cdot 10^{10}$	666	1402	276
40	9,853,350	3367	$3.32 \cdot 10^{10}$	672	4642	297
80	2,647,400	10,983	$2.91 \cdot 10^{10}$	680	14,975	296
160	737,860	40,530	$2.99 \cdot 10^{10}$	720	55,675	290
320	208,345	156,493	$3.26 \cdot 10^{10}$	848	213,865	253

6 Design Testing

We tested our hardware implementation using a Sage reference implementation, iVerilog, and an Altera Stratix V FPGA (5SGXEA7N) on a Terasic DE5-Net FPGA development board.

Parameters and PRNG Inputs. First, we chose a set of parameters, which were usually the system parameters of the cryptosystem (m, t, and n, with $k = n - mt$). In addition, we picked two design parameters, N_R and N_H, which configure the size of the processor arrays in the GF(2^m) and GF(2) Gaussian systemizers. In order to guarantee a deterministic output, we randomly picked seeds for the PRNGs and used the same seeds for corresponding tests on different platforms. Given the parameters and random seeds as input, we used Sage code to generate appropriate input data for each design module.

Sage Reference Results. For each module, we provide a reference implementation in Sage using built-in Sage functions for field arithmetic, etc. Given the parameters, seeds, and input data, we used the Sage reference implementation to generate reference results for each module.

iVerilog Simulation Results. We simulated the Verilog HDL code of each module using a "testbench" top module and the iVerilog simulator. At the end of the simulation, we stored the simulation result in a file. Finally, we compared the simulation result with the Sage reference result. If these reference and simulation results matched repeatedly for different inputs, we assumed the Verilog HDL code to be correct.

FPGA Results. After we tested the hardware design through simulation, we synthesized the design for an Altera Stratix V FPGA using the Altera Quartus 16.1 tool chain. We used a PCIe interface for communication with the FPGA. After a test finished, we wrote the FPGA output to a file. Then we compared the output from the FPGA testrun with the output of the iVerilog simulation and the Sage reference results. If the outputs matched, we assumed the hardware design to be correct.

Table 8. Performance of the key generator for parameters $m = 13$, $t = 119$, and $n = 6960$. All the numbers in the table come from compilation reports of the Altera and Xilinx tool chains respectively. For Xilinx, logic utilization is counted in LUTs.

Case	N_H	N_R	Cycles	Logic	Time × Area	Mem.	Fmax	Time
				Altera Stratix V				
logic	40	1	11,121,220	29,711	$3.30 \cdot 10^{11}$	756	240 MHz	46.43 ms
bal.	80	2	3,062,942	48,354	$1.48 \cdot 10^{11}$	764	248 MHz	12.37 ms
time	160	4	896,052	101,508	$9.10 \cdot 10^{10}$	803	244 MHz	3.68 ms
				Xilinx Virtex Ultrascale+				
logic	40	1	11,121,220	42,632	$4.74 \cdot 10^{11}$	348.5	200 MHz	55.64 ms
bal.	80	2	3,062,942	60,989	$1.87 \cdot 10^{11}$	356	221 MHz	13.85 ms
time	160	4	896,052	112,845	$1.01 \cdot 10^{11}$	375	225 MHz	3.98 ms

Table 9. Comparison with related work. Cycles and time are average values, taking into account failure cases.

Design	m	t	n	Cycles (avg.)	Freq.	Time (avg.)	Arch.
Shoufan et al. [24]	11	50	2048	$1.47 \cdot 10^7$	163 MHz[a]	90 ms	Virtex V
this work	11	50	2048	$2.72 \cdot 10^6$	168 MHz[b]	16 ms	Virtex V
Chou [7]	13	128	8192	$1.24 \cdot 10^9$	1–4 GHz[c]	1236–309 ms	Haswell
this work	13	128	8192	$4.30 \cdot 10^6$	215 MHz[a]	20 ms	Stratix V

[a] Actual frequency running on FPGAs.
[b] Fmax reported by the Xilinx tool chain.
[c] Available for a range of frequencies.

7   Evaluation

We synthesized the final design for an Altera Stratix V FPGA (5SGXEA7N) and for comparison for a Xilinx UltraScale+ VUP9 FPGA (e.g., used in the Amazon EC2 F1 instances). Based on the PQCRYPTO project [20] recommendations, the following system parameters were selected: $m = 13$, $t = 119$, $n = 6960$ and $k = 5413$ (note $k = n - mt$). These parameters were specified in [5] for a target public key size of about 1 MB. They provide a classical security level of about 266-bit which corresponds to a post-quantum security level of at least 128-bit.

Due to the large size of the permuted parity check matrix H, generating the public key K by doing matrix systemization on the binary version of H is usually the most expensive step both in logic and cycles in the key-generation algorithm. In our key generator, independently of the security parameters, the design can be tuned by adjusting N_R and N_H, which configure the size of the processor array of the GF(2^m) and GF(2) Gaussian systemizer respectively. Tables 6 and 7 show that by adjusting N_R and N_H in the two Gaussian systemizers, we can achieve a trade-off between area and performance for the key generator.

Table 8 shows performance data for three representative parameter choices: The *logic* case targets to minimize logic consumption at the cost of performance, the *time* case focuses on maximising performance at the cost of resources, and the *balanced* case (bal.) attempts to balance logic usage and execution time.

Comparison of our results with other Niederreiter key-generator implementations on FPGAs is not easy. Table 9 gives an attempt of comparing our result to the performance data given in [24]. The design in [24] occupies about 84% of the target FPGA for their entire Niederreiter-cryptosystem implementation including key generation, encryption, decryption, and IO. Our design requires only about 52% of the logic (for $N_H = 30$ and $N_R = 10$), but only for the key generation. The design in [24] practically achieves a frequency of 163 MHz while we can only report estimated synthesis results for Fmax of 168 MHz for our design. Computing a private-public key pair using the design in [24] requires about 90 ms on average (their approach for generating the Goppa polynomial is not constant time and the key-generation procedure needs to be repeated several times until the Gaussian systemization of the public key succeeds). Our design requires about 16 ms on average at 168 MHz.

We also compare our design to a highly efficient CPU implementation from [7] in Table 9. The results show that our optimized hardware implementation competes very well with the CPU implementation. In this case, we ran our implementation on an Altera Stratix V FPGA. The actual frequency that we achieved fits well to the estimated frequencies for Stratix V in Table 8.

8   Conclusion

This work presents a new FPGA-based implementation of the key-generation algorithm for the Niederreiter cryptosystem using binary Goppa codes. It is the first hardware implementation of a key generator that supports currently recommended security parameters (and many others due to tunable parameters). Our design is based on novel hardware implementations of Gaussian systemizer, Gao-Mateer additive FFT, and Fisher-Yates shuffle.

Acknowledgments. We want to thank Tung Chou for his invaluable help, in particular for discussions about the additive FFT implementation.

References

1. Augot, D., Batina, L., Bernstein, D.J., Bos, J., Buchmann, J., Castryck, W., Dunkelman, O., Güneysu, T., Gueron, S., Hülsing, A., Lange, T., Mohamed, M.S.E., Rechberger, C., Schwabe, P., Sendrier, N., Vercauteren, F., Yang, B.Y.: Initial recommendations of long-term secure post-quantum systems. Technical report, PQCRYPTO ICT-645622 (2015). https://pqcrypto.eu.org/docs/initial-recommendations.pdf. Accessed 22 June 2017
2. Bernstein, D.J.: High-speed cryptography in characteristic 2. http://binary.cr.yp.to/m.html. Accessed 17 Mar 2017

3. Bernstein, D.J., Buchmann, J., Dahmen, E. (eds.): Post-Quantum Cryptography. Springer, Heidelberg (2009)
4. Bernstein, D.J., Chou, T., Schwabe, P.: McBits: fast constant-time code-based cryptography. In: Bertoni, G., Coron, J.-S. (eds.) CHES 2013. LNCS, vol. 8086, pp. 250–272. Springer, Heidelberg (2013)
5. Bernstein, D.J., Lange, T., Peters, C.: Attacking and defending the McEliece cryptosystem. In: Buchmann, J., Ding, J. (eds.) PQCrypto 2008. LNCS, vol. 5299, pp. 31–46. Springer, Heidelberg (2008)
6. Cherkaoui, A., Fischer, V., Fesquet, L., Aubert, A.: A very high speed true random number generator with entropy assessment. In: Bertoni, G., Coron, J.-S. (eds.) CHES 2013. LNCS, vol. 8086, pp. 179–196. Springer, Heidelberg (2013)
7. Chou, T.: McBits revisited. In: Fischer, W., Homma, N. (eds.) Cryptographic Hardware and Embedded Systems. LNCS, Springer (2017)
8. Fisher, R.A., Yates, F.: Statistical Tablesfor Biological, Agriculturaland Medical Research. Oliver and Boyd, London (1948)
9. Gao, S., Mateer, T.: Additive fast fourier transforms over finite fields. IEEE Trans. Inf. Theory **56**(12), 6265–6272 (2010)
10. Grover, L.K.: A fast quantum mechanical algorithm for database search. In: Symposium on the Theory of Computing - STOC 1996, pp. 212–219. ACM (1996)
11. Guo, Q., Johansson, T., Stankovski, P.: A key recovery attack on MDPC with CCA security using decoding errors. In: Cheon, J.H., Takagi, T. (eds.) ASIACRYPT 2016. LNCS, vol. 10031, pp. 789–815. Springer, Heidelberg (2016)
12. Heyse, S., Maurich, I., Güneysu, T.: Smaller keys for code-based cryptography: QC-MDPC McEliece implementations on embedded devices. In: Bertoni, G., Coron, J.-S. (eds.) CHES 2013. LNCS, vol. 8086, pp. 273–292. Springer, Heidelberg (2013)
13. Hu, J., Cheung, R.C.C.: An application specific instruction set processor (ASIP) for the Niederreiter cryptosystem. Cryptology ePrint Archive, Report 2015/1172 (2015)
14. Karatsuba, A., Ofman, Y.: Multiplication of multidigit numbers on automata. Sov. Phys. Dokl. **7**, 595–596 (1963)
15. Massolino, P.M.C., Barreto, P.S.L.M., Ruggiero, W.V.: Optimized and scalable coprocessor for McEliece with binary Goppa codes. ACM Trans. Embed. Comput. Syst. **14**(3), 45 (2015)
16. McEliece, R.J.: A public-key cryptosystem based on algebraic coding theory. DSN Prog. Rep. **42–44**, 114–116 (1978)
17. Montgomery, P.L.: Five, six, and seven-term Karatsuba-like formulae. IEEE Trans. Comput. **54**(3), 362–369 (2005)
18. Niederreiter, H.: Knapsack-type cryptosystems and algebraic coding theory. Probl. Control Inf. Theory **15**, 19–34 (1986)
19. PKCS #11 base functionality v2.30, p. 172. ftp://ftp.rsasecurity.com/pub/pkcs/pkcs-11/v2-30/pkcs-11v2-30b-d6.pdf. Accessed 20 June 2017
20. Post-quantum cryptography for long-term security PQCRYPTO ICT-645622. https://pqcrypto.eu.org/. Accessed 17 March 2017
21. Rostovtsev, A., Stolbunov, A.: Public-key cryptosystem based on isogenies. Cryptology ePrint Archive, Report 2006/145 (2006)
22. Shor, P.W.: Algorithms for quantum computation: discrete logarithms and factoring. In: Foundations of Computer Science - FOCS 1994, pp. 124–134. IEEE (1994)
23. Shor, P.W.: Polynomial-time algorithms for prime factorization and discrete logarithms on a quantum computer. SIAM Rev. **41**(2), 303–332 (1999)

24. Shoufan, A., Wink, T., Molter, G., Huss, S., Strentzke, F.: A novel processor architecture for McEliece cryptosystem and FPGA platforms. IEEE Trans. Comput. **59**(11), 1533–1546 (2010)
25. Sidelnikov, V.M., Shestakov, S.O.: On insecurity of cryptosystems based on generalized Reed-Solomon codes. Discrete Mathe. Appl. **2**(4), 439–444 (1992)
26. Wang, W., Szefer, J., Niederhagen, R.: Solving large systems of linear equations over GF(2) on FPGAs. In: Reconfigurable Computing and FPGAs - ReConFig 2016, pp. 1–7. IEEE (2016)

Cipher & Protocol Design

Blockcipher-Based Authenticated Encryption: How Small Can We Go?

Avik Chakraborti[1](✉), Tetsu Iwata[2], Kazuhiko Minematsu[3],
and Mridul Nandi[4]

[1] NTT Secure Platform Laboratories, Tokyo, Japan
chakraborti.avik@lab.ntt.co.jp
[2] Nagoya University, Nagoya, Japan
iwata@cse.nagoya-u.ac.jp
[3] NEC Corporation, Tokyo, Japan
k-minematsu@ah.jp.nec.com
[4] Applied Statistics Unit, Indian Statistical Institute, Kolkata, India
mridul.nandi@gmail.com

Abstract. This paper presents a design of authenticated encryption (AE) focusing on minimizing the implementation size, i.e., hardware gates or working memory on software. The scheme is called COFB, for COmbined FeedBack. COFB uses an n-bit blockcipher as the underlying primitive, and relies on the use of a nonce for security. In addition to the state required for executing the underlying blockcipher, COFB needs only $n/2$ bits state as a mask. Till date, for all existing constructions in which masks have been applied, at least n bit masks have been used. Thus, we have shown the possibility of reducing the size of a mask without degrading the security level much. Moreover, it requires one blockcipher call to process one input block. We show COFB is provably secure up to $O(2^{n/2}/n)$ queries which is almost up to the standard birthday bound. We also present our hardware implementation results. Experimental implementation results suggest that our proposal has a good performance and the smallest footprint among all known blockcipher-based AE.

Keywords: COFB · AES · Authenticated encryption · Blockcipher

1 Introduction

Authenticated encryption (AE) is a symmetric-key cryptographic primitive for providing both confidentiality and authenticity. Due to the recent rise in communication networks operated on small devices, the era of the so-called Internet of Things, AE is expected to play a key role in securing these networks.

In this paper, we study blockcipher modes for AE with primary focus on the hardware implementation size. Here, we consider the overhead in size, thus the state memory size beyond the underlying blockcipher itself (including the key schedule) is the criteria we want to minimize. We observe this direction has not

© International Association for Cryptologic Research 2017
W. Fischer and N. Homma (Eds.): CHES 2017, LNCS 10529, pp. 277–298, 2017.
DOI: 10.1007/978-3-319-66787-4_14

received much attention until the launch of CAESAR competition (see below), while it would be relevant for future communication devices requiring ultra low-power operations. A general approach to reduce the entire hardware size of AE modes is to use a lightweight blockcipher [15,17,25,48,49] or to use standard AES implemented in a tiny, serialized core [37], where the latter is shown to be effective for various schemes including popular CCM [5] or OCB [32] modes, as shown in [16] and [12]. Our approach is orthogonal to these directions.

In this paper, we propose a new blockcipher AE mode which utilizes both plaintext and ciphertext feedback. Our proposal is called COFB for COmbined FeedBack, and we show that this enables essentially AE using the minimum amount of state memory while keeping the security level similar to the previous schemes. Specifically, let n denote the block size in bits of the underlying blockcipher, then our proposal needs an $n/2$-bit register for a mask in addition to the registers required for holding round keys and the internal state memory (i.e., n bits) for the blockcipher computation. Ignoring the state for the round keys, it requires $1.5n$ bit state. It has provable security up to $O(2^{n/2}/n)$ queries, based on the standard assumption that the blockcipher is a PRP (PseudoRandom Permutation). Our scheme is efficient in that the rate is 1, i.e., it makes one blockcipher call to process one input block, meaning that it is as fast as encryption-only modes.

CAESAR [3], started in 2012, attracted 57 AE schemes, and there are schemes that were designed to minimize the implementation size. The most relevant one is JAMBU [52], which can be implemented with $1.5n$-bit state memory. However, the provable security result is not published for this scheme[1], and the security claim about the confidentiality in the nonce misuse scenario was shown to be flawed [40]. We also point out that the rate of JAMBU is $1/2$, i.e., it makes two blockcipher calls to process one input block. This can be seen in our implementation results where COFB is more efficient, in terms of throughput per area, than JAMBU by a factor of two. CLOC and SILC [28,29] have provable security results and were designed to minimize the implementation size, however, they do not allow the implementation with $1.5n$-bit state and the rate is also $1/2$.

On the downside, COFB is completely serial both for encryption and decryption. However, we argue that this is a reasonable trade-off, as tiny devices are our primal target platform for COFB. We present Table 1 to show a comparison of blockcipher AE modes including COFB.

In order to instantiate our efficiency claim, we implemented COFB on hardware and evaluated it on FPGAs. The implementation results show the impressive performance figures of COFB both for size and speed. For the sake of completeness we also compare COFB with various schemes (not limited to blockcipher modes) listed in the hardware benchmark framework called ATHENa [1]. We have to warn that this is a rough comparison ignoring differences in several implementation factors (see Sect. 6). Nevertheless, we think this comparison implies a good performance of COFB among others even using the standard AES-128.

---

[1] The authenticity result was briefly presented in the latest specification [52].

Table 1. Comparison of AE modes, using an n-bit blockcipher with k-bit keys. An inverse-free mode is a mode that does not need the blockcipher inverse (decryption) function for both encryption and decryption. For JAMBU, the authenticity bound was briefly presented in [52].

Scheme	State size	Rate	Parallel	Inverse-free	Sec. proof	Ref
COFB	$1.5n + k$	1	No	Yes	Yes	This work
JAMBU	$1.5n + k$	1/2	No	Yes	Partial	[52]
CLOC/SILC	$2n + k$	1/2	No	Yes	Yes	[28, 29]
iFEED	$3n + k$	1	Only for Enc	Yes	Flawed [47]	[54]
OCB	$\geq 3n + k$	1	Yes	No	Yes	[32, 41, 42]

2   Preliminaries

Notation. We fix a positive integer n which is the block size in bits of the underlying blockcipher E_K. Typically, we consider $n = 128$ and AES-128 [7] is the underlying blockcipher, where K is the 128-bit AES key. The empty string is denoted by λ. For any $X \in \{0,1\}^*$, where $\{0,1\}^*$ is the set of all finite bit strings (including λ), we denote the number of bits of X by $|X|$. Note that $|\lambda| = 0$. For two bit strings X and Y, $X \| Y$ denotes the concatenation of X and Y. A bit string X is called a *complete* (or *incomplete*) block if $|X| = n$ (or $|X| < n$ respectively). We write the set of all complete (or incomplete) blocks as $\mathcal{B}$ (or $\mathcal{B}^<$ respectively). Let $\mathcal{B}^{\leq} = \mathcal{B}^< \cup \mathcal{B}$ denote the set of all blocks. For $B \in \mathcal{B}^{\leq}$, we define $\overline{B}$ as follows:

$$\overline{B} = \begin{cases} 0^n & \text{if } B = \lambda \\ B\|10^{n-1-|B|} & \text{if } B \neq \lambda \text{ and } |B| < n \\ B & \text{if } |B| = n \end{cases}$$

Given $Z \in \{0,1\}^*$, we define the parsing of Z into n-bit blocks as

$$(Z[1], Z[2], \ldots, Z[z]) \xleftarrow{n} Z, \tag{1}$$

where $z = \lceil |Z|/n \rceil$, $|Z[i]| = n$ for all $i < z$ and $1 \leq |Z[z]| \leq n$ such that $Z = (Z[1] \| Z[2] \| \cdots \| Z[z])$. If $Z = \lambda$, we let $z = 1$ and $Z[1] = \lambda$. We write $\|Z\| = z$ (number of blocks present in Z). We similarly write $(Z[1], Z[2], \ldots, Z[z]) \xleftarrow{m} Z$ to denote the parsing of the bit string Z into m bit strings $Z[1], Z[2], \ldots, Z[z-1]$ and $1 \leq |Z[z]| \leq m$. Given any sequence $Z = (Z[1], \ldots, Z[s])$ and $1 \leq a \leq b \leq s$, we represent the subsequence $(Z[a], \ldots, Z[b])$ by $Z[a..b]$. Similarly, for integers $a \leq b$, we write $[a..b]$ for the set $\{a, a+1, \ldots, b\}$. For two bit strings X and Y with $|X| \geq |Y|$, we define the extended xor-operation as

$$X \underline{\oplus} Y = X[1..|Y|] \oplus Y \text{ and}$$
$$X \overline{\oplus} Y = X \oplus (Y\|0^{|X|-|Y|}),$$

where $(X[1], X[2], \ldots, X[x]) \xleftarrow{1} X$ and thus $X[1..|Y|]$ denotes the first $|Y|$ bits of X. When $|X| = |Y|$, both operations reduce to the standard $X \oplus Y$.

Let $\gamma = (\gamma[1], \ldots, \gamma[s])$ be a tuple of equal-length strings. We define $\mathrm{mcoll}(\gamma) = r$ if there exist distinct $i_1, \ldots, i_r \in [1..s]$ such that $\gamma[i_1] = \cdots = \gamma[i_r]$ and r is the maximum of such integer. We say that $\{i_1, \ldots, i_r\}$ is an r-multi-collision set for γ.

Authenticated Encryption and Security Definitions. An authenticated encryption (AE) is an integrated scheme that provides both privacy of a plaintext $M \in \{0,1\}^*$ and authenticity of M as well as associate data $A \in \{0,1\}^*$. Taking a nonce N (which is a value never repeats at encryption) together with associated date A and plaintext M, the encryption function of AE, $\mathcal{E}_K$, produces a tagged-ciphertext (C, T) where $|C| = |M|$ and $|T| = t$. Typically, t is a fixed length and we assume $n = t$ throughout the paper. The corresponding decryption function, $\mathcal{D}_K$, takes (N, A, C, T) and returns a decrypted plaintext M when the verification on (N, A, C, T) is successful, otherwise returns the atomic error symbol denoted by $\perp$.

Privacy. Given an adversary $\mathcal{A}$, we define the *PRF-advantage* of $\mathcal{A}$ against $\mathcal{E}$ as $\mathbf{Adv}_{\mathcal{E}}^{\mathrm{prf}}(\mathcal{A}) = |\Pr[\mathcal{A}^{\mathcal{E}_K} = 1] - \Pr[\mathcal{A}^{\$} = 1]|$, where $\$$ returns a random string of the same length as the output length of $\mathcal{E}_K$, by assuming that the output length of $\mathcal{E}_K$ is uniquely determined by the query. The PRF-advantage of $\mathcal{E}$ is defined as

$$\mathbf{Adv}_{\mathcal{E}}^{\mathrm{prf}}(q, \sigma, t) = \max_{\mathcal{A}} \mathbf{Adv}_{\mathcal{E}}^{\mathrm{prf}}(\mathcal{A}),$$

where the maximum is taken over all adversaries running in time t and making q queries with the total number of blocks in all the queries being at most σ. If $\mathcal{E}_K$ is an encryption function of AE, we call it the *privacy advantage* and write as $\mathbf{Adv}_{\mathcal{E}}^{\mathrm{priv}}(q, \sigma, t)$, as the maximum of all nonce-respecting adversaries (that is, the adversary can arbitrarily choose nonces provided all nonce values in the encryption queries are distinct).

Authenticity. We say that an adversary $\mathcal{A}$ *forges* an AE scheme $(\mathcal{E}, \mathcal{D})$ if $\mathcal{A}$ is able to compute a tuple (N, A, C, T) satisfying $\mathcal{D}_K(N, A, C, T) \neq \perp$, without querying (N, A, M) for some M to $\mathcal{E}_K$ and receiving (C, T), i.e. (N, A, C, T) is a non-trivial forgery.

In general, a forger can make q_f forging attempts without restriction on N in the decryption queries, that is, N can be repeated in the decryption queries and an encryption query and a decryption query can use the same N. The *forging advantage* for an adversary $\mathcal{A}$ is written as $\mathbf{Adv}_{\mathcal{E}}^{\mathrm{auth}}(\mathcal{A}) = \Pr[\mathcal{A}^{\mathcal{E}} \text{ forges}]$, and we write

$$\mathbf{Adv}_{\mathcal{E}}^{\mathrm{auth}}((q, q_f), (\sigma, \sigma_f), t) = \max_{\mathcal{A}} \mathbf{Adv}_{\mathcal{E}}^{\mathrm{auth}}(\mathcal{A})$$

to denote the maximum forging advantage for all adversaries running in time t, making q encryption and q_f decryption queries with total number of queried blocks being at most σ and σ_f, respectively.

Unified Security Notion for AE. The privacy and authenticity advantages can be unified into a single security notion as introduced in [23,43]. Let $\mathcal{A}$ be an adversary that only makes non-repeating queries to $\mathcal{D}_K$. Then, we define the AE-advantage of $\mathcal{A}$ against $\mathcal{E}$ as

$$\mathbf{Adv}_{\mathcal{E}}^{\mathrm{AE}}(\mathcal{A}) = |\Pr[\mathcal{A}^{\mathcal{E}_K, \mathcal{D}_K} = 1] - \Pr[\mathcal{A}^{\$, \perp} = 1]|,$$

where $\perp$-oracle always returns $\perp$ and \$-oracle is as the privacy advantage. We similarly define $\mathbf{Adv}_{\mathcal{E}}^{\mathrm{AE}}((q, q_f), (\sigma, \sigma_f), t) = \max_{\mathcal{A}} \mathbf{Adv}_{\mathcal{E}}^{\mathrm{AE}}(\mathcal{A})$, where the maximum is taken over all adversaries running in time t, making q encryption and q_f decryption queries with the total number of blocks being at most σ and σ_f, respectively.

Blockcipher Security. We use a blockcipher E as the underlying primitive, and we assume the security of E as a PRP (pseudorandom permutation). The *PRP-advantage* of a blockcipher E is defined as $\mathbf{Adv}_E^{\mathrm{prp}}(\mathcal{A}) = |\Pr[\mathcal{A}^{E_K} = 1] - \Pr[\mathcal{A}^{\mathsf{P}} = 1]|$, where P is a random permutation uniformly distributed over all permutations over $\{0, 1\}^n$. We write

$$\mathbf{Adv}_E^{\mathrm{prp}}(q, t) = \max_{\mathcal{A}} \mathbf{Adv}_E^{\mathrm{prp}}(\mathcal{A}),$$

where the maximum is taken over all adversaries running in time t and making q queries. Here, σ does not appear as each query has a fixed length.

3 Combined Feedback Mode

Let E_K be the underlying primitive, a blockcipher, with key K. Depending on how the next input block of E_K is determined from the previous output of E_K, a plaintext block, or a ciphertext block, we can categorize different types of feedback modes. Some of the feedback modes are illustrated in Fig. 1. The first three modes are known as the *message feedback mode*, *ciphertext feedback mode*, and *output feedback mode*, respectively. The examples using the first three modes can be found in the basic encryption schemes [4] or AE schemes [5, 28, 29, 54]. The fourth mode, which uses additional (linear) operation $G : \mathcal{B} \to \mathcal{B}$, is new. We call it *combined feedback*. In the combined feedback mode, the next input block $X[i]$ of the underlying primitive E_K depends on at least two of the following three values: (i) previous output $E_K(X[i-1])$, (ii) plaintext $M[i]$, and (iii) ciphertext $C[i]$. With an appropriate choice of G, this feedback mode turns out to be useful for building small and efficient AE schemes. We provide a unified presentation of all types of feedback functions below.

Definition 1 (Feedback Function). *A function $\rho : \mathcal{B} \times \mathcal{B} \to \mathcal{B} \times \mathcal{B}$ is called a feedback function (for an encryption) if there exists a function $\rho' : \mathcal{B} \times \mathcal{B} \to \mathcal{B} \times \mathcal{B}$ (used for decryption) such that*

$$\forall Y, M \in \mathcal{B}, \quad \rho(Y, M) = (X, C) \Rightarrow \rho'(Y, C) = (X, M). \tag{2}$$

ρ *is called a plaintext or output feedback if X depends only on M or Y, respectively (e.g., the first and third mode in Fig. 1). Similarly, it is called ciphertext feedback if X depends only on C in the function ρ' (e.g., the second mode in Fig. 1). All other feedback functions are called* combined feedback.

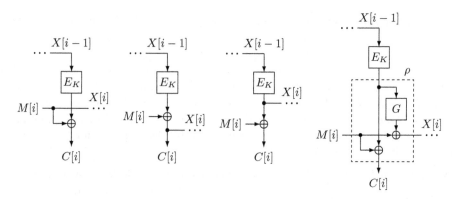

Fig. 1. Different types of feedback modes. We introduce the last feedback mode (called the combined feedback mode) in our construction.

The condition stated in Eq. (2) is sufficient for inverting the feedback computation from the ciphertext. Given the previous output block $Y = E_K(X[i-1])$ and a ciphertext block $C = C[i-1]$, we are able to compute $(X, M) = (X[i], M[i])$ by using $\rho'(Y, C)$.

In particular, when G is not the zero function nor the identity function, the combined feedback mode using this G is not reduced to the remaining three modes. It can be described as $\rho(Y, M) = (X, C) = (G(Y) \oplus M, Y \oplus M)$.

4   COFB: A Small-State, Rate-1, Inverse-Free AE Mode

In this section, we present our proposal, COFB, which has rate-1 (i.e. needs one blockcipher call for one input block), and is inverse-free, i.e., it does not need a blockcipher inverse (decryption). In addition to these features, this mode has a quite small state size, namely $1.5n + k$ bits, in case the underlying blockcipher has an n-bit block and k-bit keys. We first specify the basic building blocks and parameters used in our construction.

Key and Blockcipher. The underlying cryptographic primitive is an n-bit blockcipher, E_K. We assume that n is a multiple of 4. The key of the scheme is the key of the blockcipher, i.e. K. As mentioned we typically assume that E_K is AES-128 with $n = k = 128$, however, COFB can be instantiated with any blockcipher of any n-bit block size by appropriately defining other components.

Masking Function. We define the masking function mask : $\{0,1\}^{n/2} \times \mathbb{N}^2 \to \{0,1\}^{n/2}$ as follows:

$$\mathsf{mask}(\Delta, a, b) = \alpha^a \cdot (1 + \alpha)^b \cdot \Delta \tag{3}$$

We may write $\mathsf{mask}_\Delta(a, b)$ to mean $\mathsf{mask}(\Delta, a, b)$. Here, $\cdot$ denotes the multiplication over $GF(2^{n/2})$, and α denotes the primitive element of the field. For the primitive polynomial defining the field, we choose the lexicographically first one,

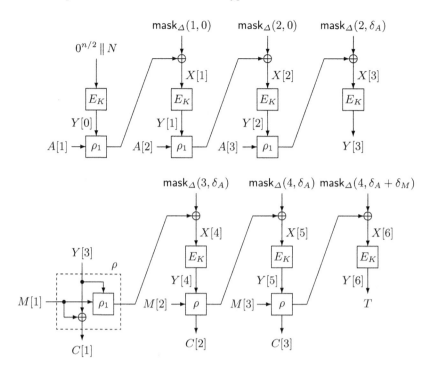

Fig. 2. Encryption of COFB for 3-block associated data and plaintext.

that is, $p(x) = x^{64} + x^4 + x^3 + x + 1$ following [6,27]. Rogaway [41] showed that for all $(a, b) \in \{0, \ldots, 2^{51}\} \times \{0, \ldots, 2^{10}\}$, the values of $\alpha^a \cdot (1 + \alpha)^b$ are distinct[2]. For other values of n, we need to identify the primitive element α of the primitive polynomial and an integer L such that $\alpha^a \cdot (1 + \alpha)^b$ are distinct for all $(a, b) \in \{0, \ldots, L\} \times \{0, \ldots, 4\}$. Then the total allowed size of a message and associated data would be at most nL bits. We need this condition to prove the security claim. In particular we have the following properties of the masking function.

Lemma 1. *For any $(a, b) \neq (a', b')$ chosen from the set $\{0, \ldots, L\} \times \{0, \ldots, 4\}$ (as described above), $c \in \{0, 1\}^{n/2}$ and a random $n/2$ bit string Δ, we have*

$$\Pr[\mathsf{mask}_\Delta(a, b) \oplus \mathsf{mask}_\Delta(a', b') = c] = \frac{1}{2^{n/2}}, \text{ and } \Pr[\mathsf{mask}_\Delta(a, b) = c] = \frac{1}{2^{n/2}}.$$

Proof of the first equation trivially follows from the fact that $\alpha^a \cdot (1 + \alpha)^b$ are distinct for all $(a, b) \in \{0, \ldots, L\} \times \{0, \ldots, 4\}$.

Similar masking functions are frequently used in other modes, such as [9,35,41], however, the masks are full n bits. The use of n-bit masking function

---

[2] If we follow the notations of [41], the right hand side of Eq. (3) could be written as $2^a 3^b \Delta$.

usually allows to redefine the AE scheme as a mode of XE or XEX tweakable blockcipher [41], which significantly reduces the proof complexity. In our case, to reduce the state size, we decided to use the $n/2$-bit masking function, and as a result the proof is ad-hoc and does not rely on XE or XEX.

Feedback Function. Let $Y \in \{0,1\}^n$ and $(Y[1], Y[2], Y[3], Y[4]) \xleftarrow{n/4} Y$, where $Y[i] \in \{0,1\}^{n/4}$. We define $G : \mathcal{B} \to \mathcal{B}$ as $G(Y) = (Y[2], Y[3], Y[4], Y[4] \oplus Y[1])$. We also view G as the $n \times n$ non-singular matrix, so we write $G(Y)$ and $G \cdot Y$ interchangeably. For $M \in \mathcal{B}^{\leq}$ and $Y \in \mathcal{B}$, we define $\rho_1(Y, M) = G \cdot Y \oplus \overline{M}$. The feedback function ρ and its corresponding ρ' are defined as

$$\rho(Y, M) = (\rho_1(Y, M), Y \oplus M),$$
$$\rho'(Y, C) = (\rho_1(Y, Y \oplus C), Y \oplus C).$$

Note that when $(X, M) = \rho'(Y, C)$ then $X = (G \oplus I)Y \oplus C$. Our choice of G ensures that $I \oplus G$ is also invertible matrix. So when Y is chosen randomly for both computations of X (through ρ and ρ'), X also behaves randomly. We need this property when we bound probability of bad events later.

Tweak Value for The Last Block. Given $B \in \{0,1\}^*$, we define $\delta_B \in \{1,2\}$ as follows:

$$\delta_B = \begin{cases} 1 & \text{if } B \neq \lambda \text{ and } n \text{ divides } |B| \\ 2 & \text{otherwise.} \end{cases} \tag{4}$$

This will be used to differentiate the cases that the last block of B is n bits or shorter, for B being associated data or plaintext or ciphertext. We also define a formatting function Fmt for a pair of bit strings (A, Z), where A is associated data and Z could be either a message or a ciphertext. Let $(A[1], \ldots, A[a]) \xleftarrow{n} A$ and $(Z[1], \ldots, Z[z]) \xleftarrow{n} Z$. We define $\mathsf{t}[i]$ as follows:

$$\mathsf{t}[i] = \begin{cases} (i, 0) & \text{if } i < a \\ (a - 1, \delta_A) & \text{if } i = a \\ (i - 1, \delta_A) & \text{if } a < i < a + z \\ (a + z - 2, \delta_A + \delta_Z) & \text{if } i = a + z \end{cases}$$

Now, the formatting function $\mathsf{Fmt}(A, Z)$ returns the following sequence:

$$((A[1], \mathsf{t}[1]), \ldots, (\overline{A[a]}, \mathsf{t}[a]), (Z[1], \mathsf{t}[a + 1]), \ldots, (\overline{Z[z]}, \mathsf{t}[a + z])),$$

where the first coordinate of each pair specifies the input block to be processed, and the second coordinate specifies the exponents of α and $1 + \alpha$ to determine the constant over $\mathrm{GF}(2^{n/2})$. Let $\mathbb{Z}_{\geq 0}$ be the set of non-negative integers and $\mathcal{X}$ be some non-empty set. We say that a function $f : \mathcal{X} \to (\mathcal{B} \times \mathbb{Z}_{\geq 0} \times \mathbb{Z}_{\geq 0})^+$ is *prefix-free* if for all $X \neq X'$, $f(X) = (Y[1], \ldots, Y[\ell])$ is not a prefix of $f(X') = (Y'[1], \ldots, Y'[\ell'])$ (in other words, $(Y[1], \ldots, Y[\ell]) \neq (Y'[1], \ldots, Y'[\ell])$). Here, for a set $\mathcal{S}$, $\mathcal{S}^+$ means $\mathcal{S} \cup \mathcal{S}^2 \cup \cdots$, and we have the following lemma.

Lemma 2. *The function* Fmt(·) *is prefix-free.*

The proof is more or less straightforward and hence we skip it.

Now we present the specifications of COFB in Fig. 3. The encryption and decryption algorithms are denoted by COFB-$\mathcal{E}_K$ and COFB-$\mathcal{D}_K$. We remark that the nonce length is $n/2$ bits, which is enough for the security up to the birthday bound. The nonce is processed as $E_K(0^{n/2} \| N)$ to yield the first internal chaining value. The encryption algorithm takes non-empty A and non-empty M, and outputs C and T such that $|C| = |M|$ and $|T| = n$. The decryption algorithm takes (N, A, C, T) with $|A|, |C| \neq 0$ and outputs M or $\perp$.

We remark that the pseudocodes of Fig. 3 are for clarity and not necessarily memory-efficient due to (say) the use of Fmt and caching multiple $Y[i]$ values at decryption. In fact, the encryption and decryption of COFB can be done with keeping one input/output state for the blockcipher and sequentially updating the $n/2$-bit mask. See Fig. 2 for an illustration.

Module Mask-Gen(K, N)

1. $Y[0] \leftarrow E_K(0^{n/2} \| N)$
2. $(Y^1[0], \ldots, Y^4[0]) \xleftarrow{n/4} Y[0]$
3. $\Delta \leftarrow Y^2[0] \| Y^3[0]$
4. **return** $(\Delta, Y[0])$

Algorithm COFB-$\mathcal{E}_K(N, A, M)$

1. $(\Delta, Y[0]) \leftarrow$ Mask-Gen(K, N)
2. $(A[1], \ldots, A[a]) \xleftarrow{n} A$
3. $(M[1], \ldots, M[m]) \xleftarrow{n} M$
4. $\ell \leftarrow a + m$
5. $((B[1], \mathsf{t}[1]), \ldots, (B[\ell], \mathsf{t}[\ell])) \leftarrow$ Fmt(A, M)
6. **for** $i = 1$ **to** ℓ
7. $X[i] \leftarrow (B[i] \oplus G \cdot Y[i-1]) \ \overline{\oplus} \ \mathsf{mask}_\Delta(\mathsf{t}[i])$
8. $Y[i] \leftarrow E_K(X[i])$
9.   **if** $i > a$ **then**
10. $C[i - a] \leftarrow Y[i-1] \oplus M[i-a]$
11. $T \leftarrow Y[\ell]$
12. **return** (C, T)

Algorithm COFB-$\mathcal{D}_K(N, A, C, T)$

1. $(\Delta, Y[0]) \leftarrow$ Mask-Gen(K, N)
2. $(A[1], \ldots, A[a]) \xleftarrow{n} A$
3. $(C[1], \ldots, C[c]) \xleftarrow{n} C$
4. $\ell \leftarrow a + c$
5. $((B[1], \mathsf{t}[1]), \ldots, (B[\ell], \mathsf{t}[\ell])) \leftarrow$ Fmt(A, C)
6. **for** $i = 1$ **to** ℓ
7.   **if** $i \leq a$ **then**
8. $X[i] \leftarrow (B[i] \oplus G \cdot Y[i-1]) \overline{\oplus} \mathsf{mask}_\Delta(\mathsf{t}[i])$
9.   **else** $X[i] \leftarrow (B[i] \oplus Y[i-1] \oplus G \cdot Y[i-1])$
             $\overline{\oplus} \ \mathsf{mask}_\Delta(\mathsf{t}[i])$
10. $Y[i] \leftarrow E_K(X[i])$
11. **for** $i = 1$ **to** c
12. $M[i] \leftarrow Y[i+a-1] \oplus C[i]$
13. $M \leftarrow (M[1], \ldots, M[c])$
14. $T' \leftarrow Y[\ell]$
15. **if** $T' = T$ **then return** M
16. **else return** $\perp$

Fig. 3. The encryption and decryption algorithms of COFB.

5   Security of COFB

We present the security analysis of COFB in Theorem 1.

Theorem 1 (Main Theorem).

$$\mathbf{Adv}^{AE}_{COFB}((q, q_f), (\sigma, \sigma_f), t) \leq \mathbf{Adv}^{prp}_{AES}(q', t') + \frac{0.5(q')^2}{2^n} + \frac{4\sigma + 0.5nq_f}{2^{n/2}}$$

$$+ \frac{q_f + (q + \sigma + \sigma_f) \cdot \sigma_f}{2^n}$$

where, $q' = q + q_f + \sigma + \sigma_f$, which corresponds to the total number of blockcipher calls through the game, and $t' = t + O(q')$.

Proof. Without loss of generality, we can assume $q' \leq 2^{\frac{n}{2}-1}$, since otherwise the bound obviously holds as the right hand side becomes more than one. The first transition we make is to use an n-bit (uniform) random permutation P instead of E_K, and then to use an n-bit (uniform) random function R instead of P. This two-step transition requires the first two terms of our bound, from the standard PRP-PRF switching lemma and from the computation to the information security reduction (e.g., see [13]). Then what we need is a bound for COFB using R, denoted by COFB-R. That is, we prove

$$\mathbf{Adv}_{\mathsf{COFB\text{-}R}}^{\mathsf{AE}}((q, q_f), (\sigma, \sigma_f), \infty) \leq \frac{4\sigma + 0.5nq_f}{2^{n/2}} + \frac{q_f + (q + \sigma + \sigma_f) \cdot \sigma_f}{2^n}. \quad (5)$$

For $i = 1, \ldots, q$, we write (N_i, A_i, M_i) and (C_i, T_i) to denote the i-th encryption query and response. Here, $A_i = (A_i[1], \ldots, A_i[a_i])$, $M_i = (M_i[1], \ldots, M_i[m_i])$, and $C_i = (C_i[1], \ldots, C_i[m_i])$. Let $\ell_i = a_i + m_i$, which denotes the total input block length for the i-th encryption query. We write $X_i[j]$ (resp. $Y_i[j]$) for $i = 1, \ldots, q$ and $j = 0, \ldots, \ell_i$ to denote the j-th input (resp. output) of the internal R invoked at the i-th encryption query, where the order of invocation follows the specification shown in Fig. 3. We remark that $X_i[0] = 0^{n/2} \| N_i$ and $Y_i[\ell_i] = T_i$ for all $i = 1, \ldots, q$. Similarly, we write Δ_i to denote $Y_i^2[0] \| Y_i^3[0]$ where $Y_i^1[0] \| \cdots \| Y_i^4[0] \xleftarrow{n/4} Y_i[0]$.

We introduce the following relaxations in the game, which only gain the advantage. First, after completing all queries and forging attempts (i.e. decryption queries), let the adversary learn all the Y-values for all encryption queries only. We remark that any X-values computed at the message processing phase (not the AD processing phase) of the i-th encryption query are immediately determined by the i-th query-response tuple, $(N_i, A_i, M_i, C_i, T_i)$ and Y_i values from the property of feedback function, and Δ-values (it is a part of $Y[0]$).

In case of the ideal oracle, all these variables corresponding to Y will be chosen uniformly and independently, where at the plaintext encryption phase $Y_i[j]$ is randomly chosen and used to determine $C_i[j]$ as $C_i[j] = Y_i[j-1] \oplus M_i[j]$, and at AD processing phase it is a dummy and has no influence to the response (C_i, T_i). For decryption queries, the ideal oracle always returns $\perp$ (here we assume that the adversary makes only fresh queries).

Coefficients-H Technique. We outline the Coefficients-H technique developed by Patarin, which serves as a convenient tool for bounding the advantage (see [39,50]). We will use this technique (without giving a proof) to prove our main theorem. Consider two oracles $\mathcal{O}_0 = (\$, \perp)$ (the ideal oracle for the relaxed game) and $\mathcal{O}_1$ (real, i.e. our construction in the same relaxed game). Let $\mathcal{V}$ denote the set of all possible views an adversary can obtain. For any view $\tau \in \mathcal{V}$, we will denote the probability to realize the view as $\mathsf{ip}_{\mathsf{real}}(\tau)$ (or $\mathsf{ip}_{\mathsf{ideal}}(\tau)$) when it is interacting with the real (or ideal respectively) oracle. We call these *interpolation probabilities*. Without loss of generality, we assume that the adversary is deterministic and fixed. Then, the probability space for the interpolation probabilities is uniquely determined by the underlying oracle. As we deal with stateless oracles, these probabilities are independent of the order of query responses in the view. Suppose we have a set of views, $\mathcal{V}_{\text{good}} \subseteq \mathcal{V}$, which we call *good* views, and the following conditions hold:

1. In the game involving the ideal oracle $\mathcal{O}_0$ (and the fixed adversary), the probability of getting a view in $\mathcal{V}_{\text{good}}$ is at least $1 - \epsilon_1$.
2. For any view $\tau \in \mathcal{V}_{\text{good}}$, we have $\mathsf{ip}_{\text{real}}(\tau) \geq (1 - \epsilon_2) \cdot \mathsf{ip}_{\text{ideal}}(\tau)$.

Then we have $|\Pr[\mathcal{A}^{\mathcal{O}_0} = 1] - \Pr[\mathcal{A}^{\mathcal{O}_1} = 1]| \leq \epsilon_1 + \epsilon_2$. The proof can be found at (say) [50]. Now we proceed with the proof of Theorem 1 by defining certain $\mathcal{V}_{\text{good}}$ for our games, and evaluating the bounds, ϵ_1 and ϵ_2.

Views. In our case, a view τ is defined by the following tuple:

$$\tau = ((N_i, A_i, M_i, Y_i)_{i \in \{1, \ldots, q\}}, (N_{i'}^*, A_{i'}^*, C_{i'}^*, T_{i'}^*, Z_{i'}^*)_{i' \in \{1, \ldots, q_f\}}),$$

where $Z_{i'}^*$ denotes the output of the decryption oracle $\mathcal{D}$ (it is always $\perp$ when we interact with the ideal oracle) for the i'-th decryption query $(N_{i'}^*, A_{i'}^*, C_{i'}^*, T_{i'}^*)$. Note that Y_i denotes $(Y_i[0], \ldots, Y_i[\ell_i]) = Y_i[0..\ell_i]$, where $\ell_i = a_i + m_i$, and a_i (resp. m_i) denotes the block length of A_i (resp. M_i). Here we implicitly use the fact that given a complete block $M_i[j]$, the mapping from $Y_i[j]$ to $C_i[j]$ is bijective and hence keeping those $Y_i[j]$ values instead of $C_i[j]$ is sufficient. Similarly we define $c_{i'}^*$ and $a_{i'}^*$, and write $\ell_{i'}^* = a_{i'}^* + c_{i'}^*$.

Let $(L_i[j], R_i[j]) \overset{n/2}{\longleftarrow} X_i[j]$ for all $i \in [1..q]$ and $j \in [1..\ell_i]$. For any i, let p_i denote the length of the longest common prefix of $\mathsf{Fmt}(A_i^*, C_i^*)$ and $\mathsf{Fmt}(A_j, C_j)$ where $N_j = N_i^*$. If there is no such j, we define $p_i = -1$. Since Fmt is prefix-free, it holds that $p_i < \min\{\ell_i^*, \ell_j\}$. We observe that p_i is unique for all $i = 1, \ldots, q_f$, as there is at most one encryption query that uses the same nonce as N_i^*.

Bad Views. Now we define a bad view. The complement of the set of bad views is defined to be the set of good views. A view is called bad if one of the following events occurs:

B1: $L_i[j] = 0^{n/2}$ for some $i \in [1..q]$ and $j > 0$.
B2: $X_i[j] = X_{i'}[j']$ for some $(i, j) \neq (i', j')$ where $j, j' > 0$.
B3: $\mathsf{mcoll}(R) > n/2$, where R is the tuple of all $R_i[j]$ values. Recall that $(L_i[j], R_i[j]) \overset{n/2}{\longleftarrow} X_i[j]$.
B4: $X_i^*[p_i + 1] = X_{i_1}[j_1]$ for some i, i_1, j_1 with p_i as defined above. Note that when $p_i \geq 0$, $X_i^*[p_i + 1]$ is determined from the values of Y.
B5: For some $Z_i^* \neq \perp$. This clearly cannot happen for the ideal oracle case.

We add some intuitions on these events. When **B1** does not hold, then $X_i[j] \neq X_{i'}[0]$ for all i, i', and $j > 0$. Hence Δ_i will be completely random. When **B2** does not hold, then all the inputs for the random function are distinct for encryption queries, which makes the responses from encryption oracle completely random in the "real" game. When **B3** does not hold, then at the right half of $X_i[j]$ we see at most $n/2$ multi-collisions. A successful forgery is to choose one of the $n/2$ multi-collision blocks and forge the left part so that the entire block collides. Forging the left part has $2^{-n/2}$ probability due to randomness of masking. Finally, when **B4** does not hold, then the $(p_i + 1)$-st input for the i-th forging attempt will be fresh with a high probability and so all the subsequent inputs will remain fresh with a high probability.

A view is called good if none of the above events hold. Let $\mathcal{V}_{\text{good}}$ be the set of all such good views. The following lemma bounds the probability of not realizing a good view while interacting with a random function (this will complete the first condition of the Coefficients-H technique).

Lemma 3.
$$\Pr_{\text{ideal}}[\tau \notin \mathcal{V}_{\text{good}}] \leq \frac{4\sigma + 0.5nq_f}{2^{n/2}}.$$

Proof (of Lemma 3). Throughout the proof, we assume all probability notations are defined over the ideal game. We bound all the bad events individually and then by using the union bound, we will obtain the final bound. We first develop some more notation. Let $(Y_i^1[j], Y_i^2[j], Y_i^3[j], Y_i^4[j]) \xleftarrow{n/4} Y_i[j]$. Similarly, we denote $(M_i^1[j], M_i^2[j]) \xleftarrow{n/2} M_i[j]$.

(1) $\Pr[\mathbf{B1}] \leq \sigma/2^{n/2}$: We fix a pair of integers (i, j) for some $i \in [1..q]$ and $j \in [1..\ell_i]$. Now, $L_i[j]$ can be expressed as

$$(Y_i^2[j-1] \| Y_i^3[j-1]) \oplus (\alpha^a \cdot (1+\alpha)^b \cdot \Delta_i) \oplus M_i^1[j]$$

for some a and b. Note that when $j > 1$, Δ_i and $Y_i[j-1]$ are independently and uniformly distributed, and hence for those j, we have $\Pr[L_i[j] = 0^{n/2}] = 2^{-n/2}$ (apply Lemma 1 after conditioning $Y_i[j-1]$). Now when $j = 1$, we have the following three possible choice: (i) $L_i[1] = (1+\alpha) \cdot \Delta_i \oplus \text{Cons}$ if $a_i \geq 2$, (ii) $L_i[1] = \alpha \cdot \Delta_i \oplus \text{Cons}$ if $a_i = 1$ and the associated data block is full, and (iii) $L_i[1] = \alpha^2 \cdot \Delta_i \oplus \text{Cons}$ if $a_i = 1$ and the associated data block is not full, for some constant Cons. In all cases by applying Lemma 1, $\Pr[\mathbf{B1}] \leq \sigma/2^{n/2}$.

(2) $\Pr[\mathbf{B2}] \leq \sigma/2^{n/2}$: For any $(i, j) \neq (i', j')$ with $j, j' \geq 1$, the equality event $X_i[j] = X_{i'}[j']$ has a probability at most 2^{-n} since this event is a non-trivial linear equation on $Y_i[j-1]$ and $Y_{i'}[j'-1]$ and they are independent to each other. Note that $\sigma^2/2^n \leq \sigma/2^{n/2}$ as we are estimating probabilities.

(3) $\Pr[\mathbf{B3}] \leq 2\sigma/2^{n/2}$: The event **B3** is a multi-collision event for randomly chosen σ many $n/2$-bit strings as Y values are mapped in a regular manner (see the feedback function) to R values. From the union bound, we have

$$\Pr[\mathbf{B3}] \leq \binom{\sigma}{n/2} \frac{1}{2^{(n/2)\cdot((n/2)-1)}} \leq \frac{\sigma^{n/2}}{2^{(n/2)\cdot((n/2)-1)}} \leq \left(\frac{\sigma}{2^{(n/2)-1}}\right)^{n/2} \leq \frac{2\sigma}{2^{n/2}},$$

where the last inequality follows from the assumption $(\sigma \leq 2^{(n/2)-1})$.

(4) $\Pr[\mathbf{B4} \wedge \mathbf{B1}^c \wedge \mathbf{B3}^c] \le 0.5nq_f/2^{n/2}$: We fix some i and want to bound the probability $\Pr[X_i^*[p_i+1] = X_{i_1}[j_1] \wedge \mathbf{B1}^c \wedge \mathbf{B3}^c]$ for some i_1, j_1. If $p_i = -1$ (i.e., N_i^* does not appear in encryption queries), then N_i^* is fresh as left $n/2$ bits of all $X_i[j]$ is non-zero for all $j > 0$ (since we also consider $\mathbf{B1}$ does not hold). So the probability is zero. Now we consider $p_i \ge 0$. The event $\mathbf{B3}^c$ implies that at most $n/2$ possible values of (i_1, j_1) are possible for which $X_i^*[p_i+1] = X_{i_1}[j_1]$ can hold. Fix any such (i_1, j_1). Now it is sufficient to bound the probability for equality for the left $n/2$ bits. We first consider the case where $j_1 = p_i + 1$. Now from the definition of p_i, $(C_i^*[p_i+1], t_i^*[p_i+1]) \ne (C_{i_1}[p_i+1], t_{i_1}[p_i+1])$. If $t_i[p_i+1] = t_{i_1}[p_i+1]$ then the bad event cannot hold with probability one. Otherwise, we obtain a non-trivial linear equation in Δ_{i_1} and apply Lemma 1, and we also use the fact that $G + I$ is non singular. A similar argument holds for the other choices of j_1. Therefore, the probability for the atomic case is at most $2^{-n/2}$, and because we have at most $q_f \cdot n/2$ chances, $\Pr[\mathbf{B4} \wedge \mathbf{B1}^c \wedge \mathbf{B3}^c]$ is at most $(n/2) \cdot q_f \cdot 1/2^{n/2}$.

Summarizing, we have

$$\Pr_{\text{ideal}}[\tau \notin \mathcal{V}_{\text{good}}] \le \Pr[\mathbf{B1}] + \Pr[\mathbf{B2}] + \Pr[\mathbf{B3}] + \Pr[\mathbf{B4} \wedge \mathbf{B1}^c \wedge \mathbf{B3}^c]$$

$$\le \frac{\sigma}{2^{n/2}} + \frac{\sigma}{2^{n/2}} + \frac{2\sigma}{2^{n/2}} + \frac{0.5nq_f}{2^{n/2}} = \frac{4\sigma + 0.5nq_f}{2^{n/2}},$$

which concludes the proof. □

Lower Bound of $\mathsf{ip}_{\text{real}}(\tau)$. We consider the ratio of $\mathsf{ip}_{\text{real}}(\tau)$ and $\mathsf{ip}_{\text{ideal}}(\tau)$. In this paragraph we assume that all the probability space, except for $\mathsf{ip}_{\text{ideal}}(*)$, is defined over the real game. We fix a good view

$$\tau = ((N_i, A_i, M_i, Y_i)_{i \in \{1,\dots,q\}}, (N_{i'}^*, A_{i'}^*, C_{i'}^*, T_{i'}^*, Z_{i'}^*)_{i' \in \{1,\dots,q_f\}}),$$

where $Z_{i'}^* = \bot$. We separate τ into

$$\tau_e = (N_i, A_i, M_i, Y_i)_{i \in \{1,\dots,q\}} \text{ and } \tau_d = (N_{i'}^*, A_{i'}^*, C_{i'}^*, T_{i'}^*, Z_{i'}^*)_{i' \in \{1,\dots,q_f\}},$$

and we first see that for a good view τ, $\mathsf{ip}_{\text{ideal}}(\tau)$ equals to $1/2^{n(q+\sigma)}$.

Now we consider the real case. Since $\mathbf{B1}$ and $\mathbf{B2}$ do not hold with τ, all inputs of the random function inside τ_e are distinct, which implies that the released Y-values are independent and uniformly random. The variables in τ_e are uniquely determined given these Y-values, and there are exactly $q+\sigma$ distinct input-output of R. Therefore, $\Pr[\tau_e]$ is exactly $2^{-n(q+\sigma)}$.

We next evaluate

$$\mathsf{ip}_{\text{real}}(\tau) = \Pr[\tau_e, \tau_d] = \Pr[\tau_e] \cdot \Pr[\tau_d|\tau_e] = \frac{1}{2^{n(q+\sigma)}} \cdot \Pr[\tau_d|\tau_e]. \tag{6}$$

We observe that $\Pr[\tau_d|\tau_e]$ equals to $\Pr[\bot_{\text{all}}|\tau_e]$, where $\bot_{\text{all}}$ denotes the event that $Z_i^* = \bot$ for all $i = 1, \dots, q_f$, as other variables in τ_d are determined by τ_e.

Let η denote the event that, for all $i = 1, \dots, q_f$, $X_i^*[j]$ for $p_i < j \le \ell_i^*$ is not colliding to X-values in τ_e and $X_i^*[j']$ for all $j' \ne j$. For $j = p_i + 1$, the above condition is fulfilled by **B4**, and thus $Y_i^*[p_i + 1]$ is uniformly random, and hence $X_i^*[p_i + 2]$ is also uniformly random, due to the property of feedback function (here, observe that the mask addition between the chain of $Y_i^*[j]$ to $X_i^*[j + 1]$ does not reduce the randomness).

Now we have $\Pr[\bot_{\text{all}}|\tau_e] = 1 - \Pr[(\bot_{\text{all}})^c|\tau_e]$, and we also have $\Pr[(\bot_{\text{all}})^c|\tau_e] = \Pr[(\bot_{\text{all}})^c, \eta|\tau_e] + \Pr[(\bot_{\text{all}})^c, \eta^c|\tau_e]$. Here, $\Pr[(\bot_{\text{all}})^c, \eta|\tau_e]$ is the probability that at least one T_i^* for some $i = 1, \ldots, q_f$ is correct as a guess of $Y_i^*[\ell_i^*]$. Here $Y_i^*[\ell_i^*]$ is completely random from η, hence using the union bound we have

$$\Pr[(\bot_{\text{all}})^c, \eta|\tau_e] \leq \frac{q_f}{2^n}.$$

For $\Pr[(\bot_{\text{all}})^c, \eta^c|\tau_e]$ which is at most $\Pr[\eta^c|\tau_e]$, the above observation suggests that this can be evaluated by counting the number of possible bad pairs (i.e. a pair that a collision inside the pair violates η) among the all X-values in τ_e and all X^*-values in τ_d, as in the same manner to the collision analysis of e.g., CBC-MAC using R. For each i-th decryption query, the number of bad pairs is at most $(q + \sigma + \ell_i^*) \cdot \ell_i^* \leq (q + \sigma + \sigma_f) \cdot \ell_i^*$. Therefore, the total number of bad pairs is $\sum_{1 \leq i \leq q_f}(q + \sigma + \sigma_f) \cdot \ell_i^* \leq (q + \sigma + \sigma_f) \cdot \sigma_f$, and we have

$$\Pr[(\bot_{\text{all}})^c, \eta^c|\tau_e] \leq \frac{(q + \sigma + \sigma_f) \cdot \sigma_f}{2^n}.$$

Combining all, we have

$$\text{ip}_{\text{real}}(\tau) = \frac{1}{2^{n(q+\sigma)}} \cdot \Pr[\tau_d|\tau_e] = \text{ip}_{\text{ideal}}(\tau) \cdot \Pr[\bot_{\text{all}}|\tau_e]$$
$$\geq \text{ip}_{\text{ideal}}(\tau) \cdot (1 - (\Pr[(\bot_{\text{all}})^c, \eta|\tau_e] + \Pr[(\bot_{\text{all}})^c, \eta^c|\tau_e]))$$
$$\geq \text{ip}_{\text{ideal}}(\tau) \cdot \left(1 - \frac{q_f + (q + \sigma + \sigma_f) \cdot \sigma_f}{2^n}\right).$$

$\square$

6 Hardware Implementation of COFB

6.1 Overview

COFB primarily aims to achieve a lightweight implementation on small hardware devices. For such devices, the hardware resource for implementing memory is often the dominant factor of the size of entire implementation, and the scalability by parallelizing the internal components is not needed. In this respect, COFB's small state size and completely serial operation is quite desirable.

For implementation aspects, COFB is simple, as it consists of a blockcipher and several basic operations (bitwise XOR, the feedback function, and the constant multiplications over $GF(2^{n/2})$). Combined with the small state size, this implies that the implementation size of COFB is largely dominated by the underlying blockcipher.

We also provide the number of clock cycles needed to process input bytes, as a conventional way to estimate the speed. Here, COFB taking a-block AD (associated data) and an m-block message needs $12(a + m) + 23$ cycles. Table 2 shows the number of average cycles per input message bytes, which we call cycles per byte (cpb), assuming AD has the same length as message and the underlying blockcipher has 128-bit block. That is, the table shows $(12 \cdot 2m + 23)/16m$.

Table 2. Clock cycles per message byte for COFB using a 128-bit blockcipher.

	Message length (Bytes)										
	16	32	64	128	256	512	1024	2048	4096	16384	32768
cpb	2.93	2.22	1.86	1.68	1.59	1.54	1.52	1.51	1.50	1.50	1.50

6.2 Hardware Architecture

We describe the hardware implementation of COFB using AES-128. This is a basic implementation without any pipelining, and employs a module architecture. We primary focus on the encryption-only circuit, however, the combined encryption and decryption circuit should have very small amount of overhead thanks to the inverse-freeness (i.e. no AES decryption routine is needed) and simplicity of the mode. Due to the similarity between the associated data and the message processing phase, the same hardware modules are used in the both phases. A single bit switch is used to distinguish between the two types of input data. The main architecture consists of the modules described below. We remark that, there is also a Finite State Machine (FSM) which controls the flow by sending signal to these modules. The FSM has a rather simple structure, and will be described in the full version. Then, the overall hardware architecture is described in Fig. 4.

1. **State Registers:** The state registers are used to store the intermediate states after each iteration. We use a 128-bit **State** register to store the 128-bit AES block state, a 64-bit Δ register to store the 64-bit mask applied to each AES input, and a 128-bit **Key** register to store the 128-bit key. The round key of AES is stored in the additional 128-bit register (**Round Key**), however, this is included in the AES module.

2. **AES Round:** AES round function module runs one AES round computation and produces a 128-bit output, using two 128-bit inputs, one from the **State** and the other from (internal) **Round Key** registers. The latter register is initialized by loading the master key, stored in the **Key** register, each time the AES function is invoked. The output of AES module is stored into the **State** register, which is the input for the next round. The entire operation is serial, while the internal round computation and the round key generation run in parallel, and needs 11 cycles to perform full AES-128 encryption.

3. **Feedback Function** ρ: The ρ module is to compute the linear feedback function ρ on the 128-bit data block and the 128-bit intermediate state value (output from the AES computation). The output is a 128-bit ciphertext and a 128-bit intermediate state (to be masked and stored to the **State** register).

4. **MaskUpdate: uMask** module updates the mask stored in Δ register. **uMask** receives the current mask value and updates it by multiplying with α or $(1+\alpha)$ or $(1+\alpha)^2$ based on the signals generated by the FSM, where signals are to indicate the end of the message and the completeness of the final block process.

Basic Implementation: We describe a basic flow of our implementation of COFB, which generally follows the pseudocode of Fig. 3. Prior to the initialization, **State** register is loaded with $0^{64} \| N$. Once **State** register is initialized, the initialization process starts by encrypting the nonce ($0^{64} \| N$) with AES. Then, 64 bits of the encrypted nonce is chopped by the "chop" function as in Fig. 4, and this chopped value is stored into the Δ register (this is initialization of Δ). After these initializations, 128-bit associated data blocks are fetched and sent to the ρ module along with the previous AES output to produce a 128 bit intermediate state. This state is partially masked with 64-bit Δ for every AES call. After all the associated data blocks are processed, the message blocks are processed in the same manner, except that the ρ function produces 128-bit ciphertext blocks in addition to the intermediate state values. Finally, after the message processing is over, the tag is generated using an additional AES call.

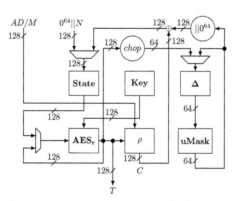

Fig. 4. Hardware circuit diagram

Combined Encryption and Decryption: As mentioned earlier, we here focus on the encryption-only circuit. However, due to the similarity between the encryption and the decryption modes, the combined hardware for encryption and decryption can be built with a small increase in the area, with the same throughput. This can be done by adding a control flow to a binary signal for mode selection.

6.3   Implementation Results

We implemented COFB on Xilinx Virtex 6 and Virtex 7, using VHDL and Xilinx ISE 13.4. AES-128 is used as the internal blockcipher. Table 3 presents the implementation results of COFB on Virtex 7 with the target device xc7vx330t and Virtex 6 with the target device xc6vlx760. We employ RTL approach and a basic iterative type architecture. The areas are listed in the number of Slice Registers, Slice LUTs and Occupied Slices. We also report frequency (MHz), Throughput (Gbps), and throughput-area efficiency. In the full version, we will show the area utilization for this basic AES-based implementation.

Table 3. Implementation results of COFB on FPGAs.

Platform	# Slice registers	# LUTs	# Slices	Frequency (MHz)	Gbps	Mbps/ LUT	Mbps/ Slice
Virtex 6	722	1075	442	267.20	2.85	2.24	6.45
Virtex 7	722	1456	555	264.24	2.82	2.22	5.08

For AES, we use the implementation available from Athena [1] maintained by George Mason University. This implementation stores all the round subkeys in a single register to make the AES implementation faster and parallelizable. However, the main motivation of COFB is to reduce hardware footprint. Hence, we change the above implementation to a sequential one such that it processes only one AES round in a single clock cycle. This in turn eliminates the need to store all the round subkeys in a single register and reduces the hardware area consumed by the AES module.

6.4   Comparison with ATHENa Database

We compare our implementation of COFB with the results published in ATHENa Database [2], taking Virtex 6 and Virtex 7 as our target platforms. We first warn that this is a rough comparison. Here, we ignore the overhead to support the GMU API and the fact that ours is encryption-only while the others are (to the best of our knowledge) supporting both encryption and decryption, and the difference in the achieved security level, both quantitative and qualitative. We acknowledge that supporting GMU API will require some additional overhead to the current figures of COFB. Nevertheless, we think the current figures of COFB suggest that small hardware implementations are possible compared with other blockcipher AE modes shown in the table, using the same AES-128, even if we add a circuit for supporting GMU API and decryption.

We also remark that it is basically hard to compare COFB using AES-128 with other non-block-cipher-based AE schemes in the right way, because of the difference in the primitives and the types of security guarantee. For example, ACORN is built from scratch and does not have any provable security result, and is subjected to several cryptanalysis [20,34,44,45]. Joltik and JAMBU-SIMON employ lightweight (tweakable) blockciphers allowing smaller implementation than AES, and Sponge AE schemes (ASCON, Ketje, NORX, and PRIMATES-HANUMAN) use a keyless permutation of a large block size to avoid key scheduling circuit and have the provable security relying on the random permutation model. In Table 4, we provide the comparison table only on the Vertex 6 platform. The comparison table on the Vertex 7 platform will be provided in the full version.

Table 4. Comparison on Virtex 6 [2]. In the "Primitive" column, SC denotes Stream cipher, (T)BC denotes (Tweakable) blockcipher, and BC-RF denotes the blockcipher's round function.

Scheme	Primitive	#LUT	#Slices	Gbps	Mbps/LUT	Mbps/Slices
ACORN [51]	SC	455	135	3.112	6.840	23.052
AEGIS [53]	BC-RF	7592	2028	70.927	9.342	34.974
AES-COPA [10]	BC	7754	2358	2.500	0.322	1.060
AES-GCM [22]	BC	3175	1053	3.239	1.020	3.076
AES-OTR [36]	BC	5102	1385	2.741	0.537	1.979
AEZ [26]	BC-RF	4597	1246	8.585	0.747	2.756
ASCON [21]	Sponge	1271	413	3.172	2.496	7.680
CLOC [29]	BC	3145	891	2.996	0.488	1.724
DEOXYS [31]	TBC	3143	951	2.793	0.889	2.937
ELmD [19]	BC	4302	1584	3.168	0.736	2.091
JAMBU-AES [52]	BC	1836	652	1.999	1.089	3.067
JAMBU-SIMON [52]	BC (non-AES)	1222	453	0.363	0.297	0.801
Joltik [30]	TBC	1292	442	0.853	0.660	0.826
Ketje [14]	Sponge	1270	456	7.345	5.783	16.107
Minalpher [46]	BC (non-AES)	2879	1104	1.831	0.636	1.659
NORX [11]	Sponge	2964	1016	11.029	3.721	10.855
PRIMATES-HANUMAN [8]	Sponge	1012	390	0.964	0.953	2.472
OCB [33]	BC	4249	1348	3.122	0.735	2.316
SCREAM [24]	TBC	2052	834	1.039	0.506	1.246
SILC [29]	BC	3066	921	4.040	1.318	4.387
Tiaoxin [38]	BC-RF	7123	2101	52.838	7.418	25.149
TriviA-ck [18]	SC	2118	687	15.374	7.259	22.378
COFB	BC	1075	442	2.850	2.240	6.450

7 Conclusion

This paper presents COFB, a blockcipher mode for AE focusing on the state size. When instantiated with an n-bit blockcipher, COFB operates at rate-1, and requires state size of $1.5n$ bits, and is provable secure up to $O(2^{n/2}/n)$ queries based on the standard PRP assumption on the blockcipher. In fact this is the first scheme fulfilling these features at once. A key idea of COFB is a new type of feedback function combining both plaintext and ciphertext blocks. We have also presented the hardware implementation results, which demonstrate the effectiveness of our approach.

Acknowledgements. The authors thank the anonymous reviewers for helpful feedback. The work by Tetsu Iwata was supported in part by JSPS KAKENHI, Grant-in-Aid for Scientific Research (B), Grant Number 26280045, and was partially carried out while visiting Nanyang Technological University, Singapore.

References

1. ATHENa: Automated Tool for Hardware Evaluation. https://cryptography.gmu.edu/athena/
2. Authenticated Encryption FPGA Ranking. https://cryptography.gmu.edu/athenadb/fpga_auth_cipher/rankings_view
3. CAESAR: Competition for Authenticated Encryption: Security, Applicability, and Robustness. http://competitions.cr.yp.to/caesar.html/
4. Recommendation for Block Cipher Modes of Operation: Methods and Techniques. NIST Special Publication 800–38A. National Institute of Standards and Technology (2001)
5. Recommendation for Block Cipher Modes of Operation: The CCM Mode for Authentication and Confidentiality. NIST Special Publication 800–38C. National Institute of Standards and Technology (2004)
6. Recommendation for Block Cipher Modes of Operation: The CMAC Mode for Authentication. NIST Special Publication 800–38B. National Institute of Standards and Technology (2005)
7. NIST FIPS 197. Advanced Encryption Standard (AES). Federal Information Processing Standards Publication, 197 (2001)
8. Andreeva, E., Bilgin, B., Bogdanov, A., Luykx, A., Mendel, F., Mennink, B., Mouha, N., Wang, Q., Yasuda, K.: PRIMATEs v1.02. Submission to CAESAR (2016). https://competitions.cr.yp.to/round2/primatesv102.pdf
9. Andreeva, E., Bogdanov, A., Luykx, A., Mennink, B., Tischhauser, E., Yasuda, K.: Parallelizable and authenticated online ciphers. In: Sako, K., Sarkar, P. (eds.) ASIACRYPT 2013. LNCS, vol. 8269, pp. 424–443. Springer, Heidelberg (2013). doi:10.1007/978-3-642-42033-7_22
10. Andreeva, E., Bogdanov, A., Luykx, A., Mennink, B., Tischhauser, E., Yasuda, K.: AES-COPA v. 2. Submission to CAESAR (2015). https://competitions.cr.yp.to/round2/aescopav2.pdf
11. Aumasson, J.-P., Jovanovic, P., Neves, S.: NORX v3.0. Submission to CAESAR (2016). https://competitions.cr.yp.to/round3/norxv30.pdf
12. Banik, S., Bogdanov, A., Minematsu, K.: Low-area hardware implementations of CLOC, SILC and AES-OTR. In: DIAC (2015)
13. Bellare, M., Kilian, J., Rogaway, P.: The security of the cipher block chaining message authentication code. J. Comput. Syst. Sci. **61**(3), 362–399 (2000)
14. Bertoni, G., Daemen, M.P.J., Van Assche, G., Van Keer, R.: Ketje v2. Submission to CAESAR (2016). https://competitions.cr.yp.to/round3/ketjev2.pdf

15. Bogdanov, A., Knudsen, L.R., Leander, G., Paar, C., Poschmann, A., Robshaw, M.J.B., Seurin, Y., Vikkelsoe, C.: PRESENT: an ultra-lightweight block cipher. In: Paillier, P., Verbauwhede, I. (eds.) CHES 2007. LNCS, vol. 4727, pp. 450–466. Springer, Heidelberg (2007). doi:10.1007/978-3-540-74735-2_31

16. Bogdanov, A., Mendel, F., Regazzoni, F., Rijmen, V., Tischhauser, E.: ALE: AES-based lightweight authenticated encryption. In: Moriai, S. (ed.) FSE 2013. LNCS, vol. 8424, pp. 447–466. Springer, Heidelberg (2014). doi:10.1007/978-3-662-43933-3_23

17. Borghoff, J., et al.: PRINCE – a low-latency block cipher for pervasive computing applications. In: Wang, X., Sako, K. (eds.) ASIACRYPT 2012. LNCS, vol. 7658, pp. 208–225. Springer, Heidelberg (2012). doi:10.1007/978-3-642-34961-4_14

18. Chakraborti, A., Nandi, M.: TriviA-ck-v2. Submission to CAESAR (2015). https://competitions.cr.yp.to/round2/triviackv2.pdf

19. Datta, N., Nandi, M.: Proposal of ELmD v2.1. Submission to CAESAR (2015). https://competitions.cr.yp.to/round2/elmdv21.pdf

20. Dey, P., Rohit, R.S., Adhikari, A.: Full key recovery of ACORN with a single fault. J. Inf. Sec. Appl. **29**, 57–64 (2016)

21. Dobraunig, C., Eichlseder, M., Mendel, F., Schläffer, M.: Ascon v1.2. Submission to CAESAR (2016). https://competitions.cr.yp.to/round3/asconv12.pdf

22. Dworkin, M.: Recommendation for block cipher modes of operation: Galois/counter mode (GCM) and GMAC. NIST Special Publication 800–38D (2011). http://csrc.nist.gov/publications/nistpubs/800-38D/SP-800-38D.pdf

23. Fleischmann, E., Forler, C., Lucks, S.: McOE: a family of almost foolproof on-line authenticated encryption schemes. In: Canteaut, A. (ed.) FSE 2012. LNCS, vol. 7549, pp. 196–215. Springer, Heidelberg (2012). doi:10.1007/978-3-642-34047-5_12

24. Grosso, V., Leurent, G., Standaert, F.-X., Varici, K., Journault, A., Durvaux, F., Gaspar, L., Kerckhof, S.: SCREAM Side-Channel Resistant Authenticated Encryption with Masking. Submission to CAESAR (2015). https://competitions.cr.yp.to/round2/screamv3.pdf

25. Guo, J., Peyrin, T., Poschmann, A., Robshaw, M.: The LED block cipher. In: Preneel, B., Takagi, T. (eds.) CHES 2011. LNCS, vol. 6917, pp. 326–341. Springer, Heidelberg (2011). doi:10.1007/978-3-642-23951-9_22

26. Hoang, V.T., Krovetz, T., Rogaway, P.: AEZ v4.2: Authenticated Encryption by Enciphering. Submission to CAESAR (2016). https://competitions.cr.yp.to/round3/aezv42.pdf

27. Iwata, T., Kurosawa, K.: OMAC: one-key CBC MAC. In: Johansson, T. (ed.) FSE 2003. LNCS, vol. 2887, pp. 129–153. Springer, Heidelberg (2003). doi:10.1007/978-3-540-39887-5_11

28. Iwata, T., Minematsu, K., Guo, J., Morioka, S.: CLOC: authenticated encryption for short input. In: Cid, C., Rechberger, C. (eds.) FSE 2014. LNCS, vol. 8540, pp. 149–167. Springer, Heidelberg (2015). doi:10.1007/978-3-662-46706-0_8

29. Iwata, T., Minematsu, K., Guo, J., Morioka, S., Kobayashi, E.: CLOC and SILC. Submission to CAESAR (2016) https://competitions.cr.yp.to/round3/clocsilcv3.pdf

30. Jean, J., Nikolić, I., Peyrin, T.: Joltik v1.3. Submission to CAESAR (2015). https://competitions.cr.yp.to/round2/joltikv13.pdf

31. Jean, J., Nikolić, I., Peyrin, T.: Deoxys v1.41. Submission to CAESAR (2016). https://competitions.cr.yp.to/round3/deoxysv141.pdf

32. Krovetz, T., Rogaway, P.: The software performance of authenticated-encryption modes. In: Joux, A. (ed.) FSE 2011. LNCS, vol. 6733, pp. 306–327. Springer, Heidelberg (2011). doi:10.1007/978-3-642-21702-9_18

33. Krovetz, T., Rogaway, P.: OCB(v1.1). Submission to CAESAR (2016). https:// competitions.cr.yp.to/round3/ocbv11.pdf

34. Lafitte, F., Lerman, L., Markowitch, O., Van Heule, D.: SAT-based cryptanalysis of ACORN. IACR Cryptology ePrint Archive 2016:521 (2016)

35. Minematsu, K.: Parallelizable rate-1 authenticated encryption from pseudorandom functions. In: Nguyen, P.Q., Oswald, E. (eds.) EUROCRYPT 2014. LNCS, vol. 8441, pp. 275–292. Springer, Heidelberg (2014). doi:10.1007/978-3-642-55220-5_16

36. Minematsu, K.: AES-OTR v3.1. Submission to CAESAR (2016). https:// competitions.cr.yp.to/round3/aesotrv31.pdf

37. Moradi, A., Poschmann, A., Ling, S., Paar, C., Wang, H.: Pushing the limits: a very compact and a threshold implementation of AES. In: Paterson, K.G. (ed.) EUROCRYPT 2011. LNCS, vol. 6632, pp. 69–88. Springer, Heidelberg (2011). doi:10.1007/978-3-642-20465-4_6

38. Nikolić, I.: Tiaoxin - 346. Submission to CAESAR (2016). https://competitions. cr.yp.to/round3/tiaoxinv21.pdf

39. Patarin, J.: Etude des Générateurs de Permutations Basés sur le Schéma du D.E.S. Phd Thèsis de Doctorat de l'Université de Paris 6 (1991)

40. Peyrin, T., Sim, S.M., Wang, L., Zhang, G.: Cryptanalysis of JAMBU. In: Leander, G. (ed.) FSE 2015. LNCS, vol. 9054, pp. 264–281. Springer, Heidelberg (2015). doi:10.1007/978-3-662-48116-5_13

41. Rogaway, P.: Efficient instantiations of tweakable blockciphers and refinements to modes OCB and PMAC. In: Lee, P.J. (ed.) ASIACRYPT 2004. LNCS, vol. 3329, pp. 16–31. Springer, Heidelberg (2004). doi:10.1007/978-3-540-30539-2_2

42. Rogaway, P., Bellare, M., Black, J.: OCB: a block-cipher mode of operation for efficient authenticated encryption. ACM Trans. Inf. Syst. Secur. 6(3), 365–403 (2003)

43. Rogaway, P., Shrimpton, T.: A provable-security treatment of the key-wrap problem. In: Vaudenay, S. (ed.) EUROCRYPT 2006. LNCS, vol. 4004, pp. 373–390. Springer, Heidelberg (2006). doi:10.1007/11761679_23

44. Salam, M.I., Bartlett, H., Dawson, E., Pieprzyk, J., Simpson, L., Wong, K.K.-H.: Investigating cube attacks on the authenticated encryption stream cipher ACORN. In: Batten, L., Li, G. (eds.) ATIS 2016. CCIS, vol. 651, pp. 15–26. Springer, Singapore (2016). doi:10.1007/978-981-10-2741-3_2

45. Salam, Md.I., Wong, K.K.-H., Bartlett, H., Simpson, L.R., Dawson, Ed., Pieprzyk, J.: Finding state collisions in the authenticated encryption stream cipher ACORN. In: Proceedings of the Australasian Computer Science Week Multiconference, p. 36 (2016)

46. Sasaki, Y., Todo, Y., Aoki, K., Naito, Y., Sugawara, T., Murakami, Y., Matsui, M., Hirose, S.: Minalpher v1.1. Submission to CAESAR (2015). https://competitions. cr.yp.to/round2/minalpherv11.pdf

47. Schroé, W., Mennink, B., Andreeva, E., Preneel, B.: Forgery and subkey recovery on CAESAR candidate iFeed. In: Dunkelman, O., Keliher, L. (eds.) SAC 2015. LNCS, vol. 9566, pp. 197–204. Springer, Cham (2016). doi:10.1007/ 978-3-319-31301-6_11

48. Shibutani, K., Isobe, T., Hiwatari, H., Mitsuda, A., Akishita, T., Shirai, T.: *Piccolo*: an ultra-lightweight blockcipher. In: Preneel, B., Takagi, T. (eds.) CHES 2011. LNCS, vol. 6917, pp. 342–357. Springer, Heidelberg (2011). doi:10.1007/ 978-3-642-23951-9_23

49. Suzaki, T., Minematsu, K., Morioka, S., Kobayashi, E.: TWINE: a lightweight block cipher for multiple platforms. In: Knudsen, L.R., Wu, H. (eds.) SAC 2012. LNCS, vol. 7707, pp. 339–354. Springer, Heidelberg (2013). doi:10.1007/978-3-642-35999-6_22

50. Vaudenay, S.: Decorrelation: a theory for block cipher security. J. Cryptol. **16**(4), 249–286 (2003)

51. Wu, H.: ACORN: A Lightweight Authenticated Cipher (v3). Submission to CAESAR (2016). https://competitions.cr.yp.to/round3/acornv3.pdf

52. Wu, H., Huang, T.: The JAMBU Lightweight Authentication Encryption Mode (v2.1). Submission to CAESAR (2016). https://competitions.cr.yp.to/round3/jambuv21.pdf

53. Wu, H., Preneel, B.: AEGIS: A Fast Authenticated Encryption Algorithm (v1.1). Submission to CAESAR (2016). https://competitions.cr.yp.to/round3/aegisv11.pdf

54. Zhang, L., Wu, W., Sui, H., Wang, P.: iFeed[AES] v1. Submission to CAESAR (2014). https://competitions.cr.yp.to/round1/ifeedaesv1.pdf

Gimli: A Cross-Platform Permutation

Daniel J. Bernstein[1(✉)], Stefan Kölbl[2], Stefan Lucks[3],
Pedro Maat Costa Massolino[4], Florian Mendel[5], Kashif Nawaz[6],
Tobias Schneider[7], Peter Schwabe[4], François-Xavier Standaert[6],
Yosuke Todo[8], and Benoît Viguier[4]

[1] University of Illinois at Chicago, Chicago, USA
djb@cr.yp.to
[2] Technical University of Denmark, Kongens Lyngby, Denmark
stek@dtu.dk
[3] Bauhaus-Universität Weimar, Weimar, Germany
Stefan.Lucks@uni-weimar.de
[4] Radboud University, Nijmegen, Netherlands
P.Massolino@cs.ru.nl,peter@cryptojedi.org,benoit@viguier.nl
[5] Graz University of Technology, Graz, Austria
florian.mendel@gmail.com
[6] Université Catholique de Louvain, Louvain-la-Neuve, Belgium
{kashif.nawaz,fstandae}@uclouvain.be
[7] Ruhr-University Bochum, Bochum, Germany
tobias.schneider-a7a@rub.de
[8] NTT Secure Platform Laboratories, Tokyo, Japan
todo.yosuke@lab.ntt.co.jp

Abstract. This paper presents GIMLI, a 384-bit permutation designed to achieve high security with high performance across a broad range of platforms, including 64-bit Intel/AMD server CPUs, 64-bit and 32-bit ARM smartphone CPUs, 32-bit ARM microcontrollers, 8-bit AVR microcontrollers, FPGAs, ASICs without side-channel protection, and ASICs with side-channel protection.

Keywords: Intel · AMD · ARM Cortex-A · ARM Cortex-M · AVR · FPGA · ASIC · Side channels · The eyes of a hawk and the ears of a fox

Author list in alphabetical order; see https://www.ams.org/profession/leaders/culture/CultureStatement04.pdf. This work resulted from the Lorentz Center Workshop "HighLight: High-security lightweight cryptography". This work was supported in part by the Commission of the European Communities through the Horizon 2020 program under project number 645622 (PQCRYPTO) and project number 645421 (ECRYPT-CSA); the Austrian Science Fund (FWF) under grant P26494-N15; the ARC project NANOSEC; the Belgian Fund for Scientific Research (FNRS-F.R.S.); the Technology Foundation STW (project 13499 TYPHOON), from the Dutch government; the Netherlands Organisation for Scientific Research (NWO) under grant 639.073.005; and the U.S. National Science Foundation under grant 1314919. "Any opinions, findings, and conclusions or recommendations expressed in this material are those of the author(s) and do not necessarily reflect the views of the National Science Foundation." Permanent ID of this document: 93eb34af666d7fa7264d94c21c18034a.

© International Association for Cryptologic Research 2017
W. Fischer and N. Homma (Eds.): CHES 2017, LNCS 10529, pp. 299–320, 2017.
DOI: 10.1007/978-3-319-66787-4_15

1   Introduction

Keccak [11], the 1600-bit permutation inside SHA-3, is well known to be extremely energy-efficient: specifically, it achieves very high throughput in moderate-area hardware. Keccak is also well known to be easy to protect against side-channel attacks: each of its 24 rounds has algebraic degree only 2, allowing low-cost masking. The reason that Keccak is well known for these features is that *most symmetric primitives are much worse in these metrics*.

Chaskey [21], a 128-bit-permutation-based message-authentication code with a 128-bit key, is well known to be very fast on 32-bit embedded microcontrollers: for example, it runs at just 7.0 cycles/byte on an ARM Cortex-M3 microcontroller. The reason that Chaskey is well known for this microcontroller performance is that *most symmetric primitives are much worse in this metric*.

Salsa20 [7], a 512-bit-permutation-based stream cipher, is well known to be very fast on CPUs with vector units. For example, [9] shows that Salsa20 runs at 5.47 cycles/byte using the 128-bit NEON vector unit on a classic ARM Cortex-A8 (iPad 1, iPhone 4) CPU core. The reason that Salsa20 and its variant ChaCha20 [6] are well known for this performance is again that *most symmetric primitives are much worse in this metric*. This is also why ChaCha20 is now used by smartphones for HTTPS connections to Google [13] and Cloudflare [27].

Cryptography appears in a wide range of application environments, and each new environment seems to provide more reasons to be dissatisfied with most symmetric primitives. For example, Keccak, Salsa20, and ChaCha20 slow down dramatically when messages are short. As another example, Chaskey has a limited security level, and slows down dramatically when the same permutation is used inside a mode aiming for a higher security level.

Contributions of this paper. We introduce GIMLI, a 384-bit permutation. Like other permutations with sufficiently large state sizes, GIMLI can easily be used to build high-security block ciphers, tweakable block ciphers, stream ciphers, message-authentication codes, authenticated ciphers, hash functions, etc.

What distinguishes GIMLI from other permutations is its *cross-platform* performance. GIMLI is designed for energy-efficient hardware *and* for side-channel-protected hardware *and* for microcontrollers *and* for compactness *and* for vectorization *and* for short messages *and* for a high security level.

We present a complete specification of GIMLI (Sect. 2), a detailed design rationale (Sect. 3), an in-depth security analysis (Sect. 4), and performance results for a wide range of platforms (Sect. 5).

Availability of implementations. We place all software and hardware implementations described in this paper into the public domain to maximize reusability of our results. They are available at https://gimli.cr.yp.to.

2 GIMLI Specification

This section defines GIMLI. See Sect. 3 for motivation.

Notation. We denote by $\mathcal{W} = \{0, 1\}^{32}$ the set of bitstrings of length 32. We will refer to the elements of this set as "words". We use

- $a \oplus b$ to denote a bitwise exclusive or (XOR) of the values a and b,
- $a \wedge b$ for a bitwise logical and of the values a and b,
- $a \vee b$ for a bitwise logical or of the values a and b,
- $a \lll k$ for a cyclic left shift of the value a by a shift distance of k, and
- $a \ll k$ for a non-cyclic shift (i.e., a shift that is filling up with zero bits) of the value a by a shift distance of k.

We index all vectors and matrices starting at zero. We encode words as bytes in little-endian form.

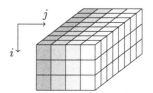

Fig. 1. State representation

The state. GIMLI applies a sequence of rounds to a 384-bit state. The state is represented as a parallelepiped with dimensions $3 \times 4 \times 32$ (see Fig. 1) or, equivalently, as a 3×4 matrix of 32-bit words.

We name the following sets of bits:

- a column j is a sequence of 96 bits such that $\mathbf{s}_j = \{s_{0,j}; s_{1,j}; s_{2,j}\} \in \mathcal{W}^3$
- a row i is a sequence of 128 bits such that $\mathbf{s}_i = \{s_{i,0}; s_{i,1}; s_{i,2}; s_{i,3}\} \in \mathcal{W}^4$

Each round is a sequence of three operations: (1) a non-linear layer, specifically a 96-bit SP-box applied to each column; (2) in every second round, a linear mixing layer; (3) in every fourth round, a constant addition.

The non-linear layer. The SP-box consists of three sub-operations: rotations of the first and second words; a 3-input nonlinear T-function; and a swap of the first and third words. See Fig. 2 for details.

The linear layer. The linear layer consists of two swap operations, namely *Small-Swap* and *Big-Swap*. *Small-Swap* occurs every 4 rounds starting from the 1st round. *Big-Swap* occurs every 4 rounds starting from the 3rd round. See Fig. 3 for details of these swaps.

The round constants. There are 24 rounds in GIMLI, numbered $24, 23, \ldots, 1$. When the round number r is $24, 20, 16, 12, 8, 4$ we XOR the round constant 0x9e377900 $\oplus\, r$ to the first state word $s_{0,0}$.

Putting it together. Algorithm 1 is pseudocode for the full GIMLI permutation. Appendix A is a C reference implementation.

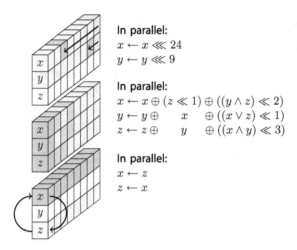

In parallel:
$$x \leftarrow x \lll 24$$
$$y \leftarrow y \lll 9$$

In parallel:
$$x \leftarrow x \oplus (z \ll 1) \oplus ((y \wedge z) \ll 2)$$
$$y \leftarrow y \oplus \quad x \quad \oplus ((x \vee z) \ll 1)$$
$$z \leftarrow z \oplus \quad y \quad \oplus ((x \wedge y) \ll 3)$$

In parallel:
$$x \leftarrow z$$
$$z \leftarrow x$$

Fig. 2. The SP-box applied to a column

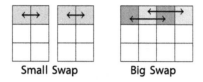

Small Swap   Big Swap

Fig. 3. The linear layer

3   Understanding the GIMLI Design

This section explains how we arrived at the GIMLI design presented in Sect. 2.

We started from the well-known goal of designing one unified cryptographic primitive suitable for many different applications: collision-resistant hashing, preimage-resistant hashing, message authentication, message encryption, etc. We found no reason to question the "new conventional wisdom" that a permutation is a better unified primitive than a block cipher. Like Keccak, Ascon [15], etc., we evaluate performance only in the forward direction, and we consider only forward modes; modes that also use the inverse permutation require extra hardware area and do not seem to offer any noticeable advantages.

Where GIMLI departs from previous designs is in its objective of being a single primitive that performs well on every common platform. We do not insist on beating all previous primitives on all platforms simultaneously, but we do insist on coming reasonably close. Each platform has its own hazards that create poor performance for many primitives; what GIMLI shows is that all of these hazards can be avoided simultaneously.

Vectorization. On common Intel server CPUs, vector instructions are by far the most efficient arithmetic/logic instructions. As a concrete example, the 12-round ChaCha12 stream cipher has run at practically the same speed as 12-round

Algorithm 1. The GIMLI permutation

Require: $\mathbf{s} = (s_{i,j}) \in \mathcal{W}^{3 \times 4}$
Ensure: GIMLI($\mathbf{s}$) $= (s_{i,j}) \in \mathcal{W}^{3 \times 4}$
  for r from 24 downto 1 inclusive **do**
    for j from 0 to 3 inclusive **do**
      $x \leftarrow s_{0,j} \lll 24$ $\triangleright$ SP-box
      $y \leftarrow s_{1,j} \lll 9$
      $z \leftarrow s_{2,j}$
      $s_{2,j} \leftarrow x \oplus (z \ll 1) \oplus ((y \wedge z) \ll 2)$
      $s_{1,j} \leftarrow y \oplus \quad x \quad \oplus ((x \vee z) \ll 1)$
      $s_{0,j} \leftarrow z \oplus \quad y \quad \oplus ((x \wedge y) \ll 3)$
    end for
                                                $\triangleright$ linear layer
    if $r \mod 4 = 0$ **then**
      $s_{0,0}, s_{0,1}, s_{0,2}, s_{0,3} \leftarrow s_{0,1}, s_{0,0}, s_{0,3}, s_{0,2}$ $\triangleright$ *Small-Swap*
    else if $r \mod 4 = 2$ **then**
      $s_{0,0}, s_{0,1}, s_{0,2}, s_{0,3} \leftarrow s_{0,2}, s_{0,3}, s_{0,0}, s_{0,1}$ $\triangleright$ *Big-Swap*
    end if

    if $r \mod 4 = 0$ **then**
      $s_{0,0} = s_{0,0} \oplus \text{0x9e377900} \oplus r$ $\triangleright$ Add constant
    end if
  end for
  return $(s_{i,j})$

AES-192 on several generations of Intel CPUs (e.g., 1.7 cycles/byte on Westmere; 1.5 cycles/byte on Ivy Bridge; 0.8 cycles/byte on Skylake), despite AES hardware support, because ChaCha12 takes advantage of the vector hardware on the same CPUs. Vectorization is attractive for CPU designers because the overhead of fetching and decoding an instruction is amortized across several data items.

Any permutation built from (e.g.) common 32-bit operations can take advantage of a $32b$-bit vector unit if the permutation is applied to b blocks in parallel. Many modes of use of a permutation support this type of vectorization. But this type of vectorization creates two performance problems. First, if b parallel blocks do not fit into vector registers, then there is significant overhead for loads and stores; vectorized Keccak implementations suffer exactly this problem. Second, a large b is wasted in applications where messages are short.

GIMLI, like Salsa and ChaCha, views its state as consisting of 128-bit rows that naturally fit into 128-bit vector registers. Each row consists of a vector of $128/w$ entries, each entry being a w-bit word, where w is optimized below. Most of the GIMLI operations are applied to every column in parallel, so the operations naturally vectorize. Taking advantage of 256-bit or 512-bit vector registers requires handling only 2 or 4 blocks in parallel.

Logic operations and shifts. GIMLI's design uses only bitwise operations on w-bit words: specifically, and, or, xor, constant-distance left shifts, and constant-distance rotations.

There are tremendous hardware-latency advantages to being able to carry out w bit operations in parallel. Even when latency is not a concern, bitwise operations are much more energy-efficient than integer addition, which (when carried out serially) uses almost $5w$ bit operations for w-bit words. Avoiding additions also allows "interleaved" implementations as in Keccak, Ascon, etc., saving time on software platforms with word sizes below w.

On platforms with w-bit words there is a software cost in avoiding additions. One way to quantify this cost is as follows. A typical ARX design is roughly balanced between addition, rotation, and xor. NORX [2] replaces each addition $a + b$ with a similar bitwise operation $a \oplus b \oplus ((a \wedge b) \ll 1)$, so 3 instructions (add, rotate, xor) are replaced with 6 instructions; on platforms with free shifts and rotations (such as the ARM Cortex-M4), 2 instructions are replaced with 4 instructions; on platforms where rotations need to be simulated by shifts (as in typical vector units), 5 instructions are replaced with 8 instructions. On top of this near-doubling in cost, the diffusion in the NORX operation is slightly slower than the diffusion in addition, increasing the number of rounds required for security.

The pattern of GIMLI operations improves upon NORX in three ways. First, GIMLI uses a third input c for $a \oplus b \oplus ((c \wedge b) \ll 1)$, removing the need for a separate xor operation. Second, GIMLI uses only two rotations for three of these operations; overall GIMLI uses 19 instructions on typical vector units, not far behind the 15 instructions used by three ARX operations. Third, GIMLI varies the 1-bit shift distance, improving diffusion compared to NORX and possibly even compared to ARX.

We searched through many combinations of possible shift distances (and rotation distances) in GIMLI, applying a simple security model to each combination. Large shift distances throw away many nonlinear bits and, unsurprisingly, turned out to be suboptimal. The final GIMLI shift distances $(2, 1, 3$ on three 32-bit words) keep 93.75% of the nonlinear bits.

32-bit words. Taking $w = 32$ is an obvious choice for 32-bit CPUs. It also works well on common 64-bit CPUs, since those CPUs have fast instructions for, e.g., vectorized 32-bit shifts. The 32-bit words can also be split into 16-bit words (with top and bottom bits, or more efficiently with odd and even bits as in "interleaved" Keccak software), and further into 8-bit words.

Taking $w = 16$ or $w = 8$ would lose speed on 32-bit CPUs that do not have vectorized 16-bit or 8-bit shifts. Taking $w = 64$ would interfere with GIMLI's ability to work within a quarter-state for some time (see below), and we do not see a compensating advantage.

State size. On common 32-bit ARM microcontrollers, there are 14 easily usable integer registers, for a total of 448 bits. The 512-bit states in Salsa20, ChaCha, NORX, etc. produce significant load-store overhead, which GIMLI avoids by (1) limiting its state to 384 bits (three 128-bit vectors), i.e., 12 registers, and (2) fitting temporary variables into just 2 registers.

Limiting the state to 256 bits would provide some benefit in hardware area, but would produce considerable slowdowns across platforms to maintain an acceptable level of security. For example, 256-bit sponge-based hashing at a 2^{100} security level would be able to absorb only 56 message bits (22% of the state) per permutation call, while 384-bit sponge-based hashing at the same security level is able to absorb 184 message bits (48% of the state) per permutation call, presumably gaining more than a factor of 2 in speed, even without accounting for the diffusion benefits of a larger state. It is also not clear whether a 256-bit state size leaves an adequate long-term security margin against multi-user attacks (see [16]) and quantum attacks; more complicated modes can achieve high security levels using small states, but this damages efficiency.

One of the SHA-3 requirements was 2^{512} preimage security. For sponge-based hashing this requires at least a 1024-bit permutation, or an even larger permutation for efficiency, such as Keccak's 1600-bit permutation. This requirement was based entirely on matching SHA-512, not on any credible assertion that 2^{512} preimage security will ever have any real-world value. GIMLI is designed for useful security levels, so it is much more comparable to, e.g., 512-bit Salsa20, 400-bit Keccak-f[400] (which reduces Keccak's 64-bit lanes to 16-bit lanes), 384-bit C-Quark [4], 384-bit SPONGENT-256/256/128 [12], 320-bit Ascon, and 288-bit Photon-256/32/32 [17].

Working locally. On the popular low-end ARM Cortex-M0 microcontroller, many instructions can access only 8 of the 14 32-bit registers. Working with more than 256 bits at a time incurs overhead to move data around. Similar comments apply to the 8-bit AVR microcontroller.

GIMLI performs many operations on the left half of its state, and separately performs many operations on the right half of its state. Each half fits into 6 32-bit registers, plus 2 temporary registers.

It is of course necessary for these 192-bit halves to communicate, but this communication does not need to be frequent. The only communication is *Big-Swap*, which happens only once every 4 rounds, so we can work on the same half-state for several rounds.

At a smaller scale, GIMLI performs a considerable number of operations within each column (i.e., each 96-bit quarter-state) before the columns communicate. Communication among columns happens only once every 2 rounds. This locality is intended to reduce wire lengths in unrolled hardware, allowing faster clocks.

Parallelization. Like Keccak and Ascon, GIMLI has degree just 2 in each round. This means that, during an update of the entire state, all nonlinear operations are carried out in parallel: a nonlinear operation never feeds into another nonlinear operation.

This feature is often advertised as simplifying and accelerating masked implementations. The parallelism also has important performance benefits even if side channels are not a concern.

Consider, for example, software using 128-bit vector instructions to apply Salsa20 to a single 512-bit block. Salsa20 chains its 128-bit vector operations: an addition feeds into a rotation, which feeds into an xor, which feeds into the next addition, etc. The only parallelism possible here is between the two shifts inside a shift-shift-or implementation of the rotation. A typical vector unit allows more instructions to be carried out in parallel, but Salsa20 is unable to take advantage of this. Similar comments apply to BLAKE [3] and ChaCha20.

The basic NORX operation $a \oplus b \oplus ((a \wedge b) \ll 1)$ is only slightly better, depth 3 for 4 instructions. GIMLI has much more internal parallelism: on average approximately 4 instructions are ready at each moment.

Parallel operations provide slightly slower forward diffusion than serial operations, but experience shows that this costs only a small number of rounds. GIMLI has very fast backward diffusion.

Compactness. GIMLI is intentionally very simple, repeating a small number of operations again and again. This gives implementors the flexibility to create very small "rolled" designs, using very little area in hardware and very little code in software; or to unroll for higher throughput.

This simplicity creates three directions of symmetries that need to be broken. GIMLI is like Keccak in that it breaks all symmetries within the permutation, rather than (as in Salsa, ChaCha, etc.) relying on attention from the mode designer to break symmetries. GIMLI puts more effort than Keccak into reducing the total cost of asymmetric operations.

The first symmetry is that rotating each input word by any constant number of bits produces a near-rotation of each output word by the same number of bits; "near" accounts for a few bits lost from shifts. *Occasionally* (after rounds 24, 20, 16, etc.) GIMLI adds an asymmetric constant to entry 0 of the first row. This constant has many bits set (it is essentially the golden ratio 0x9e3779b9, as used in TEA), and is not close to any of its nontrivial rotations (never fewer than 12 bits different), so a trail applying this symmetry would have to cancel many bits.

The second symmetry is that each round is identical, potentially allowing slide attacks. This is much more of an issue for small blocks (as in, e.g., 128-bit block ciphers) than for large blocks (such as GIMLI's 384-bit block), but GIMLI nevertheless incorporates the round number r into the constant mentioned above. Specifically, the constant is 0x93e77900 $\oplus$ r. The implementor can also use 0x93e77900 $+ r$ since r fits into a byte, or can have r count from 0x93e77918 down to 0x93e77900.

The third symmetry is that permuting the four input columns means permuting the four output columns; this is a direct effect of vectorization. Occasionally (after rounds 24, 20, 16, etc.) GIMLI swaps entries 0, 1 in the first row, and swaps entries 2, 3 in the first row, reducing the symmetry group to 8 permutations (exchanging or preserving 0, 1, exchanging or preserving 2, 3, and exchanging or preserving the halves). Occasionally (after rounds 22, 18, 14, etc.) GIMLI swaps the two halves of the first row, reducing the symmetry group to 4 permutations (0123, 1032, 2301, 3210). The same constant distinguishes these 4 permutations.

We also explored linear layers slightly more expensive than these swaps. We carried out fairly detailed security evaluations of GIMLI-MDS (replacing a, b, c, d with $s \oplus a, s \oplus b, s \oplus c, s \oplus d$ where $s = a \oplus b \oplus c \oplus d$), GIMLI-SPARX (as in [14]), and GIMLI-Shuffle (with the swaps as above). We found some advantages in GIMLI-MDS and GIMLI-SPARX in proving security against various types of attacks, but it is not clear that these advantages outweigh the costs, so we opted for GIMLI-Shuffle as the final GIMLI.

Inside the SP-box: choice of words and rotation distances. The bottom bit of the T-function adds y to z and then adds x to y. We could instead add x to y and then add the new y to z, but this would be contrary to our goal of parallelism; see above.

After the T-function we exchange the roles of x and z, so that the next SP-box provides diffusion in the opposite direction. The shifted parts of the T-function already provide diffusion in both directions, but this diffusion is not quite as fast, since the shifts throw away some bits.

We originally described rotations as taking place after the T-function, but this is equivalent to rotation taking place before the T-function (except for a rotation of the input and output of the entire permutation). Starting with rotation saves some instructions outside the main loop on platforms with rotated-input instructions; also, some applications reuse portions of inputs across multiple permutation calls, and can cache rotations of those portions. These are minor advantages but there do not seem to be any disadvantages.

Rotating all three of x, y, z adds noticeable software cost and is almost equivalent to rotating only two: it merely affects which bits are discarded by shifts. So, as mentioned above, we rotate only two. In a preliminary GIMLI design we rotated y and z, but we found that rotating x and y improves security by 1 round against our best integral attacks; see below.

This leaves two choices: the rotation distance for x and the rotation distance for y. We found very little security difference between, e.g., $(24, 9)$ and $(26, 9)$, while there is a noticeable speed difference on various software platforms. We decided against "aligned" options such as $(24, 8)$ and $(16, 8)$, although it seems possible that any security difference would be outweighed by further speedups.

4 Security Analysis

4.1 Diffusion

As a first step in understanding the security of reduced-round GIMLI, we consider the following two minimum security requirements:

- the number of rounds required to show the avalanche effect for each bit of the state.
- the number of rounds required to reach a *state full of* 1 starting from a state where only one bit is set. In this experiment we replace bitwise exclusive *or* (XOR) and bitwise logical *and* by a bitwise logical *or*.

Given the input size of the SP-box, we verify the first criterion with the Monte-Carlo method. We generate random states and flip each bit once. We can then count the number of bits flipped after a defined number of rounds.

Experiments show that 10 rounds are required for each bit to change on the average half of the state (see Table 5 in Appendix F).

As for the second criterion, we replace the T-function in the SP-box by the following operations:

$$x' \leftarrow x \vee (z \lll 1) \vee ((y \vee z) \lll 2)$$
$$y' \leftarrow y \vee x \vee ((x \vee z) \lll 1)$$
$$z' \leftarrow z \vee y \vee ((x \vee y) \lll 3)$$

By testing the 384 bit positions, we prove that a maximum of 8 rounds are required to fill up the state.

4.2   Differential Cryptanalysis

To study GIMLI's resistance against differential cryptanalysis we use the same method as has been used for NORX [1] and SIMON [20] by using a tool-assisted approach to find the optimal differential trails for a reduced number of rounds. In order to enable this approach we first need to define the valid transitions of differences through the GIMLI round function.

The non-linear part of the round function shares similarities with the NORX round function, but we need to take into account the dependencies between the three lanes to get a correct description of the differential behavior of GIMLI. In order to simplify the description we will look at the following function which only covers the non-linear part of GIMLI:

$$f(x,y,z): \quad \begin{aligned} x' &\leftarrow y \wedge z \\ y' &\leftarrow x \vee z \\ z' &\leftarrow x \wedge y \end{aligned} \tag{1}$$

where $x, y, z \in \mathcal{W}$. For the GIMLI SP-box we only have to apply some additional linear functions which behave deterministically with respect to the propagation of differences. In the following we denote $(\Delta_x, \Delta_y, \Delta_z)$ as the input difference and $(\Delta_{x'}, \Delta_{y'}, \Delta_{z'})$ as the output difference. The *differential probability* of a differential trail T is denoted as $\mathrm{DP}(T)$ and we define the weight of a trail as $w = -\log_2(\mathrm{DP}(T))$.

Lemma 1 (Differential Probability). *For each possible differential through f it holds that*

$$\begin{aligned}
\Delta_{x'} \wedge (\Delta_y \vee \Delta_z) &= 0 \\
\Delta_{y'} \wedge (\Delta_x \vee \Delta_z) &= 0 \\
\Delta_{z'} \wedge (\Delta_x \vee \Delta_y) &= 0 \\
(\Delta_x \wedge \Delta_y \wedge \neg\Delta_z) \wedge \neg(\Delta_{x'} \oplus \Delta_{y'}) &= 0 \\
(\Delta_x \wedge \neg\Delta_y \wedge \Delta_z) \wedge (\Delta_{x'} \oplus \Delta_{z'}) &= 0 \\
(\neg\Delta_x \wedge \Delta_y \wedge \Delta_z) \wedge \neg(\Delta_{x'} \oplus \Delta_{y'}) &= 0 \\
(\Delta_x \wedge \Delta_y \wedge \Delta_z) \wedge \neg(\Delta_{x'} \oplus \Delta_{y'} \oplus \Delta_{z'}) &= 0.
\end{aligned} \tag{2}$$

The differential probability *of* $(\Delta_x, \Delta_y, \Delta_z) \xrightarrow{f} (\Delta_{x'}, \Delta_{y'}, \Delta_{z'})$ *is given by*

$$DP((\Delta_x, \Delta_y, \Delta_z) \xrightarrow{f} (\Delta_{x'}, \Delta_{y'}, \Delta_{z'})) = 2^{-2 \cdot hw(\Delta_x \vee \Delta_y \vee \Delta_z)}. \tag{3}$$

A proof for this lemma is given in Appendix G. We can then use these conditions together with the linear transformations to describe how differences propagate through the GIMLI round functions. For computing the differential probability over multiple rounds we assume that the rounds are independent. Using this model we then search for the optimal differential trails with the SAT/SMT-based approach [1,20].

We are able to find the optimal differential trails up to 8 rounds of GIMLI (see Table 1). After more rounds this approach failed to find any solution in a reasonable amount of time. The 8-round differential trail is given in Table 6 in Appendix G.

Table 1. The optimal differential trails for a reduced number of rounds of GIMLI.

Rounds	1	2	3	4	5	6	7	8
Weight	0	0	2	6	12	22	36	52

In order to cover more rounds of GIMLI we restrict our search to a *good* starting difference and expand it in both directions. As the probability of a differential trail quickly decreases with the Hamming weight of the state it is likely that any high probability trail will contain some rounds with very low Hamming weight. In Table 2, we show the results when starting from a single bit difference in any of the words. Interestingly, the best trails match the optimal differential trails up to 8 rounds given in Table 1.

Table 2. The optimal differential trails when expanding from a single bit difference in any of the words.

Rounds	1	2	3	4	5	6	7	8	9
$r = 0$	0	2	6	14	28	58	102		
$r = 1$	0	0	2	6	12	26	48	88	
$r = 2$	-	0	2	6	12	22	36	66	110
$r = 3$	-	-	8	10	14	32	36	52	74
$r = 4$	-	-	-	26	28	32	38	52	74

Using the optimal differential for 7 rounds we can construct a 12-round differential trail with probability 2^{-188} (see Table 7 in Appendix G). If we look at the corresponding differential, this means we do not care about any intermediate differences; many trails might contribute to the probability. In the case of our 12-round trail we find 15800 trails with probability 2^{-188} and 20933 trails with probability 2^{-190} contributing to the differential. Therefore, we estimate the probability of the differential to be $\approx 2^{-158.63}$.

4.3 Algebraic Degree and Integral Attacks

Since the algebraic degree of the round function of GIMLI is only 2, it is important how the degree increases by iterating the round function. We use the (bit-based) division property [28, 29] to evaluate the algebraic degree, and the propagation search is assisted by mixed integer linear programming (MILP) [32]. See Appendix H.

We first evaluated the upper bound of the algebraic degree on r-round GIMLI, and the result is summarized as follows.

# rounds	1	2	3	4	5	6	7	8	9
	2	4	8	16	29	52	95	163	266

When we focus on only one bit in the output of r-round GIMLI, the increase of the degree is slower than the general case. Especially, the algebraic degree of z_0 in each 96-bit value is lower than other bits because z_0 in rth round is the same as x_6 in $(r-1)$th round. All bits except for z_0 is mixed by at least two bits in $(r-1)$th round. Therefore, we next evaluate the upper bound of the algebraic degree on four z_0 in r-round GIMLI, and the result is summarized as follows.

# rounds	1	2	3	4	5	6	7	8	9	10	11
	1	2	4	8	15	27	48	88	153	254	367

In integral attacks, a part of the input is chosen as active bits and the other part is chosen as constant bits. Then, we have to evaluate the algebraic degree involving active bits. From the structure of the round function of GIMLI, the algebraic degree will be small when 96 entire bits in each column are active. We evaluated two cases: the algebraic degree involving $s_{i,0}$ is evaluated in the first case, and the algebraic degree involving $s_{i,0}$ and $s_{i,1}$ is evaluated in the second case. Moreover, all z_0 in 4 columns are evaluated, and the following table summarizes the upper bound of the algebraic degree in the weakest column in every round.

The above result implies that GIMLI has 11-round integral distinguisher when 96 bits in $s_{i,0}$ are active and the others are constant. Moreover, when 192 bits in $s_{i,0}$ and $s_{i,1}$ are active and the others are constant, GIMLI has 13-round integral distinguisher.

# rounds		3	4	5	6	7	8	9	10	11	12	13	14
Active	0		0	0	4	8	15	28	58	89	95	96	96	96
Columns	0 and 1	0	0	7	15	30	47	97	153	190	191	191	192

5 Implementations

This section reports the performance of GIMLI for several target platforms. See Tables 3 and 4 for cross-platform overviews of hardware and software performance.

5.1 FPGA and ASIC

We designed and evaluated three main architectures to address different hardware applications. These different architectures are a tradeoff between resources, maximum operational frequency and number of cycles necessary to perform the full permutation. Even with these differences, all 3 architectures share a common simple communication interface which can be expanded to offer different operation modes. All this was done in VHDL and tested in ModelSim for behavioral results, synthesized and tested for FPGAs with Xilinx ISE 14.7. In case of ASICs this was done through Synopsis Ultra and Simple Compiler with 180 nm UMC L180, and Encounter RTL Compiler with ST 28 nm FDSOI technology.

The first architecture, depicted in Fig. 4, performs a certain number of rounds in one clock cycle and stores the output in the same buffer as the input. The number of rounds it can perform in one cycle is chosen before the synthesis process and can be 1, 2, 3, 4, 6, or 8. In case of 12 or 24 combinational rounds, optimized architectures for these cases were done, in order to have better results. The rounds themselves are computed as shown in Fig. 5. In every round there is one SP-box application on the whole state, followed by the linear layer. In the linear layer, the operation can be a small swap with round constant addition, a big swap, or no operation, which are chosen according to the two least significant bits of the round number. The round number starts from 24 and is decremented by one in each combinational round block.

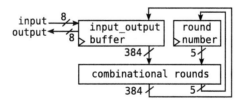

Fig. 4. Round-based architecture

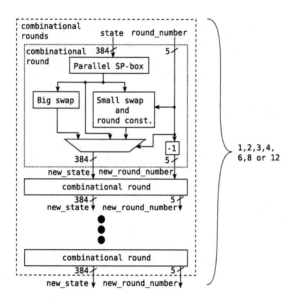

Fig. 5. Combinational round in round-based architecture

Besides the round and the optimized half and full combinational architectures, the other one is a serial-based architecture illustrated in Fig. 6. The serial-based architecture performs one SP-box application per cycle, through a circular-shift-based architecture, therefore taking in total 4 cycles. In case of the linear layer, it is still executed in one cycle in parallel. The reason of not being done in a serial based manner, is because the parallel version cost is very low.

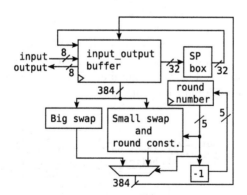

Fig. 6. Serial-based architecture

All hardware results are shown in Table 3. In case of FPGAs the lowest latency is the one with 4 combinational rounds in one cycle, and the one with best Resources×Time/State is the one with 2 combinational rounds. For ASICs the

Table 3. Hardware results for GIMLI and competitors. Gates Equivalent(GE). Slice(S). LUT(L). Flip-Flop(F). * Could not finish the place and route.

Perm.	State size	Version	Cycles	Resources	Period (ns)	Time (ns)	Res.×Time/ State
FPGA – Xilinx Spartan 6 LX75							
Ascon	320		2	732 S(2700 L+325 F)	34.570	70	158.2
GIMLI	384	12	2	1224 S(4398 L+389 F)	27.597	56	175.9
Keccak	400		2	1520 S(5555 L+405 F)	77.281	155	587.3
C-quark*	384		2	2630 S(9718 L+389 F)	98.680	198	1351.7
Photon	288		2	2774 S(9430 L+293 F)	74.587	150	1436.8
Spongent*	384		2	7763 S(19419 L+389 F)	292.160	585	11812.7
GIMLI	384	24	1	2395 S(8769 L+385 F)	56.496	57	352.4
GIMLI	384	8	3	831 S(2924 L+390 F)	24.531	74	159.3
GIMLI	384	6	4	646 S(2398 L+390 F)	18.669	75	125.6
GIMLI	384	4	6	415 S(1486 L+391 F)	8.565	52	55.5
GIMLI	384	3	8	428 S(1587 L+393 F)	10.908	88	97.3
GIMLI	384	2	12	221 S(815 L+392 F)	5.569	67	38.5
GIMLI	384	1	24	178 S(587 L+394 F)	4.941	119	55.0
GIMLI	384	Serial	108	139 S(492 L+397 F)	3.996	432	156.2
28 nm ASIC – ST 28nm FDSOI technology							
GIMLI	384	12	2	35452GE	2.2672	5	418.6
Ascon	320		2	32476GE	2.8457	6	577.6
Keccak	400		2	55683GE	5.6117	12	1562.4
C-quark	384		2	111852GE	9.9962	20	5823.4
Photon	288		2	296420GE	10.0000	20	20584.7
Spongent	384		2	1432047GE	12.0684	25	90013.1
GIMLI	384	24	1	66205GE	4.2870	5	739.1
GIMLI	384	8	3	25224GE	1.5921	5	313.7
GIMLI	384	6	4	21675GE	2.1315	9	481.2
GIMLI	384	4	6	14999GE	1.0549	7	247.2
GIMLI	384	3	8	14808GE	2.0119	17	620.6
GIMLI	384	2	12	10398GE	1.0598	13	344.4
GIMLI	384	1	24	8097GE	1.0642	26	538.5
GIMLI	384	Serial	108	5843GE	1.5352	166	2522.7
180 nm ASIC – UMC L180							
GIMLI	384	12	2	26685	9.9500	20	1382.9
Ascon	320		2	23381	11.4400	23	1671.7
Keccak	400		2	37102	22.4300	45	4161.0
C-quark	384		2	62190	37.2400	75	12062.1
Photon	288		2	163656	99.5900	200	113183.8
Spongent	384		2	234556	99.9900	200	122151.9
GIMLI	384	24	1	53686	17.4500	18	2439.6
GIMLI	384	8	3	19393	7.9100	24	1198.4
GIMLI	384	6	4	15886	12.5100	51	2070.0
GIMLI	384	4	6	11008	10.1700	62	1749.1
GIMLI	384	3	8	10106	10.0500	81	2115.8
GIMLI	384	2	12	7112	15.2000	183	3377.8
GIMLI	384	1	24	5314	9.5200	229	3161.4
GIMLI	384	Serial	108	3846	11.2300	1213	12146.0

results change as the lowest latency is the one with full combinational setting, and the one with best Resources×Time/State is the one with 8 combinational rounds for 180 nm and 4 combinational rounds for 28 nm. This difference illustrates that each technology can give different results, making it difficult to compare results on different technology.

Hardware variants that do 2 or 4 rounds in one cycle appear to be attractive choices, depending on the application scenario. The serial version needs 4.5 times more cycles than the 1-round version, while saving around 28% of the gate equivalents (GE) in the 28 nm ASIC technology, and less in the other ASIC technology and FPGA. If resource constraints are extreme enough to justify the serial version then it would be useful to develop a new version optimized for the target technology, for better results.

To compare the GIMLI permutation to other permutations in the literature, we synthesized all permutations with similar half-combinational architectures, taking exactly 2 cycles to perform a permutation. The permutations that were chosen for comparison were selected close to GIMLI in terms of size, even though in the end the final metric was divided by the permutation size to try to "normalize" the results.

The best results in Resources×Time/State are from 24-round GIMLI and 12-round Ascon-128, with Ascon slightly more efficient in the FPGA results and GIMLI more efficient in the ASIC results. Both permutation in all 3 technologies had very similar results, while Keccak-f[400] is worse in all 3 technologies. The permutations SPONGENT-256/256/128, Photon-256/32/32 and C-Quark have a much higher resource utilization in all technologies. This is because they were designed to work with little resources in exchange for a very high response time (e.g., SPONGENT is reported to use 2641 GE for 18720 cycles, or 5011 GE for 195 cycles), therefore changing the resource utilization from logic gates to time. GIMLI and Ascon are the most efficient in the sense of offering a similar security level to SPONGENT, Photon and C-Quark, with much lower product of time and logic resources.

5.2   SP-box in Assembly

We now turn our attention to software. Subsequent subsections explain how to optimize GIMLI for various illustrative examples of CPUs. As a starting point, we show in Listing 5.2 how to apply the GIMLI SP-box to three 32-bit registers x, y, z using just two temporary registers u, v.

# Rotate	# Compute x	# Compute y	# Compute z
x ← x ⋘ 24	v ← z ≪ 1	v ← y	u ← u ∧ v
y ← y ⋘ 9	x ← y ∧ z	y ← u ∨ z	u ← u ≪ 3
u ← x	x ← x ≪ 2	y ← y ≪ 1	v ← v ⊕ u
	x ← x ⊕ v	y ← y ⊕ u	z ← v ⊕ z
	x ← x ⊕ u	y ← y ⊕ v	

Listing 5.2: SP-box assembly instructions

5.3   8-bit Microcontroller: AVR ATmega

The AVR architecture provides 32 8-bit registers (256 bits). This does not allow the full 384-bit GIMLI state to stay in the registers: we are forced to use loads and stores in the main loop.

To minimize the overhead for loads and stores, we work on a half-state (two columns) for as long as possible. For example, we focus on the left half-state for rounds 21, 20, 19, 18, 17, 16, 15, 14. Before doing this, we focus on the right half-state through the end of round 18, so that the *Big-Swap* at the end of round 18 can feed 2 words (64 bits) from the right half-state into the left half-state. See Appendix C for the exact order of computation.

A half-state requires a total of 24 registers (6 words), leaving us with 8 registers (2 words) to use as temporaries. We can therefore use the same order of operations as defined in Listing 5.2 for each SP-box. In a stretch of 8 rounds on a half-state (16 SP-boxes) there are just a few loads and stores.

We provide two implementations of this construction. One is fully unrolled and optimized for speed: it runs in just 10 264 cycles, using 19 218 bytes of ROM. The other is optimized for size: it uses just 778 bytes of ROM and runs in 23 670 cycles. Each implementation requires about the same amount of stack, namely 45 bytes.

5.4   32-bit Low-End Embedded Microcontroller: ARM Cortex-M0

ARM Cortex-M0 comes with 14 32-bit registers. However orr, eor, and-like instructions can only be used on the lower registers (r0 to r7). This forces us to use the same computation layout as in the AVR implementation. We split the state into two halves: one in the lower registers, one in the higher ones. Then we can operate on each during multiple rounds before exchanging them.

5.5   32-bit High-End Embedded Microcontroller: ARM Cortex-M3

We focus here on the ARM Cortex-M3 microprocessor, which implements the ARMv7-M architecture. There is a higher-end microcontroller, the Cortex-M4, implementing the ARMv7E-M architecture; but our GIMLI software does not make use of any of the DSP, (optional) floating-point, or additional saturated instructions added in this architecture.

The Cortex-M3 features 16 32-bit registers r0 to r15, with one register used as program counter and one as stack pointer, leaving 14 registers for free use. As the GIMLI state fits into 12 registers and we need only 2 registers for temporary values, we compute the GIMLI permutation without requiring any load or store instructions beyond the initial loads of the input and the final stores of the output.

One particularly interesting feature of various ARM instruction sets including the ARMv7-M instruction set are free shifts and rotates as part of arithmetic instructions. More specifically, all bit-logical operations allow one of the inputs to be shifted or rotated by an arbitrary fixed distance for free. This was used, e.g., in [26, Sec. 3.1] to eliminate all rotation instructions in an unrolled implementation of BLAKE. For GIMLI this feature gives us the non-cyclic shifts by 1, 2, 3 and the rotation by 9 for free. We have not found a way to eliminate the rotation by 24. Each SP-box evaluation thus uses 10 instructions: namely, 9 bit-logical operations (6 xors, 2 ands, and 1 or) and one rotation.

From these considerations we can derive a lower bound on the amount of cycles required for the GIMLI permutation: Each round performs 4 SP-box evaluations (one on each of the columns of the state), each using 10 instructions, for a total of 40 instructions. In 24 rounds we thus end up with $24 \cdot 40 = 960$ instructions from the SP-boxes, plus 6 xors for the addition of round constants. This gives us a lower bound of 966 cycles for the GIMLI permutation, assuming an unrolled implementation in which all *Big-Swap* and *Small-Swap* operations are handled through (free) renaming of registers. Our implementation for the M3 uses such a fully unrolled approach and takes 1 047 cycles.

5.6   32-bit Smartphone CPU: ARM Cortex-A8 with NEON

We focus on a Cortex-A8 for comparability with the highly optimized Salsa20 results of [9]. As a future optimization target we suggest a newer Cortex-A7 CPU core, which according to ARM has appeared in more than a billion chips. Since our GIMLI software uses almost purely vector instructions (unlike [9], which mixes integer instructions with vector instructions), we expect it to perform similarly on the Cortex-A7 and the Cortex-A8.

The GIMLI state fits naturally into three 128-bit NEON vector registers, one row per vector. The T-function inside the GIMLI SP-box is an obvious match for the NEON vector instructions: two ANDs, one OR, four shifts, and six XORs. The rotation by 9 uses three vector instructions. The rotation by 24 uses two 64-bit vector instructions, namely permutations of byte positions (vtbl) using a precomputed 8-byte permutation. The four SP-boxes in a round use 18 vector instructions overall.

A straightforward 4-round-unrolled assembly implementation uses just 77 instructions for the main loop: 72 for the SP-boxes, 1 (vrev64.i32) for *Small-Swap*, 1 to load the round constant from a precomputed 96-byte table, 1 to xor the round constant, and 2 for loop control (which would be reduced by further unrolling). We handle *Big-Swap* implicitly through the choice of registers in two vtbl instructions, rather than using an extra vswp instruction. Outside the main loop we use just 9 instructions, plus 3 instructions to collect timing information and 20 bytes of alignment, for 480 bytes of code overall.

The lower bound for arithmetic is $65 \cdot 6 = 390$ cycles: 16 arithmetic cycles for each of the 24 rounds, and 6 extra for the round constants. The Cortex-A8 can overlap permutations with arithmetic. With moderate instruction-scheduling effort we achieved 419 cycles, just 8.73 cycles/byte. For comparison, [9] says that a "straightforward NEON implementation" of the inner loop of Salsa20 "cannot do better than 11.25 cycles/byte" (720 cycles for 64 bytes), plus approximately 1 cycle/byte overhead. [9] does better than this only by handling multiple blocks in parallel: 880 cycles for 192 bytes, plus the same overhead.

Table 4. Cross-platform software performance comparison of various permutations. "Hashing 500 bytes": AVR cycles for comparability with [5]. "Permutation": Cycles/byte for permutation on all platforms. AEAD timings from [8] are scaled to estimate permutaton timings.

Hashing 500 bytes	Cycles	ROM Bytes	RAM Bytes
AVR ATmega			
Spongent [5]	25 464 000	364	101
Keccak-f[400] [5]	1 313 000	608	96
GIMLI-Hash[b] (**this paper**) small	805 110	778	44
GIMLI-Hash[b] (**this paper**) fast	362 712	19 218	45

Permutation	Cycles/B	ROM Bytes	RAM Bytes
AVR ATmega			
GIMLI (**this paper**) small	413	778	44
ChaCha20 [31]	238	$-^a$	132
Salsa20 [19]	216	1 750	266
GIMLI (**this paper**) fast	213	19 218	45
AES-128 [22] small	171	1 570	$-^a$
AES-128 [22] fast	155	3 098	$-^a$
ARM Cortex-M0			
GIMLI (**this paper**)	49	4 730	64
ChaCha20 [23]	40	$-^a$	$-^a$
Chaskey [21]	17	414	$-^a$
ARM Cortex-M3/M4			
Spongent [12,24] (c-ref, our measurement)	129 486	1 180	$-^a$
Ascon [15] (opt32, our measurement)	196	$-^a$	$-^a$
Keccak-f[400] [30]	106	540	$-^a$
AES-128 [25]	34	3 216	72
GIMLI (**this paper**)	21	3 972	44
ChaCha20 [18]	13	2 868	8
Chaskey [21]	7	908	$-^a$
ARM Cortex-A8			
Keccak-f[400] (KetjeSR) [8]	37.52	$-^a$	$-^a$
Ascon [8]	25.54	$-^a$	$-^a$
AES-128 [8] many blocks	19.25	$-^a$	$-^a$
GIMLI (**this paper**) single block	8.73	480	$-^a$
ChaCha20 [8] multiple blocks	6.25	$-^a$	$-^a$
Salsa20 [8] multiple blocks	5.48	$-^a$	$-^a$
Intel Haswell			
GIMLI (**this paper**) single block	4.46	252	$-^a$
NORX-32-4-1 [8] single block	2.84	$-^a$	$-^a$
GIMLI (**this paper**) two blocks	2.33	724	$-^a$
GIMLI (**this paper**) four blocks	1.77	1227	$-^a$
Salsa20 [8] eight blocks	1.38	$-^a$	$-^a$
ChaCha20 [8] eight blocks	1.20	$-^a$	$-^a$
AES-128 [8] many blocks	0.85	$-^a$	$-^a$

^{a} no data
^{b} Sponge construction[10] with $c = 256$ bits, $r = 128$ bits and 256 bits of output.

5.7   64-bit Server CPU: Intel Haswell

Intel's server/desktop/laptop CPUs have had 128-bit vectorized integer instructions ("SSE2") starting with the Pentium 4 in 2001, and 256-bit vectorized integer instructions ("AVX2") starting with the Haswell in 2013. In each case the vector registers appeared in CPUs a few years earlier supporting vectorized floating-point instructions ("SSE" and "AVX"), including full-width bitwise logic operations, but not including shifts. The vectorized integer instructions include shifts but not rotations. Intel has experimented with 512-bit vector instructions in coprocessors such as Knights Corner and Knights Landing, and has announced a 512-bit instruction set that includes vectorized rotations and three-input logical operations, but we focus here on CPUs that are commonly available from Intel and AMD today.

Our implementation strategy for these CPUs is similar to our implementation strategy for NEON: again the state fits naturally into three 128-bit vector registers, with GIMLI instructions easily translating into the CPU's vector instructions. The cycle counts on Haswell are better than the cycle counts for the Cortex-A8 since each Haswell core has multiple vector units. We save another factor of almost 2 for 2-way-parallel modes, since 2 parallel copies of the state fit naturally into three 256-bit vector registers. As with the Cortex-A8, we outperform Salsa20 and ChaCha20 for short messages.

References

1. Aumasson, J.-P., Jovanovic, P., Neves, S.: Analysis of NORX: investigating differential and rotational properties. In: Aranha, D.F., Menezes, A. (eds.) LATIN-CRYPT 2014. LNCS, vol. 8895, pp. 306–324. Springer, Cham (2015). doi:10.1007/978-3-319-16295-9_17. 308, 309
2. Aumasson, J.-P., Jovanovic, P., Neves, S.: NORX: parallel and scalable AEAD. In: Kutyłowski, M., Vaidya, J. (eds.) ESORICS 2014. LNCS, vol. 8713, pp. 19–36. Springer, Cham (2014). doi:10.1007/978-3-319-11212-1_2. 304
3. Aumasson, J., Meier, W., Phan, R.C., Henzen, L.: The Hash Function BLAKE. Information Security and Cryptography. Springer, Heidelberg (2014). 306
4. Aumasson, J.-P., Knellwolf, S., Meier, W.: Heavy Quark for secure AEAD. In: DIAC 2012: Directions in Authenticated Ciphers (2012). 305
5. Balasch, J., Ege, B., Eisenbarth, T., Gérard, B., Gong, Z., Güneysu, T., Heyse, S., Kerckhof, S., Koeune, F., Plos, T., Pöppelmann, T., Regazzoni, F., Standaert, F.-X., Assche, G.V., Keer, R.V., van Oldeneel tot Oldenzeel, L., von Maurich, I.: Compact implementation and performance evaluation of hash functions in ATtiny devices. Cryptology ePrint Archive: Report 2012/507 (2012). https://eprint.iacr.org/2012/507/. 317
6. Bernstein, D.J.: ChaCha, a variant of Salsa20. In: SASC 2008: The State of the Art of Stream Ciphers (2008). https://cr.yp.to/chacha/chacha-20080128.pdf. 300
7. Bernstein, D.J.: The Salsa20 family of stream ciphers. In: Robshaw, M., Billet, O. (eds.) New Stream Cipher Designs. LNCS, vol. 4986, pp. 84–97. Springer, Heidelberg (2008). doi:10.1007/978-3-540-68351-3_8. 300
8. Bernstein, D.J., Lange, T.: eBACS: ECRYPT benchmarking of cryptographic systems. https://bench.cr.yp.to. Accessed 25 June 2017. 317

9. Bernstein, D.J., Schwabe, P.: NEON crypto. In: Prouff, E., Schaumont, P. (eds.) CHES 2012. LNCS, vol. 7428, pp. 320–339. Springer, Heidelberg (2012). doi:10. 1007/978-3-642-33027-8_19. 300, 316

10. Bertoni, G., Daemen, J., Peeters, M., Assche, G.V.: Cryptographic sponge functions (2011). http://sponge.noekeon.org/CSF-0.1.pdf. 317

11. Bertoni, G., Daemen, J., Peeters, M., Assche, G.: Keccak. In: Johansson, T., Nguyen, P.Q. (eds.) EUROCRYPT 2013. LNCS, vol. 7881, pp. 313–314. Springer, Heidelberg (2013). doi:10.1007/978-3-642-38348-9_19. 300

12. Bogdanov, A., Knezevic, M., Leander, G., Toz, D., Varici, K., Verbauwhede, I.: SPONGENT: the design space of lightweight cryptographic hashing (2011). https://eprint.iacr.org/2011/697. 305, 317

13. Bursztein, E.: Speeding up and strengthening HTTPS connections for Chrome on Android (2014). https://security.googleblog.com/2014/04/ speeding-up-and-strengthening-https.html. 300

14. Dinu, D., Perrin, L., Udovenko, A., Velichkov, V., Großschädl, J., Biryukov, A.: Design strategies for ARX with provable bounds: Sparx and LAX. In: Cheon, J.H., Takagi, T. (eds.) ASIACRYPT 2016. LNCS, vol. 10031, pp. 484–513. Springer, Heidelberg (2016). doi:10.1007/978-3-662-53887-6_18. 306

15. Dobraunig, C., Eichlseder, M., Mendel, F., Schläffer, M.: Ascon v1.2. Submission to the CAESAR competition (2016). https://competitions.cr.yp.to/round3/ asconv12.pdf. 302, 317

16. Fouque, P.-A., Joux, A., Mavromati, C.: Multi-user collisions: applications to discrete logarithm, Even-Mansour and PRINCE. In: Sarkar, P., Iwata, T. (eds.) ASIACRYPT 2014. LNCS, vol. 8873, pp. 420–438. Springer, Heidelberg (2014). doi:10. 1007/978-3-662-45611-8_22. 305

17. Guo, J., Peyrin, T., Poschmann, A.: The PHOTON family of lightweight hash functions. In: Rogaway, P. (ed.) CRYPTO 2011. LNCS, vol. 6841, pp. 222–239. Springer, Heidelberg (2011). doi:10.1007/978-3-642-22792-9_13. 305

18. Hülsing, A., Rijneveld, J., Schwabe, P.: ARMed SPHINCS. In: Cheng, C.-M., Chung, K.-M., Persiano, G., Yang, B.-Y. (eds.) PKC 2016. LNCS, vol. 9614, pp. 446–470. Springer, Heidelberg (2016). doi:10.1007/978-3-662-49384-7_17. 317

19. Hutter, M., Schwabe, P.: NaCl on 8-Bit AVR microcontrollers. In: Youssef, A., Nitaj, A., Hassanien, A.E. (eds.) AFRICACRYPT 2013. LNCS, vol. 7918, pp. 156–172. Springer, Heidelberg (2013). doi:10.1007/978-3-642-38553-7_9. 317

20. Kölbl, S., Leander, G., Tiessen, T.: Observations on the SIMON block cipher family. In: Gennaro, R., Robshaw, M. (eds.) CRYPTO 2015. LNCS, vol. 9215, pp. 161–185. Springer, Heidelberg (2015). doi:10.1007/978-3-662-47989-6_8. 308, 309

21. Mouha, N., Mennink, B., Herrewege, A.V., Watanabe, D., Preneel, B., Verbauwhede, I.: Chaskey: an efficient MAC algorithm for 32-bit microcontrollers. In: Joux, A., Youssef, A. (eds.) SAC 2014. LNCS, vol. 8781, pp. 306–323. Springer, Cham (2014). doi:10.1007/978-3-319-13051-4_19. 300, 317

22. Poettering, B.: AVRAES: the AES block cipher on AVR controllers (2003). http:// point-at-infinity.org/avraes/. 317

23. Samwel, N., Neikes, M.: arm-chacha20 (2016). https://gitlab.science.ru.nl/ mneikes/arm-chacha20/tree/master. 317

24. Schneider, E., de Groot, W.: spongent-avr (2015). https://github.com/weedegee/ spongent-avr. 317

25. Schwabe, P., Stoffelen, K.: All the AES you need on Cortex-M3 and M4. In: Selected Areas in Cryptology - SAC 2016. LNCS. Springer. To appear. 317

26. Schwabe, P., Yang, B.-Y., Yang, S.-Y.: SHA-3 on ARM11 processors. In: Mitrokotsa, A., Vaudenay, S. (eds.) AFRICACRYPT 2012. LNCS, vol. 7374, pp. 324–341. Springer, Heidelberg (2012). doi:10.1007/978-3-642-31410-0_20. 316

27. Sullivan, N.: Do the ChaCha: better mobile performance with cryptography (2015). https://blog.cloudflare.com/do-the-chacha-better-mobile-performance-with-cryptography/. 300

28. Todo, Y.: Structural evaluation by generalized integral property. In: Oswald, E., Fischlin, M. (eds.) EUROCRYPT 2015. LNCS, vol. 9056, pp. 287–314. Springer, Heidelberg (2015). doi:10.1007/978-3-662-46800-5_12. 310

29. Todo, Y., Morii, M.: Bit-based division property and application to SIMON family. In: Peyrin, T. (ed.) FSE 2016. LNCS, vol. 9783, pp. 357–377. Springer, Heidelberg (2016). doi:10.1007/978-3-662-52993-5_18. 310

30. Van Assche, G., Van Keer, R.: Structuring and optimizing Keccak software (2016). 317

31. Weatherley, R.: Arduinolibs (2016). https://rweather.github.io/arduinolibs/crypto.html. 317

32. Xiang, Z., Zhang, W., Bao, Z., Lin, D.: Applying MILP method to searching integral distinguishers based on division property for 6 lightweight block ciphers. In: Cheon, J.H., Takagi, T. (eds.) ASIACRYPT 2016. LNCS, vol. 10031, pp. 648–678. Springer, Heidelberg (2016). doi:10.1007/978-3-662-53887-6_24. 310

A   Appendices

The full version of the paper is online at https://gimli.cr.yp.to. See the full version for appendices.

GIFT: A Small Present
Towards Reaching the Limit of Lightweight Encryption

Subhadeep Banik[1,5]($\boxtimes$), Sumit Kumar Pandey[2], Thomas Peyrin[1,2,3],
Yu Sasaki[3], Siang Meng Sim[2], and Yosuke Todo[4]

[1] Temasek Laboratories, Nanyang Technological University, Singapore, Singapore
{bsubhadeep,thomas.peyrin}@ntu.edu.sg
[2] School of Physical and Mathematical Sciences, Nanyang Technological University,
Singapore, Singapore
emailpandey@gmail.com, SSIM011@e.ntu.edu.sg
[3] School of Computer Science and Engineering, Nanyang Technological University,
Singapore, Singapore
Sasaki.Yu@lab.ntt.co.jp
[4] NTT Secure Platform Laboratories, Tokyo, Japan
Todo.Yosuke@lab.ntt.co.jp
[5] LASEC, École Polytechnique Fédérale de Lausanne, Lausanne, Switzerland

Abstract. In this article, we revisit the design strategy of PRESENT, leveraging all the advances provided by the research community in construction and cryptanalysis since its publication, to push the design up to its limits. We obtain an improved version, named GIFT, that provides a much increased efficiency in all domains (smaller and faster), while correcting the well-known weakness of PRESENT with regards to linear hulls.

GIFT is a very simple and clean design that outperforms even SIMON or SKINNY for round-based implementations, making it one of the most energy efficient ciphers as of today. It reaches a point where almost the entire implementation area is taken by the storage and the Sboxes, where any cheaper choice of Sbox would lead to a very weak proposal. In essence, GIFT is composed of only Sbox and bit-wiring, but its natural bitslice data flow ensures excellent performances in all scenarios, from area-optimised hardware implementations to very fast software implementation on high-end platforms.

We conducted a thorough analysis of our design with regards to state-of-the-art cryptanalysis, and we provide strong bounds with regards to differential/linear attacks.

Keywords: Lightweight cryptography · Block cipher · PRESENT · GIFT

1 Introduction

In the past decade, the development of ubiquitous computing applications triggered the rapid expansion of the lightweight cryptography research field. All these applications operating in very constrained devices may require certain

© International Association for Cryptologic Research 2017
W. Fischer and N. Homma (Eds.): CHES 2017, LNCS 10529, pp. 321–345, 2017.
DOI: 10.1007/978-3-319-66787-4_16

symmetric-key cryptography components to guarantee privacy and/or authentication for the users, such as block or stream ciphers, hash functions or MACs. Existing cryptography standards such as AES [18] or SHA-2 [33] are not always suitable for these strong constraints. There have been extensive research conducted in this direction, with countless new primitives being introduced [2,4,5,12,15,22,39], many of them getting broken rather rapidly (designing a cipher with strong constraints is not an easy task). Conforming to general trend, the American National Institute for Science and Technology (NIST) recently announced that it will consider standardizing some lightweight functions in a few years [34]. Some lightweight algorithms such as PRESENT [12], PHOTON [21] and SPONGENT [11] have already been included into ISO standards (ISO/IEC 29192-2:2012 and ISO/IEC 29192-5:2016).

Comparing different lightweight primitives is a very complex task. First, lightweight encryption encompasses a broad range of use cases, from passive RFID tags (that require a very low power consumption to operate) to battery powered devices (that require a very low energy consumption to maximise its life span) or low-latency applications (for disk encryption). While it is generally admitted that a major criterion for lightweight encryption is area minimisation, the throughput/area ratio is also very important because it shows the ability of the algorithm to provide good implementation trade-offs (this ratio is also correlated to the power or energy consumption of the algorithm). Moreover, the range of the various platforms to consider is very broad, starting from tiny RFID tags to rather powerful ARM processors. Even high-end servers have to be taken into account as it is likely that these very small and constrained devices will be communicating with back-end servers [6].

While most ciphers take lightweight hardware implementations into account to some extend, PRESENT [12] is probably one of the first candidates that was exclusively designed for that purpose. Its design is inspired by SERPENT [7] and is very simple: the round function is simply composed of a layer of small 4-bit Sboxes, followed by a bit permutation layer (essentially free in hardware) and a subkey addition. PRESENT has been extensively analysed in the past decade, and while its security margin has eroded, it remains a secure cipher. One can note that the weak point of PRESENT is the tendency of linear trails to cluster and to create powerful linear hulls [10,17].

Since the publication of PRESENT, many advances have been obtained, both in terms of security analysis and primitive design. The NSA proposed in 2013 two ciphers [4], SIMON and SPECK, that can reach much better efficiency in both hardware and software when compared to all other ciphers. However, this comes at the cost that proving simple linear/differential bounds for SIMON is much more complicated than for Substitution-Permutation-Network (SPN) ciphers like PRESENT (SIMON is based on a Feistel construction, with an internal function that uses only a AND, some XORs and some rotations). Besides, no preliminary analysis or rationale was provided by the SIMON authors. Last year, the tweakable block cipher SKINNY [5] was published to compete with SIMON's efficiency for round-based implementations, while providing strong linear/differential bounds.

As of today, SIMON and SKINNY seem to have a clear advantage in terms of efficiency when compared to other designs. Yet, PRESENT remains an elegant design, that suffers from being one of the first lightweight encryption algorithm to have been published, and thus not benefiting from the many advances obtained by the research community in the recent years.

Our Contributions. In this article, we revisit the PRESENT construction, 10 years after the original publication of PRESENT. This led to the creation of GIFT, a new lightweight block cipher, improving over PRESENT in both security and efficiency. Interestingly, our cipher GIFT offers extremely good performances and even surpasses both SKINNY and SIMON for round-based implementations (see Table 1). This indicates that GIFT is probably the cipher the most suited for the very important low-energy consumption use cases. Due to its simplicity and natural bitslice organisation of the inner data flow, our cipher is very versatile and performs also very well on software, reaching similar performances as SIMON, the current fastest lightweight candidate on software.

Table 1. Hardware performances of round-based implementations of PRESENT, SKINNY, SIMON and our new cipher GIFT, synthesized with STM 90 nm Standard cell library.

	Area (GE)	Delay (ns)	Cycles	TP_{MAX} (MBit/s)	Power (μW) (@10 MHz)	Energy (pJ)
GIFT-64-128	1345	1.83	29	1249.0	74.8	216.9
SKINNY-64–128	1477	1.84	37	966.2	80.3	297.0
PRESENT 64/128	1560	1.63	33	1227.0	71.1	234.6
SIMON 64/128	1458	1.83	45	794.8	72.7	327.3
GIFT-128-128	1997	1.85	41	1729.7	116.6	478.1
SKINNY-128-128	2104	1.85	41	1729.7	132.5	543.3
SIMON 128/128	2064	1.87	69	1006.6	105.6	728.6

In more details, we have revisited the PRESENT design strategy and pushed it to its limits, while providing special care to the known weak point of PRESENT: the linear hulls. The diffusion layer of PRESENT being composed of only a bit permutation, most of the security of PRESENT relies on its Sbox. This Sbox presents excellent cryptographic properties, but is quite costly. Indeed, it is trivial to see that the PRESENT Sbox needs to have a branching number of 3, or very good differential paths would exist otherwise (with only a single active Sbox per round). We managed to remove this constraint by carefully crafting the bit permutation in conjunction with the Difference Distribution Table (DDT)/Linear Approximation Table (LAT) of the Sbox. We remark that, to the best of the authors knowledge, this is the first time that the linear layer and the Sbox are fully intricate in a SPN cipher.

In terms of performances, removing this Sbox constraint allowed us to choose a much cheaper Sbox, which is actually what composes most of the overall area cost in PRESENT. GIFT is not only much smaller, but also much faster than PRESENT. As can be seen in Table 2, GIFT is by far the cipher that uses the least total number of operation per bit up to now. In terms of security, we are able to provide strong security bounds for simple differential and linear attacks. We can even show that GIFT is very resistant against linear hulls, and the clustering effect is greatly reduced when compared to PRESENT, thus correcting its main weak point. We have conducted a thorough security analysis of our candidate with state-of-the-art cryptanalysis techniques.

Table 2. Total number of operations and theoretical performance of GIFT and various lightweight block ciphers. N denotes a NOR gate, A denotes a AND gate, X denotes a XOR gate.

Cipher	nb. of rds	gate cost (per bit per round)			nb. of op.	nb. of op.	round-based
		int. cipher	key sch.	total	w/o key sch.	w/key sch.	impl. area
GIFT-64-128	28	1 N		1 N	$3 \times 28 = 84$	$3 \times 28 = \mathbf{84}$	$1 + 2.67 \times 2 = \mathbf{6.34}$
		2 X		2 X			
SKINNY-64-128	36	1 N		1 N	$3.25 \times 36 = 117$	$3.875 \times 36 = \mathbf{139.5}$	$1 + 2.67 \times 2.875$
		2.25 X	0.625 X	2.875 X			
SIMON-64/128	44	0.5 A		0.5 A	$2 \times 44 = 88$	$3.5 \times 44 = \mathbf{154}$	$0.67 + 2.67 \times 3 = \mathbf{8.68}$
		1.5 X	1.5 X	3.0 X			
PRESENT-128	31	1 A	0.125 A	1.125 A	$4.75 \times 31 = 147.2$	$5.22 \times 31 = \mathbf{161.8}$	$1.5 + 2.67 \times 4.094$
		3.75 X	0.344 X	4.094 X			
GIFT-128-128	40	1 N		1 N	$3.0 \times 40 = 120$	$3.0 \times 40 = \mathbf{120}$	$1 + 2.67 \times 2 = \mathbf{6.34}$
		2 X		2 X			
SKINNY-128-128	40	1 N		1 N	$3.25 \times 40 = 130$	$3.25 \times 40 = \mathbf{130}$	$1 + 2.67 \times 2.25 = \mathbf{7.01}$
		2.25 X		2.25 X			
SIMON-128/128	68	0.5 A		0.5 A	$2 \times 68 = 136$	$3 \times 68 = \mathbf{204}$	$0.67 + 2.67 \times 2.5 = \mathbf{7.34}$
		1.5 X	1 X	2.5 X			
AES-128	10	4.25 A	1.06 A	5.31 A	$20.25 \times 10 = 202.5$	$24.81 \times 10 = \mathbf{248.1}$	$7.06 + 2.67 \times 19.5$
		16 X	3.5 X	19.5 X			

We end up with a very natural and clean cipher, with a simple round function and key schedule (composed of only a bit permutation, thus essentially free in hardware). The cipher can be seen in three different representations (classical 1D, bitslice 2D, and 3D), each offering simple yet different perspective on the cipher's security and opportunities for implementation improvements. GIFT comes in two versions, both with a 128-bit key: one 64-bit block version GIFT-64 and one 128-bit block version GIFT-128. The only difference between these two versions is the bit permutation to accommodate twice more state bits for GIFT-128.

In our hardware implementations of GIFT the storage composes about 75% of the total area, and the (very cheap) Sbox about 20%. Since any weaker choice of the Sbox would lead to a very insecure design, we argue that GIFT is probably very close to reaching the area limit of lightweight encryption.

Outline. We first specify GIFT in Sect. 2, and we provide the design rationale in Sect. 3. A thorough security analysis is performed in Sect. 4, while performances and implementation strategies are given in Sects. 5 and 6 for hardware and software respectively. All details are provided in the full version of the paper.

2 Specifications

In this work, we propose two versions of GIFT, GIFT-64-128 is a 28-round SPN cipher and GIFT-128-128 is a 40-round SPN cipher, both versions have a key length of 128-bit. For short, we call them GIFT-64 and GIFT-128 respectively.

GIFT can be perceived in three different representations. In this paper, we adopt the classical 1D representation, describing the bits in a row like PRESENT. It can also be described in bitslice 2D, a rectangular array like RECTANGLE [44], and even in 3D cuboid like 3D [32]. These alternative representations are detailed in the full version.

Round Function. Each round of GIFT consists of 3 steps: SubCells, PermBits, and AddRoundKey, which is conceptually similar to wrapping a gift:

1. Put the content into a box (SubCells);
2. Wrap the ribbon around the box (PermBits);
3. Tie a knot to secure the content (AddRoundKey).

Figure 1 illustrates 2 rounds of GIFT-64.

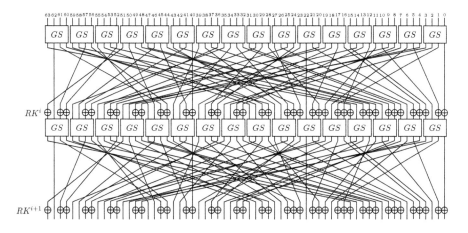

Fig. 1. 2 Rounds of GIFT-64.

Table 3. Specifications of GIFT Sbox GS.

x	0	1	2	3	4	5	6	7	8	9	a	b	c	d	e	f
$GS(x)$	1	a	4	c	6	f	3	9	2	d	b	7	5	0	8	e

Initialization. The cipher receives an n-bit plaintext $b_{n-1}b_{n-2}...b_0$ as the cipher state S, where $n = 64, 128$ and b_0 being the least significant bit. The cipher state can also be expressed as s many 4-bit nibbles $S = w_{s-1}||w_{s-2}||...||w_0$, where $s = 16, 32$. The cipher also receives a 128-bit key $K = k_7||k_6||...||k_0$ as the key state, where k_i is a 16-bit word.

SubCells. Both versions of GIFT use the same invertible 4-bit Sbox, GS. The Sbox is applied to every nibble of the cipher state. $w_i \leftarrow GS(w_i)$, $\forall i \in \{0, ..., s-1\}$. The action of this Sbox in hexadecimal notation is given in Table 3.

PermBits. The bit permutation used in GIFT-64 and GIFT-128 are given in Tables 4 and 5 respectively. It maps bits from bit position i of the cipher state to bit position $P(i)$. $b_{P(i)} \leftarrow b_i$, $\forall i \in \{0, ..., n-1\}$.

AddRoundKey. This step consists of adding the round key and round constants. An $n/2$-bit round key RK is extracted from the key state, it is further partitioned into 2 s-bit words $RK = U||V = u_{s-1}...u_0||v_{s-1}...v_0$, where $s = 16, 32$ for GIFT-64 and GIFT-128 respectively.

For GIFT-64, U and V are XORed to $\{b_{4i+1}\}$ and $\{b_{4i}\}$ of the cipher state respectively. $b_{4i+1} \leftarrow b_{4i+1} \oplus u_i$, $b_{4i} \leftarrow b_{4i} \oplus v_i$, $\forall i \in \{0, ..., 15\}$.

For GIFT-128, U and V are XORed to $\{b_{4i+2}\}$ and $\{b_{4i+1}\}$ of the cipher state respectively. $b_{4i+2} \leftarrow b_{4i+2} \oplus u_i$, $b_{4i+1} \leftarrow b_{4i+1} \oplus v_i$, $\forall i \in \{0, ..., 31\}$.

For both versions of GIFT, a single bit "1" and a 6-bit round constant $C = c_5c_4c_3c_2c_1c_0$ are XORed into the cipher state at bit position $n-1$, 23, 19, 15, 11, 7 and 3 respectively. $b_{n-1} \leftarrow b_{n-1} \oplus 1$, $b_{23} \leftarrow b_{23} \oplus c_5$, $b_{19} \leftarrow b_{19} \oplus c_4$, $b_{15} \leftarrow b_{15} \oplus c_3$, $b_{11} \leftarrow b_{11} \oplus c_2$, $b_7 \leftarrow b_7 \oplus c_1$, $b_3 \leftarrow b_3 \oplus c_0$.

Table 4. Specifications of GIFT-64 Bit Permutation.

i	0	1	2	3	4	5	6	7	8	9	10	11	12	13	14	15
$P_{64}(i)$	0	17	34	51	48	1	18	35	32	49	2	19	16	33	50	3
i	16	17	18	19	20	21	22	23	24	25	26	27	28	29	30	31
$P_{64}(i)$	4	21	38	55	52	5	22	39	36	53	6	23	20	37	54	7
i	32	33	34	35	36	37	38	39	40	41	42	43	44	45	46	47
$P_{64}(i)$	8	25	42	59	56	9	26	43	40	57	10	27	24	41	58	11
i	48	49	50	51	52	53	54	55	56	57	58	59	60	61	62	63
$P_{64}(i)$	12	29	46	63	60	13	30	47	44	61	14	31	28	45	62	15

Table 5. Specifications of GIFT-128 Bit Permutation.

i	0	1	2	3	4	5	6	7	8	9	10	11	12	13	14	15
$P_{128}(i)$	0	33	66	99	96	1	34	67	64	97	2	35	32	65	98	3
i	16	17	18	19	20	21	22	23	24	25	26	27	28	29	30	31
$P_{128}(i)$	4	37	70	103	100	5	38	71	68	101	6	39	36	69	102	7
i	32	33	34	35	36	37	38	39	40	41	42	43	44	45	46	47
$P_{128}(i)$	8	41	74	107	104	9	42	75	72	105	10	43	40	73	106	11
i	48	49	50	51	52	53	54	55	56	57	58	59	60	61	62	63
$P_{128}(i)$	12	45	78	111	108	13	46	79	76	109	14	47	44	77	110	15
i	64	65	66	67	68	69	70	71	72	73	74	75	76	77	78	79
$P_{128}(i)$	16	49	82	115	112	17	50	83	80	113	18	51	48	81	114	19
i	80	81	82	83	84	85	86	87	88	89	90	91	92	93	94	95
$P_{128}(i)$	20	53	86	119	116	21	54	87	84	117	22	55	52	85	118	23
i	96	97	98	99	100	101	102	103	104	105	106	107	108	109	110	111
$P_{128}(i)$	24	57	90	123	120	25	58	91	88	121	26	59	56	89	122	27
i	112	113	114	115	116	117	118	119	120	121	122	123	124	125	126	127
$P_{128}(i)$	28	61	94	127	124	29	62	95	92	125	30	63	60	93	126	31

Key Schedule and Round Constants. The key schedule and round constants are the same for both versions of GIFT, the only difference is the round key extraction. A round key is *first* extracted from the key state before the key state update.

For GIFT-64, two 16-bit words of the key state are extracted as the round key $RK = U||V$. $U \leftarrow k_1$, $V \leftarrow k_0$.

For GIFT-128, four 16-bit words of the key state are extracted as the round key $RK = U||V$. $U \leftarrow k_5||k_4$, $V \leftarrow k_1||k_0$.

The key state is then updated as follows, $k_7||k_6||...||k_1||k_0 \leftarrow k_1 \ggg 2||k_0 \ggg 12||...||k_3||k_2$, where $\ggg i$ is an i bits right rotation within a 16-bit word.

The round constants are generated using the same 6-bit affine LFSR as SKINNY, whose state is denoted as $(c_5, c_4, c_3, c_2, c_1, c_0)$. Its update function is defined as: $(c_5, c_4, c_3, c_2, c_1, c_0) \leftarrow (c_4, c_3, c_2, c_1, c_0, c_5 \oplus c_4 \oplus 1)$. The six bits are initialized to zero, and updated *before* being used in a given round. The values of the constants for each round are given in the table below, encoded to byte values for each round, with c_0 being the least significant bit.

Rounds	Constants
1 - 16	01,03,07,0F,1F,3E,3D,3B,37,2F,1E,3C,39,33,27,0E
17 - 32	1D,3A,35,2B,16,2C,18,30,21,02,05,0B,17,2E,1C,38
33 - 48	31,23,06,0D,1B,36,2D,1A,34,29,12,24,08,11,22,04

Remark: GIFT aims at single-key security, so we do not claim any related-key security (even though no attack is known in this model as of today). In case one wants to protect against related-key attacks as well, we advice to double the number of rounds.

3 Design Rationale

First, let us propose a subclassification for SPN ciphers.

Definition 1. *Substitution-bitPermutation network (SbPN) is a subclassification of Substitution-Permutation network, where the permutation layer (p-layer) only comprises of bit permutation. An m/n-SbPN cipher is an n-bit cipher in which substitution layer (s-layer) comprises of m-bit (Super-)Sboxes.*

For SPN ciphers like AES and SKINNY, we can shift the XOR components from the p-layer to the s-layer to form Super-Sboxes, leaving the p-layer with only bit permutation. For example, PRESENT is a 4/64-SbPN cipher, SKINNY-64 is a 16/64-SbPN cipher, and SKINNY-128 and AES are 32/128-SbPN ciphers.

Having that said, GIFT-64 is a 4/64-SbPN cipher while GIFT-128 is (probably the first of its kind) a 4/128-SbPN cipher.

3.1 The Designing of GIFT

Before we discuss the design rationale of GIFT, we would like to share some background story about GIFT, its design approach, and its comparison with another PRESENT-like ciphers.

The Origin of GIFT. It all started with a casual remark "What if the Sboxes in PRESENT are replaced with some smaller Sboxes, say the PICCOLO Sbox? It will be extremely lightweight since the core cipher only has some Sboxes and nothing else...". We quickly tested it but only to realise that the differential bounds became very low because the Sbox does not have differential branching number of 3. That is when we started analyzing the differential characteristics and studying the interaction between the linear layer and the Sbox. Surprisingly, we found that by carefully crafting the linear layer based on the properties of the Sbox, we were able to achieve the same differential bound as PRESENT without the constraint of differential branching number of 3. In addition, this result can also be applied to the improve linear cryptanalysis resistance which was lacking in PRESENT. Eventually, a small present—GIFT was created.

Design Approach. It is natural to ask how GIFT is different from the other lightweight primitives, especially the recent SKINNY family of block ciphers that was proposed at CRYPTO2016. One of the main difference is the design approach. SKINNY was designed with a high-security-reduce-area approach, that is to have a strong security property, then try to remove/reduce various components as much as possible. While GIFT adopts a small-area-increase-security approach, starting from a small area goal, we try to improve its security as much as possible.

Other PRESENT-like Ciphers. Besides PRESENT, one may also compare GIFT-64 with RECTANGLE since both are 4/64-SbPN ciphers and an improvement on the design of PRESENT. RECTANGLE was designed to be software friendly and to achieve a better resistance against the linear cryptanalysis as compared to PRESENT. However, although its bit permutation (ShiftRow) was designed to be software friendly, little analysis was done on the how differential and linear characteristics propagate through the cipher. Whereas for GIFT, we study the interplay of the Sbox and the bit permutation to achieve better differential and linear bounds. In addition, the ShiftRow of RECTANGLE achieves full diffusion in 4 rounds at best. Whereas GIFT-64 achieves full diffusion in 3 rounds like PRESENT, which can be proven to be the optimal for 4/64-SbPN ciphers.

3.2 Designing of GIFT Bit Permutation

To better understand the design rationale of the linear layer, we first look at the permutation layer of PRESENT to analyze the issue when the Sbox is replaced with another Sbox that does not have branching number of 3. Next, we show how we can solve this issue by carefully designing the bit permutation.

Linear Layer of PRESENT. The bit permutation of PRESENT is given in Table 6.

Table 6. Bit permutation of PRESENT.

i	0	1	2	3	4	5	6	7	8	9	10	11	12	13	14	15
$P(i)$	0	16	32	48	1	17	33	49	2	18	34	50	3	19	35	51
i	16	17	18	19	20	21	22	23	24	25	26	27	28	29	30	31
$P(i)$	4	20	36	52	5	21	37	53	6	22	38	54	7	23	39	55
i	32	33	34	35	36	37	38	39	40	41	42	43	44	45	46	47
$P(i)$	8	24	40	56	9	25	41	57	10	26	42	58	11	27	43	59
i	48	49	50	51	52	53	54	55	56	57	58	59	60	61	62	63
$P(i)$	12	28	44	60	13	29	45	61	14	30	46	62	15	31	47	63

It is known that the bit permutation can be partitioned into 4 independent bit permutations, mapping the output of 4 Sboxes to the input of 4 Sboxes in the next round.

For convenience, we number the Sboxes in i^{th} round as $Sb_0^i, Sb_1^i, ..., Sb_{s-1}^i$, where $s = n/4$. These Sboxes can be grouped in 2 different ways - the Quotient and Remainder groups, Qx and Rx, defined as

- $Qx = \{Sb_{4x}, Sb_{4x+1}, Sb_{4x+2}, Sb_{4x+3}\}$,
- $Rx = \{Sb_x, Sb_{q+x}, Sb_{2q+x}, Sb_{3q+x}\}$, where $q = \frac{s}{4}, 0 \le x \le q - 1$.

In PRESENT, $n = 64$ and output bits of $Qx^i = \{Sb^i_{4x}, Sb^i_{4x+1}, Sb^i_{4x+2}, Sb^i_{4x+3}\}$ map to input bits of $Rx^{i+1} = \{Sb^{i+1}_x, Sb^{i+1}_{4+x}, Sb^{i+1}_{8+x}, Sb^{i+1}_{12+x}\}$, this group mapping is defined in Table 7, where the entry (l, m) at row rw and column cl denotes that the lth output bit of the Sbox corresponding to the row rw at i^{th} round will map to the mth input bit of the Sbox corresponding to the column cl at $(i+1)^{th}$ round. For example, suppose $x = 2$, row and column start at 0, then the entry $(3, 2)$ at row 2 and column 3 means that the 3rd output bit of Sb^i_{10} maps to 2nd input bit of Sb^{i+1}_{14}, thus $P(43) = 58$ (see Table 6).

Table 7. PRESENT group mapping from Qx^i to Rx^{i+1}.

Qx^i \ Rx^{i+1}	Sb^{i+1}_x	Sb^{i+1}_{4+x}	Sb^{i+1}_{8+x}	Sb^{i+1}_{12+x}
Sb^i_{4x}	$(0,0)$	$(1,0)$	$(2,0)$	$(3,0)$
Sb^i_{4x+1}	$(0,1)$	$(1,1)$	$(2,1)$	$(3,1)$
Sb^i_{4x+2}	$(0,2)$	$(1,2)$	$(2,2)$	$(3,2)$
Sb^i_{4x+3}	$(0,3)$	$(1,3)$	$(2,3)$	$(3,3)$

PRESENT bit permutation can be realised in hardware with wires only (no logic gates required). Further, full diffusion is achieved in 3 rounds; from 1 bit to 4, then 4 to 16 and then 16 to 64. But, if there exists Hamming weight 1 to Hamming weight 1 differential transition, or $1-1$ bit differential transition, then there exists consecutive single active bit transitions.

We define $1 - 1$ bit DDT as a sub-table of the DDT containing Hamming weight 1 differences. Consider some Sbox with the following $1 - 1$ bit DDT (see Table 8). Δx and Δy denote the differential in the input and output of Sbox respectively. It is evident that this Sbox has differential branch number 2.

It is trivial to see that there exists a single active bit path which results in a differential characteristic with single active Sboxes in each round. Let the input differences be at 3rd bit of $Sb^{(i)}_{15}$. According to $1 - 1$ bit DDT (Table 8), there exists a transition from 1000 to 1000. From the group mapping (Table 7), 3rd output bit of $Sb^{(i)}_{15}$ maps to 3rd input bit of $Sb^{(i+1)}_{15}$. And then the differential continues from 3rd output bit of $Sb^{(i+1)}_{15}$ to 3rd input bit of $Sb^{(i+2)}_{15}$ and so on. Not only that, if there exists any $1 - 1$ bit transition (not necessarily $1000 \rightarrow 1000$), one can verify that there always exists some differential characteristic with single active Sbox per round for at least 4 consecutive rounds.

To overcome this problem, we propose a new construction paradigm, "Bad Output must go to Good Input" or BOGI in short. We explain this in the context of the differential of an Sbox, but the analysis is same for linear case also.

Bad Output Must Go to Good Input (BOGI). The existence of the single active bit path is because the bit permutation allows $1 - 1$ bit transition from some Sbox in i^{th} round to propagate to some Sbox in $(i + 1)^{th}$ round that

Table 8. $1 - 1$ bit DDT Example 1

Δx \ Δy	1000	0100	0010	0001
1000	2	0	0	0
0100	0	0	0	0
0010	0	0	0	0
0001	0	0	0	0

Table 9. $1 - 1$ bit DDT Example 2

Δx \ Δy	1000	0100	0010	0001
1000	0	2	2	0
0100	0	0	0	0
0010	0	0	0	0
0001	0	2	2	0

again would produce $1 - 1$ bit transition. To overcome such problem, it must be ensured that such path does not exist. In $1 - 1$ bit DDT, let us define $\Delta x = x_3 x_2 x_1 x_0$ be a good input if the corresponding row has all zero entries, else a bad input. Similarly, we define $\Delta y = y_3 y_2 y_1 y_0$ be a good output if the corresponding column has all zero entries, else a bad output. In Table 8, 1000 is both bad input and bad output, rest are good.

Consider another $1 - 1$ bit DDT in Table 9. Let GI, GO, BI, BO denote the set of good inputs, good outputs, bad inputs and bad outputs respectively. Then, in Table 9, $GI = \{0100, 0010\}$, $GO = \{1000, 0001\}$, $BI = \{1000, 0001\}$ and $BO = \{0100, 0010\}$. Or, if we represent these binary strings by integers considering the position of the "1" (rightmost position is 0) in these strings, we may rewrite $GI = \{2, 1\}$, $GO = \{3, 0\}$, $BI = \{3, 0\}$ and $BO = \{2, 1\}$.

An output belonging to BO (bad ouput) could potentially come from a single bit transition through some Sbox in this round. Thus we want to map this active output bit to some GI (good input) in the next round, which guaranteed that it will not propagate to another $1 - 1$ bit transition. As a result, it avoids single active bit path in 2 consecutive rounds.

BOGI: Let $|BO| \le |GI|$ and $\pi_1 : BO \to GI$ be an injective map. To ensure that π_1 is an injective map, it is required that $|BO| \le |GI|$ (the cardinality of the set BO must be less than or equal to the cardinality of the set GI). Let $\pi_2 : GO \to \pi_1(BO)^C$ (the complement of $\pi_1(BO)$) be another injective map. The map π_1 ensures that "Bad Output must go to Good Input". A combined map $\pi : BO \cup GO \to BI \cup GI$ is defined as $\pi(e) = \pi_1(e)$ if and only if $e \in BO$, otherwise $\pi(e) = \pi_2(e)$. For example, consider the Table 9. The injective maps $\pi_1 : \{2, 1\} \to \{2, 1\}$ and $\pi_2 : \{3, 0\} \to \{3, 0\}$ both have 2 choices which altogether make 4 choices for the combined map π. An example BOGI mapping would be $\pi(0) = 0, \pi(1) = 1, \pi(2) = 2, \pi(3) = 3$, which happens to be an identity mapping.

Any choice of π may be used to define the bit permutation. We call these πs *differential BOGI permutations* as derived from $1 - 1$ bit DDT.

Remark: Similar analysis is done for linear case also. Analogous to $1 - 1$ bit DDT, analysis is done on the basis of $1 - 1$ bit LAT and BOGI permutations are found for linear case too. We call them *linear BOGI permutations*. We can now choose any common permutation from the set of both differential and linear BOGI permutations.

BOGI Bit Permutation for GIFT. Let $\pi : \{0, 1, 2, 3\} \rightarrow \{0, 1, 2, 3\}$ be a common permutation from the set of both differential and linear BOGI permutations. Table 10 shows the group mapping.

Table 10. BOGI Bit Permutation mapping from Qx^i to Rx^{i+1}.

Qx^i \ Rx^{i+1}	Sb_x^{i+1}	Sb_{q+x}^{i+1}	Sb_{2q+x}^{i+1}	Sb_{3q+x}^{i+1}
Sb_{4x}^i	$(0, \pi(0))$	$(1, \pi(1))$	$(2, \pi(2))$	$(3, \pi(3))$
Sb_{4x+1}^i	$(1, \pi(1))$	$(2, \pi(2))$	$(3, \pi(3))$	$(0, \pi(0))$
Sb_{4x+2}^i	$(2, \pi(2))$	$(3, \pi(3))$	$(0, \pi(0))$	$(1, \pi(1))$
Sb_{4x+3}^i	$(3, \pi(3))$	$(0, \pi(0))$	$(1, \pi(1))$	$(2, \pi(2))$

Note that we made some left rotations to the rows of the bit mapping, this is because we need the inputs to each Sbox in $(i+1)^{\text{th}}$ round to be coming from 4 different bit positions.

In GIFT, we chose an Sbox that has a common BOGI permutation that is an identity mapping, that is $\pi(i) = i$. Figure 2 illustrates the group mapping from $Q0$ to $R0$ in GIFT-64. The same BOGI permutation is applied to all the q group mappings to form the final n-bit permutation for both version of GIFT.

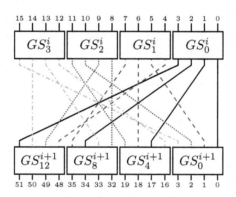

Fig. 2. Group mapping from $Q0$ to $R0$ in GIFT-64.

Some Results About Our Bit Permutation. To be concise, we leave the proofs for our results in the full version. Let $Q0, Q1, \cdots, Q(q-1)$ be q different Quotient groups and $R0, R1, \cdots, R(q-1)$ be q different Remainder groups. Then, for $0 \le x \le q - 1$,

1. The input bits of an Sbox in Rx come from 4 distinct Sboxes in Qx.
2. The output bits of an Sbox in Qx go to 4 distinct Sboxes in Rx.
3. The input bits of 4 Sboxes from the same Qx come from 16 different Sboxes.
4. The output bits of 4 Sboxes from the same Rx go to 16 different Sboxes.

Lemma 1. *When the number of Sboxes in a round is* 16 *or* 32, *the proposed bit permutation achieves an optimal full diffusion which is achievable by a bit permutation.*

Lemma 2. *In the proposed bit permutation, there does not exist any single active bit transition for two consecutive rounds in both differential and linear characteristics.*

Definition 2. *The **differential** (resp. **linear**) **score of an Sbox** is $|GI|+|GO|$ observed from $1-1$ bit DDT (resp. LAT).*

Lemma 3. *There exists differential (resp. linear) BOGI permutation for an Sbox if and only if the differential (resp. linear) score of an Sbox is at least* 4.

It is essential that our Sbox has at least score 4 for both differential and linear, and has some common BOGI permutation. These are 2 of the main criteria for the selection of GIFT Sbox.

Remark: BOGI permutation is a group mapping that is independent of the number of groups. Thus, this permutation design is scalable to any bit permutation size that is multiple of 16. This allows us to potentially design larger state size like 256-bit that is useful for designing hash functions.

3.3   Selection of GIFT Sbox

We first recall some Sbox properties and introduce a metric to estimate the hardware implementation cost of Sboxes.

Properties of Sbox. For the differential property, let $S : \mathbb{F}_2^4 \to \mathbb{F}_2^4$ denote a 4-bit Sbox. Let $\Delta_I, \Delta_O \in \mathbb{F}_2^4$ be the input and output differences, $D_S(\Delta_I, \Delta_O) = \sharp\{x \in \mathbb{F}_2^4 | S(x) \oplus S(x \oplus \Delta_I) = \Delta_O\}$, and $D_{max}(S) = \max_{\Delta_I, \Delta_O \neq 0} D_S(\Delta_I, \Delta_O)$. For the linear property, let $\alpha, \beta \in \mathbb{F}_2^4$ be the input and output masking, $L_S(\alpha, \beta) = |\sharp\{x \in \mathbb{F}_2^4 | x \bullet \alpha = S(x) \bullet \beta\} - 8|$, and $L_{max}(S) = \max_{\alpha, \beta \neq 0} L_S(\alpha, \beta)$.

Definition 3 ([36]). *Let M_i and M_o be two invertible matrices and $c_i, c_o \in \mathbb{F}_2^4$. The Sbox S' defined by $S'(x) = M_o S(M_i(x \oplus c_i)) \oplus c_o$ belongs to the affine equivalence (AE) set of S.*

It is known that both D_{max} and L_{max} are preserved under the AE class.

Definition 4 ([36]). *Let P_i and P_o be two bit permutation matrices and $c_i, c_o \in \mathbb{F}_2^4$. The Sbox S' defined by $S'(x) = P_o S(P_i(x \oplus c_i)) \oplus c_o$ belongs to the permutation-xor equivalence (PE) set of S.*

One is to note that the $1-1$ bit differential and linear transition is preserved only under the PE class. That is to say that the score of an Sbox is preserved under the PE class but not the AE class.

Heuristic Sbox Implementation. We use a simplified metric to estimate the implementation cost of Sboxes. We denote $\{\text{NOT}, \text{NAND}, \text{NOR}\}$ as N-operations[1] and $\{\text{XOR}, \text{XNOR}\}$ as X-operations, and estimate the cost of an N-operation to be 1 unit and X-operations to be 2 units. We consider the following 4 types of instruction for the construction of the Sboxes: $a \leftarrow \text{NOT}(a)$; $a \leftarrow a \text{ X } b$; $a \leftarrow a \text{ X } (b \text{ N } c)$; $a \leftarrow a \text{ X } ((b \text{ N } c) \text{ N } d)$, where a, b, c, d are distinct bits of an Sbox input. These so-called *invertible instructions* [23] allow us to implement the inverse Sbox by simply reversing the sequence of the instructions. In addition, the implementation cost of the inverse Sbox would be the same as the direct Sbox since the same set of instructions is used.

Under this metric, we found that PRESENT Sbox requires $4\text{N} + 9\text{X}$ operations, a cost of 22 units. While RECTANGLE Sbox requires $4\text{N} + 7\text{X}$ operations, a cost of 18 units. Hence, one of the criteria for our Sbox is to have implementation cost lesser than 18 units[2].

Search for GIFT Sbox. Our primary design criteria for the GIFT Sbox are:

1. Implementation cost of at most 17 units.
2. With a score of at least 4 in both differential and linear. I.e. For both differential and linear, $|GO| + |GI| \geq 4$.
3. There exists a common BOGI permutation for both differential and linear.

From the list of 302 AE Sboxes presented in [14], we generate the PE Sboxes and check its implementation cost. Our heuristic search shows that there is no optimal Sboxes [30] ($D_{max} = 4$ and $L_{max} = 4$) that satisfies all 3 criteria, hence we extended our search to non-optimal Sboxes. For Sboxes with $D_{max} = 6$ and $L_{max} = 4$, we found some Sboxes with implementation cost of 16 units. For a cost of 15 units, the best possible Sboxes (in terms of D_{max} and L_{max}) that satisfies the criteria have $D_{max} = 12$ and $L_{max} = 6$. And Sboxes with cost of at most 14 units have either $D_{max} = 16$ or $L_{max} = 8$. To maximise the resistance against differential and linear attacks while satisfying the Sbox criteria, we consider Sboxes with $D_{max} = 6$, $L_{max} = 4$ and implementation cost of 16 units.

In order to reduce the occurrence of sub-optimal differential transition, we impose two additional criteria:

4. $\#\{(\Delta_I, \Delta_O) \in \mathbb{F}_2^4 \times \mathbb{F}_2^4 | D_S(\Delta_I, \Delta_O) > 4\} \leq 2$.
5. For $D_S(\Delta_I, \Delta_O) > 4$, $wt(\Delta_I) + wt(\Delta_O) \geq 4$, where $wt(\cdot)$ is the Hamming weight.

Criteria (5) ensures that when sub-optimal differential transition occurs, there is a total of at least 4 active Sboxes in the previous and next round.

Finally, we pick an Sbox with a common BOGI permutation for differential and linear that is an identity, i.e. $\pi(i) = i$.

---

[1] We do not need to consider AND and OR because when we use these invertible instructions, it is equivalent to some other instructions that have been taken into consideration. For instance, $a \text{ XOR } (b \text{ AND } c) \equiv a \text{ XNOR } (b \text{ NAND } c)$.

[2] This "unit" metric is to facilitate the Sbox search, the Sboxes are later synthesized to obtain their GE in Sect. 5.

Properties of GIFT Sbox. Our GIFT Sbox GS can be implemented with 4N+6X operations (smaller than the Sboxes in PRESENT and RECTANGLE), has a maximum differential probability of $2^{-1.415}$ and linear bias of 2^{-2}, algebraic degree 3 and no fixed point. For the sub-optimal differential transitions with probability $2^{-1.415}$, there are only 2 such transitions and the sum of Hamming weight of input and output differentials is 4. The implementation, differential distribution table (DDT) and linear approximation table (LAT) of GS are provided in the full version.

3.4 Designing of GIFT Key Schedule

Key State Update. One of our main goals when designing the key schedule is to minimize the hardware area, and thus we chose bit permutation which is just wire shuffle and has no hardware area at all. For it to be also software friendly, we consider the entire key state rotation to be in blocks of 16-bit, and bit rotations within some 16-bit blocks. Since it is redundant to apply bit rotations within key state blocks that have not been introduced to the cipher state, we update the key state blocks only after it has been extracted as a round key.

To introduce the entire key material into the cipher state as fast as possible, the key state blocks that are extracted as the round key are chosen such that all the key material are introduced into the cipher state in the least possible number of rounds.

Adding Round Keys. To optimize the hardware performances of GIFT, we XOR the round key to only half of the cipher state. This saves a significant amount of hardware area in a round-based implementation. For it to be software friendly too, we XOR the round key at the same i-th bit positions of each nibble. This makes the bitslice implementation more efficient. In addition, since all nibbles contains some key material, the entire state will be dependent on the key after a SubCells operation.

The choice of the positions for adding the round key and 16-bit rotations were chosen to optimize the related-key differential bounds. However, we would like to reiterate that more rounds is advised to resist related-key attacks.

Round Constants. For the round constants, but instead of using a typical decimal counter, we use a 6-bit affine LFSR (like in SKINNY [5]). It requires only a single XNOR gate per update which is probably has smallest possible hardware area for a counter. Each of the 6 bits is xored to a different nibble to break the symmetry. In addition, we add a "1" at the MSB to further increase the effect.

4 Security Analysis

In this section, we provide short summary of the various cryptanalysis that we had conducted on GIFT. All details are provided in the full version.

4.1 Differential and Linear Cryptanalysis

We use Mixed Integer Linear Programming(MILP) to compute the lower bounds for the number of active Sboxes in both differential cryptanalysis [9] (DC) and linear cryptanalysis [31] (LC), the results are summaries in Table 11. The MILP solution provide us the actual differential or linear characteristics, which allow us to compute the actual differential probability and correlation contribution.

Table 11. Lower bounds for number of active Sboxes.

Cipher	DC/LC	Rounds								
		1	2	3	4	5	6	7	8	9
GIFT-64	DC	1	2	3	5	7	10	13	16	18
	LC	1	2	3	5	7	9	12	15	18
PRESENT	DC	1	2	4	6	10	12	14	16	18
	LC	1	2	3	4	5	6	7	8	9
RECTANGLE	DC	1	2	3	4	6	8	11	13	14
	LC	1	2	3	4	6	8	10	12	14
GIFT-128	DC	1	2	3	5	7	10	13	17	19
	LC	1	2	3	5	7	9	12	14	18

Recall that one of our main goals is to match the differential bounds of PRESENT, that is having an average of 2 active Sboxes per round, but with a lighter Sbox and without the constraint of differential branching number of 3. In addition, we aim for same ratio for the linear bound which was not accomplished by PRESENT. These targets were achieved at 9-round of GIFT. Hence, our DC and LC analysis and discussion focus on 9-round.

Regarding the security against DC, GIFT-64 has a 9-round differential probability of $2^{-44.415}$, taking the average per round and propagate forward, we expect that the differential probability will be lower than 2^{-63} after 14 rounds. Therefore, we believe 28-round GIFT-64 is enough to resist against DC. For GIFT-128, it has a 9-round differential probability of $2^{-46.99}$, which suggested that 26-round is sufficient to achieve a differential probability lower than 2^{-127}. Therefore, we believe 40-round GIFT-128 is enough to resist against DC.

Regarding LC, GIFT-64 has a 9-round linear hull effect of $2^{-49.997}$, which expected to require 13-round to achieve correlation potential lower than 2^{-64}. Therefore, we believe 28-round GIFT-64 is enough to resist against LC. For GIFT-128, it has a 9-round differential probability of $2^{-45.99}$, which means that we would need around 27 rounds to achieve a differential probability lower than 2^{-128}. Therefore, we believe 40-round GIFT-128 is enough to resist against LC.

Related-Key Differential Cryptanalysis. For GIFT-64, since it takes 4 rounds for the all the key material to be introduced into the cipher state, it is trivial to see that it is possible to have no active Sboxes from 1-round to 4-round. Thus we start our computation on the related-key differential bounds from 5-round onwards. From 5-round to 12-round, the probability of these differential characteristics are $2^{-1.415}, 2^{-5}, 2^{-6.415}, 2^{-10}, 2^{-16}, 2^{-22}, 2^{-27}, 2^{-33}$ respectively. Even if we suppose that the probability of 12-round characteristic is lower bounded by 2^{-33}, it is doubtful that 28 rounds are secure against related-key differential cryptanalysis. Therefore, as we describe in Sect. 2, we strongly recommend to increase the number of rounds to achieve the security against the related-key attacks.

For GIFT-128, we start our computation from 3-round onwards. From 3-round to 9-round, the probabilities are $2^{-1.415}, 2^{-5}, 2^{-7}, 2^{-11}, 2^{-20}, 2^{-25}, 2^{-31}$ respectively. Similar to GIFT-64, it is doubtful that 40 rounds are secure against related-key differential cryptanalysis.

4.2 Integral Attacks

We discuss the security against integral attacks [26]. Here the integral distinguisher is found by using the (bit-based) division property [40,42] and the key recovery is executed by using the partial-sum technique [19]. As a result, the number of rounds that we can find integral distinguishers is 9 rounds for GIFT-64, and the following is an example.

$$(A^{60}, ACAA) \xrightarrow{9R} ((UUBB)^{16})$$

Here, only 2nd bit in plaintext is constant, and bits $\{b_{4i}\}$ and $\{b_{4i+1}\}$ in 9-round ciphertexts are balanced. Note that there is no whitening key at the beginning. Therefore, we can trivially extend integral distinguishers by one round, and GIFT-64 has 10-round integral distinguishers, respectively. We can append four rounds to the 10-round integral distinguisher as the key recovery and attack 14-round GIFT-64. The attack complexity is about 2^{97} with 2^{63} chosen plaintexts.

We also evaluated the longest integral distinguisher for GIFT-128 by using the (bit-based) division property. As a result, we can find 11-round integral distinguisher. The number of rounds is improved by two rounds than that for GIFT-128. However, the number of bits in round key that is XORed every round increases from 32 bits to 64 bits. Therefore, we expect that GIFT-128 is also secure against integral attacks.

4.3 Impossible Differential Attacks

Impossible differential attacks [8,25] exploits a pair of difference Δ_1 and Δ_2 in which Δ_1 never reaches Δ_2 after some rounds.

We searched for impossible differentials by using the MILP-based tool [38]. The results show that there does not exist any impossible differentials with 1-active nibble against 7 rounds of GIFT-64. Thus full rounds are sufficient to resist the impossible differential attack.

4.4 Meet-in-the-Middle Attacks

The meet-in-the-middle (MITM) attack discussed here is a rather classical one, which separates the encryption algorithm into two independent functions [13,16].

GIFT-64-128 XORs only 32 bits out of 128 bits of the key to the state in every round. Given this property, along with splice-and-cut [1] and initial-structure (IS) [37] techniques, we choose that 8 bits of (k_6, k_7) and 8 bits of k_2, k_3 as sources of independent computations called neutral bits and separate 15 rounds as shown in Fig. 3. Note that when the backward computation reaches the plaintext, the attacker makes a query to obtain the corresponding ciphertext. Every details of the attack procedure will be explained in the full version.

Round	1	2	3	4	5	6	7	8	9	10	11	12	13	14	15
Subkey U	k_1	k_3^B	k_5	k_7^F	k_1	k_3^B	k_5	k_7^F	k_1	k_3^B	k_5	k_7^F	k_1	k_3^B	k_5
V	k_0	k_2^B	k_4	k_6^F	k_0	k_2^B	k_4	k_6^F	k_0	k_2^B	k_4	k_6^F	k_0	k_2^B	k_4
Remarks		$\longleftarrow$			IS			$\longrightarrow$			match			$\longleftarrow$	

Fig. 3. Chunk separation for 15-round MitM attack.

For each of 2^{112} non-neutral bits, the attacker computes the forward and backward chunks for 2^8 choices of neutral bits. Therefore, the time complexity is 2^{120} and the memory complexity is 2^8. This requires the knowledge of the full codebook, thus the data complexity is 2^{64}.

4.5 Invariant Subspace Attacks

Since the round constant is XORed only in the MSB of several S-boxes, invariant subspace attacks [20, 28, 29] can be a potential threat.

We exhaustively searched for the subspace transition through the GIFT S-box and confirmed that XORing the constant to MSB breaks the invariant subspace, thus GIFT resists the attack. The details are provided in the full version.

4.6 Nonlinear Invariant Attacks

Nonlinear invariant attacks [41] are weak-key attacks that can be applied when the round constant is XORed only to some particular bits of nibbles. The core idea is to find a nonlinear approximation of the round transformation with probability one. For the SPN structure, the attacks are mounted when (1) S-box has the quadratic nonlinear invariant and (2) the linear layer is represented by the multiplication with an orthogonal binary matrix.

The diffusion of GIFT (bit permutation) is orthogonal. However, it is not represented by the multiplication with an orthogonal binary matrix. Moreover, we searched for the quadratic nonlinear invariant for GIFT S-box, but there is no such invariant. Therefore, GIFT is secure against the nonlinear invariant attacks.

4.7 Algebraic Attacks

Algebraic attacks do not threaten GIFT, the analysis is provided in the full version.

5 Hardware Implementation

GIFT is surprisingly efficient and on ASIC platforms across various degrees of serialization. This is mainly due to the extremely lightweight round function that performs key addition on only half of the state and uses a bit permutation as the only diffusion mechanism. Due to page constraints, we leave the details in the full version of our paper and present the summary here.

5.1 Round Based Implementation

GIFT includes various design strategies in order to minimize gate count. GIFT employs key addition to only half of the state and so saves silicon area in the process. SKINNY uses the same mechanism, but it additionally uses an equal amount of XOR gates to add the tweak to the state, and so the number of XOR gates required to construct the roundkey addition layer is equal to that of any cipher employing full state addition.

In Table 12, we compare the hardware performances of GIFT with other lightweight ciphers. In Fig. 4 we list the individual area requirements of the respective components in GIFT.

We see that GIFT has the smallest area compared to the other ciphers. From the pie chart, we see that the storage area (which is a fixed cost) took up most of the area percentage, the cipher component (which is the variable) only make up a small percentage to the overall area.

Table 12. Comparison of performance metrics for round based implementations synthesized with STM 90 nm Standard cell library

	Area (GE)	Delay (ns)	Cycles	TP_{MAX} (MBit/s)	Power (μW) (@10 MHz)	Energy (pJ)
GIFT-64-128	1345	1.83	29	1249.0	74.8	216.9
SKINNY-64-128	1477	1.84	37	966.2	80.3	297.0
PRESENT 64/128	1560	1.63	33	1227.0	71.1	234.6
SIMON 64/128	1458	1.83	45	794.8	72.7	327.3
MIDORI 64	1542	2.06	17	1941.7	60.6	103.0
PICCOLO 64/128[a]	1868	2.32	32	889.9	79.4	254.1
RECTANGLE 64/128	1637	1.61	27	1472.2	76.2	206.0
LED 64/128	1831	5.25	50	243.8	131.3	656.5
GIFT-128-128	1997	1.85	41	1729.7	116.6	478.1
SKINNY-128-128	2104	1.85	41	1729.7	132.5	543.3
SIMON 128/128	2064	1.87	69	1006.6	105.6	728.6
MIDORI 128	2522	2.25	21	2844.4	89.2	187.3
AES128	7215	3.83	11	3038.2	730.3	803.3

([a] Piccolo implemented in dynamic key mode)

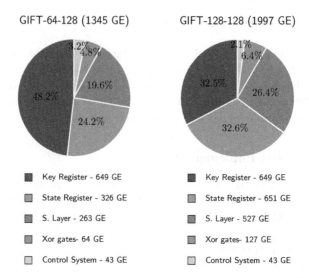

Fig. 4. Componentwise area requirements for GIFT-64-128 and GIFT-128-128

5.2   Serial Implementation

The serial implementation of GIFT-64-128 uses a mixed datapath of size 4 bits on the stateside and 16 bits on the keyside. The architecture has been explained in Fig. 5.

GIFT-128-128 uses a similar architecture: a mixture of 4 bit datapath in the stateside and a 32 bit datapath on the keyside is employed. We also implemented bit serial versions of GIFT as per the techniques outlined in [24]. In Table 13, we

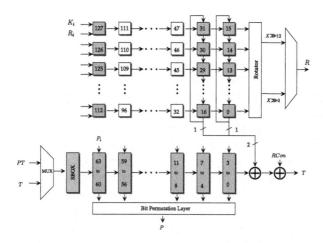

Fig. 5. Serial Implementation for GIFT-64-128 (The boxes in green denote scan flip-flops/registers)

Table 13. Comparison of performance metrics for serial implementations synthesized with STM 90 nm Standard cell library

	Degree of Serialization	Area (GE)	Delay (ns)	Cycles	TP$_{MAX}$ (MBit/s)	Power (μW) (@10 MHz)	Energy (nJ)
GIFT-64-128	4/16	1113	2.14	522	57.3	39.0	2.04
GIFT-64-128	1	930	2.67	2816	8.5	35.9	10.11
SKINNY-64-128	4	1265	1.73	756	48.9	59.2	4.48
SKINNY-64-128	1	887	0.98	3152	20.7	42.6	13.42
PRESENT 64/128	4	1158	1.94	576	57.3	58.0	3.34
SIMON 64/128	1	794	1.10	1536	37.9	44.7	6.87
LED 64/128	4	1225	2.54	1904	13.2	49.8	9.48
GIFT-128-128	4/32	1455	2.25	714	79.7	61.7	4.40
GIFT-128-128	1	1213	2.46	6528	8.0	40.3	26.30
SKINNY-128-128	8	1638	1.95	840	78.1	79.1	6.64
SKINNY-128-128	1	1110	0.81	6976	22.7	53.8	37.53
SIMON 128/128	1	1077	1.17	4480	25.1	60.5	27.10
AES 128[a]	8	2060	5.79	246	88.6	129.7	3.19

([a] AES implementation figures from [3])

list the performance comparisons of GIFT with other block ciphers. While the bit serial implementation of Simon is probably the most compact due to the nature of the design, but the performance of GIFT is comparable/better with other ciphers with similar level of serialization.

6   Software Implementation

In this section, we describe our software implementation of GIFT-64 and GIFT-128. Due to its inherent bitslice structure, it seems natural to consider that the most efficient software implementations of GIFTwill be bitslice implementations.

We leave the details of the packing/unpacking of the data and round function implementation in the full version.

Benchmarks. We have produced this bitslice implementation for AVX2 registers and we give in Table 14 the benchmarking results on a computer with a Intel Haswell processor (i5-4460U). We have benchmarked the bitslice implementations of SIMON and SKINNY (available online) on the same computer for fairness.

Comments. Bitslice implementations can be used for any parallel mode (as it is the case for most modern operating modes), but can also be used for serial modes when several users are communicating in parallel. In this setting, the

Table 14. Bitslice software implementations of GIFT and other lightweight block ciphers. Performances are given in cycles per byte, with messages composed of 2000 64-bit blocks to obtain the results.

Cipher	Speed (c/B)	Ref.	Cipher	Speed (c/B)	Ref.
GIFT-64-128	2.10	new	GIFT-128-128	2.57	new
SKINNY-64-128	2.88	[27]	SKINNY-128-128	4.70	[27]
SIMON-64-128	1.74	[43]	SIMON-128-128	2.55	[43]

implementation would be exactly the same, as our key preparation does not assume that the keys have to be the same for all blocks. In the scenario of a serial mode for a single user, then a classical table-based or VPERM implementation will probably be the most efficient option [6].

For low-end micro-controllers, it is very likely that GIFT will perform very well on this platform. RECTANGLE is very good on micro-controllers and GIFT shares the same general strategy on this regard. The key schedule being even simpler, we believe that it will actually perform even better than RECTANGLE.

Acknowledgements. The authors would like to thank the anonymous referees for their helpful comments. This work is partly supported by the Singapore National Research Foundation Fellowship 2012 (NRF-NRFF2012-06).

References

1. Aoki, K., Sasaki, Y.: Preimage attacks on one-block MD4, 63-step MD5 and more. In: Avanzi, R.M., Keliher, L., Sica, F. (eds.) SAC 2008. LNCS, vol. 5381, pp. 103–119. Springer, Heidelberg (2009). doi:10.1007/978-3-642-04159-4_7
2. Banik, S., Bogdanov, A., Isobe, T., Shibutani, K., Hiwatari, H., Akishita, T., Regazzoni, F.: Midori: a block cipher for low energy. In: Iwata, T., Cheon, J.H. (eds.) ASIACRYPT 2015. LNCS, vol. 9453, pp. 411–436. Springer, Heidelberg (2015). doi:10.1007/978-3-662-48800-3_17
3. Banik, S., Bogdanov, A., Regazzoni, F.: Atomic-AES v 2.0. Cryptology ePrint Archive, Report 2016/1005 (2016)
4. Beaulieu, R., Shors, D., Smith, J., Treatman-Clark, S., Weeks, B., Wingers, L.: The SIMON and SPECK Families of Lightweight Block Ciphers. Cryptology ePrint Archive, Report 2013/404 (2013)
5. Beierle, C., Jean, J., Kölbl, S., Leander, G., Moradi, A., Peyrin, T., Sasaki, Y., Sasdrich, P., Sim, S.M.: The SKINNY family of block ciphers and its low-latency variant MANTIS. In: Robshaw, M., Katz, J. (eds.) CRYPTO 2016. LNCS, vol. 9815, pp. 123–153. Springer, Heidelberg (2016). doi:10.1007/978-3-662-53008-5_5
6. Benadjila, R., Guo, J., Lomné, V., Peyrin, T.: Implementing lightweight block ciphers on x86 architectures. In: Lange, T., Lauter, K., Lisoněk, P. (eds.) SAC 2013. LNCS, vol. 8282, pp. 324–351. Springer, Heidelberg (2014). doi:10.1007/978-3-662-43414-7_17

7. Biham, E., Anderson, R., Knudsen, L.: Serpent: a new block cipher proposal. In: Vaudenay, S. (ed.) FSE 1998. LNCS, vol. 1372, pp. 222–238. Springer, Heidelberg (1998). doi:10.1007/3-540-69710-1_15

8. Biham, E., Biryukov, A., Shamir, A.: Cryptanalysis of Skipjack reduced to 31 rounds using impossible differentials. J. Cryptology **18**(4), 291–311 (2005)

9. Biham, E., Shamir, A.: Differential cryptanalysis of DES-like cryptosystems. In: Menezes, A.J., Vanstone, S.A. (eds.) CRYPTO 1990. LNCS, vol. 537, pp. 2–21. Springer, Heidelberg (1991). doi:10.1007/3-540-38424-3_1

10. Blondeau, C., Nyberg, K.: Links between truncated differential and multidimensional linear properties of block ciphers and underlying attack complexities. In: Nguyen, P.Q., Oswald, E. (eds.) EUROCRYPT 2014. LNCS, vol. 8441, pp. 165–182. Springer, Heidelberg (2014). doi:10.1007/978-3-642-55220-5_10

11. Bogdanov, A., Knežević, M., Leander, G., Toz, D., Varıcı, K., Verbauwhede, I.: SPONGENT: a lightweight hash function. In: Preneel, B., Takagi, T. (eds.) CHES 2011. LNCS, vol. 6917, pp. 312–325. Springer, Heidelberg (2011). doi:10.1007/978-3-642-23951-9_21

12. Bogdanov, A., Knudsen, L.R., Leander, G., Paar, C., Poschmann, A., Robshaw, M.J.B., Seurin, Y., Vikkelsoe, C.: PRESENT: an ultra-lightweight block cipher. In: Paillier, P., Verbauwhede, I. (eds.) CHES 2007. LNCS, vol. 4727, pp. 450–466. Springer, Heidelberg (2007). doi:10.1007/978-3-540-74735-2_31

13. Bogdanov, A., Rechberger, C.: A 3-subset meet-in-the-middle attack: cryptanalysis of the lightweight block cipher KTANTAN. In: Biryukov, A., Gong, G., Stinson, D.R. (eds.) SAC 2010. LNCS, vol. 6544, pp. 229–240. Springer, Heidelberg (2011). doi:10.1007/978-3-642-19574-7_16

14. Cannière, C.D.: Analysis and Design of Symmetric Encryption Algorithms. Ph.D thesis, Katholieke Universiteit Leuven Bart Preneel (promotor) (2007)

15. Cannière, C., Dunkelman, O., Knežević, M.: KATAN and KTANTAN — a family of small and efficient hardware-oriented block ciphers. In: Clavier, C., Gaj, K. (eds.) CHES 2009. LNCS, vol. 5747, pp. 272–288. Springer, Heidelberg (2009). doi:10.1007/978-3-642-04138-9_20

16. Chaum, D., Evertse, J.-H.: Cryptanalysis of des with a reduced number of rounds. In: Williams, H.C. (ed.) CRYPTO 1985. LNCS, vol. 218, pp. 192–211. Springer, Heidelberg (1986). doi:10.1007/3-540-39799-X_16

17. Cho, J.Y.: Linear cryptanalysis of reduced-round PRESENT. In: Pieprzyk, J. (ed.) CT-RSA 2010. LNCS, vol. 5985, pp. 302–317. Springer, Heidelberg (2010). doi:10.1007/978-3-642-11925-5_21

18. Daemen, J., Rijmen, V.: The Design of Rijndael: AES - The Advanced Encryption Standard. Springer, Heidelberg (2002)

19. Ferguson, N., Kelsey, J., Lucks, S., Schneier, B., Stay, M., Wagner, D., Whiting, D.: Improved cryptanalysis of rijndael. In: Goos, G., Hartmanis, J., Leeuwen, J., Schneier, B. (eds.) FSE 2000. LNCS, vol. 1978, pp. 213–230. Springer, Heidelberg (2001). doi:10.1007/3-540-44706-7_15

20. Guo, J., Jean, J., Nikolic, I., Qiao, K., Sasaki, Y., Sim, S.: Invariant subspace attack against midori64 and the resistance criteria for s-box designs. IACR Trans. Symmetric Cryptology **2016**(1), 33–56 (2016)

21. Guo, J., Peyrin, T., Poschmann, A.: The PHOTON family of lightweight hash functions. In: Rogaway, P. (ed.) CRYPTO 2011. LNCS, vol. 6841, pp. 222–239. Springer, Heidelberg (2011). doi:10.1007/978-3-642-22792-9_13

22. Guo, J., Peyrin, T., Poschmann, A., Robshaw, M.: The LED block cipher. In: Preneel, B., Takagi, T. (eds.) CHES 2011. LNCS, vol. 6917, pp. 326–341. Springer, Heidelberg (2011). doi:10.1007/978-3-642-23951-9_22. [35]

23. Jean, J., Peyrin, T., Sim, S.M.: Optimizing implementations of lightweight building blocks. Cryptology ePrint Archive, Report 2017/101 (2017)
24. Jean, J., Moradi, A., Peyrin, T., Sasdrich, P.: Bit-Sliding: A Generic Technique for Bit-Serial Implementations of SPN-based Primitives. In: To appear in Cryptographic Hardware and Embedded Systems - CHES 2017 - Taipei, Taiwan, 25–28 September 2017
25. Knudsen, L.: Deal - a 128-bit block cipher. NIST AES Proposal (1998)
26. Knudsen, L., Wagner, D.: Integral cryptanalysis. In: Daemen, J., Rijmen, V. (eds.) FSE 2002. LNCS, vol. 2365, pp. 112–127. Springer, Heidelberg (2002). doi:10.1007/3-540-45661-9_9
27. Kölbl, S.: AVX implementation of the Skinny block cipher (2016). https://github.com/kste/skinny_avx
28. Leander, G., Abdelraheem, M.A., AlKhzaimi, H., Zenner, E.: A cryptanalysis of PRINTCIPHER: the invariant subspace attack. In: Rogaway, P. (ed.) CRYPTO 2011. LNCS, vol. 6841, pp. 206–221. Springer, Heidelberg (2011). doi:10.1007/978-3-642-22792-9_12
29. Leander, G., Minaud, B., Rønjom, S.: A generic approach to invariant subspace attacks: cryptanalysis of robin, iSCREAM and zorro. In: Oswald, E., Fischlin, M. (eds.) EUROCRYPT 2015. LNCS, vol. 9056, pp. 254–283. Springer, Heidelberg (2015). doi:10.1007/978-3-662-46800-5_11
30. Leander, G., Poschmann, A.: On the classification of 4 bit S-boxes. In: Carlet, C., Sunar, B. (eds.) WAIFI 2007. LNCS, vol. 4547, pp. 159–176. Springer, Heidelberg (2007). doi:10.1007/978-3-540-73074-3_13
31. Matsui, M.: Linear cryptanalysis method for DES cipher. In: Helleseth, T. (ed.) EUROCRYPT 1993. LNCS, vol. 765, pp. 386–397. Springer, Heidelberg (1994). doi:10.1007/3-540-48285-7_33
32. Nakahara, J.: 3D: a three-dimensional block cipher. In: Franklin, M.K., Hui, L.C.K., Wong, D.S. (eds.) CANS 2008. LNCS, vol. 5339, pp. 252–267. Springer, Heidelberg (2008). doi:10.1007/978-3-540-89641-8_18
33. National Institute of Standards and Technology: Fips 180–2: Secure hash standard. http://csrc.nist.gov
34. National Institute of Standards and Technology: Lightweight cryptography (2016). https://www.nist.gov/programs-projects/lightweight-cryptography
35. Preneel, B., Takagi, T. (eds.): CHES 2011. LNCS, vol. 6917. Springer, Heidelberg (2011)
36. Saarinen, M.-J.O.: Cryptographic analysis of all 4×4-bit S-boxes. In: Miri, A., Vaudenay, S. (eds.) SAC 2011. LNCS, vol. 7118, pp. 118–133. Springer, Heidelberg (2012). doi:10.1007/978-3-642-28496-0_7
37. Sasaki, Y., Aoki, K.: Finding preimages in full MD5 faster than exhaustive search. In: Joux, A. (ed.) EUROCRYPT 2009. LNCS, vol. 5479, pp. 134–152. Springer, Heidelberg (2009). doi:10.1007/978-3-642-01001-9_8
38. Sasaki, Y., Todo, Y.: New impossible differential search tool from design and cryptanalysis aspects. In: Coron, J.-S., Nielsen, J.B. (eds.) EUROCRYPT 2017. LNCS, vol. 10212, pp. 185–215. Springer, Cham (2017). doi:10.1007/978-3-319-56617-7_7
39. Shibutani, K., Isobe, T., Hiwatari, H., Mitsuda, A., Akishita, T., Shirai, T.: Piccolo: an ultra-lightweight blockcipher. In: Preneel, B., Takagi, T. (eds.) CHES 2011. LNCS, vol. 6917, pp. 342–357. Springer, Heidelberg (2011). doi:10.1007/978-3-642-23951-9_23. [35]
40. Todo, Y.: Structural evaluation by generalized integral property. In: Oswald, E., Fischlin, M. (eds.) EUROCRYPT 2015. LNCS, vol. 9056, pp. 287–314. Springer, Heidelberg (2015). doi:10.1007/978-3-662-46800-5_12

41. Todo, Y., Leander, G., Sasaki, Y.: Nonlinear invariant attack. In: Cheon, J.H., Takagi, T. (eds.) ASIACRYPT 2016. LNCS, vol. 10032, pp. 3–33. Springer, Heidelberg (2016). doi:10.1007/978-3-662-53890-6_1

42. Todo, Y., Morii, M.: Bit-based division property and application to SIMON family. In: Peyrin, T. (ed.) FSE 2016. LNCS, vol. 9783, pp. 357–377. Springer, Heidelberg (2016). doi:10.1007/978-3-662-52993-5_18

43. Wingers, L.: Software for SUPERCOP benchmarking of SIMON and SPECK (2015). https://github.com/lrwinge/simon_speck_supercop

44. Zhang, W., Bao, Z., Lin, D., Rijmen, V., Yang, B., Verbauwhede, I.: Rectangle: a bit-slice lightweight block cipher suitable for multiple platforms. Sci. China Inf. Sci. **58**(12), 1–15 (2015)

Making Password Authenticated Key Exchange Suitable for Resource-Constrained Industrial Control Devices

Björn Haase[(⊠)] and Benoît Labrique

Endress + Hauser Conducta GmbH & Co. KG,
Dieselstr. 24, 70839 Gerlingen, Germany
Bjoern.Haase@conducta.endress.com

Abstract. Connectivity becomes increasingly important also for small embedded systems such as typically found in industrial control installations. More and more use-cases require secure remote user access increasingly incorporating handheld based human machine interfaces, using wireless links such as Bluetooth. Correspondingly secure operator authentication becomes of utmost importance. Unfortunately, often passwords with all their well-known pitfalls remain the only practical mechanism.

We present an assessment of the security requirements for the industrial setting, illustrating that offline attacks on passwords-based authentication protocols should be considered a significant threat. Correspondingly use of a Password Authenticated Key Exchange protocol becomes desirable. We review the significant challenges faced for implementations on resource-constrained devices.

We explore the design space and shown how we succeeded in tailoring a particular variant of the Password Authenticated Connection Establishment (PACE) protocol, such that acceptable user interface responsiveness was reached even for the constrained setting of an ARM Cortex-M0+ based Bluetooth low-energy transceiver running from a power budget of 1.5 mW without notable energy buffers for covering power peak transients.

Keywords: PAKE · ARM Cortex-M0 · Curve25519 · ECDH · PACE · Curve25519 · ECDH key-exchange · Elliptic-curve cryptography · Embedded devices · Elligator · Process industry · Bluetooth · Curve19119 · X19119 · Bluetooth low energy

1 Introduction and Motivation

Connectivity becomes increasingly important also for small microcontroller-based embedded systems found in industrial control installations, such as so-called field devices. More and more use-cases require secure remote user access, e.g. for maintenance and configuration involving subsystems such as industrial control units and home automation electronics. Increasingly smart phones or tablet computers are used as handheld units providing the Human Machine Interface (HMI). The continuously growing Internet of Things will only add to this development.

© International Association for Cryptologic Research 2017
W. Fischer and N. Homma (Eds.): CHES 2017, LNCS 10529, pp. 346–364, 2017.
DOI: 10.1007/978-3-319-66787-4_17

It is of great interest to provide efficient cryptographic primitives and protocols suitable also for the resource-constrained embedded CPUs typically employed in these environments. In most applications, user authentication by use of iris scanners, fingerprint analysis or based on smart cards is unfortunately not practical. On the other hand, implanted identification chips are already in wide-spread use, but mainly in the context of production animals and for some specific reason rather not for human operators.

In many circumstances, the old-fashioned password remains the only practical means for authentication of human operators. We presume that frequently the crucial weakness of the security solution is the password-based authentication protocol, namely if the protocol exposes the password to offline dictionary attacks. Astonishingly weak challenge-response-type protocols seem still to be in wide-spread use in many critical systems.

In the context of resource-constrained devices and password authentication, the aspect of efficiency becomes of utmost importance, since the computational complexity directly translates into the delay experienced by the user during the login procedure.

This article summarizes the results of research implemented in the context of securing a Bluetooth-low-energy based human-machine-interface for an industrial field device hardware.

Contribution of this work. The contribution of this work is threefold.

- We present the result of our review of PAKE protocols from the perspective of efficient implementations in small microcontrollers.
- We explore the design space for efficient implementations of one option, the PACE protocol family, considering Weierstrass curves as well as more recently suggested Montgomery or Edwards curves.
- We provide experimental results for implementations on an ARM Cortex M0+ for both, 128 and 96 bit security level.

Note regarding side-channel protection
All of the software presented in this paper avoids secret-data dependent branches and is, thus, inherently protected against timing attacks on targets for which instruction duration does not depend on the value of operands.

2 Organization of This Paper

This paper is organized as follows. First in Sect. 3 the reader is given a review of the security requirements for operator authentication in industrial control installations.

In Sect. 4 properties of different PAKE protocols are reviewed from the perspective of suitability for resource-constrained industrial control devices. As a result of this analysis the PACE protocol family suggested by Bender, Kügler and Fischlin [1] was assessed to be particularly well adapted.

In Sect. 5 the specific particularities of the PACE protocol are reviewed and the most important points with respect to efficiency are analyzed.

The subsequent Sect. 6 considers issues that show up when trying to specifically tailor the PACE protocol for the constrained setting. Optimization for efficiency includes selection of a suitable finite field used for the elliptic curve point group, a suitable elliptic curve and a matching choice of symmetric primitives.

In Sect. 7 we introduce a new Montgomery curve "Curve19119" for a legacy security level.

In Sect. 8 we describe the specific tailoring chosen for PACE in the experiments and describe our optimization strategy.

Section 9 combines both, presentation of the experimental results and comparison with other related work.

3   Security Requirements and Implementation Constraints

In industrial control installation it is common to wire many so-called field devices still by using a purely analogue interface, e.g. encoding measurement values in a current ranging from 4...20 mA. This holds even in 2017. Depending on the installation up to 90% of the instrumentation does not use any digital data transmission. This is an advantage regarding security.

Field devices often have to withstand high temperatures and humidity. One consequence is that the user interface often only allows for a few buttons and one line of LCD, not providing good usability for the operators.

This is one motivation for integrating wireless interfaces based on standards such as Bluetooth 4.0 low energy. Wireless access allows for comfort by referring the graphical user interface to a powerful handheld unit. Unfortunately many wireless standards were originally not designed for the security requirements in industry plants, where manipulation of the integrity of one single field device might result in explosions or other severe damage. Note that, for instance, the security layer of Bluetooth low energy 4.0 is not providing any protection against a passive eavesdropper! Providing protection is difficult, since any simple challenge-response protocol exposes the passwords to the risk of offline attacks.

Field devices also often face the requirement of having to be intrinsically safe with respect to the risk of explosions, for instance when used on refineries. Most strategies for intrinsic safety base on circuit-designs that limit peak currents, peak voltages and the amount of energy in buffers like capacitors or batteries. The limitation guarantees that ignition of explosive gas or dust becomes impossible. As a consequence a large portion of so-called "2-wire" field devices has to operate from 15mW to 30mW functional power for its full operation. Note that this power is constantly available but cannot be exceeded transiently since intrinsically safe barriers and interfaces prevent that any more current will be delivered. If circuitry needs transients, e.g. for a measurement circuit, this needs to be buffered locally.

An important aspect in the context of this paper is the limitation of the actual size of the energy buffers, since levels sufficient for triggering an ignition must be prevented. Batteries often may not be integrated due to the continuous maintenance requirement and the temperature rating. A typical value for the energy stored in buffer capacitors for transients is in the range of several mJ only. Note that most of the transient buffer will be allocated for the main functionality of the field device and only a small fraction will be made available for wireless transmission or for complex calculations. The algorithms and protocol implementations need to have both in mind, low power consumption on average and limited energy buffers for covering transients.

4 Review of PAKE Protocols from the Perspective of Resource-Constrained Devices

Since the initial pioneer papers from Bellovin, S.M. and M. Merritt [2] regarding key generation based on weak "user memorable" (i.e. low entropy) passwords extensive literature is available regarding the basic problem. Protocols typically are referred to by use of acronyms such as EKE [8], SPEKE [9], SRP [10], PACE [1], PAK [11, 15], AMP [7, 12] and AugPAKE [13, 16]. Many of these base on the framework of Diffie-Hellman key exchange [14].

At a first glance a plethora of protocol candidates needs to be considered for the setting of field devices. A closer look, however, exposes that unfortunately most of the protocols suggested are to be considered impractical for this setting. For applications in extremely resource-constrained devices the most suitable algorithm subset must not make use of multiplicative group operations, such that using elliptic curves becomes possible.

This special subgroup of PAKE protocols seems to be particularly difficult to construct correctly. Many protocols have been shown to be insecure. We assessed only a small subset of more carefully analyzed protocols such as AugPAKE [13, 16] or PACE [1] to be good candidates. To make matters worse, an additional aspect to consider is the issue of pending patents on protocols or efficient implementation of algorithmic sub-steps. In particular a patent applications for the AugPAKE [13, 16] protocol does apply under US020110145579A1. As a result our further analysis did concentrate on PACE [1].

5 Review of the Password-Authenticated Connection Establishment (PACE) Protocol

The PACE protocol designed by Bender, Kügler and Fischlin [1, 18] might actually rather be considered to form a tailorable family of protocols involving different steps that allow for specific implementation choices. E.g. it may be implemented on large-characteristic fields as well as on groups defined by points on elliptic curves. Correspondingly in the security analysis of the protocol [1] four alternative variants of the Map2Point sub-step of the protocol were suggested. The PACE protocol family assumes that a cyclic finite group of a large order, such as provided by points on an elliptic curve, is available. In the protocol basically four different sub-steps may be distinguished (see also Fig. 2 and 3 in [1] for the specific definitions).

- In a first step a random number "s" is exchanged between the two parties by use of purely symmetric cryptographic primitives and the weak shared secret (password) as key. It is the objective of the subsequent protocol steps to verify that both sides initiate the PACE protocol run by using the same "s" value without exposing any information on its actual value to passive or active attackers.

- In a second step of each protocol run the two parties interactively agree on a session-specific generator of the group: G = Map2Point(s). This involves usage of symmetric and asymmetric primitives and exchange of one or more messages.
- In a third step, the two parties implement a conventional Diffie-Hellman protocol for agreeing on a shared session secret by use of the session-specific generator G.
- Subsequently, in the last step, exchange of conventional authentication code messages being derived from the shared Diffie-Hellman secret are used for mutually proving that both parties share the same secret. The session key is also derived from the Diffie-Hellman result.

Efficiency analysis of PACE. With respect to computational efficiency one may neglect the computational complexity of the symmetric primitives altogether. The two dominant components within the protocol are the Map2Point sub-step and the shared secret generation by the Diffie-Hellman sub-step.

The Diffie-Hellman step in PACE works with a generator base point G that varies in each protocol execution. This implies that optimizations possible for fixed base point algorithms could not be used.

The most important factor for an efficient implementation of the PACE protocol is actually the efficiency of the Map2Point protocol sub-step. In [1] four distinct alternatives have been analyzed.

The DH2Point algorithm as used by the German government authority BSI for the German identiy card requires the equivalent of two fixed and one variable point exponentiation, possibly for patent circumvention. A very similar option is the Coin2Point alternative which is trading off a scalar multiplication against an additional message exchange.

The computational complexity may be significantly reduced if a so-called integrated mapping [27] (in [1] referred to as hash to curve h2c operation) algorithm is available for the selected curve. Such an operation maps an arbitrarily chosen scalar number to a point on the elliptic curve. Fortunately constant-time algorithms for efficient integrated mapping are available for many curves. For examples see [3, 4, 28] and references cited therein, notably the so-called Shallue-Woestijne-Ulas (SWU) algorithm. The possible performance benefit of integrated mapping is large since the order of magnitude of efficient integrated mapping algorithms accounts roughly for two field inversions only and is thus only a small fraction of two exponentiations [28].

6   Tailoring of PACE for Resource-Constrained Devices

Tailoring of PACE for an embedded target should best cover all relevant levels within the implementation pyramid: Choice of a suitable finite field, a suitable finite group, etc. In this section we focus on the asymmetric operations since they dominate the computational effort.

Giving our final result at the very beginning, we conclude that best efficiency regarding all aspects might be obtained by using Montgomery or Edwards curves such as Curve25519 constructed over fields with special primes of the form $2^n - m$ and Elligator2 as part of the Map2Point protocol.

In this paper we aim not only at presenting our final result. We also would like to present the reasoning why other approaches had been discarded in our industry setting. We also aim at giving our rough estimates regarding their respective performance disadvantages. For some applications actual implementations might be forced to use specific algorithms that might not best suited from a performance perspective and also a rough assessment might prove helpful.

6.1 Choosing the Field

Despite some impressing results for binary fields (see e.g. [6]) also on architectures such as the ARM Cortex M0, the more complex security story of constructions on top of binary extension fields [34–36] lead us to focus on prime fields quite early.

Assessment of Performance for random prime fields. We did shortly assess the penalty to expect for random primes (such as used by the Brainpool group [17, 21]) and came to the conclusion that for the 128 bit security level on a small 32 bit CPU like the ARM Cortex M0 roughly a factor of ~ 2.75 should be expected for multiplications and a factor of ~ 4 for squarings. This stems from the observation that the cost for one fully optimized Karatsuba multiplication and half a textbook multiplication for Montgomery reduction makes multiply and square operations almost equally expensive. According to our analysis the possible performance gain for the 1/2 multiplication in Montgomery reduction is almost compensated for by losing the possibility of employing the Karatsuba stages that proved highly beneficial in [5].

Assessment of Performance for the Solinas prime [23] for P-256. A very rough assessment of the potential of the Solinas prime for P-256 leads us to the expectation that the larger number of additions and conditional moves during the reduction being expensive to implement in constant time accounts for a penalty in the range of some 10% … 30% for multiply and square operations in comparison to the optimized Curve25519 prime field implementation from [5]. We expect penalties for addition and subtraction to be somewhat larger. They might reach even +100% since the nice feature of the additional "carry bit" in the last 32 bit word available for Curve25519 is missing. In our opinion this is one of the factors leading to the speed difference factor of 3 when comparing Curve25519 [5] and P-256 [26].

6.2 Selection of Appropriate Elliptic Curve Groups

Selection of appropriate elliptic curve groups impacts efficiency directly and indirectly by a number of parameters, having both, technical and legal origin, such as pending intellectual property rights. The latter aspect is of major importance for all industrial applications. Specifically industrial control devices typically are designed for world-wide installation and already the complex handling of external licenses or the mere theoretical risk of intellectual property right conflicts in a single country typically force implementers to search for circumvention approaches.

In the context of the PACE protocol family one of the major efficiency parameters is linked to the Map2Point sub-step, specifically the availability of an integrated mapping primitive.

For the NIST standard P-256 with p mod 4 == 3 SWU could be used. Unfortunately part of this algorithm seems to be covered by patents.

This drew our attention to a second set of candidate curves, specifically more recent Edwards or Montgomery curves such as Curve25519 [29]. Curve25519 has recently been standardized by ITEF [22] and independently found to be particularly suitable for the Cortex M0 by a group at the company ARM itself [25]. Moreover a patent-free mapping algorithm, Elligator2, is available [4]. For Curve25519, as a side-effect of the original design goal of avoiding secret-dependent table lookups in [29] highly efficient algorithms are available without facing penalties for variable base point scalar multiplications and with a small memory footprint.

6.3   Tailoring on the Protocol Level

The by far most important parameter on the PACE protocol level for efficiency is the choice of the Map2Point primitive. When choosing Montgomery curves as a basis, Elligator 2 is the natural choice.

When using Coin2Point for patent circumvention the complexity of PACE is roughly doubled. Note that the penalty might even be larger since the requirement of calculating full additions, precludes more memory efficient and possibly faster approaches working on x-coordinate-only point representations.

6.4   Exploring the Potential of Reduced Security Parameters

Use of a legacy-level curve for PACE might very well be appropriate, however we think that going below the 96 bit security level might not be advisable. Also we would only recommend this for a setting where sessions are short and compromised confidentiality due to lost forward security is not critical. Note that this could possibly be considered the case for some industry installations where the integrity is the main target and confidentiality is often considered to form a target of a somewhat reduced priority. We would recommend reducing security parameters only in case that the alternative would be to be thrown back to challenge-response protocols.

7   Curve19119: A Little Brother of Curve25519

Due to the high computational complexity of PAKE protocols we aimed at exploring the performance gain for a legacy security parameter. Unlike the situation for conventional Weierstrass curves there seem to be no established Montgomery curves for a security of say 80 or 96 bits. For this reason we designed a new curve using a field based on the 191 bit prime $2^{191}-19$. We refer to the curve and the associated Diffie-Hellman x-coordinate-only protocol by the acronyms Curve19119 and X19119 respectively.

Curve19119 was constructed following almost the same rigid requirement set as used for Curve25519, however for the prime $2^{191}-19$. The single exception in the construction prescription is that we imposed the additional constraint on the curve parameter "A" that "A + 2" shall be a square. Note that this allows for application of the most efficient Hisil-Wong-Carter-Dawson [20] point addition formula in extended coordinates for the isomorphic Edwards curve. Just as for Curve25519 the Montgomery curve equation reads

$$y^2 = x^3 + A x^2 + x \tag{1}$$

with A = 528418 and the base point x = 11. The candidate A = 922 has been ruled out due to the group order being smaller than $2^{(191-3)}$.

The group order of Curve19119 is 8 (2^{188} + 680582284250681071959223527) with a secure near-prime order quadratic twist. Note that actually a very similar curve with A = 281742 was suggested by Diego F. Aranha et al. [19]. This other curve, in contrast to the Curve19119 presented here, does not allow for the more efficient point addition in extended coordinates.

8 Putting It Together: PACE on the ARM Cortex M0

In the following paragraphs we will present our specific choices and elaborate on our optimization strategy. The full protocol overview of our implementation is given in Fig. 1 and uses mostly terminology from [1]. Note that the task of generating fresh entropy for random number generation is a crucial aspect but due to its complexity out of the scope of this paper. We implemented the full protocol with Curve25519. For Curve19119 we only aimed at being able to assess the performance gain and restricted the implementation effort to the most expensive component, the X19119 Diffie-Hellman part.

According to our target security level in the protocol, we take 128 bit random numbers for the values s and t and chose a 64 bit nonce n for Salsa20-20.

Review of the ARM Cortex M0 microcontroller architecture. The ARM Cortex M0 and M0+ cores (M0) are the smallest members of ARM's Cortex-M series targeting low-cost and low-power embedded devices. The important feature with respect to asymmetric cryptography operation is the 32 bit x 32 bit => 32 bit single cycle multiplier engine available in virtually all actual instances. Previous research [5] has shown that one of the key bottlenecks for efficiency is register pressure in conjunction with a comparably slow memory interface (von Neumann-Architecture with a shared address and data bus).

8.1 Symmetric Encryption

For both, random number generation and symmetric encryption we made use of Salsa20-20 [32]. We selected the conservative 20 rounds variant because the amount of payload to encrypt is small and efficiency considerations allow for the more

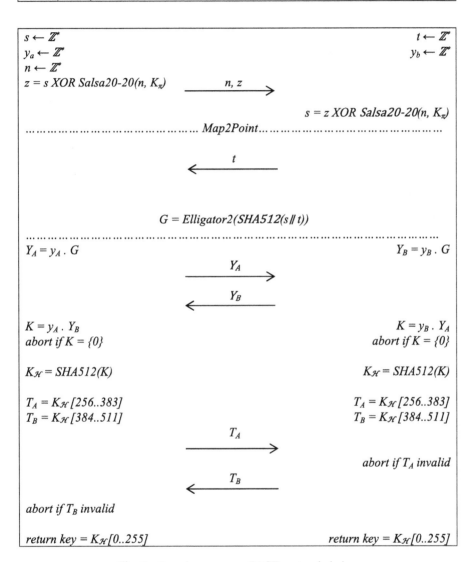

Fig. 1. Overview over our PACE protocol choices

conservative variant. We preferred Salsa20-20 because according to our assessment it was more extensively reviewed, specifically as part of the eSTREAM project than other candidates, such as Speck or Simon [33]. This choice also avoided considerations regarding cache timing attacks on the smart phone implementation for the client.

Assembly optimization strategy. The most important identified weakness of the M0 is the memory bandwidth. Luckily, the Salsa20 permutation runs in its inner loop on a set of four 32 bit words being permuted one after the other and, thus, fits into the register set. Also the 32 bit rotation operation requires only one single instruction on the M0 architecture. Our assembly code implementing the hsalsa20 permutation of the 64 byte input runs in 2628 cycles ($\sim$ 41.1 cycles/byte) and needs 404 bytes of program flash.

8.2   Cryptographic Hash

We selected SHA512. An advantage provided by using SHA512 was also that when hashing the shared secret of the Diffie-Hellman substep, the 512 bit result allowed for extracting all of, 256 bit session key and two 128 bit authentification verification messages from a single run. This avoided the need for implementing a specific symmetric message authentication code primitive.

Assembly optimization strategy. The main bottleneck for the SHA512 implementation is the fact that the small 32 bit register set of the M0 is by far too small for holding the intermediate state of the SHA512 subsystem. Also the 64 bit rotations require a large number of 32 bit shifts. The implementation is optimized for speed rather than code size by unrolling the inner loop completely. This results in a rather big memory footprint of 1448 Bytes. Hashing 10 bytes costs 22031 cycles on the M0 and for 2048 bytes of data we end up with an efficiency of 181.6 cycles per byte.

8.3   Point Verification for PACE

Both, Curve25519 and Curve19119 are of nearly prime order. Specifically, the group order is 8 times a prime. During the X25519 and X19119 scalar multiplication each of the weak points is mapped onto the neutral element and thus verification that a point is valid may be implemented subsequently by checking, after each point multiplication, that the result of the point multiplication differs from the neutral element. Insertion of a twist point does not provide the attacker any advantage according the security guarantees of X25519 and the identically constructed X19119.

8.4   Map2Point Protocol Substep

We use the Hash2Point procedure and Elligator2 as "h2c" function according to terminology from [1].

Elligator2. The implementation shares most arithmetic operations with the elliptic curve point multiplication. The most costly sub-steps are formed by one field inversion and one exponentiation with $2^{254} - 10$. Both of them are implemented in constant time by an exponentiation operation. For the exponentiation with $2^{254} - 10$ an important optimization goal was to reduce the number of temporary field elements. We came up with a solution needing 255 field squarings and 11 field multiplications.

8.5   Diffie-Hellman Protocol

Regarding Diffie-Hellman protocol, we implemented two variants, X25519 and X19119 in order to assess the potential of performance gain when reducing the security parameter from 128 bits to 96 bits.

Optimization for X25519. The optimized arithmetic on the prime field and the basic algorithm used for the X25519 protocol sub-steps is based on the strategy of [5]. We integrated only almost negligible improvements regarding the integer squaring operation. Differing from [5] we implement the conditional swap operation after each ladder step by swapping pointer variables instead of data. We expect slightly better performance and also a reduced side-channel leakage [24].

Optimization for X19119. In order to allow for a fair comparison between the legacy-level security curve Curve19119 and the highly optimized X25519 implementation from [5], an equivalent level of optimization was considered necessary. We followed the same approach that has been used as in [5]. Due to the almost identical structure of the curve construction, reduction, addition and subtraction algorithms could be re-used almost identically just as for the algorithms for the x-coordinate-only Montgomery ladder of X19119.

With respect to the optimization of Multiplication and Squaring, Curve19119 suffers from the penalty of less symmetry. For the prime $2^{255}-19$ a cascade of three refined Karatsuba stages could be used for mapping 256 bit multiplications to the 32×32 bit level in a symmetric cascade. This is possible because 256 is a power of two. For the prime $2^{191}-19$ our most efficient multiplication and squaring implementation first uses a refined Karatsuba stage for mapping 192 bit operations to 96 bit operations.

On the 96 bit level, squaring was split into a 64 bit squaring using one additional level of refined Karatsuba, two 32 bit multiplications and one 32 bit squaring. The 96 bit Multiplication correspondingly was mapped onto a 64 bit multiplication (implemented again with one level of refined Karatsuba) and 5 remaining 32 bit multiplications.

The lack of symmetry in comparison to the 256 bit case results in a slightly increased overhead due to additional memory accesses. This was only partially compensated for by reduced register pressure.

It is also worth noting that the Montgomery curve group constant "A" for Curve19119 is slightly less optimal than for Curve25519. For Curve25519 the small curve constant required within the Montgomery ladder calculations fits into 17 bits and multiplication could be implemented by using one addition and one 16 bit multiplication, while for Curve19119 18 bits length make two 16 bit multiplications necessary for each operand word.

8.6 Implementation Strategy Regarding Absence of Energy Buffers: Asynchronous Crypto Engine (ACE)

Due to the absence of large energy buffers in many field devices it turned out to be mandatory to setup a framework that allows for an "interrupt and resume" mode of operation in case of temporarily insufficient power resources.

For this reason all of the calculations of the protocol were implemented by an asynchronous crypto engine (ACE) object accounting for roughly ¾ of the PACE implementation effort. The ACE interfaces to the host application by accepting calculation tasks for complex operations and by generating an asynchronous "requested operation completed" event subsequently. The engine is periodically invoked from a power supervision system in case that the respective energy buffer charge level allows for a given number of CPU cycles to be allocated for cryptographic calculations. Details on the asynchronous calculation tasks will be given in the results section.

Note that the ACE object strategy also optimizes for stack requirements since the point within the source code where the actual calculation is triggered may be specifically chosen such that the call stack has only a low fill level.

9 Experimental Results and Discussion

In this section we will present experimental results of our implementations. We first give details regarding the hardware used for the experiments. Then we use a bottom-up approach for structuring the presentation of the results.

9.1 Environment Used for Collecting Experimental Data

The results reported here were measured on an nRF51822 microcontroller with integrated wireless transceiver from the company Nordic Semiconductors. This device includes a 32 bit ARM Cortex M0+ microcontroller, 256 kByte of flash memory and 16 kByte of RAM in addition to radio frequency circuitry suitable for the Bluetooth low energy protocol. Data flash and program memory access do not require wait states on this target platform. It does not include cache and, thus, RAM access timing does not depend on the actual address.

Specific properties of the target hardware platform. In the nRF51822 around 128/256 kByte of flash memory and 10/16 kByte of RAM memory are required alone for running the wireless protocol stack. Around 6 kByte of RAM are available for both, the communication application and security operations, both for static data and execution stack. In our setting first a Bluetooth connection is established, the PACE protocol messages are exchanged with a smart phone and the authentication calculations have to run while the wireless link is maintained. I.e. the client-side implementation of the protocol runs on a smart phone.

A particular property of the nRF51822 setting in Bluetooth operation is that the 16 MHz clock frequency cannot be divided down in small steps.

For this reason the CPU core is either "on" or "off" and consumes roughly 4.3 mA when running. Due to required operation in the industrial temperature range up to 85°C a supply voltage of 2 V is used, being larger than the necessary value for consumer temperatures. The value was obtained by current measurements for repeated X25519 protocol runs and takes into account some safety margin for process variations and current consumption increase at 85°C temperature.

In the given setting the M0 transceiver CPU interfaces to a main microcontroller of the control unit by use of a communication software layer using a serial interface. The main microcontroller of the control unit monitors the energy buffer state and allocates a certain amount of the available energy buffer budget to the Cortex M0 running the wireless interface and the security implementation.

Since the wireless interface for the HMI use-case is considered only to be an "add-on" feature most of the net functional power of 30 mW is allocated for the main field-device functionality. Only an amount of power of 1.5 mW is available for the M0 transceiver unit, a significant fraction of which being consumed by the RF receiver and transmitter unit and the Bluetooth protocol stack.

Cycle counts reported here were experimentally obtained by use of a hardware timer block in the nRF51822 controller. The cryptographic part of the software was compiled by use of the LLVM compiler with the settings recommended in [5].

9.2   Efficiency Results for Asymmetric Cryptography

Table 1 summarizes our results regarding synchronous execution of the asymmetric primitives for squaring, multiplication, addition and inversion. It also benchmarks the performance of X25519 and Curve25519 field operations against X19119 and Curve19119. The columns "*a24" and "*i16" refer to multiplication with the curve constant and a 16 bit integer respectively. The latter operation is implemented for a continuous re-randomization in projective coordinates as defense e.g. against horizontal attacks [30, 31] being out of the scope of the present paper and not activated for the X25519/X19119 speed measurements reported here.

Table 1. Cortex M0 cycle counts for prime field operations and a single point multiplication. All field operations include reduction modulo $2^{191} - 38$ and $2^{256} - 38$ respectively.

	x*x	x*y	x + y	1/x	* a24	* i16	½ ECDH
Curve19119	666	983	95	140568	144	119	1801856
Curve25519	985	1475	117	268281	190	145	3466086
relative factor	1.48	1.50	1.23	1.91	1.32	1.22	1.92

The column denoted "1/2 ECDH" refers to one run of the X25519/X19119 protocol respectively. The cycle count for X25519 is 50480 cycles lower in comparison to [5]. We expect that this is mainly due to the fact we made use of constant-time swaps of pointers by logic operations instead of swapping the full field elements as in [5].

The only other published report regarding efficiency for prime-field curves for the M0 that we are aware of is found in [26]. There 4.59 (10.73) million cycles were reported for an assembly-optimized NIST P-192 (P-256) scalar multiplication respectively. Our implementations for the M0 on the 96 bit and 128 bit security level are a factor of 2.55 and 3.1 faster respectively. We therefore assume that our implementation establishes a new speed record for an implementation for the 96 bit security level, with timing side-channel awareness. In our opinion the large difference stems mainly from the fact that the multiplication and squaring operation is much better optimized. A second important factor might be that the addition formulas for the Montgomery curve provide better performance than what is possible with P-192.

The cost of a synchronous execution of the Elligator2 algorithm costs 547338 cycles for Curve25519. We did not implement it for Curve19119, The operations required for Curve19119 are essentially the same as for Curve25519. The complexity is almost identical to two field inversions since the cost is dominated by the field squarings required by the exponentiation approach used for the constant-time algorithm. Therefore an improvement factor of equally 1.9 may be accurately predicted.

When comparing the efficiencies of X25519 and X19119, we come to the conclusion that roughly a speed improvement of 1.92 is possible for the legacy-level curve also on the PACE level.

9.3 Efficiency Figures Regarding the Asynchronous ACE Engine

The results for the most important performance figures regarding the asynchronized protocol engine are summarized in Table 2. The time values were calculated for the 16 MHz clock of our core and the energy values were calculated by using factors for the supply voltage of 2 V and the drawn current of 4.3 mA.

Table 2. Results for the asynchronized ACE protocol engine

Suboperation	Cycle count	Time	Energy/μJ
X25519 ladder step	13,486	843 μs	7.2
Elligator step "v"	271,061	16.9 ms	145.7
Elligator step "epsilon"	276,291	17.3 ms	148.5
Field inversion	268,289	16.8 ms	144.2
Short SHA512 block hash	21,560	1121 μs	11.6
Prepare random scalar for X25519	17,945	1121 μs	9.6
Complete PACE protocol run	7,588,000	474 ms	4078.6

The respective state of the PACE protocol is stored in the body of the Asynchronous Crypto Engine (ACE) object. This object also holds all intermediate results required for resuming an interrupted calculation. For storing this state and intermediates we need 264 bytes of static memory and measured an additional execution stack requirement of 432 bytes by using a stack guard pattern method. The sum of both is only slightly larger than the 548 bytes reported in [5], probably due to the inclusion of the SHA512 operations.

The total protocol including two point multiplications and the Elligator accounts for 7.588 million cycles and a dissipated energy of roughly 4 mJ respectively.

Note that this amount of energy is about four times the total energy buffer size of our explosion protected experiment hardware! Since the CPU cannot be clocked down (not unusual for wireless transceivers!) we had to go to sleep very frequently so that the energy buffer may re-charge with the average current granted to the M0 subsystem until the calculation operation may be allowed to resume. Recall also that we run the calculation while the wireless stack maintains the link to the handheld unit running the client side implementation!

The interruption of the calculation was not allowed at arbitrary points within the software but only at distinct boundaries. The biggest blocks are formed by the field inversion and the Elligator because otherwise we would have had to place all of the temporaries used during the field exponentiation in the ACE object reducing the amount of memory available. In order to limit the amount of the maximum energy chunk, the Elligator was split into two sub-blocks coined "v" and "epsilon" in line with the terminology of [4].

In total the maximum transient energy chunk is given by the inversions and the two Elligator2 sub-steps and amounts roughly to 150 µJ. We assessed the additional overhead due to the asynchronous interface to amount to roughly 3%.

9.4   Assessment of the User-Perceived Login Delay

While the biggest amount of required energy buffer size is determined by the maximum chunk size in the ACE state machine, the user-experienced duration of the login delay is controlled mainly by the granted average power. If the core would be allowed to run without interruption, the whole protocol calculation would have finished after 474 ms. This is clearly perfect from a usability perspective on the GUI interface.

However, when assuming that 5% of the total average power of 30 mW of the control unit may be allocated for the "add-on-feature" of a wireless user interface, we end up with roughly 1.5 mW. Subtracting 0.5 mW for maintaining the wireless link one ends up with 1 mW average power for the security functionality or 0.5 mA at 2 V. If the core consumes 4.3 mA it must sleep most of the time. For this reason a time stretching factor of 4.3 mA/0.5 mA of 8.6 needs to be considered, such that the actual protocol calculation needs roughly four seconds.

This is a value clearly perceivable by the user but still in an acceptable range. The times calculated theoretically such as above also roughly correspond to the times measured on the actual smart phone setting. We sometimes observe additional delay of say 0.5 s, since sometimes the ACE object needs to wait a bit until the amount of energy required for the Elligator is fully available. Wakeup-cycles of the CPU are triggered by the radio transmission periods controlled by the handheld device.

When considering a login delay of four seconds, it is obvious that there is not any room left for loosing efficiency by avoiding the burden of assembly optimizations or by choosing cryptographic primitives of lower efficiency!

The tight constraints also were the original motivation for developing the custom curve Curve19119 in the first line. It was mainly due to the performance improvements obtained in [5] that acceptable login delays were obtained without being forced to use a security parameter that is no longer state-of the art.

10 Summary

Summing up, in this paper we have explored the design-space regarding password authenticated key exchange for the domain of resource-constrained explosion protected industrial control devices.

We first reviewed PAKE protocols from the literature and came to the conclusion that the PACE protocol family is well suited for the given setting.

We then analyzed the impact of the choice of elliptic curve candidates for PACE for ARM Cortex M0 devices and came to the conclusion that best efficiency for software-based implementations on small 32 bit microcontrollers is likely to be obtained when using Montgomery or Edwards curves over prime fields using Pseudo-Mersenne primes of the form $2^n - m$.

Based on our analysis an implementation avoiding the risk of intellectual property violation without complicated licensing for the PACE protocol on NIST curves should be expected to be roughly a factor of 2.5 less efficient. The main factor is patent circumvention regarding hashing of scalars onto elliptic curves and use of the Coin2Point primitive of PACE as workaround. For curves built on top of a random prime field we derived an additional speed-reduction factor of roughly 3 accounting for the large cost of modulo reduction in a purely software-based solution on the ARM Cortex M0.

We did evaluate the performance benefit stemming from reduction of the 128 bit security parameter to roughly 96 bits and observed a speed gain in the range of 1.92. For this purpose we introduced a new elliptic curve Curve19119 and a corresponding Diffie-Hellman Protocol X19119 that we believe to setup new speed records for the 96 bit security level for constant-time implementations on Cortex M0 microcontrollers.

We used our optimized elliptic curve cryptographic algorithms in order to construct a tailored solution based on the PACE protocol family.

Finally we have shown that the scheme allows for an actual implementation in the setting of a wireless Bluetooth transceiver controller running the PACE protocol with Curve25519 in parallel to the wireless operation. For a power budget of 1.5 mW worst case login delays in the range of 4 s were attained for the 128 bit security level.

This result was obtained in an explosion-protected setting where incorporation of larger capacitors or batteries was impossible. The clue to circumvent the problem generated by the absence of notable energy buffers was definition of an asynchronous operation mode for the cryptographic algorithms. This way the amount of required energy buffer size was reduced down to 150 μJ.

Our analysis brings us to the conclusion that when working on the conventional Weierstrass curves, the limits imposed by acceptable login-delays on the user interface would most likely have forced us to reduce the security parameter to a value that might not be adequate nowadays. Ultimately this might even have driven us back to weak challenge-response protocols.

Acknowledgements. The authors acknowledge inspiring discussions with Peter Schwabe, Marc Fischlin, Florian Bachmann and Johann Heyszl. We also would like to thank Tanja Lange for drawing our attention to the possibility of advantageous application of reptiles.

Concluding remark

Concluding this paper regarding a rather complex protocol we express the hope that our contribution also might help to re-explore the potential of special types of simple challenge-response protocols. We do refer specifically to protocols that might be constructed on top of isomorphic transformations from the space of cryptographic protocols to Italian language, such as sketched in Fig. 2.

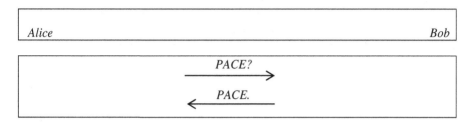

Fig. 2. Sketch of a challenge-response protocol candidate that might be beneficial.

References

1. Bender, J., Fischlin, M., Kügler, D.: Security analysis of the PACE key-agreement protocol. In: Samarati, P., Yung, M., Martinelli, F., Ardagna, Claudio A. (eds.) ISC 2009. LNCS, vol. 5735, pp. 33–48. Springer, Heidelberg (2009). doi:10.1007/978-3-642-04474-8_3
2. Bellovin, S.M., Merritt, M.: Encrypted key exchange: password-based protocols secure against dictionary attacks. In: Proceedings of the IEEE Symposium on Security and Privacy. IEEE Computer Society (1992)
3. Icart, T.: How to hash into elliptic curves. In: Halevi, S. (ed.) CRYPTO 2009. LNCS, vol. 5677, pp. 303–316. Springer, Heidelberg (2009). doi:10.1007/978-3-642-03356-8_18
4. Bernstein, D.J., Hamburg, M., Krasnova, A., Lange, T.: Elligator: Elliptic-curve points indistinguishable from uniform random strings. In: CCS 2013. ACM, New York (2013)
5. Düll, M., Haase, B., Hinterwäldler, G., Hutter, M., Paar, C., Sanchez, A.H., Schwabe, P.: High-speed Curve25519 on 8-bit, 16-bit and 32-bit microcontrollers. Des. Codes Cryptogr. **77**, 493–514 (2015)
6. De Clercq, R., Uhsadel, L., Van Herrewege, A., Verbauwhede, I.: Ultra low-power implementation of ECC on the ARM Cortex-M0+. In: DAC 2014 Proceedings of the 51st Annual Design Automation Conference on Design Automation Conference, pp. 1–6. ACM, New York (2014). https://www.cosic.esat.kuleuven.be/publications/article-2401.pdf. 15, 16
7. Kwon, T.: Summary of AMP (Authentication and key agreement via Memorable Passwords). http://grouper.ieee.org/groups/1363/passwdPK/contributions/ampsummary2.pdf
8. Bellovin, S., Merrit, M.: Augmented encrypted key exchange: a password-based protocol secure against dictionary attacks and password-file compromise. In: ACM Conference on Computer and Communications Security, pp. 244–250 (1993)
9. Jablon, D.: Strong password-only authenticated key exchange. ACM Comput. Commun. Rev. **26**(5), 5–26 (1996)
10. Wu, T.: Secure remote password protocol. In: ISOC Network and Distributed System Security Symposium (1998)

11. MacKenzie, P.: The PAK suite: protocols for password-authenticated key exchange. In: Submission to IEEE P1363.2, April 2002
12. Kwon, T.: Authentication and key agreement via memorable password. In: ISOC Network and Distributed System Security Symposium, February 2001
13. Shin, T., Kobara, K.: Efficient augmented password-only authentication and key exchange for IKEv2 (2012). https://tools.ietf.org/html/rfc6628
14. Diffie, W., Hellman, M.: New directions in cryptography. IEEE Trans. Inf. Theory 22(6), 544–654 (1976)
15. MacKenzie, P.: The PAK suite: protocols for password-authenticated key-exchange. DIMACS Technical report 2002-46 (2002)
16. Shin, S., Kobara, K., Imai, H.: Security proof of AugPAKE. Cryptology ePrint Archive: Report 2010/334, June 2010. http://eprint.iacr.org/2010/334
17. Federal Office for Information Security (BSI): Elliptic Curve Cryptography, Version 2.0, TR-03111, June 2012. https://www.bsi.bund.de
18. Federal Office for Information Security (BSI): Advanced Security Mechanism for Machine Readable Travel Document – Extended Access Control (EAC), Password Authenticated Connection Establishment (PACE), and Restricted Identification (RI), BSI-TR-03110, June 2012. https://www.bsi.bund.de
19. Aranha, D.F., Barreto, P.S.L.M., Pereira, G.C.C.F., Ricardini, J.E.: A note on high-security general-purpose elliptic curves (2013). https://eprint.iacr.org/2013/647.pdf
20. Hisil, H., Wong, K.K.-H., Carter, G., Dawson, E.: Twisted edwards curves revisited. In: Pieprzyk, J. (ed.) ASIACRYPT 2008. LNCS, vol. 5350, pp. 326–343. Springer, Heidelberg (2008). doi:10.1007/978-3-540-89255-7_20
21. Lochter, M., Merkle, J.: Elliptic curve cryptography (ECC) brainpool standard curves and curve generation, IETF RFC 5639 (2010)
22. Lepinski, M., Kent, S.: Additional diffie-hellman groups for use with IETF standards, IETF RFC 5114 (2008)
23. Solinas, J.A.: Generalized Mersenne Numbers (1999)
24. Nascimento, E., Chmielewski, L., Oswald, D., Schwabe, P.: Attacking embedded ECC implementations through cmov side channels. Selected Areas in Cryptology – SAC 2016, Springer (2016, to appear)
25. Tschofenig, H., Pegourie-Gonnard, M.: Performance of state-of-the-art cryptography on ARM-based microprocessors. In: NIST LWC Workshop (2015)
26. Wenger, E., Unterluggauer, T., Werner, M.: 8/16/32 shades of elliptic curve cryptography on embedded processors. In: Paul, G., Vaudenay, S. (eds.) INDOCRYPT 2013. LNCS, vol. 8250, pp. 244–261. Springer, Cham (2013). doi:10.1007/978-3-319-03515-4_16
27. Coron, J.-S., Gouget, A., Icart, T., Pailler, P.: Supplemental access control (PACE v2): security analysis of PACE integrated mapping (2011). https://eprint.iacr.org/2011/058.pdf
28. Brier, E., Coron, J.-S., Icart, T., Madore, D., Randiram, H., Tibouchi, M.: Efficient indifferentiable hashing into ordinary elliptic curves. http://eprint.iacr.org/
29. Bernstein, D.J.: Curve25519: new Diffie-Hellman speed records (2006). https://cr.yp.to/ecdh/curve25519-20060209.pdf
30. Clavier, C., Feix, B., Gagnerot, G., Roussellet, M., Verneuil, V.: Horizontal correlation analysis on exponentiation. In: Soriano, M., Qing, S., López, J. (eds.) ICICS 2010. LNCS, vol. 6476, pp. 46–61. Springer, Heidelberg (2010). doi:10.1007/978-3-642-17650-0_5
31. Batina, L., Chmielewski, Ł., Papachristodoulou, L., Schwabe, P., Tunstall, M.: Online template attacks. In: Meier, W., Mukhopadhyay, D. (eds.) INDOCRYPT 2014. LNCS, vol. 8885, pp. 21–36. Springer, Cham (2014). doi:10.1007/978-3-319-13039-2_2
32. Bernstein, D.J.: Salsa20 design (2005). https://cr.yp.to/snuffle/design.pdf

33. Beaulieu, R., Shors, D., Smith, J., Treatman-Clark, S., Weeks, B., Wingers, L.: Simon and speck: block ciphers for the internet of things (2015). http://csrc.nist.gov/groups/ST/lwc-workshop2015/papers/session1-shors-paper.pdf
34. Petit, C., Quisquater, J.-J.: On polynomial systems arising from a weil descent. In: Wang, X., Sako, K. (eds.) ASIACRYPT 2012. LNCS, vol. 7658, pp. 451–466. Springer, Heidelberg (2012). doi:10.1007/978-3-642-34961-4_28
35. Gaudry, P., Hess, F., Smart, N.: Constructive and destructive facets of Weil descent on elliptic curves. J. Cryptol. **15**, 19–46 (2002). http://www.hpl.hp.com/techreports/2000/HPL-2000-10.html
36. Gaudry, P.: Index calculus for abelian varieties of small dimension and the elliptic curve discrete logarithm problem. J. Symbolic Comput. **44**, 1690–1702 (2009). http://eprint.iacr.org/2004/073

Security Evaluation

Back to Massey: Impressively Fast, Scalable and Tight Security Evaluation Tools

Marios O. Choudary$^{(\boxtimes)}$ and P.G. Popescu

University Politehnica of Bucharest, Bucharest, Romania
marios.choudary@cs.pub.ro, pgpopescu@yahoo.com

Abstract. None of the existing rank estimation algorithms can scale to large cryptographic keys, such as 4096-bit (512 bytes) RSA keys. In this paper, we present the first solution to estimate the guessing entropy of arbitrarily large keys, based on mathematical bounds, resulting in the fastest and most scalable security evaluation tool to date. Our bounds can be computed within a fraction of a second, with no memory overhead, and provide a margin of only a few bits for a full 128-bit AES key.

Keywords: Side-channel attacks · Guessing entropy · Bounds · Scalability

1 Introduction

Side-channel attacks are powerful tools to extract secret information from hardware devices, such as the cryptographic microcontrollers used in banking smartcards. These attacks apply a divide-and-conquer strategy, such that they are able to target each subkey byte of a cryptographic algorithm independently. This may allow an attacker to mount a practical side-channel attack on a block cipher such as AES, when using a key of 128 or 256 bits (16 or 32 bytes, respectively), by targeting each of the 16 or 32 key bytes independently, whereas a purely brute-force search attack on the full key is computationally infeasible.

Recent advances in side-channel attacks have focused on the problem of estimating the rank of the full key of a cryptographic algorithm, after obtaining sorted lists of probabilities for the different subkeys that compose the full key (e.g. lists for the 16 subkey bytes of AES, when used with a 128-bit key).

These recent algorithms represent very useful tools for security evaluators that need to estimate the security of a given device. The algorithm proposed by Veyrat-Charvillon et al. [7] was the first method that could estimate the rank of a full 128-bit key, albeit with a considerable error margin. More recent algorithms [11–13] have reduced the bounds of this estimation to within one bit for 128-bit keys and can run within seconds of computation, after being given with a list of sorted probabilities for the individual subkeys.

We thank our God, the One God in Three Persons: Father, Son and Holy Spirit, for this work.

W. Fischer and N. Homma (Eds.): CHES 2017, LNCS 10529, pp. 367–386, 2017.
DOI: 10.1007/978-3-319-66787-4_18

But none of these algorithms can scale for large keys composing of more than 256 bytes (e.g. an RSA 2048 or 4096 bit key), while at the same time providing tight bounds. Furthermore, even for smaller key sizes (e.g. 128-bit AES key), existing approaches can deviate from the actual security metric.

In this paper, we present sound mathematically-derived bounds for the guessing entropy, which allow us to evaluate the security of devices using arbitrary large keys (even 512 bytes or more). These have no memory requirements, can be computed instantaneously and provide bounds within a few bits.

2   Background: Side-Channel Attacks and Key Enumeration

Given a physical device (e.g. a smartcard) that implements a cryptographic algorithm, such as AES, we may record side-channel traces (power consumption or electromagnetic emissions) using an oscilloscope. In this case, for each encryption of a plaintext p_i with a key $k\star$, we can obtain a leakage trace $\mathbf{x}_i$ that contains some information about the encryption operation.

For the particular case of AES and other similar block ciphers that use a substitution box (S-Box), a common target for side-channel attacks is the S-box operation $v = \text{S-box}(k \star \oplus p)$ from the first round of the block cipher. Since this operation is done for each subkey $k\star$ in part (for AES each subkey only has 8 bits), we can attack each of the subkeys separately. And by using information from the leakage traces, a side-channel attack such as DPA [1], CPA [3] or Template Attacks [2] can assign higher probabilities to the correct subkeys, leading to a very powerful brute-force search on each subkey.

After obtaining the lists of probabilities for each subkey, we may need to combine these lists in some way in order to determine what are the most likely values for the full cryptographic key. One important motivation for this is that secure devices, such as the microcontrollers used in EMV cards, need to obtain a Common Criteria certification at some assurance level (e.g. $EAL4+$). To provide such certification, evaluation laboratories may need to verify the security of devices against side-channel attacks also for the case of full-key recovery attacks, in particular where some subkeys may leak considerably different than others.

For the particular case of AES, we need to combine from 16 bytes (128-bit key) to 32 bytes (256-bit key). If the target device leaks enough information and sufficient measurements are done, then the attack may provide a probability close to one for the correct subkey value, while assigning a very small probability to the other candidate subkey values. In this case, the combination is trivial, as we only need to use the most likely value for each subkey. However, in practice, due to noise in the measurements and various security measures in secured devices, the correct value of each subkey may be ranked anywhere between the first and the last position. In this case, a trivial direct combination of all the lists of probabilities is not computationally feasible. Note that this problem arises in any scenario where we need to combine multiple lists of probabilities, not just in the case of AES, as we shall show below.

To deal with this combination problem in the context of side-channel attacks, two kinds of combination algorithms have emerged in recent years: key enumeration and rank estimation algorithms. Key enumeration algorithms [5,14] provide a method to output full keys in decreasing order of likelihood, such that we can minimize the number of keys we try until finding the correct one (which is typically verified by comparing the encryption of a known plaintext/ciphertext pair).

The other kind of algorithms, which are directly related to our paper, are the rank estimation algorithms. These algorithms provide an estimate of the full *key rank*, i.e. the number of keys we should try until finding the correct one if we were to apply a similar approach to key enumeration. The great advantage of rank estimation algorithms is that we can estimate the key rank even if this rank is very high (e.g. 2^{80} or larger), whereas enumerating such large number of keys is computationally infeasible. For security evaluations, this was until now probably the most convenient tool, since it can quickly estimate the security of a device. However, it is important that these rank estimation algorithms provide some guarantee of their bounds, since otherwise their output can be misleading.

Veyrat-Charvillon et al. [7] proposed the first efficient rank estimation algorithm for 128-bit keys, which could run in between 5 and 900 s. The main drawbacks of this algorithm are that the bounds of the rank estimation can be up to 20–30 bits apart from the real key rank and the required time to tighten the bounds increases exponentially. More recently, new algorithms [11–13] have improved the speed and tightness of the rank estimation. Among these, the histogram-based approach of Glowacz et al. [11] is probably the fastest and scales well even up to keys composed of 128 bytes (e.g. 1024-bit RSA key).

Nevertheless, none of these recent algorithms can scale efficiently to larger cryptographic keys, e.g. 2048-bit (256 bytes) or 4096-bit (512 bytes) keys, such as common RSA keys used for public key encryption. We have tested the C implementation of Glowacz et al. [11] on 256 subkey bytes and it took about 64 seconds per iteration (using the default N = 2048 bins and the merge parameter set to two, i.e. doing a pre-computation step where lists of subkey probabilities are first combined two by two; for merge = 3 the memory requirements killed the program), while for 512 subkey bytes (merge = 2) the memory requirements killed again the program[1]. The algorithm of Martin et al. [13] is also prohibitive for large keys, since it runs in $O(m^2 n \log n)$, where m is the number of subkeys and n is the number of possible values per subkey. Similarly, the PRO algorithm of Bernstein et al. [12] (which is the fastest of the two proposed by the authors) took about 5 h for 256 subkey bytes and made the evaluation platform run out of swap memory (according to their results).

In contrast, our methods presented in the following sections allow us to obtain tight bounds instantaneously for arbitrarily large keys[2]. This is the first fully scalable security evaluation method proposed to date.

---

[1] On a Intel i5 4-core CPU at 3.2 GHz, with 16 GB RAM.

[2] The only limitation being the numerical representation used by the computing machine.

A possible scenario where such scalable methods are required, is the evaluation of side-channel attacks against the key loading operation. That is, side-channel attacks which target the transfer of keys from memory to registers, rather than the cryptographic algorithm itself. This was the case for example in the attacks of Oswald and Paar against the commercial Mifare DES-Fire MF3ICD40 [6] or the attacks of Choudary and Kuhn [8] against the AVR XMEGA. Recent secure devices, such as the *A7101CGTK2: Secure authentication microcontroller* [23] support RSA encryptions with keys up to 4096 bits (512 bytes). Hence, in order to evaluate the security of these devices against full-key recovery side-channel attacks during the key loading operation, we need scalable rank estimation algorithms.

Furthermore, our methods are generally applicable, so they can be used in any other scenario where probability lists need to be combined to determine the approximate security of some system.

3   Experimental Data

In order to present and demonstrate our results, we used two distinct datasets, one from a hardware AES implementation and the other from MATLAB simulated data. The first dataset consists of $2^{20} \approx 1\,\mathrm{M}$ power-supply traces of the AES engine inside an AVR XMEGA microcontroller, obtained while the cryptographic engine was encrypting different uniformly distributed plaintexts. The traces correspond to the S-box lookup from the first round key. Each trace contains $m = 5000$ oscilloscope samples recorded at $500\,\mathrm{MS/s}$, using a Tektronix TDS7054 oscilloscope, configured at $250\,\mathrm{MHz}$ bandwidth in HIRES mode with Fastframe and $10\,\mathrm{mV/div}$ vertical resolution, using DC coupling. The XMEGA microcontroller was powered at $3.3\,\mathrm{V}$ from batteries and was run by a $2\,\mathrm{MHz}$ sinewave clock. We shall refer to this as the *real* dataset.

The second dataset consists of simulated data, generated using MATLAB. The data contains unidimensional leakage samples $\mathbf{x}_i$ produced as the hamming weight of the AES S-box output value mixed with Gaussian noise, i.e.

$$\mathbf{x}_i = \mathrm{HW}(\text{S-box}(k \oplus p_i)) + r_i, \tag{1}$$

where p_i is the plaintext byte corresponding to this trace, and r_i represents the Gaussian noise (variance 10). We shall refer to this as the *simulated* dataset.

3.1   Template Attacks

To use our datasets with the methods evaluated in this paper, we need to obtain lists of probabilities for the possible values of the 16 subkeys used with our AES implementations. To do this we use template attacks (TA) [2,8] on each subkey during the S-box lookup of the first AES round.[3]

---

[3] For the case of the real dataset, we first applied a Correlation Power Analysis (CPA) attack [3] to determine which is the leakage sample that leaks the most and then used this single sample in a template attack.

After executing a side-channel attack using a vector $\mathbf{X}$ of leakage traces (e.g. the *real* or *simulated* traces in our case), we obtain a vector of scores or probabilities $d(k|\mathbf{X}) \in \mathbb{R}^{|\mathcal{S}|}$ for each possible key byte value $k \in \{1, \ldots, |\mathcal{S}|\}$, where $|\mathcal{S}|$ is the number of possible values (typically $|\mathcal{S}| = 256$ for one AES subkey byte). In the case of template attacks we obtain real probabilities and we shall often write $P(k|\mathbf{X}) = d(k|\mathbf{X})$.[4]

After obtaining the probabilities $P_i(k|\mathbf{X})$ for each subkey byte i, we can compute the security metrics and rank estimation methods presented below.

4   Security Metrics

To evaluate the security of a device against different side-channel attacks, an evaluator will typically use some evaluation metric. Standaert et al. [4] presented several such metrics for the case of attacks that target a single subkey at a time. Among these, we present below the guessing entropy and the conditional entropy. Afterwards we show how to derive scalable and tight bounds for these metrics. These allow us to obtain very efficient methods for estimating the security of devices against full-key recovery side-channel attacks.

4.1   Guessing Entropy

In 1994, James L. Massey proposed a metric [16], known as the *Guessing Entropy*, to measure the average number of guesses that an attacker needs to find a secret after a cryptanalytic attack (such as our side-channel attacks).

Given the probability vectors $P(k|\mathbf{X})$ for each subkey obtained after a side channel attack, we can compute Massey's guessing entropy as follows. First, sort all the probability values $P(k|\mathbf{X})$, obtaining the sorted probability vector $\mathbf{p} = \{p_1, p_2, \ldots, p_{|\mathcal{S}|}\}$, where $p_1 = \max_k P(k|\mathbf{X})$, p_2 is the second largest probability and so on. Then, compute Massey's guessing entropy (GM) as:

$$\mathrm{GM} = \sum_{i=1}^{|\mathcal{S}|} i \cdot p_i. \tag{2}$$

Massey's guessing entropy represents the *statistical expectation* of the position of the correct key in the sorted vector of conditional probabilities. A similar measure is the *actual* guessing entropy (GE) [4], which provides the position of the correct key in the sorted vector of conditional probabilities. The GE is computed as follows: given the vector of sorted probabilities (or scores)

---

[4] Unprofiled side-channel attacks such as CPA often return a score vector, e.g. based on the correlation coefficient $\rho_k \in [-1, 1]$ for each possible candidate value k, which might not work very well with rank estimation methods. However, even in the unprofiled setting is possible to use other methods, such as linear regression on the fly [15] to obtain pseudo-probabilities that work well with rank estimation algorithms.

$\mathbf{p} = \{p_1, p_2, \ldots, p_{|\mathcal{S}|}\}$, return the position of the probability corresponding to the correct key $k\star$[5]:

$$GE = i, \quad p_i = P(k \star |\mathbf{X}). \tag{3}$$

As we can see from their definitions, both measures are computed from the posteriori probabilities of the keys given a set of leakage traces, but the GM computes the *expected* position of the correct key, while the GE computes the *actual* position of the correct key. For this reason, the GE requires knowledge of the correct key, while the GM does not. Furthermore, we can see that averaging the GE over many experiments we approximate precisely the GM. Therefore, if we had exact probabilities, the GM would be the expected value of the GE.

In terms of usage, the GE is the most used measure in the side-channel evaluations published so far, mainly because it represents the actual position of the correct key and also because it can be computed even when using score-based attacks which do not output probabilities for each key (e.g. by sorting the keys according to their correlation after a correlation power attack and selecting the position of the correct key).

However, if we can obtain good probabilities for the key candidates (e.g. by using template attacks), then the GM can be a better evaluation tool, because as we said, the GM represents the expected value of the GE, but also because it is less affected by minor differences between probabilities. That is, when p_1 is much larger than the other probabilities, both measures will return 1 (or close to 1). On the other hand, for all scenarios in which the key is not easy to detect and the probabilities $p_1, p_2, \ldots, p_{|\mathcal{S}|}$ are very close to each other, any minor variation in the probabilties (e.g. due to measurement errors) will lead to possibly large variations of GE, while GM will provide the correct result, i.e. the expected value (which should be around $(|\mathcal{S}| + 1)/2$ if all the probabilities are very close).

Furthermore, the GM will allow us to derive the fast, scalable and tight bounds that we present in the following sections.

In our results, we shall show the logarithm (base 2) of the guessing entropy.

4.2   Conditional Entropy

In information theory, the mutual information $I(X, Y)$ between two random variables X and Y is defined as:

$$I(X, Y) = H(X) - H(X|Y), \tag{4}$$

where

$$H(X) = -\mathbb{E} \log_2 P(X) = -\sum_{x \in \mathcal{X}} P(x) \cdot \log_2 P(x) \tag{5}$$

represents Shannon's entropy for the random variable X, and

$$H(X|Y) = \sum_{y \in \mathcal{Y}} P(y) H(X|Y = y) = -\sum_{y \in \mathcal{Y}} P(y) \sum_{x \in \mathcal{X}} P(x|y) \cdot \log_2 P(x|y) \tag{6}$$

---

[5] This measure assumes that an evaluator knows which is the correct key.

represents the conditional entropy of X given Y. In short, the conditional entropy shows how much entropy (uncertainty) remains about the variable X when the variable Y is given.

As before, we are interested in knowing how much uncertainty (entropy) remains about the random variable K (representing the secret key byte k), when a set of leakage traces (represented by the variable L) is given; this can be quantified using the conditional entropy defined above. If K represents one key byte, as in our setup, then $H(K) = 8.$[6] Using this notation we obtain the conditional entropy

$$H(K|L) = \sum_{\mathbf{X} \in \mathcal{L}} P(\mathbf{X}) H(K|L = \mathbf{X}) = -\sum_{\mathbf{X} \in \mathcal{L}} P(\mathbf{X}) \sum_{k \in \mathcal{K}} P(k|\mathbf{X}) \cdot \log_2 P(k|\mathbf{X}).$$
(7)

In practice, we can compute the conditional entropy from (7) using one of the following options[7]:

1. Compute an integral over the full leakage space, leading to the computationally-intensive form:

$$H(K|L) = -\int_{\mathbf{X} \in \mathcal{L}} P(\mathbf{X}) \sum_{k \in \mathcal{K}} P(k|\mathbf{X}) \cdot \log_2 P(k|\mathbf{X}) d\mathbf{X}.$$
(8)

2. Use Monte Carlo sampling from a limited subset of N traces:

$$H(K|L) = -\frac{1}{N} \sum_{i=1}^{N} \sum_{k \in \mathcal{K}} P(k|\mathbf{X}_i) \cdot \log_2 P(k|\mathbf{X}_i).$$
(9)

The first form is computationally intensive, as for multi-dimensional leakage traces the integral in (8) needs to be computed over a multi-dimensional space. Therefore, in our experiments we used the second form, where N is the number of iterations (usually $N = 100$) over which we computed the second summation and the probabilities $P(k|\mathbf{X}_i)$ were obtained from template attacks on each iteration.

5   Tight Bounds for Guessing Entropy

In this section, we explain how to adapt several known bounds (lower and upper) of the guessing entropy (GM) in the context of side-channel attacks, when we deal with a single list of probabilities (e.g. targeting a single subkey byte). These bounds can be used as a fast approximation of the GM (since they run in linear time, because they don't require the sorting operation that is necessary for the computation of GM), but their great advantage is in the context of multiple lists of probabilities (see next section).

---

[6] We assume all key bytes are equally likely, in the absence of leakage information.

[7] There are other ways to estimate the conditional entropy, including several variants of the Monte Carlo method. Here we focused only on the two most popular such variants.

5.1 Bounds for Massey's Guessing Entropy from Probabilities

Arikan [19] presented a lower and an upper bound for GM. We can adapt these bounds to our side-channel context using the notation from previous sections, as follows:

$$\frac{1}{1 + \ln |\mathcal{S}|} \left[\sum_{k=1}^{|\mathcal{S}|} p_k^{1/2} \right]^2 \leq \mathrm{GM} \leq \left[\sum_{k=1}^{|\mathcal{S}|} p_k^{1/2} \right]^2, \tag{10}$$

with the important remark that in the lower and upper bounds the individual probabilities $p_k = P(k|X)$ do not need to be sorted. This means that both bounds can be computed in $O(|\mathcal{S}|)$. The upper bound of Arikan has been improved in [18], by Theorem 3, yielding:

$$\mathrm{GM} \leq \frac{1}{2} \left[\sum_{k=1}^{|\mathcal{S}|} p_k^{1/2} \right]^2 + \frac{1}{2} \leq \left[\sum_{k=1}^{|\mathcal{S}|} p_k^{1/2} \right]^2.$$

Combining this with (10), we obtain the tighter relation:

$$\frac{1}{1 + \ln |\mathcal{S}|} \left[\sum_{k=1}^{|\mathcal{S}|} p_k^{1/2} \right]^2 \leq \mathrm{GM} \leq \frac{1}{2} \left[\sum_{k=1}^{|\mathcal{S}|} p_k^{1/2} \right]^2 + \frac{1}{2}. \tag{11}$$

We shall refer to these lower and upper bounds as $\mathrm{LB_{GM}}$ and $\mathrm{UB_{GM}}$, respectively.

We show the results of using these bounds on the simulated (left) and real (right) datasets in Fig. 1. We can make several observations. Firstly, the bounds are in both cases within 1–2 bits apart[8] for all values of the guessing entropy.

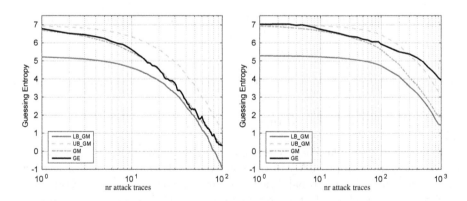

Fig. 1. GM, GE and GM bounds from probabilities for the simulated (left) and real (right) datasets, when targeting a single subkey byte. These are averaged results over 100 experiments.

---

[8] While this is not as tight as other rank estimation algorithms, we shall see later that our bounds stay tight even when using a large number of target subkey bytes and that they are always sound (due to the mathematical demonstration), while existing rank estimations can provide estimation and calculation errors.

Secondly, we see that for the simulated dataset the GM is very close to the GE, but for the real dataset the GE deviates considerably and even goes outside the upper bound of the GM. In all our experiments, we observed that the GM stays either close or below the GE. This can be explained by the fact that even if many probabilities are close to each other in value, small ordering errors can have a higher impact on GE (which only depends on the order) than on GM (which only depends on the probability values).

As we shall show later, previous rank estimation algorithms, such as the one of Glowacz et al. [11], also tend to follow more the GM rather than the GE, because they also rely on the values of probabilities rather than the exact position of the correct key, even though such algorithms also use the value of the correct key in order to position their bounds closer to the actual position of the correct key. Nevertheless, both measures can be useful. If we need the exact position of the key for a particular set of measurements, then GE is the best tool. However, the GE cannot be computed for large number of target subkeys and is also subject to the particular measurements, i.e. noise can cause the correct subkey value to be ranked very bad, even though its probability is very close to those in the top, leading to a very high GE, while the GM will show a lower value. Hence, in such scenario the GM may actually provide a better intuition since with a new set of traces (e.g. the attacker), the correct subkey value could be ranked better, leading to a smaller GE. Furthermore, the fact that the GM will in general be below the GE (or very close to it in case it is slightly above) means that relying on the GM will provide a safer conclusion from a designer perspective. That is, if the resulting GM is above a desired security level for some scenario, then we can be confident enough that the GE will either be very close or above.

From the figure, we also see that GM always stays within the bounds. This is guaranteed, given the mathematical derivation. And as we shall see, the algorithmic approaches can introduce estimation errors and provide erroneous results that are neither between our bounds nor close to the expected GE.

Besides the above differences between GM and GE, what is most important in our context, is that we can obtain very fast and scalable bounds for GM.

Finally, we mention another important difference between GM and GE, namely for the computation of GE we need knowledge of the real key (so we can compute its position), while for the GM we do not. Hence, our GM bounds allow anyone to estimate the security of a device, while previous rank estimations could only be used by evaluators having access to the real key (target) values.

5.2   Bounds from Conditional Entropy

We now show how to bound Massey's guessing entropy as a function of the conditional entropy, using Massey's inequality [16] and McEliece and Yu inequality [17]. This allows us to obtain a general relation between the guessing entropy and the conditional entropy in the context of side-channel attacks.

Let $H(K|L = \mathbf{X})$ be the conditional entropy obtained for the set of leakage traces $\mathbf{X}$. Applying Massey's inequality [16] to GM and $H(K|L = \mathbf{X})$, we obtain the following upper bound for the conditional entropy:

$$2 + \log(\text{GM} - 1) \geq H(K|L = \mathbf{X}). \tag{12}$$

Then, applying McEliece and Yu's inequality [17], we obtain a lower bound for the conditional entropy as:

$$H(K|L = \mathbf{X}) \geq \frac{2 \log |\mathcal{S}|}{|\mathcal{S}| - 1}(\text{GM} - 1). \tag{13}$$

Using (12) and (13), we obtain lower and upper bounds for GM as a function of the conditional entropy:

$$2^{H(K|L=\mathbf{X})-2} + 1 \leq \text{GM} \leq \frac{|\mathcal{S}| - 1}{2 \log |\mathcal{S}|} H(K|L = \mathbf{X}) + 1. \tag{14}$$

We refer to these as LB_{GMHK} and UB_{GMHK}, respectively.

Remark 1. The left inequality in (14) is true when $H(K|L = \mathbf{X})$ is greater than 2 bits.

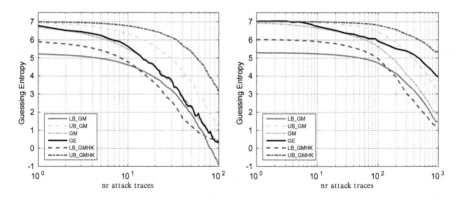

Fig. 2. GM, GE and GM bounds from probabilities and conditional entropy $H(K|L)$ for the simulated (left) and real (right) datasets, when targeting a single subkey byte. These are averaged results over 100 experiments.

We show these bounds in Fig. 2, along with the previous bounds, for both the simulated (left) and real (right) datasets. We can see that in both cases the lower bound LB_{GMHK} stays within 1 bit of GM for all values of GM, while the upper bound UB_{GMHK} deviates substantially, even more than 3 bits from the GM. Secondly, in both results we see that UB_{GM} is a much better upper bound than UB_{GMHK}. We observed this in all our experiments. Combining the best of these bounds, we can say that for the lower bound we should use the maximum between LB_{GMHK} and LB_{GM}, while for the upper bound we should use UB_{GM}.

6 Impressive Scaling: Scalable Bounds for Guessing Entropy

We now show how to scale the bounds presented in the previous section to arbitrarily many lists of probabilities, so they can be used to estimate the security of a full AES key (16–32 subkey bytes) or even RSA key (128–512 subkey bytes), while being computable in time that increases *linearly* with the number of subkeys targeted.

In the following, we shall use the notation GM^f to refer to the GM for the full key, n_s for the number of subkeys composing the full target key, and $|\mathcal{S}|^{n_s}$ for the number of possible full key values (e.g. $n_s = 16, |\mathcal{S}|^{n_s} = 2^{128}$ for AES-128).

6.1 Using Bounds of GM for Evaluation of Full Key

In Sect. 5.1, we showed how to derive tight bounds for GM from probabilities in the case of a single subkey byte. Considering the shape of the summation involved in (11), we need a way to avoid the computation of all the possible probabilities in the set of cross-probabilities from the full key space. Splitting the full sum into groups of partial sums leads to our main result:

Theorem 1 *(LB_{GM} and UB_{GM} for full key). Let $p_1^i, p_2^i, ..., p_{|\mathcal{S}|}^i$ be the probabilities for the $i = 1, 2, ..., n_s$ target subkey. Then we have*

$$\frac{1}{1 + \ln|\mathcal{S}|^{n_s}} \prod_{i=1}^{n_s} \left[\sum_{k=1}^{|\mathcal{S}|} \sqrt{p_k^i} \right]^2 \leq \mathrm{GM}^f \leq \frac{1}{2} \prod_{i=1}^{n_s} \left[\sum_{k=1}^{|\mathcal{S}|} \sqrt{p_k^i} \right]^2 + \frac{1}{2}.$$

Proof. Considering the LB_{GM} and UB_{GM} bounds for the full key, we have

$$\frac{1}{1 + \ln|\mathcal{S}|^{n_s}} \left[\sum_{k=1}^{|\mathcal{S}|^{n_s}} \sqrt{p_k^f} \right]^2 \leq \mathrm{GM}^f \leq \frac{1}{2} \left[\sum_{k=1}^{|\mathcal{S}|^{n_s}} \sqrt{p_k^f} \right]^2 + \frac{1}{2}.$$

Then, adding the fact that the new probabilities are combined as a product of n_s probabilities from target subkeys, i.e. $p_k^f = \prod_{i=1}^{n_s} p_j^i$, with $j = j(k, i) \in \{1, 2, ..., |\mathcal{S}|\}$ and factoring accordingly, we obtain that

$$\sum_{k=1}^{|\mathcal{S}|^{n_s}} \sqrt{p_k^f} = \left[\sum_{k=1}^{|\mathcal{S}|} \sqrt{p_k^1} \right] \cdot \left[\sum_{k=1}^{|\mathcal{S}|} \sqrt{p_k^2} \right] \cdots \cdot \left[\sum_{k=1}^{|\mathcal{S}|} \sqrt{p_k^{n_s}} \right]$$

i.e.

$$\sum_{k=1}^{|\mathcal{S}|^{n_s}} \sqrt{p_k^f} = \prod_{i=1}^{n_s} \left[\sum_{k=1}^{|\mathcal{S}|} \sqrt{p_k^i} \right]$$

and we are done.

UB$_{\text{GM}}$ runs in $O(|\mathcal{S}|)$ and for full key runs in $O(n_{\text{s}} \cdot |\mathcal{S}|)$, i.e. the computation time only increases *linearly* with the number of subkey bytes.

Remark 2. We can estimate the number of bits δ between our LB$_{\text{GM}}$ and UB$_{\text{GM}}$ bounds for the full key as $\delta = \log 2(\text{UB}_{\text{GM}}) - \log 2(\text{LB}_{\text{GM}}) = \log 2(\text{UB}_{\text{GM}}/\text{LB}_{\text{GM}})$. Ignoring the $1/2$ factor (which is negligible as the number of subkeys increases), we obtain the following approximation:

$$\delta \approx \log 2 \left(\frac{1 + \ln |\mathcal{S}|^{n_{\text{s}}}}{2} \right) = \log 2 \left(\frac{1 + n_{\text{s}} \cdot \ln |\mathcal{S}|}{2} \right) \text{ bits.}$$

6.2   Using Bounds of $H(K|L)$ for Evaluation of Full Key

Assuming independence between target subkeys and considering the bounds presented into (14) applied for the full key space yields

Theorem 2 (*LB$_{GMHK}$ and UB$_{GMHK}$ for full key*). *Let $H(K|L = \mathbf{X}_i)$ be the conditional entropy for the $i = 1, 2, ..., n_s$ target subkey, then*

$$2^{\sum_{i=1}^{n_s} H(K|L=\mathbf{X}_i)-2} + 1 \leq GM^f \leq \frac{|\mathcal{S}|^{n_s} - 1}{2 \log |\mathcal{S}|^{n_s}} \sum_{i=1}^{n_s} H(K|L = \mathbf{X}_i) + 1.$$

Proof. Considering (14) applied for full key space yields

$$2^{H(K^f|L^f=\mathbf{X})-2} + 1 \leq \text{GM}^f \leq \frac{|\mathcal{S}|^{n_s} - 1}{2 \log |\mathcal{S}|^{n_s}} H(K^f|L^f = \mathbf{X}) + 1,$$

where $H(K^f|L^f = \mathbf{X})$ is the joint conditional entropy for all n_s target subkeys. And because of the assumed independence between target subkeys, yields from [20, Theorem 2.6.6] that

$$H(K^f|L^f = \mathbf{X}) = \sum_{i=1}^{n_s} H(K|L = \mathbf{X}_i),$$

which gives us the wanted result.

Again, both bounds LB$_{\text{GMHK}}$ and UB$_{\text{GMHK}}$ run in $O(|\mathcal{S}|)$ and for full key in $O(n_{\text{s}} \cdot |\mathcal{S}|)$, i.e. they both scale *linearly* with the number of target subkeys.

In Fig. 3, we show our scaled bounds for GM^f for the case of targeting two subkey bytes. We computed both GM^f and GE^f by first obtaining the cross-product of probabilities between the first two subkeys in the datasets. We see again that our bounds are correct for GM^f, while GE^f deviates slightly from GM^f for the real dataset (refer to Sects. 4.1 and 5.1 for an explanation). LB$_{\text{GM}}$ and UB$_{\text{GM}}$ stay within about 2 bits in both the simulated and real experiments from Fig. 3. UB$_{\text{GMHK}}$ stays again far from GM^f, but LB$_{\text{GMHK}}$ is tighter than LB$_{\text{GM}}$ for higher values of GM^f, as we saw also in the case of a single subkey byte. This confirms that for the lower bound we should use the maximum from LB$_{\text{GM}}$ and LB$_{\text{GMHK}}$, while for the upper bound we should use UB$_{\text{GM}}$.

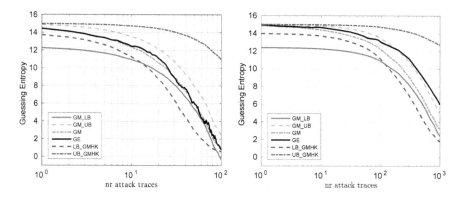

Fig. 3. GM, GE and GM bounds for the simulated (left) and real (right) datasets, when targeting two subkey bytes. These are averaged results over 100 experiments.

6.3   GM Bounds from Element Positioning

Considering the computational advantage of working with scalable bounds for GM, in [21,22], based on an inequality related to positioning an element into a sorted matrix, the authors present new scalable bounds for GM as follows:

$$\prod_{i=1}^{n_s} \mathrm{GM}_i \leq \mathrm{GM}^f \leq |\mathcal{S}|^{n_s} - \prod_{i=1}^{n_s} \left(|\mathcal{S}| - \mathrm{GM}_i\right),$$

where GM_i is the guessing entropy of the $i = 1, 2, ..., n_s$ target subkey.

In order to answer the authors, which left the improvement of these bound as open question, we accepted the challenge and refined both bounds. But because we observed (see Fig. 7 in Appendix) that these improved bounds are still much weaker than the $\mathrm{LB_{GM}}$ and $\mathrm{UB_{GM}}$ bounds, we leave the results and proofs of this part in Appendix.

6.4   GM Bounds Versus the FSE 2015 Rank Estimation

As mentioned in Sect. 2, several algorithms [7,11–13] have been proposed in recent years to estimate the rank of the correct full key. Among them, the rank estimation of Glowacz et al. [11], to which we shall refer as FSE15 from now on, is probably the fastest and scales well for keys up to 128 bytes (e.g. 1024-bit RSA key). For this reason, in Fig. 4, we compare our GM bounds to the results of FSE15 (using their C implementation) for the case of two subkeys, for both the simulated (left) and real (right) datasets. The results show that the FSE15 bounds generally stay within our GM bounds in both data sets, but for the real data set they go slightly beyond our bounds, following the GE^f.

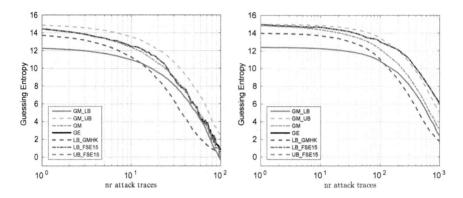

Fig. 4. GM, GE GM bounds and FSE15 bounds for the simulated (left) and real (right) datasets, when targeting two subkey bytes. These are averaged results over 100 experiments.

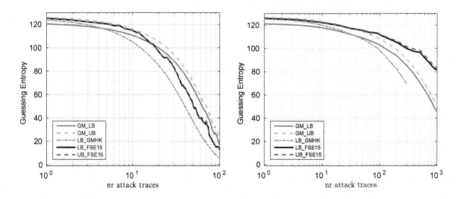

Fig. 5. GM bounds and FSE15 bounds for the simulated (left) and real (right) datasets, when targeting 16 subkey bytes. These are averaged results over 100 experiments.

In Fig. 5, we compare our GM bounds and the FSE15 bounds for the full 16-byte AES key, again for the simulated (left) and real (right) datasets. From this figure, we see that our GM bounds are tight even for the full 128-bit AES key (16 subkeys), LB_{GM} and UB_{GM} staying within 5 bits of each other in both experiments. From the experiments on the real dataset, we also see that LB_{GMHK} fails once the guessing entropy decreases below 70 bits, due to numerical limitations[9] when computing the bound at this point. Comparing our bounds to the FSE15 bounds in the simulated data set, we can see that for higher values of GM^f, the FSE15 bounds stay within our GM bounds, but afterwards they start to deviate, due to the deviation of GE^f from GM^f. A similar pattern is observed with the real data set.

---

[9] We used MATLAB R2015b.

From these experiments, we can see that the FSE15 bounds follow the GE, while our GM bounds follow the GM, and in general the FSE15 bounds stay within our GM bounds, due to the GE being close to the GM. Depending on the requirements, one may prefer to use one tool or the other. However, while less tight than the FSE15 bounds, our GM bounds have the advantage of being scalable to arbitrarily large number of subkeys, while any of the previous rank estimation algorithms, including the FSE15 bounds are limited due to memory and computation time to some maximum size.

6.5   GM Bounds Versus Rank Estimation Algorithms

Given the development of several rank estimation algorithms in the recent years [7,9–13,21], we provide in Table 1 a comparison of these algorithms with our GM bounds in terms of computation time, memory requirements, tightness and accuracy for different key sizes.

Table 1. Comparing GM bounds with rank estimation algorithms.

Method	Good	Bad
FSE '15 [11]	Very fast (<1 s) for up to $n_s = 128$. Very tight bounds	Not scalable for $n_s \geq 256$ (slow)
Asiacrypt '15 [13]	Tight bounds (similar to FSE'15). Fast for $n_s = 16$ (1–4 s)	Memory can be prohibitive for large key sizes. Not scalable: $O(n_s{}^2|\mathcal{S}|\log|\mathcal{S}|)$ (very slow for large key size)
Eurocrypt '15 [10]	Success Rate (SR) for full key as function of time complexity. Time: $O(n_s \cdot Nmax^2)$	No method to go from SR to key rank for a given set of leakage traces. Not scalable for tighter bounds (would require large Nmax)
PRO [12]	Fast for $n_s = 16$ (about 7 s). Tight bounds as function of α (can be slow)	Can run out of RAM for large keys ($\alpha = 2^{13}$). Takes about 5 h for large keys, not scalable
Eurocrypt '13 [7]	Bounds within 6 bits for key ranks smaller than 2^{30}, when targetting a 128-bit key	Run time: 5 s–900 s. Bound up to 20–30 bits for large key ranks ($2^{50} - 2^{100}$). Memory: 4k – 83 MB. Weak bounds (40 bit) for small key rank
CARDIS '14 (Ye) [9]	Acceptable bound, unclear for 16-bit (close to Eurocrypt'13)	Computationally intensive. Scalability may be bad (not evaluated)
CT-RSA '17 [21]	Fast and scalable: $O(n_s \cdot (|\mathcal{S}|\log|\mathcal{S}|))$	Weak lower bound. Very weak upper bound
LB$_{GM}$ and UB$_{GM}$	Guaranteed bounds for GM. Fastest method to date. Scales to arbitrarily large n_s: $O(n_s \cdot |\mathcal{S}|)$. Tight bounds (5 bits for 128-bit key). Constant (negligible) memory	

7   Conclusion

In this paper we have presented the first fully scalable, tight, fast and sound method for estimating the guessing entropy from arbitrarily many lists of probabilities. This method, based on mathematically-derived bounds, allows us to estimate within a few bits the guessing entropy for a 128-bit key, but can also be used to estimate the guessing entropy for cryptographic keys of 1024 bytes (8192 bits) and much larger, which is not possible with any of the previous rank estimation algorithms due to memory or running time limitations.

As an illustration of this capability, we show in Fig. 6, the computation of our bounds for a 1024-byte (8192-bit) key[10]. For simplicity and easier reproducibility, we have used the simulated dataset, where we have replicated the 16 lists of probabilities (one for each target subkey byte) 64 times, so we get 1024 lists of probabilities[11]. The plot shows our LB_{GM} and UB_{GM} bounds for this case. Note in the right side, that the margin between our bounds is about 11.5 bits, which is expected from Remark 2. We leave this figure as a reference for future methods, as none of the previous ones could be used to obtain this plot.

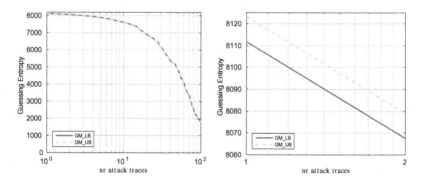

Fig. 6. LB_{GM} and UB_{GM} bounds for a 1024-byte (8192-bit) key, computed from 1024 lists of probabilities. We used a logarithmic Y-axis, as in the rest of the figures. On the right, we show a zoom for $n_a = 1$ and $n_a = 2$ attack traces only.

Acknowledgement. This work has partially been funded by University Politehnica of Bucharest, through the Excellence Research Grants Program, UPB - GEX. Identifiers: UPB - EXCELENȚĂ - 2016, *Noi metode pentru modelarea consumului de energie în dispozitivele electronice* and *Managementul Eficient al Datelor în Sisteme Distribuite Moderne bazat pe Noi Limite ale Entropiei (acronym:* **BigDataH***)*, Contract numbers: 17&18/26.09.2016.

---

[10] Computed using symbolic variables and variable precision arithmetic features of MATLAB, within 13 seconds per iteration.

[11] However, the computation of our bounds would work equally well for any set of lists of probabilities.

References

1. Kocher, P., Jaffe, J., Jun, B.: Differential power analysis. In: Wiener, M. (ed.) CRYPTO 1999. LNCS, vol. 1666, pp. 388–397. Springer, Heidelberg (1999). doi:10. 1007/3-540-48405-1_25
2. Chari, S., Rao, J.R., Rohatgi, P.: Template attacks. In: Kaliski, B.S., Koç, K., Paar, C. (eds.) CHES 2002. LNCS, vol. 2523, pp. 13–28. Springer, Heidelberg (2003). doi:10.1007/3-540-36400-5_3
3. Brier, E., Clavier, C., Olivier, F.: Correlation power analysis with a leakage model. In: Joye, M., Quisquater, J.-J. (eds.) CHES 2004. LNCS, vol. 3156, pp. 16–29. Springer, Heidelberg (2004). doi:10.1007/978-3-540-28632-5_2
4. Standaert, F.-X., Malkin, T.G., Yung, M.: A unified framework for the analysis of side-channel key recovery attacks. In: Joux, A. (ed.) EUROCRYPT 2009. LNCS, vol. 5479, pp. 443–461. Springer, Heidelberg (2009). doi:10.1007/ 978-3-642-01001-9_26
5. Veyrat-Charvillon, N., Gérard, B., Renauld, M., Standaert, F.-X.: An optimal key enumeration algorithm and its application to side-channel attacks. In: Knudsen, L.R., Wu, H. (eds.) SAC 2012. LNCS, vol. 7707, pp. 390–406. Springer, Heidelberg (2013). doi:10.1007/978-3-642-35999-6_25
6. Oswald, D., Paar, C.: Breaking Mifare DESFire MF3ICD40: power analysis and templates in the real world. In: Preneel, B., Takagi, T. (eds.) CHES 2011. LNCS, vol. 6917, pp. 207–222. Springer, Heidelberg (2011). doi:10.1007/ 978-3-642-23951-9_14
7. Veyrat-Charvillon, N., Gérard, B., Standaert, F.-X.: Security evaluations beyond computing power. In: Johansson, T., Nguyen, P.Q. (eds.) EUROCRYPT 2013. LNCS, vol. 7881, pp. 126–141. Springer, Heidelberg (2013). doi:10.1007/ 978-3-642-38348-9_8
8. Choudary, O., Kuhn, M.G.: Efficient template attacks. In: Francillon, A., Rohatgi, P. (eds.) CARDIS 2013. LNCS, vol. 8419, pp. 253–270. Springer, Cham (2014). doi:10.1007/978-3-319-08302-5_17
9. Ye, X., Eisenbarth, T., Martin, W.: Bounded, yet sufficient? How to determine whether limited side channel information enables key recovery. In: Joye, M., Moradi, A. (eds.) CARDIS 2014. LNCS, vol. 8968, pp. 215–232. Springer, Cham (2015). doi:10.1007/978-3-319-16763-3_13
10. Duc, A., Faust, S., Standaert, F.-X.: Making masking security proofs concrete. In: Oswald, E., Fischlin, M. (eds.) EUROCRYPT 2015. LNCS, vol. 9056, pp. 401–429. Springer, Heidelberg (2015). doi:10.1007/978-3-662-46800-5_16
11. Glowacz, C., Grosso, V., Poussier, R., Schüth, J., Standaert, F.-X.: Simpler and more efficient rank estimation for side-channel security assessment. In: Leander, G. (ed.) FSE 2015. LNCS, vol. 9054, pp. 117–129. Springer, Heidelberg (2015). doi:10. 1007/978-3-662-48116-5_6
12. Bernstein, D.J., Lange, T., van Vredendaal, C.: Tighter, faster, simpler side-channel security evaluations beyond computing power. https://eprint.iacr.org/2015/221
13. Martin, D.P., O'Connell, J.F., Oswald, E., Stam, M.: Counting keys in parallel after a side channel attack. In: Iwata, T., Cheon, J.H. (eds.) ASIACRYPT 2015. LNCS, vol. 9453, pp. 313–337. Springer, Heidelberg (2015). doi:10.1007/ 978-3-662-48800-3_13
14. Poussier, R., Standaert, F.-X., Grosso, V.: Simple key enumeration (and rank estimation) using histograms: an integrated approach. In: Gierlichs, B., Poschmann, A.Y. (eds.) CHES 2016. LNCS, vol. 9813, pp. 61–81. Springer, Heidelberg (2016). doi:10.1007/978-3-662-53140-2_4

15. Choudary, M.O., Poussier, R., Standaert, F.-X.: Score-based vs. probability-based enumeration – a cautionary note. In: Dunkelman, O., Sanadhya, S.K. (eds.) INDOCRYPT 2016. LNCS, vol. 10095, pp. 137–152. Springer, Cham (2016). doi:10.1007/978-3-319-49890-4_8

16. Massey, J.L.: Guessing and entropy. In: IEEE ISIT, p. 204 (1994)

17. McEliece, R.J., Yu, Z.: An inequality on entropy. In: IEEE ISIT 1995, p. 329 (1995). ISBN: 0-7803-2453-6

18. Boztaş, S.: Comments on "An inequality on guessing and its application to sequential decoding". IEEE Trans. Inf. Theory **43**(6), 2062–2063 (1997)

19. Arikan, E.: An inequality on guessing and its application to sequential decoding. IEEE Trans. Inf. Theory **42**(1), 99–105 (1996)

20. Cover, T.M., Thomas, J.A.: Elements of Information Theory, 2nd edn. Wiley (2006). ISBN: 0-471-24195-4

21. David, L., Wool, A.: A bounded-space near-optimal key enumeration algorithm for multi-subkey side-channel attacks. In: Handschuh, H. (ed.) CT-RSA 2017. LNCS, vol. 10159, pp. 311–327. Springer, Cham (2017). doi:10.1007/978-3-319-52153-4_18

22. David, L., Wool, A.: A bounded-space near-optimal key enumeration algorithm for multi-dimensional side-channel attacks. Cryptology ePrint Archive, Report 2015/1236 (2015). http://eprint.iacr.org/2015/1236

23. NXP A710x family: Secure authentication microcontroller. http://www.nxp.com/products/identification-and-security/secure-authentication-and-anti-counterfeit-technology/secure-authentication-microcontroller:A710X_FAMILY. Accessed 11 Oct 2016

A   GM bounds from element positioning

Considering the computational advantage of working with scalable bounds for GM, in [21,22], based on an inequality related to positioning an element into a sorted matrix, the authors present new scalable bounds for GM as follows:

$$\prod_{i=1}^{n_s} \mathrm{GM}_i \leq \mathrm{GM}^f \leq |\mathcal{S}|^{n_s} - \prod_{i=1}^{n_s} (|\mathcal{S}| - \mathrm{GM}_i), \tag{15}$$

where GM_i is the guessing entropy of the $i = 1, 2, ..., n_s$ target subkey.

In order to answer the authors, which left the improvement of these bound as open question, we accept the challenge and refine both bounds as follows.

First, for the upper bound, we may observe that the base inequality involved here, representing the positioning of an element into a sorted matrix built from the combination of products of elements of two vectors x and y, see [22] Fig. 3, i.e.

$$ij \leq rank(x_i, y_j) \leq n^2 - (n - i)(n - j), \quad i, j = 1, 2, ...n$$

is weak and its meaning is unclear (the position of an element could not go so far). A more meaningful form of this inequality is a tighter one, like

$$ij \leq rank(x_i, y_j) \leq n^2 - (n - i + 1)(n - j + 1) + 1$$

and considering its right hand side applied for our context reveals an improved upper bound for GM. But this improvement is almost unnoticeable in our experiments, so we will not use it for the following discussions.

Now, for the lower bound we define as $I_1, I_2, ..., I_m$ nonempty, pairwise disjoint subsets of $\{1, 2, ..., n_s\}$, with $\cup_j I_j = \{1, 2, ..., n_s\}$, $j = 1, 2, ...m$, $m \leq n_s$ and with the same number of elements ($|I_1| = |I_2| = ... = |I_m| = n_s/m$).

We further define as GM_{I_j} the guessing entropy of the combined target subkeys from the subset I_j, $j = 1, 2..., m$. We have the following

Theorem 3 *(EP bounds for GM). Considering the above we have*

$$\prod_{i=1}^{n_s} GM_i \leq \prod_{j=1}^{m} GM_{I_j} \leq GM^f.$$

Proof. The left hand side of the inequality follows directly from the combination of the left hand sides of the inequality of [21, Theorem 2] particularized for $d = j$, with $j = 1, 2, ..., m$, i.e. from inequalities

$$\prod_{i \in I_j} \mathrm{GM}_i \leq \mathrm{GM}_{I_j}, \quad j = 1, 2, ...m.$$

For the right hand side of the inequality we notice that grouping the target subkeys into subgroups of the same size, yields lists of probabilities per the new target subkeys of the same size, so we can still apply the left hand side of the generalized base inequality form [21] in order to obtain the wanted result.

It is easy to observe that the previous result is a refinement of the lower bound presented into [21, 22]. Also we can refine furthermore the result by using a good grouping strategy. For example in practice $n_s = 16$ so a lower bound will arrive from grouping into 2 groups of 8 elements, then a weaker lower bound will be derived by grouping into 4 groups of 4 elements, and so on until we group each individual element, which is the lowest bound, i.e.

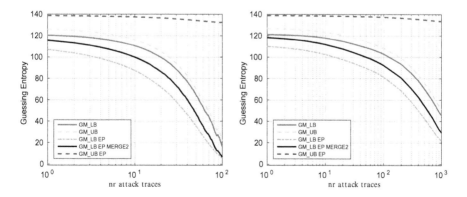

Fig. 7. GM bounds and EP bounds for the simulated (left) and real (right) datasets, when targeting 16 subkey bytes. These are averaged results over 100 experiments.

Corollary 1.

$$\prod_{i=1}^{n_s} GM_i = \prod_{j=1}^{n_s} GM_{I_j} \leq \prod_{j=1}^{8} GM_{I_j} \leq \prod_{j=1}^{4} GM_{I_j} \leq \prod_{j=1}^{2} GM_{I_j} \leq GM^f.$$

Because of the computational limitations, in our experiments we have only considered grouping as much as two elements per group, i.e. two subkeys. In Fig. 7, we compare these bounds, with our GM bounds. We see that even after merging, the two EP bounds are weaker than our LB_{GM} and UB_{GM} bounds.

Fast Leakage Assessment

Oscar Reparaz[(✉)], Benedikt Gierlichs, and Ingrid Verbauwhede

Department of Electrical Engineering, imec-COSIC, KU Leuven,
Kasteelpark Arenberg 10, 3001 Leuven-Heverlee, Belgium
{oscar.reparaz,benedikt.gierlichs,ingrid.verbauwhede}@esat.kuleuven.be

Abstract. We describe a fast technique for performing the computationally heavy part of leakage assessment, in any statistical moment (or other property) of the leakage samples distributions. The proposed technique outperforms by orders of magnitude the approach presented at CHES 2015 by Schneider and Moradi. We can carry out evaluations that before took 90 CPU-days in 4 CPU-*hours* (about a 500-fold speedup). As a bonus, we can work with exact arithmetic, we can apply kernel-based density estimation methods, we can employ arbitrary preprocessing functions such as absolute value to power traces, and we can perform information-theoretic leakage assessment. Our trick is simple and elegant, and lends itself to an easy and compact implementation. We fit a prototype implementation in about 130 lines of C code.

Keywords: Leakage assessment · Efficient computation · Side-channel analysis · Countermeasure

1 Introduction

Implementations of cryptographic protocols and algorithms often need to be protected against side-channel attacks. This is true for devices all along the range from tiny embedded compute platforms, where an adversary is able to perform local attacks (power [KJJ99], EM [QS01, GMO01], etc.), to cloud infrastructure, where an attacker is able to perform remote attacks (timing attacks [BB03], cache attacks [Per05], etc.). There is a large variety of countermeasures, some are ad-hoc, others are supported by theory, some protect against specific attacks, others protect against families of attacks, etc. However, most countermeasures have in common that it is not easy to implement them properly, and thus the effectiveness of their implementation needs to be carefully validated. This is done by physical testing. The most common, classical approach is to apply relevant attacks and assess the effort that is required to break the implementation. An advantage of this approach is that one gets a good view on the security level provided by the implementation. A disadvantage is that the approach can be extensive, time consuming and costly. Indeed, an attack may comprise many steps (sample preparation, data acquisition, pre-processing, analysis, post-processing, key enumeration) and for each step there are many possible techniques, and there are many relevant attacks.

© International Association for Cryptologic Research 2017
W. Fischer and N. Homma (Eds.): CHES 2017, LNCS 10529, pp. 387–399, 2017.
DOI: 10.1007/978-3-319-66787-4_19

Leakage assessment is a fundamentally different approach. It was introduced by Coron, Naccache and Kocher [CKN00, CNK04] after the publication of Differential Power Analysis [KJJ99] as a procedure to assess side-channel information leakage. In brief, leakage assessment techniques allow to assess whether a device leaks information that might be exploitable by side-channel attacks. The approach gained momentum in security evaluations of countermeasures against side-channel attacks in academia [BGN+14, SM15, DCE16] after it resurfaced in publications by Cryptography Research Inc. [GJJR11, CDG+13]. Leakage assessments (especially non-specific ones, see Sect. 2) are easy to carry out and can be very sensitive.

Previous Work. Schneider and Moradi present formulae for leakage assessment at any order traversing the dataset only once [SM15]. They base their approach on the work of Pébay [P08]. The works of Durvaux and Standaert [DS16] and Ding et al. [DCE16] are orthogonal to this paper, and can benefit from the techniques we describe.

Our Contribution. We present a computational trick that serves to accelerate the computationally heavy part of leakage assessment, in any statistical moment or other property of the leakage samples distributions, by orders of magnitude compared to [SM15].

2   Leakage Assessment

There is essentially only one approach to leakage assessment: it is Test Vector Leakage Assessment (TVLA) by Cryptography Research (CRI).

The main idea is to check whether two well chosen data inputs (the test vectors) lead to distinguishable side-channel information. One says that the device leaks if the side-channel information is distinguishable. The test should be repeated with a few pairs of input data to increase confidence. If the side-channel information is not distinguishable one has learned little, in particular one must not conclude that the device does not leak. Even when the device is deemed leaking, one does not necessarily learn that key-extraction is easy.

In the remainder we focus on (local) power analysis attacks, where the side-channel information is typically referred to as power traces or curves. It is straightforward to adapt the technique to other sources of information leakage, e.g. binary cache hit/miss.

Applying TVLA one chooses two inputs, A and B. One obtains measurement traces from the processing of A or B. Practice has shown that tests are very sensitive and pick up all kinds of systematic effects, therefore the measurement process should be as randomized as possible. For example, measurements of groups A and B should be randomly interleaved.

One ends up with two sets of measurements and computes a suitable statistic or metric to determine if the samples in the two sets come from the same distribution or not [GJJR11, CDG+13, MOBW13]. For instance, using Welch's two-tailed t-test with confidence level 99.999% one determines that the device leaks if the threshold ±4.5 is exceeded.

The TVLA proposals by CRI distinguish specific and non-specific tests. In specific tests one checks for leakage of one or a few chosen intermediate values. One chooses the inputs A and B such that a "substantial" difference occurs only for the chosen intermediate values while all other intermediate values appear to be similar or random. This typically requires to know the key used by the implementation. In non-specific tests one checks for leakage of any intermediate value. Due to fundamental properties of cryptographic algorithms it often suffices to choose two different inputs A and B.

To enhance the power of the assessment and to increase coverage of special cases that are hard to anticipate, CRI proposed fixed versus random testing. One input is fixed at the chosen value, the other input takes uniformly distributed random values (in specific tests the domain can be restricted).

Durvaux and Standaert [DS16] argue that fixed versus fixed testing with two different well chosen inputs can lead to faster leakage detection.

Anyhow, what we propose in the next section is orthogonal to this and hence may serve to improve all flavors of leakage assessment.

3 Fast Leakage Assessment

The focus of this paper is on how one uses the measurement samples to compute the test statistic. A simple approach could be to first obtain all measurements and store them for instance on a hard disk. Then one reads the measurements and uses chosen algorithms to compute the required moments of the distributions and finally the statistic. A different approach could be to interleave data acquisition and computation of statistical moments. There are different algorithms with different properties: some algorithms require multiple passes through the data set, some algorithms are single pass; some algorithms are numerically more stable than others. In general, one wants to use algorithms that are efficient and numerically stable. Typically one ends up using so-called update algorithms. For each new sample, these algorithms update a number of intermediate results that allow to compute the final value without having to pass through the data set again. See [SM15] for a discussion.

Key Idea. The first key observation for our work is that all solutions and algorithms discussed in the side-channel analysis-related literature directly compute moments or statistics from samples. The second key observation is that, in order to compute a distribution's mean, one only needs a sample distribution histogram, and not the whole sample set. The same holds for variance, and actually for any statistical moment or other property of the sampled distribution.

Our main idea is hence a divide and conquer step: we first compute the histogram describing the sample distribution for each class, for each time sample. Only this step requires access to the traces. Note that this step is typically performed quite fast. It boils down to read/write memory accesses and counter increments by one. Then, using only the histograms, we compute all necessary statistical moments and the t-statistic, or other properties and metrics.

Notation. We assume that an evaluator takes N side-channel leakage traces $t_i[n]$. The time index n ranges from 1 to the trace length L. The trace index i ranges from 1 to the number of traces N. Each time sample within a trace is an integral value from the set $\{0, 1, \ldots, 2^Q - 1\} = [0, 2^Q) \cap \mathbb{Z}$, where Q is the number of quantization bits used to sample the side-channel signal. (In typical oscilloscopes, $Q = 8$ bits.) The array $c[i]$ stores the class index corresponding to the i-th trace. We assume there are just two classes $c[i] \in \{0, 1\}$, $\forall i$ (fixed and random, for instance).

Procedure. The procedure works as follows:

Step 1. Initialize two families of histograms $H_0[n]$ and $H_1[n]$. Each family is actually a $L \times 2^Q$ matrix of counters. Row n stores the histogram for trace distribution at time sample n.

Step 2. For each trace $t_i[n]$, $n = 1, \ldots, L$ belonging to class $c[i] \in \{0, 1\}$, update the corresponding histograms as $H_{c[i]}[n][t_i[n]] \leftarrow H_{c[i]}[n][t_i[n]] + 1$.

Step 3. From the two histogram families H_0 and H_1, compute the necessary moments and the t-statistic value.

Why this Works. This procedure works since histogram families H_i carry all the information about the (estimated) class-conditional distributions. From those histograms, it becomes easy to compute means or any other statistical moment or property of the distributions. For example, we can compute the sample mean $m_0[n]$ at time sample n in step 3 from H_0 as:

$$m_0[n] = \frac{1}{\sum_{i=0}^{2^Q-1} H_0[n][i]} \sum_{i=0}^{2^Q-1} i \cdot H_0[n][i]. \tag{1}$$

In a similar way, we can compute all necessary statistical moments to calculate the t-statistic value at any order only from the histograms H_i.

4   Implementation

We wrote a C99 shared library named libfastld, with no external dependencies except math.h, implementing the previous methodology. Our approach is simple: it fits in around 130 lines of source code. Our interface is simple as well: the implementation provides a function

```
void add_curve(fastld_t *ctx, uint8_t *curve, uint8_t class);
```

that processes one curve array and updates the corresponding histograms in the state ctx according to the trace class. This curve can be discarded after calling add_curve. Afterwards, the state is processed in step 3 to yield a t-statistic curve. Our current implementation first pre-processes histograms at arbitrary order (by first centering and then exponentiating each histogram) and then uses the Welford method to estimate the variance [Knu81, Sect. 4.2.2.A]. Then, from variances and means the t-statistic is constructed.

We decided to use 32-bit unsigned integers for matrix counters. This means we can iterate step 2 over 2^{32} ($\approx$ 4 billion) traces without problems. This seemed to us like a comfortable maximum number of traces for our current evaluations. We could have used 16-bit counters for better performance, but this requires more care not to overflow (theoretically possible after $2^{16} \approx 65$ k measurements). In our case, measurements are quantized with $Q = 8$ bits.

Which Algorithm to Use for Variance Computation? For the moments computation step, we are not forced to use single-pass algorithms. This step is performed based on a histogram, and not on the whole trace dataset. Therefore, multiple-pass algorithms are cheap to compute, can provide very good numerical stability and can lend themselves to an easy implementation [TFC83].

(Recall that the distribution estimation phase, step 1, is single-pass. Thus, once we acquire a trace and update the corresponding histogram, we can throw away the trace.)

5   Performance Analysis

5.1   Analytical

Separation of Tasks. We effectively decouple two tasks:

1. estimating measurement distributions, and
2. computing distribution parameters (statistical moments).

The first task is performed in step 2. This step produces a compact representation of measurement distributions (namely, two sets of histograms). The running time of this step depends on the number of traces, and only this step. The computational effort in step 2 is just one counter increment per time sample per trace. This is the key advantage of this method: the computational work per trace is minimal.

The resulting histograms are used in step 3 to perform the second task. Previous approaches, such as Schneier and Moradi [SM15] perform both tasks at the same time. We will see that performing the moment estimation from the histogram information brings advantages.

5.2   Empirical

First Dataset. Our dataset comprises $N = 10^6$ traces of $L = 3000$ samples long. We assume traces are provided one-at-a-time. (If traces are made transposed, this may accelerate the process, but we are interested in on-the-fly algorithms.) Our dataset is synthetic: the distribution of each time sample is uniform at random in $\{0, \ldots, 255\}$. We compile the implementation from Sect. 4 with gcc version 4.9.2 and optimization flags -O3. Our benchmark platform is a Core i5 desktop workstation running at 3.3 GHz.

Running Times. The update of histograms (Step 2 in Sect. 3) takes 9.8 s to process the $N = 10^6$ traces. This makes roughly a trace processing bandwidth of 305 MB/s. After step 2, we compute the first 10 statistical moments (Step 3 in Sect. 3) in 0.8 s. Note that the distribution of this synthetic dataset is the worst possible for cache efficiency. Thus, these figures can be taken as worst-case. Traces coming from an actual device will likely follow a distribution more amenable to cache accesses in step 2.

Memory Requirements. For traces $L = 3000$ time samples long the size required to hold the two histogram families H_0 and H_1 is about 6 MB, which just fits into the L2 cache of modern processors.

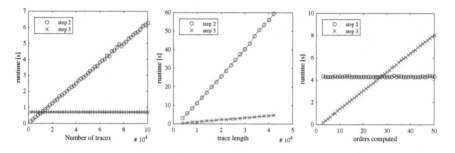

Fig. 1. Left: running times for step 2 and step 3, as the number of traces grows, for $L = 5000$ and five statistical moments computed. Center: running times as the trace length grows, for $N = 100\ 000$ traces and five statistical moments computed. Right: running times as the number of statistical moments computed grows, for $N = 100\ 000$ and $L = 5000$.

5.3   Scaling

Scaling of Running Times. The method proposed in Sect. 3 scales well in several directions. It is easy to see that the running time of step 2 is linear in the number of traces, and the running time of step 3 is constant. In Fig. 1, left, we plot the empirical running time of step 2 and 3 as the number of traces grows. Traces are $L = 5000$ time samples long and step 3 computes the first five statistical moments. We can see that indeed the dependency of the running time of step 2 is linear, and the time spent on step 3 is independent of the number of traces. In Fig. 1, center, we plot running times as a function of the trace length, for a fixed number of traces ($N = 100\ 000$) and five statistical moments. We can see that the running times of both steps depend linearly on the trace length. Finally in Fig. 1, right, we plot the running times as a function of the number of statistical moments computed. Step 2 runs in time independent of the number of computed moments, and the running time for step 3 is linear in the number of computed moments. In this case, we fix the number of traces $N = 100\ 000$ and the trace length $L = 5000$.

Memory Scaling. It is easy to see that memory requirements scale linearly with the trace length L. Interestingly, they are constant with the number of traces N. The number of computed statistical moments incurs little influence on the memory requirements as well. There is an exponential dependency on Q, albeit for a typical oscilloscope we may safely assume $Q = 8$. The number of bytes required to store the histogram families is obviously $2 \times L \times 2^Q \times W$ if we use W-byte counters.

6 Discussion

6.1 Comparison with Other Approaches

As a rough benchmark, the work of Schneider and Moradi requires around 9 h to compute up to the fifth order from a dataset of 100 million traces of 3 000 time samples using 24 cores [SM15, Sect. 4.3]. This makes around 7.8×10^{-3} s per trace per core, which is roughly 800 times slower than our approach. We note that this is a very crude benchmark: the benchmarking platforms are substantially different and many other variables are as well different. Nevertheless, it serves as evidence that the approach presented in this paper outperforms previous work by several orders of magnitude.

We also implemented the update formulae of Schneider and Moradi and benchmarked with the same dataset. The results can be found in Appendix A.

Table 1. Scaling. A cell marked with "—" means "same content as the cell above".

Method	Ops. per trace	Time per trace $L = 3000$	Finalization step $L = 3000$
[SM15], orders 1–5	$14L$ RW + $66L$ MUL + L DIV + $31L$ ADD	7.8×10^{-3} s	0 s (virtually free)
This paper, orders 1–5	$2L$ RW + L ADD	1.45×10^{-5} s	0.3 s
This paper, orders 1–10	—	—	0.8 s
This paper, orders 1–50	—	—	4.6 s
This paper, orders 1–100	—	—	9.4 s

Operation Count Scaling. Here we describe how the operation count scales for both methods. The results are condensed in Table 1. We should note that operations for the [SM15] method are performed on double-precision floating point arithmetic, while for our method are performed using 32-bit integers. The operation count of the [SM15] method was a back-of-the-envelope calculation based on the update formulas in [SM15, Sect. A.1].

If restricted to computing the first five statistical moments, the [SM15] method requires the following operation count per trace per timesample: about

14 double-precision floating-point read-write operations, about 66 floating-point multiplications, 1 floating-point division and about 31 floating-point additions. The number of operations in this case highly depends on the number of statistical moments one would like to compute.

In contrast, the method proposed in this paper requires just two 32-bit memory read-write operations and one integer addition for step 2, per time sample per trace. The computation per trace is constant, independent of the statistical moments one is interested to compute. Our method requires a finalization step that takes less than $1\,$s for $L = 3000$ traces, and does not depend on N and thus can be amortized. This means that our method outperforms the [SM15] method for sufficiently many traces.

Memory Scaling. For both methods, memory requirements are not usually the bottleneck. Both methods require linearly more memory as the number of time samples L grows. The [SM15] method requires memory linear in the number of statistical moments computed, and our method requires memory exponential in the quantization steps of the oscilloscope, often $Q = 8$.

6.2   Parallelization

The algorithm described in Sect. 3 is embarrassingly parallel. The work of step 2 can be split across several processors trivially. Step 3 can be as well distributed: each processor gets a different time-slice. However, we believe parallelization will be applied seldom. In our case, our implementation is single-threaded because multi-threading was not deemed necessary. Step 2 is no longer the most consuming step in our evaluation chain.

6.3   Bonuses

Bonus: Exact Arithmetic. In the extreme case, one can perform the whole computation of step 3 in rational arithmetic (that is, working in $\mathbb{Q}$). Thus, we have the ability to compute the *exact* value for the (square of the) t-statistic, eliminating any round-off or numeric stability issue. Since we work with exact values, the choice of estimator to compute statistical moments is superfluous, since they will all yield the intended exact result.

The penalty in computational effort is very low. There is no impact on the running time of the dominating step 2, and only slight on step 3. We have implemented step 3 in rational arithmetic using the GNU's Multiple Precision Arithmetic library (GMP) with mpq_t rational integer types. (This requires obviously linking against GMP. This is only required for using exact arithmetic.) The final square root floating point computation in the denominator is performed with at least 128-bit precision, but this is not really necessary. We can very well compare t^2 against $(4.5)^2$ to fail or pass a device.

We repeated the experiment with the dataset from Sect. 4. Step 3 now takes around $81\,$s. This is a one-time effort. We believe this is a useful feature, especially for evaluation labs where extra assurance is desirable. When using exact arithmetic one does not have to worry about the choice of algorithm for variance, numeric stability or errors.

Bonus: Kernel-Based Estimation. It is well-known that kernel-based density estimation methods may lead to more accurate estimations, especially when the sample size is scarce (few traces). We note that kernel-based estimations are very easy to plug in our method. One can apply the kernels directly to the histograms (output of step 2), instead to each trace individually. Then, the evaluator only has to modify accordingly step 3. This fact can be helpful if the evaluator wants to experiment with a family of kernels (say, different kernel bandwidths). She can experiment with different parameters *a posteriori*, once traces have been collected and thrown away in step 2.

Bonus: Arbitrary Pre-processing Function. Sometimes, one is interested in using a different pre-processing function other than centering and exponentiating. In some noisy cases, it is advisable to use for example absolute difference [BGRV15] rather than the theoretically optimum centered product [PRB09] (assuming HW leakage behavior and Gaussian noise).

The evaluator can apply an arbitrary pre-processing function of his choice after step 2 and before step 3. For example, the evaluator can inject the absolute value pre-processing function. This is not trivial to do in the approach of Schneier and Moradi. (One could develop the Taylor expansion for $|x|$ to approximate with a polynomial, but this incurs an error due to truncation.)

Bonus: Information-Theoretic Leakage Detection. From the histograms, it is also possible to perform an information-theory based leakage detection test, using for instance a two-sample Kolmogorov–Smirnov test (this tool was previously used for instance by Whitnall and Oswald [WOM11]) or mutual information [MOBW13]. We note that for mutual information it is possible to apply a kernel density estimation method *after* the histograms H_0 and H_1 have been estimated (due to linearity), resulting in a fast estimation.

Bonus: Cropping Detection. It is important to detect if there is cropping while acquiring power traces when performing a leakage detection test. Typical oscilloscopes output a saturated value when sampling a value out of range. When performing leakage detection tests with cropped (saturated) values, the obtained t-value is unreliable and should be discarded. (Normally, with saturated samples the t-statistic grows very much. It is easy to explain this: saturated samples carry a small variance, shrinking the denominator and thus the t-value grows.) One should ideally check that there is no cropping while measuring. However, in the case that such check is missing, our method after step 2 allows to detect if any of the traces were cropped (maybe the evaluator did a mistake, or some event (mis)happened), *after* trace collection. It is however impossible to recover from this mistake; that is, it is impossible to "remove" cropped traces once the histograms of step 2 have been filled, meaning that traces must be acquired again. Nevertheless, we think this can bring extra assurance whether to trust the evaluation or not. This can be implemented in step 3 as follows: verify that the histogram does not take the extremal values (in our case, 0 and $2^Q - 1$). We found this feature useful in our own experience.

6.4 DPA Attacks

In principle one could port the same principles from Sect. 3 to plain DPA attacks. However, the gain is not so strong, since one should keep in general one histogram per plaintext value, instead of just two. Naively the memory requirements are significantly higher. Of course, if the evaluator can choose texts this can be significantly lowered.

6.5 Deployment

The technique presented in this paper is mature and was used in several evaluations performed in the last three years in our lab. Among others, it was used in the evaluation of recently proposed higher-order masking schemes such as [BGN+14, CBRN14, CBR+15, CRB+16] and other publications [CN16, CBG+17].

7 Conclusion

In this paper we presented a simple methodology to significantly alleviate the computation effort required to perform a leakage assessment. Our method is extremely simple and compact to implement (about 130 lines of C code), but has a significant impact on the running time of a leakage assessment. We can lower the running time of leakage assessment evaluations by several orders of magnitude .

Acknowledgments. This work was supported in part by the Research Council KU Leuven: C16/15/058. In addition, this work was supported by the Flemish Government, FWO G.00130.13N, FWO G.0876.14N and Thresholds G0842.13; by the Hercules Foundation AKUL/11/19; through the Horizon 2020 research and innovation programme under grant agreement 644052 HECTOR and Cathedral ERC Advanced Grant 695305. Benedikt Gierlichs is Postdoctoral Fellow of the Fund for Scientific Research - Flanders (FWO).

A   Benchmark of Schneider and Moradi

Here we repeat the analysis from Sect. 5.3 for the method of Schneider and Moradi. We evaluate both methods in the same machine, with the same toolchain and with software written by the same person. Nevertheless, the purpose of this section is only exploratory, and it is possible that a more optimized implementation of either method yields better performance.

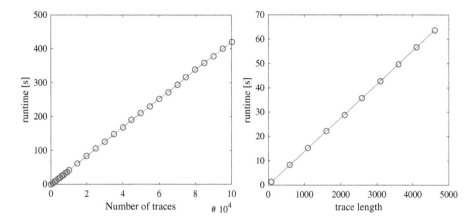

Fig. 2. Method of Schneider and Moradi. Left: running times as the number of traces grows, for $L = 3000$ and five statistical moments computed. Right: running times as the trace length grows, for $N = 100\,000$ traces and five statistical moments computed.

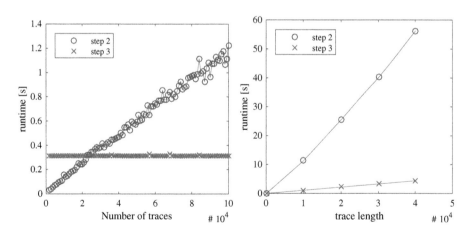

Fig. 3. Method presented in this paper. Left: running times as the number of traces grows, for $L = 3000$ and five statistical moments computed. Right: running times as the trace length grows, for $N = 100\,000$ traces and five statistical moments computed. Note that the number of traces in the right picture is an order of magnitude larger than that of Fig. 2.

We compute t-statistics up to the fifth order. In Fig. 2 we plot the evolution of running times for the method of Schneider and Moradi. For completeness, we repeat in Fig. 3 the performance of the method presented in this paper for parameters that match Fig. 2.

The difference in running time between methods is expected to grow substantially as the statistical order increases. However, estimations of higher-order statistical moments are very sensitive to noise and thus are rarely done in today's evaluations.

References

[BB03]   Brumley, D., Boneh, D.: Remote timing attacks are practical. In: Proceedings of the 12th USENIX Security Symposium. USENIX Association (2003)

[BGN+14] Bilgin, B., Gierlichs, B., Nikova, S., Nikov, V., Rijmen, V.: Higher-order threshold implementations. In: Sarkar, P., Iwata, T. (eds.) ASIACRYPT 2014. LNCS, vol. 8874, pp. 326–343. Springer, Heidelberg (2014). doi:10.1007/978-3-662-45608-8_18

[BGRV15] Balasch, J., Gierlichs, B., Reparaz, O., Verbauwhede, I.: DPA, bitslicing and masking at 1 GHz. In: Güneysu and Handschuh [GH15], pp. 599–619

[CBG+17] De Cnudde, T., Bilgin, B., Gierlichs, B., Nikov, V., Nikova, S., Rijmen, V.: Does coupling affect the security of masked implementations? In: Guilley, S. (ed.) COSADE 2017. LNCS, vol. 10348, pp. 1–18. Springer, Cham (2017)

[CBR+15] Cnudde, T., Bilgin, B., Reparaz, O., Nikov, V., Nikova, S.: Higher-order threshold implementation of the AES S-Box. In: Homma, N., Medwed, M. (eds.) CARDIS 2015. LNCS, vol. 9514, pp. 259–272. Springer, Cham (2016). doi:10.1007/978-3-319-31271-2_16

[CBRN14] De Cnudde, T., Bilgin, B., Reparaz, O., Nikova, S.: Higher-order glitch resistant implementation of the PRESENT S-Box. In: Ors, B., Preneel, B. (eds.) BalkanCryptSec 2014. LNCS, vol. 9024, pp. 75–93. Springer, Cham (2015). doi:10.1007/978-3-319-21356-9_6

[CDG+13] Cooper, J., DeMulder, E., Goodwill, G., Jaffe, J., Kenworthy, G., Rohatgi, P.: Test vector leakage assessment (TVLA) methodology in practice. In: International Cryptographic Module Conference (2013)

[CKN00]   Coron, J.-S., Kocher, P., Naccache, D.: Statistics and secret leakage. In: Frankel, Y. (ed.) FC 2000. LNCS, vol. 1962, pp. 157–173. Springer, Heidelberg (2001). doi:10.1007/3-540-45472-1_12

[CN16]   De Cnudde, T., Nikova, S.: More efficient private circuits II through threshold implementations. In: Maurine, P., Tunstall, M. (eds.) International Workshop on Fault Diagnosis and Tolerance in Cryptography 2016, Volume Conference Publishing Service, pp. 114–124, Santa Barbara, CA, USA. IEEE (2016)

[CNK04]   Coron, J.-S., Naccache, D., Kocher, P.C.: Statistics and secret leakage. ACM Trans. Embedded Comput. Syst. 3(3), 492–508 (2004)

[CRB+16] De Cnudde, T., Reparaz, O., Bilgin, B., Nikova, S., Nikov, V., Rijmen, V.: Masking AES with $d+1$ shares in hardware. In: Gierlichs, B., Poschmann, A.Y. (eds.) CHES 2016. LNCS, vol. 9813, pp. 194–212. Springer, Heidelberg (2016). doi:10.1007/978-3-662-53140-2_10

[DCE16] Ding, A.A., Chen, C., Eisenbarth, T.: Simpler, faster, and more robust T-test based leakage detection. In: Standaert, F.-X., Oswald, E. (eds.) COSADE 2016. LNCS, vol. 9689, pp. 163–183. Springer, Cham (2016). doi:10.1007/978-3-319-43283-0_10

[DS16] Durvaux, F., Standaert, F.-X.: From improved leakage detection to the detection of points of interests in leakage traces. In: Fischlin, M., Coron, J.-S. (eds.) EUROCRYPT 2016. LNCS, vol. 9665, pp. 240–262. Springer, Heidelberg (2016). doi:10.1007/978-3-662-49890-3_10

[GH15] Güneysu, T., Handschuh, H. (eds.): CHES 2015. LNCS, vol. 9293. Springer, Heidelberg (2015)

[GJJR11] Goodwill, G., Jun, B., Jaffe, J., Rohatgi, P.: A testing methodology for side channel resistance validation. In: NIST Non-invasive Attack Testing Workshop (2011)

[GMO01] Gandolfi, K., Mourtel, C., Olivier, F.: Electromagnetic analysis: concrete results. In: Koç, Ç.K., Naccache, D., Paar, C. (eds.) CHES 2001. LNCS, vol. 2162, pp. 251–261. Springer, Heidelberg (2001). doi:10.1007/3-540-44709-1_21

[KJJ99] Kocher, P., Jaffe, J., Jun, B.: Differential power analysis. In: Wiener, M. (ed.) CRYPTO 1999. LNCS, vol. 1666, pp. 388–397. Springer, Heidelberg (1999). doi:10.1007/3-540-48405-1_25

[Knu81] Knuth, D.E.: The Art of Computer Programming, Volume II: Seminumerical Algorithms, 2nd edn. Addison-Wesley, Boston (1981)

[MOBW13] Mather, L., Oswald, E., Bandenburg, J., Wójcik, M.: Does my device leak information? an *a priori* statistical power analysis of leakage detection tests. In: Sako, K., Sarkar, P. (eds.) ASIACRYPT 2013. LNCS, vol. 8269, pp. 486–505. Springer, Heidelberg (2013). doi:10.1007/978-3-642-42033-7_25

[P08] Pébay, P.: Formulas for robust, one-pass parallel computation of covariances and arbitrary-order statistical moments. Technical report SAND2008-6212, Sandia National Laboratory (2008)

[Per05] Percival, C.: Cache missing for fun and profit. In: Proceedings of BSDCan 2005 (2005)

[PRB09] Prouff, E., Rivain, M., Bevan, R.: Statistical analysis of second order differential power analysis. IEEE Trans. Comput. **58**(6), 799–811 (2009)

[QS01] Quisquater, J.-J., Samyde, D.: ElectroMagnetic Analysis (EMA): measures and counter-measures for smart cards. In: Attali, I., Jensen, T. (eds.) E-smart 2001. LNCS, vol. 2140, pp. 200–210. Springer, Heidelberg (2001). doi:10.1007/3-540-45418-7_17

[SM15] Schneider, T., Moradi, A.: Leakage assessment methodology - a clear roadmap for side-channel evaluations. In: Güneysu and Handschuh [GH15], pp. 495–513

[TFC83] LeVeque, R.J., Chan, T.F., Golub, G.H.: Algorithms for computing the sample variance: analysis and recommendations. Am. Stat. **37**(3), 242–247 (1983)

[WOM11] Whitnall, C., Oswald, E., Mather, L.: An exploration of the kolmogorov-smirnov test as a competitor to mutual information analysis. In: Prouff, E. (ed.) CARDIS 2011. LNCS, vol. 7079, pp. 234–251. Springer, Heidelberg (2011). doi:10.1007/978-3-642-27257-8_15

FPGA Security

Your Rails Cannot Hide from Localized EM: How Dual-Rail Logic Fails on FPGAs

Vincent Immler[✉], Robert Specht, and Florian Unterstein

Fraunhofer Institute for Applied and Integrated Security (AISEC),
Munich, Germany
{vincent.immler,robert.specht,florian.unterstein}@aisec.fraunhofer.de

Abstract. Protecting cryptographic implementations against side-channel attacks is a must to prevent leakage of processed secrets. As a cell-level countermeasure, so called DPA-resistant logic styles have been proposed to prevent a data-dependent power consumption.

As most of the DPA-resistant logic is based on dual-rails, properly implementing them is a challenging task on FPGAs which is due to their fixed architecture and missing freedom in the design tools.

While previous works show a significant security gain when using such logic on FPGAs, we demonstrate this only holds for power-analysis. In contrast, our attack using high-resolution electromagnetic analysis is able to exploit local characteristics of the placement and routing such that only a marginal security gain remains, therefore creating a severe threat.

To further analyze the properties of both attack and implementation, we develop a custom placer to improve the default placement of the analyzed AES S-box. Different cost functions for the placement are tested and evaluated w.r.t. the resulting side-channel resistance on a Spartan-6 FPGA. As a result, we are able to more than double the resistance of the design compared to cases not benefiting from the custom placement.

1 Introduction

Physical attacks based on power analysis, called DPA [20], have been subject to extensive research and initiated the development of DPA countermeasures at different levels of abstraction. Some introduce noise, e.g., [12,23] or randomize the order of operations, i.e., shuffling, e.g., [16,23]. More application-specific attempts to increase the resistance are done by manipulating the underlying cryptographic algorithm to randomize its intermediate values, i.e., masking at the algorithmic level, e.g., [29,30]. Others, so called "hiding" countermeasures, try to solve the problem by avoiding data-dependencies in the power consumption. These countermeasures at the cell-level, called DPA-resistant logic styles, ideally remove the data-dependent power consumption and thereby equalize it.

When considering the various proposals in this domain [3,13,15,19,22,26, 28,33,43,44], one identifies that most of them are based on dual-rail precharge (DRP) logic or duplication schemes. Both no longer represent a bit as a single value but instead as complementary rails of $(\mathtt{true},\mathtt{false}) = (t, f)$, such that

© International Association for Cryptologic Research 2017
W. Fischer and N. Homma (Eds.): CHES 2017, LNCS 10529, pp. 403–424, 2017.
DOI: 10.1007/978-3-319-66787-4_20

regardless of the operation, each bit-flip is compensated by an inverse bit-flip. However, both approaches are fundamentally different as explained later on in more detail: Using a simplified view, DRP styles can be considered as a function $f_{DRP}(t, f)$ and duplication schemes as a compound function of $f_{DUP}(t)$ and $f_{DUP}^{-1}(f)$ which leads to different implementations as sketched in Fig. 1.

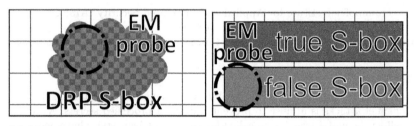

(a) S-box implementing the inseparable function $f_{DRP}(t, f)$ (DRP logic).

(b) S-box implementing $f_{DUP}(t)$ and $f_{DUP}^{-1}(f)$ separately (duplication scheme).

Fig. 1. Resulting FPGA floor plan to illustrate different dual-rail styles. The on-chip positioning of a probe used for the EM analysis is indicated by a circle.

To properly implement either one, several design flaws must be avoided such as *glitches* [24]. Another, the *early propagation* (EP) effect [37] is typically prevented by a synchronization mechanism, e.g., an enable signal. Moreover, to achieve equal power consumption between the dual-rails, it is necessary to minimize their *routing imbalances* [39], as they result in different capacitive loads when switching which can be exploited by a DPA attack. Therefore, some routing techniques have been proposed such as [11, 26, 41] to diminish the load imbalances in either the ASIC or FPGA design process. Most dual-rail mitigation techniques work reasonably-well when assuming a power-based side-channel, e.g., by measuring the voltage over a shunt resistor (including parasitics), thereby treating the leakage of a device as a whole. The local placement and routing imbalances are therefore not sufficiently considered as part of a design or evaluation process. From a practical point of view, power-analysis also requires the PCB to be modified in most cases. Moreover, decoupling capacitances tend to be increasingly more integrated recently in the chip itself which makes the use of the power-based side-channel more difficult.

An often preferred alternative are side-channels based on Electro-Magnetic (EM) emanation. Various publications have shown different options on how to measure the emanation. Mainly two approaches exist, the off-chip measurement [7, 32], i.e., the probe is positioned slightly above the chip package and on-chip (or on-surface) measurement [17, 31, 35, 42], i.e., the chip is partially depackaged to position the probe directly on top of the die's surface. By positioning a suitable EM probe in proximity to the area of interest, spatial information of the implementation can be explored [17, 31]. This is also known as localized EM and is due to previous results a promising candidate to measure dual-rails independently from each other, thereby possibly bypassing this countermeasure.

Our Contribution. A natural question that arises is by how much better on-chip EM attacks perform when compared to power measurements, as local placement and routing characteristics could possibly be more easily extracted using a localized EM attack. To start answering this question, we first survey the existing logic styles for FPGA platforms and argue that previous security evaluations did not fully assess the properties of the underlying designs, i.e., the density of the placement and local routing imbalances.

Afterwards, we practically investigate if the available DRP logics can still be assumed secure when subject to a localized EM attack. As a result, we show that only a barely noticeable security gain of any DRP logic remains when compared to a SingleRail implementation using the default placement of the Xilinx ISE tools. To the best of the authors' knowledge, we are the first to publicly perform such attacks on dual-rails using high-resolution equipment, i.e., with a probe diameter of $150\,\mu$m at a very low distance of $\leq 50\,\mu$m.[1]

To fairly compare the security of dual-rails using a power- and an EM-based analysis, we present a systematic evaluation methodology based on a correlation based leakage test which is complemented by an information theoretic approach. It is additionally supplemented by considering the Signal-to-Noise-Ratio (SNR).

As the next contribution we focus on the placement of the secure logic, more specifically its density and its possible influence on the resistance towards an EM-based analysis. As target design and platform, we selected an AES S-box to be realized on a Spartan-6 FPGA. Its local placement using ISE defaults is improved by means of a custom placer based on simulated annealing. A new and previous cost function are evaluated for the placer. Our experimental results show that increasing the density of the placement using our own cost function helps to reduce the amount of extractable leakage by an EM-based analysis.

State-of-the-Art. Secure logic styles primarily follow two competing concepts on FPGAs: DRP logic and duplication schemes. DRP logic gates operate in two phases, i.e., precharge and evaluation, which are controlled by the clock signal as seen later on in Fig. 6b. Proposed candidates include: WDDL [40], BCDL [28], DPLnoEE [3], and AWDDL [26], as listed in Table 1.

Unfortunately, none of the DRP proposals include a thorough analysis based on a localized EM attack to answer the fundamental question, if dual-rails could be measured separately, e.g., by measuring differing orientations of the emanated field of the rails, therefore possibly bypassing this countermeasure. Another issue is local placement and routing imbalances. Especially large nets with multiple sinks cause a "messy" routing with the following properties: not all dual-rails can be fully balanced due to the lack of precise timing information from the Xilinx tools as stated in [26], also one cannot assume that balanced dual-rails remain balanced across several devices using the same design due to device-specific variation as shown in [43], cross-coupling of lines adds another uncertainty that may lead to leakage and inter-dependency of lines within an FPGA [6,9].

---

[1] We omitted results from probes with $100\,\mu$m and $250\,\mu$m due to similarity reasons. In contrast, a probe with $3\,$mm was almost equivalent to a power-based measurement.

Table 1. Survey on dual-rail logic styles for reconfigurable hardware.

Reference	Design properties				Device under test		Evaluation
	EP	Glitch	Route	Place	Platform	Target	Setup
DRP logic							
BCDL [28]	✓	✓	x	?	Stratix II	AES	Power
WDDL [33,40]	x	✓	x	*	Stratix	DES	off-chip EM
DPLnoEE [3]	*	✓	x	?	Stratix I	AES	Power[a]
AWDDL [26]	✓	✓	*	?	Virtex 5	AES	Power
Duplication schemes							
DWDDL [44]	x	✓	x	?	Spartan 3E	AES	Power
Part. SDDL [19]	✓	x	*	?	Spartan 3E	AES	Power
PA-DPL [13,14]	✓	x	*	*	Virtex 5	AES	off-chip EM
[15]	✓	✓	x	?	Virtex 5	AES	off-chip EM
GliFreD [43]	✓	✓	*	?	Spartan 6	AES	Power

✓ : addressed   x: problematic   *:partially considered   ?:not considered   [a]EM on capacitor

Regardless of these obstacles, some work has been done in hardening DRP logic on FPGAs. In [34], different placement strategies are investigated. Each is based on constraints of the Quartus-II tools. Since the evaluation is done using a power-based DPA only, analyzing local effects of the various placements more closely has not been possible.

In another work [26], the authors investigate if rails can be balanced using a custom routing algorithm. Although the leakage is reduced by their router, the authors report that it cannot be completely avoided since the Xilinx tools only report worst-case values that differ from reality. Moreover, the placement was not considered at all. Since this is the foundation for an optimized routing, verifying its properties prior to the routing would have been necessary. Again, results are only based on a power-analysis. Table 1 summarizes additional DRP logic styles and indicates the strong need for an on-chip EM analysis.

In contrast to DRP logic, duplication schemes are typically realized as follows: For a given circuit, a complementary one is created which leads to a dual-copy of a fully placed-and-routed circuit which has been shown, can often be broken due to non-dual glitches in the original and dual part of the circuit [24,43].

In terms of implementing them, they have the advantage of using duplicated routes that are shifted in horizontal or vertical direction [15,43]. The balancing aspect is therefore derived from the fact that routes of equivalent shape using identical hardware resources are likely to yield balanced capacitive loads. However, the resulting distance between true/false is typically large, e.g., at least a tile and often more than that [13,44]. Considering localized EM attacks this may be a significant issue. Moreover, the only known duplication scheme to address both glitches and early-propagation is GliFreD [43] which results in a massive Flip-Flop (FF) overhead compared to DRP logic styles. Furthermore, it has only

been evaluated using power-analysis. Table 1 includes other candidates of duplication schemes and lists their conceptual weaknesses with respect to their design
properties. Hence, they are not considered in depth as part of our work.

One minor exception of duplication schemes we would like to address is the
work of [14] which analyzes various placement strategies of PA-DPL [13] by using
on-chip EM measurements. However, their measurement setup is incomparable
to ours (cf. Sect. 5.3). As an example, the diameter of their coil is by orders of
magnitude larger (1 mm) than ours (150 μm). This may have prevented a more
detailed analysis, since no differences for the tested placements were observed.

In the direction of EM-based analysis, we would like to refer to [17,18,31,35]
to illustrate the advancements over previous EM-based approaches. Aforementioned references indicate that localized EM attacks are more powerful than
power measurements. However, they did not carry out a thorough comparison.
Hence, we also investigate the practical limits of localized EM in terms of resolution vs. the given routing architecture and technology size of a Xilinx Spartan 6.

2   Dual-Rail Routing and Placement

Let us recall selected properties of dual-rail styles and how they relate to a localized EM attack. As outlined before, both DRP logic and duplications schemes
create complementary rails to achieve a constant number of switches independent
from the processed data, ideally resulting in equalized power consumption.

This appears as a valid approach when neglecting the design challenges to
properly implement them. However, even under idealized assumptions, carrying
out a localized EM attack could prove more resourceful than a power-based
measurement, as a wise positioning of the probe may lead to an asymmetric
view on the rails as illustrated in Fig. 2a. As the signal strength picked up by
the probe depends on its distance to the emanating source, it appears likely
that due to an unequal signal strength of **true** and **false** that they no longer
compensate each other. The resulting residue then reflects the properties of the
stronger signal which exhibits the same behavior of a SingleRail implementation.

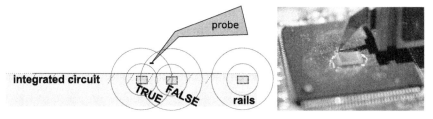

(a) Artistic illustration of a local EM attack.   (b) Probe positioned on die.

Fig. 2. Introductory material on high-resolution, localized EM analysis.

Clearly, the success of this depends on the resolution of the attack relative to
the density of the placement and routing of the logic. It is therefore not possible

to analyze this problem independently from placement and routing characteristics. Hence, they must be considered and optimized, too.

For duplication schemes, the situation is as sketched in Fig. 1b. For a given S-box, a complementary copy is created resulting in symmetrically placed and routed logic. While achieving a high level of uniformity, at the same time the distance between true and false is typically large, often multiple tiles of an FPGA. Please also note that due to the divided approach of duplication schemes, both rails *and* the computing LUTs of the true and false paths are fully separated.

For DRP logic as depicted in Fig. 1a, the situation is completely different. Since both true and false path must be jointly routed to each Look-Up-Table (LUT), each rail must be routed individually and cannot be copied. Ideally, depending on the quality of the placement and routing capabilities, one would be able to route a dual-rail much closer to each other when compared to duplication schemes. However, at the same time, where this is not possible, local non-uniformities (larger distances between still balanced dual-rails, cf. Fig. 3b) or even imbalances would occur (rails with unequal capacitive loads, cf. Fig. 3c).

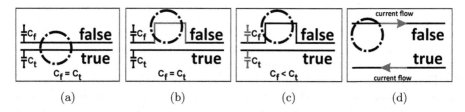

(a)   (b)   (c)   (d)

Fig. 3. Different routing characteristics. (3a) "Ideal" dual-rail (3b) Non-uniformity (3c) Imbalance (3d) Large distance between rails and different orientation of the emanated field due to current flow.

Since computing true and false rails of DRP logic takes place within the same slice (or same LUT), we expect that the remaining non-uniformities and imbalances are much more difficult to exploit when compared to a duplication scheme where both computation and dual-rail routing are split. We therefore focus on the resistance of DRP styles and compare their effectiveness as a countermeasure under a power- and localized EM-attack setting. To do so, we first introduce the topic of placement and its optimizations, to also compare a low and high-density placement, as a higher density should help mitigate the aforementioned effects.

3   Placement on FPGAs

Commonly available FPGAs share similarities in their fabrics, i.e., the underlying structure of hardware resources. For Xilinx FPGAs, the reoccurring structure implementing the majority of logic is called a *tile*. Each tile typically comprises two *slices*, whereas each slice contains 4 LUTs, several multiplexors, and FFs. In between each tile and slice, different routing resources are available.

As a first step to implement the designated logic on FPGAs, its representation as a hardware description language is mapped onto the device using device-specific libraries. Subsequently, the logic must be placed such that the hardware resources are not exceeded. On a global level, partitioning the logic is often done using quadratic placement, especially on ASICs. On a local level, i.e., modules of reasonable size this is often done using simulated annealing [38]. In general, this is termed the "placement problem" [27] and known to be np-complete, i.e., placing logic within a certain rectangular area P based on some minimized cost function $C(p)$ is only practically feasible using approximative approaches.

P is defined by its boundaries $x_{high}, x_{low}, y_{high}, y_{low}$. The list of gates G and nets V is a graph $G = (V, E)$. The cost function $C(p) = C(V, E)$ represents the sum of the expected wirelength for each net. Determining the wirelength $WL(e)$ can be done using different approaches, as discussed in Sect. 3.2. In addition to that, it is possible to assign weights $w(e)$ to each net for, e.g., critical nets. The resulting cost function is then denoted as: $C(p) = \sum_{e \in E} w(e)WL(e)$.

The placement problem can now be formalized as: given P, a list of gates and nets $G = (V, E) = (FV \cup MV, E)$ with FV as fixed gates and MV as movable gates, and a cost function $C(V, E)$. Determine (x_i, y_i) such that for each $v_i \in MV$: (i) it is placed within P and (ii) no pair of v_i, v_j overlaps with $\forall v_i, v_j$ (iii) $C(p)$ is minimal.

3.1 Simulated Annealing

Simulated annealing [2] resembles a cooling process to allow larger changes in the beginning as long as the temperature is high. While cooling down, the magnitude of changes becomes smaller with each iteration. Thereby, an approximative global optimum is found by avoiding local minima/maxima.

For the placement region P, an initial random placement p_0 is realized. Its quality is determined by the cost function $C(p_0)$. For a given temperature T_0 in the beginning, the subsequent iterations start to move around logic gates. Each new placement is again evaluated by $C(p)$. Degradations are only accepted with a probability of $e^{-\frac{C(p_{new}) - C(p_{old})}{T}}$, i.e., the acceptance rate of optimizing towards the wrong direction decreases. This process continues until an exit criterion is fulfilled, e.g., a certain temperature, iteration count or quality of placement.

3.2 Cost Functions

As part of this work, we adapted the cost function of Versatile-Place-and-Route (VPR) [2] which is based on the Half-Perimeter-Wire-Length (HPWL). Moreover, we define our own cost function called Same-Slice-Same-Tile (SSST). Both are also illustrated in Fig. 4 and explained hereafter.

HPWL. The function $q(n) \cdot$ HPWL which we use is a modified version of the linear congestion function of [2]. The original equation is

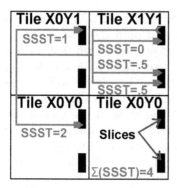

(a) Same Slice Same Tile.

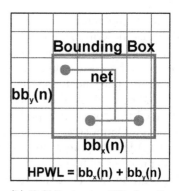

(b) Half-Perimeter-Wirelength.

Fig. 4. Illustration of different cost functions of the custom placer.

$$C_{lc}(p) = \sum_{n=1}^{N_{nets}} q(n)\Big[\frac{bb_x(n)}{C_{av,x}(n)} + \frac{bb_y(n)}{C_{av,y}(n)}\Big] \tag{1}$$

whereas N_{nets} is the number of nets between the to-be-placed instances. $bb_x(n)$ and $bb_y(n)$ are the side lengths in x or y direction of the specific bounding box of a net n, as sketched in Fig. 4b. A bounding box is the smallest rectangle that fits each instance of a net. Hence, $HPWL = bb_x(n) + bb_y(n)$.

$q(n)$ is a specific factor to balance nets with many pins. The respective values have been taken from [5]. $C_{av,x}(n)$ and $C_{av,y}(n)$ reflect the routing channel capacity to, e.g., make certain wires more expensive than others. However, since the Xilinx Spartan 6 is assumed to provide a symmetric channel/wire layout in arbitrary direction, we simplify the cost function to:

$$C_{HPWL}(p) = \sum_{n=1}^{N_{nets}} q(n)\big[bb_x(n) + bb_y(n)\big] \tag{2}$$

SSST. Since our goal is to not only make an optimized routing but also to create a placement of highest density, we define our own cost function

$$C_{SSST}(p) = \sum_{n=1}^{N_{nets}} \sum_{m=1}^{N_{sinks}} P(m) \tag{3}$$

whereas $\sum_{m=1}^{N_{sinks}} P(m)$ is the sum over all wirelengths of a net with

$$P(m) = \begin{cases} 0, & \text{if} \quad \text{Source and sink are within the same } slice \\ 0.5, & \text{if} \quad \text{Source and sink are within the same } tile \\ d(\text{Tile}(s), \text{Tile}(m)), & \text{else} \end{cases} \tag{4}$$

The function $d(.,.)$ represents the Manhattan distance[2] between the tile in which the source of the net is placed and the tile in which the sink is. Figure 4a illustrates the properties of the SSST-metric.

4   Custom Placer and Design Implementation

In the following subsection, we describe the implementation of our custom placer. Subsequently, we use this placer to work on the design presented in Sect. 4.2.

4.1   Custom Placer

Since our device-under-test (DUT) for the design is a Xilinx Spartan-6 FPGA, we could make use of the RapidSmith library [21]. The resulting workflow is outlined in Fig. 5 and is based on the Xilinx Design Language (XDL). For our use case, we fully process the design (as depicted in Fig. 6a) up to the ncd right before bitgen, using the standard Xilinx ISE tools.

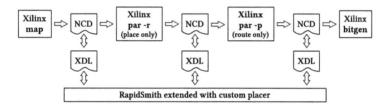

Fig. 5. Workflow using the RapidSmith library and the custom placer

The only modifications we made to the design are (i) to put all elements requiring improved placement into a closed group which is area constrained, (ii) to keep the input PIN positions of the LUTs locked, and (iii) to put LUTs of each logic gate into the same slice using either the pair (A,B) or (C,D) of LUTs.

Once the design is processed by ISE, it is converted to its XDL representation and imported to RapidSmith. The S-box is detected by its hierarchy name and confined to the region P using the same boundaries as for the constraints of the ISE toolchain. Afterwards, the primitive sites within this region are identified to check if the designated logic could be placed using the given site (e.g., SLICEL).

To relocate the already placed logic, it is necessary to remove the nets and extract the logic from its given XDL hierarchy. A group of "relocatable" logic is created to allow their repositioning. Another abstract group is created to keep track of how they are interconnected, i.e., the nets. The initial placement of the ISE tools is considered as p_0, i.e., the start of the simulated annealing is well-defined and not a random placement. Subsequently, the annealing is carried out as described in Sect. 3.1 using the cost functions of Fig. 4a and b.

---

[2] $\mathrm{d} = \mathrm{abs}(x_s - x_m) + \mathrm{abs}(y_s - y_m)$, i.e., the rectangular distance over the grid.

Once the annealing stops (after less than a minute), the logic is placed back on the primitive sites. Please note, since relocating the logic was performed by making "valid moves" only, there is no legalization step required (in contrast to quadratic placement). The thus placed logic is then interconnected using the routing capabilities of the ISE tools and the `bit` files are generated.

4.2 Design Implementation

For the analysis, we made an exemplary design which in addition to the control logic consists in an AES S-box [1]. We have taken the area-optimized S-box by Canright [4] which is a typical design for an S-box hardware implementation.

As logic styles, we selected the following: SingleRail, WDDL [40], DPL-noEE [3], and AWDDL [26], as they can all be realized using the same routing which leads to an unambiguous comparison.[3] For each style, we instantiated the S-box logic by 2-input gates. A block diagram of the design is shown in Fig. 6a.

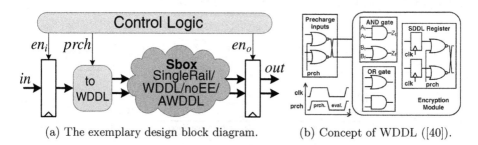

(a) The exemplary design block diagram.   (b) Concept of WDDL ([40]).

Fig. 6. Basic properties of the implemented design.

Since we aim at evaluating only the leakage associated to the combinatorial circuit, we must exclude the leakage of the output register (see [25]). We therefore implement the design as follows: At a certain clock cycle, the control logic disables *prch* signal and the "to WDDL" conversion unit propagates the input to the S-box thereby initializing the evaluation phase. In the next half of the clock cycle the control logic enables *prch* signal and the precharge phase is started.

In a common DRP circuit en_o should be active at the start of precharge in order to store the output of the combinatorial circuit (here the AES S-box). Therefore, the control logic does not enable en_o signal and the register does not store the S-box output.[4] Over these two (evaluation and precharge) phases either power consumption or electro-magnetic emanation of the FPGA are measured.

To implement the logic and achieve the same routing for them, we use the following procedure. Using AWDDL as a start, we implement WDDL and DPL-noEE by changing only the LUT contents in the XDL file which is possible due to

---

[3] Our results can also be mapped onto BCDL [28] since it is similar to DPLnoEE.

[4] At a later point in time, en_o becomes active in order to check the correct functionality of the circuit. This is not covered by the recorded power and EM traces.

the 2-input AWDDL gates. For the SingleRail variant, we additionally disable the FALSE rail of WDDL and adjusted the "toWDDL" conversion accordingly.

Now, different sets of placements are created. Each comprises all four logics and uses the procedure to achieve the same routing within each set:

- **Set 1:** Default ISE placement using constraints
- **Set 2a:** Customized placement optimized towards HPWL
- **Set 2b:** Customized placement optimized towards SSST

The resulting placement metrics according to the cost functions are summarized in Table 2. For both Set 2a and 2b, one can see that an improvement over the ISE defaults is achieved. Each design of each set is then subject to the power and EM measurement using the same bit file. The measurement setups are described hereafter and preceed the practical investigations of Sect. 6.

Table 2. Results of the respective cost functions for different designs of the S-box.

Design type	HPWL	SSST
Set 1 (default placement)	5860.0	3198.0
Set 2a (optimized towards HPWL)	3241.6	2308.0
Set 2b (optimized towards SSST)	3540.8	1781.0

5   Measurement Setups

In the following, we briefly present the properties of our measurement setups.

5.1   Notations

For a specific side channel experiment we collect the set I of traces with N being the number of collected traces. One trace I of length T is represented by its samples $I = (i_0, ..., t_T)$ which have been acquired over time. The plaintext is denoted as $P = p_0||...||p_{15}$ and the key as $K = k_0||k_1||...||k_{15}$. The target intermediate value of the AES S-box is defined by $v_{i,n} = \mathrm{SBOX}(k_{i,n} \oplus p_{i,n})$ for the subkey and plaintext of target byte $i \in [0, 15]$ and trace number $n \in [1, ..., N]$.

We denote $\oplus$ as the bitwise XOR-operator, V as the set of all possible intermediate values v, and $|\cdot|$ as the number of elements in a set. Whenever accessing a single value of a trace with number n, point in time t, and intermediate value v we denote this as $i_{n,t}^v$. I_v denotes the set of traces for the intermediate value v.

5.2   Signal-to-Noise-Ratio (SNR)

When investigating the properties of a measurement campaign from a security point of view, we are mostly interested in the *effectiveness* of distinguishing the targeted values. For this purpose, the SNR definition by Mangard et al. in [23] has often been used. It is expressed by

$$\mathrm{SNR_M} = \frac{\mathrm{Var}(\mathrm{E}[\boldsymbol{I}_{X0}], ..., \mathrm{E}[\boldsymbol{I}_{X|\boldsymbol{V}|}])}{\mathrm{E}[\mathrm{Var}(\boldsymbol{I}_{X0}), ..., \mathrm{Var}(\boldsymbol{I}_{X|\boldsymbol{V}|})]} \qquad \forall\, X_j \in \boldsymbol{V} \qquad (5)$$

and denoted as $\mathrm{SNR_M}$ in the following. It is known to be a useful tool to identify the points in time that have leakage in their first statistical moment.

5.3   High Resolution EM Measurement Setup

As a device under test, we use a decapsulated Spartan 6 FPGA, which is clocked at 8 MHz. For the FPGA as shown in Fig. 2a, we rasterize an area of 2730 µm × 1600 µm with the probe at a distance to the surface of ≤50 µm. In total, we use 120 (15 × 8) equally-spaced positions to acquire measurements within this area.

For the FPGA as shown in Fig. 2b, we rasterize an area of 2730 µm × 1600µm with an equally-spaced 15 × 8 grid (120 measurement positions in total) and the probe at a distance of ≤5 µm to the die surface. For the measurement, we use a Langer ICR HH150-6 near-H-field (horizontal) probe with a coil diameter of 150 µm. The maximum bandwidth of the probe is 6 GHz with a built-in 30 dB preamplifier. In addition to that, we use another 30 dB amplifier such that the resulting signal is amplified by 60 dB in total.

With this setup synchronized to the device's clock, we collected 10 000 traces for each target design and position at a rate of 5 GS/s using a LeCroy WavePro 725 Zi. The resulting mean and $\mathrm{SNR_M}$ for WDDL are shown in Fig. 7a.

5.4   Power Measurement Setup

Aside from the change in the measurement approach, the setup is kept the same for the power-based measurement, i.e., the same FPGA using the same designs. Instead of the H-field probe and amplifiers, a differential probe (LeCroy AP033) measures the voltage drop across a 10 Ω shunt resistor.

With this setup, we collected a total of 100 000 traces for each target design using the same clock frequency and samplingrate. As an example, the resulting mean and $\mathrm{SNR_M}$ for WDDL are shown in Fig. 7b

6   Practical Investigations

In this chapter we present the concept of our practical investigations and the results for the power and high resolution EM measurements.

6.1   Concept of Investigations

To guarantee comparable results between the four logic styles, we adhere to the following requirements: (*i*) only identical bit files are used for the comparison of power and high resolution EM measurement (*ii*) the same routing is realized for all logic styles (*iii*) the improvement over the SingleRail logic is only considered

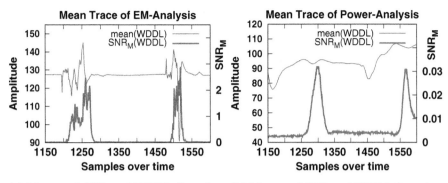

(a) Mean and SNR_M of WDDL (based on localized EM measurement)

(b) Mean and SNR_M of WDDL (based on power measurement over shunt)

Fig. 7. Basic properties of the design and comparison of the measurement setups.

within the same measurement method. Hence, Figs. 8 and 9 are based on the same `bit` files with the same routing using the default ISE placement (Set 1).

To fairly compare the properties of the implementations and analyze their leakage, we selected three metrics. The first is a correlation based leakage test proposed by Durvaux et al. [8], which works very similar to a CPA with profiled power model. To carry out the test, the traces are split into two sets, the profiling set I_p and an attack set I_a. The profiling set is used to estimate the power consumption model m of the device by calculating the mean for each point in time for each element in V, according to

$$m_v = \frac{1}{|I_p(v)|} \sum_{n \in |I_p(v)|} I_{p,n} \tag{6}$$

As a result, a power model is created which is based on practical measurements. It therefore better reflects the actual properties of the device when compared to "black-box" power models, e.g., Hamming weight or Hamming distance. $I_p(v)$ and $I_a(v)$ denotes the selection of all traces with the internal value v.

Afterwards the correlation vector $\boldsymbol{corr}$ is computed by correlating each trace of the attack set I_a with the corresponding value of $\boldsymbol{m}_i = (m(0,i), ..., m(|I_a|, i))$, as shown in Eq. 7. In this case, $m(n,i)$ denotes the element of m_v for the intermediate value v of trace number n and target byte i.

$$corr_{t,i} = \rho(\boldsymbol{m}_i, i_{a,t}) \tag{7}$$

To quantify the achieved security complexity, we make use of the properties of the Pearson correlation coefficient, as the measurements to disclosure are proportional to $(\max(\boldsymbol{corr})^2)$. Based on this behavior we define the security gain as: secgain $= (\frac{\max(\boldsymbol{corr}_1)}{\max(\boldsymbol{corr}_2)})^2$. The thus created power model and resulting correlation coefficient leads to the detection of first order leakage.

To complement our correlation-based analysis, we use the mutual information (MI) which is an information theoretic (IT) metric proposed by [10, 36] independently. It has the advantage of detecting leakages at arbitrary order. Hence, it captures the amount of information available to the worst-case adversary. We use it to directly calculate the mutual information between a given trace and the S-box input, as shown in Eq. 8, for each point in time t and target byte i.

$$mi_{t,i} = H(I_t) - H(I_t|v_i) \tag{8}$$

Since our goal is to also compare power and high resolution EM measurements, we additionally include the results of SNR_M as third metric.

6.2   Power Measurement Results for Default ISE Placement (Set 1)

By carrying out a power-based side-channel attack first, we confirm the results of previous publications such as [26] and showcase the correct behavior of our implementations. According to our concept, we perform the correlation based leakage test which leads to the curves as shown in Fig. 8. The results are based on a default ISE placement (Set 1) with the described technique to ensure the same routing amongst all the considered candidates. Each evaluated implementation shows two correlation peaks which correspond to evaluation and precharge phase.

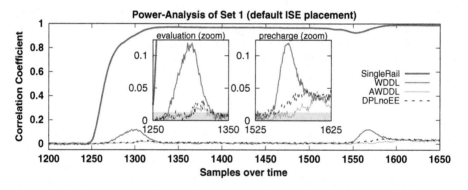

Fig. 8. Correlation based leakage test of a power measurement for AWDDL, DPLnoEE, WDDL, and SingleRail of the default placement

The obtained correlations are well above the significance threshold of 0.012, defined by Mangard et al. [23]. The insignificant region is indicated by the grey area inside the boxes of Fig. 8. Clearly visible is the strong correlation of the SingleRail variant that climbs up to 0.99. It is, as expected, orders of magnitude higher when compared to the dual-rail logics. WDDL shows a maximum correlation of 0.119, DPLnoEE of 0.048, and AWDDL of 0.046 respectively.

Based on this metric, the WDDL design – due to its data-dependent time-of-evaluation and time-of-precharge – has the highest leakage of the dual rail styles. DPLnoEE and AWDDL show a similar leakage in the evaluation phase.

As claimed by [26], the leakage of AWDDL is marginally lower in the precharge phase when compared to DPLnoEE. The plots also show a leakage of AWDDL that is shifted in time which is owed to its self-timed behavior. A massive leakage is observed for the SingleRail implementation that spreads over both evaluation and precharge phase. This is probably due to parasitics of the power measurement setup. The resulting security gains are:

- SingleRail → WDDL: $\left(\frac{0.990}{0.119}\right)^2 = 69.2$
- WDDL → DPLnoEE: $\left(\frac{0.119}{0.048}\right)^2 = 6.15$
- DPLnoEE → AWDDL: $\left(\frac{0.048}{0.046}\right)^2 \approx 1$ (difference below significance interval)

To complement our analysis we applied the information theoretic metric, too. They confirm the results of the correlation based leakage test and are summarized in Table 3. As a next step, we investigate if similar security gains can be obtained if the device under test is subject to a localized-EM attack.

6.3   Localized-EM Measurement for Default ISE Placement (Set 1)

Using the same design files and same DUT, we also performed high resolution, localized EM measurements. This leads to Fig. 9 for the correlation based test. Again, we indicated the insignificant region by a grey area inside the plot.

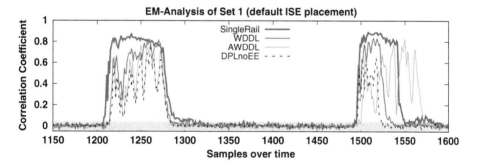

Fig. 9. Leakage test of a localized EM measurement for the considered logic styles at the position of the highest correlation using the default ISE placement.

It is striking that during the evaluation phase all correlation curves peak at very similar levels. Considering both phases, the SingleRail implementation has its highest peak at 0.89, followed by WDDL and AWDDL at 0.83, and DPLnoEE at 0.77. We would like to highlight that only 10 000 traces were necessary to create these results. Deriving the respective security gains, we get

- SingleRail → WDDL: $\left(\frac{0.889}{0.836}\right)^2 = 1.13$
- WDDL → DPLnoEE: $\left(\frac{0.836}{0.768}\right)^2 = 1.18$
- DPLnoEE → AWDDL: $\left(\frac{0.768}{0.829}\right)^2 \approx 0.858$

which shows a barely noticeable security gain when using a high resolution, localized EM attack. Since the same `bit` files were used this is clearly owed to the superior measurement acquisition. Again, the results of the information theoretic metric are added to Table 3.

It is remarkable that under this setting, AWDDL performs worse when compared to DPLnoEE. This is owed to the fact that DPLnoEE gates directly go to precharge once one of the inputs goes to precharge. In contrast, AWDDL goes to precharge only when both inputs are in precharge. Therefore, the propagation wave of AWDDL spreads over time which leads to the presented result, i.e., the leakage of AWDDL continues even after that of the SingleRail has stopped.

6.4   Comparing Localized EM and Power Measurements

In this section we compare the results (as given in Table 3) of the power and localized EM measurements, both of which are using the same `bit` files (cf. Sects. 6.2 and 6.3). Hence, routing and placement is the same for both measurements and all considered logic styles (Set 1). Therefore, the only substantial differences can only be caused by the specifics of the measurement setups.

Table 3. Summary of the practical evaluations for the default ISE placement.

Design	Attack	$\mathrm{SNR_M}$	max($corr$)	max(secgain)	max(MI)
SingleRail		54.16	0.990	←		2.99
WDDL	Power	0.032	0.119		463.2	0.057
AWDDL		0.011	0.046	←		0.030
DPLnoEE		0.013	0.048			0.032
SingleRail		4.06	0.889	←		2.93
WDDL	EM	2.89	0.836		1.34	2.57
AWDDL		1.80	0.829			1.96
DPLnoEE		1.37	0.768	←		1.95

When evaluating the results w.r.t. the obtained security gain, it is striking that they differ significantly between power (about a factor of 463) and localized EM measurements (about a factor of 1.34). This strongly supports the argument that localized EM attacks are a severe threat to dual-rail logic on FPGAs.

For the SingleRail implementation, it is surprising that the total leakage appears to only be captured by a power measurement, resulting in a much higher $\mathrm{SNR_M}$ of 54.16 when compared to the localized EM measurement (4.06). However, this changes drastically when inspecting the numbers for DRP logic as the results of localized EM outperform the power-based by orders of magnitude.

Another approach to substantiate the impact of our results is the capability of the setups in distinguishing the true and false rail. To analyze this, we need to consider two scenarios: (i) In case the rails are inseparable, one would expect to see a significant increase in the leakage when deactivating one of the rails since the balancing aspect is lost. (ii) If the opposite is true, i.e., the rails are separable, then the leakage should be approximately the same when deactivating one of the rails since from the beginning on, there would have been no difference.

This can be studied by observing the behavior when switching from the SingleRail implementation to any of the dual-rail variants. For the power measurements we are within scenario (i), as the correlation significantly differs when performing the switch between SingleRail and dual-rail. For the local EM measurements we are within scenario (ii), as the magnitude of correlation remains the same regardless of the fact whether it is a SingleRail or a dual-rail variant.

All observations are backed by the IT analysis that verifies the claimed behavior of the different measurement methods. Under this scenario, both measurement methods perform equally when considering the SingleRail implementation, indicating that aside from the difference in SNR_M, the full leakage is extracted.

As a next step, we investigate if this situation can be improved by means of an increased density of the placement. The goal of this is to increase the density up to the point where distinguishing the rails is no longer possible.

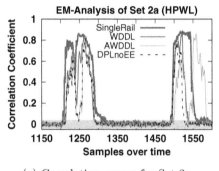   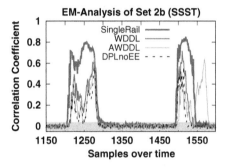

(a) Correlation curves for Set 2a.   (b) Correlation curves for Set 2b.

Fig. 10. Correlation based leakage test of a high resolution EM measurement.

6.5   Security Analysis of the Custom Placement

To improve the situation under a localized EM attack, we investigate the impact of the previously described placement improvements. We repeated our measurements using these files and carried out the same tests. For HPWL and SSST, the results of this test are illustrated in Fig. 10a and b respectively.

Again, for the sake of fair comparison, we realized the same routing within the HPWL (Set2a) and SSST (Set2b) designs. We therefore *only* compare the results of the placement and the security improvement from a SingleRail to dual-rail version. Otherwise, the effect of the routing could not be excluded.

Considering the results for HPWL, one can see that for Fig. 10a almost no improvement is achieved. In contrast, the SSST-based placement shows an improvement at a factor of about 2.24. Taking the results of Table 2 into account, it is evident that by using the SSST cost function one achieves a more dense placement up to the point where the power of the used EM attack is degrading (Table 4).

Table 4. Summary of the EM analysis for the customized placements.

Design	Attack	SNR_M	max($corr$)	max(secgain)	max(MI)
HPWL					
SingleRail		2.82	0.881	←	2.76
WDDL	EM	3.04	0.867	**1.15**	2.12
AWDDL		1.70	0.863		2.21
DPLnoEE		1.92	0.823	←	1.96
SSST					
SingleRail		3.23	0.851	←	2.31
WDDL	EM	1.54	0.720	**2.24**	1.73
AWDDL		1.29	0.653		1.20
DPLnoEE		1.36	0.569	←	1.14

However, since an optimal placement is likely not to be found analytically (which could further improve the resistance), only improving the placement as a countermeasure is insufficient. We therefore analyzed also a masked version of AWDDL. These supplementary results are shown in Fig. 11 of the Appendix.

7   Conclusion

In this work we have shown that verifying DRP logics on FPGAs only by a power-based side-channel analysis is insufficient. While their security gain is remarkable in this setting, it is not when considering high-resolution, localized EM measurements. We therefore suggest to always include a thorough EM-based analysis in future proposals of such logic styles.

To compensate for the significant loss in security under an EM-based attack, we investigated if the situation improves when adapting the placement. This is achieved by a custom placer using simulated annealing using a novel cost function. Our practical investigations confirm that by using a more dense placement, the security doubles when compared to the default ISE setting.

While generally assuming that a single countermeasure is insufficient and combining multiple countermeasures is needed, we demonstrate that for dual-rails on FPGAs this may result in a wrong systematic, as they may be rendered mostly useless, especially if not taking care of the placement.

Even though we did not specifically consider duplication schemes, we expect that our findings apply to them as well, since the minimum distance between their `true` and `false` is typically large, i.e., more than one tile. This needs to be confirmed by future evaluations, also considering triple-rail logics such as [22].

References

1. Federal Information Processing Standards Publication (FIPS 197). Advanced Encryption Standard (AES) (2001)
2. Betz, V., Rose, J.: VPR: A New Packing, Placement and Routing Ttool for FPGA Research
3. Bhasin, S., Guilley, S., Flament, F., Selmane, N., Danger, J.-L., Evaluation, C.E.: An approach towards robust dual-rail precharge logic. In: WESS 2010, p. 6. ACM (2010)
4. Canright, D.: A very compact S-box for AES. In: Rao, J.R., Sunar, B. (eds.) CHES 2005. LNCS, vol. 3659, pp. 441–455. Springer, Heidelberg (2005). doi:10.1007/11545262_32
5. Cheng, C.-L.E.: RISA: accurate and efficient placement routability modeling. In: Proceedings of the 1994 IEEE/ACM International Conference on Computer-aided Design, ICCAD 1994, Los Alamitos, CA, USA. IEEE Computer Society Press
6. Cnudde, T.D., Bilgin, B., Gierlichs, B., Nikov, V., Nikova, S., Rijmen, V.: Does coupling affect the security of masked implementations? Cryptology ePrint Archive, Report 2016/1080 (2016)
7. De Mulder, E., Buysschaert, P., Ors, S., Delmotte, P., Preneel, B., Vandenbosch, G., Verbauwhede, I.: Electromagnetic analysis attack on an FPGA implementation of an elliptic curve cryptosystem. In: The International Conference on Computer as a Tool, EUROCON 2005, vol. 2, pp. 1879–1882, November 2005
8. Durvaux, F., Standaert, F.-X.: From improved leakage detection to the detection of points of interests in leakage traces. In: Fischlin, M., Coron, J.-S. (eds.) EUROCRYPT 2016. LNCS, vol. 9665, pp. 240–262. Springer, Heidelberg (2016). doi:10.1007/978-3-662-49890-3_10
9. Giechaskiel, I., Eguro, K.: Information Leakage Between FPGA Long Wires. CoRR (2016)
10. Gierlichs, B., Batina, L., Tuyls, P., Preneel, B.: Mutual information analysis. In: Oswald, E., Rohatgi, P. (eds.) CHES 2008. LNCS, vol. 5154, pp. 426–442. Springer, Heidelberg (2008). doi:10.1007/978-3-540-85053-3_27
11. Guilley, S., Hoogvorst, P., Mathieu, Y., Pacalet, R.: The "Backend Duplication" method. In: Rao, J.R., Sunar, B. (eds.) CHES 2005. LNCS, vol. 3659, pp. 383–397. Springer, Heidelberg (2005). doi:10.1007/11545262_28
12. Güneysu, T., Moradi, A.: Generic side-channel countermeasures for reconfigurable devices. In: Preneel, B., Takagi, T. (eds.) CHES 2011. LNCS, vol. 6917, pp. 33–48. Springer, Heidelberg (2011). doi:10.1007/978-3-642-23951-9_3
13. He, W., de la Torre, E., Riesgo, T.: A precharge-absorbed DPL logic for reducing early propagation effects on FPGA implementations. In: ReConFig 2011. IEEE Computer Society (2011)
14. He, W., Herrmann, A.: Placement security analysis for side-channel resistant dual-rail scheme in FPGA. In: Proceedings of the Second Workshop on Cryptography and Security in Computing Systems, CS2 2015 (2015)
15. He, W., Otero, A., de la Torre, E., Riesgo, T.: Automatic generation of identical routing pairs for FPGA implemented DPL logic. In: ReConFig 2012. IEEE (2012)
16. Herbst, C., Oswald, E., Mangard, S.: An AES smart card implementation resistant to power analysis attacks. In: Zhou, J., Yung, M., Bao, F. (eds.) ACNS 2006. LNCS, vol. 3989, pp. 239–252. Springer, Heidelberg (2006). doi:10.1007/11767480_16

17. Heyszl, J., Mangard, S., Heinz, B., Stumpf, F., Sigl, G.: Localized electromagnetic analysis of cryptographic implementations. In: Dunkelman, O. (ed.) CT-RSA 2012. LNCS, vol. 7178, pp. 231–244. Springer, Heidelberg (2012). doi:10.1007/978-3-642-27954-6_15

18. Heyszl, J., Merli, D., Heinz, B., Santis, F., Sigl, G.: Strengths and limitations of high-resolution electromagnetic field measurements for side-channel analysis. In: Mangard, S. (ed.) CARDIS 2012. LNCS, vol. 7771, pp. 248–262. Springer, Heidelberg (2013). doi:10.1007/978-3-642-37288-9_17

19. Kaps, J.-P., Velegalati, R.: DPA resistant AES on FPGA using partial DDL. In: FCCM 2010, pp. 273–280. IEEE Computer Society (2010)

20. Kocher, P.C., Jaffe, J., Jun, B.: Differential power analysis. In: Wiener, M. (ed.) CRYPTO 1999. LNCS, vol. 1666, pp. 388–397. Springer, Heidelberg (1999). doi:10.1007/3-540-48405-1_25

21. Lavin, C., Padilla, M., Lamprecht, J., Lundrigan, P., Nelson, B., Hutchings, B., Wirthlin, M.: Rapidsmith - a library for low-level manipulation of partially placed-and-routed FPGA designs. Technical report, Brigham Young University, September 2012

22. Lomné, V., Maurine, P., Torres, L., Robert, M., Soares, R., Calazans, N.: Evaluation on FPGA of triple rail logic robustness against DPA and DEMA. In: DATE 2009, pp. 634–639. IEEE (2009)

23. Mangard, S., Oswald, E., Popp, T.: Power Analysis Attacks: Revealing the Secrets of Smart Cards. Springer, New York (2007)

24. Mangard, S., Schramm, K.: Pinpointing the side-channel leakage of masked AES hardware implementations. In: Goubin, L., Matsui, M. (eds.) CHES 2006. LNCS, vol. 4249, pp. 76–90. Springer, Heidelberg (2006). doi:10.1007/11894063_7

25. Moradi, A., Eisenbarth, T., Poschmann, A., Paar, C.: Power analysis of single-rail storage elements as used in MDPL. In: Lee, D., Hong, S. (eds.) ICISC 2009. LNCS, vol. 5984, pp. 146–160. Springer, Heidelberg (2010). doi:10.1007/978-3-642-14423-3_11

26. Moradi, A., Immler, V.: Early propagation and imbalanced routing, How to diminish in FPGAs. In: Batina, L., Robshaw, M. (eds.) CHES 2014. LNCS, vol. 8731, pp. 598–615. Springer, Heidelberg (2014). doi:10.1007/978-3-662-44709-3_33

27. Nam, G.-J., Villarrubia, P.G.: Placement: introduction/problem formulation. In: Alpert, C.J., Mehta, D.P., Sapatnekar, S.S. (eds.) Handbook of Algorithms for Physical Design Automation, 1st edn, pp. 277–287. Auerbach Publications, Boca Raton (2008)

28. Nassar, M., Bhasin, S., Danger, J.-L., Duc, G., Guilley, S.: BCDL: a high speed balanced DPL for FPGA with global precharge and no early evaluation. In: DATE 2010, pp. 849–854. IEEE (2010)

29. Nikova, S., Rijmen, V., Schläffer, M.: Secure hardware implementation of nonlinear functions in the presence of glitches. J. Cryptol. 24(2), 292–321 (2011)

30. Oswald, E., Mangard, S., Pramstaller, N., Rijmen, V.: A side-channel analysis resistant description of the AES S-box. In: Gilbert, H., Handschuh, H. (eds.) FSE 2005. LNCS, vol. 3557, pp. 413–423. Springer, Heidelberg (2005). doi:10.1007/11502760_28

31. Peeters, E., Standaert, F.-X., Quisquater, J.-J.: Power and electromagnetic analysis: improved model, consequences and comparisons. Integr. VLSI J. 40, 52–60 (2007)

32. Quisquater, J.-J., Samyde, D.: ElectroMagnetic analysis (EMA): measures and counter-measures for smart cards. In: Attali, I., Jensen, T. (eds.) E-smart 2001. LNCS, vol. 2140, pp. 200–210. Springer, Heidelberg (2001). doi:10.1007/3-540-45418-7_17

33. Sauvage, L., Guilley, S., Danger, J.-L., Mathieu, Y., Nassar, M.: Successful attack on an FPGA-based WDDL DES cryptoprocessor without place and route constraints. In: Proceedings of the Conference on Design, Automation and Test in Europe, DATE 2009 (2009)

34. Sauvage, L., Nassar, M., Guilley, S., Flament, F., Danger, J.-L., Mathieu, Y.: DPL on stratix II FPGA: What to expect? In: ReConFig 2009, pp. 243–248. IEEE Computer Society (2009)

35. Specht, R., Heyszl, J., Kleinsteuber, M., Sigl, G.: Improving non-profiled attacks on exponentiations based on clustering and extracting leakage from multi-channel high-resolution EM measurements. In: Mangard, S., Poschmann, A.Y. (eds.) COSADE 2014. LNCS, vol. 9064, pp. 3–19. Springer, Cham (2015). doi:10.1007/978-3-319-21476-4_1

36. Standaert, F.-X., Malkin, T.G., Yung, M.: A unified framework for the analysis of side-channel key recovery attacks. In: Joux, A. (ed.) EUROCRYPT 2009. LNCS, vol. 5479, pp. 443–461. Springer, Heidelberg (2009). doi:10.1007/978-3-642-01001-9_26

37. Suzuki, D., Saeki, M.: Security evaluation of DPA countermeasures using dual-rail pre-charge logic style. In: Goubin, L., Matsui, M. (eds.) CHES 2006. LNCS, vol. 4249, pp. 255–269. Springer, Heidelberg (2006). doi:10.1007/11894063_21

38. Swartz, W.: Placement using simulated annealing. In: Alpert, C.J., Mehta, D.P., Sapatnekar, S.S. (eds.) Handbook of Algorithms for Physical Design Automation, pp. 311–325. Auerbach Publications, Baco Raton (2008)

39. Tiri, K., Hwang, D., Hodjat, A., Lai, B.-C., Yang, S., Schaumont, P., Verbauwhede, I.: Prototype IC with WDDL and differential routing – DPA resistance assessment. In: Rao, J.R., Sunar, B. (eds.) CHES 2005. LNCS, vol. 3659, pp. 354–365. Springer, Heidelberg (2005). doi:10.1007/11545262_26

40. Tiri, K., Verbauwhede, I.: A logic level design methodology for a secure DPA resistant ASIC or FPGA implementation. In: DATE 2004, pp. 246–251. IEEE Computer Society (2004)

41. Tiri, K., Verbauwhede, I.: Place and route for secure standard cell design. In: CARDIS 2004, pp. 143–158. Kluwer (2004)

42. Unterstein, F., Heyszl, J., De Santis, F., Specht, R.: Dissecting leakage resilient PRFs with multivariate localized em attacks - a practical security evaluation on FPGA. In: Constructive Side-Channel Analysis and Secure Design: 8th International Workshop, April 13–14, 2017, Paris, France. Springer International Publishing (2017)

43. Wild, A., Moradi, A., Güneysu, T.: GliFreD: Glitch-Free Duplication - Towards Power-Equalized Circuits on FPGAs (2015)

44. Yu, P., Schaumont, P.: Secure FPGA circuits using controlled placement and routing. In: CODES+ISSS 2007, pp. 45–50. ACM (2007)

Appendix

For the sake of completeness, we present the results of a simple boolean masked version of AWDDL as an example in Fig. 11, using the default placement of

ISE. Both power and localized EM attack have been carried out. The first order correlation based leakage test did (as expected) not show any leakage.

In contrast, using the mutual information, it was still possible for both designs to extract leakage. Hence, additional countermeasures would be required.

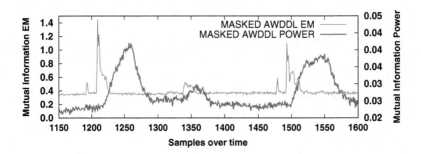

Fig. 11. Mutual information of the evaluation and precharge phases over time.

How to Break Secure Boot on FPGA SoCs Through Malicious Hardware

Nisha Jacob[1]([✉]), Johann Heyszl[1],
Andreas Zankl[1], Carsten Rolfes[1], and Georg Sigl[1,2]

[1] Fraunhofer Institute for Applied and Integrated Security (AISEC),
Munich, Germany
{nisha.jacob,johann.heyszl,
andreas.zankl,carsten.rolfes}@aisec.fraunhofer.de
[2] Technische Universität München, EI SEC, Munich, Germany
sigl@tum.de

Abstract. Embedded IoT devices are often built upon large system on chip computing platforms running a significant stack of software. For certain computation-intensive operations such as signal processing or encryption and authentication of large data, chips with integrated FPGAs, FPGA SoCs, which provide high performance through configurable hardware designs, are used. In this contribution, we demonstrate how an FPGA hardware design can compromise the important secure boot process of the main software system to boot from a malicious network source instead of an authentic signed kernel image. This significant and new threat arises from the fact that the CPU and FPGA are connected to the same memory bus, so that FPGA hardware designs can interfere with secure boot routines on FPGA SoCs that are without any interruption on regular SoCs. An enabling factor is that integrated hardware designs are likely bought from external partners and there is a realistic lack of security review at the system integrators. This facilitates flaws or even unwanted functionality in such hardware designs. We perform a proof of concept on a Xilinx Zynq-7000 FPGA SoC, and the threat can be generalized to other devices. We also present as effective mitigation, an easy-to-review and re-usable wrapper module which prevents any unauthorized memory access by included hardware designs.

Keywords: FPGA SoCs · Secure boot · Hardware design · Outsourced · Threat

1 Introduction

We are currently experiencing a rapid increase in the number of embedded devices being used in the context of the Internet-of-Things (IoT) and cyber physical systems. The application domains of such systems range from automotive, aviation, infrastructure, to industrial production and even home appliances. Across all domains, embedded systems are mostly build on powerful high-volume System on Chips (SoCs) running a mixture of open-source and closed source

© International Association for Cryptologic Research 2017
W. Fischer and N. Homma (Eds.): CHES 2017, LNCS 10529, pp. 425–442, 2017.
DOI: 10.1007/978-3-319-66787-4_21

software, and include network communication interfaces. Such devices perform critical tasks, however, are at the same time physically accessible for attackers in many cases. Fortunately, several security mechanisms have been developed to counteract possible attacks based on physical access. The arguably most important and widely adopted countermeasure is a secure boot mechanism which ensures that only authentic and unmodified software can be run right from the start of the first code within the CPU. This prevents attackers from manipulating software images and restarting devices into a manipulated behaviour. As such, it can be seen as the foundation of all further software security measures. Some applications of embedded systems require high computational capabilities for signal processing or cryptographic operations. At the same time, devices often remain in the field for many years which means that updates of the functionality are likely required. For such cases, FPGA manufacturers such as Xilinx have produced SoC chips known as FPGA SoCs which include configurable hardware logic on the same chip as a conventional CPU architecture. Embedded systems built using such devices (e.g. [26]) are able to support significant computational capabilities through hardware acceleration while both, software as well as hardware can be updated in the field.

However, this additional configurable hardware may lead to severe security issues. Configurable hardware within FPGA SoCs is typically connected to high-bandwidth memory buses of the main CPU which means that hardware blocks may possibly access memory regions which are access-managed by the software system. This has severe consequences for the system, because this may easily corrupt the security of the entire system. We have in the past seen similar attack vectors in the PC world which were successful. For instance, external high-speed interfaces have been misused to directly access internal memory [12,24]. Fortunately, countermeasures such as Input Output Memory Management Units (IOMMUs) have also been developed against such attacks [3] which handle the memory management of peripherals with direct access to memory and thereby prevent unauthorised memory accesses. In our opinion, however, such threats are now possible from a new direction i.e., through the integrated hardware. In order to understand the reasons for this, it is important to realize that hardware designs (e.g. cryptographic accelerators) will possibly come from 'external' sources. This is simply cheaper and provides a faster time-to-market. Open-source software is used for similar reasons. Even large ASIC SoCs for short-lived consumer-grade routers/modems are designed with outsourced hardware modules, which means that the following threat also applies to ASICs in such cases. For example, the Elastic Compute Cloud (EC2) from Amazon Web Services (AWS) now includes an instance with integrated FPGAs (EC2 F1 instance) where IP cores can be used from a dedicated IP market place [15]. While designers of embedded systems will likely have sufficient software expertise within their team, they will, in many cases, lack proper hardware engineering expertise along with the required extensive tooling for hardware development and verification. If hardware is sourced from elsewhere, it is hence questionable whether the embedded system designers/integrators will be able to properly review the hardware code to check for unwanted functionality or possible attacks. In many cases, hardware blocks will even be delivered as a synthesized netlist which more or less prohibits proper review. The problem is that malicious functionality could be part of such hardware modules.

Previous contributions have already highlighted some of the issues arising from this where unwanted additional functionality in hardware blocks leaks or corrupts sensitive information. E.g. Kutzner et al. [19] describe how an AES core could be maliciously modified such that the key of the last round is output instead of the cipher text. Other contributions have demonstrated how cryptographic keys could be leaked via intentional side-channels such as the power consumption [21] or over the wireless channel [17]. King et al. [18] and Yang et al. [29] show how a privilege escalation of applications can be achieved at run-time using malicious hardware blocks. For this, King et al. modify the data cache and MMU of the Leon processor, while Yang et al., modify the register that holds the privilege bit of the OpenRISC processor. Li et al. [20] describe how a hardware core, which is originally purposed for memory tracing in the context of software debugging, may include unwanted functionality to inject code into the running system. As a proof of concept, Li et al. demonstrate how a log-in password check of a Linux Operating System (OS) can successfully be circumvented by a hardware core scanning and manipulating the memory on the Xilinx Zynq-7000. Jacob et al. [23] show how public authentication keys can be overwritten by a malicious hardware core in FPGA SoCs so that the devices accepts malicious system updates.

In this work, we show that even the secure boot process, one of the most important and basic security features of embedded systems, can be compromised by malicious hardware blocks in the FPGA on FPGA SoCs. We describe a proof of concept on the Xilinx Zynq-7000 device and explain why even later models which include IOMMUs (and are fit to counteract attacks such as described by Li et al. [20] and Jacob et al. [23]) will likely be susceptible to such attacks. Our proof of concept system includes a conventional software stack along with an additional hardware block for the FPGA. The included unwanted hardware functionality overwrites parameters of the second stage boot loader, U-boot, during the secure boot so that an *unauthorized* kernel image is retrieved and booted over the network instead of the local *authorized* image even though all previous boot stages are properly verified prior to that. In our opinion, it will not be realistic for general design teams to acquire the necessary hardware expertise to prevent this. Hence, we developed an efficient countermeasure, which provides full re-usability, and is easy-to-review because of the small code size, that protects against all unauthorized memory accesses through hardware cores while raising an alarm at every attempt. It is a simple hardware wrapper for the AXI bus interface which is easy to wrap around all outsourced hardware cores with memory access and is configured through every access from software. It can be seen as a stripped-down IOMMU which instead works straight from configuration (without requiring the software to explicitly enable or configure it, which is usually done after boot in the OS) and has a smaller set of functionality, thus, trusted code base.

The paper is organised as follows. Section 2 reviews the security of embedded systems generally. Section 3 outlines the attack on the secure boot process. Section 4 describes the Xilinx Zynq device and boot sequence along with a generalization to other devices. Section 5 presents the proof of concept along with a discussion. Section 6 presents the countermeasure.

2   On the Security of Embedded Systems

To highlight the importance of a secure boot process we review popular security mechanisms for embedded systems in this section. They can be divided into three general kinds of security measures built on top of each other.

Hardware Security. Since many IoT embedded systems are in physical reach of potential attackers, security must be rooted in the hardware of respective devices. Hardware security mechanisms for instance include protection against physical tampering, which can be achieved by using tamper-proof casings with light sensors to detect break-ins. Chip-internal tamper detection sensors typically monitor clock and voltage inputs to prevent fault-injection attacks [4]. In case of a tamper event, critical data is e.g. cleared and the system is shut down. Many SoCs for embedded systems include dedicated secure memory for keys and/or certificates. This helps to refrain from storing such information on external memories. Another important aspect of hardware security is to protect debug interfaces using e.g. passwords so that read-out and/or corruption of data and software is prevented in the field [13].

Secure System Startup. One of the most important security mechanisms is a secure boot process. In this process, all executed code is verified for integrity and authenticity using cryptographic means before execution. This means that right after the system startup, the running software can be trusted, which is the required foundation for all later security mechanisms. For a secure boot, a chain-of-trust is established which starts from the very first code that is executed from within the CPUs internal hardwired ROM (also including respective keying material), commonly called the hardware root-of-trust [10]. Given that attackers have physical access, a trusted boot process using Trusted Platform Modules (TPMs) on the contrary, cannot provide this assurance, since the external TPM can always be manipulated by malicious software on the main CPU (comparable to a man-in-the-middle attack). Using similar functions as secure boot, secure update processes allow updates in-the-field from authentic sources by checking authenticity and integrity as well as decrypting confidential data using cryptographic methods. Both require a secure storage for the respective key material.

Runtime Security. After the device startup, all assets such as cryptographic keys, processed data and control functions must be protected against run-time attacks on the software. This only makes sense if the running software is trusted from the start (i.e. secure boot). Popular mechanisms include different kinds of software isolation and virtualization to prevent corrupted processes (e.g. after successful exploits) from accessing sensitive or higher-privilege information. Memory isolation can be achieved through the OS or a hypervisor. Both need hardware support in the form of a Memory Management Unit (MMU) and/or IOMMUs [3]. Trusted execution environments [25] provide an additional privilege level for processes where sensitive processes including their memory regions e.g. keys, and even peripherals, can be put into a secure world to prevent access by corrupted processes from the normal world.

Through this work we would like to highlight that even if we have an FPGA SoC with a secure hardware root-of-trust and a secure boot process, as well as runtime protection (by isolation of software components), we still have a major risk that the system may be compromised. This risk comes from the reconfigurable hardware. We show that protection mechanisms such as a secure boot, MMU, or privilege levels do not help against such threats.

3   Attacking the Secure Boot on FPGA SoCs

In this section, we outline the general idea of an attack on the secure boot process in the context of FPGA SoCs. The main underlying observation for all secure boot processes is that the verification of the authenticity and integrity of a software image is either not done in-place, or, more importantly, the process which performs the verification and later hands off control to the subsequent stage is inherently not atomic in the sense that it could be interrupted by manipulations. This is an issue that we generally want to highlight and which is of particular relevance for embedded systems built upon FPGA SoCs. In most cases of conventional SoCs, there is no reason to believe that a manipulation of the memory is happening while the CPU is executing the secure boot code, since no-one besides the CPU is accessing the memory. However, in the case of FPGA SoCs, hardware cores on the FPGA have access to the shared memory bus. Hence, such cores, once loaded, present as immediate additional actors on those buses and may manipulate memory content while the CPU is not 'aware' of this. Specifically, such hardware cores, once loaded, are able to manipulate the boot process such that a malicious software image is executed instead of an authentic one. This can be achieved by the hardware secretly overwriting parts of a running bootloader. We present a proof of concept on the Xilinx Zynq-7000 FPGA SoC.

It is important to note that the malicious functionality in the hardware, for the reasons explained in the introduction, is part of an FPGA configuration file and contains authentic signatures. It is also important to note that it often makes sense to load the FPGA before starting the software system so that the hardware acceleration is e.g. available to verify large software images to reduce software startup times in secure boot scenarios.

4   Relevant Properties of the Xilinx Zynq-7000

We chose the Xilinx Zynq-7000 device for our practical proof of concept since it is a popular choice for contemporary embedded system designs. Also, the insights are generalizable to later models as well as devices from different manufacturers.

The Xilinx Zynq-7000 is an FPGA SoC consisting of a dual core ARM Cortex A9 CPU and a Xilinx 7-series FPGA fabric on the same die. The processing system includes a MMU and two-level cache. A small on-chip RAM of 256KB is available for the storage of sensitive information or code. A larger external DDR memory can be accessed via the memory controllers. The main memory bus is an ARM AMBA AXI bus system. External communication is supported through CAN, I2C, Ethernet and USB interfaces. The device includes a hard-core AES and HMAC implementation which are used during the decryption and authenticity verification of images and configuration files to be run on the Zynq-7000. The ARM trusted execution environment known as TrustZone is available for runtime security of the software system. A one-bit hardware setting divides all processes and peripherals into either a secure, or a normal world.

4.1   Secure Boot Process on the Xilinx Zynq-7000

Figure 1 depicts the boot process on the Zynq-7000 FPGA SoC. It consists of five stages after power-up:

1. BootROM (non-accessible internal hardwired code)
2. First Stage Bootloader (FSBL)
3. FPGA configuration (bitstream)
4. Second stage bootloader (i.e. U-boot)
5. Operating System (OS)

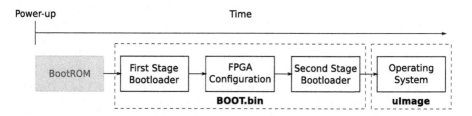

Fig. 1. Overview of boot process on Xilinx Zynq-7000

The FSBL, bitstream and second stage bootloader are packed into a single boot image i.e., BOOT.bin as separate partitions. Each partition within the boot image is separately encrypted and authenticated. Figure 2 depicts the structure of such a partition. It contains the payload as the main part. For AES/HMAC-based authentication and integrity checks, the HMAC key as well as the HMAC digest are appended to the payload before encryption. Xilinx uses the MAC-then-encrypt order of encryption and authentication i.e., the message digest of each partition is first computed followed by its encryption. The key for the AES encryption can either be stored in the battery-backed RAM or in eFuses of the chip. The selection of the AES key source can be enforced by setting the corresponding eFuse. If the optional RSA algorithm is used for authentication, an RSA signature verification is computed in software and the signature as well as the certificate are appended to the partition. The hash of the RSA public key, which is used to validate the certificate, is stored in an on-chip eFuse array.

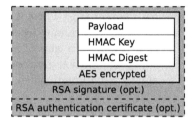

Fig. 2. Content of an authenticated and encrypted boot partition

After power-up, the CPU executes the hardwired instructions from the internal BootROM which is a small and inaccessible read-only memory of 128KB. It also initializes the clocks and configures the first ARM processor core along with the necessary peripherals to fetch the FSBL from Non-Volatile Memory (NVM) based on the boot mode stating the source where the FSBL can be fetched (i.e. SD card, QSPI flash, NAND flash or NOR flash). The boot mode is determined by the voltage levels on the chip's external pin[1]. The BootROM code then copies the FSBL from the NVM to the 192KB[2] on-chip memory (which is typically large enough). The FSBL code is decrypted and authenticated using the AES/HMAC core on the fly while copying it to the internal memory. Upon successful verification of the HMAC, control is handed off to the FSBL and it is executed from the same internal memory. The FSBL is a Xilinx-specific bootloader which initializes clocks, GPIOs, DDR controller and the FPGA fabric. Following the initializations, the FSBL loads subsequent partitions. Xilinx provides a template of the FSBL code, which can be customized. The FSBL controls the decryption and authentication of the bitstream and second stage bootloader. If a bitstream is part of the boot image, this is loaded next. (The bitstream may alternatively be loaded at a later stage of boot through the U-boot or the OS. This, however, is uncommon since it requires additional code to be inserted into the U-boot or later OS instead of using the Xilinx template. Also, hardware acceleration

---

[1] Those pins are accessible to possible attackers but no unauthorized images can be started.

[2] The rest of the on-chip memory is reserved for the BootROM code until control is handed off to the FSBL.

would not be available for the verification of the OS image.). The bitstream is decrypted and authenticated using AES/HMAC while it is loaded into the FPGA configuration memory. If the verification fails, the FPGA containing an unauthentic configuration is not activated. As a next step, the second stage bootloader, e.g., U-boot is decrypted and authenticated. As the on-chip memory is not large enough for typical loaders, the decrypted U-boot is stored on the external DDR memory. If the verification is successful, control is then handed off to U-boot. After initialization of the platform (processor, clocks, memory) and reservation of memory, U-boot enters the main loop where it decrypts and authenticates the kernel image. U-boot then reads the kernel image header and jumps to the address of the kernel header, handing off control to the OS.

As can be devised, a secure chain-of-trust is established starting from the BootROM code. If any of the partitions cannot be successfully verified, the system goes into a secure lockdown mode. In case of a lockdown, the AES key in the BBRAM is cleared and the configuration memory of the FPGA is cleared (the keys and settings in the eFuses remain untouched).

5   Proof of Concept: Breaking the Secure Boot on Xilinx Zynq-7000

In this section, we describe our proof of concept where we practically break the secure boot process of the Xilinx Zynq-7000 FPGA SoC using a hardware module. The investigation was carried on a Zedboard Rev. D development board with 512MB of external DDR memory. The FSBL v2015.4, u-boot-xlnx v2016.1 and linux-xlnx v2016.1 from Xilinx are used [27]. The Xilinx tool *bootgen* is used to encrypt and compute the message digests of each partition. Each partition of the boot image is decrypted and authenticated using the on-chip AES/HMAC. The AES encryption key is stored in the battery-backed RAM.

Hardware Module. As a likely scenario for the proof of concept, we chose a hardware module similar to a cryptographic accelerator which we connect to the AXI bus of the Xilinx Zynq-7000. In our case this module only XORs two input values, which can be seen as a placeholder for several meaningful cryptographic operations. We use an interface which is typical for high-speed hardware accelerators and consists of a low-speed slave interface for configuration and control (i.e. source address, destination address, length, and enable signal) as well as a high-speed master interface for data transfer [5,6,11]. The master interface is DMA-like and, hence, reduces the load on the processing system by not requiring the CPU for data input/output. The CPU only passes the configuration information after which the module starts to perform its core function whilst accessing data directly from the memory. Upon completion, a flag is set to alert the processor.

In addition to this, the module also contains unwanted functionality. Using the high-speed data interface, the module progressively scans the external DDR memory and maliciously alters its content. It specifically scans the U-boot binary in the DDR memory for the kernel boot parameters. After finding the target memory location, the boot parameters are modified to load an unauthorized kernel image from a remote server over the network instead of booting from the verified source. For this unwanted functionality, our example hardware module requires 117 LUTs and 46 Slices in addition to the original functionality. This hardware overhead will likely pass unnoticed since e.g. a high-speed AES-GCM core for the same family of FPGAs and including a similar interface requires 22.7 k LUTs and 6.9 k Slices [5] for example, which is larger by orders of magnitude. Another smaller example of a SHA-384/512 core (excluding the interface) for the same FPGA family still requires 2.5 k LUTs and 700 Slices [14], which is also significantly larger.

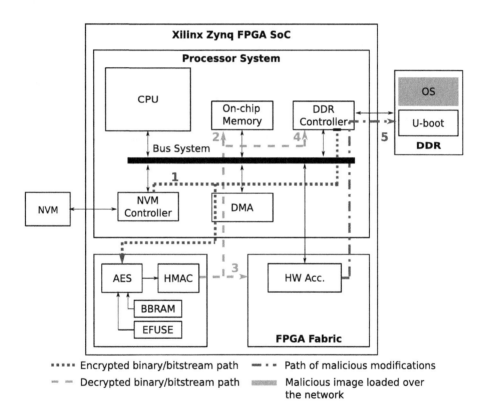

Fig. 3. Secure boot attack on Xilinx Zynq-7000 FPGA SoC

Sequence of Events During the Attack. Figure 3 depicts the Xilinx Zynq-7000 FPGA SoC and highlights the data flow of the encrypted and decrypted images during the secure boot process as it is described in Section 4. The numbers in the figure indicate the sequence of events during the attacked boot process. In step 1 (dotted grey path), the encrypted and authenticated partitions are read from NVM (our system boots from an SD-card) or DDR memory and piped through the AES/HMAC cores for verification[3]. Boot steps 2–4 (dashed green paths) depict the successive loading of the FSBL, bitstream and U-boot respectively, as described in Section 4.1. Following the successful verification and loading of the bitstream to the FPGA, U-boot is verified and loaded to the external DDR memory and control is handed-over. As soon as the hardware is activated after the successful verification of the HMAC, the malicious core starts to scan the external DDR memory for a particular U-boot setting which is to be modified. This is the actual attack and depicted as step 5 in Figure 3.

```
fi.sdboot=if mmcinfo; then echo Boot
from SD env variables to RAM... && lo
ad mmc 0 ${devicetree_load_address} $
{devicetree_image} && zynqaes ${devic
etree_load_address} ${devicetree_size
}$ ${devicetree_dest_address} $device
tree_len$ &&load mmc 0 ${ramdisk_load
_address} ${ramdisk_image} && zynqaes
 ${ramdisk_load_address} $ramdisk_siz
e$ ${ramdisk_dest_address} $ramdisk_l
en$ &&load mmc 0 ${kernel_load_addres
s} ${kernel_image} && zynqaes ${kerne
l_load_address} $kernel_size$ ${kerne
l_dest_address} $kernel_len$ &&bootm
${kernel_load_address} ${ramdisk_load
_address} ${devicetree_load_address};
```
(a) Authentic image

```
fi.sdboot=if mmcinfo; then echo Boot
from SD env variables to RAM... && bo
otp 0x2000000 10.148.95.25:dt.dtb &&
bootp 0x4000000 10.148.95.25:ur.gz&&
bootp 0x2080000 10.148.95.25:uI &&boo
tm 0x4000000 0x2080000 0x2000000;vice
tree_len$ &&load mmc 0 ${ramdisk_load
_address} ${ramdisk_image} && zynqaes
 ${ramdisk_load_address} $ramdisk_siz
e$ ${ramdisk_dest_address} $ramdisk_l
en$ &&load mmc 0 ${kernel_load_addres
s} ${kernel_image} && zynqaes ${kerne
l_load_address} $kernel_size$ ${kerne
l_dest_address} $kernel_len$ &&bootm
${kernel_load_address} ${ramdisk_load
_address} ${devicetree_load_address};
```
(b) Corrupted image

Fig. 4. Excerpt of the .rodata section of the U-boot image

Figure 4a shows an excerpt of the trusted U-boot image which contains strings representing the boot parameters in the .rodata section of the image. In step 5 explained above explained, the hardware module searches for the SD card boot parameters i.e., `fi.sdboot=` (see Figure 4a). Upon locating the string, the following original boot parameters from the authentic image, which are used to load and verify the kernel image on the SD card, are overwritten:

`load mmc 0 <dest_addr> <filename>`
`zynqaes <src_addr> <src_len> <dest_addr> <dest_len>`

The `load` command is used to transfer the encrypted and authenticated kernel image from the SD card to the DDR memory. The `zynqaes` command then routes this image from the DDR memory to the AES-HMAC core for decryption and authentication. The malicious functionality overwrites these commands with the following bootp command:

`bootp <dest_addr> <sever_IP_addr>:<filename>`

---

[3] Encrypted partitions may first be copied from NVM to DDR in order to accelerate data transfer.

The `bootp` command downloads a file from the specified server IP address to the DDR memory[4]. Once the image is downloaded to the DDR memory from the remote server, the kernel is booted. For this, the malicious core also writes a regular U-boot boot command, which specifies the locations where the `bootp` command had placed the kernel image, uramdisk and devicetree in the DDR memory, as follows:

`bootm <kernel_addr> <ramdisk_addr> <devicetree_addr>`

Figure 4b shows the same excerpt as Figure 4a, with the described malicious modifications highlighted in grey. (In our set-up, the kernel image (`uI`), device-tree (`dt.dtb`) and uramdisk (`ur.gz`) are three separate images and, hence, successively loaded.) Note that the U-boot code after the overwritten section of code is corrupted. This is highlighted in red in Figure 4b but does not make a difference as control is handed off to the OS after the `bootm` command.

Through the last command, control is handed-off and the malicious kernel image is booted without the system or secure boot process having any chance to detect the manipulation.

Regarding timing, the module is clocked at 100 MHz. Each read operation to the external memory takes 70 ns. Insertion of the malicious code takes 3.6 µs. Straight after activation, the core begins to scan the memory starting from the address 0×4000000, which is the default address where the U-boot is stored. This address is static and publicly accessible from the default implementation of the FSBL provided by Xilinx or the U-boot code which is open-source. The overall attack (scanning and overwriting) takes 5.5 ms. Note that the scanning would even be faster if the hardware core uses a full memory mapped AXI interface or an AXI-stream interface which support burst data transfers.

To summarize, we were able to carry out the proof of concept attack successfully and have shown that secure boot, which is a critical protection mechanism for embedded systems, can be compromised using malicious hardware in the FPGA of FPGA SoCs.

Note that for this proof of concept, the RSA authentication of images was not enabled and only the AES-HMAC was used for decryption and authentication. However, the same attack can be carried out when RSA is enabled without any modifications to the malicious functionality.

5.1   Discussions and Generalizations

There are several interesting aspects of the described successful attack which require a more detailed discussion. This helps understanding and highlights generalizations to other devices.

IOMMUs. In general, IOMMUs or System MMUs (as called by ARM), are designed to protect the system against threats such as the one demonstrated in this contribution where bus peripherals access shared memory resources without

---

[4] Alternative U-boot commands that could be used to load a file from a remote server are `tftpboot` and `dhcp`.

proper authorization. IOMMUs are hardware cores which, when properly configured, control bus access rights of such peripherals. They are even available in newer (and partly more expensive) FPGA SoCs such as the Xilinx UltraScale+ [28] and Altera Stratix 10 [1]. However, IOMMUs are typically initialized by the OS, which is the last stage in the boot process. Hence, we conclude that the availability of IOMMUs on FPGA SoCs will not generally prevent the described attack because this would require an earlier configuration. We advise the use of the countermeasure presented in the next section instead.

ARM TrustZone. ARM TrustZone prevents unauthorized accesses from the normal world to secure world resources (e.g. memory regions) through the use of the TrustZone bit, which is implemented in all system parts (MMU, bus participants, CPU). However, it is e.g. likely that cryptographic cores are placed within TrustZone, which allows them unlimited access which may lead to an attack as described. Even if an IP core is not within TrustZone, it is still able to compromise boot, since U-boot is typically not running in TrustZone. So while TrustZone is an important security feature, it is not an effective countermeasure against this attack.

Static Access Restrictions on Xilinx Devices. The Zynq-7000 allows to statically restrict the access of peripherals to the memory at design time. This means that under no operational circumstances, the hardware may access certain excluded memory regions. A similar feature is also offered by Microsemi for the SmartFusion2 FPGA SoCs [22]. However, this would pose a drastic limitation for designs since for most cases, the final use of a hardware module such as a cryptographic accelerator will be determined by software and it will be beneficial if all memory regions can be accessed. For example, a cryptographic core that is used for run-time integrity checking of software requires access to all memory regions.

On the Xilinx Zynq UltraScale+ series, a XMPU module can be used to restrict the access of masters on the bus. This access configuration can optionally be locked at boot time (recommended method by Xilinx [28]). This, however, means that the settings can only be changed after a power-on-reset using a modified and signed image. Alternatively, if this setting is not locked at boot time, the configuration can be changed at run-time. In our opinion, a static configuration will not likely be used for acceleration-type cores since it poses as an unfavorable restriction to designs. Instead the countermeasures presented in the next section is advised.

Generalization. We used the Xilinx Zynq-7000 for a proof of concept. It is currently being deployed and will likely stay in the field for many years. And even though the Zynq Ultrascale+ includes IOMMUs and XMPU, the Zynq-7000 will remain attractive for new designs due to lower costs. Also, as described above, the availability of IOMMUs does not by default prevent the described threats. They also need to be configured properly before the FPGA is loaded.

The order of the boot of FPGA and software system influences the vulnerability of the boot process. In case of FPGA SoCs from Altera, three cases of boot [2] are available: (i) the CPU boots and configures the FPGA during its boot sequence (similar to Zynq-7000), (ii) the FPGA is configured first and the CPU boot sequence is controlled by the FPGA, and (iii) the FPGA and CPU boot independently. The first case is the same with the same issue, the second is even worse as the FPGA is configured first. In the last, the FPGA and CPU are booted independently so the success will depend on whether the FPGA boots before the OS or during the CPU. In all cases, devices like, e.g. Stratix V and Arria 10 have no IOMMU and are vulnerable at run-time at least.

Microsemi on the contrary offers non-volatile FPGA SoCs, which means that the FPGA is ready to be used directly after power-up and there is no configuration of the FPGA from external memory as is the case with standard SRAM-based FPGA SoCs from Xilinx and Altera. Hence, the threat is imminent from the very start of the system.

To summarize the above cases, whenever the FPGA is configured early during the boot sequence, and this is often the case, a secure boot process can be compromised by a malicious core in the FPGA and the use of the countermeasure described in the next section is advised.

Virtual vs. Physical Memory Addressing. There is no virtual addressing before the OS is loaded. Hence, attacks such as the presented one do not have to take address mappings into account and can rely on direct physical addressing instead.

Finding the Location of the Code to be Overwritten. One of the key factors for attack vectors as the one described in this contribution is to estimate the location of the code which is to be overwritten. The less precise this is, the more code needs to be searched which takes more time. Interestingly, the location of the respective U-boot image depends only on a few factors and can be determined using publicly accessible information. Within the U-boot image, the presented attack overwrites U-boot environment variables which are located in the .rodata section of the image in the form of strings. By being part of the U-boot image, the variables are authenticated. (Technically, there are cases where such variables are instead retrieved from other, unauthentic external memories, and are loaded onto the heap in RAM at run-time. However, this option is completely unreasonable in the context of secure embedded systems since attackers with physical access may easily modify them [16]. Hence, we assume that U-boot is compiled such that it does not read environment variables from external memory.)

U-boot is generally unaware where the previous bootloader, in our case the FSBL, was loaded. Hence, after the basic initialization, U-boot checks the current value of the program counter to determine the location. By default, the FSBL loads the U-boot binary to start at address 0×4000000. There are regions in DDR memory, which need to be preserved to store the kernel image, device-tree and uramdisk. Hence, if U-boot detects that the previous loader has put it into those regions, it relocates itself to a predefined region before continuing execution. The relocation offset is usually at the end of the RAM so that one big continuous part of the memory remains for the OS. By analysing the

U-boot code (which is open-source), the offset address can be retrieved[5]. In our practical investigation, we found that the initialization before the relocation takes approximately 37 ms. Afterwards, the remaining part of the initialization is done, which takes approximately 400 ms on our example setup. Finally the kernel is loaded as a last step. From this we see that an attack could target the initial location of the U-boot during the 37 ms until it is relocated, or the final location during the 400 ms of further initialization.

Timing and Durations. The available time to perform a search for the specific string to be overwritten depends on whether it is done before or after the relocation, as described above. Our presented hardware module is able to scan up to 2.1 MB of memory, and successfully modify the specific boot parameters during the shorter time of 37 ms before relocation. For comparison, the size of a standard U-boot is about 3 MB which already hints at the high likeliness of success. Our practical investigations have indeed shown, that for both cases, the attack could be performed successfully.

Caches. The CPU caches are enabled by U-boot and could possibly influence the outcome of such attacks if the respective code to be overwritten is cached while it is overwritten in the RAM. This would lead to the case that the original data is possibly written back from cache in case of a later cache eviction. However, we did not encounter such situations and suspect that the targeted part of the U-boot image, the boot environment variables, are not accessed, thus, not cached until they are used shortly before handing over control to the OS kernel.

6   Wrapper Countermeasure

In this section, we propose a general countermeasure to protect systems against unauthorized memory access from hardware cores within the FPGA part of FPGA SoCs. For this purpose, we developed a flexible and lightweight security-enhanced hardware wrapper for cores with an AXI interface[6].

Cores can be easily integrated into the wrapper and subsequently connected to the AXI bus. The wrapper stores access commands and prevents the core from accessing other memory regions than designated by software driving it through the command interface. In principle it can be regarded as a stripped-down IOMMU. However, functionality is restricted to a minimum to support easy review, and a small trusted code base for easy re-use. Also, the wrapper is working with restricted default settings from the very start of the FPGA and does not rely on the OS configuring it (contrary to IOMMUs).

Typically, a software process using a hardware core writes configuration information (source address, destination address, length, enable) to the core via the core's slave interface. Based on this information the core performs its function

---

[5] The U-boot command `bdinfo` outputs the relocation offset on a running system.
[6] The source code for the wrapping module can be retrieved from https://github.com/Fraunhofer-AISEC/axi-firewall.

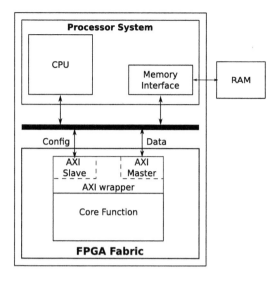

Fig. 5. Hardware core with security-enhanced wrapper

using the master interface for memory access. Figure 5 depicts a system architecture of an FPGA SoC including a core which is wrapped with our proposed design. Our wrapper uses the received configuration information to monitor the AXI-transactions of the master interface and only allows access to the memory range specified by the software process while leveraging the time during the AXI handshake to enforce the access commands. In a typical AXI transaction, the address channel is first set followed by the data channel. A transaction begins with the master sending the address of the memory location to be read/written along with an address valid signal. It then waits until the slave responds with an address ready signal. Next, the slave sends a data valid signal and the master responds with a data ready signal following which valid data can then be read/written to the memory. The wrappers checks the address issued by the master while it waits for the slaves' address ready response signal. If the wrapped underlying core attempts to access memory outside of the allowed range, an alarm signal is set. Thereby aborting a transaction before any valid data could be read/written to the memory while not affecting the performance of legitimate transactions. The wrapper also checks the length of data read/written as per the current configuration. If the core attempts to read or write more data, the remaining transactions are dropped and an alarm is raised. Furthermore, the wrapper also ensures that the core is only functional when a software process has explicitly set the enable signal, which prevents the core from performing accesses while technically in idle state. If the core tries to initiate any unauthorised transactions, an alarm is raised. Thus the core is not able to enable itself or modify its configuration settings.

The alarm signal can be connected to the interrupt controller or a separate tamper detection unit. Currently, all subsequent transactions are blocked after an alarm is raised. However, based on the criticality of the system, other actions can be taken such as e.g. putting the system into a secure lockdown mode. The wrapper also includes a 2-bit error output code to indicate the cause of the alarm which is listed in Table 1.

Table 1. Wrapper error codes

Error code	Description
00	No error
01	Exceeded permitted number of transactions
10	Out-of-range write
11	Out-of-range read

For cores that may require access to both the secure and normal world e.g., run-time integrity monitors, the TrustZone setting may not be fixed at boot (through the FSBL). In such cases, cores with a master interface may set the TrustZone security bit themselves and are, hence, free to access the secure world memory without explicit permission. Our wrapper, however, sets the security bit of the master interface to normal world by default unless explicitly reconfigured through software which prevents this.

Our proposed wrapper requires a hardware overhead of 133 LUTs and 55 Slices which is a low overhead compared to the given security gain in our opinion. There is no cycle count penalty during operation.

In a previous contribution, Brunel et al. [7] have developed a secure AXI bridge which is similar to a full IOMMU core for SoCs. The downside in our view is that it requires significantly more hardware resources and contains a significantly larger amount of source code to review. Coburn et al., [8] and Cotret et al. [9] present a post-boot run-time protection core similar to TrustZone. This is achieved by storing system wide or processor specific (for MPSoCs) security policies in large look-up-tables or BRAMS resulting in a significant overhead in area and latency. In contrast, the proposed wrapper protects devices against malicious hardware IP cores. Further, the wrapper reuses the configuration information passed to it from the firmware and leverages the time between the AXI handshaking for the enforcement. Hence minimizing the overhead in terms of area, performance, latency and maintenance of the security policies.

Xilinx provides a module known as the XMPU which can be used to dynamically restrict memory access from early boot stages onwards [28] but is only available for the Zynq Ultrascale+ devices. Unfortunately, the sources of the module are not publicly available. In contrast, our AXI-wrapper can be used for any IP cores with memory access and is not restricted to any manufacturer or device. Also, as the source code of the wrapper is small in size and public, it can be easily reviewed and re-used.

7 Conclusion

We successfully demonstrated the feasibility and practical impact of attacks on the secure boot process of FPGA SoCs through hardware on the FPGA. In a time where services such as the Amazon AWS EC2 F1 instances and embedded systems based on FPGA SoCs entice the broader use of hardware from IP vendors, the trust level of such outsourced hardware is difficult to determine. Hence, in our opinion, hardware cores including unwanted functionality such as the one described here, could become more common in hardware IP marketplaces. Hence, to prevent attacks against secure boot such as the one we presented and protect against similar attacks through unauthorized memory accesses from hardware cores generally, we propose to use our efficient wrapping module as a countermeasure. Alternatively, a strict restriction in the boot order (FPGA last) and early configuration of IOMMUs would be necessary.

References

1. Altera Corporation. Stratix 10 secure device manager provides best-in-class FPGA and SoC security (2015)
2. Altera Corporation. Arria 10 SoC boot user guide (2016)
3. AMD. I/O Memory Management Unit (2011). http://developer.amd.com/wordpress/media/2012/10/48882.pdf
4. Bar-El, H., Choukri, H., Naccache, D., Tunstall, M., Whelan, C.: The sorcerer's apprentice guide to fault attacks. Cryptology ePrint Archive, Report 2004/100 (2004). http://eprint.iacr.org/2004/100
5. BarcoSilex. BA415-AES-GCM 10 to 100 Gbps IP core (2015). http://www.xilinx.com/products/intellectual-property/1-4sw1c9.html
6. BarcoSilex. BA413-SHA1, SHA2 and HMAC IP core (2016). http://www.barco-silex.com/ip-cores/encryption-engine/BA413
7. Brunel, J., Pacalet, R., Ouaarab, S., Duc, G.: SecBus, a software/hardware architecture for securing external memories. In: 2nd IEEE International Conference on Mobile Cloud Computing, Services, and Engineering, MobileCloud 2014, Oxford, United Kingdom, April 8–11, 2014, pp. 277–282 (2014)
8. Coburn, J., Ravi, S., Raghunathan, A., Chakradhar, S.: SECA: security-enhanced communication architecture. In: Proceedings of the 2005 International Conference on Compilers, Architectures and Synthesis for Embedded Systems, CASES 2005, New York, pp. 78–89. ACM (2005)
9. Cotret, P., Devic, F., Gogniat, G., Badrignans, B., Torres, L.: Security enhancements for FPGA-based MPSoCs: A boot-to-runtime protection flow for an embedded linux-based system. In: 7th International Workshop on Reconfigurable and Communication-Centric Systems-on-Chip (ReCoSoC), York, United Kingdom, July 9–11, 2012, pp. 1–8 (2012)
10. Wilkins, D.: UEFI firmware security best practices. UEFI Plugfest (2014)
11. Ensilica. Ensilica eSi - SHA-256 (2013). http://www.ensilica.com/wp-content/uploads/eSi-SHA-256.pdf
12. Gamma International. Tactical IT intrusion portfolio: FINFIREWIRE (2011). https://wikileaks.org/spyfiles/files/0/293_GAMMA-201110-FinFireWire.pdf

13. Gonzalvo, B., Bourbao, E., Majéric, F., Bossue, L.: JTAG combined attacks. In: 2016 8th IFIP International Conference on New Technologies, Mobility and Security (NTMS). IEEE (2016)
14. Helion. HTSHA-FAST64: Fast SHA-384/512 hashing (2016). http://www.xilinx.com/products/intellectual-property/1-8dyf-612.html
15. Barr, J.: Developer preview – EC2 instances (F1) with programmable hardware. Amazon Web Services (2016)
16. Oh, J.W.: Reverse engineering flash memory for fun and benefit. Blackhat (2014)
17. Jin, Y., Makris, Y.: Hardware trojans in wireless cryptographic ICs. IEEE Des. Test Comput. **27**(1), 26–35 (2010)
18. King, S.T., Tucek, J., Cozzie, A., Grier, C., Jiang, W., Zhou, Y.: Designing and implementing malicious hardware. In: Proceedings of the 1st Usenix Workshop on Large-Scale Exploits and Emergent Threats, LEET 2008, Berkeley, pp. 5:1–5:8. USENIX Association (2008)
19. Kutzner, S., Poschmann, A.Y., Stöttinger, M.: Hardware trojan design and detection: a practical evaluation. In: Proceedings of the Workshop on Embedded Systems Security, WESS 2013, New York, pp. 1:1–1:9. ACM (2013)
20. Li, L.W., Duc, G., Pacalet, R.: Hardware-assisted memory tracing on new SoCs embedding FPGA fabrics. In: Proceedings of the 31st Annual Computer Security Applications Conference, ACSAC 2015, New York, pp. 461–470. ACM (2015)
21. Lin, L., Kasper, M., Güneysu, T., Paar, C., Burleson, W.: Trojan side-channels: lightweight hardware trojans through side-channel engineering. In: Clavier, C., Gaj, K. (eds.) CHES 2009. LNCS, vol. 5747, pp. 382–395. Springer, Heidelberg (2009). doi:10.1007/978-3-642-04138-9_27
22. Microsemi Corporation. SmartFusion2 and IGLOO2 FPGA security and reliability (2015)
23. Jacob, N., Rolfes, C., Zankl, A., Heyszl, J., Sigl, G.: Compromising FPGA SoCs using malicious hardware blocks. In: Design Automation and Test in Europe, DATE 2017, Lausanne, Switzerland, March (2017)
24. Sevinsky, R.: Funderbolt adventures in thunderbolt DMA attacks. BlackHat (2013)
25. Murdoch, S.J.: Introduction to Trusted Execution Environments (TEE). University of Cambridge (2014)
26. Xilinx Inc. The roads must roll: Zynq SoC will be used to build intelligent transport system in Singapore (2015). https://forums.xilinx.com/t5/Xcell-Daily-Blog/The-Roads-Must-Roll-Zynq-SoC-will-be-used-to-build-Intelligent/ba-p/600630
27. Xilinx Inc. Xilinx Github (2016). https://github.com/Xilinx
28. Xilinx Inc. UG 1085: Zynq UltraScale+ MPSoC: Technical reference manual, February (2017)
29. Yang, K., Hicks, M., Dong, Q., Austin, T.M., Sylvester, D.: A2: analog malicious hardware. In: IEEE Symposium on Security and Privacy, SP 2016, San Jose, CA, USA, May 22–26, 2016, pp. 18–37 (2016)

Emerging Attacks II

Illusion and Dazzle: Adversarial Optical Channel Exploits Against Lidars for Automotive Applications

Hocheol Shin, Dohyun Kim, Yujin Kwon, and Yongdae Kim[✉]

Korea Advanced Institute of Science and Technology, Dajeon, Republic of Korea
{h.c.shin,dohyunjk,dbwls8724,yongdaek}@kaist.ac.kr

Abstract. With the advancement in computing, sensing, and vehicle electronics, autonomous vehicles are being realized. For autonomous driving, environment perception sensors such as radars, lidars, and vision sensors play core roles as the eyes of a vehicle; therefore, their reliability cannot be compromised. In this work, we present a spoofing by relaying attack, which can not only induce illusions in the lidar output but can also cause the illusions to appear closer than the location of a spoofing device. In a recent work, the former attack is shown to be effective, but the latter one was never shown. Additionally, we present a novel saturation attack against lidars, which can completely incapacitate a lidar from sensing a certain direction. The effectiveness of both the approaches is experimentally verified against Velodyne's VLP-16.

Keywords: Attack · Autonomous car · Sensor · Lidar · Saturating · Spoofing

1 Introduction

Of late, in the automotive industry, there is a trend shift towards autonomous vehicles. Most of the major automotive manufacturers have researched and/or invested in this technology and even companies outside the vehicular domain are considering autonomous vehicles as profitable future business ventures. In realizing autonomous vehicles, especially environment perception sensors such as radars, object-recognizing cameras, ultrasonic sensors, and lidars are critical; major sensor manufacturers (e.g. Velodyne, IBEO, and Mobileye) are attracting as much attention as the vehicle manufacturers.

Among the various environment perception sensors, the lidar, the target sensor in this work, has its own advantages that cannot be found in the other sensors. Compared to the current automotive radars and cameras, lidars have a considerably higher resolution and precision. Lidars can work both at daytime and nighttime unlike cameras, and can also recognize lanes, license plates, and street signs due to their retro-reflective surfaces [3]. These exclusive strengths render the lidar essential in autonomous driving platforms; they can be found on almost all autonomous vehicles except Tesla [17].

© International Association for Cryptologic Research 2017
W. Fischer and N. Homma (Eds.): CHES 2017, LNCS 10529, pp. 445–467, 2017.
DOI: 10.1007/978-3-319-66787-4_22

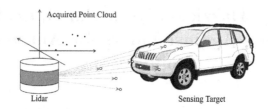

Fig. 1. Simplified illustration of a three-layer lidar operation.

Although they are beneficial, lidars may be vulnerable to intentional external interferences, because they must be exposed to the outside. If the lidar in an autonomous vehicle is deceived by an attacker, it can lead to lethal outcomes, similar to a blind driver or a driver viewing illusions. Despite these risks, security against such threats are not being considered in the design of automotive lidars. In fact, during Black Hat Europe 2015, Petit et al. presented a work on remotely tempering a camera (Mobileye C2-270) and a lidar (IBEO LUX 3), with light [30]. Against the target lidar, they successfully induced multiple fake dots—sensed points that are not from real objects, but generated by the injected signal—in a wall-like shape by relaying and replaying the received lidar pulses with an intentionally added delay; they even induced multiple copies of the wall-like shape by repeating the waveform. However, they were only able to induce fake dots, further than the location of spoofer (this has even been specified as a limitation of their work). This is a critical limitation as an attack because the further the object is, the lesser is its effect on the victim vehicle. Therefore, at the time of spoofing, the most threatening object to the victim vehicle would not be the induced fake dots, but the attacker herself.

In this work, we have addressed such limitations. We demonstrated that it is possible to induce fake dots *closer* than the spoofer location. We also detail the *actual* attack process, which is considerably more complex than that of the previous work, such that the described process and parametric setup would be sufficient for other researchers to reproduce this work. Note that, inducing closer fake dots would not be possible without such detailed understanding of the process. Apart from the aforementioned contributions, we present a novel saturation attack against the lidars. By illuminating the lidar with a strong light of the same wavelength as that the lidar uses, we can actually erase the existing objects in the sensed output of the lidar. This approach was inspired by the work of Park et al., wherein they blinded a drop sensor in a medical infusion pump and rendered it unable to sense the fluid drops [29]. We also discovered that curved reception glass, which a number of off-the-shelve lidars adopt, can pose a severe threat to the lidar due to refraction/reflection. The target lidar we used to show the effectiveness of our attack was Velodyne's VLP-16, which was never analyzed previously. In addition, we discuss practical aspects of the presented attacks along with several detailed scenarios. We also present multiple approaches to mitigate our attacks, and their limitations. Our contributions can be summarized as follows:

- We present the process of inducing fake dots closer than the spoofer location. This was considered to be impossible in the previous work.
- We introduce a saturation attack against the lidars, which can incapacitate a lidar from detecting objects.
- We present the attack process in considerable details for reproducibility.
- We discuss, in-depth, the resolution of problems pertaining to the deployment of attacks in reality, with detailed attack scenarios.

The remainder of this paper is organized as follows. Section 2 provides the required backgrounds for understanding this work. Section 3 presents the attack schemes for both attacks, and Sect. 4 the attack results. Sections 5 and 6 include the discussions and the related works, respectively. Finally, we conclude the study in Sect. 7.

2 Background

2.1 Lidar

Lidar is an *active remote sensing* method, or a sensor using this method to measure the distances to nearby objects. Here, *active sensing* is a way of analyzing the target of interest by exposing it to the energy (or signal) intentionally transmitted by the sensor itself. It is distinguished from the opposite, *passive sensing*, which examines the target of interest only by receiving energy from it. *Remote sensing* is a way of analyzing the target of interest without physical contact; examples include the telescope, radar, and seismometer.

The lidar was devised shortly after the advent of the laser, as a laser ranging device for the lunar laser ranging experiment [2]. Since then, it has been widely applied in fields such as meteorology [11], agriculture [40], topography [43], and altimetry [23]. Since the adoption of the lidar as one of the sensory systems for the test vehicle in the *DARPA*-funded Autonomous Land Vehicle project [31], its usage has expanded to advanced driver assistance systems [4,8] and autonomous driving platforms [10,14].

Limiting the scope of the environment perception sensors to automotive systems, there are roughly two types of lidars: *scanning* and *solid-state*. Scanning lidars are mainly composed of a/multiple laser transceiver(s) and a moving rotary system for scanning; they acquire an around-view by rotating the laser transceiver. However, the moving parts of scanning lidars contribute to its high cost and are limited in their reliability/durability. In contrast, solid-state lidars do not require moving parts for steering their laser beams. Although affordable solid-state lidars with acceptable performances are the ultimate goal of lidar manufacturers, currently, scanning lidars are dominant in the market due to lack of technical advancements, and solid-state lidars with equivalent performances are generally considered as the next-generation lidars [1,12,33]. Therefore, we confine our interest to scanning lidars only; in most cases, scanning lidars are denoted as lidars, for the rest of this work.

The working of a lidar is similar to that of a pulsed radar, and is quite simple. First, a lidar transmits a laser pulse, while spinning. When the transmitted pulse hits an object, a part of the transmitted energy reflects back to the lidar, as an echo. Note that, there can be multiple echoes, when the object does not fully block the transmitted pulse, possibly resulting in multiple echoes. Then, the echo(es) are received by the lidar, and the elapsed time (Δt) is measured. As light has a known constant speed (c) in air, the lidar can derive the distance (l) to the object using the following equation:

$$l = c\Delta t/2 \tag{1}$$

The lidar can also determine the direction in which the pulse is transmitted, from the rotation angle of its spin. Knowing both the direction and the distance, the lidar can *map* points. The lidar rotates to cover its field of view, resulting in a point cloud, i.e., the set of all the measured points. Multi-layer lidars either have multiple copies of this system with vertical slant angles between them or they also scan vertically. Figure 1 illustrates the operation of a multi-layer lidar.

As the pulses are transmitted periodically, there are ambiguities in determining the elapsed time of the received echoes. Assuming that an echo was received, after the last pulse was transmitted, and that the elapsed time is Δt, the echo can either be that of the last transmitted pulse or of one of the previous pulses'. Denoting the Pulse Repetition Time (PRT) as T, the elapsed time can be any of $\Delta t + nT$. Therefore, to limit uncertainties, lidars and pulsed radars define the *receiving time* (Δt_{max}) and *dead time* (D). Whenever a pulse is transmitted, a lidar waits for its echoes, for the duration of the receiving time, and every echo received in that interval is considered as that of the last transmitted pulse. After the receiving time ends, the lidar ignores all the incoming pulses for the duration of the dead time; then, the next pulse is transmitted. This establishes the relationship, $\Delta t_{max} + D = T$; the *maximum distance* (l_{max}) of a lidar can be derived using Eq. (1) to be $l_{max} = c\Delta t_{max}/2$. Figure 2 illustrates these relationships.

Additionally, for a lidar, a wide receiving angle (size of the receiver aperture) is not required, if it is precisely calibrated. Only the echoes falling into the receiving angle can effectively affect the sensing result. The receiving aperture needs to cover the direction of the pulse transmission only during the maximum round-trip time (Δt_{max}) of the light pulse. Thus, we can derive the minimum required receiving angle (Θ_R [°]) from the rotating speed (ω [°/s]) and the maximum distance of the lidar, as per the following equation:

$$\Theta_R = \Delta t_{max} \cdot \omega = \frac{2l_{max}}{c} \cdot \omega \ [°] \tag{2}$$

Because the rotating speed of a lidar is numerically much smaller than that of light ($\omega \ll c$), and the maximum distance is in the range of several hundred meters, the minimum required receiving angle is very small. For example, this value is only 0.0048° [1] for the Velodyne's VLP-16.

---

[1] $2 \cdot 100/3e8$ [s] $\times 360 \cdot 20$ [°/s]. Note that 20 Hz is the maximum update rate of VLP-16.

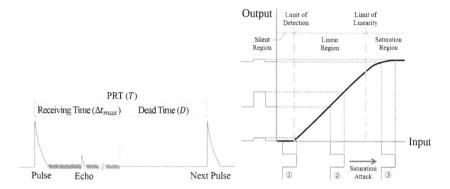

Fig. 2. Relationship between the PRT, receiving time, and dead time.

Fig. 3. Typical transition curve of a sensor and input-output relationships in the three regions of the curve: the *silent* (①), *linear* (②), and *saturation* (③) regions.

2.2   Sensor Attacks

Although it is not long since sensor attacks drew significant attention from the security academia, several researchers have studied various approaches in compromising the sensors and defending them. Given diverse types of attack channels for sensor attacks, Shin et al. [34] classified them into three types: *regular, transmission*, and *side* channel. Regular channel attacks target the sensing structure using the same type of physical quantity sensed by the victim sensor, e.g. sound wave for a microphone. Side channel attacks likewise target the sensing structure as in regular channel attacks, but use a physical quantity other than the one sensed by the target sensor, as in the case where Son et al. [37] affected gyroscope sensing results with acoustic stimuli. Lastly, transmission channel attacks influence the channel connecting the sensing structure and the other parts of the system. For example, Foo Kune et al. intentionally induced electromagnetic interference (EMI) in the wire connecting an analog sensor and an amplifier to overwrite the sensor output [9]. For the rest of this paper, we focus on the regular channel attack, because the following two types of attacks against lidars all belong to that type.

Sensor Saturating

All sensors can be viewed as a form of transducers because they convert one type of inbound physical quantity into another type (mostly electric). Although it is ideal for transducers (particularly for sensors) to have linear transition curve, a certain degree of nonlinearity is inevitable. Figure 3 depicts a typical sensor transition curve, and its input range can be divided into three regions. First, the *silent* region is an input range below the threshold of the sensor. The threshold also can be called the "Limit of Detection", because input signals below the threshold will not be detected. Thus, the output of the sensor will be the same as that for a zero input signal, which is natural because every sensor has a limited sensitivity. Second is the *linear* region, which is the intended operation region or the dynamic range of the sensor. By design, all sensors should be guaranteed to work in this region, because the output is proportional to the input only in this region. As the input increases over the "Limit of Linearity", the *saturation* region starts. In this region, the curve again becomes nonlinear, and the sensor cannot reflect the input changes well.

The principle of saturating is to push the overall level of the input signal (②) into the saturation region (③), in order to render the sensor unable to reflect the variations in the legitimate input signal. As shown in Fig. 3, an attacker can incapacitate a sensor by exposing it to excessive stimuli (② → ③).

Sensor Spoofing

Different from saturating, whose goal is the denial-of-service (DoS), the goal of the sensor spoofing is to deceive the victim sensor. The attacker deceives the victim sensor by exposing it to the attacking signal which simulates the circumstance that the attacker wants the sensor to believe. Simulating a fake circumstance exploits the *semantic gap* between what the circumstance really is and how the sensor perceives it to be. For example, an earthquake and a child shaking a seismometer are totally different, but it can seem similar to the sensor. Therefore, fabricating reality itself, e.g. spoofing a smoke detector by generating a real smoke, is not considered sensor spoofing.

For active sensors, in particular, sensor spoofing can be performed in more specialized forms. As mentioned in Sect. 2.1, active sensors expose the target of examination to their own energy; an active sensor can take a particular waveform (ping waveform) to differentiate its echoes from the other inbound signals. Therefore, the attacker should first acquire the ping waveform, and then *relay* it after an intentionally inserted delay to affect the victim sensor; this is called *sensor spoofing by relaying*. Besides, the received ping waveform can be duplicated during relaying, to amplify the effect.

The advantage of sensor spoofing is that it is not easy for the victim sensor to determine whether it is real or not. In many cases, it is almost impossible to detect the attack without external aids.

3   Attack Methods

3.1   Target System

We assume that the target is a scanning lidar system exposed to the exterior due to its role as an environment perception sensor. Although we focus on lidars for autonomous driving applications because attacking them leads to the most severe outcomes, the following attack schemes can also be applied to lidars for other types of applications, as long as they operate similarly.

For the case of inducing fake dots closer than the spoofer location, we assume one more condition: the ping waveform remains unchanged or at least changes predictably. We confirmed that most of the real-world lidar products for autonomous applications would meet this condition. We could not find any product with a random ping waveform as part of the specification. This can be cross-confirmed by measurements. We analyzed the Velodyne VLP-16 to confirm that it has a consistent ping waveform, and we could also infer that the IBEO LUX 3 had consistent ping waveform by examining the work of Petit et al. [30].

3.2   Attack Model

We list different models for the two types of attacks: saturating and spoofing. This is because the required attacker capabilities are different for each.

Saturating: The attacker can inject an attacking light into the target sensor remotely. The attacking equipment can transmit light, whose wavelength is the same as that used by the target, with sufficient intensity to saturate the target receiver. This includes the ability to aim and focus onto the target sensor.

Spoofing by Relaying: In addition to the ability to inject an attacking light into the target sensor, the attacker can receive a signal from the target. Thus, the attacker has both a receiver and transmitter to receive and inject.

Fig. 4. Lidars with curved reception glasses. Velodyne's VLP-16, HDL-32E, IBEO's LUX Mini, and Quarnergy's M8 (from left).

3.3   Saturating

As described in Sect. 2.2, saturating renders the victim sensor unable to reflect the input signal changes. This line of attack is powerful, because saturation itself is unavoidable. The victim systems can easily detect the attack[2], but cannot prevent the sensor from saturating. As the size of the sensor output curve's linear region is limited, irrespective of its size, its output will start to saturate at a certain input strength. This also applies to lidars, and by exploiting it, attackers can effectively perform DoS attacks. As the medium used for the attack is light, saturating against lidars can also be called *blinding*.

Lidars can be saturated by exposing the target lidar to an intensive light source with the same wavelength as that used by the lidar. We observed numerous induced fake dots with a weak light source, and the complete blinding of a certain direction with a strong light source. The effect of saturating will be described and illustrated in detail, in Sect. 4.2. The following points are characteristics common to the saturation attacks against lidars:

---

[2] However, we could not find any function alerting the occurrence of saturation.

Stealthiness against Drivers and Pedestrians: In order to not hinder human driving and for eye safety, lidars use infrared (IR) lasers for their operation. The invisibility of the medium also assists stealthiness in saturating. Even if the target lidar is saturated by a high-intensity IR light source, human drivers and pedestrians would be unaware, rendering the attack effective.

Receiving Angle: As mentioned in Sect. 2.1, a wide receiving angle is not essential for lidars to sense objects in the field of view. Therefore, lidar receivers typically have much smaller receiving angles compared to the angle of view (360° for the case of VLP-16) of the lidar. This can limit the effect of saturating, because the attacking light comes from a certain direction, when the lidar is rotating. As a result, saturating cannot affect target's field of view universally, but disturbs only a fan-shaped part of it; the angle of disturbance would be proportional to the receiving angle. Referring to Eq. (2), the minimum receiving angle for meeting the specification is sufficient to render saturating impractical. In reality, however, we found that the receiving angles of lidars are much larger than required, rendering them significantly more vulnerable to saturating, even without adopting multiple light sources to widen the angle of disturbance.

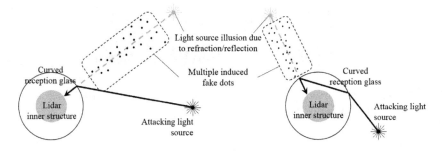

Fig. 5. Speculations of how the oblique incidence of light onto a curved reception glass induces fake dots in a direction different from that of the actual light source.

Curved Reception Glass: Due to the small receiving angles of scanning lidars, it can only affect the sectors in the direction of the attacker. However, we found that an oblique incidence of strong light onto the curved reception glass of VLP-16 can cause the appearance of fake dots in directions other than that of the attacking light source. In addition to VLP-16, there are several lidars with curved reception glasses e.g. the Velodyne HDL-32E, IBEO LUX mini, and Quarnergy M8 (Fig. 4). Although we are not 100% sure because we were only able to conduct a non-destructive analysis, the above-mentioned occurrence is most likely due to refraction or reflection on the curved glass surface. Figure 5 illustrates these speculations. Fake dots in directions other than the direction of the attacker can be a severe threat to the victim, because the detected points have different significances according to their directions on roads. For example, an autonomous vehicle should not be hindered by vehicles on the other lanes, even if they are very close. Now assume the attacker vehicle is located slightly ahead of the

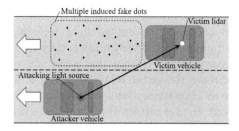

Fig. 6. Attack scenario exploiting a curved reception glass. The attacker and victim vehicles are heading the same direction, and the attacker obliquely illuminates the victim's lidar with a strong light source.

victim's vehicle in the lane next to the victim's; exploiting the above effect, the attacker can generate fake dots in front of the victim, where nothing exists in fact. Figure 6 depicts this attack scenario.

3.4 Spoofing by Relaying

Our approach for spoofing by relaying is basically the same as the principle used in the relaying attack method proposed by Petit et al. [30]. In this work, however, we also provide a method to generate fake dots *closer* than the attacker position. This was listed as one of the limitations of the Petit et al.'s work. We first start with the ideal process to understand how spoofing by relaying works in general, then discuss the actual process.

Ideal Attack Process
Lidars measure distances by measuring the round-trip time of the flight of light. A fired laser pulse flies until it meets an object, and is then reflected back to the lidar. Ideally, the procedure for spoofing by relaying is to mimic this process:

1. Prepare an attack tool composed of a receiver, an adjustable delay component, and a transmitter of the same wavelength as that used by the lidar.
2. Aim at the target lidar with the attack equipment.
3. Receive the target lidar pulse signal using the receiver.
4. Add the required delay using the delay component.
5. Fire a laser pulse back to the target lidar using the transmitter.

Theoretically, this process would induce only one fake dot, and the required delay (d_i) in step 4 to generate a fake dot at a distance (l) can be determined as follows. Let the distance between the spoofer and the victim lidar be l_s; $l_s \leq l$ because we cannot add a negative delay. Therefore, d_i should be the delay, which makes an echo appear $l - l_s$ further than the spoofer, i.e. the round-trip time of light for the distance, $l - l_s$. Using Eq. (1), it is derived as,

$$d_i = \frac{2(l - l_s)}{c} \tag{3}$$

Although the basic procedure is as mentioned above, there are two other points to be considered. One is the limited lidar receiving angle. Even if the attacker fires attacking pulses to the victim lidar, they cannot affect the victim, when the victim's receiver is not facing the attack direction. Therefore, the attacking pulse should reach the victim lidar, while it is still within the receiving angle. The other is the lidar receiving time; as discussed in Sect. 2.1, lidars ignore echoes with delays larger than a certain threshold derived from their range, i.e. the maximum measurable distance. Only echoes that fall within the receiving time can affect the measurement. This applies to the attacker also; therefore, the attacker should fire back to the target lidar within the receiving time. For example, VLP-16 has a range of 100 m, which results in a receiving time of $(2 \times 100 \, \text{m})/(3 \times 10^8 \, \text{m/s}) = 667 \, \text{ns}$. Therefore, in order to affect the measurement of the VLP-16, an attacker should fire back at least within 667 ns.

Actual Attack Process
Although theoretically, the attack process is as discussed above, the actual process is quite different. First, the laser pulse from the lidar diverges. Accordingly, the attacker receiver obtains multiple adjacent laser pulses; however, only a part of these pulses exactly head in the direction of the receiver. This enables the attacker to detect the target's laser pulse a few PRTs (T) in advance, compared to the case where the laser pulses do not diverge at all. Next, irrespective of how close the receiver and transmitter are placed in the attack tool, they are apart by a certain distance. Let us assume that they are arranged horizontally; as the horizontal resolution of scanning lidars are typically high, the laser pulse heading to the receiver and the pulse to the transmitter is not temporally the same. Consequently, there is a time difference (S) between the detection of a

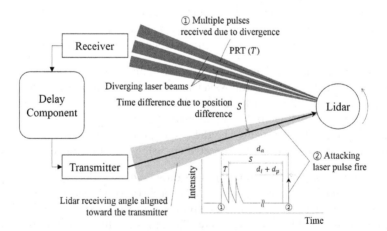

Fig. 7. Actual attack process: As the lidar rotates, multiple laser pulses, temporally separated by the PRT (T), are first captured by the attacker receiver (①). Then, after the actual required delay (d_a), the attacking laser pulse is fired (②). The graph below displays the temporal arrangement of events.

laser pulse by the receiver and the firing of a pulse toward the transmitter. Note that the round-trip time of light would have almost no effect, because the speed of light is much faster than the rotating speed of the lidar.

Owing to the above-mentioned phenomena, the required delay to induce a fake dot at a certain distance differs from Eq. (3) due to the time differences, T and S. Assuming that the receiver is illuminated by the lidar, before the transmitter and denoting the signal processing/propagation delay as d_p,

$$d_a = d_i + nT + S + d_p \tag{4}$$

The time differences (T and S) are compensated by adding them to the ideal delay, because the delay component is triggered by the first received pulse. The delay d_p can be compensated likewise, because it is a constant delay which can be measured in advance. Note that, n multiplied by T is for the case, where the delay component is triggered multiple PRTs in advance. In addition, although $n, S \to 0$ as the distance between the lidar and the spoofer increases, attackers can enlarge n and S by increasing the receiver aperture size and the receiver-transmitter separation, respectively. Figure 7 illustrates this process. This can be used for making a virtually *negative-valued delay* to generate fake dots closer than the attacker location. Assuming that $l < l_s$ in Eq. (3), d_i becomes negative. However, d_a will remain positive, because $T, S \gg |d_i|$.

A Notable Characteristics of Spoofing by Relaying Attack

– Stealthiness against Drivers and Pedestrians: As in saturating, spoofing attempts are invisible to human eyes.
– Inducing Multiple Fake Dots: If the lidar rotates at a constant speed, an attacker can generate multiple fake dots with one attack tool. This can be done by periodically firing back the attacking pulses, immediately after the first attacking pulse, with the same period as the PRT. The PRT of the target lidar can be approximately derived from the specification, and then, minutely adjusted by measurements. Let us denote the angular horizontal resolution of the target lidar, whose rotating speed is constant, as r_H [°], and the update rate as f [Hz]. Then, the theoretical interval between consecutive pulses can be derived as follows:

$$1 \left/ \left(\frac{360}{r_H} \times f \right) \right. = \frac{r_H}{360f} \text{ [s]} \tag{5}$$

Note that this is irrespective of the distance between the lidar and the attacker.
– Receiving Angle: Similar to saturating, a small receiving angle limits the maximum number of fake dots inducible by a fixed spoofer. Therefore, to increase the number of fake dots the attacker should utilize multiple transmitters.
– Curved Reception Glass: Although we did not experimentally confirm if spoofing attack using refraction/reflection on the curved glass is possible because we could not obtain a pulse laser source that was sufficiently strong, we expect

the oblique incidence of a strong laser pulse to readily induce fake dots in sectors, other than the direction of the attacker. If this is possible, it will expose the victim vehicle to threats far more dangerous than that of saturating.

4   Experiments

In this section, we present equipment used and experimental setups for them. In addition, experimental results are provided with figures. Note that further details for the experiments, including videos and raw lidar packet capture for the attack, can be found in the appendices.

Table 1. VLP-16 specification

# of Vert. Layers	16	Light Wavelength	903nm
Update rate	5/10/20 Hz	Angular resolution	0.1/0.2/0.4° (hor.) 2° (ver.)
Range	100 m	Field of view	-15° ~ 15° (ver.) 360° (hor.)

4.1   Experimental Setup

Target Lidar: We selected Velodyne's VLP-16 [42] for verifying our attack methods. It is the lightest and the latest in the product lineup, and targeted for various mobile usages such as autonomous vehicles, UAVs, and robotics. Its specification related to this paper, is summarized in Table 1. Note that, the VLP-16 has an adjustable update rate and horizontal resolution, and they are in a trade-off relationship. For our case, they were set to lower values: 5 Hz and 0.1°, respectively[3]. To check the effect of the attacks we required a visualizer for the sensing result. We used Velodyne's official visualization software, VeloView [27], which visualizes the sensing result in real time by parsing the UDP packet stream from VLP-16, and supports recording into pcap files and replaying them.

Attack Tool for Saturating: For saturating, only a light source is required. We used a 30 mW, 905 nm laser module (≈ USD 40) as the weak light source, and a power-adjustable 800 mW, 905 nm laser module (≈ USD 350) as the strong one. Product names and pictures can be found in the appendices.

Attack Tool for Spoofing: The attack tool is as depicted in Fig. 7. We used an OSRAM SFH 213 FA (≈ USD 1) photodiode (PD) with additional comparator circuitry for the receiver[4], and an OSRAM SPL PL90 (≈ USD 16) pulsed laser diode (PLD) with a PCO-7110-40-4 (≈ USD 300) PLD driver from Directed Energy Inc. Note that, both of the PD and the PLD are not standalone; the PLD driver is required to generate the high-current pulses, essential for firing the laser pulses. For the delay component, we used an Agilent 33250 A function generator with external-trigger mode in the burst n-cycle pulse output setup.

---

[3] Raw packet captures for 10 Hz & 0.2° can also be found in the appendices.

[4] Its detailed circuit diagram is given in the appendices.

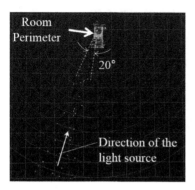

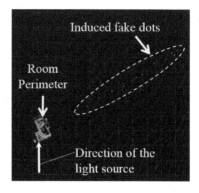

Fig. 8. VeloView output during exposure to a weak light source. Fake dots are observable only in the direction of the light source. The maximum angle between the dots was measured to be 20°.

Fig. 9. VeloView output during oblique exposure to a strong light source. Fake dots are observable in a direction other than the light source.

4.2 Saturating

For saturating, we illuminated the VLP-16 with the aforementioned light sources. As mentioned in Sect. 3.3, invisible light is one of the strengths of this attack. Thus, we used an IR viewer [32] to aim the light.

Weak Light Source: When the lidar was illuminated by a weak light source, we could observe numerous randomly-located fake dots, as depicted in Fig. 8. Because the experiment was conducted in a basement, every dot outside the room perimeter is apparently fake. As discussed in Sect. 3.3, induced fake dots were observed only in the direction of the light source. We suppose that the overall increase in the noise floor due to the injected light is the cause of the induced fake dots. The VLP-16 seems to have an absolute threshold for detecting echoes, and the raised noise floor might almost reach this threshold, causing the noise fluctuations lead to numerous fake dots.

Strong Light Source (Direct): We switched the light source to a strong one, and directly illuminated the lidar. We discovered that the lidar became completely blind in a sector, in the field of view (Fig. 10). We could also observe multiple fake dots as in the case of the weak light source and a severe degradation in the received signal strength in the direction of illumination.

Strong Light Source (Oblique): We obliquely illuminated the lidar, and observed fake dots in a direction other than that of the light source, as in Fig. 9. We also experimentally confirmed that curved glasses can change the incoming direction of the obliquely incident light. Details can be found in the appendices.

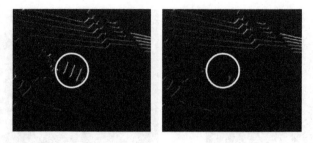

Fig. 10. VeloView output before (left) and after (right) exposure to a strong light source. We placed a metal plate $(41 \times 42\,\text{cm}^2)$ in front of the lidar.

4.3   Spoofing by Relaying

We performed spoofing by relaying using the attack tool described in Sect. 4.1. We first aimed the attack tool on the lidar to receive its pulses. When the incoming pulses are captured by the PD, the comparator converts them into a series of 5 V pulses. Then, these pulses are fed to the function generator, which is triggered by the first received pulse. The function generator waits for a predefined delay, and transmits a predefined number of copies of the output pulse to the PLD driver. Finally, the PLD driver lets the PLD fire laser pulses as signaled.

To induce multiple fake dots (Sect. 3.4), the intervals between the output pulses have to be matched to the PRT of the target lidar. Although the PRT can be derived using Eq. (5), the real value subtly varies. We analyzed the target lidar signal and found that the best approximation was 55.296 μs, whereas the theoretical value was 55.556 μs. We observed that the measured PRT remained the same over time and over various distances between the spoofer and the lidar. After determining the actual PRT, we encountered a problem in applying it as the output pulse interval. The smallest supported PRT of the PLD, OSRAM SPL PL90, was only 100 μs; therefore, to circumvent this problem, we set the output pulse interval as double of the actual PRT, $110.592 = 2 \cdot 55.296\,\mu s$. Then, we measured the delay d_a; it was determined by setting the *cycle*—a function generator parameter to determine how many times the output pulses will be repeated after the inserted delay per a trigger—value to one, and gradually increasing the delay parameter of the function generator until a fake dot appeared. When the distance between the spoofer and lidar was approximately 5m, the delay was measured to be 663.3 μs. We could also conclude that the ping waveform of the VLP-16 was only a single laser pulse; else, we could not have observed any fake dot. Once we observed a fake dot by a single pulse, we gradually increased the cycle value. However, no matter how large the cycle was, no more than ten fake dots were observable. This may be because the receiving angle of the VLP-16 for the PLD used is approximately 2.0° [5], which corresponds to ten fake dots[6].

---

[5] This is considerably smaller than the case in Fig. 8. The differences in the light source strength and beam diameter may be the cause.

[6] As we fired attacking pulses for every two target lidar pulses, $10 \cdot 2 \cdot 0.1° = 2.0°$. Note that 0.1° was the horizontal resolution of VLP-16 then.

Figure 11 shows the induced fake dots. Note that this scheme works outdoor under sunlight. Refer to the appendices for the details.

In Sect. 3.4, we present a method by which an attacker could induce fake dots closer than the spoofer. To confirm this, we gradually reduced the value of d_a until the induced fake dots were located between the spoofer and the lidar. Figure 12 displays the induced fake dots located between the spoofer and the lidar. The lidar-to-spoofer distance and the delay were 12 m and 1.959 μs, respectively.

We note that the exact value of d_a is not essential for inducing fake dots. In reality, a sufficiently large cycle would suffice. We observed multiple fake dots, when the cycle was set as 30, even with the delay parameter of the function generator set as zero. This is because whenever the cycle is increased by one, it is equivalent to adding a delay of 2·PRT. With the zero delay of the function generator, no delay other than d_p will be added. Therefore, the total delay for the m-th pulse will be just $2mT + d_p$ from Eq. (4). At a certain value among m's (denote it m'), the relation, $2m'T + d_p \approx d_a = nT + S + d_p$, satisfies, which is equivalent to inducing a fake dot with $d_i = 0$ in Eq. (4). From that on, the pulses will start inducing fake dots.

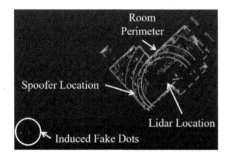

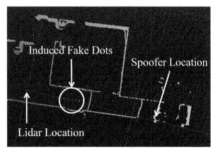

Fig. 11. VeloView output of the multiple induced fake dots.

Fig. 12. VeloView output of the fake dots closer than the spoofer. Note that the redder a dot, the closer it is to the lidar.

5   Discussion

5.1   Practical Consideration for Attack Deployment

Aiming Problem: Aiming is one of the main obstacles in deploying attacks in practice. When the target vehicle moves, the attacker has to track the target lidar with the attack tool. However, advanced attackers may circumvent this difficulty by adopting the following approaches: Lidars are typically located at a fixed position on the vehicle, i.e. on the center of the roof or on the corners. Further, there are many cases on the road, when vehicles run straight with a constant speed. Therefore, an attacker may mount the attack tool on a vehicle with an accurate motorized mount, and deliberately follow/precede the target vehicle such that the relative speed becomes zero. This can render the situation almost similar to a stationary case. Next, attackers may adopt an optical system such as a *beam expander* [24] to widen the attacking beam width or spread the beam with an appropriate optical system such as concave lenses for a flashlight-like effect. Note that in this case, the decrease in light intensity due to expansion does not affect the effectiveness of the attack, because lidars are designed to mainly sense reflected lights, considerably weaker than direct illumination. Even if a weak light intensity matters, attackers can utilize stronger light sources. Attackers can also install a *trap* on the road. With the attacking transceiver installed and calibrated in advance, the attacker can render the problem similar to a stationary case, because the speed of the victim vehicle is considerably slower than the rotating speed of the lidar and the speed of light.

Parameter Setting: Unlike in laboratory, attackers do not have access to the target sensor output, in reality. Therefore, the attacker cannot determine the best parameters for the attack tool. However, this would not be a serious issue because of the following reasons: First, most vehicles are mass produced, and are identical in terms of their sensors. Therefore, the attacker can obtain multiple types of vehicles, and analyze them to acquire the essential information for deploying the attacks, e.g. the PRT(s) and lidar position(s). Further, a precisely calibrated attack tool will work, regardless of the circumstances, and this calibration can be done in advance. Because real echoes and intentionally generated attack pulses are indistinguishable, spoofing by relaying will work as long as the transmitter and receiver are suitably aligned in the same direction. With such a calibrated attack tool aimed at the victim lidar, the only variable is the distance between the attacker and the target vehicle, which the attacker can measure by adopting additional sensors.

5.2   Potential Countermeasures

Redundancy and Fusion: If a vehicle is equipped with multiple lidars having an overlapping field of view, the effect of saturating and spoofing can be mitigated to a certain extent. However, this directly increases the cost, and is not a definitive solution because attackers can blind multiple lidars simultaneously. Besides, it is also not easy to detect spoofing, when fake dots are induced in non-overlapped zones. Likewise, the fusion of multiple types of sensors cannot be an ultimate solution either. Radars [44], cameras [30,44], and ultrasonic sensors [44] have all been revealed to be vulnerable to either blinding/jamming or spoofing.

Saturation Detection: As discussed in Sect. 3.3, attempts to intentionally saturate a lidar can be easily detected, and the victim vehicle can adopt fail-safe mode. For example, it can abandon sensor outputs from the direction of the attack and move to the roadside, while slowing down. However, the victim will be unable to drive because saturation itself is inevitable. Further, on crowded roads, the fail-safe maneuver might rather endanger the victim vehicle.

Reducing the Receiving Angle: According to the calculation and measurement in Sects. 2.1 and 4.3 respectively, the receiving angle of VLP-16 (2.0°) is considerably larger than the minimum required size (0.0048°) for meeting the specifications. Therefore, reducing the receiving angle can mitigate the effect of saturating and spoofing. Both the angle of the region blinded by saturation and the maximum number of inducible fake points by spoofing can be reduced. However, reducing the receiving angle is not easy, because it is in a trade-off relationship with the lidar sensitivity [25]. Further, it would be difficult to reduce the receiving angle to the minimum required value due to the design margins.

Random-Direction Pinging: Transmitting pulses in random directions can mitigate the effect of spoofing, because it is no longer possible to induce multiple fake dots by a single spoofer. However, it is practically difficult to apply this approach to current lidars with rotating scanners. Randomly rotating the scanners will severely degrade the reliability and durability of the lidar. Even current lidars have reliability issues due to their moving parts [1]. Further, the update rate, a key performance figure, will be reduced.

To avoid the problem of random rotation, lidars may maintain the current scan-by-spinning but transmit pulses at random instants. However, this will directly lead to update rate decreases. Lidars using this approach should spin faster to reach the required update rate, which may again lead to reliability issues. Currently, in our opinion, the best cost/performance effective mitigation against the induction of multiple (closer) fake dots is to electrically perturb PRTs while keeping the rotating speed constant. Such slightly perturbed PRTs will not severely degrade the performance/reliability, but will effectively prevent the attacker from predicting pulse-firing instants blocking aforementioned two types of threats.

Randomizing the Ping Waveform: Transmitting pulses with randomized waveforms and rejecting pulses different from the transmitted one can fundamentally prevent spoofing from inducing fake dots closer than the spoofer. Further, this also can help mitigate inter-lidar interference. Approaches of this type have been intensively studied for military radars [26]. However, this cannot prevent all spoofing attempts, because attackers can still induce fake dots further than the spoofer location.

Mitigating Curved Glass Effects: The best approach for removing unwanted effect of the curved reception glasses is to get rid of them. Indeed, several lidars (e.g. IBEO LUX 2010 and Velodyne HDL-64E) do not have them. Even if curved glasses are essential for the operation, designers may mitigate their adverse effect by carefully selecting glass materials or designing glass curvature so that obliquely incident attacking light cannot reach central receiving structures.

5.3   Other Points

Fatality of Induced Fake Dots: Unlike the case of the IBEO LUX 3 [30], where it was possible to generate many fake dots spanning 30° approximately, only up to ten fake dots were induced in the VLP-16. As previously noted, the ten fake dots correspond to an object 2.0° wide. This may not appear important initially, but its significance cannot be underestimated; for example, the size of an object spanning 2.0°, 55 m away from the lidar would be 1.9 m wide, which is almost as wide as most vehicles. As per the data from UK Department for Transport [39], 55 m is the *braking distance* for a car driving at 60mph. Because the braking distance is the distance required solely for braking, even autonomous vehicles have no room for checking the authenticity of the observed dots, but need to immediately activate emergency braking or evasive maneuvers. Such sudden actions are sufficient to endanger the surrounding vehicles.

Increasing the Number of Induced Fake Dots: As revealed in the experiment, the number of fake dots by one attack tool is limited due to the size of the receiving angle. However, by adopting multiple attack tools, they can be increased. Further, attackers can also induce a larger shape to the victim lidar by orchestrating multiple attack tools.

Comparison with the Previous Work: Although we have improved upon the previous work in many aspects, there are a certain issues that have not been dealt with or were inferior in the outcome. However, we emphasize that the target lidar was different; as noted before, the IBEO LUX 3 was used in the previous work, whereas the Velodyne VLP-16 was used in our case. We did not deal with the induction of multiple dots in a single direction. VLP-16 has three modes of operation: *last*, *strongest*, and *dual*. Among the three, only the dual mode allows up to two dots per direction; the other two modes permit only one dot. Therefore, for the last and strongest modes, inducing multiple dots in a single direction was fundamentally impossible. For the dual mode, to induce two dots in one angle, two attack pulses should not deviate more than 667ns. However, as discussed in Sect. 4.3, this small deviation was not possible under our single-PLD setup due to the smallest supported PRT of the PLD used. As Petit et al. used the same single PLD, the operation scheme of IBEO LUX 3 seems to differ from that of VLP-16. Further, we did not deal with the tracking/recognition of the induced fake dots. This was because Velodyne does not provide such a functionality for any of its products, whereas IBEO does, and there were no suitable alternatives. Finally, as previously mentioned, the difference in the spanning angle of the induced fake dots seems solely because of the difference between the receiving angles of the two lidars. If the receiving angle of LUX 3 had not been that large, it would not have been possible to observe such a wide span of the induced dots because the transmitter was also fixed in the previous work.

6   Related Work

Automotive Security: With the abrupt increase in the proportion of electronics in modern vehicles, vehicles are no longer safe zones against hacking threats. Since Koscher et al. first demonstrated the feasibility of vehicle hacking [16], numerous researchers have discovered vulnerabilities in vehicular networks and control units [18], demonstrated the feasibility of remote hacking [5,19], and even the hacking of real vehicles [20]. To cope with these new threats, various approaches have been proposed as defensive measures [6,7,13,18,22,41]. However, most works in this field focus on compromising and defending the structurally vulnerable control area network buses. In comparison, researches on vehicular sensor security are rare, despite its criticality for (semi-)autonomous vehicles. We have already discussed the contributions and limitations of Petit et al. [30] in Sect. 1; this work was the first in revealing that the vehicular sensors for autonomous driving can be easily tempered by external stimuli. Another notable work is that of Yan et al., who performed a comprehensive security analysis on environment perception sensors mounted on a real vehicle, the Tesla Model S [44]. They succeeded in jamming and spoofing the ultrasonic sensors, and only in jamming the mm-wave radar. They also demonstrated, like Petit et al., that cameras are extremely vulnerable to exposure to a strong light source. However, the lidar was not dealt with, because the Model S does not have one. Finally, Shoukry et al. spoofed an anti-lock braking (ABS) sensor, another vehicular sensor that is a type of magnetic encoder [35]. They installed an attacking actuator next to the target sensor, and canceled the legitimate magnetic field from the sensor by emitting its reverse waveform. Then, they added the spoofing waveform, and it was injected without any disturbance. By simulation, they showed that by this attack, the ABS system would be unable to brake properly.

Sensor Attacks: Park et al. caused a medical infusion pump to over/under infuse fluids by injecting an IR laser to its drop sensor [29]. They illuminated the receiver of the drop sensor to render it unable to sense any fluid drops, which in turn led to over-infusion. To the best of our knowledge, this was the first attempt at inducing a critical high-level malfunction by saturating. With a *side* channel attack, Son et al. incapacitated a flying drone by inducing massive fluctuations in the gyroscope outputs with acoustic stimuli [37]. Trippel et al. further developed this idea over a DoS attack; they succeeded in controlling an RC car driven by a smartphone's accelerometer output, only with the injection of acoustic stimuli to the MEMS-based accelerometer [38]. Finally, as an example of *transmission* channel attack, Foo Kune et al. injected fake sensor outputs by inducing EMI to the wire connecting an analog sensor and an amplifier [9]. They demonstrated that this can be exploited to induce malfunctions in implantable medical devices such as pacemakers and cardiac defibrillators.

Defenses against Sensor Attacks: To counter the aforementioned threats to sensors, several approaches have been proposed. Shoukry et al. proposed an active sensor spoofing defense scheme called PyCRA [36]. This is a spoofing detection scheme that detects spoofing attempts by turning off the active sensor transmitter at random instants such that the attacker cannot react to the sudden changes. When the sensor is attacked, the spoofing signal can be detected because no incoming signal is expected. However, the PyCRA cannot be applied to lidars or radars because it assumes the channel between the transmitter and receiver to be fixed, whereas lidars and radars have continuously changing channels because targets can be located anywhere. Further, Shin et al. pointed out that the PyCRA has a critical problem to be applied to analog-digital systems [34], because it can either lead to an arms race between the attacker and the defender or requires too many resources to be secure. For redundancy and fusion, most works in this field focus on sensor reliability/precision enhancements rather than on the security; relatively fewer works focus on security [15, 21, 28]. However, redundancy and fusion have limitations, as discussed in Sect. 5.2.

7   Conclusion

Lidars are undoubtedly one of the core sensors in autonomous vehicles. Being the eyes of safety-critical systems, such as cars, their reliability is critical and cannot be compromised, because it can endanger human lives. In this work, we have presented and experimentally verified two types of attacks that can severely degrade the reliability of lidars. Although we have listed many mitigative approaches in the discussion, they are either technically/economically infeasible or are not definitive solutions to the presented attacks. We do not advocate the complete abandonment of the transition toward autonomous driving, because we believe that its advantages can outweigh the disadvantages, if realistic adversarial scenarios are appropriately mitigated. However, such considerations are currently absent; therefore, automakers and device manufacturers need to start considering these future threats before too late.

Acknowledgment. This work was supported by the Advanced Technology R&D Center of Hyundai AutoEver.

References

1. Ackerman, E.: Velodyne Says It's Got a "Breakthrough" in Solid State Lidar Design. http://spectrum.ieee.org/cars-that-think/transportation/sensors/velodyne-announces-breakthrough-in-solid-state-lidar-design. Accessed 24 Feb 2017
2. Alley, C.O., Bender, P.L., Dicke, R.H., Faller, J.E., Franken, P.A., Plotkin, H.H., Wilkinson, D.T.: Optical radar using a corner reflector on the Moon. J. Geophys. Res. **70**(9), 2267–2269 (1965). http://dx.doi.org/10.1029/JZ070i009p02267
3. Beasley, E.: LiDAR and Autonomous Technology. http://velodynelidar.com/blog/lidar-autonomous-technology/. Accessed 9 Mar 2017
4. Bhatia, P.: Vehicle Technologies to Improve Performance and Safety. Technical report, University of California Transportation Center (2003). https://escholarship.org/uc/item/4zw4m05k
5. Checkoway, S., McCoy, D., Kantor, B., Anderson, D., Shacham, H., Savage, S., Koscher, K., Czeskis, A., Roesner, F., Kohno, T., et al.: Comprehensive experimental analyses of automotive attack surfaces. In: Proceedings of 20th USENIX Security Symposium. USENIX Association (2011)
6. Cho, K.T., Shin, K.G.: Fingerprinting electronic control units for vehicle intrusion detection. In: Proceedings of 25th USENIX Security Symposium, pp. 911–927. USENIX Association (2016)

7. Dagan, T., Wool, A.: Parrot, a software-only anti-spoofing defense system for the can bus. In: ESCAR EUROPE (2016)
8. Distner, M., Bengtsson, M., Broberg, T., Jakobsson, L.: City safety a system addressing rear-end collisions at low speeds. In: Proceedings of the 21st International Technical Conference on the Enhanced Safety of Vehicles (2009)
9. Kune, D.F., Backes, J., Clark, S., Kramer, D., Reynolds, M., Fu, K., Kim, Y., Xu, W.: Ghost talk: Mitigating EMI signal injection attacks against analog sensors. In: IEEE Symposium on Security and Privacy. IEEE (2013)
10. Ford Mediacenter: Ford First Automaker to Test Autonomous Vehicle at Mcity, University of Michigans Simulated Urban Environment. https://media. ford.com/content/fordmedia/fna/us/en/news/2015/11/13/ford-first-automaker-to-test-autonomous-vehicle-at-mcity.html. Accessed 23Feb 2017
11. Goyer, G., Watson, R.: The laser and its application to meteorology. Bull. Am. Meteorol. Soc. **44**(9), 564–575 (1963)
12. Higgins, S.: Solid-State LiDAR: A New Era of 3D Scanning. http://www. spar3d.com/blogs/the-other-dimension/vol13no50-solid-state-lidar-a-new-era-of-3d-scanning/. Accessed 24 Feb 2017
13. Hoppe, T., Kiltz, S., Dittmann, J.: Security threats to automotive CAN networks – Practical examples and selected short-term countermeasures. In: Harrison, M.D., Sujan, M.-A. (eds.) SAFECOMP 2008. LNCS, vol. 5219, pp. 235–248. Springer, Heidelberg (2008). doi:10.1007/978-3-540-87698-4_21
14. Huynh, T.: Google self-driving car: everything you need to know. http://www. techradar.com/news/car-tech/google-self-driving-car-everything-you-need-to-know-1321548. Accessed 23 Feb 2017
15. Ivanov, R., Pajic, M., Lee, I.: Attack-resilient sensor fusion for safety-critical cyber-physical systems. ACM Trans. Embed. Comput. Syst. **15**(1), 21 (2016)
16. Koscher, K., Czeskis, A., Roesner, F., Patel, S., Kohno, T., Checkoway, S., McCoy, D., Kantor, B., Anderson, D., Shacham, H., et al.: Experimental security analysis of a modern automobile. In: IEEE Symposium on Security and Privacy, pp. 447–462. IEEE (2010)
17. Lambert, F.: Tesla still has no plans to use LiDAR in consumer vehicles, but does use the tech for 'ground truthing'. https://electrek.co/2016/11/02/tesla-no-plan-for-lidar-self-driving-cars/. Accessed 9 Mar 2017
18. Miller, C., Valasek, C.: Adventures in automotive networks and control units. In: DEF CON 21 (2013)
19. Miller, C., Valasek, C.: A survey of remote automotive attack surfaces. In: Black Hat USA (2014)
20. Miller, C., Valasek, C.: Remote exploitation of an unaltered passenger vehicle. In: Black Hat USA (2015)
21. Montgomery, P.Y., Humphreys, T.E., Ledvina, B.M.: Receiver-autonomous spoofing detection: experimental results of a multi-antenna receiver defense against a portable civil GPS spoofer. In: Proceedings of the ION International Technical Meeting (2009)
22. Müter, M., Asaj, N.: Entropy-based anomaly detection for in-vehicle networks. In: IEEE Intelligent Vehicles Symposium, pp. 1110–1115. IEEE (2011)
23. NASA: Planetary Laser Altimetry. https://tharsis.gsfc.nasa.gov/index.php. Accessed 23 Feb 2017
24. Newport Corp: Optics: How to Build a Beam Expander. http://assets.newport. com/webdocuments-en/images/how_to_build_a_beam_expander_5.pdf
25. Osta, P.V.: The Basics of Microscopy. http://www.vanosta.be/microscopy.htm

26. Pace, P.E.: Detecting and Classifying Low Probability of Intercept Radar. Artech House, Boston (2009)
27. ParaView: VeloView (2017). http://www.paraview.org/VeloView/. Accessed 05 Mar 2017
28. Park, J., Ivanov, R., Weimer, J., Pajic, M., Lee, I.: Sensor attack detection in the presence of transient faults. In: Proceedings of the ACM/IEEE Sixth International Conference on Cyber-Physical Systems (2015)
29. Park, Y., Son, Y., Shin, H., Kim, D., Kim, Y.: This ain't your dose: Sensor spoofing attack on medical infusion pump. In: 10th USENIX Workshop on Offensive Technologies. USENIX Association (2016)
30. Petit, J., Stottelaar, B., Feiri, M., Kargl, F.: Remote attacks on automated vehicles sensors: experiments on camera and LiDAR. In: Black Hat Europe (2015)
31. Pomerleau, D.A.: ALVINN, an autonomous land vehicle in a neural network. Carnegie Mellon University, Computer Science Department, Technical report (1989)
32. Public Lab: Near-Infrared Camera (2017). https://publiclab.org/wiki/near-infrared-camera. Accessed 06 Mar 2017
33. Quanergy Systems Inc.: Quanergy S3 Solid State LiDAR, the World's First Affordable Solid State LiDAR Sensor, to Begin Full Scale Manufacturing in 2017. http://www.businesswire.com/news/home/20170103005387/en/Quanergy-S3-Solid-State-LiDAR-Worlds-Affordable. Accessed 24 Feb 2017
34. Shin, H., Son, Y., Park, Y., Kwon, Y., Kim, Y.: Sampling race: Bypassing timing-based analog active sensor spoofing detection on analog-digital systems. In: 10th USENIX Workshop on Offensive Technologies. USENIX Association (2016)
35. Shoukry, Y., Martin, P., Tabuada, P., Srivastava, M.: Non-invasive spoofing attacks for anti-lock braking systems. In: Bertoni, G., Coron, J.-S. (eds.) CHES 2013. LNCS, vol. 8086, pp. 55–72. Springer, Heidelberg (2013). doi:10.1007/978-3-642-40349-1_4
36. Shoukry, Y., Martin, P., Yona, Y., Diggavi, S., Srivastava, M.: PyCRA: Physical challenge-response authentication for active sensors under spoofing attacks. In: Proceedings of the 22nd ACM SIGSAC Conference on Computer and Communications Security, pp. 1004–1015. ACM (2015)
37. Son, Y., Shin, H., Kim, D., Park, Y., Noh, J., Choi, K., Choi, J., Kim, Y.: Rocking drones with intentional sound noise on gyroscopic sensors. In: Proceedings of 24th USENIX Security Symposium, pp. 881–896. USENIX Association (2015)
38. Trippel, T., Weisse, O., Xu, W., Honeyman, P., Fu, K.: WALNUT: Waging doubt on the integrity of MEMS accelerometers with acoustic injection attacks. In: IEEE European Symposium on Security and Privacy. IEEE (2017)
39. UK Department for Transport: The Highway Code - General rules, techniques and advice for all drivers and riders (103 to 158) - Rule 126. https://www.gov.uk/guidance/the-highway-code/general-rules-techniques-and-advice-for-all-drivers-and-riders-103-to-158#rule126
40. USDA: ARS study helps farmers make best use of fertilizers. https://www.ars.usda.gov/news-events/news/research-news/2010/ars-study-helps-farmers-make-best-use-of-fertilizers/. Accessed 23 Feb 2017
41. Van Herrewege, A., Singelee, D., Verbauwhede, I.: CANAuth - A simple, backward compatible broadcast authentication protocol for CAN bus. In: ECRYPT Workshop on Lightweight Cryptography (2011)
42. Velodyne: Velodyne LiDAR Puck (2017). http://velodynelidar.com/docs/datasheet/63-9229_Rev-C_VLP16_Datasheet_Web.pdf. Accessed 05 Mar 2017

43. Vosselman, G., Maas, H.G.: Airborne and Terrestrial Laser Scanning. Whittles Publishing, Dunbeath (2010)
44. Yan, C., Xu, W., Liu, J.: Can you trust autonomous vehicles: contactless attacks against sensors of self-driving vehicle. In: DEF CON 24 (2016)

Appendices

Due to space limitation, appendices are posted to the website below:
https://sites.google.com/view/ches17illusionanddazzle.

Hacking in the Blind: (Almost) Invisible Runtime User Interface Attacks

Luka Malisa$^{(\boxtimes)}$, Kari Kostiainen, Thomas Knell, David Sommer, and Srdjan Capkun

Department of Computer Science, ETH Zürich, Switzerland
{luka.malisa,kari.kostiainen,david.sommer,srdjan.capkun}@inf.ethz.ch,
knellt@student.ethz.ch

Abstract. We describe novel, adaptive user interface attacks, where the adversary attaches a small device to the interface that connects user input peripherals to the target system. The device executes the attack when the authorized user is performing safety-, or security-critical operations, by modifying or blocking user input, or injecting new events. Although the adversary fully controls the user input channel, to succeed he needs to overcome a number of challenges, including the inability to directly observe the state of the user interface and avoiding being detected by the legitimate user. We present new techniques that allow the adversary to do user interface state estimation and fingerprinting, and thus attack a new range of scenarios that previous UI attacks do not apply to. We evaluate our attacks on two different types of platforms: e-banking on general-purpose PCs, and dedicated medical terminals. Our evaluation shows that such attacks can be implemented efficiently, are hard for the users to detect, and would lead to serious violations of input integrity.

1 Introduction

Modern malware can reside in various places — on the device itself, but also on connected peripherals (e.g., BIOS or hard drive). One type of such malware resides in user interface devices, such as a keyboard or a mouse [19]. The goal of such malicious peripherals is to inject pre-programmed sequences of user input that, e.g., install some form of malware to the device itself. However, installing malware or introducing system misconfigurations, such as adding an administrative account, can be prevented by security hardening (e.g., Windows Embedded Lockdown features [16]), or by existing malware-detection approaches.

A significantly stealthier alternative is to attack systems *only* through their user interfaces (UIs). Such attacks exploit a fundamental property of any device designed to operate under user control; irrespective of applied security hardening techniques, the device *must continue* to accept user input.

As user input cannot be simply blocked, various UI attacks have been proposed. Current state-of-the-art are BadUSB-style attacks [19], where the goal of

© International Association for Cryptologic Research 2017
W. Fischer and N. Homma (Eds.): CHES 2017, LNCS 10529, pp. 468–489, 2017.
DOI: 10.1007/978-3-319-66787-4_23

the malicious peripheral is to inject simple, *pre-programmed* sequences of keyboard and mouse input [11], commonly while the user is not active. However, due to the lack of system state awareness, such approaches are restricted to executing only simple attacks (e.g., add new account, install malware). For example, the BadUSB malware does not know in which state the system is currently in, and launching such attacks that inject user input at the wrong time could result either in attack failure, or in users trivially detecting them.

We therefore pose the following question: *"Can an adversary improve the state-of-the-art UI attacks, and expand the set of applicable attack scenarios?"*. We observe that if the malware could infer the system state, and the precise attack launch time, stealthy and more powerful attacks become possible.

We present a new class of adaptive runtime user interface attacks, where the adversary infers the system state, violates the integrity of user input at a specific point in time, *while the device is operated by the legitimate user*, causing precise and stealthy runtime UI attacks without any malware running on the device. Contrary to existing works, our attack does not blindly inject input events, but rather hijacks the input channel of a currently active user, and enables new attack scenarios (e.g., compromise integrity of e-banking payment) that are not achievable with existing UI attacks. The attack is hard for the user to detect, it can result in serious safety or security violations, and the users are led to believe that they accidentally caused the damage themselves.

The first part of the attack is conventional. The adversary gains temporary physical access to the target system and attaches a small attack device (e.g., similar to the NSA cottonmouth [1]) in between an input device and the system.

In the second part of the attack lies its novelty. Contrary to existing approaches, our attack device observes the constant stream of user input events and, based on this information, determines when the user is about to perform a critical operation, and when the UI attack should be launched. Although the attack device has full visibility and control of the user input channel, it *cannot directly observe the state of the target system*, as the device has no system feedback (e.g., access monitor output). In particular, the adversary does not know the current state of the UI or the mouse pointer location, and must therefore, given user input, infer the most likely system state and correct attack timing.

To successfully realize our UI attacks, we had to overcome technical challenges. Once the adversary has determined the correct time to attack, the attack device injects a series of precise and fast input events. While the adversary is able to freely manipulate the input channel, the user receives instant visual feedback — the legitimate user is part of the system control loop. Therefore, we designed novel attack techniques, including state tracking and fingerprinting, that are both accurate (low false positives), and stealthy (give little visual indication to the user). To demonstrate the attack, we implemented it on a small embedded device, and evaluated it on general-purpose PCs and medical terminals.

On PC platforms, we tested our attack on UIs of real-world e-banking websites. We can accurately fingerprint UIs in a reliable (90% attack success rate) and stealthy (90% of users did not notice our attack) manner, that is surprisingly

| Pacemaker Programmer | Industrial Robot | E-Banking Websites | Malicious Proxy Device | Touchscreen | Malicious Peripherals |

Fig. 1. (Left) Examples of critical user interfaces on dedicated terminals and general-purpose PCs. Attacking such UIs can lead to various safety and security violations. (Right) the adversary attaches an attack device to an user input interface.

tolerant to noise (users habitually clicking around, pressing "tabs" to navigate between elements, different browsers and screen resolutions). For dedicated terminals, we tested the attack on a simulated UI of a medical implant programmer. We show that we can accurately perform system state tracking, and that the attacks are very hard to detect (93–96% success rate).

Performing such attacks is not possible using existing UI attacks, *unless* the malware resorts to injecting malicious software onto the target device; a step that we never resort to. We emphasize that our attack approach is applicable to a wide range of attack scenarios, including different user input methods and UIs, where the adversary has to perform the attack under target state uncertainty. Our attack approach is easy to deploy, as it requires only brief and non-invasive access to the system (e.g., attaching a USB device takes seconds).

One way to detect the attack is that the user notices the subtle visual changes on the user interface while the attack is active (e.g., medical device settings are modified). However, our user studies show that the vast majority of users fail to notice the attack. Preventing this attack likely requires different approaches, e.g., authentication of input devices, design of protective measures on user interfaces, and this work motivates the development of such solutions. Since our attack is invisible to traditional malware detection, it operates under uncertainty without any feedback from the system, and it gives little visual indication to the user, we call it *hacking in the blind*. To summarize, we make the following contributions:

- *New attack approach.* We propose a novel way to attack systems through their user interfaces. The attack is quick to deploy, hard for users to notice, and invisible to existing malware detection.
- *New attack techniques.* We developed a novel user interface tracking and fingerprinting techniques.
- *Attack prototype.* We implemented the attack on a small embedded device.
- *User studies.* We conducted both user studies on two case UIs (online banking and implant programmer) to evaluate attack detection rates.
- *Analysis of protective measures.* We analyze possible countermeasures and point out their limitations.

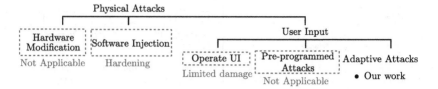

Fig. 2. Classification of physical attack techniques and their limitations to our setting.

2   Problem Statement

The goal of the adversary is to attack a security-critical user interface (Fig. 1), and we focus on attack scenarios where the adversary has brief physical access to the target system, prior to its usage. In this section we discuss limitations of known physical and user interface attacks and describe our adversary model.

2.1   Limitations of Known Attacks

There are various kinds of physical attack, and Fig. 2 provides a categorization of common attack techniques.

Hardware modification. One could argue that, in case the attacker has even brief physical access to a device, that the device should already be considered as trivially compromised. However, this is often not the case, due to two practical reasons. First, the attacker often can not shut the device down, without being noticed. This would prevent the attacker from opening the device and injecting advanced hardware backdoors or performing similar hardware modifications. Second, the attacker may simply not have sufficient time to perform such attacks. For example, in case of the hospital, we observed that the intensive care ward was never left unattended for extended periods of time.

Software injection. Another approach that relies on physical access is local injection of malicious code. For example, many terminals can be configured such that unsigned code cannot be executed from, e.g., connected USB devices.

Operate user interface. User input can not be simply blocked, and an attack approach that leverages this fact is to manipulate the device directly through its user interface. For example, if the adversary has physical access to the target device, and can operate its UI, the adversary can perform all the operations that the legitimate user is entitled to. Such attacks have two limitations. First, unauthorized use can be addressed with user authentication (e.g., devices could be screen locked). Second and more importantly, on security-critical UIs, the damage of such attacks is typically limited. For example, certain medical devices are only connected to patients when operated by doctors, and such attacks are less severe than runtime attacks that modify the operation of the terminal during its use. Similarly, e-banking sites are protected using second-factor authentication, that the attacker does not necessarily have access to.

Pre-programmed attacks. Another class of UI attacks rely on external devices connected to the target system. In such cases, no malware is present on the target system, and the purpose of the attack device is to either passively intercept user input or to actively inject pre-programmed sets of commands. A hardware key logger that collects user input is an example of a passive attack. BadUSB [19] is an example of a pre-programmed attack where a malicious input device (keyboard) injects keystrokes into the target system. Such attacks leverage keyboard shortcuts that, e.g., open a console or an administrative window and modify system settings. Such attacks do not apply to hardened terminals, as they rarely have console programs, and the user, or an adversary that controls user input, cannot "escape" the application UI to modify system settings beyond what the application enables. As the adversary does not know the current system state, such attacks can not be used to compromise (e.g., hijack) an e-banking user session, without resorting to installing malware to the device.

2.2   Our Goal: Adaptive Runtime Attacks

The focus of our work is on *adaptive runtime UI attacks*, that overcome the limitations of the above discussed techniques. We explore UI attacks that work even if hardware modifications are not practical and software injection can be prevented. Our goal is to design runtime UI attacks that are more damaging and accurate than pre-programmed attacks or operating the device through its UI.

Adversary model. We assume an adversary that gains temporary access to the target device prior to device usage, attaches a small attack device that sits in-between user input peripherals and the device (Fig. 1), and leaves the premises. If the input device is external (e.g., USB mouse), the adversary can attach the attack device to the USB port that connects it to the target system. The adversary can also simply replace an external input peripheral with one that contains the attack device. Most PCs have open ports for UI peripherals, and our survey (https://goo.gl/arp2DU) shows that many terminals use external peripherals, also connected to easily accessible ports.

   Besides installing the attack device, the adversary does not interact with the target device in any other way. In particular, we assume that the adversary cannot observe current system state (the user interface might be locked, or password protected). If the device is used via two input devices (e.g., mouse and keyboard), the adversary can connect both of them to the same attack device. The attack device can observe, delay, and block all events from the connected user input devices as well as inject new events. We assume that, in the terminal case, the adversary knows the target application UI (its states and state transitions).

Example attack targets. We explore attacks in two different contexts (general-purpose PCs and dedicated terminals) that represent different types of attack targets. The UI of a dedicated terminal device typically consists of a single application, that occupies the entire screen, and that the user cannot escape out of. Terminal devices often have fixed screen resolutions. On the other hand, general-purpose PCs have many applications with various UIs. The application UIs are managed by windowing systems that have various screen resolutions.

3   Hacking in the Blind

The installed attack device observes user events from the connected input device(s) and launches the attack by modifying user input or injecting new input events when the legitimate user is performing a security-critical operation.

While the attack device can intercept all user input events, their interpretation may have two forms of uncertainty. First, the adversary may not know the state of the target device UI (e.g., because the UI was locked when the attack device was installed). We call this *state uncertainty*. Second, the adversary may not be able to interpret all received user input events without ambiguity. In particular, mouse events are relative to the mouse cursor location that may be unknown to the adversary. We call this *location uncertainty*. In contrast to mouse input, touchscreen events do not have location uncertainty as touchscreen clicks are reported to the operating system in terms of their absolute (x, y) coordinates.

The primary challenge in our approach is to launch the attack accurately under such uncertainty, without any feedback from the target device (hacking in the blind). The best attack strategy depends on the attack platform (general-purpose PC vs. dedicated terminal), application user interface configuration, the type of the input device, and the level of stealthiness the adversary wants to achieve. We first discuss simple attack strategies, and then move on to present our two main attack techniques: state tracking and UI fingerprinting.

3.1   Simple Techniques

If the adversary manages to reduce (or remove) both location and state uncertainty, attacking the device user interface becomes easier. Assuming that the adversary knows both the current user interface state, the mouse cursor location, and complete model of the UI, each event can be interpreted unambiguously. For example, if an adversary knows the complete user interface configuration of a terminal, can easily track both mouse movement and state transitions in the user interface. In PCs, building such a model is typically not possible. Below we list simple methods that can help the adversary to reduce uncertainty.

Reducing state uncertainty. A simple technique to learn the state of the system is to wait for a reboot. If the attack device can determine when the terminal is booted, it knows that the target device UI is in a known state. While PCs are routinely restarted, many terminals run for long periods of time.

Reducing location uncertainty. A simple technique to determine the mouse cursor location is to actively move the mouse (i.e., inject movement events) towards a corner of the screen. For example, if the mouse is moved up and left sufficiently, the adversary knows with certainty that the mouse cursor is located at the top-left corner of the screen. Moving the mouse while the system is idle may not be possible, if the target device user interface is locked.

Summary. We assume a strong adversary, that in many scenarios has to perform the attack under location uncertainty, state uncertainty or both, and next we

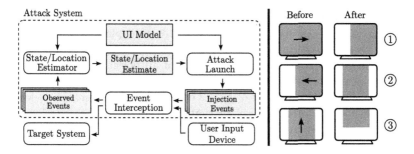

Fig. 3. (Left) Overview of our attack system. (Right) Movement event handling. Movement can reduce the uncertainty area size (1) and (3) or change its location (2).

design attack techniques to handle both. We first describe state tracking that is applicable to terminals, where the adversary can build a complete model of the target system UI. After that, we describe UI fingerprinting that allows attack state detection on PC platforms, where such model creation is infeasible.

3.2   State Tracking

Starting from this section, we describe a state tracking approach that enables the adversary to launch accurate attacks despite of uncertainty. State tracking is applicable to terminals, where the adversary can build a complete model of the target system UI (e.g., typically on dedicated terminals, the target application UI constitutes the complete target system UI). A noteworthy property of the system is that it estimates user interface state and mouse location *fully passively*, and thus enables implementation of stealthy attacks. We proceed by giving a high-level overview of the attack system (Fig. 3).

The attack device contains a static model of the target system UI that the adversary constructed before the device deployment and it has two main components. The first one is a *State and Location Estimator* that determines the most likely user interface state (and mouse cursor location) based on the observed user events and the UI model. The estimation process can begin from a known, or an unknown UI state, at an arbitrary moment and it tracks mouse and keyboard events. The second component is an *Attack Launcher* that injects precise input events while the legitimate user is performing a safety-critical operation.

User interface model. The UI model contains user interface states, their elements (buttons, text boxes, sliders, etc.) and state transitions. For each state, the model includes the locations and the types of the input elements and the possible state transition that the element triggers. One of the states is defined as the start state and one or more states are defined as the target states. The goal of the attack is to modify safety-critical inputs (*target elements*) on the target states. Typically the target state includes also a confirmation element that the user clicks to confirm the safety-critical operation.

State and location estimation. Here we describe our state and location estimation algorithm for mouse and keyboard. Later we explain how the same algorithm can be used to estimate state for touchscreens (only state uncertainty).

The algorithm operates by keeping track of all possible user interface state and mouse location combinations. For each possible state and location, the algorithm maintains a *state tracker* object. The state trackers contain an identifier of the state and an *uncertainty area* that determines the possible location of the mouse in that state instance. Additionally, the algorithm assigns a probability for each tracker object that represent the likelihood that the terminal user interface and the mouse cursor are in this state and location.

The estimation algorithm maintains the tracker objects in a list. If the estimation begins from a known state, we start with only one tracker, to which we assign 100% probability. If it begins from an unknown state, we create one tracker per possible system state and assign them equal probabilities. Assuming no prior knowledge on the mouse location, we set the mouse uncertainty area to cover the entire screen in each tracker during initialization.

The state and location estimation is an event-driven process. Based on the received user input events, we create new trackers, or update and delete existing ones. For each mouse movement event, we update the mouse uncertainty area in each tracker. For every mouse click, we consider all possible outcomes of the click, including transitions to new states, as well as remaining in the same state. We create new *child trackers* with updated uncertainty areas, add the children to the list, and remove the *parent tracker*. When we observe a user event sequence that indicates interaction with a specific UI element, we update the probabilities of each tracker accordingly. We explain these steps in detail below.

Movement event handling. When the mouse uncertainty area is the entire device screen, any mouse movement reduces the size of the uncertainty area. For example, if the user moves the mouse to the right, the area becomes smaller, as the mouse cursor can no longer reside in the leftmost part of the screen (Fig. 3). If the mouse is moved to a direction where the uncertainty area border is not on the edge of the screen, the mouse movement does not reduce the size of the uncertainty area, but only causes its location to be updated. Any mouse movement towards a direction where the uncertainty area is on the border of the screen, reduces the size of the uncertainty area further. For each received mouse movement event, we update the uncertainty areas in all trackers.

Click event handling. When we observe a mouse click event, the estimation algorithm considers all possible outcomes for each tracker, that are determined by the current mouse uncertainty area (Fig. 4, left). For each possible outcome we create new child trackers and update their mouse uncertainty areas as follows.

If the user interface remains in the same state, the updated mouse area for the child is the original area of the parent, from which we remove the areas of the UI elements that cause transitions to other states. For each state transition, the mouse area is calculated as the intersection of the parent area and the area of the user input element that caused the transition. Once the updated mouse uncertainty areas are calculated for each child tracker, we remove the parent from the list, and add the children. We repeat the process for each tracker on the list, and we note that, as a result of this process, the list may contain multiple trackers for the same state with different mouse uncertainty areas.

The probability of a child tracker is calculated by multiplying the probability of its parent with a *transition probability*. We consider two options for assigning transition probabilities, as shown in Fig. 4 (right):

- *Equal transitions.* Our first option is to consider all possible state transitions equally likely. E.g., if the mouse uncertainty area contains two buttons, each of them causing a separate state transition, and parts of the screen where a click does not cause a state transition, we assign each of them $1/3$ probability.
- *Element area.* Our second option is to calculate the transition probabilities based on the surface of the user interface element covered by the mouse uncertainty area. For example, if the uncertainty area covers a larger area over one button than another, we assign it bigger transition probability.

The transition probabilities can be enhanced with *a priori probabilities* of UI element interactions. For example, based on prior experience on comparable UIs, the adversary can estimate that "OK" is pressed twice as likely as "Cancel".

Element detection. Finally, we identify user interaction with certain UI elements based on sequences of observed input events. For example, an event sequence that begins with a button down event, followed by movement left or right that exceeds a given threshold, followed by a button up event is an indication of slider usage. Similarly, text input from the keyboard indicates likely interaction with a text field, and a click indicates interaction with a button.

When we observe such event sequences (slider movement, text input, button click), we update the probabilities of the possible trackers on the list. One possible approach would be to remove all trackers from the list where interaction with the identified element is not possible (e.g., a button click is not possible under the mouse uncertainty area), and we could then increase the probabilities of the remaining trackers equally. Such an approach could yield fast results, but also provide erroneous state estimations. If the user provides text input on a user interface state that does not contain editable text fields or if text highlighting is mistaken for slider movement, the algorithm would remove the correct state from the list. We adopt a safer approach where we consider trackers with the identified elements more likely and scale up their probabilities, and keep the remaining trackers and scale down their probabilities.

Target state detection. Our algorithm continues the state tracking process until two criteria are met. First, we have identified the target state with a probability that exceeds a threshold. After each click event and detected element we sum the probabilities for all trackers that represent the same state to check if any of them exceeds the threshold. Second, the mouse uncertainty area must be small enough to launch the attack. We combine the mouse uncertainty areas from all matching trackers and consider the uncertainty area sufficiently small when its size is smaller than the size of the confirmation element.

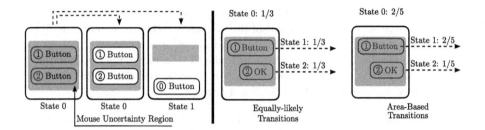

Fig. 4. Click event handling (left), and transition probabilities (right).

State estimation for touchscreen. Using a touchscreen instead of a mouse does not affect our algorithm. Typically touchscreens report click events in absolute coordinates, hence using a touchscreen corresponds to the case where the mouse location is known, but the starting state is not. Determining the possible transitions after a click is trivial, since there can be at most one intersection of a clicking point with the area of an element in a specific state.

3.3   User Interface Fingerprinting

In this section we describe UI fingerprinting that is applicable to adaptive UI attacks on general-purpose PC platforms. On a high level, our UI fingerprinting approach works as follows. The attack device keeps a history of all events observed in the last t minutes (in our experiments, $t = 5\,\mathrm{min}$ produced good results). For every observed mouse click event, the attack device takes the target application UI model, analyzes the event history and asks the following question: *"Is the user interacting with the critical UI?"*. Similarly to our state tracking approach, we also require a UI model for fingerprinting. However, the model is simpler as no UI transitions are modeled.

In Fig. 5, we illustrate our fingerprinting approach on a concrete example. The critical UI in this case is simple, and consists of three elements: two text-boxes and a button. We require one text-box to be filled out, while the other is optional. The latest event (at time t_0) the attack device observes is a mouse click. The attack device assumes the click was performed on the confirmation element, and traverses the event history backwards in time to see if the user was indeed interacting with the critical UI, according to the specified model.

The first encountered event is a mouse move, so the device moves the mouse uncertainty region accordingly. The following two events are a click and a key press, so the device creates two trackers (the uncertainty region was over two different elements), and shrinks the uncertainty region over the corresponding elements. The next event is another move, followed by a click and a keyboard press. In the lower tracker, the click would have originated over no element, but in the upper tracker, both required text-boxes would be filled, at which point the attack device concludes that the user is interacting with the targeted UI state.

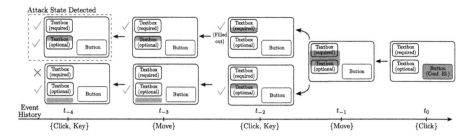

Fig. 5. Fingerprinting UI example. For every observed click, the attack device traverses the event history and checks if the user is currently interacting with the target UI.

3.4   Attack Launch Techniques

Once the attack device has identified the attack state with sufficiently small uncertainty area, it is ready to launch the attack. In a simple approach, the adversary moves the mouse cursor over one of the attack elements, modifies its value, moves the cursor over the confirmation button, and clicks it. The process is fast and the user has little chances of preventing the attack. However, the user is likely to notice it. For example, if a doctor never clicked the confirm button, the doctor is unlikely to implant the pacemaker into a patient. For this reason, we focus on more subtle attack launch techniques. Below we describe two such techniques and in Sects. 4 and 5 we evaluate their user detection.

Element-driven attack. The adversary first identifies that the user interacts with one of the target elements. This can be easily done when the mouse uncertainty area is smaller than the target element. Once the user has modified the value of the target element, the adversary waits a small period of time and during it tracks the mouse movement, then quickly moves the mouse cursor back to the target element, modifies its value, and returns the mouse cursor to its location. After that, the adversary lets the legitimate user confirm the safety-critical operation. The technique only requires little mouse movement, but the modified value remains visible to the user for a potentially long time, as the adversary does not know when the user will confirm the safety-critical operation.

Confirmation-driven attack. The adversary identifies that the system is on the attack state and lets the user to set the attack element values uninterrupted. When the user clicks the confirmation button, the attack activates. The adversary blocks the incoming click event, moves the mouse cursor over one of the attack elements, modifies its value, moves the mouse cursor back over the confirmation button, and then passes the click event to the target system. The adversary then changes the modified attack element back to its original value. In this technique, the mouse cursor may have to be moved more, but the modified attack element settings remain visible to the user only for a brief period of time.

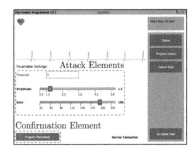

Fig. 6. Attack device prototype. We implemented the full attack.

Fig. 7. Case study UI: custom cardiac implant programmer.

3.5 Attack Device Protoype

We built a full prototype of the attack device by implementing the entire attack system in C++ and deployed it on two BeagleBone Black boards (Fig. 6). The two boards communicate over ethernet, as each board has only one set of USB ports and we evaluate an attack where the adversary controls both mouse and keyboard input. A custom attack device would consists of a single embedded device. The boards have processing power comparable to a modern low-end smartphone (1 GHz CPU, 512 MB RAM).

The boards are conveniently powered through USB, and no external power supplies are required. Each board intercepts one USB device (keyboard and mouse, respectively), and the two boards communicate through a short ethernet cable. We emphasize that the complete attack software is running on the boards themselves, and no remote communication with the attacker is either required or performed. We purposefully optimized the C++ code for execution speed.

4 Case Study: Pacemaker Programmer UI

To evaluate our state tracking based attack on terminals, we focus on a simulated pacemaker programmer (Fig. 7). We also performed a case-study on e-banking user interfaces, on 20 domain experts, and we refer the reader to Sect. 5 for details. A video of our attack is available at https://goo.gl/kdkRDC.

We implemented the user interface based on the publicly available documentation of an existing cardiac implant programmer [5]. Such a programmer terminal is used by doctors to configure medical implant settings. For example, when a doctor prepares a pacemaker for implantation, she configures its settings based on the heart condition of the receiving patient. The terminal can also be used to monitor the operation of the implant and potentially update its settings.

The model of this user interface consists of approximately ten states and contains three types of user input elements: buttons, text fields and sliders. All state transitions are triggered by button clicks. The attack elements are the user input elements that are used to configure the pacemaker settings. Threshold is set using a text field (keyboard), while amplitude and rate are set using slider

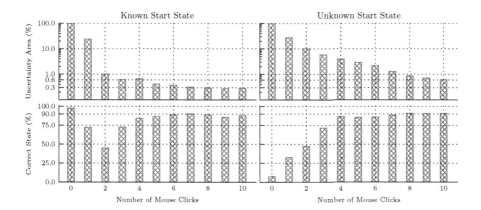

Fig. 8. State tracking accuracy of our attack system.

elements (mouse), see Fig. 7. All attack elements are on the same state. The model creation was a manual process that took a few hours.

We implemented the user interface using HTML5/JavaScript, and the UI serves two different purposes. First, we use it to demonstrate the attack and evaluate attack detection on-site. For this use, we run the user interface on a standard PC, instead of a terminal (Fig. 6). Second, we use the same UI to collect user traces and evaluate the detection of different attack variants online.

Trace collection. To evaluate the tracking algorithm we collected online user traces for the programmer UI. We recruited participants using the global crowd sourcing platform CrowdFlower. In the instructions, we asked the participants to find saved patient data that matches a given medical condition, copy that patient's pacemaker settings to the programming screen, and finally, to program the device by pressing the confirmation element. We recorded all user input during the task, but no private information on study participants was collected.

In total 400 contributors completed the task. We observed that approximately 7% of user input gestures were over non-existent elements (e.g., users clicked when the mouse cursor was not over a button).

Estimation accuracy. We ran our estimator on all our traces (Fig. 8). As our algorithm is event-based, after each click we measured (a) the size of the mouse uncertainty area, expressed as percentage of the overall screen, and (b) the probability that we correctly estimate the real state the user is currently in.

We say that our algorithm correctly estimates the current state, when it assigns the highest probability for the correct state among all states. As all our traces start from the same state, to evaluate the situation where the tracking begins from an unknown state, we cut the first 10% from all our evaluation traces. As tracking options we used the element-area transition probabilities together with element detection (scaling parameter 0.95) and a priori probabilities that we obtained by profiling the training traces.

First, we discuss the case where the state tracking begins from a known start state (shown left in Fig. 8). The uncertainty area is the full screen at first and the probability for estimating the correct state is 100% (known start state). As the estimation algorithm gathers more user input events, the uncertainty area size reduces quickly and already after three clicks the area is less than 1% of the screen size. The estimation probability decreases first, as the first click adds uncertainty to the tracking process, but after additional click events, the estimation probability increases steadily, and after ten clicks the algorithm can estimate the correct state with 90% probability.

Next, we consider the scenario where the state tracking begins from an unknown target system state (shown right in Fig. 8). In the beginning, the uncertainty area is the entire screen and the probability for the state estimate is low, as all states are equally likely. As the tracking algorithm gathers more user events, the uncertainty area reduces, but not as fast as in the case of known start state. The uncertainty area becomes less than 1% of the screen size after eight clicks. The probability for the correct state estimate increases and after ten clicks we can estimate the correct state with approximately 90% probability.

We conclude that in both cases we can identify the correct system state with high probability after observing only ten clicks and the uncertainty area becomes very small (below 1%, equals to a small, 50×50 pixel rectangle). If the user enters the attack state after ten clicks, we can launch the attack accurately.

We compared the performance of our different tracking options, and we noticed that the they performed comparably. Element detection gave a major accuracy increase, while a priori probabilities did not improve accuracy significantly.

Attack launch success rate. To evaluate if our system successfully detects the correct time to launch the attack, we ran our algorithm on all the user traces we recorded from our user study. In 83% of all traces, our system correctly identified the attack launch time, namely right after the user programs the pacemaker. In 16% of the traces, our system did not identify a suitable attack time and, as a result, no attack would be launched. Only in 1% of the traces our system launched the attack at the wrong time. We conclude that our system correctly identifies the attack launch time in most cases.

Estimation overhead. To analyze how fast our state and location estimation algorithm runs, we measured the runtime overhead of processing each user input event from the collected traces. The algorithm was run on the two BeagleBone boards with element tracking enabled, using equal transition probabilities.

Both mouse and keyboard events require little computation. The processing overhead per event is very small (below 0.5 ms) and such events can be easily processed in real-time. Mouse click events require more computation, as those cause generation of new trackers, and the processing delay is relative to the number of state trackers that the algorithm maintains. Figure 9 shows the average processing delay for mouse clicks from our evaluation traces. When we

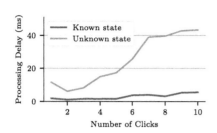

Fig. 9. The device per-event overhead increases as the algorithm accumulates more trackers, but is overall low.

Attack group	Attack succeeded	Task completed
1. Element, text, 5 ms	50%	84
2. Element, text, 62 ms	37%	84
3. Element, text, 125 ms	48%	86
4. Element, slider, 5 ms	12%	80
5. Element, slider, 62 ms	9%	83
6. Element, slider, 125 ms	6%	86
7. Confirmation, text, 10 ms	93%	81
8. Confirmation, text, 125 ms	96%	79
9. Confirmation, text, 250 ms	93%	78
10. Confirmation, slider, 10 ms	95%	85
11. Confirmation, slider, 125 ms	90%	82
12. Confirmation, slider, 250 ms	95%	79
Total		987

Fig. 10. Attack detection results.

start tracking from a known state, the overhead increases slightly over time, but remains under 7 ms per event. When we start tracking from an unknown state, the algorithm accumulates significantly more trackers, and thus the processing overhead increases faster. After ten clicks, processing a single input event takes approximately 43 ms on our test platform. From the analyzed traces we observe that the interval between consecutive mouse clicks is typically in the order of seconds. This gives the attack device ample time to process incoming click events.

We conclude that our implementation is fast. Mouse and keyboard events are processed in real-time and the processing overhead for mouse clicks is significantly smaller than the typical interval between clicks. The UI remains responsive, with no "processing lag" that would indicate an attack is taking place. Our attack device can also be significantly minimized in terms of hardware. Based on our results, even less powerful devices than our own would be sufficient.

Online attack detection user study. To evaluate how many users would detect our attacks, we conducted two user studies. Here we describe the first, large-scale online study. We recruited 1200 new study participants, that we divided into 12 groups. We tested two element-driven attack variants: one where we modify a text element and another where we modify a slider. We also tested two confirmation-driven attack variants: one with text and another with slider input. For each four attack variant we tested three separate speeds of the attack.

We provided the same task description as before, but depending on the group, we launched an attack during the task. Once the task was over, we asked the participants: *"Do you think you programmed the pacemaker correctly?"*.

If a participant noticed the UI manipulation, she had three possible ways to act on it. First, she was able to program the pacemaker again with the correct values. Second, the participant could report that the device was not programmed correctly in the post-test question. Third, the she could write to the freeform feedback that she noticed something suspicious in the application user interface.

In total 987 participants completed the task. We consider that the attack succeeded when the participant did none of the above mentioned three actions.

The results are shown in Fig. 10. The success rate for the element-driven text attacks was 37–50% and for the element-driven slider attacks 6–12%, depending on the speed of the attack. The success rate for the confirmation-driven text attacks was 93–96% and for the confirmation-driven slider attacks 90–95%.

All the tested confirmation-driven attacks had high success rates (over 90%). In the element-driven attacks the user interface manipulation remains visible longer for the user, and this is a possible explanation why the attacks do not succeed equally well. We conclude that confirmation-driven attacks are a better strategy for the adversary and focus the rest of our analysis on those.

We compared the success rates of text and slider manipulation on confirmation-driven attacks, but found no statistically significant difference ($\chi^2(1, N = 484) = 0.12$), $p = 0.73$). We also compared the success rates of different attacks speeds on confirmation-driven text attacks ($\chi^2(2, N = 238) = 0.42$), $p = 0.81$) and slider attacks ($\chi^2(2, N = 246) = 2.20$), $p = 0.33$), but found no significant difference. This implies that the adversary has at least a few hundred milliseconds time to perform the user interface manipulation without sacrificing its success rate.

We analyzed all freeform text responses, and none of the users associated the observed UI changes with a malicious attack. Only two users commented on the changing values of UI elements and both attributed them to a software glitch.

On-site user study. Our study participants were not domain experts, i.e., users that would commonly operate a pacemaker programmer. We therefore performed a on-site user study on two medical professionals (one doctor, one nurse). Both participants failed to detect our attack, and were under the impression they programmed the pacemaker correctly.

5 Case Study: Online Banking UI

In this section we describe our experiments on e-banking user interface. To evaluate how successful our attack is in fingerprinting UIs and compromising the integrity of e-banking payments, we performed a separate on-site user study, similar to the previous on-site attack detection study. We created partial local replicas of three major e-banking websites (we only copied the payment parts of the sites). The replicas were nearly the same as their online counterparts, with minor differences introduced through the replication process.

Recruitment and procedure. We recruited 20 domain experts, where each participant was required to be a regular e-banking user of one of the three banks we replicated the websites of, and use either Chrome of Firefox during e-banking sessions. Each participant was presented a sheet of paper with the following instructions steps. (1) Open the browser you usually use for e-banking. (2) Click on your e-banking site link, located in the browser bookmarks. (3) Imagine you already performed the login procedure, as the replica website requires no login. (4) Navigate to the payment site, and (5) make a payment to the account provided on the study sheet. (6) To complete the task, close the browser.

The attack device was already installed to the laptop and was hidden from sight. First step of our attack was to automatically detect that the user is interacting with a critical UI (payment information is filled in), and which of the three banks was being used. The second step was to detect when the "Confirm payment" button was clicked. The attack device then inserted mouse and keyboard input that changed the payment field containing the amount of money transmitted, and injected a javascript snippet through the URL bar that masked the changed value in the upcoming "Payment confirmation" screen. The javascript was only needed to mask the website so that the user has a harder time noticing the attack. The whole attack was done in approximately 0.5 s, and a video which demonstrates our attack is available at: https://goo.gl/kdkRDC. After completing the user study, we presented each participant with an exit questionnaire: *"1. Was the payment experience comparable to your regular e-banking experience?"* and *"2. What do you think the user study was about?"*

Results. Our attack successfully detected the precise point in time when the users were interacting with the critical UI (making a payment) in 90% of the cases. Our attack failed in only 10% of the cases (two users). In both cases the attack state detection succeeded, but the attack input injection failed due to implementation flaws, that were corrected after the study.

90% of participants positively answered to the first question, noting that it was similar to their regular e-banking experience. Out of those, some users noted that the UI looked slightly different, which was due to the imperfections introduced by our replication process. Only 10% noted that the experience was not the same, due to the missing second-factor authentication step. Out of 20 participants, 30% had no idea about the true nature of the user study. Another 30% suspected that some form of attack was performed (phishing, key-logging, removal of second-factor authentication), while another 30% thought the study was a usability test. Only two users detected our attack, and correctly guessed the true nature of the study. We conclude that our attack was stealthy.

Discussion. We did not perform any security priming in our user study, however we acknowledge that the role-playing bias of study participant not using their real e-banking could be present. Users might have been less careful, because they knew that their own money is not at risk. At the same time, our study setup introduces another bias. Since the study was performed under our supervision, some study participants may have been more alert than if they would have done the online payment on their own.

We tested our attack on various browsers, e-banking sites and screen resolutions as well as browser window locations, and we conclude that our attacks can successfully perform UI fingerprinting and e-banking session hijacking, with no false positives, and very low false negatives. Furthermore, we showed that our attacks were not detected by the majority of users.

The user study was performed on our custom laptop, and the e-banking website were replicas. At no point did we require the study participants to disclose any kind of private information, such as their e-banking credentials.

6   Countermeasures

In this section we analyze possible countermeasures and their limitations.

Trusted input devices. One way to address our attacks is to mandate usage of trusted input devices. We call a user input device *trusted*, when it securely shares a key with the target system, as then all traffic can be encrypted and authenticated which prevents the adversary from observing, injecting, or replaying events. However, deployment of secure input devices is challenging. For example, doctors need be able to operate medical terminals at all times, even in case of trusted peripherals breaking down.

Increased user feedback. The UI can provide visual feedback on each change of attack elements [12]. For example, the UI can draw a border around a recently edited element to keep it visible. In a confirmation-driven attack, the user would see the border, but as the adversary changes the attack element value back to the original, the content of the user interface element would appear as expected. Noticing that an attack happened may be difficult for the user.

Change rate limiting. The user interface could limit the rate at which the values of the UI elements can be changed. However, our study results show that the majority of users do not notice even relatively slow UI manipulations that take 250 ms. Finding a rate limit that efficiently prevents user interface manipulation attacks, but does not prevent legitimate user interactions is challenging.

Randomized user interfaces. Another way to address our attacks is to randomize parts of the safety-critical system user interface. While UI randomization [13, 23, 26] can complicate, or even prevent our attacks, it also increases the chances of human error. In contrast to smartphone screen lock, on safety-critical terminals an increased error rate is typically not acceptable. For example, medical devices consider lack of UI consistency a critical safety violation [10].

Continuous user authentication. While traditional user authentication systems require the user to log in once, continuous authentication systems monitor user input over a period of time to detect if the usage deviates from a previously recorded user profile. Many such systems track mouse velocity, acceleration and movement direction [6, 22], together with click events [6, 22], angle-based curvature metrics and click-pause measurements [28].

The proposed systems [17, 21, 28] need to observe the impostor for significant amount of time (e.g., 12 consecutive seconds [21]). Our attacks require only brief mouse movement and one or few clicks, and the attacks can be performed well under a second. Our state estimation works fully passively, and current continuous authentication systems are not directly applicable to detecting them.

Summary. We conclude that all the reviewed countermeasures have limitations. Finding better protective measures that are both effective and practical to deploy remains an open problem.

7   Discussion

In this section we discuss the applicability of the proposed approach to other scenarios and directions for future work.

Attacks in the wild. Attacks similar to ours may already be taking place in the wild. For example, the NSA cottonmouth project [1] is a malicious USB connector that can both inject and observe user input. Such and similar devices are ideally suited to perform our attacks.

User interface complexity. We experimented our attacks on a terminal user interface that consists of approximately ten states. We consider this typical UI complexity for embedded dedicated-purpose terminals. We also experimented our attack on real (and replica) online banking websites. We believe that these examples capture different types of security-critical user interfaces.

System output. In our attack scenario, the adversary has only access to the user input channel. An attack device that is attached to an interface that connects a touchscreen to the terminal mainboard is an example of a scenario where the adversary may be able to access the system output channel as well. Video interfaces can have high bandwidths and running image recognition algorithms on a small embedded device in real-time may be challenging.

User presence. We tailored our attack for the case, where the legitimate user is operating the device. The presence of the legitimate user both helps and complicates our attack. Observing specific input events (e.g., mouse clicks that presumably take place over buttons) help the adversary to determine the current user interface state. At the same time, the adversary must inject the attack events in a subtle manner to avoid user detection. If the attack is performed without the user presence (i.e., when the system is idle), a different strategy is needed. Exploring such state estimation strategies is an interesting future work.

Mouse transfer function. In our attack prototype, we assumed there was no mouse transfer function, and that the physical mouse movement directly corresponded to the on-screen cursor movement. However, if present, such functions can be inferred and accounted for [20].

8   Related Work

USB attacks. Key loggers are small devices that the adversary can attach between a keyboard and the target system. The key logger records user input and the adversary collects the device later to learn any entered user secrets such as passwords. Such attacks are limited to passive information leakage, while our approach enables active runtime attacks with severe safety implications.

A malicious user input device, or a smartphone that impersonates one [27], can attack PC platforms by executing pre-programmed attack sequences [7,9,15]. For example, a malicious keyboard can issue dedicated key sequence to open a terminal and execute malicious system commands. The input device might also be able to copy malicious code to the target system. Such attacks are typically not possible on hardened embedded terminals where the user cannot escape the application UI, and installation and execution of unsigned code is prevented.

An attack that sounds similar to our attack approach is Mousejacking [2]. However, in the Mousejack attack, the attacker does gain access to legitimate user input, but is only able to blindly inject fake events into the input channel.

USB firewalls. In recent research, USB firewall architectures have been proposed [3, 24, 25]. Similar to network firewalls, these approaches include packet filtering functionality (e.g., in the OS kernel), and can prevent a USB peripheral of one class masquerading as an instance of another class (e.g., mass storage device masquerades as keyboard). Such measures do not prevent our attacks, where all injected USB packets match the device class of the benign peripheral.

USB fingerprinting. Researchers have demonstrated fingerprinting of PCs based on their USB communication timing patterns [4]. Similar approach could be applied to fingerprint USB input devices. The processing delays that our attack incur are so small that users cannot observe them, but it remains an open question if timing-based fingerprinting could be used to detect the attack.

Terminal protection. Software-based attestation is a technique that allows a host platform to verify the software configuration of a connected peripheral [14]. Such attestation would not address the variant of our attack where the attack device sits between the benign peripheral and the terminal. Power analysis can be used to identify unknown (malicious) software processes running on embedded terminals, such as medical devices [8]. Such approaches would not detect our attack where no malicious code is running on the terminal. Our prototype is susceptible to power-analysis as it draws power from the host USB connection. However, the device could easily be designed to include an on-board battery.

User interface attacks. In systems where multiple applications or websites share the same display, the user can be tricked to interact with false UI elements. For example, a malicious website may be able to draw an overlay over a button that causes the user click the button unintentionally. Such attacks are called clickjacking [12] or UI redressing [18]. In our attack scenario, the adversary can only modify and injects user events.

9   Conclusions

In this paper we have presented hacking in the blind, a novel approach to attack systems through input integrity violation under uncertainty about the target system state. In the attack, the adversary installs an attack device between a user input device and the target system, and the attack is launched when the authorized user is performing a security-critical operation, by modifying or injecting new user input events. Our approach is easy to deploy on the location, invisible to traditional malware detection, difficult for the user to notice, and surprisingly robust to noise. Many of the attack variants we tested had success rate over 90%. We analyzed several countermeasures and noticed that all of them have limitations. We conclude that our attack presents a serious threat to many safety-critical terminals and PC applications.

References

1. Nsa cottonmouth project. https://nsa.gov1.info/dni/nsa-ant-catalog/usb/index.html
2. Mousejack technical details (2017). https://www.bastille.net/research/vulnerabilities/mousejack/technical-details
3. Angel, S., Wahby, R.S., Howald, M., Leners, J.B., Spilo, M., Sun, Z., Blumberg, A.J., Walfish, M.: Defending against malicious peripherals (2015). http://arxiv.org/abs/1506.01449
4. Bates, A.M., Leonard, R., Pruse, H., Lowd, D., Butler, K.R.: Leveraging usb to establish host identity using commodity devices. In: Network and Distributed System Security Symposium (NDSS) (2014)
5. Biotronik. Cardiac rhythm management. http://goo.gl/jvCuzC
6. Cai, Z., Shen, C., Guan, X.: Mitigating behavioral variability for mouse dynamics: a dimensionality-reduction-based approach. Trans. Hum.-Mach. Syst. **44**(2) (2014)
7. Chen, K.: Reversing and exploiting an apple firmware update. In: Black Hat USA (2009)
8. Clark, S.S., Ransford, B., Rahmati, A., Guineau, S., Sorber, J., Xu, W., Wattsupdoc, K.: Power side channels to nonintrusively discover untargeted malware on embedded medical devices. In: USENIX Workshop on Health Information Technologies (HealthTech) (2013)
9. Crenshaw, A.: Plug and prey: malicious USB devices (2011)
10. Graham, M., Kubose, T., Jordan, D., Zhang, J., Johnson, T.R., Patel, V.L.: Heuristic evaluation of infusion pumps: implications for patient safety in intensive care units. J. Med. Inf. **73**, 771–779 (2004)
11. Hak5. USB rubber ducky (2017). http://usbrubberducky.com/
12. Huang, L.-S., Moshchuk, A., Wang, H.J., Schechter, S., Jackson, C.: Clickjacking: attacks and defenses. In: USENIX Security Symposium (2012)
13. Intel. Identity protection technology with PKI - technology overview (2013). https://goo.gl/TtgzXW
14. Li, Y., McCune, J.M., Perrig, A.: SBAP: software-based attestation for peripherals. In: Trust and Trustworthy Computing (TRUST) (2010)
15. Maskiewicz, J., Ellis, B., Mouradian, J., Shacham, H.: Mouse trap: exploiting firmware updates in USB peripherals. In: Workshop on Offensive Technologies (WOOT) (2014)
16. Microsoft. Lockdown features (windows embedded industry 8.1) (2014). https://goo.gl/JcXC9X
17. Mondal, S., Bours, P.: A computational approach to the continuous authentication biometric system. Inf. Sci. **304**, 28–53 (2015)
18. Niemietz, M.: UI redressing: attacks and countermeasures revisited. In: CONFidence (2011)
19. Nohl, K., Lell, J.: BadUSB - on accessories that turn evil. In: Black Hat USA (2014)

20. Quinn, P., Cockburn, A., Casiez, G., Roussel, N., Gutwin, C.: Exposing and understanding scrolling transfer functions. In: Proceedings of the 25th Annual ACM Symposium on User Interface Software and Technology, pp. 341–350. ACM (2012)
21. Shen, C., Cai, Z., Guan, X., Du, Y., Maxion, R.: User authentication through mouse dynamics. IEEE Trans. Inf. Forensics Secur. 8(1), 16–30 (2013)
22. Shen, C., Cai, Z., Guan, X., Sha, H., Du, J.: Feature analysis of mouse dynamics in identity authentication and monitoring. In: IEEE International Conference on Communications (ICC) (2009)
23. G. P. Store. Lockdown pro. https://play.google.com/store/apps/details?id=appplus.mobi.lockdownpro
24. Tian, D.J., Bates, A., Butler, K.: Defending against malicious usb firmware with goodUSB. In: Annual Computer Security Applications Conference (ACSAC) (2015)
25. Tian, J., Scaife, N., Bates, A., Butler, K., Traynor, P.: Making USB great again with USBFILTER. In: To appear in USENIX Security Symposium (2016)
26. von Zezschwitz, E., Koslow, A., De Luca, A., Hussmann, H.: Making graphic-based authentication secure against smudge attacks. In: International Conference on Intelligent User Interfaces (IUI) (2013)
27. Wang, Z., Stavrou, A.: Exploiting smart-phone USB connectivity for fun and profit. In: Annual Computer Security Applications Conference (ACSAC) (2010)
28. Zheng, N., Paloski, A., Wang, H.: An efficient user verification system via mouse movements. In: Computer and Communications Security (CCS) (2011)

On the Security of Carrier Phase-Based Ranging

Hildur Ólafsdóttir, Aanjhan Ranganathan[(⊠)], and Srdjan Capkun

ETH Zurich, Zurich, Switzerland
`raanjhan@inf.ethz.ch`

Abstract. Multicarrier phase-based ranging is fast emerging as a cost-optimized solution for a wide variety of proximity-based applications due to its low power requirement, low hardware complexity and compatibility with existing standards such as ZigBee and 6LoWPAN. Given potentially critical nature of the applications in which phase-based ranging can be deployed (e.g., access control, asset tracking), it is important to evaluate its security guarantees. Therefore, in this work, we investigate the security of multicarrier phase-based ranging systems and specifically focus on distance decreasing relay attacks that have proven detrimental to the security of proximity-based access control systems (e.g., vehicular passive keyless entry and start systems). We show that phase-based ranging, as well as its implementations, are vulnerable to a variety of distance reduction attacks. We describe different attack realizations and verify their feasibility by simulations and experiments on a commercial ranging system. Specifically, we successfully reduced the estimated range to less than 3 m even though the devices were more than 50 m apart. We discuss possible countermeasures against such attacks and illustrate their limitations, therefore demonstrating that phase-based ranging cannot be fully secured against distance decreasing attacks.

Keywords: Secure ranging · Proximity verification · Phase-based ranging

1 Introduction

The use of proximity and location information is ubiquitous today in a wide range of applications [20,38]. For example, proximity-based access tokens (e.g., contactless smart cards, key fobs) are prevalent today in a number of systems [17,34] including public transport ticketing, parking and highway toll fee collection, payment systems, electronic passports, physical access control and personnel tracking. Furthermore, modern automobiles use passive keyless entry systems (PKES) to unlock, lock or start the vehicle. The vehicle automatically identifies and unlocks when the key fob is in proximity, and there is no need for the user to remove the key from his pocket. By eliminating the need for user interaction, PKES-like systems also offer better protection in scenarios, e.g., where the user forgets to lock the car manually. With the advent of modern cyber physical autonomous systems and the internet of things, the need for proximity and location information is only bound to increase.

© International Association for Cryptologic Research 2017
W. Fischer and N. Homma (Eds.): CHES 2017, LNCS 10529, pp. 490–509, 2017.
DOI: 10.1007/978-3-319-66787-4_24

Numerous ranging techniques [23] that use radio communication signals have been developed in the recent years. Some techniques are based on estimating the change in the physical characteristics of the signal such as amplitude, phase and frequency. For example, ranging systems based on received signal strength (RSS) [7,42] rely on the free-space path-loss propagation model to estimate the distance between two entities. Other ranging techniques estimate distance based on the time-of-flight (e.g., roundtrip time of flight (RTOF), time-difference-of-arrival (TDOA)) [44] of the radio frequency signal.

Most of these ranging techniques are inherently insecure. For example, an attacker can fake the signal strength in an RSS-based ranging system. Similarly, in an ultrasonic ranging system, an attacker can gain an advantage by relaying messages over the faster radio-frequency channel [39]. Recently, it was shown that the PKES systems used in automobiles are also vulnerable to relay attacks [15]. In a relay attack, the attacker uses two proxy devices to relay the communications between two legitimate entities without requiring any knowledge of the actual data being transmitted; therefore independent of any cryptographic primitives implemented. Researchers were able to unlock the car and drive away even though the legitimate key was several hundred meters away from the car. Similar relay attacks were demonstrated on other radio-frequency based access tokens (NFC phones [16], Google Wallet [35]), even though the communication range for many such contactless systems is limited to a few centimeters.

Multicarrier phase-based ranging [8] is fast emerging as a cost-optimized solution for a wide variety of proximity-based applications. The low hardware complexity and their low power consumption make them suitable for power-constrained wireless sensor system applications. For example, the advent of internet of things has seen an increasing number of *smart and networked* devices being deployed ubiquitously where low power consumption is a key requirement. Today, multicarrier phase-based ranging solutions [1,6,41] that are compliant with prominent standards such as WiFi, ZigBee [5] and 6LoWPAN [21] are already being commercialized (e.g., warehouse monitoring, child-monitoring). Given the widespread deployment of 802.11 WiFi networks, several indoor localization and ranging schemes [4,12,41,43] that use the carrier-phase of the radio signals have been proposed. For example, Chronos [41] leverages the carrier phase information of the 802.11 WiFi signals to implement a centimetre-level localization and ranging system using commodity WiFi cards. The implications of distance modification attacks in scenarios where these systems are deployed in security-critical applications like access control to automobiles, critical infrastructure, and medical devices are significant and have not been investigated so far.

Therefore, in this work, we investigate the security of carrier phase-based ranging systems and demonstrate their vulnerability to distance modification attacks by exploiting the inherent physical properties of the signal. We focus on attacks which result in a decrease of the measured distance since these have been shown to be most relevant in a majority of security applications. Specifically, we make the following contributions: (i) We show that phase-based ranging, as well as its implementations, are vulnerable to a variety of distance reduction attacks.

To this extent, we describe three different attack realizations with varying degree of attacker complexity and evaluate their effectiveness under various conditions. We demonstrate the attack on a commercial multicarrier phase-ranging system and show that it is feasible to reduce the estimated distance significantly. Specifically, through our experiments we successfully reduced the estimated range to less than 3 m even though the devices were more than 50 m apart. We discuss possible countermeasures against these distance decreasing relay attacks and illustrate their limitations. We show how implementing countermeasures such as e.g., estimating rough time-of-flight, pseudorandom frequency hopping etc. only increases the system complexity without fully securing against distance decreasing attacks.

2   Background

2.1   Phase-Based Ranging

In phase-based ranging, two devices A and B measure the distance between them by estimating the phase difference between a received continuous wave signal and a local reference signal. For example, if device A (verifier) is measuring its distance to device B (prover), then the verifier begins ranging by transmitting a continuous wave carrier signal. The prover locks its local oscillator to this incoming signal and transmits it back to the verifier. The verifier measures the distance based on the difference in the phase of the received signal and its reference signal as shown in Fig. 1a. If the distance d between the verifier and the prover is less than the signal's wavelength i.e., $\frac{2 \cdot f}{c}$, where f is the frequency of the signal and c is the speed of light, the measured phase difference θ will be $\theta = 4\pi \cdot \frac{d \cdot f}{c}$. In order to unambiguously measure distances greater than the

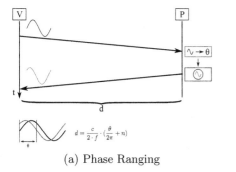

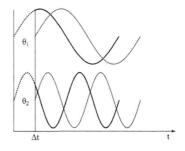

(a) Phase Ranging   (b) Multicarrier Phase Ranging

Fig. 1. (a) The prover locks its local oscillator to the verfier's signal and transmits it back to the verifier. The verifier then measures the distance based on the difference in the phase of the received signal and its reference signal. (b) Two signals of different frequencies that travel the same amount of time will experience a different phase shift.

signal's wavelength, it is necessary to keep track of the number of whole cycles elapsed. Therefore, the equation for measuring d becomes,

$$d = \frac{c}{2 \cdot f} \cdot (\frac{\theta}{2\pi} + n) \qquad (1)$$

where n is an integer which reflects the number of whole cycles elapsed. The need for keeping track of n is eliminated by using continuous wave signals of different frequencies.

2.2 Multicarrier Phase Ranging

Multicarrier phase ranging systems eliminates the whole cycle ambiguity by transmitting continuous wave signals at different frequencies (Fig. 1b). For example, the verifier first transmits a signal with a frequency f_1 to which the prover locks its local oscillator and retransmits the signal back to the verifier. At the verifier, the measured phase difference between the received signal from the prover and the verifier's own signal for this frequency (θ_1) is given by (from Eq. 1),

$$\theta_1 = 2\pi \cdot (\frac{2 \cdot d \cdot f_1}{c} + n) \qquad (2)$$

The verifier then transmits a continuous wave signal with a frequency f_2 and measures the phase difference (θ_2) as previously.

$$\theta_2 = 2\pi \cdot (\frac{2 \cdot d \cdot f_2}{c} + n) \qquad (3)$$

The distance d between the verifier and the prover can be unambiguously measured by combining Eqs. 2 and 3:

$$d = \frac{c}{4\pi} \cdot \frac{\theta_2 - \theta_1}{f_2 - f_1} \qquad (4)$$

Phase Slope Method: In real-world, using only two frequencies to measure the phase differences results in poor ranging accuracy. Therefore, it is typical for the verifier to measure the phase differences on more than two frequencies, thereby improving the system's resolution and accuracy. The phase difference measurements (θ_i) for each frequency (f_i) can be expressed in the form of $\theta_i = \frac{4\pi}{c} \cdot f_i \cdot d + N$.

If the phase differences are plotted on a phase vs frequency curve, the slope of the curve represents the distance d between the verifier and the prover (Fig. 2). In other words, the above equation can be seen as a straight line with the distance proportional to the slope of the line, $d = \frac{c}{4\pi} \cdot slope$. Figure 2a shows the measured phase differences vs frequency for two different distances. The phase-differences are straightened as is shown in Fig. 2b to calculate the effective slope and estimate the distance between the verifier and the prover.

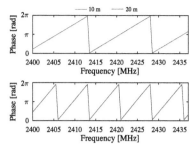
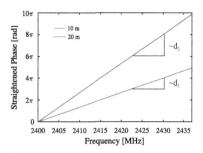

(a) The phase of the received signal.

(b) The straightened phase of the received signal.

Fig. 2. Phase versus frequency if the prover is 10 and 20 m away from the verifier.

2.3 Commercial Phase Ranging Systems

Due to their low-complexity and low power requirement, multicarrier phase ranging is fast emerging as a cost-optimized solution for a wide variety of applications. For example, multicarrier phase ranging has been proposed for the positioning of ultra-high frequency RFID systems [24,25]. More recently, Atmel released a radio transceiver [6] specifically targeting low-power applications and complying with standards such as ZigBee [5] and 6LoWPAN [21]. The radio transceiver AT86RF233 is designed for use in industry, scientific and medical (ISM) band applications and implements multicarrier phase-based ranging technique for distance measurement. Further more, leveraging the proliferation of 802.11 WiFi networks and the availability of carrier phase information directly from the network cards [18], several indoor localization schemes [4,12] have been proposed recently. For example, Chronos [41] leverages the carrier phase information of the 802.11 WiFi signals to implement an indoor localization and ranging system using commodity WiFi cards with centimeter-level precision.

The ranging procedure in these systems is typically divided into control and ranging signals. The control messages are all transmitted using the same preset frequency and is used to set up the necessary parameters and time synchronization for the ranging to take place. In addition, the verifier and prover exchange the results of the ranging using the control channel. The frequencies of the continuous wave signals used in the ranging ranges from 2.324–2.527 GHz with configurable hop sizes of 0.5, 1, 2, 4 MHz.

3   Security of Phase Ranging Systems

In this section, we investigate the security of phase ranging systems with a focus on the physical-layer distance decreasing attacks as these attacks have been shown to be detrimental to a number of security critical applications (e.g., NFC payment systems [16,35], keyless entry systems in automobiles [15]).

3.1   Distance Decreasing Relay Attacks

We consider two devices, a verifier and a prover that are able to communicate over a wireless radio link. The devices implement multicarrier phase measurement for ranging. The verifier measures and verifies the distance claimed by the prover. The verifier is trusted and is assumed to be honest. In this setting, distance decreasing attacks can be mounted in two ways: (i) by a dishonest prover trying to cheat on its distance to the verifier, referred to as an internal attack and (ii) by an external attacker who aims to shorten the distance between the verifier and the honest prover, referred to as a "distance-decreasing relay attack".

There are several ways for a dishonest or a malicious prover to mount an internal attack. For example, a malicious prover can cheat on the distance by not locking on to the correct phase when the verifier transmits its interrogating signal (from Fig. 1a). The malicious prover can simply respond with a signal that is phase incoherent with the verifier's reference signal; thus resulting in a different distance estimate at the verifier. Such internal attacks can only be prevented by distance bounding [9] and implementing distance bounding [29,31,33] require a number of hardware-software modifications that are incompatible with the existing design of phase ranging systems. In this work, we focus on external attackers under the assumption that both the verifier and the prover are trusted and honest. Such a scenario is most applicable to e.g., passive keyless entry systems where the key fob and the car are both trusted and assumed to be honest. However, we note that the presented attacks in this paper can be used by a dishonest prover to decrease its distance to the verifier without any loss of generality.

Additionally, it is important that the verifier and the prover exchange data that is cryptographically generated. Otherwise, it would be trivial for an unauthorized device to recreate the ranging signals and appear legitimate to the verifier. Throughout this paper, we assume that the verifier and the prover generate and exchange cryptographic data in order to prevent unauthorized ranging attempts.

3.2   Phase-Slope Rollover Attack

Recall that in a multicarrier phase ranging system, distance d is measured based on the estimated phase differences between two or more carrier frequency signals (Eq. 4). Thus, the maximum measurable distance i.e., the largest value of distance d_{max} that can be estimated using multicarrier phase-ranging system, depends on the maximum measurable phase difference $\Delta\theta_{max}$ between the two frequency signals. Given that the phase values range from 0 to 2π, the maximum measurable phase difference between any two frequencies is $\Delta\theta_{max} = 2\pi$. Substituting the values in Eq. 4 the maximum measurable distance is given by,

$$d_{max} = \frac{c}{4\pi} \cdot \frac{\Delta\theta_{max}}{\Delta f}$$
$$d_{max} = \frac{c}{2} \cdot \frac{1}{\Delta f}$$

$$(5)$$

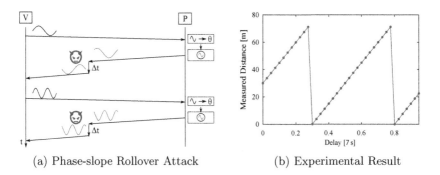

(a) Phase-slope Rollover Attack   (b) Experimental Result

Fig. 3. (a) The verifier's signal travels unaltered from the verifier to the prover. Then the prover locks onto the incoming signal and transmits a signal with the same phase back. The attacker intercepts the prover's signal and *delays each frequency by the same amount*. The verifier calculates an incorrect distance measurement based on the attacker's signal. (b) The verifier and prover are located 30 m from each other and the frequency hop size is 2 MHz (roll over happens at every 500 ns/75 m). The figure shows the measured distance at the verifier when an attacker uniformly delays all the frequencies by the same amount.

For example, if the frequency hop size is 2 MHz (Δf), the maximum distance measurable without any ambiguity is 75 m after which the measured distance rolls over to 0 m. Similarly for frequency hop sizes of 0.5, 1, 2, 4 MHz, the maximum measurable distances are 300, 150, 75 and 37.5 m respectively, beyond which there is a rollover.

In our phase-slope rollover attack, we demonstrate how an attacker can leverage the maximum measurable distance property of the phase ranging system in order to execute the distance decreasing relay attack. The phase-slope rollover attack is illustrated in Fig. 3a. The attacker is assumed to be closer to the verifier than the prover. For illustrative simplicity, here we assume that the prover is far away from the verifier or in other words, the verifier and the prover are not in communication range. During a phase-slope rollover attack, the attacker simply relays (amplify and forward) the verifier's interrogating signal to the prover. The prover determines the phase of the interrogating signal and re-transmits a response signal that is phase-locked with the verifier's interrogating signal. The attacker receives the prover's response signal and forwards it to the verifier, however with a time delay (Δt). The attacker chooses the time delay such that measured phase differences $\Delta\theta$ between the carrier frequency signals reaches its maximum value of 2π and rolls over. Considering the previous example of a system with the frequency hop size of 2 MHz, the measured phase differences $\Delta\theta$ rolls over every 500 ns. Figure 3b shows how the measured distance by the verifier changes depending on the delay Δt introduced by the attacker. In Sect. 4, we demonstrate the feasibility of such an attack on a commercial phase-based ranging system using a experimental setup. Furthermore, we show that an attacker can decrease the estimated distance to the minimum possible distance measurable (depends on sampling rate) by the system irrespective of the true distance of the prover.

3.3   RF Cycle Slip Attack

In this section, we describe an alternative way for an attacker to decrease the estimated distance of multicarrier phase ranging systems. In this attack, the attacker manipulates the phase of individual carrier frequencies in order to achieve the required phase difference between the carrier frequencies that will result in a reduced distance estimate at the verifier. This is in contrast to the phase-slope rollover attack described previously, where the attacker simply delays all the carrier frequencies by Δt until the effective phase difference between the carrier frequencies exceed the maximum value and rolls over.

In a RF cycle slip attack, the attacker delays each carrier frequency f_i by Δt_i. Recall that at the verifier, phase difference θ_i is measured between the prover's response signal and the verifier's reference signal for frequency f_i. Thus, an attacker can alter θ_i by delaying individual carrier signals by an amount that causes each phase measurement to change to a value θ_i'. The attacker chooses the new phase, θ_i', for each frequency such that the slope of the phase vs frequency graph decreases and thus decreasing the measured distance. Figure 4b illustrates the delays needed for individual carrier frequencies to cause a particular distance estimate by the verifier. One of the drawbacks of this method is that the attacker needs very high sampling rate. Alternatively, the attacker can use analog delay lines [26,40] to realize such a relay attack hardware.

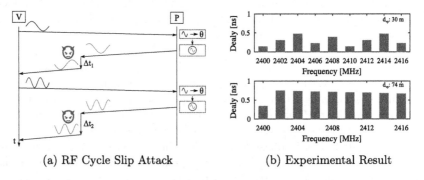

(a) RF Cycle Slip Attack   (b) Experimental Result

Fig. 4. (a) The verifier's signal travels unaltered from the verifier to the prover. Then the prover locks onto the incoming signal and transmits a signal with the same phase back. The attacker intercepts the prover's signal and *delays each frequency individually.* The verifier calculates an incorrect distance measurement based on the attacker's signal. (b) The delay of each frequency the attacker needs to introduce to decrease the distance to 1 m from 30 and 74 m respectively. Here d_{vp} is prover-verifier distance.

3.4   On-the-fly Phase Manipulation Attack

In this section, we present a *real-time phase manipulation* attack, in which the attacker is not required to delay the prover's response signal. In this attack, the attacker manipulates the phase of the prover's response signal by mixing it with specially crafted signal which results in an appropriate phase difference at the verifier. It is important to note that the real-time phase manipulation attacks keeps any possible data exchanged intact independent of the modulation scheme used.

Figure 5 illustrates the real-time phase manipulation attack. The prover receives the interrogating signal and re-transmits a phase-locked response signal back to the verifier. The prover's response $s_P(t)$ can be expressed as $s_P(t) = \cos(2\pi ft + \theta_{ap})$, where f is the signal frequency and θ_{ap} is the received phase of the prover's signal at the attacker. The attacker receives the prover's signal $s_P(t)$ and mixes it with a specially crafted signal $s_{if}(t) = \cos(4\pi ft + \theta_A)$ before relaying the signal to the verifier. Note that the crafted signal has twice the frequency of the prover's response signal. This is to account for the frequency conversion that occurs during mixing of two signals. The attacker's signal $s_A(t)$ (after filtering high frequency components) that is finally relayed to the verifier can be derived as follows:

$$
\begin{aligned}
s_A(t) &= s_{if}(t) \otimes s_P(t) \\
&= \cos(2\pi ft + \theta_{ap}) \otimes \cos(4\pi ft + \theta_A) \\
&\stackrel{LP}{=} \frac{1}{2} \cos\left(2\pi ft + \theta_A - \theta_{ap}\right)
\end{aligned}
\tag{6}
$$

From Eq. 6, we observe that the relayed signal $s_A(t)$ is identical to the prover's response signal except that it is shifted in phase. Recall that (Eq. 4), in a multi-carrier phase ranging system, the measured distance depends on the change in phase difference measurements between each carrier frequency. Thus, in order to modify the measured distance, the attacker needs to manipulate the phase of each carrier frequency such that it results in a reduced distance estimate. In

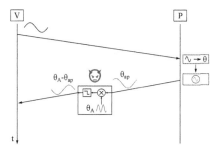

Fig. 5. Attacker phase shifts the prover's signal by first mixing it with a signal of twice the frequency and then low-pass filters the result before transmitting it to the verifier.

other words, the attacker has to choose θ_A such that $\theta_A - \theta_{ap}$ results in a phase difference estimate that corresponds to the reduced distance. In order to configure θ_A, the attacker must have apriori knowledge of the phase of the prover's signal when received at the attacker's location (θ_{ap}). The attacker can detect the phase of the verifier's signal when it received it and if the attacker knows the distance between the attacker and the prover, the attacker can estimate θ_{ap}. An alternative method for the attacker would be to actually detect (e.g., using a phase-locked loop) the phase of the prover's response signal. However, this would introduce unnecessary delays[1] in the relaying hardware thus making it less favourable for the attacker.

4   Experimental Evaluation

In this section, we evaluate the feasibility of the above described distance decreasing relay attacks using both commercial phase-ranging systems and simulations. First, we demonstrate the distance decrease relay attack on the commercially available Atmel AT86RF233 radio transceiver [6,32] that implements multicarrier phase-based ranging technique. Furthermore, we evaluate the feasibility of the attacks in different environmental conditions (e.g., noise, communication range) using simulations.

Table 1. Atmel hardware configuration for the attack

Parameter	Value
Frequency hop Δf	2 MHz
Ranging frequency range	2.403–2.443 GHz
Control message frequency	2.4 GHz
No. of frequencies	20
Signal strength	−17 dBm

4.1   Practical Demonstration of the Attack

Figure 6a shows the experimental setup used in evaluating the feasibility of executing the distance decreasing relay attack on the Atmel phase-ranging system. Our setup consists of two multicarrier phase ranging devices based on Atmel AT86RF233 radio transceiver. One device (1) acts as the prover while the other device (3) takes the role of the verifier. The verifier continuously measures the distance between the prover and itself and outputs the result to the connected laptop (4). The laptop was configured to continuously log the distance measurements. We used Atmel's default setup for configuring the ranging parameters[2] and list them in Table 1.

---

[1] Due to the settling time of PLLs.
[2] For the 50 m attack the transmit power of the Atmel devices was increased to −10 dBm.

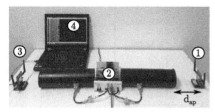

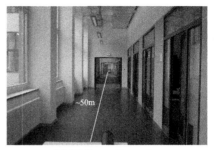

(a) Our Experimental Setup   (b) Hallway Location

Fig. 6. (a) Two Atmel AT86RF233 multicarrier phase ranging devices that function as the prover (1) and verifier (3), a laptop (4) that records the estimated distances and the attacker's hardware (2) comprising of a USRP [2] and two directional antennas. (b) Hallway in which the experiment took place.

Attacker Hardware. The attacker's hardware (2) consists of an USRP [2] and two directional antennas, one used for receiving the prover's response signal and the other for transmitting the attacker's signal to the verifier. The attacker setup was placed close to the verifier while the prover was placed at different distances to the verifier. We implemented the phase-slope rollover attack described in Sect. 3.2 in which the attacker delays all the carrier frequencies until the effective phase difference between the frequencies exceed the maximum value of 2π and rolls over. The verifier's interrogating signal was left unmodified and the attacker manipulated (delayed and amplified) only the prover's response signal. In order to minimize the processing delay due to the attacker's hardware, all processing was done directly on the USRP's FPGA, that included receiving, delaying and transmitting the signal. In other words, the host computer of the USRP was bypassed completely and the signal processing was done solely in the FPGA of the USRP. The delay from receiving to transmitting, caused by the USRP hardware, was 536.22 ns with a standard deviation of 1.83 ns. The USRP's host computer was only used to trigger the relay attack and for specifying the amount of delay to introduce into the prover's response signal. The delay was made configurable from the host and tuned at runtime to achieve the desired attack objective.

Experimental Results. We placed the prover at distances 30 m, 40 m and 50 m away from the verifier in an empty hallway. The prover and verifier were in communication range during the experiment and thus were able to estimate their true distance in the absence of the attacker. The results of our experiment are shown in Fig. 7. As can be observed, without the presence of the attacker (solid line), the verifier and the prover estimate their true distance. When the attack is triggered, the verifier's estimated distance begins to reduce. The gradual reduction is due to the verifier averaging the range estimates over a number of samples. We note that the experiment was carried out in a corridor (see Fig. 6b)

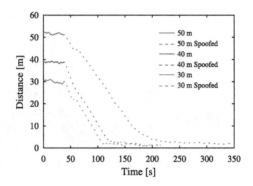

Fig. 7. Effectiveness of the distance decreasing relay attack where the prover and verifier are located 30, 40 and 50 m apart and the attacker attempts to decrease the distance.

with significant interference from other ISM band systems (e.g., WiFi). Even in such conditions, our attacker was able to reduce the distance estimate by more than 50 m.

Rollover Using Only Amplification. If two phase-ranging devices are further away from each other than the maximum unambiguous distance that they can measure an attacker can cause a roll-over by simply amplifying their signals. We simulated such and attack on the Atmel AT86RF233 radio transceivers. We placed the devices at roughly 53 m apart. When the devices were configured to use a frequency hop size of 2 MHz they correctly estimated their position. However, when configured to use a hop size of 4 MHz they incorrectly measured a distance of 15–16 m, which is consistent with the rollover being 37.5 m. Such an attack is simple to implement but of course the attacker can only reduce the distance rather than spoof the devices to a particular distance since the measured distance will be determined by the devices actual distance.

4.2   Theoretical Evaluation

In this section, we evaluate the effectiveness of the distance decreasing relay attack under various channel conditions using simulations.

Simulation Setup. For the simulations, we implemented the verifier, the prover and the attacker in Matlab. The multicarrier phase-ranging system was modelled exactly as described in Sect. 2.2. Similar to real-world phase ranging systems, the verifier uses multiple carrier frequencies in the ISM band as the interrogating signal. The range of frequencies used were 2.40–2.48 GHz with a configurable frequency hop of 1 MHz or 2 MHz. The phase of the verifier's interrogating signal is selected randomly for each frequency hop to simulate real-world behaviour. The prover measures the phase of the verifier's signal as in a real system and generates its response signal that is phase synced to the verifier's interrogating

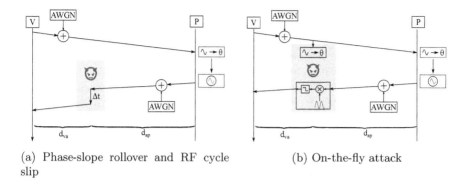

(a) Phase-slope rollover and RF cycle slip   (b) On-the-fly attack

Fig. 8. Simulation Setup: d_{va} and d_{ap} are the verifier-attacker distance and attacker-prover distance respectively. For the Phase-slope rollover attack (a) all frequencies are delayed equally but for the RF cycle slip attack each carrier frequency is uniquely delayed. In the on-the-fly attack (b), the attacker estimates the phase of the verifier's signal and uses it and knowledge of the distance to the prover to estimate the phase of the prover's signal when it arrives at the attacker. The attacker then mixes and low-pass filters the prover's signal to achieve the desired phase shift.

signal. For evaluating the effectiveness of the attack under noisy channel conditions, white Gaussian noise is added to both the verifier's and the prover's signal. The distances between the verifier, prover and the attacker were simulated by introducing propagation delays in the signal. For example, in order to simulate a verifier-prover distance of 30 m, the signals were temporally shifted by 100 ns before they were processed by the verifier or the prover.

The attacker was modelled depending on the type of attack evaluated. In the scenario of the phase-slope rollover and the RF cycle slip attack (Fig. 8a), the attacker only received and delayed the response signal from the prover appropriately before relaying it to the verifier. In the case of on-the-fly phase manipulation attack (Fig. 8b), the attacker estimates the phase of the verifier's signal to be able to estimate the phase of the prover's signal when it reaches the attacker. The attacker then mixes the received response signal with his locally generated signal as described in Sect. 3.4 to generate a attack signal that is appropriately shifted in phase in order to reduce the distance estimate while preserving the carrier frequency. The attack signal is low-pass filtered and relayed to the verifier.

Effect of Channel Noise. We evaluated the effectiveness of the various distance decreasing attacks described in Sect. 3 under different noise conditions. The evaluations were averaged over 100 different iterations for each SNR value in the set [0–30] dB. We compared the error in the estimated distance in an adversarial and non-adversarial scenario. The non-adversarial setting was simulated with the prover located 1 m away from the verifier without any attacker present. In the adversarial scenario, an attacker located 1 m away from the verifier relayed the signals between the verifier and the prover. The verifier and the prover were assumed to be out of communication range. Additive white Gaussian noise was

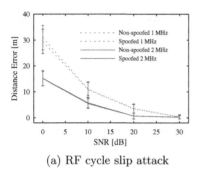

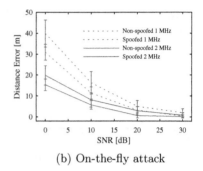

(a) RF cycle slip attack   (b) On-the-fly attack

Fig. 9. Distance measurement errors in a non-adversarial and during an attack. In the adversarial setting the prover and verifier are not in communications range. The non-adversarial measurements are when prover is located 1 m away from the verifier. During an RF cycle slip attack (a), the prover is located 30 m away from the verifier and during the OTF attack (b), the prover is located 74 m away from the verifier. The attacker tries to reduce this distance to 1 m in both the scenarios.

added to both the verifier's interrogating signal and the prover's response signal. Figure 9a and b shows the results for the RF cycle slip attacker and On-the-fly phase manipulation attacker respectively. We simulated the attacks for the commonly used frequency hop size of 1 MHz and 2 MHz. As seen in Fig. 9a for the RF cycle slip attack, there is little difference in the distance error between the adversarial and non-adversarial setting. However, the on-the-fly phase manipulation attacker performs slightly worse than the non-adversarial setting. This is because the attacker must estimate the verifier's phase under noisy conditions and any error in this estimation results in an incorrect phase shift.

Effect of Interference from the Prover. In certain scenarios, it is common that the verifier and the prover are in communication range and the verifier also receives the legitimate response signals in addition to the attacker's signals. In this set of experiments, we evaluated the effect of interference caused by the legitimate prover signals on the ability of the attacker to reduce the estimated distance. The amplitude and phase of the received signal at the verifier will depend on both the amplitude and phase of the attacker and the prover signals. For example, if the prover's signal is weaker than the attacker's, the effect on the estimated distance due to the legitimate prover's signal will be minimal. Figure 10 shows the deviation in the distance calculated by the verifier for different verifier-prover distances. In our simulations, the attacker was located 1 m away from the verifier and the prover's distance from the verifier was varied. The attacker's objective was always to force the estimated distance to be 1 m. It can be seen that the effect is negligible even if the prover is located at a distance of 10 m from the verifier.

Random Phase Manipulation Attack. An attacker can simply introduce a random phase change to the prover's signal, by either randomly delaying the phase of individual carrier frequencies or introducing a random phase change in the

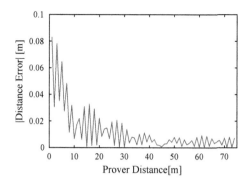

Fig. 10. The effect on measured distance when the verifier and prover are in communications range and the attacker does not correct for the effect from the prover's signal. The attacker is located 1 m away from the verifier and tries to decrease all true prover-verifier distances to 1 m.

on-the-fly attack. A naive phase-ranging system might simply try to linearly fit a slope to the measured phase which will result in an incorrect distance. Depending on the true distance of the prover and verifier, the attacker might thus achieve a distance reduction by simply randomly manipulating the phase. However, a verifier should be able to detect that the received phase is abnormal and thus surmise that any distance calculated from it would be incorrect.

5   Effectiveness of Countermeasures

In this section, we discuss possible countermeasures and their effectiveness in preventing the distance decrease attacks described previously.

5.1   Frequency Hopping

In order to execute the distance decreasing attack, the attacker must know the correct carrier frequency or be capable of re-transmitting the entire set of frequencies used for ranging. So, an obvious countermeasure would be to implement pseudo-random frequency hopping. In other words, the verifier and the prover change carrier frequencies based on a shared secret during the ranging process. However, it would be ineffective against attackers capable of listening and transmitting over the entire range of frequencies used by the system. With the widespread availability of low-cost, high-bandwidth amplifiers [11], it is reasonable to assume that the attacker would be capable of executing these attacks over the entire range of frequencies used by the multicarrier phase ranging system. Moreover, the attacker can listen to the verifier's interrogating signal that is necessary for the prover to lock and retransmit its response, thereby easily detecting the next frequency used by the verifier and prover to execute the ranging. Thus, a large bandwidth or a pseudo-random frequency hop sequence would be ineffective in preventing distance decreasing attacks.

5.2   Rough Time-of-Flight Estimation

An alternative countermeasure would be to realize a rough time-of-flight estimation. The verifier and the prover can implement a challenge-response mechanism i.e., the verifier modulates challenges in the interrogating signal that is transmitted to the prover. The prover demodulates the challenge, computes a corresponding response and modulates them back on the phase-locked response signal that the prover transmits back to the verifier. Assuming that the signals travel at the speed of light and knowing the prover's processing time, the verifier can estimate a coarse distance by measuring the time elapsed between transmitting the challenges and receiving the responses. It is well established that the precision of the time estimate depends on the system bandwidth [8]. Commercially available phase-ranging radio transceivers today are capable of exchanging data at a maximum rate of 2 Mbps. Assuming that the transceivers can estimate time-of-flight at this data rate, the maximum achievable precision is 500 ns, which translates to a distance estimate of 150 m. This means that, the system would potentially detect attacks in scenarios where the prover is greater than 150 m away from the verifier.

It is important to note that the time-of-flight estimate would only guarantee whether the prover is within, for example 150 m. This still leaves a lot of room for an attacker to execute a distance decreasing attack as phase-ranging would still be required in addition to rough time-of-flight for precise distance estimates. For example, the attacker can still reduce the estimated distance to 1 m even in scenarios where the prover is located 100 m away from the verifier. In order to improve the precision of the time-of-flight estimate, it is necessary to increase the system bandwidth. Given that one of the main advantages of multicarrier phase ranging is its low-complexity and cost, increasing the bandwidth for better time-of-flight estimate will potentially make the phase-ranging system redundant.

5.3   Phase-Shifted Response Signal

Even though implementing a time-of-flight estimation prevents rollover attacks, it is ineffective against an attacker capable of on-the-fly phase manipulation. As

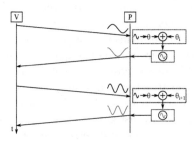

Fig. 11. The prover adds a phase offset to the received phase, which is known to the verifier.

described previously, in an on-the-fly phase manipulation attack, the attacker does not reduce the estimated distance by delaying the signals. The attacker mixes a locally generated intermediate frequency signal with the response signal in real-time to generate the attack signal (Fig. 11). In order to generate the intermediate frequency signal, the attacker must know the phase of the incoming response signal. The attacker can estimate the phase of the incoming response signal based on the prover's distance. The prover can potentially leverage this requirement for the attacker and introduce additional phase-shifts in its response signals. The phase-shifts introduced by the prover can be agreed apriori with the verifier and can be accounted for during the distance estimation. The attacker cannot guess the phase-shift that the prover introduces and thereby cannot generate a corresponding mixing signal to execute the distance reduction attack and thereby will result in large fluctuations in the measured phase difference across the carrier frequencies. Recall that, in an non-adversarial setting, the phase difference between the carrier frequencies would vary linearly.

However, an attacker can always detect the phase of the response signal and accordingly generate the mixing signal. Due to the required precision of the phase estimates, the verifier and the prover transmit their interrogating and response signals for a long duration of time 60–100 μs, in order to allow the phase-locked loop to converge to a precise value. This gives significant time for the attacker to detect the phase of the response signal and generate the necessary mixing signal for the distance decreasing attack. Furthermore, it is important to note that, this technique does not prevent the rollover attacks and hence has to be combined with rough time-of-flight estimation technique. This further increases the complexity of the system, thereby making other ranging techniques such as UWB-IR better suited for security critical applications.

6 Related Work

In this section, we discuss relevant related work in physical-layer security of wireless ranging systems beginning with the works closest to ours. Physical-layer attacks exploits the physical properties of the radio communication system and are therefore independent of any higher layer cryptographic protocols implemented. Several attacks ranging from simply relaying the signal between two legitimate nodes to injecting messages at the physical layer were demonstrated in the past. Clulow et al. [10] introduced physical-layer attacks such as early detect and late commit attacks. In an early detect attack, the attacker predicts the data bit before receiving the entire symbol while in a late commit attack, the attacker leverages the ability of the receiver to decode the bit even though the entire symbol has not been correctly received. The feasibility of these attacks on a ISO 14443 RFID was demonstrated in [19]. For short and medium-distance precision ranging and localisation, ultra-wide band (UWB) and chirp spread spectrum (CSS) emerged as the most prominent techniques [36] and were standardized in IEEE 802.15.4a [22] and ISO/IEC 24730-5 [3]. Flury et al. [14] evaluated the security of impulse radio ultra wide-band PHY layer. The authors demonstrated an effective distance decrease of 140 m for the mandatory modes of the standard. Poturalski et al. [27,28] introduced the Cicada attack on the impulse radio ultra wide-band PHY. In this attack, a malicious transmitter continuously transmits a "1" impulse with power greater than that of an honest transmitter. This degrades the performance of energy detection based receivers resulting in distance reduction and possibly denial of service. Ranganathan et al. [30] investigated the security of CSS-based ranging systems and demonstrated that an attacker would be able to effectively reduce the distance estimated by more than 600 m.

To the best of our knowledge, the security of phase ranging systems have not been evaluated in literature. However, there have been several works [13,24, 32,37,45] that evaluated novel high precision distance measurement techniques using carrier phase of a signal.

7   Conclusion

In this work, we investigated the security of multicarrier phase-based ranging systems and demonstrated its vulnerability to distance decreasing relay attacks. We demonstrated both through simulations and real world experiments that phase-based ranging is vulnerable to a variety of distance reduction attacks. We showed that an attacker can reduce the distance measured by a multicarrier phase-based ranging system to any arbitrary value and thus compromise its security. Specifically, we successfully reduced the estimated range to less than 3 m even though the devices were more than 50 m apart. We discussed possible countermeasures that can make it more costly and difficult for an attacker. However, these countermeasures increase the system complexity, do not fully secure against distance decreasing attacks and can be easily circumvented by strong attackers.

References

1. Rf ranging. http://www.rfranging.com/. Accessed 9 Apr 2016
2. Usrp n210. https://www.ettus.com/. Accessed 9 Apr 2016
3. ISO/IEC 14443: Identification cards - Contactless integrated circuit cards - Proximity cards - Part 2: Radio frequency power and signal interface (2010)
4. Abrudan, T.E., Haghparast, A., Koivunen, V.: Time synchronization and ranging in OFDM systems using time-reversal. IEEE Trans. Instrum. Meas. **62**, 3276–3290 (2013)
5. Alliance, Z.: Zigbee specification. ZigBee document 053474r13 (2006). http://www.zigbee.org
6. Atmel: Atmel avr2152: Rtb evaluation application software user's guide (2013)
7. Bahl, P., Padmanabhan, V.N.: RADAR: an in-building RF-based user location and tracking system (2000)
8. Bensky, A.: Wireless Positioning Technologies and Applications. Artech House, Norwood (2007)
9. Brands, S., Chaum, D.: Distance-bounding protocols. In: Helleseth, T. (ed.) EUROCRYPT 1993. LNCS, vol. 765, pp. 344–359. Springer, Heidelberg (1994). doi:10.1007/3-540-48285-7_30

10. Clulow, J., Hancke, G.P., Kuhn, M.G., Moore, T.: So near and yet so far: distance-bounding attacks in wireless networks. In: Buttyán, L., Gligor, V.D., Westhoff, D. (eds.) ESAS 2006. LNCS, vol. 4357, pp. 83–97. Springer, Heidelberg (2006). doi:10. 1007/11964254_9

11. Datasheets, M.P.A.: Minicircuits products

12. Exel, R.: Carrier-based ranging in ieee 802.11 wireless local area networks. In: 2013 IEEE Wireless Communications and Networking Conference (WCNC). IEEE (2013)

13. Farnsworth, B.D., Taylor, D.W.: High precision narrow-band RF ranging. In: Proceedings of the 2010 International Technical Meeting of The Institute of Navigation (2001)

14. Flury, M., Poturalski, M., Papadimitratos, P., Hubaux, J.P., Boudec, J.Y.L.: Effectiveness of distance-decreasing attacks against impulse radio ranging (2010)

15. Francillon, A., Danev, B., Capkun, S.: Relay attacks on passive keyless entry and start systems in modern cars (2011)

16. Francis, L., Hancke, G., Mayes, K., Markantonakis, K.: Practical NFC peer-to-peer relay attack using mobile phones. In: Ors Yalcin, S.B. (ed.) RFIDSec 2010. LNCS, vol. 6370, pp. 35–49. Springer, Heidelberg (2010). doi:10.1007/978-3-642-16822-2_4

17. Gupta, S.K.S., Mukherjee, T., Venkatasubramanian, K., Taylor, T.B.: Proximity based access control in smart-emergency departments (2006)

18. Halperin, D., Hu, W., Sheth, A., Wetherall, D.: Tool release: gathering 802.11 n traces with channel state information. ACM SIGCOMM Comput. Commun. Rev. **41**, 53 (2011)

19. Hancke, G.P., Kuhn, M.G.: Attacks on time-of-flight distance bounding channels (2008)

20. Hazas, M., Scott, J., Krumm, J.: Location-aware computing comes of age (2004)

21. Shelby, Z., Bormann, C.: 6LoWPAN: The Wireless Embedded Internet, vol. 43. Wiley, New York (2011)

22. The Institute of Electrical and Electronic Engineers: IEEE 802.15.4a-2007 Wireless Medium Access Control (MAC) and Physical Layer (PHY) Specifications for Low-Rate Wireless Personal Area Networks (WPANs) (2007)

23. Liu, H., Darabi, H., Banerjee, P., Liu, J.: Survey of wireless indoor positioning techniques and systems (2007)

24. Miesen, R., Kirsch, F., Groeschel, P., Vossiek, M.: Phase based multi carrier ranging for UHF RFID. In: 2012 IEEE International Conference on Wireless Information Technology and Systems (ICWITS) (2012)

25. Miesen, R., Parr, A., Schleu, J., Vossiek, M.: 360 degree carrier phase measurement for UHF RFID local positioning. In: 2013 IEEE International Conference on RFID-Technologies and Applications (RFID-TA). IEEE (2013)

26. Moon, Y., Choi, J., Lee, K., Jeong, D.K., Kim, M.K.: An all-analog multiphase delay-locked loop using a replica delay line for wide-range operation and low-jitter performance. IEEE J. Solid-State Circuits **35**, 377–384 (2000)

27. Poturalski, M., Flury, M., Papadimitratos, P., Hubaux, J.P., Boudec, J.Y.L.: The cicada attack: degradation and denial of service in IR ranging (2010)

28. Poturalski, M., Flury, M., Papadimitratos, P., Hubaux, J.P., Boudec, J.Y.L.: Distance Bounding with IEEE 802.15.4a: Attacks and Countermeasures (2011)

29. Ranganathan, A., Danev, B., Capkun, S.: Proximity verification for contactless access control and authentication systems. In: Proceedings of the 31st Annual Computer Security Applications Conference. ACM (2015)

30. Ranganathan, A., Danev, B., Francillon, A., Capkun, S.: Physical-layer attacks on chirp-based ranging systems. In: Proceedings of the Fifth ACM Conference on Security and Privacy in Wireless and Mobile Networks, WISEC 2012 (2012)
31. Ranganathan, A., Tippenhauer, N.O., Škorić, B., Singelée, D., Čapkun, S.: Design and implementation of a terrorist fraud resilient distance bounding system. In: Foresti, S., Yung, M., Martinelli, F. (eds.) ESORICS 2012. LNCS, vol. 7459, pp. 415–432. Springer, Heidelberg (2012). doi:10.1007/978-3-642-33167-1_24
32. Rapinski, J., Smieja, M.: Zigbee ranging using phase shift measurements. J. Navig. **68**, 665–677 (2015)
33. Rasmussen, K.B., Capkun, S.: Realization of RF distance bounding. In: USENIX Security Symposium (2010)
34. Rasmussen, K.B., Castelluccia, C., Heydt-Benjamin, T.S., Capkun, S.: Proximity-based access control for implantable medical devices (2009)
35. Roland, M.: Applying recent secure element relay attack scenarios to the real world: Google wallet relay attack. Computing Research Repository (2012)
36. Sahinoglu, Z., Gezici, S.: Ranging in the IEEE 802.15.4a Standard (2006)
37. Salido-Monzú, D., Martin-Gorostiza, E., Lazaro-Galilea, J., Domingo-Perez, F., Wieser, A.: Multipath mitigation for a phase-based infrared ranging system applied to indoor positioning. In: 2013 International Conference on Indoor Positioning and Indoor Navigation (IPIN). IEEE (2013)
38. Schiller, J., Voisard, A.: Location-Based Services. Elsevier, San Francisco (2004)
39. Sedighpour, S., Capkun, S., Ganeriwal, S., Srivastava, M.B.: Distance enlargement and reduction attacks on ultrasound ranging (2005)
40. Springer, A., Gugler, W., Huemer, M., Koller, R., Weigel, R.: A wireless spread-spectrum communication system using saw chirped delay lines (2001)
41. Vasisht, D., Kumar, S., Katabi, D.: Decimeter-level localization with a single WiFi access point. In: 13th USENIX Symposium on Networked Systems Design and Implementation (NSDI 16) (2016)
42. Xiang, Z., Song, S., Chen, J., Wang, H., Huang, J., Gao, X.: A wireless LAN-based indoor positioning technology. IBM J. Res. Dev. **48**, 617–626 (2004)
43. Xiong, J., Sundaresan, K., Jamieson, K.: Tonetrack: leveraging frequency-agile radios for time-based indoor wireless localization. In: Proceedings of the 21st Annual International Conference on Mobile Computing and Networking. ACM (2015)
44. Technologies, Z.: Sapphire Dart Ultra-Wideband (UWB) Real Time Locating System (2010)
45. Zhang, Y., Qi, W., Zhang, S.: The unambiguous distance in a phase-based ranging system with hopping frequencies. arXiv preprint arXiv:1403.1923 (2014)

Side Channel Analysis II

Single-Trace Side-Channel Attacks on Masked Lattice-Based Encryption

Robert Primas$^{(\boxtimes)}$, Peter Pessl, and Stefan Mangard

IAIK, Graz University of Technology, Graz, Austria
rprimas@gmail.com, {peter.pessl,stefan.mangard}@iaik.tugraz.at

Abstract. Although lattice-based cryptography has proven to be a particularly efficient approach to post-quantum cryptography, its security against side-channel attacks is still a very open topic. There already exist some first works that use masking to achieve DPA security. However, for public-key primitives SPA attacks that use just a single trace are also highly relevant. For lattice-based cryptography this implementation-security aspect is still unexplored.

In this work, we present the first single-trace attack on lattice-based encryption. As only a single side-channel observation is needed for full key recovery, it can also be used to attack masked implementations. We use leakage coming from the Number Theoretic Transform, which is at the heart of almost all efficient lattice-based implementations. This means that our attack can be adapted to a large range of other lattice-based constructions and their respective implementations.

Our attack consists of 3 main steps. First, we perform a template matching on all modular operations in the decryption process. Second, we efficiently combine all this side-channel information using belief propagation. And third, we perform a lattice-decoding to recover the private key. We show that the attack allows full key recovery not only in a generic noisy Hamming-weight setting, but also based on real traces measured on an ARM Cortex-M4F microcontroller.

Keywords: Lattice-based cryptography · Side-channel analysis · Single-trace attack · Number theoretic transform

1 Introduction

The current public-key infrastructure is threatened by progress towards large-scale quantum computing. Constructions based on RSA, DLP, or ECC, will succumb to Shor's algorithm [32], which is able to defeat these systems in polynomial time. While estimates on the availability of powerful enough quantum computers vary greatly–they range from 15 years [18] to never [31]–the threat is still taken very seriously. This is demonstrated by, e.g., NIST's current call for post-quantum secure proposals [19] and official recommendations regarding post-quantum security from the NSA [20].

© International Association for Cryptologic Research 2017
W. Fischer and N. Homma (Eds.): CHES 2017, LNCS 10529, pp. 513–533, 2017.
DOI: 10.1007/978-3-319-66787-4_25

When it comes to possible post-quantum secure algorithms, lattice-based cryptography appears to be a promising option and has garnered a lot of attention over the past decade. It proved to be versatile and efficient, as there already exist practical lattice-based constructions offering basic services such as public-key encryption, digital signatures, and key exchange. Furthermore, lattices also serve as the basis for new primitives such as homomorphic encryption.

A very popular building block for lattice-based constructions is the ring-variant of the Learning with Errors problem, RLWE [16]. Recent implementations of RLWE-based public-key encryption, e.g., [7,24,29], have shown that its performance can compete with (or even exceed) that of RSA and ECC-based systems on a large set of platforms.

While these results demonstrate practicality, the implementation-security aspect of lattice-based cryptography is still a vastly unexplored and open topic. Just like any other cryptographic algorithm, an unprotected implementation of RLWE-based encryption will succumb to side-channel attacks such as Kocher's Differential Power Analysis (DPA) [14]. Due to the large number of linear operations in the en- and decryption process, masking [5] appears to be a natural fit for protecting lattice-based cryptosystems against DPA. In fact, there already exist masked implementations of lattice-based encryption [21,26–28]. They also show that this countermeasure can be implemented with (relatively) little resource overhead.

However, especially for public-key primitives the Simple Power Analysis (SPA) security aspect is also of high importance. This is demonstrated by, e.g., the large number of single-trace attacks targeting implementations of RSA and ECC. Yet, for lattice-based cryptography this aspect has never been analyzed thus far. As implementation techniques for RLWE-based schemes differ drastically from those of established public-key constructions, there are new potential venues for such single-trace attacks.

Our Contribution. In this work, we are first to show that single-trace attacks are indeed a threat to implementations of lattice-based cryptography. We present a new side-channel attack on lattice-based encryption that can, given sufficient leakage, recover the private key using just the side-channel observation of a single decryption. Hence, it can also be applied to masked implementations to recover each individual share, recombine them, and still perform full decryption-key recovery.

Our attack targets the computation of the Number Theoretic Transform (NTT), which is an essential building block for almost all efficient implementations of lattice-based cryptography. Thus, the attack can be ported to not only different implementations of encryption, but also to implementations of other lattice-based constructions. Furthermore, the NTT is not the first target for a DPA attack and was thus less protected in earlier works [21].

Our attack is comprised of 3 main steps. First, we perform a side-channel template matching [6] on each modular operation performed during the inverse NTT in the decryption process. In the second step, we combine the information (probabilities of intermediates) of every operation in the entire NTT. We do so by representing the FFT-like structure of the NTT as a graph and then applying the belief propagation algorithm (BP). While the use of BP in context of side-channel attacks is not new [12,13,36], it hasn't been used in the context of public-key encryption yet. In our setting, a simple implementation of BP would require an impractical amount of time. Thus, we designed several optimizations that are targeted specifically at the NTT analysis. In our third and final step, we combine the knowledge of some secret intermediate values with the public key in order to reveal the private key. Concretely, we recover the full decryption key by first reducing the size of the public key and then performing a lattice decoding.

We evaluate our single-trace key-recovery attack in two different settings. First, we determine the success rate in a generic Hamming-weight leakage model. There, our attack has a high success rate, i.e., > 0.9, with noise parameters of up to $\sigma_l = 0.4$. Second, to verify our findings in practice we use real traces from EM measurements of an ARM Cortex-M4F software implementation. In this latter scenario, we were always able to recover the decryption key. Finally, we also show that our attack performs similarly well even if masking is used.

Outline. In Sect. 2, we recall lattice-based encryption, efficient implementations, as well as proposed side-channel protection mechanisms. Then, in Sect. 3 we recall soft-analytical side-channel attacks and belief propagation as its main tool. The three steps of the attack are then described in the following sections. The first step, a side-channel analysis of the NTT, is given in Sect. 4. Then, in Sect. 5 we efficiently combine all information using belief propagation. The third and final step, i.e., lattice decoding, is given in Sect. 6. We present and discuss the outcome and performance of our attack in Sect. 7.

2 Lattice-Based Encryption and Implementation

In this section, we recall lattice-based encryption, efficient implementation techniques, and previous works on side-channel countermeasures.

2.1 Lattice-Based Public-Key Encryption

In this work, we use the RLWE-based public-key encryption scheme proposed by Lyubashevsky, Peikert, and Regev [16]. It operates with polynomials over the ring $\mathcal{R}_q = \mathbb{Z}_q[x]/\langle x^n + 1 \rangle$ and is parameterized by the tuple (n, q, σ). n denotes the dimension of the polynomials, q is the modulus for the base field $\mathbb{Z}_q$, and σ is the standard deviation for a discrete Gaussian distribution D_σ. We use boldface lowercase letters to interchangeably denote polynomials in $\mathcal{R}_q$ as well as their respective coefficient vectors. We now recall the basic encryption scheme.

Key generation. For key-pair generation, two polynomials $\mathbf{r}_1$ and $\mathbf{r}_2$ are sampled from the discrete Gaussian distribution D_σ. Next, the public key $\mathbf{p}$ is computed as $\mathbf{p} = \mathbf{r}_1 - \mathbf{a}\mathbf{r}_2$. The uniformly-random polynomial $\mathbf{a}$ is either a global domain parameter or is also included in the public key. $\mathbf{r}_2$ is the private key, $\mathbf{r}_1$ is simply discarded.

Encryption. First, the plaintext $\mathbf{m}$ is encoded as $\overline{\mathbf{m}} \in \mathcal{R}_q$. In a simple variant of encoding, the bits of $\mathbf{m}$ are simply multiplied by $q/2$. Then, three error polynomials $\mathbf{e}_1, \mathbf{e}_2, \mathbf{e}_3 \in D_\sigma$ are sampled. The ciphertext is a pair of polynomials $(\mathbf{c}_1, \mathbf{c}_2)$ with $\mathbf{c}_1 = \mathbf{a}\mathbf{e}_1 + \mathbf{e}_2$ and $\mathbf{c}_2 = \mathbf{p}\mathbf{e}_1 + \mathbf{e}_3 + \overline{\mathbf{m}}$.

Decryption. The private key $\mathbf{r}_2$ is used to compute $\mathbf{m}^\star = \mathbf{c}_1\mathbf{r}_2 + \mathbf{c}_2$. The original message $\mathbf{m}$ is then retrieved by feeding $\mathbf{m}^\star$ to a decoder. There, one computes the distance of each coefficient in $\mathbf{m}^\star$ to $q/2$. If this distance is $< q/4$, then the decoder outputs 1, otherwise 0.

The above scheme only offers CPA security [8]. Recently, Oder et al. [21] presented an extension that also offers protection against adaptive chosen-ciphertext attacks (CCA2). However, the core encryption and decryption algorithms are identical, which is why we do not further discuss their CCA2 transformation here.

2.2   Efficient Implementation

There already exists a somewhat large body of work targeting efficient implementation of the above encryption scheme. They range from FPGAs to low-resource microcontrollers and desktop CPUs (e.g., [7,11,15,23,24,29]).

In our work we use the parameter set $(n = 256, q = 7681, \sigma = 4.51)$, which was introduced by Göttert et al. [11] and is used by all of the above implementations. The concrete security level provided by this instance is still under debate and estimates vary (see, e.g., [2,10,21]). However, all our later analysis can be extended to other parameters.

Number Theoretic Transform (NTT). If q is prime, n a power of two, and $q \equiv 1 \bmod 2n$ (which is the case for virtually all previously proposed parameter sets), then there exist primitive n-th roots of unity ω_n in $\mathbb{Z}_q$. This fact allows to efficiently compute polynomial multiplication in $\mathcal{R}_q$ by means of the Number Theoretic Transform (NTT).

The NTT is essentially a Discrete Fourier Transform (DFT) in a prime field $\mathbb{Z}_q$ instead of over the complex numbers $\mathbb{C}$. Thus, this transformation is efficiently computed using the same optimizations found in, e.g., the Cooley-Tukey FFT, and runs in time $\mathcal{O}(n \log n)$. The basic building block is a butterfly, which is comprised of a modular multiplication with a certain power of the chosen primitive root, a modular addition, and a modular subtraction. A total of $n \log_2(n)/2$ butterflies are computed during the NTT, as shown in Fig. 1 with the example of a 4-coefficient NTT. The required powers of the primitive root, i.e., $\omega_n^0 \ldots \omega_n^{n/2}$, are typically called *twiddle factors*. The inverse transformation (INTT) is computed by simply invoking the NTT with $\omega_n^{-1} \bmod q$. We denote $\widetilde{\mathbf{a}}$ as the NTT transformed of $\mathbf{a}$.

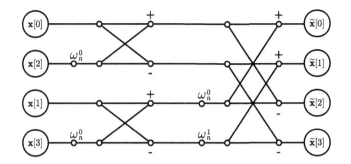

Fig. 1. A 4-coefficient NTT network comprised of 4 butterflies.

Multiplication of two polynomials $\mathbf{a}$, $\mathbf{b}$ can now be implemented as $\mathbf{c} = \text{INTT}(\text{NTT}(\mathbf{a}) * \text{NTT}(\mathbf{b}))$, where $*$ denotes a point-wise multiplication[1]. Thus, a product can be computed in time complexity $\mathcal{O}(n \log n)$ (compared to $\mathcal{O}(n^2)$ for non-ring-based LWE constructions). This is one of the main arguments behind the choice of the particular ring[2] $\mathcal{R}_q = \mathbb{Z}_q[x]/\langle x^n + 1\rangle$.

As proposed by Roy et al. [29], the encryption scheme described in Sect. 2.1 can be optimized by keeping the ciphertext in the NTT domain, i.e., transmitting $(\tilde{\mathbf{c}}_1, \tilde{\mathbf{c}}_2)$. This requires that the same primitive root ω_n is used for both encryption and decryption. Thus, it must be agreed upon and is public.

2.3   Side-Channel Protection of RLWE Encryption

Implementation security of lattice-based primitives is still a very new and open topic. Yet, there already exists some previous work that studies potential protection mechanisms. We now discuss these proposals.

Masking. Due to the linearity of the main operations, i.e., polynomial addition and multiplication, the masking countermeasure [5] is a natural fit for lattice-based public-key encryption. As proposed by Reparaz et al. [27,28] and shown in Fig. 2, the private key $\mathbf{r}_2$ can be split into two shares $\mathbf{r}_2'$, $\mathbf{r}_2''$ such that $\mathbf{r}_2 = \mathbf{r}_2' + \mathbf{r}_2''$ mod q. Then, polynomial multiplications, additions, and the inverse NTT can be computed on each share individually.

The final decoding step, i.e., recovering $\mathbf{m}$ from $\mathbf{m}^*$, is nonlinear and requires more care. Reparaz et al. designed a masked decoder which outputs two binary shares of the message, i.e., $\mathbf{m} = \mathbf{m}' \oplus \mathbf{m}''$, which can then be used as a shared key in a protected implementation of, e.g., the AES.

---

[1] This explanation is slightly simplified and omits, e.g., the scaling required for the negative-wrapped convolution. For a more thorough explanation, we refer to [29].

[2] There do exist proposals that are consciously avoiding the ring $\mathcal{R}_q$ and thus cannot use the NTT [3,4]. Still, NTT-enabled variants are the large majority.

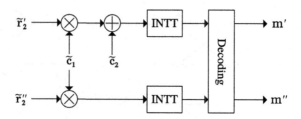

Fig. 2. Basic masking scheme for decryption

Shuffling and Blinding. In addition to masking, Oder et al. [21] propose to use further countermeasures. First, they suggest to use shuffling to protect the point-wise operations, i.e., point-wise addition and multiplication. They state that these operations are the most likely target for a DPA attack. Hence, the NTT is still computed in an unshuffled manner.

And second, they also use a randomization technique previously proposed by Saarinen [30]. They pick random values $a, b \in [1, q-1]$ and then multiply the coefficients $a \cdot \widetilde{c}_1, b \cdot \widetilde{r}_2$ and $ab \cdot \widetilde{c}_2 \bmod q$. Due to the linearity of the NTT, the mask can be removed by multiplying the output of the INTT with $(ab)^{-1} \bmod q$.

Additively Homomorphic Masking. In a later work, Reparaz et al. [26] present a different masking approach which exploits the additively homomorphic property of LWE. This, however, has some caveats. First, Reparaz et al. do not claim theoretical first-order security. And second, decoding errors are more likely. This makes their method incompatible with the CCA2-transformation presented by Oder et al. [21]. Due to these reasons, we do not further analyze the susceptibility of this approach to our attack.

3   Soft-Analytical Side-Channel Attacks

In this section, we describe Soft-Analytical Side-Channel Attacks (SASCA), which were proposed by Veyrat-Charvillon et al. [36] and are one of our main attack tools. The main goal of SASCA is to bridge the gap between divide-and-conquer approaches such as Kocher's Differential Power Analysis (DPA) [14] and algebraic/analytical side-channel attacks [25]. DPA offers low time and memory complexity as well as high noise tolerance, but is suboptimal in terms of data complexity (number of observed traces). Algebraic attacks are better in this second regard, but are very sensitive to errors and often require exact information.

Veyrat-Charvillon et al. first perform a side-channel template matching [6] on all intermediates computed during an AES encryption. For each intermediate T, the template matching returns a vector of conditional probabilities $\Pr(T = t|\ell)$, where ℓ denotes the observed side-channel leakage and t runs through all realizations of the random variable T. Then, they construct a factor graph of the AES and its specific implementation. This graph models the relationship between all intermediates. Finally, they use the belief propagation algorithm (BP) on this graph and the corresponding conditional probabilities to efficiently combine the information of all leakage points. We now give a brief description of this BP algorithm.

3.1 Belief Propagation

The belief propagation algorithm, originally proposed by Pearl et al. [22], allows to efficiently compute the marginalization of a function given its factorization. Our description and notation is largely based on that of MacKay [17, Chap. 26]. Given a function P^* of a set of N variables $\mathbf{x} \equiv \{x_n\}_{n=1}^N$ which is the product of M factors:

$$P^*(\mathbf{x}) = \prod_{m=1}^M f_m(\mathbf{x}_m),$$

where each of the factors $f_m\ (\mathbf{x}_m)$ is a function of a subset $\mathbf{x}_m$ of $\mathbf{x}$ and the x_n are defined over a domain $\mathcal{D}$, the problem of marginalization is defined as computing the marginal function Z_n of any variable x_n:

$$Z_n(x_n) = \sum_{\{x_{n'}\}, n' \neq n} P^*(\mathbf{x}),$$

or its normalized marginal $P_n(x_n) = Z_n(x_n)/Z$ with the normalization constant $Z = \sum_{\mathbf{x}} \prod_{m=1}^M f_m(\mathbf{x})$. The computational cost of marginalization is believed to grow exponentially with the number of variables N. The BP algorithm aims at reducing it by exploiting the factorization of the given function. BP is based on the message-passing principle. It requires a representation of the given function as a bipartite factor graph consisting of variable nodes and factor nodes. A variable node represents one of the variables $x_i \in \mathbf{x}$, whereas a factor node corresponds to one of the factors f_m. Edges are drawn between x_i and f_m iff the factor f_m depends on the variable x_i. The number of variables f_m depends on is the factors degree $\deg(f_m)$. The BP algorithm can be used to determine the marginal functions by iteratively executing the following two steps:

From variable to factor:

$$\mathfrak{q}_{n \to m}(x_n) = \prod_{m' \in \mathcal{M}(n) \backslash \{m\}} \mathfrak{r}_{m' \to n}(x_n), \tag{1}$$

where $\mathcal{M}(n)$ denotes the set of factors in which n participates.

From factor to variable:

$$\mathfrak{r}_{m \to n}(x_n) = \sum_{x_m \backslash n} f_m(\mathbf{x}_m) \prod_{n' \in \mathcal{N}(m) \backslash m} \mathfrak{q}_{n' \to m}(x_n), \tag{2}$$

where $\mathcal{N}(m)$ denotes the indices of the variables that the m-th factor depends on and $\mathbf{x}_{m \backslash n}$ denotes the set of variables in $\mathbf{x}_m$ without x_n.

After convergence, the marginal function $Z_n(x_n)$ can be computed as:

$$Z_n(x_n) = \prod_{m \in \mathcal{M}(n)} \mathfrak{r}_{m \to n}(x_n),$$

and the normalized marginals can be obtained from: $P_n(x_n) = Z_n(x_n)/Z$, where the normalizing constant Z is given by: $Z = \sum_{x_n} Z_n(x_n)$

If the factor graph is tree-like (acyclic), then the above algorithm returns the exact marginals. Unfortunately, in many real life applications the factor graphs contains cycles. To overcome this problem, the so called *loopy* BP algorithm has been proposed. It uses the same update rules and also iterates until convergence is reached, but uses a slightly different initialization. While it is not guaranteed that the loopy BP algorithm will return correct values or even converge, it usually gives sufficiently precise approximations of the marginals in many real-world applications. The exact conditions under which the loopy BP algorithm converges are still unknown. However, some sufficient conditions that ensure BP convergence have been stated by, e.g., Su et al. [35].

4   Attack Step 1: Side-Channels in an NTT Butterfly

After having covered all required preliminaries, we now start the description of our attack. As the first step of the attack, we exploit side-channel leakage during the computation of the inverse NTT in the decryption algorithm. Concretely, we first perform a profiling and then, for the actual attack, we match the recorded templates at each modular operation. As outcome, we obtain information in form of a probability vector for each such operation.

In order to understand how much information a side-channel adversary can realistically expect in this first step, and to also allow attack evaluation in a realistic scenario, we performed a side-channel analysis of the NTT on a real device. We now discuss our targeted implementation and platform, the measurement setup, and some results of this analysis. We additionally introduce a generic and simpler Hamming-weight leakage model, which will later be used in addition to real traces. First, however, we explain the choice of the NTT as the primary target for our attack.

4.1   The NTT as Side-Channel Target

The Number Theoretic Transform (NTT) is a main building block of virtually all efficient instantiations and implementations of lattice-based cryptography. Yet, thus far it has not been target of any side-channel analysis.

One potential reason is that the point-wise operations, i.e., multiplications and additions while computing $\tilde{\mathbf{c}}_1 * \tilde{\mathbf{r}}_2 + \tilde{\mathbf{c}}_2$, are the prime target for DPA attacks as they allow easy coefficient-wise prediction of intermediates [21]. However, this makes it tempting to use less protection in other parts, i.e., the NTT.

Also, the NTT is an interesting target for algebraic side-channel attacks. As seen in Fig. 1, it is comprised of many potentially leaking modular operations which are additionally connected by relatively simple algebraic rules. This makes it possible to combine the information of all leaking computations.

4.2 Measurement Setup and Implementation

We performed side-channel measurements on a Texas Instruments MSP432 (ARM Cortex-M4F) microcontroller on a MSP432P401R LaunchPad development board. A Cortex-M4F was also used by many other (protected) implementations of RLWE encryption [7,21,27].

We exploit the EM side channel. As shown in Fig. 3, we placed a Langer RF-B 3-2 near-field probe in proximity to the external core-voltage regulation circuitry. This setup does not require any on-chip spatial profiling. Also, we expect similar outcomes for a power analysis. Our microcontroller was clocked at its maximum possible frequency of 48 MHz.

Fig. 3. EM probe placed near the voltage-regulation circuitry of an ARM Cortex-M4F

We base our analysis on the implementation techniques used in the open-sourced Cortex-M4F implementation of de Clercq et al. [7], which is also the basis of the masked software implementation of Reparaz et al. [27]. They implemented modular multiplication with division, i.e., $a \bmod q = a - q \lfloor a/q \rfloor$, and use the integrated hardware multiplier and divider. On our platform, the multiplication runs in constant time, but the DIV instruction does not. Reduction after addition and subtraction is implemented using ARM conditional statements (IT instruction), which run in constant time.

4.3 Real-Device Side-Channel Analysis

The NTT is comprised of repeated applications of a butterfly. It is a reasonable assumption that all invocations utilize the same hardware, e.g., on-chip multiplier and divider, which results in loop-invariant leakage. To simplify our later analysis and attack evaluation, we thus opt for the following approach. We analyzed the butterfly operations, i.e., modular multiplication and addition/subtraction, independently. For the analysis, the operands were preloaded into registers and no leakage of loading and storing in memory was used. We prerecorded a set number of traces for each possible operand combination. For attack evaluation, we pick a random key, perform encryption/decryption, and for each of the $n \log_2(n)/2 = 1024$ butterflies invoked during decryption randomly pick one of the prerecorded traces that corresponds to the processed intermediate. We now describe our results for each operation in the butterfly.

Modular Addition and Subtraction. de Clercq et al. implement modular addition and subtraction with conditional ARM statements. While these run in constant time, they still leak their state through other side-channels. With a template matching, we were able to correctly classify virtually all, i.e., > 0.99, of the taken branches. In the following, we simply assume that an attacker can correctly detect whether a reduction happened or not. Alternatively, one could also include the probability that a reduction happened in the later analysis.

Modular Multiplication. In a butterfly, one of the inputs is multiplied by a known twiddle factor ω. There are $qn/2 = 983\,168$ possible operand/twiddle factor combinations, for each of them we prerecorded 100 traces. Thus, we use roughly 100 million traces for evaluation. For the attack, for each multiplication we randomly pick one out of the 100 traces corresponding to the processed value.

In the analysis, we use two steps to recover information on the unknown input. First, we exploit that the runtime of division is data dependent. We found that it depends on the bit size of the dividend, i.e., the value that is reduced (the divisor is the constant q). By measuring this time, which we do with a simple thresholding in the side-channel trace, we can immediately assign the intermediate to one out of several disjoint sets.

In the second step, we perform a side-channel template matching [6] to further narrow down the operand. For each multiplication, we use 99 (remaining) traces to build templates for each currently possible operand. The points-of-interest used for template building were determined with a t-test [9]. We then match all templates with the previously picked trace and compute the probability vector required for the next step of our attack.

In order to give a sense on the informativeness of our traces we use the metric proposed in [34], i.e., give the average entropy left in the probability vectors conditioned on the leakage $\Pr(T = t | \ell)$. Without leakage, we have an entropy of $\log_2(q) \approx 12.9$ bit. After performing the template matching, the average entropy decreases to roughly 7 bit. However, we observed that the outcome somewhat correlates with the value of the used twiddle factor. With $\omega_n^0 = 1$ we have a remaining entropy of about 10 bits. With larger values, we generally achieve better results.

4.4   A Simplified Model

In order to allow reproducibility, we additionally analyze the performance of our attack with a more generic and simpler model, namely the common noisy Hamming weight leakage model. That is, apart from knowing if a reduction happened after addition/subtraction, for each modular multiplication an attacker gets two samples of the form:

$$l = (\text{HW}(a) + \mathcal{N}(0, \sigma_l)) || (\text{HW}(a\omega_n^i \bmod q) + \mathcal{N}(0, \sigma_l))$$

a is the unknown input and ω_n^i the used twiddle factor. HW denotes the Hamming weight function and $\mathcal{N}$ the Gaussian distribution with standard deviation σ_l. For the experiments, we perform a 2-variate template matching on these simulated traces.

5   Attack Step 2: Belief Propagation in the NTT

In the above template matching, the adversary obtains side-channel information on each computed butterfly. In the second step of the attack, we now combine all this information over the entire (I)NTT. We efficiently do so by using belief propagation. We construct a factor-graph representation of the NTT, include the side-channel information in this graph, and then run BP until convergence is reached. With the constructed factor graph the runtime of a straight-forward BP implementation is impractical. Thus, we present optimizations designed specifically for the NTT factor-graph, which decrease the runtime drastically.

5.1   Factor-Graph Construction

A factor graph is a bipartite graph containing variable nodes and factor nodes. For modeling the NTT, we add one variable node x for each input/output of a butterfly. With $n = 256$, we thus have $n(\log_2(n) + 1) = 2\,304$ variable nodes.

   We then add three types of factor nodes: f_{ADD}, f_{SUB}, and f_{MUL}. As seen in Fig. 4, each type of factor occurs once per butterfly. Thus, there are a total of $3n \log_2(n)/2 = 3072$ factor nodes in the NTT model. Evidently, there are cycles in the graph shown in Fig. 4, so the loopy BP algorithm is needed.

   f_{MUL} is only connected to x_2 and thus has degree 1. Its purpose is to add the side-channel information gathered from the modular multiplication of x_2 with the known twiddle factor ω. We performed a template matching in Step 1 and therefore are given vector of probabilities conditioned on the leakage l. Thus we have:

$$f_{\text{MUL}}(x_{i_2}) = \Pr(x_2 = x_{i_2}|l)$$

   The factors f_{ADD} and f_{SUB} represent the modular addition and subtraction, respectively. They are connected to both butterfly-input nodes x_1 and x_2, and one of the two output nodes x_3 or x_4. Thus, their degree is 3. These factors model how variable nodes inside a butterfly are related, e.g., that $x_3 = x_1 + x_2\omega \bmod q$. Furthermore, we use these factors to include whether

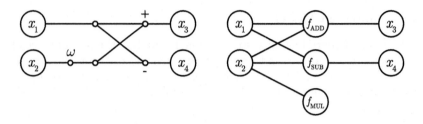

Fig. 4. Butterfly network (left) and our corresponding factor graph (right)

a reduction happened after addition or subtraction, respectively. For addition with subsequent reduction step, we have:

$$f_{\mathrm{ADD}}(x_{i_1}, x_{i_2}, x_{i_3}) = \begin{cases} 1 \text{ if } x_{i_1} + x_{i_2}\omega \equiv x_{i_3} \bmod q \text{ and } x_{i_1} + (x_{i_2}\omega \bmod q) \geq q \\ 0 \text{ otherwise} \end{cases}$$

If no reduction happened, then the second clause $x_{i_1} + (x_{i_2}\omega \bmod q) > q$ is simply negated. For subtraction with subsequent reduction, we have:

$$f_{\mathrm{SUB}}(x_{i_1}, x_{i_2}, x_{i_4}) = \begin{cases} 1 \text{ if } x_{i_1} - x_{i_2}\omega \equiv x_{i_4} \bmod q \text{ and } x_{i_1} - (x_{i_2}\omega \bmod q) < 0 \\ 0 \text{ otherwise} \end{cases}$$

Other Leakage Points. The factor-graph representation of the NTT is flexible, thus it can be modified to accommodate other leaking operations. One could, e.g., additionally include side-channel information of loading and storing in memory or leakage on operands of modular addition and subtraction.

5.2 BP Runtime Estimation Without Optimization

As it turns out, the runtime of a straight-forward implementation of BP on our constructed factor graph is impractically high. It depends on the number of iterations, the number of variable nodes and the size of their domain $\mathcal{D}$, as well as the number of factor nodes and their degree.

Each iteration of BP involves the invocation of the update rules $\mathfrak{q}$ (variable to factor, Eq. 1) and $\mathfrak{r}$ (factor to variable, Eq. 2) for all variable nodes and factor nodes, respectively. In our case the number of required iterations is small, e.g., ≤ 25, and therefore does not have a significant impact on the asymptotic runtime. The runtime of $\mathfrak{q}$ is also fairly low.

However, the same cannot be said for $\mathfrak{r}$. For a factor f with degree $\deg(f)$ and its inputs $x_1, \ldots, x_{\deg(f)}$ with domain $\mathcal{D}$, one can compute the update rule given in Eq. 2 by simply looping over all $|\mathcal{D}|^{\deg(f)}$ possible input combinations of f. In our scenario, we have factors $f_{\mathrm{ADD}}, f_{\mathrm{SUB}}$ with $\deg(f) = 3$ and variable nodes with domain size $|\mathcal{D}| = q = 7681$. When additionally multiplying with the number of f_{ADD} and f_{SUB} in our factor graph, then we reach a runtime of $\approx 2^{49}$ for a single iteration. Reducing from cubic to quadratic runtime can be done by only considering triplets where f_{ADD}, f_{SUB} can be 1, but this still amounts to $\approx 2^{37}$ operations. Obviously, both numbers are not very practical and optimizations are needed.

5.3 Runtime Optimizations

In Algorithm 1, we show an optimization that can decrease the runtime of $\mathfrak{r}$ for all factor nodes of degree 3 in the factor graph, i.e. f_{ADD} and f_{SUB}, drastically. We show it on the example of a factor node of type f_{ADD}. A slight variation of the presented algorithm can be used to optimize f_{SUB}.

Algorithm 1. Efficient BP for Modular Addition

Input:

$\quad \mathfrak{q}_a, \mathfrak{q}_b, \mathfrak{q}_c \qquad$ Incoming messages from summands and result node

$\quad$ Reduction $\qquad$ True if a reduction step was executed

Output:

$\quad \mathfrak{r}_a, \mathfrak{r}_b, \mathfrak{r}_c \qquad$ Outgoing messages for summands and result node

1: $\tilde{\mathbf{a}} = \mathrm{FFT}_{2q}(\mathfrak{q}_a)$, $\tilde{\mathbf{b}} = \mathrm{FFT}_{2q}(\mathfrak{q}_b)$, $\tilde{\mathbf{c}} = \mathrm{FFT}_{2q}(\mathfrak{q}_c)$
2: $\mathbf{t}_a = \mathrm{IFFT}_{2q}(\mathrm{CONJ}(\tilde{\mathbf{b}}) * \tilde{\mathbf{c}})$
3: $\mathbf{t}_b = \mathrm{IFFT}_{2q}(\mathrm{CONJ}(\tilde{\mathbf{a}}) * \tilde{\mathbf{c}})$
4: $\mathbf{t}_c = \mathrm{IFFT}_{2q}(\tilde{\mathbf{a}} * \tilde{\mathbf{b}})$
5: **if** Reduction **then**
6: $\quad \mathfrak{r}_a = \mathbf{t}_a[q \ldots 2q - 1]$, $\mathfrak{r}_b = \mathbf{t}_b[q \ldots 2q - 1]$, $\mathfrak{r}_c = \mathbf{t}_c[q \ldots 2q - 1]$
7: **else**
8: $\quad \mathfrak{r}_a = \mathbf{t}_a[0 \ldots q - 1]$, $\mathfrak{r}_b = \mathbf{t}_b[0 \ldots q - 1]$, $\mathfrak{r}_c = \mathbf{t}_c[0 \ldots q - 1]$

Our optimization uses the fact that update rules for input/output distributions of modular additions/subtractions can be efficiently expressed in matrix-vector notation. Consider the addition $a + b = c \bmod q$, with $\mathfrak{q}_a, \mathfrak{q}_b, \mathfrak{q}_b$ the incoming messages from the corresponding variable nodes. Each such message is a q-dimensional vector assigning a probability to each value in $\mathcal{D}$, we say that $a_i = \mathfrak{q}_{a_i} = \Pr(a = i)$. The output $\mathfrak{r}_c$ depends on $\mathfrak{q}_a, \mathfrak{q}_b$ and an entry $c_k^* = \mathfrak{r}_{c_k}$ can be computed as the sum over all $a_i b_j$ with $i + j \equiv k \bmod q$. The whole update can be written in matrix-vector notation:

$$
\begin{bmatrix}
a_0 & a_{q-1} & \cdots & a_2 & a_1 \\
a_1 & a_0 & a_{q-1} & & a_2 \\
\vdots & a_1 & a_0 & \ddots & \vdots \\
a_{q-2} & & \ddots & \ddots & a_{q-1} \\
a_{q-1} & a_{q-2} & \cdots & a_1 & a_0
\end{bmatrix}
\cdot
\begin{bmatrix}
b_0 \\
b_1 \\
\vdots \\
b_{q-2} \\
b_{q-1}
\end{bmatrix}
=
\begin{bmatrix}
c_0^* \\
c_1^* \\
\vdots \\
c_{q-2}^* \\
c_{q-1}^*
\end{bmatrix},
$$

where the columns of the left matrix are circular shifts of q_a. The above equation can be rewritten as a circular convolution $q_a \star q_b$, which can be efficiently computed using the FFT and the circular convolution theorem. Thus, we have :

$$r_c = q_a \star q_b = \mathrm{IFFT}_q(\mathrm{FFT}_q(q_a) * \mathrm{FFT}_q(q_b)).$$

The update rules for r_a and r_b can be obtained similarly by additionally using complex conjugations CONJ, as shown in Algorithm 1. Recall that we also include whether a reduction happened during modular addition and subtraction. This can be efficiently done by replacing the q-coefficient FFT with a $2q$-coefficient FFT and by using only either the upper or lower half of the IFFT output.

The runtime of computing r for the degree-3 factor nodes is now reduced to $\mathcal{O}(q \log q)$, since the only runtime relevant operations are FFTs. This allows us to perform one iteration of the BP algorithm for our whole factor graph in about one minute using a single core of an Intel Core i7-5600U CPU.

5.4   BP on Subgraphs

In our experiments, we found that applying BP to the whole NTT factor graph does not yield satisfactory results. While we can narrow down values, the outcome was not sufficient for key recovery. Yet, we were able to identify two problems and show how to circumvent them by applying BP only to subgraphs.

Uneven availability of side-channel information. The template attack on multiplication is a primary source of information. Yet, multiplications are not spread evenly across the NTT, as illustrated in Fig. 5a (also compare to Fig. 1). Each cell of this figure corresponds to one variable node. White variables are multiplied with a twiddle factor, black ones are not. Due to the lack of multiplications and its side-channel information in the top-right corner, the BP algorithm cannot recover these variable with high-enough certainty.

Varying outcome of the template attack. As already pointed out in Sect. 4.3, the performance of the template attack depends on the used twiddle factor. In the first NTT layer, one always multiplies with $\omega_n^0 = 1$. Even if this multiplication is not optimized out, the fact that no reduction is performed leads to little leakage.

We circumvent these two problems by applying BP not on the whole NTT graph, but instead only on disjoint subgraphs. As depicted in Fig. 5b, we have subgraphs FG 1, FG 2, and FG 3. These do not include the first layer and have a higher ratio of observed to unobserved variables (compared to the full graph). Thus, applying BP to these subgraphs gives significantly better results.

After convergence is reached on all 3 graphs, we perform a classification, i.e., pick the most likely value, on certain variable nodes. Concretely, we use variables from layer 6 (output of layer 5 and input of layer 6). This is the last layer of FG 1 and variables in later layers are usually recovered with higher confidence. As shown in Fig. 5c, we use the 192 variables with indices 32...128 and 160...255.

If masking is used, then we have to perform BP twice to get the intermediates in both invocations of the INTT. The unmasked intermediates can be computed by simply adding the recovered values of both INTTs.

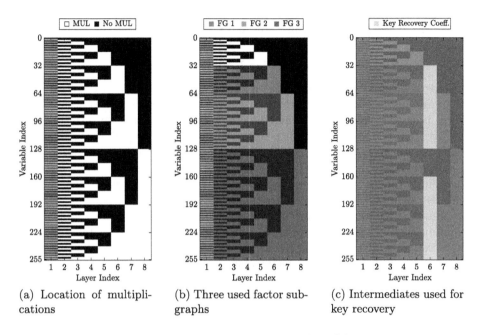

(a) Location of multiplications

(b) Three used factor subgraphs

(c) Intermediates used for key recovery

Fig. 5. Representation of the NTT and used factors

6 Attack Step 3: Lattice Decoding

Due to applying BP only on subgraphs, we cannot recover the full INTT input $\tilde{\mathbf{c}}_1 * \tilde{\mathbf{r}}_2 + \tilde{\mathbf{c}}_2$. Hence, the decryption key $\tilde{\mathbf{r}}_2$ (or equivalently $\mathbf{r}_2$) cannot be determined with simple linear algebra and another step is needed. In this third and final attack step, we combine the recovered intermediates with the public key. First, we create linear equations in the intermediates and $\mathbf{r}_2$ and use them to decrease the rank of the lattice spanned by the public key $(\mathbf{a}, \mathbf{p})$. Then, we use lattice-basis reduction and decoding to find $\mathbf{r}_2$ in the reduced-rank lattice.

6.1 Generating Linear Equations in the Key

We use the recovered intermediates to construct linear equations in the private key $\mathbf{r}_2$. Polynomial multiplication in $\mathcal{R}_q$ can be written as a matrix-vector product. We write the INTT output as $\mathbf{m}^\star = \mathbf{c}_1\mathbf{r}_2 + \mathbf{c}_2 = \mathbf{C}_1\mathbf{r}_2 + \mathbf{c}_2$, where the columns of matrix $\mathbf{C}_1$ are nega-cyclic rotations of $\mathbf{c}_1$. All operations inside the (I)NTT are linear, thus this system can be transformed to describe any of its intermediates. Concretely, we transform it such that it describes the recovered values of the sixth INTT layer.

We transform the system by performing a partial reversal of the INTT. We revert 3 butterfly stages by computing $x_1 = (x_3 + x_4)/2 \bmod q$ and $x_2 = (x_3 - x_4)/(2\omega)$ (cf. Fig. 4). We end up with a system of form $\mathbf{C}'_1 \mathbf{r}_2 + \mathbf{c}'_2 = \mathbf{x}$, with $\mathbf{x}$ being the 192 recovered intermediates and $\mathbf{C}'_1$, $\mathbf{c}'_2$ the transformed coefficients.

6.2   Key Recovery Using Lattice Reduction

The decryption key $\mathbf{r}_2$ is finally recovered by combining the above system with the information embedded in the public key $(\mathbf{a}, \mathbf{p})$. Recall that $\mathbf{p} = \mathbf{r}_1 - a\mathbf{r}_2$. As $\mathbf{r}_1$ is small (it is sampled from a discrete Gaussian distribution with small σ), we have that $\mathbf{p} \approx -a\mathbf{r}_2$. Thats is, $\mathbf{p}$ is close to the vector $-a\mathbf{r}_2$ which is part of the q-ary lattice spanned by the columns of $\mathbf{A}$ (the matrix consisting of nega-cyclic rotations of $\mathbf{a}$). Hence, the recovery of $\mathbf{r}_2$ can be seen as a bounded-distance decoding problem. The chosen system-parameters (n, q, σ) ensure that solving this decoding problem is not feasible without further information.

However, by incorporating the linear equations from above the problem can be reduced to a size that is solvable. We substitute the 192 equations $\mathbf{C}'_1 \mathbf{r}_2 + \mathbf{c}'_2 = \mathbf{x}$ into $\mathbf{p} = \mathbf{r}_1 - \mathbf{A}\mathbf{r}_2$ to get some $\mathbf{p}' = \mathbf{r}_1 - \mathbf{A}'\mathbf{r}'_2$. The number of columns of $\mathbf{A}'$, and hence the rank of the spanned lattice, is now reduced to $256 - 192 = 64$.

We then search for the closest vector to $\mathbf{p}'$ by solving a shortest-vector problem. Concretely, we search for the error term $\mathbf{r}_1$ (or $-\mathbf{r}_1$) as an unusually short vector in the lattice generated by $(\mathbf{A}'\|\mathbf{p}')$. This approach of solving the lattice decoding problem is described by, e.g., Albrecht et al. [1]. The short vector is recovered using the BKZ lattice basis reduction algorithm, we use the implementation provided by Shoup's NTL [33]. We invoke BKZ with a blocksize of 25, but abort reduction as soon as a candidate for $\mathbf{r}_1$, i.e., a vector with a small enough norm, is found.

After that, one can compute the private key $\mathbf{r}_2$ by solving the linear system $\mathbf{p} = \mathbf{r}_1 - a\mathbf{r}_2$ for both recovered $\mathbf{r}_1$ and $-\mathbf{r}_1$. The correct $\mathbf{r}_2$ is the one that follows the distribution used for key generation. That is, we pick the smaller out of the two solutions.

Performance of Decoding. We tested the correctness and performance of this key-recovery approach by performing well over 1 000 experiments. In each of them we use the correct intermediates (cf. Fig. 5c) and only perform the decoding step. All our experiments were successful. The average runtime on a single core of a Xeon E5-2699v4 CPU is approximately 45 s.

This decoding approach is not limited to using exactly 192 recovered intermediates, it can be invoked with any number of coefficients. However, the runtime of decoding will increase if fewer values are available. For instance, with 160 recovered intermediates the average runtime is 5 min and thus still well within practicality. Below that, however, it increases drastically. With 150 values, it reaches multiple hours. Experiments with 146 or fewer coefficients were not successful after 1 full day of computation.

7 Attack Results and Conclusion

Our attack consists of subsequent execution of the three attack steps described in the previous sections. We now present the outcome. First, we evaluate the attack using real traces. We illustrate an exemplary outcome and give a success rate. Then, we give the success rate for the Hamming-weight model with varying noise-parameter σ_l, both with and without masking applied.

7.1 Real Device

With real traces obtained from the setup described in Sect. 4, we have the following results. Figure 6 illustrates an exemplary outcome of template-matching and the subsequent belief propagation on the subgraph FG 3 (cf. Sect. 5.4). For each variable node, we color-code the entropy of the probability vector. For black nodes, the probability distribution is close to uniform, whereas for white nodes one value has reached probability close to 1. After 1 iteration (Fig. 6a), the probability distributions essentially correspond to the direct output of the template matching. After 20 iterations of BP (Fig. 6c), the network has converged and almost all intermediates are determined with very high probability.

Lattice decoding is successful if all of the 192 intermediates used for key-recovery are correct. After observing Fig. 6, it should not come as a surprise that all our key-recovery experiments in the real-trace setting were successful. The success rate, i.e., the probability that all used coefficients are correct, is 1.

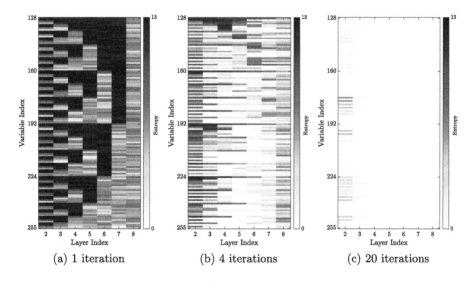

(a) 1 iteration   (b) 4 iterations   (c) 20 iterations

Fig. 6. FG 3: entropy after set number of iterations of BP

7.2 Hamming-Weight Model

In order to get a broader and more generic analysis of our attack, we also tested it with a noisy Hamming-weight model (cf. Sect. 4.4). We rerun all tests with varying noise parameter σ_l. The outcome is illustrated in Fig. 7, where we show the success rate and the average entropy (after template matching) for each tested value of σ_l. We give the entropy to allow at least a rough comparison to the real-trace setting.

In the non-masked case, we have a high single-trace success rate up to $\sigma_l = 0.4$ or 0.5, then it drops drastically. Note, however, that an attacker that can observe multiple decryptions can decrease the observed σ_l by averaging the traces. In the masked setting, key-recovery is successful if the correct intermediates are recovered in both invocations of the inverse NTT (see Fig. 2). Only then their sum is equal to the unmasked value. Thus, the expected success rate is squared, which is confirmed by our results. Obviously, averaging cannot be done if masking is used.

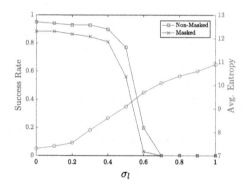

Fig. 7. Success rates in the Hamming-weight leakage model

7.3 Conclusion

Our attack clearly shows that SPA security of lattice-based schemes cannot be neglected and that relying on masking alone is not sufficient. Implementation techniques that are vastly different to established constructions such as RSA and ECC open up new venues in this regard. In fact, the regular structure of the NTT allows to efficiently combine leakage of the entire decryption process. Furthermore, each recovered intermediate can be used to decrease the difficulty of key-recovery with the public key. And while this work focuses on lattice-based encryption, our attack can be adapted to any other implementation of lattice-based cryptography which employs the NTT.

When it comes to potential countermeasures, masking appears to be effective against DPA, yet it does not prevent our attack. Thus, additional countermeasures should be implemented and will now be discussed.

Possible Countermeasures. One of the first measures to strengthen an implementation against SPA attacks is to ensure a constant runtime and control flow. In our side-channel analysis of a real device, we exploit timing differences stemming from the DIV operation invoked during modular reduction. There do exist constant-time alternatives, as already shown by Oder et al. [21].

Like many other algebraic attacks, our key recovery can be thwarted by employing shuffling. Concretely, the operations inside the NTT, e.g., the order in which the butterflies are processed within one NTT layer, need to be shuffled. Shuffling only point-wise operations, as proposed by Oder et al., clearly does not hamper our attack. Other hiding countermeasures, such as the random insertion of dummy operations inside the NTT, can also make our attack harder.

Oder et al. also propose to use a blinding countermeasure (cf. Sect. 2.3). Our attack still applies, but needs an additional step and potentially a different selection of recovered intermediates. Concretely, it requires that a sufficient amount of the INTT output coefficients are recoverable or can be computed from the recovered intermediates. Then, one can test if the distribution of the unblinded INTT output, i.e., after multiplication with $ab^{-1} \bmod q$, corresponds to that of a valid $\mathbf{m}^\star$ (centered around 0 and $q/2$). For a non-masked implementation, or if the same blinding values a, b are reused for both shares, then one can run through all $q - 1$ possibilities of $ab \bmod q$. If different a, b are used for both shares, then one needs to try all $(q - 1)^2$ combinations. With our parameters, this can be easily done within a minute. When using 64 output coefficients, this always returned the correct blinding values in our tests. Hence, this countermeasure does not significantly increase single-trace security. It, however, prevents averaging in the non-masked scenario.

Acknowledgements. This work has been supported by the Austrian Research Promotion Agency (FFG) under project SCALAS (grant number 845589) and under the COMET K-Project DeSSnet (grant number 862235).

References

1. Albrecht, M.R., Fitzpatrick, R., Göpfert, F.: On the efficacy of solving LWE by reduction to unique-SVP. In: Lee, H.-S., Han, D.-G. (eds.) ICISC 2013. LNCS, vol. 8565, pp. 293–310. Springer, Cham (2014). doi:10.1007/978-3-319-12160-4_18
2. Albrecht, M.R., Player, R., Scott, S.: On the concrete hardness of learning with errors. J. Math. Cryptol. **9**(3), 169–203 (2015)
3. Bernstein, D.J., Chuengsatiansup, C., Lange, T., van Vredendaal, C.: NTRU prime. IACR Cryptology ePrint Archive **2016**, 461 (2016)
4. Bos, J.W., Costello, C., Ducas, L., Mironov, I., Naehrig, M., Nikolaenko, V., Raghunathan, A., Stebila, D.: Frodo: take off the ring! practical, quantum-secure key exchange from LWE. In: Weippl, E.R., Katzenbeisser, S., Kruegel, C., Myers, A.C., Halevi, S. (eds.) CCS 2016, pp. 1006–1018. ACM (2016)
5. Chari, S., Jutla, C.S., Rao, J.R., Rohatgi, P.: Towards sound approaches to counteract power-analysis attacks. In: Wiener, M. (ed.) CRYPTO 1999. LNCS, vol. 1666, pp. 398–412. Springer, Heidelberg (1999). doi:10.1007/3-540-48405-1_26

6. Chari, S., Rao, J.R., Rohatgi, P.: Template attacks. In: Kaliski, B.S., Koç, K., Paar, C. (eds.) CHES 2002. LNCS, vol. 2523, pp. 13–28. Springer, Heidelberg (2003). doi:10.1007/3-540-36400-5_3

7. de Clercq, R., Roy, S.S., Vercauteren, F., Verbauwhede, I.: Efficient software implementation of ring-lwe encryption. In: Nebel, W., Atienza, D. (eds.) DATE 2015, pp. 339–344. ACM (2015)

8. Fluhrer, S.R.: Cryptanalysis of ring-lwe based key exchange with key share reuse. IACR Cryptology ePrint Archive **2016**, 85 (2016)

9. Gierlichs, B., Lemke-Rust, K., Paar, C.: Templates vs. stochastic methods. In: Goubin, L., Matsui, M. (eds.) CHES 2006. LNCS, vol. 4249, pp. 15–29. Springer, Heidelberg (2006). doi:10.1007/11894063_2

10. Göpfert, F., van Vredendaal, C., Wunderer, T.: A quantum attack on lwe with arbitrary error distribution. Cryptology ePrint Archive, Report 2017/221 (2017)

11. Göttert, N., Feller, T., Schneider, M., Buchmann, J., Huss, S.: On the design of hardware building blocks for modern lattice-based encryption schemes. In: Prouff, E., Schaumont, P. (eds.) CHES 2012. LNCS, vol. 7428, pp. 512–529. Springer, Heidelberg (2012). doi:10.1007/978-3-642-33027-8_30

12. Grosso, V., Standaert, F.-X.: ASCA, SASCA and DPA with enumeration: which one beats the other and when? In: Iwata, T., Cheon, J.H. (eds.) ASIACRYPT 2015. LNCS, vol. 9453, pp. 291–312. Springer, Heidelberg (2015). doi:10.1007/978-3-662-48800-3_12

13. Grosso, V., Standaert, F.: Masking proofs are tight (and how to exploit it in security evaluations). IACR Cryptology ePrint Archive **2017**, 116 (2017)

14. Kocher, P., Jaffe, J., Jun, B.: Differential power analysis. In: Wiener, M. (ed.) CRYPTO 1999. LNCS, vol. 1666, pp. 388–397. Springer, Heidelberg (1999). doi:10.1007/3-540-48405-1_25

15. Liu, Z., Seo, H., Sinha Roy, S., Großschädl, J., Kim, H., Verbauwhede, I.: Efficient ring-LWE encryption on 8-bit AVR processors. In: Güneysu, T., Handschuh, H. (eds.) CHES 2015. LNCS, vol. 9293, pp. 663–682. Springer, Heidelberg (2015). doi:10.1007/978-3-662-48324-4_33

16. Lyubashevsky, V., Peikert, C., Regev, O.: On ideal lattices and learning with errors over rings. In: Gilbert, H. (ed.) EUROCRYPT 2010. LNCS, vol. 6110, pp. 1–23. Springer, Heidelberg (2010). doi:10.1007/978-3-642-13190-5_1

17. MacKay, D.J.C.: Information Theory, Inference, and Learning Algorithms. Cambridge University Press, New York (2003)

18. Mariantoni, M.: Building a superconducting quantum computer. Invited Talk at PQCrypto 2014, October 2014. https://www.youtube.com/watch?v=wWHAs-HA1c

19. NIST. Post-Quantum crypto standardization, December 2016. http://csrc.nist.gov/groups/ST/post-quantum-crypto/call-for-proposals-2016.html

20. NSA/IAD. CNSA Suite and Quantum Computing FAQ, January 2016. https://www.iad.gov/iad/library/ia-guidance/ia-solutions-for-classified/algorithm-guidance/cnsa-suite-and-quantum-computing-faq.cfm

21. Oder, T., Schneider, T., Pöppelmann, T., Güneysu, T.: Practical cca2-secure and masked ring-lwe implementation. IACR Cryptology ePrint Archive **2016**, 1109 (2016)

22. Pearl, J.: Reverend bayes on inference engines: a distributed hierarchical approach. In: Proceedings of the Second AAAI Conference on Artificial Intelligence, AAAI 1982, pp. 133–136. AAAI Press (1982)

23. Pöppelmann, T., Güneysu, T.: Towards practical lattice-based public-key encryption on reconfigurable hardware. In: Lange, T., Lauter, K., Lisoněk, P. (eds.) SAC 2013. LNCS, vol. 8282, pp. 68–85. Springer, Heidelberg (2014). doi:10.1007/978-3-662-43414-7_4

24. Pöppelmann, T., Oder, T., Güneysu, T.: High-performance ideal lattice-based cryptography on 8-bit atxmega microcontrollers. In: Lauter, K., Rodríguez-Henríquez, F. (eds.) LATINCRYPT 2015. LNCS, vol. 9230, pp. 346–365. Springer, Cham (2015). doi:10.1007/978-3-319-22174-8_19

25. Renauld, M., Standaert, F.-X.: Algebraic side-channel attacks. In: Bao, F., Yung, M., Lin, D., Jing, J. (eds.) Inscrypt 2009. LNCS, vol. 6151, pp. 393–410. Springer, Heidelberg (2010). doi:10.1007/978-3-642-16342-5_29

26. Reparaz, O., Clercq, R., Roy, S.S., Vercauteren, F., Verbauwhede, I.: Additively homomorphic ring-LWE masking. In: Takagi, T. (ed.) PQCrypto 2016. LNCS, vol. 9606, pp. 233–244. Springer, Cham (2016). doi:10.1007/978-3-319-29360-8_15

27. Reparaz, O., Roy, S.S., de Clercq, R., Vercauteren, F., Verbauwhede, I.: Masking ring-lwe. J. Cryptogr. Eng. **6**(2), 139–153 (2016). Extended journal version of [28]

28. Reparaz, O., Roy, S.S., Vercauteren, F., Verbauwhede, I.: A masked ring-LWE implementation. In: Güneysu, T., Handschuh, H. (eds.) CHES 2015. LNCS, vol. 9293, pp. 683–702. Springer, Heidelberg (2015). doi:10.1007/978-3-662-48324-4_34

29. Roy, S.S., Vercauteren, F., Mentens, N., Chen, D.D., Verbauwhede, I.: Compact ring-LWE cryptoprocessor. In: Batina, L., Robshaw, M. (eds.) CHES 2014. LNCS, vol. 8731, pp. 371–391. Springer, Heidelberg (2014). doi:10.1007/978-3-662-44709-3_21

30. Saarinen, M.-J.O.: Arithmetic coding and blinding countermeasures for lattice signatures. J. Cryptogr. Eng. 1–14 (2017)

31. Shamir, A.: Financial cryptography: past, present, and future. Invited Talk at Financial Cryptography 2016, February 2016. https://www.lightbluetouchpaper.org/2016/02/22/financial-cryptography-2016/#comment-1456744

32. Shor, P.W.: Polynomial-time algorithms for prime factorization and discrete logarithms on a quantum computer. SIAM Rev. **41**(2), 303–332 (1999)

33. Shoup, V.: NTL: a library for doing number theory. http://www.shoup.net/ntl/

34. Standaert, F.-X., Malkin, T.G., Yung, M.: A unified framework for the analysis of side-channel key recovery attacks. In: Joux, A. (ed.) EUROCRYPT 2009. LNCS, vol. 5479, pp. 443–461. Springer, Heidelberg (2009). doi:10.1007/978-3-642-01001-9_26

35. Su, Q., Wu, Y.C.: On convergence conditions of gaussian belief propagation. IEEE Trans. Signal Process. **63**(5), 1144–1155 (2015)

36. Veyrat-Charvillon, N., Gérard, B., Standaert, F.-X.: Soft analytical side-channel attacks. In: Sarkar, P., Iwata, T. (eds.) ASIACRYPT 2014. LNCS, vol. 8873, pp. 282–296. Springer, Heidelberg (2014). doi:10.1007/978-3-662-45611-8_15

A Systematic Approach to the Side-Channel Analysis of ECC Implementations with Worst-Case Horizontal Attacks

Romain Poussier[1](✉), Yuanyuan Zhou[1,2], and François-Xavier Standaert[1]

[1] ICTEAM/ELEN/Crypto Group, Université catholique de Louvain,
Louvain-la-Neuve, Belgium
romain.poussier@uclouvain.be
[2] Brightsight BV, Delft, The Netherlands

Abstract. The wide number and variety of side-channel attacks against scalar multiplication algorithms makes their security evaluations complex, in particular in case of time constraints making exhaustive analyses impossible. In this paper, we present a systematic way to evaluate the security of such implementations against horizontal attacks. As horizontal attacks allow extracting most of the information in the leakage traces of scalar multiplications, they are suitable to avoid risks of overestimated security levels. For this purpose, we additionally propose to use linear regression in order to accurately characterize the leakage function and therefore approach worst-case security evaluations. We then show how to apply our tools in the contexts of ECDSA and ECDH implementations, and validate them against two targets: a Cortex-M4 and a Cortex-A8 micro-controllers.

1 Introduction

State of the art. The secure implementation of Elliptic Curve Cryptography (ECC) is an important ingredient in modern information systems. In this paper, we are concerned with side-channel attacks against scalar multiplication implementations which have been the focus of continuous interest over the last 20 years. This literature informally divides these attacks in two main categories: attacks using a *Divide and Conquer* (DC) approach and attacks using an *Extend and Prune* (EP) approach – which we next survey.

Attacks that belong to the first category aim at recovering the scalar bits independently and are therefore simple to analyze. They associate a probability or a score to each scalar bit. The scalar is trivially recovered if all the correct bits have the highest probability. If it is not the case, computational power can be used to mitigate the lack of side-channel information thanks to key enumeration [30,35,38]. If the key is beyond computational reach (e.g. beyond 2^{60}), rank estimation (which requires the knowledge of the key and is therefore only accessible to evaluators, not to concrete adversaries) allows estimating the computational security level of a leaking implementation [6,20,30,39].

© International Association for Cryptologic Research 2017
W. Fischer and N. Homma (Eds.): CHES 2017, LNCS 10529, pp. 534–554, 2017.
DOI: 10.1007/978-3-319-66787-4_26

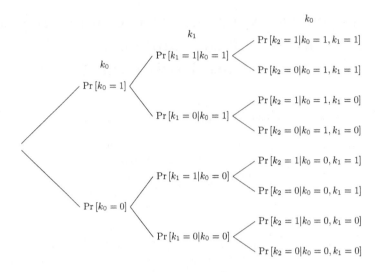

Fig. 1. Conditional probability tree for a 3 bits scalar $k = (k_0, k_1, k_2)$.

Attacks using an EP approach recover the scalar bits in a recursive manner. Recovering the i-th bit requires to first recover all the previous ones. For a n-bit scalar, EP attacks can be seen as a probability tree with 2^n leaves where each level corresponds to a different bit. Figure 1 illustrates such a probability tree for $n = 3$, where each node corresponds to the conditional probability of a bit given that the previous ones are correctly recovered. In this context, a first attack strategy is to only look at the most probable tree path. We refer to this method as first-order Success Rate (1-O SR). This strategy fails if not enough side-channel information is available for at least one of the bits. In such a case, the aforementioned enumeration algorithms cannot be applied due to the conditional dependencies. Yet, a recent study [27] describes a method to apply key enumeration/rank estimation on EP attacks[1].

According to these two classes, we now describe the state of the art on side-channel attacks against scalar multiplications. For each of them, we describe its overall modus operandi, we show its associated class and we finally exhibit a countermeasure (if existing).

The first attacks discovered on scalar multiplication, such as timing and Simple Power Analysis [25,26] (SPA), aimed at finding different patterns that depend on a scalar bit value. Such differences occur if the scalar multiplication or the elliptic curve operations are irregular, which makes the timing pattern of

---

[1] Instead of only looking at the most probable path, it assumes that the tree can be divided into three parts. The first part corresponds to the bits which the adversary is certain to have recovered correctly. The second part contains the (computationally feasible) paths on which the adversary has partial information. The final part is the exhaustive remaining part of the tree on which the adversary has no information. Enumeration is done on this sub-tree using a Pollard-like method.

the leaking implementations dependent on all the scalar bits. As a consequence, an adversary has to recover the scalar in a recursive manner and these attacks belong to the EP class. Using a regular scalar multiplication as further described in Sect. 2 naturally thwarts them.

Later on, (vertical) Differential Power Analysis (DPA) [26] and Correlation Power Analysis (CPA) [7] were applied to scalar multiplications [13,32]. Such methods aim at recovering the scalar bits iteratively using several side-channel leakages traces of a scalar multiplication with a fixed scalar and several known inputs. Thanks to the inputs knowledge, the scalar bits are recovered by guessing one internal value that depends on the input and the guessed bits. Independently of the distinguisher (e.g. correlation, difference of means,...), we refer to all attacks using this framework as DPA. Here again, guessing the internal value associated with a scalar bit requires that all the previous bits have been correctly recovered. Hence, DPA also belongs to the EP class. Since this method requires leakages on several executions with a fixed scalar, scalar randomization techniques [12,13] are efficient countermeasures. Protocols using a scalar nonce such as ECDSA [36] are naturally protected against DPA.

Next, Template Attacks (TA) [8] were introduced as a powerful tool to extract all the information available in some leakage traces. In the context of scalar multiplication, it has been first introduced against ECDSA [31]. From the prior knowledge of the input, the attack computes 2^d templates in order to recover the first d bits of the scalar nonce. The actual bit of the nonce is then found with templates matching. The secret key is finally recovered using lattice techniques [5,34] from several partially known nonces and their associated signatures. Interestingly, since such TA do not recover the whole scalar, they neither belong to the EP nor DC classes.

Alternatively, Online Template Attacks (OTA) [2,16] were introduced to recover the full scalar. This method interleaves the templates building and the attack phases, thus requiring more online access to the target device. As the iterative template building requires the knowledge of the current internal state which depends on the previous bits, OTA belongs to the EP class. Since both TA and OTA require the knowledge of the input, point randomization techniques [13,23] are effective. Using the fact that $(X, Y, Z) = (\lambda^2 X, \lambda^3 Y, \lambda Z)$ in Jacobian coordinates (see Sect. 2), an option to randomize the input is to change its coordinates at the beginning of each scalar multiplication using a random λ.

Horizontal Differential Power Attacks (HDPA) [3,11] are another powerful alternative to TA. From the posterior knowledge of the input, the scalar bits are recovered by guessing several internal values that depend on both the input and the guessed bits (instead of only one in the case of DPA). As guessing the internal values associated with a particular bit requires the knowledge of the previous ones, HDPA belongs to the EP class. As for TA, point randomization is effective against HDPA.

Finally, Horizontal Collision Attacks (HCA) [3,4,10,14,21,40] have been proposed in order to bypass the point randomization countermeasures. These attacks require the scalar multiplication to exhibit different operand input/output collisions that depend on the scalar bit values. Being able to detect such collisions from a trace allows recovering the scalar bits. Up to our knowledge, only one collision attack defeats the Montgomery scalar multiplication implemented as further described in Sect. 2.2 by Algorithm 1 [21]. The collision is able to find whether two consecutive scalar bits are the same or not. Given this information, the scalar is finally recovered using a modified version of the Baby-Step/Giant-Step algorithm. If they target a regular scalar multiplication, HCA belong to the DC class, since the position of the collisions in the leakage traces depends only on the current scalar bit value in this case. In case of irregular algorithms, this position depends on the previous bits and HCA then belong to the EP class. In general, countermeasures aiming at increasing the noise level (e.g. shuffling, random delays, ...) are the only effective ones against the attack presented in [21]. In this respect, one drawback of these attacks (from the adversary's viewpoint) is that they only exploit a very small part of the available information compared to HDPA and TA (which implies that the amount of noise needed to hide the collisions is more limited).

We additionally mention that all the aforementioned attacks (except the TA) ignore the leakages due to the direct manipulation of the scalar bits during the scalar multiplication (such as discussed in [9,22,33]). Exploiting these leakages is an orthogonal concern to this study and is therefore out of the scope of our investigations.

Our contribution. Based on this broad state of the art, our goal is to further investigate and systematize the security evaluation of scalar multiplication implementations against HDPA. Our motivations in this context are threefold:

First of all, such attacks can potentially exploit most of the informative samples provided by a leaking implementation, and are therefore a natural candidate for approaching their worst-case security level, which we aim for.

Second, most of the HDPA literature is based on the correlation distinguisher and assumes an a priori leakage model. Yet, given our goal to approach the worst-case security level of scalar multiplication implementations, it is natural to study efficient solutions allowing a better characterization of the leakages. In view of its broad applicability in the context of block cipher implementations, linear regression appears as an excellent candidate for this purpose [37], and we therefore study its applicability in our asymmetric setting.

Third, and quite importantly, only few practical experiments have been reported on the application of HDPA against actual implementations of scalar multiplication algorithms. We contribute to this issue by providing the results of experiments against two (more or less challenging) targets: the first one is a low frequency ARM Cortex M4 micro-controller (without interrupts), the second one runs a Linux operating system in background and runs at high frequency. While successful attacks against this second target have been published for block ciphers [1,29], no public report discusses their vulnerabilities in the ECC case. We also illustrate the application of framework to both ECDH and ECDSA.

The rest of the paper is organized as followed. Section 2 introduces the notations and the necessary background on elliptic curve cryptosystems and implementations. Section 3 describes the generic view we consider for regular scalar multiplication along with the systematic security evaluation method. Finally, Sects. 4 and 5 respectively show the experimental results for the application of this framework against our two targets.

2   Background

2.1   Notations

We use capital letters for random variables and small caps for their realizations. We use sans serif font for functions (e.g. F) and calligraphic fonts for sets (e.g. $\mathcal{A}$). We use capital bold letters for matrices (e.g. $\mathbf{M}$) and small bold caps for vectors (e.g. $\mathbf{v}$). We denote the conditional probability of a random variable A given B with $\Pr[A|B]$.

2.2   Elliptic Curves Cryptography (ECC)

Let $\mathbb{F}_p$ be a finite field with a characteristic bigger than 3. We define by $\mathcal{E}(\mathbb{F}_p)$ the set of points $(x, y) \in \mathbb{F}_p^2$ (called affine coordinates) that satisfy the Weierstrass equation $y^2 = x^3 + ax + b$, $(a, b) \in \mathbb{F}_p^2$ with discriminant $\Delta = -16(4a^3 + 27b^2) \neq 0$. $\mathcal{E}(\mathbb{F}_p)$ along with a point at infinity which form an Abelian additive group. The addition over $\mathcal{E}(\mathbb{F}_p)$ requires field additions, subtractions, multiplications and one inversion. We denote by $+$ the addition of two points P and Q, and by $[k]P$ the k-times repeated additions $P + P + \ldots + P$ with $k \in \mathbb{N}$ (called scalar multiplication).

Scalar Multiplication. Most elliptic curve cryptosystems require to compute a scalar multiplication $[k]P$ from a number $k \in [1, |{<}P{>}| - 1]$ and a curve point P, where $|{<}P{>}|$ is the order of the subgroupgenerated by P. In each case, k is a sensitive variable unknown from the attacker which can be a private key (e.g. for ECDH key exchange) or directly linked to it (e.g. for ECDSA). As a result, the scalar multiplication represents an important source of potential side-channel leakages. In order to thwart the most basic side-channel attacks, scalar multiplication algorithms avoid conditional branching and have a regular execution independently of the bits of k. In the following we will consider the (left to right) Montgomery ladder [24] as described by Algorithm 1. We now view the n-bit scalar as a binary vector $\mathbf{k} = (k_0, \ldots, k_{n-1})$ (where k_0 is the most significant bit).

Jacobian Coordinates. In general, field inversions are costly compared to additions, subtractions and multiplications. Moving from affine coordinates to Jacobian coordinates allows avoiding the inversion when performing an addition or a doubling over $\mathcal{E}(\mathbb{F}_p)$. The Jacobian plan $\mathcal{J}$ over $\mathbb{F}_p^3$ is defined as $\{(X, Y, Z) \in \mathbb{F}_p^3 \text{ s.t. } \forall \lambda \in \mathbb{F}_p, (X, Y, Z) = (\lambda^2 X, \lambda^3 Y, \lambda Z)\}$. The set of points $\mathcal{E}_{\mathcal{J}}(\mathbb{F}_p)$ defined

---

Algorithm 1. Montgomery ladder.

Input: $P, \mathbf{k} = (k_0, ..., k_{n-1})$
Output: $[k]P$
   $R_0 \leftarrow \mathcal{O}$
   $R_1 \leftarrow P$
   for $i = 0$ to $n - 1$ **do**
      $R_{1-k_i} \leftarrow R_{1-k_i} + R_{k_i}$
      $R_{k_i} \leftarrow [2]R_{k_i}$
   end for
   return R_0

---

by the equation $Y^2 = X^3 + aXZ^4 + bZ^6$ defines an elliptic curve over the Jacobian plan. The Jacobian point (X, Y, Z), $Z \neq 0$ corresponds to the affine point $(X/Z^2, Y/Z^3)$. The point at infinity in affine coordinates corresponds to the point $(\lambda^2, \lambda^3, 0)$ in Jacobian coordinates.

Given two points P and Q in $\mathcal{E}_{\mathcal{J}}(\mathbb{F}_p)$ with $P \neq \pm Q$, the formulas for the addition $P + Q$ and doubling $P + P$ are respectively given by Algorithms 2 and 3. As it is important for the rest of the paper, we stress the fact that an addition over $\mathcal{E}_{\mathcal{J}}(\mathbb{F}_p)$ (resp. a doubling) requires 16 field multiplications (resp. 10).

Algorithm 2. Addition over $\mathcal{E}_{\mathcal{J}}(\mathbb{F}_p)$.

Input: $P = (X_1, Y_1, Z_1), Q = (X_2, Y_2, Z_2), P \neq \pm Q$
Output: $P + Q = (X_3, Y_3, Z_3)$
   $\mathsf{Z}_1 \leftarrow Z_1^2, \mathsf{Z}_2 \leftarrow Z_2^2, U_1 \leftarrow X_1\mathsf{Z}_2, U_2 \leftarrow X_2\mathsf{Z}_1, \mathsf{H} \leftarrow U_1 - U_2, S_1 \leftarrow Y_1\mathsf{Z}_2 Z_2, S_2 \leftarrow$
   $Y_2\mathsf{Z}_1 Z_1, R \leftarrow S_1 - S_2, \mathsf{H} \leftarrow \mathsf{H}^2, G \leftarrow \mathsf{H}\mathsf{H}, V \leftarrow U_1\mathsf{H}$
   $X_3 \leftarrow R^2 + G - 2V$
   $Y_3 \leftarrow R(V - X_3) - S_1 G$
   $Z_3 \leftarrow Z_1 Z_2 \mathsf{H}$
   return (X_3, Y_3, Z_3)

Algorithm 3. Doubling over $\mathcal{E}_{\mathcal{J}}(\mathbb{F}_p)$.

Input: $P = (X_1, Y_1, Z_1)$
Output: $P + P = (X_2, Y_2, Z_2)$
   $\mathsf{X} \leftarrow X_1^2, \mathsf{Y} \leftarrow Y_1^2, \mathsf{Z} \leftarrow Z_1^2, M \leftarrow 3\mathsf{X} + a\mathsf{Z}^2, T \leftarrow \mathsf{Y}^2, S \leftarrow 4X_1\mathsf{Y}$
   $X_2 \leftarrow M^2 - 2S$
   $Y_2 \leftarrow M(S - X_2) - 8T$
   $Z_2 \leftarrow 2Y_1 Z_1$
   return (X_2, Y_2, Z_2)

Note that the Montgomery ladder algorithm is typically reflective of the state of the art implementations of ECC secure against SPA. In the following, we further considered implementations protected with scalar randomization in order to avoid DPA attacks. So our focus is on single-trace attacks which naturally goes with our worst-case information extraction motivation.

3   Systematic Approach

In this section we describe a systematic method for the worst-case security analysis of scalar multiplications. We first give an abstract view of regular scalar multiplications. We then use this abstraction to specify the amount of informative points in our leakage traces. We finally show how these informative points can be extracted and combined to attack the scalar bits, and show how this method applies on two ECC primitives, namely ECDH and ECDSA.

3.1   Generic Scalar Multiplication Architecture

As explained in Sect. 2.2, elliptic curve cryptosystems require to compute a scalar multiplication. Section 1 also discussed the regularity requirements of the scalar multiplication implementations, which implies that they can be described as a fixed and predictable sequence of operations. In this context, all operations that affect the internal state depending on the scalar bit value contain sensitive information. In order to quantify this information, we will next describe the scalar multiplication based on different levels, depicted in Fig. 2. At the top level, a regular binary scalar multiplication is an iterative processing of the scalar bits. Each bit handling is itself composed of a fixed number of additions and doublings. Then, each addition (resp. doubling) contains a fixed number of field operations (such as field additions, subtractions and multiplications). Finally, each field operation is composed of a fixed number of register operations (such as register additions, subtractions and multiplications). As a result, and for an n-bit scalar, the sequence of register operations that can be exploited by an adversary can be divided into n parts that depend on the scalar bit index. Independently of the kind of operation, we assume that each part contains N register operations. We therefore have that a regular binary scalar multiplication leads to n sequences of N sensitive operations of which the results are stored in registers. We denote as $\mathbf{r}_i = (r_i^j)$, $j \in [0, N-1]$ the N intermediate computation results occurring during the manipulation of the i-th scalar bit[2]. Eventually, each of these computations will lead to side-channel leakages denoted as $\mathbf{l}_i = (l_i^j)$, $j \in [0, N-1]$.

3.2   Information Extraction

From the previous abstract view of the scalar multiplication and its associated leakages, the next step is to extract the information. Given a leakage l on a register r, we compute the probability $\Pr[l|r = x]$, $x \in [0, 2^{|r|} - 1]$ that the observed leakage comes from the manipulation of the value x by r (where $|r|$ denotes the size of the register in bits). While using templates would be optimal, their computational complexity is exponential in $|r|$ as it requires to estimate $2^{|r|}$ Probability Density Functions (PDF) per register (e.g. $2^{|r|}$ means and variances

---

[2] Note that this is an abstract view. In practice, an operation can have more than one register input/output. In such case, one can count this operation as corresponding to several registers or only use one of them.

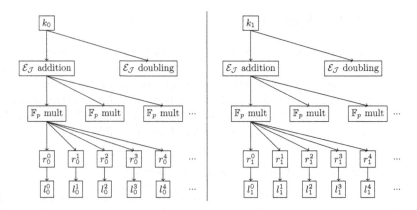

Fig. 2. Level view of a regular scalar multiplication. First level (top): scalar bit handling. Second: elliptic curve arithmetic. Third: Field arithmetic. Fourth: register operations. Fifth: leakages on register operations

for Gaussian templates). Therefore, and as a more efficient alternative, we use linear regression [37] with a linear basis containing the $|r|$ bits of the registers. The latter decreases the profiling complexity from $O(2^{|r|})$ to $O(|r|)$, which is particularly interesting in the case of a $r = 32$-bit architecture (as we will investigate). Yet, this admittedly comes at the cost of a potential information loss in case the leakage function has informative non-linear terms (which we will briefly discuss in Sects. 4 and 5).

We denote by $\lceil \mathbf{k} \rceil_i$ the first i bits of $\mathbf{k}$. We denote by $r_i^j(P, \lceil \mathbf{k} \rceil_i)$ the internal value processed by the register operation r_i^j when the input point is P and the first i bits of $\mathbf{k}$ are equal to $\lceil \mathbf{k} \rceil_i$. Similarly, we denote by $l_i^j(P, \lceil \mathbf{k} \rceil_i)$ the leakage corresponding to its manipulation. Using N_{prof} leakages from random inputs (P^q) and random scalars ($\mathbf{k}^q$), $q \in [0, N_{prof} - 1]$, we compute the $N_{prof} \times 33$ matrix $\mathbf{A}$ where the q-th line is the binary representation of $r_i^j(P^q, \lceil \mathbf{k}^q \rceil_i)$ appended with a constant 1. From $\mathbf{A}$ and the vector $\mathbf{l}_i^j = (l_i^j(P^q, \lceil \mathbf{k}^q \rceil_i))$, $q \in [0, N_{prof} - 1]$ containing the N_{prof} leakages, we compute the linear basis $\mathbf{b}$ that characterizes l_i^j using Eq. 1 (where A^T denotes the transpose of $\mathbf{A}$):

$$\mathbf{b} = (\mathbf{A}^T \mathbf{A})^{-1} \mathbf{A}^T \mathbf{l}_i^j. \tag{1}$$

Assuming that the noise follows a Gaussian distribution, the variance σ^2 is computed using a second set of traces (in order to avoid overfitting) as shown by Eq. 2. Note that we assume independence between the noise and the value processed by the register [28].

$$\sigma^2 = (\mathbf{l}_i^j - \mathbf{A}\mathbf{b})^T \cdot (\mathbf{l}_i^j - \mathbf{A}\mathbf{b}). \tag{2}$$

From $\mathbf{b}$ and σ^2, the probability that a leakage l_i^j comes from the manipulation of x by r_i^j is then given by Eq. 3, where $\mathcal{N}_{\mu, \sigma^2}(l)$ denotes the evaluation in l of the normal density function with mean μ and variance σ^2, and $(x)_2$ denotes the binary decomposition of x appended with 1:

$$\Pr\left[l_i^j \mid x\right] = \mathcal{N}_{(x)_2 \cdot b, \sigma^2}(l_i^j). \tag{3}$$

3.3 Information Combination

Now that we are able to identify and extract the information, we aim at combining it to attack the scalar bits. As shown in Sect. 2, HDPA belong to the EP class. In order to exploit the information on a specific bit, a hypothesis on the values of the previous ones must be made.

From the knowledge of input P and the knowledge of the first $i-1$ bits, the likelihood that the bit i is equal to 1 (resp. 0) is computed by guessing all the register values $r_i^j(P, \lceil \mathbf{k} \rceil_{i-1} || 1)$ (resp. $r_i^j(P, \lceil \mathbf{k} \rceil_{i-1} || 0)$ and combining their likelihoods. Given the leakages $\mathbf{l}_i$ on the i-th bit, Eq. 4 gives the probability that the leakages come from the first $i-1$ bits being equal to $\lceil \mathbf{k} \rceil_{i-1}$ and the i-th bit being equal to $v \in \{0, 1\}$ (where $||$ denotes the concatenation):

$$\Pr\left[\mathbf{l}_i \mid \lceil \mathbf{k} \rceil_i = \lceil \mathbf{k} \rceil_{i-1} || v\right] = \prod_{j=0}^{N-1} \Pr\left[l_i^j \mid r_i^j(P, \lceil \mathbf{k} \rceil_{i-1} || v)\right]. \tag{4}$$

This formula assumes that the leakages l_i^j are independent (which simplifies the profiling phase as we only consider univariate samples). While this assumption may not be perfectly correct, we verified experimentally that considering multivariate samples did not improve the efficiency of our attacks in the next section, and therefore assume it to be sufficiently correct for simplicity. Extending this framework to attack k by chunks of d bits is straightforward. Given a d bits hypothesis vector $\mathbf{v}$, Eq. 5 extends the previous equation to attack d bits at a time, where $\mathbf{v}_{|j}$ denotes the j first elements of $\mathbf{v}$:

$$\Pr\left[\mathbf{l}_i, ..., \mathbf{l}_{i+d-1} \mid \lceil \mathbf{k} \rceil_{i+d-1} = \lceil \mathbf{k} \rceil_{i-1} || \mathbf{v}\right] = \prod_{j=0}^{d-1} \Pr\left[\mathbf{l}_{i+j} \mid \lceil \mathbf{k} \rceil_{i-1} || \mathbf{v}_{|j}\right]. \tag{5}$$

When there is no ambiguity, we will refer to $\Pr\left[\mathbf{l}_i, ..., \mathbf{l}_{i+d-1} \mid \lceil \mathbf{k} \rceil_{i+d-1} = \lceil \mathbf{k} \rceil_{i-1} || \mathbf{v}\right]$ as $\Pr_{\lceil \mathbf{k} \rceil_{i-1} || \mathbf{v}}$ for readability reasons.

3.4 ECDH vs. ECDSA

In the rest of the paper we always assume that $\mathbf{k}$ is attacked by chunks of d bits. For simplicity, we assume that $n_d = \frac{n}{d} \in \mathbb{N}$ and we rewrite $\mathbf{k} = (\mathbf{k}_0, ..., \mathbf{k}_{n_d-1})$ being viewed as binary vectors of d elements.

ECDH. In order to attack ECDH, the attacker has to recover the full scalar in one trace. He starts by attacking the first d bits using Eq. 5. Using a leakage from a known input, he computes the likelihoods $\text{Pr}_{\mathbf{v}}$ for all the 2^d scalar hypotheses $\mathbf{v} \in \{0, 1\}^d$. He then selects the hypothesis $\mathbf{k}_0^* = \text{argmax}_{\mathbf{v}}(\text{Pr}_{\mathbf{v}})$ that maximizes the likelihood as being the correct guess. The following scalar guesses are selected iteratively according the previous results as $\mathbf{k}_i^* = \text{argmax}_{\mathbf{v}}(\text{Pr}_{\mathbf{k}_0^*||...||\mathbf{k}_{i-1}^*||\mathbf{v}})$, with $\mathbf{v} \in \{0, 1\}^d$. The iterative process ends when the adversary has obtained a full scalar hypothesis $\mathbf{k}^* = (\mathbf{k}_0^*, ..., \mathbf{k}_{n_d-1}^*)$.

The attack trivially succeeds if $\mathbf{k}^* = \mathbf{k}$, which corresponds to a 1-O SR. If this is not the case, one can use computational power to mitigate the lack of information by enumerating through the other paths [27]. In this study we only look at the 1-O SR as our focus is on optimal information extraction (rather than exploitation).

Eventually, the chunk size d is a parameter chosen by the adversary. It increases the attack complexity exponentially in d, but allows increasing linearly the amount of leakage samples exploited by the adversary.

ECDSA. As for ECDH, a potential strategy to attack the ECDSA scalar nonce is to recover all its bits. Another option is to use the algebraic relation between the nonce and the secret key. Using lattice techniques, one can attack the secret key by recovering partial on the first d bits of several nonces. This strategy fails if at least one of the nonces' partial information is not recovered properly. As a consequence, the attacker has to make sure that the d-bit partial information of each nonce is correct. As the attack on the first d bits does not suffer from the conditional dependencies, one can turn the previously estimated likelihoods into true probabilities by applying Bayes' theorem, as in Eq. 6. From these probabilities, the adversary decides to ignore all the results having a probability lower

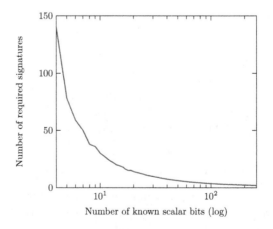

Fig. 3. Complexity of the lattice-based attack against ECDSA. Left: number of nonces (y axis) needed when having d bits of partial information per nonce (x axis).

than a given threshold to maximize the success of the lattice attack.

$$\Pr\left[\mathbf{k}_0 = \mathbf{v} \,\middle|\, \mathbf{l}_0, ..., \mathbf{l}_{d-1}\right] = \frac{\Pr_{\mathbf{v}}}{\sum_{\mathbf{v}^* \in \{0,1\}^d} \Pr_{\mathbf{v}^*}}. \tag{6}$$

To give more insight on the side-channel requirements of a lattice-based attack against ECDSA, Fig. 3 shows how many nonces are needed (y axis) in function of the partial information d (x axis). As we can see, the number of required nonces decreases exponentially when d increases. It confirms the need of being able to extract most of the information and to discard the wrong results in a meaningful way. We use the fplll [15] library v4.0.4 with block sizes of 20 and 30 (only for 4 bits leaked case) to perform the experiments.

4   Experimental Results on Cortex-M4

In this section we apply previous systematic approach to attack ECC implementations in a 32-bit Cortex-M4 micro-controller. We first describe our implementation, device and the measurement setup. We then follow our evaluation framework step by step and discuss experimental results.

4.1   Target Implementation

We implemented the finite field and elliptic curve arithmetic in assembly on both chips. We chose the NIST P-256 curve [36]. Our attack framework is independent of the choice of curve, as its only requirement is the regularity of the implementation. We thus focused on achieving constant time without optimizations. We implemented the Montgomery ladder as described in Sect. 2.2 using Jacobian coordinates. We used the addition and doubling formulas from Algorithms 2 and 3. The whole scalar multiplication runs in approximately 17,000,000 clock cycles.

Field additions and subtractions are implemented in a straightforward manner using carry additions and subtractions. Field multiplications are done using the Long Integer Multiplication (LIM) followed by a modular reduction. More details on the implementation can be found in eprint version of the paper, such as a description of the assembly long integer multiplication.

4.2   Device and Setup

Our first target is a 32-bit ARM Cortex-M4 micro-controller from the atmel SAM4C-EK evaluation kit[3]. It proceeds most instructions in constant time and does not have any programs running in parallel that could disturb the signal. Moreover, this micro-controller runs at 100 MHz which makes it a relatively easy target for power acquisition.

---

[3] http://infocenter.arm.com/help/topic/com.arm.doc.ddi0439b/DDI0439B_cortex_m4_r0p0_trm.pdf http://www.atmel.com/tools/SAM4C-EK.aspx.

We monitored the voltage variation using a 4.7 Ω resistor inserted in the supply circuit of the chip. We performed the trace acquisition using a Lecroy WaveRunner HRO 66 ZI oscilloscope running at 200 megasamples per second. For each scalar multiplication execution, we triggered the measurement at the beginning of the execution and recorded the processing of the first 123 bits of the scalar. Each trace contains 40,000,000 time samples and weighs 320,000,000 mega-bytes (written in double precision format).

Since the device does not suffer from any interruptions, the power traces are directly used without any preprocessing.

4.3   Identifying and Extracting the Information

Among all the register operations $\mathbf{r}_i$ available for a given bit, we target only the higher 32-bit result of each umull and umaal instructions. This choice allows our attack to remain implementation-independent (since those intermediate results will indeed appear in most implementations). As shown by the doubling and addition formulas in Sect. 2.2, an addition plus a doubling consist in 25 field multiplications (the curve uses $a = -3$, thus the multiplication by a is done using subtractions). Each field multiplication itself consists in 64 32-bits register multiplications. As a result, we attack the implementation using $N = 25 \times 64 = 1,600$ leakage samples per scalar bit.

In order to efficiently identify the time positions of the corresponding registers r_i^j, we use the unprofiled correlation and partial SNR described below. They exploit a set of $N_{poi} = 8,000$ traces **l** acquired using random known inputs (P^q) and scalars $(\mathbf{k}^q)$, $q \in [0, N_{poi} - 1]$. We denote by $\mathbf{l}[t]$ vector of size N_{poi} containing the N_{poi} leakages of the t-th time sample of each trace.

Unprofiled Correlation. Given the N_{poi} internal values $r_i^j = r_i^j(P^q, \lceil \mathbf{k}^q \rceil_i)$ and a leakage model M, we apply the Pearson's correlation ρ on each time sample. That is, we compute $\rho(\mathsf{M}(r_i^j), \mathbf{l}[t])$, $t \in [0; 40,000,000]$. We used the Hamming weight function for M. The time sample showing the highest correlation is selected as the time sample of r_i^j. The disadvantage of using unprofiled correlation for the POI research is the requirement of a leakage model. However, it allows using the information from the full 32 bits of the internal values r_i^j.

Partial Signal to Noise Ratio (SNR). Computing the standard SNR is not suitable to identify a specific register as any bijective relation between two registers will make them impossible to distinguish. Moreover, a 32-bit SNR would require more than 2^{32} leakages samples in the case of our 32-bit devices. Using partial SNR allows avoiding these issues at the cost of a controlled information lost. For this purpose, the 32-bit values of r_i^j are first truncated to x bits. Each trace is then labeled according to its truncated value and split into 2^x sets $\mathcal{S}_i$. For each time sample, the partial SNR is finally computed as $\frac{\mathsf{var}(\mathsf{mean}(\mathcal{S}_i))}{\mathsf{mean}(\mathsf{var}(\mathcal{S}_i))}$ where var and mean respectively denote the sample variance and mean functions. The time sample showing the highest SNR ratio is selected as the time sample of r_i^j. While partial SNR does not rely on a leakage model, it suffers from algorithmic noise because of the truncation process (which reduces the information exploited). That is, since the remaining $32 - x$ bits are not taken into account when creating the sets $\mathcal{S}_i$, the actual signal is reduced. However, ignoring the value of this remaining bits allows avoiding the bijection issue. In order to illustrate the bijection issue, one can take the AES as an example. Computing the full SNR related to the plaintext m XORed with the key k doesn't allow differentiating whether we are before or after the S-box computation. This means an SNR spike will be exhibited for both $x \oplus k$ and $\mathsf{S}(m \oplus k)$, where S denotes the AES S-box. However, computing a partial SNR on e.g. only 4 bits of $x \oplus k$ instead of the 8 bits will break the bijection between the input and the output of the S-Box. As a result, it will allow discriminating between the input and the output of the S-box in the partial SNR spike.

Optimizations. Applying one of these two methods on the full trace for all r_i^j's is very time consuming as we have $123 \times 1,600$ registers to characterize over 40,000,000 time samples. However, we know that the time order of the register is $(r_0^0, ..., r_0^{N-1}, r_1^0, ...r_i^j, ...r_{n-1}^{N-1})$. Using that knowledge, we can first search r_0^0 among the first W time samples. Using correlation, we select r_0^0's position by computing a p-value with a threshold of 5 [17]. If r_0^0 has not been found, we move the window to the next W time samples and repeat this process until r_0^0 is found. Once this temporal location is found, we search r_0^1 similarly, by setting the initial offset of the window at r_0^0. This process is iterated until all the registers are found. We set the window value W to 20,000, chosen to be slightly higher than $\frac{40,000,000}{123 \times 25}$ (the time samples divided by the number of field multiplications).

Extraction. Once the temporal locations of all the registers are found, we apply linear regression on each of them to extract the information as described in Sect. 3.2, using a set of $N_{prof} = 10,000$ traces. Note that for this simple device, the leakage model was found to be close to Hamming weight and the linear leakage model is not expected to cause a significant information loss. Yet, the formal analysis of this statement with leakage certification tools is an interesting scope for further research [18,19].

4.4   Information Combination

Using the maximum likelihood approach of Sect. 3.3, we attack the first 123 bits of the Cortex-M4 implementation with the 1-O SR described in Sect. 3.4. We used a new set of traces that has not been used to identify nor to extract the information for this purpose. As a first experiment, we compute the success rate of recovering the 123 bits using all the information. Secondly, we simulate an implementation with less information by reducing the number N of register per scalar bit. In that case, we study how using computational power by increasing the chunk's size d can mitigate the lack of information. Finally, we study how the number N of informative registers impacts the success rate of the attack.

Our first experiment is to look at the success rate using all the information. In that case we have $N = 1,600$ registers per scalar bit. We achieved a success rate of 0.85 using a chunk's size of 1 bit. It shows that such a device would require much more algorithmic noise to be protected against worst case attacks (e.g. using random delays, shuffling...).

As using all the information allows recovering all the 123 bits with a high success rate, we next simulate a less informative implementation by using $N = 600$. In such a case, increasing the chunk size d is an option to increase success rate. As stated in Sect. 3.4, the number of points of interest increases linearly with the size of d at the cost of an exponential time complexity increase. Figure 4 shows the impact of the chunk size on the success rate. As we can see, the success rate increases linearly with d. We also see that the slope of the curve is lower than 1. This is explained by the fact that the number of points of interest for the bits of indexes $(0, 1, ..., d-1)$ of each chunk is equal to $(dN, (d-1)N, ..., N)$. That is, only the first chunk's bit fully benefits from increasing d, while the last one does not get any improvement.

As a last experiment, we study the impact of the number of target register N on the success rate. Figure 5 shows the evolution of the success rate in function of N for different values of d. Independently of d, the success rate increases exponentially with N.

From these experiments, we conclude that as general in side-channel analysis, the information extraction phase of the attacks is the most critical one, since it is the one causing the exponential security loss. Computational power can then be used as a useful (sometimes necessary) complementary ingredient to mitigate a possible lack of information.

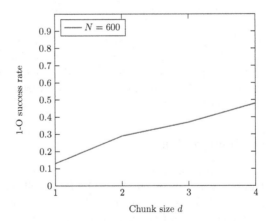

Fig. 4. First-order success rate of the 123-bit recovery on the Cortex-M4 depending on the chunk size d for different $N = 600$.

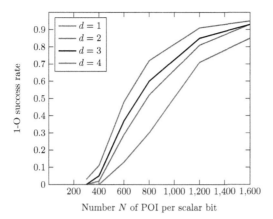

Fig. 5. first-order success rate of the 123-bit recovery on the Cortex-M4 depending on the number of poi N for different values of d.

5   Experimental Results on Cortex-A8

In this section we show the attack results on the Cortex-A8 micro-controller. As in the previous section, we first describe the device and measurement setup. We then show the application of the framework against this target along with the results. The scalar multiplication is implemented the same way in Jacobian coordinates as described in Sect. 4.1.

5.1   Device and Setup

Our second target is a 32-bit AM335x 1GHz ARM Cortex-A8 linux-based single board computer[4]. As opposed to the previous target, this one is way more challenging [1,29]. As it is running a full version of Ubuntu 14.04 and more than 100 processes are running in the background while we execute our assembly Montgomery ladder scalar multiplication implementation via SSH from the host PC. The CPU has instruction cache and 13-stage ARM pipeline, all those factors introduce a lot of noise and interruptions. Moreover, the high (1 GHz) frequency also add more obstacles in terms of side channel measurements.

We measured the EM emission using a Langer HV100-27 magnetic near field probe. As in [1,29], we got the best EM signal when the probe is around the capacitor *C65*. During the measurements, we set the CPU frequency to the highest 1 GHz and the CPU frequency governor to *'Performance'*. We measured the EM traces using a Lecroy WaveRunner 620Zi oscilloscope at a sampling rate of 10 GS/s. For each scalar multiplication execution, we also triggered the measurement at the beginning of the execution and recorded the processing of the first 4 bits of the scalar, so that each trace contains 2,000,000 sample points. As mentioned in [1,29], the traces contain long interruptions that randomly appear

---

[4] http://infocenter.arm.com/help/topic/com.arm.doc.ddi0344k/DDI0344K_cortex_a8_r3p2_trm.pdf https://beagleboard.org/black.

due to the Linux system. We eliminated these interruptions by running the program with the "nohup" command via SSH without any elevating techniques. While this technique removes the big interruptions, the traces still contain many smaller ones.

5.2   Preprocessing

In order to deal with the small interruptions, the traces have to be preprocessed. The overall synchronization iterates over three steps. The first one consists in synchronizing the traces around a particular field multiplication. The second step is to cut the traces around the synchronized area into slices. Finally, each slice is added to the set of preprocessed traces by concatenation. These three steps are repeated for each field multiplication.

Synchronization. While the last two steps of the preprocessing are straightforward, the synchronization part deserves more insight. We use a correlation-based alignment method to synchronize the EM traces per field multiplication operation. This method works in three steps that are depicted in Fig. 6. The left (resp. right) part of the figure shows the traces before (resp. after) synchronization.

- Firstly, a searching interval A that contains the operation to be synchronized is selected among all the traces. This is shown by the red window.
- Secondly, a second smaller reference interval B_q specific to each trace q is chosen, shown by the yellow window on the three traces in Fig. 6(a).
- For each trace, we finally find the portion to be synchronized by using the second window B_q to search over the whole interval A. The right portion is selected as the one having the maximum correlation with the reference interval. If the correlation is lower than a given threshold (arbitrarily chosen by the attacker), the trace is assumed not good enough and is thus discarded.

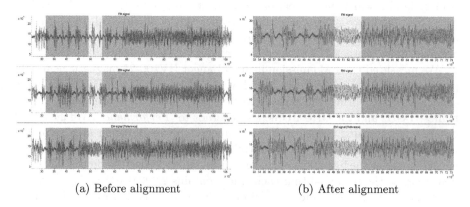

(a) Before alignment   (b) After alignment

Fig. 6. Three EM traces before and after alignment

Once the traces are synchronized, we identify and extract the information the same way as in the previous section on the Cortex-M4 with a different number of traces. We used $N_{poi} = N_{prof} = 100,000$ traces to both identify and extract the information. As will be clear next, a linear leakage model was sufficient to obtain positive results even for this more challenging device. However, as in the previous section, analyzing the quality of this model with leakage certification tools would certainly be worth further investigations.

5.3   Information Combination

As for the experiment on the Cortex-M4, we use the maximum likelihood approach of Sect. 3.3 to attack the first 4 bits of the Cortex-A8 implementation. This time, we assume we are attacking an ECDSA secret key and use the probabilistic approach of Sect. 3.4 on ECDSA. We used a new set of 2,200 traces that has not been used to identify nor to extract the information.

Our first experiment simply looks at the 1-O SR. In that case, we recovered the 4 bits with a success rate of 0.8155. As shown by Fig. 3, we know that 140 ECDSA nonces are required to recover the secret key with 4 bits of partial information. As no error on the partial information is tolerated, the success rate of the key recovery is equal to $0.8155^{140} \approx 3.9 \cdot 10^{-13}$. This confirms the strong need of a sound way to discriminate the wrong results.

Motivated by this first experiment, we next studied how we can automatically remove the wrong attack results. This is achieved by setting a probability threshold under which some attack traces will be discarded. That is, an attack trace is considered as invalid if the probability given by formula 6 for the most likely partial nonce after the attack is below a given threshold. Intuitively, the higher the threshold is, the more confident we are in having a successful partial nonce recovery, which comes at the cost of increasing the number of discarded attack traces. Table 1 shows how the success rate evolves in function of the probability threshold over the 2,200 attack traces. As we can see, using a threshold

Table 1. Evolution of the ECDSA scalar and key recovery success rate in function of the threshold.

Threshold	Scalar 1-O SR	Key 1-O SR	# discarded result	# remaining result
0.5	0.8174349612	$3.9 \cdot 10^{-13}$	9	2,191
0.75	0.8462296698	$5.5 \cdot 10^{-13}$	171	2,029
0.9	0.8680042239	$2.5 \cdot 10^{-9}$	306	1,894
0.99	0.9025578563	$5.8 \cdot 10^{-7}$	558	1,642
0.9999	0.956596	0.002	1,025	1,175
0.99999	0.980366	0.062	1,235	965
0.9999999	0.991708	0.312	1,597	613
0.999999999	0.9942363112	0.445	1,853	347
0.9999999999	1	1	1,958	242

of 0.5 does not discard much results and thus does not increase the probability to recover the ECDSA secret key. However, the first-order success rate increases when setting a higher probability threshold. We finally achieve a perfect success rate using a threshold of 0.9999999999. Using this value, 1,958 of the attack results were discarded, thus keeping 242 of them. As only 140 correct scalars are needed to recover the ECDSA secret key, we achieve a success rate of 1.

6 Conclusion

This paper provides a generic evaluation framework for HDPA against scalar multiplication algorithms, instantiates it with state of the art tools for pre-processing, POI detection, profiling and information extraction, and applies it to concrete implementations reflective of the variety of targets that can be used for embedded cryptographic applications. In view of the limited experimental reports available on the topic, we hope these implementation and systematization efforts can be used to clarify the practicality of such advanced attacks in practice, even against challenging targets running at high clock frequencies, and therefore argue for their integration as a part of current certification practices.

From a designer's point of view, our results also highlight that implementations of scalar multiplications on commercial platforms with scalar randomization activated are generally at risk, in view of the huge amount of informative samples such implementations provide. Straightforward solutions to improve this situation include performance optimizations (since implementations with less cycles inevitably leak less to the horizontal adversary) and the addition of noise. Yet, our analysis of an ARM Cortex-A8 running at 1 GHz (a presumably noisy target) suggests that this may not be enough. In this respect, the systematic implementation of point randomization seems strictly necessary to reach high security levels, the evaluation of which (with a systematic evaluation framework as we described in this paper) is an interesting scope for further research, in order to better assess its worst-case security.

Acknowledgements. François-Xavier Standaert is a research associate of the Belgian Fund for Scientific Research. This work has been funded in parts by the European Commission through the H2020 project 731591 (acronym REASSURE) and the ERC project 724725 (acronym SWORD). Yuanyuan Zhou would like to thank Brightsight management board for the support and his colleagues for fruitful discussions.

References

1. Balasch, J., Gierlichs, B., Reparaz, O., Verbauwhede, I.: DPA, bitslicing and masking at 1 GHz. In: Güneysu, T., Handschuh, H. (eds.) CHES 2015. LNCS, vol. 9293, pp. 599–619. Springer, Heidelberg (2015). doi:10.1007/978-3-662-48324-4_30
2. Batina, L., Chmielewski, Ł., Papachristodoulou, L., Schwabe, P., Tunstall, M.: Online template attacks. In: Meier, W., Mukhopadhyay, D. (eds.) INDOCRYPT 2014. LNCS, vol. 8885, pp. 21–36. Springer, Cham (2014). doi:10.1007/978-3-319-13039-2_2

3. Bauer, A., Jaulmes, E., Prouff, E., Wild, J.: Horizontal and vertical side-channel attacks against secure RSA implementations. In: Dawson, E. (ed.) CT-RSA 2013. LNCS, vol. 7779, pp. 1–17. Springer, Heidelberg (2013). doi:10.1007/978-3-642-36095-4_1

4. Bauer, A., Jaulmes, E., Prouff, E., Wild, J.: Horizontal collision correlation attack on elliptic curves. In: Lange, T., Lauter, K., Lisoněk, P. (eds.) SAC 2013. LNCS, vol. 8282, pp. 553–570. Springer, Heidelberg (2014). doi:10.1007/978-3-662-43414-7_28

5. Benger, N., Pol, J., Smart, N.P., Yarom, Y.: "Ooh Aah.. Just a Little Bit": a small amount of side channel can go a long way. In: Batina, L., Robshaw, M. (eds.) CHES 2014. LNCS, vol. 8731, pp. 75–92. Springer, Heidelberg (2014). doi:10.1007/978-3-662-44709-3_5

6. Bernstein, D.J., Lange, T., van Vredendaal, C.: Tighter, faster, simpler side-channel security evaluations beyond computing power. IACR Cryptology ePrint Archive, 2015:221 (2015)

7. Brier, E., Clavier, C., Olivier, F.: Correlation power analysis with a leakage model. In: Joye, M., Quisquater, J.-J. (eds.) CHES 2004. LNCS, vol. 3156, pp. 16–29. Springer, Heidelberg (2004). doi:10.1007/978-3-540-28632-5_2

8. Chari, S., Rao, J.R., Rohatgi, P.: Template attacks. In: Kaliski, B.S., Koç, K., Paar, C. (eds.) CHES 2002. LNCS, vol. 2523, pp. 13–28. Springer, Heidelberg (2003). doi:10.1007/3-540-36400-5_3

9. Chen, C.-N.: Memory address side-channel analysis on exponentiation. In: Lee, J., Kim, J. (eds.) ICISC 2014. LNCS, vol. 8949, pp. 421–432. Springer, Cham (2015). doi:10.1007/978-3-319-15943-0_25

10. Clavier, C., Feix, B., Gagnerot, G., Giraud, C., Roussellet, M., Verneuil, V.: ROSETTA for single trace analysis. In: Galbraith, S., Nandi, M. (eds.) INDOCRYPT 2012. LNCS, vol. 7668, pp. 140–155. Springer, Heidelberg (2012). doi:10.1007/978-3-642-34931-7_9

11. Clavier, C., Feix, B., Gagnerot, G., Roussellet, M., Verneuil, V.: Horizontal correlation analysis on exponentiation. In: Soriano, M., Qing, S., López, J. (eds.) ICICS 2010. LNCS, vol. 6476, pp. 46–61. Springer, Heidelberg (2010). doi:10.1007/978-3-642-17650-0_5

12. Clavier, C., Joye, M.: Universal exponentiation algorithm a first step towards *Provable* SPA-resistance. In: Koç, Ç.K., Naccache, D., Paar, C. (eds.) CHES 2001. LNCS, vol. 2162, pp. 300–308. Springer, Heidelberg (2001). doi:10.1007/3-540-44709-1_25

13. Coron, J.-S.: Resistance against differential power analysis for elliptic curve cryptosystems. In: Koç, Ç.K., Paar, C. (eds.) CHES 1999. LNCS, vol. 1717, pp. 292–302. Springer, Heidelberg (1999). doi:10.1007/3-540-48059-5_25

14. Danger, J.-L., Guilley, S., Hoogvorst, P., Murdica, C., Naccache, D.: Improving the big mac attack on elliptic curve cryptography. In: Ryan, P.Y.A., Naccache, D., Quisquater, J.-J. (eds.) The New Codebreakers. LNCS, vol. 9100, pp. 374–386. Springer, Heidelberg (2016). doi:10.1007/978-3-662-49301-4_23

15. The FPLLL development team. fplll, a lattice reduction library (2016).https://github.com/fplll/fplll

16. Dugardin, M., Papachristodoulou, L., Najm, Z., Batina, L., Danger, J.-L., Guilley, S.: Dismantling real-world ECC with horizontal and vertical template attacks. In: Standaert, F.-X., Oswald, E. (eds.) COSADE 2016. LNCS, vol. 9689, pp. 88–108. Springer, Cham (2016). doi:10.1007/978-3-319-43283-0_6

17. Durvaux, F., Standaert, F.-X.: From improved leakage detection to the detection of points of interests in leakage traces. In: Fischlin, M., Coron, J.-S. (eds.) EUROCRYPT 2016. LNCS, vol. 9665, pp. 240–262. Springer, Heidelberg (2016). doi:10.1007/978-3-662-49890-3_10
18. Durvaux, F., Standaert, F.-X., Pozo, S.M.D.: Towards easy leakage certification: extended version. J. Cryptograph. Eng. **7**(2), 129–147 (2017)
19. Durvaux, F., Standaert, F.-X., Veyrat-Charvillon, N.: How to certify the leakage of a chip? In: Nguyen, P.Q., Oswald, E. (eds.) EUROCRYPT 2014. LNCS, vol. 8441, pp. 459–476. Springer, Heidelberg (2014). doi:10.1007/978-3-642-55220-5_26
20. Glowacz, C., Grosso, V., Poussier, R., Schüth, J., Standaert, F.-X.: Simpler and more efficient rank estimation for side-channel security assessment. In: Leander, G. (ed.) FSE 2015. LNCS, vol. 9054, pp. 117–129. Springer, Heidelberg (2015). doi:10.1007/978-3-662-48116-5_6
21. Hanley, N., Kim, H.S., Tunstall, M.: Exploiting collisions in addition chain-based exponentiation algorithms using a single trace. In: Nyberg, K. (ed.) CT-RSA 2015. LNCS, vol. 9048, pp. 431–448. Springer, Cham (2015). doi:10.1007/978-3-319-16715-2_23
22. Heyszl, J., Mangard, S., Heinz, B., Stumpf, F., Sigl, G.: Localized electromagnetic analysis of cryptographic implementations. In: Dunkelman, O. (ed.) CT-RSA 2012. LNCS, vol. 7178, pp. 231–244. Springer, Heidelberg (2012). doi:10.1007/978-3-642-27954-6_15
23. Joye, M., Tymen, C.: Protections against differential analysis for elliptic curve cryptography — an algebraic approach —. In: Koç, Ç.K., Naccache, D., Paar, C. (eds.) CHES 2001. LNCS, vol. 2162, pp. 377–390. Springer, Heidelberg (2001). doi:10.1007/3-540-44709-1_31
24. Joye, M., Yen, S.-M.: The montgomery powering ladder. In: Kaliski, B.S., Koç, K., Paar, C. (eds.) CHES 2002. LNCS, vol. 2523, pp. 291–302. Springer, Heidelberg (2003). doi:10.1007/3-540-36400-5_22
25. Kocher, P.C.: Timing attacks on implementations of Diffie-Hellman, RSA, DSS, and other systems. In: Koblitz, N. (ed.) CRYPTO 1996. LNCS, vol. 1109, pp. 104–113. Springer, Heidelberg (1996). doi:10.1007/3-540-68697-5_9
26. Kocher, P.C., Jaffe, J., Jun, B., Rohatgi, P.: Introduction to differential power analysis. J. Cryptograph. Eng. **1**(1), 5–27 (2011)
27. Lange, T., Vredendaal, C., Wakker, M.: Kangaroos in side-channel attacks. In: Joye, M., Moradi, A. (eds.) CARDIS 2014. LNCS, vol. 8968, pp. 104–121. Springer, Cham (2015). doi:10.1007/978-3-319-16763-3_7
28. Lerman, L., Poussier, R., Bontempi, G., Markowitch, O., Standaert, F.-X.: Template attacks vs. machine learning revisited (and the curse of dimensionality in side-channel analysis). In: Mangard, S., Poschmann, A.Y. (eds.) COSADE 2014. LNCS, vol. 9064, pp. 20–33. Springer, Cham (2015). doi:10.1007/978-3-319-21476-4_2
29. Longo, J., Mulder, E., Page, D., Tunstall, M.: SoC It to EM: electromagnetic side-channel attacks on a complex system-on-chip. In: Güneysu, T., Handschuh, H. (eds.) CHES 2015. LNCS, vol. 9293, pp. 620–640. Springer, Heidelberg (2015). doi:10.1007/978-3-662-48324-4_31
30. Martin, D.P., O'Connell, J.F., Oswald, E., Stam, M.: Counting keys in parallel after a side channel attack. In: Iwata, T., Cheon, J.H. (eds.) ASIACRYPT 2015. LNCS, vol. 9453, pp. 313–337. Springer, Heidelberg (2015). doi:10.1007/978-3-662-48800-3_13
31. Medwed, M., Oswald, E.: Template attacks on ECDSA. In: Chung, K.-I., Sohn, K., Yung, M. (eds.) WISA 2008. LNCS, vol. 5379, pp. 14–27. Springer, Heidelberg (2009). doi:10.1007/978-3-642-00306-6_2

32. Messerges, T.S., Dabbish, E.A., Sloan, R.H.: Power analysis attacks of modular exponentiation in smartcards. In: Koç, Ç.K., Paar, C. (eds.) CHES 1999. LNCS, vol. 1717, pp. 144–157. Springer, Heidelberg (1999). doi:10.1007/3-540-48059-5_14
33. Nascimento, E., Chmielewski, L., Oswald, D., Schwabe, P.: Attacking embedded ECC implementations through cmov side channels. IACR Cryptology ePrint Archive, 2016:923 (2016)
34. Nguyen, P.Q., Shparlinski, I.E.: The insecurity of the elliptic curve digital signature algorithm with partially known nonces. Des. Codes Crypt. **30**(2), 201–217 (2003)
35. Poussier, R., Standaert, F.-X., Grosso, V.: Simple key enumeration (and Rank Estimation) using histograms: an integrated approach. In: Gierlichs, B., Poschmann, A.Y. (eds.) CHES 2016. LNCS, vol. 9813, pp. 61–81. Springer, Heidelberg (2016). doi:10.1007/978-3-662-53140-2_4
36. NIST FIPS PUB. 186-2: Digital signature standard (dss). National Institute for Standards and Technology (2000)
37. Schindler, W., Lemke, K., Paar, C.: A stochastic model for differential side channel cryptanalysis. In: Rao, J.R., Sunar, B. (eds.) CHES 2005. LNCS, vol. 3659, pp. 30–46. Springer, Heidelberg (2005). doi:10.1007/11545262_3
38. Veyrat-Charvillon, N., Gérard, B., Renauld, M., Standaert, F.-X.: An optimal key enumeration algorithm and its application to side-channel attacks. In: Knudsen, L.R., Wu, H. (eds.) SAC 2012. LNCS, vol. 7707, pp. 390–406. Springer, Heidelberg (2013). doi:10.1007/978-3-642-35999-6_25
39. Veyrat-Charvillon, N., Gérard, B., Standaert, F.-X.: Security evaluations beyond computing power. In: Johansson, T., Nguyen, P.Q. (eds.) EUROCRYPT 2013. LNCS, vol. 7881, pp. 126–141. Springer, Heidelberg (2013). doi:10.1007/978-3-642-38348-9_8
40. Walter, C.D.: Sliding windows succumbs to big mac attack. In: Koç, Ç.K., Naccache, D., Paar, C. (eds.) CHES 2001. LNCS, vol. 2162, pp. 286–299. Springer, Heidelberg (2001). doi:10.1007/3-540-44709-1_24

Sliding Right into Disaster: Left-to-Right Sliding Windows Leak

Daniel J. Bernstein[2(✉)], Joachim Breitner[3(✉)], Daniel Genkin[3,4(✉)],
Leon Groot Bruinderink[1(✉)], Nadia Heninger[3(✉)], Tanja Lange[1(✉)],
Christine van Vredendaal[1(✉)], and Yuval Yarom[5(✉)]

[1] Technische Universiteit Eindhoven, Eindhoven, Netherlands
{L.Groot.Bruinderink,c.v.vredendaal}@tue.nl, tanja@hyperelliptic.org
[2] University of Illinois at Chicago, Chicago, USA
djb@cr.yp.to
[3] University of Pennsylvania, Philadelphia, USA
{joachim,danielg3,nadiah}@cis.upenn.edu
[4] University of Maryland, College Park, USA
[5] University of Adelaide and Data61, CSIRO, Adelaide, Australia
yval@cs.adelaide.edu.au

Abstract. It is well known that constant-time implementations of modular exponentiation cannot use sliding windows. However, software libraries such as Libgcrypt, used by GnuPG, continue to use sliding windows. It is widely believed that, even if the complete pattern of squarings and multiplications is observed through a side-channel attack, the number of exponent bits leaked is not sufficient to carry out a full key-recovery attack against RSA. Specifically, 4-bit sliding windows leak only 40% of the bits, and 5-bit sliding windows leak only 33% of the bits.

In this paper we demonstrate a complete break of RSA-1024 as implemented in Libgcrypt. Our attack makes essential use of the fact that Libgcrypt uses the left-to-right method for computing the sliding-window expansion. We show for the first time that the direction of the encoding matters: the pattern of squarings and multiplications in left-to-right sliding windows leaks significantly more information about the exponent than right-to-left. We show how to extend the Heninger-Shacham algorithm for partial key reconstruction to make use of this information and obtain a very efficient full key recovery for RSA-1024. For RSA-2048 our attack is efficient for 13% of keys.

Keywords: Left-to-right sliding windows · Collision entropy · Cache attack · Flush+Reload · RSA-CRT

1 Introduction

Modular exponentiation in cryptosystems such as RSA is typically performed starting from the most significant bit (MSB) in a left-to-right manner. More efficient implementations use precomputed values to decrease the number of

© International Association for Cryptologic Research 2017
W. Fischer and N. Homma (Eds.): CHES 2017, LNCS 10529, pp. 555–576, 2017.
DOI: 10.1007/978-3-319-66787-4_27

multiplications. Typically these windowing methods are described in a right-to-left manner, starting the recoding of the exponent from the least significant bit (LSB), leading to the potential disadvantage that the exponent has to be parsed twice: once for the recoding and once of the exponentiation.

This motivated researchers to develop left-to-right analogues of the integer recoding methods that can be integrated directly with left-to-right exponentiation methods. For example, the only method for sliding-window exponentiation in the Handbook of Applied Cryptography [16, Chap. 14.6] is the left-to-right version of the algorithm. Doche [7] writes "To enable 'on the fly' recoding, which is particularly interesting for hardware applications" in reference to Joye and Yen's [14] left-to-right algorithm.

Given these endorsements, it is no surprise that many implementations chose a left-to-right method of recoding the exponent. For example, Libgcrypt implements a left-to-right exponentiation with integrated recoding. Libgcrypt is part of the GnuPG code base [2], and is used in particular by GnuPG 2.x, which is a very popular implementation of the OpenPGP standard [6] for applications such as encrypted email and files. Libgcrypt is also used by various other applications; see [1] for a list of frontends.

It is known that exponentiation using sliding-window methods leaks information, specifically the pattern of squarings and multiplications, through cache-based side-channel attacks. However, it is commonly believed that for window width w only about a fraction $2/(w+1)$ bits would leak: each window has 1 bit known to be 1, and each gap has on average 1 bit known to be 0, compared to $w+1$ bits occupied on average by the window and the gap.

Libgcrypt 1.7.6, the last version at the time of writing this paper, resists the attacks of [9,15], because the Libgcrypt maintainers accepted patches to protect against chosen-ciphertext attacks and to hide timings obtained from loading precomputed elements. However, the maintainers refused a patch to switch from sliding windows to fixed windows; they said that this was unnecessary to stop the attacks. RSA-1024 in Libgcrypt uses the CRT method and $w = 4$, which according to the common belief reveals only 40% of all bits, too few to use the key-recovery attack [11] by Heninger and Shacham. RSA-2048 uses CRT and $w = 5$, which according to the common belief reveals only 33% of all bits.

1.1 Contributions

In this paper we show that the common belief is incorrect for the left-to-right recoding: this recoding actually leaks many more bits. An attacker learning the location of multiplications in the left-to-right squarings-and-multiplications sequence can recover the key for RSA-1024 with CRT and $w = 4$ in a search through fewer than 10000 candidates for most keys, and fewer than 1000000 candidates for practically all keys. Note that RSA-1024 and RSA-1280 remain widely deployed in some applications, such as DNSSEC. Scaling up to RSA-2048 does not stop our attack: we show that 13% of all RSA-2048 keys with CRT and $w = 5$ are vulnerable to our method after a search through 2000000 candidates.

We analyze the reasons that left-to-right leaks more bits than right-to-left and extensive experiments show the effectiveness of this attack. We further improve the algorithm by Heninger and Shacham to make use of less readily available information to attack RSA-2048, and prove that our extended algorithm efficiently recovers the full key when the side channel leaks data with a *self-information* rate greater than $1/2$.

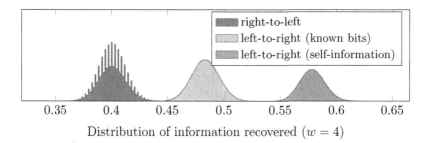

Distribution of information recovered ($w = 4$)

Fig. 1. The sequence of squares and multiplies of left-to-right windowed exponentiation contains much more information about the exponent than from exponentiation in the other direction, both in the form of known bits (red) and information-theoretic bits (green). Recovering close to 50% of the information about the key allows an efficient full key recovery attack. (Color figure online)

To illustrate the real-world applicability of this attack, we demonstrate how to obtain the required side-channel data (the pattern of squarings and multiplications) from the modular-exponentiation routine in Libgcrypt version 1.7.6 using a Flush+Reload [24,25] cache-timing attack that monitors the target's cache-access patterns. The attack combines a small number of traces (at most 20) using the same secret RSA key, and does not depend on further front end details.

1.2 Targeted Software and Current Status

Software and Hardware. We target Libgcrypt version 1.7.6, which is the latest version at the time of writing this paper. We compiled Libgcrypt using GCC version 4.4.7 and the -O2 optimization level. We performed the attack on an HP-Elite 8300 desktop machine, running Centos 6.8 with kernel version 3.18.41-20. The machine has a 4-core Intel i5-3470 processor, running at 3.2 GHz, with 8 GiB of DDR3-1600 CL-11 memory.

Current Status. We have disclosed this issue to the Libgcrypt maintainers and are working with them to produce and validate a patch to mitigate our attack. The vulnerability has been assigned CVE-2017-7526. A new version of Libgcrypt will be released simultaneously with the publication of this paper.

2   Preliminaries

2.1   RSA-CRT

RSA signature key generation is done by generating two random primes p, q. The public key is then set to be (e, N) where e is a (fixed) public exponent and $N = pq$. The private key is set to be (d, p, q) where $ed \equiv 1 \pmod{\phi(n)}$ and $\phi(n) = (p - 1)(q - 1)$. RSA signature of a message m is done by computing $s = h(m)^d \bmod N$ where h is a padded cryptographically secure hash function. Signature verification is done by computing $z = s^e \bmod N$ and verifying that z equals $h(m)$. A common optimization for RSA signatures is based on the Chinese Remainder Theorem (CRT). Instead of directly computing $s = h(m)^d \bmod N$ directly, the signer computes $s_p = h(m)^{d_p} \bmod p$, $s_q = h(m)^{d_q} \bmod q$ (where d_p and d_q are derived from the secret key) and then combines s_p and s_q into s using the CRT. The computations of s_p and s_q work with half-size operands and have half-length exponents, leading to a speedup of a factor $2 - 4$.

2.2   Sliding Window Modular Exponentiation

In order to compute an RSA signature (more specifically the values of s_p and s_q defined above), two modular exponentiation operations must be performed. A modular exponentiation operation gets as inputs base b, exponent d, and modulus p and outputs $b^d \bmod p$. A common method used by cryptographic implementations is the sliding window method, which assumes that the exponent d is given in a special representation, the windowed form. For a window size parameter w, the windowed form of d is a sequence of digits $d_{n-1} \cdots d_0$ such that $d = \sum_{i=0}^{n-1} d_i 2^i$ and d_i is either 0 or an odd number between 1 and $2^w - 1$.

Algorithm 1 performs the sliding window exponentiation method, assuming that the exponent is given in a windowed form, in two steps: It first precomputes the values of $b^1 \bmod p, b^3 \bmod p, \cdots, b^{2^w - 1} \bmod p$ for odd powers of b. Then, the algorithm scans the digits of d from the most significant bit (MSB) to the least significant bit (LSB). For every digit, the algorithm performs a squaring operation (Line 6) on the accumulator variable a. Finally, for every non-zero digit of d, the algorithm performs a multiplication (Line 8).

2.3   Sliding Window Conversion

The representation of a number d in (sliding) windows is not unique, even for a fixed value of w. In particular, the binary representation of d is a valid window form. However, since each non-zero digit requires a costly multiplication operation, it is desirable to reduce the number of non-zero digits in d's sliding windows.

Right-to-Left Sliding Windows. One approach to computing d's sliding windows (with fewer of non-zero digits) scans d's binary representation from the least significant bit (LSB) to the most significant bit (MSB) and generates d's sliding

---

Algorithm 1. Sliding window modular exponentiation.

Input: Three integers b, d and p where $d_n \cdots d_1$ is a windowed form of d.
Output: $a \equiv b^d \pmod{p}$.
1: **procedure** MOD_EXP(b, d, p)
2:     $b_1 \leftarrow b$, $b_2 \leftarrow b^2 \bmod p$, $a \leftarrow 1$
3:     **for** $i \leftarrow 1$ **to** $2^{w-1} - 1$ **do**   ▷ precompute table of small powers of b
4:         $b_{2i+1} \leftarrow b_{2i-1} \cdot b_2 \bmod p$
5:     **for** $i \leftarrow n$ **to** 1 **do**
6:         $a \leftarrow a \cdot a \bmod p$
7:         **if** $d_i \neq 0$ **then**
8:             $a \leftarrow a \cdot b_{d_i} \bmod p$
9:     **return** a
10: **end procedure**

---

windows from the least significant digit (right) to the most significant digit (left). For every clear bit, a zero digit is appended to the left of the windowed form. For each set bit, a non-zero digit is appended whose value is the w-bit integer ending at the current bit. The next $w - 1$ digits in the windowed form are set to be zero digits. The scan resumes from the leftmost bit unused so far. Finally, any leading zeroes in the window form are truncated.

For example, let $w = 3$, and $d = 181$, which is $\underline{1\,0\,1\,1}\,0\,\underline{1\,0\,1}$ in binary. The windows are underlined. This yields the sliding window form 10030005.

Left-to-Right Windowed Form. An alternative approach is the left-to-right windowed form, which scans the bits of d the most to least significant bit and the windowed form is generated from the most significant digit to the least significant one. Similar to the right-to-left form, for every scanned clear bit a zero digit is appended to the right of the windowed form. When a set bit is encountered, since we require from digits to be odd, the algorithm cannot simply set the digit to be the w-bit integer starting at the current bit. Instead, it looks for the longest integer u that has its most significant bit at the current bit, terminates in a set bit, and its number of bits k is at most w bits long. The algorithm sets the next $k - 1$ digits in the windowed form to be zero, sets the subsequent digit to be u and resumes the scan from the next bit unused so far. As before, leading zeroes in the sliding window form are truncated.

Using the $d = 181$ and $w = 3$ example, the left-to-right sliding windows are $\underline{1\,0\,1}\,\underline{1\,0\,1}\,0\,\underline{1}$ and the corresponding windowed form is 500501

Left-to-Right vs. Right-to-Left. While both the methods produce a windowed form whose average density (the ratio between the non-zero digits and the total form length) is about $1/(w + 1)$, generating the windowed form using the right-to-left method guarantees that every non-zero digit is followed by at least $w - 1$ zero digits. This is contrast to the left-to-right method, where two non-zero digits can be as close as adjacent. As explained in Sect. 3, such consecutive non-zero digits can be observed by the attacker, aiding key recovery for sliding window exponentiations using the left-to-right windowed form.

Algorithm 2. Left-to-right sliding window modular exponentiation.

Input: Three integers b, d and p where $d_n \cdots d_1$ is the binary representation of d.

Output: $a \equiv b^d \pmod{p}$.

  1: **procedure** MOD_EXP(b, d, p)
  2:     $b_1 \leftarrow b$, $b_2 \leftarrow b^2$, $a \leftarrow 1$, $z \leftarrow 0$
  3:     **for** $i \leftarrow 1$ **to** $2^{w-1} - 1$ **do**   ▷ precompute table of small odd powers of b
  4:        $b_{2i+1} \leftarrow b_{2i-1} \cdot b_2 \bmod p$
  5:     $i \leftarrow n$
  6:     **while** $i \neq 1$ **do**   ▷ main loop for computing $b^d \bmod p$
  7:        $z \leftarrow z + $ COUNT_LEADING_ZEROS$(d_i \cdots d_1)$
  8:        $i \leftarrow i - z$ ▷ i is the leftmost unscanned set bit of d
  9:        $l \leftarrow \min(i, w)$
10:        $u \leftarrow d_i \cdots d_{i-l+1}$
11:        $t \leftarrow $ COUNT_TRAILING_ZEROS(u)
12:        $u \leftarrow $ SHIFT_RIGHT(u, t) ▷ remove trailing zeroes by shifting u to the right
13:        **for** $j \leftarrow 1$ **to** $z + l - t$ **do**
14:           $a \leftarrow a \cdot a \bmod p$
15:        $a \leftarrow a \cdot b_u \bmod p$ ▷ notice that u is always odd
16:        $i \leftarrow i - l$
17:        $z \leftarrow t$
18:     **return** a
19: **end procedure**

2.4 GnuPG's Sliding Window Exponentiation

While producing the right-to-left sliding window form requires a dedicated procedure, the left-to-right form can be generated "on-the-fly" during the exponentiation algorithm, combining the generation of the expansion and the exponentiation itself in one go. Consequently, the left-to-right sliding window form [16, Algorithm 14.85], shown in Algorithm 2, is the prevalent method used by many implementations, including GnuPG.

Every iteration of the main loop (Line 6) constructs the next non-zero digit u of the windowed from by locating the location i of leftmost set bit of d which was not previously handled (Line 8) and then removing the trailing zeroes from $d_i \cdots d_{i-w+1}$. It appends the squaring operations needed in order to handle the zero windowed form digits preceding u (Line 13) before performing the multiplication operation using u as the index to the precomputation table (thus handling u), and keeping track of trailing zeroes in z.

3 Sliding Right Versus Sliding Left Analysis

In this section, we show how to recover some bits of the secret exponents, assuming that the attacker has access to the square-and-multiply sequence performed by Algorithm 2. We show that more bits can be found by applying this approach to the square-and-multiply sequence of the left-to-right method compared to that of the right-to-left method. At high level, our approach consists of two main steps. In the first step, we show how to directly recover some of the bits of the exponent by analyzing the sequence of squaring and multiplication operations performed by Algorithm 2. This step shows that we are capable of directly recovering an average of 48% of the bits of d_p and d_q for 1024-bit RSA with $w = 4$, the window size used by Libgcrypt for 1024-bit RSA. However, the number of remaining unknown bits required for a full key recovery attack is still too large to brute force. In Sect. 3.4 we show that applying a modified version of the techniques of [11] allows us to recover the remaining exponent bits and obtain the full private key, if at least 50% of the bits are recovered.

3.1   Analyzing the Square and Multiply Sequence

Assume the attacker has access to the sequence $S \in \{s, m\}^*$ corresponding to the sequence of square and multiply operations performed by Algorithm 2 executed on some exponent d. Notice that the squaring operation (Line 13) is performed once per bit of d, while the multiplication operation is performed only for some exponent bits. Thus, we can represent the attacker's knowledge about S as a sequence $s \in \{0, 1, \underline{1}, x, \underline{x}\}^*$ where $0, 1$ indicate known bits of d, x denotes an unknown bit and the positions of multiplications are underlined. For $y \in \{0, 1, \underline{1}, x, \underline{x}\}$ we denote by y^i the i-times repetition of y times.

Since at the start of the analysis all the bits are unknown, we convert S to the sequence s as follows: every sm turns into a $\underline{x}$, all remaining s into x. As a running example, the sequence of squares and multiplies $S = $ smsssssssmsmssssssm is converted into $D_1 = \underline{x}$xxxxxxx$\underline{x}$x$\underline{x}$xxxxx$\underline{x}$.

To obtain bits of d from S_1, the attacker applies the rewrite rules in Fig. 2.

Rule 0: $\underline{x} \rightarrow \underline{1}$

Rule 1: $\underline{1}x^i\underline{1}x^{w-i-1} \rightarrow \underline{1}x^i\underline{1}0^{w-i-1}$ for $i = 0, \cdots, w - 2$

Rule 2:   xxx$\underline{11} \rightarrow$ 1xx$\underline{11}$

Rule 3: $\underline{1}x^i x^{w-1}\underline{1} \rightarrow \underline{1}0^i x^{w-1}\underline{1}$ for $i > 0$

Fig. 2. Rules to deduce known bits from a square-and-multiply sequence

Rule 0: Multiplication bits. Because every digit in the windowed form is odd, a multiplication always happens at bits that are set.

Applied to D_1 we obtain $D_2 = \underline{1}$xxxxxx$\underline{11}$xxxx$\underline{1}$.

Rule 1: Trailing zeros. The algorithm tries to include as many set bits as possible in one digit of the windowed form. So when two multiplications are fewer than w bits apart, we learn that there were no further set bits available to include in the digit corresponding to the second multiplication. Rule 1 sets the following bits to zero accordingly.

Applied to D_2 we obtain $D_3 = \underline{1}$xxxxxx$\underline{11}$000x$\underline{1}$.

Rule 2: Leading one. If we find two immediately consecutive multiplications, it is clear that as the algorithm was building the left digit, there were no trailing zeroes in $u = d_i \cdots d_{i-l+1}$, i.e. $t = 0$ in Line 11. This tells us the precise location of d_i, which we know is set.

Applied to D_3 we obtain $D_4 = \underline{1}$xxx1xx$\underline{11}$000x$\underline{1}$.

Rule 3: Leading zeroes. Every set bit of d is included in a non-zero digit of the windowed form, so it is at most $w - 1$ bits to the left of a multiplication. If two consecutive multiplications are more than w bits apart, we know that there are zeroes in between.

Applied to D_4 we obtain $D_5 = \underline{1}$0001xx$\underline{11}$000x$\underline{1}$.

Larger Example. Consider the bit string

010000111110010100110011010100110000110001111110001110010000$1001.

The corresponding sequence of square and multiply operations (using $w = 4$) evolves as follows as we apply the rules:
```
xxxxxxxxxxxxxxxxxxxxxxxxxxxxxxxxxxxxxxxxxxxxxxxxxxxxxxxxxxxxxxxxxx
x1xxxxxxx1xxx1xxxx1xxx1xx1xxxx11xxxxx1xxxxxx1x1xxxxx1xx1xxxxxxx1
x100xxxxx1xxx1xxxx1xxx1xx10xxx11000xx10xxxxx1x100xxx1xx10xxxxxx1
x100xxxxx1xxx1xxxx1xxx1xx101xx11000xx10xxxxx1x100xxx1xx10xxxxxx1
x10000xxx1xxx10xxx1xxx1xx101xx11000xx1000xxx1x100xxx1xx10000xxx1.
```

Out of the 64 bits, 34 become known through this analysis.

Iterative Application. The previous examples shows that by applying rules iteratively, we can discover a few more bits. In particular, for a window where a leading one is recovered (Rule 2), one may learn the leading bit of the preceding window. Iterating Rule 2 in the example above gives 3 more known leading bits:

```
x10000xxx1xxx101xx11xx11x101xx11000xx1000xxx1x100xxx1xx10000xxx1.
```

This iterative behavior is hard to analyze and occurs rarely in practice. Therefore the following analysis disregards it. Note that the algorithm of Sect. 3.4 does use the additional bits.

3.2 Analyzing Recovery Rules

In this section we analyze the number of bits we are theoretically expected to recover using Rules 0–3 described in the previous section. The analysis applies to general window size w and the bit string length n.

Renewal processes with rewards. We model the number of bits recovered as a renewal reward process [21]. A renewal process is associated with interarrival times $\underline{X} = (X_1, X_2, \dots)$ where the X_i are independent, identically distributed and non-negative variables with a common distribution function F and mean μ. Let

$$S_n = \sum_{i=1}^{n} X_i, \quad n \in \mathbb{N},$$

where $\underline{S} = (0, S_1, S_2, \dots)$ is the sequence of arrival times and

$$N_t = \sum_{n=1}^{\infty} \mathbf{1}(S_n \le t), \quad t \in \mathbb{R}^+$$

is the associated counting process. Now let $\underline{Y} = (Y_1, Y_2, \dots)$ be an i.i.d. sequence associated with $\underline{X}$ in the sense that Y_i is the reward for the interarrival X_i. Note that even though both $\underline{X}$ and $\underline{Y}$ are i.i.d., X_i and Y_i can be dependent. Then the stochastic process

$$R_t = \sum_{i=1}^{N_t} Y_i, \quad t \in \mathbb{R}^+,$$

is a renewal reward process. The function $r(t) = \mathbb{E}(R_t)$ is the renewal reward function. We can now state the *renewal reward theorem* [17]. Since $\mu_X < \infty$ and $\mu_Y < \infty$ we have for the renewal reward process

$$R_t/t \to \mu_Y/\mu_X \text{ as } t \to \infty \text{ with probability } 1,$$
$$r(t)/t \to \mu_Y/\mu_X \text{ as } t \to \infty.$$

This is related to our attack in the following way. The n bit locations of the bit string form an interval of integers $[1, n]$, labeling the leftmost bit as 1. We set $X_1 = b + w - 1$, where b is the location of the first bit set to 1, that is, the left boundary of the first window. Then the left boundary of the next window is independent of the first $b + w - 1$ bits. The renewal process examines each window independently. For each window X_i we gain information about *at least* the multiplication bit. This is the reward Y_i associated with X_i. The renewal reward theorem now implies that for bit strings of length n, the expected number of recovered bits will converge to $\frac{n\mu_Y}{\mu_X}$.

Recovered bit probabilities. In the remainder of this section we analyze the expected number of bits that are recovered (the reward) in some number of bits (the renewal length) by the rules of Sect. 3.1. Then by calculating the probability of each of these rules' occurrence, we can compute the overall number of recovered bits by using the renewal reward theorem. Note that Rule 0 (the bits set to $\underline{1}$) can be incorporated into the other rules by increasing their recovered bits by one.

Rule 1: Trailing zeroes. The first rule applies to short windows. Recall that we call a window a "short window" whenever the length between two multiplications is less than $w - 1$.

Let $0 \le j \le w - 2$ denote the length between two multiplications. (A length of $w - 1$ is a full-size window.) The probability of a short window depends on these j bits, as well as $w - 1$ bits after the multiplication: the multiplication bit should be the right-most 1-bit in the window. The following theorem (which we prove in the full version of this paper) gives the probability of a short window.

Theorem 1. *Let X be an interarrival time. Then the probability that $X = w$ and we have a short window with reward $Y = w - j$, $0 \leq j \leq w - 2$ is*

$$p_j = \frac{1 + \sum_{i=1}^{j} 2^{2i-1}}{2^{j+w}}$$

We see in the proof that the bits $y_{w-j-1}, \ldots, y_{w-2}$ can take any values. Also since bit $y_{w-j-2} = 0$ is known, we have a renewal at this point where future bits are independent.

Rule 2: Leading one. As explained in Sect. 3.1, this rule means that when after renewal an ultra-short window occurs (a 1 followed by $w - 1$ zeroes) we get an extra bit of information about the previous window. The exception to this rule is if the previous window was also an ultra-short window. In this case the $\underline{1}$ of the window is at the location of the multiplication bit we would have learned and therefore we do not get extra information. As seen in the previous section, an ultra-short window occurs with probability $p_0 = 1/2^w$ If an ultra-short window occurs after the current window with window-size $1 \leq j \leq w - 1$, we therefore recover $(w - j) + 1$ bits (all bits of the current window plus 1 for the leading bit) with probability $p_j p_0$ and $(w - j)$ with probability $p_j(1 - p_0)$.

Rule 3: Leading zeroes. The last way in which extra bits can be recovered is the leading zeroes. If a window of size $w - d$ is preceded by more than d zeroes, then we can recover the excess zeroes. Let X_0 be a random variable of the length of a bit string of zeros until the first 1 is encountered. Then X_0 is geometrically distributed with $p = 1/2$. So $\mathbb{P}[X_0 = k] = (1/2)^k \cdot (1/2) = (1/2)^{k+1}$. This distribution has mean $\mu_X = 1$.

Let X_w be a random variable representing the length of the bit string from the first 1 that was encountered until the multiplication bit. For general window length of w, we have

$$\mathbb{P}[X_w = k] = \begin{cases} \frac{1}{2^{w-1}} & k = 1 \\ \frac{1}{2^{w-k+1}} & k > 1 \end{cases}$$

Now the distribution of the full bit string is the sum of the variables X_0 and X_w. We have that $\mathbb{P}[X_0 + X_w = k] = \sum_{i=1}^{\min(k,w)} \mathbb{P}[X_w = i] \cdot \mathbb{P}[X_0 = k - i]$.

Notice that this rule only recovers bits if the gap between two multiplications is at least $w - 1$. This means that these cases are independent of Rule 1.

There is a small caveat in this analysis: the renewal length is unclear. In the case that we have a sequence of zeroes followed by a short window of size $j < w$, we are implicitly conditioning on the $w - j$ bits that follow. This means we cannot simply renew after the $\underline{1}$ and since we also cannot distinguish between a short and regular window size, we also cannot know how much information we have on the bits that follow.

We solve this by introducing an upper and lower bound. For the upper bound the recovered bits remains as above and the renewal at $X_0 + w$. This is an obvious upper bound. This means that for a sequence of zeroes followed by a short window of size j, we assume a probability of 1 of recovering information on the $w - j$ bits that follow the sequence. We get an average recovered bits of

$$\overline{R} = \sum_{k=w}^{\infty} \sum_{i=1}^{\min(k,w)} (k - i + 1) \cdot \mathbb{P}[X_w = i] \cdot \mathbb{P}[X_0 = k - i],$$

and a renewal length of

$$\overline{N} = \sum_{k=w}^{\infty} \sum_{i=1}^{\min(k,w)} (k + w - i) \cdot \mathbb{P}[X_w = i] \cdot \mathbb{P}[X_0 = k - i].$$

For the lower bound we could instead assume a probability of 0 of recovering information on the $w - j$ bits. We can however get a tighter bound by observing that the bits that follow this rule are more likely a 0 than a 1 and we are more likely to recover a 0 at the start of a new window then we are a 0. Therefore bound the renewal at $X_0 + X_w$ and throw away the extra information. Similar formulas can be derived for the lower bounds $\underline{R}$ and $\underline{N}$.

From this, we can calculate the expected renewal length for fixed w, by summing over all possible renewal lengths with corresponding probabilities. We can do the same for the expected number of recovered bits per renewal. Finally, we are interested in the expected total number of recovered bits in a n-bit string. We calculate this by taking an average number of renewals (by dividing n by the expected renewal length) and multiply this with the number of recovered bits per window. Since we have upper and lower bounds for both the renewal length and recovered bits for Rule 3, we also get lower and upper bounds for the expected total number of recovered bits.

Recovered Bits for Right-to-Left. The analysis of bit recovery for right-to-left exponentiation is simpler. The bit string is an alternation of X_0 and X_w (see Rule 3), where $X_w = w$ and X_0 is geometrically distributed with $p = 1/2$. Therefore the expected renewal length N and the expected reward R are

$$N = \sum_{i=0}^{\infty} (w + i) \cdot \mathbb{P}[X_0 = i] = w + 1 \quad \text{and} \quad R = \sum_{i=0}^{\infty} (1 + i) \cdot \mathbb{P}[X_0 = i] = 2.$$

Then by the renewal reward theorem, we expect to recover $\frac{2n}{w+1}$ bits.

3.3   Experimental Verification

To experimentally validate our analysis, we sampled n-bit binary strings uniformly at random and used Algorithm 2 to derive the square and multiply sequence. We then applied Rules 0–3 from Sect. 3.1 to extract known bits.

Case $n = 512$, $w = 4$. Figure 1 shows the total fraction of bits learned for right-to-left exponentiation compared to left-to-right exponentiation, for $w = 4$, over 1,000,000 experiments with $w = 4$ and $n = 512$, corresponding to the our target Libgcrypt's implementation for 1024-bit RSA. On average we learned

251 bits, or 49%, for left-to-right exponentiation with 512-bit exponents. This is between our computed lower bound of $\beta_L = 245$ (from a renewal length of $\underline{N} = 4.67$ bits and reward of 2.24 bits on average per renewal) and upper bound $\beta_U = 258$ (from a renewal length of $\overline{N} = 4.90$ bits and reward of 2.47 bits per renewal). The average number of recovered bits for right-to-left exponentiation is $204 \approx \frac{2n}{w+1}$ bits, or 40%, as expected.

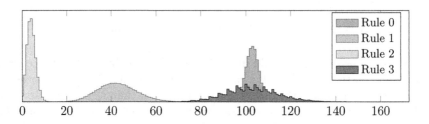

Fig. 3. We generated 100,000 random 512-bit strings and generated the square and multiply sequence with $w = 4$. We then applied Rules 0–3 successively to recover bits of the original string. We plot the distribution of the number of recovered bits in our experiments.

Figure 3 shows the distribution of the number of new bits learned for each rule with left-to-right exponentiation by successively applying Rules 0–3 for 100,000 exponents. Both Rule 0 and Rule 3 contribute about $205 \approx \frac{2n}{w+1}$ bits, which is equal both to our theoretical analysis and is also the number of bits learned from the right-to-left exponentiation. The spikes visible in Rule 3 are due to the fact that we know that any least significant bits occurring after the last window must be 0, and we credit these bits learned to Rule 3. The number of bits learned from this final step is equal to $n \bmod w$, leading to small spikes at intervals of w bits.

Case $n = 1024$, $w = 5$. For $n = 1024$ and $w = 5$, corresponding to Libgcrypt's implementation of 2048-bit RSA, we recover 41.5% of bits on average using Rules 0–3. This is between our lower bound of $\beta_L = 412$ (from a lower bound average renewal length of $\underline{N} = 5.67$ bits, and expected 2.29 bits on average per renewal) and upper bound of $\beta_U = 436$ (from an average renewal length of $\overline{N} = 5.89$ bits with an average reward of 2.51 bits per renewal). Note that the reward per renewal is about the same as in the first case ($n = 512, w = 4$), but the average renewal length is higher. This means that we win fewer bits for this case.

3.4   Full RSA Key Recovery from Known Bits

Once we have used the recovered sequence of squares and multiplies to derive some information about the bits of the Chinese remainder theorem coefficients $d_p = d \bmod (p - 1)$ and $d_q = d \bmod (q - 1)$, we can use a modified version of the branch and prune algorithm of Heninger and Shacham [11] to recover the remaining unknown bits of these exponents to recover the full private key.

The algorithm will recover the values d_p and d_q from partial information. In order to do so, we use the integer forms of the RSA equations

$$ed_p = 1 + k_p(p - 1)$$
$$ed_q = 1 + k_q(q - 1)$$

which these values satisfy for positive integers $k_p, k_q < e$.

RSA Coefficient Recovery. As described in [12,26], k_p and k_q are initially unknown, but are related via the equation $(k_p - 1)(k_q - 1) \equiv k_p k_q N \bmod e$. Thus we need to try at most e pairs of k_p, k_q. In the most common case, $e = 65537$. As described in [26], incorrect values of k_p, k_q quickly result in no solutions.

LSB-Side Branch and Prune Algorithm. At the beginning of the algorithm, we have deduced some bits of d_p and d_q using Rules 0–3. Given candidate values for k_p and k_q, we can then apply the approach of [11] to recover successive bits of the key starting from the least significant bits. Our algorithm does a depth-first search over the unknown bits of d_p, d_q, p, and q. At the ith least significant bit, we have generated a candidate solution for bits $0 \ldots i-1$ of each of our unknown values. We then verify the equations

$$ed_p = 1 + k_p(p - 1) \bmod 2^i$$
$$ed_q = 1 + k_q(q - 1) \bmod 2^i$$
$$pq = N \bmod 2^i \tag{1}$$

and prune a candidate solution if any of these equations is not satisfied.

Analysis. Heuristically, we expect this approach to be efficient when we know more than 50% of bits for d_p and d_q, distributed uniformly at random. [11,18] We also expect the running time to grow exponentially in the number of unknown bits when we know many fewer than 50% of the bits. From the analysis of Rules 0–3 above, we expect to recover 48% of the bits. While the sequence of recovered bits is not, strictly speaking, uniformly random since it is derived using deterministic rules, the experimental performance of the algorithm matched that of a random sequence.

Experimental Evaluation for $w = 4$. We ran 500,000 trial key recovery attempts for randomly generated d_p and d_q with 1024-bit RSA and $w = 4$. For a given trial, if the branching process passed 1,000,000 candidates examined without finding a solution, we abandoned the attempt. Experimentally, we recover more than 50% of the bits 32% of the time, and successfully recovered the key in 28% of our trials. For 50% or 512 bits known, the median number of examined candidates was 182,738. We recovered 501 bits on average in our trials using Rules 0–3; at this level the median number of candidates was above 1 million.

Experimental Evaluation for $w = 5$. We experimented with this algorithm for 2048-bit RSA, with $w = 5$. The number of bits that can be derived unconditionally using Rules 0–3 is around 41% on average, below the threshold where we expect the Heninger-Shacham algorithm to terminate for 1024-bit exponents. The algorithm did not yield any successful key recovery trials at this size.

4   RSA Key Recovery from Squares and Multiplies

The sequence of squares and multiplies encodes additional information about the secret exponent that does not translate directly into knowledge of particular bits. In this section, we give a new algorithm that exploits this additional information by recovering RSA keys directly from the square-and-multiply sequence. This gives a significant speed improvement over the key recovery algorithm described in Sect. 3.4, and brings an attack against $w = 5$ within feasible range.

4.1   Pruning from Squares and Multiplies

Our new algorithm generates a depth-first tree of candidate solutions for the secret exponents, and prunes a candidate solution if it could not have produced the ground-truth square-and-multiply sequence obtained by the side-channel attack. Let $\mathrm{SM}(d) = s$ be the deterministic function that maps a bit string d to a sequence of squares and multiplies $s \in \{s, m\}^*$.

In the beginning of the algorithm, we assume we have ground truth square-and-multiply sequences s_p and s_q corresponding to the unknown CRT coefficients d_p and d_q. We begin by recovering the coefficients k_p and k_q using brute force as described in Sect. 3.4. We will then iteratively produce candidate solutions for the bits of d_p and d_q by generating a depth-first search tree of candidates satisfying Eq. 1 starting at the least significant bits. We will attempt to prune candidate solutions for d_p or d_q at bit locations i for which we know the precise state of Algorithm 2 from the corresponding square and multiply sequence s, namely when element i of s is a multiply or begins a sequence of w squares. To test an i-bit candidate exponent d_i, we compare $s' = \mathrm{SM}(d_i)$ to positions 0 through $i - 1$ of s, and prune d_i if the sequences do not match exactly.

4.2   Algorithm Analysis

We analyze the performance of this algorithm by computing the expected number of candidate solutions examined by the algorithm before it recovers a full key. Our analysis was inspired by the information-theoretic analysis of [18], but we had to develop a new approach to capture the present scenario.

Let $p_s = \Pr[\mathrm{SM}(d_i) = s]$ be the probability that a fixed square-and-multiply sequences s is observed for a uniformly random i-bit sequence d_i. This defines the probability distribution D_i of square-and-multiply sequences for i-bit inputs.

In order to understand how much information a sequence s leaks about an exponent, we will use the *self-information*, defined as $I_s = -\log p_s$. This is the analogue of the number of bits known for the algorithm given in Sect. 3.4. As with the bit count, we can express the number of candidate solutions that generate s in terms of I_s: $\#\{d \mid \mathrm{SM}(d) = s\} = 2^i p_s = 2^i 2^{-I_s}$. For a given sequence s, let I_i denote the self-information of the least significant i bits.

Theorem 2. (Heuristic). *If for the square-and-multiply sequences s_{p_i} and s_{q_i}, we have $I_i > i/2$ for almost all i, then the algorithm described in Sect. 4.1 runs in expected linear time in the number of bits of the exponent.*

Proof. (Sketch). In addition pruning based on s, the algorithm also prunes by verifying the RSA equations up to bit position i. Let $\mathrm{RSA}_i(d_p, d_q) = 1$ if $(ed_p - 1 + k_p)(ed_q - 1 + k_q) = k_p k_q N \bmod 2^i$ and 0 otherwise. For random (incorrect) candidates d_{p_i} and d_{q_i}, $\Pr[\mathrm{RSA}_i(d_{p_i}, d_{q_i})] = 1/2^i$.

As in [11], we heuristically assume that, once a bit has been guessed wrong, the set of satisfying candidates for d_{p_i} and d_{q_i} behave randomly and independently with respect to the RSA equation at bit position i.

Consider an incorrect guess at the first bit. We wish to bound the candidates examined before the decision is pruned. The number of incorrect candidates satisfying the square-and-multiply constraints and the RSA equation at bit i is

$$\#\{d_{p_i}, d_{q_i}\} \le \#\{d_{p_i} \mid \mathrm{SM}(d_{p_i}) = s_{p_i}\} \cdot \#\{d_{q_i} \mid \mathrm{SM}(d_{q_i}) = s_{q_i}\} \cdot \Pr[\mathrm{RSA}_i(d_{p_i}, d_{q_i})]$$
$$= 2^i 2^{-I_i} \cdot 2^i 2^{-I_i} \cdot 2^{-i} = 2^{i-2I_i} \le 2^{i \cdot (1-2c)}$$

with $I_i/i \ge c$ for some $c > 1/2$.

In total, there are $\sum_i \#\{d_{p_i}, d_{q_i}\} \le \sum_i 2^{i \cdot (1-2c)} \le 1/(1 - 2^{1-2c})$ candiates.

But *any* of the n bits can be guessed wrongly, each producing a branch of that size. Therefore, the total search tree has at most $n \cdot (1 + \frac{1}{1-2^{1-2c}})$ nodes.

A similar argument also tells us about the expected size of the search tree, which depends on the *collision entropy* [20]

$$H_i = -\log \sum_{s \in \{s,m\}^i} p_s^2$$

of the distribution D_i of distinct square-and-multiply sequences. This is the log of the probability that two i-bit sequences chosen according to D_i are identical.

For our distribution D_i, the H_i are approximately linear in i. We can define the *collision entropy rate* $H = H_i/i$ and obtain an upper bound for the expected number of examined solutions, which we prove in the full version of the paper:

Theorem 3. *The expected total number of candidate solutions examined by Algorithm 2 for n-bit d_p an d_q is*

$$E\left[\sum_i \#\{d_{p_i}, d_{q_i}\}\right] \le n\left(1 + \frac{1 - 2^{n \cdot (1-2H)}}{1 - 2^{1-2H}}\right).$$

Entropy calculations. We calculated the collision entropy rate by modeling the leak as a Markov chain. For $w = 4$, $H = 0.545$, and thus we expect Algorithm 2 to comfortably run in expected linear time. For $w = 5$, $H = 0.461$, and thus we expect the algorithm to successfully terminate on some fraction of inputs. We give more details on this computation in the full version of this paper.

4.3 Experimental Evaluation for $w = 4$

We ran 500,000 trials of our sequence-pruning algorithm for randomly generated d_p and d_q with 1024-bit RSA and plot the distribution of running times in Fig. 4.

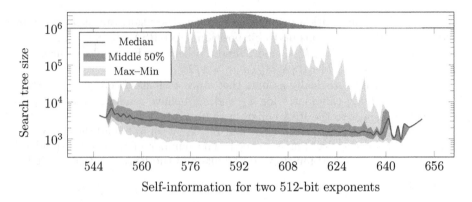

Fig. 4. We attempted 500,000 key recovery trials for randomly generated 1024-bit RSA keys with $w = 4$. We plot the distribution of the number of candidates tested by the algorithm against the self-information of the observed square-and-multiply sequences, measured in bits. The histogram above the plot shows the distribution of self-information across all the trials.

For a given trial, if the branching process passed 1,000,000 candidates examined without finding a solution, we abandoned the attempt. For each trial square-and-multiply sequence s, we computed the number of bit sequences that could have generated it. From the average of this quantity over the 1 million exponents generated in our trial, the collision entropy rate in our experiments is $H = 0.547$, in line with our analytic computation above. The median self-information of the exponents generated in our trials was 295 bits; at this level the median number of candidates examined by the algorithm was 2,174. This can be directly compared to the 251 bits recovered in Sect. 3, since the self-information in that case is exactly the number of known bits in the exponent.

4.4   Experimental Evaluation for $w = 5$

We ran 500,000 trials of our sequence-pruning algorithm for 2048-bit RSA and $w = 5$ with randomly generated d_p and d_q and plot the distribution of running times in Fig. 5. 8.6% of our experimental trials successfully recovered the key before hitting the panic threshold of 1 million tries. Increasing the allowed tree size to 2 million tries allowed us to recover the key in 13% of trials. We experimentally estimate a collision entropy rate $H = 0.464$, in line with our analytic computation. The median self-information for the exponents generated in our trials is 507 bits, significantly higher than the 420 bits that can be directly recovered using the analysis in Sect. 3.

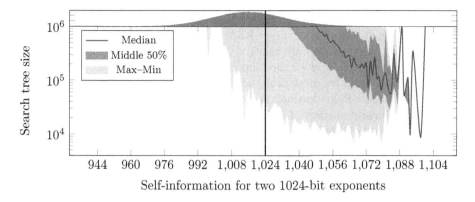

Fig. 5. We attempted 500,000 key recovery trials for randomly generated 2048-bit RSA keys with $w = 5$, and plot the distribution of search tree size by the self-information. The vertical line marks the 50% rate at which we expect the algorithm to be efficient.

5   Attacking Libgcrypt

In the previous section we showed how an attacker with access to the square-and-multiply sequence can recover the private RSA key. To complete the discussion we show how the attacker can obtain the square-and-multiply sequence.

5.1   The Side-Channel Attack

To demonstrate the vulnerability in Libgcrypt, we use the Flush+Reload attack [25]. The attack, which monitors shared memory locations for access by a victim, consists of two phases. The attacker first evicts a monitored location from the cache, typically using the x86 `clflush` instruction. He then waits for a short while, before measuring the time to access the monitored location. If the victim has accessed the memory location during the wait, the contents of the memory location will be cached, and the attacker's access will be fast. Otherwise, the attacker causes the contents to be retrieved from the main memory and his access takes longer. By repeating the attack, the attacker creates a trace of the victim accesses to the monitored location over time. Flush+Reload has been used in the past to attack modular exponentiation [3,25], as well as other cryptographic primitives [4,5,13,19,24] and non-cryptographic software [10,28].

Mounting the Flush+Reload attack on Libgcrypt presents several challenges. First, as part of the defense against the attack of Yarom and Falkner [25], Libgcrypt uses the multiplication code to perform the squaring operation. While this is less efficient than using a dedicated code for squaring, the use of the same code means that we cannot identify the multiply operations by probing a separate multiply code. Instead we probe code locations that are used between the operations to identify the call site to the modular reduction.

The second challenge is achieving a sufficiently high temporal resolution. Prior side-channel attacks on implementations of modular exponentiation use large (1024–4096 bits) moduli [8,9,15,25,27], which facilitate side-channel attacks [22]. In this attack we target RSA-1024, which uses 512-bit moduli. The operations on these moduli are relatively fast, taking a total of less than 2500 cycles on average to compute a modular multiplication. To be able to distinguish events of this length, we must probe at least twice as fast, which is close to the limit of the Flush+Reload attack and would results in a high error rate [3]. We use the amplification attack of Allan et al. [3] to slow down the modular reduction. We target the code of the subtraction function used as part of the modular reduction. The attack increases the execution time of the modular reduction to over 30000 cycles.

Our third challenge is that even with amplification, there is a chance of missing a probe [3]. To reduce the probability of this happening, we probe two memory locations within the execution path of short code segments. The likelihood of missing both probes is small enough to allow high-quality traces.

Overall, we use the Flush+Reload attack to monitor seven victim code location. The monitored locations can be divided into three groups. To distinguish between the exponentiations Libgcrypt performs while signing, we monitor locations in the entry and exit of the exponentiation function. We also monitor a location in the loop that precomputes the multipliers to help identifying these multiplications. To trace individual modular multiplications, we monitor locations within the multiply and the modular reduction functions. Finally, to identify the multiplication by non-zero multipliers, we monitor locations in the code that conditionally copies the multiplier and in the entry to the main loop of the exponentiation. The former is accessed when Libgcrypt selects the multiplier before it performs the multiplication. The latter is accessed after the multiplication when the next iteration of the main loop starts. We repeatedly probe these locations once every 10000 cycles, allowing for 3–4 probes in each modular multiply or square operation.

5.2 Results

To mount the attack, we use the FR-trace software, included in the Mastik toolkit [23]. FR-trace provides a command-line interface for performing the Flush+Reload and the amplification attacks we require for recovering the square-and-multiply sequences of the Libgcrypt exponentiation. FR-trace waits until there is activity in any of the monitored locations and collects a trace of the activity. Figure 6 shows a part of a collected activity trace.

Recall that the Flush+Reload attack identifies activity in a location by measuring the time it takes to read the contents of the location. Fast reads indicate activity. In the figure, monitored locations with read time below 100 cycles indicate that the location was active during the sample.

Because multiplications take an average 800 cycles, whereas our sample rate is once in 10000 cycles, most of the time activity in the multiplication code is contained within a single sample. In Fig. 6 we see the multiplication operations as "dips" in the multiplication trace (dotted black).

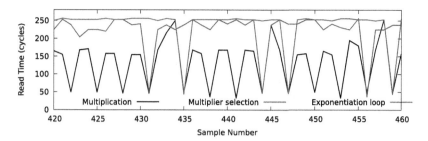

Fig. 6. Libgcrypt activity trace.

Each multiplication operation is followed by a modular reduction. Our side-channel amplification attack "stretches" the execution of the modular reduction and it spans over more than 30000 cycles. Because none of the memory addresses traced in the figure is active during the modular reduction, we see gaps of 3–4 samples between periods of activity in any of the other monitored locations.

To distinguish between multiplications that use one of the precomputed multipliers and multiplications that square the accumulator by multiplying it with itself, we rely on activity in the multiplier selection and in the exponentiation loop locations. Before multiplying with a precomputed multiplier, the multiplier needs to be selected. Hence we would expect to see activity in the multiplier selection location just before starting the multiply, and due to the temporal granularity of the attack we are likely to see both events in the same sample. Similarly, after performing the multiplication and the modular reduction, we expect to see activity in the beginning of the main exponentiation loop. Again, due to attack granularity, this activity is likely to occur within the same sample as the following multiplication. Thus, because we see activity in the multiplier selection location during sample 431 and activity in the beginning of the exponentiation loop in the following multiplication (sample 435), we can conclude that the former multiplication is using one of the precomputed multipliers.

In the absence of errors, this allows us to completely recover the sequence of square and multiplies performed and with it, the positions of the non-zero digits in the windowed representation of the exponent.

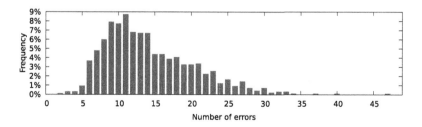

Fig. 7. Distribution of the number of errors in captured traces.

However, capture errors do occur, as shown in Fig. 7. To correct these, we capture multiple traces of signatures using the same private key. On average there are 14 errors in a captured trace. We find that in most cases, manually aligning traces and using a simple majority rule is sufficient to recover the complete square-and-multiply sequence. In all of the cases we have tried, combining twenty sequences yielded the complete sequence.

Acknowledgments. Yuval Yarom performed part of this work as a visiting scholar at the University of Pennsylvania. This work was supported by the Netherlands Organisation for Scientific Research (NWO) under grant 639.073.005; by the Commission of the European Communities through the Horizon 2020 program under project number 645622 (PQCRYPTO) and project number 645421 (ECRYPT-CSA); by the National Science Foundation under grants 1314919, 1408734, 1505799, 1513671, 1319880 and 14–519. by a gift from Cisco; by an Endeavour Research Fellowship from the Australian Department of Education and Training; by the 2017-2018 Rothschild Post-doctoral Fellowship; by the Blavatnik Interdisciplinary Cyber Research Center (ICRC); by the Check Point Institute for Information Security; by the Israeli Centers of Research Excellence I-CORE program (center 4/11); by the Leona M. & Harry B. Helmsley Charitable Trust; by the Warren Center for Network and Data Sciences; by the financial assistance award 70NANB15H328 from the U.S. Department of Commerce, National Institute of Standards and Technology; and by the Defense Advanced Research Project Agency (DARPA) under Contract #FA8650-16-C-7622.

Permanent ID of this document: `8016c16382e6f3876aa03bef6e4db5ff`. Date: 2017.06.26.

References

1. GnuPG Frontends. https://www.gnupg.org/related_software/frontends.html
2. GNU Privacy Guard. https://www.gnupg.org
3. Allan, T., Brumley, B.B., Falkner, K., van de Pol, J., Yarom, Y.: Amplifying side channels through performance degradation. In: 32nd Annual Computer Security Applications Conference (ACSAC), Los Angeles, CA, US, December 2016
4. Benger, N., van de Pol, J., Smart, N.P., Yarom, Y.: "Ooh Aah.. Just a Little Bit": a small amount of side channel can go a long way. In: Batina, L., Robshaw, M. (eds.) CHES 2014. LNCS, vol. 8731, pp. 75–92. Springer, Heidelberg (2014). doi:10.1007/978-3-662-44709-3_5
5. Groot Bruinderink, L., Hülsing, A., Lange, T., Yarom, Y.: Flush, Gauss, and reload – a cache attack on the BLISS lattice-based signature scheme. In: Gierlichs, B., Poschmann, A.Y. (eds.) CHES 2016. LNCS, vol. 9813, pp. 323–345. Springer, Heidelberg (2016). doi:10.1007/978-3-662-53140-2_16
6. Callas, J., Donnerhacke, L., Finney, H., Shaw, D., Thayer, R.: OpenPGP message format. RFC 4880, November 2007
7. Doche, C.: Exponentiation. In: Handbook of Elliptic and Hyperelliptic Curve Cryptography., pp. 144–168. Chapman and Hall/CRC (2005). doi:10.1201/9781420034981.pt2
8. Genkin, D., Shamir, A., Tromer, E.: RSA Key extraction via low-bandwidth acoustic cryptanalysis. In: Garay, J.A., Gennaro, R. (eds.) CRYPTO 2014. LNCS, vol. 8616, pp. 444–461. Springer, Heidelberg (2014). doi:10.1007/978-3-662-44371-2_25

9. Genkin, D., Pachmanov, L., Pipman, I., Tromer, E.: Stealing keys from PCs using a radio: cheap electromagnetic attacks on windowed exponentiation. In: Güneysu, T., Handschuh, H. (eds.) CHES 2015. LNCS, vol. 9293, pp. 207–228. Springer, Heidelberg (2015). doi:10.1007/978-3-662-48324-4_11

10. Gruss, D., Spreitzer, R., Mangard, S.: Cache template attacks: automating attacks on inclusive last-level caches. In: 24th USENIX Security Symposium, pp. 897–912, Washington, DC, US, August 2015

11. Heninger, N., Shacham, H.: Reconstructing RSA private keys from random key bits. In: Halevi, S. (ed.) CRYPTO 2009. LNCS, vol. 5677, pp. 1–17. Springer, Heidelberg (2009). doi:10.1007/978-3-642-03356-8_1

12. İnci, M.S., Gulmezoglu, B., Irazoqui, G., Eisenbarth, T., Sunar, B.: Cache attacks enable bulk key recovery on the cloud. In: Gierlichs, B., Poschmann, A.Y. (eds.) CHES 2016. LNCS, vol. 9813, pp. 368–388. Springer, Heidelberg (2016). doi:10.1007/978-3-662-53140-2_18

13. Irazoqui, G., Inci, M.S., Eisenbarth, T., Sunar, B.: Wait a Minute! A fast, Cross-VM Attack on AES. In: Stavrou, A., Bos, H., Portokalidis, G. (eds.) RAID 2014. LNCS, vol. 8688, pp. 299–319. Springer, Cham (2014). doi:10.1007/978-3-319-11379-1_15

14. Joye, M., Yen, S.-M.: Optimal left-to-right binary signed-digit recoding. IEEE Trans. Comput. **49**(7), 740–748 (2000). doi:10.1109/12.863044

15. Liu, F., Yarom, Y., Ge, Q., Heiser, G., Lee, R.B.: Last-level cache side-channel attacks are practical. In: IEEE Symposium on Security and Privacy 2015. IEEE (2015)

16. Menezes, A.J., van Oorschot, P.C., Vanstone, S.A.: Handbook of Applied Cryptography. CRC Press, Boca Raton (1996)

17. Moder, J.J., Elmaghraby, S.E.: Handbook of Operations Research: Models and Applications, vol. 1. Van Nostrand Reinhold Co., New York (1978)

18. Paterson, K.G., Polychroniadou, A., Sibborn, D.L.: A coding-theoretic approach to recovering noisy RSA keys. In: Wang, X., Sako, K. (eds.) ASIACRYPT 2012. LNCS, vol. 7658, pp. 386–403. Springer, Heidelberg (2012). doi:10.1007/978-3-642-34961-4_24

19. van de Pol, J., Smart, N.P., Yarom, Y.: Just a little bit more. In: Nyberg, K. (ed.) CT-RSA 2015. LNCS, vol. 9048, pp. 3–21. Springer, Cham (2015). doi:10.1007/978-3-319-16715-2_1

20. Rényi, A.: On measures of entropy and information. In: Proceedings of the Fourth Berkeley Symposium on Mathematical Statistics and Probability, vol. 1, pp. 547–561, Berkeley (1961)

21. Ross, S.M.: Stochastic Processes. Probability and Mathematical Statistics. Wiley, New York (1983). ISBN 0-471-09942-2

22. Walter, C.D.: Longer keys may facilitate side channel attacks. In: Matsui, M., Zuccherato, R.J. (eds.) SAC 2003. LNCS, vol. 3006, pp. 42–57. Springer, Heidelberg (2004). doi:10.1007/978-3-540-24654-1_4

23. Yarom, Y.: Mastik: a micro-architectural side-channel toolkit, September 2016. http://cs.adelaide.edu.au/yval/Mastik/Mastik.pdf

24. Yarom, Y., Benger, N.: Recovering OpenSSL ECDSA nonces using the Flush+Reload cache side-channel attack. Cryptology ePrint Archive, Report 2014/140, February 2014

25. Yarom, Y., Falkner, K.: Flush+Reload: a high resolution, low noise, L3 cache side-channel attack. In: 25th USENIX Security Symposium, pp. 719–732, San Diego, CA, US (2014)

26. Yarom, Y., Genkin, D., Heninger, N.: CacheBleed: a timing attack on openSSL constant time RSA. In: Gierlichs, B., Poschmann, A.Y. (eds.) CHES 2016. LNCS, vol. 9813, pp. 346–367. Springer, Heidelberg (2016). doi:10.1007/978-3-662-53140-2_17

27. Zhang, Y., Juels, A., Reiter, M.K., Ristenpart, T.: Cross-VM side channels and their use to extract private keys. In: 19th ACM Conference on Computer and Communications Security (CCS), pp. 305–316, Raleigh, NC, US, October 2012

28. Zhang, Y., Juels, A., Reiter, M.K., Ristenpart, T.: Cross-tenant side-channel attacks in PaaS clouds. In: Computer and Communications Security (CCS), Scottsdale, AZ, US (2014)

Encoding Techniques

Faster Homomorphic Function Evaluation Using Non-integral Base Encoding

Charlotte Bonte[1], Carl Bootland[1], Joppe W. Bos[2], Wouter Castryck[1,3],
Ilia Iliashenko[1], and Frederik Vercauteren[1,4(✉)]

[1] imec-Cosic, Department of Electrical Engineering, KU Leuven, Leuven, Belgium
{charlotte.bonte,carl.bootland}@esat.kuleuven.be,
iliailiashenko@gmail.com
[2] NXP Semiconductors, Leuven, Belgium
joppe.bos@nxp.com
[3] Laboratoire Paul Painlevé, Université de Lille-1, Villeneuve-d'Ascq, France
wouter.castryck@gmail.com
[4] Open Security Research, Shenzhen, China
frederik.vercauteren@gmail.com

Abstract. In this paper we present an encoding method for real numbers tailored for homomorphic function evaluation. The choice of the degree of the polynomial modulus used in all popular somewhat homomorphic encryption schemes is dominated by security considerations, while with the current encoding techniques the correctness requirement allows for much smaller values. We introduce a generic encoding method using expansions with respect to a non-integral base, which exploits this large degree at the benefit of reducing the growth of the coefficients when performing homomorphic operations. This allows one to choose a smaller plaintext coefficient modulus which results in a significant reduction of the running time. We illustrate our approach by applying this encoding in the setting of homomorphic electricity load forecasting for the smart grid which results in a speed-up by a factor 13 compared to previous work, where encoding was done using balanced ternary expansions.

1 Introduction

The cryptographic technique which allows an untrusted entity to perform arbitrary computation on encrypted data is known as fully homomorphic encryption. The first such construction was based on ideal lattices and was presented by Gentry in 2009 [24]. When the algorithm applied to the encrypted data is known in advance one can use a *somewhat homomorphic encryption* (SHE) scheme which

This work was supported by the European Commission under the ICT programme with contract H2020-ICT-2014-1 644209 HEAT, and through the European Research Council under the FP7/2007-2013 programme with ERC Grant Agreement 615722 MOTMELSUM. The second author is also supported by a PhD fellowship of the Research Foundation - Flanders (FWO).

W. Fischer and N. Homma (Eds.): CHES 2017, LNCS 10529, pp. 579–600, 2017.
DOI: 10.1007/978-3-319-66787-4_28

only allows to perform a limited number of computational steps on the encrypted data. Such schemes are significantly more efficient in practice.

In all popular SHE schemes, the plaintext space is a ring of the form $R_t = \mathbb{Z}_t[X]/(f(X))$, where $t \geq 2$ is a small integer called the coefficient modulus, and $f(X) \in \mathbb{Z}[X]$ is a monic irreducible degree d polynomial called the polynomial modulus. Usually one lets $f(X)$ be a cyclotomic polynomial, where for reasons of performance the most popular choices are the power-of-two cyclotomics $X^d + 1$ where $d = 2^k$ for some positive integer k, which are maximally sparse. In this case arithmetic in R_t can be performed efficiently using the fast Fourier transform, which is used in many lattice-based constructions (e.g. [8–10,34]) and most implementations (e.g. [3,6,7,25,26,29,32]).

One interesting problem relates to the *encoding* of the input data of the algorithm such that it can be represented as elements of R_t and such that one obtains a meaningful outcome after the encrypted result is decrypted and decoded. This means that addition and multiplication of the input data must agree with the corresponding operations in R_t up to the depth of the envisaged SHE computation. An active research area investigates different such encoding techniques, which are often application-specific and dependent on the type of the input data. For the sake of exposition we will concentrate on the particularly interesting and popular setting where the input data consists of finite precision real numbers θ, even though our discussion below is fairly generic. The main idea, going back to Dowlin et al. [19] (see also [20,27,31]) and analyzed in more detail by Costache et al. [16], is to expand θ with respect to a base b

$$\theta = a_r b^r + a_{r-1} b^{r-1} + \cdots + a_1 b + a_0 + a_{-1} b^{-1} + a_{-2} b^{-2} + \cdots + a_{-s} b^{-s} \quad (1)$$

using integer digits a_i, after which one replaces b by X to end up inside the Laurent polynomial ring $\mathbb{Z}[X^{\pm 1}]$. One then reduces the digits a_i modulo t and applies the ring homomorphism to R_t defined by

$$\iota : \mathbb{Z}_t[X^{\pm 1}] \to R_t : \begin{cases} X \mapsto X, \\ X^{-1} \mapsto -g(X) \cdot f(0)^{-1}, \end{cases}$$

where we write $f(X) = Xg(X) + f(0)$ and it is assumed that $f(0)$ is invertible modulo t; this is always true for cyclotomic polynomials, or for factors of them. The quantity $r + s$ will sometimes be referred to as the *degree* of the encoding (where we assume that $a_r a_{-s} \neq 0$). For power-of-two-cyclotomics the homomorphism ι amounts to letting $X^{-1} \mapsto -X^{d-1}$, so that the encoding of (1) is given by[1] $a_r X^r + a_{r-1} X^{r-1} + \cdots + a_1 X + a_0 - a_{-1} X^{d-1} - a_{-2} X^{d-2} - \cdots - a_{-s} X^{d-s}$.

Decoding is done through the inverse of the restriction $\iota|_{\mathbb{Z}_t[X^{\pm 1}]_{[-\ell,m]}}$ where

$$\mathbb{Z}_t[X^{\pm 1}]_{[-\ell,m]} = \left\{ a_m X^m + a_{m-1} X^{m-1} + \ldots + a_{-\ell} X^{-\ell} \mid a_i \in \mathbb{Z}_t \text{ for all } i \right\}$$

is a subset of Laurent polynomials whose monomials have bounded exponents. If $\ell + m + 1 = d$ then this restriction of ι is indeed invertible as a $\mathbb{Z}_t$-linear map. The

---

[1] In fact in [16] it is mentioned that inverting X is only possible in the power-of-two cyclotomic case, but this seems to be overcareful.

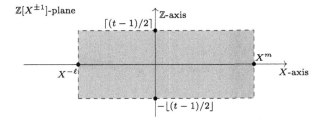

Fig. 1. Box in which to stay during computation, where $\ell + m + 1 = d$.

precise choice of ℓ, m depends on the data encoded. After applying this inverse, one replaces the coefficients by their representants in $\{-\lfloor (t-1)/2 \rfloor, \ldots, \lceil (t-1)/2 \rceil\}$ to end up with an expression in $\mathbb{Z}[X^{\pm 1}]$, and evaluates the result at $X = b$. Ensuring that decoding is correct to a given computational depth places constraints on the parameters t and d, in order to avoid ending up outside the box depicted in Fig. 1 if the computation were to be carried out directly in $\mathbb{Z}[X^{\pm 1}]$. In terms of R_t we will often refer to this event as the 'wrapping around' of the encoded data modulo t or $f(X)$, although we note that this is an abuse of language. In the case of power-of-two cyclotomics, ending up above or below the box does indeed correspond to wrapping around modulo t, but ending up at the left or the right of the box corresponds to a mix-up of the high degree terms and the low degree terms.

The precise constraints on t and d not only depend on the complexity of the computation, but also on the type of expansion (1) used in the encoding. Dowlin et al. suggest to use balanced b-ary expansions with respect to an odd base $b \in \mathbb{Z}_{\geq 3}$, which means that the digits are taken from $\{-(b-1)/2, \ldots, (b-1)/2\}$. Such expansions have been used for centuries going back at least to Colson (1726) and Cauchy (1840) in the quest for more efficient arithmetic.

If we fix a precision, then for smaller b the balanced b-ary expansions are longer but the coefficients are smaller, this implies the need for a larger d but smaller t. Similarly for larger bases the expansions become shorter but have larger coefficients leading to smaller d but larger t. For the application to somewhat homomorphic encryption considered in [6,16] the security requirements ask for a very large d, so that the best choice is to use as small a base as possible, namely $b = 3$, with digits in $\{\pm 1, 0\}$. Even for this smallest choice the resulting lower bound on t is very large and the bound on d is much smaller than that coming from the cryptographic requirements. To illustrate this, we recall the concrete figures from the paper [6], which uses the Fan-Vercauteren (FV) somewhat homomorphic encryption scheme [23] for privacy-friendly prediction of electricity consumption in the setting of the smart grid. Here the authors use $d = 4096$ for cryptographic reasons, which is an optimistic choice that leads to 80-bit security only (and maybe even a few bits less than that [1]). On the other hand using balanced ternary expansions, correct decoding is guaranteed as soon as $d \geq 368$, which is even a conservative estimate. This eventually leads to the

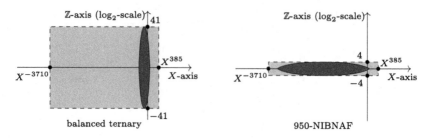

Fig. 2. Comparison of the amount of plaintext space which is actually used in the setting of [6], where $d = 4096$. More precise figures to be found in Sect. 4.

huge bound $t \gtrsim 2^{107}$, which is overcome by decomposing R_t into 13 factors using the Chinese Remainder Theorem (CRT). This is then used to homomorphically forecast the electricity usage for the next half hour for a small apartment complex of 10 households in about half a minute, using a sequential implementation.

The discrepancy between the requirements coming from correct decoding and those coming from security considerations suggests that other possible expansions may be better suited for use with SHE. In this paper we introduce a generic encoding technique, using very sparse expansions having digits in $\{\pm 1, 0\}$ with respect to a *non-integral* base $b_w > 1$, where w is a sparseness measure. These expansions will be said to be of 'non-integral base non-adjacent form' with window size w, abbreviated to w-NIBNAF. Increasing w makes the degrees of the resulting Laurent polynomial encodings grow and decreases the growth of the coefficients when performing operations; hence lowering the bound on t. Our encoding technique is especially useful when using finite precision real numbers, but could also serve in dealing with finite precision complex numbers or even with integers, despite the fact that b_w is non-integral (this would require a careful precision analysis which is avoided here).

We demonstrate that this technique results in significant performance increases by re-doing the experiments from [6]. Along with a more careful precision analysis which is tailored for this specific use case, using 950-NIBNAF expansions we end up with the dramatically reduced bound $t \geq 33$. It is not entirely honest to compare this to $t \gtrsim 2^{107}$ because of our better precision analysis; as explained in Sect. 4 it makes more sense to compare the new bound to $t \gtrsim 2^{42}$, but the reduction remains huge. As the reader can see in Fig. 2 this is explained by the fact that the data is spread more evenly across the plaintext space during computation. As a consequence we avoid the need for CRT decomposition and thus reduce the running time by a factor 13, showing that the same homomorphic forecasting can be done in only 2.5 s.

Remark. An alternative recent proposal for encoding using a non-integral base can be found in [15], which targets efficient evaluation of the discrete Fourier transform on encrypted data. Here the authors work exclusively in the power-of-two cyclotomic setting $f(X) = X^d + 1$, and the input data consists of complex numbers θ which are expanded with respect to the base $b = \zeta$, where ζ is a primitive $2d$-th root of unity, i.e. a root of $f(X)$; a similar idea was used in [12].

One nice feature of this approach is that the correctness of decoding is not affected by wrapping around modulo $f(X)$. To find a sparse expansion they use the LLL algorithm [28], but for arbitrary complex inputs the digits become rather large when compared to w-NIBNAF.

2   Encoding Data Using w-NIBNAF

Our approach in reducing the lower bound on the plaintext modulus t is to use encodings for which many of the coefficients are zero. In this respect, a first improvement over balanced ternary expansions is obtained by using the non-adjacent form (NAF) representations which were introduced by Reitweisner in 1960 for speeding up early multiplication algorithms [33]. We note that independent work by Cheon et al. [11] also mentions the advantages of using NAF encodings.

Definition 1. *The* non-adjacent form (NAF) representation *of a real number θ is an expansion of θ to the base $b = 2$ with coefficients in $\{-1, 0, 1\}$ such that any two adjacent coefficients are not both non-zero.*

The NAF representation has been generalized [13]: for an integer $w \geq 1$ (called the 'window size') one can ensure that in any window of w consecutive coefficients at most one of them is non-zero. This is possible to base $b = 2$ but for $w > 2$ one requires larger coefficients.

Definition 2. *Let $w \geq 1$ be an integer. A w-NAF representation of a real number θ is an expansion of θ with base 2 and whose non-zero coefficients are odd and less than 2^{w-1} in absolute value such that for every set of w consecutive coefficients at most one of them is non-zero.*

We see that NAF is just the special case of w-NAF for $w = 2$. Unfortunately, due to the fact that the coefficients are taken from a much larger set, using w-NAF encodings in the SHE setting actually gives larger bounds on both t and d for increasing w. Therefore this is not useful for our purposes.

Ideally, we want the coefficients in our expansions to be members of $\{\pm 1, 0\}$ with many equal to 0, as this leads to the slowest growth in coefficient sizes, allowing us to use smaller values for t. This would come at the expense of using longer encodings, but remember that we have a lot of manoeuvring space on the d side. One way to achieve this goal is to use a *non-integral* base $b > 1$ when computing a non-adjacent form. We first give the definition of a non-integral base non-adjacent form with window size w (w-NIBNAF) representation and then explain where this precise formulation comes from.

Definition 3. *A sequence $a_0, a_1, \ldots, a_n, \ldots$ is a w-balanced ternary sequence if it has $a_i \in \{-1, 0, 1\}$ for $i \in \mathbb{Z}_{\geq 0}$ and satisfies the property that each set of w consecutive terms has no more than one non-zero term.*

Definition 4. *Let $\theta \in \mathbb{R}$ and $w \in \mathbb{Z}_{>0}$. Define b_w to be the unique positive real root of the polynomial $F_w(x) = x^{w+1} - x^w - x - 1$. A w-balanced ternary sequence $a_r, a_{r-1}, \ldots, a_1, a_0, a_{-1}, \ldots$ is a w-NIBNAF representation of θ if*

$$\theta = a_r b_w^r + a_{r-1} b_w^{r-1} + \cdots + a_1 b_w + a_0 + a_{-1} b_w^{-1} + \cdots .$$

Below we will show that every $\theta \in \mathbb{R}$ has at least one such w-NIBNAF representation and provide an algorithm to find such a representation. But let us first state a lemma which shows that b_w is well-defined for $w \geq 1$.

Lemma 1. *For an integer $w \geq 1$ the polynomial $F_w(x) = x^{w+1} - x^w - x - 1$ has a unique positive real root $b_w > 1$. The sequence $b_1, b_2, \ldots$ is strictly decreasing and $\lim_{w \to \infty} b_w = 1$. Further, $(x^2 + 1) \mid F_w(x)$ for $w \equiv 3 \bmod 4$.*

The proof is straightforward and given in Appendix A. The first few values of b_w are as follows

$$b_1 = 1 + \sqrt{2} \approx 2.414214, \qquad b_2 \approx 1.839287,$$
$$b_3 = \tfrac{1}{2}(1 + \sqrt{5}) \approx 1.618034, \qquad b_4 \approx 1.497094,$$

where we note that b_3 is the golden ratio ϕ.

Since we are using a non-integral base, a w-NIBNAF representation of a fixed-point number has infinitely many non-zero terms in general. To overcome this one approximates the number by terminating the w-NIBNAF representation after some power of the base. We call such a terminated sequence an *approximate w-NIBNAF representation*. There are two straightforward ways of deciding where to terminate: either a fixed power of the base is chosen so that any terms after this are discarded giving an easy bound on the maximal possible error created, or we choose a maximal allowed error in advance and terminate after the first power which gives error less than or equal to this value.

Algorithm 1 below produces for every $\theta \in \mathbb{R}$ a w-NIBNAF representation in the limit as ϵ tends to 0, thereby demonstrating its existence. It takes the form of a greedy algorithm which chooses the closest signed power of the base to θ and then iteratively finds a representation of the difference. Except when θ can be written as $\theta = h(b_w)/b_w^q$, for some polynomial h with coefficients in $\{\pm 1, 0\}$ and $q \in \mathbb{Z}_{\geq 0}$, any w-NIBNAF representation is infinitely long. Hence, we must terminate Algorithm 1 once the iterative input is smaller than some pre-determined precision $\epsilon > 0$.

We now prove that the algorithm works as required.

Lemma 2. *Algorithm 1 produces an approximate w-NIBNAF representation of θ with an error of at most ϵ.*

Proof. Assuming that the algorithm terminates, the output clearly represents θ to within an error of at most size ϵ. First we show that the output is w-NIBNAF. Suppose that the output, on input θ, b_w, ϵ, has at least two non-zero terms, the first being a_d. This implies either that $b_w^d \leq |\theta| < b_w^{d+1}$ and $b_w^{d+1} - |\theta| > |\theta| - b_w^d$

Algorithm 1. GreedyRepresentation

Input: θ – the real number to be represented,
b_w – the w-NIBNAF base to be used in the representation,
ϵ – the precision to which the representation is determined.
Output: An approximate w-NIBNAF representation $a_r, a_{r-1}, \ldots$ of θ with
        error less than ϵ, where $a_i = 0$ if not otherwise specified.

$\sigma \leftarrow \mathrm{sgn}(\theta)$
$t \leftarrow |\theta|$
while $t > \epsilon$ **do**
    $r \leftarrow \lceil \log_{b_w}(t) \rceil$
    if $b_w^r - t > t - b_w^{r-1}$ **then**
        $r \leftarrow r - 1$
    $a_r \leftarrow \sigma$
    $\sigma \leftarrow \sigma \cdot \mathrm{sgn}(t - b_w^r)$
    $t \leftarrow |t - b_w^r|$
Return $(a_i)_i$.

---

or $b_w^{d-1} < |\theta| \le b_w^d$ and $b_w^d - |\theta| \le |\theta| - b_w^{d-1}$. These conditions can be written as $b_w^d \le |\theta| < \frac{1}{2}b_w^d(1 + b_w)$ and $\frac{1}{2}b_w^{d-1}(1 + b_w) \le |\theta| \le b_w^d$ respectively, showing that

$$\big||\theta| - b_w^d\big| < \max\left\{ b_w^d - \tfrac{1}{2}b_w^{d-1}(1 + b_w),\ \tfrac{1}{2}b_w^d(1 + b_w) - b_w^d \right\} = \tfrac{1}{2}b_w^d(b_w - 1).$$

The algorithm subsequently chooses the closest power of b_w to this smaller value, suppose it is b_w^ℓ. By the same argument with θ replaced by $|\theta| - b_w^d$ we have that either $b_w^\ell \le \big||\theta| - b_w^d\big|$ or $\frac{1}{2}b_w^{\ell-1}(1 + b_w) \le \big||\theta| - b_w^d\big|$ and since b_w^ℓ is larger than $\frac{1}{2}b_w^{\ell-1}(1+b_w)$ the maximal possible value of ℓ, which we denote by $\ell_w(d)$, satisfies

$$\ell_w(d) = \max\left\{ \ell \in \mathbb{Z} \mid \tfrac{1}{2}b_w^{\ell-1}(1 + b_w) < \tfrac{1}{2}b_w^d(b_w - 1) \right\}.$$

The condition on ℓ can be rewritten as $b_w^\ell < b_w^{d+1}(b_w - 1)/(b_w + 1)$ which implies that $\ell < d + 1 + \log_{b_w}((b_w - 1)/(b_w + 1))$ and thus

$$\ell_w(d) = d + \left\lceil \log_{b_w}\left(\frac{b_w - 1}{b_w + 1} \right) \right\rceil,$$

so that the smallest possible difference is independent of d and equal to

$$s(w) := d - \ell_w(d) = -\left\lceil \log_{b_w}\left(\frac{b_w - 1}{b_w + 1} \right) \right\rceil = \left\lfloor \log_{b_w}\left(\frac{b_w + 1}{b_w - 1} \right) \right\rfloor.$$

We thus need to show that $s(w) \ge w$. As w is an integer this is equivalent to

$$\log_{b_w}\left(\frac{b_w + 1}{b_w - 1} \right) \ge w \iff b_w^w \le \frac{b_w + 1}{b_w - 1} \iff b_w^{w+1} - b_w^w - b_w - 1 \le 0$$

which holds for all w since $F_w(b_w) = 0$. Note that our algorithm works correctly and deterministically because when $|\theta|$ is exactly half-way between two powers of b_w we pick the larger power. This shows that the output is of the desired form.

Finally, to show that the algorithm terminates we note that the k'th successive difference is bounded above by $\frac{1}{2}b_w^{d-(k-1)s(w)}(b_w - 1)$ and this tends to 0 as k tends to infinity. Therefore after a finite number of steps (at most $\lceil (d - \log_{b_w}(2\epsilon/(b_w - 1)))/s(w) \rceil + 1$) the difference is smaller than or equal to ϵ and the algorithm terminates. $\square$

The process of encoding works as described in the introduction, i.e. we follow the approach from [16,19] except we use an approximate w-NIBNAF representation instead of the balanced ternary representation. Thus to encode a real number θ we find an approximate w-NIBNAF representation of θ with small enough error and replace each occurrence of b_w by X, after which we apply the map ι to end up in plaintext space R_t. Decoding is almost the same as well, only that after inverting ι and lifting the coefficients to $\mathbb{Z}$ we evaluate the resulting Laurent polynomial at $X = b_w$ rather than $X = 3$, computing the value only to the required precision. Rather than evaluating directly it is best to reduce the Laurent polynomial modulo $F_w(X)$ (or modulo $F_w(X)/(X^2+1)$ if $w \equiv 3 \bmod 4$) so that we only have to compute powers of b_w up to w (respectively $w - 2$).

Clearly we can also ask Algorithm 1 to return $\sum_i a_i X^i \in \mathbb{Z}_t[X^{\pm 1}]$, this gives an encoding of θ with maximal error ϵ. Since the input θ of the algorithm can get arbitrarily close to but larger than ϵ, the final term can be $\pm X^h$ where $h = \lfloor \log_{b_w}(2\epsilon/(1 + b_w)) \rfloor + 1$. If we are to ensure that the smallest power of the base to appear in any approximate w-NIBNAF representation is b_w^s then we require that if b_w^{s-1} is the nearest power of b_w to the input θ then $|\theta| \leq \epsilon$ so that we must have $\frac{1}{2}b_w^{s-1}(1 + b_w) \leq \epsilon$ which implies the smallest precision we can achieve is $\epsilon = b_w^{s-1}(1 + b_w)/2$. In particular if we want no negative powers of b_w then the best precision possible using the greedy algorithm is $(1 + b_w^{-1})/2 < 1$.

Remark. If one replaces b_w by a smaller base $b > 1$ then Algorithm 1 still produces a w-NIBNAF expansion to precision ϵ: this follows from the proof of Lemma 2. The distinguishing feature of b_w is that it is maximal with respect to this property, so that the resulting expansions become as short as possible.

3   Analysis of Coefficient Growth During Computation

After encoding the input data it is ready for homomorphic computations. This increases both the number of non-zero coefficients as well as the size of these coefficients. Since we are working in the ring R_t there is a risk that our data wraps around modulo t as well as modulo $f(X)$, in the sense explained in the introduction, which we should avoid since this leads to erroneous decoding. Therefore we need to understand the coefficient growth more thoroughly. We simplify the analysis in this section by only considering multiplications and what constraint this puts on t, it is then not hard to generalize this to include additions.

Worst case coefficient growth for w-NIBNAF encodings. Here we analyze the maximal possible size of a coefficient which could occur from computing with w-NIBNAF encodings. Because fresh w-NIBNAF encodings are just approximate w-NIBNAF representations written as elements of R_t we consider finite w-balanced ternary sequences and the multiplication endowed on them from R_t. Equivalently, we consider multiplication in the $\mathbb{Z}[X^{\pm 1}]$-plane depicted in Fig. 1. As we ensure in practice that there is no wrap around modulo $f(X)$ this can be ignored in our analysis.

To start the worst case analysis we have the following lower bound; note that the d we use here is *not* that of the degree of $f(X)$.

Lemma 3. *The maximal absolute size of a term that can appear in the product of p arbitrary w-balanced ternary sequences of length $d + 1$ is at least*

$$B_w(d,p) := \sum_{k=0}^{\lfloor \lfloor p\lfloor d/w\rfloor/2\rfloor/(\lfloor d/w\rfloor+1)\rfloor} (-1)^k \binom{p}{k}\binom{p-1+\lfloor p\lfloor d/w\rfloor/2\rfloor - k\lfloor d/w\rfloor - k}{p-1}.$$

A full proof of this lemma is given in Appendix A but the main idea is to look at the largest coefficient of m^p where m has the maximal number of non-zero coefficients, $\lfloor d/w\rfloor +1$, all being equal to 1 and with exactly $w-1$ zero coefficients between each pair of adjacent non-zero coefficients. The (non-zero) coefficients of m^p are variously known in the literature as extended (or generalized) binomial coefficients or ordinary multinomials; we denote them here by $\binom{p}{k}_n$ defined via

$$\left(1 + X + X^2 + \ldots + X^{n-1}\right)^p = \sum_{k=0}^{\infty} \binom{p}{k}_n X^k,$$

[18,21,22,35]. In particular the maximal coefficient is the (or a) central one and we can write $B_w(d,p) = \binom{p}{k}_n$ where $k = \lfloor p\lfloor d/w\rfloor/2\rfloor$ and $n = \lfloor d/w\rfloor + 1$.

We note that the w-NIBNAF encoding, using the greedy algorithm with precision $\frac{1}{2}$, of $b_w^{d+w-(d \bmod w)}(b_w - 1)/2$ is m so in practice this lower bound is achievable although highly unlikely to occur.

We expect that this lower bound is tight, indeed we were able to prove the following lemma, the proof is also given in Appendix A.

Lemma 4. *Suppose w divides d, then $B_w(d,p)$ equals the maximal absolute size of a term that can be produced by taking the product of p arbitrary w-balanced ternary sequences of length $d + 1$.*

We thus make the following conjecture which holds for all small values of p and d we tested and which we assume to be true in general.

Conjecture 1. *The lower bound $B_w(d,p)$ given in Lemma 3 is exact for all d, that is the maximal absolute term size which can occur after multiplying p arbitrary w-balanced ternary sequences of length $d + 1$ is $B_w(d,p)$.*

This conjecture seems very plausible since as soon as one multiplicand does not have non-zero coefficients exactly w places apart the non-zero coefficients start to spread out and decrease in value.

To determine $B_w(d,p)$ for fixed p define $n := \lfloor d/w \rfloor + 1$, then we can expand the expression for $B_w(d,p)$ as a 'polynomial' in n of degree $p-1$ where the coefficients depend on the parity of n, see [5] for more details. The first few are:

$$B_w(d,1) = 1, \qquad\qquad\qquad\qquad B_w(d,2) = n,$$

$$B_w(d,3) = \tfrac{1}{8}(6n^2 + 1) - \tfrac{(-1)^n}{8}, \qquad\qquad B_w(d,4) = \tfrac{1}{3}(2n^3 + n),$$

$$B_w(d,5) = \tfrac{1}{384}(230n^4 + 70n^2 + 27) - \tfrac{(-1)^n}{384}(30n^2 + 27),$$

$$B_w(d,6) = \tfrac{1}{20}(11n^5 + 5n^3 + 4n).$$

Denoting the coefficient of n^{p-1} in these expressions by ℓ_p, it can be shown (see [2] or [5]) that $\lim_{p\to\infty} \sqrt{p}\ell_p = \sqrt{6/\pi}$ and hence we have

$$\lim_{p\to\infty} \log_2(B_w(d,p)) - (p-1)\log_2(n) + \tfrac{1}{2}\log_2\left(\tfrac{\pi p}{6}\right) = 0$$

or equivalently $B_w(d,p) \sim_p \sqrt{6/\pi p}\, n^{p-1}$. Thus we have the approximation

$$\log_2(B_w(d,p)) \approx (p-1)\log_2(n) - \tfrac{1}{2}\log_2\left(\tfrac{\pi p}{6}\right)$$

which for large enough n (experimentally we found for $n > 1.825\sqrt{p-1/2}$) is an upper bound for $p > 2$. For a guaranteed upper bound we refer to Mattner and Roos [30] where they state, for $n, p \in \mathbb{Z}_{>0}$ with $n \geq 2$, if $p \neq 2$ or $n \in \{2,3,4\}$ then $B_w(d,p) \leq \sqrt{6/(\pi p(n^2-1))}\,n^p$. This upper bound is in fact a more precise asymptotic limit than that above which only considers the leading coefficient.

Statistical analysis of the coefficient growth. Based on the w-NIBNAF encodings of random numbers in $N \in [-2^{40}, 2^{40}]$, we try to get an idea of the amount of zero and non-zero coefficients in a fresh encoding without fractional part, obtained by running Algorithm 1 to precision $(1+b_w^{-1})/2$. We also analyze how these proportions change when we perform multiplications. We plot this for different values of w to illustrate the positive effects of using sparser encodings. As a preliminary remark note that the w-NIBNAF encodings produced by Algorithm 1 applied to $-N$ and N are obtained from one another by changing all the signs, so the coefficients -1 and 1 are necessarily distributed evenly.[2]

We know from the definition of a w-NIBNAF expansion that at least $w-1$ among each block of w consecutive coefficients of the expansion will be 0, so we expect for big w that the 0 coefficient occurs a lot more often than ± 1. This is clearly visible in Fig. 3. In addition we see an increasing number of 0 coefficients and decreasing number of ± 1 coefficients for increasing w. Thus both the absolute and the relative sparseness of our encodings increase as w increases.

---

[2] This is a desirable property leading to the maximal amount of cancellation during computation. While this does not affect our worst case analysis, in practice where the worst case is extremely unlikely this accounts for a considerable reduction of the size of the coefficient modulus t. If in some application the input encodings happen to be biased towards 1 or -1 then one can work with respect to the *negative* base $-b_w < -1$, by switching the signs of all the digits appearing at an odd index.

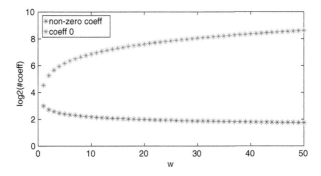

Fig. 3. Plot of $\log_2(\#\text{coeff})$ on the vertical axis against w on the horizontal axis averaged over $10\,000$ w-NIBNAF encodings of random integers in $\left[-2^{40}, 2^{40}\right]$.

Table 1. Comparison between the previous encoding techniques and w-NIBNAF

	Balanced ternary	1-NIBNAF	2-NAF	2-NIBNAF
Zero coefficients	32.25%	48.69%	65.23%	70.46%
Non-zero coefficients	67.76%	51.31%	34.77%	29.54%

Since the balanced ternary encoding of [16, 19] and the 2-NAF encoding [33], only have coefficients in $\{0, \pm 1\}$ it is interesting to compare them to 1-NIBNAF and 2-NIBNAF respectively. We compare them by computing the percentage of zero and non-zero coefficients, in $10\,000$ encodings of random integers N in $\left[-2^{40}, 2^{40}\right]$. We compute this percentage up to an accuracy of 10^{-2} and consider for our counts all coefficients up to and including the leading coefficient, further zero coefficients are not counted. When we compare the percentages of zero and non-zero coefficients occurring in 1-NIBNAF and balanced ternary in Table 1 we see that for the balanced ternary representation, the occurrences of 0, 1 and -1 coefficients are approximately the same, while for 1-NIBNAF the proportion of 0 coefficients is larger than that of 1 or -1. Hence we can conclude that 1-NIBNAF encodings will be sparser than the balanced ternary encodings even though the window size is the same. For 2-NIBNAF we also see an improvement in terms of sparseness of the encoding compared to 2-NAF.

The next step is to investigate what happens to the coefficients when we multiply two encodings. From Fig. 4 we see that when w increases the maximal size of the resulting coefficients becomes smaller. So the plots confirm the expected result that sparser encodings lead to a reduction in the size of the resulting coefficients after one multiplication. Next, we investigate the behaviour for an increasing amount of multiplications. In Fig. 5 one observes that for a fixed number of multiplications the maximum coefficient, considering all coefficients in the resulting polynomial, decreases as w increases and the maximum degree of the polynomial increases as w increases. This confirms that increasing the degree of the polynomial, in order to make it more sparse, has the desirable

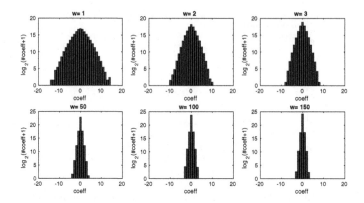

Fig. 4. Plot of $\log_2(\#\text{coeff}+1)$ on the vertical axis against the respective value of the coefficient on the horizontal axis for the result of 10 000 multiplications of two w-NIBNAF encodings of random numbers between $\left[-2^{40}, 2^{40}\right]$.

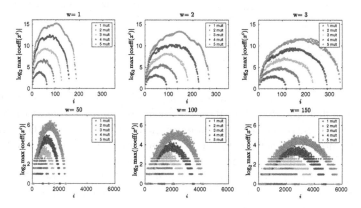

Fig. 5. $\log_2$ of the maximum absolute value of the coefficient of x^i seen during 10 000 products of two w-NIBNAF encodings of random numbers in $\left[-2^{40}, 2^{40}\right]$ against i.

effect of decreasing the size of the coefficients. Figure 5 also shows that based on the result of one multiplication we can even estimate the maximum value of the average coefficients of x^i for a specific number of multiplications by scaling the result for one multiplication.

To summarize, we plot the number of bits of the maximum coefficient of the polynomial that is the result of a certain fixed amount of multiplications as a function of w in Fig. 6. From this figure we clearly see that the maximal coefficient decreases when w increases and hence the original encoding polynomial is sparser. In addition we see that the effect of the sparseness of the encoding on the size of the resulting maximal coefficient is bigger when the amount of multiplications increases. However the gain of sparser encodings decreases as w

becomes bigger. Furthermore, Fig. 6 shows that the bound given in Lemma 3 is much bigger than the observed upper bound we get from 10 000 samples.

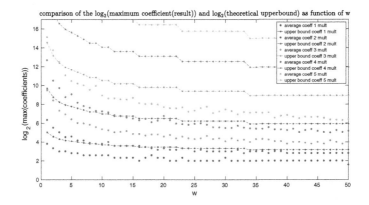

Fig. 6. $\log_2$ of the observed and theoretical maximum absolute coefficient of the result of multiplying w-NIBNAF encodings of random numbers in $\left[-2^{40}, 2^{40}\right]$ against w.

4   Practical Impact

We encounter the following constraints on the plaintext coefficient modulus t while homomorphically computing with polynomial encodings of finite precision real numbers. The first constraint comes from the correctness requirement of the SHE scheme: the noise inside the ciphertext should not exceed a certain level during the computations, otherwise decryption fails. Since an increase of the plaintext modulus expands the noise this places an upper bound on the possible t which can be used. The second constraint does not relate to SHE but to the circuit itself. After any arithmetic operation the polynomial coefficients tend to grow. Given that fact, one should take a big enough plaintext modulus in order to prevent or mitigate possible wrapping around modulo t. This determines a lower bound on the range of possible values of t. In practice, for deep enough circuits these two constraints are incompatible, i.e. there is no interval from which t can be chosen. However, the plaintext space R_t can be split into smaller rings $R_{t_1}, \ldots, R_{t_k}$ with $t = \prod_{i=1}^{k} t_i$ using the Chinese Remainder Theorem (CRT). This technique [8] allows us to take the modulus big enough for correct evaluation of the circuit and then perform k threads of the homomorphic algorithm over $\{R_{t_i}\}_i$. These k output polynomials will then be combined into the final output, again by CRT. This approach needs k times more memory and time than the case of a single modulus. Thus the problem is mostly about reducing the number of factors of t needed.

An a priori lower bound on t can be derived using the worst case scenario in which the final output has the maximal possible coefficient, which was ana-lyzed in Sect. 3. If we use w-NIBNAF encodings for increasing values of w then this lower bound will decrease, eventually leading to fewer CRT factors; here a concern is not to take w too large to prevent wrapping around modulo $f(X)$. In practice though, we can take t considerably smaller because the worst case occurs with a negligible probability, which even decreases for circuits having a bigger multiplicative depth. Moreover, we can allow the least significant coefficients of the fractional part to wrap around modulo t with no harm to the final results.

In this section we revisit the homomorphic method for electricity load forecasting described in [6] and demonstrate that by using w-NIBNAF encodings, by ignoring the unlikely worst cases, and by tolerating minor precision losses we can reduce the number of CRT factors from $k = 13$ to $k = 1$, thereby enhancing its practical performance by a factor 13. We recall that [6] uses the Fan-Vercauteren SHE scheme [23], along with the group method of data handling (GMDH) as a prediction tool; we refer to [6, Sect. 3] for a quick introduction to this method. Due to the fact that 80% of electricity meter devices in the European Union should be replaced with smart meters by 2020, this application may mitigate some emerging privacy and efficiency issues.

Experimental setup. For comparison's sake we mimic the treatment in [6] as closely as possible. In particular we also use the real world measurements obtained from the smart meter electricity trials performed in Ireland [14]. This dataset [14] contains observed electricity consumption of over 5000 residential and commercial buildings during 30 min intervals. We use aggregated consumption data of 10 buildings. Given previous consumption data with some additional information, the GMDH network has the goal of predicting electricity demand for the next time period. Concretely, it requires 51 input parameters: the 48 previous measurements plus the day of the week, the month and the temperature. There are three hidden layers with 8, 4, 2 nodes, respectively. A single output node provides the electricity consumption prediction for the next half hour. Recall that a node is just a bivariate quadratic polynomial evaluation.

The plaintext space is of the form $R_t = \mathbb{Z}_t[X]/(X^{4096} + 1)$, where the degree $d = 4096$ is motivated by the security level of 80 bits which is targetted in [6]; recent work by Albrecht [1] implies that the actual level of security is slightly less than that. Inside R_t the terms corresponding to the fractional parts and those corresponding to the integral parts come closer together after each multiplication. Wrapping around modulo $X^{4096} + 1$, i.e. ending up at the left or at the right of the box depicted in Fig. 1, means that inside R_t these integer and fractional parts start to overlap. In this case it is no longer possible to decode correctly. We encode the input data using approximate w-NIBNAF representations with a fixed number of integer and fractional digits. When increasing the window size w one should take into account that the precision of the corresponding encodings changes as well. To maintain the same accuracy of the algorithm it is important to keep the precision fixed, hence for bigger w's the smaller base b_w should result in an increase of the number of coefficients used by an encoding. Starting with the balanced ternary expansion (BTE), for any $w > 2$, the numbers $\ell(w)_i$ and $\ell(w)_f$ of integer and fractional digits should be expanded

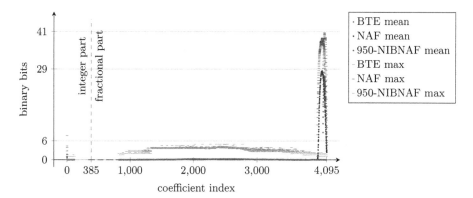

Fig. 7. The mean and the maximal size per coefficient of the resulting polynomial.

according to $\ell(w)_i = (\ell(\text{BTE})_i - 1) \cdot \log_{b_w} 3 + 1$, $\ell(w)_f = -\lfloor \log_{b_w} e_f \rfloor$, where e_f is the maximal error of an approximate w-NIBNAF representation such that the prediction algorithm preserves the same accuracy. Empirically we found that the GMDH network demonstrates reasonable absolute and relative errors when $\ell(\text{BTE})_i^{\text{inp}} = 4$ and $e_f^{\text{inp}} = 1$ for the input and $\ell(\text{BTE})_i^{\text{pol}} = 2$ and $e_f^{\text{pol}} = 0.02032$ for the coefficients of the nodes (quadratic polynomials).

Results. The results reported in this section are obtained running the same software and hardware as in [6]: namely, FV-NFLlib software library [17] running on a laptop equipped with an Intel Core i5-3427U CPU (running at 1.80 GHz). We performed 8560 runs of the GMDH algorithm with BTE, NAF and 950-NIBNAF. The last expansion is with the maximal possible w such that the resulting output polynomial still has discernible integer and fractional parts. Correct evaluation of the prediction algorithm requires the plaintext modulus to be bigger than the maximal coefficient of the resulting polynomial. This lower bound for t can be deduced either from the maximal coefficient (in absolute value) appearing after any run or, in case of known distribution of coefficient values, from the mean and the standard deviation. In both cases increasing window sizes reduce the bound as depicted in Fig. 7. Since negative encoding coefficients are used, 950-NIBNAF demands a plaintext modulus of 7 bits which is almost 6 times smaller than for BTE and NAF.

As expected, w-NIBNAF encodings have longer expansions for bigger w's and that disrupts the decoding procedure in [6,16]. Namely, they naively split the resulting polynomial into two parts of equal size. As one can observe in Fig. 7, using 950-NIBNAF, decoding in this manner will not give correct results. Instead, the splitting index i_s should be shifted towards zero, i.e. to 385. To be specific [6, Lem. 1] states that i_s lies in the interval $(d_i + 1, d - d_f)$ where $d_i = 2^{r+1}(\ell(w)_i^{\text{inp}} + \ell(w)_i^{\text{pol}}) - \ell(w)_i^{\text{pol}}$ and $d_f = 2^{r+1}(\ell(w)_f^{\text{inp}} + \ell(w)_f^{\text{pol}}) - \ell(w)_f^{\text{pol}}$. Indeed, this is the worst case estimation which results in the maximal $w = 74$ for the current network configuration.

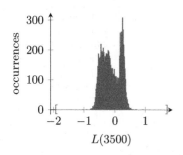

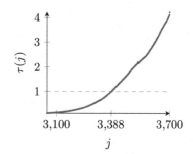

Fig. 8. The distribution of $L(3500)$ over 8560 runs of the GMDH algorithm and an approximation of its prediction interval in red.

Fig. 9. The expected precision loss after ignoring fractional coefficients less than j.

However the impact of the lower coefficients of the fractional part can be much smaller than the precision required by an application. In our use case the prediction value should be precise up to $e_f^{\text{inp}} = 1$. We denote the aggregated sum of lower coefficients multiplied by corresponding powers of the w-NIBNAF base as $L(j) = \sum_{i=j-1}^{i_s} a_i b_w^{-i}$. Then the omitted fractional coefficients a_i should satisfy $|L(i_c)| < 1$, where i_c is the index after which coefficients are ignored.

To find i_c we computed $L(j)$ for every index j of the fractional part and stored those sums for each run of the algorithm. For fixed j the distribution of $L(j)$ is bimodal with mean $\mu_{L(j)}$ and standard deviation $\sigma_{L(j)}$ (see Fig. 8). Despite the fact that this unknown distribution is not normal, we naively approximate the prediction interval $[\mu_{L(j)} - 6\sigma_{L(j)}, \mu_{L(j)} + 6\sigma_{L(j)}]$ that will contain the future observation with high probability. It seems to be a plausible guess in this application because all observed $L(j)$ fall into that region with a big overestimate according to Fig. 8. Therefore i_c is equal to the maximal j that satisfies $\tau(j) < 1$, where $\tau(j) = \max(|\mu_{L(j)} - 6\sigma_{L(j)}|, |\mu_{L(j)} + 6\sigma_{L(j)}|)$.

As Fig. 9 shows, i_c is equal to 3388. Thus, the precision setting allows an overflow in any fractional coefficient a_j for $j < 3388$. The final goal is to provide the bound on t which is bigger than any a_j for $j \geq 3388$. Since the explicit distributions of coefficients are unknown and seem to vary among different indices, we rely in our analysis on the maximal coefficients occurring among all runs. Hence, the plaintext modulus should be bigger than $\max_{j \geq 3388}\{a_j\}$ over all resulting polynomials. Looking back at Fig. 7, one can find that $t = 33$ suffices.

As mentioned above t is constrained in two ways: from the circuit and from the SHE correctness requirements. In our setup the ciphertext modulus is $q \approx 2^{186}$ and the standard deviation of noise is $\sigma = 102$, which together impose that $t \leq 396$ [6]. This is perfectly compatible with $t = 33$, therefore 950-NIBNAF allows us to omit the CRT trick and work with a single modulus, reducing the sequential timings by a factor 13. In the parallel mode it means that 13 times less memory is needed.

Table 2. GMDH implementation with 950-NIBNAF and BTE [6]

	t	CRT factors	timing for one run
950-NIBNAF	$2^{5.044}$	1	2.57 s
BTE (this paper)	$2^{41.627}$	5	12.95 s
BTE [6]	$2^{103.787}$	13	32.5 s

Additionally, these plaintext moduli are much smaller than the worst case estimation from Sect. 3. For 950-NIBNAF we take $d \in [542, 821]$ according to the encoding degrees of input data and network coefficients. Any such encoding contains only one non-zero coefficient. Consequently, any product of those encodings has only one non-zero coefficient which is equal to ± 1. When all monomials of the GMDH polynomial result in an encoding with the same index of a non-zero coefficient, the maximal possible coefficient of the output encoding will occur. In this case the maximal coefficient is equal to the evaluation of the GMDH network with all input data and network coefficients being just 1. It leads to $t = 2 \cdot 6^{15} \simeq 2^{39.775}$.

One further consequence of smaller t is that one can reconsider the parameters of the underlying SHE scheme. Namely, one can take smaller q and σ that preserve the same security level and require a smaller bound on t instead of 396 taken above. Given $t = 33$ from above experiments, q reduces to 2^{154} together with $\sigma \approx 5$ that corresponds to smaller sizes of ciphertexts and faster SHE routines, where σ is taken the minimal possible to prevent the Arora-Ge attack [4] as long as each batch of input parameters is encrypted with a different key. Unfortunately, it is not possible to reduce the size of q by 32 bits in our implementation due to constraints of the FV-NFLlib library.

5   Conclusions

We have presented a generic technique to encode real numbers using a non-integral base. This encoding technique is especially suitable for use when evaluating homomorphic functions since it utilizes the large degree of the defining polynomial imposed by the security requirements. This leads to a considerably smaller growth of the coefficients and allows one to reduce the size of the plaintext modulus significantly, resulting in faster implementations. We show that in the setting studied in [6], where somewhat homomorphic function evaluation is used to achieve a privacy-preserving electricity forecast algorithm, the plaintext modulus can be reduced from about 2^{103} when using a balanced ternary expansion encoding, to $33 \simeq 2^{5.044}$ when using the encoding method introduced in this paper (non-integral base non-adjacent form with window size w), see Table 2. This smaller plaintext modulus means a factor 13 decrease in the running time of this privacy-preserving forecasting algorithm: closing the gap even further to making this approach suitable for industrial applications in the smart grid.

References

1. Albrecht, M.R.: On dual lattice attacks against small-secret LWE and parameter choices in HElib and SEAL. In: Coron, J.-S., Nielsen, J.B. (eds.) EUROCRYPT 2017. LNCS, vol. 10211, pp. 103–129. Springer, Cham (2017). doi:10.1007/978-3-319-56614-6_4

2. Aliev, I.: Siegel's lemma and sum-distinct sets. Discrete Comput. Geom. **39**(1–3), 59–66 (2008)

3. Alkim, E., Ducas, L., Pöppelmann, T., Schwabe, P.: Post-quantum key exchange - a new hope. In: USENIX Security Symposium. USENIX Association (2016)

4. Arora, S., Ge, R.: New algorithms for learning in presence of errors. In: Aceto, L., Henzinger, M., Sgall, J. (eds.) ICALP 2011. LNCS, vol. 6755, pp. 403–415. Springer, Heidelberg (2011). doi:10.1007/978-3-642-22006-7_34

5. Bootland, C.: Central Extended Binomial Coefficients and Sums of Powers. In preparation

6. Bos, J.W., Castryck, W., Iliashenko, I., Vercauteren, F.: Privacy-friendly forecasting for the smart grid using homomorphic encryption and the group method of data handling. In: Joye, M., Nitaj, A. (eds.) AFRICACRYPT 2017. LNCS, vol. 10239, pp. 184–201. Springer, Cham (2017). doi:10.1007/978-3-319-57339-7_11

7. Bos, J.W., Costello, C., Naehrig, M., Stebila, D.: Post-quantum key exchange for the TLS protocol from the ring learning with errors problem. In: IEEE S&P, pp. 553–570. IEEE Computer Society (2015)

8. Bos, J.W., Lauter, K., Loftus, J., Naehrig, M.: Improved security for a ring-based fully homomorphic encryption scheme. In: Stam, M. (ed.) IMACC 2013. LNCS, vol. 8308, pp. 45–64. Springer, Heidelberg (2013). doi:10.1007/978-3-642-45239-0_4

9. Brakerski, Z., Gentry, C., Vaikuntanathan, V.: (Leveled) fully homomorphic encryption without bootstrapping. In: Goldwasser, S. (ed.) ITCS 2012, pp. 309–325. ACM, Janary 2012

10. Brakerski, Z., Vaikuntanathan, V.: Fully homomorphic encryption from ring-LWE and security for key dependent messages. In: Rogaway, P. (ed.) CRYPTO 2011. LNCS, vol. 6841, pp. 505–524. Springer, Heidelberg (2011). doi:10.1007/978-3-642-22792-9_29

11. Cheon, J.H., Jeong, J., Lee, J., Lee, K.: Privacy-preserving computations of predictive medical models with minimax approximation and non-adjacent form. In: Proceedings of WAHC 2017. LNCS (2017)

12. Cheon, J.H., Kim, A., Kim, M., Song, Y.: Homomorphic encryption for arithmetic of approximate numbers. Cryptology ePrint Archive, Report 2016/421 (2016). http://eprint.iacr.org/2016/421

13. Cohen, H., Miyaji, A., Ono, T.: Efficient elliptic curve exponentiation using mixed coordinates. In: Ohta, K., Pei, D. (eds.) ASIACRYPT 1998. LNCS, vol. 1514, pp. 51–65. Springer, Heidelberg (1998). doi:10.1007/3-540-49649-1_6

14. Commission for Energy Regulation. Electricity smart metering customer behaviour trials (CBT) findings report. Technical Report CER11080a (2011). http://www.cer.ie/docs/000340/cer11080(a)(i).pdf

15. Costache, A., Smart, N.P., Vivek, S.: Faster homomorphic evaluation of Discrete Fourier Transforms. IACR Cryptology ePrint Archive (2016)

16. Costache, A., Smart, N.P., Vivek, S., Waller, A.: Fixed point arithmetic in SHE schemes. In SAC 2016. LNCS. Springer (2016)

17. CryptoExperts.   FV-NFLlib   (2016).   https://github.com/CryptoExperts/FV-NFLlib

18. de Moivre, A.: The Doctrine of Chances. Woodfall, London (1738)
19. Dowlin, N., Gilad-Bachrach, R., Laine, K., Lauter, K., Naehrig, M., Wernsing, J.: Manual for using homomorphic encryption for bioinformatics. Technical report, MSR-TR-2015-87, Microsoft Research (2015)
20. Dowlin, N., Gilad-Bachrach, R., Laine, K., Lauter, K.E., Naehrig, M., Wernsing, J.: Cryptonets: Applying neural networks to encrypted data with high throughput and accuracy. In: Balcan, M., Weinberger, K.Q. (eds.) International Conference on Machine Learning, vol. 48, pp. 201–210 (2016). www.JMLR.org
21. Eger, S.: Stirling's approximation for central extended binomial coefficients. Am. Math. Mon. **121**, 344–349 (2014)
22. Euler, L.: De evolutione potestatis polynomialis cuiuscunque $(1 + x + x^2 + x^3 + x^4 + \text{etc.})^n$. Nova Acta Academiae Scientarum Imperialis Petropolitinae, vol. 12, pp. 47–57 (1801)
23. Fan, J., Vercauteren, F.: Somewhat practical fully homomorphic encryption. IACR Cryptology ePrint Archive 2012/144 (2012)
24. Gentry, C.: Fully homomorphic encryption using ideal lattices. In: Mitzenmacher, M. (ed.) 41st ACM STOC, pp. 169–178. ACM Press, May/June (2009)
25. Göttert, N., Feller, T., Schneider, M., Buchmann, J., Huss, S.: On the design of hardware building blocks for modern lattice-based encryption schemes. In: Prouff, E., Schaumont, P. (eds.) CHES 2012. LNCS, vol. 7428, pp. 512–529. Springer, Heidelberg (2012). doi:10.1007/978-3-642-33027-8_30
26. Güneysu, T., Oder, T., Pöppelmann, T., Schwabe, P.: Software speed records for lattice-based signatures. In: Gaborit, P. (ed.) PQCrypto 2013. LNCS, vol. 7932, pp. 67–82. Springer, Heidelberg (2013). doi:10.1007/978-3-642-38616-9_5
27. Lauter, K., López-Alt, A., Naehrig, M.: Private computation on encrypted genomic data. In: Aranha, D.F., Menezes, A. (eds.) LATINCRYPT 2014. LNCS, vol. 8895, pp. 3–27. Springer, Cham (2015). doi:10.1007/978-3-319-16295-9_1
28. Lenstra, A.K., Lenstra, H.W., Lovász, L.: Factoring polynomials with rational coefficients. Math. Ann. **261**, 515–534 (1982)
29. Lyubashevsky, V., Micciancio, D., Peikert, C., Rosen, A.: SWIFFT: A modest proposal for FFT hashing. In: Nyberg, K. (ed.) FSE 2008. LNCS, vol. 5086, pp. 54–72. Springer, Heidelberg (2008). doi:10.1007/978-3-540-71039-4_4
30. Mattner, L., Roos, B.: Maximal probabilities of convolution powers of discrete uniform distributions. Stat. Probab. Lett. **78**(17), 2992–2996 (2008)
31. Naehrig, M., Lauter, K.E., Vaikuntanathan, V.: Can homomorphic encryption be practical? In: Cachin, C., Ristenpart, T. (eds.) ACM Cloud Computing Security Workshop - CCSW, pp. 113–124. ACM (2011)
32. Pöppelmann, T., Güneysu, T.: Towards practical lattice-based public-key encryption on reconfigurable hardware. In: Lange, T., Lauter, K., Lisoněk, P. (eds.) SAC 2013. LNCS, vol. 8282, pp. 68–85. Springer, Heidelberg (2014). doi:10.1007/978-3-662-43414-7_4
33. Reitwiesner, G.W.: Binary arithmetic. In: Advances in Computers, vol. 1, pp. 231–308. Academic Press (1960)
34. Stehlé, D., Steinfeld, R.: Making NTRU as secure as worst-case problems over ideal lattices. In: Paterson, K.G. (ed.) EUROCRYPT 2011. LNCS, vol. 6632, pp. 27–47. Springer, Heidelberg (2011). doi:10.1007/978-3-642-20465-4_4
35. Swanepoel, J.W.: On a generalization of a theorem by Euler. J. Number Theory **149**, 46–56 (2015)

A   Proofs

Lemma 1. *For an integer $w \geq 1$ the polynomial $F_w(x) = x^{w+1} - x^w - x - 1$ has a unique positive root $b_w > 1$. The sequence $b_1, b_2, \ldots$ is strictly decreasing and $\lim_{w \to \infty} b_w = 1$. Further, $(x^2 + 1) \mid F_w(x)$ for $w \equiv 3 \mod 4$.*

Proof. For $w \geq 1$, $F'_w(x) = (w+1)x^w - wx^{w-1} - 1 = (x-1)((w+1)x^{w-1} + x^{w-2} + \cdots + 1)$ so that for $x \geq 0$ there is only one turning point of $F_w(x)$, at $x = 1$. Further, $F''_w(x) = (w+1)wx^{w-1} - w(w-1)x^{w-2}$, which takes the value $2w > 0$ at $x = 1$, so the turning point is a minimum. Since $F_w(0) = -1$ and $\lim_{x \to \infty} F_w(x) = \infty$ we conclude that there is a unique positive root of $F_w(x)$, $b_w > 1$, for any $w \geq 1$. Further, we have that $F_{w+1}(x) = xF_w(x) + x^2 - 1$ so that $F_{w+1}(b_w) = b_w^2 - 1 > 0$ so that $b_{w+1} < b_w$ and hence the sequence b_w is strictly decreasing and bounded below by 1 so must converge to some limit, say $b_\infty \geq 1$. If $b_\infty > 1$ then as b_w is the positive solution to $x - 1 = (x + 1)/x^w$ and, for $x \geq b_\infty > 1$, $\lim_{w \to \infty} (x+1)/x^w = 0$ we see that $b_\infty = \lim_{w \to \infty} b_w = 1$, a contradiction. Hence $b_\infty = 1$ as required. Finally we see that $F_w(x) = x(x-1)(x^{w-1}+1) - (x^2+1)$ and for $w = 4k+3$ that $x^{w-1} + 1 = 1 - (-x^2)^{2k+1} = (x^2 + 1) \sum_{i=0}^{2k} (-x^2)^i$ and hence $(x^2 + 1) \mid F_{4k+3}(x)$. $\qquad\square$

Recall that to find a lower bound on the maximal absolute coefficient size we consider w-balanced ternary sequences and to each sequence (a_i) we have the corresponding polynomial $\sum_i a_i X^i$ in R_t. As we only look at the coefficients and their relative distances we can simply assume that to each w-balanced ternary sequence $c_0, c_1, \ldots, c_d$ of length $d + 1$ we have the associated polynomial $c_0 + c_1 X + \ldots + c_d X^d$ of degree d. Multiplication of polynomials thus gives us a way of multiplying (finite) w-balanced ternary sequences. In the rest of this appendix we use the polynomial and sequence notation interchangeably.

Lemma 3. *The maximal absolute size of a term that can appear in the product of p arbitrary w-balanced ternary sequences of length $d + 1$ is at least*

$$B_w(d, p) := \sum_{k=0}^{\lfloor \lfloor p\lfloor d/w \rfloor/2 \rfloor/(\lfloor d/w \rfloor+1) \rfloor} (-1)^k \binom{p}{k} \binom{p - 1 + \lfloor p\lfloor d/w \rfloor/2 \rfloor - k\lfloor d/w \rfloor - k}{p - 1}.$$

Proof. Consider the product of p sequences all of which are equal to $m = 10 \cdots 010 \cdots 010 \cdots 0$ of length $d + 1$, having $n := \lfloor d/w \rfloor + 1$ non-zero terms (all being 1) and between each pair of adjacent non-zero terms there are exactly $w - 1$ zero terms. Note that n is the maximal number of non-zero terms possible.

As polynomials we have that $m = \sum_{i=0}^{n-1} X^{iw} = \frac{1-X^{nw}}{1-X^w}$, and hence we have

$$
m^p = \left(\frac{1-X^{nw}}{1-X^w}\right)^p = (1-X^{nw})^p \cdot (1-X^w)^{-p}
$$

$$
= \left(\sum_{i=0}^{p}(-1)^i \binom{p}{i} X^{inw}\right) \left(\sum_{j=0}^{\infty} \binom{p-1+j}{p-1} X^{jw}\right)
$$

$$
= \sum_{\ell=0}^{\infty} \left(\sum_{k=0}^{\lfloor \ell/n \rfloor}(-1)^k \binom{p}{k}\binom{p-1+\ell-kn}{p-1}\right) X^{\ell w},
$$

where we have used the substitution $(i, j) \rightarrow (k, \ell) = (i, in + j)$. Since we know that m^p has degree $p(n-1)w$ we can in fact change the infinite sum over ℓ to a finite one from $\ell = 0$ to $p(n-1)$. To give the tightest lower bound we look for the maximal coefficient of m^p. It is well known that this maximal coefficient occurs as the central coefficient, namely of x^ℓ where ℓ is any nearest integer to $p(n-1)/2$ and this gives us $B_w(d, p)$. $\square$

Lemma 4. *Suppose w divides d, then $B_w(d, p)$ equals the maximal absolute size of a term that can be produced by taking the product of p arbitrary w-balanced ternary sequences of length $d + 1$.*

Proof. Let $S_w(d, p)$ be the set of all sequences that are the product of p arbitrary w-balanced ternary sequences of length $d + 1$. To prove the lemma we bound all the terms of any sequence in $S_w(d, p)$. For $i = 0, \ldots, pd$ define

$$
m_w(d, p, i) = \max\{ |a_i| \mid a_i \text{ is the } i\text{'th term of a sequence in } S_w(d, p) \}.
$$

Define $B_w(d, p, \ell) := \sum_{k=0}^{\lfloor \ell/n \rfloor}(-1)^k \binom{p}{k}\binom{p-1+\ell-kn}{p-1}$, the coefficient of $X^{\ell w}$ in m^p. We will prove by induction on p that $m_w(d, p, i) \le B_w(d, p, \lfloor i/w \rfloor)$. We will use the notation $C_i(f)$ for a polynomial f to denote the coefficient of X^i in $f(X)$; this is defined to be zero if $i > \deg(f)$ or $i < 0$. Thus in this notation $B_w(d, p, \ell) = C_{\ell w}((1-X^{nw})^p/(1-X^w)^p)$. The base case $p = 1$ is straight forward, all the $m_w(d, p, i)$ are equal to 1 by the definition of a w-balanced ternary sequence. We therefore suppose that $m_w(d, p-1, i) \le B_w(d, p-1, \lfloor i/w \rfloor)$ for $0 \le i \le (p-1)d$. Consider a product of p w-balanced ternary sequences of length $d + 1$. It can be written as $f(X)e(X)$ where $f(X) \in S_w(d, p-1)$ and $e(X) \in S_w(d, 1)$. We know that if $f(X) = \sum_{i=0}^{(p-1)d} a_i X^i$ then $|a_i| \le m_w(d, p-1, i)$ and if $e(X) = \sum_{j=0}^{d} \alpha_j X^j$ that $(fe)(X) = f(X)e(X) = \sum_{k=0}^{pd} \left(\sum_{i=\max(0,k-d)}^{\min((p-1)d,k)} a_i \alpha_{k-i}\right) X^k$, and due to the form of $e(X)$ we see that $|C_k(fe)| \le \sum_{j=1}^{n_k} |a_{i_j}| \le \sum_{j=1}^{n_k} m_w(d, p-1, i_j)$ for some $n_k \le n$, $\max(0, k-d) \le i_1 < i_2 < \cdots < i_{n_k} \le \min((p-1)d, k)$ and $i_{j+1} - i_j \ge w$ for $j = 1, \ldots, n_k - 1$.

The final condition on the i_j implies that the $\lfloor i_j/w \rfloor$ are distinct and since $m_w(d, p-1, i)$ is bounded above by $B_w(d, p-1, \lfloor i/w \rfloor)$, which depends only on

$\lfloor i/w \rfloor$, we can recast this as

$$|C_k(fe)| \le \sum_{j=1}^{n_k} B_w(d, p-1, \ell_j) = \sum_{j=1}^{n_k} C_{\ell_j w} \left(\left(\frac{1-X^{nw}}{1-X^w} \right)^{p-1} \right)$$

where $\max(0, \lfloor k/w \rfloor - (n-1)) \le \ell_1 < \ell_2 < \cdots < \ell_{n_k} \le \min((p-1)(n-1), \lfloor k/w \rfloor)$ where we have used that $d/w = n - 1$ is an integer.

Since $\lfloor k/w \rfloor - (\lfloor k/w \rfloor - (n-1)) + 1 = n$ we see that to make n_k as large as possible the ℓ_j must be the (at most n) consecutive integers in this range subject also to $0 \le \ell_1$ and $\ell_{n_k} \le (p-1)(n-1)$. Thus taking a maximum over all possible f and e we have

$$m_w(d, p, k) \le \sum_{\ell=\lfloor k/w \rfloor - (n-1)}^{\lfloor k/w \rfloor} C_{\ell w} \left(\left(\frac{1-X^{nw}}{1-X^w} \right)^{p-1} \right)$$

$$= \sum_{j=0}^{n-1} C_{\lfloor k/w \rfloor w} \left(\left(\frac{1-X^{nw}}{1-X^w} \right)^{p-1} X^{w(n-1-j)} \right)$$

$$= C_{\lfloor k/w \rfloor w} \left(\left(\frac{1-X^{nw}}{1-X^w} \right)^{p} \right) = B_w(d, p, \lfloor k/w \rfloor),$$

which proves the inductive step. To finish the proof we note as before that the maximal value of $B_w(d, p, \lfloor k/w \rfloor)$ for $0 \le k \le pd$ is reached, for example, when $\lfloor k/w \rfloor = \lfloor p \lfloor d/w \rfloor / 2 \rfloor$ and in this case we have $B_w(d, p)$ as required.   □

Hiding Secrecy Leakage in Leaky Helper Data

Matthias Hiller[1]($^{(\boxtimes)}$) and Aysun Gurur Önalan[2]

[1] Fraunhofer AISEC, Munich, Germany
`matthias.hiller@aisec.fraunhofer.de`
[2] Chair of Security in Information Technology,
Technical University of Munich, Munich, Germany

Abstract. PUFs provide cryptographic keys for embedded systems without dedicated secure memory. Practical PUF implementations often show a bias in the PUF responses, which leads to secrecy leakage in many key derivation constructions. However, previously proposed mitigation techniques remove the bias at the expense of discarding large numbers of PUF response bits. Instead of removing the bias from the input sequence, this work reduces the secrecy leakage through the helper data. We apply the concept of wiretap coset coding to add randomness to the helper data such that an attacker cannot isolate significant information about the key anymore.

Examples demonstrate the effectiveness of coset coding for different bias parameters by computing the exact leakage for short code lengths and applying upper bounds for larger code lengths. In our case study, we compare a secrecy leakage mitigation design with coset coding and Differential Sequence Coding (DSC). It reduces the number of required PUF response bits by 60% compared to state-of-the-art debiasing approaches.

Keywords: Physical Unclonable Functions (PUFs) · Fuzzy extractor · Secrecy leakage · Coding theory · Wiretap channel · Coset coding

1 Introduction

Silicon Physical Unclonable Functions (PUFs) measure physical manufacturing variations inside integrated circuits to derive a unique behavior for each device. Typical silicon PUFs can be implemented in a standard CMOS manufacturing process such that they provide cryptographic keys for embedded devices without dedicated secure key storage in non-volatile memory [1]. This makes them a suitable solution to protect a wide span of devices, starting from lightweight IoT sensors up to complex high-end circuits such as FPGAs.

PUF responses are noisy and often not fully random such that postprocessing steps are necessary to derive stable and secure cryptographic keys from PUFs. The syndrome encoder computes helper data that is stored off-chip, e.g. in unsecured external non-volatile memory. The helper data maps the PUF response to codewords of an Error-Correcting Code (ECC) to enable error correction,

© International Association for Cryptologic Research 2017
W. Fischer and N. Homma (Eds.): CHES 2017, LNCS 10529, pp. 601–619, 2017.
DOI: 10.1007/978-3-319-66787-4_29

but it must not leak information about the derived key. Several error correction schemes were proposed and implemented over the last decade, e.g. [2–10].

Early work such as [11] already acknowledged the fact that PUF implementations can have imperfections that result in a reduced entropy of the PUF response. As the field matured, the security implications of the imperfections in the PUF responses, and especially bias, were analyzed and addressed in more detail [5, 10, 12–15].

Looking at a fuzzy commitment [16] in Fig. 1 there are two ways to reduce the leakage within this setting: The approaches in [5, 10] reshape the input distribution in a debiasing step such that an unbiased sequence is processed in the syndrome encoder. This comes at the expense that the unbiased sequence is significantly shorter than the input PUF response. In contrast, we operate on the ECC encoding to mask the leakage on the secret. While [7] proposed a method to store multiple instances of helper data and thus hide the correct value, we create the ambiguity within one single instance of helper data in this work.

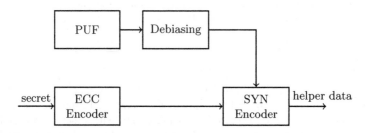

Fig. 1. Helper data generation for a fuzzy commitment and a biased PUF

Another recent line of work relaxed the security argument from an information theoretical setting to a complexity theoretical argument [17–20] where no secrecy leakage is observed. However, to be able to quantify the actual statistical correlation, we stay in the stricter information theoretical setting in the following.

1.1   Contributions

- We show that the problem of secure key storage with PUFs relates closely to the wiretap channel [21]. To the best of our knowledge, we are therefore the first to apply coset coding [22] to PUFs. Instead of embedding only the secret key, we add mask bits that are encoded by the ECC together with the secret key and thus contribute to the helper data as well. Due to the bias, the helper data inevitably leaks information about the key and the mask. Since the attacker is not able to isolate the leakage on the key, this leakage cannot be exploited.
- Examples demonstrate and quantify the leakage reduction that is achieved by assigning mask bits for coset coding. We compute the exact leakage for short

code lengths and apply an upper bound for long code lengths for Reed–Muller (RM) codes and a wide range of bias parameters.
- We provide design parameters for a practical design with Differential Sequence Coding (DSC) and compare it to state-of-the-art debiasing approaches with Index-Based Syndrome coding (IBS) and the von Neumann corrector (VN). The comparison shows that our approach reduces the number of PUF response bits by 60% for a moderately biased PUF with a bias of 0.54 and only has a negligible secrecy leakage of less than 0.06 bit for the entire key.

1.2 Organization

Section 2 introduces the state of the art related to this work. The wiretap channel and corresponding codes which are the foundation of our new leakage reduction method are summarized in Sect. 3. Section 4 describes the correspondence between the wiretap channel model and PUF key storage, and Sect. 5 introduces coset coding for PUFs. The new approach is compared to the state of the art in Sect. 6. Section 7 concludes this work.

1.3 Notation

Capital letters indicate random variables or values that are functions of random variables, while small letters represent numbers and specific instantiations of random variables. Matrices are given by bold capital letters, and calligraphic letters represent sets. C is a codeword of a linear ECC $\mathcal{C}$ with code length n, code size k, minimum distance d, generator matrix $\mathbf{G}$, and parity check matrix $\mathbf{H}$ [23]. The helper data W is computed from PUF response X and secret S. Superscripts define the lengths of vectors.

Let $\mathbb{E}[\cdot]$ be the expectation operator and $\Pr[\cdot]$ the probability of an event. Further, let $\mathrm{hw}(\cdot)$ be the Hamming weight of a vector.

2 State of the Art Debiasing Approaches for PUFs

A simple approach of removing bias is to XOR multiple PUF response bits [24], which reduces the bias for independent and identically distributed (i.i.d) PUF responses according to the piling-up lemma [25]. However, each XOR also reduces the number of PUF response bits so that only a fraction of the input length remains and the output error probability is increased at the same time. Therefore, we take a closer look at more sophisticated alternatives, namely Index-Based Syndrome Coding (IBS) and the von Neumann Corrector (VN) in the following.

For high input bit error probabilities in the range $> 20\%$, the multi-bit symbol-based approach discussed in [26] can also be used to generate keys from biased PUFs without secrecy leakage.

2.1   Index-Based Syndrome Coding

IBS computes pointers to reliable PUF response bits and stores the pointers in helper data [5]. Going back to Fig. 1, the IBS pointer generation acts as debiasing and syndrome encoding at once. IBS decreases the output error probability but it cannot correct any errors. To enable error correction, IBS is typically concatenated with ECCs such as BCH or Reed–Muller codes [23].

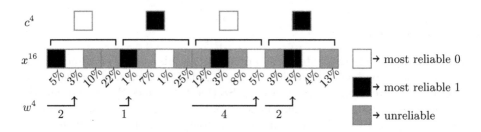

Fig. 2. Helper data generation with index-based syndrome coding

Figure 2 shows an example for helper data generation with IBS. The PUF response sequence is divided into blocks of fixed size q (here, $q = 4$). The ECC encoder maps k-bit secrets into n-bit codewords C^n. The inputs of the IBS encoder are a codeword bit C_i, a block of PUF response bits X^q and reliability information, e.g. the bit error probability, for each of the PUF bits. It generates a pointer W^s, $s = \lceil \log q \rceil$ to index the bit which is equal to the secret bit with the highest probability. The other bits of the block are discarded. This process is repeated for each C_i. The indexing operation selects the PUF response bits according to the distribution of input C. As proven in [5], IBS does not leak secret information for i.i.d PUF response bits as long as no additional reliability information is published. Complementary IBS adds an intermediate error correction step to increase the efficiency of IBS [6]. However, it was shown in [9], that larger block sizes are required for more efficient indexing of reliable PUF response bits.

2.2   Von Neumann Corrector

In [10], another debiasing step was proposed to overcome the leakage caused by biased PUF responses. It is based on the von Neumann (VN) corrector [27] and evaluates pairs of consecutive PUF response bits. (1,0) and (0,1) pairs occur with the same probability but differ in the order of the numbers such that a uniform random process is sampled while the pairs (1,1) and (0,0) are ignored. Figure 3 shows the helper data generation with the VN corrector as debiasing scheme and the fuzzy commitment as syndrome encoder [16].

The encoder scans the PUF response X^m sequentially and maps it to a sequence T^n ($m > n$). If two consecutive PUF bits of X^m differ, the first bit

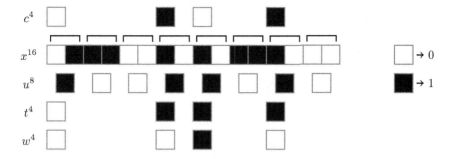

Fig. 3. Helper data generation with the fuzzy commitment and the von Neumann corrector

is added to the debiased output T^n and the position of the pair is stored as additional helper data U^l, as shown in Fig. 3. For i.i.d PUF response bits, the VN approach provides perfectly random outputs. The efficiency of the approach is enhanced in [10] by searching X^m in multiple passes for patterns of different size. For the fuzzy commitment, helper data W^n is computed as XOR between T^n and the codeword C^n. Neither W^n nor U^l leak secret information. However, a high number of discarded PUF response bits causes an overhead in PUF size. In addition, an implementation of the multi-pass version would require either multiple readouts of the PUF or buffering the entire PUF response.

IBS and the VN corrector both address only the debiasing and syndrome coding blocks in Fig. 1. In the following, we also take the ECC encoder into account.

3   Wiretap Channel and Coset Codes

Before going into our new leakage countermeasure for PUFs, we briefly discuss the information theoretical problem that forms the foundation of our work. In 1975, Wyner introduced the wiretap channel model which represents a communication system that is wiretapped by an adversary [21], as shown in Fig. 4.

Alice encodes a k-bit secret message S^k to an n-bit codeword C^n and transmits it to Bob through the main channel. Due to noise, Bob receives a distorted version Y^n of C^n and recovers message $\hat{S}^k$. The attacker Eve also observes a noisy version Z^n of C^n through the wiretapper's channel.

The challenge is to develop a coding scheme that allows a reliable communication from Alice to Bob while preventing Eve from recovering any information. In a reliable system, Bob can decode message $\hat{S}^k$ from his received vector Y^n correctly with a high probability. For security reasons, we need to limit the information that Z^n provides to Eve about S^k. The delicate challenge is to encode the message such that it has just enough structure to be decoded correctly by Bob while it still must resemble ambiguous to Eve. Note that the wiretap channel has to be noisier than the main channel to be able to achieve any secret

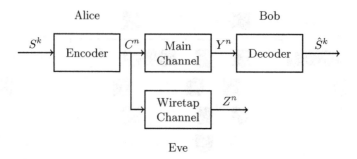

Fig. 4. The wiretap channel

communication at all. The current research field of physical-layer security also makes extensive use of the wiretap channel model [28,29].

The basic idea of wiretap coding is to introduce randomness to the encoding process by assigning multiple codewords to each message. Alice selects a message S^k and encodes it as a codeword of code $\mathcal{C}_1$. Instead of a bijective and deterministic encoding, $\mathcal{C}_1$ contains a set of multiple possible codewords for each message and the encoder selects one of the corresponding codewords at random.

Bob recovers the message correctly, if $\mathcal{C}_1$ contains a sufficient amount of redundancy such that the error probability

$$P_e = \Pr[\hat{S}^k \neq S^k] < \epsilon_1 \tag{1}$$

for an $\epsilon_1 > 0$. For large block lengths, it was shown that there exist codes such that $\lim_{n \to \infty} P_e = 0$ [28].

Eve's channel has a higher noise level so that she has multiple possible solutions instead of one unique solution for the decoding problem. If the code is designed properly, codeword candidates for all possible 2^k messages are suitable, and ideally equiprobable, for her received message Z^n. In other words, according to [28]

$$\lim_{n \to \infty} \frac{1}{n} I(S^k; Z^n) = 0 \tag{2}$$

The noise level on the main channel determines the amount of redundancy that has to be spent to achieve a reliable decoding for Bob. The difference between the noise levels of the main channel and the wiretap channel defines the maximum size of the secret information S^k that can be transmitted from Alice to Bob in n transmitted symbols while keeping Eve ignorant. However, determining the noise levels can be challenging in practice.

The secrecy capacity C_S is thus given by [28]

$$C_S = I(C; Y) - I(C; Z) \tag{3}$$

Most wiretap codes discussed in the information theory community use random codes, where random numbers are generated and then assigned to different codebooks. Random coding arguments are highly suitable to prove that a problem can be solved with some asymptotic behavior or to show that a problem cannot be solved better than some bound. However storing and searching large random codebooks, e.g. with more than 2^{32} entries, in an embedded system is not feasible. After understanding the general theoretical behavior of a problem by analyzing the behavior of random codes, work on deterministic algorithms is the next step to bring an approach closer towards implementations in practical systems.

In 1984, Ozarow and Wyner proposed a practical wiretap coding scheme called coset coding [22]. A coset of a set is computed by adding a constant to all elements of the original set [23]. In coset coding, a coset is selected according to the secret message. Then, the encoder selects one element of the coset at random as transmitted message. Coset coding achieves secrecy for a wiretap channel model where the main channel is noiseless and the wiretapper observes the message through a binary erasure channel, which is a stochastic channel that replaces a transmitted symbol with an erasure symbol with a given fixed probability. Later, this scheme was extended to other channel models, e.g. Binary Symmetric Channels (BSCs) in [30].

Let $\mathbf{G}_1$ be a $k_1 \times n$ generator matrix of linear code $\mathcal{C}_1$ and $\mathbf{H}_1$ be the parity check matrix of the same code. Similarly, $\mathbf{G}_2$ and $\mathbf{H}_2$ are the generator and parity check matrices of a linear code $\mathcal{C}_2 \subset \mathcal{C}_1$ with message length k_2 and code length n. The code space $\mathcal{C}_1$ is partitioned into 2^k sets containing cosets of $\mathcal{C}_2$, where $k = k_1 - k_2$.

$$\mathbf{G}_1 = \begin{bmatrix} \mathbf{G}_2 \\ \mathbf{G} \end{bmatrix} \tag{4}$$

A uniform random vector R^{k_2} is added as mask to disguise the secret message S^k. The encoding is formalized by

$$C^n = \begin{bmatrix} R^{k_2} & S^k \end{bmatrix} \cdot \begin{bmatrix} \mathbf{G}_2 \\ \mathbf{G} \end{bmatrix} \tag{5}$$

$$= R^{k_2} \cdot \mathbf{G}_2 + S^k \cdot \mathbf{G} \tag{6}$$

The coset $S^k \cdot \mathbf{G}$ contains the secret message while codeword $R^{k_2} \cdot \mathbf{G}_2$ adds randomness to prevent Eve from decoding code $\mathcal{C}$ correctly.

The effectiveness of the coset coding countermeasure is measured by the mutual information $I(S^k; Z^n)$. However, computing the exact mutual information in Eq. 2 is practically infeasible for large codes. Chen and Han Vinck provide an upper bound on the information leakage for the case that the main channel and the wiretapper's channel both are BSCs and linear codes are used for the coset coding construction [30]. For a main channel with bit error probability p_m and a wiretap channel with a bit error probability of p_w, the secrecy leakage is bounded by

$$I(S^k; Z^n) \leq \log\left(2^n P_{\mathcal{C}_2}(p_w)\right), \tag{7}$$

where

$$P_{\mathcal{C}_2}(p_w) = \frac{1}{|\mathcal{C}_2|} \sum_{c^n \in \mathcal{C}_2} p_w^{\mathrm{hw}(c^n)} (1 - p_w)^{(n - \mathrm{hw}(c^n))} \tag{8}$$

for code space $\mathcal{C}_2$ with cardinality $|\mathcal{C}_2|$ and elements c^n with Hamming weight $\mathrm{hw}(c^n)$. Note that code $\mathcal{C}$ is important for the reliability while the secrecy leakage in Eq. 7 only depends on $\mathcal{C}_2$.

Equation 8 iterates over all codewords. A good code design minimizes the product $p_w^{\mathrm{hw}(c^n)}(1-p_w)^{(n-\mathrm{hw}(c^n))}$ to tighten the bound in Eq. 7. Since the error probability p_w is given by the channel, one can only optimize the code. p_w is smaller than $(1-p_w)$ such that the Hamming weight $\mathrm{hw}(c^n)$ of the codewords in $\mathcal{C}_2$ is maximized. When $\mathcal{C}_1$ is partitioned into $\mathcal{C}$ and $\mathcal{C}_2$, it is therefore important to assign components with high Hamming weights to $\mathcal{C}_2$ to maximize the impact of the mask.

4   Wiretap Channel Model for PUFs

To apply coset coding to PUFs, we first need to show that key derivation with PUFs also corresponds to the wiretap channel model.

In the following, we apply the fuzzy commitment scheme [16]. However the code-offset fuzzy extractor or the syndrome construction, both [2], or systematic low leakage coding [8] could also be used in a similar way. Figure 5 shows the PUF key generation and reproduction with an attacker that has access to the public helper data.

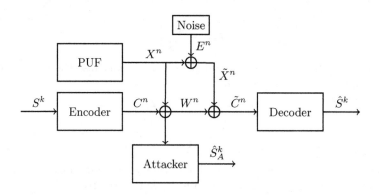

Fig. 5. Fuzzy commitment PUF model with an attacker

The ECC encoder maps the secret S^k to a codeword C^n and the fuzzy commitment XORs C^n with PUF response X^n to generate helper data W^n. W^n is public, so both the legitimate decoder and the attacker can access it. The legitimate receiver observes a noisy version of the PUF response $\tilde{X}^n = X^n \oplus E^n$ with error pattern E^n. If the distortion is within the error correction capability of code $\mathcal{C}_1$, the decoder can recover the secret successfully with a high probability. The attacker tries to extract information regarding the secret from the helper data W^n.

To map this PUF model to the wiretap channel model, one has to leave the procedure-centric view which is typically applied in PUF key generation and look at the information flows. The source outputs secret S^k, while $\hat{S}^k$ and $\hat{S}^k_A$ are the inputs of the sinks at the receiver and the attacker side. In both cases, the information is modified on the way from the source to the sink.

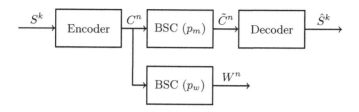

Fig. 6. Wiretap channel model for PUFs

Figure 6 shows the wiretap channel model for PUFs, where the main and wiretapper's channels are modeled as BSCs. Bob's ECC decoder receives a noisy codeword $\tilde{C}^n$ with error pattern E^n, i.e., $\tilde{C}^n = C^n \oplus E^n$. In Fig. 5, X^n is added twice to the codeword which is transmitted over the main channel, so that only the noise E^n remains.

$$\tilde{C}^n = C^n \oplus X^n \oplus \tilde{X}^n \tag{9}$$
$$= C^n \oplus X^n \oplus X^n \oplus E^n \tag{10}$$
$$= C^n \oplus E^n \tag{11}$$

The attacker's path in Fig. 6 does not show a decoder since we assume an unbounded attacker. Therefore, W^n must not leak any information regardless of any subsequent processing steps.

W^n also is a distorted version of C^n, since

$$W^n = C^n \oplus X^n \tag{12}$$

The PUF response X^n is interpreted as the wiretapper's error pattern that is added to codeword C^n in the wiretap channel. Assuming independent errors for each position, the error patterns E^n and X^n can therefore be modeled by BSCs with crossover probabilities $p_m = \frac{1}{n} \mathbb{E}[E^n]$ and $p_w = \frac{1}{n} \mathbb{E}[X^n]$, respectively.

So, we have shown that secure key storage with PUFs can also be interpreted as a wiretap channel. In contrast to the wireless wiretap channel setting, the PUF setting has the advantage that p_w can be measured and characterized precisely in practice, as e.g. in [31].

5   Wiretap Coset Codes for PUFs

This section introduces coset coding to PUFs as a new practical tool to address helper data leakage, based on an example first and then provides a generic approach.

Let the PUF response bits X^n be i.i.d with $\Pr[x = 1] = b$, $b \in [0, 1]$. Then, the probability distribution of X^n is a binomial distribution with $\mathrm{hw}(x^n)$ successes out of n Bernoulli trials with success probability b.

$$\Pr[X^n = x^n] = b^{\mathrm{hw}(x^n)} \cdot (1 - b)^{(n - \mathrm{hw}(x^n))} \tag{13}$$

If $b \neq 0.5$, the response bits are said to be biased and information leakage through the helper data is observed, e.g. [15]. In the following, we discuss a toy example to explain the leakage and its mitigation for a biased PUF.

Let us consider a fuzzy commitment scheme and 4-bit PUF responses X^4 with bias $b = 0.25$. For error correction, exemplarily a $(4, 3, 2)$ error detecting code is applied whose generator matrix is given by

$$\mathbf{G}_1 = \begin{pmatrix} 1\,1\,1\,1 \\ 0\,0\,1\,1 \\ 0\,1\,0\,1 \end{pmatrix}$$

Let us assume that for a specific instance helper data $w^4 = 0001$ is stored and observed by the attacker. Table 1 shows all key candidates and assigns the conditional probability of occurrence for the given helper data to each candidate.

Table 1. Probability of different key candidates for the given helper data $w^4 = 0001$ and bias $b = 0.25$.

s^3	c^4	x^4	$\Pr[X^4 = x^4]$	$\Pr[S^3 = s^3 \mid W^4 = w^4]$
0 0 0	0 0 0 0	0 0 0 1	$0.75^3 \cdot 0.25$	0.225
0 0 1	0 1 0 1	0 1 0 0	$0.75^3 \cdot 0.25$	0.225
0 1 0	0 0 1 1	0 0 1 0	$0.75^3 \cdot 0.25$	0.225
0 1 1	0 1 1 0	0 1 1 1	$0.75 \cdot 0.25^3$	0.025
1 0 0	1 1 1 1	1 1 1 0	$0.75 \cdot 0.25^3$	0.025
1 0 1	1 0 1 0	1 0 1 1	$0.75 \cdot 0.25^3$	0.025
1 1 0	1 1 0 0	1 1 0 1	$0.75 \cdot 0.25^3$	0.025
1 1 1	1 0 0 1	1 0 0 0	$0.75^3 \cdot 0.25$	0.225

Recalling the notation from Sect. 3, we start with secret length $k = 3$ and no masking, so $k_2 = 0$. The first three columns show the mapping between the key candidates s^3, codewords c^4 and PUF responses x^4. Key candidates s^3 are encoded to codewords c^4 by $\mathbf{G}_1$, i.e. $c^4 = s^3 \cdot \mathbf{G}_1$. For a given w^4, there is an exact one-to-one mapping between a PUF response x^4 and a secret s^3, since

$$x^4 = w^4 \oplus c^4 = w^4 \oplus s^3 \cdot \mathbf{G}_1. \tag{14}$$

The probabilities of all x^4 are listed in the fourth column of the table.

The fifth column shows that one half of the possible PUF responses contains three zeros and a single one, while the other half contains one zero and three ones. Due to the bias towards zero, the PUF responses with more ones, highlighted in gray in the table, have a lower probability of occurrence than the other half. This gives the attacker an advantage to guess the secret correctly.

Previous work focused on debiasing the PUF response to avoid leakage. In contrast, we now assign multiple PUF responses to each key candidate.

By interpreting the first bit of each key candidate as mask, so $k_2 = 1$, we reduce k to $k = 2$. Now, we obtain four different key candidates whereas each candidate can be derived from two different PUF responses. For example, key candidates $s^3 = 000$ and $s^3 = 100$ now both lead to $s^2 = 00$ whose corresponding PUF responses are $x^4 = 0001$ and $x^4 = 1110$. So,

$$\Pr[s^2 = 00|W^4 = 0001] = \Pr[s^3 = 000|W^4 = 0001] \tag{15}$$
$$+ \Pr[s^3 = 100|W^4 = 0001]$$
$$= 0.25. \tag{16}$$

After shortening s^3 to s^2 and interpreting the first bit as mask, all four key candidates $s^2 \in \{00, 01, 10, 11\}$ occur with probability 0.25. As a result, the probability $\Pr[S^2 = s^2|W^4 = 0001]$ is uniformly distributed and the attacker has no advantage from observing the helper data.

Generalizing the example, let $\mathbf{G}_1$ be the generator matrix of an (n, k_1, d) linear block code $\mathcal{C}_1$. We mask k secret key bits with k_2 mask bits according to Eq. 4. Again, $\mathbf{G}_1$ is constructed as

$$\mathbf{G}_1 = \begin{bmatrix} \mathbf{G}_2 \\ \mathbf{G} \end{bmatrix} \tag{17}$$

where $\mathbf{G}_2$ is a $k_2 \times n$ generator matrix encoding the mask bits and $\mathbf{G}$ is $k \times n$ generator matrix encoding the secret key bits. As in the wiretap coset codes, $\mathcal{C}_1$ has a generator matrix G_1 and is partitioned by cosets of $\mathcal{C}_2$ with generator matrix G_2.

Applying k_2 mask bits maps 2^{k_2} PUF responses to each key. As the number of assigned PUF responses increases, $\Pr[S^k|W^n]$ gets closer to a uniform distribution which prevents the attacker from deriving secret information. Therefore, increasing the number of mask bits reduces the information leakage.

The mutual information $I(S^k; W^n)$ between the secret and the helper data quantifies the leakage. So, the leakage is upper bounded by

$$I(S^k; W^n) = H(S^k) - H(S^k|W^n) \tag{18}$$
$$\leq k - \tilde{H}_\infty(S^k|W^n) \tag{19}$$

The conditional min entropy[1] $\tilde{H}_\infty(S^k|W^n)$ is given by [2]

$$\tilde{H}_\infty(S^k|W^n) = -\log_2\left(\underset{w^n}{\mathbb{E}}\left[\max_{s^k}\Pr_{S^k|W}[s^k|w^n]\right]\right). \tag{20}$$

The distribution of probability $P_{S^k|W}(s^k|w^n)$ was already discussed in detail in the previous example and Table 1. Now, we iterate over all w^n and in each iteration all values x^n with $x^n = c^n \oplus w^n$ for $c^n \in C_1$, are listed. According to $\Pr[X^n = x^n]$ for the listed x^n, $\max_{s^k} \Pr[S^k|W^n = w^n]$ is computed. For larger code length, computing $\tilde{H}_\infty(S^k|W^n)$ becomes infeasible, but it can be bounded, e.g. according to [15].

6   Evaluation

After introducing the new leakage countermeasure for biased PUFs, this section evaluates its effectiveness. In Sect. 6.1, we compute and discuss the exact leakage for small codes with $n = 8$. Bounded results for a larger code with length $n = 64$ are provided in Sect. 6.2. Section 6.3 compares our approach to the state of the art in a practical setting.

In the following, we analyze coset code designs based on Reed–Muller (RM) codes [23]. RM codes are a popular code class that was already used several times in the PUF context, e.g. [3,4,6,32]. They have a highly regular structure and are well-suited for compact hardware implementations. $\mathrm{RM}(r, m)$ codes with parameters r and m have code length $n = 2^m$, message length $k = \sum_{i=0}^{r}\binom{m}{i}$, and code distance $d = 2^{(m-r)}$. Area-optimized FPGA implementations of RM codes for PUF error correction can be found e.g. in [4,32].

The generator matrix $\mathbf{G}$ of an $\mathrm{RM}(r, m)$ code, is built from m base vectors $v_{(i)}^n$ of length $n = 2^m$ and the all ones vector $v_{(0)}^n$ of form

$$v_{(0)}^n = 11111111\cdots11111111$$
$$v_{(m)}^n = 00000000\cdots11111111$$
$$\vdots$$
$$v_{(3)}^n = 00001111\cdots00001111$$
$$v_{(2)}^n = 00110011\cdots00110011$$
$$v_{(1)}^n = 01010101\cdots01010101$$

For $r' = \{1, ..., r\}$ all linear combinations of r' base vectors $v_{(1)}^n$ to $v_{(m)}^n$ are added to $\mathbf{G}$. Note that combining r' base vectors always results in a vector with Hamming weight $d = 2^{(m-r')}$. The generator matrix consists of $v_{(0)}^n$ and all linear combinations of 1 to r vectors in the set $\{v_{(1)}^n, v_{(2)}^n \cdots v_{(m)}^n\}$.

---

[1] Please be aware that referenced publications from different communities vary in their definitions of the conditional min-entropy. We use the definition in [2] and not the one that is used in [28].

6.1   Exact Computations for Short Codes

Figure 7 presents the results for different bias values b in terms of total leakage according to Eqs. 19 and 20. To show the impact of coset coding, we used RM codes and a fuzzy commitment. Increasing the number of mask bits reduces the total leakage, as expected. $b = 0.5$ refers to a uniform distribution of PUF response bits so the leakage is always 0. High b values refer to a high bias, which cause an increased secrecy leakage.

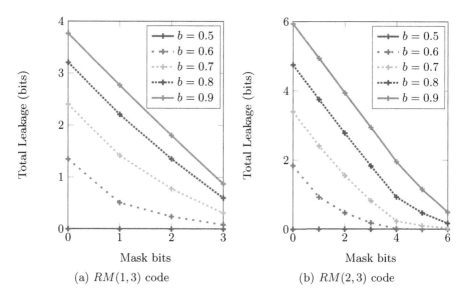

(a) $RM(1,3)$ code   (b) $RM(2,3)$ code

Fig. 7. Computed total information leakage of wiretap coset coding for PUFs with bias b and RM(1, 3) and RM(2, 3) codes.

The RM(1,3) code in Fig. 7a has parameters (8,4,4) such that it carries 4 information bits if no bits are assigned to the mask. Depending on the bias, between 1.3 and 3.8 of the 4 secret bits are leaked. As expected, the total leakage is reduced as more secret bits are interpreted as mask bits.

The first row of its generator matrix **G** has Hamming weight 8 while the other three rows have a Hamming weight of 4. The steepness of the curves changes after one bit is assigned to the mask which is consistent with the behavior given in Eq. 7, where the Hamming weight also plays a critical role in reducing the leakage.

The second example, presented in Fig. 7b, is an RM(2, 3) code with parameters (8,7,2). It shows significantly more secrecy leakage for high b since it also contains more information that could be leaked. In contrast to the first example, the RM(2, 3) code is able to generate nearly leakage-free secret bits. For example for $b = 0.6$, after interpreting 3 bits as mask only less than 0.2 bit leak in total about the remaining 4 secret bits.

The curves have three areas of different steepness because the generator matrix has three more rows with Hamming weight 2 in addition to the four rows of the RM(1,3) code. Therefore, each additional bit after 4 mask bits has less impact than the bits 1 to 4.

6.2 Upper Bounds for Long Codes

After discussing fundamental properties of coset coding with short code lengths in the previous section, this section shows the secrecy leakage reduction through coset coding for a code length of 64, which is also used in practical implementations.

The exhaustive computation discussed in the previous subsection becomes infeasible for longer code lengths. We therefore upper bound the leakage with the bound presented in [30]. From a security point of view, it is important to prove that the leakage is lower than a given threshold. In the following, we set this threshold to less than 1 bit total leakage. The previous figures demonstrated that this strongly depends on the bias at the input.

Figure 8 realigns the plots such that all start at a secrecy leakage around one. The offset in x direction is given by m. The RM(2,6) code has parameters (64,22,16) and the bias is narrowed down to parameters between $b = 0.52$ and $b = 0.60$. When interpreting the results, it is important to take into account that the results are conservative upper bounds and the actual values are always lower.

For a small bias of $b = 0.52$, roughly 4 mask bits are sufficient. Going to $b = 0.56$ already requires more than 11 mask bits. However, even for $b = 0.60$ the bias can be brought down close to zero.

6.3 Comparison with the State of the Art

Several previous publications demonstrated that code concatenation or a combination of error reduction and ECC facilitate to achieve key error probabilities of 10^{-6} for low implementation complexities [3–6,9]. In addition, we have shown in Sect. 6.1 that codes with a high ratio of key bits per codeword bit show more promising masking properties. We therefore follow general experience of previous work and coset coding specific behavior to refrain from providing a stand-alone wiretap coset coding solution and directly combine it with Differential Sequence Coding (DSC) [9].

DSC stores differential pointers U_i that indicate reliable PUF bits X, as shown in Fig. 9. Each reliable PUF bit is mapped to a codeword bit C_i while unreliable PUF response bits are ignored. If the indexed PUF response bit is likely to be equal to its corresponding codeword bit, the inversion bit V_i is set to zero. Otherwise it is set to one. The pointers and the inversion bits are stored as helper data.

It was shown in [9] that DSC performs very efficient error reduction for unbiased PUFs. For biased PUFs, two new aspects have to be considered: First, the inversion bits V start to leak secret information, and second the bias even

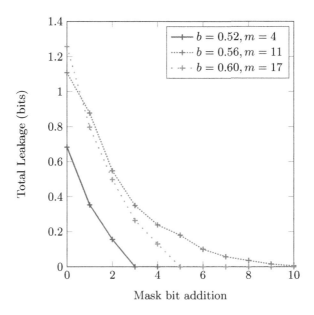

Fig. 8. Bounded total information leakage of wiretap coset coding for PUFs with bias b and $RM(2, 6)$. m refers to the initial offset of mask bits.

increases if the PUF response is reduced to its more reliable bits. This relation between bias and reliability was discussed in detail in [12].

To mitigate this leakage and derive a reliable key, we combine DSC and coset coding in this work. First, S^k is encoded to C^n by coset encoding, and then C^n is embedded into reliable PUF responses X^m by DSC.

Table 2 presents the result of DSC + wiretap RM coset coding (CC) and compares it with previous leakage mitigation approaches. We computed all results in Table 2 for an SRAM PUF with average bit error $P_{in} = 10\%$, i.i.d PUF response bits with bias 0.54 and reliability distribution according to [4,12]. A key error probability $P_e \leq 10^{-6}$ is targeted for 128 bit key length. The error correction relies on two ECC stages. We used repetition codes with parameters (n_3, k_3, n_3) as inner codes for the code-offset fuzzy extractor, VN and IBS. For DSC, the

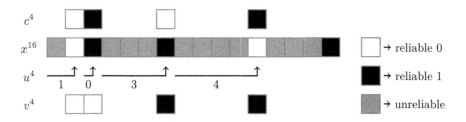

Fig. 9. Helper data generation with differential sequence coding

Table 2. Design comparison of a code-offset fuzzy extractor, DSC, IBS, VN debiasing and DSC with wiretap coset coding for an SRAM PUF with $P_{in} = 10\%$ and $b = 0.54$, and $P_e \leq 10^{-6}$ and 128 bit key length.

Design	Fuz Ext	DSC	IBS	VN	CC + DSC	CC + DSC
Codes	Rep + BCH	RM	Rep + BCH	Rep + BCH	RM	RM
Parameters			7 bits per block	3 passes	30 mask bits	25 mask bits
Number of Blocks z	2	4	2	4	2	4
Inner Code (n_3, k_3, n_3)	(3,1,3)	$(2.5, 1)^*$	(5,1,5)	(8,1,8)	$(2.75, 1)^*$	$(5.75, 1)^*$
Outer Code (n_1, k_1, d_1)	(255,99,47)	(64,42,8)	(127,64,21)	(63,36,11)	(128,99,8)	(64,57,4)
Secret Size S^k	198	168	128	144	138	128
PUF Size X^m	1,530	640	1,778	2,471	704	1,472
Key Error Probability P_e	5.4×10^{-7}	3.5×10^{-7}	4.6×10^{-7}	9.7×10^{-8}	2.5×10^{-7}	6.6×10^{-7}
Secrecy Leakage $I(S^k; W^n)$	≤ 65.5	≤ 37.1	0	0	≤ 0.06	≤ 0.01

inner repetition code is replaced by DSC with the rate $(n_3, 1)$, denoted by a star. The code-offset fuzzy extractor, and IBS and VN debiasing schemes use BCH codes as outer code with (n_1, k_1, d_1) whereas wiretap coset coding uses RM codes. z refers to the number of BCH or RM codewords that are used to generate the entire key.

First of all, the Fuzzy Extractor and DSC results without debiasing clearly demonstrate that there exists significant leakage, even for the relatively low bias of 0.54. Removing this leakage with the state-of-the-art approaches IBS or VN increases the number of PUF bits from 640 with DSC to 1,778 and 2,471, respectively, which is an increase of over 1,100 PUF response bits or 178%.

Our new approach with DSC and wiretap coset coding only requires 704 PUF response bits for a negligible upper bounded total leakage of 0.06. Therefore, the debiasing overhead is reduced by almost 170% from 178% to 10%, or roughly 1,000 PUF bits such that the overall number of PUF response bits is reduced by 60% compared to IBS and VN.

We also provide a more conservative value for a secrecy leakage ≤ 0.01. As already discussed in Sects. 6.1 and 6.2, the efficiency of coset coding decreases as the number of mask bits increases. Removing the last 0.05 bit in the conservative estimate of the secrecy leakage doubles the number of PUF response bits.

7   Conclusion

Biased PUF responses lead to secrecy leakage. We introduce wiretap coset coding to PUFs to mitigate the leakage through the helper data. In contrast to previous work that eliminates the bias at the input, we modify the ECC.

This work applies the wiretap channel model to PUFs to reduce the secrecy leakage with coset coding. The typical one-to-one mapping between information and codeword is changed to a one-to-many mapping so that all secrets show a similar probability again for a given helper data candidate.

The exact secrecy leakage can be computed for short codes while bounds also provide leakage results for longer codes. Our design for a practical scenario reduces the overall number of required PUF response bits by roughly $1,000$ or 60% compared to the reference approaches VN and IBS.

Acknowledgements. The authors would like to thank Georg Sigl and Vincent Immler for the helpful comments and discussions.

References

1. Herder, C., Yu, M., Koushanfar, F., Devadas, S.: Physical unclonable functions and applications: a tutorial. Proc. IEEE **102**(8), 1126–1141 (2014)
2. Dodis, Y., Reyzin, L., Smith, A.: Fuzzy extractors: how to generate strong keys from biometrics and other noisy data. In: Cachin, C., Camenisch, J.L. (eds.) EUROCRYPT 2004. LNCS, vol. 3027, pp. 523–540. Springer, Heidelberg (2004). doi:10.1007/978-3-540-24676-3_31
3. Bösch, C., Guajardo, J., Sadeghi, A.-R., Shokrollahi, J., Tuyls, P.: Efficient helper data key extractor on FPGAs. In: Oswald, E., Rohatgi, P. (eds.) CHES 2008. LNCS, vol. 5154, pp. 181–197. Springer, Heidelberg (2008). doi:10.1007/978-3-540-85053-3_12
4. Maes, R., Tuyls, P., Verbauwhede, I.: Low-overhead implementation of a soft decision helper data algorithm for SRAM PUFs. In: Clavier, C., Gaj, K. (eds.) CHES 2009. LNCS, vol. 5747, pp. 332–347. Springer, Heidelberg (2009). doi:10.1007/978-3-642-04138-9_24
5. Yu, M., Devadas, S.: Secure and robust error correction for physical unclonable functions. IEEE Des. Test Comput. **27**(1), 48–65 (2010)
6. Hiller, M., Merli, D., Stumpf, F., Sigl, G.: Complementary IBS: application specific error correction for PUFs. In: IEEE International Symposium on Hardware-Oriented Security and Trust (HOST), pp. 1–6 (2012)
7. Skoric, B., de Vreede, N.: The spammed code offset method. IEEE Trans. Inf. Forensics Secur. **9**(5), 875–884 (2014)
8. Hiller, M., Yu, M., Pehl, M.: Systematic low leakage coding for physical unclonable functions. In: ACM Symposium on Information, Computer and Communications Security (ASIACCS), pp. 155–166 (2015)
9. Hiller, M., Yu, M., Sigl, G.: Cherry-picking reliable PUF bits with differential sequence coding. IEEE Trans. Inf. Forensics Secur. **11**(9), 2065–2076 (2016)
10. Maes, R., van der Leest, V., van der Sluis, E., Willems, F.: Secure key generation from biased PUFs: extended version. J. Cryptographic Eng. **6**(2), 121–137 (2016)
11. Guajardo, J., Kumar, S.S., Schrijen, G.-J., Tuyls, P.: FPGA intrinsic PUFs and their use for IP protection. In: Paillier, P., Verbauwhede, I. (eds.) CHES 2007. LNCS, vol. 4727, pp. 63–80. Springer, Heidelberg (2007). doi:10.1007/978-3-540-74735-2_5
12. Maes, R.: An accurate probabilistic reliability model for silicon PUFs. In: Bertoni, G., Coron, J.-S. (eds.) CHES 2013. LNCS, vol. 8086, pp. 73–89. Springer, Heidelberg (2013). doi:10.1007/978-3-642-40349-1_5

13. Koeberl, P., Jiangtao, L., Rajan, A., Wei, W.: Entropy loss in PUF-based key generation schemes: the repetition code pitfall. In: IEEE International Symposium on Hardware-Oriented Security and Trust (HOST), pp. 44–49 (2014)
14. Delvaux, J., Gu, D., Schellekens, D., Verbauwhede, I.: Helper data algorithms for PUF-based key generation: overview and analysis. IEEE Trans. Comput. Aided Des. Integr. Circuits Syst. **34**(6), 889–902 (2015)
15. Delvaux, J., Gu, D., Verbauwhede, I., Hiller, M., Yu, M.-D.M.: Efficient fuzzy extraction of PUF-induced secrets: theory and applications. In: Gierlichs, B., Poschmann, A.Y. (eds.) CHES 2016. LNCS, vol. 9813, pp. 412–431. Springer, Heidelberg (2016). doi:10.1007/978-3-662-53140-2_20
16. Juels, A., Wattenberg, M.: A fuzzy commitment scheme. In: ACM Conference on Computer and Communications Security (CCS), pp. 28–36 (1999)
17. Fuller, B., Meng, X., Reyzin, L.: Computational fuzzy extractors. In: Sako, K., Sarkar, P. (eds.) ASIACRYPT 2013. LNCS, vol. 8269, pp. 174–193. Springer, Heidelberg (2013). doi:10.1007/978-3-642-42033-7_10
18. Herder, C., Ren, L., van Dijk, M., Yu, M., Devadas, S.: Trapdoor computational fuzzy extractors and stateless cryptographically-secure physical unclonable functions. IEEE Trans. Dependable Secure Comput. (2016)
19. Huth, C., Becker, D., Guajardo, J., Duplys, P., Güneysu, T.: Securing systems with scarce entropy: LWE-based lossless computational fuzzy extractor for the IoT, IACR eprint archive (2016)
20. Colombier, B., Bossuet, L., Fischer, V., Hely, D.: Key reconciliation protocols for error correction of silicon PUF responses. IEEE Trans. Inf. Forensics Secur. **12**(8), 1988–2002 (2017)
21. Wyner, A.D.: The wire-tap channel. Bell Syst. Tech. J. **54**(8), 1355–1387 (1975)
22. Ozarow, L.H., Wyner, A.D.: Wire-tap channel II. In: Beth, T., Cot, N., Ingemarsson, I. (eds.) EUROCRYPT 1984. LNCS, vol. 209, pp. 33–50. Springer, Heidelberg (1985). doi:10.1007/3-540-39757-4_5
23. MacWilliams, F.J., Sloane, N.J.A.: The Theory of Error-Correcting Codes. North-Holland (1977)
24. Aysu, A., Gulcan, E., Moriyama, D., Schaumont, P., Yung, M.: End-to-end design of a PUF-based privacy preserving authentication protocol. In: Güneysu, T., Handschuh, H. (eds.) CHES 2015. LNCS, vol. 9293, pp. 556–576. Springer, Heidelberg (2015). doi:10.1007/978-3-662-48324-4_28
25. Matsui, M.: Linear cryptanalysis method for DES cipher. In: Helleseth, T. (ed.) EUROCRYPT 1993. LNCS, vol. 765, pp. 386–397. Springer, Heidelberg (1994). doi:10.1007/3-540-48285-7_33
26. Yu, M., Hiller, M., Devadas, S.: Maximum likelihood decoding of device-specific multi-bit symbols for reliable key generation. In: IEEE International Symposium on Hardware-Oriented Security and Trust (HOST), pp. 38–43 (2015)
27. von Neumann, J.: Various techniques used in connection with random digits. Appl. Math Series **12**, 36–38 (1951)
28. Bloch, M., Barros, J.: Physical-Layer Security: From Information Theory to Security Engineering. Cambridge University Press, Cambridge (2011)
29. Bloch, M., Hayashi, M., Thangaraj, A.: Error-control coding for physical-layer secrecy. Proc. IEEE **103**(10), 1725–1746 (2015)
30. Chen, Y., Han Vinck, A.J.: On the binary symmetric wiretap channel. In: International Zurich Seminar on Communications, pp. 17–20 (2010)

31. Katzenbeisser, S., Kocabaş, Ü., Rožić, V., Sadeghi, A.-R., Verbauwhede, I., Wachsmann, C.: PUFs: myth, fact or busted? A security evaluation of physically unclonable functions (PUFs) cast in silicon. In: Prouff, E., Schaumont, P. (eds.) CHES 2012. LNCS, vol. 7428, pp. 283–301. Springer, Heidelberg (2012). doi:10.1007/978-3-642-33027-8_17

32. Hiller, M., Kürzinger, L., Sigl, G., Müelich, S., Puchinger, S., Bossert, M.: Low-area Reed decoding in a generalized concatenated code construction for PUFs. In: IEEE Computer Society Annual Symposium on VLSI (ISVLSI) (2015)

Efficient Implementations

Very High Order Masking: Efficient Implementation and Security Evaluation

Anthony Journault$^{(\boxtimes)}$ and François-Xavier Standaert

ICTEAM/ELEN/Crypto Group, Université catholique de Louvain,
Louvain-la-Neuve, Belgium
{anthony.journault,fstandae}@uclouvain.be

Abstract. In this paper, we study the performances and security of recent masking algorithms specialized to parallel implementations in a 32-bit embedded software platform, for the standard AES Rijndael and the bitslice cipher Fantomas. By exploiting the excellent features of these algorithms for bitslice implementations, we first extend the recent speed records of Goudarzi and Rivain (presented at Eurocrypt 2017) and report realistic timings for masked implementations with 32 shares. We then observe that the security level provided by such implementations is uneasy to quantify with current evaluation tools. We therefore propose a new "multi-model" evaluation methodology which takes advantage of different (more or less abstract) security models introduced in the literature. This methodology allows us to both bound the security level of our implementations in a principled manner and to assess the risks of overstated security based on well understood parameters. Concretely, it leads us to conclude that these implementations withstand worst-case adversaries with $> 2^{64}$ measurements under falsifiable assumptions.

1 Introduction

The masking countermeasure is among the most investigated solutions to improve the security of cryptographic implementations against side-channel analysis. Concretely, masking amounts to perform cryptographic operations on secret shared data, say with d shares. Very summarized, it allows amplifying the noise in the physical measurements (hence the security level) exponentially in d, at the cost of quadratic (in d) performance overheads [27,38]. As discussed in [25], these performance overheads may become a bottleneck for the deployment of secure software implementations, especially as the number of shares increases – which is however needed if high security levels are targeted [15].

In this respect, two recent works from Eurocrypt 2017 tackled the challenge of improving the performances of masked implementations. In the first one, Goudarzi and Rivain leveraged the intuition that bitslice implementations are generally well suited to improve software performances, and described optimizations leading to fast masked implementations of the AES (and PRESENT), beating all state-of-the-art implementations based on polynomial representations [22]. In the second one, Barthe et al. introduced new masking algorithms

© International Association for Cryptologic Research 2017
W. Fischer and N. Homma (Eds.): CHES 2017, LNCS 10529, pp. 623–643, 2017.
DOI: 10.1007/978-3-319-66787-4_30

that are perfectly suited for parallel (bitslice) implementations and analyzed the formal security guarantees that can be expected from them [5].

Building on these two recent works, our contributions are in four parts:

First, since the new masking algorithms of Barthe et al. are natural candidates for bitslice implementations, we analyze their performance on a 32-bit ARM Cortex M4 processor. Our results confirm that they allow competing with the performances of Goudarzi and Rivain with limited optimization efforts.

Second, we put forward the additional performance gains that can be obtained when applying the algorithms of Barthe et al. to bitslice ciphers with limited non-linear gates, such as the LS-design Fantomas from FSE 2014 [23].

Third, and since our implementations can run with very high number of shares (we focus on the case with $d = 32$), we question their security evaluation. For this purpose, we start from the observation that current evaluation methodologies (e.g., based on leakage detection [10,16,21,33,44] or on launching high order attacks [35,39,49]) are not sufficient to gain quantitative insights about the security level of these implementations (and the risks of errors in these evaluations). Hence, we introduce a new "multi-model" methodology allowing to mitigate these limitations. This methodology essentially builds on the fact that by investigating the security of the masked implementations in different security models, starting from the most abstract "probing model" of Ishai et al. [27], following with the intermediate "bounded moment model" of Barthe et al. [5] and ending with the most concrete "noisy leakage model" of Prouff and Rivain [38], one can gradually build a confident assessment of the security level.

Finally, we apply our new multi-model methodology to our implementations of the AES and Fantomas, and discuss its limitations. Its application allows us to claim so far unreported security levels (e.g., against adversaries exploiting more than 2^{64} measurements) and to conclude that, in front of worst-case adversaries taking advantage of all the exploitable leakage samples in an implementation, performance improvements naturally lead to security improvements.

2   Background

In this section, we recall the parallel masking scheme we aim to study, and the two block ciphers we choose to work with, namely the AES and Fantomas.

2.1   Barthe et al.'s Parallel Masking Algorithm

Masking is a popular side-channel countermeasure formalized by the seminal work of Ishai et al. [27]. Its main idea is to split all the key dependent data (often called sensitive variables) in different pieces which are randomly generated. More formally, masking consists in sharing a sensitive value s such that:

$$s = s_1 \oplus s_2 \oplus \cdots \oplus s_d.$$

In the case of Boolean masking we will consider next, $\oplus$ is the XOR operation, each share s_i is a random bit and d is the number of shares. In order to apply masking to a block cipher, one essentially needs a way to perform secure multiplications and to refresh the shares. In the case of the bitslice implementations we will consider next, this amounts to perform secure AND gates and XORing with fresh random values. For this purpose, we will use the algorithms proposed by Barthe et al. at Eurocrypt 2017 [5]. Namely, and following their notations, we denote as $a = (a_1, a_2, \cdots, a_d)$ a vector of d shares, by $\mathsf{rot}(a, n)$ the rotation of vector a by n positions. Moreover, the bitwise addition and multiplication operations (i.e., the XOR and AND gates) between two vectors a and b are denoted as $a \oplus b$ and $a \cdot b$, respectively. Based on these notations, the refreshing algorithm is given by Algorithm 1 for any number of shares d. Its time complexity is constant in the number of shares d and requires d bits of fresh uniform randomness.

Algorithm 1. Parallel Refreshing Algorithm

Input: Shares a satisfying $\bigoplus_i a_i = a$, uniformly random vector r
Output: Refreshed shares b satisfying $\bigoplus_i b_i = a$
  $b = a \oplus r \oplus \mathsf{rot}(r, 1)$
  return b

For readability, we next give the multiplication algorithm for the case $d = 4$ in Algorithm 2. Its description for any d can be found in [5]. The time complexity of the algorithm is linear in the number of shares d and it requires $d \cdot \lceil \frac{d-1}{4} \rceil$ bits of randomness. Intuitively, this algorithm can be viewed as a combination of different steps: (1) the loading (and possible rotation) of the input share(s), (2) a partial product phase between the shares, (3) the loading and rotation of the fresh randomness, and (4) a compression phase where partial products are XORed together, interleaved with the addition of fresh randomness.

Algorithm 2. Parallel Multiplication Algorithm for $d = 4$

Input: Shares a and b satisfying $\bigoplus_i a_i = a$ and $\bigoplus_i b_i = b$, unif. rand. vector r
Output: Shares x satisfying $\bigoplus_i x_i = a \cdot b$
  $c_1 = a \cdot b$
  $c_2 = a \cdot \mathsf{rot}(b, 1)$
  $c_3 = \mathsf{rot}(a, 1) \cdot b$
  $d_1 = c_1 \oplus \mathsf{r}$
  $d_2 = d_1 \oplus c_2$
  $d_3 = d_2 \oplus c_3$
  $d_4 = d_3 \oplus \mathsf{rot}(\mathsf{r}, 1)$
  $x = d_4$
  return x

2.2 Target Algorithms

The AES Rijjndael [13] is a 128-bit block cipher operating on bytes and allowing three different key sizes (128, 192 and 256 bits). We will focus on the 128-bit variant that has 10 rounds. Each round is composed of the succession of 4 operations: SubBytes (which is the non-linear part), ShiftRows, MixColumns and AddRoundKey (except for the last round where MixColumns is removed). Each round key is generated thanks to a key schedule algorithm. Operations will be detailed in the implementation section. The AES' robustness over the years and widespread use makes it a natural benchmark to compare implementations.

Fantomas is an instance of LS-Design [23], of which the main goal is to make Boolean masking easy to apply. It is a 128-bit cipher iterating 12 rounds based on the application of an 8-bit bitslice S-box followed by a 16-bit linear layer (usually stored in a table and called the L-box), together with a partial round constant addition and a key addition. The internal state of Fantomas can be seen as an 8×16-bit matrix where the S-box is applied on the columns and the L-box is applied on the rows. The precise description of the S-box and L-box are provided in the extended version of this work available on the IACR ePrint.

We note that another instance of LS-design (namely Robin) has been recently cryptanalyzed by Leander et al. [29] and Todo et al. [47]: both attacks highlight a dense set of weak keys in the algorithm and can be thwarted by adding full round constants in each round [28]. Despite there is no public indication that a similar attack can be applied to Fantomas, we considered a similar tweak as an additional security margin (and denote this variant as Fantomas*).

2.3 Target Device and Measurement Setups

Our implementations are optimized for a 32-bit ARM Cortex-M4 processor clocked at 100 MHz and embedded in the SAM4C-EK evaluation board [1]. Of particular interest for our experiments, this device has an embedded True Random Number Generator (TRNG) which provides 32 bit of randomness every 80 clock cycles. We recall the description of the ARM processor and instructions set given in [22]. The processor is composed of sixteen 32-bit purpose registers labeled from R0 to R15. Registers R0 to R12 are the variable registers (available for computations), R13 contains the stack pointer, R14 contains the link register and R15 is the program counter. The ARM instructions can be classified in three distinct sets: the data instructions such as AND, XOR, OR, LSR, MOV, ..., which cost 1 clock cycle; the memory instructions such as STR, LDR,..., which cost 2 clock cycles (with the thumb extension); and the branching instructions such as B, BL, BX, ..., which cost from 2 to 4 clock cycles. A useful property of the ARM assembly is the barrel shifter. It allows applying one of the following instructions on one of the operands of any data instruction for free: the logical shift (right LSR and left LSL), the arithmetic shift right ASR and the rotate-right ROR.

As for our security evaluations, we performed power analysis attacks using a standard setup measuring voltage variations across a resistor inserted in the supply circuit, with acquisitions performed using a Lecroy WaveRunner HRO 66 oscilloscope running at 625 Msamples/second and providing 8-bit samples.

3   Efficient Implementations

We designed our implementations in a modular manner, starting with building blocks such as refreshing and multiplication algorithms, and then building more complex components such as the S-boxes, rounds, and full cipher upon the previous ones. This adds flexibility to the implementation (i.e., we can easily change one of the building blocks, for example the random number generator) and enables simple cycle counts for various settings. Following this strategy, we first describe the implementation of cipher independent operations, and then discuss optimizations that specifically relate to the AES and Fantomas*.

3.1   Cipher Independent Components

We start by setting up the parameters of our parallel masking scheme and then depict the implementation of the refreshing and multiplication algorithms.

Given the register size r of a processor, parallel masking offers different trade-offs to store the shares of a masked implementation. In the following, we opted for the extreme solution where the number of shares d equals r (which minimizes the additional control overheads needed to store the shares of several intermediate values in a single register). In our 32-bit ARM processor example, this implies that we consider a masked implementation with 32 shares.

More precisely, let $\boldsymbol{s} = (s_1, \cdots s_{32})$ be a 32-bit word where each s_i for $1 \leq i \leq 32$ is a bit and s be a sensitive bit. We have that $s = \bigoplus_{i=1}^{32} s_i$. Concretely, our implementations will store such vectors of 32 shares corresponding to a single bit of sensitive data in single registers. This allows us to take advantage of the parallelization offered by bitwise operations such as XOR, AND, OR, ... That is, let $\perp$ be such a bitwise operator and $\boldsymbol{s}^a$, $\boldsymbol{s}^b$ two 32-bit words, we have:

$$\boldsymbol{s}^a \perp \boldsymbol{s}^b = (s_1^a \perp s_1^b, \cdots, s_{32}^a \perp s_{32}^b).$$

In practice, for a block cipher of size n with key size k, its internal state will therefore be represented and stored as $n + k$ 32-bit words in our parallel masking setting. The initial key sharing (performed once in a leak-free environment) is done as usual by ensuring that the s_i's are random bits for $2 \leq i \leq d$ and $s_1 = s \oplus s_2 \oplus \cdots \oplus s_d$. These shares are then refreshed with Algorithm 1 before each execution. And the un-sharing can finally be done by computing the value $\bigoplus_{i=1}^{32} s_i$, or equivalently by computing the Hamming weight modulo 2 of $\boldsymbol{s}$.

One natural consequence of this data representation is that it requires the block cipher description to be decomposed based on Boolean operations. Bit-slice ciphers such as Fantomas* are therefore very suitable in this context, since directly optimized to minimize the complexity of such a decomposition.

Refreshing and Multiplication Algorithms. Since only requiring simple AND, XOR and rotation operations, these algorithms have naturally efficient implementations on our target device. The only particular optimization we considered is to keep all intermediate values in registers whenever possible, in order to minimize the overheads due to memory transfers. (An ARM pseudo-code for the multiplication with $d = 4$ is given in the ePrint version). The random values needed for the refreshings are first loaded and kept in registers. We then compute the c_i's and d_i's together instead of successively as in Algorithm 2, allowing to save costly load and store instructions. Eventually, the randomness was produced according to two different settings. In the first one, we generated it on-the-fly thanks to the embedded TRNG of our board which costs $RC = 80$ clock cycles per 32-bit word. In the second one, we considered a cheaper PRG following the setting of [22], which costs $RC = 10$ cycles per 32-bit word. Based on these figures, the refreshing algorithm is implemented in 28 (resp. 98) clock cycles and the multiplication algorithm in 197 (resp. 757) clock cycles.

3.2   Cipher Dependent Components

We now describe how we implemented the AES Rijndael and Fantomas* in bitslice mode rather than in based on their (more) usual byte representation.

AES Components. The AES S-box is an 8-bit permutation which can be viewed as the composition of an inverse in $\mathbb{F}_{2^8}$ and an affine function. A well-known method to mask this S-box, first proposed by Rivain and Prouff in [42], is to decompose the inversion in a chain of squarings and multiplications. Yet, this decomposition is not convenient in our parallel masking setting since not based on binary operations. Hence, a better starting point for our purposes is the binary circuit put forward by Boyar and Peralta in 2010 [8]. It requires 83 XOR, 32 AND and 4 NOT gates. Recently, Goudarzi and Rivain re-arranged some operations of this circuit in order to improve their implementation of a masked bitsliced AES [22]. We therefore implemented the AES S-box thanks to the latter representation, with each AND replaced by a secure multiplication and the XORs transposed using the corresponding ARM assembly instructions.

Following, and thanks to our internal state representation, the ShiftRows operation is easy to implement: it just consists in a re-ordering of the data which is achieved by a succession of load and store instructions.

The AES MixColumns operation is slightly more involved. The usual representation of MixColumns is based on a matrix product in $\mathbb{F}_{2^8}$, as depicted in the following, where c_i and d_i for $0 \leq i \leq 3$ are bytes:

$$\begin{pmatrix} 02\ 03\ 01\ 01 \\ 01\ 02\ 03\ 01 \\ 01\ 01\ 02\ 03 \\ 03\ 01\ 01\ 02 \end{pmatrix} \times \begin{pmatrix} c_1 \\ c_2 \\ c_3 \\ c_4 \end{pmatrix} = \begin{pmatrix} d_1 \\ d_2 \\ d_3 \\ d_4 \end{pmatrix}.$$

The multiplication by 01 is trivial and the one by 03 can be split into $02 \oplus 01$, which only leaves the need of a good multiplication by 02 (sometimes called the xtimes function). This function is usually performed thanks to pre-computed tables [13], but it can also be achieved solely with binary instructions. Let $b = (b_0, \cdots, b_7)$ be a byte with $b_i \in \{0,1\}$ for $0 \leq i \leq 7$. We recall that the AES field is defined as $\mathbb{F}_{2^8} \equiv \mathbb{F}_2[x]/(x^8 + x^4 + x^3 + x + 1)$. Using this polynomial, the xtimes can be turned into the following Boolean expression:

$$\mathsf{xtimes}(b) = \mathsf{xtimes}(b_0, \cdots, b_7) = (b_1, b_2, b_3, b_4 \oplus b_0, b_5 \oplus b_0, b_6, b_7 \oplus b_0, b_0). \quad (1)$$

For the parallel masking scheme, each bit b_i is again replaced by a 32-bit word. So in practice, we simply implement Mixcolumns by small pieces: for each byte c_i we load the eight 32-bit words, compute all the products by 02 thanks to Eq. (1), and store the results in a temporary memory slot. Eventually, we recombine the temporary values by XORing them to obtain the right output.

Fantomas* components. Fantomas*'s 8-bit S-box is an unbalanced Feistel network built from 3- and 5-bit S-boxes originally proposed in the MISTY block cipher (see [34], Sect. 2.1 and [23]). It can be decomposed in 11 AND gates, 25 XOR gates and 5 NOT gates. Since the S-box is bitsliced, the implementation of the parallel scheme is straightforward. Namely, each W_i in the algorithm is a 32-bit word encoding one secret bit in 32 shares. As for the AES S-box, ANDs are replaced by secure multiplications and XORs are applied directly.

The Fantomas* linear layer so-called L-box can be represented as a 16×16 binary matrix M (given in the ePrint version). Let V a 16×1-bit vector of the internal state of Fantomas*. Applying the L-box consists in doing the product $M * V$, which corresponds to executing XOR gates between the bits of V, defined by the entries of the matrix M. Since the XOR is a bitwise and linear operation, the L-box can again be computed directly in the parallel masking context (where a bit in the vector V simply becomes a 32-bit word of shares). In practice, as in the original publication of Fantomas* [23], we split M in two 16×8 matrices: a left one and a right one. This allows us to work independently with the first 8 bits and the last 8 bits of V. For this purpose, we load eight 32-bit words and compute the XORs between them corresponding to the left/right parts of M, and store these intermediate values in a temporary memory slot. Eventually, one has just to XOR the results of these two products to recover the output.

3.3 Performance Evaluation

Table 1 provides the total number of total clock cycles for both the AES and Fantomas* in our two settings for the randomness generation. The S-box column reports the percentage of clock cycles spent in the evaluation of the S-box (excluding the randomness generation and refreshings). The linear layer column reports the percentage of clock cycles spent in the evaluation of the linear parts (i.e., ShiftRows, MixColumns and AddRoundKey for the AES; the L-boxes, key and round constant additions for Fantomas*). The rand. column reports the percentage of clock cycles spent in the generation of fresh random numbers (including the refresh operations and random values needed in the multiplication). Note that in order to make our results comparable with the ones of Goudarzi and Rivain, we did not consider the evaluation of the AES key schedule and simply assumed that the round keys (or the master key for Fantomas*) were pre-computed, stored in a shared manner and refreshed before each execution of the ciphers. Besides, and as in this previous work (Sect. 6.2), we systematically refreshed one of the inputs of each multiplication in order to avoid flaws related to the multiplication of linearly-related inputs.[1] The masked AES implementation in [22] is evaluated on a device similar to ours with up to 10 shares. Using their cost formulas, we can extrapolate the number of clock cycles of their implementation for $d = 32$ shares as approximately $3,821,312$ cycles (considering $RC = 10$), which highlights that the linear complexity of our multiplication algorithm indeed translates into excellent concrete performances. The further comparison of our (share-based) bitslicing approach with the (algorithm-based) one in [22] is an interesting scope for further research. In this respect, we note the focus of our codes was on regularity and simplicity, which allowed fast development times while also leaving room for further optimizations.

Table 1. Performance evaluation results for $d = 32$.

	Total # of cycles	S-box %	Linear Layer %	rand. %
AES ($RC = 10$)	2,783,510	25.16	1.99	72.66
AES ($RC = 80$)	9,682,710	7.23	0.6	91.91
Fantomas* ($RC = 10$)	1,217,616	23.95	4.6	68.56
Fantomas* ($RC = 80$)	4,134,096	7.06	1.38	90.74

As expected, using the bitslice cipher Fantomas* rather than the standard AES Rijndael allows reducing the cycle counts by an approximate factor 2. This is essentially due to the fact that the overall number of secure multiplications of the latter is roughly twice lower (2112 against 5120 multiplications).

This benchmarking highlights that the time spent in the linear layers in very high order (parallel) masked implementations is negligible: efforts are spent in the S-box executions and (mostly) the randomness generation. It suggests various tracks for improved designs, ranging from the minimization of the non-linear components thanks to powerful linear layers, the reduction of the randomness requirements in secure multiplications or the better composition of linear & non-linear gadgets (see Sects. 4.1 and 4.3), and the design of efficient RNGs.

4   Side-Channel Security Evaluation

The previous section showed that bitslice implementations of masking schemes lead to excellent performances, as already hinted by Goudarzi and Rivain [22], and that the parallel refreshing and multiplication algorithms of Barthe et al. in [5] are perfectly suited to them. Thanks to these advances, we are able to obtain realistic timings for very high order masked implementations.

---

[1] We used the iteration of $\lceil \frac{d-1}{3} \rceil$ simple refreshing gadgets (given Algorithm 1) for this purpose, which is conjectured to be composable in [5] (and therefore comparable to the refreshing used in [22]). As will be discussed in Sects. 4.1 and 4.3, this very direct strategy leaves ample room for further optimization efforts.

Quite naturally, such very high order implementations raise the complementary challenge that they are not trivial to evaluate. In particular, since one can expect that they lead to very high security levels (if their shares' leakages are independent and sufficiently noisy), an approach based on "launching attacks" is unlikely to provide any meaningful conclusion. That is, unsuccessful attacks under limited evaluation time and cost do not give any indication of the actual security level (say 2^x) other than that the evaluator was unable to attack in complexity 2^y, with potentially $2^x \gg 2^y$. In the following, we introduce a new methodology for this purpose, based on recent progresses in the formal analysis of masking exploiting different proof techniques and leakage models.

4.1   Rationale: A Multi-model Approach

The core idea of our following security evaluation is to exploit a good separation of duties between the different leakage models and metrics that have been introduced in the literature. More precisely, we will use the probing model of Ishai et al. to guarantee an "algorithmic security order" [27], the bounded moment model of Barthe et al. to guarantee a "physical security order" [5], and the noisy leakage model of Prouff and Rivain to evaluate concrete security levels [38].

Step 1. The probing model, composability and formal methods. In general, the first important step when evaluating a masked implementation is to study its security against (abstract) t-probing attacks. In this model, the adversary is able to observe t wires within the implementation (usually modeled as a sequence of operations). From a theoretical point of view, it has been shown in [14] that (under conditions of noise and independence considered in the following steps), probing security is a necessary condition for concrete (noisy leakage) security against (e.g., power or electromagnetic) side-channel attacks. It has also been shown in [5] that it is equally relevant in the case of parallel implementation we study here (i.e., that it is also a necessary condition in this context).

From a practical point of view, the probing security of simple gadgets such as given by Algorithms 1 and 2 is given in their original papers, and the main challenge for their application to complete ciphers is their composability. That is, secure implementations must take into account the fact that using the output of a computational gadget (e.g., an addition or multiplication) as the input of another computational gadget may provide additional information to the adversary. Such an additional source of leakage is essentially prevented by adding refreshing gadgets. There exists two strategies to ensure that the refreshings in an implementation are sufficient. First, one can use probing-secure computational gadgets, test implementations with formal methods such as [3], and add refreshing gadgets whenever a composition issue is spotted by the tool. This solution theoretically leads to the most efficient implementations, but is limited by the complexity of analyzing full implementations at high orders. Second, one can impose stronger (local) requirements to the computational gadgets, such as the Strong Non Interference (SNI) property introduced in [4]. Those gadgets are generally more expensive in randomness, but save the designers/evaluators from the task of analyzing their implementation globally. As mentioned in Sect. 3.3 we exploited a rough version of this second strategy, by applying an SNI refreshing to one input of every multiplication. As discussed in [7] (e.g., when masking the AES S-box based on a polynomial representation in Sect. 7.2), it is actually possible to obtain SNI circuits with less randomness thanks to a clever combination of SNI and NI gadgets. The investigation of such optimizations in the case of bitslice implementations is an interesting open problem.

Step 2. The bounded moment model and Welch's T-test. Given that probing security is guaranteed for an implementation, the next problem is to guarantee the shares' leakages physical independence. In other words, the evaluator needs to test whether the leakage function does "re-combine" the shares in some way that is not detectable by abstract probing attacks. From a theoretical viewpoint, this recombination can be captured by a reduction of the security order in the bounded moment model [5]. Concretely, it may be due to defaults such as computational glitches [31,32] and memory transitions [2,11].

From a practical point of view, the security order in the bounded moment leakage model can be estimated thanks to so-called "moment-based security evaluations". One option for this purpose is to launch high order attacks such as [35,39,49]. In recent years, and alternative and increasingly popular solution for this purpose has been to exploit simple(r) leakage-detection tests [10,16,21, 33,44]. We will next rely on the recent discussion and tools from [46].[2]

Step 3. The noisy leakage model and concrete evaluations. Eventually, once a designer/evaluator is convinced that his target implementation guarantees a certain security order, it remains to evaluate the amount of noise in the implementation. Indeed, from a theoretical point of view, a secure masking scheme is expected to amplify the impact of the noise in any side-channel attack (and therefore the worst-case measurement complexity) exponentially in the number of shares. This concrete security is reflected by the noisy leakage model [38].

From a practical point of view, the noise condition for secure masking (and the resulting noisy leakage security) can be captured by an information theoretic or security analysis [45]. In this respect, it is important to note that this condition depends on both the physical noise of the operations in the target implementation and the number of such operations. When restricting the evaluation to divide-and-conquer attacks, which is the standard strategy to exploit physical leakages [30], this number of operations drops to the number of exploitable operations (i.e., the operations that depend on an enumerable part of the key). We will next consider this standard adversarial setting.[3]

Besides, as mentioned at the beginning of the section, one may expect that the security level of a very high order masked implementation is beyond the evaluator's measurement (and time, memory) capacities. In this context, rather than trying to launch actual attacks we will rely on the (standard cryptographic)

---

[2] Note that nothing prevents using the bounded moment model to analyze abstract implementations: as shown in [5] it may also allow explaining the security of certain types of countermeasures that cannot be captured by probing security.

[3] More advanced strategies include algebraic/analytical side-channel attacks, which may require considering slight additional (constant) security margins [24,41,48].

strategy of bounding the attack complexity based on the adversary's power. For this purpose, we will use the tools recently introduced in [15, 26] which show that such bounds can be obtained from the information theoretic analysis of the leakage function (i.e., a characterization of the individual shares' leakages).

Wrapping up. The main observation motivating our rationale is that security against side-channel attacks can be gradually built by exploiting existing leakage models, starting from the most abstract probing model, following with the intermediate bounded moment model, and finishing with the most physical noisy leakage model. In this respect, one great achievement of recent research in side-channel analysis is that each of those theoretical leakage models has a concrete counterpart allowing its practical evaluation. Namely, the probing security of an algorithm (represented as a sequence of operations) is challenged by formal methods or guaranteed by composable gadgets, bounded moment security is tested thanks to moment-based distinguishers or leakage-detection tools, and noisy leakage security is quantified thanks to information theoretic metrics which eventually bound standard security metrics such as the success rate.

Cautionary note. Because of place constraints, the following sections will not recall the technical details of the tools used in our evaluations (i.e., Welch's T-test, linear regression and the mutual information metric). We rather specify all the parameters used and link to references for the description of the tools.

4.2   Bounded Moment Security and Security Order

Noise-Efficient Leakage Detection Test. As we rely on SNI refreshings to ensure the composability of our masked implementations, the first step in our evaluation is to evaluate the extent to which the shares' physical leakages are independent.[4] As mentioned in the previous subsection, this independence is reflected by a security order in the bounded moment model, which can be estimated thanks to leakage detection. For this purpose, we used a variant of leakage detection test recently introduced in [46], Sect. 3.2. As with the standard detection tools, its main idea is to consider two leakage classes: one corresponding to a fixed plaintext and key, the other corresponding to random (or fixed [16]) plaintext(s) and a fixed key. The test then tries to detect a differences between these classes at different orders (i.e., after raising the leakage samples to different powers). The only specificity of this "noise-efficient" variation is that it mitigates the exponential amplification of the noise due to masking by averaging the traces before raising them to some power, thus reducing the evaluation time and storage. Such an averaging is possible because of our evaluation setting where masks are known. It admittedly makes the test completely qualitative (i.e., the number of traces needed to detect is not correlated with the security level that we discuss in the next subsection). Yet, in view of the noise level of our implementation, it was the only way to detect high order leakages somewhat efficiently.

---

[4] Analyzing the SNI security of a software code (rather than an abstract implementation as usually done in masking gadget proofs) would further increase the relevance of the composability argument and is an interesting scope for further research.

Unfortunately, and even using this tweak, the complexity of the leakage detection is still exponential in the number of shares and therefore hardly achievable at order 32 (see again [46]). As a result, we studied reduced-order implementations with limited number of shares/randomness. Similarly to reduced-round versions in block cipher cryptanalysis, the goal of such implementations is to extrapolate the attacks' behavior based on empirically verifiable but weakened versions of our implementations. In particular, we used such implementations to verify the extent to which the shares are recombined by the physical leakages. Since the implementations considered for this purpose are similar to the one using 32 shares (see next), the hope is that they give the evaluator an estimate of the "security order reduction factor" f caused by physical defaults (e.g., [2] showed that transition-based leakages reduce this order by a factor two).

Concretely, we analyzed both tweaked implementations with $d = 2$ and $d = 4$ shares (thanks to an adapted software) and the implementation with 32 shares where only 2 (resp. 4) bits of the random numbers generated were actually random – the other 30 (resp. 28) bits being kept constant. All tests gave consistent results and no leakage of order below the expected 2 (resp. 4) was detected. For illustration, the result of a leakage detection test for the Fantomas* S-box with $d = 4$ shares (tweaked implementation) is given in Fig. 1. We used 120,000 different traces, each of them repeated 50 times, for a total of 6,000,000 measurements. The top of the figure shows the average trace, the bottom of the figure is the result of the detection test at order 4, where we see that the standard threshold of 4.5 is passed for a couple of samples. We additionally checked that those samples correspond to the multiplications performed during the S-box execution. By contrast, we could not spot evidence of lower order leakages (for which detection plots are given in the ePrint version). We insist that testing such reduced-order implementations does not offer formal guarantees that no flaw may happen for the full version with 32 random shares.[5] Nevertheless, (i) the fact that we observed consistent results for the $d = 2$ and $d = 4$ cases is reassuring; (ii) we may expect that some physical defaults (such as couplings [9]) become less critical with larger number of shares, since the shares will be more physically separated in this case; and (iii) most importantly, we will use the factor f as a parameter of our security evaluations, allowing a good risk assessment.

Robustness Against Transition-Based Leakages. The results of the previous detection tests are (positively) surprising since one would typically expect that the transition-based leakages discussed in [2] reduce the security order in the bounded moment model from the optimal $o = d - 1$ to $o = \lceil d/2 \rceil - 1$. For example, assuming a sharing $s = s_1 \oplus s_2$, observing the Hamming distance between the shares s_1 and s_2 would provide the adversary with leakages of the form $\mathsf{HD}(s_1, s_2) = \mathsf{HW}(s_1 \oplus s_2) = s$. By contrast, in our parallel implementation setting, no such transitions could be detected. While we leave the full analysis of this phenomenon (e.g., with formal methods) as an open problem, we next

---

[5] Note also that the variant of leakage detection with averaging used here makes the interpretation of such flaws less easy to interpret with the tools of [15] (Sect. 4.2).

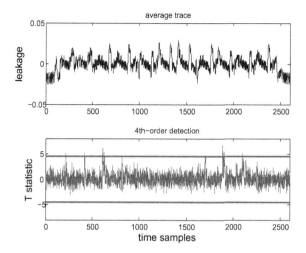

Fig. 1. Noise-efficient leakage detection with 6M traces (50x averaging).

provide preliminary explanations why this positive result is at least plausible. For this purpose, we first observe that the multiplication Algorithm 2 essentially iterates three types of operations: partial products, compressions and refreshings; and it ensures that any pair of partial products $(a_i \cdot b_j, a_j \cdot b_i)$ is separated from the other pairs (and the $a_i \cdot b_i$ partial products) by a refreshing. As already hinted in [5], the distances between such pairs of intermediate results do not lead to additional information to the adversary. So the main source of transition-based leakages would be based on intermediate results separated by refreshings. In this respect, we note that our implementation was designed so that intermediate results are produced progressively according to the previous "compute partial products – compress – refresh" structure, which additionally limits the risk that many unrefreshed intermediates remain in the registers. Eventually, we checked that intermediate results in successive clock cycles do not lead to detectable transition-based leakages in the bounded moment model thanks to simulations. So intuitively, we can explain the absence of such transition-based leakages by the fact that our parallel manipulation of the shares mitigates them.[6]

Summarizing, as any hypothesis test, leakage detection offers limited theoretical guarantees that no lower-order leakages could be detected with more measurements. Yet, our experiments do not provide any evidence of strong recombinations of the shares' leakages via transitions or other physical defaults, which can be explained by algorithmic features. Hence, in the following, we will consider two possible settings for our evaluations: the empirically observed one, assuming a security order 31 in the bounded moment model, and a more conservative one, assuming a security order 15 in the bounded moment model.

---

[6] When decreasing technology sizes, this gain may come with higher risk of couplings between the shares (as also mentioned in [5] and recently discussed in [9]).

4.3 Noisy Leakage Security and Information Theoretic Analysis

Assuming the security order of our implementations to be 31 (as observed experimentally) or 15 (taking a security margin due to a risk of physical defaults that we could not spot), we now want to evaluate the security level of these implementations in the noisy leakage model, based on an information theoretic and security analysis. For this purpose, our next investigations will follow three main steps. First we will estimate the deterministic and noisy parts of the leakage function corresponding to our measurements, thanks to linear regression [43]. This will additionally lead to an estimation of our implementations' Signal to Noise Ratio (SNR). Second, we will use this estimation of the leakage function to quantify the information leakage of our Boolean encodings (assuming security orders 31 and 15, as just motivated), using the numerical integration techniques from [15]. Finally, we will take advantage of the tightness of masking security proofs recently put forward in [26], in order to bound the complexity of multivariate (aka horizontal) attacks taking advantage of all the leakage samples computationally exploitable by a divide-and-conquer side-channel adversary.

Linear Regression and Noise Level. For this first step, we again considered a simplified setting where the evaluator has access to the masks during his profiling phase. Doing so, he is able to efficiently predict the 32 bits of the bus in our ARM Cortex device, and therefore to estimate the leakage function for various target operations thanks to linear regression. More precisely, and given a sensitive value s and its shares vector $\boldsymbol{s}$ considered in our masking scheme, linear regression allows estimating the true leakage function $\hat{\mathsf{L}}(\boldsymbol{s}) \approx \hat{\mathsf{D}}(\boldsymbol{s}) + \hat{N}$, with $\hat{\mathsf{D}}(\boldsymbol{s})$ the deterministic part of the leakages and $\hat{N}$ a noise random variable. As frequently considered in the literature, we used a linear basis (made of the 32 bits of the bus and a constant element) for this purpose. Such a model rapidly converged towards close to Hamming weight leakages, with estimated SNR of 0.05 for the best sample (defined as the variance of $\hat{\mathsf{D}}(\boldsymbol{s})$ divided by the variance of $\hat{N}$).

Encoding Leakage. Given the previous sensitive value s, its shares vector $\boldsymbol{s}$ considered in our masking scheme, and a leakage function L leading to samples $l = \mathsf{L}(\boldsymbol{s})$, a standard metric to capture the informativeness of these leakages is the Mutual Information [45], defined as follows:

$$\mathrm{MI}(S; \mathsf{L}(\boldsymbol{S})) = \mathrm{H}[S] + \sum_{s \in S} \Pr[s] \cdot \sum_{l \leftarrow \mathsf{L}} \mathsf{f}(l|s) \cdot \log_2 \Pr[s|l].$$

In this equation, $\mathrm{H}[S]$ is the entropy of the sensitive variable S and $\mathsf{f}(l|s)$ the conditional Probability Density Function (PDF) of the leakages $\mathsf{L}(\boldsymbol{s})$ given the secret s. Assuming Gaussian noise, it can be written as a mixture model:

$$\mathsf{f}(l|s) = \sum_{\boldsymbol{s} \in S^{d-1}} \mathcal{N}\left(l|(s, \boldsymbol{s}), \sigma_n^2\right) \cdot$$

The conditional probability $\Pr[s|l]$ is then computed thanks to Bayes' theorem as:

$$\Pr[s|l] = \frac{f(l|s)}{\sum_{s^* \in \mathcal{S}} f(l|s^*)}.$$

Unfortunately, what we obtained thanks to linear regression is not the true leakage function $\mathsf{L}(s)$ but only its estimate $\hat{\mathsf{L}}(s)$. Hence, what we will compute in the following is rather the Hypothetical Information (HI), defined as:

$$\mathrm{HI}(S; \hat{\mathsf{L}}(\boldsymbol{S})) = \mathrm{H}[S] + \sum_{s \in \mathcal{S}} \Pr[s] \cdot \sum_{l \leftarrow \hat{\mathsf{L}}} \hat{\mathsf{f}}(l|s) \cdot \log_2 \hat{\Pr}[s|l].$$

Formally, it corresponds to the amount of information that would be leaked from an implementation of which the leakages would be exactly predicted by $\hat{\mathsf{L}}(s)$. Admittedly, we cannot expect that $\mathrm{HI}(S; \hat{\mathsf{L}}(\boldsymbol{S})) = \mathrm{MI}(S; \mathsf{L}(\boldsymbol{S}))$ in practice (e.g., since we used a linear basis rather than a full one in our regression).[7] However, we note that the information leakages of a masked implementation depend only on their security order and SNR, not on variations of the leakage function's shape. So small errors on $\hat{\mathsf{L}}$ should not affect our conclusions. Furthermore, in our parallel setting the addition of significant non-linear terms in the regression basis would also directly decrease the security order because it would re-combine the shares in a non-linear manner (see [5]). Since the previous moment-based evaluation did not detect such re-combinations, a linear leakage model is also well motivated from this side. We finally note that adding quadratic terms in our basis could be a way to capture the reduction of the security order from 31 to 15. Yet, for efficiency, we next reflect such reductions of the security order by simply (and pessimistically) reducing the number of random shares in $\boldsymbol{s}$.

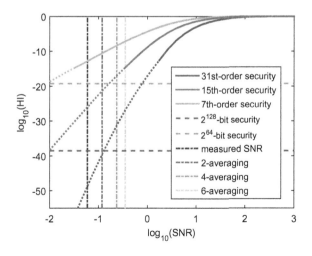

Fig. 2. Information theoretic analysis of the encoding.

---

[7] Yet, we can test that it is close enough thanks to leakage certification [17, 18].

The result of such an information theoretic evaluation for our Boolean encoding is given in Fig. 2, where we plot the HI in log scale, for various SNRs. Of particular interest are the measured SNR and the SNRs with (2, 4 and 6×) averaging, which would correspond to the noise level of sensitive shares vectors appearing multiple times in the implementation, therefore allowing the adversary to reduce the noise of these leakage samples by averaging (which we will discuss next). We also plotted the curves corresponding to the security orders 31, 15 and 7 (i.e., corresponding to a flaw parameter $f = 1, 2$ and 4). Remarkably, we see that for the measured SNR, the leakage of a single encoding secure of order 31 would lead to an HI below 2^{-128}. Since the masking proofs in [15] show that the measurement complexity of any side-channel attack is inversely proportional to (and bounded by) this information leakage, it implies that a simple attack exploiting a single leakage sample corresponding to a 32-tuple of parallel shares would not be successful even with the full AES/Fantomas* codebook. Similarly, a 15th-order secure implementation would be secure with up to a comfortable $10^{26} \approx 2^{82}$ measurements. Table 2 provides an alternative view of these findings and lists experimental HI values for different levels of averaging.

Table 2. Experimental bounds on $\log_{10}(\text{HI})$ for the encoding.

SNR	Measured	×2	×3	×4	×5	×6	×7
Security order 31	−48		−39	−34	−31	−29	−27	−25
Security order 15	−26		−22	−19	−17	−16	−15	−14

Worst-Case Security Level. While the previous figure and table show that an adversary exploiting a single 32-tuple of parallel shares, assuming security order 31 (or 15) and the SNR estimated in the previous section, will not be able to perform efficient key recoveries, it has been recently put forward in [6] and more formally discussed in [26] that optimal side-channel adversaries are actually much more powerful. Namely, such adversaries can theoretically exploit all the 32-tuples in the implementation, and if some of these tuples are manipulated multiple times, average their leakages in order to improve their SNR.

In order to take such a possibility into account in our security evaluations, we therefore started by inspecting the codes of our implementations in order to determine (1) the number of linear and non-linear operations that can be targeted by a divide-and-conquer attack (for illustration, we considered an adversary targeting a single S-box), and (2) the number of such operations for which one of the operands is repeated x times in the code. The result of such a code inspection is given in Table 3. Note that the table includes the count of the SNI refreshings added to one input of each multiplication, which we reported as 32 (resp. 11) additional linear operations for the AES (resp. Fantomas*).[8]

---

[8] This assumes that the iteration of simple refreshing gadgets to obtain an SNI refreshing is tweaked so that the tuple of shares to refresh is only XORed once, at the end of the iteration. It therefore slightly differs from the proposal in [5]. We leave the investigation of such a variant as an interesting scope for further research.

Table 3. S-box code inspection for the AES and Fantomas*.

Cipher	Operations	Total #	2-rep.	3-rep.	4-rep.	5-rep.	6-rep.	7-rep.
AES	Linear	115	20	55	18	12	10	0
	Non-lin.	32	2	16	2	7	5	0
Fantomas*	Linear	41	13	18	10	0	0	0
	Non-lin.	11	1	5	5	0	0	0

Thanks to the tools in [26], we then bounded the measurement complexity of adversaries taking advantage of a single tuple (considered in the previous section), all the tuples, and all the tuples with averaging in Fig. 3. Concretely, the second adversary is simply captured by relying on an "Independent Operation Leakage" assumption which considers (pessimistically for the designer) that the information of all the 32-tuples of shares in the implementation is independent and therefore can be summed. Taking the example of the Fantomas* S-box, it means that this adversary can exploit the information of 41 encodings for the linear operations, and 11*32 encodings for the non-linear ones (where the factor 32 comes from the linear cost of the parallel multiplication algorithm, of which the leakage was bounded in [38]). And the third adversary is captured by adapting the encoding leakages depending on the number of repetitions allowed by the code. Taking the example of the linear operations in Fantomas*, it means that this adversary can exploit the information of 13 encodings with double SNR, 18 encodings with triple SNR, ... The latter is admittedly pessimistic too since it considers an averaging based on the most repeated operand only. Besides, it assumes that sensitive values manipulated multiple times will leak according to the same model (which is not always the case in practice [19]). The main observations of this worst-case security evaluation are threefold:

First, the security levels reached for the two first adversaries are significantly higher than previously reported thanks to "attack-based evaluations". In particular, we reach the full codebook (measurement) security if the security order was 31 (as empirically estimated) and maintain $> 2^{64}$ measurement security if this order was only 15. In this respect, we insist that this order is the *only* parameter which could lead to an overstated security level (i.e., all the other assumptions in our evaluations are pessimistic for the designer). Quite naturally, the figure also exhibits that masked implementations with lower orders (e.g., 8 or 4) cannot offer strong security guarantees in case of SNRs in the 0.01 range.

Second, the impact of averaging is much more critical, since the adversary then essentially cancels the exponential increase of the noise that is the expected payload of the masking countermeasure. Roughly, for an implementation secure of order d, doubling the SNR thanks to 2-averaging reduces the security by an approximate factor 2^d. By contrast, multiplying the number of target d-tuples (without averaging) by α only reduces the security by a factor α.

Third, in front of these optimal adversaries, Fantomas* offers (slightly) more security than the AES despite we assume the same information leakages for their

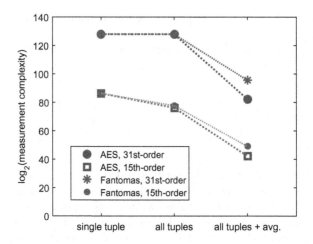

Fig. 3. Measurement complexity bounds for different attacks.

encodings. This gain is essentially due to the fact that Fantomas* implementations are slightly more efficient, effectively reducing the opportunities for the adversary to exploit many leakage samples and to average them.

Towards Mitigating Averaging Attacks. As a conclusion of this paper, we first observe that our experiments raise interesting optimization problems for finding new representations of block cipher S-boxes, minimizing the number of non-linear operations and the multiple manipulation of the same intermediate values during their execution. Besides, and quite fundamentally, Fig. 3 recalls that the security of the masking countermeasure is the result of a tradeoff between an amount of physical noise (reflected by the SNR) and an amount of digital noise (reflected by the shares' randomness) in the implementations. In this respect, there is a simple way to mitigate the previous "averaging attacks", namely to add refreshing gadgets to prevent the repetition of the same sensitive values multiple times in an implementation. Remarkably, the systematic refreshing that we add to one input of each multiplication does contribute positively to this issue. For example, we show in the ePrint version that the number of repetitions in our codes increases if one removes these refreshings. By extending this approach brutally (i.e., by refreshing all the intermediate tuples in an implementation so that they are never used more than twice: once when generated, once when used), one can therefore mitigate the "all tuples + avg." adversary of Fig. 3. But most interestingly, the latter observations suggest the search for good tradeoffs between physical and digital noise as a fundamental challenge for sound masking. That is, how to efficiently ensure composability as mentioned in Sect. 4.1 (first step) and prevent the averaging attacks in this section?

Acknowledgments. François-Xavier Standaert is an associate researcher of the Belgian Fund for Scientific Research (FNRS-F.R.S.). This work has been funded in parts by the INNOVIRIS project SCAUT and by the European Commission through the ERC project 724725 and the H2020 project REASSURE.

References

1. http://www.atmel.com/tools/sam4c-ek.aspx
2. Balasch, J., Gierlichs, B., Grosso, V., Reparaz, O., Standaert, F.-X.: On the cost of lazy engineering for masked software implementations. In: Joye, M., Moradi, A. (eds.) CARDIS 2014. LNCS, vol. 8968, pp. 64–81. Springer, Cham (2015). doi:10. 1007/978-3-319-16763-3_5
3. Barthe, G., Belaïd, S., Dupressoir, F., Fouque, P.-A., Grégoire, B., Strub, P.-Y.: Verified proofs of higher-order masking. In: Oswald and Fischlin [37], pp. 457–485
4. Barthe, G., Belaïd, S., Dupressoir, F., Fouque, P.-A., Grégoire, B., Strub, P.-Y., Zucchini, R.: Strong non-interference and type-directed higher-order masking. In: Weippl, E.R., Katzenbeisser, S., Kruegel, C., Myers, A.C., Halevi, S. (eds.) ACM CCS 2016, pp. 116–129. ACM (2016)
5. Barthe, G., Dupressoir, F., Faust, S., Grégoire, B., Standaert, F.-X., Strub, P.-Y.: Parallel implementations of masking schemes and the bounded moment leakage model. In: Coron and Nielsen [12], pp. 535–566
6. Battistello, A., Coron, J.-S., Prouff, E., Zeitoun, R.: Horizontal side-channel attacks and countermeasures on the ISW masking scheme. In: Gierlichs and Poschmann [20], pp. 23–39
7. Belaïd, S., Benhamouda, F., Passelègue, A., Prouff, E., Thillard, A., Vergnaud, D.: Randomness complexity of private circuits for multiplication. In: Fischlin, M., Coron, J.-S. (eds.) EUROCRYPT 2016. LNCS, vol. 9666, pp. 616–648. Springer, Heidelberg (2016). doi:10.1007/978-3-662-49896-5_22
8. Boyar, J., Peralta, R.: A new combinational logic minimization technique with applications to cryptology. In: Festa, P. (ed.) SEA 2010. LNCS, vol. 6049, pp. 178–189. Springer, Heidelberg (2010). doi:10.1007/978-3-642-13193-6_16
9. De Cnudde, T., Bilgin, B., Gierlichs, B., Nikov, V., Nikova, S., Rijmen, V.: Does coupling affect the security of masked implementations? Cryptology ePrint Archive, Report 2016/1080 (2016). http://eprint.iacr.org/2016/1080
10. Cooper, J., De Mulder, E., Goodwill, G., Jaffe, J., Kenworthy, G., Rohatgi, P.: Test vector leakage assessment (TVLA) methodology in practice (extended abstract). ICMC 2013. http://icmc-2013.org/wp/wp-content/uploads/2013/09/goodwillkenworthtestvector.pdf
11. Coron, J.-S., Giraud, C., Prouff, E., Renner, S., Rivain, M., Vadnala, P.K.: Conversion of security proofs from one leakage model to another: a new issue. In: Schindler, W., Huss, S.A. (eds.) COSADE 2012. LNCS, vol. 7275, pp. 69–81. Springer, Heidelberg (2012). doi:10.1007/978-3-642-29912-4_6
12. Coron, J.-S., Nielsen, J.B. (eds.): EUROCRYPT 2017. LNCS, vol. 10210. Springer, Cham (2017). doi:10.1007/978-3-319-56617-7
13. Daemen, J., Rijmen, V.: The Design of Rijndael: AES - The Advanced Encryption Standard. Information Security and Cryptography. Springer, Heidelberg (2002). doi:10.1007/978-3-662-04722-4
14. Duc, A., Dziembowski, S., Faust, S.: Unifying leakage models: from probing attacks to noisy leakage. In: Nguyen and Oswald [36], pp. 423–440

15. Duc, A., Faust, S., Standaert, F.-X.: Making masking security proofs concrete - or how to evaluate the security of any leaking device. In: Oswald and Fischlin [37], pp. 401–429

16. Durvaux, F., Standaert, F.-X.: From improved leakage detection to the detection of points of interests in leakage traces. In: Fischlin, M., Coron, J.-S. (eds.) EURO-CRYPT 2016. LNCS, vol. 9665, pp. 240–262. Springer, Heidelberg (2016). doi:10.1007/978-3-662-49890-3_10

17. Durvaux, F., Standaert, F.-X., Del Pozo, S.M.: Towards easy leakage certification. In: Gierlichs and Poschmann [20], pp. 40–60

18. Durvaux, F., Standaert, F.-X., Veyrat-Charvillon, N.: How to certify the leakage of a chip? In: Nguyen and Oswald [36], pp. 459–476

19. Gérard, B., Standaert, F.-X.: Unified and optimized linear collision attacks and their application in a non-profiled setting: extended version. J. Cryptogr. Eng. **3**(1), 45–58 (2013)

20. Gierlichs, B., Poschmann, A.Y. (eds.): CHES 2016. LNCS, vol. 9813. Springer, Heidelberg (2016). doi:10.1007/978-3-662-53140-2

21. Goodwill, G., Jun, B., Jaffe, J., Rohatgi, P.: A testing methodology for side channel resistance validation. In: NIST Non-Invasive Attack Testing Workshop (2011). http://csrc.nist.gov/news_events/non-invasive-attack-testing-workshop/papers/08_Goodwill.pdf

22. Goudarzi, D., Rivain, M.: How fast can higher-order masking be in software? In: Coron and Nielsen [12], pp. 567–597

23. Grosso, V., Leurent, G., Standaert, F.-X., Varıcı, K.: LS-Designs: bitslice encryption for efficient masked software implementations. In: Cid, C., Rechberger, C. (eds.) FSE 2014. LNCS, vol. 8540, pp. 18–37. Springer, Heidelberg (2015). doi:10.1007/978-3-662-46706-0_2

24. Grosso, V., Standaert, F.-X.: ASCA, SASCA and DPA with enumeration: which one beats the other and when? In: Iwata, T., Cheon, J.H. (eds.) ASIACRYPT 2015. LNCS, vol. 9453, pp. 291–312. Springer, Heidelberg (2015). doi:10.1007/978-3-662-48800-3_12

25. Grosso, V., Standaert, F.-X., Faust, S.: Masking vs. multiparty computation: how large is the gap for AES? J. Cryptogr. Eng. **4**(1), 47–57 (2014)

26. Grosso, V., Standaert, F.-X.: Masking proofs are tight (and how to exploit it in security evaluations). Cryptology ePrint Archive, Report 2017/116 (2017). http://eprint.iacr.org/2017/116

27. Ishai, Y., Sahai, A., Wagner, D.: Private circuits: securing hardware against probing attacks. In: Boneh, D. (ed.) CRYPTO 2003. LNCS, vol. 2729, pp. 463–481. Springer, Heidelberg (2003). doi:10.1007/978-3-540-45146-4_27

28. Journault, A., Standaert, F.-X., Varici, K.: Improving the security and efficiency of block ciphers based on LS-designs. Des. Codes Cryptogr. **82**(1–2), 495–509 (2017)

29. Leander, G., Minaud, B., Rønjom, S.: A generic approach to invariant subspace attacks: cryptanalysis of Robin, iSCREAM and Zorro. In: Oswald and Fischlin [37], pp. 254–283

30. Mangard, S., Oswald, E., Standaert, F.-X.: One for all - all for one: unifying standard differential power analysis attacks. IET Inf. Secur. **5**(2), 100–110 (2011)

31. Mangard, S., Popp, T., Gammel, B.M.: Side-channel leakage of masked CMOS gates. In: Menezes, A. (ed.) CT-RSA 2005. LNCS, vol. 3376, pp. 351–365. Springer, Heidelberg (2005). doi:10.1007/978-3-540-30574-3_24

32. Mangard, S., Pramstaller, N., Oswald, E.: Successfully attacking masked AES hardware implementations. In: Rao and Sunar [40], pp. 157–171

33. Mather, L., Oswald, E., Bandenburg, J., Wójcik, M.: Does my device leak information? An *a priori* statistical power analysis of leakage detection tests. In: Sako, K., Sarkar, P. (eds.) ASIACRYPT 2013. LNCS, vol. 8269, pp. 486–505. Springer, Heidelberg (2013). doi:10.1007/978-3-642-42033-7_25

34. Matsui, M.: New block encryption algorithm MISTY. In: Biham, E. (ed.) FSE 1997. LNCS, vol. 1267, pp. 54–68. Springer, Heidelberg (1997). doi:10.1007/BFb0052334

35. Moradi, A., Standaert, F.-X.: Moments-correlating DPA. In: Proceedings of the 2016 ACM Workshop on Theory of Implementation Security, TIS 2016, pp. 5–15. ACM, New York (2016)

36. Nguyen, P.Q., Oswald, E. (eds.): EUROCRYPT 2014. LNCS, vol. 8441. Springer, Heidelberg (2014). doi:10.1007/978-3-642-55220-5

37. Oswald, E., Fischlin, M. (eds.): EUROCRYPT 2015. LNCS, vol. 9056. Springer, Heidelberg (2015). doi:10.1007/978-3-662-46800-5

38. Prouff, E., Rivain, M.: Masking against side-channel attacks: a formal security proof. In: Johansson, T., Nguyen, P.Q. (eds.) EUROCRYPT 2013. LNCS, vol. 7881, pp. 142–159. Springer, Heidelberg (2013). doi:10.1007/978-3-642-38348-9_9

39. Prouff, E., Rivain, M., Bevan, R.: Statistical analysis of second order differential power analysis. IEEE Trans. Comput. **58**(6), 799–811 (2009)

40. Rao, J.R., Sunar, B. (eds.): CHES 2005. LNCS, vol. 3659. Springer, Heidelberg (2005). doi:10.1007/11545262

41. Renauld, M., Standaert, F.-X., Veyrat-Charvillon, N.: Algebraic side-channel attacks on the AES: why time also matters in DPA. In: Clavier, C., Gaj, K. (eds.) CHES 2009. LNCS, vol. 5747, pp. 97–111. Springer, Heidelberg (2009). doi:10.1007/978-3-642-04138-9_8

42. Rivain, M., Prouff, E.: Provably secure higher-order masking of AES. In: Mangard, S., Standaert, F.-X. (eds.) CHES 2010. LNCS, vol. 6225, pp. 413–427. Springer, Heidelberg (2010). doi:10.1007/978-3-642-15031-9_28

43. Schindler, W., Lemke, K., Paar, C.: A stochastic model for differential side channel cryptanalysis. In: Rao and Sunar [40], pp. 30–46

44. Schneider, T., Moradi, A.: Leakage assessment methodology - extended version. J. Cryptogr. Eng. **6**(2), 85–99 (2016)

45. Standaert, F.-X., Malkin, T.G., Yung, M.: A unified framework for the analysis of side-channel key recovery attacks. In: Joux, A. (ed.) EUROCRYPT 2009. LNCS, vol. 5479, pp. 443–461. Springer, Heidelberg (2009). doi:10.1007/978-3-642-01001-9_26

46. Standaert, F.-X.: How (not) to use Welch's t-test in side-channel security evaluations. Cryptology ePrint Archive, Report 2017/138 (2017). http://eprint.iacr.org/2017/138

47. Todo, Y., Leander, G., Sasaki, Y.: Nonlinear invariant attack. In: Cheon, J.H., Takagi, T. (eds.) ASIACRYPT 2016. LNCS, vol. 10032, pp. 3–33. Springer, Heidelberg (2016). doi:10.1007/978-3-662-53890-6_1

48. Veyrat-Charvillon, N., Gérard, B., Standaert, F.-X.: Soft analytical side-channel attacks. In: Sarkar, P., Iwata, T. (eds.) ASIACRYPT 2014. LNCS, vol. 8873, pp. 282–296. Springer, Heidelberg (2014). doi:10.1007/978-3-662-45611-8_15

49. Waddle, J., Wagner, D.: Towards efficient second-order power analysis. In: Joye, M., Quisquater, J.-J. (eds.) CHES 2004. LNCS, vol. 3156, pp. 1–15. Springer, Heidelberg (2004). doi:10.1007/978-3-540-28632-5_1

PRESENT Runs Fast

Efficient and Secure Implementation in Software

Tiago B.S. Reis[(✉)], Diego F. Aranha, and Julio López

Institute of Computing, University of Campinas, Campinas, Brazil
`tiagob.reis@gmail.com`

Abstract. The PRESENT block cipher was one of the first hardware-oriented proposals for implementation in extremely resource-constrained environments. Its design is based on 4-bit S-boxes and a 64-bit permutation, a far from optimal choice to achieve good performance in software. As a result, most software implementations require large lookup tables in order to meet efficiency goals. In this paper, we describe a new portable and efficient software implementation of PRESENT, fully protected against timing attacks. Our implementation uses a novel decomposition of the permutation layer, and bitsliced computation of the S-boxes using optimized Boolean formulas, not requiring lookup tables. The implementations are evaluated in embedded ARM CPUs ranging from microcontrollers to full-featured processors equipped with vector instructions. Timings for our software implementation show a significant performance improvement compared to the numbers from the FELICS benchmarking framework. In particular, encrypting 128 bits using CTR mode takes about 2100 cycles on a Cortex-M3, improving on the best Assembly implementation in FELICS by a factor of 8. Additionally, we present the fastest masked implementation of PRESENT for protection against timing and other side-channel attacks in the scenario we consider, improving on related work by 15%. Hence, we conclude that PRESENT can be remarkably efficient in software if implemented with our techniques, and even compete with a software implementation of AES in terms of latency while offering a much smaller code footprint.

1 Introduction

The need for secure and efficient implementations of cryptography for embedded systems has been an active area of research since at least the birth of public-key cryptography. While considerable progress has been made over the last years, with development of many cryptographic engineering techniques for optimizing and protecting implementations of both symmetric [24] and asymmetric algorithms [9], the emergence of the Internet of Things (IoT) brings new challenges. The concept assumes an extraordinary amount of devices connected to the Internet and among themselves in local networks. Devices range from simple radio-frequency identification (RFID) tags to complex gadgets like smartwatches, home appliances and smartphones; and fulfill a wide variety of roles, from the automation of simple processes to critical tasks such as traffic control and environmental surveillance [5].

© International Association for Cryptologic Research 2017
W. Fischer and N. Homma (Eds.): CHES 2017, LNCS 10529, pp. 644–664, 2017.
DOI: 10.1007/978-3-319-66787-4_31

In a certain sense, the IoT is already here, as the number of devices storing and exchanging sensitive data rapidly multiplies. Realizing the scale in which security issues arise in this scenario poses challenges in terms of software security, interoperable authentication mechanisms, cryptographic algorithms and protocols. The possible proliferation of weak proprietary standards is particularly worrying, aggravated by the fact that IoT devices are many times physically exposed or widely accessible via the network, which opens up new possibilities of attacks making use of side-channel leakage. These leaks occur through operational aspects of a concrete realization of the cryptographic algorithm, such as the execution time of a program [14,25]. Consequently, securely implementing cryptographic algorithms in typical IoT devices remains a relevant research problem for the next few years, which is further complicated by the limited availability of resources such as RAM and computational power in these devices.

In order to fulfill the need for cryptographic implementations tailored for resource-constrained embedded devices, many different *lightweight* algorithms have been proposed for various primitives. One such proposal is the PRESENT block cipher [11], a substitution-permutation network designed by Bogdanov *et al.* and published in CHES 2007, that has received a great deal of attention from the cryptologic community and was standardized by ISO for lightweight cryptographic methods [37]. The block cipher has two versions: PRESENT-80 with an 80-bit key, and PRESENT-128 with a 128-bit key, both differing only by the key schedule, being one of its main design goals to optimize the hardware implementation. In this work, we focus on this block cipher, providing an alternative formulation of the original PRESENT algorithm. We discuss why our formulation is expected to be more efficient in software and provide implementation results that support this claim. Also, we analyze the impact of using a second-order masking scheme as a side-channel leakage countermeasure.

Our Contributions. We introduce a new portable and secure software implementation of PRESENT that leads to significant performance improvement compared to previous work. The main idea consists in optimizing the computation of permutation P in two consecutive rounds, by replacing it with two more efficient permutations P_0 and P_1 in alternated rounds. In this work, side-channel resistance is implemented through constant time execution and masking countermeasures. Our implementations are evaluated on embedded ARM processors, but the techniques should remain efficient across platforms. Extensive experimental results provided on both Cortex-M microcontrollers and more powerful Cortex-A processors indicate that we obtained the fastest side-channel resistant implementation of PRESENT for our target architectures.

Organization. Section 2 reviews related work on software implementation of PRESENT and Sect. 3 describes the original specification of the block cipher. Novel techniques for efficient software implementation are discussed in Sect. 4, security properties and side-channel countermeasures in Sect. 5. Section 6 describes our target platforms, relevant aspects about our implementation and present the performance figures we obtained, before comparing them with results from the open research literature. Conclusions are drawn in Sect. 7.

2   Related Work

The design of PRESENT [11] has motivated an extensive amount of research in the cryptologic community, both in terms of cryptanalysis and engineering aspects. The main results in these regards are summarized here.

Starting from the cryptanalytic results, many techniques have been explored to break PRESENT's security claims [10,15,27,38], and, yet, the best full-round attack found is a biclique attack [27] able to recover the secret key based on $2^{79.76}$ encryptions of PRESENT-80 or $2^{127.91}$ encryptions of PRESENT-128. Although the result is technically a proof that PRESENT is not an ideally secure block cipher, it actually helps building up confidence in the cipher design. After extensive research efforts, the best known attack still requires almost as much computational effort as a brute-force attack.

Regarding the efficient implementation of PRESENT, one of the most comprehensive works is the PhD thesis by Axel Poschmann, one of PRESENT's designers [33]. The author discusses a plethora of implementation results, both in hardware and in software, for a wide selection of architectures, ranging from 4-bit to 64-bit devices. For the software implementations, the author presents different versions optimized for either code size or speed. He focuses on implementing the S-box as a lookup table, which is potentially vulnerable to timing attacks in processors equipped with cache memory. Hence, the optimizations introduced to improve the S-box performance cannot be used in our work, because we are concerned with side-channel security.

In [31], Papapagiannopoulos *et al.* present efficient bitsliced implementations of PRESENT, along with implementations for other block ciphers, having as target architecture the ATtiny family of AVR microcontrollers. This work employs an extension [17] of Boyar-Peralta heuristics [13] to minimize the complexity of digital circuits applied to PRESENT, providing a set of 14 instructions to compute the S-box. Bao *et al.* [6] adapt the approach to implement the inverse S-box in 15 instructions for the LED cipher, which shares the same substitution layer with PRESENT.

Similarly to [31], Benadjila *et al.* [7] also provide bitsliced implementations for many different block ciphers, including PRESENT, but this time for Intel x86 architectures. One of the primary focuses of this work is the usage of SIMD instructions to speed up the implementations through vectorization.

It is also important to cite the work of Dinu *et al.* [18], which implements and optimizes PRESENT alongside with twelve other different block ciphers for three different platforms: 8-bit ATmega, 16-bit MSP430 and 32-bit ARM Cortex-M3. Their best results for PRESENT were obtained through a table-based implementation that merges the permutation layer and the substitution layer of the cipher in some instances. Since the Cortex-M3 is also one of the target architectures for our work, it is relevant to observe actual figures in this case. For this platform, the authors report an execution time of 16,919 clock cycles for encrypting 128 bits of data in CTR mode and 270,603 cycles for running the key schedule, encrypting and decrypting 128 bytes of data in CBC mode.

Out of all the aforementioned works, none of them discusses side-channel security and many even explicitly state the usage of large tables to compute the PRESENT S-box, which is a well-known source of side-channel leakage [12]. However, there are some researchers who address this issue. For example, [22] presents a bitsliced implementation for PRESENT that uses a masking scheme to provide second-order protection against side-channel attacks. The authors use a device endowed with a Cortex-M4 processor and report an execution time of 6,532 cycles to encrypt one 64-bit block, excluding the time consumed by the random number generator in the masking routine. They also provide experimental evidence for the effectiveness of masking as a side-channel attack countermeasure in ARM-based architectures. It is worth noting, however, that the masking scheme used by the authors only aims to protect the S-box computation, hence leaving the key unmasked and the algorithm open to possible attacks that might target specific sections of the code.

At last, we mention the paper [32], which applies a technique called Threshold Implementation to counteract differential power analysis attacks and glitches on hardware circuitry. This alternative masking scheme, originally proposed by Nikova *et al.* [29], has the advantage of not requiring the generation of random bits for computing operations between shares of secret information, but demands the evaluation of multiple S-boxes which can become computationally expensive in software.

3   The PRESENT Block Cipher

The PRESENT block cipher [11] is a substitution-permutation network (SPN) that encrypts a 64-bit block using a key with 80 or 128 bits. The key is first processed by the key schedule to generate 32 round keys $subkey_1, ..., subkey_{32}$ with 64 bits each. To encrypt a given block of data, it repeats the following steps over 31 rounds: the block is XORed with the corresponding round key; each contiguous set of 4 bits in the block is substituted according to the output of the substitution box (S-box) S; and then the 64 bits are rearranged by a permutation P. After the final round, the block is XORed with $subkey_{32}$. A high-level description of PRESENT encryption is given in Algorithm 1.

The S-box S acts over every 4 bits of the block, as specified in Table 1. Although the most straightforward way to implement the S-box in software is by using a lookup table, [31] shows how to simulate one evaluation of this function by performing 14 Boolean operations over the 4 input bits. Listing 1.1 contains a C-language implementation of the S-box and also of the inverse of this S-box, which can be useful for the decryption algorithm. The S-box was directly obtained from [31] using the extended Boyar-Peralta heuristics [13]. We computed the inverse S-box using the same approach with software from Brian Gladman [21]. Our inverse S-box has 15 instructions and reproduces the same number obtained by Bao *et al.* [6], in which the function was not explicitly given.

Algorithm 1. PRESENT encryption of one message block.

Input: A 64-bit block of plaintext B, a key K.
Output: A 64-bit block of ciphertext C.
1: $subkey = (subkey_1, subkey_2, ..., subkey_{32}) \leftarrow keySchedule(K)$
2: $C \leftarrow B$
3: **for** $i = 1$ **to** 31 **do**
4:     $C \leftarrow C \oplus subkey_i$
5:     $C \leftarrow S(C)$
6:     $C \leftarrow P(C)$
7: **end for**
8: $C \leftarrow C \oplus subkey_{32}$
9: **return** C

Table 1. PRESENT S-box, given in hexadecimal notation.

x	0	1	2	3	4	5	6	7	8	9	A	B	C	D	E	F
$S(x)$	C	5	6	B	9	0	A	D	3	E	F	8	4	7	1	2

Listing 1.1. Bitsliced implementation in C for both the direct and inverse S-boxes of the PRESENT block cipher.

```
/* Each macro takes as input 4 words and transforms
 * them in-place according to the S-box function
 * or its inverse.
 */

#define PRESENT_SBOX(x0,x1,x2,x3)           \
    T1 = x2 ^ x1;    T2 = x1 & T1;          \
    T3 = x0 ^ T2;    T5 = x3 ^ T3;          \
    T2 = T1 & T3;    T1 = T1 ^ T5;          \
    T2 = T2 ^ x1;    T4 = x3 | T2;          \
    x2 = T1 ^ T4;    x3 = ~x3;              \
    T2 = T2 ^ x3;    x0 = x2 ^ T2;          \
    T2 = T2 | T1;    x1 = T3 ^ T2;          \
    x3 = T5;

#define PRESENT_INV_SBOX(x0,x1,x2,x3)   \
    T0 = ~x3;        T1 = x2 ^ x0;          \
    T2 = x2 & x0;    T3 = x1 ^ T2;          \
    T4 = x3 ^ T1;    x3 = T0 ^ T3;          \
    T0 = T1 & x3;    T1 = x2 ^ T0;          \
    T2 = T4 | T1;    x0 = T3 ^ T2;          \
    T5 = T4 ^ T1;    T2 = T3 & T5;          \
    x2 = T4 ^ T2;    x1 = T2 ^ (~T1);       \
```

The permutation P is specified by Eq. 1 below and moves the i-th bit of the state to the position $P(i)$:

$$P(i) = \begin{cases} 16i \mod 63, & \text{if } i \neq 63, \\ 63, & \text{if } i = 63. \end{cases} \tag{1}$$

From the definition of P, one can easily verify that $P^2 = P^{-1}$. By looking at Fig. 1, another interesting property of this permutation can be noticed: if the 64-bit state of the cipher is stored in four 16-bit registers, the application of the permutation P aligns the state in a way that the concatenation of the i-th bit of each of the four registers of the permuted state corresponds to 4 consecutive bits of the original state. These properties will be explored by the technique proposed later.

$$B = \begin{bmatrix} 00 & 01 & 02 & 03 & 04 & 05 & 06 & 07 & 08 & 09 & 10 & 11 & 12 & 13 & 14 & 15 \\ 16 & 17 & 18 & 19 & 20 & 21 & 22 & 23 & 24 & 25 & 26 & 27 & 28 & 29 & 30 & 31 \\ 32 & 33 & 34 & 35 & 36 & 37 & 38 & 39 & 40 & 41 & 42 & 43 & 44 & 45 & 46 & 47 \\ 48 & 49 & 50 & 51 & 52 & 53 & 54 & 55 & 56 & 57 & 58 & 59 & 60 & 61 & 62 & 63 \end{bmatrix},$$

$$P(B) = \begin{bmatrix} 00 & 04 & 08 & 12 & 16 & 20 & 24 & 28 & 32 & 36 & 40 & 44 & 48 & 52 & 56 & 60 \\ 01 & 05 & 09 & 13 & 17 & 21 & 25 & 29 & 33 & 37 & 41 & 45 & 49 & 53 & 57 & 61 \\ 02 & 06 & 10 & 14 & 18 & 22 & 26 & 30 & 34 & 38 & 42 & 46 & 50 & 54 & 58 & 62 \\ 03 & 07 & 11 & 15 & 19 & 23 & 27 & 31 & 35 & 39 & 43 & 47 & 51 & 55 & 59 & 63 \end{bmatrix}.$$

Fig. 1. Matrix representation of the 64-bit input block B and its permutation $P(B)$, both split into four 16-bit rows.

4   Efficient Implementation

The main novelty introduced in this work lies in the techniques devised to efficiently implement the PRESENT block cipher in software, which are now described. First, we limit the scope to PRESENT-80, the version using an 80-bit key, which is better suited for lightweight applications due to a smaller memory footprint. The encryption and decryption routines are exactly the same for the 128-bit version, the only difference is in the key schedule, which should not be a critical section of the algorithm in terms of performance. In fact, applying the same techniques exposed here to PRESENT-128, provides, within a 5% margin, the same time measurements for all scenarios we consider.

Algorithm 2 specifies our proposal for implementing encryption of a single block with PRESENT. Essentially, every two applications of permutation P are replaced by evaluations of permutations P_0 and P_1, which satisfy the property that $P_1 \circ P_0 = P^2$, a fact that preserves the correctness of the modified algorithm. The way P_0 and P_1 act upon the cipher state is represented in Fig. 2, and code in the C programming language to implement both permutations follows in Listing 1.2. On the description of this algorithm, we use the function S_{BS}, which we define as being the same S-box used for PRESENT, but taking as inputs state bits whose indexes are congruent modulo 16 instead of every four consecutive bits. In other words, this S-box interprets the state of the cipher as four 16-bit words and operates on them in a bitsliced fashion.

Algorithm 2. Our proposal for PRESENT encryption of one message block.

Input: A 64-bit block of plaintext B, a key K.
Output: A 64-bit block of ciphertext C.
1: $subkey = (subkey_1, subkey_2, ..., subkey_{32}) \leftarrow keySchedule(K)$
2: $C \leftarrow B$
3: **for** $i = 1$ **to** 15 **do**
4:     $C \leftarrow C \oplus subkey_{2i-1}$
5:     $C \leftarrow P_0(C)$
6:     $C \leftarrow S_{BS}(C)$
7:     $C \leftarrow P_1(C)$
8:     $C \leftarrow C \oplus P(subkey_{2i})$
9:     $C \leftarrow S_{BS}(C)$
10: **end for**
11: $C \leftarrow C \oplus subkey_{31}$
12: $C \leftarrow P(C)$
13: $C \leftarrow S_{BS}(C)$
14: $C \leftarrow C \oplus subkey_{32}$
15: **return** C

We need to observe two facts to prove the equivalence between Algorithms 1 and 2. First, the S-box S in Algorithm 1 acts on the same quadruplets of bits that S_{BS} acts on Algorithm 2, since both P_0 and P bitslice the state over 16-bit words. Then note that $P(P(X \oplus subkey_i) \oplus subkey_{i+1}) = P^2(X \oplus subkey_i) \oplus P(subkey_{i+1}) = P_1(P_0(X \oplus subkey_i)) \oplus P(subkey_{i+1})$, being that leftmost term exactly the transformation undergone by state X over rounds i and $i+1$ on Algorithm 1 and the rightmost term the transformation undergone by state X over rounds i and $i+1$, for i odd, on Algorithm 2, when we disregard the S-box step on both algorithms. Since the S-boxes operate equivalently and, without S-boxes, the algorithms are also equivalent, the proof is concluded.

Now, at first glance, it may not be clear why our alternative version for PRESENT is faster than the original one, but there are two main advantages. The first one is due to complexity in software. Permutations P_0 and P_1 are simply more software friendly, requiring less operations to be implemented, when compared to the permutation P. An evidence to corroborate this fact was obtained from the source code generator for bit permutations provided by Jasper Neumann in [28], estimating a cost of 14 clock cycles to execute either P_0 or P_1 and a cost of 24 cycles to execute P, when implemented optimally.

Listing 1.2. Efficient implementation in C of the permutations P_0 and P_1 of our proposal for PRESENT encryption.

```
/* The following macros permute two 64-bit blocks
 * simultaneously, using an auxiliary variable t
 * and storing one block on the high 16-bit word
 * of the 32-bit variables X0, X1, X2 and X3, and
 * the other block on the low 16-bit word of the
 * same variables.
 */

#define PRESENT_PERMUTATION_P0(X0,X1,X2,X3) \
    t = (X0^(X1>>1)) & 0x55555555;          \
    X0 = X0^t; X1 = X1^(t<<1);              \
    t = (X2^(X3>>1)) & 0x55555555;          \
    X2 = X2^t; X3 = X3^(t<<1);              \
    t = (X0^(X2>>2)) & 0x33333333;          \
    X0 = X0^t; X2 = X2^(t<<2);              \
    t = (X1^(X3>>2)) & 0x33333333;          \
    X1 = X1^t; X3 = X3^(t<<2);              \

#define PRESENT_PERMUTATION_P1(X0,X1,X2,X3) \
    t = (X0^(X1>>4)) & 0x0F0F0F0F;          \
    X0 = X0^t; X1 = X1^(t<<4);              \
    t = (X2^(X3>>4)) & 0x0F0F0F0F;          \
    X2 = X2^t; X3 = X3^(t<<4);              \
    t = (X0^(X2>>8)) & 0x00FF00FF;          \
    X0 = X0^t; X2 = X2^(t<<8);              \
    t = (X1^(X3>>8)) & 0x00FF00FF;          \
    X1 = X1^t; X3 = X3^(t<<8);              \
```

The second advantage of our proposal involves the application of the S-box. A careful analysis of Algorithm 2 leads to the conclusion that, at lines 6, 9 and 13, where the S-box is applied, the state of the variable C is not the same as the state to which the S-box is applied in Algorithm 1. At line 6, the state has undergone an extra P_0 permutation in relation to the original formulation; and at lines 9 and 13 the state has undergone an extra evaluation of P. By looking at Figs. 1 and 2, it stands clear that, if the ciphertext is stored into four 16-bit registers, both P and P_0 organize the state in such a way that every four consecutive bits are aligned in columns throughout those four registers, similarly to what would be seen in a fully bitsliced implementation. Therefore, an implementation following the structure in Algorithm 2 can make use of bitwise operations to simulate the S-box step, calculating sixteen S-box applications simultaneously.

The same rationale may be applied to generate other alternative versions of the PRESENT encryption algorithm. Figure 3 illustrates different versions of PRESENT obtained by interchanging S-box applications and permutations. In this figure, S represents the S-box applied over every four consecutive bits of the state and S_{BS} represents the S-box computed in a bitsliced fashion.

$$B = \begin{bmatrix} 00\ 01\ 02\ 03\ 04\ 05\ 06\ 07\ 08\ 09\ 10\ 11\ 12\ 13\ 14\ 15 \\ 16\ 17\ 18\ 19\ 20\ 21\ 22\ 23\ 24\ 25\ 26\ 27\ 28\ 29\ 30\ 31 \\ 32\ 33\ 34\ 35\ 36\ 37\ 38\ 39\ 40\ 41\ 42\ 43\ 44\ 45\ 46\ 47 \\ 48\ 49\ 50\ 51\ 52\ 53\ 54\ 55\ 56\ 57\ 58\ 59\ 60\ 61\ 62\ 63 \end{bmatrix},$$

$$P_0(B) = \begin{bmatrix} 00\ 16\ 32\ 48\ 04\ 20\ 36\ 52\ 08\ 24\ 40\ 56\ 12\ 28\ 44\ 60 \\ 01\ 17\ 33\ 49\ 05\ 21\ 37\ 53\ 09\ 25\ 41\ 57\ 13\ 29\ 45\ 61 \\ 02\ 18\ 34\ 50\ 06\ 22\ 38\ 54\ 10\ 26\ 42\ 58\ 14\ 30\ 46\ 62 \\ 03\ 19\ 35\ 51\ 07\ 23\ 39\ 55\ 11\ 27\ 43\ 59\ 15\ 31\ 47\ 63 \end{bmatrix},$$

$$P_1(B) = \begin{bmatrix} 00\ 01\ 02\ 03\ 16\ 17\ 18\ 19\ 32\ 33\ 34\ 35\ 48\ 49\ 50\ 51 \\ 04\ 05\ 06\ 07\ 20\ 21\ 22\ 23\ 36\ 37\ 38\ 39\ 52\ 53\ 54\ 55 \\ 08\ 09\ 10\ 11\ 24\ 25\ 26\ 27\ 40\ 41\ 42\ 43\ 56\ 57\ 58\ 59 \\ 12\ 13\ 14\ 15\ 28\ 29\ 30\ 31\ 44\ 45\ 46\ 47\ 60\ 61\ 62\ 63 \end{bmatrix}.$$

Fig. 2. Matrix representation of the 64-bit input block B and its permutations $P_0(B)$ and $P_1(B)$, all of them divided into four 16-bit rows.

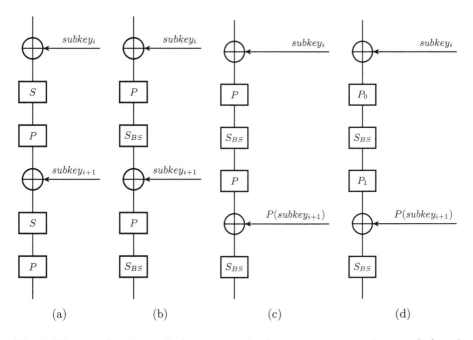

Fig. 3. Diagram showing equivalent ways to implement two consecutive rounds (i and $i + 1$) of PRESENT for encryption. The original specification for the block cipher corresponds to the leftmost diagram and the rightmost one corresponds to the version proposed here with alternating P_0 and P_1 permutations.

One last observation to further improve performance of the implementation in a 32-bit architecture is that two blocks of plaintext can be encrypted in CTR mode at once, organizing the state such that 32 S-boxes are calculated simultaneously instead of only 16. For a 64-bit architecture, the same strategy can be carried out to encrypt four blocks at once.

All of the algorithmic observations and implementation techniques discussed here extend directly to the decryption routine, as shown by Algorithm 3. The inversion of encryption is particularly simplified by the fact that P_0 and P_1 are involutory permutations, that is, $P_0^{-1} = P_0$ and $P_1^{-1} = P_1$. The involutory property of P_0 and P_1 has yet another advantage. Since $P_1 \circ P_0 = P^2$ and $P^2 = P^{-1}$, it follows that $P = P_0 \circ P_1$, what might be used to reduce the code size of the implementation, because the permutation P does not need to be implemented provided that P_0 and P_1 have already been coded.

Algorithm 3. Our proposal for PRESENT decryption of one message block.

    Input: A 64-bit block of ciphertext C, a key K.
    Output: A 64-bit block of plaintext B.
  1: $subkey = (subkey_1, subkey_2, ..., subkey_{32}) \leftarrow keySchedule(K)$
  2: $B \leftarrow C$
  3: $B \leftarrow B \oplus subkey_{32}$
  4: $B \leftarrow S_{BS}^{-1}(B)$
  5: $B \leftarrow P^{-1}(B)$
  6: $B \leftarrow B \oplus subkey_{31}$
  7: **for** $i = 15$ **to** 1 **do**
  8:      $B \leftarrow S_{BS}^{-1}(B)$
  9:      $B \leftarrow B \oplus subkey_{2i}$
10:      $B \leftarrow P_1(B)$
11:      $B \leftarrow S_{BS}^{-1}(B)$
12:      $B \leftarrow P_0(B)$
13:      $B \leftarrow B \oplus P(subkey_{2i-1})$
14: **end for**
15: **return** B

At last, it is important to notice that our proposal has the drawback of applying the permutation P to some of the round keys. Although, since typically many blocks of message are encrypted or decrypted with the same key, the key schedule routine should have a low impact on the algorithm's practical performance, since it is executed only once for several executions of encryption/decryption routines.

5   Side-Channel Countermeasures

As commented previously, there has been extensive work on the cryptanalysis of PRESENT and the lack of significant advances provides evidence that the cipher is likely to fulfill the desired security goals. However, even if the block cipher design is ideally secure, a careless implementation may leak sensitive data during execution and undermine the security of the algorithm with its insecure realization.

Particularly, a major concern is side-channel attacks, that is, attacks which are crafted based on information obtained from the physical implementation of a cryptographic primitive. For instance, an attacker may gather data such as execution time of an algorithm [14,19,25], power consumption [30], sound produced by the hardware [20] or even magnetic radiation emitted during the computation [26] and, through these data, the attacker may gain access to sensitive information processed by the device under analysis.

It is worth noting that side-channel attacks are limited to situations where the attacker has physical access to the hardware executing the implementation or at least can interact with the device through the network. It is not completely unreasonable to ignore the possibility of such attacks when the implementation of the algorithm is physically protected from the attacker or not accessible for any kind of interaction, but reality tends to go in the opposite direction in the IoT context. In this scenario, devices are frequently accessible to the attacker by either physical means or through the network and typically lack tamper-resistance countermeasures for protecting the hardware from external influence.

5.1 Protecting Against Timing Attacks

The focus is primarily on timing attacks, since they are entirely within the scope of software implementation, and appear to be the most practical side-channel attack. Furthermore, protecting software implementations from more invasive side-channel attacks is very challenging, since the software countermeasures can be typically circumvented by an invasive attacker. Recent work has developed static analysis tools to detect variances in execution time correlated with secret information at a rather low level [2,34], allowing implementers to formally guarantee constant execution time of their code or at least implement mitigations.

In practice, the main sources of timing vulnerabilities are memory accesses and conditional branches depending on secret data. Conditional branching, by definition, may cause different instructions to be executed among different runs of a program, which, by its turn, may cause the execution time of the algorithm to depend on sensitive data given as input. The effect of branch misprediction in more sophisticated processors may further interfere with pipelined datapaths and provoke significant variations [1]. In a similar way, if a processor is equipped with cache memory, the execution time may leak information about the rate of cache misses or hits during memory accesses, and, clearly, if these accesses depend on sensitive data, this implementation becomes susceptible to side-channel attacks [8]. Therefore, by avoiding these situations, a software implementation can encrypt a message block in constant time, independently of characteristics about the inputs (plaintext message or cryptographic key). This runtime property is called *isochronicity*.

5.2   Masking the Implementation

Ensuring that code runs in constant time is sufficient to render timing attacks impractical, although other side-channel leakages might still be exploited. Another family of techniques for improving side-channel resistance is called *secret sharing*, or *masking*, which consists in splitting sensitive variables occurring in the computation into $d + 1$ shares (or masks) in order to unlink the correlation between environmental information and the secret data being processed. A masking technique based on $d + 1$ masks is said to be a d-th order masking and can only be broken by an attacker who manages to obtain leakage related to at least $d + 1$ intermediate variables of the algorithm. It is possible to prove that the difficulty for a side-channel attack to succeed, in practice, increases exponentially with d and, hence, the masking order can be considered a sound criterion to evaluate the robustness of the implementation against side-channel analysis [16].

The literature presents different alternatives to implement a masked encryption algorithm [32], but analysis will be restricted to the proposal given by Ishai *et al.* in [23], which appears to be the most appropriate for a fast software implementation. In this proposal, the masked state of a sensitive variable m with $d+1$ *shares* is

$$m = \bigoplus_{i=0}^{d} m_i = m_0 \oplus m_1 \oplus \ldots \oplus m_d, \tag{2}$$

where each m_i is a share of the secret and all shares form together a masked secret. In order to create a masked implementation on the variable m, one can randomly generate the d masks $m_1, m_2, ..., m_d$ and calculate m_0 such that Eq. 2 holds.

From this definition, we can derive ways to calculate different operations over the masks. The following list contains all operations necessary to implement a masked version of PRESENT.

1. A NOT operation over a masked secret has to be carried out as a NOT operation performed on an odd number of masks to preserve the relationship in Eq. 2. A single mask can just as well be negated:

$$\neg m = \neg m_0 \oplus m_1 \oplus \ldots \oplus m_d.$$

2. An XOR operation between masked secrets $a = \bigoplus_{i=0}^{d} a_i$ and $b = \bigoplus_{i=0}^{d} b_i$ can be performed by calculating the XOR of all corresponding masks:

$$a \oplus b = \bigoplus_{i=0}^{d} (a_i \oplus b_i).$$

3. An AND operation between two masked secrets is more complicated and can be computed as follows: for every pair (i, j), $1 \leq i < j \leq d + 1$, generate

a random bit $z_{i,j}$. Then, compute $z_{i,j} = (z_{i,j} \oplus a_i b_i) \oplus a_j b_i$. Now, for every $1 \leq i \leq d+1$, the i-th share may be computed as

$$m_i = a_i b_i \oplus \bigoplus_{i \neq j} z_{i,j}.$$

4. An OR operation might be calculated using the logical identity $OR(a,b) = \neg(\neg a \cdot \neg b)$, which depends only on operations previously defined.

The nonlinear operations OR and AND stand out as the most expensive ones, requiring $O(d^2)$ calls to a random bit generator and memory to store a matrix z of $O(d^2)$ entries. This is the main drawback of the technique in resource-constrained devices and makes the use of high-order masking impractical in many scenarios.

6   Implementation Details and Results

6.1   Target Architecture

Currently, there is a vast variety of processors under consideration for integration to the IoT. The focus given in this work is on some representatives of the ARM architecture, since it is the world leader in the market of microprocessors and, thus, attracts relevant academic work as well as commercial interest. More specifically, our implementations were benchmarked on the following platforms:

- **Cortex-M0+:** Arduino Zero powered by an Atmel SAMD21G18A ARM Cortex-M0+ CPU, clocked at 48MHz.
- **Cortex-M3:** Arduino Due powered by an Atmel SAM3X8E ARM Cortex-M3 CPU, clocked at 84MHz.
- **Cortex-M4:** Teensy 3.2 board containing a MK20DX256VLH7 Cortex-M4 CPU, clocked at 72 MHz.
- **Cortex-A7/A15:** ODROID-XU4 board containing a Samsung Exynos5422 2GHz Cortex-A15 and Cortex-A7 octa-core CPU.
- **Cortex-A53:** ODROID-C2 board containing an Amlogic 64-bit ARM 2GHz Cortex-A53 (ARMv8) quad-core CPU.

Members of the Cortex-M [4] family are commonly used in embedded applications, being found on devices ranging from medical instrumentation equipment to domestic household appliances. The design of these processors is optimized for cost and energy efficiency, making them relatively low-end when compared to the other targets.

As for the members of Cortex-A [3] family, they are more computationally powerful than the Cortex-M processors, being able to execute complex tasks such as running a robust operating system or a high-quality multimedia task. These processors have access to the NEON engine, a powerful Single Instruction Multiple Data (SIMD) extension, and may have sophisticated out-of-order execution.

6.2   Main Results

In order to discuss our results, the code size and speed of our implementations are measured in two scenarios based on what is proposed in the FELICS framework [18], such that results can be comparable in a fair and reliable manner.

Scenario 1 simulates a communication protocol established in sensor networks or between IoT devices. It is assumed here that the device possesses the master key stored in RAM, calculates the key schedule and then proceeds to encrypt and decrypt 128 bytes of sensitive data using the CBC mode of operation. Due to the employment of the CBC mode, the suggested trick of encrypting more than one block in parallel does not work, since this mode of operation forces dependencies between consecutive input blocks. Hence, it stands clear that it is not the optimal scenario to use our techniques, but we still chose to implement it exactly as described in [18] for the sake of comparison.

Scenario 2 simulates an authentication protocol in which the block cipher is used to encrypt 128 bits of data in CTR mode of operation. The round keys are assumed to be stored in memory and, consequently, no key schedule is required. This is a very appropriate stance to employ all of the optimizations proposed so far, since the CTR mode encrypts and decrypts blocks of input independently.

Results for both scenarios are expressed in Tables 2 and 3. All the measurements were based on code fully written in C language, compiled by GCC 6.3.1 in the case of the Cortex-A family and by GCC 4.8.4 for the Cortex-M family, using the flag -O3 for optimized speed results. The isochronicity property of the constant time implementations was validated using the FlowTracker static analysis tool [34]. FlowTracker performs information flow analysis from function inputs marked as secret to branch instructions and memory addresses, effectively detecting and thwarting timing attacks. This tool analyzes compiled code at the LLVM Intermediate Representation level, thus closer to the platform-specific native code. All timings for Cortex-M processors were reproduced to a reasonable degree in the ARM Cortex-M Prototyping System (MPS2), an FPGA-based board with support to microcontrollers ranging from the Cortex-M0 to M7. However, we only report timings collected in the widely available platforms to simplify comparisons with future competing implementation efforts.

One of the main observations attained from these measurements is that the cost to protect the implementations with masking is high, especially in lower-end processors. In our case, a second-order masking was used and the time consumed by the random number generator was disregarded. Still, a slowdown of up to 6.8 times was observed in the case of the Cortex-M0+. For higher-end processors, however, the slowdown can be inferior to a 4-factor. Throughout all processors, a sensible increase in code size due to masking is observed.

Another fact to notice is that, as expected, even when differences in input size are taken into account, the performance of PRESENT in Scenario 2 is substantially better than the performance in Scenario 1, mainly due to the choice of mode of operation. In Scenario 1, using the CBC mode, only decryption can be parallelized, and encryption ends up being roughly twice as slow as in CTR mode.

Table 2. Performance results for Scenario 1 – key schedule, encryption and decryption of 128 bytes in CBC mode – of side-channel resistant implementations of PRESENT, encompassing both isochronous (constant time) and second-order masking countermeasures.

Processor	Code size [bytes]	Key schedule [cycles]	Encryption [cycles]	Decryption[cycles]
Isochronous implementation				
Cortex-M0+	1436	6381	46429	23445
Cortex-M3	1320	5043	29442	16291
Cortex-M4	1328	3464	22993	11731
Cortex-A7	2732	3232	21027	10657
Cortex-A15	1792	1740	14780	7050
Cortex-A53	2484	1554	13583	3726
Masked implementation				
Cortex-M0+	8056	7145	332079	204690
Cortex-M3	7048	4628	197601	122521
Cortex-M4	9216	3413	186556	100417
Cortex-A7	9248	2657	116004	64041
Cortex-A15	9248	1894	59474	29130
Cortex-A53	8452	1943	39983	12848

Table 3. Performance results for Scenario 2 – encryption of 128 bits in CTR mode – of side-channel resistant implementations of PRESENT, encompassing both isochronous (constant time) and second-order masking countermeasures.

Processor	Code size [bytes]	Execution time [cycles]
Isochronous implementation		
Cortex-M0+	2524	3183
Cortex-M3	2476	2116
Cortex-M4	2612	1599
Cortex-A7	2456	1708
Cortex-A15	2456	960
Cortex-A53	2536	1052
Masked implementation		
Cortex-M0+	12392	21744
Cortex-M3	9728	12387
Cortex-M4	11012	11096
Cortex-A7	13322	7482
Cortex-A15	13322	3688
Cortex-A53	18028	3681

6.3   Vector Implementation Using NEON

For the platforms with access to NEON instructions, parallelism within the PRESENT encryption algorithm can also be explored for enhancing performance. In particular, it is relevant to mention that the NEON instructions VTBL and VTBX allow the computation of fast table lookups by performing register operations, without the need of memory accesses.

Besides the original formulation of the algorithm, that implements S-boxes as lookup tables, we were also able to evaluate the performance of a different proposal mentioned in [33] and attributed to Gregor Leander. The idea is similar to ours, in principle, since it decomposes the permutation P into two others. However, Leander's decomposition aims to allow a faster lookup table-based implementation, which is the opposite direction we are looking for. Still, even using the NEON instructions to implement the lookup tables used in Leander's method, our formulation was found to be faster.

NEON implementations can process eight blocks simultaneously due to the support of 128-bit registers, in the same fashion as processing two blocks in parallel in 32-bit processors or four blocks in parallel using 64-bit ones. For this reason, neither scenario used previously is appropriate to evaluate vector implementations. Scenario 1 does not support parallelism due to the mode of operation employed and Scenario 2 processes only 128 bits of data, which is only two blocks of input, not making use of the full capacity of processing eight blocks at once.

For this reason, we chose to analyze the performance of our NEON implementations under a third scenario, in which we run the key schedule, encrypt and decrypt 128 bytes of data. These results are reported in Tables 4 and 5, alongside with the results of the native implementation, without vector instructions, to provide a baseline for comparison.

By analyzing the results, we notice that the NEON instructions were able to provide a meaningful speedup for the 32-bit processors. For the 64-bit Cortex-A53, however, the efficiency of native instructions associated with the possibility of processing four blocks in parallel beats the vector implementation by a small margin. Naturally, these implementations have a substantial impact on code size when compared to Table 2.

Notice also that the only difference introduced by this third scenario compared to Scenario 1 is the choice of the mode of operation. It further illustrates how much better CTR performs in this case, in which we can make use of the parallelism intrinsic to the encryption routine.

6.4   Comparison with Related Work

Although many implementation results for PRESENT are published, we focus here on comparing our metrics to the works of [18, 22], which are, to the best of our knowledge, the most efficient publicly available implementations of PRESENT in similar platforms to the ones we use.

Table 4. Performance results for isochronous execution of the key schedule, encryption and decryption of 128 bytes of data in CTR mode, using both serial and vectorized code.

Processor	Code size [bytes]	Key schedule [cycles]	Encryption+Decryption [cycles]
Serial implementation			
Cortex-M0+	2524	6381	47884
Cortex-M3	2476	5043	31830
Cortex-M4	2612	3464	26785
Cortex-A7	2456	2732	27161
Cortex-A15	2456	1740	14169
Cortex-A53	2536	1554	7406
Vector implementation using NEON			
Cortex-A7	2798	2299	14274
Cortex-A15	2798	1533	8083
Cortex-A53	3908	1552	7322

Table 5. Performance results for execution of the key schedule, encryption and decryption of 128 bytes of data in CTR mode, using both serial and vectorized code, protected by second-order masking.

Processor	Code size [bytes]	Key schedule [cycles]	Encryption+Decryption [cycles]
Serial implementation			
Cortex-M0+	12392	7145	345619
Cortex-M3	9728	4628	205244
Cortex-M4	11012	3413	192454
Cortex-A7	13322	2657	119542
Cortex-A15	13322	1894	58635
Cortex-A53	18028	1943	23207
Vector implementation using NEON			
Cortex-A7	2798	2671	76286
Cortex-A15	2798	1948	28633
Cortex-A53	3908	1941	28343

In [18], a series of implementations is presented for many block ciphers which are benchmarked on a Cortex-M3 processor. For a scenario identical to the Scenario 2 we described, they report an execution time of 16,786 clock cycles and a code size of 3,568 bytes. Our results are almost 8 times better considering the execution time, and over 30% better regarding the code size. They also measure these metrics for Scenario 1, in which they report the usage of 270,603 cycles of execution and 2,528 bytes of code, which is slower and more space-consuming than our implementation, but by a smaller margin, since the CBC mode of operation employed in this case does not benefit from some of the optimizations.

The work of [22] showcases a bitsliced implementation of PRESENT on a Cortex-M4, protected by a second-order masking. It claims to be able to encrypt one input block in 6,532 cycles. We argue that our results are better, since, even if there is no penalty caused by the tight coupling with a mode of operation, it would encrypt 128 bits of data in 13,064 cycles, which is slower than the 11,096 cycles we achieved for the same processor on Scenario 2. Furthermore, since this implementation has a bitslice factor of 32, it cannot actually encrypt only 128 bits of data without having to do extra work, whereas our implementation is not only faster, but more flexible in the sense that it allows small amounts of data to be efficiently encrypted.

It is also relevant to take into consideration performance results from other block ciphers to gauge how useful our techniques may be in practice. In particular, we take a closer look at AES, arguably the most extensively used block cipher today and which has been originally praised for its good performance in software [35]. The current state-of-the-art implementations for AES on Cortex-M processor are from [36], in which several different results are presented. Table 6 compares our results to theirs when encrypting 128 bits of data through CTR mode in constant time. We notice that PRESENT is slower than AES on Cortex-M3, but slightly faster on Cortex-M4 and, on both processors, PRESENT's code footprint is several times smaller.

Table 6. Comparison between our results for PRESENT and results from [36] for AES when encrypting 128 bits of data in CTR mode, in constant time.

Implementation	Code size [bytes]	Execution time [cycles]
AES on Cortex-M3	12120	1617
PRESENT on Cortex-M3	2476	2116
AES on Cortex-M4	12120	1618
PRESENT on Cortex-M4	2612	1599

7   Conclusion

In this work, we presented a novel technique for accelerating encryption and decryption using the PRESENT block cipher. Our modified algorithm is expected to be faster in software when compared to the original PRESENT specification for many platforms and, indeed, our experimental data supports that we were able to significantly outperform state-of-the-art results for processors within the ARM Cortex-M family. This makes PRESENT competitively efficient even when compared to secure implementations of widely used software-oriented ciphers such as AES.

Furthermore, our proposal has the advantage to be readily implemented in constant time, which is relevant in contexts where there is concern regarding side-channel attacks. For further side-channel security, we implemented and analyzed the performance impact of a second-order masking scheme.

At last, we show that our technique can also be applied to vector implementations – using the ARM-NEON extension, for example – to achieve even higher performance gains in some compatible platforms.

Acknowledgements. The authors gratefully acknowledge financial support from LG Electronics Inc. during the development of this research, under the project *"Efficient and Secure Cryptography for IoT"*. The third author also acknowledges financial support from CNPq: a research productivity scholarship.

References

1. Aciiçmez, O., Koç, C.K., Seifert, J.P.: On the power of simple branch prediction analysis. In: Proceedings of the 2nd ACM Symposium on Information, Computer and Communications Security, ASIACCS 2007, pp. 312–320. ACM, New York (2007). doi:10.1145/1229285.1266999
2. Almeida, J.B., Barbosa, M., Barthe, G., Dupressoir, F., Emmi, M.: Verifying constant-time implementations (2016)
3. ARM: Cortex-A Series Family. https://www.arm.com/products/processors/cortex-a/index.php. Accessed June 2016
4. ARM: Cortex-M Series Family. https://www.arm.com/products/processors/cortex-m/index.php. Accessed June 2016
5. Atzori, L., Iera, A., Morabito, G.: The internet of things: a survey. Comput. Netw. **54**(15), 2787–2805 (2010). doi:10.1016/j.comnet.2010.05.010
6. Bao, Z., Luo, P., Lin, D.: Bitsliced implementations of the PRINCE, LED and RECTANGLE block ciphers on AVR 8-Bit microcontrollers. In: Qing, S., Okamoto, E., Kim, K., Liu, D. (eds.) ICICS 2015. LNCS, vol. 9543, pp. 18–36. Springer, Cham (2016). doi:10.1007/978-3-319-29814-6_3
7. Benadjila, R., Guo, J., Lomné, V., Peyrin, T.: Implementing lightweight block ciphers on x86 architectures. In: Lange, T., Lauter, K., Lisoněk, P. (eds.) SAC 2013. LNCS, vol. 8282, pp. 324–351. Springer, Heidelberg (2014). doi:10.1007/978-3-662-43414-7_17
8. Bernstein, D.J.: Cache-timing attacks on AES (2005). http://cr.yp.to/papers.html#cachetiming
9. Bernstein, D.J.: Curve25519: new Diffie-Hellman speed records. In: Yung, M., Dodis, Y., Kiayias, A., Malkin, T. (eds.) PKC 2006. LNCS, vol. 3958, pp. 207–228. Springer, Heidelberg (2006). doi:10.1007/11745853_14

10. Blondeau, C., Nyberg, K.: Links between truncated differential and multidimensional linear properties of block ciphers and underlying attack complexities. In: Nguyen, P.Q., Oswald, E. (eds.) EUROCRYPT 2014. LNCS, vol. 8441, pp. 165–182. Springer, Heidelberg (2014). doi:10.1007/978-3-642-55220-5_10

11. Bogdanov, A., Knudsen, L.R., Leander, G., Paar, C., Poschmann, A., Robshaw, M.J.B., Seurin, Y., Vikkelsoe, C.: PRESENT: an ultra-lightweight block cipher. In: Paillier, P., Verbauwhede, I. (eds.) CHES 2007. LNCS, vol. 4727, pp. 450–466. Springer, Heidelberg (2007). doi:10.1007/978-3-540-74735-2_31

12. Bonneau, J., Mironov, I.: Cache-Collision timing attacks against AES. In: Goubin, L., Matsui, M. (eds.) CHES 2006. LNCS, vol. 4249, pp. 201–215. Springer, Heidelberg (2006). doi:10.1007/11894063_16

13. Boyar, J., Peralta, R.: A new combinational logic minimization technique with applications to cryptology. In: Festa, P. (ed.) SEA 2010. LNCS, vol. 6049, pp. 178–189. Springer, Heidelberg (2010). doi:10.1007/978-3-642-13193-6_16

14. Cheval, V., Cortier, V.: Timing attacks in security protocols: symbolic framework and proof techniques. In: Focardi, R., Myers, A. (eds.) POST 2015. LNCS, vol. 9036, pp. 280–299. Springer, Heidelberg (2015). doi:10.1007/978-3-662-46666-7_15

15. Cho, J.Y.: Linear cryptanalysis of reduced-round PRESENT. In: Pieprzyk, J. (ed.) CT-RSA 2010. LNCS, vol. 5985, pp. 302–317. Springer, Heidelberg (2010). doi:10.1007/978-3-642-11925-5_21

16. Coron, J.-S., Prouff, E., Rivain, M., Roche, T.: Higher-order side channel security and mask refreshing. In: Moriai, S. (ed.) FSE 2013. LNCS, vol. 8424, pp. 410–424. Springer, Heidelberg (2014). doi:10.1007/978-3-662-43933-3_21

17. Courtois, N., Hulme, D., Mourouzis, T.: Solving circuit optimisation problems in cryptography and cryptanalysis. IACR Cryptology ePrint Archive 2011, 475 (2011). http://eprint.iacr.org/2011/475

18. Dinu, D., Corre, Y.L., Khovratovich, D., Perrin, L., Großschädl, J., Biryukov, A.: Triathlon of lightweight block ciphers for the internet of things. IACR Cryptology ePrint Archive 2015, 209 (2015). http://eprint.iacr.org/2015/209

19. Doychev, G., Köpf, B.: Rational protection against timing attacks. In: Fournet, C., Hicks, M.W., Viganò, L. (eds.) IEEE 28th Computer Security Foundations Symposium, CSF 2015, Verona, Italy, 13–17 July 2015, pp. 526–536. IEEE (2015). doi:10.1109/CSF.2015.39

20. Genkin, D., Shamir, A., Tromer, E.: RSA key extraction via low-bandwidth acoustic cryptanalysis. In: Garay, J.A., Gennaro, R. (eds.) CRYPTO 2014. LNCS, vol. 8616, pp. 444–461. Springer, Heidelberg (2014). doi:10.1007/978-3-662-44371-2_25

21. Gladman, B.: Serpent S Boxes as Boolean Functions. http://www.gladman.me.uk/

22. Groot, W., Papagiannopoulos, K., Piedra, A., Schneider, E., Batina, L.: Bitsliced masking and ARM: friends or foes? In: Bogdanov, A. (ed.) LightSec 2016. LNCS, vol. 10098, pp. 91–109. Springer, Cham (2017). doi:10.1007/978-3-319-55714-4_7

23. Ishai, Y., Sahai, A., Wagner, D.: Private circuits: securing hardware against probing attacks. In: Boneh, D. (ed.) CRYPTO 2003. LNCS, vol. 2729, pp. 463–481. Springer, Heidelberg (2003). doi:10.1007/978-3-540-45146-4_27

24. Käsper, E., Schwabe, P.: Faster and timing-attack resistant AES-GCM. In: Clavier, C., Gaj, K. (eds.) CHES 2009. LNCS, vol. 5747, pp. 1–17. Springer, Heidelberg (2009). doi:10.1007/978-3-642-04138-9_1

25. Kocher, P.C.: Timing attacks on implementations of Diffie-Hellman, RSA, DSS, and other systems. In: Koblitz, N. (ed.) CRYPTO 1996. LNCS, vol. 1109, pp. 104–113. Springer, Heidelberg (1996). doi:10.1007/3-540-68697-5_9

26. Kuhn, M.G.: Electromagnetic eavesdropping risks of flat-panel displays. In: Martin, D., Serjantov, A. (eds.) PET 2004. LNCS, vol. 3424, pp. 88–107. Springer, Heidelberg (2005). doi:10.1007/11423409_7

27. Lee, C.: Biclique cryptanalysis of PRESENT-80 and PRESENT-128. J. Supercomput. **70**(1), 95–103 (2014). doi:10.1007/s11227-014-1103-3

28. Neumann, J.: Code generator for bit permutations. http://programming.sirrida. de/calcperm.php

29. Nikova, S., Rechberger, C., Rijmen, V.: Threshold implementations against side-channel attacks and glitches. In: Ning, P., Qing, S., Li, N. (eds.) ICICS 2006. LNCS, vol. 4307, pp. 529–545. Springer, Heidelberg (2006). doi:10.1007/11935308_38

30. O'Flynn, C., Chen, Z.D.: Side channel power analysis of an AES-256 bootloader. In: CCECE, pp. 750–755. IEEE (2015)

31. Papapagiannopoulos, K.: High throughput in slices: the case of PRESENT, PRINCE and KATAN64 ciphers. In: Saxena, N., Sadeghi, A.-R. (eds.) RFID-Sec 2014. LNCS, vol. 8651, pp. 137–155. Springer, Cham (2014). doi:10.1007/978-3-319-13066-8_9

32. Poschmann, A., Moradi, A., Khoo, K., Lim, C., Wang, H., Ling, S.: Side-channel resistant crypto for less than 2, 300 GE. J. Cryptol. **24**(2), 322–345 (2011). doi:10.1007/s00145-010-9086-6

33. Poschmann, A.Y.: Lightweight cryptography: cryptographic engineering for a pervasive world. Ph.D. thesis, Ruhr University Bochum (2009). http://d-nb.info/996578153

34. Rodrigues, B., Pereira, F.M.Q., Aranha, D.F.: Sparse representation of implicit flows with applications to side-channel detection. In: CC, pp. 110–120. ACM (2016)

35. Schneier, B., Kelsey, J., Whiting, D., Wagner, D., Hall, C., Ferguson, N., Kohno, T., Stay, M.: The twofish team's final comments on AES selection. https://www.schneier.com/academic/paperfiles/paper-twofish-final.pdf. Accessed Mar 2017

36. Schwabe, P., Stoffelen, K.: All the AES you need on Cortex-M3 and M4. In: Avanzi, R., Heys, H. (eds.) Selected Areas in Cryptology - SAC 2016. LNCS. Springer, Heidelberg (2016). To appear

37. For Standardization, I.O.: ISO/IEC 29192-2:2012. https://www.iso.org/standard/56552.html. Accessed Feb 2017

38. Wang, M.: Differential cryptanalysis of PRESENT. IACR Cryptology ePrint Archive 2007, 408 (2007). http://eprint.iacr.org/2007/408

FourQ on Embedded Devices with Strong Countermeasures Against Side-Channel Attacks

Zhe Liu[1,2], Patrick Longa[3(✉)], Geovandro C.C.F. Pereira[2], Oscar Reparaz[4], and Hwajeong Seo[5]

[1] SnT, University of Luxembourg, Luxembourg City, Luxembourg
[2] IQC, University of Waterloo, Waterloo, Canada
{zhelu.liu,geovandro.pereira}@uwaterloo.ca
[3] Microsoft Research, Redmond, USA
plonga@microsoft.com
[4] imec-COSIC KU Leuven, Leuven, Belgium
oscar.reparaz@esat.kuleuven.be
[5] Hansung University, Seoul, Korea
hwajeong84@gmail.com

Abstract. This work deals with the energy-efficient, high-speed and high-security implementation of elliptic curve scalar multiplication and elliptic curve Diffie-Hellman (ECDH) key exchange on embedded devices using FourQ and incorporating strong countermeasures to thwart a wide variety of side-channel attacks. First, we set new speed records for *constant-time* curve-based scalar multiplication and DH key exchange at the 128-bit security level with implementations targeting 8, 16 and 32-bit microcontrollers. For example, our software computes a static ECDH shared secret in ~6.9 million cycles (or 0.86 s @8 MHz) on a low-power 8-bit AVR microcontroller which, compared to the fastest Curve25519 and genus-2 Kummer implementations on the same platform, offers 2× and 1.4× speedups, respectively. Similarly, it computes the same operation in ~496 thousand cycles on a 32-bit ARM Cortex-M4 microcontroller, achieving a factor-2.9 speedup when compared to the fastest Curve25519 implementation targeting the same platform. Second, we engineer a set of side-channel countermeasures taking advantage of FourQ's rich arithmetic and propose a secure implementation that offers protection against a wide range of sophisticated side-channel attacks. Finally, we perform a differential power analysis evaluation of our software running on an ARM Cortex-M4, and report that no leakage was detected with up to 10 million traces. These results demonstrate the potential of deploying FourQ on low-power applications such as protocols for IoT.

Keywords: Elliptic curves · FourQ · ECDH · Embedded devices · IoT · Energy efficiency · Side-channel attacks · Strong countermeasures

1 Introduction

Elliptic curve cryptography (ECC) is a popular public-key system that has become an attractive candidate to enable strong cryptography on constrained

© International Association for Cryptologic Research 2017
W. Fischer and N. Homma (Eds.): CHES 2017, LNCS 10529, pp. 665–686, 2017.
DOI: 10.1007/978-3-319-66787-4_32

devices. Its reduced key sizes and great performance are nicely matched by its solid security foundation based on the elliptic curve discrete logarithm problem (ECDLP). Hence, it is foremost relevant to research ECC-based mechanisms that could ameliorate efficiency and power limitations with the goal of making ECC suitable for constrained applications.

FourQ [16] is a high-performance elliptic curve that provides about 128 bits of security and enables efficient and secure scalar multiplications. Implementations based on this curve have been shown to achieve the fastest computations of variable-base, fixed-base and double scalar multiplications to date on a large variety of x64 and ARMv7–A processors [16,36]. This performance trait is especially attractive for IoT, when devices need to keep clock frequencies to a minimum (in order to fulfill limited power budgets) and yet need to minimize the impact on the device's response time. Moreover, FourQ's high speed is expected to have a direct positive impact in energy savings, since reduced computing time typically translates to lower energy consumption.

Side-Channel Attacks. Protection against side-channel attacks [32,33] represents another important aspect of the security in embedded devices. These attacks, which have been the focus of intense research since Kocher' seminal paper [33], can be classified as: *passive* attacks (a.k.a. side-channel analysis (SCA)), such as differential side-channel analysis (DSCA) [32], timing [33], correlation [6], collision [23] and template [8] attacks, among many other variants; and *active* attacks (a.k.a. fault attacks). Refer to [3,20] for detailed taxonomies of attacks and countermeasures. Certainly, most of these attacks can be rendered ineffective (or greatly limited in impact) by restricting the lifespan of secrets, for instance, by using *fully* ephemeral ECDH key exchange[1]. However, some protocols such as those based on static ECDH or ephemeral ECDH with cached public keys can be subjected to these attacks and, thus, might require additional defenses. In this work, we focus on *passive attacks*.

Our Contributions. We present the first implementations of FourQ-based scalar multiplication and ECDH key exchange on 8, 16, and 32-bit microcontrollers (MCUs), and demonstrate that this curve can deliver the fastest curve-based computations on embedded IoT devices, potentially helping to achieve stringent design goals in terms of response time and energy (see Sects. 3 and 4). For example, a static ECDH shared key is computed $2\times$, $1.8\times$, and $2.9\times$ faster than the fastest Curve25519 implementations on 8-bit AVR, 16-bit MSP430X, and 32-bit ARM Cortex-M4 MCUs, respectively.

In addition, we present, to the best of our knowledge, the first *publicly-available* design and implementation of an elliptic curve-based system that

---

[1] In some contexts, the term "ephemeral ECDH" is used even when public keys are cached and reused for a certain period of time. We stress that using fresh private and public keys per each key exchange (which we refer to as "fully ephemeral ECDH") greatly increases resilience against side-channel attacks and limits the attack surface.

includes defenses against a wide variety of passive attacks (see Sect. 5). Our protected scalar multiplication and ECDH algorithms, which include a set of efficient countermeasures that have been especially tailored for FourQ, are designed to minimize the risk of timing attacks, simple and differential side-channel analysis (SSCA/DSCA), correlation and collision attacks, and specialized attacks such as the doubling attack [23], the refined power attack (RPA) [25], zero-value point attacks (ZVP) [1], same value attacks (SVA) [38], exceptional procedure attacks [29], invalid point attacks [5], and small subgroup attacks. To assess the soundness of our algorithms, we carry out a differential power analysis evaluation on an STM32F4Discovery board containing a popular ARM Cortex-M4 MCU. We perform leakage detection tests and correlation power analysis attacks to verify that indeed the implemented countermeasures substantially increase the required attacker effort for unprofiled vertical attacks (see Sect. 6).

Previous works in the literature presenting protected ECC implementations only include basic countermeasures against a subset of the attacks we deal with in this paper [40,55]. Moreover, reported implementations (other than implementations exclusively protected against timing attacks [19]) have not been publicly released. Our software for ARM Cortex-M4 has been made publicly available as part of the FourQlib library [17]:

> https://github.com/Microsoft/FourQlib.

Likewise, the implementations for AVR and MSP are available at:

> https://github.com/geovandro/microFourQ-AVR, and
> https://github.com/geovandro/microFourQ-MSP.

Disclaimer. No software implementation can guarantee 100% side-channel security. In some cases, certain powerful attacks such as template attacks [8] can be carried out using a single target trace, making any randomization or masking technique useless [42]. Moreover, the issue gets more complicated for embedded devices that lack access to a good source of randomness. Since many SCA attacks closely depend on the underlying hardware, it is recommended to include additional countermeasures at the software and hardware levels depending on the targeted platform. Also, note that hardware countermeasures are usually required to properly deal with most sophisticated invasive attacks.

2   Preliminaries: FourQ

FourQ, introduced by Costello and Longa in 2015 [16], is defined by the complete twisted Edwards [4] equation $\mathcal{E}/\mathbb{F}_{p^2} : -x^2 + y^2 = 1 + dx^2y^2$, where the quadratic extension field $\mathbb{F}_{p^2} = \mathbb{F}_p(i)$ for $i^2 = -1$ and $p = 2^{127} - 1$, and $d = 125317048443780598345676279555970305165 \cdot i + 4205857648805777768770$. The prime order subgroup $\mathcal{E}(\mathbb{F}_{p^2})[N]$, where N is the 246-bit prime corresponding to $\#\mathcal{E}(\mathbb{F}_{p^2}) = 392 \cdot N$, is used to carry out cryptographic computations. In this subgroup, the neutral element is given by $\mathcal{O}_{\mathcal{E}} = (0,1)$.

Algorithm 1. FourQ's scalar multiplication on $\mathcal{E}(\mathbb{F}_{p^2})[N]$ (from [16]).

Input: Point $P \in \mathcal{E}(\mathbb{F}_{p^2})[N]$ and integer scalar $m \in [0, 2^{256})$.
Output: $[m]P$.

Compute endomorphisms and precompute lookup table:
1: Compute $\phi(P)$, $\psi(P)$ and $\psi(\phi(P))$.
2: Compute $T[u] = P + [u_0]\phi(P) + [u_1]\psi(P) + [u_2]\psi(\phi(P))$ for $u = (u_2, u_1, u_0)_2$ in $0 \le u \le 7$. Write $T[u]$ in coordinates $(X + Y, Y - X, 2Z, 2dT)$.

Scalar decomposition and recoding:
3: Decompose m into the multiscalar (a_1, a_2, a_3, a_4) as in [16, Prop. 5].
4: Recode (a_1, a_2, a_3, a_4) into $(d_{64}, \ldots, d_0)$ and $(m_{64}, \ldots, m_0)$ using [16, Alg. 1].
   Write $s_i = 1$ if $m_i = -1$ and $s_i = -1$ if $m_i = 0$.

Main loop:
5: $Q = s_{64} \cdot T[d_{64}]$
6: **for** $i = 63$ **to** 0 **do**
7:     $Q = [2]Q + s_i \cdot T[d_i]$
8: **return** Q

FourQ is equipped with *two* efficiently computable endomorphisms, ψ and ϕ, which give rise to four-dimensional decompositions. The computation of a constant-time, exception-free variable-base scalar multiplication with the form $[m]P$, where m is an integer in $[1, 2^{256})$ and P is a point from $\mathcal{E}(\mathbb{F}_{p^2})[N]$, proceeds as follows (see Algorithm 1). First, one needs to prepare an 8-point precomputed table at Steps 1–2 and execute the decomposition and recoding algorithms at Steps 3–4. As before, let a scalar m be any integer in $[1, 2^{256})$. FourQ's decomposition [16, Prop. 5] maps m to a set of *multiscalars* $(a_1, a_2, a_3, a_4) \in \mathbb{Z}^4$ such that $0 \le a_i < 2^{64}$ for $i = 1, ..., 4$ and such that a_1 is odd. These multiscalars are then recoded using [16, Alg. 1] to a representation consisting of exactly 65 "signed digit-columns" d_j and "sign masks" m_j for $j = 0, ..., 64$. Finally, the evaluation stage consists of an initial point loading and a single loop of 64 iterations, where each iteration consists of exactly one doubling and one addition.

2.1   Cofactor Elliptic Curve Diffie-Hellman Key Exchange

In this section, we describe the ECDH key exchange using FourQ in *two* variants: (i) using 64-byte public keys, and (ii) using compressed 32-byte public keys. Let's first define the following function denoted by "DH" [34]:

function DH(m, P)
    Check that P is on the curve. If not, return "FAILED".
    Compute $Q = [392]P$ and $T = [m]Q$.
    If $T = (0, 1)$ return "FAILED".
    Return T in affine coordinates.

Note that the function DH validates the input point P against the curve equation in order to thwart invalid point attacks. The multiplication by 392, which is not required to be computed in constant-time, clears the cofactor and guarantees that the point Q belongs to $\mathcal{E}(\mathbb{F}_{p^2})[N]$, as required by Algorithm 1 for the computation of $[m]Q$. This measure protects against small subgroup attacks.

An ECDH key exchange with 64-byte public keys can then be carried out as follows. Two users, Alice and Bob, pick random integers m_A and m_B (resp.) in the range $[0, 2^{256})$, and then compute the public keys $A = [m_A]G$ and $B = [m_B]G$ (resp.), where G is the generator. After exchanging public keys, Alice computes $K_A = \mathrm{DH}(m_A, B)$ and Bob computes $K_B = \mathrm{DH}(m_B, A)$. The y-coordinate of the value $K = K_A = K_B$ can then be used as the shared secret.

ECDH Key Exchange with 32-Byte Public Keys. It is possible to reduce the size of the public keys to only 32 bytes with the approach described next.

An element $y = a + b \cdot i \in \mathbb{F}_{p^2}$ encoded as $y = (a_0, ..., a_{126}, 0, b_0, ..., b_{126})$ is defined as "negative" if and only if $a_{126} = 1$, or if $b_{126} = 1$ and $a = 0$. We define Compress(P) as the function that takes as input a point $P = (x, y) \in E$ and encodes it as the 256-bit string $\underline{P} = (x, y)$, which is the 255-bit encoding of y followed by a sign bit; this sign bit is $\overline{1}$ if and only if x is negative. We define Expand(S) as the function that takes a 256-bit string S and recovers $P = (x, y)$ as follows: parse the first 255 bits as y, compute $u/v = (y^2 - 1)/(dy^2 + 1)$, and compute $\pm x = \sqrt{u/v}$, where the $\pm$ is chosen so that the sign of x matches the 256-th bit of the string S. Refer to [18, Appendix A] and [34, Appendix B] for low-level details about the decompression procedure.

The ECDH key exchange mechanism then proceeds as follows [34]. Alice and Bob pick random integers m_A and m_B (resp.) in the range $[0, 2^{256})$, and then compute the public keys $\underline{A} = \mathrm{Compress}([m_A]G)$ and $\underline{B} = \mathrm{Compress}([m_B]G)$ (resp.). After exchanging public keys, Alice computes $K_A = \mathrm{DH}(m_A, \mathrm{Expand}(\underline{B}))$ and Bob computes $K_B = \mathrm{DH}(m_B, \mathrm{Expand}(\underline{A}))$. As before, the y-coordinate of the value $K = K_A = K_B$ is the shared secret.

3   Implementation Details on AVR, MSP and ARM

In this section, we briefly describe relevant implementation aspects for *three* popular MCUs: 8-bit AVR ATmega, 16-bit MSP430X, and 32-bit ARM Cortex-M4. For more details, refer to the extended version of the paper [35].

3.1   Implementation of Arithmetic over $\mathbb{F}_{(2^{127}-1)^2}$

In contrast to traditional ECC curves, which are defined over a prime field $\mathbb{F}_p$, FourQ is defined over the quadratic extension field $\mathbb{F}_{p^2}$ for $p = 2^{127} - 1$. Let $a = a_0 + a_1 \cdot i, b = b_0 + b_1 \cdot i \in \mathbb{F}_{p^2}$. Operations in $\mathbb{F}_{p^2}$ are computed as follows

$$a \pm b = (a_0 \pm b_0) + (a_1 \pm b_1) \cdot i,$$
$$a \times b = (a_0 \cdot b_0 - a_1 \cdot b_1) + ((a_0 + a_1) \cdot (b_0 + b_1) - a_0 \cdot b_0 - a_1 \cdot b_1) \cdot i,$$
$$a^2 = (a_0 + a_1) \cdot (a_0 - a_1) + (2a_0 \cdot a_1) \cdot i,$$
$$a^{-1} = a_0 \cdot (a_0^2 + a_1^2)^{-1} - a_1 \cdot (a_0^2 + a_1^2)^{-1} \cdot i,$$

where operations on the right are carried out in $\mathbb{F}_p$. Naïvely, multiplication requires three integer multiplications, three modular reductions, two field additions and three field subtractions, whereas squaring requires only two integer multiplications, two modular reductions, two field additions and one field subtraction.

We improve the performance of multiplication and squaring in $\mathbb{F}_{p^2}$ by transforming field additions into simple integer additions. This is possible because our integer multiplication accepts inputs in the extended range $[0, 2^{128})$. For the case of Cortex-M4, we speed up multiplication in $\mathbb{F}_{p^2}$ by exploiting lazy reduction, which allows the elimination of one modular reduction by delaying the reductions of the products until the very end of the computation.

Field inversions a^{-1} (mod p) are computed via Fermat's Little Theorem as a^{p-2} (mod p), using a fixed multiplication-and-squaring chain with 126 field squarings and 10 field multiplications in order to have a constant-time execution.

Modular reduction is particularly efficient on FourQ. Let $r = a + b$ be the result of adding two operands in $\mathbb{F}_p$. To reduce this result, one only needs to reset the 128-th bit of r and then perform an addition between that top bit and the updated value of r, i.e., given $0 \le r < 2 \cdot (2^{127} - 1)$, compute $a + b$ (mod p) as r (mod $2^{127}) + (r \gg 127)$. For example, assume that the intermediate result r of the addition is stored in the 16 AVR registers r0:r15. Then, modular reduction can be efficiently implemented using AVR assembly as follows

MOV r16, r15 $\rightarrow$ ANDI r15, 0x7F $\rightarrow$ ADD r16, r16 $\rightarrow$ ADC r0, 0 $\rightarrow \cdots \rightarrow$ ADC r15, 0

A similar procedure applies to reductions after multiplications and squarings, with the difference that reduction is, in these cases, applied to an intermediate result with double precision (i.e., 32 bytes). Specifically, given an input $0 \le r < (2^{127} - 1)^2$, the fast reduction algorithm requires two consecutive rounds computing $r \leftarrow r$ (mod $2^{127}) + (r \gg 127)$.

3.2 Implementation on 8-Bit AVR ATmega

AVR microcontrollers have a modified Harvard architecture that features 32 8-bit general-purpose registers denoted by r0:r31. From this pool of registers, the last three pairs, called X (r27:r26), Y (r29:r28), and Z (r31:r30), are used as 16-bit address pointers to load and store data from memory. The AVR instruction set supports a total of 133 instructions, and each instruction has a fixed latency; for example, ordinary arithmetic/logical instructions such as addition (ADD) and addition with carry (ADC) are executed in a single clock cycle, while unsigned multiplication (MUL) as well as load/store instructions take two clock cycles.

For our benchmarks, we used the IAR Embedded Workbench – AVR 6.80.7, which features an assembler and a cycle-accurate graphical simulator, and targeted the ATxmega256A3 model. This specific microcontroller has 256 KB of programmable flash memory, 16 KB of SRAM and 4 KB of EEPROM, and operates at a maximum frequency of 32 MHz.

Finite Field Operations. For the 128-bit integer multiplication, we use 2-level Karatsuba in a recursive way, with the low level 32-bit multiplications implemented in product-scanning form. For the 128-bit squaring, we employ the Sliding Block Doubling (SBD) method [49]. In order to minimize the use of load/store instructions, integer multiplication and squaring were integrated with the modular reduction at the assembly level. Modular reduction over the prime $p = 2^{127} - 1$ as well as the arithmetic over $\mathbb{F}_{p^2}$ were implemented as described in Sect. 3.1.

3.3   Implementation on 16-Bit MSP430X

The ultra-low power MSP430X is a representative 16-bit microcontroller that includes support for 27 core instructions and 16 registers (r0:r15). It also includes an external 16-bit or 32-bit hardware multiplier that operates in parallel to the CPU. The multiplier offers three different modes: MPY (unsigned multiplication), MPYS (signed multiplication) and MAC (unsigned multiply-and-accumulate). In general, other instructions take one cycle when working with general-purpose registers.

   In our benchmarks, we targeted the MSP430FR5969 model, which is suitable for use in wireless sensor nodes. This MCU features 2 KB of SRAM and 64 KB of FRAM (code) memory, and operates at up to 16 MHz. We followed the same methodology for cycle count acquisition that was employed for AVR using the IAR Embedded Workbench (MSP430 6.50.1).

Finite Field Operations. We make extensive use of the 16-bit MAC operation available in the targeted MSP430X microcontroller. This operation, which computes $16 \times 16 + 32 \to 33$-bit, was used as basic block to realize a 128-bit integer multiplication in a column-wise way [26]. Squaring was implemented using the SBD method, as in the case of AVR. Modular reduction and the arithmetic over $\mathbb{F}_{p^2}$ were implemented as described in Sect. 3.1.

3.4   Implementation on 32-Bit ARM Cortex–M4

Cortex-M4 [2] is part of the increasingly popular ARM Cortex-M family, which includes a wide range of 32-bit RISC ARM microcontrollers. It supports the ARMv7E-M instruction set, which comprises Thumb-2 instructions and additional saturating/SIMD instructions called the "DSP extension". The Cortex-M4 architecture has a 3-stage pipeline with branch speculation, includes 16 32-bit registers (r0:r15), and supports a mix of 16 and 32-bit operations corresponding to Thumb-2. Field arithmetic can take advantage of the powerful single-cycle multiply and multiply-and-accumulate instructions from the DSP extension: UMUL, UMLAL, and UMAAL. These instructions compute the product 32×32-bit $\to 64$-bit (UMUL), plus a 64-bit accumulation with a single 64-bit value (UMLAL) or plus a 64-bit accumulation with two 32-bit values (UMAAL).

To evaluate the performance of our implementation, we use an STM32F4Discovery board [52] that contains a 32-bit ARM Cortex-M4F STM32F407VGT6 microcontroller. This MCU has 1 MB of flash memory, 192 KB of SRAM and 64 KB of CCM (core coupled memory) data RAM, and can be clocked at a frequency of up to 168 MHz. Compilation was performed with the GNU ARM Embedded toolchain and GNU GCC v4.9.2.

Finite Field Operations. Integer multiplication was implemented using the schoolbook method and the efficient MAC instructions. The computation of a field multiplication is then completed with the execution of the modular reduction described in Sect. 3.1. However, in the case of multiplication in $\mathbb{F}_{p^2}$ we do much better by applying lazy reduction on a basic schoolbook multiplication that computes $a \times b$ as $(a_0 \cdot b_0 - a_1 \cdot b_1) + (a_0 \cdot b_1 + a_1 \cdot b_0) \cdot i$ for elements $a = a_0 + a_1 \cdot i, b = b_0 + b_1 \cdot i \in \mathbb{F}_{p^2}$.

4   Results and Analysis of Constant-Time Implementations

In this section, we summarize implementation results for 8-bit AVR, 16-bit MSP430X, and 32-bit ARM Cortex-M4 microcontrollers. Our FourℚQ implementations are based on Algorithm 1 for the case of variable-base scalar multiplication. For the case of fixed-base scalar multiplication, we use the modified LSB-set comb method from [21, Algorithm 5], which requires a table with $v \cdot 2^{w-1}$ points (v and w denote the number of internal tables and their window size, respectively).

The implemented algorithms guarantee regular, exception-free execution (see Sect. 2) and run in constant-time. Hence, they are protected against timing and exceptional procedure attacks. Note that cache attacks do not apply to the targeted AVR ATmega MCU, since its architecture does not support the use of cache memory. Although the MSP430FR MCU family presents some form of integrated caching, it is activated when the MCU operates at a higher frequency than the access frequency of the FRAM [54] (i.e., the FRAM can be operated at up to 8 MHz without use of this cache). Since we fix the frequency at 8 MHz, our software runs in constant-time with no risk of timing leakage. Finally, the targeted Cortex-M4 STM32F4 MCU includes a cache memory to accelerate flash memory accesses [53]. However, our software does not use flash memory to store the precomputed tables and, therefore, cache attacks do not apply.

At the high-level, we implemented the ECDH schemes described in Sect. 2.1, which are protected against invalid point and small subgroup attacks.

Results. Table 1 summarizes the results for variable-base and fixed-base scalar multiplication, static ECDH and fully ephemeral ECDH key exchange for the three targeted microcontrollers. In the case of ECDH with FourQ, we evaluate the use of both 32 and 64-byte public keys. For comparison, we include two efficient alternatives that have been deployed on various microcontrollers: the "μKummer" implementation by Renes et al. [46] using the genus-2 Kummer surface by Gaudry and Schost [24], and the "Curve25519" implementations by Düll et al. [19] and De Santis et al. [48]. The Kummer surface enables fast static DH key exchange with a small footprint. However, it does not support efficient, exception-free fixed-base algorithms which inject a significant speedup in settings such as ephemeral DH key exchange, signature key generation and signing. μKummer's DH public keys are also 50% larger (compared to options that use 32-byte public keys). In the case of Curve25519, although this curve supports efficient fixed-base computations via its isomorphic Edwards form, Curve25519 implementations typically target static ECDH and, thus, do not offer this optimization option (as is the case of [19, 48]).

As can be seen in Table 1, our FourQ-based implementations set new speed records for scalar multiplication and ECDH by a large margin on all of the targeted platforms. In particular, for variable-base computations, FourQ is $2.1\times$, $1.9\times$, and $3\times$ faster than Curve25519 on AVR, MSP430X, and Cortex-M4, respectively. These results are roughly the same when considering static ECDH. Similarly, for the case of ephemeral ECDH our implementations are between $2.4\times$ and $3.9\times$ faster than Curve25519 implementations without fixed-base support. When compared against μKummer on AVR, FourQ achieves roughly factor-1.4 speedup for computing variable-base scalar multiplication and static ECDH. This gap has a significant increase to factor-2 speedup when considering the case of ephemeral ECDH. Note that the Kummer surface has not been implemented on MSP430X and Cortex-M4 MCUs.

As consequence of the reduction in computing time, our implementations allow a significant reduction in energy costs. For example, following [44] we estimate that our software demands 41.65mJ of energy to compute a fully ephemeral ECDH key exchange with 32-byte public keys (or, equivalently, $\sim$162,064 key exchanges for the life of a double AA battery) on a MICAz sensor node containing an 8-bit AVR MCU. When comparing against similar calculations for other curves, we observe that our FourQ implementation on AVR is able to run $2.7\times$ and $1.9\times$ more key exchanges than Curve25519 and μKummer (resp.) for the same battery budget.

Table 1. Performance (in cycles) of scalar multiplication and ECDH operations on 8-bit AVR ATmega, 16-bit MSP430X, and 32-bit ARM Cortex-M4 microcontrollers for different state-of-the-art implementations. Cycle counts are rounded to the nearest 10^2 cycles.

Source	Scalar multiplication		ECDH	
	Fixed-base	Random	Static	Ephemeral
8-bit AVR ATmega				
Curve25519 [19]	13,900,400[a]	13,900,400	13,900,400[c]	27,800,800[b,c]
μKummer [46]	9,513,500[a]	9,513,500	9,739,100[d]	19,027,100[b,d]
FourQ (this work)	**2,980,700**	**6,505,300**	**6,886,400[e]**	**9,870,500[e]**
			7,221,300[c]	**10,206,500[c]**
16-bit MSP430X (16-bit multiplier) @8 MHz				
Curve25519 [19]	7,933,300[a]	7,933,300	7,933,300[c]	15,866,600[b,c]
FourQ (this work)	**1,851,300**	**4,280,400**	**4,527,900[e]**	**6,379,200[e]**
			4,826,100[c]	**6,677,400[c]**
32-bit ARM Cortex-M4				
Curve25519 [48]	1,423,700[a]	1,423,700	1,423,700[c]	2,847,400[b,c]
FourQ (this work)	**232,900**	**469,500**	**496,400[e]**	**729,900[e]**
			542,900[c]	**776,600[c]**

[a] Montgomery ladder is used for fixed-base and variable-base scalar multiplication.
[b] Estimated, since authors only provided counts for static ECDH.
[c,d,e] Public key sizes are 32, 48 and 64 bytes, respectively.

5   Side-Channel Countermeasures

This section begins with a description of countermeasures especially tailored for FourQ. Then, we present our protected scalar multiplication algorithm and cover implementation aspects of table lookups and a protected ECDH key exchange scheme. Finally, we discuss the rationale behind our protected algorithms.

5.1   Specialized Side-Channel Countermeasures for FourQ

The use of randomization, if done properly, greatly increases the effort needed to perform DSCA and other similar attacks, both in terms of data complexity (number of measurements needed [7]) and computational effort (time to perform the attack [47]). In an ECC scalar multiplication operation there is ample room for randomization of internal computations, especially on curves such as FourQ because of its rich underlying mathematical structure. Coron proposed *three* randomization techniques to protect ECC against DPA attacks: scalar randomization, point blinding and projective coordinate randomization [15]. Other popular methods include key splitting [10], and random curve and field isomorphisms [30].

Next, we describe especially-tailored scalar randomization and point blinding techniques optimized for use with FourQ.

Scalar Randomization. The typical approach is to randomize the scalar m by adding a multiple of the curve order $\#E$ using a random value r, i.e., computing $m' = m + r \cdot \#E$. It is well known that this randomization can be ineffective if the prime p has a special structure [9,10,41,50]. Indeed, when p is a pseudo-Mersenne prime with the form $2^k - c$ for small c, by Hasse's theorem the binary representation of the top half of the curve order $\#E$ consists of either only 1's or a 1 followed by 0's and, thus, the most significant bits of $m + r\#E$ are those of m. As consequence, the random value r must be greater than $\approx k/2$ as a minimum requirement, which means that the cost of protected implementations of curves such as Curve25519 increase by at least 50% when using this countermeasure.

We avoid this significant performance degradation by specializing the GLV-based scalar randomization by Ciet et al. [11] to FourQ. Our explicit counter-measure is described below.

Proposition 1 (Scalar Randomization). *Let the multiscalars (a'_1, a'_2, a'_3, a'_4) $= (a_1, a_2, a_3, a_4) + \mathbf{c}$ be the decomposition result of a given integer m, as defined in [16, Prop. 5], where $\mathbf{c} = 5\mathbf{b}_2 - 3\mathbf{b}_3 + 2\mathbf{b}_4$ is a vector in the lattice of zero decompositions $\mathcal{L}$ and $\mathbf{B} = (\mathbf{b}_1, \mathbf{b}_2, \mathbf{b}_3, \mathbf{b}_4)$ is the Babai optimal basis in [16, Prop. 3]. Let $\mathbf{V} = (\mathbf{v}_1, \mathbf{v}_2, \mathbf{v}_3, \mathbf{v}_4) = (\mathbf{b}_2 - \mathbf{b}_3 + \mathbf{b}_4, 2\mathbf{b}_2 - \mathbf{b}_3 + \mathbf{b}_4, \mathbf{b}_1 + \mathbf{b}_2 + \mathbf{b}_4, \mathbf{b}_1 + 2\mathbf{b}_2 - \mathbf{b}_3 + \mathbf{b}_4)$ be a matrix of four independent vectors in $\mathcal{L}$ such that $||\mathbf{v}_i||_\infty < 2^{62}$ for $i = 1, \ldots, 4$, and let $\mathbf{r} = (r_1, r_2, r_3, r_4)$ be a vector with random integer elements in $[0, 2^{16})$. Then, the multiscalar set $(a'_1, a'_2, a'_3, a'_4) + \mathbf{r} \cdot (\mathbf{v}_1, \mathbf{v}_2, \mathbf{v}_3, \mathbf{v}_4)$ is a valid decomposition of m with all four randomly-generated coordinates less than 2^{80}.*

Refer to the extended version of the paper [35] for the proof of Proposition 1.

Proposition 1 specifies the countermeasure procedure with $4 \times 16 = 64$ bits of randomization. This brings enough entropy to provide security against several attacks, especially when combined with additional countermeasures (see Sect. 5.2), while requiring a relatively low overhead in comparison with other curves (the cost of FourQ's scalar multiplication is only increased by 25% in this case).

Point Blinding. The typical approach is to compute $[m]P$ as $[m](P + R) - S$ for a randomly-generated secret point R and a precomputed point $S = [m]R$. To avoid the cost of an extra scalar multiplication, Coron suggests that R and S are updated at each new execution using $R = [(-1)^b 2]R$ and $S = [(-1)^b 2]S$ for a random bit b. Nevertheless, the method still requires storage for two points and the computation of a full scalar multiplication if the value of m is changed.

It is possible to do better using the extended-binary-based-method with RIP (called "EBRIP") due to Mamiya et al. [37]. In this case, $[m]P$ is computed as

$([m]P + R) - R$ using a random point R. The value in parenthesis is computed by splitting m in t portions of equal length and running a t-way simultaneous scalar multiplication in which R is represented as $[(1\bar{1}\bar{1}\ldots\bar{1})_2]R$.

Adapting EBRIP to FourℚQ is straightforward: it suffices to assume $t = 4$ and adjust the precomputed values which, in the case of FourℚQ, use the endomorphisms. The details are shown in Algorithm 2. The overhead of the method is small: the number of precomputations increases from 8 to 16 points (adding 8 extra point additions to the cost), and a final correction subtracting R is required at the end of scalar multiplication.

We note that typical update functions for blinding points offer poor randomization, making them an easy target of collision-like attacks [23, 41]. We improve resilience against these attacks with an inexpensive change to the new update function $R = [(-1)^b 3]R$ for a random bit b.

5.2   Protected Scalar Multiplication

Algorithm 2 details our scalar multiplication routine with SCA countermeasures, including the scalar randomization and point blinding techniques described above. Note that we also make extensive use of projective coordinate randomization [15]. This technique is a form of multiplicative masking: in our case, a non-zero element $r \in \mathbb{F}_{2^{127}-1}$ is applied to points (X, Y, Z) in homogeneous projective coordinates to obtain the equivalent *randomized* tuple $(r{\cdot}X, r{\cdot}Y, r{\cdot}Z)$.

Protected ECDH Key Exchange. In order to use Algorithm 2, the function DH described in Sect. 2.1 only needs minor changes and the inclusion of a blinding point B. We assume that a fresh blinding point is generated during key generation, and the value passed and updated each time the protected ECDH function is invoked. The modified function is shown below.

   function DH_SCA(m, P, B)
      Check that P and B are on the curve. If not, return "FAILED".
      Compute $Q = [392]P$.
      Compute $T = [m]Q$ and update B using Algorithm 2.
      If $T = (0, 1)$ return "FAILED", else return T and B in affine.

The function DH_SCA can be directly used in place of the function DH in the ECDH key exchange schemes using 32 and 64-byte public keys that were described in Sect. 2.1. As explained before, these functions are protected against invalid point and small subgroup attacks.

Reducing Table Lookup Leakage. Table lookups are common to many ECC algorithms (including the proposed routine) and, hence, their secure implementation is crucial. Most works in the literature use *constant-time* table lookups, which simply perform a linear pass over the whole table, masking out the correct result using logical instructions. This masking typically employs masks that are all 0's or 1's, which may be relatively easy to distinguish through SPA.

Algorithm 2. SCA-protected FourQ's scalar multiplication on $\mathcal{E}(\mathbb{F}_{p^2})[N]$.

Input: Point $P = (x_P, y_P)$, blinding point $R = (x_R, y_R) \in \mathcal{E}(\mathbb{F}_{p^2})[N]$, integer scalar m and random value $s \in [0, 2^{256})$, a random bit b, and random values $[r_{81}, r_{80}, \ldots, r_0] \in \mathbb{F}_p^{82}$.

Output: $[m]P$ and updated point R.

Randomize input points and update blinding point R:

1: Set $R = (r_{81} \cdot x_R, r_{81} \cdot y_R, r_{81})$.

2: Compute $R = [(-1)^b 3]R$.

3: Set $P = (r_{80} \cdot x_P, r_{80} \cdot y_P, r_{80})$.

Compute endomorphisms and precompute lookup table:

4: Compute $\phi(P)$, $\psi(P)$ and $\psi(\phi(P))$.

5: Compute $T[u] = -R + [u_0]P + [u_1]\phi(P) + [u_2]\psi(P) + [u_3]\psi(\phi(P))$ for $u = (u_3, u_2, u_1, u_0)_2$ in $0 \leq u \leq 15$. Write $T[u]$ in coordinates (X, Y, Z).

Scalar decomposition, randomization and recoding:

6: Decompose m into the multiscalar (a_1, a_2, a_3, a_4) as in [16, Prop. 5].

7: Randomize (a_1, a_2, a_3, a_4) as in Proposition 1 and recode to digit-columns $(d_{79}, \ldots, d_0)$ s.t. $d_i = a_1[i] + 2a_2[i] + 4a_3[i] + 8a_4[i]$ for $i = 0, \ldots, 79$.

Main loop:

8: $Q = R$

9: **for** $i = 79$ **to** 0 **do**

10:    $S = (r_i \cdot X_{T[d_i]}, r_i \cdot Y_{T[d_i]}, r_i \cdot Z_{T[d_i]})$.

11:    $Q = [2]Q + S$

12: **return** $(Q - R)$ and R in affine coordinates.

One way to reduce the potential leakage is by using masks with the same Hamming weight. For example, one could use the masking strategy shown below (to extract $T[d]$ from a 16-point table T, as required at Step 10 of Algorithm 2).

```
v = 0xAA...A, S ← T[0]    // Table index (d) is between 0 and 15
for i = 1 to 15
    d--    // While d >= 0 mask = 0x55...5, else mask = 0xAA...A
    mask = ((top_bit(d) - 1) & ~ v)|(~ (top_bit(d) - 1) & v)
    S ← ((mask & (S^T[i]))^S)^(v & (S^T[i]))
return S = T[d]
```

In this case, the bulk of the extraction procedure is carried out with the new mask values 0x55...5 (used to update S with the current table entry) and 0xAA...A (used to keep the current value of S). Operations over these masks are expected to produce traces that are more difficult to distinguish from each other. Note, however, that this does not eliminate all the potential leakage. For example, a sophisticated attacker might try to reveal the secret digit by observing the operation (top_bit(d) - 1) inside the derivation of mask, which produces intermediate all-0 or all-1 values. Nevertheless, this operation happens only once per iteration (in contrast to the multiple, word-wise use of the other masks), so the strategy above does reduce the attack surface significantly.

Another potential attack is to apply a horizontal attack on the table outputs. By default, our routine applies projective coordinate randomization after each point extraction (at Step 10). When horizontal collision-correlation attacks apply, one could reduce the potential leakage by doing a full table randomization at each iteration and before point extraction. This technique should also increase the effectiveness of the countermeasures described above.

Analysis of the Protected Algorithms. First, it is easy to see that the SCA-protected scalar multiplication in Algorithm 2 inherits the properties of regularity and completeness from Algorithm 1 when using complete twisted Edwards formulas [28]. This means that computations work for any possible input point in $\mathcal{E}(\mathbb{F}_{p^2})$ and any 32-byte scalar string, which thwarts exceptional procedure attacks [29]. Likewise, [16, Proposition 5] and Proposition 1 lend themselves to constant-time implementations of the scalar decomposition and randomization. This, together with field, extension field and table lookup operations implemented with no secret-dependent branches and no secret-memory addresses, guarantees protection against timing [33] and cache attacks [43]. E.g., refer to Sect. 3 for details about our constant-time implementations of the $\mathbb{F}_p$ and $\mathbb{F}_{p^2}$ arithmetic for several MCUs. Additionally, note that the use of regular, constant-time algorithms also protects against SSCA attacks such as SPA [32]. In some platforms, however, some computations might have distinctive operand-dependent power/EM signatures even when the execution flow is constant. Our frequent coordinate randomization and the techniques for minimizing table lookup leakage discussed before should make SSCA attacks exploiting such leakage impractical.

The use of point blinding effectively protects against RPA [25], ZVP [1] and SVA [38] attacks, since the attacker is not able to freely use the input point P to generate special values or collisions during intermediate computations. Poorly-randomized update functions for the blinding point has been the target of collision attacks [23]. We first note that intermediate values in the EBRIP algorithm [37] have the form $R + Q$ or $[2]R + Q$ for some point Q and blinding point R. Therefore, a naïve update function such as $R = [(-1)^b 2]R$ for a random bit b allows an attacker to find collisions since an updated blinding value $[2]R$ generates values that match those of the preceding scalar multiplication. The easy change to the function $R = [(-1)^b 3]R$ at Step 2 of Algorithm 2 eliminates the possibility of such collisions, since values calculated with $[3]R$ and $[6]R$ do not appear in a preceding computation.

Our combined use of different randomization techniques, namely randomization of projective coordinates at different stages (Steps 1, 3 and 10), randomization of the scalar and blinding of the base point, injects a high level of randomization to intermediate computations. This is expected to reduce leakage that could be useful to carry out correlation, collision-correlation and template attacks. Moreover, in some cases our especially-tailored countermeasures for FourQ offer better protection in comparison with other elliptic curves. For example, Feix et al. [22] presents vertical and horizontal collision-correlation attacks on ECC implementations with scalar randomization and point blinding countermeasures. They essentially exploit that randomizing with multiples of the order is ineffective on curves such as the NIST curves and Curve25519, as we explain in Sect. 5.1. Our 64-bit scalar randomization does not have this disadvantage and is more cost effective.

As previously discussed, some attacks could target collisions between the precomputed values in Step 5 of Algorithm 2 and their secret use at Step 11 after point extraction (for example, using techniques from [27]). One way to increase resilience against this class of attacks is by randomizing the full table before each point extraction using coordinate randomization, and minimizing the attack surface through some clever masking via a linear pass over the full table (this in order to thwart attacks targeting memory accesses [40]). However, other more sophisticated countermeasures might be required to protect against recent one-trace template attacks that inspect memory accesses [39]. We remark that some variants of these attacks are only adequately mitigated at lower abstraction levels, i.e., the underlying hardware architecture should be noisy enough such that these attacks become impractical.

Performance. To assess the performance impact of our countermeasures, we refactored our implementation for ARM Cortex-M4 (Sect. 3.4) using the algorithms proposed in this section. In summary, our software computes a static ECDH shared secret in about 1.18 and 1.14 million cycles using 32 and 64-byte public keys, respectively. Therefore, the strong countermeasures induce a roughly 2× slowdown in comparison with the constant-time-only implementation. Notably, these results are still up to 1.25x faster than the fastest constant-time-only Curve25519 results (see Table 1). We comment that, if greater protection is required, adding full table randomization before point extraction at Step 10 of Algorithm 2 increases the cost of static ECDH to 2.60 and 2.55 million cycles, resp.

6   Side-Channel Evaluation: Case Study with Cortex–M4

The main goal of the evaluation is to assess the DPA security of the implementation. Our randomization techniques are meant to protect mainly against vertical DPA attacks (cf. [12] for this notation). In a vertical DPA attack, the adversary collects many traces corresponding to the multiplication of a known varying input point with a secret scalar. This situation matches, for example, ECDH key exchange protocols. Vertical DPA attacks are probably the easiest to carry out.

Assumptions. We assume that the adversary cannot distinguish values from a single side-channel measurement. In particular, the (small) table indices cannot be retrieved from a single measurement. This assumption is common in practice (cf. [31, Sect. 4.1] or [45, Sect. 3.1]) and is usually provided by the underlying hardware. Note that masking does not make sense if this assumption is violated, since then it would be trivial to unmask all the required shares to reconstruct the secrets. Masking needs a minimum level of noise to be meaningful [7,51].

Platform. Our platform is a 32-bit ARM Cortex-M4 STM32F100RB processor with no dedicated security features. We acquire EM traces from a decoupling capacitor in the power line with a Langer RF-5U EM probe and 20 dB amplification. This platform is very low noise: DPA on an unprotected byte-oriented AES implementation succeeds with 15 traces. We give a comfortable setting to the evaluator: he has access to the source code and the code contains extra routines for triggering that allow precise alignment of traces.

The EM traces comprise two inner iterations of the main loop (Step 9 in Algorithm 2) as we show in Fig. 1.

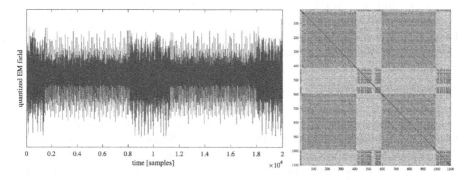

Fig. 1. Left: exemplary EM trace. Right: cross correlation of a single trace.

Methodology. We use two complementary techniques: leakage detection and key-recovery attacks. Failing a leakage detection test [13,14] is a necessary, yet not sufficient, condition for key-extracting attacks to work. When an implementation passes a leakage detection test, no data dependency is detected, and hence key-recovery attacks will not work. For key-recovery attacks, we resort to standard CPA attacks [6]; the device behavior is modeled as Hamming weight of register values. As an intermediate targeted sensitive variable we choose the point Q after execution of Step 11 in Algorithm 2. We first test each randomizing countermeasure described in Sect. 5.1 in isolation (all others switched off); later the full Algorithm 2 is evaluated. To test the effectiveness of each countermeasure, we first perform the analysis when the countermeasure is switched off. In this situation, a key-recovery attack is expected to work and a leakage detection test is expected to fail. This serves to confirm that the setup is indeed sound. Then, we repeat the same evaluation when the countermeasure is switched on. The analysis is expected not to show leakage and the CPA attacks are expected to fail. This means that the countermeasure (and *only* it) is effective.

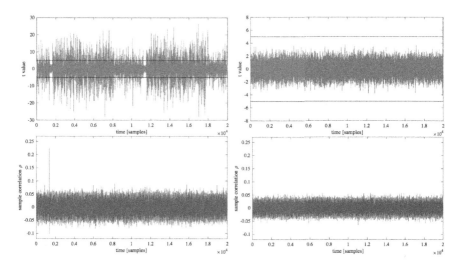

Fig. 2. Top row: fixed-vs-random leakage detection test on the input point. Bottom: CPA attacks. Left column: no countermeasure enabled. Right column: point blinding on/coord. randomization off/scalar randomization off.

No countermeasure. In the first scenario we switch off all countermeasures by fixing the PRNG output to a constant value known to the evaluator. In Fig. 2 top left, we plot the result of a non-specific leakage detection test (fix-vs-random on input point) for $5,000$ traces. We can see that the t-statistic clearly exceeds the threshold $C = \pm 4.5$, indicating severe leakage. In Fig. 2, bottom left, we plot the result of a key-recovery CPA attack (red for correct subkey hypothesis, green for others). The attack works (sample correlation ρ for the correct subkey hypothesis stands out at $\rho \approx 0.22$).

Point blinding. Here we test the point blinding countermeasure in isolation. We take $5,000$ traces when the point blinding countermeasure is switched on. The evaluator does not know the initial PRNG seed that feeds the masks. In Fig. 2, top right, we plot the t-statistic value of the non-specific fix-vs-random leakage detection test on the input point. The t-statistic does not surpass the threshold C. Thus, no first-order leakage is detected.

The results of the CPA attack are in Fig. 2, bottom right. The attack does not recover the key, as expected. (In this CPA attack and subsequent ones, the evaluator computes predictions averaging over 2^{10} independent random PRNG seeds, for each subkey hypothesis. This is possible since the evaluator has access to the source code).

Projective coordinate randomization. We use the same test fixture (fix-vs-random on input point) to test the projective coordinate randomization. In Fig. 3, top left, we plot the result of the leakage detection test. No first-order leakage is detected. The DPA attack is unsatisfactory as Fig. 3, bottom left, shows.

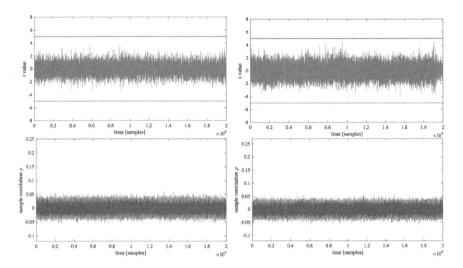

Fig. 3. Left: point blinding off/coord. randomization on/scalar randomization off. Right: point blinding off/coord. randomization off/scalar randomization on.

Scalar randomization. Here we perform a fix-vs-random test on the key when the input point is kept fix. In this way, we hope to detect leakages coming from an incomplete randomization of the key. In Fig. 3, top right, we plot the result of this leakage detection test. No first-order leakage is detected. For the CPA attack, we keep the key fixed (secret) and vary the input basepoint. The CPA attack does not work, as Fig. 3, bottom right, shows.

All countermeasures switched on. The implementation is meant to be executed with all the countermeasures switched on. We took 10 million traces and performed a fix-vs-random leakage detection test. No first-order leakage was detected (Fig. 4).

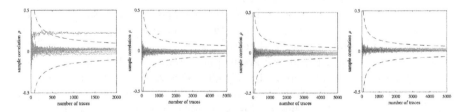

Fig. 4. Evolution of ρ as function of number of traces. Left to right (point blinding/coord. randomization/scalar randomization): off/off/off, on/off/off, off/on/off, off/off/on.

Acknowledgments. We would like to thank Craig Costello for helping in the design of the scalar randomization countermeasure, and Diego F. Aranha, Pedro R.N. Pedruzzi, Joost Renes and the reviewers for their valuable comments. Geovandro Pereira was partially supported by NSERC, CryptoWorks21, and Public Works and Government Services Canada. Oscar Reparaz was partially supported by the Research Council KU Leuven C16/15/058. Hwajeong Seo was supported by the ICT R&D program of MSIP/IITP (B0717-16-0097, Development of V2X Service Integrated Security Technology for Autonomous Driving Vehicle).

References

1. Akishita, T., Takagi, T.: Zero-value point attacks on elliptic curve cryptosystem. In: Boyd, C., Mao, W. (eds.) ISC 2003. LNCS, vol. 2851, pp. 218–233. Springer, Heidelberg (2003). doi:10.1007/10958513_17

2. ARM Limited: Cortex-M4 technical reference manual (2009–2010). http://infocenter.arm.com/help/topic/com.arm.doc.ddi0439b/DDI0439B_cortex_m4_r0p0_trm.pdf

3. Avanzi, R.M.: Side channel attacks on implementations of curve-based cryptographic primitives. IACR Cryptology ePrint Archive, Report 2005/017 (2005). http://eprint.iacr.org/2005/017

4. Bernstein, D.J., Birkner, P., Joye, M., Lange, T., Peters, C.: Twisted Edwards curves. In: Vaudenay, S. (ed.) AFRICACRYPT 2008. LNCS, vol. 5023, pp. 389–405. Springer, Heidelberg (2008). doi:10.1007/978-3-540-68164-9_26

5. Biehl, I., Meyer, B., Müller, V.: Differential fault attacks on elliptic curve cryptosystems. In: Bellare, M. (ed.) CRYPTO 2000. LNCS, vol. 1880, pp. 131–146. Springer, Heidelberg (2000). doi:10.1007/3-540-44598-6_8

6. Brier, E., Clavier, C., Olivier, F.: Correlation power analysis with a leakage model. In: Joye, M., Quisquater, J.-J. (eds.) CHES 2004. LNCS, vol. 3156, pp. 16–29. Springer, Heidelberg (2004). doi:10.1007/978-3-540-28632-5_2

7. Chari, S., Jutla, C.S., Rao, J.R., Rohatgi, P.: Towards sound approaches to counteract power-analysis attacks. In: Wiener, M. (ed.) CRYPTO 1999. LNCS, vol. 1666, pp. 398–412. Springer, Heidelberg (1999). doi:10.1007/3-540-48405-1_26

8. Chari, S., Rao, J.R., Rohatgi, P.: Template attacks. In: Kaliski, B.S., Koç, Ç.K., Paar, C. (eds.) CHES 2002. LNCS, vol. 2523, pp. 13–28. Springer, Heidelberg (2003). doi:10.1007/3-540-36400-5_3

9. Ciet, M.: Aspects of fast and secure arithmetics for elliptic curve cryptography. Ph.D. thesis, Université Catholique de Louvain, Louvain-la-Neuve (2003)

10. Ciet, M., Joye, M.: (Virtually) Free randomization techniques for elliptic curve cryptography. In: Qing, S., Gollmann, D., Zhou, J. (eds.) ICICS 2003. LNCS, vol. 2836, pp. 348–359. Springer, Heidelberg (2003). doi:10.1007/978-3-540-39927-8_32

11. Ciet, M., Quisquater, J.-J., Sica, F.: Preventing differential analysis in GLV elliptic curve scalar multiplication. In: Kaliski, B.S., Koç, Ç.K., Paar, C. (eds.) CHES 2002. LNCS, vol. 2523, pp. 540–550. Springer, Heidelberg (2003). doi:10.1007/3-540-36400-5_39

12. Clavier, C., Feix, B., Gagnerot, G., Roussellet, M., Verneuil, V.: Horizontal correlation analysis on exponentiation. In: Soriano, M., Qing, S., López, J. (eds.) ICICS 2010. LNCS, vol. 6476, pp. 46–61. Springer, Heidelberg (2010). doi:10.1007/978-3-642-17650-0_5

13. Cooper, J., DeMulder, E., Goodwill, G., Jaffe, J., Kenworthy, G., Rohatgi, P.: Test Vector Leakage Assessment (TVLA) methodology in practice. In: International Cryptographic Module Conference (2013)
14. Coron, J.-S., Kocher, P., Naccache, D.: Statistics and secret leakage. In: Frankel, Y. (ed.) FC 2000. LNCS, vol. 1962, pp. 157–173. Springer, Heidelberg (2001). doi:10. 1007/3-540-45472-1_12
15. Coron, J.-S.: Resistance against differential power analysis for elliptic curve cryptosystems. In: Koç, Ç.K., Paar, C. (eds.) CHES 1999. LNCS, vol. 1717, pp. 292–302. Springer, Heidelberg (1999). doi:10.1007/3-540-48059-5_25
16. Costello, C., Longa, P.: FourQ: four-dimensional decompositions on a Q-curve over the Mersenne prime. In: Iwata, T., Cheon, J.H. (eds.) ASIACRYPT 2015. LNCS, vol. 9452, pp. 214–235. Springer, Heidelberg (2015). doi:10.1007/ 978-3-662-48797-6_10. Full version: https://eprint.iacr.org/2015/565
17. Costello, C., Longa, P.: FourQlib (2015–2017). https://github.com/Microsoft/ FourQlib
18. Costello, C., Longa, P.: SchnorrQ: Schnorr signatures on FourQ. MSR Technical report (2016). https://www.microsoft.com/en-us/research/wp-content/uploads/ 2016/07/SchnorrQ.pdf
19. Düll, M., Haase, B., Hinterwälder, G., Hutter, M., Paar, C., Sánchez, A.H., Schwabe, P.: High-speed Curve25519 on 8-bit, 16-bit, and 32-bit microcontrollers. Des. Codes Crypt. **77**(2–3), 493–514 (2015)
20. Fan, J., Verbauwhede, I.: An updated survey on secure ECC implementations: attacks, countermeasures and cost. In: Naccache, D. (ed.) Cryptography and Security: From Theory to Applications. LNCS, vol. 6805, pp. 265–282. Springer, Heidelberg (2012). doi:10.1007/978-3-642-28368-0_18
21. Faz-Hernández, A., Longa, P., Sánchez, A.H.: Efficient and secure algorithms for GLV-based scalar multiplication and their implementation on GLV-GLS curves (extended version). J. Cryptogr. Eng. **5**(1), 31–52 (2015)
22. Feix, B., Roussellet, M., Venelli, A.: Side-channel analysis on blinded regular scalar multiplications. In: Meier, W., Mukhopadhyay, D. (eds.) INDOCRYPT 2014. LNCS, vol. 8885, pp. 3–20. Springer, Cham (2014). doi:10.1007/ 978-3-319-13039-2_1
23. Fouque, P.-A., Valette, F.: The doubling attack – *why upwards is better than downwards*. In: Walter, C.D., Koç, Ç.K., Paar, C. (eds.) CHES 2003. LNCS, vol. 2779, pp. 269–280. Springer, Heidelberg (2003). doi:10.1007/978-3-540-45238-6_22
24. Gaudry, P., Schost, E.: Genus 2 point counting over prime fields. J. Symb. Comput. **47**(4), 368–400 (2012)
25. Goubin, L.: A refined power-analysis attack on elliptic curve cryptosystems. In: Desmedt, Y.G. (ed.) PKC 2003. LNCS, vol. 2567, pp. 199–211. Springer, Heidelberg (2003). doi:10.1007/3-540-36288-6_15
26. Gouvêa, C.P.L., López, J.: Software implementation of pairing-based cryptography on sensor networks using the MSP430 microcontroller. In: Roy, B., Sendrier, N. (eds.) INDOCRYPT 2009. LNCS, vol. 5922, pp. 248–262. Springer, Heidelberg (2009). doi:10.1007/978-3-642-10628-6_17
27. Hanley, N., Kim, H., Tunstall, M.: Exploiting collisions in addition chain-based exponentiation algorithms using a single trace. In: Nyberg, K. (ed.) CT-RSA 2015. LNCS, vol. 9048, pp. 431–448. Springer, Cham (2015). doi:10.1007/ 978-3-319-16715-2_23
28. Hisil, H., Wong, K.K., Carter, G., Dawson, E.: Twisted Edwards curves revisited. In: Pieprzyk, J. (ed.) ASIACRYPT 2008. LNCS, vol. 5350, pp. 326–343. Springer, Heidelberg (2008). doi:10.1007/978-3-540-89255-7_20

29. Izu, T., Takagi, T.: Exceptional procedure attack on elliptic curve cryptosystems. In: Desmedt, Y.G. (ed.) PKC 2003. LNCS, vol. 2567, pp. 224–239. Springer, Heidelberg (2003). doi:10.1007/3-540-36288-6_17

30. Joye, M., Tymen, C.: Protections against differential analysis for elliptic curve cryptography — an algebraic approach —. In: Koç, Ç.K., Naccache, D., Paar, C. (eds.) CHES 2001. LNCS, vol. 2162, pp. 377–390. Springer, Heidelberg (2001). doi:10.1007/3-540-44709-1_31

31. Joye, M., Yen, S.-M.: The montgomery powering ladder. In: Kaliski, B.S., Koç, Ç.K., Paar, C. (eds.) CHES 2002. LNCS, vol. 2523, pp. 291–302. Springer, Heidelberg (2003). doi:10.1007/3-540-36400-5_22

32. Kocher, P., Jaffe, J., Jun, B.: Differential power analysis. In: Wiener, M. (ed.) CRYPTO 1999. LNCS, vol. 1666, pp. 388–397. Springer, Heidelberg (1999). doi:10.1007/3-540-48405-1_25

33. Kocher, P.C.: Timing attacks on implementations of Diffie-Hellman, RSA, DSS, and other systems. In: Koblitz, N. (ed.) CRYPTO 1996. LNCS, vol. 1109, pp. 104–113. Springer, Heidelberg (1996). doi:10.1007/3-540-68697-5_9

34. Ladd, W., Longa, P., Barnes, R.: Curve4Q. Internet-Draft, draft-ladd-cfrg-4q-01 (2016–2017). https://www.ietf.org/id/draft-ladd-cfrg-4q-01.txt

35. Liu, Z., Longa, P., Pereira, G., Reparaz, O., Seo, H.: FourQ on embedded devices with strong countermeasures against side-channel attacks. IACR Cryptology ePrint Archive, Report 2017/434 (2017). http://eprint.iacr.org/2017/434

36. Longa, P.: FourQNEON: faster elliptic curve scalar multiplications on ARM processors. In: Avanzi, R., Heys, H. (eds.) Selected Areas in Cryptography - SAC 2016. LNCS. Springer (2016, to appear). http://eprint.iacr.org/2016/645

37. Mamiya, H., Miyaji, A., Morimoto, H.: Efficient countermeasures against RPA, DPA, and SPA. In: Joye, M., Quisquater, J.-J. (eds.) CHES 2004. LNCS, vol. 3156, pp. 343–356. Springer, Heidelberg (2004). doi:10.1007/978-3-540-28632-5_25

38. Murdica, C., Guilley, S., Danger, J., Hoogvorst, P., Naccache, D.: Same values power analysis using special points on elliptic curves. In: Schindler, W., Huss, S.A. (eds.) COSADE 2012. LNCS, vol. 7275, pp. 183–198. Springer, Heidelberg (2012). doi:10.1007/978-3-642-29912-4_14

39. Nascimento, E., Chmielewski, L., Oswald, D., Schwabe, P.: Attacking embedded ECC implementations through cmov side channels. In: Selected Areas in Cryptology – SAC 2016. Springer (2016, to appear)

40. Nascimento, E., López, J., Dahab, R.: Efficient and secure elliptic curve cryptography for 8-bit AVR microcontrollers. In: Chakraborty, R.S., Schwabe, P., Solworth, J. (eds.) SPACE 2015. LNCS, vol. 9354, pp. 289–309. Springer, Cham (2015). doi:10.1007/978-3-319-24126-5_17

41. Okeya, K., Sakurai, K.: Power analysis breaks elliptic curve cryptosystems even secure against the timing attack. In: Roy, B., Okamoto, E. (eds.) INDOCRYPT 2000. LNCS, vol. 1977, pp. 178–190. Springer, Heidelberg (2000). doi:10.1007/3-540-44495-5_16

42. Oswald, E., Mangard, S.: Template attacks on masking—resistance is futile. In: Abe, M. (ed.) CT-RSA 2007. LNCS, vol. 4377, pp. 243–256. Springer, Heidelberg (2006). doi:10.1007/11967668_16

43. Page, D.: Theoretical use of cache memory as a cryptanalytic side-channel. Technical report CSTR-02-003, Department of Computer Science, University of Bristol (2002). http://www.cs.bris.ac.uk/Publications/Papers/1000625.pdf

44. Piotrowski, K., Langendoerfer, P., Peter, S.: How public key cryptography influences wireless sensor node lifetime. In: Proceedings of the Fourth ACM Workshop on Security of Ad hoc and Sensor Networks, pp. 169–176. ACM (2006)

45. Prouff, E., Rivain, M.: A generic method for secure SBox implementation. In: Kim, S., Yung, M., Lee, H.-W. (eds.) WISA 2007. LNCS, vol. 4867, pp. 227–244. Springer, Heidelberg (2007). doi:10.1007/978-3-540-77535-5_17

46. Renes, J., Schwabe, P., Smith, B., Batina, L.: μKummer: Efficient hyperelliptic signatures and key exchange on microcontrollers. In: Gierlichs, B., Poschmann, A.Y. (eds.) CHES 2016. LNCS, vol. 9813, pp. 301–320. Springer, Heidelberg (2016). doi:10.1007/978-3-662-53140-2_15

47. Reparaz, O., Gierlichs, B., Verbauwhede, I.: Selecting time samples for multivariate DPA attacks. In: Prouff, E., Schaumont, P. (eds.) CHES 2012. LNCS, vol. 7428, pp. 155–174. Springer, Heidelberg (2012). doi:10.1007/978-3-642-33027-8_10

48. Santis, F.D., Sigl, G.: Towards side-channel protected X25519 on ARM Cortex-M4 processors. Software Performance Enhancement for Encryption and Decryption, and Benchmarking (SPEED-B) (2016)

49. Seo, H., Liu, Z., Choi, J., Kim, H.: Multi-precision squaring for public-key cryptography on embedded microprocessors. In: Paul, G., Vaudenay, S. (eds.) INDOCRYPT 2013. LNCS, vol. 8250, pp. 227–243. Springer, Cham (2013). doi:10.1007/978-3-319-03515-4_15

50. Smart, N.P., Oswald, E., Page, D.: Randomised representations. IET Inf. Secur. 2(2), 19–27 (2008)

51. Standaert, F.-X., Veyrat-Charvillon, N., Oswald, E., Gierlichs, B., Medwed, M., Kasper, M., Mangard, S.: The world is not enough: another look on second-order DPA. In: Abe, M. (ed.) ASIACRYPT 2010. LNCS, vol. 6477, pp. 112–129. Springer, Heidelberg (2010). doi:10.1007/978-3-642-17373-8_7

52. STMicroelectronics: STM32F4DISCOVERY: Discovery kit with STM32F407VG MCU, data brief (2016). http://www.st.com/content/ccc/resource/technical/document/data_brief/09/71/8c/4e/e4/da/4b/fa/DM00037955.pdf/files/DM00037955.pdf/jcr:content/translations/en.DM00037955.pdf

53. STMicroelectronics: Reference manual: STM32F405/415, STM32F407/417, STM32F427/437 and STM32F429/439 advanced ARM-based 32-bit MCUs (2017). http://www.st.com/content/ccc/resource/technical/document/reference_manual/3d/6d/5a/66/b4/99/40/d4/DM00031020.pdf/files/DM00031020.pdf/jcr:content/translations/en.DM00031020.pdf

54. Texas Instruments: User's guide: MSP430FR58xx, MSP430FR59xx, MSP430FR68xx, and MSP430FR69xx family (2012–2017). http://www.ti.com.cn/cn/lit/ug/slau367m/slau367m.pdf

55. Wenger, E., Unterluggauer, T., Werner, M.: 8/16/32 shades of elliptic curve cryptography on embedded processors. In: Paul, G., Vaudenay, S. (eds.) INDOCRYPT 2013. LNCS, vol. 8250, pp. 244–261. Springer, Cham (2013). doi:10.1007/978-3-319-03515-4_16

Bit-Sliding: A Generic Technique for Bit-Serial Implementations of SPN-based Primitives

Applications to AES, PRESENT and SKINNY

Jérémy Jean[1]([⊠]), Amir Moradi[2]([⊠]),
Thomas Peyrin[3,4]([⊠]), and Pascal Sasdrich[2]([⊠])

[1] ANSSI Crypto Lab, Paris, France
Jeremy.Jean@ssi.gouv.fr
[2] Horst Görtz Institute for IT Security,
Ruhr-Universität Bochum, Bochum, Germany
{Amir.Moradi,Pascal.Sasdrich}@rub.de
[3] Temasek Laboratories, Nanyang Technological University, Singapore, Singapore
Thomas.Peyrin@ntu.edu.sg
[4] School of Physical and Mathematical Sciences,
Nanyang Technological University, Singapore, Singapore

Abstract. Area minimization is one of the main efficiency criterion for lightweight encryption primitives. While reducing the implementation data path is a natural strategy for achieving this goal, Substitution-Permutation Network (SPN) ciphers are usually hard to implement in a bit-serial way (1-bit data path). More generally, this is hard for any data path smaller than its Sbox size, since many scan flip-flops would be required for storage, which are more area-expensive than regular flip-flops.

In this article, we propose the first strategy to obtain extremely small bit-serial ASIC implementations of SPN primitives. Our technique, which we call *bit-sliding*, is generic and offers many new interesting implementation trade-offs. It manages to minimize the area by reducing the data path to a single bit, while avoiding the use of many scan flip-flops.

Following this general architecture, we could obtain the first bit-serial and the smallest implementation of AES-128 to date (1560 GE for encryption only, and 1738 GE for encryption and decryption with IBM 130 nm standard-cell library), greatly improving over the smallest known implementations (about 30% decrease), making AES-128 competitive to many ciphers specifically designed for lightweight cryptography. To exhibit the generality of our strategy, we also applied it to the PRESENT and SKINNY block ciphers, again offering the smallest implementations of these ciphers thus far, reaching an area as low as 1065 GE for a 64-bit block 128-bit key cipher. It is also to be noted that our bit-sliding seems to obtain very good power consumption figures, which makes this implementation strategy a good candidate for passive RFID tags.

Keywords: Bit-serial implementations · Bit-slide · Lightweight cryptography

© International Association for Cryptologic Research 2017
W. Fischer and N. Homma (Eds.): CHES 2017, LNCS 10529, pp. 687–707, 2017.
DOI: 10.1007/978-3-319-66787-4_33

1   Introduction

Due to the increasing importance of pervasive computing, lightweight cryptography has attracted a lot of attention in the last decade among the symmetric-key community. In particular, we have seen many improvements in both primitive design and their hardware implementations. We currently know much better how a lightweight encryption scheme should look like (small block size, small nonlinear components, very few or even no XORs gates for the linear layer, etc.).

Lightweight cryptography can have different meanings depending on the applications and the situations. For example, for passive RFID tags, power consumption is very important, and for battery-driven devices energy consumption is a top priority. Power and energy consumption depend on both the area and throughput of the implementation. In this scenario, so-called round-based implementations (i.e., one cipher round per clock cycle) are usually the most efficient trade-offs with regards to these metrics. For example, the tweakable block cipher SKINNY [6] was recently introduced with the goal of reaching the best possible efficiency for round-based implementations.

Yet, for the obvious reason that many lightweight devices are very strongly constrained, one of the most important measurement remains simply the implementation area, regardless of the throughput. It was estimated in 2005 that only a maximum of 2000 GE can be dedicated to security in an RFID tag [19]. While these numbers might have evolved a little since then, it is clear that area is a key aspect when designing/implementing a primitive. In that scenario, round-based implementations are far from being optimal since the data path is very large. In contrast, the serial implementation strategy tries to minimize the data path to reduce the overall area. Some primitives even specialized for this type of implementation (e.g., LED [15], PHOTON [14]), with a linear layer crafted to be cheap and easy to perform in a serial way.

In 2013, the National Security Agency (NSA) published two new ciphers [5], SIMON (tuned for hardware) and SPECK (tuned for software) targeting very low-area implementations. SIMON is based on a simple Feistel construction with just a few rotations, ANDs and XORs to build the internal function. The authors showed that SIMON's simplicity easily allows many hardware implementation trade-offs with regards to the data path, going as low as a 1-bit-serial implementation.

For Substitution-Permutation Network (SPN) primitives, like AES [12] or PRESENT [7], the situation is more complex. While they can usually provide more confidence concerning their security, they are known to be harder to implement in a bit-serial way. To the best of the authors' knowledge, as of today, there is no bit-serial implementation of an SPN cipher, mainly due to the underlying structure organized around their Sbox and linear layers. While this construction offers efficient and easy implementation trade-offs, it seems nontrivial to build an architecture with a dapa path below the Sbox size. Thus, there remains a gap to bridge between SPN primitives and ciphers with a general SIMON-like structure.

Our Contributions. In this article, we provide the first general bit-serial Application-Specific Integrated Circuit (ASIC) implementation strategy for SPN ciphers. Our technique, that we call *bit-sliding*, allows implementations to use small data paths, while significantly reducing the number of costly scan flip-flops (FF) used to store the state and key bits.

Although our technique mainly focuses on 1-bit-serial implementations, it easily scales and supports many other trade-offs, e.g., data paths of 2 bits, 4 bits, etc. This agility turns to be very valuable in practice, where one wants to map the best possible implementation to a set of constraints combining a particular scenario and specific devices. We applied our strategy to AES, and together with other minor implementation tricks, we obtained extremely small AES-128 implementations on ASIC: only 1560 Gate Equivalent (GE) for encryption (incl. 75% for storage), and 1738 GE for encryption and decryption using IBM 130 nm library (incl. 67% for storage).[1] By comparison, using the same library, the smallest ASIC implementation of AES-128 previously known requires 2182 GE for encryption [22] (incl. 64% of storage), and 2402 GE for encryption and decryption [3] (incl. 55% of storage).[2] Our results show that AES-128 could almost be considered as a lightweight cipher.

Since our strategy is very generic, we also applied it to the cases of PRESENT and SKINNY, again obtaining the smallest known implementations. More precisely, for the 64-bit block 128-bit key versions and using the IBM 130 nm library, we could reach 1065 GE for PRESENT and 1054 GE for SKINNY compared to the to-date smallest PRESENT-128 with 1230 GE [31]. Our work shows that the gap between the design strategy of SIMON and a classical SPN is smaller than previously thought, as SIMON can reach 958 GE for the same block/key sizes.

In terms of power consumption, it turns out that bit-sliding provides good results when compared to currently known implementation strategies. This makes it potentially interesting for passive RFID tags for which power is a key constraint. However, as for any bit-serial implementation, due to the many cycles required to execute the circuit, the energy consumption figures will not be as good as one can obtain with round-based implementations.

We emphasize that for fairness, we compare the various implementations to ours using five standard libraries: namely, UMC 180 nm, UMC 130 nm, UMC 90 nm, NanGate 45 nm and IBM 130 nm.

2   Bit-Sliding Implementation Technique

We describe in this section the conducting idea of our technique, which allows to significantly decrease the area required to *serially* implement any SPN-based cryptographic primitive. To clearly expose our strategy, we first describe the general structure of SPN primitives in Sect. 2.1 and we recall the most common

---

[1] The same library used to benchmark SIMON area footprints in [5].

[2] We note that the 2400 GE reported in [22] are done on a different library, namely UMC 180 nm. The numbers we report here are obtained by re-synthesizing the code from [22] on IBM 130 nm.

types of hardware implementation trade-offs in Sect. 2.2. Then, in Sect. 2.3, we explain the effect of reducing the data path of an SPN implementation, in particular how the choice of the various flip-flops used for state storage strongly affects the total area. Finally, we describe our bit-sliding implementation strategy in Sect. 2.4 and we tackle the problem of bit-serializing any Sbox in Sect. 2.5. Applications of these techniques to AES-128 and PRESENT block ciphers are conducted in the subsequent sections of the paper (the case of SKINNY is provided in the long version of the paper [17]). For completeness, we provide in Sect. 2.6 a quick summary of previous low-area implementations of SPN ciphers such as AES-128 and PRESENT.

2.1   Substitution-Permutation Networks

Even though our results apply to any SPN-based construction (block cipher, hash function, stream cipher, public permutation, etc.), for simplicity of the description, we focus on block ciphers.

A *block cipher* corresponds to a keyed family of permutations over a fixed domain, $E : \{0,1\}^k \times \{0,1\}^n \to \{0,1\}^n$. The value k denotes the key size in bits, n the dimension of the domain on which the permutation applies, and for each key $K \in \{0,1\}^k$, the mapping $E(K, \cdot)$, that we usually denote $E_K(\cdot)$, defines a permutation over $\{0,1\}^n$.

From a high-level perspective, an SPN-based block cipher relies on a round function f that consists of the mathematical composition of a nonlinear permutation S and a linear permutation P, which can be seen as a direct application of Shannon's confusion (nonlinear) and diffusion (linear) paradigm [27].

From a practical point of view, the problem of implementing the whole cipher then reduces to implementing the small permutations S and P, that can either be chosen for their good cryptographic properties, and/or for their low hardware or software costs. In most known ciphers, the nonlinear permutation $S : \{0,1\}^n \to \{0,1\}^n$ relies on an even smaller permutation called Sbox, that is applied several times in parallel on independent portions on the internal n-bit state. We denote by s the bit-size of these Sboxes. Similarly, the linear layer often comprises identical functions applied several times in parallel on independent portions on the internal state. We denote by l the bit-size of these functions.

2.2   Implementation Trade-Offs

We usually classify ASIC implementations of cryptographic algorithms in three categories: round-based implementations, fully unrolled implementations and serial implementations. A round-based implementation typically offers a very good area/throughput trade-off, by providing the cryptographic functionalities (e.g., encryption and decryption). The idea is this case consists in simply implementing the full round function f of the block cipher in one clock cycle and to reuse the circuit to produce the output of the cipher. In contrast, to minimize the latency a fully unrolled implementation would implement *all* the rounds at the expense of a much larger area, essentially proportional to the number of the cipher rounds (for instance PRINCE [8] or MANTIS [6] have been designed to satisfy such low-latency requirements). Finally, serial implementations (the focus of this article) trade throughput by only implementing a small fraction of the round function f, for applications that require to minimize the area as much as possible.

2.3   Data Path Reduction and Flip-Flops

From round-based to serial implementations, the data path is usually reduced. In the case of SPN primitives, reducing this data path is natural as long as the application independence of the various sub-components of the cipher (s-bit Sboxes and l-bit linear functions) is respected. This is the reason why all the smallest known SPN implementations are serial implementations with an s-bit data path (l being most of the time a multiple of s). Many trade-offs lying between an s-bit implementation and a round-based implementation can easily be reached. For example, in the case of AES, depending on the efficiency targets, one can trivially go from a byte-wise implementation, to a row- or column-wise implementation, up to a full round-based implementation.

The data path reduction in an ASIC implementation offers area reduction at two levels. First, it allows to reduce the number of sub-components to implement (n/s Sboxes in the case of a round-based implementation versus only a single Sbox for a s-bit serial implementation), directly reducing the total area cost. Second, it offers an opportunity to reduce the number of scan flip-flops (scan FF), at the benefit of regular flip-flops (FF) for storage. A scan FF contains a 2-to-1 multiplexer to select either the data input or the scan input. This scan feature allows to drive the FF data input with an alternate source of data, thus greatly increasing the possibilities for the implementer about where the data navigates. In short: in an ASIC architecture, when a storage bit receives data only from a single source, regular FF can be used. If another source must potentially be selected, then a scan FF is required (with extra multiplexers in case of multiple sources). However, the inner multiplexer comes at a non-negligible price, as scan FF cost about 20–30% more GE than regular ones.

2.4   The Bit-Sliding Strategy

Because of the difference between scan FF and regular FF, when minimizing the area is the main goal, there is a natural incentive in trying to use as many regular FF as possible. In other words, the data should flow in such a way that many storage bits only have a single input source. This is hard to achieve with a classical s-bit data path, since the data usually moves from all bits of an Sbox to all bits of another Sbox. Thus, the complex wiring due to the cipher specifications impacts all the Sbox storage bits at the same time. For example, in the case of AES, the ShiftRows forces most internal state storage bits to use scan FFs.

This is where the bit-sliding strategy comes into play. When enabling the bit-serial implementation by reducing the data path from s bits to a single bit, we make the data bits *slide*. All the complex data wiring due to the cipher specifications becomes handled only by the very first bit of the cipher state. Therefore, this first bit has to be stored in a scan FF, while the other bits can simply use regular FF. Depending on the cipher sub-components, other state bits should also make use of scan FF, but the effect is obviously stronger as the size of the Sbox grows larger.

We emphasize that minimizing the ratio of scan FF is really the relevant way to look at the problem of area minimization. Most previous works concentrated on the optimization of the ciphers sub-components. Yet, in the case of lightweight cryptography where implementations are already very optimized for area, these sub-components represent a relatively small portion of the total area cost, in opposition to the storage costs. For example, for our PRESENT implementations, the storage represents about 80–90% of the total area cost. For AES-128, the same ratio is about 65–75%.

2.5   Bit-Serializing Any Sbox

A key issue when going from an s-bit data path to a single bit data path, is to find a way to implement the Sbox in a bit-serial way. For some ciphers, like PICCOLO [28] or SKINNY [6], this is easy as their Sbox can naturally be decomposed into an iterative 1-bit data path process. However, for most ciphers, this is not the case and we cannot assume such a decomposition always exists.

We therefore propose to emulate this bit-serial Sbox by making use of s scan FFs to serially shift out the Sbox output bits at each clock cycle, while reusing the classical s-bit data path circuit of the entire Sbox to store its output.

Although the cost of this strategy is probably not optimal (extra regular FFs should change to scan FF), we nevertheless argue that this is not a real issue since the overall cost of this bit-serial Sbox implementation is very small when compared to the total area cost of the entire cipher. Moreover, this strategy has the important advantage that it is very simple to put into place and that it generically works for any Sbox.

2.6   Previous Serial SPN Implementations

Most of the existing SPN ciphers such as AES or PRESENT have been implemented using word-wise serialization, with 4- or 8-bit data paths. For AES, after two small implementations of the encryption core by Feldhofer et al. [13] in 2005 and Hämäläinen et al. [16] in 2006, one can emphasize the work by Moradi et al. [22] in 2011, which led to an encryption-only implementation of AES-128 with 2400 GE for the UMC 180 nm standard-cell library. More recently, a follow-up work by Banik et al. [2] added the decryption functionality, while keeping the overhead as small as possible: they reached a total of 2645 GE on STM 90 nm library. According to our estimations (see Sect. 3), this implementation requires around 2760 GE on UMC 180 nm, which therefore adds decryption to [22] for a small overhead of about 15%. In [3] Banik et al. further improved this to 2227 GE on STM 90 nm (about 2590 GE on UMC 180 nm).

As for PRESENT, the first result appeared in the specifications [7], where the authors report a 4-bit serial implementation using about 1570 GE on UMC 180 nm. In 2008, Rolfes et al. [25] presented an optimization reaching about 1075 GE on the same library, which was further decreased to 1032 GE by Yap et al. [31].

Finally, we remark that bit-serial implementations of SKINNY and GIFT [4] have already been reported, which are based on the work described in this article.

3   Application to AES-128

3.1   Optimizations of the Components

Since its standardization, the AES has received many different kind of contributions including the attempts to optimize its implementations on many platforms. We review here the main results that we use in our implementations, which specifically target two internal components of the AES: the 8-bit Sbox from SubBytes and the matrix multiplication applied in the MixColumns.

SubBytes. One crucial design choice of any SPN-based cipher lies in the Sbox and its cryptographic strength. In the AES, Daemen and Rijmen chose to rely on the algebraic inversion in the field $GF(2^8)$ for its good resistance to classical differential and linear cryptanalysis. Based on this strong mathematical structure, Satoh et al. in [26] used the tower field decomposition to implement the field inversion using only 2-bit operations, later improved by Mentens et al. in [21]. Then, in 2005, Canright reported a smaller implementation of the combined Sbox and its inverse by enumerating all possible normal bases to perform the decomposition, which resulted in the landmark paper [10]. In our serial implementation supporting both encryption and decryption, we use this implementation.

However, when the inverse Sbox is not required, especially for inverse-free mode of operations like CTR that do not require the decryption operation, the implementation cost can be further reduced. Indeed, Boyar, Matthews and Peralta have shown in [9] that solving an instance of the so-called Shortest Linear Program NP-hard problem yields optimized AES Sbox implementations. In particular, they introduce a 115-operation implementation of the Sbox, further refined to 113 logical operations in [11], which is, to the best of our knowledge, the smallest known to date. We use this implementation in our encryption-only AES cores, which allows to save 20–30 GE over Canright's implementation.

We should also refer to [29], where the constructed Sbox with small footprint needs in average 127 clock cycles. The work has been later improved in [30], where the presented Sbox finishes the operation after at most 16 (in average 7) clock cycles. Regardless of the vulnerability of such a construction to timing attacks [20], we could not use them in our architecture due to their latency higher than 8 clock cycles.

MixColumns. Linear layers of SPN-based primitives have attracted lots of attention in the past few years, mostly from the design point of view. Here, we are interested in finding an efficient implementation of the fixed MixColumns transformation, which can either be seen as multiplication by a 4×4 matrix over $GF(2^8)$ or by a 32×32 matrix over $GF(2)$. For 8-bit data path, similar to previous works like [1,2,33], we have considered the 32×32 binary matrix to implement the MixColumns. An already-reported strategy can implement it in 108 XORs, but we tried to slightly improve this by using a heuristic search tool from [18], which yielded two implementations using 103 and 104 XORs, where the 104-XOR one turned to be more area efficient.

3.2 Bit-Serial Implementations of AES-128 Encryption

We first begin by describing an implementation that only supports encryption, and then complete it to derive one that achieves both encryption and decryption.

Data Path. The design architecture of our bit-serial implementation of AES-128 is shown in Fig. 1. The entire 128-bit state register forms a shift register, which is triggered at every clock cycle. The white register cells indicate regular FFs, while the gray ones scan FFs. The plaintext bits are serially fed from most significant bit (MSB) down to least significant bit (LSB) of the Bytes 0,4,8,12,1,5,9,13,2,6,10,14,3,7,11,15. In other words, during the first 128 clock cycles, first 8 bits (MSB downto LSB) of plaintext Byte 0 and then that of Byte 4 are given till the 8 bits (MSB downto LSB) of plaintext Byte 15.

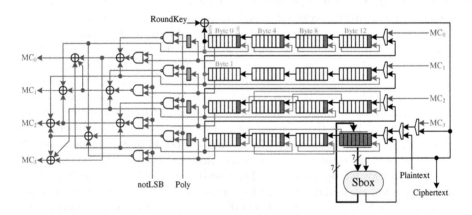

Fig. 1. Bit-serial architecture for AES-128 (encryption only, data path).

The AddRoundKey is also performed in a bit serial form, i.e., realized by one 2-input XOR gate. For each byte, during the first 7 clock cycles, the AddRoundKey result is fed into the rotating shift register, and at the 8th clock cycle, the Sbox output is saved at the last 8 bits of the shift register and at the same time the rest of the state register is shifted. Therefore, we had to use scan FFs for the last 8 bits of the state shift register (see Fig. 1). For the Sbox module, as stated before, we made use of the 113-gate description given in [11] by Cagdas Calik. After 128 clock cycles, the SubBytes is completely performed.

The ShiftRows is also performed bit-serially. The scan FFs enable us to perform the entire ShiftRows in 8 clock cycles. We should emphasize that we have examined two different design architectures. In our design, in contrast to [2,3,22], the state register is always shifted without any exception. This avoids extra logic to enable and disable the registers. In [3], an alternative solution is used, where each row of the state register is controlled by clock gating. Hence, by freezing the first row, shifting the second row once, the third row twice and the forth row three times, the ShiftRows can be performed. We have examined this fashion in our bit-serial architecture as well. It allows us to turn 9 scan FFs to regular FFs, but it needs 4 clock gating circuits and the corresponding control logic. For the bit-serial architecture, it led to more area consumption. We discuss this architecture in Sect. 3.4, when we extend our serial architecture to higher bit lengths.

For the MixColumns, we also provide a bit-serial version. More precisely, each column is processed in 8 clock cycles, i.e., the entire MixColumns is performed in 32 clock cycles. In order to enable such a scenario, when processing a column, we need to store the MSB of all four bytes, which are used to determine whether the extra reduction for the xtime (i.e., multiplication by 2 in $GF(2^8)$ under AES polynomial) is required. The green cells in Fig. 1 indicate the extra register cells which are used for this purpose. The input of the green register cells come from the 2nd MSB of column bytes. Therefore, these registers should store the MSB one clock cycle before the operation on each column is started. During the ShiftRows and at the 8th clock cycle of MixColumns on each column, these registers are enabled. This enables us to fulfill our goal, i.e., always clocking the state shift register. The bit-serial MixColumns circuit needs two control signals: Poly, which provides the bit representation of the AES polynomial 0x1B serially (MSB downto LSB) and notLSB, which enables xtime for the LSB.

Therefore, one full round of the AES is performed in $128 + 8 + 32 = 168$ clock cycles. During the last round, MixColumns is ignored, and the last AddRound-Key is performed while the ciphertext bits are given out. Therefore, the entire encryption takes $9 \times 168 + 128 + 8 + 128 = 1776$ clock cycles. Similar to [2,3,22], while the ciphertext bits are given out, the next plaintext can be fed inside. Therefore, similar to their reported numbers, the clock cycles required to fed plaintext inside are not counted.

Key Path. The key register is similar to the state register and is shifted one bit per clock cycle, and gives one bit of the RoundKey to be used by AddRoundKey (see Fig. 2). The key schedule is performed in parallel to the AddRoundKey and SubBytes, i.e., in 128 clock cycles. In other words, while the RoundKey bit is given out the next RoundKey is generated. Therefore, the key shift register needs to be frozen during ShiftRows and MixColumns operations, which is done by means of clock gating. As shown in Fig. 2, the entire key register except the last one is made by regular FFs, which led to a large area saving. During key

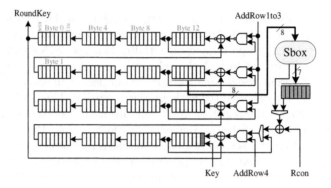

Fig. 2. Bit-serial architecture for AES-128 (encryption only, key path).

schedule, the Sbox module, which is shared with the data path,[3] is required 4 times. We instantiate 7 extra scan FFs, those marked by green, which save 7 bits of the Sbox output and can shift serially as well. It is noteworthy that 4 of such register cells are shared with the data path circuit to store the MSBs required in MixColumns.[4] At the first clock cycle of the key schedule, the Sbox is used and its output is stored in the dedicated green register. It is indeed a perfect sharing of the Sbox module between the data path and key path circuits. During every 8 clock cycles, the Sbox is used by the key path at the first clock cycle and by the data path at the last clock cycle. During the first 8 clock cycles, the Sbox output $S(\text{Byte}_{13})$ is added to Byte_0, which is already the first byte of the next Roundkey. Note that the RoundConstant Rcon is also provided serially by the control logic. During the next 16 clock cycles, by means of AddRow4 signal, $S(\text{Byte}_{13}) \oplus \text{Byte}_0 \oplus \text{Byte}_4$ and $S(\text{Byte}_{13}) \oplus \text{Byte}_0 \oplus \text{Byte}_4 \oplus \text{Byte}_8$ are calculated, which are the next 2 bytes of the next RoundKey. The next 8 clock cycles, Byte_{12} is fed unchanged into the shift register, that is required to go through the Sbox later. This process is repeated 4 times and at the last 8 clock cycles, i.e., clock cycles 121 to 128, by means of AddRow1to3, the last XORs are performed to make the Bytes 12, 13, 14, and 15 of the next RoundKey. During the next 8+32 clock cycles, when the data path circuit is performing ShiftRows and MixColumns, the entire key shift register is frozen.

3.3   Bit-Serial AES-128 Encryption and Decryption Core

Data Path. In order to add decryption, we slightly changed the architecture (see Fig. 3). First, we replaced the last 7 regular FFs by scan FFs, where Byte_0 is stored. Then, as said before, we made use of Canright AES Sbox [10].

The encryption functionality of the circuit stays unchanged, while the decryption needs several more clock cycles. After serially loading the ciphertext bits, at the first 128 clock cycles, the AddRoundKey is performed. Afterwards, the

---

[3] Eight 2-to-1 MUX at the Sbox input are not shown.

[4] It requires four 2-to-1 MUX which are not shown.

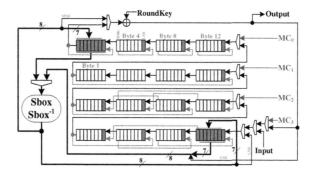

Fig. 3. Bit-serial architecture for `AES-128` (encryption and decryption, data path).

ShiftRows^{-1} should be done. To do so, we perform the ShiftRows three times since ShiftRows^3 = ShiftRows^{-1}. This helps us to not modify the design architecture, i.e., no extra scan FF or MUX. Therefore, the entire ShiftRows^{-1} takes $3 \times 8 = 24$ clock cycles. The next SubBytes^{-1} and AddRoundKey are performed at the same time. For the first clock cycle, the Sbox inverse is stored in 7 scan FFs, where Byte$_0$ is stored, and the same time the XOR with the RoundKey bit and the shift in the sate register happen. In the next 7 clock cycles, the AddRoundKey is performed. This is repeated 16 times, i.e., 128 clock cycles. For the MixColumns^{-1}, we followed the principle used in [3] that MixColumns^3 = MixColumns^{-1}. In other words, we repeat the MixColumns process explained above 3 times, in $3 \times 32 = 96$ clock cycles. Note that for simplicity, the MixColumns circuit is not shown in Fig. 3. At the last decryption round, first the ShiftRows^{-1} is performed, in 24 clock cycles, and afterwards, when the SubBytes^{-1} and AddRoundKey are simultaneously performed, the plaintext bits are given out. Therefore, the entire decryption takes $128 + 9 \times (24 + 128 + 96) + 24 + 128 = 2512$ clock cycles. Note that the state register, similar to the encryption-only variant, is always active.

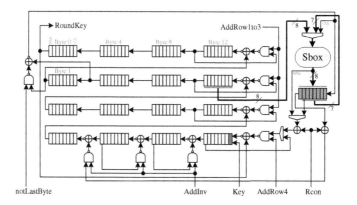

Fig. 4. Bit-serial architecture for `AES-128` (encryption and decryption, key path).

Key Path. Enabling the inverse key schedule in our bit-serial architecture is a bit more involved than in the data path. According to Fig. 4, we still make use of only one scan FF and the rest of the key shift register is made by regular FFs. We only extended the 7 green scan FFs to 8. At the first 8 clock cycles, $Byte_1 \oplus Byte_5$ is serially computed and shifted into the green scan FFs, and at the 8th clock cycle the entire 8-bit Sbox output is stored in the green scan FFs. Within the next 16 clock cycles, the key state is just rotated. During the next 8 clock cycles, the green scan FFs are serially shifted out and its XOR results with $Byte_0$ is stored. At the same time, by means of `AddInv` signal, $Byte_0 \oplus Byte_4$, $Byte_4 \oplus Byte_8$, and $Byte_8 \oplus Byte_{12}$ are serially computed, that are the first 4 bytes of the next RoundKey upwards. For sure, RoundConstant is also provided (serially) in reverse order (by the control logic). This process is repeated 4 times with one exception. At the last time, i.e., at Clock cycles 97 to 104, by means of the `notLastByte` signal, the XOR is bypassed when the green scan FFs are serially loaded. This is due to the fact that such an XOR has already been performed. Hence, the key scheduleinv takes again 128 clock cycles, and is synchronized with the AddRoundKey of the data path circuit. During other clock cycles, where ShiftRows^{-1} and MixColumns^{-1} are performed, the key shift register is disabled.

3.4 Extension to Higher Bit Lengths

We could relatively easily extend our design architecture(s) to higher bit lengths. More precisely, instead of shifting 1 bit at every clock cycle, we can process either 2, 4, or 8 bits. The design architectures stay the same, but every computing module provides 2, 4, or 8 bits at every clock cycle. More importantly, the number of scan FFs increases almost linearly. For the 2-bit version, the 9 scan FFs that enabled ShiftRows must be doubled. Its required number of clock cycles is also half of the 1-bit version, i.e., 888 for encryption and 1256 for decryption.

However, we observed that in 4-bit (resp. 8-bit) serial version almost half (resp. full) of the FFs of the state register need to be changed to scan FF, that in fact contradicts our desire to use as much regular FFs as possible instead of scan FFs. In these two settings (4- and 8-bit serial), we have achieved more efficient designs if the ShiftRows is realized by employing 4 different clock gating, each of which for a row in state shift register. This allows us to avoid replacing 36 (resp. 72) regular FFs by scan FF. This architecture forces us to spend 4 more clock cycles during MixColumns since not all state registers during ShiftRows are shifted, and the MSB for the MixColumns cannot be saved beforehand. Therefore, for the 4-bit version, the AddRoundKey and SubBytes are performed in 32 clock cycles, the ShiftRows in 6 cycles, and the MixColumns in $4 \times (1 + 2) = 12$ cycles, hence $9 \times (32 + 6 + 12) + 32 + 6 + 32 = 520$ clock cycles for the entire encryption.

For the decryption, the ShiftRows^{-1} does not need to be performed as ShiftRows^3, and it can also be done in 6 clock cycles. However, the MixColumns^{-1} still requires to apply 3 times MixColumns, i.e., $3 \times 12 = 36$ cycles. Thus, the entire decryption needs $32 + 9 \times (6 + 32 + 36) + 6 + 32 = 736$ clock cycles.

In the 8-bit serial version, since the Sbox is required during the entire 16 clock cycles of SubBytes, we had to disable the state shift register 4 times to allow the

Sbox module to be used by the key schedule. Since MixColumns now computes the entire column in 1 clock cycle, there is no need for extra registers (as well as clock cycles) to save the MSBs. Therefore, AddRoundKey and SubBytes need 20 clock cycles, ShiftRows 3 clock cycles, and MixColumns 4 clock cycles, i.e., $9 \times (20 + 3 + 4) + 20 + 3 + 16 = 282$ clock cycles in total. The first step of decryption is AddRoundKey, but at the same time the next RoundKey should be provided. In order to simplify the control logic, the first sole AddRoundKey also takes 20 clock cycles, and MixColumns^{-1} 12 clock cycles. Hence, the entire decryption is performed in $20 + 9 \times (3 + 20 + 12) + 3 + 16 = 354$ clock cycles.

Compared to [2,3,22], our design is different with respect to how we handle the key schedule. For example, our entire key state register needs only 8 scan FFs; we could reduce the area, but with a higher number of clock cycles. It is noteworthy that we have manually optimized most of the control logic (e.g., generation of Rcon) to obtain the most compact design.

Table 1. AES-128 implementations for a data path of δ bits @ 100 KHz.

Func.	δ	UMC180		UMC130		UMC90		Ngate45		IBM130		Latency	Ref.
	bits	GE	μW	GE	μW	GE	μW	GE	μW	GE	μW	Cycles	
NAND	μm^2	9.677		5.120		3.136		0.798		5.760			
Enc	1	1727	3.510	1902	0.845	1596	0.666	1982	100.2	1560	0.823	1776	**New**
Enc	2	1796	3.640	1992	0.904	1667	0.699	2054	104.6	1625	0.842	888	**New**
Enc	4	1920	4.040	2168	1.040	1784	0.800	2146	111.4	1731	0.892	520	**New**
Enc	8	2112	3.990	2360	1.020	1968	0.784	2337	122.2	1912	0.874	282	**New**
Enc	8	2400	6.240	3574	1.270	2292	0.768	2768	136.6	2182	0.984	226	[22]
EncDec	1	1917	3.670	2142	0.944	1794	0.713	2171	112.1	1738	0.852	1776/2512	**New**
EncDec	2	2028	3.920	2269	0.972	1916	0.761	2286	119.8	1855	0.922	888/1256	**New**
EncDec	4	2212	4.590	2509	1.200	2097	0.942	2436	130.4	2069	1.070	520/736	**New**
EncDec	8	2416	4.490	2713	1.170	2329	0.945	2621	142.3	2293	1.070	282/354	**New**
EncDec	8	2577	3.560	2893	0.915	2332	0.645	2793	139.1	2402	0.753	246/326	[3]
EncDec	8	2772	5.860	3233	1.280	2639	0.832	3105	160.2	2503	1.110	226/226	[2]

3.5 Results

The synthesis result of our designs under five different standard cell libraries and the corresponding power consumption values – estimated at 100 KHz – are shown in Table 1. We have also shown that of the designs reported in [2,3,22]. It should be noted that we had access to their designs and did the syntheses by our considered libraries. It can be seen that in all cases our constructions outperform the smallest designs reported in literature. The numbers listed in Table 1 obtained under the highest optimization level (for area) of the synthesizer. For all designs (including [2,3,22]), we further forced the synthesizer to make use of the dedicated scan FFs of the underlying library when needed. It can be seen that all of our designs need smaller area footprints compared to the other designs.

In case of the estimated power consumption, our designs also outperform the others except the one in [3]. However, as an important observation by increasing the δ, the estimated power consumption is increased. We should highlight that our target is the smallest footprint, and our designs would not provide better results if either area×time or energy is considered as the metric.

Based on the results presented in Table 1, it can be seen that comparing the area based on GE in different libraries does not make much sense. For instance, the synthesis results reported in [2,3] that are based on STM 65 nm and STM 90 nm libraries cannot be compared with that of another design under a different library. Indeed, such a huge difference comes from the definition of GE, i.e., the relative area of the NAND gate compared to the other gates: an efficient NAND gate (compared to the other gates in the library) will yield larger GE numbers than an inefficient one. The area of the NAND gate under our considered libraries are also listed in Table 1. The designs synthesized by Nangate 45 nm show almost the highest GE numbers, that is due to its extremely small NAND gate. More interestingly, using IBM 130 nm, it shows the smallest GE numbers while the results with UMC 130 nm (with the same technology size) are amongst the largest ones. One reason is the larger NAND gate in IBM 130 nm.

4 Application to PRESENT

4.1 Optimization of the Components

Substitution Layer. To help the synthesizer reach an area-optimized implementation, we use the tool described in [18] to look for an efficient implementation of the PRESENT Sbox. We have found several ones that allow to significantly decrease the area of the Sbox, in comparison to a LUT-based VHDL description: namely, while the LUT description yields an area equivalent to 60–70 GE, our Sbox implementation decreases it to about 20–30 GE. In our serial implementations described below, we have selected the PRESENT Sbox implementation described in [18] using 21.33 GE on UMC 180 nm In our serial implementations described below, we have selected the PRESENT Sbox implementation described in [18] using 21.33 GE on UMC 180 nm, which is the world's smallest known implementation to date of the PRESENT S-box, about 1 GE smaller than the one provided in [32].

Permutation Layer. The diffusion layer of PRESENT is designed as a bit permutation that is cheap and efficient in hardware, particularly for round-based architectures since then the permutation simply breaks down to wired connections. However, for serialized architectures, such as for our bit-sliding technique, the bit permutation seems to be an obstacle. Although the permutation layer has some underlying structure, adapting it for a bit-serial implementation seems nontrivial. However, we present in the following an approach that allows to decompose the permutation into two independent operations that can be easily performed in a bit-serial fashion. We note that a two-stage decomposition of the PRESENT permutation has also been described in [23]. The first operation performs a local permutation at the bit-level, whereas the second operation performs a global permutation at the nibble-level, comparable to ShiftRows in the AES.

Local Permutation. Essentially, the local permutation sorts all bits of a single row of the state (in its matrix representation) according to their significance as show in Fig. 5. Hence, given four nibbles 0,1,2,3 (with bit-order: MSB downto LSB), the first nibble will contain the most significant bits (in order 0,1,2,3) after the sorting operation, whereas the fourth nibble will hold the least significant bits. Fortunately, this operation can be applied to each row individually and independently. As a direct consequence, only one row of the state register needs to implement the local permutation, which can then be applied to the state successively.

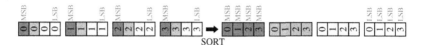

Fig. 5. Local Permutation (SORT). Re-ordering of bits according to their significance.

Global Permutation. After the local permutation has been performed on all rows of the state, all bits are sorted according to their significance and, for instance, the first column will contain all MSBs. However, for a correct implementation of the permutation layer, the bits should be sorted row-wise instead of column-wise. Therefore, the global permutation restores the correct ordering by rearranging the nibbles as shown in Fig. 6, which can also be visualized as a mirroring of the state to its diagonal. Then, either by swapping two nibbles or by holding a nibble in its position, the global permutation can be mapped to structures that are very similar to the ShiftRows operation of AES or SKINNY and we can adapt some design strategies.

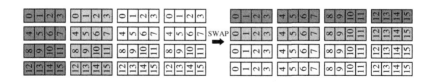

Fig. 6. Global Permutation (SWAP). Column- and row-wise re-ordering of nibbles.

4.2 Bit-Serial Implementations of PRESENT

Data Path. We illustrate in Fig. 7 the basic architecture of our bit-serial implementation of PRESENT. Similar to the bit-serial AES design described in Sect. 3, the 64-bit state of PRESENT is held in a shift register and shifted at every clock cycle. Again, the white cells represent regular FFs, while the gray ones indicate the positions of scan FFs. During the initialization phase, the plaintext is provided starting from its MSB to its LSB of each nibble in the order of 0,1,2,3,4,5,6,7,8,9,10,11,12,13,14,15. Hence, each nibble is provided within 4 clock cycles, starting from MSB to LSB and the entire plaintext is stored in the state register after 64 clock cycles starting from Nibble_0 to Nibble_{15}.

Similar to our bit-serial AES implementation, the addition of the round key is performed in a bit serial fashion using a single 2-input XOR gate. However, since PRESENT has a 64-bit state of 16 nibbles, only during the first 3 clock cycles, the result of the XOR-operation is fed into the state register. At the 4th clock cycle, the Sbox is applied and the result is saved in the last 4 bits of the state register (using the indicated scan FFs) while the remaining part of the state is shifted.

At the 16th clock cycle, the first stage of the permutation (local permutation) is applied to the last row in parallel to the 4th Sbox operation. The red lines in Fig. 7 indicate the data flow that realizes the sorting of the bits according to their significance. Since this operation could be interleaved with the continuous shifting of the state register, we could save a few scan FFs for the last row.

After 64 clock cycles, the round key has been added, all 16 Sboxes have been evaluated, and each row has been sorted according to the local permutation. To finalize the round computation, the second stage of the permutation (global permutation) is performed in 4 clock cycles by means of the blue lines in Fig. 7. In total, a full round of the cipher is performed in $4 \times 16 + 4 = 68$ clock cycles. After 31 rounds (2108 clock cycles), the ciphertext is returned as the result of the final key addition, whereby the next plaintext can be loaded into the state register simultaneously.

Key Path. The state register of the key update function is implemented as shift register, which is shifted and rotated one bit per clock cycle, similar to the state of the data path (see Fig. 8 for the 80-bit version). At each clock cycle, one bit of the round key is extracted and given to the data path module.

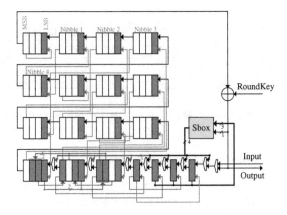

Fig. 7. Bit-serial architecture for PRESENT (encryption only, data path).

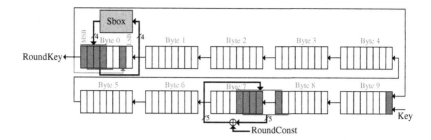

Fig. 8. Bit-serial architecture for `PRESENT-80` (encryption only, key path).

Besides, in order to derive the next round key, the current state has to be rotated by 61 bits to the left which can be done in parallel to the round key addition and Sbox computation of the data path. However, these operation takes 64 clock cycles in total, and the rotation of the round key needs only 61 clock cycles. Hence, we have to stop the shifting of the key register using a gated clock signal. However, since we would loose synchronization between key schedule and round function for the last 3 bits of the round key, we have to partition the key register into a higher (7 bits) and a lower part (73 bits). Then, after 61 clock cycles, the lower part is stopped, while the higher part still is rotated using an additional scan FF (see blue line in Fig. 8) to provide the remaining 3 bits of the round key. Then, while the data path module performs the finalization of the permutation layer, the remaining 4 bits of the higher part are rotated to restore the correct order of the bits. In addition, during the last clock cycle, the round constant is added as well as the Sbox is applied (which is shared with the data path module[5]). Eventually, the key register holds the next round key and is synchronized with the round function in order to continue with the next round.

4.3 Extension to Higher Bit Lengths

In this section, we discuss necessary changes of our architectures to extend and scale the data path to higher bit lengths in order to increase the throughput and decrease the latency.

2-Bit Serial. Expansion of our 1-bit serial data path to a 2-bit serial one is straightforward. Essentially, every component is adapted such that it provides 2 bits at a time, i.e., the state register is shifted for two bits per clock cycle, while the Sbox is applied every 2 clock cycles. Similarly, the local permutation is performed every 8 clock cycles, and the finalization of the permutation takes another 2 clock cycles. Hence, an entire round is computed within $16 \times 2 + 2 = 34$ clock cycles, which is exactly half of the clock cycles of the 1-bit serial architecture.

---

[5] Again, necessary 2-to-1 MUX at the inputs are not shown.

Unfortunately, adaption of the key path to a 2-bit serial one is more complex. In particular the rotation of 61 bits is difficult since shifting 2 bits at a time does not allow a rotation of an odd number of bits. In order to overcome this issue, we decided to distinguish between odd and even rounds. During an odd round we use a rotation of 60 bits, while during even rounds the key state is rotated by 62 bits. However, this approach implies the need for additional multiplexers in order to select the correct round key as well as the correct positions to inject the round constant and the Sbox computation. Apart from that, the key state register is shifted 2 bits per clock cycle, still uses a gated clock signal for the lower part and a rotation of the most significant bits (eight or six, depending on the round) for synchronization.

4-Bit Serial. Further, we considered extending the data path to 4 bits using our bit-sliding technique and replacing all FFs of the state registers by scan FFs. Unfortunately, the bit permutation layer prevents an efficient scaling of our approach, which would result in an architecture that is even larger than the results reported in the literature (for nibble-serial implementations). In particular, the decomposition of the permutation layer, that allowed us an efficient realization for 1- and 2-bit serial data paths, is rather inefficient for nibble-serial structures. Although the global permutation could be realized using only scan FFs for the entire state, the local permutation would require additional multiplexers for the last row of the state. Eventually, performing the entire permutation in a single clock cycle after the substitution layer (as it is done in existing nibble-serial architectures), would be possible solely using scan FFs and without the need of further multiplexers. Hence, although our bit-sliding approach offers outstanding results for 1- and 2-bit serial data paths, it does not scale for larger structures and classical approaches appear to be more efficient.

4.4   Results

In Table 2 we report synthesis results and estimated power consumption of our designed architectures using the aforementioned five standard cell libraries based on various technologies (from 45 nm to 180 nm). We also report the results for the design published in [31] which is, to the best of our knowledge, the smallest PRESENT architecture reported in the literature. We emphasize again that we had access to the design sources from [31] and performed the syntheses using our considered libraries with the same set of parameters as for our architectures. It can be seen that our constructions outperform the smallest designs reported in the literature in terms of area and power.

Table 2. Encryption-only `PRESENT` implementations for a data path of δ bits @ 100 KHz.

Key	δ	UMC180		UMC130		UMC90		Ngate45		IBM130		Latency	Ref.
	bits	GE	μW	GE	μW	GE	μW	GE	μW	GE	μW	Cycles	
80	1	934	1.82	1006	0.44	872	0.32	1113	55.43	847	0.43	2252	**New**
80	2	1004	2.05	1096	0.47	949	0.33	1191	59.33	913	0.45	1126	**New**
80	4	1032	3.13	1088	0.53	990	0.33	1279	59.69	942	0.49	516	[31]
128	1	1172	2.41	1268	0.59	1090	0.43	1397	69.26	1065	0.57	2300	**New**
128	2	1265	2.61	1366	0.61	1189	0.44	1499	74.92	1150	0.58	1150	**New**
128	4	1344	4.00	1416	0.67	1289	0.53	1672	77.54	1230	0.71	528	[31]

5   Conclusion

In this paper, we have introduced a new ASIC implementation strategy, so-called bit-sliding, that allows to obtain efficient bit-serial implementations of SPN ciphers. Apart from the area savings due to a small data path, the bit-sliding strategy reduces the proportion of scan-flip flops to store the cipher state and key, greatly improving the performances compared to state-of-the-art area-optimized implementations.

We have successfully applied bit-sliding to `AES-128`, `PRESENT` and `SKINNY`, and in some cases reduced the area figures by more than 25%. Even though area optimization was our main objective, it turns out that power consumption figures are also improved, which indicates that bit-sliding can be used especially for passive RFID tags, where area and power consumption are the key measures to optimize, notably affecting the proximity requirements.

However, as for any bit-serial implementation, it is to be noted that energy consumption necessarily increases when compared to round-based implementations, due to the higher latency. Therefore, depending on the area available for security on the device, bit-sliding might not be the best choice for battery-driven devices. All in all, this work shows that for some scenarios, `AES-128` can be considered as a lightweight cipher and can now easily fit in less than 2000 GE.

Acknowledgements. The authors would like to thank the anonymous referees for their helpful comments. The authors would like to thank B. Jungk for early discussions and his input on the bitserial implementations of `PRESENT`. Additionally, we would like to thank S. Banik, A. Bogdanov and F. Regazzoni for providing us their implementation of `AES` from [2,3]. We also thank H. Yap, K. Khoo, A. Poschmann and M. Henricksen for sharing with us their implementation of `PRESENT` described in [32]. This work is partly supported by the Singapore National Research Foundation Fellowship 2012 (NRF-NRFF2012-06).

References

1. Banik, S., Bogdanov, A., Regazzoni, F.: Exploring energy efficiency of lightweight block ciphers. In: Dunkelman, O., Keliher, L. (eds.) SAC 2015. LNCS, vol. 9566, pp. 178–194. Springer, Cham (2016). doi:10.1007/978-3-319-31301-6_10

2. Banik, S., Bogdanov, A., Regazzoni, F.: Atomic-AES: a compact implementation of the AES encryption/decryption core. In: Dunkelman, O., Sanadhya, S.K. (eds.) INDOCRYPT 2016. LNCS, vol. 10095, pp. 173–190. Springer, Cham (2016). doi:10.1007/978-3-319-49890-4_10

3. Banik, S., Bogdanov, A., Regazzoni, F.: Atomic-AES v 2.0. IACR Cryptology ePrint Archive 2016:1005 (2016)

4. Banik, S., Pandey, S.K., Peyrin, T., Sasaki, Y., Sim, S.M., Todo, Y.: GIFT: a small PRESENT. In: Cryptographic Hardware and Embedded Systems - CHES 2017, Taipei, Taiwan, September 25–28, 2017 (2017)

5. Beaulieu, R., Treatman-Clark, S., Shors, D., Weeks, B., Smith, J., Wingers, L.: The SIMON and SPECK lightweight block ciphers. In: 2015 52nd ACM/EDAC/IEEE on Design Automation Conference (DAC), pp. 1–6. IEEE (2015)

6. Beierle, C., et al.: The SKINNY family of block ciphers and its low-latency variant MANTIS. In: Robshaw, M., Katz, J. (eds.) CRYPTO 2016. LNCS, vol. 9815, pp. 123–153. Springer, Heidelberg (2016). doi:10.1007/978-3-662-53008-5_5

7. Bogdanov, A., Knudsen, L.R., Leander, G., Paar, C., Poschmann, A., Robshaw, M.J.B., Seurin, Y., Vikkelsoe, C.: PRESENT: an ultra-lightweight block cipher. In: Paillier, P., Verbauwhede, I. (eds.) CHES 2007. LNCS, vol. 4727, pp. 450–466. Springer, Heidelberg (2007). doi:10.1007/978-3-540-74735-2_31

8. Borghoff, J., Canteaut, A., Güneysu, T., Kavun, E.B., Knežević, M., Knudsen, L.R., Leander, G., Nikov, V., Paar, C., Rechberger, C., Rombouts, P., Thomsen, S.S., Yalçin, T.: PRINCE – a low-latency block cipher for pervasive computing applications. In: Wang, X., Sako, K. (eds.) ASIACRYPT 2012. LNCS, vol. 7658, pp. 208–225. Springer, Heidelberg (2012). doi:10.1007/978-3-642-34961-4_14

9. Boyar, J., Matthews, P., Peralta, R.: Logic minimization techniques with applications to cryptology. J. Cryptol. **26**(2), 280–312 (2013)

10. Canright, D.: A very compact S-Box for AES. In: Rao, J.R., Sunar, B. (eds.) CHES 2005. LNCS, vol. 3659, pp. 441–455. Springer, Heidelberg (2005). doi:10.1007/11545262_32

11. CMT: Circuit Minimization Team. http://www.cs.yale.edu/homes/peralta/CircuitStuff/CMT.html

12. Daemen, J., Rijmen, V.: The Design of Rijndael: AES - The Advanced Encryption Standard. Springer, Heidelberg (2002)

13. Feldhofer, M., Wolkerstorfer, J., Rijmen, V.: AES implementation on a grain of sand. IEE Proc. Inf. Secur. **152**(1), 13–20 (2005)

14. Guo, J., Peyrin, T., Poschmann, A.: The PHOTON family of lightweight hash functions. In: Rogaway, P. (ed.) CRYPTO 2011. LNCS, vol. 6841, pp. 222–239. Springer, Heidelberg (2011). doi:10.1007/978-3-642-22792-9_13

15. Guo, J., Peyrin, T., Poschmann, A., Robshaw, M.J.B.: The LED block cipher. [24], pp. 326–341

16. Hamalainen, P., Alho, T., Hannikainen, M., Hamalainen, T.D.: Design and implementation of low-area and low-power AES encryption hardware core. In: 9th EUROMICRO Conference on Digital System Design: Architectures, Methods and Tools, DSD 2006, pp. 577–583. IEEE (2006)

17. Jean, J., Moradi, A., Peyrin, T., Sasdrich, P.: Bit-sliding: a generic technique for bit-serial implementations of SPN-based primitives - applications to AES, PRESENT and SKINNY. Cryptology ePrint Archive, Report 2017/600 (2017)
18. Jean, J., Peyrin, T., Sim, S.M.: Optimizing implementations of lightweight building blocks. Cryptology ePrint Archive, Report 2017/101 (2017)
19. Juels, A., Weis, S.A.: Authenticating pervasive devices with human protocols. In: Shoup, V. (ed.) CRYPTO 2005. LNCS, vol. 3621, pp. 293–308. Springer, Heidelberg (2005). doi:10.1007/11535218_18
20. Kocher, P.C.: Timing attacks on implementations of Diffie-Hellman, RSA, DSS, and other systems. In: Koblitz, N. (ed.) CRYPTO 1996. LNCS, vol. 1109, pp. 104–113. Springer, Heidelberg (1996). doi:10.1007/3-540-68697-5_9
21. Mentens, N., Batina, L., Preneel, B., Verbauwhede, I.: A systematic evaluation of compact hardware implementations for the Rijndael S-Box. In: Menezes, A. (ed.) CT-RSA 2005. LNCS, vol. 3376, pp. 323–333. Springer, Heidelberg (2005). doi:10. 1007/978-3-540-30574-3_22
22. Moradi, A., Poschmann, A., Ling, S., Paar, C., Wang, H.: Pushing the limits: a very compact and a threshold implementation of AES. In: Paterson, K.G. (ed.) EUROCRYPT 2011. LNCS, vol. 6632, pp. 69–88. Springer, Heidelberg (2011). doi:10.1007/978-3-642-20465-4_6
23. Poschmann, A.: Lightweight cryptography - cryptographic engineering for a pervasive world. Cryptology ePrint Archive, Report 2009/516 (2009)
24. Preneel, B., Takagi, T. (eds.): CHES 2011. LNCS, vol. 6917. Springer, Heidelberg (2011)
25. Rolfes, C., Poschmann, A., Leander, G., Paar, C.: Ultra-lightweight implementations for smart devices – security for 1000 gate equivalents. In: Grimaud, G., Standaert, F.-X. (eds.) CARDIS 2008. LNCS, vol. 5189, pp. 89–103. Springer, Heidelberg (2008). doi:10.1007/978-3-540-85893-5_7
26. Satoh, A., Morioka, S., Takano, K., Munetoh, S.: A compact Rijndael hardware architecture with S-Box optimization. In: Boyd, C. (ed.) ASIACRYPT 2001. LNCS, vol. 2248, pp. 239–254. Springer, Heidelberg (2001). doi:10.1007/3-540-45682-1_15
27. Shannon, C.E.: Communication theory of secrecy systems. Bell Syst. Techn. J. **28**(4), 656–715 (1949)
28. Shibutani, K., Isobe, T., Hiwatari, H., Mitsuda, A., Akishita, T., Shirai, T.: Piccolo: an ultra-lightweight blockcipher. [24], pp. 342–357
29. Wamser, M.S.: Ultra-small designs for inversion-based s-boxes. In: 17th Euromicro Conference on Digital System Design, DSD 2014, Verona, Italy, August 27–29, 2014, pp. 512–519. IEEE Computer Society (2014)
30. Wamser, M.S., Holzbaur, L., Sigl, G.: A petite and power saving design for the AES s-box. In: 2015 Euromicro Conference on Digital System Design, DSD 2015, Madeira, Portugal, August 26–28, 2015, pp. 661–667. IEEE Computer Society (2015)
31. Yap, H., Khoo, K., Poschmann, A., Henricksen, M.: EPCBC - a block cipher suitable for electronic product code encryption. In: Lin, D., Tsudik, G., Wang, X. (eds.) CANS 2011. LNCS, vol. 7092, pp. 76–97. Springer, Heidelberg (2011). doi:10.1007/978-3-642-25513-7_7
32. Yap, H., Khoo, K., Poschmann, A., Henricksen, M.: EPCBC - a block cipher suitable for electronic product code encryption. In: Lin, D., Tsudik, G., Wang, X. (eds.) CANS 2011. LNCS, vol. 7092, pp. 76–97. Springer, Heidelberg (2011). doi:10.1007/978-3-642-25513-7_7
33. Zhang, X., Parhi, K.K.: High-speed VLSI architectures for the AES algorithm. IEEE Trans. Very Large Scale Integr. (VLSI) Syst. **12**(9), 957–967 (2004)

Author Index

Anceau, Stéphanie 175
Aranha, Diego F. 644

Banik, Subhadeep 321
Bernstein, Daniel J. 299, 555
Bleuet, Pierre 175
Bonte, Charlotte 579
Bootland, Carl 579
Bos, Joppe W. 579
Breitner, Joachim 555

Cagli, Eleonora 45
Capkun, Srdjan 468, 490
Castryck, Wouter 579
Chakraborti, Avik 277
Chou, Tung 213
Choudary, Marios O. 367
Clavier, Christophe 24
Clédière, Jessy 175
Coron, Jean-Sébastien 93

Daemen, Joan 137
Dumas, Cécile 45

Eisenbarth, Thomas 69

Forte, Domenic 189

Genkin, Daniel 555
Gierlichs, Benedikt 387
Goudarzi, Dahmun 154
Groot Bruinderink, Leon 555
Gross, Hannes 115

Haase, Björn 346
Hamburg, Mike 3
Heninger, Nadia 555
Heyszl, Johann 425
Hiller, Matthias 601
Hülsing, Andreas 232
Hutter, Michael 3

Iliashenko, Ilia 579
Immler, Vincent 403

Irazoqui, Gorka 69
Iwata, Tetsu 277

Jacob, Nisha 425
Jean, Jérémy 687
Journault, Anthony 623

Kim, Dohyun 445
Kim, Yongdae 445
Knell, Thomas 468
Kölbl, Stefan 299
Kostiainen, Kari 468
Kwon, Yujin 445

Labrique, Benoît 346
Lange, Tanja 555
Liu, Zhe 665
Longa, Patrick 665
López, Julio 644
Lucks, Stefan 299

Maingault, Laurent 175
Malisa, Luka 468
Mangard, Stefan 115, 513
Marson, Mark E. 3
Massolino, Pedro Maat Costa 299
Mendel, Florian 299
Minematsu, Kazuhiko 277
Moghimi, Ahmad 69
Moradi, Amir 687

Nandi, Mridul 277
Nawaz, Kashif 299
Niederhagen, Ruben 253

Ólafsdóttir, Hildur 490
Önalan, Aysun Gurur 601

Pandey, Sumit Kumar 321
Pereira, Geovandro C.C.F. 665
Pessl, Peter 513
Peyrin, Thomas 321, 687
Popescu, P.G. 367

Poussier, Romain   534
Primas, Robert   513
Prouff, Emmanuel   45

Rainard, Jean-luc   175
Ranganathan, Aanjhan   490
Reis, Tiago B.S.   644
Reparaz, Oscar   387, 665
Reynaud, Léo   24
Rijneveld, Joost   232
Rivain, Matthieu   154
Rolfes, Carsten   425
Rossi, Mélissa   3

Sasaki, Yu   321
Sasdrich, Pascal   687
Schanck, John   232
Schneider, Tobias   299
Schwabe, Peter   232, 299
Seo, Hwajeong   665
Shakya, Bicky   189
Shin, Hocheol   445
Sigl, Georg   425
Sim, Siang Meng   321
Sommer, David   468

Specht, Robert   403
Standaert, François-Xavier   299, 534, 623
Szefer, Jakub   253

Tehranipoor, Mark M.   189
Todo, Yosuke   299, 321
Tucoulou, Rémi   175

Unterstein, Florian   403

van Vredendaal, Christine   555
Verbauwhede, Ingrid   387
Vercauteren, Frederik   579
Vergnaud, Damien   154
Viguier, Benoît   299
Vivek, Srinivas   154

Wang, Wen   253

Xu, Xiaolin   189

Yarom, Yuval   555

Zankl, Andreas   425
Zhou, Yuanyuan   534